W9-AAE-260

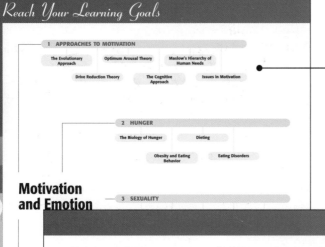

Reach Your Learning Goals

1 APPROACHES TO MOTIVATION

The Evolutionary Approach | Optimum Arousal Theory | Maslow's Hierarchy of Human Needs

Drive Reduction Theory | The Cognitive Approach | Issues in Motivation

2 HUNGER

The Biology of Hunger | Dieting

Obesity and Eating Behavior | Eating Disorders

Motivation and Emotion

3 SEXUALITY

Chapter Map

Combines the section maps into a visual summary of the chapter's main topics.

---

① *Describe psychological approaches to emotion.*

- Motivation gives our behavior, thoughts, and feelings a purpose. Motivated behavior is energized, directed, and sustained. Early evolutionary theorists considered motivation to be based on instinct, the innate biological pattern of behavior that is assumed to be universal throughout a species. The idea that some of our motivation is unlearned and involves physiological factors is still present today. The evolutionary psychology view emphasizes that various aspects of motivation that provided evolutionary advantages were passed down through the genes from generation to generation.
- A drive is an aroused state that occurs because of a physiological need. A need is a deprivation that energizes the drive to eliminate or reduce the deprivation. Drive reduction theory was proposed as an explanation of motivation, with the goal of drive reduction being homeostasis, the body's tendency to maintain an equilibrium.
- Optimum arousal theory focuses on the Yerkes-Dodson law, which states that performance is best under conditions of moderate rather than low or high arousal. Moderate arousal often serves us best when we tackle life's tasks, but there are times when low or high arousal is linked with better performance. Sensation seeking is one aspect of the motivation for high arousal that psychologists study.
- The contemporary view of motivation emphasizes cognitive factors, including such information processing abilities as attention, memory, and problem solving. Psychologists debate how extensively motivation is influenced by conscious versus unconscious thought. Intrinsic motivation, based on internal factors such as self-determination, curiosity, challenge, and effort, is one of the most widely

② *Explain the physiological basis of hunger and the nature of eating behavior.*

- Interest in the stomach's role was stimulated by Cannon's classic research, but stomach signals are not the only factors that affect hunger. Glucose (blood sugar) is an important factor in hunger, probably because the brain is critically dependent on sugar for energy. Rodin's work helped clarify the role of insulin and glucose in hunger. Leptin, a protein secreted by fat cells, decreases food intake and increases energy expenditure. The hypothalamus plays an important role in regulating hunger. The lateral hypothalamus is involved in stimulating eating, the ventromedial hypothalamus in restricting eating. Today, neuroscientists are exploring the roles that neurotransmitters and neural circuits play in hunger.
- Obesity is a serious and pervasive problem in the United States. Heredity, basal metabolism, set point, and fat cells are biological factors involved in obesity. Obese persons are more responsive to external cues than normal-weight persons are; although, there are individuals at all weight levels who respond more to external than to internal stimuli. Self-control is an important cognitive factor in eating behavior. Time and place affect eating, as does the type of food available. Our early ancestors ate natural fruits to satisfy nutritional needs, but today we fill up on the empty calories in candy and soda. The dramatic increase in obesity in the late twentieth century underscores the significance of environmental factors in obesity as increasing numbers of people eat high-fat foods and lead sedentary lives.
- Dieting for weight loss and restrained eating for weight control are common in American society. Most diets don't work, although some people do lose weight when [...] important [...] am. Many [...] ven if they [...] hin can be [...] However,

---

Reach Your Learning Goals

Restates the chapter's learning goals and provides a bulleted review that matches up in a one-to-one fashion with the bulleted review statements in the *Review and Sharpen Your Thinking* sections. Use it as a guide to help you organize your study of the chapter, *not* as a substitute for reading and studying the chapter.

---

positive or negative, primary or mixed, polar opposites, and intensity. Both Plutchik's and Tompkins' lists of basic emotions reflect an evolutionary perspective. The two-dimensional approach to classifying emotions argues that there are just two broad dimensions of emotional experi-

ences: positive affectivity and negative affectivity. Positive emotions likely play an important role in well-being through adaptation, growth, social connection, and building personal and social resources.

Key Terms

motivation, p. 425
instinct, p. 425
drive, p. 425
need, p. 425
homeostasis, p. 426
Yerkes-Dodson law, p. 426
intrinsic motivation, p. 428
extrinsic motivation, p. 428
hierarchy of needs, p. 429

self-actualization, p. 429
basal metabolism rate (BMR), p. 433
set point, p. 433
anorexia nervosa, p. 436
bulimia nervosa, p. 437
estrogens, p. 437
androgens, p. 438

human sexual response pattern, p. 438
pheromones, p. 440
need for achievement, p. 447
attribution theory, p. 447
need for affiliation, p. 452
emotion, p. 455
polygraph, p. 456

James-Lange theory, p. 456
Cannon-Bard theory, p. 457
two-factor theory of emotion, p. 459
facial feedback hypothesis, p. 462
display rules, p. 464
catharsis, p. 467

Key Terms List

Includes all terms that are defined in the chapter and page references for their definitions, so that you can check your understanding and recall of essential vocabulary.

Apply Your Knowledge

1. Ask your friends to define the word *motivation*. Think about the way your friends define motivation and the way psychologists approach motivation. What are the similarities? What are the differences? Are your friends likelier to say they have too much motivation or not enough? Why might that be?

2. Do a web search for the word *hunger*. What kinds of sites are listed first? How do the topics that these sites cover compare with the discussion of hunger in the text? Do the sites give you any insight into the role of environment in hunger?

3. Imagine that someone offered you a pill that would double the size of your lateral hypothalamus but make your androgen levels go down to half their current level. How might this pill affect your eating and sexual behavior? Would you take the pill?

4. How much of our interpretation of emotions depends on verbal or nonverbal cues? Try the following exercise: Watch a movie that you're not familiar with and find a scene with a number of people in it. First watch the scene with the sound off and try to guess what emotions are being experienced by each person; describe the nonverbal cues that led you to your conclusions. Find a different scene, and listen to it without watching to guess what emotions are being experienced; describe the verbal cues that you used. Then, watch both scenes with the sound on. Were verbal or nonverbal cues more useful?

Connections  mhhe.com/ santrock7

For extra help in mastering the material in this chapter, see the review sections and practice quizzes in the Student Study Guide, the CD-ROM, and the Online Learning Center.

Apply Your Knowledge

Strengthen your grasp of key concepts and exercise your thinking skills with activities and web-based exercises.

Marginal Connections

Tell you where to find additional help in the form of review questions and activities in the Study Guide, *Making the Grade* CD, or the Online Learning Center for *Psychology,* 7e.

IMPORTANT:

HERE IS YOUR REGISTRATION CODE TO ACCESS
YOUR PREMIUM McGRAW-HILL ONLINE RESOURCES.

For key premium online resources you need THIS CODE to gain access. Once the code is entered, you will be able to use the Web resources for the length of your course.

If your course is using **WebCT** or **Blackboard**, you'll be able to use this code to access the McGraw-Hill content within your instructor's online course.

Access is provided if you have purchased a new book. If the registration code is missing from this book, the registration screen on our Website, and within your WebCT or Blackboard course, will tell you how to obtain your new code.

Registering for McGraw-Hill Online Resources

TO gain access to your McGraw-Hill web resources simply follow the steps below:

(1) USE YOUR WEB BROWSER TO GO TO:　**http://www.mhhe.com/santrockp7**

(2) CLICK ON **FIRST TIME USER**.

(3) ENTER THE REGISTRATION CODE* PRINTED ON THE TEAR-OFF BOOKMARK ON THE RIGHT.

(4) AFTER YOU HAVE ENTERED YOUR REGISTRATION CODE, CLICK **REGISTER**.

(5) FOLLOW THE INSTRUCTIONS TO SET-UP YOUR PERSONAL UserID AND PASSWORD.

(6) WRITE YOUR UserID AND PASSWORD DOWN FOR FUTURE REFERENCE.
KEEP IT IN A SAFE PLACE.

TO GAIN ACCESS to the McGraw-Hill content in your instructor's **WebCT** or **Blackboard** course simply log in to the course with the UserID and Password provided by your instructor. Enter the registration code exactly as it appears in the box to the right when prompted by the system. You will only need to use the code the first time you click on McGraw-Hill content.

Thank you, and welcome to your McGraw-Hill online Resources!

0-07-249412-3 SANTROCK: PSYCHOLOGY, 7E

Psychology

Psychology

SEVENTH EDITION

John W. Santrock

University of Texas at Dallas

Boston   Burr Ridge, IL   Dubuque, IA   Madison, WI   New York   San Francisco   St. Louis
Bangkok   Bogotá   Caracas   Kuala Lumpur   Lisbon   London   Madrid   Mexico City
Milan   Montreal   New Delhi   Santiago   Seoul   Singapore   Sydney   Taipei   Toronto

McGraw-Hill Higher Education 🌀
A Division of The **McGraw-Hill** Companies

This book is printed on recycled, acid-free paper containing 10% postconsumer waste.

1 2 3 4 5 6 7 8 9 0 VNH/VNH 0 9 8 7 6 5 4 3 2

ISBN 0-07-249412-3

Editor-in-Chief: *Thalia Dorwick*
Publisher: *Steve Rutter*
Senior sponsoring editor: *Melissa Mashburn*
Senior developmental editors: *Judith Kromm and Rebecca Smith*
Senior marketing manager: *Chris Hall*
Managing editor, production: *Melissa Williams*
Senior production supervisor: *Pam Augspurger*
Design manager: *Jean Mailander*
Illustrators: *John & Judy Waller and EPS, Inc.*
Art manager: *Robin Mouat*
Compositor: *The GTS Companies*
Typeface: *9.5/12 Meridien*
Printer: *Von Hoffmann Press*

Cover Image: © *Moonrunner Design*

The credits section for this book is on pages C-1–C-4 which constitutes an extension of the copyright page.

Library of Congress Cataloging-in-Publication Data

Santrock, John W.
    Psychology / John W. Santrock.-7th ed.
        p. cm.
        Includes bibliographical references and indexes.
        ISBN 0-07-249412-3
        1. Psychology. I. Title.
    BF121.S265
        150—dc21   2002
                        2002074338

INTERNATIONAL EDITION ISBN 0-07-119886-5
Copyright © 2000. Exclusive rights by The McGraw-Hill Companies, Inc. for manufacture and export. This book cannot be re-exported from the country to which it is consigned by McGraw-Hill. The International Edition is not available in North America.

www.mhhe.com

Find Balance!

Balance scientific research with real-world applications.

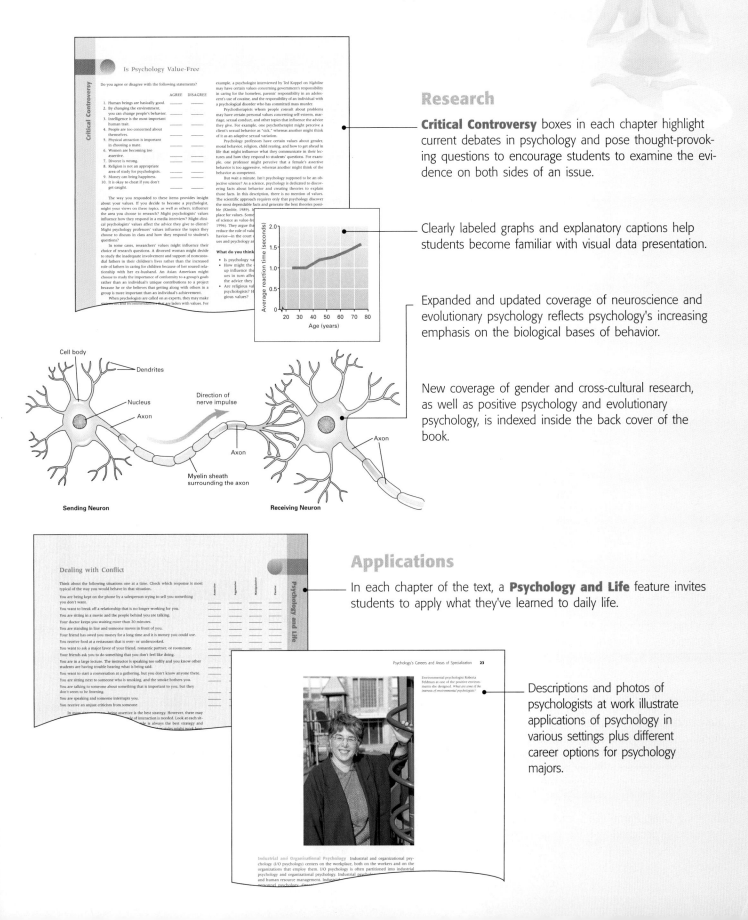

Research

Critical Controversy boxes in each chapter highlight current debates in psychology and pose thought-provoking questions to encourage students to examine the evidence on both sides of an issue.

Clearly labeled graphs and explanatory captions help students become familiar with visual data presentation.

Expanded and updated coverage of neuroscience and evolutionary psychology reflects psychology's increasing emphasis on the biological bases of behavior.

New coverage of gender and cross-cultural research, as well as positive psychology and evolutionary psychology, is indexed inside the back cover of the book.

Applications

In each chapter of the text, a **Psychology and Life** feature invites students to apply what they've learned to daily life.

Descriptions and photos of psychologists at work illustrate applications of psychology in various settings plus different career options for psychology majors.

Stay Focused and Learn!

Students need help finding the key ideas in introductory psychology. Santrock's unique **learning system** keeps students **focused** on these ideas so they learn and remember fundamental psychological concepts.

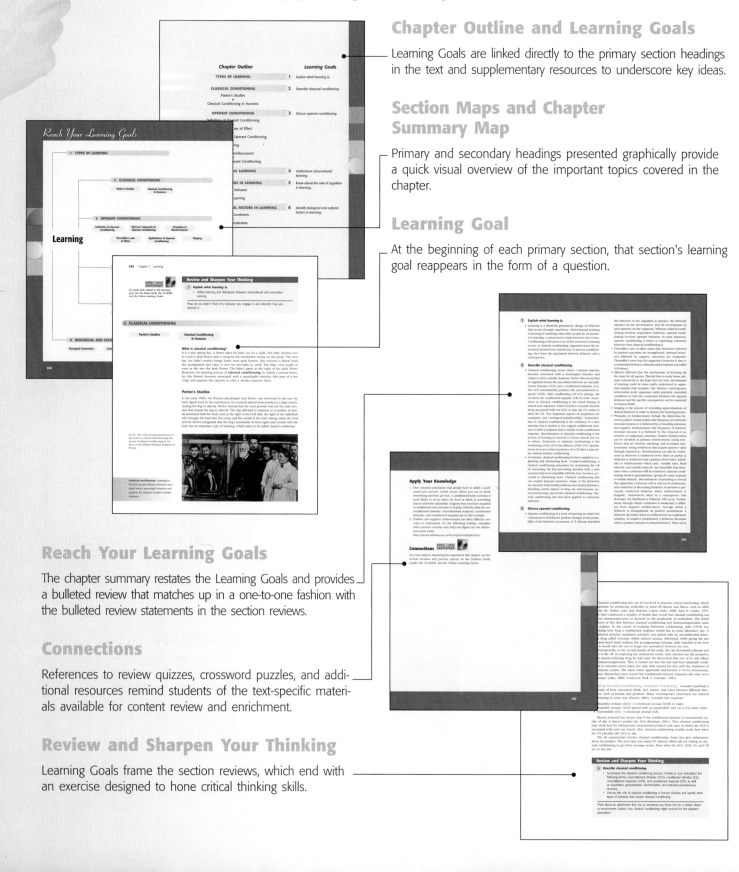

Chapter Outline and Learning Goals

Learning Goals are linked directly to the primary section headings in the text and supplementary resources to underscore key ideas.

Section Maps and Chapter Summary Map

Primary and secondary headings presented graphically provide a quick visual overview of the important topics covered in the chapter.

Learning Goal

At the beginning of each primary section, that section's learning goal reappears in the form of a question.

Reach Your Learning Goals

The chapter summary restates the Learning Goals and provides a bulleted review that matches up in a one-to-one fashion with the bulleted review statements in the section reviews.

Connections

References to review quizzes, crossword puzzles, and additional resources remind students of the text-specific materials available for content review and enrichment.

Review and Sharpen Your Thinking

Learning Goals frame the section reviews, which end with an exercise designed to hone critical thinking skills.

Make Connections and Succeed!

Supplementary print and media resources include a variety of review and assessment tools that carry through the text's emphasis on key ideas, reinforcing learning and enhancing student **success.**

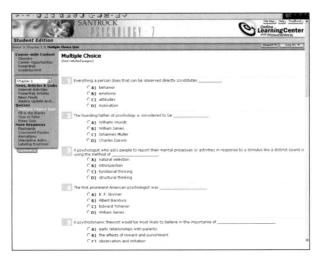

Online Learning Center

www.mhhe.com/Santrockp7

Student Resources Chapter outlines and practice quizzes are keyed to the text Learning Goals. The student section of the website also contains flashcards, interactive review exercises, and access, via **PowerWeb,** to current news about psychology, research tools, and many other valuable study tools.

Instructor Resources Teaching resources on this password-protected site include the Instructor's Course Planner, Image Bank, PowerPoint files, and Web links to additional resources.

Student Study Guide

A guided review of the chapter is organized by text section and Learning Goals, as are the three practice tests provided for each chapter. As in the text, **Connections** direct students to other text-correlated resources for additional help in mastering key ideas and concepts.

Instructor's Course Planner

The same Learning Goals that reinforce the key ideas in the text and Study Guide frame the teaching suggestions in this valuable manual. Chapter overviews, lecture/discussion suggestions, and goal reinforcement activities are a few of the resources provided in the Instructor's Course Planner.

Student CD-ROM

Free CD-ROM gives students more practice review tests and a learning style assessment in an easy-to-use format.

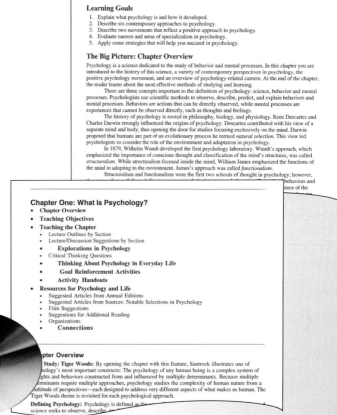

With special appreciation to my wife, Mary Jo

About the Author

JOHN W. SANTROCK received his Ph.D. from the University of Minnesota in 1973. He taught at the University of Charleston and the University of Georgia before joining the psychology department at the University of Texas at Dallas. He was recently a member of the editorial board of *Developmental Psychology*. His research on father custody is widely cited and used in expert witness testimony to promote flexibility and alternative considerations in custody disputes. John has also authored these exceptional McGraw-Hill texts: *Child Development*, Ninth Edition, *Life-Span Development*, Eighth Edition, *Children*, Seventh Edition, *Adolescence*, Ninth Edition, and *Educational Psychology*.

Brief Contents

Contents

CHAPTER 12   Personality 474

CHAPTER 13   Psychological Disorders 516

CHAPTER 14   Therapies 560

CHAPTER 15   Stress, Coping, and Health 600

CHAPTER 16   Social Psychology 644

Preface

Since I started teaching psychology in 1967, my motivation and love for introducing students to this relevant science have not wavered. This commitment to relevance and to science not only has been a foundation of my teaching, but it is also the heart of this book. In this edition, I've kept the theme of psychology as a relevant science and, in line with current trends in the discipline, increased the emphasis on the biological aspects of psychology and on the positive changes psychology can help us achieve in our lives. These themes, together with a stronger focus on the key ideas in psychology, are the main features of this revision of **Psychology.**

Psychology: The Relevant Science

Many students come into the introductory psychology class asking why they should study psychology when their major is physics or computer science or French. To a psychologist the answer is obvious: It will help you to understand yourself and others better. Psychology is relevant to almost every aspect of daily life. What psychologists have learned from memory research, for example, can be used to study more effectively, no matter what the subject is. Principles of learning can be applied to change undesirable behavior in children. Knowledge of sensation and perception can be used to more effectively design computers. Research on stress, coping, and health can help people to live fuller, happier lives.

Writing the preface for the seventh edition of *Psychology*, I am convinced that the science of psychology is more relevant today than ever. After September 11, 2001, psychologists and psychiatrists were called on to counsel not only people whose lives were directly affected by the attacks on the World Trade Center and the Pentagon, but also students, teachers, parents, and others who were struggling to understand, as we were, what could trigger such hostility and violence toward Americans. Psychology teaches us about the roots of aggression and the influence of groups on individual behavior. It also suggests strategies for handling stress, whatever the source. Nothing is more relevant to contemporary life.

In addition to relevance, this edition continues to stress the scientific nature of the discipline. A hallmark of the book has always been its focus on research, the foundation of all sciences. Here the latest research findings are discussed, along with the classic studies that established psychology as an objective science. More than 600 citations come from sources published since January 2000, including many from 2002. Also, numerous new graphs show students how scientific data can be presented visually.

Neuroscience and Biological Influences on Behavior

The growing emphasis on neuroscience and genetics as the means to understand the effects of biology on behavior is also reflected in this edition. Evolutionary psychology, another area of increasing interest, receives increased attention as well. Knowing that students often have difficulty understanding why it is important to learn biology in a course on psychology, I've taken particular care to present these topics in a psychological context and to underscore the complex relationship between biology, environment, and behavior wherever appropriate. Neuroscientist Lawrence Cauller provided outstanding guidance for incorporating stronger biological neuroscience content in this edition.

Positive Psychology

Currently, there is a movement in psychology to focus attention on the positive contributions psychology can make to everyday life. Proponents of positive psychology, notably Mihaly Csikszentmihalyi, share the belief that for much of the twentieth century the discipline concentrated on the negative aspects of life and that it's time to emphasize the positive side of psychology. Positive psychology offers all of us the opportunity to take control of our lives and find balance. For this edition, I have revised many of the chapter-opening vignettes and examples in the text to highlight positive outcomes and, with Csikszentmihalyi's expert guidance, incorporated material on positive psychology throughout the book.

Focus on Key Ideas

The most significant instructional challenge facing introductory psychology teachers today is ensuring that students master the core content of the course. For students overwhelmed by information from lectures, textbooks, the Internet, and other media, it is more difficult than ever to find the main ideas in their courses. To address these challenges and help students achieve the best possible outcome, I have developed a learning system for this edition that emphasizes basic concepts and ideas, encourages review, and promotes critical thinking. This system frames the presentation in the text *and* the supplements, providing a truly integrated package that reinforces learning and gives instructors the tools they need to assess students' grasp of core concepts and ideas.

The learning system has several components, all centered on three to six key ideas per chapter. These ideas are encapsulated in learning goals, which correspond with the chapter's main headings, as shown at the opening of each chapter. The learning goals reappear at several places in the chapter: as a question at the beginning of a new topic, in a guided review at the end of the section, and again in a summary at the end of the chapter. Content maps of the section and subsection headings accompany the learning goal question at the beginning of each major section. Together with a complete chapter map at the end of the chapter, the section maps provide a visual guide to the core concepts that support the learning goals.

To encourage students to apply what they've learned, and increase the likelihood that they will remember the material, the learning system includes critical thinking questions keyed to the learning goals in the "Review and Sharpen Your Thinking" sections. Additionally, "What Do You Think?" exercises accompany each of the new Critical Controversy boxes and at least three critical thinking exercises follow the review section at the end of each chapter in a section titled, "Apply Your Knowledge." For students who have access to the Web, the end-of-chapter exercises include at least one Web-based activity.

To help students make the best use of the student supplements, notes in the margins of the text remind students where to go to check their grasp of key concepts and ideas or to find practice quizzes, weekly news updates, and links to additional resources. Incorporating the learning goals and maps in the student supplements reinforces the lessons from the text and eliminates the confusion many students have about how to use the supplements to boost their performance in the course.

Changes in Coverage

Instructors who have used previous editions of this text will find much in the seventh edition that's different and much that hasn't changed. In addition to increased emphasis on neuroscience, genetics, evolutionary psychology, and positive psychology, the seventh edition contains increased coverage of diversity, controversies, and careers in psychology. This material is presented where appropriate throughout the book.

The table of contents and chapter sequence remain the same as in the sixth edition, except that human development now falls closer to the beginning of the book (Chapter 4). With this change, instructors can cover a topic of high student interest early in the course, while the principles of genetics (Chapter 3) are still fresh in students' minds, and later incorporate the material in their discussions of learning, cognition, and language.

Although the number of chapters and their topics are unchanged, the substance and presentation in each chapter have been revised thoroughly. Some of the detail that is less relevant today than it once was has been pruned to make room for cutting-edge research and some of the presentation was reconceptualized to focus on the key ideas reflected in the learning goals. Although there isn't enough space here to list all of the changes in this edition, here are the highlights:

CHAPTER 1 What Is Psychology?

- Expanded, updated coverage of the evolutionary psychology approach and a new section on positive approaches to psychology, including the humanistic movement and the positive psychology movement
- Expanded treatment of psychology's careers including descriptions of the work that different types of psychologists do
- New section added on how to get the most out of psychology focusing on study habits and skills

CHAPTER 2 Psychology's Scientific Methods

- New opening discussion of attitudes central to the scientific approach and on collaboration in science
- Introduction of James Pennebaker's research as an extended example of the scientific method and positive psychology
- Reorganized section on research methods focusing on descriptive, correlational, and experimental research and including new coverage of positive and negative correlations and their interpretation, and recent research on bias and the placebo effect
- New introduction to data analysis and interpretation with explanation of descriptive statistics and inferential statistics

CHAPTER 3 Biological Foundations of Behavior

- Reorganized chapter now starts with a discussion of the characteristics of the nervous system, focusing on complexity, integration, adaptability, and electrochemical transmission
- Revised presentation of neuron structure and function, including new material on drugs, neurotransmitters, and neural networks
- Updated coverage of functioning in the left and right hemispheres of the brain and many new drawings of the brain
- Separate section on the endocrine system
- Expanded and updated discussion of neurogenesis
- New section on genetics and evolution

CHAPTER 4 Human Development

- Nature and nurture section now includes a discussion of genotype and phenotype, as well as a subsection on optimal experiences
- Added coverage on the brain and how it changes from infancy to adulthood
- Revised discussion of socioemotional development in childhood includes the effects of divorce, positive parenting, ethnic and cultural differences, and gender development
- New sections on positive psychology and development in childhood, adolescence, and adulthood
- Expanded discussion of biological aspects of aging, including new figures on telomeres and aging, and updated information on Alzheimer's disease
- Updated coverage of cognitive changes and aging, including new figures on longitudinal changes in six intellectual abilities and on the relation of age to reaction time
- Discussion of John Gottman's work on what makes a successful marriage, and of Laura Carstensen's research on emotion, social networks, and aging, including new figures on aging and remembering emotional material

CHAPTER 5 Sensation and Perception

- Completely revised discussion of how we sense and perceive the world now includes transduction, bottom-up and top-down processing, new examples of signal detection theory, and selective attention
- New coverage on parallel processing in the visual cortex and on the process of binding in neural pathways and how it functions in visual perception
- Cochlear implants and sound localization added to discussion of the auditory system
- Discussion of parallel processing in touch
- Expanded coverage of pain including new discussion of the "fast" and "slow" pain pathways, plus pain control and treatment
- New section on human factors and perception, including recent research of Susan Lederman and Roberta Klatsky, and of Robert McCann at NASA

CHAPTER 6 States of Consciousness

- Neuroscience coverage incorporated in sections on consciousness, stages of sleep, and psychoactive drugs
- Greater coverage of circadian rhythms, including the suprachiasmatic nucleus
- New coverage of the role of sleep in the storage and maintenance of long-term memory
- Addition of recent research on sleep deprivation in adolescents and older adults
- New section on sleep and disease

- Inclusion of new research on dream content across cultures
- Expanded and updated material on the activation-synthesis theory of dreaming
- Most recent data on trends in adolescent drug use (Johnston, O'Malley, & Bachman, 2001)

CHAPTER 7 Learning

- Expanded and clarified discussion of classical conditioning, including new examples such as fear of the dentist and how it varies across cultures, a new section on the role of classical conditioning in health problems, and applications to consumer psychology
- Expanded, improved, easier-to-understand examples of positive and negative reinforcement
- Expanded and easier-to-understand examples in comparing punishment and negative reinforcement
- Expanded applications of operant conditioning, including the use of shaping and behavior modification in the classroom

CHAPTER 8 Memory

- Revised coverage of memory encoding includes the effects of divided attention
- New discussion of recent research on how verbal working memory can be impaired by negative emotion, and on how writing about negative emotional events can improve working memory
- Revised coverage of memory storage includes new sections on prospective memory and on connectionist networks and memory, plus a discussion of long-term potentiation
- Revised discussion of forgetting includes Ebbinghaus' Forgetting Curve, decay and transience, and a new section on motivated forgetting
- Complete reorganization of memory and study strategy section to correspond to organization of the section on memory

CHAPTER 9 Thinking and Language

- Expanded coverage of concepts, including new sections on the functions and structures of concepts
- New section on expertise, including four ways that experts solve problems differently than novices do
- Earlier discussion of the like between cognition and language
- Revised section on language acquisition and development includes material on the level of maternal speech to infants and its effects on vocabulary development in infants, a new figure on language milestones, a discussion of how young children find the boundaries between words, and recent research on how long it takes to become competent at a second language

CHAPTER 10 Intelligence

- Intelligence testing now cohesively discussed in opening section
- New section on neuroscience and intelligence with subsections on head and brain size, information-processing speed, electrical activity in the brain, and energy consumption in the brain
- Added sections on theories of multiple and emotional intelligence, including a comparison of Gardner's, Sternberg's, and Mayer/Salovy theories of intelligence
- New section on the influence of heredity and environment includes the research of Craig Ramey and colleagues, as well as gender and cultural comparisons

CHAPTER 11 Motivation and Emotion

- Section on motivation theory now includes the evolutionary approach to motivation, arousal and sensation seeking, expanded coverage of intrinsic and extrinsic motivation, and a discussion of the importance of self-generated goals
- Hunger section includes expanded and updated discussion of blood chemistry and the role of leptin in obesity, new material on neurotransmitters in the section on brain processes and hunger, new data on obesity in the U. S., and more coverage of anorexia nervosa and bulimia nervosa
- Social cognitive motivation section now includes a cross-cultural comparison of math achievement in the United States, Japan, and Taiwan, achievement applications in the workplace and in sports, and discussions of the motivation for affiliation and well-being
- Section on emotion includes a new discussion of the roles of neural circuits and neurotransmitters, including Joseph LeDoux's concept of direct and indirect pathways for fear in the brain, and of the links between emotion and the brain's hemispheres
- New focus on positive emotions, including Barbara Frederickson's research on how they might enhance people's well-being and David Buss's ideas on the evolved mechanisms that can produce a deep sense of happiness

CHAPTER 12 Personality

- Issues in the study of personality now at beginning of chapter
- Social cognitive theory section revised to include discussions of personal control, locus of control, and optimism
- New figure showing the link between self-efficacy and smoking cessation
- New discussion of changes in self-esteem across the life span, including new figure based on 2002 research study

- Section on personality assessment expanded to include discussion of the big five factors, locus of control, and the selection of employees

CHAPTER 13 Psychological Disorders

- The multiaxial system in *DSM-IV* covered in greater depth, including a new figure on the major categories of psychological disorders, organized according to Axis I and Axis II
- Introduction of concept of etiology, new discussion of the etiology of anxiety disorders, and expanded discussion of post-traumatic stress disorder
- Added material on the hidden observer concept applied to dissociative disorders
- Updated discussion of mood disorders, including new coverage on neurobiological abnormalities, new material on the depressive realism view of depression, and several new figures
- New section on suicide, including coverage of suicide rates across cultures
- Expanded discussion of schizophrenia, including recent information about heredity and schizophrenia as well as neurobiological factors and case studies

CHAPTER 14 Therapies

- Substantially reorganized chapter with biological therapies now covered in the first section
- Updated discussion and figures on the effects of drug therapies, including Prozac and Risperdal
- New sections on cognitive behavior therapy and using cognitive therapy to treat psychological disorders
- New section on sociocultural approaches and issues, including new coverage of the community mental health movement

CHAPTER 15 Stress, Coping, and Health

- Reorganization of stress discussion to focus on sources—including the workplace—and responses—including gender differences with a new section on stress and illness includes coverage of the link between positive emotions and health
- New section on coping strategies with new coverage of problem-focused and emotion-focused coping, optimism, and positive thinking, and the role of religion in helping people cope with stress
- Section on healthful living updated with new coverage of the role of the antidepressant Zyban in helping people quit smoking, as well as the effective rates of other approaches, such as nicotine patches

CHAPTER 16 Social Psychology

- Revised social influence section with expanded discussion of symptoms of groupthink and strategies for avoiding groupthink, as well as a discussion of leadership styles in women and men
- Expanded, updated discussion of prejudice focusing on the reasons people develop prejudice
- Updated section on social interaction, including discussion of neurotransmitters and aggression, recent information on children's TV viewing habits and possible links to aggression, and updated coverage of trends in altruism among U.S. college students
- In relationships section, addition of recent research on gender and relationships, new research on loneliness, stress, and health, and new discussion of loneliness and technology

Print and Media Supplements

For the Student

PowerWeb This unique online tool provides students with current articles, curriculum-based materials, weekly updates with assessment, informative and timely world news, Web links, research tools, study tools, and interactive exercises. A PowerWeb access card is packaged FREE with each new copy of the text.

Making the Grade Student CD-ROM Packaged FREE with the text, this user-friendly CD-ROM gives students an opportunity to test their comprehension of the course material in a manner that is comfortable and beneficial. The CD-ROM opens with a Learning Style/Study Skills questionnaire that students can use to identify the best way for them to study. Also included are practice tests that cover topics in the introductory psychology course, an Internet primer, and a statistics primer.

New! In-Psych Student CD-ROM *In-Psych* sets a new standard for introductory psychology multimedia. The CD-ROM is organized according to the text chapter outlines and features more than sixty interactive exercises chosen to illustrate especially difficult core introductory psychology concepts. Each exercise showcases one of three types of media assets: an audio clip, a video clip, or a simulation lab. *In-Psych* also includes a pre-test, follow-up assignments, Web resources, chapter quizzes, a student research guide, and an interactive timeline that puts events, key figures, and psychology research in historical perspective. (Available in December 2002)

Student Study Guide Designed to reinforce the key ideas in the text, the student study guide contains the following features for each chapter of the text: chapter overview, learning objectives, guided review (for each section), three practice tests, essay questions, crossword puzzle, learning goal checklist, and diagram labeling exercises.

Psych On-Line This supplement is designed to help students get the most out of the Internet for psychology research and provides general resource locations. Psychology sites are grouped by topic with a brief explanation of each site. Included in this booklet are a number of general resource sites for students seeking help.

Online Learning Center for Students The official website for the text contains chapter outlines, practice quizzes that can be emailed to the professor, key term flashcards, interactive exercises, internet activities, Web links to relevant psychology sites, drag-and-drop labeling exercises, Internet primer, career appendix, and a statistics primer. www.mhhe.com/Santrockp7

For the Instructor

Instructor's Manual This manual provides many useful tools to enhance your teaching. In each chapter you will find teaching objectives, chapter overviews, key terms, Teaching the Chapter, lecture/discussion suggestions, goal reinforcement classroom activities, Experiencing Psychology boxed feature, critical thinking questions, video/media suggestions, and references and sources of bibliographical information.

Test Item Files Two Test Item Files provide instructors with the widest variety of questions to last the life of this edition. The questions in the Test Item Files are also available on *Brownstone*, a powerful but accessible test-generating program that McGraw-Hill offers on a hybrid CD-ROM. With *Brownstone*, instructors can easily select questions and print tests and answer keys. Instructors can also customize questions, headings, and instructions; add or import their own questions; and print tests in a choice of printer-supported fonts.

In-Class Activities Manual By Patricia A. Jarvis, Cynthia R. Nordstrom, and Karen B. Williams, Illinois State University. Geared to instructors of large introductory psychology courses, this activities manual covers every major topic in the course. Nineteen chapters include fifty-eight separate activities, all of which have been used successfully in the authors' classes. Each activity includes a short description of the demonstration, the approximate time needed to complete the activity, the materials needed, step-by-step procedures, practical tips, and suggested readings related to the activity. The manual also includes teaching tips for the novice and experienced instructor on how to prepare an effective syllabus, what to consider when structuring a large section, how to select and manage a teaching assistant, and other key topics.

PowerPoint Lectures Available on the Internet, these presentations cover the key points of the chapter and include charts and graphs from the text. Helpful lecture guidelines are provided in the Notes section for each slide. These presentations can be used as they are, or can be modified to meet your needs.

Overhead Transparencies More than seventy key images from the text are available to the instructor upon adoption. A separate package, *Introductory Psychology Transparency Set*, provides more than one hundred additional images illustrating key concepts in general psychology.

Online Learning Center for Instructors The password-protected instructor side of the text website contains the Instructor's Manual, a sample chapter from the text, PowerPoint Presentations, Web links, and other teaching resources. www.mhhe.com/Santrockp7

PageOut™ Build your own course website in less than an hour. You don't have to be a computer whiz to create a website. Especially with an exclusive McGraw-Hill product called PageOut. It requires no prior knowledge of HTML, no long hours of coding, and no design skills on your part. With Page-Out even the most inexperienced computer user can quickly and easily create a professional-looking course website. Simply fill in templates with your information and with content provided by McGraw-Hill, choose a design, and you've got a website specifically designed for your course. Best of all, it's FREE! Visit us at www.pageout.net to find out more.

Instructor's Resource CD-ROM This comprehensive CD-ROM includes the contents of the Instructor's Manual, Test Item Files, an image gallery, and PowerPoint slides. The Presentation Manager provides an easy-to-use interface for the design and delivery of multimedia classroom presentations.

Acknowledgments

Many people guided this revision of *Psychology*. The McGraw-Hill team of Steve DeBow, President, Thalia Dorwick, Editor in Chief, Steve Rutter, Publisher, Melissa Mashburn, Senior Editor, and Chris Hall, Senior Marketing Manager, all played key roles and spent long hours in the planning and publication process for this edition. They provided me with an enormously talented trio of developmental editors who have made the seventh edition a much better book. Judith Kromm, Rebecca Smith, and Sylvia Shepard should feel that this is their book as much as it is my book. Their recommendations and revisions are deeply appreciated.

In-Depth Reviewers of the Seventh Edition

I benefited considerably from the advice and analysis provided by a number of in-depth reviewers of the book's 7th edition. The following individuals provided this input:

Mihaly Csikszentmihalyi, Claremont Graduate University (positive psychology)
Larry Cauller, University of Texas at Dallas (neuroscience)
Susan Swithers, Purdue University (Chapters 3 and 5 and author of end-of-chapter exercises)
John Mitterer, Brock University (author of many of the Critical Controversy boxes)
Meredith Stanford-Pollack, University of Massachusetts at Lowell (diversity)
Saera Khan, Western Washington University (illustrations)

Reviewers of the Seventh Edition

The following psychologists also helped to make the seventh edition a much better text through their thoughtful reviews:

Richard Anderson, Bowling Green State University
Jim Backlund, Kirtland Community College
Stella B. Baldwin, Wake Technical Community College
Pearl Berman, Indiana University of Pennsylvania
Joy L. Berrenberg, University of Colorado at Denver
Frederick M. Brown, Penn State University
Richard Cavasina, California University of Pennsylvania
George A. Cicala, University of Delaware
Pamela Costa, Tacoma Commmunity College
Donna Dahlgren, Indiana University Southeast
Leta Fenell, Chesapeake College
Roseanne L. Flores, Hunter College
Bety Jane Fratzke, Indiana Wesleyan University
Robert Gallen, Indiana University of Pennsylvania
J. P. Garofalo, University of Pittsburgh
Michael Kaye Garza, Brookhaven College
Roderick C. Gillis, University of Miami
Leslie Grout, Hudson Valley Community College
Arthur Gutman, Florida Institute of Technology
Christine Harness, University of Wisconsin, Milwaukee
James R. Heard, Antelope Valley College
Paul Hernandez, South Texas Community College
Karen Jordan, University of Illinois at Chicago
Kevin Keating, Broward Community College
Saera Khan, Western Washington University
Brian Kim, University of Maryland, College Park
Michele K. Lewis, Northern Virginia Community College, Annandale
Wanda McCarthy, Northern Kentucky University
Diane Martichuski, University of Colorado at Boulder
Glenn E. Meyer, Trinity University
Fred Miller, Oregon Health Sciences University, Portland Community College
Richard Miller, Western Kentucky University
Ann Miner, Indiana University of Pennsylvania
Arthur G. Olguin, Santa Barbara City College
Barbara Radigan, Community College of Allegheny County, Allegheny Campus
Pamela Regan, California State University, Los Angeles

Bob Riesenberg, Whatcom Community College
Susan J. Shapiro, Indiana University East
John E. Sparrow, University of New Hampshire,
    Manchester
Meredith Stanford-Pollock, University of
    Massachusetts at Lowell
Susan Swithers, Purdue University
Jeremy Turner, The University of Tennessee at Martin
David Wasieleski, Valdosta State University
Marek Wosinski, Arizona State University

Reviewers of Previous Editions

The following psychologists shared their comments and ideas or contributed content for previous editions of *Psychology*: Valerie Ahl, University of Wisconsin-Madison; Susan Amato, Boise State University; Jim Backlund, Kirtland Community College; James Bartlett, University of Texas-Dallas; Jackson Beatty, UCLA; Ludy Benjamin, Texas A&M; John Best, Eastern Illinois University; Michelle Boyer-Pennington, Middle Tennessee State University; Charles Brewer, Clemson University; Richard Brislin, University of Hawaii; David Buss, University of Texas, Austin; James Calhoun, University of Georgia; Lillian Comas-Diaz, Transcultural Mental Health Institute; Mihaly Csikszentmihalyi, Claremont Graduate University; Florence Denmark, Pace University; Ellen Dennehy, University of Texas, Dallas; Kim Dielmann, University of Central Arkansas; G. William Domhoff, University of California, Santa Cruz; James Francis, San Jacinto College; Stanley Gaines, Pomona College; Robert Gifford, University of Victoria; James Greer, Louisiana State University; Jean Berko Gleason, Boston University; Richard Halgin, University of Massachusetts, Amherst; John Harvey; University of Iowa; N.C. Higgins, University of North British Columbia; James J. Johnson, Illinois State University; James Jones, University of Delaware; Seth Kalichman, Georgia State University; Laura King, Southern Methodist University; Paul R. Kleinginna, Georgia Southern University; Linda Kline, California State University, Chico; Karen Kopera-Frye, The University of Akron; Phil Kraemer, University of Kentucky; Eric Landrum, Boise State University; Gary D. Laver, California Polytechnic State University, San Luis Obispo; Marta Losonczy, Salisbury State University; Karen E. Luh, University of Wisconsin, Madison; Jerry Marshall, University of Central Florida; Vicki Mays, University of California, Los Angeles; David Mostofsky, Boston University; Carol Nemeroff, Arizona State University; David Neufeldt, Hutchinson Community College; Illene Noppe, University of Wisconsin, Green Bay; Cindy Nordstrom, Illinois State University; Alice O'Toole, University of Texas, Dallas; Raymond Paloutzian, Westmont College; David Penn, Louisiana State University; James Pennebaker, University of Texas, Austin; Jeffrey Pedroza, Lansing Community College; Lawrence A. Pervin, Rutgers University; Michelle Perry, University of Illinois at Urbana, Champaign; Vincent Punzo, Earlham College; Ed Raymaker, Eastern Main Technical College; Daniel Schacter, Harvard University; Judith A. Sheiman, Kutztown University; Paula Shear, University of Cincinnati; Cynthia Sifonis, University of Illinois; Charles M. Slem, California Polytechnic State University, San Luis Obispo; Steven Smith, Texas A&M; Keith E. Stanovich, University of Toronto; Barry Stein, Tennessee Technological University; Jutta M. Street, Wake Technical Community College; Roger M. Tarpy, Jr., Bucknell University; Christopher Taylor, University of Arizona; Leonard Williams, Rowan University; Michael Zickar, Bowling Green State University.

1

What Is Psychology?

The chapter themes and corresponding learning goals listed here preview the most important ideas in the chapter. The chapter themes are the primary section titles. The learning goals will help you to review each of the main ideas and, at the end of the chapter, they will help you to make sure you know the key points in each section. The maps at the beginning of each primary section provide a visual guide to the section themes. Use the complete chapter map at the end of the chapter as a visual guide to help you recall the material covered in the chapter.

Chapter Outline

EXPLORING PSYCHOLOGY

Studying the Mind and Behavior
▼
A Quest for Answers to Ancient Questions
▼
Early Scientific Approaches to Psychology

CONTEMPORARY APPROACHES TO PSYCHOLOGY

The Behavioral Approach
▼
The Psychodynamic Approach
▼
The Cognitive Approach
▼
The Behavioral Neuroscience Approach
▼
The Evolutionary Psychology Approach
▼
The Sociocultural Approach

A POSITIVE APPROACH TO PSYCHOLOGY

The Humanistic Movement
▼
The Positive Psychology Movement

PSYCHOLOGY'S CAREERS AND AREAS OF SPECIALIZATION

Careers in Psychology
▼
Areas of Specialization in Psychology

HOW TO GET THE MOST OUT OF PSYCHOLOGY

Good Study Habits
▼
Thinking Critically
▼
The Book's Learning Tools

Learning Goals

1 Explain what psychology is and how it developed.

2 Describe six contemporary approaches to psychology.

3 Describe two movements that reflect a positive approach to psychology.

4 Evaluate careers and areas of specialization in psychology.

5 Apply some strategies that will help you succeed in psychology.

Who could have predicted the startling success of golfer Eldrick—better known as Tiger—Woods? In 2000, at the age of 24, Woods became the youngest person ever to win golf's four major championships: the Master's, the U.S. Open, the PGA, and the British Open.

At the age of 6 months, Tiger Woods sat in his high chair watching his father hit golf balls into a net in the garage. At 18 months of age, he played his first hole of golf (410 yards, par four) and finished in 11 shots (8 to reach the green)! When Tiger was 2 years old, a sports announcer predicted, "This young boy is going to be to golf what Jimmy Connors and Chris Evert are to Tennis" (Strege, 1997).

Tiger's triumphs raise an interesting question for psychologists: What factors enable some children to achieve greatness? Is it possible for parents, coaches, and others to shape a child's life and turn him or her into a champion? Did Tiger's parents play an important role in his development as a great golfer? The only child of doting parents, Tiger was coached and encouraged to excel. He won his first major tournament at the age of 8.

Some parents, though, try to get their children to become champions in a particular sport, using similar strategies to those of Tiger's parents, and the children end up being miserable and the parents frustrated. What other factors could be involved in Tiger's success as a golf champion beyond supportive parenting and excellent coaching? Might Tiger have a special mix of genes and athletic skills that most others don't have?

In this chapter, we explore these questions, first by surveying the roots of psychological science and the development of different approaches to the study of human behavior. Second, we explore a variety of career opportunities available to individuals with degrees in psychology. And, third, to help you get the most out of this book and to understand psychology more clearly, we discuss some study strategies and ways to think critically, both in class and in everyday life.

Tiger Woods, one of the world's leading golfers. *What do you think might have motivated Tiger to become a great golfer?*

1 EXPLORING PSYCHOLOGY

| **Studying the Mind and Behavior** | **A Quest for Answers to Ancient Questions** | **Early Scientific Approaches to Psychology** |

What is psychology and how did it develop?

What motivates people such as Tiger Woods to become the best in the world at what they do is one of the many questions that psychologists study. What else do psychologists do?

Imagine that you are seated at a dinner table next to someone you have never met. What comes to mind when you find out she is a psychologist? Many people would say that she analyzes people's problems. When my wife is asked what her husband does for a living, she says that he is a psychologist. She commonly hears another question, "Does he psychoanalyze you all of the time?" When people find out I am a psychologist, I can see by their reaction that they are thinking, "Uh, oh, I'd better be on my guard or he will find out what I am really like."

Many psychologists do analyze people's problems and try to help them cope more effectively. However, many psychologists are researchers, not therapists. No single image captures psychologists' varied activities. Consider the following descriptions of some contemporary psychologists at work:

- A research psychologist trained in cognitive psychology painstakingly constructs the thousands of steps in a computer program that, presented with hundreds of sentences, will learn language as an infant does.
- Another research psychologist trained in physiological psychology and neuroscience injects epinephrine into a rat that has learned a maze to determine how the hormone affects the rat's memory.
- A clinical psychologist probes a depressed client's thoughts for clues about the cause of the depression and thinks about ways to help the client become psychologically healthier.
- A psychologist interested in gender and women's issues teaches at a community college and works with her college and the community to eliminate sexual harassment.
- An organizational psychologist has a consulting firm that advises corporations on ways to improve communication and work productivity.
- A researcher works at Educational Testing Service to ferret out possible cultural bias in psychological tests.
- A forensic psychologist is a trial consultant who prepares witnesses to testify and teaches attorneys how to present themselves to jurors.

These are but a few of the many different portraits of psychologists. As you read further, you will discover that psychology is a diverse field and that psychologists have wide-ranging interests.

Studying the Mind and Behavior

Psychology may strike you as being simple common sense, but researchers often turn up the unexpected in human behavior. For example, it may seem obvious that couples who live together (cohabit) before marriage have a better chance of making the marriage last. After all, practice makes perfect, doesn't it? But researchers have actually found a higher rate of success for couples who marry before living together (Nock, 1995). It also might seem obvious that we would experience more stress and be less happy if we had to function in many different roles than if we functioned in only one role. However, women who engage in multiple roles (such as wife, mother, and career woman) report more satisfaction with their lives than women who engage in a single role or fewer roles (such as wife or wife and mother)(Watkins & Subich, 1995). As you can see, psychology doesn't accept assumptions at face value, however reasonable they sound. Psychology is a rigorous discipline that tests assumptions (Pittenger, 2003).

Formally defined, **psychology** is the scientific study of behavior and mental processes. There are three key terms in this definition: science, behavior, and mental processes. To understand what psychology is, you need to know what each of these terms means.

psychology The scientific study of behavior and mental processes.

As a **science,** psychology uses systematic methods to observe, describe, predict, and explain behavior. Scientific methods are not casual. Researchers carefully and precisely plan and conduct their studies (Elms, Kantowitz, & Roediger, 2003). In psychology, it is desirable to obtain results that *describe* the behavior of many different people. For example, researchers might construct a questionnaire on sexual attitudes and give it to 500 individuals. They might spend considerable time devising the questions and determining the backgrounds of the people chosen to participate in the survey. The researchers may try to *predict* the sexual activity of college students based on their liberal or conservative attitudes or on their sexual knowledge, for example. After the psychologists have analyzed their data, they also will want to *explain* why any change in behavior occurred. They might ask, "Is the reason an increased fear of sexually transmitted diseases?" Because psychologists use the same research methods as physicists, biologists, and other scientists, psychology is a *scientific* discipline.

Let's now examine what behavior and mental processes are. **Behavior** is everything we do that can be directly observed—two people kissing, a baby crying, a college student riding a motorcycle.

Mental processes are trickier to define than behavior; they are the thoughts, feelings, and motives that each of us experiences privately but that cannot be observed directly. Though we cannot directly see thoughts and feelings, they are nonetheless real. They include *thinking* about kissing someone, a baby's *feelings* when its mother leaves the room, and a college student's *memory* of a motorcycle ride.

Controversy is also a part of science. As scientists conduct research and uncover new findings, they refine or even discard ideas. Healthy debate characterizes the field of psychology, and a new psychological perspective has sometimes arisen when one scientist questions the views of another. Such ongoing debate and controversy are signs of a vigorous, healthy discipline. In each chapter of this text, you will find a Critical Controversy box that focuses on a current debate in psychology.

A Quest for Answers to Ancient Questions

Psychology seeks to answer questions that people have been asking for thousands of years:

How do our senses perceive the world?
What is the connection between thinking and behavior?
How do we learn? What is memory?
Are we in conscious control of our lives, or is behavior determined by unconscious forces?
Why does one person grow and flourish, whereas another person struggles in life?
What makes some people smarter than others?
Do dreams matter?
Why do some children so strongly resemble their parents in how they think and act? How do some children turn out so differently?
Can people learn to be happier and more optimistic?

The questions are old, but the science is young. From the time human language included the word *why* and became rich enough to let people talk about the past, we have been creating myths to explain why things are the way they are. Ancient myths attributed most important events to the pleasure or displeasure of the gods: When a volcano erupted, the gods were angry; if two people fell in love, they had been hit by Cupid's arrows. Gradually, myths gave way to philosophy, the rational investigation of the underlying principles of being and knowledge. People attempted to explain events in terms of natural rather than supernatural causes (Viney & King, 2003).

Historians believe that the idea of an independent human mind may have developed around the sixth century B.C. In India, for example, the Buddha said that it was our own sensations and perceptions that combined to form our human thoughts. The

science In psychology, the use of systematic methods to observe, describe, predict, and explain behavior.

behavior Everything we do that can be directly observed.

mental processes The thoughts, feelings, and motives that each of us experiences privately but that cannot be observed directly.

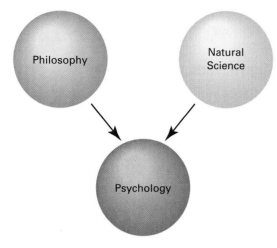

FIGURE 1.1 **Psychology's Beginnings**
Psychology's seeds were sown in the nineteenth century by merging ideas from philosophy and natural sciences such as biology and physiology. *Why did psychology emerge as a hybrid offspring from these areas?*

Chinese sage Confucius (551–479 B.C.) believed that the power of thought and decision lay within us (Hunt, 1993).

In the Western tradition, philosophy came of age in ancient Greece in the fourth and fifth centuries B.C. Socrates, Plato, Aristotle, and others debated the nature of thought and behavior, including the possible link between the mind and the body. Later philosophers, especially René Descartes, argued that the mind and body were completely separate and focused their attention on the mind. Psychology grew out of this tradition of thinking about the mind and body.

Philosophy was not the only discipline from which psychology emerged. Psychology also has roots in the natural sciences of biology and physiology (Benjamin, 1999). The intellectual atmosphere when psychology emerged as a science in the late nineteenth century was dominated by the work of the British naturalist Charles Darwin (1809–1882).

In 1859, Darwin published his ideas in *On the Origin of Species.* He proposed the principle of **natural selection,** an evolutionary process that favors organisms that are best adapted to reproduce and survive. He believed that organisms reproduce at rates that would cause enormous increases in the population of most species, yet noted that populations remain nearly constant. Darwin reasoned that an intense, constant struggle for food, water, and resources must occur among the young born in each generation, because many of the young do not survive. Those that do survive to adulthood pass their genes on to the next generation. Darwin concluded that organisms with biological features that led to more successful reproduction were better represented in subsequent generations. Over the course of many generations, organisms with these characteristics would constitute a larger percentage of the population. Eventually this process could modify a whole population. If environmental conditions changed, however, other characteristics might become favored by natural selection, moving the process in a different direction.

Psychology has recently rediscovered Darwin's evolutionary theory and applied it to behavior. There is an especially strong interest today in interpreting behavior in terms of its adaptive value to evolutionary development (Cosmides & others, 2003; Larsen & Buss, 2002).

Along with Darwin, nineteenth-century physiologists gave the new field of psychology a boost. The German physiologist Johannes Müller and others proposed that an important role of the brain is to associate incoming sensory information with appropriate motor responses.

Thus, by the late nineteenth century, conditions were ripe for psychology to emerge as a scientific discipline, a hybrid offspring of philosophy and natural science (see figure 1.1). Indeed, as we will see shortly, it was a philosopher-physician who

mhhe com/ *Philosophers in Ancient*
santrockp7 *Greece had some ideas that were very different from our own. See the Online Learning Center's Around the Globe feature for a brief discussion of Ancient Greek ideas of causation.*

natural selection The principle that the organisms that are best adapted to their environment are the most likely to survive, reproduce, and pass on their genes to their offspring.

WILHELM WUNDT (1832–1920)
Founded the first psychology laboratory
(with his co-workers) in 1879 at the
University of Leipzig in Germany.

WILLIAM JAMES (1842–1910)
What was his functionalist approach like?

structuralism An early school of psychology that attempted to discover basic elements (structures) of the human mind.

functionalism An early school of psychology that emphasized the interaction between the mind and the outside environment.

put the pieces of the philosophy–natural science puzzle together to create the academic discipline of psychology.

Early Scientific Approaches to Psychology

Psychology has always varied somewhat from country to country, depending on the interests of psychologists in each country and the priorities of their cultures. The German physiologist Wilhelm Wundt (1832–1920) is most often regarded as the founding father of modern psychology, but it was William James (1842–1910), perhaps more than any other person, who gave it an American stamp.

Some historians like to say that modern psychology was born in December, 1879 at the University of Leipzig, when Wundt and two young students performed an experiment to measure the time lag between the instant at which a person heard a sound and the instant at which that person actually pressed a telegraph key to signal that he had heard. The experiment was one of many attempts to measure human behavior through physiological measurement.

What was so special about this experiment? Wundt's experiment was about the workings of the brain: He was trying to measure the amount of time it took the human brain and nervous system to translate information into action. At the heart of this experiment was the idea that mental processes could be studied quantitatively —that is, that mental processes could be measured. This focus ushered in the new science of psychology.

Structuralism   The main research conducted by Wundt and his collaborators focused on trying to discover basic elements or "structures" of mental processes (Hergenhahn, 2001). For example, they described three different dimensions of *feeling:* pleasure/displeasure, tension/relaxation, and excitement/depression. A student of Wundt's, E. B. Titchener (1867–1927), gave Wundt's approach the label of **structuralism** because of its focus.

The most common method used in the study of mental structures was *introspection* (literally, "looking inside"). For this type of experiment, a person was placed in a laboratory setting and was asked to think (introspect) about what was going on mentally as various events took place. For example, the individual might be subjected to a sharp, repetitive clicking sound and asked to report whatever conscious feelings the clicking produced. What made this method scientific was the systematic, detailed self-reports required of the person in the controlled laboratory setting.

These studies focused mainly on sensation and perception because they were the easiest processes to break down into component parts. For example, Titchener used the introspective method to study taste. He trained participants to identify and record their taste sensations. The outcome was the identification of four components of taste: bitter, sweet, salty, and sour. In the long run, though, conscious introspection was not a very productive method of exploring the basic elements of human behavior.

Functionalism   In contrast to structuralism, which focused on describing the components of the mind, **functionalism** emphasized the functions of mind and behavior in adapting to the environment. The structuralists were not interested in the person's interaction with the environment, but this was a major theme of the functionalists. Thus, in a way, the structuralists were looking *inside* the mind, searching for its structures, whereas the functionalists were looking more at what was going on in the person's interaction with the *outside* world.

William James and other functionalists did not believe in the existence of elementary, rigid structures of the mind. James saw the mind as flexible and fluid, characterized by constant change and adaptation in response to a flow of information. He called this flow a *stream of consciousness.*

The following review should help you to reach the learning goals related to this initial exploration of the field of psychology.

Review and Sharpen Your Thinking

1 *Explain what psychology is and how it developed.*
- Define psychology, and explain the three terms contained in the definition.
- Describe the contributions of philosophy and natural science to psychology.
- Define structuralism and functionalism, and explain how they differ.

Are there some questions about your mind and behavior that a deeper understanding of psychology might help you answer?

mhhe.com/
santrockp7

For study tools related to this learning goal, see the Study Guide, the CD-ROM, and the Online Learning Center.

CONTEMPORARY APPROACHES TO PSYCHOLOGY 2

The Behavioral Approach   **The Cognitive Approach**   **The Evolutionary Psychology Approach**

The Psychodynamic Approach   **The Behavioral Neuroscience Approach**   **The Sociocultural Approach**

How do contemporary psychologists approach the study of behavior?

The two approaches we have just discussed—structuralism and functionalism—are no longer considered among psychology's main approaches. However, psychology has reframed some aspects of these approaches. Psychologists still have an interest in the structures of the brain and how they function. They also stress the importance of the person's interaction with the environment. Psychologists today realize that human thought and behavior are influenced by many factors, including common biological heritage, biological variations from person to person, and experience. In addition to immediate environmental influences, such as our physical and social surroundings, psychologists also recognize the broader influence of culture.

Efforts to understand the complexity of mental processes and behavior have given rise to a number of broad approaches in psychology. The following sections will introduce six contemporary approaches: behavioral, psychodynamic, cognitive, behavioral neuroscience, evolutionary psychology, and sociocultural. Knowing about these approaches is important because many of the debates and controversies in psychology reflect differences in researchers' perspectives. In addition, much of the research discussed later in the text can be understood more clearly against the background of one or more of these approaches.

As you consider the six approaches and how they might illuminate human thought and behavior, keep three ideas in mind:

1. Although psychology may often seem to focus on the individual, human beings *Social* are profoundly social. They need other people to satisfy their wants and needs. Parents, teachers, peers, friends, and partners in close relationships play important roles in our socially connected lives (Borstein & Bradley, 2003; Collins & others, 2000). How we treat others and they us, whether caring or hurting, stirs our thoughts and emotions.

2. Theories can help us to understand human behavior in general, but there is *Unique* still enormous individual variation. No two lives play out in the same way. Roommates, parents and children, teachers and students, friends and lovers soon discover their differences. One task of psychology is to chart not only our commonalities but also what makes us unique (Stanovich, 2001). Your mixture of genes and experiences cannot be duplicated. Even in these days of animal cloning and the

potential for human cloning, experience uniquely imprints each person's life (Gottlieb, 2002; Moore, 2001).

3. Keep in mind that one approach is not necessarily better than the other. Some approaches are more useful in some situations and at certain times in the development of the field. Individual psychologists may become invested in a particular approach, but all six approaches provide valid ways of looking at human behavior. Just as blueprints, floor plans, and photographs are all valid ways of looking at a house, some approaches are better for some purposes than others. For instance, a floor plan is more useful than a photograph for deciding how much lumber to buy. Similarly, the behavioral neuroscience approach is more useful than the sociocultural approach for explaining the fundamental aspects of perception. At the same time, the sociocultural approach is more useful than the behavioral neuroscience approach for understanding how to reduce prejudice and discrimination.

The Behavioral Approach

The **behavioral approach** emphasizes the scientific study of observable behavioral responses and their environmental determinants. In other words, the behavioral approach focuses on interactions with the environment that can be seen and measured. The principles of the behavioral approach also have been widely applied to help people change their behavior for the better. The psychologists who adopt this approach are called *behaviorists*. Under the intellectual leadership of John B. Watson (1878–1958) and B. F. Skinner (1904–1990), behaviorism dominated psychological research during the first half of the twentieth century.

Many studies with a behavioral approach take place in experimental laboratories under carefully controlled conditions. When behaviorism was in its infancy, virtually all behavioral studies were conducted in the laboratory, although today many take place outside the laboratory in natural settings, such as schools and homes.

Skinner emphasized that what we *do* is the ultimate test of who we are. He believed that rewards and punishments determine our behavior. For example, a child might behave in a well-mannered fashion because her parents have rewarded this behavior. An adult might work hard at a job because of the money he gets for his effort. We do these things, say behaviorists, not because of an inborn motivation to be competent people but rather because of the environmental conditions we have experienced and continue to experience (Skinner, 1938).

Contemporary behaviorists still emphasize the importance of observing behavior to understand an individual and continue to use the rigorous sorts of experimental methods advocated by Watson and Skinner (Martin & Pear, 2002; Watson & Tharp, 2003). They also continue to stress the importance of environmental determinants of behavior (Baldwin & Baldwin, 2001; Spiegler & Guerremont, 2003). However, not every behaviorist accepts the earlier behaviorists' rejection of thought processes (often called cognition).

Social cognitive theory, as proposed by Albert Bandura (1925–), stresses that behavior is determined not only by environmental conditions but also by how thoughts modify the effects of environment on behavior (Bandura, 1986, 2001). Bandura believes that imitation is one of the main ways in which we learn about our world. To reproduce a model's behavior, we must enter and store the information in memory, which is a mental (cognitive) process. Thus social cognitive theorists have broadened the scope of behaviorism to include not only observed behavior but also the ways in which the mind processes information about the environment.

In one of Bandura's (1965) experiments, children watched a film in which a model was rewarded, punished, or experienced no consequences for being aggressive. Bandura observed how aggressive the children were after they watched the film. He found that children who watched the model being rewarded for being aggressive were subsequently more aggressive themselves than were children who saw the model being punished or receiving no consequences for being aggressive.

behavioral approach Emphasizes the scientific study of behavior and asserts that behavior is shaped by the environment.

social cognitive theory Stresses that behavior is determined not only by environmental conditions but also by how thoughts modify the impact of environment on behavior.

What can the behavioral approach tell us about Tiger Woods? Behaviorists would tell us not to look inside Tiger to try to find out what makes him a great golfer. According to behaviorists, motives and feelings cannot be directly observed, so they won't help us understand his behavior. Behaviorists would examine Tiger's learning history. If Tiger was praised by his parents and golf instructor for his extensive practice and achievements, he might have worked even harder on his golf game. Social cognitive theorists such as Bandura would stress that Tiger developed his golf skills through extensive observational learning. They also would suggest that Tiger developed positive expectations and the self-confidence to become a great golfer through interactions with others.

The Psychodynamic Approach

The **psychodynamic approach** emphasizes unconscious thought, conflict between biological instincts and society's demands, and early family experiences. This approach argues that unlearned biological instincts, especially sexual and aggressive impulses, influence the way people think, feel, and behave. These instincts, buried deep within the unconscious mind, are often at odds with society's demands. Although Sigmund Freud (1856–1939), the founding father of the psychodynamic approach, saw much of psychological development as instinctual, he believed that early relationships with parents are the chief forces that shape an individual's personality. Freud's (1917) theory was the basis for the therapeutic technique that he termed *psychoanalysis*. His approach was controversial when he introduced it in Vienna at the beginning of the twentieth century. However, his ideas flourished, and many clinicians still find value in his insights about human behavior.

Unlike the behavioral approach, the psychodynamic approach focuses almost exclusively on clinical applications rather than on experimental research. For this reason, psychodynamic theories always have been controversial and difficult to validate. Nonetheless, they are an important part of psychology. Today's psychodynamic the-

psychodynamic approach Emphasizes the unconscious aspects of the mind, conflict between biological instincts and society's demands, and early family experiences.

SIGMUND FREUD (1856–1939)
What was the nature of his psychoanalytic approach?

ories tend to place less emphasis on sexual instincts and more on cultural experiences as determinants of behavior.

What can the psychodynamic approach tell us about Tiger Woods? The psychodynamic approach suggests that Tiger is likely to be unaware of why he became a great golfer and why he behaves the way he does. It also suggests that his early experiences with his parents likely formed his outgoing personality and ability to get along with others.

The Cognitive Approach

According to cognitive psychologists, your brain hosts or embodies a "mind," whose mental processes allow you to remember, make decisions, plan, set goals, and be creative (Anderson, 2000; Neisser, 2000; Sternberg, 2003). The **cognitive approach,** then, emphasizes the mental processes involved in knowing: how we direct our attention, how we perceive, how we remember, and how we think and solve problems. For example, cognitive psychologists want to know how we solve algebraic equations, why we remember some things for only a short time but remember others for a lifetime, and how we can use imagery to plan for the future.

Cognitive psychologists view the mind as an active and aware problem-solving system (Baddeley, 1998; Simon, 1996). This positive view contrasts with the behavioral view, which portrays behavior as controlled by external environmental forces. The cognitive view also contrasts with pessimistic views (such as those of Freud) that see human behavior as being controlled by instincts or other unconscious forces. In the cognitive view, an individual's mental processes are in control of behavior through memories, perceptions, images, and thinking (Leahy, 2001; Medin, Ross, & Markham, 2001).

One area of cognitive research that occasionally gets attention in news coverage of criminal trials is eyewitness identification. The potential bias in eyewitness identification was revealed in an experiment in which students in an introductory psychology class were asked to view 10 "criminals" (actually graduate and upperclass undergraduate White males) for 25 seconds each (Brown, Deffenbacher, & Sturgill, 1977). The experimenter told the class to observe the "criminals" carefully because they would have to pick out the "criminals" from mug shots later. Ninety minutes later the students looked at 15 mug shots and were asked whether each person had appeared earlier in front of the class. Five of the 15 mug shots were of people who actually had appeared. These five "criminals" were correctly identified 72 percent of the time. However, the ten "noncriminals" were incorrectly identified as having appeared in front of the class 45 percent of the time. This study indicates that people in mug shots might be falsely accused and reflects how inaccurate our memories sometimes can be.

What can the cognitive approach tell us about Tiger Woods? Cognitive psychologists would be impressed with Tiger's ability to process information, especially his ability to concentrate and focus his attention. They also would be interested in his ability to remember how to swing a golf club so accurately time after time. Cognitive psychologists might be intrigued by Tiger's ability to solve problems and make decisions, not only while playing in a golf tournament, but also in his daily life.

The Behavioral Neuroscience Approach

The **behavioral neuroscience approach** emphasizes that the brain and nervous system are central to understanding behavior, thought, and emotion. Neuroscientists believe that thoughts and emotions have a physical basis in the brain. Electrical impulses zoom throughout the brain's cells, releasing chemical substances that enable us to think, feel, and behave. Our remarkable human capabilities would not be possible without the brain and nervous system, which constitute the most complex, intricate, and elegant system imaginable.

cognitive approach Focuses on the mental processes involved in knowing: how we direct our attention, perceive, remember, think, and solve problems.

behavioral neuroscience approach Views understanding the brain and nervous system as central to understanding behavior, thought, and emotion.

Enormous strides have been made in understanding the brain and its role in psychological matters in recent years (Kolb & Whishaw, 2001; Zillmer & Spiers, 2001; Wilson, 2003). Much of what we know about the brain comes from research on animals that have simpler brains with far fewer nerve cells than humans (Changeux & Chavillion, 1995). Consider the memory of the sea slug, a tiny snail with only about 10,000 nerve cells. The sea slug is a slow creature, but if given an electric shock to its tail, it withdraws the tail quickly—and even more quickly if the tail was previously shocked. In a primitive way, the sea slug remembers. The memory is written in chemical code. Shocking the sea slug's tail releases a chemical that basically reminds the organism that the tail was previously shocked. This memory informs the nerve cells to send out chemical commands to retract the tail (Kandel & Schwartz, 1982). As nature builds complexity out of simplicity, so the mechanism used by the sea slug may work in the human brain as well. In humans, the memory might come from the sight of a close friend, a dog's bark, or the sound of a car horn. Chemicals called *neurotransmitters* are the ink with which memories are written.

What can the behavioral neuroscience approach tell us about Tiger Woods? Neuroscientists are intrigued by the neural circuitry that underlies virtually all behaviors. They would be interested in the brain processes that underlie Tiger's amazing athletic skills. They would attempt to explain how Tiger's brain coordinates so many things so quickly to allow him to strike a golf ball so smoothly and competently.

Neuroscientists have studied the memory of the sea slug, a tiny snail with only about 10,000 nerve cells. *How did they investigate the sea slug's memory?*

The Evolutionary Psychology Approach

Although Darwin introduced the theory of evolution by natural selection in the middle of the nineteenth century, his ideas about evolution only recently became a popular framework for explaining behavior. One of psychology's newest approaches, the **evolutionary psychology approach** emphasizes the importance of adaptation, reproduction, and "survival of the fittest" in explaining behavior. Evolution favors organisms that are best adapted to survive and reproduce in a particular environment. The evolutionary psychology approach focuses on the conditions that allow individuals to survive or fail. In this view, natural selection favors behaviors that

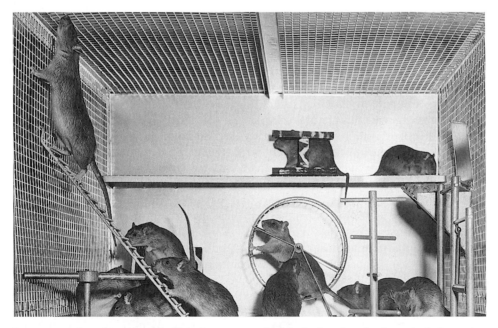

In one research study, an "enriched" environment rewired the brains of rats by dramatically increasing their neural connections and neurochemical activity (Rosenzweig, Bennett, & Diamond, 1972). In psychology and life, both biological and environmental processes matter. *Can you think of other ways scientists might study how "enriched" environments might influence behavior?*

evolutionary psychology approach
Emphasizes the importance of functional purpose and adaptation in explaining why behaviors are formed, are modified, and survive.

In Xinjiang, China, a woman prepares for horseback courtship. Her suitor must chase her, kiss her, and evade her riding crop—all on the gallop. A new marriage law took effect in China in 1981. The law sets a minimum age for marriage—22 years for males, 20 years for females. Late marriage and late childbirth are critical efforts in China's attempt to control population growth. *What do you think about such laws?*

The tapestry of American culture has changed dramatically in recent years. Nowhere is the change more noticeable than in the increasing ethnic diversity of America's citizens. Ethnic minority groups—African American, Latino, Native American, and Asian, for example—made up approximately one-third of individuals under the age of 17 in the United States in the year 2000. Two of psychology's challenges are to become more sensitive to race and ethnic origin and to provide improved services to ethnic minority individuals. *What might these communication strategies be like?*

increase the organism's reproductive success and ability to pass its genes to the next generation.

David Buss (1995, 2000) argues that, just as evolution shapes our physical features, such as body shape and height, it also pervasively influences how we make decisions, how aggressive we are, our fears, and our mating patterns. Thus it is argued that the way we adapt in our world today can be traced to problems animals and early humans faced in adapting to their evolutionary environments.

Steven Pinker (1999) also believes that evolutionary psychology is an important approach to understanding behavior. According to Pinker, the way the mind works can be summarized by three points: (1) the mind computes, (2) the mind was designed to compute by evolution, and (3) these computations are performed by specialized brain systems that natural selection has designed to achieve specific kinds of goals, such as survival. Thus, in Pinker's view, the mind analyzes sensory input in ways that would have benefited prehistoric human hunters and gatherers. People with minds that understood causes and effects, who could build tools, set traps, and avoid poisonous mushrooms, had the best chance of surviving and having offspring that would someday invent mathematics and make movies about robots.

Evolutionary psychologists believe that their approach provides an umbrella that unifies the diverse fields of psychology. Not all psychologists agree. Some argue that it is unlikely that one approach can unify the diverse, complex field of psychology (Graziano, 1995). Others stress that the evolutionary approach does not adequately account for cultural diversity (Paludi, 2002). But the evolutionary psychology approach is young, and its future may be fruitful (Cosmides & others, 2003).

What can the evolutionary psychology approach tell us about Tiger Woods? The evolutionary approach would stress that Tiger's golfing abilities are the result of a long evolutionary process in which genes involving excellent hand-eye motor coordination survived and were passed down from generation to generation. This approach also would call attention to the adaptive behavior that allows Tiger to function competently in his world.

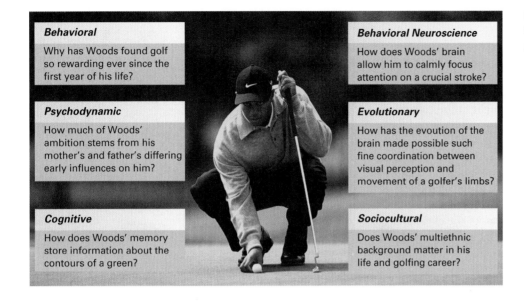

FIGURE 1.2 **Questions About Tiger Woods Derived from Six Psychological Approaches**

Behavioral
Why has Woods found golf so rewarding ever since the first year of his life?

Behavioral Neuroscience
How does Woods' brain allow him to calmly focus attention on a crucial stroke?

Psychodynamic
How much of Woods' ambition stems from his mother's and father's differing early influences on him?

Evolutionary
How has the evoution of the brain made possible such fine coordination between visual perception and movement of a golfer's limbs?

Cognitive
How does Woods' memory store information about the contours of a green?

Sociocultural
Does Woods' multiethnic background matter in his life and golfing career?

The Sociocultural Approach

The **sociocultural approach** examines the ways in which the social and cultural environments influence behavior. The sociocultural approach argues that a full understanding of a person's behavior requires knowing about the cultural context in which the behavior occurs. For instance, in some cultures, such as in the United States, it may be entirely acceptable for a woman to be assertive, but, in another culture, such as in Iran, the same behavior may be considered inappropriate.

An example of the sociocultural approach is the research of Harold Stevenson and his colleagues (1990; Stevenson, 1995), who compared the math achievement of U.S. children with that of their counterparts in China, Taiwan, and Japan. In these studies, the Asian students consistently outperformed U.S. students. And the longer they were in school, the wider the gap was between Asian and American students' math achievement. Stevenson believes that U.S. parents and schools should raise expectations to improve their students' performance.

The sociocultural approach focuses not only on comparisons of behavior across countries but also on the behavior of people from different ethnic and cultural groups within a country (Matsumoto, 2001). Thus there is increasing interest in the behavior of African Americans, Latinos, and Asian Americans, especially in terms of the factors that have restricted or enhanced their ability to adapt and cope with living in a predominantly White society (Banks, 2002, 2003).

What can the sociocultural approach tell us about Tiger Woods? The sociocultural approach would be especially interested in Tiger's multiethnic background and how this might have hindered or helped the development of his skills and behavior. In an interview with Oprah Winfrey, Woods said that he made up the term *Cablinasian* when he was a young boy, so that he could respond to frequent inquiries about his ethnicity. He chose this unusual term because he did not want to ignore any aspect of his heritage (his mother's ethnic heritage is Thai and Chinese; his father's is Native American, African American, and White Anglo-American). The sociocultural approach also would be interested in the achievement context of the American culture and how this influenced his motivation.

Figure 1.2 can help you to remember how psychologists with a sociocultural approach would think about Tiger Woods as a golf phenomenon. For comparison, the figure also includes questions that psychologists who adopt a different approach might pose about Woods.

The sociocultural approach can provide insights into behavior that other approaches do not adequately explain, such as altruism. See the Critical Controversy box for a discussion of this topic.

sociocultural approach Emphasizes social and cultural influences on behavior

Can Humans Really Be Altruistic?

If there was a silver lining in the dark cloud of September 11, 2001, it was that firefighters, police officers, emergency medical personnel, and many ordinary individuals altruistically risked their own lives to help other people caught in the collapse of the twin towers of the World Trade Center in New York City. Altruistic behavior is often defined as voluntary behavior that is intended to benefit others and is not motivated by any expectation of personal gain. The most extreme form of altruism is giving one's life to save someone else, as many of those who responded to the September 11th attack did.

Altruism poses an important problem for the evolutionary psychology approach (Caporael, 2001). According to Charles Darwin's theory of evolution, behaviors that favor an organism's reproductive success are likely to be passed on to future generations. In fact, altruistic behavior *reduces* a person's chances of reproductive success. Therefore, altruists should be at a clear disadvantage compared to those who act more selfishly, ensuring the propagation of their own genes. Over many generations, selfish behavior should be favored and altruistic behavior should die out.

Referring to altruistic behavior among social insects, Darwin (1859/1979) himself wrote about one circumstance that is difficult for evolutionary theory to explain. Worker bees, born without the ability to reproduce, spend their lives caring for the offspring of the queen bee in their hive. Natural selection predicts that sterile worker bees should become extinct over time. How, then, could there be such a thing as a sterile worker bee?

Seen through the Darwinian lens of the "survival of the fittest," human altruism also appears implausible. The concept of *kin selection* provides one way to reconcile altruism with evolutionary theory. According to this concept, our genes survive not just when we reproduce but also when our relatives reproduce. Kin selection includes the idea of *inclusive fitness,* which is measured by the number of our own direct descendants and those of our relatives, in proportion to their degree of relationship with us. The worker bees in a hive turn out to be genetically related to the queen bee and, hence, to all of the other bees in the hive, including any eggs the queen bee lays. Thus, even though a worker bee has no direct offspring, its inclusive fitness is high when the hive thrives. The theory of kin selection can explain why some people forgo having their own children and choose instead to care for relatives and relatives' children. What this theory cannot explain is altruism directed toward people outside the family and especially toward strangers.

In contrast to the evolutionary psychology approach, the sociocultural approach attempts to explain altruistic behavior as being the result of social and cultural experiences (Dovidio & Penner, 2001; Gergen, 1994). According to this approach, each of us is a product of many culturally and socially derived relationships, which continually unfold over time. Because our relationships within our culture are open-ended and adaptable

Firefighters helping victims of the September 11, 2001, terrorist attack on the World Trade Center in New York City. *Why are humans altruistic?*

rather than rigidly determined by our genes, genuine acts of altruism are possible. Simply put, if our culture teaches us to be kind without regard for our own gain, then we can become true altruists.

By providing a theory that emphasizes the importance of adaptation and natural selection in explaining all behavior, the evolutionary psychology approach has much to recommend it (Belk & Ruse, 2000). It fo/rces us to look at our capacity for selfishness and to refine our notions of kindness and altruism. Yet the sociocultural approach is attractive because it stresses that people can be genuinely altruistic. This possibility is what we think about when we think about the firefighters, police officers, and other people who lost their lives on September 11, 2001. In the end, this contrast in views may well serve to sharpen our understanding of what it is to be fully human.

What do you think?

- Are people ever truly altruistic? Or are they operating according to selfish motives?
- Have you ever acted in a truly altruistic fashion? Or could your behavior be explained by theories of kin selection?
- What kind of research might settle the question of whether humans are capable of genuine altruism?

Review and Sharpen Your Thinking

2   Describe six contemporary approaches to psychology.

- Define each of the six approaches in your own words.
- Some approaches emphasize what is going on inside of the person. Others focus on the outside environment. Compare the approaches in this regard.

Suppose you could talk with a psychologist from each of the six approaches. Think about the members of your family and other people you know. Write down at least one question you might want to ask about the thoughts and behaviors of these people.

mhhe.com/
santrockp7

For study tools related to this learning goal, see the Study Guide, the CD-ROM, and the Online Learning Center.

A POSITIVE APPROACH TO PSYCHOLOGY 3

The Humanistic Movement

The Positive
Psychology Movement

Can psychology make us happier?

If you are like most people, you probably associate psychology with problems, such as depression, violence, and eating disorders. Psychologists, too, sometimes think that their field focuses too much on the negative and not enough on the positive aspects of behavior.

Psychology deals with both the positive and negative aspects of life. When the tone of psychology was believed to be too negative, two movements emerged to focus on the positive effects psychology can have on people's lives. One of these movements (humanistic) appeared in the middle of the twentieth century; the other (positive psychology) began gaining momentum at the beginning of the twenty-first century. Let's explore these two movements.

The Humanistic Movement

The **humanistic movement** emphasizes a person's positive qualities, the capacity for positive growth, and freedom to choose an destiny. Humanistic psychologists stress that people have the ability to control their lives and avoid being manipulated by the environment (Maslow, 1971; Rogers, 1961). They believe that, rather than being driven by unconscious sexual and aggressive impulses, as the psychodynamic approach dictates, or by external rewards, as the behavioral approach emphasizes, people can choose to live by higher human values, such as altruism and free will. Humanistic psychologists also think that people have a tremendous potential for conscious self-understanding and that the way to help others achieve self-understanding is by being warm, nurturant, and supportive of them. Many aspects of this optimistic approach to defining human nature appear in clinical practice today.

The Positive Psychology Movement

The end of an old century and the beginning of a new one can stimulate reflections on what was and visions of what could be and should be. In 2000, two influential American psychologists, Mihaly Csikszentmihalyi and Martin Seligman, edited a special issue of the journal *American Psychologist* on the theme of positive psychology (Seligman & Csikszentmihalyi, 2000).

humanistic movement An emphasis on a person's capacity for personal growth, freedom to choose a destiny, and positive qualities.

positive psychology movement A strong emphasis on the experiences that people value subjectively (such as happiness), positive individual traits (such as the capacity for love), and positive group and civic values (such as responsibility).

Humanists believe that we have a natural tendency to be loving toward each other and that each of us has the capacity to be a loving person.

Mihaly Csikszentmihalyi, one of the main architects of the current positive psychology movement.

Their analysis of psychology in the twentieth century was that it had become far too negative, focusing on what can go wrong in people's lives rather than on what they can do competently. Too often, they said, psychology has characterized people as passive and victimized.

Seligman, Csikszentmihalyi, and others hope to usher in a new focus on the positive things that psychology can accomplish (Diener, 2000; Nakamura & Csikszentmihalyi, 2001; Seligman, 2001). They describe the **positive psychology movement** as giving a stronger emphasis to and conducting more research on three general topics (Seligman & Csikszentmihalyi, 2000):

1. Experiences that people value subjectively, such as hope, optimism, and happiness
2. Positive individual traits, such as the capacity for love, work, creativity, talent, and interpersonal skills
3. Positive group and civic values, such as responsibility, nurturance, civility, and tolerance

This is a worthwhile goal. Throughout this book I talk about the positive potential of psychology and the ways in which it can enable individuals and groups to take more control of their own lives and to live them in a more fulfilling way. I also frequently link theory with specific applications that demonstrate psychology's contributions in these positive settings.

Review and Sharpen Your Thinking

3 **Describe two movements that reflect a positive approach to psychology.**

   • Explain the nature of the humanistic movement.
   • Describe the positive psychology movement.

Think about what you read in the newspaper and see on television and at the movies. Does the information focus more on the negative or the positive aspects of people's lives? Why might the media present more negative than positive stories? Are they just giving their readers and viewers what they want? Are there ways in which the positive psychology movement could help to change the media's negative orientation?

4 PSYCHOLOGY'S CAREERS AND AREAS OF SPECIALIZATION

> Careers in Psychology

> Areas of Specialization in Psychology

What types of careers are available to psychology majors?

Psychologists don't spend all of their time in a laboratory, white-smocked with clipboard in hand, observing rats and crunching numbers. Some psychologists spend their days seeing people with problems; others teach at universities and conduct research. Still others work in business and industry, designing more efficient criteria for hiring. In short, psychology is a field with many areas of specialization.

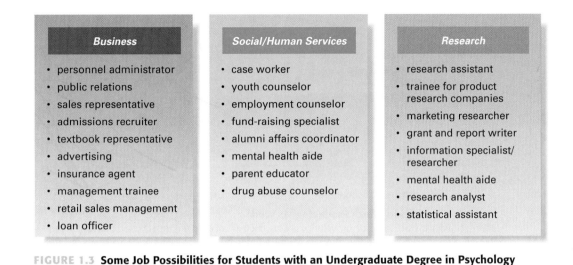

Business	Social/Human Services	Research
• personnel administrator	• case worker	• research assistant
• public relations	• youth counselor	• trainee for product research companies
• sales representative	• employment counselor	• marketing researcher
• admissions recruiter	• fund-raising specialist	• grant and report writer
• textbook representative	• alumni affairs coordinator	• information specialist/researcher
• advertising	• mental health aide	• mental health aide
• insurance agent	• parent educator	• research analyst
• management trainee	• drug abuse counselor	• statistical assistant
• retail sales management		
• loan officer		

FIGURE 1.3 **Some Job Possibilities for Students with an Undergraduate Degree in Psychology**

Careers in Psychology

Have you ever thought about majoring in psychology? Students who major in psychology often find that the subject matter is highly interesting. You already have encountered some interesting topics in this chapter, including the brain's role in behavior and analyzing the lives of people such as Tiger Woods from a psychological perspective. In the remaining chapters of this book, you will encounter hundreds more truly fascinating inquiries in psychology.

Not only do you gain considerable knowledge and understanding of the mind and behavior by majoring in psychology, but majoring in psychology equips you with a rich and diverse portfolio of skills that serve you well in many different types of work, both practical and professional. A psychology major helps you improve your skills in research, measurement and computing, problem solving and critical thinking, and writing (Hayes, 1997). Integrating these skills, which span the arts and sciences, provides you with unique qualifications. Even if you are not a psychology major and do not plan to major in psychology, this course and others in psychology can give you a richer, deeper understanding of many areas of life.

Psychology also pays reasonably well (Sternberg, 1997). Psychologists earn well above the median salary in the United States. It is unlikely that you would live in a palatial mansion because you majored in psychology, but it is also unlikely that you would go broke. A psychology major enables you to improve peoples' lives, to understand yourself and others, possibly to advance the state of knowledge in the field, and to have an enjoyable time while you are doing these things.

An undergraduate degree in psychology can give you access to a variety of jobs. For a list of some of the job possibilities in business, social and human services, and research, see figure 1.3. If you choose a career in psychology, you can greatly expand your opportunities (and your income) by getting a graduate degree, either a master's or a doctorate. For example, Anna Marie Apanovitch has a Ph.D. in experimental psychology and is now a senior marketing analyst at Bayer Corporation (O'Connor, 2001). She is part of a team that does objective, cost-effective analysis of different marketing programs for various drugs, such as aspirin. She says that the skills she learned in psychology serve her well in her marketing position. She especially believes psychology helped her become a better critical thinker and communicator.

Where do psychologists work? Slightly more than one-third are teachers, researchers, or counselors at colleges or universities. Most other psychologists work in clinical and private practice settings (see figure 1.4).

Anna Marie Apanovitch obtained a Ph.D. in experimental psychology and today is a senior marketing analyst for Bayer Corporation. Psychology provides excellent training for a wide range of careers, as exemplified by Anna Marie Apanovitch's job. She believes that it is important for students to think about their long-term career options and the skills they will need in performing those jobs and then to work on building up the skills at every opportunity. *Are there some careers in psychology that interest you?*

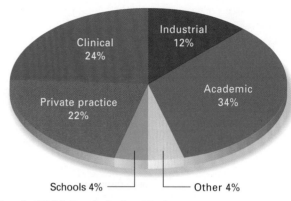

FIGURE 1.4 Settings in Which Psychologists Work
More psychologists work in academic settings (34%), such as colleges and universities, than any other. However, clinical (24%) and private practice (22%) settings, both contexts in which many psychologists in the mental health professions work, together make up almost half of the total settings.

Areas of Specialization in Psychology

If you were to go to graduate school to earn an advanced degree in psychology, you would be required to specialize in a particular area. Following is a list of some of the specialties: clinical and counseling; experimental; behavioral neuroscience and comparative; developmental; social; personality; health; community; school and educational; industrial and organizational; environmental; cross-cultural; psychology of women; forensic; and sport. Some of these categories are not mutually exclusive. For example, some social psychologists are also experimental psychologists.

Clinical and Counseling Psychology Clinical and counseling psychology is the most widely practiced specialization in psychology. Clinical and counseling psychologists diagnose and treat people with psychological problems (Corey & Corey, 2002; James & Gilliland, 2003). Counseling psychologists sometimes deal with people who have less serious problems. For instance, counseling psychologists may work with students, advising them about personal problems and career planning.

A clinical psychologist typically has a doctoral degree in psychology, which requires 3 to 4 years of graduate work and 1 year of internship in a mental health facility. Clinical psychologists are different from psychiatrists. *Psychiatry* is a branch of medicine practiced by physicians with a doctor of medicine (M.D.) degree who subsequently specialize in abnormal behavior and psychotherapy. Clinical psychologists and psychiatrists alike are interested in improving the lives of people with mental health problems. One important distinction is that psychiatrists can prescribe drugs, whereas clinical psychologists cannot.

Some clinical psychologists specialize in working with a certain age group. Luis Vargas is a clinical child psychologist at the University of New Mexico Children's Psychiatric Hospital. He is interested in cultural issues that affect the assessment and treatment of children from diverse backgrounds. Luis is especially motivated to find better ways to conduct therapy with Latino children and youth who have become juvenile delinquents or who have abused drugs.

Luis Vargas (*left*) conducting a child therapy session

Experimental Psychology Experimental psychologists use an experimental strategy in their work and often conduct basic research. Among the key aspects of behavior that experimental psychologists study are sensation and perception, cognitive processes (such as memory), learning, motivation, and emotion (Klein, 2002; Meyers, 2003).

Jim Stevenson is an experimental psychologist who works at the National Aeronautics and Space Administration (NASA). He also is blind. Stevenson's research interests focus on how sound can be added to graphic displays and the different ways in which the ears hear patterns.

"Well, you don't look like an experimental psychologist to *me*."
© The New Yorker Collection 1994 Sam Gross from Cartoonbank.com. All rights reserved.

Behavioral Neuroscience and Comparative Psychology

Behavioral neuroscientists and comparative psychologists focus on biological processes, especially the brain's role in behavior (Pinel, 2003; Rains, 2002). Many of these scientists use animals in their research and investigate a range of topics, from how the brain processes information to the effects of hormones on behavior. Comparative psychology is a branch of psychology that studies animal behavior.

Joseph LeDoux is a neuroscientist at New York University. His research is aimed at understanding the biological underpinnings of emotions such as fear. As part of his research program, LeDoux studies the ways in which the brain forms, stores, and retrieves memories of life's significant events, especially traumatic ones (LeDoux, 2000, 2002). He hopes that his research will help improve the understanding of anxiety disorders.

Developmental Psychology

Developmental psychology is concerned with how people become who they are, from conception to death. In particular, developmental psychologists focus on the biological and environmental factors that contribute to human development. For many years the major emphasis of developmentalists was on child development. However, an increasing number of today's developmental psychologists show a strong interest in adult development and aging (Santrock, 2002). Their inquiries range across the biological, cognitive, and social domains of life.

Joseph LeDoux, a neuroscientist who studies the brain's role in emotions.

Laura Carstensen is a developmental psychologist at Stanford University and also is director of the Institute for Gender and Women there. Carstensen's research has documented that older adults become more selective about the people with whom they interact (Carstensen, Pasupathi, & Nesselroade, 2002; Fung, Carstensen, & Lang, 2001). Because older adults place a high value on emotional satisfaction, they often spend more time with a few people with whom they have had rewarding relationships than with people they don't know very well in large social gatherings.

Social Psychology

Social psychology deals with people's social interactions, relationships, social perceptions, and attitudes (Aronson, Wilson, & Akert, 2002). Social psychologists believe we can better understand mind and behavior if we know something about how people function in groups.

Roy Baumeister is a social psychologist at Case Western Reserve University. His diverse research interests include the extent to which self-esteem influences behavior, why some people fail to control their behavior, how people perform under pressure, and why people seem to be attracted more to the negative than to the positive in life (Baumeister, 1997; Baumeister, Bratslavsky, & Finkenauer, 2000).

Personality Psychology

Personality psychology focuses on the relatively enduring traits and characteristics of individuals. Personality psychologists study such topics as self-concept, aggression, moral development, gender roles, and inner or outer directedness (Ashcroft, 2003; Feist & Feist, 2002).

Laura Carstensen (*right*), a developmental psychologist who studies the socioemotional lives of older adults.

Rodney Hammond (*left*), a community psychologist, talking with an adolescent about strategies for coping with stress and avoiding high-risk situations.

William Revelle, a personality psychologist at Northwestern University, researches the biological foundations of personality (Baehr, Revelle, & Eastman, 2000). He also studies how certain personality traits might be linked with the extent to which people are motivated and how they think (Revelle, 2000).

Health Psychology Health psychology is a multidimensional approach to health that emphasizes psychological factors, lifestyle, and the nature of the health care delivery system. Many health psychologists study the roles of stress and coping in people's lives (Baum, Revenson, & Singer, 2001). Health psychologists may work in physical or mental health areas. Some are members of multidisciplinary teams that conduct research or provide clinical services.

Jeannette Ickovics is a health psychologist at Yale University. Her research focuses on sexually transmitted diseases in females. In one study, she focused on the behaviors that place adolescent girls at risk for pregnancy and also put them at risk for sexually transmitted diseases (Ickovics, 2001). In this study, many of the adolescent girls who became pregnant had a history of sexually transmitted diseases and multiple and high-risk sex partners.

Community Psychology Community psychology focuses on providing accessible care for people with psychological problems. Community-based mental health centers are one means of delivering such services as outreach programs to people in need, especially those who traditionally have been underserved by mental health professionals (Dalton, Elias, & Wandersman, 2001; Duffy, 2003). Community psychologists view human behavior in terms of adaptation to resources and the specific situation. They work to create communities that are more supportive of residents by pinpointing needs, by providing needed services, and by teaching people how to gain access to resources that are already available. Community psychologists are also concerned about *prevention*. They try to prevent mental health problems by identifying high-risk groups and then intervening with appropriate services and by stimulating new opportunities in the community.

Rodney Hammond is a community psychologist. Today, he trains psychologists at Wright State University in Ohio and directs a federally funded program to prevent homicide and violence among ethnic minority youth. He and his associates teach at-risk youth how to use social skills to manage conflict effectively (Hammond, 2001). Rodney's message to undergraduate students: "If you are interested in people and problem solving, psychology is a great way to combine the two."

School and Educational Psychology School and educational psychology is concerned with children's learning and adjustment in school. School psychologists in elementary and secondary school systems test children, make recommendations about educational placement, and work on educational planning teams. Educational psychologists work at colleges and universities, teach classes, and do research on teaching and learning (Santrock, 2001).

Michael Pressley is an educational psychologist at Notre Dame University. His research focuses on ways to improve children's reading. For example, he has found that children's reading improves when they use effective reading strategies, such as monitoring what they have read for meaning and periodically summarizing what they have read (Pressley, 2000).

Environmental psychologist Roberta Feldman in one of the positive environments she designed. *What are some of the interests of environmental psychologists?*

Industrial and Organizational Psychology Industrial and organizational psychology (I/O psychology) centers on the workplace, both on the workers and on the organizations that employ them. I/O psychology is often partitioned into industrial psychology and organizational psychology. Industrial psychology involves personnel and human resource management. Industrial psychology is increasingly referred to as personnel psychology. Organizational psychology examines the social and group influences of the organization (Goldstein & Ford, 2002; Muchinsky, 2003).

Leatta Hough, an I/O psychologist, is a cofounder of Personnel Decisions Research Institute in Minneapolis. She conducts research on personnel testing used to select job applicants and helps businesses develop better resources for their employees. She especially "is interested in predicting behavior in the world of work" (Hough, 2001).

Environmental Psychology Environmental psychology is the study of transactions between people and the physical environment. Environmental psychologists explore the effects of physical settings in most major areas of psychology, including perception, cognition, learning, development, abnormal behavior, social relations, and others (Bell & others, 2001). Topics that an environmental psychologist might study range from how different building and room arrangements influence behavior to strategies for getting people to reduce behavior that harms the environment.

Roberta Feldman is an environmental psychologist who also has a degree in architecture. Her research and applied interests focus on the design of buildings and communities that people can feel are their own (Feldman, 1999). To accomplish this,

Feldman listens to peoples' ideas about what they want, not what architects and developers think they need.

Cross-Cultural Psychology   Cross-cultural psychology is the study of culture's role in understanding behavior, thought, and emotion (Matsumoto, 2001). Cross-cultural psychologists compare the nature of psychological processes in different cultures, with a special interest in whether psychological phenomena are universal or culture-specific. The International Association for Cross-Cultural Psychology promotes research on cross-cultural comparisons and awareness of culture's role in psychology.

Harry Triandis is a cross-cultural psychologist at the University of Illinois. He is especially interested in the extent to which people from different cultures are oriented either toward the individual or toward the group. For example, his research and thorough observations reveal that many people from the United States are oriented more toward the individual and are more competitive with other people than are many people from Asian countries such as China and Japan, who are oriented more toward the group (Triandis, 2000, 2001).

Psychology of Women   The psychology of women emphasizes the importance of promoting research on and the study of women. This field emphasizes the importance of integrating information about women with current psychological knowledge and beliefs and applying the information to society and its institutions (Worrell, 2002). The Division of the Psychology of Women of the American Psychological Association was formed in 1973.

Rosalind Barnett conducts research on women's issues at the Murray Research Center of Radcliffe College. She is especially interested in how work and family demands and challenges affect the lives of women (Barnett, 2002). In one ongoing project, Barnett is studying the career and family aspirations and expectations of newly entering female and male freshmen at Tufts University (Barnett & James, 2001). The intent of the study is to understand the factors linked with choosing both traditional and nontraditional majors and careers.

Forensic Psychology   Forensic psychology is the field of psychology that applies psychological concepts to the legal system (Wrightsman & others, 2002). Social and cognitive psychologists increasingly conduct research on topics related to psychology and law. Forensic psychologists are hired by legal teams to provide input about many aspects of a trial. For example, forensic psychologists were members of the legal teams in the trials of O. J. Simpson and Timothy McVeigh.

Sheila Deitz is a forensic psychologist in Englewood, Colorado. She conducts research on how juries make decisions and applies this information as an expert witness in the courtroom. Deitz is a consultant to attorneys in such areas as preparation of questions to defendants and the creation of mock juries.

Sport Psychology   Sport psychology is the field of psychology that applies psychology's principles to improving sport performance and enjoying sport participation (Leunes & Nation, 2002). Sport psychology is a relatively new field, but it is rapidly gaining acceptance. At the 2000 Olympics, more than twenty sport psychologists worked with U.S. athletes and coaches.

Jay Brunza served as Tiger Woods' personal sport psychologist during Tiger's amateur career and continued to work with Tiger during his early professional career. Brunza trained Tiger to use visualization (imagining a positive situation and outcome) to improve his game. He also helped Tiger learn how to concentrate more effectively and to keep his emotions in check.

To reflect on whether a career in psychology might be in your future, see the Psychology and Life box.

Is Psychology in Your Future?

Instructions

Students who are successful as psychology majors have a profile that is related to the questions below. Answer true or false to each item.

	True	False
1. I often think about what makes people do what they do.	____	____
2. I like reading about new findings that scientists have discovered doing behavioral research.	____	____
3. I am often skeptical when someone tries to persuade me about behavioral claims, unless there is evidence to back up the claim.	____	____
4. I like the prospect of measuring behavior and doing statistics to determine meaningful differences.	____	____
5. I can usually come up with multiple explanations to account for behavior.	____	____
6. I think I could come up with ideas to research to help explain behaviors I am curious about.	____	____
7. I am often approached by others who want me to listen to their problems and share my ideas about what to do.	____	____
8. I don't get especially frustrated if I can't get answers to my questions.	____	____
9. I am usually careful with details.	____	____
10. I enjoy writing and speaking about things I am learning.	____	____
11. I like to solve puzzles.	____	____
12. I feel comfortable that psychology can provide me with an education that will lead to a good job.	____	____

Scoring and Interpretation

If you answered "true" to a majority of the items, psychology is a major that likely matches up well with your interests. Although the items are not a perfect predictor of whether you will enjoy majoring in and pursuing a career in psychology, they can give you an indication of whether you might benefit from finding out more about what psychologists do and what is involved in becoming a psychologist. Your psychology professor or a career counselor at your college likely can inform you about the best way to pursue a career in psychology.

Review and Sharpen Your Thinking

4 *Evaluate careers and areas of specialization in psychology.*

- Describe the kinds of career opportunities that are available to people with an undergraduate degree in psychology.
- List and discuss the areas of specialization in psychology.

Think of a career other than psychology that you might enter. In what ways might studying psychology be useful in that career?

mhhe.com/
santrockp7

For study tools related to this learning goal, see the Study Guide, the CD-ROM, and the Online Learning Center.

5 HOW TO GET THE MOST OUT OF PSYCHOLOGY

| Good Study Habits | Thinking Critically | The Book's Learning Tools |

What study habits and skills can help me in this course?

Very likely, you are taking other courses besides psychology. You will have a lot of reading and studying to do, and you probably will have to take a number of tests. What are some good strategies for succeeding in this and other courses?

Good Study Habits

Mastering good study habits will help you not only in psychology and in school but also in your career and personal life. Here we focus on five important strategies for success: time management, study environment, reading effectiveness, attentiveness in class, and test preparation.

Plan and Manage Your Time Effectively   Learning takes time. You will benefit enormously in this course and others if you become a great time manager. If you waste too much time, for instance, you will find yourself poorly prepared the night before an important exam. If you manage time well, you will have time to relax before exams and other deadlines. Time management can help you to be more productive and less stressed, with a better balance between work and play.

One week has 168 hours. Students vary in how they invest those hours. A typical full-time college student sleeps 50 hours, attends class between 12 and 20 hours, and spends 11 hours a week eating. Students divide the remaining hours between study, work and family obligations, and leisure pursuits.

You might find it helpful to fill out a term calendar with dates for the tests in your courses. Many students benefit from keeping a weekly calendar to see how they are allocating their time. Students who consistently get A's in courses often report that they study 2 to 3 hours outside class for every hour they are in class (Santrock & Halonen, 2002). Thus, if you are in class 15 hours a week and you want to get A's, a rule of thumb is to study 30 to 45 hours a week outside of class.

A good strategy for managing your time is to space out your study in a particular course rather than cramming it all into one or two study sessions just before the test. On a weekly schedule, block out at least 1 hour a day for 6 days to read this book and study your notes for this course. Then you will be better prepared when the time comes for each test, and you won't have to cram.

It is a good idea to plan not only for the term and the week but also for tomorrow. Great time managers identify the most important things to do each day and allocate enough time to get them done. Figuring out what is most important involves setting priorities. An effective way to set priorities is to create a manageable to-do list. Set a goal of making a to-do list for the next day every night or, at the latest, early in the morning. Figure 1.5 shows one student's to-do list.

Choose the Most Effective Study Environment   Too many distractions can keep you from studying or remembering what you have studied. Select your place of study carefully, paying close attention to the features of the environment that will let you do your best work.

"Doctor, have you any advice to offer a young man who would love to be a physician but whose crowded schedule simply doesn't permit time for medical school?" ©The New Yorker Collection 1990, Robert Weber, from cartoonbank.com. All Rights Reserved.

To Do

The Most Important:

1. Study for Psychology Test

Next Two:

2. Go to English and History classes

3. Make appointment to see advisor

Task	Time	Done
Study for psychology test	Early morn., night	
Call home	Morning	
Go to English class	Morning	
Buy test book	Morning	
Call Ann about test	Morning	
Make advisor appt.	Afternoon	
Go to history class	Afternoon	
Do exercise workout	Afternoon	

FIGURE 1.5 **Example of a To-Do List**

Some students find that their studying is more effective when they do it in the same place. Ideally, the area should be well lighted, without glare, and should be a comfortable temperature. A quiet location will let you concentrate much better than a noisy one. Noise is a major distraction to effective study. Turn off the stereo, radio, or TV while you are studying to minimize distraction.

Maximize Your Reading Effectiveness Many students approach the challenge of reading the text as just so many pages to plow through. There is a difference between *reading to read* (to complete the required number of pages) and *reading to learn*. Reading to learn from a text improves if you approach the text as a conversation the author is having with you about the concepts of psychology. As in any effective conversation, you must pay attention, figure out how the parts of the conversation fit together, and make some judgments as you go about understanding the author's intent.

The following strategies can help you to maximize your ability to understand and retain what you read:

- *Preview and plan.* Look at the number of pages you have to read and plan how to read the assignment. If the task is very long, determine at what points it would be appropriate to take breaks. For example, I have divided each chapter into three to five main sections, so a good time to take a break in your reading might be after you have read one or two main sections.
- *Skim.* Look at the reading assignment and determine what main ideas will be covered. Look at the main headings. Read the paragraphs that introduce new

What type of learner are you? Take the Learning Styles Assessment on the CD-ROM and find out.

sections. Examine the chapter reviews and summary. When you skim, you begin to build a foundation for the main ideas of the chapter.

- *Read to comprehend.* There is no way around the effort and hard work involved in learning the material in a textbook. However, there are some things that you can do to increase your understanding of what you read:
    1. Pay attention to the sections of the reading assignment as meaningful units. Take one section at a time. Read each one until you are satisfied that you know the ideas.
    2. Don't skip over what you don't understand. Find a classmate who is willing to discuss the ideas that are challenging.
    3. Work on your reading speed. Practice taking in more words as your eyes sweep the line of print. Don't mouth the words as you read because that only slows you down.
- *Read to retain.* Most students need to read assignments more than once if they are going to learn the material. Thinking about personal examples that illustrate concepts is a good memory aid. Periodically ask yourself the meaning of what you have been reading.
- *Review.* After you have used the aforementioned strategies, you will need to review the material you have read at least several times before you take a test. Just because you have read a chapter once, don't think that you will be able to remember everything in it that is important. At the end of each major section in this book, you will find review questions and, at the end of the chapter, a summary of the chapter's main ideas for an overall review.

Be a Good Listener and Concentrate in Class   You need to do more than just memorize or passively absorb new information in class. To do well in most classes, including this one, you need to go to class, listen carefully, and take good notes.

A good strategy is to treat each and every class hour as an important learning experience. To carry out this strategy, you obviously have to be there. It also helps to prepare for the class by reading about the topic(s) that will be covered prior to the class.

In preparing for a lecture, motivate yourself by telling yourself that it is important for you to stay alert and listen carefully. Make sure you get sufficient sleep the night before so that you will be able to maximize your learning in class the next day. Many students find that a regular exercise program increases their alertness and ability to concentrate in class and when they are studying.

Take notes in class, but don't try to write down everything the instructor says. As you listen to a lecture, focus on the main ideas and take notes about them. If you miss an idea, get together later with one or more students in the class to find out what the idea was. Many students find it helpful to review their notes right after class, because the material in the lecture will be fresher in their minds than if they wait several days or more to review them.

Prepare Effectively for the Test   In most cases, your grade in a course will depend on how well you do on the exams given periodically during the term. At the beginning of the term, find out what kinds of tests your instructor will be giving. Will they be all multiple-choice items? Will there be essay questions? Will the exams be a mixture of these or include other types of items, such as true-false?

A good strategy is to complete all of your textbook reading several days before the exam. All of your classroom notes should be in order so you can easily review them. If you have been studying on a regular basis, you should be in a good position to consolidate what you have learned for the test.

Some students find it helpful to develop their own questions about what they think will be covered on the test and practice answering them. You may also find it

For more study tips go to the PowerWeb section **mhhe com/ santrockp7** *of the Online Learning Center and click on Study Tips. Use the* Notes *feature of the Online Learning Center to take notes while online.*

helpful to study in a small group with other students in the class, who may be able to contribute information that you missed or did not adequately understand.

When you take a test, you will have to remember information. If you have practiced good study skills day after day and week after week leading up to the test, your ability to remember information will be enhanced when you take the test. In chapter 8, I discuss a number of strategies for remembering effectively.

Getting the most out of psychology involves remembering ideas and concepts. It also involves thinking critically about these ideas and concepts.

Thinking Critically

Thinking critically is an important aspect of psychology, as it is in all disciplines. The ability to critically evaluate information is essential to all areas of daily life (Halpern, 2002, 2003). For example, if you were planning to buy a car, you might want to collect information about different makes and models and evaluate their features and costs before deciding which one to test-drive. This would be an exercise in critical thinking.

Critical thinking is not a spectator sport (Halpern, 2000). You need to regularly practice your critical thinking skills on a wide variety of problems to keep them sharp. Let's practice them.

What Is Critical Thinking?

People don't change.
Love is blind.
Birds of a feather flock together.
Communicating with spirits is possible.

Such statements about human nature spark the psychologist's curiosity and skepticism, which is the tendency to doubt the validity of claims in the absence of evidence. Psychologists try to sort fact from fancy by critically questioning the nature of mind and behavior.

Are you a critical thinker? What does it mean to be a critical thinker? Understanding the complex nature of mind and behavior requires **critical thinking,** the process of thinking reflectively and productively and evaluating the evidence. Thinking critically means asking yourself how you know something. Too often we have a tendency to recite, define, describe, state, and list rather than analyze, infer, connect, synthesize, criticize, create, evaluate, think, and rethink (Brooks & Brooks, 2001). Following is a brief sampling of some thinking strategies that can stimulate you to think reflectively and productively:

- *Be open-minded.* Explore options and avoid narrow thinking.
- *Be intellectually curious.* Wonder, probe, question, and inquire. Also be alert for problems and inconsistencies.
- *Be intellectually careful.* Check for inaccuracies and errors, be precise, and be organized.
- *Look for multiple determinants of behavior.* People have a tendency to explain things as having a single cause. After all, that's a lot easier than having to analyze the complexity of, say, mind and behavior and come up with multiple explanations. However, one of psychology's important lessons is that mind and behavior have multiple determinants. For example, if someone asked what causes a person to be a good critical thinker, the person might respond, "Being open-minded." Having an open mind is one of critical thinking's multiple dimensions, but it does not *cause* critical thinking. When another person is asked what causes critical thinking, the individual might respond, "Practice." Yet another person might say, "An inquiring, critical thinking mentor." Like all aspects of mind and behavior, critical thinking has many dimensions.

critical thinking The process of thinking reflectively and productively, as well as evaluating evidence.

Why does the science of psychology urge you to be skeptical of astrology?

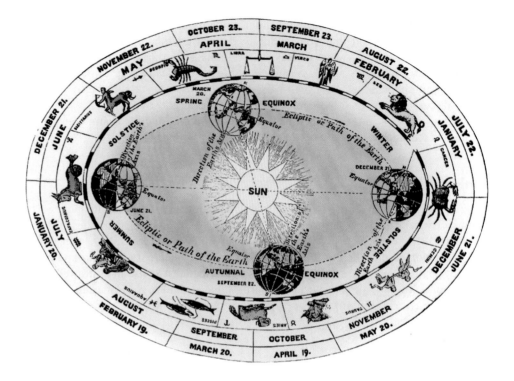

- *Think like a scientist.* Scientific thinkers examine the available evidence about some aspect of mind and behavior, evaluate how strongly the data (information) supports their hunches, analyze disconfirming evidence, and carefully consider whether they have explored all of the possible factors and explanations. It is important to underscore how critical it is to look for biases in the way people think and behave. For example, a person who is wildly enthusiastic about the remarkable effects of exercise on health when responding to survey questions about health awareness might sell exercise videos on the side. In the discussion of the scientific method in the next chapter, I explore more systematically how to think like a scientist. And in the next section, you will read about the healthy skepticism of scientific thinkers and how they require sound evidence before accepting information as valid.

Maintaining a Healthy Skepticism   The failure to think critically ranges from taking advice based on horoscopes to believing that eating a ground-up portion of a tiger's sexual organ will increase the human male's sexual potency. Critical thinking expert Diane Halpern (1998) explained why she is concerned that so many people fail to engage in critical thinking. Approximately 75 percent of Americans read their horoscope, and many of them believe that it is personally meant for them (Lister, 1992). Some phone their psychics and pay exorbitant fees for advice that ranges from how to invest their money to whether or not a loved one should be disconnected from life-support systems. They spend large sums of money on remedies for which there is no evidence of effectiveness or safety. In a survey of college students, virtually 100 percent believed in at least one of the following (Messer & Griggs, 1989):

- channeling (the ability to enter a trance state and communicate with someone in another place and time, even centuries ago)
- clairvoyance (the ability to perceive remote events that are not visible to normal sight)
- precognition ("knowing" events before they occur)
- telepathy (the extrasensory transfer of thought from one person to another)

- psychic healing (performing miracle cures instantaneously through contact with a higher spiritual being)
- psychic surgery (a brand of faith healing in which sleight of hand is relied on to achieve a miracle, such as removing dead or diseased tissue)
- crystal power (use of quartz crystals for healing)
- psychokinesis (being able to move objects without actually touching them)
- astral travel
- levitation
- the Bermuda Triangle mystery
- unidentified flying objects (UFOs)
- plant consciousness
- auras
- ghosts

Why should you be skeptical when you hear that eating a ground-up penis of a tiger will increase the human male's sexual potency?

If you believe in any of these phenomena, psychologists urge you to be more skeptical. Remember that thinking like a scientist means that you demand to see the evidence for such phenomena as channeling, crystal power, and plant consciousness. There is no scientific evidence for the existence of any of the previously listed phenomena, only personal anecdotes and coincidences—and those do not meet science's criteria of objectivity and public verifiability.

When you think like a scientist, you will be skeptical of astrology, channeling, crystal power, and anything else that claims access to wondrous powers and supernatural forces (Ward & Grashial, 1995). If something sounds too good to be true, think through the claims logically and demand to see the evidence. A failure to think critically and to demand scientific evidence often underlies our purchase and use of highly touted, ineffective health care products (Halpern, 1998). For example, there is a widespread belief around the world today that a man who ingests the ground penis of a tiger will have more sexual potency. This belief is so pervasive that it has resulted in poaching of rare wild tigers and other endangered species. Males who believe that this works think like this: Tigers (presumably) have a great sex life; thus eating a tiger's sexual organ will improve my sex life. You should be able to see what is wrong with this kind of thinking, especially in the absence of any evidence to support it.

Thinking Critically About Controversies   As I indicated earlier in the chapter, psychology is full of controversies. How might psychology benefit from these controversies? Psychology has advanced as a field because it does not accept simple explanations and because psychologists do not always agree with each other about why mind and behavior work the way they do: We have reached a more accurate understanding of mind and behavior *because* psychology fosters controversies and *because* psychologists think deeply and reflectively and examine the evidence on both sides.

What are some of psychology's controversies? Here is a brief sample:

- Are memories of sexual abuse real or imagined?
- Can intelligence be increased?
- Is alcoholism a biologically based disease or a learned behavior?
- Is it better to treat depression with drugs or with psychotherapy?

Controversies are usually not totally resolved on one side or the other. Often the resolution comes down to a matter of degree. For example, some cases of sexual abuse may be imagined, whereas others are real; and certain aspects of abuse may be more likely to be imagined than others.

In this book I call your attention to a number of controversies. Because it is important for you to think critically about controversies, each chapter has a Critical Controversy box that presents a controversial issue in contemporary psychology.

a.

b.

c.

FIGURE 1.6 **Chapter Learning Goals and Map System**

d.

The Book's Learning Tools

This book provides important study tools to help you learn about psychology more effectively. I described the book's learning tools in a student preface prior to this chapter: Studying the student preface will give you an understanding of how to learn more effectively from this book. Here I briefly mention the most important study tools in the text.

An extensive learning system is built into the book. Using it will help you to learn the material more easily. Key aspects of the learning system are the *learning goals, chapter maps,* and *review* sections, all of which are linked together.

The Learning Goals and Chapter Map System At the beginning of each chapter, you will see three to five learning goals that preview the chapter's main themes and underscore the most important ideas in the chapter (see figure 1.6a). Then, following each main heading in the text, you will come across the relevant learning goal, rephrased as a question. Also, at the beginning of each major section, you will see a map that includes the main heading and sub-headings for that particular section (see figure 1.6b). This provides a visual preview of what you will be reading in the section. At the end of each major section, you will come to the heading Review and Sharpen Your Thinking (see figure 1.6c). The first part restates the section's learning goal and asks you to review each of the main topics in the section. The bulleted review statements are correlated with the map at the beginning of the section. Finally, at the end of the chapter, a map of the entire chapter gives you a visual reminder of the main topics (see figure 1.6d). Here, a section called Reach Your Learning Goals, restates the chapter's learning goals and verbally summarizes the material related to each learning goal. This information is provided in bulleted form and matches up in a one-to-one fashion with the bulleted statements in each of the chapter's section reviews.

Thus the Learning Goals and chapter maps are integrated in each chapter from beginning to end. One learning strategy is to look at a bulleted item in Review and Sharpen Your Thinking within a chapter, try to answer the item, and then turn to the corresponding bullet in the Reach Your Learning Goals section at the end of the chapter to see if your answer is on track.

Keep in mind that, although the Reach Your Learning Goals section is an organized, systematic review of the entire chapter, it is *not* a substitute for reading and studying the chapter. Rather, use it as a guide to help you organize your study of the chapter.

FIGURE 1.7 Key Terms

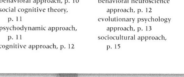

psychology The scientific study of behavior and mental processes.

Key Terms

psychology, p. 5	behavioral approach, p. 10	behavioral neuroscience	humanistic movement,
science, p. 6	social cognitive theory,	approach, p. 12	p. 17
behavior, p. 6	p. 11	evolutionary psychology	positive psychology
mental processes, p. 6	psychodynamic approach,	approach, p. 13	movement, p. 18
natural selection, p. 7	p. 11	sociocultural approach,	critical thinking, p. 29
structuralism, p. 8	cognitive approach, p. 12	p. 15	
functionalism, p. 8			

Thinking   As you read through each chapter, you will be asked many questions to encourage you to think more deeply and reflect on the topic at hand. Also, the second part of Review and Sharpen Your Thinking at the end of each major section includes one or more questions to stimulate your thinking about a topic in the section you have just read. In many cases, the thought questions are personalized so that you will be able to relate them to your own life or to people you know.

In addition, as we indicated earlier in the chapter, in each chapter you will read an in-depth Critical Controversy highlighting an important contemporary topic in psychology about which there is spirited debate. You will be asked a number of questions to encourage you to think critically about each of the controversies.

Further, the Psychology and Life box in each chapter is intended to stimulate you to think about applications of a psychology topic to the real world. Many of these features ask you to think about how you can apply what you have learned to your own life.

Key Terms   Key Terms are bold-faced, defined in the margin, and listed and page-referenced at the end of the chapter. In the Glossary at the end of the book you will find definitions for all key terms, along with a reference to the page on which the term is introduced (see figure 1.7).

Connections to Other Resources   In the margins of the book you will see notes directing you to other resources that will help you to review and learn more about psychology. These resources include the Student Study Guide, the CD-ROM that came with the book, and the On-Line Learning Center for the book. These resources include quizzes, Internet activities, and many other activities. A general reminder about the additional available study resources appears at the end of the chapter.

Review and Sharpen Your Thinking

5 *Apply some strategies that will help you succeed in psychology.*

- Discuss some good study habits.
- Describe the nature of critical thinking.
- Identify the study tools in this book.

Why do you think so many people believe in astrology?

mhhe●com/
santrockp7

For study tools related to this learning goal, see the Study Guide, the CD-ROM, and the Online Learning Center.

What Is Psychology?

1 EXPLORING PSYCHOLOGY

Studying the Mind and Behavior

A Quest for Answers to Ancient Questions

Early Scientific Approaches to Psychology

2 CONTEMPORARY APROACHES TO PSYCHOLOGY

The Behavioral Approach

The Cognitive Approach

The Evolutionary Psychology Approach

The Psychodynamic Approach

The Behavioral Neuroscience Approach

The Sociocultural Approach

3 A POSITIVE APPROACH TO PSYCHOLOGY

The Humanistic Movement

The Positive Psychology Movement

4 PSYCHOLOGY'S CAREERS AND AREAS OF SPECIALIZATION

Careers in Psychology

Areas of Specialization

5 HOW TO GET THE MOST OUT OF PSYCHOLOGY

Good Study Habits

Thinking Critically

The Book's Learning Tools

At the beginning of the chapter, we stated five learning goals and encouraged you to review material related to these goals at the end of each major section (see pages 9, 16, 17, 25, and 33). Use the following summary for additional review.

1 ***Explain what psychology is and how it developed.***

- Psychology is the scientific study of behavior and mental processes. Science uses systematic methods to observe, describe, predict, and explain. Behavior includes everything organisms do that can be observed. Mental processes are thoughts, feelings, and motives.
- Psychology emerged from two disciplines: philosophy and natural science. The idea that the mind is not a physical entity came from philosophy. The natural sciences of biology and physiology contributed the evolutionary approach to the study of behavior and the suggestion that the brain has an important role in behavior.
- Structuralism emphasized the study of the conscious mind and its structures. Wilhelm Wundt founded the first laboratory in psychology in 1879, searching for the mind's elemental structures, and E. B. Titchener named the approach "structuralism." Functionalism focused on the functions of the mind in adapting to the environment. William James was the leading functionalist theorist.

2 ***Describe six contemporary approaches to psychology.***

- The contemporary approaches to psychology are behavioral, psychodynamic, cognitive, behavioral neuroscience, evolutionary psychology, and sociocultural. The behavioral approach emphasizes the scientific study of observable behavioral responses and their environmental determinants. Social cognitive theory is a contemporary behavioral approach. The psychodynamic approach emphasizes unconscious thought, the conflict between biological instincts and society's demands, and early family experiences. The cognitive approach emphasizes the mental processes involved in knowing. The behavioral neuroscience approach emphasizes that the brain and nervous system are central to understanding behavior. The evolutionary psychology approach stresses the importance of adaptation, reproduction, and "survival of the fittest." The sociocultural approach focuses on the social and cultural determinants of behavior.
- John B. Watson and B. F. Skinner were important early behaviorists. Sigmund Freud was the founding father of the psychodynamic approach.

- Psychodynamic, cognitive, behavioral neuroscience, and evolutionary psychology approaches emphasize what is going on inside the person. Behavioral and sociocultural approaches focus on the outside environment.

3 ***Describe two movements that reflect a positive approach to psychology.***

- The humanistic movement emphasizes a person's capacity for positive growth, freedom to choose a destiny, and positive qualities.
- The positive psychology movement is a recent one. It argues that psychology has been too negative and needs to focus more on the positive aspects of people, such as their optimism, creativity, and civic values.

4 ***Evaluate careers and areas of specialization in psychology.***

- Majoring in psychology can open up many career opportunities. Careers range from conducting therapy with people who have mental problems to teaching and conducting research at a university to advertising and public relations.
- Areas of specialization in psychology include clinical and counseling psychology, experimental psychology, behavioral neuroscience and comparative psychology, developmental psychology, social psychology, personality psychology, health psychology, community psychology, school and educational psychology, industrial and organizational psychology, environmental psychology, cross-cultural psychology, the psychology of women, forensic psychology, and sport psychology.

5 ***Apply some strategies that will help you succeed in psychology.***

- Developing good study habits includes planning and time management, choosing a conducive study environment, maximizing reading effectiveness, being a good listener and concentrating in class, and preparing effectively for tests.
- Critical thinking involves thinking reflectively and productively and evaluating the evidence. It is important to

maintain a healthy skepticism about anything that appears to be magical and wondrous. Demand to see the logical evidence before believing in something involving psychology. Psychology is full of controversies, and it is important to think critically about these controversies.

Most controversies are not completely resolved on one side or the other.

- This book's learning tools include a learning goals and chapter map system, critical thinking questions, and key terms.

Key Terms

psychology, p. 5
science, p. 6
behavior, p. 6
mental processes, p. 6
natural selection, p. 7
structuralism, p. 8
functionalism, p. 8

behavioral approach, p. 10
social cognitive theory, p. 11
psychodynamic approach, p. 11
cognitive approach, p. 12

behavioral neuroscience approach, p. 12
evolutionary psychology approach, p. 13
sociocultural approach, p. 15

humanistic movement, p. 17
positive psychology movement, p. 18
critical thinking, p. 29

Apply Your Knowledge

1. Why are psychology and philosophy considered different disciplines? Research some of the questions addressed by both fields and what approaches each discipline uses to answer these questions.

2. Visit the website of a major book retailer and enter "psychology" as a search term. Examine descriptions of the five to seven most popular psychology books listed. How well do the themes covered represent your perceptions of what psychology is? How well do they represent the approaches to psychology discussed in the text? Are any perspectives over- or underrepresented? Why do you think that is?

3. In the faculty directory for your school (or for another institution), look up the psychology faculty. Select several faculty

members and discover what their area of specialization is (careful, it may not be the same as the classes they teach). How do you think their backgrounds might affect the way they teach their classes?

4. Ask three of your friends to describe how they prepared for the last exam they took. Using the study strategies discussed in the text, analyze your friends' study habits, including the things that they're doing well, and the things that they might improve on. Do the same for yourself. Are there some tasks that everyone has trouble with, or are study habits highly individual?

Connections

For extra help in mastering the material in this chapter, see the review sections and practice quizzes in the Student Study Guide, the CD-ROM, and the Online Learning Center.

2 Psychology's Scientific Methods

Chapter Outline

Learning Goals

EXPLORING PSYCHOLOGY AS A SCIENCE   **1**

A Scientific Approach
▼
Collaboration
▼
The Scientific Method

Explain what makes psychology a science.

TYPES OF RESEARCH   **2**

Descriptive Research
▼
Correlational Research
▼
Experimental Research

Discuss the three types of research that are used in psychology.

ANALYZING AND INTERPRETING DATA   **3**

Descriptive Statistics
▼
Inferential Statistics

Distinguish between descriptive statistics and inferential statistics.

FACING UP TO RESEARCH CHALLENGES   **4**

Conducting Ethical Research
▼
Minimizing Bias
▼
Being a Wise Consumer of Information About Psychology

Discuss some research challenges that involve ethics, bias, and information.

In 1881, at the age of 19, Mary Whiton Calkins left home to attend Smith College, a new women's college in Massachusetts (Furumoto, 1991; Scarborough & Furumoto, 1987). In 1887, she began to teach at another new women's college, Wellesley, that was committed to the idea that women could and should study science. Shortly after Calkins went to Wellesley, the college decided to found a program in experimental psychology like the ones being founded in men-only colleges. Wellesley asked Mary Calkins to educate herself in the subject and organize the program.

Calkins hesitated. She had taken one psychology course at Smith, but it had been mainly philosophical and provided no background in experimental science. She lived only a few miles from Harvard University, so she went to William James, the preeminent American psychologist of the time, and asked to study with him. James was willing, but the president and overseers of Harvard forbade women to study at Harvard.

After several years of struggle and negotiation, Calkins eventually was allowed to study with William James. She also studied psychology at Clark University. In the 1890s, Calkins established the new psychology program at Wellesley College.

MARY CALKINS (1863–1930).
What important role did she play in the early history of psychology?

In a career that lasted nearly 40 years, Calkins was an important voice in psychology, as well as the first woman president of the American Psychological Association. For some years, she did experimental research on the nature of memory. In later years, she became more interested in other research methods and in theories about the self.

Mary Calkins' story reminds us that the key to learning about psychology is knowing and using scientific methods. Scientific methods are what differentiates a discipline such as psychology from a discipline such as philosophy. Philosophers seek truth by thinking about thinking and by discussing thinking. Psychologists use scientific methods to seek truth.

Calkins' story also alerts us to the fact that for many years women and people from non-White ethnic backgrounds were largely excluded or steered away from becoming researchers in psychology. As you will see later in the chapter, excluding them was bad for science and for society. Today we are fortunate that capable people from every background are encouraged to apply the scientific method to the study of human behavior and to conduct all forms of research in psychology.

1 EXPLORING PSYCHOLOGY AS A SCIENCE

A Scientific Approach **Collaboration** **The Scientific Method**

What sets psychology and other sciences apart from other disciplines?
Science is not defined by *what* it investigates but by *how* it investigates. Whether you study photosynthesis, butterflies, Saturn's moons, or the reasons that people bite their fingernails, the way you study the question is what makes your approach scientific or not. You can obtain a better understanding of science by knowing what it means to take a scientific approach, realizing the importance of collaboration, and learning about the scientific method.

A Scientific Approach

Central to the scientific approach are four attitudes: curiosity, skepticism, objectivity, and a willingness to think critically.

Being curious is basic to science. Mary Calkins was enormously curious, with broad-ranging interests. Curiosity leads to asking questions. Among the questions Mary Calkins asked were "Do people remember numbers better when they are paired

Science is not defined by what it studies but by how it investigates it. Photosynthesis, butterflies, Saturn's moons, and relationships among people all can be studied in a scientific manner. *What are some areas of psychology other than relationships among people that science can appropriately be used to investigate?*

with vivid colors than with more neutral colors?" and "What is the most accurate description of the self?"

Being skeptical is also essential to science. Skeptical people question things that other people take for granted. They wonder whether a supposed fact is really true. Calkins and other female psychologists began to doubt that information collected by males from male participants would be the same as information collected by females from female participants. Skeptical people ask what evidence there is for an idea and question whether the evidence is really strong enough to be accepted as accurate and factual.

Science also means *being objective*. Scientists believe that one of the best ways to be objective is to conduct research studies (Pittenger, 2003). For example, to find out whether people remember numbers better if they are linked with vivid colors, Mary Calkins (1896) conducted an experiment. She found that people did indeed remember numbers better when they were associated with vivid colors. She also discovered in her study that the single most important determinant of remembering numbers was simply how frequently the participants were exposed to the number/color pairs.

It is sometimes said that experience is the most important teacher. We do get a great deal of knowledge from subjective, personal experience. We generalize from what we observe and frequently turn memorable encounters into lifetime "truths." But how valid are these conclusions? As individuals, we often misinterpret what we see and hear. You can probably think of many situations in which you thought that other people read you the wrong way, just as they might have felt that you misread them. Our personal judgments are often based on a need to protect our egos and self-esteem (McMillan, 2000; McMillan & Wergin, 2002).

Being objective means trying to see things as they really are, not just as we would like them to be. It means using methods of decision making that keep us in touch with the real world.

Last but not least, science involves *thinking critically*. In chapter 1, we saw that thinking critically consists of thinking reflectively, thinking productively, and evaluating the evidence. Critical thinkers question what some people say are "facts." They test the "facts." They examine research to see how sound its support of an idea really is.

These four attitudes are all ideals. No scientist possesses them all at every moment in life. But the closer we embrace these attitudes, the better we are able to use the basic tools of scientific theory and objective observation. They reduce the likelihood that information will be based on unreliable personal beliefs, opinions, and emotions. As you go through this book, practice using these scientific attitudes. You also would do well to call on these attitudes whenever you hear people discussing "facts" and arguing about issues.

mhhe com/ santrockp7 *Your instructor might assign journal articles to read in addition to the text. See, for example, Reading 2 (Science and Pseudoscience) in the PowerWeb section of the Online Learning Center.*

Research journals are the core of information in virtually every academic discipline. Those shown here are some of the increasing number of research journals that publish information about psychology.

Collaboration

Science is a collaborative effort. Even when different groups of scientists seem to be competing to answer a particular question first, they are part of a collective effort to increase an overall body of knowledge. More than that, no scientific finding has much impact until a community of scientists agrees through the process of peer review that the finding is true and important.

Within colleges and universities, psychologists share their findings with their colleagues and open their research to evaluation. Conferences conducted by national and international societies also allow psychologists to share and discuss their findings.

Research psychologists share their work by publishing it in scientific and academic journals. In contrast to other types of periodicals, these journals publish mainly scholarly research and information—usually in a specific field, such as the psychology of the workplace or human development. Journals gather and preserve the core information of the discipline of psychology.

Many journals are highly selective about what they publish. Every journal has a board of experts that evaluates articles submitted for publication. Before an article is accepted, the experts carefully assess its value to the field, the quality of its research methods and argument, and the clarity of its writing. The best journals maintain high standards, and some accept only 10 to 20 percent of the articles that are submitted to them.

The Scientific Method

One of the hallmarks of taking a scientific approach involves adopting the scientific method in studying topics in psychology (Langston, 2002; Salkind, 2003). Indeed, most of the studies psychologists publish in research journals follow the scientific method. The scientific method is essentially a four-step process:

1. Conceptualize a problem
2. Collect research information (data)
3. Analyze data
4. Draw conclusions

theory A broad idea or set of closely related ideas that attempt to explain and predict observations.

This process is based on two key ideas: theory and hypothesis. A **theory** is a broad idea or set of closely related ideas that attempt to explain certain observations. Theories try to explain why certain things have happened. They can also be used to make predictions about future observations. If your friend's new car stops dead in the street, you might have a theory to explain why it happened. Your theory probably includes the idea that there is an engine somewhere inside the car that is supposed to make it go. Your theory might also include the ideas that engines run on gasoline and that other parts of the car, such as the brakes, are designed to prevent the car from moving. This theory gives you a framework for trying to figure out why your friend's car isn't running.

In psychology, theories serve a similar purpose. They help to organize and connect observations and research. The overall meaning of the large numbers of research studies that are always being conducted in psychology would be difficult to grasp if theories did not provide a structure for summarizing and understanding them and putting them in a context with other research studies. In addition, good, testable theories generate interesting research questions and allow researchers to make observations that might answer those questions.

The second key idea underlying the scientific method is central to the process of testing a theory. A **hypothesis** is an idea that is arrived at logically from a theory. It is a prediction that can be tested. For example, if your theory about the car includes the idea of gasoline, you can test the hypothesis that a lack of gasoline caused the car to stop. You would simply add gas to the tank. If you observe that the car runs again after you add the fuel, you might conclude that your hypothesis is correct.

The relationship between theories and hypotheses is not necessarily as straightforward as this simple example indicates. A theory can generate many hypotheses. If more and more hypotheses related to a theory turn out to be true, the theory gains in credibility. One reason that so many scientists hold the theory of evolution in high esteem is that it has been able to predict many observations.

On the other hand, if some of the hypotheses derived from a theory are not supported by observation, the theory will have to be revised. In fact, entirely new theories have arisen when researchers have found that no existing theory explains the facts that they have observed. Sigmund Freud's theory that no significant changes take place in adulthood is an example of a theory that has been revised. For example, Erik Erikson (1968) observed that changes take place throughout the adult years, beginning with an increased motivation for intimacy during the 20s and 30s.

Essentially, then, the scientific method is a process of developing and testing theories. Scientists do not regard theories as being exactly, entirely, and permanently correct. A theory is judged by its ability to generate hypotheses that predict important events and behaviors. Depending on how well it predicts, a theory gains or loses support. Some theories sound great at first, but testing shows them to be worthless. Other theories start out sounding less useful but are shaped and improved in the course of testing.

A good example of the links between theory and hypothesis and the research process that binds them together is the work of James Pennebaker, a research psychologist at the University of Texas at Austin (where he also got his undergraduate degree in psychology). He is interested in the connection between emotions and health (Pennebaker & Graybeal, 2001). You may be interested to learn how his research proceeded through the four steps of the scientific method. Notice how deeply theory and hypothesis were integrated in Pennebaker's research.

1. Conceptualize a Problem   Pennebaker's thinking about emotions and health began in a very personal way. He had gotten married just after finishing college, and a few years later his marriage was in trouble. After about a month of deep depression and emotional isolation, he began to write privately every day about his problems. After about a week of writing, he says, "I noticed my depression lifting. For the first time in years—perhaps ever—I had a sense of meaning and direction. I fundamentally understood my deep love for my wife and the degree to which I needed her" (Pennebaker, 1997).

Some years later, he looked back on that experience and wondered why his private writing had helped him. He became interested in a theory of catharsis that had

hypothesis An idea that is a testable prediction, often arrived at logically from a theory.

James Pennebaker (*right*) discussing the value of writing about emotional experiences with participants in one of his research studies.

been developed by Freud and the psychodynamic psychologists nearly a hundred years before.

As we will see in chapters 11 and 14, the theory of catharsis says that by expressing pent-up emotions, a person can often eliminate those emotions, along with unwanted physical symptoms of stress and anxiety. This is the basis of psychotherapy—a process in which individuals experience relief by talking about their problems with a therapist.

Pennebaker's personal experience led him to ask whether this theory of catharsis should perhaps be modified. For example, to experience the benefits of emotional release, was it really necessary to talk to a psychotherapist? (After all, therapists can be expensive!) In fact, was it really necessary to be speaking to anyone at all? Could people with emotional troubles achieve the same relief by writing? And could people actually improve their physical health simply by writing about their problems?

To explore these ideas further, Pennebaker needed to express his questions in more specific and concrete terms. He began by developing a hypothesis that he could test through concrete, objective observations. For example, exactly what did he mean by "writing about emotions"? Also, what did he mean by "physical health"? He needed to translate these ideas into operational definitions. An **operational definition** is an objective description of how a research variable is going to be observed and measured. Operational definitions eliminate some of the fuzziness and loose ends that easily creep into thinking about a problem. By being very specific about what measurements define concepts, operational definitions also clarify concepts for other scientists.

In 1983, Pennebaker and a graduate student, Sandra Beall, decided to test the following hypothesis:

> If people write about their negative emotions and the situations that caused them, people will reduce their stress and be more healthy in the future.

operational definition A circumstance or behavior defined in such a way that it can be objectively observed and measured.

To operationally define writing about emotions, they decided to instruct student volunteer participants to write continuously for 15 minutes each day on 4 consecutive days about an upsetting or traumatic experience and to express how they felt about the experience when it happened and how they felt about it while writing. To operationally define health, they decided to record the number of illness visits that their participants made to the student health center before, during, and after the study.

2. Collect Research Information (Data)   The second step of the scientific method is to actually collect research information (data). Among the important decisions to be made about collecting data are whom to choose as the participants and which research methods to use. I explore a number of research methods in some detail shortly, so I focus here on the research participants.

Will the participants be people or animals? Will they be children, adults, or both? Will they be females, males, or both? Will they be of a single ethnicity, such as Anglo-American, or will they come from a diversity of ethnic groups?

When psychologists conduct a study, they usually want to be able to draw conclusions that will apply to a larger group of people (or animals) than the participants they actually study. Thus an investigator might conduct a study of 300 married couples in Los Angeles, California, in which the husband shows a history of abusing the wife, but the researcher may have the goal of applying the results to all married couples with a history of wife abuse in the United States. The entire group about which the investigator wants to draw conclusions is the **population.** In this particular study of spousal abuse, the population is all couples in the United States in which men abuse their wives. The subset of the population chosen by the investigator for study is a **sample.** In this spousal abuse study, the sample is the 300 couples in Los Angeles. By surveying a sample of the population, the researcher avoids the difficulties involved in trying to find and survey all American husbands who abuse their wives.

The target population to which the investigator wants to generalize varies with the study. For example, in a study of the effects of televised violence on boys' aggression, the population might be all 3- to 5-year-old boys in the United States. In a study of how people think critically, the population might be all humans. In a study of whether chimpanzees have language, the population might be all chimpanzees. Generalization from the sample to the population can be made only if the sample is representative—or "typical"—of the population. For example, a disproportionate number of the 300 couples in the study of spousal abuse might have income in the poverty range and be Anglo-Americans. We would have to be cautious about generalizing the results of this study to the entire American population of couples in which the husbands abuse their wives, especially to such couples in higher income brackets and from other ethnic groups.

To more closely mirror the population, an investigator would use a **random sample,** a sample that gives every member of the population an equal chance of being selected. In the study of spousal abuse, a representative sample would reflect the population's age, socioeconomic status, age at marriage, geographic location, religion, and so forth. A random sampling provides much better grounds for generalizing the results to a population than a nonrandom sample.

Investigators do not always use appropriate sampling methods (Dooley, 2001; Heiman, 1995). Surveys by newspapers and magazines often ask people to mail or call in their opinions. However, the people who respond probably feel more strongly about the issue than do those who do not respond. In addition, the readers may feel differently about an issue than the population as a whole. For example, when a magazine such as *Playboy* asks its readers for their opinions on sexual attitudes, the results are likely to show far more permissiveness than if a random sample of adults in the United States were asked about their sexual attitudes.

You may be getting the impression that psychological research is worthless if it is not based on a random sample. However, random sampling is important in some types of research, much less important in others. If a researcher wants to know how often spousal abuse occurs in the United States, obtaining a random sample is

population The entire group that the investigator wants to learn about.

sample The subset of the population that the investigator has chosen for study.

random sample A sample in which every member of the population has an equal chance of being selected.

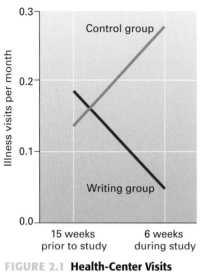

FIGURE 2.1 Health-Center Visits Before and After Writing about Emotional Experiences

Summarize the scientific method applied to James Pennebaker's study of emotional writing and health. *Do you think writing about your emotional experiences might improve your health? Explain.*

important. However, in many research studies, psychologists are interested in studying specific aspects of behavior under specific conditions, in which case they deliberately do not obtain a random sample. In these studies, they might want people with certain characteristics to be well represented. Say that a researcher is interested in discovering whether having been married before is related to the incidence and nature of spousal abuse that a wife experiences. That researcher might study 50 couples in which the wife had been married before and 50 couples in which she had not, without worrying about whether these couples represent all the couples in the United States.

It also should be pointed out that in many areas of psychology, generalization comes from similar findings across a number of studies rather than from random sampling within a single study. Imagine five or six studies conducted with varied samples—maybe one in Los Angeles with low-income and middle-income ethnic minority participants; another in Athens, Georgia, with middle-income White participants; and others with somewhat similar or different participant characteristics. If all the studies find that frequent conflict and one or more incidents of physical abuse in a previous marriage are related to spousal abuse, then we gain better confidence that these findings can be generalized to the population as a whole.

Pennebaker's sample was not random (Pennebaker, Kiecolt-Glaser, & Glaser, 1988). At the time of this research, he was teaching at Southern Methodist University (SMU), where introductory psychology students were given credit for participating in psychological research. His sample was a group of 46 students who volunteered to be his participants. Because a sample of students at SMU is not likely to be very representative of people in general, Pennebaker needed to be cautious about generalizing from the sample. Whatever results he got from this research, he would want to try similar experiments on other samples (for example, older people, nonstudents, people in other countries) before he generalized about most humans.

3. Analyze Data Once psychologists collect measurable research data, they use mathematical (statistical) procedures to understand what the data mean (Moore, 2001; Sanocki, 2001). Later in the chapter, I examine two types of statistical procedures in some detail.

In his research, Pennebaker used a number of statistical procedures to determine whether students' health benefited from writing about emotional experiences. For example, he analyzed information about how often the students who wrote about their emotional experiences used the health center. As shown in figure 2.1, the two groups—the group who wrote about their emotional experiences and those who did not (control group)—visited the health center about equally prior to the experiment. However, after the writing group wrote about their emotional experiences, they visited the health center considerably less than the control group. Psychologists often use graphs, like the one shown in figure 2.1, to illustrate their results.

4. Draw Conclusions Pennebaker's research was set up so he could draw conclusions by comparing two groups: a group of students who wrote about their emotional trauma and another group of students who wrote about other things. When he and Sandra Beall examined their results, they found that the participants who wrote about their feelings made significantly fewer illness visits to the student health center afterward than those who did not write about their emotions.

Conclusions might also be made by connecting the research findings back to the hypothesis and its underlying theory. The results of Pennebaker's study were exciting. They confirmed the hypothesis and suggested that emotional "cathartic" writing actually causes improvements in a person's physical health. The results also suggested that the general theory of emotional catharsis should be modified to account for the fact that it can be achieved through writing, as well as talking, and does not require the presence of a therapist.

It is important to keep in mind that a revision of theory usually occurs only after a number of studies produce similar results. Before we change a theory, we want to be sure that the research is reliable. *Reliability* is the extent to which scientific research yields a consistent, reproducible result. In the case of Pennebaker's work, reliability would not be established until other experiments were performed to test the same basic idea under different conditions and with different samples of participants.

Pennebaker and others performed later studies with further interesting results. One study redefined "health" operationally in terms of certain measurements of participants' blood samples (Pennebaker, Kiecolt-Glaser, & Glaser, 1988). It found that the emotional writing led to improvements in the immune system. Another study involved a group of unemployed middle-aged engineers who were deeply angry after having been suddenly fired by a corporation for which some of them had worked for 30 years (Spera, Buhrfeind, & Pennebaker, 1994). This study found that emotional writing led many of the engineers to overcome their frustration and find new jobs, whereas engineers who did not do the writing remained angry and unemployed.

Other studies have shown that writing about emotions does not necessarily have the same results for everyone. Emotional writing may or may not work for you as an individual. But, if you are interested, the Psychology and Life box on page 48, "Writing Might Improve Your Health," gives suggestions about how to do it.

Review and Sharpen Your Thinking

1   Explain what makes psychology a science.

- Discuss the four attributes of a scientific attitude.
- Explain the need for collaboration in science.
- Name and describe the four main steps in the scientific method. Include the role of theory and hypothesis in your description.

Create an operational definition of *happy.* List several measurements that you might use to assess happiness.

mhhe●com/
santrockp7

For study tools related to this learning goal, see the Study Guide, the CD-ROM, and the Online Learning Center.

TYPES OF RESEARCH   2

Descriptive Research   **Correlational Research**   **Experimental Research**

How do psychologists collect research data?

As you have seen, research information (or data) is an important step in the scientific method. The collection of data is the fundamental means of testing hypotheses. This section describes the major ways that data about behavior and mental processes can be gathered. There are three basic types of research used in psychology: descriptive, correlational, and experimental. Each has strengths and weaknesses.

Descriptive Research

Some important psychological theories have grown out of descriptive research, which serves the purpose of observing and recording behavior. For example, a psychologist might observe the extent to which people are altruistic or aggressive toward each other. By itself, descriptive research cannot prove what causes some phenomenon, but it can reveal important information about people's behaviors and attitudes. Descriptive research methods include observation, surveys and interviews, standardized tests, and case studies.

Writing Might Improve Your Health

Research by James Pennebaker and others has demonstrated that writing about your emotions can improve your physical health. Pennebaker (1997) suggests that you experiment to find a method that works best for you.

What to Write

You don't need to write about the biggest trauma in your life. Write about issues that currently bother you and preoccupy your thinking. Write about things that you may not be telling others out of fear of embarrassment or punishment. Write as objectively as you can about an experience that troubled you. Also express your emotions. Write as deeply as you can about your feelings.

How to Write It

Just start and keep writing. Don't worry about spelling or making good sentences. If you get stuck, go back and repeat what you were writing before you got stuck.

When and Where to Write

Emotional writing is not the same as keeping a journal of various events and thoughts as they occur. Write when you feel like writing. Write when you feel prepared to get into the writing on an emotional level. Find a place where you won't be interrupted or distracted.

What to Do with Your Writing

Keep the writing to yourself. Don't plan to show it to anyone. Don't write for an audience, which may cause you to hold back or feel that you need to justify yourself.

What to Expect

Writing about your emotions is not a cure-all. It's not a substitute for tackling problems that may keep you angry, sad, or frustrated. If you are in the midst of turmoil over the death of a loved one or the end of a long-term relationship, your writing may not make you instantly feel better, but it probably will help you see things in better perspective. You may feel sad or depressed for a few hours or even a day or so after writing. However, most people feel relieved, happier, and more content soon after.

Observation Scientific observation requires an important set of skills. Unless we are trained observers and practice our skills regularly, we might not know what to look for, we might not remember what we saw, we might not realize that what we are looking for is changing from one moment to the next, and we might not communicate our observations effectively (Billman, 2003).

Recall how James Pennebaker's interest in catharsis grew out of his own experience during a time of depression. Suppose we had been observing him back then and it was up to us to decide whether or not he was truly depressed. What constitutes depressed behavior? How do we know it when we see it? Does it involve a blank emotionless stare, a saddened look? To distinguish a person who is depressed from a person who is not, how long should we say that the person's blank stares and saddened looks must last?

For observations to be effective, they have to be systematic (Leary, 2001). We have to have some idea of what we are looking for. We have to know whom we are observing, when and where we will observe, and how the observations will be made. And in what form will they be recorded? In writing? Tape recording? Video?

To see the importance of observing systematically, consider the story of a horse named Hans, who was a clever animal. Hans had been trained by a retired math teacher, Mr. von Osten, to communicate by tapping his forefoot and moving his head. A head nod meant "yes," a shake "no." Mr. von Osten developed a code for verbal information in which each letter was represented by a pair of numbers. The letter *A* was coded as one tap, pause, one tap; the letter *I* was three taps, pause, two taps. Once Hans learned to tap his foot or move his head when questioned, he was given simple math problems and then fed a piece of bread or carrot for correct responses.

By the end of his training, Hans could spell words spoken to him, and he excelled in math.

Hans became a hero in Germany—his picture was on liquor bottles and toys. Experts were so impressed that an official commission of 13 scientists, educators, and public officials examined the horse, testing him to see if he really could do all of the things claimed. They came away even more impressed and issued a statement saying that there was no evidence of any intentional influence or aid on the part of Hans' questioners. According to the experts, Hans could reason and "talk."

But one scientist was not so sure that Hans was as intelligent as he had been portrayed. Oskar von Pfungst, a very sharp observer, had detected that Hans always faced his questioner. Von Pfungst hypothesized that this positioning might have something to do with Hans' math ability.

The scientist set up a very simple experiment to test this hypothesis. He wrote numbers on a card and held them up one at a time, asking Hans to tap out the numbers written on each card. Half of the cards von Pfungst held so that only Hans, not von Pfungst, could see what was on them. With the cards von Pfungst could see, Hans was his usual brilliant self, getting 92 percent of the answers correct. But for the numbers von Pfungst could not see, Hans was no longer a brilliant horse, getting only 8 percent correct.

Von Pfungst repeated the experiment over and over again with nearly the same results. He then carefully observed Hans with his other questioners, including Hans' owner, Mr. von Osten. As soon as they stated the problem to Hans, most questioners would turn their heads and upper bodies slightly. When Hans had made the correct number of foot taps, the questioners would move their heads upward.

When he learned of these observations, Mr. von Osten was stunned. Despite his years of work with the horse, he had never dreamed that Hans had learned to "read" him. Von Osten commented that he actually was angry at the horse and felt betrayed by him.

Thus we can see that what sometimes seems to be the truth may be a false impression. Furthermore, even experts can be fooled if they don't make appropriate use of other research procedures to check their observations.

If we are going to make observations, where should we make them? We have two choices: the laboratory and the everyday world.

Laboratory Observation When we observe scientifically, we often need to control certain factors that determine behavior but are not the focus of our inquiry (Crano & Brewer, 2002; Hoyle & Judd, 2002). For this reason much of psychology's research is conducted in a *laboratory*, a controlled setting with many of the complex factors of the "real world" removed.

An experiment conducted by Albert Bandura (1965), in which children behaved more aggressively after observing a model being rewarded for aggression, was briefly described in chapter 1. Bandura conducted this study in a laboratory with adults the child did not know. Thus he controlled when the child witnessed aggression, how much aggression the child saw, and what form the aggression took. Bandura would not have had as much control over the experiment or as much confidence in the results if the study had been conducted in the children's homes and if familiar people had been present, such as the child's parents, siblings, or friends.

Laboratory research does have some drawbacks. First, it is almost impossible to conduct research without the participants' knowing they are being studied. Second, the laboratory setting is unnatural and therefore can cause the participants to behave unnaturally.

Another drawback of laboratory research is that people who are willing to come to a university laboratory may not fairly represent groups from diverse cultural backgrounds. Those who are unfamiliar with university settings and with the idea of "helping science" may be intimidated by the setting.

THE FAR SIDE   By GARY LARSON

A researcher codes the behavior of children in a play group as part of a research study. *What are some advantages and disadvantages of laboratory research?*

Cross-cultural studies have to take into account cultural differences in values that can distort results.

mhhe.com/ **santrockp7**

Still another problem is that some aspects of mind and behavior are difficult if not impossible to examine in the laboratory. Laboratory studies of certain types of stress, for example, may even be unethical.

Naturalistic Observation Naturalistic observation provides insight that we sometimes cannot achieve in the laboratory (Langston, 2002). **Naturalistic observation** means observing behavior in real-world settings, making no effort to manipulate or control the situation. Psychologists conduct naturalistic observations at sporting events, day-care centers, work settings, malls, and other places people live in and frequent. Suppose that you wanted to study the level of civility on your campus. Most likely, you would want to include some naturalistic observation of how people treat one another in places like the cafeteria or the library reading room.

Naturalistic observation was used in one study that focused on the relationship between caregiving behavior and the positive development of toddlers from 18 to 30 months of age (Wachs & others, 1993). The study was conducted in Egypt. Twice a month, researchers observed children and the caregivers in the children's homes for a period of 30 minutes, noting such behaviors as how frequently the caregivers talked with the children and guided their play. They also observed the number of vocalizations made by the children and the amount of time they spent playing with objects. As had been found in studies of Western families, the more the Egyptian caregivers talked with and guided young children's play, the more alert, vocal, and actively involved in play the children were (Bukatko & Daehler, 2001).

naturalistic observation Observations of behavior in real-world settings with no effort to manipulate or control the situation.

Jane Goodall was a young woman when she made her first trip to the Gombe Research Center in Tanzania, Africa. Fascinated by chimpanzees, she dreamed about a career that would allow her to explore her hunches about the nature of chimpanzees. A specialist in animal behavior, she embarked on a career in the bush that involved long and solitary hours of careful, patient observation. Her observations spanned 30 years, years that included her marriage, the birth of her son, untold hardship, and inestimable pleasure. Due to her efforts, our understanding of chimpanzees in natural settings dramatically improved. *What are some other aspects of behavior that could be studied by using naturalistic observation?*

Surveys and Interviews   Sometimes the best and quickest way to get information about people is to ask them for it. One technique is to interview them directly. A related method that is especially useful when information from many people is needed is the survey, sometimes referred to as a questionnaire. A standard set of questions is used to obtain people's self-reported attitudes or beliefs about a particular topic. In a good survey, the questions are clear and unbiased, allowing respondents to answer unambiguously.

Surveys and interviews can be used to study a wide range of topics from religious beliefs to sexual habits to attitudes about gun control. Surveys and interviews can be conducted in person or over the telephone. Some surveys also are now being conducted over the Internet.

"Would you say Attila is doing an excellent job, a good job, a fair job, or a poor job?" Drawing by Chas Addams; ©1982 The New Yorker Magazine, Inc.

Some survey and interview questions are unstructured and open-ended, such as "Could you elaborate on your optimistic tendencies?" or "How fulfilling would you say your marriage is?" They allow for unique responses from each person surveyed. Other survey and interview questions are more structured and ask about more specific things. For example, a structured survey or interview question might ask, "How many times have you talked with your partner about a personal problem in the past month: 0, 1–2, 3–5, 6–10, 10–30, every day?"

One problem with surveys and interviews is the tendency of participants to answer questions in a way that they think is socially acceptable or desirable rather than telling what they truly think or feel. For example, a person might exaggerate the amount of communication that goes on in a relationship in order to impress the interviewer.

One example of a survey conducted by the Gallup organization (1999) asked parents their beliefs about the most important problems facing schools. Forty-three percent cited drugs, 40 percent sex, 39 percent discipline in the classroom, 28 percent violence, and 25 percent social pressure among students to be popular. The survey was based on telephone interviews with a randomly selected sample of 338 U.S. parents. Recall the discussion of random sampling earlier in the chapter. When surveys are conducted on a national basis, as Gallup polls are, random sampling is considered to be an important aspect of the survey process.

David Sirota is an industrial-organizational psychologist who uses smaller scale surveys in his work. He diagnoses an organization's problems by surveying people in the organization through questionnaires or informal interviews with individuals and small groups. He might ask, "Why do employees stay with the company?" or "What helps them produce quality products or quality service?" or "Do they have the right training and the right equipment?" or "How does management treat employees?" He also frequently surveys the company's customers, asking how well the company is meeting their needs.

Industrial-organizational psychologist David Sirota (standing) discussing the development of a survey with other researchers.

Standardized Tests   A **standardized test** requires people to answer a series of written or oral questions or sometimes both. A standardized test has two distinct features: an individual's answers are tallied to yield a single score, or set of scores, that reflects something about that individual; and the individual's score is compared with the scores of a large group of similar people to determine how the individual responded relative to others (Aiken, 2003; Cohen & Swerdlik, 2002). One widely used standardized test in psychology is the Stanford-Binet intelligence test, which is described in chapter 10.

Scores on standardized tests are often stated in percentiles. Suppose you scored in the 92nd percentile on the Scholastic Assessment Test (SAT). This score would mean that 92 percent of a large group of individuals who previously took the test received scores lower than yours.

standardized test An oral or written assessment for which an individual receives a score indicating how the individual reponded relative to others.

Standardized tests require individuals to answer a series of written or oral questions. The individual on the left is being given a standardized test of intelligence.

The main advantage of standardized tests is that they provide information about individual differences among people (Domino, 2000; Walsh & Betz, 2001). One problem with standardized tests is that they do not always predict behavior in nontest situations. Another problem is that standardized tests are based on the belief that a person's behavior is consistent and stable, yet personality and intelligence—two primary targets of standardized testing—can vary with the situation. For example, a person may perform poorly on a standardized intelligence test in an office setting but score much higher at home, where he or she is less anxious.

This criticism is especially relevant for members of minority groups, some of whom have been inaccurately classified as mentally retarded on the basis of their scores on intelligence tests (Valencia & Suzuki, 2001). In addition, cross-cultural psychologists caution that many psychological tests developed in Western cultures might not be appropriate in other cultures (Cushner & Brislin, 1995). People in other cultures may have had experiences that cause them to interpret and respond to questions much differently from the people on whom the test was standardized.

Case Study A **case study,** or case history, is an in-depth look at a single individual. Case studies are performed mainly by clinical psychologists when, for either practical or ethical reasons, the unique aspects of an individual's life cannot be duplicated and tested in other individuals (Dattilio, 2001). A case study provides information about one person's fears, hopes, fantasies, traumatic experiences, upbringing, family relationships, health, or anything that helps the psychologist understand the person's mind and behavior. For example, we could have observed Pennebaker during the period of his deep depression and used our observations as the basis of a case study.

Traumatic experiences have produced some truly fascinating case studies in psychology. Consider the following: A 26-year-old schoolteacher met a woman with whom he fell intensely in love. But several months after their love affair began, the schoolteacher became depressed, drank heavily, and talked about suicide. The suicidal ideas progressed to images of murder and suicide. His actions became bizarre. On one occasion he punctured the tires of his beloved's car. On another he stood on the side of the road where she passed frequently in her car, extending his hand in his pocket so that she would think he was holding a gun. Only eight months after meet-

case study An in-depth look at a single individual.

ing her, the teacher shot her while he was a passenger in the car that she was driving. Soon after the act, he ran to a telephone booth to call his priest. The girlfriend had died (Revitch & Schlesinger, 1978).

This case reveals how depressive moods and bizarre thinking can precede violent acts, such as murder. Other vivid case studies appear later in this book, among them a modern-day wild child named Genie, who lived in near isolation during her childhood, and a woman named Eve with three personalities. They don't indicate how everyone will react in similar circumstances, but they give us an idea of the range of possibilities in human behavior and some of the effects of different experiences.

Another, more positive example of a case study is the analysis of India's spiritual leader Mahatma Gandhi by psychodynamic theorist Erik Erikson (1969). Erikson studied Gandhi's life in great depth to discover insights about how his positive spiritual identity developed, especially during his youth. In putting the pieces of Gandhi's identity development together, Erikson described the contributions of culture, history, family, and various other factors that might affect the way other people develop an identity.

Case histories provide dramatic, in-depth portrayals of people's lives, but remember that we must be cautious when generalizing from this information. The subject of a case study is unique, with a genetic makeup and personal history that no one else shares. In addition, case studies involve judgments of unknown reliability. Psychologists who conduct case studies rarely check to see whether other psychologists agree with their observations.

Correlational Research

In **correlational research,** the goal is to describe the strength of the relationship between two or more events or characteristics. The more strongly the two events are correlated (or related or associated), the more effectively we can predict one event from the other (Vernoy & Kyle, 2003). This form of research is a key method of data analysis, which, you may recall, is the third step in the scientific method.

The degree of relationship between two variables is expressed as a numerical value called a *correlational coefficient.* Let's assume that we have data on the relationship between how long your instructor lectures (the *X* variable) and the number of times students yawn (the *Y* variable). For the sake of this example, let's assume these data produce a correlation coefficient (represented by the letter *r*) of +.70. Remember this number, as it will soon be used to illustrate what a correlation coefficient tells you about the relationship between two events or characteristics.

For the moment, however, you need to know only that the number tells you the strength of the relationship between the two factors. The rule is simple: The closer the number is to 1.00, the stronger the correlation; conversely, the closer the number is to .00, the weaker the correlation. Figure 2.2 offers guidelines for interpreting correlational numbers. But perhaps you are wondering about the significance of the plus sign in the correlation coefficient of +.70 that we have calculated in our classroom study.

Positive and Negative Correlations   The numeric value of a correlation coefficient always falls within the range from +1.00 to −1.00, but the negative numbers do not indicate a lower value than positive numbers. A correlation of +.65 is just as strong as a correlation of −.65. The plus and minus sign do have different meanings, however, which you will learn about in a moment. The most important point is that you must avoid the temptation to attach value judgments to correlational signs. A positive correlation is not "good" or "desirable" and a negative correlation is not "bad" or "undesirable."

As you can see, there are two parts to a correlation coefficient: the number and the sign. Remember that the plus or minus sign tells you nothing about the strength

Mahatma Gandhi was the spiritual leader of India in the middle of the twentieth century. Erik Erikson conducted an extensive case study of his life to determine what contributed to his identity development. *What are some limitations of the case study approach?*

1.00	Perfect relationship; the two factors always occur together
.76–.99	Very strong relationship; the two factors occur together very often
.51–.75	Strong relationship; the two factors occur together frequently
.26–.50	Moderate relationship; the two factors occur together occasionally
.01–.25	Weak relationship; the two factors seldom occur together
.00	No relationship; the two factors never occur together

FIGURE 2.2 Guidelines for Interpreting Correlational Numbers

correlational research Research with the goal of describing the strength of the relationship between two or more events or characteristics.

FIGURE 2.3 Scatter Plots Showing Positive and Negative Correlations
A positive correlation is a relationship in which two factors vary in the same direction, as shown in the two scatter plots on the left. A negative correlation is a relationship in which two factors vary in opposite directions, as shown in the two scatter plots on the right.

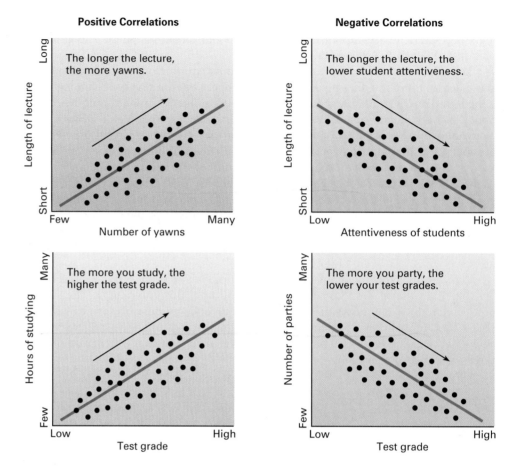

Let's return to the example about the relationship between how long your professor lectures and the number of times students yawn. As mentioned earlier, those two variables produced a correlation coefficient of +.70. What does the number .70 tell us? That these two factors happen together frequently. And what does the positive sign indicate? That the two factors vary in the same direction. As the amount of time your professor lectures increases, so does the number of yawns.

of the correlation. A correlation coefficient of −.87 is closer to −1.00, and thus indicates a stronger correlation, than the coefficient of +.45 is to +1.00.

What the plus or minus sign does tell you is the direction of the relationship between the two variables. A *positive correlation* is a relationship in which the two factors vary in the same direction. Both factors tend to increase together, or both factors tend to decrease together. Either relationship represents a positive correlation. A *negative* correlation, in contrast, is a relationship in which the two factors vary in opposite directions. As one factor increases, the other factor decreases. Thus a correlation of +.15 would indicate a weak positive correlation, and a −.74 would indicate a strong negative correlation. Examples of scatter plots showing positive and negative correlations appear in figure 2.3.

Let's return to the example about the relationship between how long your professor lectures and the number of times students yawn. As mentioned earlier, those two variables produced a correlation coefficient of +.70. What does the number .70 tell us? That these two factors happen together frequently. And what does the positive sign indicate? That the two factors vary in the same direction. As the amount of time your professor lectures increases, so does the number of yawns.

An example of a negative correlation in this situation might be the relationship between how long your instructor lectures and the level of student attentiveness. As the length of time your instructor lectures increases, the level of student attentiveness decreases. These two factors vary in opposite directions and thus have a negative correlation.

Correlation and Causation In trying to make sense of the world, people often make a big mistake about correlation. Look at the terms in bold type in the following newspaper headlines:

Researchers **Link** Coffee Consumption to Cancer of Pancreas
Scientists Find **Connection** Between Ear Hair and Heart Attacks
Psychologists Discover **Relationship** Between Marital Status and
    Health
Researchers Identify **Association** Between Loneliness and Social Skills
Parental Discipline **Tied** to Personality Disorders in Children

Reading these headlines, the general public would tend to jump to the conclusion that coffee causes cancer, ear hair causes heart attacks, and so on. But all of the words in bold type are synonymous only with correlation, not with causality. *Correlation does not equal causation.*

As you read about the findings of psychological studies, or findings in other sciences, guard against making the same mistake. Remember, correlation means only that two factors seem to occur together. Being able to predict one event based on the occurrence of another event does not necessarily tell us anything about the cause of either event (Sprinthall, 2003).

Why, then, do researchers even bother doing correlational studies? Why don't they simply conduct experiments, which provide the most compelling evidence of causality? There are several reasons. For instance, it would be unethical to carry out an experiment in which expectant mothers are directed to smoke varying numbers of cigarettes to see how cigarette smoke affects birth weight and fetal activity level. Also, the issue under investigation may be post hoc (after the fact) or historical, such as studying the childhood backgrounds of people who are abusive parents. Further, sometimes the factors simply cannot be manipulated experimentally, such as the effects of the September 11, 2001, attack on the World Trade Center on the residents of New York City.

To ensure that you understand the difference between correlation and causation, let's consider another example. Imagine a study in which it is found that people who make a lot of money have higher self-esteem than their counterparts who make less money. We could interpret this correlation to mean that making a lot of money causes high self-esteem. But we need to consider two other interpretations (see figure 2.4). One is that developing high self-esteem causes people to make a lot of money. Another interpretation is that a third factor, such as education, social upbringing, or genetic tendencies, causes the correlation between making a lot of money and high self-esteem.

Throughout this book you will read about numerous correlational research studies. Keep in mind how easy it is to assume causality when two events or characteristics are merely correlated.

Correlational methods permit research in situations that cannot be experimentally manipulated, such as disasters like the 2001 attack on the World Trade Center in New York. *What are some other examples of situations for which correlational methods might be well suited?*

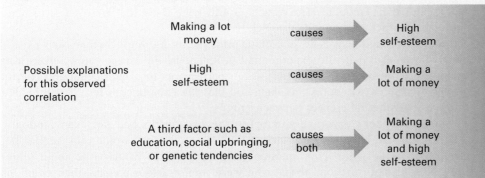

Observed Correlation: As people make a lot of money, their self-esteem increases.

Possible explanations for this observed correlation

Making a lot money — causes → High self-esteem

High self-esteem — causes → Making a lot of money

A third factor such as education, social upbringing, or genetic tendencies — causes both → Making a lot of money and high self-esteem

An observed correlation between two events cannot be used to conclude that one event causes the second event. Other possibilities are that the second event causes the first event or that a third event causes the correlation between the first two events.

FIGURE 2.4 Possible Explanations of Correlational Data

Experimental Research

Both Mary Calkins and James Pennebaker used experimental research to find answers to their questions about human behavior. So do many other research psychologists who are interested in determining causes of behavior—that is, why people do what they do (Myers & Hansen, 2002). An **experiment** is a carefully regulated procedure in which one or more factors believed to influence the behavior being studied are manipulated while all other factors are held constant.

If the behavior under study changes when a factor is manipulated, we say that the manipulated factor has caused the behavior to change. In other words, the experiment has demonstrated cause and effect. The cause is the factor that was manipulated, and the effect is the behavior that changed because of the manipulation. Nonexperimental research methods (descriptive and correlational research) cannot establish cause and effect because they do not involve manipulating factors in a controlled way.

Independent and Dependent Variables Experiments have two types of changeable factors, or variables: independent and dependent. An **independent variable** is a manipulated, influential, experimental factor. It is a potential cause. The label *independent* is used because this variable can be manipulated independently of other factors to determine its effect. Researchers have a vast array of options open to them in selecting independent variables, and one experiment may include several independent variables (Shaughnessy, Zechmeister, & Zechmeister, 2003).

In Pennebaker's first experiment, the independent variable was writing about emotions. Pennebaker manipulated this variable by asking different participants to write about their problems in different ways. For example, he asked some participants to write objectively about an emotional situation, without indulging their feelings. He asked other participants to both describe an experience and write how they felt about it. He also asked other participants to write about a topic that was unrelated to emotional events.

A **dependent variable** is a factor that can change in an experiment in response to changes in the independent variable. As researchers manipulate the independent variable, they measure the dependent variable for any resulting effect.

In Pennebaker's first experiment, the dependent variable was the number of visits that the student made to the health center during the several months after writing about an emotional experience. He found that the number of visits depended on the sort of writing that the student was asked to do.

Experimental and Control Groups Experiments can involve one or more experimental groups and one or more control groups. An **experimental group** is a group whose experience is manipulated. A **control group** is as much like the experimental group as possible and is treated in every way like the experimental group except for the manipulated factor. The control group thus serves as a baseline against which the effects of the manipulated condition can be compared.

In Pennebaker's studies, the experimental groups were those that were asked to write about their emotions. The control groups were those that were asked to write about some other, nonemotional topic.

Random assignment is an important principle in deciding whether each participant will be placed in the experimental group or in the control group. **Random assignment** means that researchers assign participants to experimental and control groups by chance. It reduces the likelihood that the experiment's results will be due to any preexisting differences between groups.

In Pennebaker's experiment, suppose the participants had not been randomly assigned but had been allowed to choose which group they would join—either the group that would write about emotions or the group that would write about something else. In that situation, people who were comfortable expressing their emotions might choose to join the first group, and people who were not comfortable expressing their emotions might choose to be in the second group. As a result, any differ-

experiment A carefully regulated procedure in which one or more factors believed to influence the behavior being studied are manipulated and all other factors are held constant.

independent variable The manipulated, influential, experimental factor in an experiment.

dependent variable The factor that can change in an experiment in response to changes in the independent variable.

experimental group A group in a research study whose experience is manipulated.

control group A comparison group that is treated in every way like the experimental group except for the manipulated factor.

random assignment Assignment of participants to experimental and control groups by chance.

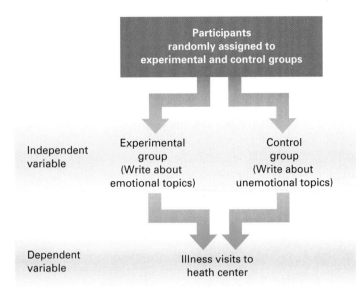

FIGURE 2.5 Random Assignment and Experimental Design

ence between the groups in terms of health at the end of the experiment might owe nothing to the effects of writing but simply reflect the effects of a person's comfort in expressing emotions (see figure 2.5).

Pennebaker randomly assigned each participant to either the experimental group that wrote about emotional experiences or a control group that wrote about a non-emotional topic. The independent variable (which is always the manipulated variable) was the type of writing the students did (about the emotion situation or about something else). The dependent variable was the number of illness visits that students paid to the health center after the writing. The design of this experiment allowed Pennebaker to argue that the emotional writing caused better health.

Some Cautions About Experimental Research   Although experimental research is a powerful tool for discovering the causes of behavior, experimental research must be done cautiously, with safeguards (Elmes, Kantowitz, & Roediger, 2003; Kantowitz, Roediger, & Elmes, 2001; Vadum & Rankin, 1998). Expectations and biases on the part of the people involved in the experiment can tarnish results (Rosnow & Rosenthal, 2002).

Experimenter Bias   Experimenters may subtly (and often unknowingly) influence their research participants. **Experimenter bias** occurs when the experimenter's expectations influence the outcome of the research.

In a classic study, Robert Rosenthal (1966) turned college students into experimenters. They were randomly assigned rats from the same litter. However, half of the students were told that their rats were "maze bright," whereas the other half were told that their rats were "maze dull." The students then conducted experiments to test their rats' ability to navigate mazes. The results were stunning. The so-called maze-bright rats were more successful than the maze-dull rats at running the mazes. The only explanation for the results is that the college students' expectations affected the performance of the rats. In subsequent studies, researchers have demonstrated that experimenters' expectations influence not only rodent behavior but human behavior as well (Rosenthal, 1994).

Research Participant Bias and the Placebo Effect   Like the experimenters, research participants may have expectations about what they are supposed to do and how they should behave that affect the results of experiments (Christiansen, 2001). **Research participant bias** occurs when the behavior of research participants during the experiment is influenced by how they think they are supposed to behave.

experimenter bias The influence of the experimenter's own expectations on the outcome of the research.

research participant bias The influence of research participants' expectations on their behavior within an experiment.

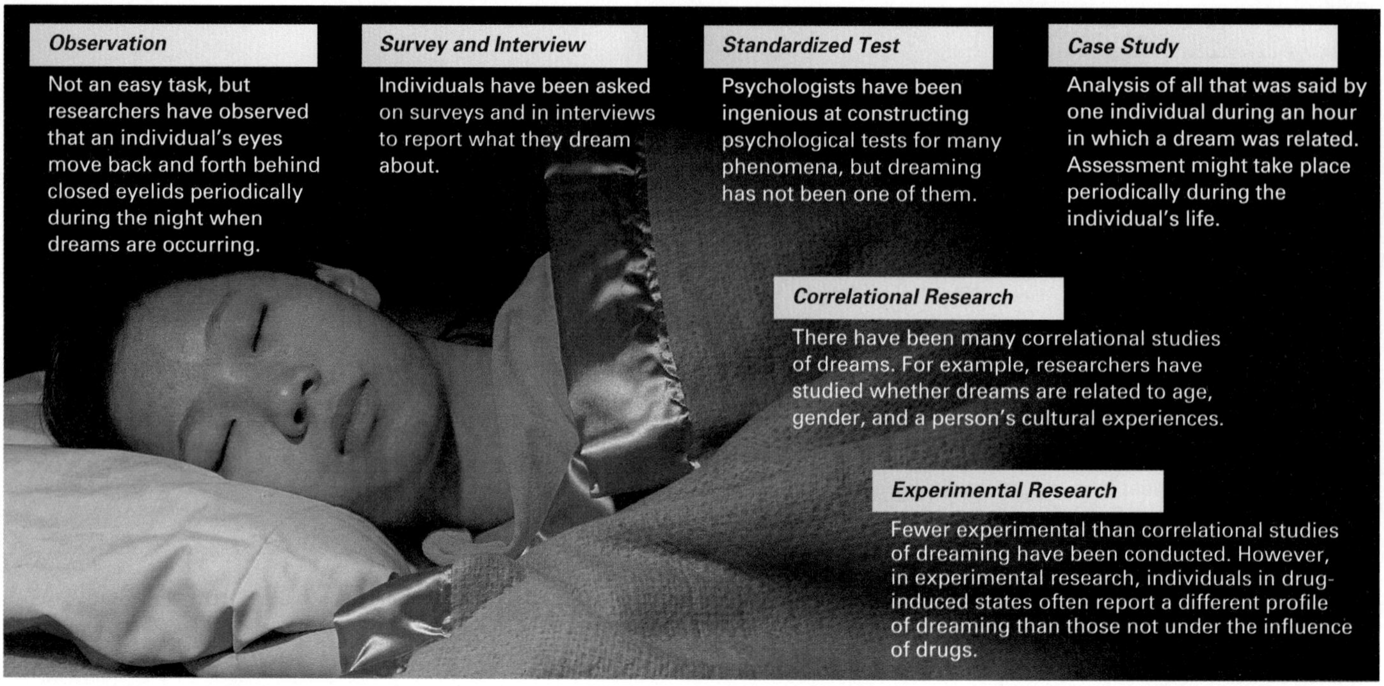

Observation	Survey and Interview	Standardized Test	Case Study
Not an easy task, but researchers have observed that an individual's eyes move back and forth behind closed eyelids periodically during the night when dreams are occurring.	Individuals have been asked on surveys and in interviews to report what they dream about.	Psychologists have been ingenious at constructing psychological tests for many phenomena, but dreaming has not been one of them.	Analysis of all that was said by one individual during an hour in which a dream was related. Assessment might take place periodically during the individual's life.

Correlational Research

There have been many correlational studies of dreams. For example, researchers have studied whether dreams are related to age, gender, and a person's cultural experiences.

Experimental Research

Fewer experimental than correlational studies of dreaming have been conducted. However, in experimental research, individuals in drug-induced states often report a different profile of dreaming than those not under the influence of drugs.

FIGURE 2.6 Psychology's Research Methods Applied to Dreaming

placebo An innocuous, inert substance or condition that may be given to participants instead of a presumed active agent, such as a drug, to determine if it produces effects similar to those of the active agent.

placebo effect The influence of participants' expectations, rather than the experimental treatment, on experimental outcome.

double-blind experiment An experiment that is conducted so that neither the experimenter nor the participants are aware of which participants are in the experimental group and which are in the placebo control group until after the results are calculated.

For example, in one study, the researchers first assessed participants' sensitivity to pain (Levine, Gordon, & Fields, 1979). Then they gave the participants an injection of a painkiller, or so the participants thought. Actually, they received a **placebo,** an innocuous, inert substance that has no specific physiological effect. (A placebo can be given to participants instead of the presumed active agent, such as a drug, to determine if it produces the effects thought to characterize the active agent.) Subsequently, when the experimenter administered painful stimuli, the participants perceived less pain than they had in the earlier assessment of their sensitivity to pain. This experiment demonstrated a **placebo effect,** which occurs when participants' expectations, rather than the experimental treatment, produce an experimental outcome.

In many studies, the researchers deliberately make use of the placebo effect to test a drug's effectiveness (Wilens & others, 2001). For example, in one recent study, 204 adults with social phobia (having an intense fear of being humiliated or embarrassed in social situations) were randomly assigned either to an experimental group in which the participants were given a drug, sertraline, or to a control group, in which they received a placebo (Van Ameringen & others, 2001). After 20 weeks, those who took sertraline showed less social phobia than their counterparts who took the placebo.

Another way to make sure that neither the experimenter's nor the participants' expectations affect the outcome is to design a **double-blind experiment.** In this design, neither the experimenter nor the participants are aware of which participants are in the experimental group and which are in the control group until the results are calculated. The study of drug treatment for social phobia just described was conducted in a double-blind manner (Van Ameringen & others, 2001). Both the experimenter, who administered the drug, and the participants were kept in the dark about which individuals were receiving the drug and which were receiving a placebo that merely looked like the drug. Thus the experimenter could not make subtle gestures signaling who was receiving the drug and who was not. This was the same method that Oskar von Pfungst used to ensure that he was not subtly signaling the horse Hans to respond in a certain way to the number written on a card. A double-blind study allows researchers to tease apart the actual effects of the independent variable from the possible effects of the experimenter's and the participants' expectations about it.

At this point you have read about several different types of research in psychology. For another look how these research methods differ, see figure 2.6.

Review and Sharpen Your Thinking

2 *Discuss the three types of research that are used in psychology.*

- Name and describe four kinds of descriptive research and identify at least one advantage of each kind of study.
- State the goal of correlational research and explain the significance of the correlation coefficient.
- Discuss the experimental method, including its components. Include in your discussion the potential pitfalls of the experimental method and how to avoid them.

You have learned that correlation does not equal causation. Develop an example of two variables (two sets of observations) that are correlated but that you believe almost certainly have no causal tie between them.

For study tools related to this learning goal, see the Study Guide, the CD-ROM, and the Online Learning Center.

ANALYZING AND INTERPRETING DATA 3

Descriptive Statistics   Inferential Statistics

How do psychologists analyze and interpret research data?

As you saw in the previous discussion of the scientific method, after psychologists collect data, they analyze and interpret it. To do this, they call on *statistics*, which are mathematical methods used to report data. There are two basic categories of statistics: descriptive statistics, which are used to describe and summarize data, and inferential statistics, which are used to draw conclusions about those data.

Descriptive Statistics

Most psychological studies generate considerable numerical data. Just simply listing all of the scores generated by a study—for each individual in the study—is often not very meaningful. **Descriptive statistics** are the mathematical procedures researchers have developed to describe and summarize sets of data in a meaningful way. Descriptive statistics show us the "big picture"—that is, the overall characteristics of the data and the significant variations among them (Sanocki, 2001).

Measures of Central Tendency If you want to describe an "average" value for a set of scores, you would use a measure of central tendency. A *measure of central tendency* is a single number that tells you the overall characteristics of a set of data. The three measures of central tendency are the mean, the median, and the mode.

The **mean** is what people often think of as the average, although it is only one type of average. The mean is calculated by adding all the scores and then dividing by the number of scores. It is a good indicator of the central tendency for a group of scores; it is the measure of central tendency that is used most often.

The mean is not so helpful, however, when a group of scores contains a few extreme scores. Consider the annual earnings for the two groups of five people shown in the table that follows. Group 1 lists the earnings of five ordinary people. Group 2 is composed of the earnings of four ordinary people plus the approximate earnings of movie director Steven Spielberg. Now look at the means that have been calculated for the two groups. The vast difference between them is due to the one extreme score. In such a situation, one of the other two measures of central tendency, median or mode, would give a more accurate picture of the data overall.

descriptive statistics Mathematical procedures that are used to describe and summarize samples of data in a meaningful way.

mean A statistical measure of central tendency that is calculated by adding all the scores and then dividing by the number of scores.

Mean $22,000

Group 1		Group 2	
	$19,000		$19,000
	19,000		19,000
	23,000		23,000
	24,000		24,000
	25,000		45,000,000
Mean	$22,000	*Mean*	$9,017,000
Median	$23,000	*Median*	$23,000
Mode	$19,000	*Mode*	$19,000

The **median** is the score that falls exactly in the middle of the distribution of scores after they have been arranged (or ranked) from highest to lowest. When you have an odd number of scores (say, 5 or 7 scores), the median is the score with the same number of scores above it as below it. In the table, each group has a median income of $23,000. Notice that, unlike the mean, the median is unaffected by extreme scores. The medians are the same for both groups ($23,000), but their means are extremely different ($22,000 versus $9,017,000). Of course, if there is an even number of scores, there is no "middle" score. This problem is dealt with by averaging the scores that "share" the middle location.

The **mode** is the score that occurs most often in a set of data. In our present example, the mode is $19,000, which occurs twice in each group. All of the other annual incomes occur only once. The mode is the least used measure of central tendency. The mode can be useful, for example, in cases in which information is desired about preference or popularity. Consider a teacher who wants to know the most popular or least popular child in her classroom. She might create a questionnaire and ask students which of their classmates they like the most or the least. The most frequently nominated child would be the mode in these instances.

Measures of Variability   In addition to revealing the central characteristics of a sample, statistics can also give us *measures of variability*, which describe how much the scores in a sample vary from one another. Imagine that you are the owner of three computer stores that all have the same annual earnings of $1,200,000. However, these three stores fluctuate widely in their monthly earnings. Store 1 consistently produces a monthly income of about $10,000. Store 2 generates no income some months but produces $200,000 of income in other months. Store 3 loses money the first 9 months of every year but makes enormous profits during October, November, and December. You would be correct in saying that the mean annual earnings of each of your stores is $1,200,000. But business planning would be easier if you could also represent the individual fluctuations in the earnings of your three stores. Measures of variability can be very helpful in this regard.

Two common measures of variability are the range and the standard deviation. The **range** is the distance between the highest and the lowest scores. The ranges in the monthly incomes of your three stores could be something like this:

Store 1: $10,500 − $9,500 = $1,000
Store 2: $200,000 − $0 = $200,000
Store 3: $500,000 − (−$50,000) = $550,000

The difference between $1,000 and $550,000 a month—and thus the range of monthly earnings at your stores—is huge. The differences reflect the vastly different cash flow at each of the three stores.

median A statistical measure of central tendency that falls exactly in the middle of a distribution of scores after they have been arranged (or ranked) from highest to lowest.

mode A statistical measure of central tendency, the score that occurs most often.

range A statistical measure of variability that is the distance between the highest and lowest scores.

research is conducted in an ethical way; another is to recognize and try to overcome researchers' deeply buried personal biases. Researchers are not the only ones who face challenges, however. So do you. Every time you encounter information about psychology, whether in the popular media or in academic journals, you face the challenge of evaluating the information objectively and making sure that you are not jumping to the wrong conclusions.

Conducting Ethical Research

Ethics is an important part of your understanding of the science of psychology. Even if you never have any formal exposure to psychology after you take this course, you will find that scientific research in psychology and related disciplines affects your everyday life. For one thing, decision makers in business, government, schools, and many other institutions use the results of psychological research to help people lead happier, healthier, more productive lives.

Psychological research affects our pocketbooks as well, at least indirectly. Very often, psychological research is supported by government grants. Because the allocation of grant money is highly competitive—not only within the scientific community but also between science and other government-sponsored projects—our society as a whole must continually decide which lines of research are the most beneficial. In recent years, for example, our priorities have shifted to educational research in the wake of a series of school shootings, declining test scores, and other problems that youth face.

In addition, the explosion in technology has forced society to grapple with looming ethics questions that were unimaginable only a few decades ago (Kimmel, 1996). Fertility research, which enables previously sterile couples to have children, might also allow prospective parents "to call up and order" the characteristics they prefer in their children—which might someday tip the balance of males and females in the world. This same line of research has led to the spectacle of frozen embryos being passed about in the courts as part of divorce settlements. Should embryos leftover from procedures for increasing fertility be saved or discarded?

Ethics in psychological research may affect you more personally if you serve at some point, as is quite likely, as a participant in a study. In that event, you need to know about your rights as a participant and about the responsibilities researchers have in assuring that these rights are safeguarded. Participants' experiences can have life-altering consequences for them if researchers fail to consider their well-being. For example, one investigation of young dating couples asked them to complete a questionnaire that coincidentally stimulated some of the participants to think about potentially troublesome issues (Rubin & Mitchell, 1976). One year later, when the researchers followed up with the original sample, 9 of 10 participants said they had discussed their answers with their dating partners. In most instances, the discussions helped to strengthen the relationships. But in some cases, the participants used the questionnaire as a springboard to discuss problems or concerns previously hidden. One participant said, "The study definitely played a role in ending my relationship with Larry." In this case, the couple had different views about how long they expected to be together. She was thinking of a short-term dating relationship only, whereas he was thinking in terms of a lifetime. Their answers to the questions brought the disparity in their views to the surface and led to the end of their relationship. Researchers have a responsibility to anticipate the personal problems their study might cause and to at least inform the participants of the possible fallout.

If you ever become a researcher in psychology yourself, you need an even deeper understanding of ethics. You may never become a researcher in the field of psychology, but you may carry out one or more experimental projects in psychology courses. Even smart, conscientious students frequently do not consider the rights of the participants who serve in their experiments. A student might think, "I volunteer in a home for the mentally retarded several hours a week. I can use the residents of the home in my study to see if a particular treatment helps improve their memory for everyday tasks." But without proper permissions, the most well-meaning, kind, and considerate studies still violate the rights of the participants.

Ethics Guidelines   Safeguarding the rights of research participants is a challenge because the potential harm is not always obvious. At first glance, you might not imagine that a questionnaire on dating relationships among college students would have any substantial impact or that an experiment involving treatment of memory loss would be anything but beneficial. But psychologists increasingly recognize the lasting harm that might come to the participants in a psychological study.

Today, colleges and universities have review boards that evaluate the ethical nature of research conducted at their institutions. Proposed research plans must pass the scrutiny of a research ethics committee before the research can be initiated.

In addition, the American Psychological Association (APA) has developed ethics guidelines for its members. The code of ethics instructs psychologists to protect their participants from mental and physical harm. The participants' best interests need to be kept foremost in the researcher's mind (Rosnow, 1995). APA's guidelines address four important issues:

- **Informed consent.** All participants must know what their participation will involve and what risks might develop. For example, participants in a study on dating should be told beforehand that a questionnaire might stimulate thoughts about issues in their relationships that they have not considered. Participants also should be informed that in some instances a discussion of the issues might improve their relationships but that in others it might worsen the relationships and even end them. Even after informed consent is given, participants must retain the right to withdraw from the study at any time and for any reason.

- **Confidentiality.** Researchers are responsible for keeping all of the data they gather on individuals completely confidential and, when possible, completely anonymous.

- **Debriefing.** After the study has been completed, participants should be informed of its purpose and the methods that were used. In most cases, the experimenter also can inform participants in a general manner beforehand about the purpose of the research without leading participants to behave in a way that they think that the experimenter is expecting. When preliminary information about the study is likely to affect the results, participants can at least be debriefed after the study has been completed.

- **Deception.** This is an ethical issue that psychologists debate extensively (Hoyle & Judd, 2002). In some circumstances, telling the participants beforehand what the research study is about substantially alters the participants' behavior and invalidates the researcher's data. For example, suppose a psychologist wants to know whether bystanders will report a theft. A mock theft is staged, and the psychologist observes which bystanders report it. Had the psychologist informed the participants beforehand that the study intended to discover the percentage of bystanders who will report a theft, the whole study would have been undermined. And so the researcher deceives participants about the purpose of the study, perhaps leading them to believe that it has some other purpose. In all cases of deception, however, the psychologist must ensure that the deception will not harm the participants and that the participants will be told the true nature of the study (debriefed) as soon as possible after the study is completed (Chastain & Landrum, 1999).

The federal government also takes a role in ensuring that research involving human participants is conducted ethically. It has an office devoted to ensuring the well-being of participants in research studies. Over the years, the Federal Office for Protection from Research Risks has been faced with many challenging and controversial decisions—among them informed consent rules for research on mental disorders, regulations governing research on pregnant women and fetuses, ethical issues regarding AIDS vaccine research, and ramifications of surreptitious egg and embryo swapping by some fertility researchers (now convicted on felony charges).

The Ethics of Research with Animals For generations, psychologists have used animals in some research. Animal studies have provided a better understanding of and solutions for many human problems (Leavitt, 2000). Neal Miller, who has made important discoveries about the effects of biofeedback on health, listed the following areas in which animal research has benefited humans (Miller, 1985):

- Psychotherapy techniques and behavioral medicine
- Rehabilitation of neuromuscular disorders
- Alleviation of the effects of stress and pain
- Drugs to treat anxiety and severe mental illness
- Methods for avoiding drug addiction and relapse
- Treatments to help premature infants gain weight so they can leave the hospital sooner
- Methods used to alleviate memory deficits in old age

Only about 5 percent of APA members use animals in their research. Rats and mice account for 90 percent of all psychological research with animals. How widespread is abuse to animals in psychological research? Animal welfare and rights activists would have you believe that abuse to these animals is extensive. It is true that researchers sometimes use procedures that would be unethical with humans, but they are guided by a set of standards for housing, feeding, and maintaining the psychological and physical well-being of their animal subjects. Researchers are required to weigh potential benefits of the research against possible harm to the animal and to avoid inflicting unnecessary pain. Animal abuse simply is not as common as animal activist groups charge. Stringent ethical guidelines must be followed, whether animals or humans are the subjects in psychological research (Herzog, 1995).

Values Questions are asked not only about the ethics of psychology but also about its values, its standards for judging what is worthwhile and desirable. Some psychologists argue that psychology should be value-free and morally neutral. From their perspective, the psychologist's role as a scientist is to present facts as objectively as possible.

Others believe that because psychologists are human, they cannot possibly be value-free, even if they try to be. Indeed, some people even argue that psychologists should take stands on value-laden issues. For example, if research shows that day care in the first year of life is harmful to children's development, shouldn't psychologists support reforms to improve day care or support mandates to have businesses give parents up to a year of paid leave after their child is born? The underlying question is psychologists' scientific responsibilities versus their responsibilities to society as a whole. To think further about psychology and values, see the Critical Controversy box.

Minimizing Bias

The debate over the place of values in psychology continues. But psychologists have generally come to agree that another type of personal objectivity is desirable when doing research. Psychological studies are most useful when they are conducted without bias or prejudice toward any particular group of people—especially biases based on sex or gender and on culture or ethnicity.

Is Psychology Value-Free

Do you agree or disagree with the following statements?

	AGREE	DISAGREE
1. Human beings are basically good.	‾‾‾	‾‾‾
2. By changing the environment, you can change people's behavior.	‾‾‾	‾‾‾
3. Intelligence is the most important human trait.	‾‾‾	‾‾‾
4. People are too concerned about themselves.	‾‾‾	‾‾‾
5. Physical attraction is important in choosing a mate.	‾‾‾	‾‾‾
6. Women are becoming too assertive.	‾‾‾	‾‾‾
7. Divorce is wrong.	‾‾‾	‾‾‾
8. Religion is not an appropriate area of study for psychologists.	‾‾‾	‾‾‾
9. Money can bring happiness.	‾‾‾	‾‾‾
10. It is okay to cheat if you don't get caught.	‾‾‾	‾‾‾

The way you responded to these items provides insight about your values. If you decide to become a psychologist, might your views on these topics, as well as others, influence the area you choose to research? Might psychologists' values influence how they respond in a media interview? Might clinical psychologists' values affect the advice they give to clients? Might psychology professors' values influence the topics they choose to discuss in class and how they respond to student's questions?

In some cases, researchers' values might influence their choice of research questions. A divorced woman might decide to study the inadequate involvement and support of noncustodial fathers in their children's lives rather than the increased role of fathers in caring for children because of her soured relationship with her ex-husband. An Asian American might choose to study the importance of conformity to a group's goals rather than an individual's unique contributions to a project because he or she believes that getting along with others in a group is more important than an individual's achievement.

When psychologists are called on as experts, they may make statements and recommendations that are laden with values. For example, a psychologist interviewed by Ted Koppel on *Nightline* may have certain values concerning government's responsibility in caring for the homeless, parents' responsibility in an adolescent's use of cocaine, and the responsibility of an individual with a psychological disorder who has committed mass murder.

Psychotherapists whom people consult about problems may have certain personal values concerning self-esteem, marriage, sexual conduct, and other topics that influence the advice they give. For example, one psychotherapist might perceive a client's sexual behavior as "sick," whereas another might think of it as an adaptive sexual variation.

Psychology professors have certain values about gender, moral behavior, religion, child rearing, and how to get ahead in life that might influence what they communicate in their lectures and how they respond to students' questions. For example, one professor might perceive that a female's assertive behavior is too aggressive, whereas another might think of the behavior as competent.

But wait a minute. Isn't psychology supposed to be an objective science? As a science, psychology is dedicated to discovering facts about behavior and creating theories to explain those facts. In this description, there is no mention of values. The scientific approach requires only that psychology discover the most dependable facts and generate the best theories possible (Kimble, 1989). In the pure world of science, there is no place for values. Some critics, though, question whether a view of science as value-free is realistic (Seligman, Olson, & Zanna, 1996). They argue that—although psychologists often strive to reduce the role of values as they seek to discover facts about behavior—in the court of life, which is psychology's setting, values and psychology are sometimes difficult to disentangle.

What do you think?

- Is psychology value-free? Explain.
- How might the culture in which psychologists grow up influence their values, and how might those values in turn affect their choice of research topics and the advice they give to clients in psychotherapy?
- Are religious values appropriate study material for psychologists? How might psychologists study religious values?

Gender Bias For centuries, society has had a strong gender bias, a preconceived notion about the abilities of women and men that prevented individuals from pursuing their own interests and achieving their potential. Mary Calkins' story at the beginning of the chapter is just one example of the barriers women have faced in the academic world and in their careers. But gender bias also has had a less obvious effect within psychology (Etaugh & Bridges, 2001; Shields & Eyssell, 2001).

Too often psychological research has had a gender bias (Kimmel & Crawford, 2002; Paludi, 2002). For too long, the female experience has been subsumed under the male experience (Tetreault, 1997). Conclusions are often drawn about females' attitudes and behaviors from research done with males as the only participants.

Florence Denmark and her colleagues (1988) argue as well that too often, when gender differences are found, they are unduly magnified. For example, a researcher might report in a study that 74 percent of the men had high achievement expectations versus only 67 percent of the women and go on to talk about the differences in some detail. In reality, this might be a rather small difference. It also might disappear if the study were repeated or the study were found to have methodological problems that don't allow such strong interpretations.

Researchers giving females equal rights in research have raised some new questions (Tetreault, 1997):

- How might gender bias influence the choice of hypotheses, participants, and research design? For example, the most widely known theory of moral development was proposed by a male (Lawrence Kohlberg) in a male-dominant society (the United States), and males were the main participants in research used to support the theory for many years.
- How might research on topics of primary interest to females, such as relationships, feelings, and empathy, challenge existing theory? For example, in the study of moral development, the highest level has often been portrayed as based on a principle of "justice for the individual" (Kohlberg, 1976). However, more recent theorizing notes that individuality and autonomy tend to be male concerns and suggests that a principle based on relationships and connections with others be added to our thinking about high-level moral development (Gilligan, 1982, 1996).
- How has research that has exaggerated gender differences between females and males influenced the way that people think about females? For example, some researchers believe that gender differences in mathematics have often been exaggerated and have been fueled by societal bias (Hyde & Mezulis, 2001; Hyde & Plant, 1995). Such exaggeration of differences can lead to negative expectations for females' math performance.

Cultural and Ethnic Bias The realization that psychological research needs to include more people from diverse ethnic groups has also been building (Graham, 1992). Historically, people from ethnic minority groups (African American, Latino, Asian American, and Native American) have been discounted from most research in the United States and simply thought of as variations from the norm, or average. Because their scores don't always fit neatly into measures of central tendency, minority individuals have been viewed as confounds, or "noise" in data. Consequently, researchers have deliberately excluded them from the samples they have selected (Ryan-Finn, Cause, & Grove, 1995). Given the fact that individuals from diverse ethnic groups have been excluded from psychological research for so long, we might reasonably conclude that people's real lives are perhaps more varied than research data have indicated in the past (Ponterotto & others, 2001; Stevenson, 1995).

Researchers also have tended to overgeneralize about ethnic groups (Trimble, 1989). **Ethnic gloss** is using an ethnic label, such as "African American" or "Latino," in a superficial way that portrays an ethnic group as being more homogeneous than it really is. For example, a researcher might describe a research sample like this: "The

ethnic gloss Involves using an ethnic label, such as "African American" or "Latino," in a superficial way that portrays the ethnic group as more homogeneous than it really is.

Look at the two photographs, one of all White males, the other of a diverse group of females and males from different ethnic groups, including some White individuals. Consider a topic in psychology, such as parenting, love, or cultural values. *If you were conducting research on this topic, might the result of the study be different depending on whether the participants in your study were the individuals in the photograph on the left or those on the right?*

participants were 20 Latinos and 20 Anglo-Americans." A more complete description of the Latino group might be something like this: "The 20 Latino participants were Mexican Americans from low-income neighborhoods in the southwestern area of Los Angeles. Twelve were from homes in which Spanish is the dominant language spoken, 8 from homes in which English is the main language spoken. Ten were born in the United States, 10 in Mexico. Ten described themselves as Mexican American, 5 as Mexican, 3 as American, 2 as Chicano, and 1 as Latino." Ethnic gloss can cause researchers to obtain samples of ethnic groups that are not representative of the group's diversity, which can lead to overgeneralization and stereotyping.

One psychologist interested in obtaining better research information about gender and ethnicity is Pam Reid, a professor of psychology at the University of Michigan (Reid & Zalk, 2002). She also is a research scientist for the University of Michigan Institute for Research on Women and Gender. Her research focuses on the ways in which gender, socioeconomic status, and ethnicity are involved in the development of social skills. Currently, Reid and her students are working on a research study to determine why middle school girls from various ethnic backgrounds stop taking classes in mathematics. Reid points out that many psychological findings have been based on research with middle-socioeconomic-status European Americans. Taking into account the expectations, attitudes, and behaviors of diverse ethnic groups can only enrich psychological theory and practice.

Being a Wise Consumer of Information About Psychology

Television, radio, newspapers, and magazines all frequently report on psychological research that is likely to be of interest to the general public. Much of the information has been published in professional journals or presented at national meetings, and most major colleges and universities have a media relations department that contacts the press about current research by their faculty.

You should be aware, however, that not all psychological information that is presented for public consumption comes from professionals with excellent credentials and reputations at colleges or universities or in applied mental health settings (Stanovich, 2001). Because journalists, television reporters, and other media personnel are not usually trained in psychological research, they often have trouble sorting through the widely varying material they find and making sound decisions about the best information to present to the public.

Pam Reid (*standing*) with students she mentors at the University of Michigan. Pam says that she took introductory psychology as an elective when she was an undergraduate and fell in love with it, a love that she still maintains.

In addition, the media often focus on sensationalistic and dramatic psychological findings to capture your attention. They tend to go beyond what actual research articles and clinical findings really say.

Even when the media present the results of excellent research, they have trouble adequately informing people about what has been found and the implications for people's lives. For example, this entire book is designed to carry out the task of carefully introducing, defining, and elaborating on key concepts and issues, research, and clinical findings. The media, however, do not have the luxury of so much time and space to detail and specify the limitations and qualifications of research. They often have only a few minutes or a few lines to summarize as best they can the complex findings of a study or a psychological concept.

In the end, you have to take responsibility for evaluating the reports on psychological research that you encounter in the media. To put it another way, you have to consume psychological information wisely. Five guidelines follow.

Distinguish Between Group Results and Individual Needs People who learn about psychological research through the media are likely to apply the results to their individual circumstances. Yet most research focuses on groups, and individual variations in participants' responses are seldom emphasized. As a result, the ill-informed consumer of psychological research may get the wrong idea about the "normality" of his or her circumstances. For example, researchers interested in the effects of divorce on an adult's ability to cope with stress might conduct a study of 50 divorced women and 50 married women. They might conclude that the divorced women, as a group, cope more poorly with stress than the married women in the study do. In this particular study, however, some of the divorced women were likely to be coping better than some of the married women. Indeed, of the 100 women in the study, the 2 or 3 women who were coping the best with stress may have been divorced women. It would be accurate to report the findings as showing that divorced women (as a group) coped less effectively with stress than married women (as a group) did. But it would not be sensible to conclude, after reading a summary of the results of the study, that your divorced sister may not be coping with stress as well as she thinks and recommend that she see a therapist.

The failure of the media to distinguish adequately between research on groups and the individual needs of consumers is not entirely their fault. Researchers have not made the difference clear, either. They often fail to examine the overlap in the data on the groups they are comparing and look for only the differences. And then too often they highlight only these differences in their reports as well.

Remember, if you read a report in a research journal or the media that states that the divorced women coped more poorly with stress than the married women did, you cannot conclude that all divorced women coped more poorly with stress. The only conclusion that you can reasonably draw is that more married women coped better than divorced women did.

Overgeneralizing from a Small Sample Media presentations of psychological information often don't have the space or time to go into details about the nature of the sample used in the study. Sometimes you will get basic information about the sample's size—whether it is based on 10 participants, 50 participants, or 200 participants, for example. If you can't learn anything else about the sample, at least pay attention to its number.

Small or very small samples require caution in generalizing to a larger population of individuals. For example, a sample of only 10 or 20 divorced women may have some unique characteristics that would make the study's finding inapplicable to many women. The women in the sample might all have high incomes, be White, be childless, live in a small southern town, and be undergoing psychotherapy. Divorced women who have moderate to low incomes, are from other ethnic backgrounds, have children, are living in different contexts, and are not undergoing psychotherapy might have given very different responses.

Look for Answers Beyond a Single Study The media might identify an interesting piece of research or a clinical finding and claim that it is something phenomenal with far-reaching implications. Although such pivotal studies do occur, they are rare. It is safer to assume that no single study will provide conclusive answers to an important question, especially answers that apply to all people. In fact, in most psychological domains that prompt many investigations, conflicting results are common. Answers to questions in research usually emerge after many scientists have conducted similar investigations that yield similar conclusions.

If one study reports that a particular therapy conducted by a particular therapist has been especially effective with divorced adults, you should not conclude that the therapy will work as effectively with all divorced adults and with other therapists until more studies are conducted. Remember that you should not take a report of one research study as the absolute, final answer to a problem.

Attributing Causes Where None Have Been Found Drawing causal conclusions from correlational studies is one of the most common mistakes made by the media. When a true experiment has not been conducted—that is, when participants have not been randomly assigned to treatments or experiences—two variables or factors might have only a noncausal relationship to each other (Leavitt, 2001). Remember from the discussion of correlation earlier in the chapter that causal interpretations cannot be made when two or more factors are simply correlated. We cannot say that one causes the other.

In the case of divorce, imagine that you read this headline: "Low income causes divorced women to have a high degree of stress." You can instantly conclude that the story is about a correlational study, not an experimental study. The word "causes" is used in error. Why? Because for ethical and practical reasons, women participants cannot be randomly assigned to become divorced or stay married, and divorced women cannot be randomly assigned to be poor or rich. A more accurate heading would probably be "Low-income divorced women have a high degree of stress," meaning that the researchers found a correlation between being divorced, having a low income, and having a lot of stress. Be skeptical of words indicating causation until you know more about the research they are describing.

Consider the Source of Psychological Information Remember that studies conducted by psychologists are not automatically accepted by the rest of the research community. The researchers usually must submit their findings to a journal for review by their colleagues, who make a decision about whether to publish the paper or not depending on the care taken in conducting the research. Although the quality of research and findings is not uniform among all psychology journals, in most cases journals submit the findings to far greater scrutiny than the popular media do (Stanovich, 2001).

Within the media, though, you can usually draw a distinction. The reports of psychological research in respected newspapers, such as the *New York Times* and *Washington Post*, as well as in credible magazines such as *Time* and *Newsweek*, are far more trustworthy than reports in tabloids, such as the *National Inquirer* and *Star.* But regardless of the source—serious publication, tabloid, or even academic journal—you are responsible for reading the details of the research behind the findings that are presented and analyzing the study's credibility.

Review and Sharpen Your Thinking

4 *Discuss some research challenges that involve ethics, bias, and information.*

- Describe researchers' ethical responsibilities to the humans and animals they study.
- Explain how gender, cultural, and ethnic bias can affect the outcome of a research study.
- Make a list of the things to keep in mind when you come across information pertaining to psychological research.

In the next few days, look through several newspapers and magazines for reports about psychological research. Also notice what you see and hear on television about psychology. Try applying the guidelines for being a wise consumer of information about psychology to these media reports.

mhhe.com/
santrockp7

For study tools related to this learning goal, see the Study Guide, the CD-ROM, and the Online Learning Center.

1 EXPLORING PSYCHOLOGY AS A SCIENCE

A Scientific Approach   Collaboration   The Scientific Method

Psychology's Scientific Methods

2 TYPES OF RESEARCH

Descriptive Research   Correlational Research   Experimental Research

3 ANALYZING AND INTERPRETING DATA

Descriptive Statistics   Inferential Statistics

4 FACING UP TO RESEARCH CHALLENGES

Conducting Ethical Research   Minimizing Bias   Being a Wise Consumer of Information about Psychology

1 *Explain what makes psychology a science.*

- A scientific attitude involves being curious, being skeptical, being objective, and thinking critically.
- Science is a collaborative effort in which colleagues share their findings, making them open for evaluation. Research psychologists usually publish their work in academic journals.
- The scientific method is essentially a four-step process: (1) conceptualize a problem, (2) collect research information (data), (3) analyze data, and (4) draw conclusions. Step 1 often involves a theory, which is a possible explanation for past observations that also can be used to predict future observations. Using a theory to generate a hypothesis or testable assumption, a researcher can collect and analyze data and then draw conclusions about the validity of the hypothesis.

2 *Discuss the three types of research that are used in psychology.*

- Descriptive research has the purpose of systematically observing and recording behavior. Four types of descriptive research are observation (in a laboratory or a naturalistic setting), surveys based on questionnaires and interviews, standardized tests, and case studies.
- In correlational research, the goal is to describe the strength of the relationship between two or more events or characteristics. A correlation coefficient is the numerical value that expresses the degree of relationship between two variables. An important point to remember is that correlation does not equal causation.
- Experimental research involves conducting an experiment, a systematic controlled study in which one or more factors believed to influence the behavior being studied are manipulated while all other factors are held constant. An experiment can determine cause and effect. An independent variable in an experiment is a manipulated, influential, experimental factor. A dependent variable is a factor that can change in an experiment in response to changes in the independent variable. Experiments can involve one or more experimental groups and one or more control groups. The experimental group is the group whose experience is being manipulated. The control group is a comparison group that is treated in every way like the experimental group except for the factor being manipulated. In random assignment, researchers assign participants to experimental and control groups by chance. Experimenter and research partici-

pant bias are potential pitfalls in experimental research. To reduce research participant bias, researchers may give a placebo to some participants. In a double-blind experiment, neither the experimenter nor the participant is aware of which participants are in the experimental or the control group until the results are analyzed.

3 *Distinguish between descriptive statistics and inferential statistics.*

- Descriptive statistics are used to describe and summarize samples of data in a meaningful way. Two types of descriptive statistics are measures of central tendency (mean, median, and mode) and measures of variability (range and standard deviation).
- Inferential statistics are used to draw conclusions about the data that have been collected. Inferential statistics aim to uncover statistical significance, which means that the differences observed between two groups are so large that they are highly unlikely to be the result of mere chance.

4 *Discuss some research challenges that involve ethics, bias, and information.*

- Researchers' ethical responsibilities include seeking participants' informed consent; ensuring their confidentiality; debriefing them about the purpose and potential personal consequences of participating; and avoiding unnecessary deception of participants. In animal research, ethical responsibilities include protecting subjects from unnecessary pain and discomfort while weighing the potential benefits of research against the possible harm to the animals.
- Psychologists need to guard against gender, cultural, and ethnic bias in research. Research in which only males or only middle-socioeconomic-status European Americans participated cannot be generalized to the population as a whole. Gender bias and ethnic bias can lead to inaccurate conclusions in psychological studies.
- Being a wise consumer of information about psychology means distinguishing between group results and individual needs; not overgeneralizing based on a small sample; understanding that a single study usually is not the defining word about an issue or a problem; not making causal conclusions from correlational studies; and evaluating the source of the information and its credibility.

Key Terms

theory, p. 42
hypothesis, p. 43
operational definition, p. 44
population, p. 45
sample, p. 45
random sample, p. 45
naturalistic observation,
   p. 50

standardized test, p. 51
case study, p. 52
correlational research, p. 53
experiment, p. 56
independent variable, p. 56
dependent variable, p. 56
experimental group, p. 56
control group, p. 56

random assignment, p. 56
experimenter bias, p. 57
research participant bias,
   p. 57
placebo, p. 58
placebo effect, p. 58
double-blind experiment,
   p. 58

descriptive statistics, p. 59
mean, p. 59
median, p. 60
mode, p. 60
range, p. 60
standard deviation, p. 61
inferential statistics, p. 62
ethnic gloss, p. 67

Apply Your Knowledge

1. Look back at the section, Maintaining a Healthy Skepticism, in chapter 1 (pp. 30–31). Find a website dedicated to one of the phenomena listed in this section. Using the four attributes of a scientific attitude, critically examine the claims made on the website. Describe the theory, the hypothesis, the data, and the analysis. Can you find all of this information on the website? If not, how would a scientist respond to the website?

2. Consider the following questions that might interest a psychologist. Describe a study you would use to address each of these questions, including what kind of research method you would employ.

   a. What percentage of people wash their hands after using the restroom?

   b. Does background music make people buy more at the grocery store?

   c. Is there a relationship between anger and car accidents?

   d. Do antidepressants work?

3. Visit the library at your school and find an article in a psychology journal. Describe what kind of study was done—was it descriptive, correlational, or an experiment? If it was an experiment, what were the independent and dependent variables? What kind of statistics did the researchers use? Can you tell if the results are statistically significant?

4. Much of the experimental research in psychology has been conducted using undergraduate students. How might this choice influence the interpretation of the results to other groups, such as children or older adults? Describe some of the special ethical issues that might be involved in using children and older adults in psychological experiments.

Connections

For extra help in mastering the material in this chapter, see the review sections and practice quizzes in the Student Study Guide, the CD-ROM, and the Online Learning Center.

3

Biological Foundations of Behavior

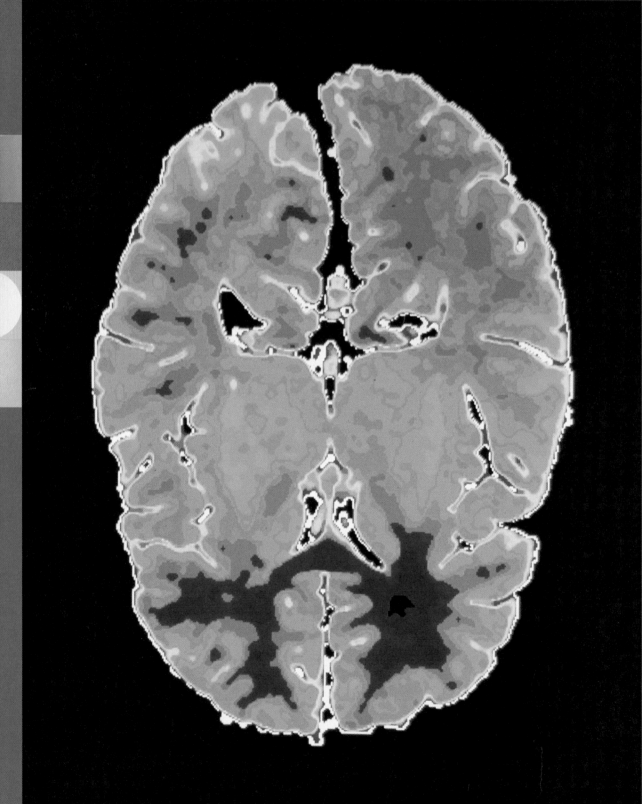

Learning Goals

1 Discuss the nature and basic functions of the nervous system.

2 Explain what neurons are and how they process information.

3 Identify the brain's levels and structures, and summarize the functions of its structures.

4 State what the endocrine system is and how it affects behavior.

5 Describe the brain's capacity for recovery and repair.

6 Explain how genetics and evolutionary psychology increase our understanding of behavior.

When Brandi Binder was just 6 years old, surgeons at the University of California at Los Angeles removed the right side of her cerebral cortex (the outermost part and highest level of the brain) in an effort to subdue frequent seizures caused by very severe and uncontrollable epilepsy.

Epileptic seizures like the ones experienced by Brandi are the result of electrical "brainstorms" that flash uncontrollably from one side of the brain to the other. Nerve cells on one side become overactive and stimulate overactivity in nerve cells on the other side. The excess stimulation produces a seizure in which the individual loses consciousness and goes into convulsions. In severe cases, seizures can occur numerous times during the day. Physicians have discovered that by severing the connection between the two sides of the brain or by removing the side of the brain in which the overactivity originates, they can eliminate the seizures or at least reduce their severity. Although not without risks and disadvantages, such surgery may greatly improve an individual's quality of life.

After her surgery, Brandi Binder had almost no control over muscles on the left side of her body, the side controlled by the right side of her brain. She needed years of therapy to regain abilities that she lost with the right side of her brain. At age 13, however, Brandi was an A student. She also loved music, math, and art, all of which are commonly associated with the brain's right side.

Brandi's story illustrates how amazingly adaptive and flexible the brain is, especially at an early age. In Brandi's case, the

Brandi Binder is evidence of the brain's great power, flexibility, and resilience. Despite having had the right side of her cortex removed, Brandi engages in many activities often portrayed as right-brain activities. She loves music, math, and art; she is shown here working on one of her paintings.

left side of her brain took over functions that are based on the right side. Although her recuperation has not been 100 percent— she never regained the use of her left arm, for example—her recovery is remarkable. Her story shows that if there is a way to compensate for damage, the brain will find it (Nash, 1997).

It is not by coincidence that the human brain is so versatile. It has evolved over millions of years from a small, fairly primitive organ into a very complex network capable of coordinating our body functions, our thoughts, our emotions, and our behaviors. Evolutionary psychologists emphasize that behaviors that increase an organism's reproductive success and enhance the ability to pass one's genes on to the next generation eventually prevail in nature over behaviors that do not promote the organism's survival. From their point of view, the complex human brain has evolved because its increased complexity in some individuals enabled them to behave in ways that gave them and their descendants a better chance of survival—for example, by being able to anticipate adversity and plan for ways to avoid it or cope with it.

This chapter examines important biological foundations of human behavior. The main focus is the nervous system and its command center—the brain.

It also explores the genetic and evolutionary processes that have a significant influence on who we are as individuals and how we behave.

1 THE NERVOUS SYSTEM

| Characteristics | Pathways in the Nervous System | Divisions of the Nervous System |

What is the nervous system and what does it do?

The **nervous system** is the body's electrochemical communication circuitry. The field that studies the nervous system is called *neuroscience,* and the people who study it are *neuroscientists.*

The human nervous system is made up of billions of interconnected cells, and it is likely the most intricately organized aggregate of matter on planet Earth (Campbell, Reece, & Mitchell, 2002). A single cubic centimeter of the human brain consists

nervous system The body's electrochemical communication circuitry, made up of billions of neurons.

of well over 50 million nerve cells, each of which communicates with many other nerve cells in information processing networks that make the most elaborate computer seem primitive.

Characteristics

The brain and nervous system guide our interaction with the world around us, move the body through the world, and direct our adaptation to our environment. Several extraordinary characteristics allow the nervous system to direct our behavior: complexity, integration, adaptability, and electrochemical transmission.

Complexity   The brain and nervous system are enormously complex. The brain itself is composed of billions of nerve cells. The orchestration of all of these cells to allow people to sing, dance, write, talk, and think is an awe-inspiring task. As Brandi Binder paints a piece of art, her brain is carrying out a huge number of tasks—involved in breathing, seeing, thinking, moving—in which extensive assemblies of nerve cells are participating.

Integration   Neuroscientist Steven Hyman (2001) calls the brain the *great integrator*. By this, he means that the brain does a wonderful job of pulling information together. Sounds, sights, touch, taste, hearing, genes, environment—the brain integrates all of these as we function in our world.

The brain and the nervous system have different levels and many different parts. Brain activity is integrated across these levels through countless interconnections of brain cells and extensive pathways that link different parts of the brain. Each nerve cell communicates, on average, with 10,000 others, making up miles and miles of connections (Bloom, Nelson, & Lazerson, 2001; Johnson, 2003). Consider what happens when a mosquito bites your arm. How does your brain know you were bitten and where? Bundles of interconnected nerve cells relay information about the bite from your arm through the nervous system in a very orderly fashion to the highest level of the brain.

Indeed, behaving in just about any way requires a lot of connections in your brain. Brandi Binder's painting does not occur because of what is going on in a single brain cell or a single part of her brain but rather because of the coordinated, integrated effort of many different nerve cells and parts of her brain.

Adaptability   The world around us is constantly changing. To survive, we must adapt to new conditions (Bloom, Nelson, & Lazerson, 2001). Our brain and nervous system together serve as our agent in adapting to the world. Although nerve cells reside in certain brain regions, they are not fixed and immutable structures. They have a hereditary, biological foundation, but they are constantly adapting to changes in the body and the environment (Wilson, 2003).

The term **plasticity** denotes the brain's special capacity for modification and change. The experiences that we have contribute to the wiring or rewiring of the brain (Blair, 2002; Greenough, 2000; Nash, 1997; Scharfman, 2002). For example, each time a baby tries to touch an object or gazes intently at a face, electrical impulses and chemical messengers shoot through the baby's brain, knitting brain cells together into pathways and networks.

The brain's plasticity is nowhere more evident than in Brandi Binder's case. After she lost much of the right side of her brain, the left side took over many functions that often are thought to reside only in the right side.

Electrochemical Transmission   The brain and the nervous system function essentially as an information processing system, powered by electrical impulses and chemical messengers. When people speak to each other, they use words. When neurons communicate with each other, they use chemicals.

plasticity The brain's special capacity for modification and change.

The electrochemical communication system works effectively in most people to allow us to think and act. However, when the electrochemical system is short-circuited, as in the case of Brandi's epilepsy, the flow of information is disrupted, the brain is unable to channel information accurately, and the person cannot effectively engage in mental processing and behavior. Epileptic seizures are the result of abnormal electrical discharges in the brain. Just as an electrical surge during a lightning storm can disrupt the circuits in a computer, the electrical surge that produces an epileptic seizure disrupts the brain's information processing circuits. The brains of individuals with epilepsy work effectively to process information between seizures, unless the seizures occur with such regularity that they cause brain damage. In about 75 percent of epilepsy cases, seizures do not cause structural damage to the brain.

Pathways in the Nervous System

As we interact with and adapt to the world, the brain and the nervous system receive and transmit sensory input, integrate the information received from the environment, and direct the body's motor activities. Information flows into the brain through sensory input, becomes integrated within the brain, and then moves out of the brain to be connected with motor output (Enger & Ross, 2003).

This flow of information through the nervous system occurs in specialized pathways that are adapted for different functions. These pathways are made up of afferent nerves, neural networks, and efferent nerves. **Afferent nerves,** or sensory nerves, carry information to the brain. The word *afferent* comes from the Latin word meaning "bring to." These sensory pathways communicate information about external and bodily environments from sensory receptors into and throughout the brain.

Efferent nerves, or motor nerves, carry the brain's output. The word *efferent* is derived from the Latin word meaning "bring forth." These motor pathways communicate information from the brain to the hands, feet, and other areas of the body that allow a person to engage in motor behavior.

Most information processing occurs when information moves through **neural networks** in the central nervous system. The function of these networks of nerve cells is to integrate sensory input and motor output (Peng, Qiao, & Xu, 2002). For example, as you read your class notes, the afferent input from your eye is transmitted to your brain, then passed through many neural networks, which translate (process) your black pen scratches into neural codes for letters, words, associations, and meaning. Some of the information is stored in the neural networks for future associations, and, if you read aloud, some is passed on as efferent messages to your lips and tongue. Neural networks make up most of the brain.

Divisions of the Nervous System

When the nineteenth-century American poet and essayist Ralph Waldo Emerson said, "The world was built in order and the atoms march in tune," he must have had the human nervous system in mind. This truly elegant system is highly ordered and organized for effective function.

Figure 3.1 shows the two primary divisions of the human nervous system: the central nervous system and the peripheral nervous system. The **central nervous system (CNS)** is made up of the brain and spinal cord. More than 99 percent of all nerve cells in our body are located in the CNS. The **peripheral nervous system (PNS)** is the network of nerves that connects the brain and spinal cord to other parts of the body. The functions of the peripheral nervous system are to bring information to and from the brain and spinal cord and to carry out the commands of the CNS to execute various muscular and glandular activities.

The peripheral nervous system itself has two major divisions: the somatic nervous system and the autonomic nervous system. The **somatic nervous system** consists of sensory nerves, whose function is to convey information from the skin and muscles to the CNS about conditions such as pain and temperature, and motor nerves,

---

afferent nerves Sensory nerves that transport information to the brain.

efferent nerves Motor nerves that carry the brain's output.

neural networks Clusters of neurons that are interconnected to process information.

central nervous system (CNS) The brain and spinal cord.

peripheral nervous system (PNS) The network of nerves that connects the brain and spinal cord to other parts of the body. It is divided into the somatic nervous system and the autonomic nervous system.

somatic nervous system Division of the PNS consisting of sensory nerves, whose function is to convey information to the CNS, and motor nerves, whose function is to transmit information to the muscles.

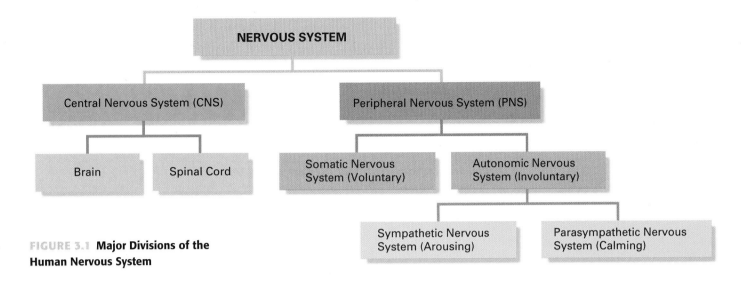

FIGURE 3.1 **Major Divisions of the Human Nervous System**

whose function is to tell muscles what to do. The function of the **autonomic nervous system** is to take messages to and from the body's internal organs, monitoring such processes as breathing, heart rate, and digestion. The autonomic nervous system also is divided into two parts: the **sympathetic nervous system** arouses the body and the **parasympathetic nervous system** calms the body.

To better understand the various divisions of the nervous system, let's see what they do in a particular situation. Imagine that you are preparing to ask a judge to dismiss a parking ticket. As you are about to enter the courtroom, you scan a note card one last time to remember what you plan to say. Your *peripheral nervous system* carries the written marks from the note card to your central nervous system. Your *central nervous system* processes the marks, interpreting them as words, while you memorize key points and plan ways to keep the judge friendly. After studying the notes several minutes longer, you jot down an additional joke that you hope will amuse her. Again your *peripheral nervous system* is at work, conveying to the muscles in your arm and hand the information from your brain that enables you to make the marks on the paper. The information that is being transmitted from your eyes to your brain and to your hand is handled by the *somatic nervous system*. This is your first ticket hearing, so you are a little anxious. Your stomach feels queasy, and your heart begins to thump. This is the *sympathetic* division of the *autonomic nervous system* functioning as you become aroused. You regain your confidence after reminding yourself that you were parked in a legal spot. As you relax, the *parasympathetic* division of the *autonomic nervous system* is working.

mhhe.com/
santrockp7

For study tools related to this learning goal, see the Study Guide, the CD-ROM, and the Online Learning Center.

Review and Sharpen Your Thinking

1 ***Identify the parts of the nervous system and explain their role in behavior.***

- Identify the fundamental characteristics of the brain and nervous system.
- Name and describe the pathways that allow the nervous system to carry out its three basic functions.
- Outline the divisions of the nervous system and explain their roles.

Try this exercise without looking at Figure 3.1. Suppose you (1) saw a person coming toward you, (2) realized it was someone famous, (3) got excited, (4) waved and shouted, (5) suddenly realized it was not a famous person, and (6) became suddenly calm again. Which part of your nervous system would have been heavily involved at each of these six points?

autonomic nervous system Division of the PNS that communicates with the body's internal organs. It consists of the sympathetic and parasympathetic nervous systems.

sympathetic nervous system The division of the autonomic nervous system that arouses the body.

parasympathetic nervous system The division of the autonomic nervous system that calms the body.

2 NEURONS

Specialized Cell Structure

Synapses and Neurotransmitters

The Neural Impulse

Neural Networks

What are neurons and how do they communicate?

Within each division of the nervous system, much is happening at the cellular level. Nerve cells, chemicals, and electrical impulses work together to transmit information at speeds of up to 330 miles per hour. As a result, information can travel from your brain to your hands (or vice versa) in a matter of milliseconds (Krogh, 2000; Martini, 2001).

There are two types of cells in the nervous system: neurons and glial cells. **Neurons** are the nerve cells that actually handle the information processing function.

The human brain contains about 100 billion neurons. The average neuron is as complex as a small computer and has as many as 10,000 physical connections with other cells. To have even the merest thought requires millions of neurons acting simultaneously (Carter, 1998).

Glial cells provide support and nutritional benefit functions in the nervous system (Lemke, 2001; Meller & others, 2002). Glial cells are not specialized to process information in the way that neurons are, although there are many more of them in the nervous system than there are neurons. In one study, neurons placed in a solution containing glial cells grew more rapidly and prolifically than neurons floating in the same solution without glial cells (Kennedy & Folk-Seang, 1986). This study indicates that glial cells function in a supportive or nutritive role for neurons.

Specialized Cell Structure

Not all neurons are alike. They are specialized to handle different information processing functions. However, all neurons do have some common characteristics. Most neurons are created very early in life, but their shape, size, and connections can change throughout the life span. Thus the way neurons function reflects a major characteristic of the nervous system that we described at the beginning of the chapter: plasticity. They are not fixed and immutable but can change. Every neuron has a cell body, dendrites, and axon (see figure 3.2).

The **cell body** contains the nucleus, which directs the manufacture of substances that the neuron needs for growth and maintenance.

Dendrites receive and orient information toward the cell body. One of the most distinctive features of neurons is the tree-like branching of their dendrites. Most nerve cells have numerous dendrites, which increase their surface area, allowing each neuron to receive input from many other neurons.

The **axon** is the part of the neuron that carries information away from the cell body toward other cells. Although very thin (1/10,000th of an inch), axons can be very long, with many branches. In fact, some extend more than three feet—all the way from the top of the brain to the base of the spinal cord.

Covering all surfaces of neurons, including the dendrites and axons, are very thin cellular membranes that are much like the surface of a bubble. The neuronal membranes are semipermeable, meaning that they contain tiny holes or *channels* that allow only certain substances to pass into and out of the neurons.

A **myelin sheath,** a layer of fat cells, encases and insulates most axons. By insulating axons, myelin sheaths speed up transmission of nerve impulses (Mattson, 2002; Paus & others, 2001). Multiple sclerosis, a degenerative disease of the nervous system in which a hardening of myelin tissue occurs, disrupts neuronal communication.

neuron Nerve cell that is specialized for processing information. Neurons are the basic units of the nervous system.

glial cells Provide support and nutritional benefits in the nervous system.

cell body Part of the neuron that contains the nucleus, which directs the manufacture of substances that the neuron needs for growth and maintenance.

dendrites Branches of a neuron that receive and orient information toward the cell body; most neurons have numerous dendrites.

axon The part of the neuron that carries information away from the cell body to other cells; each neuron has only one axon.

myelin sheath A layer of fat cells that encases and insulates most axons. The myelin sheath speeds up the transmission of nerve impulses.

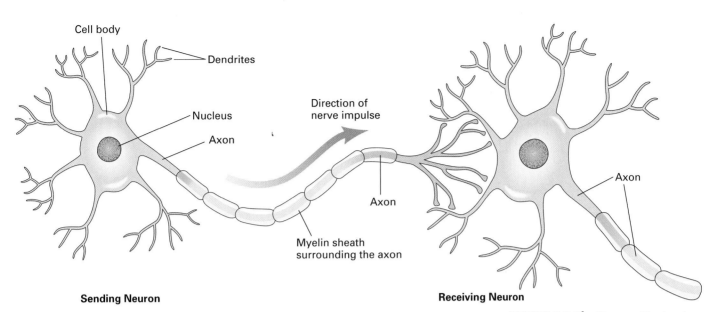

Cell body

Dendrites

Nucleus

Direction of
nerve impulse

Axon

Axon

Axon

Myelin sheath
surrounding the axon

Sending Neuron

Receiving Neuron

FIGURE 3.2 **The Neuron** The drawing shows the parts of a neuron and the connection between one neuron and another. Note the cell body, branching of dendrites, and the axon with a myelin sheath.

The myelin sheath developed as the brain evolved. As brain size increased, it became necessary for information to travel over longer distances in the nervous system. Axons without myelin sheaths are not very good conductors of electricity. With the insulation of myelin sheaths, they transmit electrical impulses and convey information much more rapidly. We can compare the myelin sheath's development to the evolution of freeways as cities grew. A freeway is a shielded road. It keeps fast-moving, long-distance traffic from getting snarled by slow local traffic.

The Neural Impulse

A neuron sends information through its axon in the form of brief impulses, or waves, of electricity. In old movies you might have seen telegraph operators tapping out messages one click at a time over a telegraph wire to the next telegraph station. That is what neurons do. To transmit information to other neurons, a neuron sends impulses ("clicks") through its axon to the next neuron. As you reach to turn this page, hundreds of such impulses will stream down the axons in your arm to tell your muscles just when to flex and how vigorously. By changing the rate and timing of the signals or "clicks," the neuron can vary its message.

How does a neuron—a living cell—generate electrical impulses? To answer this question, we need to further examine the nature of a neuron and the fluids in which it floats. A neuron is like a balloon filled with one kind of fluid and surrounded by a slightly different kind of fluid. The axon is a piece of the "balloon" that has been stretched to form a long, hollow tube. The axon tube is so thin that a few dozen axons in a bundle would be about as thick as a human hair. Floating in the fluids inside and outside the tube are electrically charged particles called *ions.*

Some of these ions, notably sodium and potassium, carry positive charges. Negatively charged ions of chlorine and other elements also are present. The cell membrane prevents negative and positive ions from randomly flowing into or out of the cell. The neuron creates electrical signals by moving positive and negative ions back and forth through its outer membrane. How does the movement of ions across the membrane occur? It's fairly simple. Embedded in the membrane—the wall of our balloon—are hundreds of thousands of small gates, called *ion channels,* that open and close to let the ions pass into and out of the cell. Normally, when the neuron is resting, not transmitting information, the ion channels are closed, and a slight negative charge is present along the inside of the cell membrane. On the outside of the cell membrane, the charge is positive. Because of the difference in charge, the membrane

FIGURE 3.3 **The Resting Potential**
An oscilloscope measures the difference in electrical potential between two electrodes. When one electrode is placed inside an axon at rest and one is placed outside, the electrical potential inside the cell is −70 millivolts (mV) relative to the outside. This potential difference is due to the separation of positive (+) and negative (−) charges along the membrane.

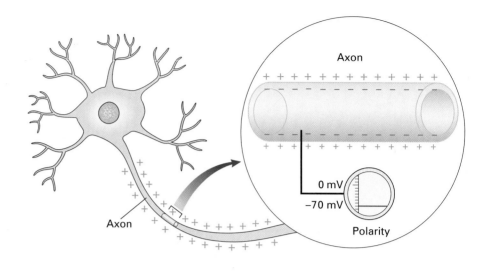

FIGURE 3.4 **The Action Potential**
An action potential is a wave of localized depolarization that travels down the axon as the ion channels in the axon membrane open and close. (*a*) The action potential causes a change in electrical potential as it moves along the axon. (*b*) The movements of sodium ions (Na⁺) and potassium ions (K⁺) into and out of the axon cause the electrical changes.

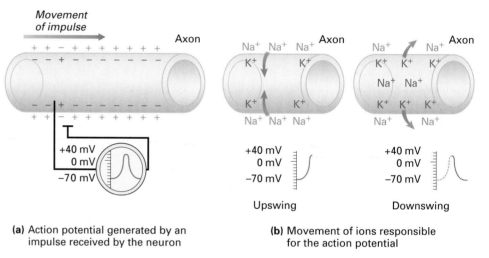

(a) Action potential generated by an impulse received by the neuron

(b) Movement of ions responsible for the action potential

resting potential The term given to the stable, negative charge of an inactive neuron.

action potential The term used to describe the brief wave of electrical charge that sweeps down the axon during the transmission of a nerve impulse.

all-or-none principle Once an electrical impulse reaches a certain level of intensity, it fires and moves all the way down the axon without losing any of its intensity.

of the resting neuron is said to be *polarized*, like the ends of a flashlight battery. **Resting potential** is the term given to the stable, negative charge of an inactive neuron (see figure 3.3). That potential, by the way, is about −70 millivolts, which is only about 1/14th of a volt, so 14 neurons could make up a 1-volt battery. An electric eel's 8,400 neurons could generate 600 volts!

A neuron becomes activated when an incoming impulse, in reaction to, say, a pinprick or the sight of someone's face, raises the neuron's voltage threshold, and the sodium gates at the base of the axon open briefly. This action allows positively charged sodium ions to flow into the neuron, creating a more positively charged neuron and *depolarizing* the membrane by decreasing the charge difference between the fluids inside and outside of the neuron. Then potassium channels open, and positively charged potassium ions move out through the neuron's semipermeable membrane. This returns the neuron to a negative charge. Then the same process occurs as the next group of channels flip open briefly. And so it goes all the way down the axon, just like a long row of cabinet doors opening and closing in sequence.

The term **action potential** is used to describe the brief wave of positive electrical charge that sweeps down the axon (see figure 3.4). An action potential lasts only about 1/1,000th of a second, because the sodium channels can stay open for only a very brief time. They quickly close again and become reset for the next action potential. When a neuron sends an action potential, it is commonly said to be "firing."

The action potential abides by the **all-or-none principle:** Once the electrical impulse reaches a certain level of intensity, it fires and moves all the way down the

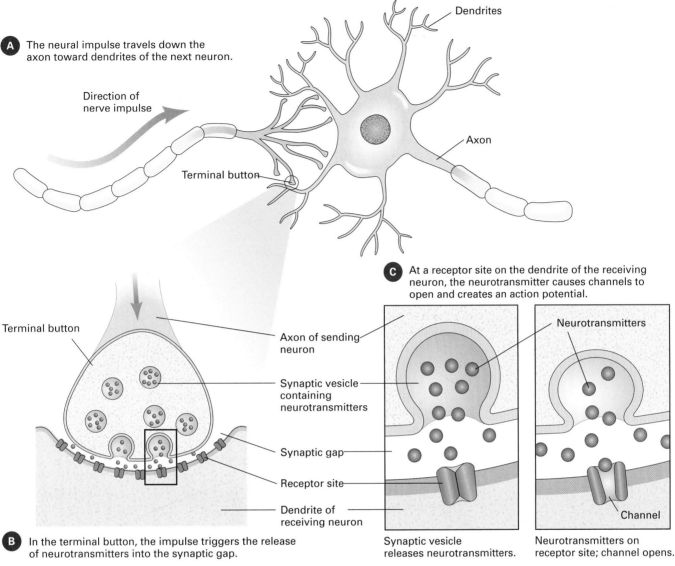

A The neural impulse travels down the axon toward dendrites of the next neuron.

Direction of nerve impulse

Dendrites

Axon

Terminal button

Terminal button

Axon of sending neuron

Synaptic vesicle containing neurotransmitters

Synaptic gap

Receptor site

Dendrite of receiving neuron

B In the terminal button, the impulse triggers the release of neurotransmitters into the synaptic gap.

C At a receptor site on the dendrite of the receiving neuron, the neurotransmitter causes channels to open and creates an action potential.

Neurotransmitters

Channel

Synaptic vesicle releases neurotransmitters.

Neurotransmitters on receptor site; channel opens.

FIGURE 3.5 How Synapses and Neurotransmitters Work (*a*) The axon of the *presynaptic* (sending) neuron meets dendrites of the *postsynaptic* (receiving) neuron. (*b*) This is an enlargement of one synapse, showing the synaptic gap between the two neurons, the terminal button, and the synaptic vesicles containing a neurotransmitter. (*c*) This is an enlargement of the receptor site. Note how the neurotransmitter opens the channel on the receptor site, triggering the neuron to fire.

axon without losing any of its intensity. The impulse traveling down an axon can be compared to the burning fuse of a firecracker. It doesn't matter whether a match or blowtorch was used to light the fuse; once the fuse has been lit, the spark travels quickly and with the same intensity down the fuse.

Synapses and Neurotransmitters

What happens when a neural impulse reaches the end of the axon? Neurons do not touch each other directly, but they manage to communicate. The story of the connection between one neuron and another is one of the most intriguing and highly researched areas of contemporary neuroscience (Bi & Poo, 2001). Figure 3.5 gives an overview of how this connection between neurons takes place.

Synaptic Transmission **Synapses** are tiny junctions between neurons; the gap between neurons is referred to as a *synaptic gap*. Most synapses lie between the axon of one neuron and the dendrites or cell body of another neuron. Before the electrical impulse can cross the synaptic gap, it must be converted into a chemical signal.

synapses Tiny junctions between two neurons, generally where the axon of one neuron meets the dendrites or cell body of another neuron.

Each axon branches out into numerous fibers that end in structures called *terminal buttons.* Stored in minute synaptic vesicles (sacs) within the terminal buttons are substances called **neurotransmitters.** As their name suggests, neurotransmitters transmit or carry information across the synaptic gap to the next neuron. When a nerve impulse reaches the terminal button, it triggers the release of neurotransmitter molecules from the synaptic vesicles. The neurotransmitter molecules flood the synaptic gap. Their movements are random, but some of them bump into receptor sites in the next neuron. If the shape of the receptor site corresponds to the shape of the neurotransmitter molecule, the neurotransmitter acts like a key to open the receptor site, so that the neuron can receive the electrical signals coming from the previous neuron. After delivering its message, the neurotransmitter is reabsorbed by the axon that released it to await the next neural impulse.

Think of the synapse as a river that blocks a road. A grocery truck (the action potential) arrives at one bank of the river, crosses by ferry, and continues its journey to market. Similarly, a message in the brain is "ferried" across the synapse by a neurotransmitter, which pours out of the terminal button just as the message approaches the synapse.

Neurochemical Messengers   There are many different neurotransmitters. Each one plays a specific role and functions in a specific pathway. Whereas some neurotransmitters stimulate or excite neurons to fire, others can inhibit neurons from firing (Heim & Nemeroff, 2002). Some neurotransmitters are both excitatory and inhibitory, depending on what is needed. As the neurotransmitter moves across the synaptic gap to the receiving neuron, its molecules might spread out or be confined to a small space. The molecules might come in rapid sequence or be spaced out. The receiving neuron integrates this information before reacting to it.

Most neurons secrete only one type of neurotransmitter, but often many different neurons are simultaneously secreting different neurotransmitters into the synaptic gaps of a single neuron. At any given time, a neuron is receiving a mixture of messages from the neurotransmitters. At its receptor sites, the chemical molecules bind to the membrane and either excite the neuron, bringing it closer to the threshold at which it will fire, or inhibit the neuron from firing. Usually the binding of an excitatory neurotransmitter from one neuron will not be enough to trigger an action potential in the receiving neuron. Triggering an action potential often takes a number of neurons sending excitatory messages simultaneously or fewer neurons sending rapid-fire excitatory messages.

So far, researchers have identified more than 50 neurotransmitters, each with a unique chemical makeup. The rapidly growing list likely will grow to more than 100 (Johnson, 2003). In organisms ranging from snails to whales, neuroscientists have found the same neurotransmitter molecules that our own brains use. Many animal venoms, such as that of the black widow spider, actually are neurotransmitter-like substances that do their harm by disturbing neurotransmission. To get a better sense of what neurotransmitters do, let's consider just six that have major effects on our behavior.

Acetylcholine   *Acetylcholine (ACh)* usually stimulates the firing of neurons and is involved in the action of muscles, learning, and memory (Devi & Silver, 2000; McIntyre & others, 2002). ACh is found throughout the central and peripheral nervous systems. The venom of the black widow spider causes ACh to gush through the synapses between the spinal cord and skeletal muscles, producing violent spasms. The drug curare, which some South American Indians apply to the tips of poison darts, blocks receptors for ACh, paralyzing muscles. In contrast, nicotine stimulates acetylcholine receptors. Individuals with Alzheimer's disease, a degenerative brain disorder that involves a decline in memory, have an acetylcholine deficiency. Some of the drugs that alleviate the symptoms of Alzheimer's disease do so by compensating for the loss of the brain's supply of acetylcholine.

neurotransmitters Chemicals that carry information across the synaptic gap from one neuron to the next.

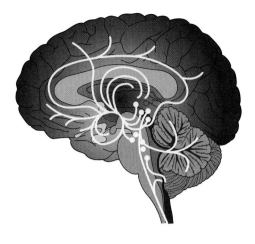

FIGURE 3.6 Serotonin Pathways
Each of the neurotransmitters in the brain
has specific pathways in which they function.
Shown here are the pathways for serotonin.

GABA   *GABA* (gamma aminobutyric acid) is found throughout the central nervous system. It is believed to be the neurotransmitter in as many as one-third of the brain's synapses. GABA is important in the brain because it keeps many neurons from firing (Bou-Flores & Berger, 2001; Ryan, 2001). In this way it helps to control the preciseness of the signal being carried from one neuron to the next. Low levels of GABA are linked with anxiety. Valium and other antianxiety drugs increase the inhibiting effects of GABA.

Norepinephrine   *Norepinephrine* usually inhibits the firing of neurons in the central nervous system, but it excites the heart muscle, intestines, and urogenital tract. Stress stimulates the release of norepinephrine (Zaimovic & others, 2000). This neurotransmitter also helps to control alertness. Too little norepinephrine is associated with depression, too much with agitated, manic states. For example, amphetamines and cocaine cause hyperactive, manic states of behavior by rapidly increasing brain levels of norepinephrine.

Recall from the beginning of the chapter that one of the most important characteristics of the brain and nervous system is integration. In the case of neurotransmitters, they may work in teams of two or more. For example, norepinephrine works with acetylcholine to regulate states of sleep and wakefulness.

Dopamine   *Dopamine* mainly inhibits. It helps to control voluntary movement (Jakel & Marangos, 2000). Dopamine also affects sleep, mood, attention, and learning. Stimulant drugs, such as cocaine and amphetamines, produce excitement, alertness, elevated mood, decreased fatigue, and sometimes increased motor activity mainly by activating dopamine receptors.

Low levels of dopamine are associated with Parkinson's disease, in which physical movements deteriorate (Malapani, Deweer, & Gibbon, 2002). Although the actor Michael J. Fox contracted Parkinson's disease in his late 20s, the disease is uncommon before the age of 30 and becomes more common as people age. High levels of dopamine are associated with schizophrenia, a severe mental disorder that is discussed in chapter 14.

Serotonin   *Serotonin* also primarily inhibits. Serotonin is involved in the regulation of sleep, mood, attention, and learning. In regulating states of sleep and wakefulness, it teams with acetylcholine and norepinephrine. Lowered levels of serotonin are associated with depression (Kanner & Balabanov, 2002; Wagner & Ambrosini, 2001). The antidepressant drug Prozac works by increasing brain levels of serotonin. Figure 3.6 shows the brain pathways for serotonin.

Endorphins   *Endorphins* are natural opiates that mainly stimulate the firing of neurons. Endorphins shield the body from pain and elevate feelings of pleasure. A long-distance

FIGURE 3.7 An Example of a Neural Network Inputs (information from the environment and sensory receptors—as when someone looks at a person's face) become embedded in extensive connections between neurons in the brain, which leads to outputs (such as remembering the person's face).

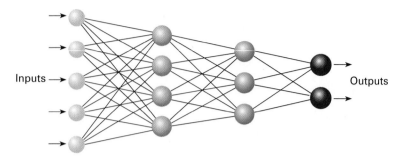

runner, a woman giving birth, and a person in shock after a car wreck all have elevated levels of endorphins (Jamurtas & others, 2000).

As early as the fourth century B.C., the Greeks used wild poppies to induce euphoria. More than 2,000 years later, the magical formula behind opium's addictive action was finally discovered. In the early 1970s, scientists found that opium plugs into a sophisticated system of natural opiates that lie deep within the brain's pathways (Pert, 1999; A. B. Pert & Snyder, 1973; Spetea & others, 2002). Morphine (the most important narcotic of opium) mimics the action of endorphins by stimulating receptors in the brain involved with pleasure and pain.

Drugs and Neurotransmitters   Most drugs that influence behavior do so mainly by interfering with the work of neurotransmitters (Beatty, 2001; Mader, 2003). Drugs can mimic or increase the effects of a neurotransmitter, or they can block those effects. An **agonist** is a drug that mimics or increases a neurotransmitter's effects. For example, the drug morphine mimics the actions of endorphins by stimulating receptors in the brain associated with pleasure and pain. An **antagonist** is a drug that blocks a neurotransmitter's effects. For example, alcohol blocks serotonin activity (Fils-Aime & others, 1996).

Neural Networks

So far in the coverage of neurons, I have focused mainly on how a single neuron functions and on how a nerve impulse travels from one neuron to another. Now let's look at how large numbers of neurons work together to integrate incoming information and coordinate outgoing information.

At the beginning of the chapter, I briefly described neural networks as clusters of neurons that are interconnected to process information. Figure 3.7 shows a simplified drawing of a neural network or pathway (McIntosh, 2000). By looking at this diagram, you can get an idea of how the activity of one neuron is linked with many others.

Some neurons have short axons and communicate with other nearby neurons. Other neurons have long axons and communicate with circuits of neurons some distance away. Researchers have found that these neural networks are not static (Carlson, 2000; Meyer & van Vreeswijk, 2002). They can be altered through changes in the strength of synaptic connections.

Any piece of information, such as a name, might be embedded in hundreds or even thousands of connections between neurons (Lee & Farhat, 2001). In this way, such human activities as being attentive, memorizing, and thinking are distributed over a wide range of connected neurons (Bartlett, 2002). The strength of these connected neurons determines how well you remember the information (Golden, 2002; Krause & others, 2000; McClelland & Rumelhart, 1986).

Let's see how the neural network concept might explain a typical memory, such as the name of a new acquaintance. Initially, the processing of the person's face might activate a small number of weak neuronal connections that make you remember a

agonist A drug that mimics or increases a neurotransmitter's effects.

antagonist A drug that blocks a neurotransmitter's effects.

general category ("interesting woman" or "attractive man"). However, repeated experience with that person will increase the strength and possibly the number of those connections. So you may remember the person's name as the neurons activated by the name become connected with the neurons that are activated by the face. Chapter 8 explores the nature of memory at greater length.

Review and Sharpen Your Thinking

2   *Explain what neurons are and how they process information.*
- Differentiate between neurons and glial cells, and describe the functions of the parts of a neuron.
- Explain what a neural impulse is and how it is generated.
- Discuss how a neural impulse is transmitted from one neuron to another.
- Describe the function of neural networks.

Why is it important to have so many connections and to have integration between neurons?

mhhe com/
santrockp7

For study tools related to this learning goal, see the Study Guide, the CD-ROM, and the Online Learning Center.

STRUCTURES OF THE BRAIN AND THEIR FUNCTIONS   3

How the Brain and Nervous System Are Studied

The Cerebral Cortex

Integration of Function in the Brain

Levels of Organization in the Brain

The Cerebral Hemispheres and Split-Brain Research

How is the brain organized?

The extensive and intricate networks of neurons that we have just studied are not visible to the naked eye. Fortunately, technology is available to help neuroscientists form pictures of the structure and organization of neurons and the larger structures they make up without harming the organism being studied. This section explores some of the techniques that are used in brain research and discusses what they have shown us about the structures and functions of the brain. Special attention is given to the cerebral cortex, the highest region of the brain.

How the Brain and Nervous System Are Studied

Much of our early knowledge of the human brain comes from clinical studies of individuals who suffered brain damage from injury or disease or who had brain surgery to relieve another condition (like Brandi Binder). Modern discoveries have relied largely on technology that enables researchers to "look inside" the brain while it is at work. Let's examine some of these techniques.

Brain Lesioning   *Brain lesioning* is an abnormal disruption in the tissue of the brain resulting from injury or disease. The study of naturally occurring brain lesions in humans has provided considerable information about how the brain functions.

Neuroscientists also produce lesions in laboratory animals to determine the effects on the animal's behavior (Krauss & Jankovic, 2002). These lesions may be made by surgically removing brain tissue, destroying tissue with a laser, or eliminating tissue by injecting it with a drug. Sometimes transient lesions can be made

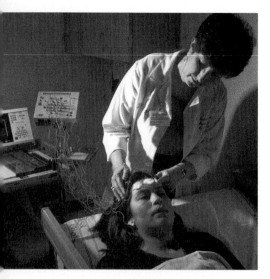

FIGURE 3.8 An EEG Recording
The electroencephalograph (EEG) is widely used in sleep research. It has led to some major breakthroughs in understanding sleep by showing how the brain's electrical activity changes during sleep.

EEGs are also used to study normal brains. (Around the Globe)

mhhe com/
santrockp7

by administering a drug that temporarily inactivates an area of the brain. The organism's behavior can be studied while the area is inactivated; after the effects of the drug have worn off, brain activity in the area returns to normal (Gazzaniga, Ivry, & Mangun, 2001).

Staining A central interest in neuroscience is to identify the pathways of connectivity in the brain and nervous system that allow information to get from one place to another (Sorensen & others, 2002). This is not an easy task because of the complexity and extent of the interconnections. Much of the progress in charting these neural networks has come about through the use of stains, or dyes, that are selectively absorbed by neurons. One commonly used stain is horseradish peroxidase. A stain will coat only a small portion of neurons so that neuroscientists, using high-powered microscopes, can see which neurons absorb the stains and determine how they are connected.

Electrical Recording Also widely used is the *electroencephalograph (EEG)*, which records the electrical activity of the brain. Electrodes placed on the scalp detect brainwave activity, which is recorded on a chart known as an electroencephalogram (see figure 3.8). This device has been used to assess brain damage, epilepsy, and other problems (Meador, 2002; Wallace & others, 2001).

Not every recording of brain activity is made with surface electrodes. In *single-unit recording*, which provides information about a single neuron's electrical activity, a thin probe is inserted in or near an individual neuron (Seidemann & others, 1996). The probe transmits the neuron's electrical activity to an amplifier so that researchers can "see" the activity.

Brain Imaging For years X rays have been used to reveal damage inside or outside our bodies, both in the brain and in other locations. But a single X ray of the brain is hard to interpret because it shows a two-dimensional image of the three-dimensional interior of the brain. A newer technique called *computerized tomography*

FIGURE 3.9 PET Scan This PET scan of the left half of the brain contrasts the different areas used in aspects of language activity: generating words, hearing words, seeing words, and speaking words.

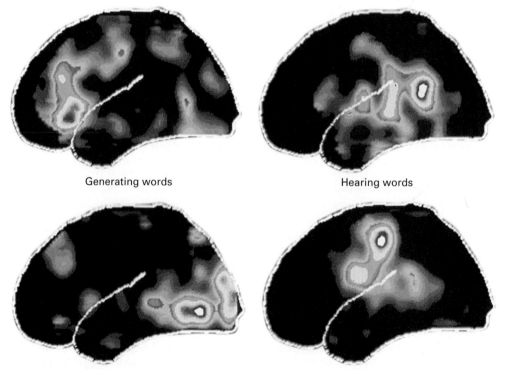

Generating words

Hearing words

Seeing words

Speaking words

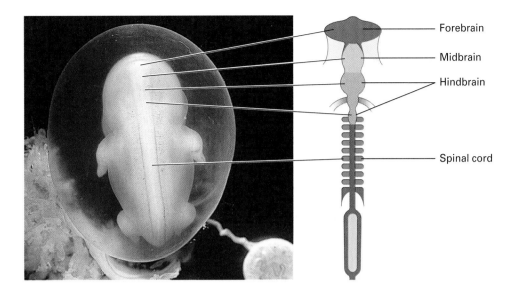

Forebrain

Midbrain

Hindbrain

Spinal cord

FIGURE 3.10 Embryological Development of the Nervous System
The photograph shows the primitive, tubular appearance of the nervous system at 6 weeks in the human embryo. The drawing shows the major brain regions and spinal cord as they appear early in the development of a human embryo.

(CT scan) produces a three-dimensional image obtained from X rays of the head that are assembled into a composite image by a computer. The CT scan provides valuable information about the location and extent of damage involving stroke, language disorder, or loss of memory.

Positron-emission tomography (PET scan) measures the amount of glucose in various areas of the brain, then sends this information to a computer for analysis. Because glucose levels vary with the levels of activity throughout the brain, tracing the amounts of glucose generates a picture of activity levels throughout the brain (Siebner & others, 2002). Figure 3.9 shows PET scans of people's brain activity while they are hearing, seeing, speaking, and thinking.

Another technique, *magnetic resonance imaging (MRI)*, involves creating a magnetic field around a person's body and using radio waves to construct images of the person's tissues and biochemical activities. MRI provides very clear pictures of the brain's interior, does not require injecting the brain with a substance, and, unlike X rays, does not pose a problem of radiation overexposure (Petersen, 2001; Niku & Lu, 2002).

In one recent study, Susan Tapert, a neuroscientist who is interested in the brain dysfunction produced by alcoholism, and her colleagues used MRI to determine the effects of alcoholism on the brain (Tapert & others, 2001). They compared MRI brain scans of two groups of young women, one of which had a history of heavy drinking, the other no history of alcohol problems. Both groups of women had abstained from alcohol for the previous 24 hours. As they completed a memory task in which they had to remember the location of an object on a screen, they underwent MRI brain scans. The young women who had a history of heavy drinking did more poorly on the memory task, and the MRI scans revealed more sluggish brain activity.

Levels of Organization in the Brain

As a human embryo develops inside its mother's womb, the nervous system begins forming as a long, hollow tube on the embryo's back. At 3 weeks or so after conception, cells making up the tube differentiate into a mass of neurons, most of which then develop into three major regions of the brain: the hindbrain, which is adjacent to the top part of the spinal cord; the midbrain, which rises above the hindbrain; and the forebrain, which is the uppermost region of the brain (see figure 3.10).

Hindbrain   The **hindbrain,** located at the skull's rear, is the lowest portion of the brain. The three main parts of the hindbrain are the medulla, cerebellum, and pons. Figure 3.11 shows the location of these brain structures.

hindbrain The lowest level of the brain, consisting of the medulla, cerebellum, and pons.

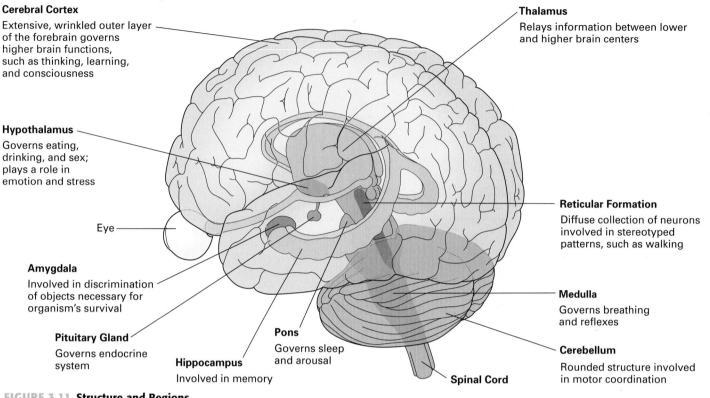

Cerebral Cortex
Extensive, wrinkled outer layer of the forebrain governs higher brain functions, such as thinking, learning, and consciousness

Hypothalamus
Governs eating, drinking, and sex; plays a role in emotion and stress

Eye

Amygdala
Involved in discrimination of objects necessary for organism's survival

Pituitary Gland
Governs endocrine system

Hippocampus
Involved in memory

Pons
Governs sleep and arousal

Spinal Cord

Thalamus
Relays information between lower and higher brain centers

Reticular Formation
Diffuse collection of neurons involved in stereotyped patterns, such as walking

Medulla
Governs breathing and reflexes

Cerebellum
Rounded structure involved in motor coordination

FIGURE 3.11 **Structure and Regions in the Human Brain**

The _medulla_ begins where the spinal cord enters the skull. It helps to control our breathing and regulates reflexes that allow us to maintain an upright posture.

The _cerebellum_ extends from the rear of the hindbrain, just above the medulla. It consists of two rounded structures thought to play important roles in motor coordination (Middleton & Strick, 2001). Leg and arm movements are coordinated by the cerebellum, for example. When we play golf, practice the piano, or learn a new dance, the cerebellum is hard at work. If a higher portion of the brain commands us to write the number 7, it is the cerebellum that integrates the muscular activities required to do so. Damage to the cerebellum impairs the performance of coordinated movements. When this damage occurs, people's movements become uncoordinated and jerky. Extensive damage to the cerebellum even makes it impossible to stand up.

The _pons_ is a bridge in the hindbrain. It contains several clusters of fibers involved in sleep and arousal.

Midbrain The **midbrain,** located between the hindbrain and forebrain, is an area in which many nerve-fiber systems ascend and descend to connect the higher and lower portions of the brain. In particular, the midbrain relays information between the brain and the eyes and ears. The ability to attend to an object visually, for example, is linked to one bundle of neurons in the midbrain. Parkinson's disease, a deterioration of movement that produces rigidity and tremors, damages a section near the bottom of the midbrain.

Two systems in the midbrain are of special interest. One is the **reticular formation** (see figure 3.11), a diffuse collection of neurons involved in stereotyped patterns of behavior such as walking, sleeping, or turning to attend to a sudden noise (Soja & others, 2001). The other system consists of small groups of neurons that use the neurotransmitters serotonin, dopamine, and norepinephrine. Although these groups contain relatively few cells, they send their axons to a remarkable variety of brain regions, perhaps explaining their involvement in high-level, integrative functions (Shier, Butler, & Lewis, 1999).

A region called the **brain stem** includes much of the hindbrain (it does not include the cerebellum) and midbrain and is so-called because it looks like a stem.

midbrain Located between the hindbrain and forebrain, a region in which many nerve-fiber systems ascend and descend to connect the higher and lower portions of the brain.

reticular formation A midbrain system that consists of a diffuse collection of neurons involved in stereotypical behaviors such as walking, sleeping, or turning to attend to a sudden noise.

brain stem The region of the brain that includes most of the hindbrain (excluding the cerebellum) and the midbrain.

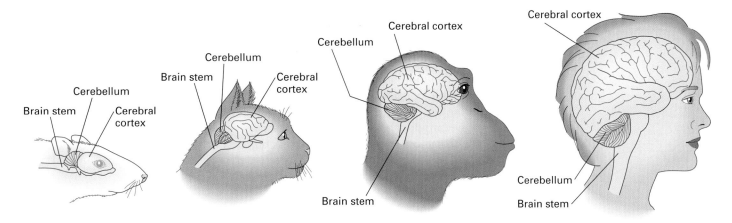

FIGURE 3.12 The Brain in Different Species Note how much larger the cerebral cortex becomes as we go from the brain of a rat to the brain of a human.

Embedded deep within the brain, the brain stem connects with the spinal cord at its lower end and then extends upward to encase the reticular formation in the midbrain. The most ancient part of the brain, the brain stem evolved more than 500 million years ago (Carter, 1998). It is much like the entire-brain of present-day reptiles and thus is often referred to as the "reptilian brain." Clumps of cells in the brain stem determine alertness and regulate basic survival functions such as breathing, heartbeat, and blood pressure.

Forebrain   You try to understand what all of these terms and parts of the brain mean. You talk with friends and plan a party for this weekend. You remember that it has been 6 months since you went to the dentist. You are confident you will do well on the next exam in this course. All of these experiences and millions more would not be possible without the **forebrain,** the highest level of the human brain.

Before we explore the structures and function of the forebrain, though, let's stop for a moment and examine how the brain evolved. The brains of the earliest vertebrates were smaller and simpler than those of later animals. Genetic changes during the evolutionary process were responsible for the development of more complex brains with more parts and more interconnections (Carlson, 2001). Figure 3.12 compares the brains of a rat, cat, chimpanzee, and human. In the chimpanzee's brain, and especially the human's brain, the hindbrain and midbrain structures are covered by a forebrain structure called the cerebral cortex (Goldsmith & Zimmerman, 2001). The human hindbrain and midbrain are similar to those of other animals, so it is the forebrain structures that mainly differentiate the human brain from the brains of animals such as rats, cats, and monkeys. The human forebrain's most important structures are the limbic system, thalamus, basal ganglia, hypothalamus, and cerebral cortex.

Limbic System   The **limbic system,** a loosely connected network of structures under the cerebral cortex, is important in both memory and emotion. Its two principal structures are the amygdala and hippocampus (see figure 3.11).

The *amygdala* (from the Latin for "almond" shape) is located within the base of the temporal lobe. It is involved in the discrimination of objects that are necessary for the organism's survival, such as appropriate food, mates, and social rivals. Neurons in the amygdala often fire selectively at the sight of such stimuli, and lesions in the amygdala can cause animals to attempt to eat, fight, or mate with inappropriate objects such as chairs. The amygdala also is involved in emotional awareness and expression through its many connections with higher and lower regions of the brain (Davidson, 2000).

The *hippocampus* has a special role in the storage of memories (Bannerman & others, 2002). Individuals who suffer extensive hippocampal damage cannot retain any new conscious memories after the damage. It is fairly certain, though, that memories are not stored "in" the limbic system. Instead, the limbic system seems to determine what parts of the information passing through the cortex should be "printed" into durable, lasting neural traces in the cortex.

forebrain The highest level of the brain. Key structures in the forebrain are the limbic system, thalamus, basal ganglia, hypothalamus, and cerebral cortex.

limbic system Loosely connected network of structures—including the amygdala and hippocampus—that play important roles in memory and emotion.

Thalamus The **thalamus** is a forebrain structure that sits at the top of the brain stem in the central core of the brain (see figure 3.11). It serves as a very important relay station, functioning much like a server in a computer network. That is, an important function of the thalamus is to sort information and send it to the appropriate places in the forebrain for further integration and interpretation (Castro-Alamancos & Calcagnotto, 2001). For example, one area of the thalamus receives information from the cerebellum and projects it to the motor area of the cerebral cortex. Indeed, most neural input to the cerebral cortex goes through the thalamus. While one area of the thalamus works to orient information from the sense receptors (hearing, seeing, and so on), another region seems to be involved in sleep and wakefulness, having ties with the reticular formation.

Basal Ganglia Above the thalamus and under the cerebral cortex lie large clusters, or *ganglia,* of neurons called basal ganglia. The **basal ganglia** work with the cerebellum and the cerebral cortex to control and coordinate voluntary movements. Basal ganglia enable people to engage in habitual behaviors such as riding a bicycle. Individuals with damage to basal ganglia suffer from either unwanted movement, such as constant writhing or jerking of limbs, or too little movement, as in the slow and deliberate movements of those with Parkinson's disease (Borand & others, 2002).

Hypothalamus The **hypothalamus,** a small forebrain structure located just below the thalamus, monitors three pleasurable activities—eating, drinking, and sex—as well as emotion, stress, and reward (see figure 3.11 for the location of the hypothalamus). As is discussed later, the hypothalamus also helps direct the endocrine system. Perhaps the best way to describe the function of the hypothalamus is as a regulator of the body's internal state. It is sensitive to changes in the blood and neural input, and it responds by influencing the secretion of hormones and neural outputs. For example, if the temperature of circulating blood near the hypothalamus is increased by just 1 or 2 degrees, certain cells in the hypothalamus start increasing their rate of firing. As a result, a chain of events is set in motion. Increased circulation through the skin and sweat glands occurs immediately to release this heat from the body. The cooled blood circulating to the hypothalamus slows down the activity of some of the neurons there, stopping the process when the temperature is just right—37.1° Celsius. These temperature-sensitive neurons function like a finely tuned thermostat in maintaining the body in a balanced state.

The hypothalamus also is involved in emotional states and stress, playing an important role as an integrative location for handling stress. Much of this integration is accomplished through the hypothalamus's action on the pituitary gland, an important endocrine gland located just below it.

If certain areas of the hypothalamus are electrically stimulated, a feeling of pleasure results. In a classic experiment, James Olds and Peter Milner (1954) implanted an electrode in the hypothalamus of a rat's brain. When the rat ran to a corner of an enclosed area, a mild electric current was delivered to its hypothalamus. The researchers thought the electric current would cause the rat to avoid the corner. Much to their surprise, the rat kept returning to the corner. Olds and Milner believed they had discovered a pleasure center in the hypothalamus. Olds (1958) conducted further experiments and found that rats would press bars until they dropped over from exhaustion just to continue to receive a mild electric shock to their hypothalamus. One rat pressed a bar more than 2,000 times an hour for a period of 24 hours to receive the stimulation to its hypothalamus (see figure 3.13). Today researchers agree that the hypothalamus is involved in pleasurable feelings but that other areas of the brain, such as the limbic system and a bundle of fibers in the forebrain, are also important in the link between the brain and pleasure.

The Olds studies have implications for drug addiction. In the Olds studies, the rat pressed the bar mainly because it produced a positive, rewarding effect (pleasure),

thalamus Forebrain structure that functions as a relay station to sort input and direct it to different areas of the cerebral cortex. It also has ties to the reticular formation.

basal ganglia Located above the thalamus and under the cerebral cortex, these large clusters of neurons work with the cerebellum and the cerebral cortex to control and coordinate voluntary movements.

hypothalamus Forebrain structure involved in regulating eating, drinking, and sex; directing the endocrine system through the pituitary gland; and monitoring emotion, stress, and reward.

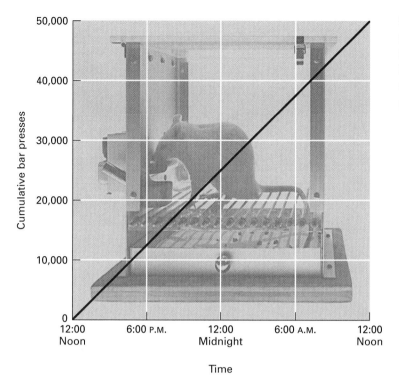

FIGURE 3.13 **Results of the Experiment by Olds (1958) on the Role of the Hypothalamus in Pleasure** The graphed results for one rat show that it pressed the bar more than 2,000 times an hour for a period of 24 hours to receive stimulation to its hypothalamus. One of the rats in Olds and Milner's experiments is shown pressing the bar.

not because it wanted to avoid or escape a negative effect (pain). Cocaine users talk about the drug's ability to heighten pleasure in food, in sex, and in a variety of activities, highlighting the reward aspects of the drug (Restak, 1988).

The Cerebral Cortex

The **cerebral cortex** is the highest region of the forebrain and is the most recently developed part of the brain in the evolution scheme. It is in the cerebral cortex that the highest mental functions, such as thinking and planning, take place. The neural tissue that makes up the cerebral cortex is the largest part of the brain in volume (about 80 percent) and covers the lower portions of the brain like a large cap. In humans, the cerebral cortex is greatly convoluted with lots of grooves and bulges, which considerably enlarge its surface area (compared to a brain with a smooth surface). The cerebral cortex is highly connected with other parts of the brain. Literally millions of axons connect the neurons of the cerebral cortex with those located elsewhere in the brain.

Lobes The wrinkled surface of the cerebral cortex is divided into two halves called *hemispheres* (see figure 3.14). Each hemisphere is subdivided into four regions—the frontal lobe, the parietal lobe, the temporal lobe, and the occipital lobe (see figure 3.15).

The **occipital lobe,** at the back of the head, responds to visual stimuli. Different areas of the occipital lobes are connected to process information about such aspects of visual stimuli as their color, shape, and motion. A stroke or wound in the occipital lobe can cause blindness or, at a minimum, wipe out a portion of the person's visual field.

The **temporal lobe,** the portion of the cerebral cortex just above the ears, is involved in hearing, language processing, and memory. The temporal lobes have a number of connections to the limbic system. For this reason, people with damage to the temporal lobes cannot file experiences into long-term memory.

The **frontal lobe,** the portion of the cerebral cortex behind the forehead, is involved in the control of voluntary muscles, intelligence, and personality. One fas-

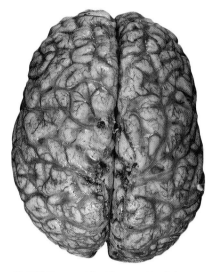

FIGURE 3.14 **The Human Brain's Hemispheres** The two halves (hemispheres) of the human brain can be seen clearly in this photograph.

cerebral cortex Highest level of the forebrain, where the highest mental functions, such as thinking and planning, take place.

occipital lobe The part of the cerebral cortex at the back of the head that is involved in vision.

temporal lobe The portion of the cerebral cortex just above the ears that is involved in hearing, language processing, and memory.

frontal lobe The part of the cerebral cortex just behind the forehead that is involved in the control of voluntary muscles, intelligence, and personality.

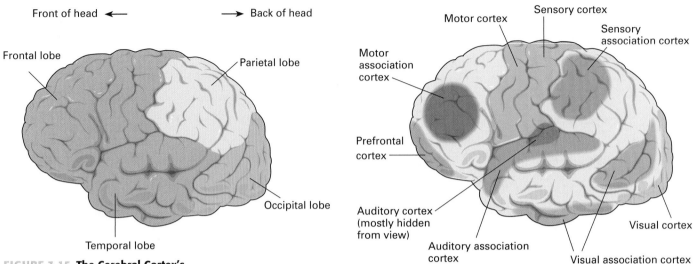

FIGURE 3.15 **The Cerebral Cortex's Lobes and Association Areas** The cerebral cortex (*left*) is roughly divided into four lobes: occipital, temporal, frontal, and parietal. The cerebral cortex (*right*) also consists of the motor cortex and sensory cortex. Further, the cerebral cortex includes association areas, such as the visual association cortex, auditory association cortex, and sensory association cortex.

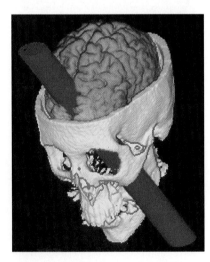

A computerized reconstruction of Phineas T. Gage's accident, based on measurements taken of his skull.

parietal lobe Area of the cerebral cortex at the top of the head that is involved in registering spatial location, attention, and motor control.

cinating case study illustrates how damage to the frontal lobe can significantly alter personality. Phineas T. Gage, a 25-year-old foreman who worked for the Rutland and Burlington Railroad, met with an accident on September 13, 1848. Phineas and several co-workers were using blasting powder to construct a roadbed. The crew drilled holes in the rock and gravel, poured in the blasting powder, and then tamped down the powder with an iron rod. While Phineas was still tamping it down, the powder blew up, driving the iron rod up through the left side of his face and out through the top of his head. Though the wound in his skull healed in a matter of weeks, Phineas became a different person. He had been a mild-mannered, hardworking, emotionally calm individual prior to the accident, well liked by all who knew him. Afterward, he became obstinate, moody, irresponsible, selfish, and incapable of participating in any planned activities. Damage to the frontal lobe of his brain dramatically altered Phineas's personality.

Without intact frontal lobes, humans are emotionally shallow, distractible, listless, and so insensitive to social contexts that they may belch with abandon at dinner parties (Hooper & Teresi, 1992). Individuals with frontal lobe damage become so distracted by irrelevant stimuli that they often cannot carry out some basic directions. In one such case, an individual, when asked to light a candle, struck a match correctly but instead of lighting the candle, he put the candle in his mouth and acted as if he was smoking it (Luria, 1973).

The frontal lobes of humans are especially large when compared with those of other animals. For example, the frontal cortex of rats barely exists; in cats, it occupies a paltry 3.5 percent of the cerebral cortex; in chimpanzees, 17 percent; and in humans, approximately 30 percent. Some neuroscientists maintain that the frontal cortex is an important index of evolutionary advancement (Hooper & Teresi, 1992).

An important part of the frontal lobes is the *prefrontal cortex,* which is at the front of the motor cortex (see figure 3.15). The prefrontal cortex is believed to be involved in higher cognitive functions, such as planning and reasoning (Manes & others, 2002). Some neuroscientists refer to the prefrontal cortex as an executive control system because of its role in monitoring and organizing thinking (Owen, 1997).

The **parietal lobe,** located at the top and toward the rear of the head, is involved in registering spatial location, attention, and motor control. Thus the parietal lobes are at work when you are judging how far you have to throw a ball to get it to someone else, when you shift your attention from one activity to another (turn your attention away from the TV to a noise outside), and when you turn the pages of this book. The brilliant physicist Albert Einstein said that his reasoning often was best when he imagined objects in space. It turns out that his parietal lobes were 15 percent larger than average (Witelson, Kigar, & Harvey, 1999).

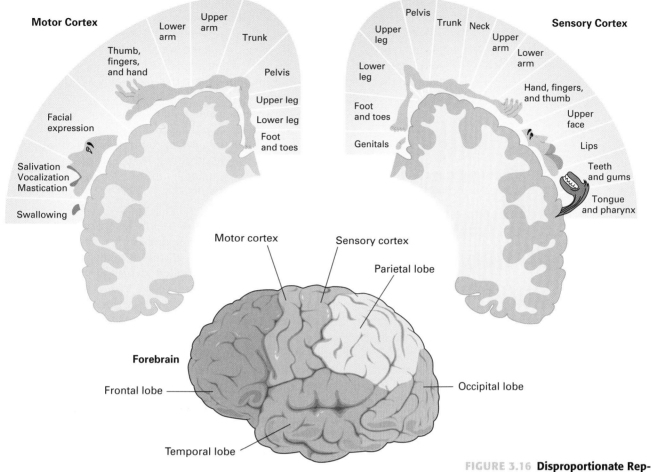

FIGURE 3.16 **Disproportionate Representation of Body Parts in the Motor and Sensory Areas of the Cortex** The amount of cortex allotted to a body part is not proportionate to the body part's size. Instead, the brain has more space for body parts that require precision and control. Thus the thumb, fingers, and hand require more brain tissue than does the arm.

In closing this discussion of the cerebral cortex's lobes, a word of caution is in order about going too far in localizing function within a particular lobe. Although I have attributed specific functions to a particular lobe (such as vision in the occipital lobe), there is considerable integration and connection between any two or more lobes and between lobes and other parts of the brain.

Sensory Cortex and Motor Cortex   Two other important regions of the cerebral cortex are the sensory cortex and the motor cortex (see figure 3.15). The **sensory cortex** processes information about body sensations. It is located at the front of the parietal lobes. The **motor cortex,** just behind the frontal lobes, processes information about voluntary movement.

The map in figure 3.16 shows which parts of the sensory and motor cortex are associated with different parts of the body. It is based on research done by Wilder Penfield (1947), a neurosurgeon at the Montreal Neurological Institute. He worked with patients who had severe epilepsy and often performed surgery to remove portions of the epileptic patients' brains. However, he was concerned that removing a portion of the brain might impair some of the individuals' functions. Penfield's solution was to map the cortex during surgery by stimulating different cortical areas and observing the responses of the patients, who were given a local anesthetic so they would remain awake during the operation. He found that, when he stimulated certain sensory and motor areas of the brain, different parts of a patient's body moved. For both sensory and motor areas, there is a point-to-point relation between a part of the body and a location on the cerebral cortex. In figure 3.16, the face and hands are given proportionately more space than other body parts because the face and

sensory cortex Area of the cerebral cortex that processes information about body sensations.

motor cortex Area of the cerebral cortex that processes information about voluntary movement.

hands are capable of finer perceptions and movements than are other body areas and, therefore, need more cerebral cortex representation.

The point-to-point mapping of sensory fields onto the cortex's surface is the basis of our orderly and accurate perception of the world (Fox, 1996). When something touches your lip, for example, your brain knows what body part has been touched because the nerve pathways from your lip are the only pathways that project to the lip region of the sensory cortex.

One familiar example of what happens when these neural pathways get connected the wrong way is seen in Siamese cats. Many Siamese cats have a genetic defect that causes the pathways from the eyes to connect to the wrong parts of the visual cortex during development. The result is that these cats spend their lives looking at things cross-eyed in an effort to "straighten out" the visual image of their visual cortex.

The Association Cortex   Embedded in the brain's lobes, the association cortex makes up 75 percent of the cerebral cortex (see figure 3.15). Processing information about sensory input and motor output is not all that is taking place in the cerebral cortex. The **association cortex** (sometimes called *association areas*) is the region of the cerebral cortex that integrates this information. The highest intellectual functions, such as thinking and problem solving, occur in the association cortex.

Interestingly, damage to a specific part of the association cortex often does not result in a specific loss of function. With the exception of language areas (which are localized), loss of function seems to depend more on the extent of damage to the association cortex than on the specific location of the damage. By observing brain-damaged individuals and using a mapping technique, scientists have found that the association cortex is involved in linguistic and perceptual functioning.

The largest portion of the association cortex is located in the frontal lobe, directly under the forehead. Damage to this area does not lead to sensory or motor loss. Indeed, it is this area that may be most directly related to thinking and problem solving. Early studies even referred to the frontal lobe as the center of intelligence, but research suggests that frontal lobe damage may not result in a lowering of intelligence. Planning and judgment are often associated with the frontal lobe. Personality also may be linked to the frontal lobe. Recall the misfortune of Phineas Gage, whose personality radically changed after he experienced frontal lobe damage.

The Cerebral Hemispheres and Split-Brain Research

At the beginning of the discussion of the cerebral cortex, I indicated that it is divided into two halves—left and right (see figure 3.14). Do these hemispheres have different functions? In 1861, French surgeon Paul Broca saw a patient who had received an injury to the left side of his brain about 30 years earlier. The patient became known as Tan, because *Tan* was the only word he could speak. Tan suffered from *aphasia*, a language disorder associated with brain damage. Tan died several days after Broca evaluated him, and an autopsy revealed that the injury was to a precise area of the left hemisphere. Today we refer to this area of the brain as *Broca's area*, and we know that it plays an important role in the production of speech. Another area of the brain's left hemisphere that has an important role in language is *Wernicke's area*, which, if damaged, causes problems in comprehending language. Figure 3.17 shows the locations of Broca's area and Wernicke's area.

Today, there continues to be considerable interest in the degree to which the brain's left hemisphere or right hemisphere is involved in various aspects of thinking, feeling, and behavior (Corballis, Funnell, & Gazzaniga, 2002; Spence & others, 2002). For many years scientists speculated that the **corpus callosum,** the large bundle of axons that connects the brain's two hemispheres, had something to do with relaying information between the two sides (see figure 3.18). Roger Sperry (1974)

association cortex Region of the cerebral cortex in which the highest intellectual functions, including thinking and problem solving, occur (also called association areas).

corpus callosum A large bundle of axons that connect the brain's two hemispheres.

confirmed this in an experiment in which he cut the corpus callosum in cats. He also severed certain nerves leading from the eyes to the brain. After the operation, Sperry trained the cats to solve a series of visual problems with one eye blindfolded. After the cat learned the task, say with only its left eye uncovered, its other eye was blindfolded and the animal was tested again. The "split-brain" cat behaved as if it had never learned the task. It seems that the memory was stored only in the left hemisphere, which could no longer directly communicate with the right hemisphere.

Further evidence of the corpus callosum's function has come from studies of patients who, like Brandi Binder before surgery, have severe, even life-threatening, forms of epilepsy. Epilepsy is caused by electrical "brainstorms" that flash uncontrollably across the corpus callosum. In one famous case, neurosurgeons severed the corpus callosum of an epileptic patient now known as W. J. in a final attempt to reduce his unbearable seizures. Sperry (1968) examined W. J. and found that the corpus callosum functions the same in humans as in animals—cutting the corpus callosum seemed to leave the patient with "two separate minds" that learned and operated independently.

The right hemisphere, it turns out, receives information only from the left side of the body, and the left hemisphere receives information only from the right side of the body. When you hold an object in your left hand, for example, only the right hemisphere of your brain detects the object. When you hold an object in your right hand, only the left hemisphere of the brain detects the object (see figure 3.19). In a normally functioning corpus callosum, both hemispheres receive this information.

In people with intact brains, specialization of function occurs in some areas. Following are the main areas in which the brain tends to divide its functioning into one hemisphere or the other (Gazzaniga, Ivry, & Mangun, 2001; Springer & Deutsch, 1998):

- *Verbal processing.* The most extensive research on the brain's two hemispheres has focused on language. Speech and grammar are localized to the left hemisphere. A common misconception, though, is that *all* language processing is carried out in the brain's left hemisphere. However, such aspects of language as appropriate use of language in different contexts, metaphor, and much of our sense of humor reside in the right hemisphere.
- *Nonverbal processing.* The right hemisphere is more dominant in processing nonverbal information, such as spatial perception, visual recognition, and emotion

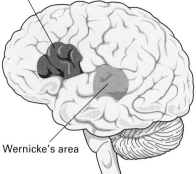

FIGURE 3.17 Broca's Area and Wernicke's Area Broca's area is located in the brain's left hemisphere, and it is involved in the control of speech. Individuals with damage to Broca's area have problems saying words correctly. Also shown is Wernicke's area, a portion of the left hemisphere that is involved in understanding language. Individuals with damage to this area cannot comprehend words; that is, they hear the words but don't know what they mean.

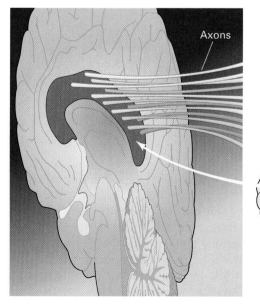

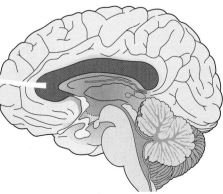

FIGURE 3.18 The Corpus Callosum The corpus callosum is a thick band of about 80 million axons that connect the brain cells in one hemisphere to those in the other. In healthy brains, the two sides engage in a continuous flow of information via this neural bridge.

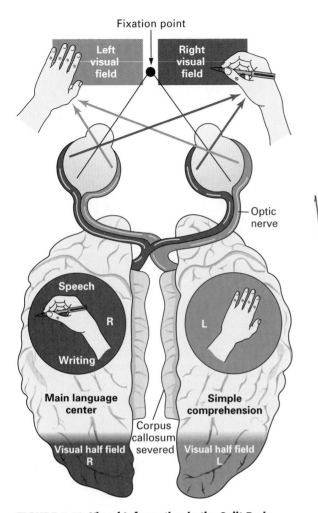

FIGURE 3.19 Visual Information in the Split Brain
In a split-brain patient, information from the visual field's left side projects only to the right hemisphere. Information from the visual field's right side projects only to the left hemisphere. Because of these projections, stimuli can be presented to only one of a split-brain patient's hemispheres.

(Corballis, Funnell, & Gazzaniga, 2002). For example, the right hemisphere is mainly at work when we are processing information about people's faces (O'Toole, 2002). The right hemisphere also may be more involved in processing information about emotions, both when we express emotions ourselves and when we recognize others' emotions (Heller, Etienne, & Miller, 1997).

Because differences in the functioning of the brain's two hemispheres are known to exist, people commonly use the phrases *left-brained* and *right-brained* as a way of categorizing themselves and others. Such generalizations have little scientific basis. The most common myth about hemispheric specialization is that the left brain is logical and the right brain is creative. The left-brain, right-brain myth started with the publication of Roger Sperry's classic split-brain studies. As Sperry's findings made their way into the media, they became oversimplified and people were labeled either right-brained (artistic) or left-brained (logical).

Sperry did discover that the *left* hemisphere is superior in the kind of logic used to prove geometric theorems. But in everyday life, our logic problems involve integrating information and drawing conclusions. In these instances, the *right* hemisphere is crucial. In most complex activities in which people engage, an interplay occurs between the brain's two hemispheres (Hoptman & Davidson, 1994). For example, in reading, the left hemisphere comprehends syntax and grammar, which the right does not. However, the right brain is better at understanding a story's intonation and emotion. A similar interplay is observed in music and art. Pop psychology assigns both music and art to the right brain. The right hemisphere is better at some musical skills, such as recognizing chords. But the left hemisphere is better at others, such as distinguishing which of two sounds came first.

Enjoying or creating music requires the use of both hemispheres. One positive result of the left-brain–right-brain myth is a perception that more right-brain activities and exercises should be incorporated into school programs (Edwards, 1979). In schools that rely heavily on rote learning to instruct students, children probably would benefit from exercises in intuitive thought and holistic thinking. But a deficiency in school curricula has nothing at all to do with left-brain, right-brain specialization.

In sum, some specialization of functions exists in both the left hemisphere (processing of certain verbal information) and the right hemisphere (processing of certain nonverbal information) of the brain. However, in many complex tasks in which humans engage in their everyday lives, integration across the hemispheres is common.

To think further about the functioning of the left and right hemispheres, see the Critical Controversy box, which explores similarities and differences in men's and women's brains.

Integration of Function in the Brain

How do all of the regions of the brain cooperate to produce the wondrous complexity of thought and behavior that characterizes humans? Neuroscience still doesn't have answers to such questions as how the brain solves a murder mystery or writes a poem or essay. But we can get a sense of integrative brain function by considering something like the act of escaping from a burning building.

Imagine you are sitting at your desk writing letters when fire breaks out behind you. The sound of crackling flames is relayed from your ear, through the thalamus, to the auditory cortex, and on to the auditory association cortex. At each stage, the stim-

Are There "His" and "Hers" Brains?

Does gender matter when it comes to brain structure and function? Human brains are much alike, whether the brain belongs to a man or a woman. However, researchers have found some differences between the male brain and the female brain (Blum, 1998; Goldstein & others, 2001; Kimura, 2000; Raz & others, 2001). Among differences discovered so far are

- One part of the hypothalamus responsible for sexual behavior is larger in men than in women (Swaab & others, 2001).
- Portions of the corpus callosum—the band of tissues through which the brain's two hemispheres communicate—are larger in women than in men (de Lacoste-Utamsing & Holloway, 1982; Le Vay, 1994). Might this difference mean that men and women process information differently? In one study, women were likelier to use both brain hemispheres to process language, whereas men were likelier to use only the left hemisphere (Shaywitz & others, 1995). Despite this difference, the two sexes performed equally well on the task, which involved sounding out words. The researchers concluded that nature has given the brain different routes to the same ability.
- It has been reported that men lose brain tissue earlier in the aging process than women do and that overall they lose more of it (Carter, 1998). Further reports suggest that men are especially prone to tissue loss in the frontal (thinking, reasoning) and temporal (hearing) lobes, but women are prone to tissue loss in the parietal lobe (spatial location) and hippocampus (memory; Nystrand, 1996). Such results, as well as many others in the effort to chart sex differences and similarities in human brains, require further research before being fully accepted as reliable and valid by the scientific community.

Differences in the ways in which men's and women's brains function likely evolved over time. Some of the differences appear to be the result of a division of labor dating to early hunter-gatherer civilizations. For example, men are better than women at spatial-navigational skills, such as map reading, judging distances, and dart throwing (Kimura, 2000; Majeres, 1999). However, some psychologists point out that in many

cases such differences are small and that the differences do not mean that all men are better than all women at such tasks (Hyde & Mezulis, 2002). Debate about whether there are gender differences and about how big or small the differences are for many human skills continues to flourish.

In one recent neuroimaging study, an area of the parietal lobe that functions in visuospatial skills was larger in men than in women (Frederikse & others, 2000). Women, on the other hand, have a better memory for words and objects and are better at fine motor skills (Halpern, 1997, 2001). These abilities may have evolved through making clothes and preparing food.

Are these brain differences truly innate, driven by "nature" through evolution, genetic programming, and hormones in the womb? Or might they be more a consequence of environment, the result of societal influences that stereotypically define sex-specific roles and characteristics, in effect shaping our brains in accordance with these roles? Some psychologists argue that the latter explanation accounts for male/female differences in math and verbal achievement (Eagly, 2001). However, many questions regarding men's and women's brains are exceedingly complex and likely cannot be answered by strictly biological or environmental arguments.

Also, according to psychologist Diane Halpern (2000, 2001), the fact that there are differences between the brains of women and men does not mean that one sex's brain is better, any more than one sex's genitals are better. Different does not mean deficient. People can be different without being unequal in ability.

What do you think?

- Could sex differences in the brain be the result rather than the cause of behavioral differences? Explain.
- Have differences in women's and men's brains likely been exaggerated in light of the substantial similarities in their brains? Might the media be involved in any exaggerations? Explain.
- Because of differences in the brains of males and females, should males and females be educated differently? Explain.

ulus is processed to extract information, and, at some stage, probably at the association cortex level, the sounds are finally matched with something like a neural memory representing sounds of fires you have heard previously. The association "fire" sets new machinery in motion. Your attention (guided in part by the reticular formation) shifts to the auditory signal being held in your association cortex, and on to your auditory association cortex, and simultaneously (again guided by reticular systems) your head turns toward the noise. Now your visual association cortex reports in: "Objects matching flames are present." In other regions of the association cortex, the visual and auditory reports are synthesized ("We have things that look and sound like fire"), and neural associations representing potential actions ("flee") are activated. However, firing the neurons that code the plan to flee will not get you out of the chair. The basal ganglia must become engaged, and from there the commands will arise to set the brain stem, motor cortex, and cerebellum to the task of actually transporting you out of the room.

Which part of your brain did you use to escape? Virtually all systems had a role; each was quite specific, and together they generated the behavior. By the way, you would probably remember this event because your limbic circuitry would likely have started the memory formation process when the significant association "fire" was first triggered. The next time the sounds of crackling flames reach your auditory association cortex, the associations triggered would include those of this most recent escape. In sum, considerable integration of function takes place in the brain (Gevins, 1999; Miller & Cohen, 2001).

For study tools related to this learning goal, see the Study Guide, the CD-ROM, and the Online Learning Center.

Review and Sharpen Your Thinking

3 *Identify the brain's levels and structures, and summarize the functions of its structures.*

- Specify four techniques that are used to study the brain and the nervous system.
- Outline the levels of organization in the human brain.
- Discuss the areas of the cerebral cortex and their functions.
- Explain how split-brain research has increased our understanding of the way the cerebral hemispheres function.
- Describe the integration of function in the brain.

In your experience, does human behavior differ in important ways from the behavior of other animals? What tasks are human brains able to accomplish that other animals may not be able to?

4 THE ENDOCRINE SYSTEM

What is the endocrine system and how does it affect behavior?

The **endocrine system** is a set of glands that regulate the activities of certain organs by releasing their chemical products into the bloodstream. In the past, the endocrine system was considered separate from the nervous system. However, today neuroscientists know that these two systems are often interconnected.

Hormones are the chemical messengers that are manufactured by the endocrine glands. Hormones travel more slowly than nerve impulses. The bloodstream conveys hormones to all parts of the body, and the membrane of every cell has receptors for one or more hormones.

The endocrine glands consist of the pituitary gland, the thyroid and parathyroid glands, the adrenal glands, the pancreas, and the ovaries in women and the testes in men (see figure 3.20). In much the same way that the brain's control of muscular activity is constantly monitored and altered to suit the information received by the brain, the action of the endocrine glands is continuously monitored and changed by nervous, hormonal, and chemical signals (Mader, 2003). Recall from earlier in the chapter that the autonomic nervous system regulates processes such as respiration, heart rate, and digestion. The autonomic nervous system acts on the endocrine glands to produce a number of important physiological reactions to strong emotions such as rage and fear.

The **pituitary gland,** a pea-sized gland that sits at the base of the skull, controls growth and regulates other glands (see figure 3.21). The anterior (front) part of the pituitary is known as the master gland, because almost all of its hormones direct the activity of target glands elsewhere in the body. In turn, the anterior pituitary gland is controlled by the hypothalamus.

endocrine system A set of glands that regulate the activities of certain organs by releasing hormones into the bloodstream.

hormones Chemical messengers manufactured by the endocrine glands.

pituitary gland An important endocrine gland at the base of the skull that controls growth and regulates other glands.

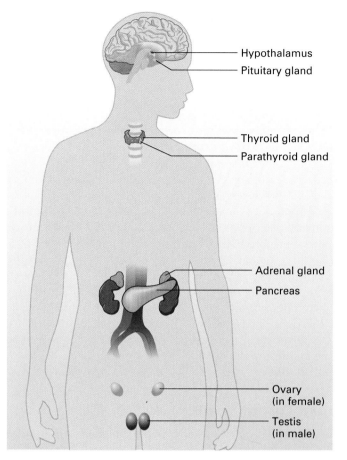

FIGURE 3.20 The Major Endocrine Glands The pituitary gland releases hormones that regulate the hormone secretions of the other glands. The pituitary gland is itself regulated by the hypothalamus.

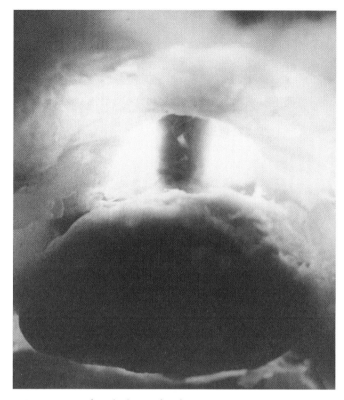

FIGURE 3.21 The Pituitary Gland The pituitary gland, which hangs by a short stalk from the hypothalamus, regulates the hormone production of many of the body's endocrine glands. Here it is enlarged 30 times.

The **adrenal glands** are instrumental in regulating moods, energy level, and the ability to cope with stress. Each adrenal gland secretes epinephrine (also called adrenaline) and norepinephrine (also called noradrenaline). Unlike most hormones, epinephrine and norepinephrine act quickly. Epinephrine helps a person get ready for an emergency by acting on smooth muscles, the heart, stomach, intestines, and sweat glands. In addition, epinephrine stimulates the reticular formation, which in turn arouses the sympathetic nervous system, and this system subsequently excites the adrenal glands to produce more epinephrine. Norepinephrine also alerts the individual to emergency situations by interacting with the pituitary and the liver. You may remember that norepinephrine functions as a neurotransmitter when it is released by neurons. In the adrenal glands, norepinephrine is released as a hormone. In both instances, norepinephrine conveys information—in the first instance to neurons, in the second to glands (Raven & Johnson, 2002).

Review and Sharpen Your Thinking

4 *State what the endocrine system is and how it affects behavior.*

- Describe the endocrine system, its glands, and their functions.

Is the behavior of animals such as rats, rabbits, and bulls more likely to be strongly controlled by hormones than that of humans? In answering this question, think about the differences in the structures of the brains of humans and those animals that were described earlier in the chapter.

mhhe com/
santrockp7

For study tools related to this learning goal, see the Study Guide, the CD-ROM, and the Online Learning Center.

adrenal glands Important endocrine glands that are instrumental in regulating moods, energy level, and the ability to cope with stress.

5 BRAIN DAMAGE, PLASTICITY, AND REPAIR

> The Brain's Plasticity and Capacity for Repair

> Brain Tissue Implants

If the brain is damaged through injury or illness, does it have the capacity to repair itself, or can its functions be restored surgically?

Recall from the discussion of the brain's important characteristics earlier in the chapter that plasticity is an example of the brain's remarkable adaptability. Neuroscientists have studied plasticity especially following brain damage, charting the brain's ability to repair itself. Brain damage can produce horrific effects, including paralysis, sensory loss, memory loss, and personality deterioration. When such damage occurs, can the brain recover some or all of its functions? Recovery from brain damage varies considerably from one case to another depending on the age of the individual and the extent of the damage (Garraghty, 1996; Sofroniew & Mobley, 2001). In the case of Brandi Binder, described at the beginning of the chapter, considerable plasticity was present, and the left hemisphere of her cerebral cortex took over many typically right-hemisphere functions after the right hemisphere was surgically removed because of epilepsy. Other people are less fortunate. There is hope that one day surgeons will be able to implant healthy tissue and restore function lost as a result of illness or injury. I discuss this area of research shortly.

The Brain's Plasticity and Capacity for Repair

The human brain shows the most plasticity in young children before the functions of the cortical regions become entirely fixed (Kolb, 1989). For example, if the speech areas in an infant's left hemisphere are damaged, the right hemisphere assumes much of this language function. However, after age 5, damage to the left hemisphere can permanently disrupt language ability. The brain's plasticity is further discussed in chapter 4 on development throughout the life span.

A key factor in recovery is whether some or all of the neurons in an affected area are just damaged or completely destroyed (Black, 1998; Carlson, 2001). If the neurons have not been destroyed, brain function often becomes restored over time.

There are three ways in which repair of the damaged brain might take place:

- *Collateral sprouting,* in which the axons of some healthy neurons adjacent to damaged cells grow new branches (Chung & Chung, 2001).
- *Substitution of function,* in which the damaged region's function is taken over by another area or areas of the brain. This is what happened to Brandi Binder.
- *Neurogenesis.* This is the term given to the generation of new neurons. One of the long-standing beliefs in neuroscience regarding plasticity was that all of the neurons an individual will ever have are present soon after birth. However, neuroscientists have recently found that human adults can generate new neurons (Kempermann & Gage, 1999). Researchers also discovered that adult monkeys' brains can create thousands of new neurons each day (Gould & others, 1999). Some researchers believe there is good evidence that neurogenesis is much more pervasive than previously thought (Hsu & others, 2001). However, other neuroscientists argue that the evidence is weak (Rakic, 2002). If researchers can discover how new neurons are generated, possibly the information can be used to fight degenerative diseases of the brain, such as Alzheimer's disease and Parkinson's disease (Gage, 2000).

Brain Tissue Implants

The brain naturally recovers some functions lost following damage, but not all. In recent years, considerable excitement has been generated about *brain grafts,* implants

Actress Patricia Neal suffered a stroke when she was 39 years of age. The stroke paralyzed one of her legs and left her unable to read, write, or speak. However, an intensive rehabilitation program and the human brain's plasticity allowed her to recover her functioning to the point that she resumed her career as an actress 4 years later. *What is the nature of the human brain's plasticity and capacity for repair?*

of healthy tissue into damaged brains (Rossi, Saggiorato, & Strata, 2002). The potential success of brain grafts is much better when brain tissue from the fetal stage (an early stage in prenatal development) is used. The neurons of the fetus are still growing and have a much higher probability of making connections with other neurons than do the neurons of adults. In a number of studies, researchers have damaged part of an adult rat's (or some other animal's) brain, waited until the animal recovered as much as possible by itself, and assessed its behavioral deficits. Then they took the corresponding area of a fetal rat's brain and transplanted it into the damaged brain of the adult rat. In these studies, the rats that received the brain transplants demonstrated considerable behavioral recovery (Dunnett, 1989).

Might such brain grafts be successful with humans suffering from brain damage? Research suggests that they might, but finding donors is a problem (Lindvall, 2001). Aborted fetuses are a possibility, but using them as a source of graft tissue raises ethical issues. Another type of treatment has been attempted with individuals who have Parkinson's disease, a neurological disorder that affects about a million people in the United States. Parkinson's disease impairs coordinated movement to the point that just walking across a room can be a major ordeal. In one recent study, brain grafts of embryonic dopamine neurons from aborted fetuses into individuals with Parkinson's disease resulted in a decrease of negative symptoms in individuals under 60 years of age but not in patients over 60 (Freed & others, 2001).

In another study, neuronal cells were transplanted into stroke victims (Kondziolka & others, 2000). The motor and cognitive skills of 12 patients who had experienced strokes improved markedly after the healthy neuronal cells were implanted in the midbrain.

The potential for brain grafts also exists for individuals with Alzheimer's disease, which is characterized by progressive decline in intellectual functioning resulting from the degeneration of neurons that function in memory. Such degenerative changes can be reversed in rats (Gage & Bjorklund, 1986). As yet, though, no successful brain grafts have been reported for Alzheimer's patients.

Review and Sharpen Your Thinking

5   *Discuss the brain's capacity for recovery and repair.*

- State the factors that favor recovery of function in damaged brains and list three ways in which the brain may recover.
- Discuss the possibility of repairing damaged brains with tissue grafts.

Suppose someone has suffered a mild form of brain damage. What questions might you ask to determine whether the person's brain will likely be able to either compensate or repair itself?

mhhe com/
santrockp7

For study tools related to this learning goal, see the Study Guide, the CD-ROM, and the Online Learning Center.

GENETIC AND EVOLUTIONARY BLUEPRINTS OF BEHAVIOR   6

Chromosomes, Genes, and DNA   The Study of Genetics   Genetics and Evolution

How do genetics and evolutionary psychology increase our understanding of behavior?

As you saw at the beginning of this chapter, genetic and evolutionary processes favor organisms that have adapted for survival. Successful adaptations can be physical, as in the case of the brain's increasing complexity, or behavioral, as in the choice of a suitable mate for raising a family.

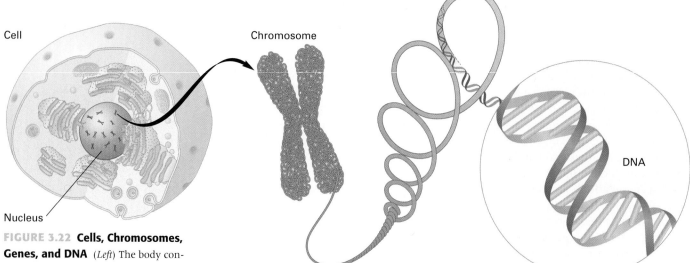

Cell

Nucleus

Chromosome

DNA

FIGURE 3.22 Cells, Chromosomes, Genes, and DNA (*Left*) The body contains trillions of cells, which are the basic structural units of life. Each cell contains a central structure, the nucleus. (*Middle*) Chromosomes and genes are located in the nucleus of the cell. Chromosomes are made up of threadlike structures composed mainly of DNA molecules. (*Right*) A gene is a segment of DNA that contains the hereditary code. The structure of DNA resembles a spiral ladder.

chromosomes Threadlike structures that contain genes and DNA. Humans have 23 chromosome pairs in the nucleus of every cell. Each parent contributes one chromosome to each pair.

deoxyribonucleic acid (DNA) A complex molecule that contains genetic information; makes up chromosomes.

genes The units of hereditary information. They are short segments of chromosomes, composed of DNA.

dominant-recessive genes principle If one gene of a pair governing a given characteristic (such as eye color) is dominant and one is recessive, the dominant gene overrides the recessive gene. A recessive gene exerts its influence only if both genes in a pair are recessive.

Chromosomes, Genes, and DNA

You began life as a single cell, a fertilized human egg, weighing about one 20-millionth of an ounce. From this single cell, you developed into a human being made up of trillions of cells. The nucleus of each human cell contains 46 **chromosomes,** which are threadlike structures that come in 23 pairs, one member of each pair coming from each parent. Chromosomes contain the remarkable substance **deoxyribonucleic acid,** or **DNA,** a complex molecule that contains genetic information. **Genes,** the units of hereditary information, are short segments of chromosomes, composed of DNA. Genes act like blueprints for cells. They enable cells to reproduce and manufacture the proteins that are necessary for maintaining life. The relationship among chromosomes, genes, and DNA is illustrated in figure 3.22.

When the approximately 30,000 genes from one parent combine at conception with the same number of genes from the other parent, the number of possibilities is staggering. Although scientists are still a long way from unraveling all the mysteries about the way genes work, some aspects of the process are well understood, starting with the fact that every person has two genes for each characteristic governed by principles of heredity (Lewis, 2003; Lewis & others, 2002).

In some gene pairs, one gene is dominant over the other. If one gene of a pair is dominant and one is recessive, according to the **dominant-recessive genes principle,** the dominant gene overrides the recessive gene. A recessive gene exerts its influence only if both genes of a pair are recessive. If you inherit a recessive gene from only one parent, you may never know you carry the gene. In the world of dominant-recessive genes, brown eyes, farsightedness, and dimples rule over blue eyes, nearsightedness, and freckles. If you inherit a recessive gene for a trait from both of your parents, you will show the trait. That's why two brown-eyed parents can have a blue-eyed child: Each parent would have a dominant gene for brown eyes and a recessive gene for blue eyes. Because dominant genes override recessive genes, the parents have brown eyes. However, the child can inherit a recessive gene for blue eyes from each parent. With no dominant gene to override them, the recessive genes make the child's eyes blue.

Unlike eye color, complex human characteristics such as personality and intelligence are likely influenced by many different genes. The term *polygenic inheritance* is used to describe the influences of multiple genes on behavior.

The Study of Genetics

Historically speaking, genetics is a relatively young science. Its origins go back to the mid-nineteenth century, when an Austrian monk named Gregor Mendel studied heredity in generations of pea plants. By cross-breeding plants with different charac-

The Human Genome Project and Your Genetic Future

The Human Genome Project, begun in the 1970s, has made stunning progress in mapping the human genome. Goals for the year 2003 are to identify all of the genes in human DNA and determine the sequence of 3 billion chemical base pairs that make up human DNA (U.S. Department of Energy, 2001). Among the surprise discoveries of the Human Genome Project is that humans have only about 30,000 genes—it was previously thought that we had 50,000 to 100,000. The project also has revealed that human DNA is about 98 percent identical to chimpanzee DNA (U.S. Department of Energy, 2001).

The Human Genome Project has already linked specific DNA variations with increased risk of a number of diseases and conditions, including Huntington's disease (in which the central nervous system deteriorates), some forms of cancer, asthma, diabetes, hypertension, and Alzheimer's disease (Davies, 2001). Other documented DNA variations affect the way people react to certain drugs.

Every individual carries a number of DNA variations that might predispose that person to a serious physical disease or mental disorder. Identifying these flaws could enable doctors to estimate an individual's disease risks, recommend healthy lifestyle regimens, and prescribe the safest and most effective drugs. A decade or two from now, parents of a newborn baby may be able to leave the hospital with a full genome analysis of their offspring that reveals various disease risks.

A positive result from the Human Genome Project. Shortly after Andrew Gobea was born, his cells were genetically altered to prevent his immune system from failing.

However, mining DNA variations to discover health risks might increasingly threaten an individual's ability to obtain and hold jobs, obtain insurance, and keep genetic profiles private. For example, should an airline pilot or neurosurgeon who one day may develop a disorder that makes the hands shake be required to leave that job early?

Answering the following questions should encourage you to think further about some of the issues involved in our genetic future (NOVA, 2001):

1. Would you want yourself or a loved one to be tested for a gene that increases your risk for a disease but does not determine whether you will actually develop the disease?
2. Would you want yourself and your mate tested before having offspring to determine your risk for having a child who is likely to contract various diseases?
3. Should testing of fetuses be restricted to traits that are commonly considered to have negative outcomes, such as Huntington's disease?
4. Should altering a newly conceived embryo's genes to improve qualities such as intelligence, appearance, and strength be allowed?
5. Should employers be permitted access to your genetic information?
6. Should life insurance companies have access to your genetic information?

teristics and noting the characteristics of the offspring, Mendel discovered predictable patterns of heredity and laid the foundation for modern genetics. Today researchers continue to apply Mendel's methods, as well as modern technology, in their quest to expand our knowledge of genetics. This section discusses three ways to study genetics: molecular genetics, selective breeding, and behavioral genetics.

Molecular Genetics The field of *molecular genetics* involves actual manipulation of genes using technology to determine their effect on behavior. There is currently a great deal of enthusiasm about the use of molecular genetics to discover the specific locations on genes that determine an individual's susceptibility to many diseases and other aspects of health and well-being (Dolfin, 2002; Mader, 2003).

The term *genome* is used to describe the complete set of instructions for making an organism. It contains the master blueprint for all cellular structures and activities for the life span of the organism. To read about the Human Genome Project and its possible applications, see the Psychology and Life box.

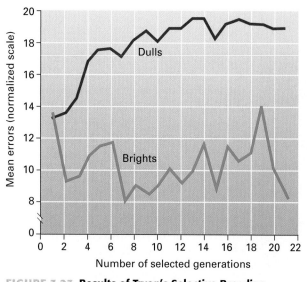

FIGURE 3.23 Results of Tryon's Selective Breeding Experiment with Maze-Bright and Maze-Dull Rats

Selective Breeding *Selective breeding* is a genetic method in which organisms are chosen for reproduction based on how much of a particular trait they display. Mendel developed this technique in his studies of pea plants. A more recent example involving behavior is the classic selective breeding study conducted by Robert Tryon (1940). He chose to study maze-running ability in rats. After he trained a large number of rats to run a complex maze, he then mated the rats that were the best at maze running ("maze bright") with each other and the ones that were the worst ("maze dull") with each other. He continued this process with 21 generations of rats. As can be seen in figure 3.23, after several generations, the maze-bright rats significantly outperformed the maze-dull rats.

Selective breeding studies have demonstrated that genes are an important influence on behavior, but that does not mean that experience is unimportant (Pinel, 2003). For example, in another study, maze-bright and maze-dull rats were reared in one of two environments: (1) an impoverished environment that consisted of a barren wire-mesh group cage, or (2) an enriched environment that contained tunnels, ramps, visual displays, and other stimulating objects (Cooper & Zubeck, 1958). When they reached maturity, only the maze-dull rats that had been reared in an impoverished environment made more maze-learning errors than the maze-bright rats.

Selective breeding is practiced at the Repository for Germinal Choice in Escondido, California, which was founded by Dr. Robert Graham as a sperm bank for Nobel Prize winners and other bright individuals with the intent of producing geniuses. The sperm is available to women whose husbands are infertile. What are the odds that the sperm bank will yield that special combination of factors required to produce a creative genius? Twentieth-century Irish-born playwright George Bernard Shaw once told a story about a beautiful woman who wrote to him, saying that, with her body and his mind, they could produce wonderful offspring. Shaw responded by saying that, unfortunately, the offspring might get his body and her mind!

What do you think about the Nobel Prize winners'–sperm bank? Is it right to breed for intelligence? Does it raise visions of the German genetics program of the 1930s and 1940s, based on the Nazis' belief that certain traits were superior? The Nazis tried to produce children with such traits and killed people without them. Or does the sperm bank merely provide a social service for couples who cannot conceive a child, couples who want to maximize the probability that their offspring will have good genes?

Behavior Genetics *Behavior genetics* is the study of the degree and nature of heredity's influence on behavior. Behavior genetics is less invasive than molecular genetics and selective breeding. Using methods such as the *twin study,* behavior geneticists examine the extent to which individuals are shaped by their heredity and their environmental experiences (Wahlsten, 2000).

In the most common type of twin study, the behavioral similarity of identical twins is compared with the behavioral similarity of fraternal twins. *Identical twins* develop from a single fertilized egg that splits into two genetically identical embryos, each of which becomes a person. *Fraternal twins* develop from separate eggs and separate sperm, making them genetically no more similar than nontwin siblings. They may even be of different sexes.

By comparing groups of identical and fraternal twins, behavior geneticists capitalize on the fact that identical twins are more similar genetically than are fraternal twins. In one twin study, 7,000 pairs of Finnish identical and fraternal twins were compared on the personality traits of extraversion (being outgoing) and neuroticism (being psychologically unstable; Rose & others, 1988). The identical twins were much more alike than the fraternal twins on both of these personality traits, suggesting that genes influence both traits.

Dr. Graham with the frozen sperm of a Nobel Prize–winning donor.

What is the nature of the twin-study method?

One problem with twin studies is that adults might stress the similarities of identical twin children more than those of fraternal twins, and identical twins might perceive themselves as a "set" and play together more than fraternal twins do. If so, observed similarities in identical twins might be more strongly influenced by environmental factors than usually thought.

In another type of twin study, researchers evaluate identical twins who have been reared in separate environments. If their behavior is similar, the assumption is that heredity has played an important role in shaping their behavior. This strategy is the basis for the Minnesota Study of Twins Reared Apart, directed by Thomas Bouchard and his colleagues (1996). They bring identical twins who have been reared apart to Minneapolis from all over the world to study their behavior. They ask thousands of questions about their family and childhood environment, personal interests, vocational orientation, and values. Detailed medical histories are obtained, including information about their diet, smoking, and exercise habits.

One pair of twins in the Minnesota study, Jim Springer and Jim Lewis, were separated at 4 weeks of age and did not see each other again until they were 39 years old. They had an uncanny number of similarities, even though they had lived apart. For example, they both worked as part-time deputy sheriffs, had vacationed in Florida, had owned Chevrolets, had dogs named Toy, and had married and divorced women named Betty. Both liked math but not spelling. Both were good at mechanical drawing. Both put on 10 pounds at about the same time in their lives, and both started suffering headaches at 18 years of age. They did have a few differences. For example, one expressed himself better orally, and the other was more proficient at writing. One parted his hair over his forehead, the other wore his hair slicked back with sideburns.

Critics argue that some of the separated twins in the Minnesota study had been together several months prior to their adoption, that some had been reunited prior to their testing (in some cases for a number of years), that adoption agencies often put identical twins in similar homes, and that even strangers who spend several hours together are likely to come up with some coincidental similarities (Adler, 1991). Still, even in the face of such criticism, it seems unlikely that all of the similarities in the identical twins reared apart could be due to experience alone.

Behavior geneticists also use *adoption studies* to try to determine whether the behavior of adopted children is more like that of their biological parents or their adopted parents. Another type of adoption study compares biological and adopted siblings. In

The Jim twins: how coincidental? Springer (*right*) and Lewis were unaware of each other for 39 years.

one study, the educational levels attained by biological parents were better predictors of the adopted children's IQ scores than were the IQs of the children's adoptive parents (Scarr & Weinberg, 1983). Because of the stronger genetic link between the adopted children and their biological parents, the implication is that heredity plays an important role in intelligence. However, there are numerous studies that document the critical role of environment in intelligence, as well (Sternberg, 1997).

Genetics and behavior, especially the way heredity and environment interact, are discussed further in chapter 4.

Genetics and Evolution

Often we can see the effects of genetics by observing family resemblances. For example, you might have your mother's dark hair and your father's long legs. Evolutionary influences are not as easy to see, because we share physical and psychological characteristics with every other human, such as a cerebral cortex in our brain that allows us to think and plan. We also share certain problems that we have to solve and adapt to, such as how to protect ourselves from harm, how to nourish our bodies, how to find a compatible mate, and how to rear our children. In the evolutionary scheme, some individuals were more successful at solving these problems and adapting effectively than others (Cummings, 2003; Goldsmith & Zimmerman, 2001). Those who were successful passed on their genes to the next generation. Those were less successful did not.

In the evolutionary psychology view, psychological functions evolved to become specialized. Thus, just as the cerebellum became functionally specialized in coordinating movement, so it might be that specialized psychological functions evolved (Buss, 2000). Among the specialized psychological functions that evolutionary psychologists study are

- Development of a fear of strangers between 3 and 24 months of age, as well as fears of snakes, spiders, heights, open spaces, and darkness (Marks, 1987)
- Perceptual adaptations for tracking motion (Ashida, Seiffert, & Osaka, 2001)
- Children's imitation of high-status rather than low-status models (Bandura, 1977)
- The worldwide preference for mates who are kind, intelligent, and dependable (Buss & others, 1990)

Evolutionary psychologists believe that these specialized functions developed because they helped humans adapt and solve problems in past evolutionary environments (Cosmides & others, 2003). In later chapters, I examine what evolutionary psychologists have to say about other psychological topics.

Before leaving the topic of evolutionary psychology, it is important to mention that some critics believe it places too much emphasis on biological foundations of behavior. For example, Albert Bandura (1998), whose social cognitive theory was described in chapter 1, acknowledges the importance of human adaptation and change. However, he rejects what he calls "one-sided evolutionism," in which social behavior is the product of evolved biology. Bandura recommends a bidirectional view. In this view, evolutionary pressures created changes in biological structures for the use of tools, which enabled organisms to manipulate, alter, and construct new environmental conditions. Environmental innovations of increasing complexity, in turn, produced new selection pressures for the evolution of specialized biological systems for consciousness, thought, and language.

Human evolution gave us body structures and biological potentialities, not behavioral dictates, according to scientists such as Steven Jay Gould (1981). Having evolved, advanced biological capacities can be instrumental in producing diverse cultures—aggressive or peaceful, for example. And Russian American scientist Theodore Dobzhansky (1977) reminds us that the human species has selected for learnability and plasticity, which allows us to adapt to diverse contexts. Most, if not all, psychologists would agree that the interaction of biology and environment is the basis for our own development as human beings. Chapter 4 further explores the influence of biology and environment on human development.

Review and Sharpen Your Thinking

6 *Explain how genetics and evolutionary psychology increase our understanding of behavior.*

- Discuss the structures and functions of chromosomes, genes, and DNA.
- Describe three methods for studying genetics.
- Explain how evolution might direct human behavior.

What ethical issues regarding genetics and behavior might arise in the future?

mhhe com/
santrockp7

For study tools related to this learning goal, see the Study Guide, the CD-ROM, and the Online Learning Center.

Biological Foundations of Behavior

1   THE NERVOUS SYSTEM

Characteristics

Pathways in the Nervous System

Divisions of the Nervous System

2   NEURONS

Specialized Cell Structure

Synapses and Neurotransmitters

The Neural Impulse

Neural Networks

3   STRUCTURES OF THE BRAIN AND THEIR FUNCTIONS

How the Brain and Nervous System Are Studied

The Cerebral Cortex

Integration of Function in the Brain

Levels of Organization in the Brain

The Cerebral Hemispheres and Split-Brain Research

4   THE ENDOCRINE SYSTEM

5   BRAIN DAMAGE, PLASTICITY, AND REPAIR

The Brain's Plasticity and Capacity for Repair

Brain Tissue Implants

6   GENETIC AND EVOLUTIONARY BLUEPRINTS OF BEHAVIOR

Chromosomes, Genes, and DNA

The Study of Genetics

Genetics and Evolution

1 Discuss the nature and basic functions of the nervous system.

- The nervous system is the body's electrochemical communication circuitry. Four important characteristics of the brain and nervous system are complexity, integration, adaptability, and electrochemical transmission. The brain's special ability to adapt and change is called plasticity.
- The flow of information in the nervous system occurs in specialized pathways of nerve cells. Three of these pathways involve sensory input, motor output, and neural networks.
- The nervous system is divided into two main parts: central (CNS) and peripheral (PNS). The CNS consists of the brain and spinal cord. The PNS has two major divisions: somatic and autonomic. The autonomic nervous system consists of two main divisions: sympathetic and parasympathetic.

2 Explain what neurons are and describe how they process information.

- Neurons are cells that specialize in processing information. They make up the communication network of the nervous system. Glial cells perform supportive and nutritive functions for neurons. The three main parts of the neuron are the cell body, dendrite (receiving part), and axon (sending part). A myelin sheath encases and insulates most axons and speeds up transmission of neural impulses.
- A neuron sends information along its axon in the form of brief electric impulses, or waves. Resting potential is the term given to the stable, slightly negative charge of an inactive neuron. When the electrical signals exceed a certain activation threshold, positively charged sodium ions rush into the neuron. The brief wave of electrical charge that sweeps down the axon is called the action potential. The neuron returns to a resting potential as positively charged potassium ions move out of it, returning the neuron to a negative charge. The action potential abides by the all-or-none principle: Its strength does not change during transmission.
- To go from one neuron to another, information must be converted from an electrical impulse to a chemical messenger called a neurotransmitter. At the synapse where neurons meet, neurotransmitters are released into the narrow gap that separates them. There some neurotransmitter molecules attach to receptor sites on the receiving neuron, where they stimulate another electrical impulse. Neurotransmitters can be excitatory or inhibitory depending on the nature of the neural impulse. Neurotransmitters include acetylcholine, GABA, norepinephrine, dopamine, serotonin, and endorphins. Most drugs that influence behavior do so mainly by mimicking neurotransmitters or interfering with their activity.
- Neural networks are clusters of neurons that are interconnected to process information.

3 Identify the brain's levels and structures and the functions of its structures.

- The main techniques used to study the brain are brain lesioning, staining, electrical recording, and brain imaging.
- The three major levels of the brain are the hindbrain, midbrain, and forebrain. The hindbrain is the lowest portion of the brain. The three main parts of the hindbrain are the medulla (involved in controlling breathing and posture), cerebellum (involved in motor coordination), and pons (involved in sleep and arousal).
- From the midbrain many nerve-fiber systems ascend and descend to connect to higher and lower levels of the brain. The midbrain contains the reticular formation, which is involved in stereotypical patterns of behavior (such as walking, sleeping, or turning to a sudden noise), and small groups of neurons that communicate with many areas in the brain. The brain stem consists of much of the hindbrain (excluding the cerebellum) and the midbrain.
- The forebrain is the highest level of the brain. The key forebrain structures are the limbic system, thalamus, basal ganglia, hypothalamus, and cerebral cortex. The limbic system is involved in memory and emotion through its two structures, the amygdala (which plays roles in survival and emotion) and the hippocampus (which functions in the storage of memories). The thalamus is a forebrain structure that serves as an important relay station for processing information. The basal ganglia are forebrain structures that help to control and coordinate voluntary movements. The hypothalamus is a forebrain structure that monitors eating, drinking, and sex; directs the endocrine system through the pituitary gland; and is involved in emotion, stress, and reward.
- The cerebral cortex makes up most of the outer layer of the brain. Higher mental functions, such as thinking and planning, take place in the cerebral cortex. The wrinkled surface of the cerebral cortex is divided into hemispheres. Each hemisphere is divided into four lobes: occipital, temporal, frontal, and parietal. There is considerable integration and connection between the brain's lobes. The sensory cortex processes information about body sensa-

tions. The motor cortex processes information about voluntary movement. Penfield (1947) pinpointed specific areas in the brain that correspond to specific parts of the body and also mapped sensory fields onto the cortex's surface. The association cortex, which makes up 75 percent of the cerebral cortex, is instrumental in integrating information, especially about the highest intellectual functions.

- A controversial topic is the extent to which the left and right hemispheres of the brain are involved in different functions. Two areas in the left hemisphere that involve specific language functions are Broca's area (speech) and Wernicke's area (comprehending language). The corpus callosum is a large bundle of fibers that connects the two hemispheres. Researchers have studied what happens when the corpus callosum has to be severed, as in some cases of severe epilepsy. Research suggests that the left brain is more dominant in processing verbal information (such as language), and the right brain in processing nonverbal information (such as spatial perception, visual recognition, and emotion). Nonetheless, in a normal individual whose corpus callosum is intact, both hemispheres of the cerebral cortex are involved in most complex human functioning.

- It is extremely important to remember that generally brain function is integrated and involves connections between different parts of the brain. Pathways of neurons involved in a particular function, such as memory, are integrated across different parts and levels of the brain.

4 State what the endocrine system is and how it affects behavior.

- The endocrine glands release hormones directly into the bloodstream for distribution throughout the body. The pituitary gland is the master endocrine gland. The adrenal glands play important roles in moods, energy level, and ability to cope with stress.

5 Describe the brain's capacity for recovery and repair.

- The human brain has considerable plasticity, although this plasticity is greater in young children than later in development. Three ways in which a damaged brain might repair itself are collateral sprouting, substitution of function, and neurogenesis.

- Brain grafts are implants of healthy tissue into damaged brains. Brain grafts are more successful when fetal tissue is used.

6 Explain how genetics and evolutionary psychology increase our understanding of behavior.

- Chromosomes are threadlike structures that come in 23 pairs, one member of each pair coming from each parent. Chromosomes contain the genetic substance deoxyribonucleic acid (DNA). Genes, the units of hereditary information, are short segments of chromosomes composed of DNA. The dominant-recessive genes principle states that if one gene of a pair is dominant and one is recessive, the dominant gene overrides the recessive gene.

- Three methods that are used to study heredity's influence are molecular genetics, selective breeding, and behavior genetics. Two methods used by behavior geneticists are twin studies and adoption studies.

- Several key points in evolutionary psychology center on the idea that nature selects behaviors that increase an organism's reproductive success, the importance of adaptive behavior, and specialization of functions. Evolutionary psychologists believe that just as parts of the brain have become specialized in function through the process of evolution, so have mental processes and behavior. Critics stress that it is important to recognize how evolutionary advances allow humans to choose and select their environments, rather than being completely under the control of their evolutionary past.

Key Terms

nervous system, p. 78
plasticity, p. 79
afferent nerves, p. 80
efferent nerves, p. 80
neural network, p. 80
central nervous system (CNS), p. 81

peripheral nervous system (PNS), p. 81
somatic nervous system, p. 81
autonomic nervous system, p. 81
sympathetic nervous system, p. 81

parasympathetic nervous system, p. 81
neurons, p. 82
glial cells, p. 82
cell body, p. 82
dendrite, p. 82
axon, p. 82

myelin sheath, p. 82
resting potential, p. 84
action potential, p. 84
all-or-none principle, p. 84
synapse, p. 85
neurotransmitter, p. 86
agonist, p. 88

Apply Your Knowledge

1. Consider the four characteristics of the nervous system. Suppose you had to do without one of them. Which would you choose, and what would be the consequences for your behavior?

2. Do a search on the World Wide Web for "nutrition" and "the brain." Examine the claims made by one or more of the websites. Based on what you learned in the chapter about how the nervous system works, how could nutrition affect brain function? Based on what you know about being a scientist, how believable are the claims on the website?

3. Imagine that you could make one part of your brain twice as big as it is right now. Which part would it be, and how do you think your behavior would change as a result? What if you had to make another part of your brain half its current size? Which part would you choose to shrink, and what would be the effects be?

4. Ephedra is a drug contained in a number of formulas marketed to enhance athletic performance. Among the actions of ephedra is stimulation of areas that normally respond to epinephrine and norepinephrine. Think about the two different kinds of actions (neurotransmitter and hormone) these chemicals normally have in the nervous system, and describe the kinds of side effects you might expect from taking ephedra. In particular, why might taking ephedra be very dangerous?

5. It's not unusual to read headlines announcing that genes are responsible for a troublesome behavior (for example, "Next time you pig out, blame it on the genes," *Los Angeles Times*, October 19, 2000, or "Men are born fighters," *Times* (London), October 19, 2001). How would you interpret statements like these in light of the material discussed in the text?

Connections

For extra help in mastering the material in this chapter, see the review sections and practice quizzes in the Student Study Guide, the CD-ROM, and the Online Learning Center.

4 Human Development

Chapter Outline

Learning Goals

EXPLORING HUMAN DEVELOPMENT   **1**

What Is Development?
▼
Do Early Experiences Rule Us for Life?
▼
How Do Nature and Nurture Influence Development?

Explain how psychologists think about development.

CHILD DEVELOPMENT   **2**

Prenatal Development
▼
Physical Development in Childhood
▼
Cognitive Development in Childhood
▼
Socioemotional Development in Childhood
▼
Positive Psychology and Children's Development

Describe children's development from conception to adolescence.

ADOLESCENCE   **3**

Positive Psychology and Adolescents
▼
Physical Development in Adolescence
▼
Cognitive Development in Adolescence
▼
Socioemotional Development in Adolescence
▼
At-Risk Youth

Identify the most important changes that occur in adolescence.

ADULT DEVELOPMENT AND AGING   **4**

Physical Development in Adulthood
▼
Cognitive Development in Adulthood
▼
Socioemotional Development in Adulthood
▼
Positive Psychology and Aging

Discuss adult development and the positive dimensions of aging.

Zhang Liyin was playing in a kindergarten class in Beijing, China, when a coach from a sports school spotted her. The coach invited her to attend the school. Zhang was selected because of her broad shoulders, narrow hips, straight legs, symmetrical limbs, open-minded attitude, vivaciousness, and outgoing personality.

Zhang's parents accepted the invitation, and now she attends the sports school in the afternoon. Attending the sports school is a privilege given to only 260,000 of China's 200 million students from elementary school to college age. These schools are the only road to Olympic stardom in China. China spends lavishly on its sports schools but has precious few neighborhood playgrounds and only one gymnasium for every 3.5 million people.

Today, at age 6, Zhang is standing on the balance beam, stretching her arms outward as she gets ready to perform a back flip. She wears the bright red gymnastic suit of the elite—a suit given to only the 10 best girls in her class of 6- to 8-year-olds. But her face wears a fearful expression. She can't drum up enough confidence to do the flip. Maybe it is because she has had a rough week. A purple bruise decorates one leg; a nasty gash disfigures the other.

Because of her young age, Zhang stays at home during the mornings and goes to sports school from noon until 6 p.m. If she continues to perform well, next year, at age 7, she will live and study at the sports school like many of its other students. The development of these children is closely monitored. If at any point a child shows a decline in potential, the child is asked to leave the sports school.

The skills in three areas of development—physical, cognitive, and socioemotional—that won Zhang Liyin her place at the sports school is the topic of this chapter. Like Zhang Liyin, each of us develops physically, cognitively, and socioemotionally. In this chapter, development is divided into three main time frames: childhood, adolescence, and adulthood. As you read each section, pay attention to how physical, cognitive, and socioemotional aspects of development typically change from one phase of life to another. And keep in mind that some people may develop more slowly or more quickly and to a different degree in these areas than other people do.

The training of future Olympians in the sports schools of China. Six-year-old Zhang Liyin (*third from the left*) hopes someday to become an Olympic gymnastics champion. Attending the sports school is considered an outstanding privilege; only 260,000 of China's 200 million students are given this opportunity.

What Is Development?	**Do Early Experiences Rule Us for Life?**	**How Do Nature and Nurture Influence Development?**

How do psychologists think about development?

Not every child is as physically skilled as Zhang Liyin, but, as children, we all traveled some common paths. For example, whether you are likely to become a famous person or simply a good one, most likely you walked at about the age of 1, talked at about the age of 2, engaged in fantasy play as a young child, and began to think more logically as an older child. Yet each of us also is unique. No one else in the world has the same fingerprints as you, for example. Let's explore the reason for these differences.

What Is Development?

Development refers to the pattern of change in human capabilities that begins at conception and continues throughout the life span. Most development involves growth, although it also consists of decline (for example, processing information becomes less quick for older adults). Researchers who study development are intrigued by its universal characteristics and by its individual variations. The pattern of development is complex because it is the product of several processes:

- *Physical processes* involve changes in an individual's biological nature. Genes inherited from parents, the hormonal changes of puberty and menopause, and changes throughout life in the brain, height and weight, and motor skills all reflect the developmental role of biological processes. Psychologists refer to such biological growth processes as *maturation*. Zhang Liyin has a body build and exceptional motor skills that allow her to perform well in gymnastics.
- *Cognitive processes* involve changes in an individual's thought, intelligence, and language. Observing a colorful mobile as it swings above a crib, constructing a sentence about the future, imagining oneself as a movie star, memorizing a new telephone number—all these activities reflect the role of cognitive processes in development. The sports school helps to develop Zhang Liyin's cognitive skills by requiring her to take academic classes for part of the day.
- *Socioemotional processes* involve changes in an individual's relationships with other people, changes in emotions, and changes in personality. An infant's smile in response to her mother's touch, a girl's development of assertiveness, an adolescent's joy at the senior prom, a young man's aggressiveness in sport, and an older couple's affection for each other all reflect the role of socioemotional processes. Among the reasons that Zhang Liyin was chosen to attend the sports school were her vivaciousness and outgoing attitude, which involve socioemotional processes.

Remember as you read about physical, cognitive, and socioemotional processes that they are intricately interwoven, as figure 4.1 shows. For example, socioemotional processes shape cognitive processes, cognitive processes promote or restrict socioemotional processes, and physical processes influence cognitive processes. Although the three processes of development are discussed in separate sections of the chapter, keep in mind that you are studying the development of an integrated human being in whom body, mind, and emotion are interdependent.

In the case of Zhang Liyin, the combination of physical, cognitive, and socioemotional skills is what led her to being chosen to attend a sports school in China. As she grows up, an important issue will be whether her cognitive and socioemotional skills suffer because she spends so much time developing her physical skills.

development The pattern of change in human capabilities that begins at conception and continues throughout the life span.

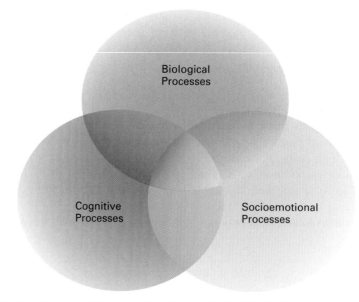

FIGURE 4.1 Developmental Changes Are the Result of Biological, Cognitive, and Socioemotional Processes These processes are interwoven as individuals develop.

Do Early Experiences Rule Us for Life?

As psychologists study development, they debate whether early experiences or later experiences are more important (Santrock, 2002). Some psychologists believe that unless infants experience warm, nurturant caregiving in the first year or so of life, they will not develop to their full potential (Berlin & Cassidy, 2000; Bowlby, 1989). Psychologists are not the only ones who think that way. The ancient Greek philosopher Plato was sure that infants who were rocked frequently became better athletes. Nineteenth-century New England ministers told parents in Sunday sermons that the way they handled their infants would determine their children's future character. This *early-experience* doctrine suggests that after a period of early development, we become relatively fixed and permanent in our makeup. It rests on the belief that each life is an unbroken trail on which a psychological quality can be traced back to its origin (Kagan, 1992, 2000)

In contrast, some psychologists emphasize the power of later experience and liken development in later years to the ebb and flow of a river. The *later-experience* advocates argue that children are malleable and that sensitive caregiving is just as important later as it is earlier (Lewis, 1997). A number of life-span developmentalists, who focus on both children and adults, stress that too little attention has been given to adult development (Baltes, 2000; Birren & Schaie, 2001). They argue that although early experiences are important contributors to development, they are not necessarily more important than later experiences.

The life of Alice Walker provides one example of the ability to continue developing past childhood. She grew up knowing the brutal effects of poverty and racism. Born in 1944, she was the eighth child of Georgia sharecroppers who earned $300 a year. When Walker was 8, her brother accidently shot her in the left eye with a BB gun. By the time her parents got her to the hospital a week later (they did not have a car), she was blind in that eye, and it had a disfiguring layer of scar tissue.

As an adolescent, Walker became acutely aware of the bias and discrimination shown toward her and her family. She had a dream of going to Senegal, Africa, to search for her roots and an identity. As the civil rights movement grew in the United States in the late 1950s and early 1960s, she shifted her focus, seeking her identity by putting herself into the heart and heat of the movement. In that context, her identity flourished and expanded. Despite the early counts against her, Walker went on to become an essayist, poet, award-winning novelist, short-story writer, and social activist. Like her characters (especially the women), she overcame her pain and anger. Walker turned poverty and trauma into a rich literary harvest, including a Pulitzer Prize–winning book, *The Color Purple*.

Undoubtedly, Alice Walker's early experiences helped to provide a foundation for her compassionate view of humanity and motivated many of her efforts. But her harsh experiences early in life did not prevent her from continuing to grow and eventually achieving great success as a writer.

Recall from chapter 2 that case studies such as this analysis of Alice Walker's life have unique aspects that are often difficult to generalize to many people. So let's explore correlational research that addresses the early/later experience issue, focusing on adolescent depression. One research study examined the link between parents' relationships with their young daughters between the ages of 3 to 5 and the daughters' depression in adolescence (Gjerde, Block, & Block, 1991). It found that the adolescent girls were more likely to be depressed when the parents had been overly controlling, had demanded high achievement, and had not adequately nurtured the girls when they were 3 to 5 years of age. These results demonstrate the importance of early experience. But other research studies show that stressful experiences in adolescence—such as making low grades, breaking up with a boyfriend, or dealing with a parent's death—are also related to depression in adolescent girls (Compas & others, 2001). Thus depression in adolescent girls appears to be linked to both early and later experiences.

Most developmentalists do not take extreme positions on the issue of early versus later experience (Lerner, 2000, 2002; Santrock, 2001). They believe that, although early experience can create a foundation for later experience, both make important contributions to development.

Alice Walker won the Pulitzer Prize for her book *The Color Purple*. Like many of the characters in her book (especially the women), Walker overcame early experiences with poverty and pain to become a very competent adult.

How Do Nature and Nurture Influence Development?

In chapter 3 I examined the relationship between genetics and behavior. Although genes play an important role in human behavior, genes alone do not determine who we are. Genes exist within the context of a complex environment that is necessary for an organism to even exist. Environment includes all of the surrounding physical and social conditions and influences that affect the development of living things. Biologists who study even the simplest animals agree that separating the effects of the animals' genes from the effects of their environment is virtually impossible (Lewis, 2003).

Genotype and Phenotype Genetic material may be expressed differently depending on the environment. Thus a person's observable and measurable characteristics might not reflect their genetic heritage very precisely because of the experiences they have had.

To account for this gap between genes and behavior, scientists make a distinction between genotype and phenotype. **Genotype** is the individual's genetic heritage, the actual genetic material. **Phenotype** is the way an individual's genotype is expressed in observable, measurable characteristics. Phenotypes include physical characteristics (such as height, weight, and eye color) and psychological characteristics (such as intelligence and personality).

For each genotype, a range of phenotypes can be expressed. An individual can inherit the genetic potential to grow very large, but good nutrition will also be important to achieving that potential. Or suppose that we could identify all of the genes that contribute to making a person introverted (shy) or extraverted (outgoing). Would *measured* introversion or extraversion be predictable from knowledge of specific

genotype An individual's genetic heritage, the actual genetic material.

phenotype The expression of an individual's genotype in observable, measurable characteristics.

genes? The answer is no, because introversion and extraversion are characteristics that are influenced not only by heredity but also by experience. For example, parents might guide a shy child to become more social.

Exploring Nature and Nurture Related to the distinction between genotype and phenotype is a broader distinction between nature and nurture. The term **nature** is often used to refer to an organism's biological inheritance. The term **nurture** is often used to refer to an organism's environmental experiences. The interaction of nature and nurture, of genes and environment, influences every aspect of mind and behavior to a degree. Neither factor operates alone (Gottlieb, 2002; Moore, 2001; Mader, 2003).

At one time, psychologists argued about what percentage of human development was due to nature and what percentage was due to nurture. That debate no longer seems productive (Johnson, 2000; Tamarin, 2002). Nor is it accurate to say that our genes "turn on" all at once, around conception or birth, after which we take our genetic legacy into the world to see how far it carries us. Throughout the life span, in many different environments, either genes produce the proteins that affect experience and human development or they don't produce these proteins, depending on how harsh or nourishing those environments are (Commoner, 2002).

Psychologists are starting to agree that many complex behaviors have some genetic loading that makes people likely to develop in a particular way. But our actual development also depends on what we experience in our environment. And that environment is complex, as is the mixture of genes that we inherit. Environmental influences range from the things we lump together under "nurture" (such as parenting, family dynamics, peer relations, schooling, and neighborhood quality) to biological encounters (such as viruses, birth complications, and even cellular activities).

As with the question on the role of early experience, most developmentalists do not take an extreme position on nature versus nurture. Development is not all one or the other (Lerner, 2002). It is an *interaction* of the two. Heredity and environment operate together to produce temperament, height, weight, ability to pitch a baseball, reading ability, and so on (Gottlieb, 2000, 2002). If Zhang Liyin becomes an Olympic champion in gymnastics, will it be because of her heredity or her environment? The answer is both. According to William Greenough (2001), who studies heredity and environment issues, "The interaction of heredity and environment is so extensive that to ask which is more important, nature or nurture, is like asking which is more important to a rectangle, height or width?"

Optimal Experiences Some psychologists believe we can develop beyond what our genetic inheritance and our environment give us. They argue that a key aspect of development involves seeking optimal experiences in life (Massimini & Delle Fave, 2000). They cite examples of people who go beyond simple biological adaptation to actively pick and choose from the environment the things that serve their purposes. These individuals build and construct their own lives, authoring a unique developmental path.

In our effort to experience our lives in optimal ways, we develop *life themes* that involve activities, social relationships, and life goals (Csikszentmihalyi & Beattie, 1979; Csikszentmihalyi & Rathunde, 1998; Nakamura & Csikszentmihalyi, 2002). One example of an optimal life theme is to make the decision to go beyond selfish reproduction and competition in order to foster understanding, tolerance, and cooperation among all human beings.

Some people are more successful at constructing optimal life experiences than others. Among individuals who have succeeded are Albert Schweitzer, Mother Teresa, Martin Luther King, Jr., and Mahatma Gandhi. These people looked for and found meaningful life themes as they developed. Their lives were not restricted to simple biological survival or passive acceptance of environmental dictates.

nature An organism's biological inheritance.

nurture An organism's environmental experience.

Review and Sharpen Your Thinking

1 **Explain how psychologists think about development.**

- Name and describe the three main developmental processes.
- Discuss the influence of early and later experiences on human development.
- Evaluate the influences of nature and nurture on development.

Your development as a human being is determined by multiple factors. Think about what you are like as a person today and reflect on the processes in your development that made you who you are.

For study tools related to this learning goal, see the Study Guide, the CD-ROM, and the Online Learning Center.

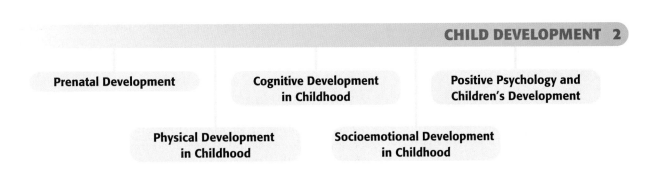

CHILD DEVELOPMENT 2

Prenatal Development

Cognitive Development in Childhood

Positive Psychology and Children's Development

Physical Development in Childhood

Socioemotional Development in Childhood

How do children develop from conception to adolescence?

How children develop has special importance because children are the future of any society. Our journey through childhood begins with conception and continues through the elementary school years. The focus of this section is on the three fundamental developmental processes—physical, cognitive, and socioemotional. The nature and nurture theme is revisited along the journey, and the importance of taking a positive view of childhood is explored.

Prenatal Development

Many special things have taken place in your life since you were born. But imagine . . . at one time you were a microscopic organism floating in a sea of fluid in your mother's womb. As the nineteenth-century American poet-essayist Samuel Taylor remarked, "The history of man for nine months preceding his birth is probably far more interesting and contains more stunning events than all the years that follow."

The Course of Prenatal Development *Conception* occurs when a single sperm cell from the male penetrates the female's ovum (egg). This process is also called *fertilization*. A *zygote* is a fertilized egg.

Prenatal development is divided into three periods:

- *Germinal period: weeks 1 and 2.* The germinal period begins with conception. The fertilized egg, a zygote, is a single cell with 23 chromosomes from the mother and 23 from the father. After 1 week and many cell divisions, the zygote is made up of 100 to 150 cells. By the end of 2 weeks, the mass of cells attaches to the uterine wall.
- *Embryonic period: weeks 3 through 8.* Before most women even know they are pregnant, the rate of cell differentiation intensifies, support systems for the cells form, and the beginnings of organs appear. In the 3rd week the neural tube, which eventually becomes the spinal cord, starts to form. At about 21 days, eyes begin to appear, and by 24 days the cells of the heart begin to differentiate.

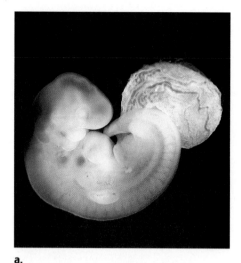

a.

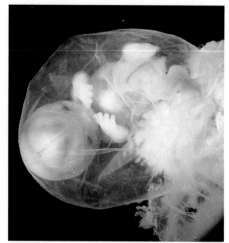

b.

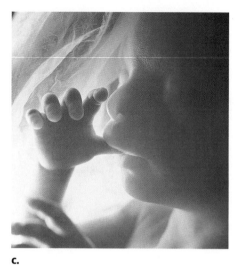

c.

FIGURE 4.2 From Embryo to Fetus

(*a*) At about 4 weeks, an embryo is about 0.2 inches (less than 1 centimeter) long. The head, eyes, and ears begin to show; the head and neck are half the length of the body; the shoulders will be located where the whitish arm buds are attached.

(*b*) At 8 weeks the developing individual is about 1.6 inches (4 centimeters) long and has reached the end of its embryonic phase. It has become a fetus. Everything that will be found in the fully developed human being has now begun to form. The fetal stage is a period of growth and perfection of detail. The heart has been beating for a month, and the muscles have just begun their first exercises.

(*c*) At 4½ months, the fetus is just over 7 inches (about 18 centimeters) long. When the thumb comes close to the mouth, the head may turn, and lips and tongue begin their sucking motions—a reflex for survival.

During the 4th week, arm and leg buds emerge (see figure 4.2a). At 5 to 8 weeks, the heart begins to beat, arms and legs become more differentiated, the face starts to form, and the intestinal tract appears (see figure 4.2b).

- *Fetal period: months 2 through 9.* Organs mature to the point at which life can be sustained outside the womb, and muscles begin their first exercises. The mother feels the fetus move for the first time. At 6 months after conception, the eyes and eyelids are completely formed, a fine layer of hair covers the fetus, the grasping reflex appears, and irregular breathing begins. By 7 to 9 months, the fetus is much longer and weighs considerably more. In addition, the functioning of various organs steps up.

In 9 short months, a single cell has developed the capacity to live and function as a human being, with the potential for further physical, cognitive, and socioemotional changes. Sometimes, however, normal development is disrupted.

Threats to the Fetus Some pregnant women tiptoe about in the belief that everything they do has a direct effect on the unborn child. Others behave more casually, assuming their experiences have little effect. The truth lies somewhere between these extremes. Although it floats in a comfortable, well-protected environment, the fetus is not totally immune to the larger environment surrounding the mother (Bailey, Forget, & Koren, 2002; Fifer & Grose-Fifer, 2002).

A *teratogen* (from the Greek word *tera*, meaning "monster") is any agent that causes a birth defect. The drug heroin is an example of a teratogen. Babies born to users of heroin are at risk for many problems, including premature birth, low birth weight, physical defects, breathing problems, and death.

Heavy drinking by pregnant women can also have devastating effects on their offspring (Bookstein & others, 2002; May & Gossage, 2001). *Fetal alcohol syndrome (FAS)* is a cluster of abnormalities that occur in children born to mothers who are heavy drinkers. These abnormalities include a small head (microcephaly) and defective limbs, face, and heart. Most FAS children are also below average in intelligence. Concern has increased about the well-being of the fetus when pregnant women drink even small amounts of alcohol. The best advice is that a woman who is pregnant or anticipates becoming pregnant should not drink any alcohol (Streissguth, 1997).

A variety of other problems may short-circuit prenatal development. Full-term infants, who have grown in the womb for 38 to 42 weeks between conception and delivery, have the best chances of normal development in childhood. A *preterm infant*, who is born prior to 38 weeks after conception, is at greater risk. Whether a preterm infant will have developmental problems is a complex issue, however. Very small preterm infants are likelier than their larger counterparts to have developmental problems (Hack & others, 2002; Watemberg & others, 2002). Also, preterm infants who grow up in poverty are likelier to have developmental problems than are those who live in better socioeconomic conditions. Indeed, many larger preterm infants from middle- and high-income families do not have developmental problems. Nonetheless, more preterm infants than full-term infants have learning disorders (Kopp, 1984).

Researchers are continuing to study ways to improve the lives of preterm infants. Tiffany Field's (1998, 2001) research has led to a surge of interest in the role that massage might play in improving the developmental outcomes of premature infants. In one study, massaging infants for 15-minutes three times a day led to 47 percent more weight gain than standard medical treatment (Field & others, 1986) (see figure 4.3). The massaged infants also were more active and alert, and they performed better on developmental tests. Field and her colleagues have also demonstrated the benefits of massage therapy with cocaine babies (Scafidi & Field, 1996) and with infants of depressed mothers (Field & others, 1996).

Prenatal and newborn development sets the stage for development in childhood. The changes in every realm of childhood—physical, cognitive, and socioemotional—set the foundation for our development as adults.

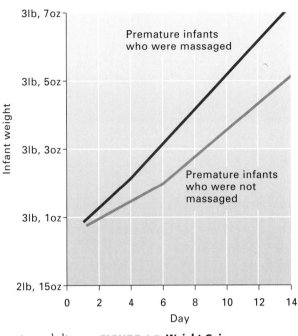

FIGURE 4.3 Weight Gain Comparison of Premature Infants Who Were Massaged or Not Massaged The graph shows that the mean daily gain of premature infants who were massaged was greater than that of premature infants were not massaged.

Physical Development in Childhood

People grow and develop physically throughout life, but at no other time will so many physical changes occur as fast as during infancy (the developmental period from birth to about 18 to 24 months of age; Fogel, 2001). During infancy, children change from virtually immobile beings to creatures who toddle as fast as their legs can carry them.

Reflexes   Newborns are not empty headed. They come into the world equipped with several genetically "wired" reflexes. For example, they have no fear of water, but they naturally hold their breath and contract their throats to keep water out.

Some of the reflexes that newborns possess persist throughout life—coughing, blinking, and yawning, for example. Others disappear in the months following birth as higher brain functions mature and infants develop voluntary control over many behaviors.

Some reflexes that weaken or disappear by 6 or 7 months of age are

- *Grasping.* When the infant's palms are touched, the infant grasps tightly with its fingers (although not the thumb).
- *Sucking.* When an object touches the infant's mouth, the infant automatically begins sucking.
- *Stepping.* When the infant is held above a surface with its feet lowered to touch the surface, the infant moves its feet as if to walk.
- *Startle.* When sudden stimulation occurs, such as hearing a loud noise or being dropped, the infant startles, arches its back, throws back its head, and flings out its arms and legs and then rapidly closes them to the center of its body.

Motor and Perceptual Skills   At birth, the newborn has a gigantic head, relative to the rest of the body, that flops around uncontrollably. Within 12 months, the infant becomes capable of sitting upright, standing, stooping, climbing, and often walking. During the 2nd year, growth decelerates, but rapid gains occur in such activities as running and climbing. Figure 4.4 shows the average ages at which infants reach various motor milestones.

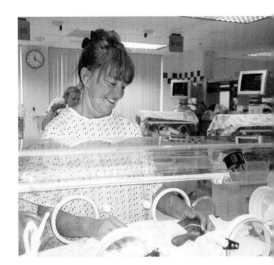

Tiffany Field massages a newborn infant. Her research has demonstrated the power of massage in improving the developmental outcome of at-risk infants. Under her direction, the Touch Research Institute in Miami, Florida, investigates the role of touch in a number of domains of health and well-being.

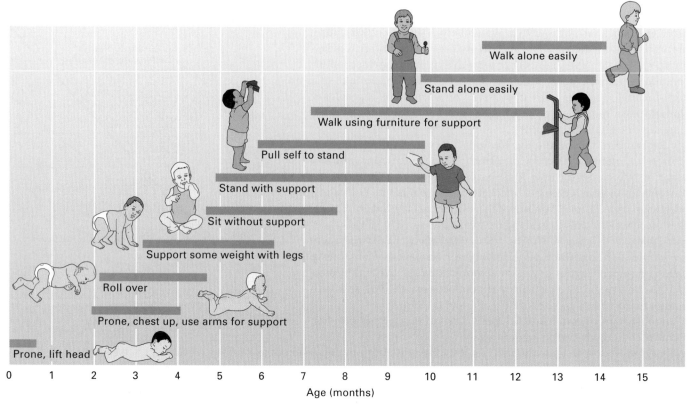

Walk alone easily

Stand alone easily

Walk using furniture for support

Pull self to stand

Stand with support

Sit without support

Support some weight with legs

Roll over

Prone, chest up, use arms for support

Prone, lift head

| 0 | 1 | 2 | 3 | 4 | 5 | 6 | 7 | 8 | 9 | 10 | 11 | 12 | 13 | 14 | 15 |

Age (months)

FIGURE 4.4 Developmental Accomplishments in Gross Motor Skills During the First 15 Months

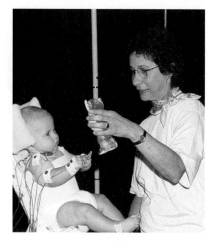

Esther Thelen is shown conducting a research study on infant motor and perceptual development. The focus of this study was to discover how infants coordinate their motor and perceptual skills to reach for and grasp an object. A computer device is used to monitor the infant's arm movements and to track muscle patterns.

The study of motor development has seen a renaissance in the past decade. Historically, researchers, such as Arnold Gesell (1934), assumed that motor milestones were like the ones shown in figure 4.4, unfolding as part of a genetic plan. However, psychologists now recognize that motor development is not the consequence of nature or nurture alone. The focus of research has shifted to discovering *how* motor skills develop and away from simply describing the age at which they develop (Lochman, 2000).

In addition, when infants are motivated to do something, they may create a new motor behavior (Thelen, 1995, 2000). That new behavior is the result of many converging factors: the developing nervous system, the body's physical properties and its movement possibilities, the goal the infant is motivated to reach, and environmental support for the skill.

Psychologists also believe that motor skills and perceptual skills are vitally linked (Smitsman, 2002). Babies are continually coordinating their movements with information they perceive through their senses to learn how to maintain their balance, reach for objects in space, and move across various surfaces and terrains (Thelen & Smith, 1998). Consider what happens when a baby sees an attractive object across the room. She must perceive the current state of her body and learn how to use her limbs to get to the goal. Although infants' movements at first are awkward and uncoordinated, they soon learn to move in ways that are appropriate for reaching their goals.

Action also educates perception. For example, watching an object while holding and touching it helps infants to learn about its texture, size, and hardness. Moving from place to place in the environment teaches babies how objects and people look from different perspectives and whether surfaces will support their weight (Gibson, 2001).

The Brain As an infant walks, talks, runs, shakes a rattle, smiles, and frowns, his or her brain is changing dramatically. At birth and in early infancy, the brain's 100 billion neurons have only minimal connections. But, as the infant ages from birth to 2 years, the dendrites of the neurons branch out, and the neurons become far more interconnected (see figure 4.5). The infant's brain literally is ready and waiting for

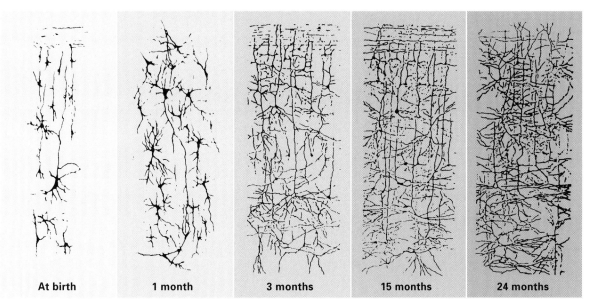

At birth **1 month** **3 months** **15 months** **24 months**

FIGURE 4.5 **Dendritic Spreading** Note the increase in connections among neurons over the course of the first 2 years of life.

the experiences that will create the connections (Eliot, 2001; Greenough, 2001; M. H. Johnson, 2000, 2001, 2002).

Recall from chapter 3 that a *myelin sheath* encases most axons. The sheath insulates neurons and helps nerve impulses travel faster. Myelination, the process of encasing axons with fat cells, begins prenatally and continues after birth. Myelination for visual pathways occurs rapidly after birth and is completed in the first 6 months. Auditory myelination is not completed until 4 to 5 years of age. Some aspects of myelination continue into adolescence.

Another important aspect of the brain's development in childhood is the dramatic increase in *synaptic connections* (Ramey & Ramey, 2000). Recall from chapter 3 that a synapse is a gap between neurons that is bridged by chemical neurotransmitters. Researchers have discovered that nearly twice as many synapses are available as will ever be used (Huttenlocher & Dabholkar, 1997). The connections that are made become stronger and will survive; the unused ones will be replaced by other neural pathways or disappear. In the language of neuroscience, these unused connections will be "pruned." Figure 4.6 vividly illustrates the dramatic growth of synapses during infancy in the visual, auditory, and prefrontal cortex areas of the brain and their later pruning.

Brain scanning techniques, such as MRI and CAT (which were discussed in chapter 3) are improving detection of developmental changes in the brain (Petersen, 2001). Using these techniques, scientists recently have discovered that children's brains undergo dramatic anatomical changes between the ages of 3 and 15 (Thompson & others, 2000). By repeatedly obtaining brain scans of the same children for up to 4 years, they found that the amount of brain material in some areas can nearly double within as little as a year, followed by a drastic loss of tissue as unneeded cells are purged and the brain continues to reorganize itself. The overall size of the brain did not show dramatic growth, but local patterns within the brain changed dramatically. From 3 to 6 years of age the most rapid growth takes place in the frontal lobe areas, which are involved in planning and organizing new actions and in maintaining attention to tasks (Thompson & others, 2000).

Of course, if the dendrites and synapses are not being stimulated by a wealth of new experiences, children's brains are less likely to develop normally (Blair, 2002). Thus, as in other areas of development, nature and nurture operate together.

FIGURE 4.6 Synaptic Density in the Human Brain from Infancy to Adulthood The graph shows the dramatic increase and then pruning in synaptic density in three regions of the brain: visual cortex, auditory cortex, and prefrontal cortex. Synaptic density is believed to be an important indication of the extent of connectivity between neurons.

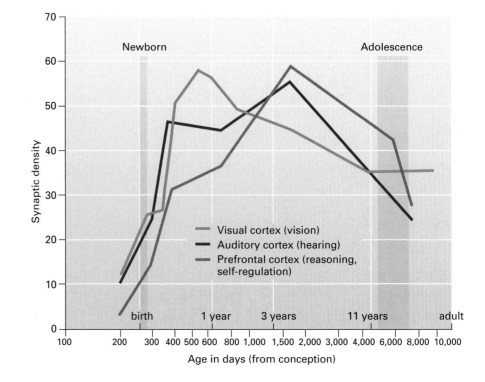

Cognitive Development in Childhood

As amazing as physical development is in childhood, it is easily matched by cognitive development. As you read earlier in the chapter, cognitive processes involve thought, intelligence, and language. Cognitive development refers to how these processes change as people mature.

Until the mid-1900s, American psychologists had no useful theory for explaining how children's minds change as they age. Psychologists who were interested in the topic had to view it through the lens of behaviorism, which emphasizes that children merely receive information from the environment, or through the lens of the IQ testing approach, which emphasizes individual differences in children's intelligence. But then Jean Piaget (1896–1980), the famous Swiss developmental psychologist, changed the way we think about children's minds. When Piaget's ideas were introduced in the United States in the 1960s, American psychologists embraced his view that children *actively construct* their cognitive world as they go through a series of stages.

Piaget's Theory of Cognitive Development In Piaget's view, children actively construct their cognitive world, using schemas to make sense of what they experience. A **schema** is a concept or framework that already exists at a given moment in a person's mind and that organizes information and provides a structure for interpreting it. Schemas are expressed as various behaviors and skills that the child can exercise in relation to objects or situations. For example, sucking is an early, simple schema. Later, more complex schemas might include licking, blowing, crawling, hiding, and so forth. Piaget's interest in schemas had to do with how they help in organizing and making sense out of current experience. In chapter 8 you will see how schemas also help us to understand why people don't remember the past in an exact way but reconstruct it instead.

Piaget (1952) said that two processes are responsible for how people use and adapt their schemas:

- **Assimilation** occurs when individuals incorporate new information into existing knowledge. That is, people *assimilate* the environment into a schema. For example, a schema in the child's mind might provide the information that

schema A concept or framework that already exists at a given moment in a person's mind and that organizes and interprets information.

assimilation Occurs when individuals incorporate new information into existing knowledge.

Sensorimotor Stage	**Preoperational Stage**	**Concrete Operational Stage**	**Formal Operational Stage**
The infant constructs an understanding of the world by coordinating sensory experiences with physical actions. An infant progresses from reflexive, instinctual action at birth to the beginning of symbolic thought toward the end of the stage.	The child begins to represent the world with words and images. These words and images reflect increased symbolic thinking and go beyond the connection of sensory information and physical action.	The child can now reason logically about concrete events and classify objects into different sets.	The adolescent reasons in more abstract, idealistic, and logical ways.
Birth to 2 Years of Age	*2 to 7 Years of Age*	*7 to 11 Years of Age*	*11 Years of Age Through Adulthood*

FIGURE 4.7 **Piaget's Four Stages of Cognitive Development**

some objects can be picked up. The first time a child realizes that she might pick up a set of keys, she is assimilating the category "keys" into the schema of "picking up."

- **Accommodation** occurs when individuals adjust their schemas to new information. That is, people *accommodate* their schemas to the environment. For example, a child might possess the schema of "picking up." With experience, the child might learn that some things can be picked up easily between two fingers, that other things might require both hands and strong use of the arms, and that still other things cannot be picked up at all because they are too hot, for example, or too heavy. Thus the schema "picking up" becomes modified into different schemas that *accommodate* the realities of different types of objects.

Assimilation and accommodation develop over time and many repetitions of experience. Consider the schema of "sucking." Newborns reflexively suck everything that touches their lips. Their experience in sucking various objects allows them to assimilate those objects into other schemas of taste, texture, shape, and so on. After several months of experience, though, they accommodate the sucking schema by being more selective with it. For example, they discover that some objects, such as fingers and the mother's breasts, can be sucked, whereas others, such as fuzzy blankets, are better not.

Another important element of Piaget's theory is his observation that we go through four stages in understanding the world (see figure 4.7). Each of the stages is age-related and consists of distinct ways of thinking. In Piaget's view, it is not simply knowing more information that makes a child's thinking more advanced with each stage. Rather, it is the different way of understanding the world that makes one stage more advanced than another. The child's cognition is qualitatively different from one stage to the next.

Sensorimotor Stage   The first Piagetian stage, the **sensorimotor stage,** lasts from birth to about 2 years of age. In this stage, infants construct an understanding of the world by coordinating sensory experiences (such as seeing and hearing) with motor (physical) actions—hence the term *sensorimotor*. As newborns they have little more than reflexive patterns with which to work. By the end of this stage, 2-year-olds show complex sensorimotor patterns and are beginning to use symbols in their thinking.

Imagine how you might experience the world if you were a 5-month-old infant. You are in a playpen filled with toys. One of the toys, a monkey, falls out of your grasp and rolls behind a larger toy, a hippopotamus. Would you know the monkey

accommodation Occurs when individuals adjust their schemas to new information.

sensorimotor stage The first Piagetian stage of cognitive development (birth to about 2 years of age), in which infants construct an understanding of the world by coordinating sensory experiences (such as seeing and hearing) with motor (physical) actions.

FIGURE 4.8 Object Permanence
Piaget thought that object permanence was one of infancy's landmark cognitive accomplishments. For this 5-month-old boy, out of sight is literally out of mind. The infant looks at the toy dog (*top*), but when his view of the toy is blocked (*bottom*), he does not search for it. In a few more months, he will search for hidden toys, reflecting the presence of object permanence.

preoperational stage The second Piagetian stage of cognitive development (approximately 2 to 7 years of age) in which thought becomes more symbolic, egocentric, and intuitive rather than logical; but the child cannot yet perform operations.

is behind the hippopotamus, or would you think it is completely gone? Piaget believed that "out of sight" literally was "out of mind" for young infants. At 5 months of age, you would not have reached for the monkey when it fell behind the hippopotamus. By 8 months of age, though, infants begin to understand that out of sight is not out of mind. At this point, you probably would have reached behind the hippopotamus to search for the monkey, coordinating your senses with your movements.

Object permanence is Piaget's term for this crucial accomplishment: understanding that objects and events continue to exist even when they cannot directly be seen, heard, or touched. The most common way to study object permanence is to show an infant an interesting toy and then cover the toy with a sheet or a blanket. If infants understand that the toy still exists, they try to uncover it (see figure 4.8). Object permanence continues to develop throughout the sensorimotor period. For example, when infants initially understand that objects exist even when out of sight, they look only briefly for them. By the end of the sensorimotor stage, infants engage in a more prolonged and sophisticated search for an object.

From sensorimotor cognition—which involves the ability to organize and coordinate sensations with physical movements and includes the realization of object permanence—we move on to a second, more symbolic cognitive stage.

Preoperational Stage Piaget's second stage of cognitive development, the **preoperational stage,** lasts from approximately 2 to 7 years of age. Preoperational thought is more symbolic than sensorimotor thought. In preschool years, children begin to represent their world with words, images, and drawings. Thus their thoughts begin to exceed simple connections of sensorimotor information and physical action.

The type of symbolic thinking that children are able to accomplish during this stage is limited, however. For one thing, they still cannot perform *operations,* by which Piaget meant mental representations that are "reversible." Preoperational children have difficulty understanding that reversing an action may restore the original conditions from which the action began. For example, the preoperational child may know that 4 plus 2 equals 6 but not understand that the reverse, 6 minus 2 equals 4, is also necessarily true according to the principle of reversibility. Or a preoperational child may walk a short distance to his friend's house each day but always gets a ride home. If you asked him to walk home one day he would probably reply that he did not know the way because he had never walked home before.

A well-known test of whether a child can think "operationally" is to present a child with two identical beakers, A and B, filled with liquid to the same height (see figure 4.9). Next to them is a third beaker, C. Beaker C is tall and thin, whereas beakers A and B are short and wide. The liquid is poured from B into C, and the child is asked whether the amounts in A and C are the same. The 4-year-old child invariably says that the amount of liquid in the tall, thin beaker (C) is greater than that in the short, wide beaker (A). The 8-year-old child consistently says the amounts are the same. The 4-year-old child, a preoperational thinker, cannot mentally reverse the pouring action; that is, she cannot imagine the liquid going back from container C to container B. Piaget said that such a child has not grasped the concept of *conservation,* a belief in the permanence of certain attributes of objects or situations in spite of superficial changes.

The child's thought in the preoperational stage is also limited in that it is egocentric. By *egocentrism,* Piaget meant the inability to distinguish between one's own perspective and someone else's perspective. Piaget and Barbel Inhelder (1969) initially studied young children's egocentrism by devising the three-mountains task (see figure 4.10). The child walks around the model of the mountains and becomes familiar with what the mountains look like from different perspectives. The child can see that different objects are on the mountains as well. The child is then seated on one side of the table on which the mountains are placed. The experimenter takes a doll and moves it to different locations around the table, at each location asking the child to select one photo from a series of photos that most accurately reflects the view the

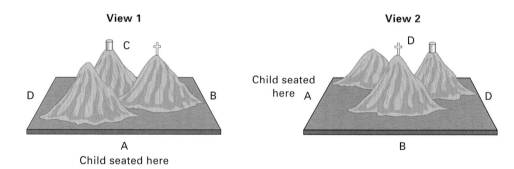

FIGURE 4.9 Piaget's Conservation Task The beaker test determines whether a child can think operationally—that is, can mentally reverse actions and understand conservation of the substance. (*a*) Two identical beakers are presented to the child, each containing the same amount of liquid. As the child watches, the experimenter pours the liquid from B into C, which is taller and thinner than A and B. (*b*) The experimenter then asks the child whether beakers A and C have the same amount of liquid. The preoperational child says no. When asked to point to the beaker that has more liquid, the child points to the tall, thin beaker.

doll is seeing. Children in the preoperational stage often pick the photo that shows the view they have rather than the view the doll has.

Another limitation of preoperational thought that Piaget identified is that it is *intuitive*. When he asked children why they knew something, they often did not give logical answers but offered personal insights or guesses instead. Preoperational children do not seem to be bothered by the absence of logic in their thinking. As Piaget observed, they often seem very sure that they know something, even though they do not use logical reasoning to arrive at the answer.

Overall, then, preoperational thought is more symbolic than sensorimotor thought, but it is egocentric and intuitive rather than logical, and it does not include the ability to perform operations. But in reaching a basic level of operational understanding, the child progresses to the third of Piaget's cognitive stages.

Concrete Operational Stage Piaget's **concrete operational stage** occurs from approximately 7 to 11 years of age. Concrete operational thought involves using operations and replacing intuitive reasoning with logical reasoning in concrete situations. Classification skills are present, but abstract thinking is not yet developed.

FIGURE 4.10 The Three-Mountains Task View 1 shows the child's perspective from where he or she is sitting. View 2 is an example of a photograph the child would be shown mixed in with others from different perspectives. The experimenter asks the child to identify the photograph in which the view of the mountains looks as it would look from position B. To correctly identify the photo, the child has to take the perspective of a person sitting at spot B. Invariably, a child who thinks in a preoperational way cannot perform this task. When asked what a view of the mountains looks like from position B, the child selects a photograph taken from location A, the child's own view at the time.

concrete operational stage The third Piagetian stage of cognitive development (approximately 7 to 11 years of age) in which thought becomes operational, replacing intuitive thought with logical reasoning in concrete situations.

Initial Presentation	Manipulation	Preoperational Child's Answer	Concrete Operational Child's Answer
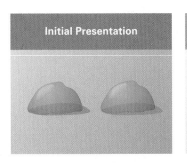	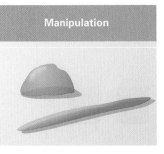		
Two identical balls of clay are shown to the child. The child agrees that they are equal.	The experimenter changes the shape of one of the balls and asks the child whether they still contain equal amounts of clay.	No, the longer one has more.	Yes, they still have equal amounts.

FIGURE 4.11 **Preoperational and Concrete Operational Children: The Clay Example**

Earlier you read about the beaker task, which preoperational children cannot do. Another well-known task for demonstrating operational thinking involves two identical balls of clay (see figure 4.11). As the child watches, the experimenter rolls one ball into a long, thin rod and leaves the other ball in its original spherical shape. Then the child is asked if more clay is in the ball or in the long, thin rod. By the time children reach 7 to 8 years of age, most answer that the amount of clay is the same. To solve this problem correctly, children have to recall that the ball was rolled into the shape of a rod and imagine the rod being returned to its original round shape—imagination that involves a reversible mental action. In this experiment and in the beaker experiment, the child who performs concrete operational thinking is able to mentally coordinate several characteristics or dimensions of an object rather than focusing on a single one. In the clay example, the preoperational child is likely to focus on either height or width. The child who has reached the stage of concrete operational thought coordinates information about both dimensions.

Many of the concrete operations identified by Piaget are related to the properties of objects. One important skill at this stage of reasoning is the ability to classify or divide things into different sets or subsets and to consider their interrelations. Figure 4.12 shows an example of a classification task that concrete operational children can perform.

FIGURE 4.12 **Classification Involving a Family Tree** One way to determine if children possess classification skills is to see if they can understand a family tree of four generations (Furth & Wachs, 1975). This family tree suggests that the grandfather (A) has three sons (B, C, & D), each of whom has two sons (E through J), and that one of these sons (J) has three sons (K, L, & M). A child who comprehends this classification system can move up and down a level (vertically), across a level (horizontally), and up and down and across a level (obliquely) within the system. A child who thinks in a concrete operational way understands that person J can, at the same time, be father, brother, and grandson, for example. A preoperational child cannot perform this classification and says that a father cannot fulfill the other roles.

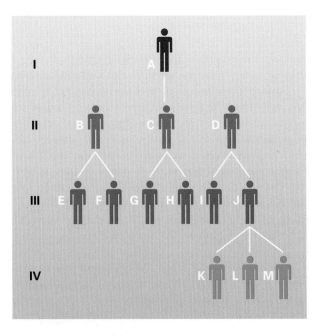

In sum, concrete operational thought involves operational thinking, classification skills, and logical reasoning in concrete, but not abstract, contexts. According to Piaget, reasoning in abstract contexts develops in the fourth and final cognitive stage.

Formal Operational Stage In Piaget's theory, individuals enter the **formal operational stage** of cognitive development at 11 to 15 years of age, and this stage continues through the adult years. Formal operational thought is more abstract, idealistic, and logical than concrete operational thought.

Unlike elementary school children, adolescents are no longer limited to actual concrete experience as the anchor of thought. They can conceive hypothetical possibilities, which are purely abstract.

Thought also becomes more idealistic. Adolescents often compare themselves and others to ideal standards. And they think about what an ideal world would be like, wondering if they couldn't carve out a better world than the one the adult generation has handed to them.

At the same time at which adolescents think more abstractly and idealistically, they also think more logically. Adolescents begin to think more the way a scientist thinks, devising plans to solve problems and systematically testing solutions. Piaget gave this type of problem solving an imposing title: *hypothetical-deductive reasoning*. The phrase denotes adolescents' ability to develop hypotheses, or best hunches, about ways to solve problems, such as an algebraic equation. It also denotes their ability to systematically deduce or conclude the best path to follow to solve the problem. In contrast, prior to adolescence, children are likelier to solve problems in a trial-and-error fashion.

Thus, over the course of Piaget's four developmental stages, a person progresses from sensorimotor cognition to abstract, idealistic, and logical thought. Piaget based his stages on careful observation of children's behavior, but there is always room to evaluate theory and research. Let's consider the current thinking about Piaget's ideas about the development of cognition.

Evaluating Piaget Piaget opened up a new way of looking at how children's minds develop. We owe him for a long list of masterful concepts that have enduring power and fascination (Scholnick, 1999). These include the concepts of schemas, assimilation, accommodation, cognitive stages, object permanence, egocentrism, and conservation. We also owe Piaget for the currently accepted vision of children as active constructive thinkers who manufacture (in part) their own development.

But just as other psychological theories have been criticized and amended, so have Piaget's (Bjorklund, 2000; Brynes, 2001; Smith, 2002). For example, researchers have found that some cognitive abilities emerge earlier in some children than Piaget thought (Bremmer, 2002; Lacerda, Von Hofsten, & Heimann, 2000). Renee Baillargeon (1997) has documented that infants as young as 4 months of age know that objects continue to exist even when hidden (which Piaget did not think was possible until 8 months of age). Also, memory and other forms of symbolic activity occur by at least the first half of the first year (much earlier than Piaget thought possible; Mandler, 1998). Nor does formal operational thought emerge as consistently in early adolescence as Piaget envisioned. Many adolescents and even adults do not reason as logically as Piaget proposed. Thus infants are more cognitively competent than Piaget thought, and adolescents and adults are less competent.

Piaget has also been criticized on broader grounds. He was interested in examining the human species and general ways in which all people go through cognitive stages at particular ages. Not surprisingly, he has been criticized for ignoring individual differences.

In another broad criticism, information-processing psychologists argue that Piaget's view places too much emphasis on grand stages and not enough on smaller, precise steps in solving problems. Information-processing psychologists believe that children's minds can be best understood by focusing more on their thinking strate-

Jean Piaget, the famous Swiss developmental psychologist, changed the way we think about the development of children's minds.

formal operational stage The fourth and final Piagetian stage of cognitive development (emerging from about 11 to 15 years of age) in which thinking becomes more abstract, idealistic, and logical.

Erik Erikson with his wife, Joan, an artist. Erikson generated one of the most important developmental theories of the twentieth century.

gies and skills, as well as on their speed and efficiency in processing information (Siegler, 1998).

The sociocultural perspective gives us yet another view of the shortcomings of Piaget's work. Piaget did not believe that culture and education play important roles in children's cognitive development. However, researchers have found that the age at which children acquire conservation skills is related to some extent to whether or not their culture provides relevant practice (Cole, 1999; Cole & Cole, 2003). The Russian psychologist Lev Vygotsky (1962) recognized that cognitive development does not occur in a sociocultural vacuum. In Vygotsky's view, the goal of cognitive development is to learn the skills that will allow you to be competent in your culture. Thus it is important to be guided and assisted by skilled members of the culture, much like being a cognitive apprentice (Rogoff, 1998). Vygotsky's view has become increasingly popular in educational psychology because of its emphasis on collaborative learning through interaction with skilled others (Rowe & Wertsch, 2002).

Today, children's cognitive development is approached from several perspectives (Flavell, Miller, & Miller, 2002; Thomas, 2001). Yet, even though some of his ideas have been modified, Piaget still stands head and shoulders above all others in this field. It was his great work that let us see that children's minds change and develop in orderly, sequential ways (Scholnick & others, 1999).

Socioemotional Development in Childhood

As children grow and develop, they are socialized by and socialize others, such as parents, siblings, peers, and teachers. Their small world widens as they grow older. In this section, you will learn about these aspects of children's socioemotional development: Erikson's theory of socioemotional development, attachment between infants and their caregivers, temperament, parenting, the wider social world, Kohlberg's theory of moral development, and gender development.

Erikson's Theory of Socioemotional Development   Erik Erikson (1902–1994) spent his early life in Europe. After working as a psychoanalyst under Sigmund Freud's direction, he came to the United States and taught at Harvard University. Although he accepted some of Freud's beliefs, he disagreed with others. For example, Freud argued that *psychosexual* stages are the key to understanding development; Erikson said that *psychosocial* stages are the key. In addition, Freud stressed that personality is shaped mainly in the first 5 years of life. By contrast, Erikson emphasized lifelong development.

Erikson's theory of life-span development proposes eight psychosocial stages of development, from infancy through old age. In Erikson's (1968) view, the first four stages take place in childhood, the last four in adolescence and adulthood (see figure 4.13). Each stage represents a developmental task or crisis that a person must negotiate. Each stage also marks a potential turning point toward greater personal competence or greater weakness and vulnerability. The more successfully people resolve the issues at each stage, the more competent they are likely to become.

Erikson's Childhood Stages   Erikson's adolescence and adult stages are examined later in the chapter. His four childhood stages are as follows:

1. *Trust versus mistrust* occurs during approximately the first 1½ years of life. Trust is built when a baby's basic needs—such as comfort, food, and warmth—are met. If infants' needs are not met by responsive, sensitive caregivers, the result is mistrust. Trust in infancy sets the stage for a lifelong expectation that the world will be a good and pleasant place to live.
2. *Autonomy versus shame and doubt* occurs from about 1½ through 3 years of age. In this stage children can develop either a positive sense of independence and autonomy or negative feelings of shame and doubt. In seeking autonomy, they are likely to develop a strong sense of independence.

Erikson's Stages	Developmental period	Characteristics
Trust versus mistrust	Infancy (Birth to 1 ½ years)	A sense of trust requires a feeling of physical comfort and minimal amount of fear about the future. Infants' basic needs are met by responsive, sensitive caregivers.
Autonomy versus shame and doubt	Toddlerhood (1 ½ to 3 years)	After gaining trust in their caregivers, infants start to discover that they have a will of their own. They assert their sense of autonomy, or independence. They realize their will. If infants are restrained too much or punished too harshly, they are likely to develop a sense of shame and doubt.
Initiative versus guilt	Early childhood (preschool years, ages 3–5)	As preschool children encounter a widening social world, they are challenged more and need to develop more purposeful behavior to cope with these challenges. Children are now asked to assume more responsibility. Uncomfortable guilt feelings may arise, though, if the children are irresponsible and are made to feel too anxious.
Industry versus inferiority	Middle and late childhood (elementary school years, 6 years–puberty)	At no other time are children more enthusiastic than at the end of early childhood's period of expansive imagination. As children move into the elementary school years, they direct their energy toward mastering knowledge and intellectual skills. The danger at this stage involves feeling incompetent and unproductive.
Identity versus identity confusion	Adolescence (10–20 years)	Individuals are faced with finding out who they are, what they are all about, and where they are going in life. An important dimension is the exploration of alternative solutions to roles. Career exploration is important.
Intimacy versus isolation	Eary adulthood (20s, 30s)	Individuals face the developmental task of forming intimate relationships with others. Erikson described intimacy as finding oneself yet losing oneself in another person.
Generativity versus stagnation	Middle adulthood (40s, 50s)	A chief concern is to assist the younger generation in developing and leading useful lives.
Integrity versus despair	Late adulthood (60s–)	Individuals look back and evaluate what they have done with their lives. The retrospective glances can either be positive (integrity) or negative (despair).

FIGURE 4.13 Erikson's Eight Stages of Human Development

3. *Initiative versus guilt* occurs from 3 to 5 years of age, the preschool years. During these years, children's social worlds are widening, and they are being challenged to develop purposeful behavior to cope with the challenges. When asked to assume more responsibility for themselves, children can develop initiative. When allowed to be irresponsible or made to feel anxious, they can develop too much guilt. But Erikson believed that young children are resilient. He said that a sense of accomplishment quickly compensates for most guilt feelings.

4. *Industry versus inferiority* occurs from about the age of 6 until puberty. Children can achieve industry by mastering knowledge and intellectual skills. When they do not, they can feel inferior. For example, Erikson believed that at the end of the period of expansive imagination that occurs in early childhood, children are ready to turn their energy to learning academic skills. If they do not, they can develop a sense of being incompetent and unproductive.

Erikson did not believe that the proper resolution to a stage is always completely positive. For example, developing trust is good, but one cannot trust all people under all circumstances and survive. For optimal development to take place, however, positive resolutions should dominate.

Evaluating Erikson's Theory   At a time when people believed that most development takes place in childhood, Erikson charted development as a lifelong challenge. His insights also helped to move us away from Freud's focus on sexuality and toward an understanding of the importance of successfully resolving different socioemotional tasks at different points in our lives. Erikson's ideas changed the way we think about some periods of development (Marcia, 2001). For example, Erikson encouraged us to look at adolescents not just as sexual beings, but as individuals seeking to find out who they are and searching to find their niche in the world.

But, like Piaget's theory, Erikson's also has been criticized. As was mentioned in chapter 2, Erikson himself mainly practiced case study research. Critics argue that a firmer research base for Erikson's entire theory has not been developed. However, research on specific stages of the theory reveals that there are important developmental tasks at certain points in our lives.

Critics also say that Erikson's attempt to capture each stage with a single concept sometimes leaves out other important developmental tasks. For example, Erikson said that the main task for young adults is resolve the conflict between intimacy and isolation. However, another important developmental task in early adulthood involves careers and work.

Such criticisms do not tarnish Erikson's monumental contributions, however. He, like Piaget, is a giant in developmental psychology.

Attachment in Infancy   The word *attachment* usually refers to a strong relationship between two people in which each person does a number of things to continue the relationship. Many types of people are attached: relatives, lovers, a teacher and a student. In the language of developmental psychology, however, **attachment** is the close emotional bond between the infant and its caregiver.

Theories about infant attachment abound. Freud believed that the infant becomes attached to the person or object who feeds the infant and thus provides oral satisfaction. For most infants, this is the mother.

But researchers have questioned the importance of feeding in infant attachment. Harry Harlow (1958) separated infant monkeys from their mothers at birth and placed them in cages in which they had access to two artificial "mothers." One of the mothers was made of wire, the other of cloth. Each mother could be outfitted with a feeding mechanism. Half of the infant monkeys were fed by the wire mother, half by the cloth mother. The infant monkeys nestled close to the cloth mother and spent little time on the wire one, even if it was the wire mother that gave them milk (see figure 4.14). This study clearly demonstrates that what the researchers described as "contact comfort," not feeding, is the crucial element in the attachment process.

Another famous study grew out of the field of *ethology,* which involves the study of the function and evolution of behavior. One of ethology's founders was the European zoologist Konrad Lorenz (1903–1989). Lorenz (1965) examined attachment behavior in geese. He separated the eggs laid by one goose into two groups. He returned one group of eggs to the goose to be hatched; the other group was hatched in an incubator. The goslings in the first group performed as predicted; they followed

attachment The close emotional bond between an infant and its caregiver.

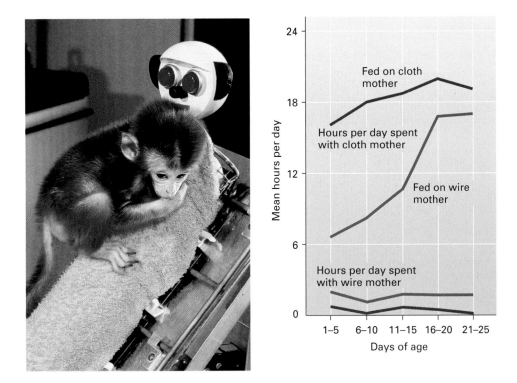

**FIGURE 4.14 Contact Time with
Wire and Cloth Surrogate Mothers**
Regardless of whether the infant monkeys were fed by a wire or a cloth mother,
they overwhelmingly preferred to spend
contact time with the cloth mother.

their mother as soon as they hatched. But those in the second group, who saw Lorenz first after hatching, followed him everywhere as if he were their mother (see figure 4.15). Lorenz marked the goslings and then placed both groups under a box. Mother goose and "mother" Lorenz stood nearby as the box was lifted. Each group of goslings went directly to its "mother." Lorenz called this process **imprinting,** the tendency of an infant animal to form an attachment to the first moving object it sees and/or hears.

For goslings, the critical period for imprinting is the first 36 hours after birth. Human infants appear to have a longer, more flexible "sensitive period" for attachment. A number of developmental psychologists believe that attachment to the caregiver during the first year provides an important foundation for later development. John Bowlby (1969, 1989), for instance, believes the infant and the mother instinctively form an attachment. He believes the newborn is innately equipped to stimulate the caregiver to respond; it cries, clings, smiles, and coos. Later the infant crawls, walks, and follows the mother. The infant's goal is to keep the mother nearby. Research on attachment supports Bowlby's view that the infant's attachment to its caregiver intensifies at about 6 to 7 months (Schaffer & Emerson, 1964).

Some babies have more positive attachment experiences than others (Levy, 1999). Mary Ainsworth (1979) believes that the difference depends on how sensitive the caregiver is to the infant's signals. She uses the term **secure attachment** to describe how infants use the caregiver, usually the mother, as a secure base from which to explore the environment. Infants who are securely attached are likelier to have mothers who are responsive and accepting and who express affection toward them than are infants who are insecurely attached (Waters & others, 1995). The securely attached infant moves freely away from the mother but also keeps tabs on her location by periodically glancing at her. The securely attached infant responds positively to being picked up by others and, when put back down, happily moves away to play. An insecurely attached infant, in contrast, avoids the mother or is ambivalent toward her. The insecurely attached infant fears strangers and is upset by minor, everyday sensations.

Not all developmentalists believe that a secure attachment in infancy is the only path to competence in life. Jerome Kagan (1998, 2000), for example, believes that

imprinting The tendency of an infant animal to form an attachment to the first moving object it sees and/or hears.

secure attachment An important aspect of socioemotional development in which infants use the caregiver, usually the mother, as a secure base from which to explore the environment.

FIGURE 4.15 "Mother" Lorenz
Konrad Lorenz, a pioneering student of animal behavior, is followed through the water by three imprinted greylag geese. Lorenz described imprinting as rapid, innate learning within a critical period that involves attachment to the first moving object seen. For goslings, the critical period is the first 36 hours after birth.

In the Hausa culture, siblings and grandmothers provide a significant amount of care for infants. *How might this practice affect attachment?*

infants are highly resilient and can adapt to wide variations in parenting style. Kagan and others stress that genetics and temperament play more important roles in a child's social competence. For example, inheriting a low tolerance for stress, rather than having an insecure attachment bond, might be responsible for the inability of a child to get along with peers.

Another criticism of attachment theory is that it ignores the evidence that in some cultures infants show strong attachments to many people, not just their primary caregiver (Thompson, 2000). In the African Hausa culture, both grandmothers and siblings provide a significant amount of care to infants (Harkness & Super, 1995). Infants in agricultural societies tend to form attachments to older siblings who are assigned a major responsibility for younger siblings' care. The attachments formed by infants in group care in Israeli kibbutzim provide another variation.

Psychologists accept the importance of competent, nurturant caregivers in an infant's development (Bornstein & Tamis-LeMonda, 2001). Still at issue, though, is whether secure attachment, especially to a single caregiver, is critical (Rosen & Burke, 1999).

Temperament   One of the factors that some psychologists believe is critical to understanding child development is **temperament,** which refers to an individual's behavioral style and characteristic way of responding. Psychiatrists Alexander Chess and Stella Thomas (1977) identify three basic types or clusters of temperament in children:

- The *easy child,* who generally is in a positive mood, quickly establishes regular routines in infancy, and adapts easily to new experiences
- The *difficult child,* who tends to react negatively and cry frequently, engages in irregular daily routines, and is slow to accept new experiences
- The *slow-to-warm-up child,* who has a low activity level, is somewhat negative, shows low adaptability, and displays a low intensity of mood

Other researchers propose different dimensions as the core of temperament, such as *emotionality* (tendency to be distressed), *sociability* (tendency to prefer the company of others to being alone), and *activity level* (tempo and vigor of movement; Buss & Plomin, 1987). Thus agreement about the basic core dimensions of temperament has not been reached (Sanson, Smart, & Hemphill, 2002; Wachs & Kohnstamm, 2001; Wachs & Bates, 2002).

temperament An individual's behavioral style and characteristic way of responding.

Many parents don't believe in the importance of temperament until they have their second child (Putnam, Sanson, & Rothbart, 2002). Parents typically view the firstborn child's behavior as a result of the way they have raised the child. However, management strategies that worked with the first child might be frustratingly ineffective with the second child. Such differences in children's temperament, which appear very early in their lives, support the belief that nature as well as nurture influence development.

Parenting Even though many American children spend a great deal of time in child care in their early years and nearly all American children spend many hours in school as they grow older, parents are still the main caregivers for most children.

Parenting Styles Ideas about the best way to rear children have gone through a lot of changes over the years and may vary across cultures. At one time, and in some cultures still, parents were advised to impose strict discipline along the lines of such adages as "Spare the rod and spoil the child" and "Children should be seen and not heard." But attitudes toward children—and how best to parent them—have changed to encompass more nurturing and caring.

Diana Baumrind (1971, 1991) believes parents interact with their children in one of four basic ways:

- **Authoritarian parenting** is a restrictive, punitive style in which the parent exhorts the child to follow the parent's directions and to value hard work and effort. The authoritarian parent firmly limits and controls the child with little verbal exchange. In a difference of opinion about how to do something, for example, the authoritarian parent might say, "You do it my way or else. No backtalk." Authoritarian parenting is associated with children's social incompetence. Children of authoritarian parents often fail to initiate activity, have poor communication skills, and compare themselves with others.
- **Authoritative parenting** encourages children to be independent but still places limits and controls on their behavior. Extensive verbal give-and-take is allowed, and parents are warm and nurturant toward the child. An authoritative parent might put his arm around the child in a comforting way and say, "You know you should not have done that; let's talk about how you can handle the situation better next time." Children whose parents are authoritative tend to be socially competent, self-reliant, and socially responsible.
- **Neglectful parenting** is a style in which parents are uninvolved in their child's life. Ask such parents, "It's 10 P.M. Do you know where your child is?" and they are likely to answer, "No." Yet children have a strong need for their parents to care about them. Children whose parents are neglectful might develop a sense that other aspects of the parents' lives are more important than they are. Children whose parents are neglectful tend to be less competent socially, not to handle independence well, and, especially, to show poor self-control.
- **Indulgent parenting** is a style in which parents are involved with their children but place few limits on them. Such parents let their children do what they want. Some parents deliberately rear their children in this way because they believe the combination of warm involvement with few restraints will produce a creative, confident child. But children whose parents are indulgent often rate poorly in social competence. They often fail to learn respect for others, expect to get their own way, and have difficulty controlling their behavior. One boy whose parents deliberately reared him in an indulgent manner moved his parents out of their bedroom suite and took it over for himself. At nearly 18 years old he had still not learned to control his behavior; when he couldn't get something he wanted, he still threw temper tantrums. As you might expect, he wasn't popular with his peers.

Figure 4.16 summarizes Baumrind's parenting styles and their child outcomes.

authoritarian parenting A restrictive, punitive style in which the parent exhorts the child to follow the parent's directions and value hard work and effort.

authoritative parenting A parenting style that encourages children's independence (but still places limits and controls on their behavior), includes extensive verbal give-and-take, and warm and nurturant interactions with the child.

neglectful parenting A parenting style in which parents are uninvolved in their child's life.

indulgent parenting A parenting style in which parents are involved with their children but place few limits on them.

FIGURE 4.16 Parenting Styles and Child Outcomes

Style	Parental Behavior	Common Outcome in Children
Authoritarian	Restrict and punish. Orders not to be questioned. Little verbal exchange.	Anxiety about social comparison, lack of initiative, poor communication skills.
Authoritative	Encourage independence within limits. Extensive verbal give-and-take. Warmth, nurturance.	Social competence, self-reliance, social responsibility.
Neglectful	Little involvement in the child's life. Unaware of what the child is doing.	Anxiety about social comparison, lack of initiative, poor communication skills.
Indulgent	Involved with the child but without placing demands. Highly permissive.	Anxiety about social comparison, lack of initiative, poor communication skills.

Although Baumrind's findings are useful, they leave many questions about parenting unanswered, and there is more to understanding parent-child relationships than parenting style (Crouter & others, 1999; Lamb & others, 1999). One key issue is whether parenting style is really a product of the parents alone. For many years the socialization of children was viewed as a straightforward, one-way matter of indoctrination—telling small children about the use of spoons and potties, the importance of saying thank you, and not killing the baby brother. The basic philosophy was that children had to be trained to fit into the social world, so their behavior had to be shaped into that of a mature adult. However, as research on temperament suggests, the young child is not like the inanimate blob of clay from which a sculptor builds a statue. Through the process of *reciprocal socialization,* children socialize their parents just as parents socialize their children. For example, children's smiles usually elicit positive overtures by parents. However, when children are difficult and aggressive, their parents are more likely to punish them. Or consider adolescents: They promote guilt feelings in parents, just as parents promote guilt feelings in them. In other words, parenting styles may be influenced by children's behavior.

A recent controversy about parenting focuses on the nature versus nurture issue. To examine this issue, see the Critical Controversy box.

Divorce The divorce rate in the United States is very high. As a result, as shown in figure 4.17, the United States has a higher percentage of children growing up in single-parent families (many of which are the result of divorce) than other industrialized countries have (Rice, 2000).

Many children are highly vulnerable to stress during the experience of divorce (Kitzmann & Gaylord, 2002). Research shows that children from divorced families

FIGURE 4.17 Single-Parent Families in Different Countries

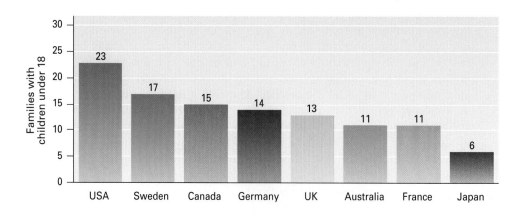

Parents Bring Up Their Children, Don't They?

In a provocative book, *The Nurture Assumption*, Judith Harris (1998) argues that what parents do does not make a difference in their children's behavior. Spank them. Hug them. Read to them. Ignore them. Harris says it won't influence how they turn out. She argues that children's genes and their peers are far more important than parents in children's development.

Harris (1998) explores the factors that influence an adult's personality, such as being shy or outgoing. Citing a number of twin studies (how these are conducted was discussed in chapter 3), she presents evidence that heredity explains about 50 percent of an adult's personality. In other words, she believes that 50 percent of your personality is due to the genes you inherited from your parents.

Harris, though, does not claim that the environment in which children grow up is unimportant in the development of personality. After all, children's genes, or their nature, account for only half of adult personality, in her view. Rather, she argues that children learn from many sources and that their learning is specific to certain contexts. Although children imitate their parents to learn how to behave at home, they imitate other people to learn how to behave outside the home. Harris singles out children's peer relations as an especially important aspect of the nurture part of the nature-nurture equation. Harris even believes that children would develop into the same types of adults if we left them in their homes, schools, neighborhoods, peer groups, and culture but switched their parents around.

How far-fetched is Harris' view? Some psychologists believe that it is more plausible than it first appears. One argument is that humans evolved to learn from any source, not just parents (Rowe, 1994). Such a general learning mechanism means that children might learn cultural innovations even if their parents do not. For example, the children of immigrants learn a second language faster and more completely than do their parents (Johnson & Newport, 1989). This likely would not occur if children learned only from their parents.

What is the theme of Judith Harris' controversial book? What is the nature of the controversy?

As you might imagine, not everyone agrees with Harris' view (Vandell, 2000). Critics say Harris is right that genes matter, and that she is right that peers matter, but that she is wrong in saying that parents do not matter. They argue that in arriving at her view, Harris ignored research studies documenting the importance of parents in children's development (Maccoby, 2000). For example, many studies reveal that when parents abuse their children, the children have problems in regulating their emotions, in becoming securely attached to others, in developing competent peer relations, and in adapting to school. Such children also develop anxiety and depression disorders (Azar, 2002; Cicchetti & Toth, 1998; Rogosch & others, 1995).

Studies of positive intervention especially have the ability to demonstrate whether parenting plays an important role in children's development (Bornstein & Bradley, 2003; Collins & others, 2000; Maccoby, 2002). In one study, training low-income mothers to respond sensitively to their infants both changed the negative responses of mothers when their infants became irritable and reduced the likelihood that distressed infants would avoid their mothers (Van den Boom, 1994). In another study, parents' participation in 16-week discussion groups on effective parenting just prior to their children's entry into kindergarten resulted in better school adjustment and higher academic achievement for their children than for children whose parents attended discussion groups without the effective parenting emphasis (Cowan & Cowan, 2001, 2002).

What do you think?

- Do you think that your personality was formed more by nature or nurture? In other words, was your personality shaped more by your genes or by your life experiences?
- Do you believe that your personality has been influenced more by your parents or by your peers and other social contexts?

are more poorly adjusted (are more likely to have psychological problems, such as being overly aggressive or depressed) than their counterparts from nondivorced families (Amato & Keith, 1991). Those who have experienced multiple divorce are at an even greater risk. What percentage of children from divorced families have adjustment problems? The consensus is approximately 25 percent, compared to only 10 percent of children in nondivorced families (Hetherington, 1999, 2000; Hetherington & Stanley-Hagan, 2002). Remember, however, that approximately 80 percent of children in divorced families do not have adjustment problems, which runs counter to stereotypical beliefs about children of divorce. Among the factors that predict better adjustment for children in divorced families are harmony between the divorced parents, authoritative parenting, good schools, and the child's possession of an easy rather than a difficult temperament (Hetherington & Kelly, 2002).

Positive Parenting   You already have examined some important aspects of positive parenting, especially an authoritative parenting style. Another aspect is recognizing that *parenting* takes time and effort. Today, suggestions that parenting can be done quickly and with little or no inconvenience are quite common (Sroufe, 2000). This attitude underlies the idea of playing Mozart recordings to enrich infants and young children's brains. Some parents who do so may be seeking a shortcut to their children's intellectual development. Judith Harris' book, *The Nurture Assumption*, tends to support this idea. And 1-minute bedtime stories are popular with parents who know reading to their children is important but do not want to spend a lot of time doing it (Walsh, 2000). Why did the quick-parenting idea catch on? One reason may be that people who do not spend much time with their children find support for their neglect and relief from a sense of guilt. Researchers have found that competent parenting takes time and effort (Bornstein 2002; Edwards & Liu, 2002; Teti & Candelaria, 2002).

Another aspect of positive parenting is coaching children about how to control their emotions (Katz, 1999). "Emotion-coaching parents" monitor their children's emotions, view their children's negative emotions as opportunities for teaching about emotion, and provide guidance in effectively dealing with emotions. In research, emotion-coaching parents have been observed to reject their children less, praise them more, and be more nurturant toward them than "emotion-dismissing parents" (Gottman, Katz, & Hooven, 1997). The children of the emotion-coaching parents in this research were better at toning down the intensity of their negative emotions and at focusing their attention and had fewer behavior problems than the children of emotion-dismissing parents.

Another aspect of positive parenting is using strategies for raising a moral child. The goal is to raise a child who is considerate of others, understands the difference between right and wrong, and is less likely to lie, cheat, or steal. Following are the positive parenting strategies that have most often been found to be helpful in raising a moral child (Eisenberg & Murphy, 1995; Eisenberg & Valiente, 2002).

- Parents are warm and supportive rather than punitive.
- Parents use reasoning the child can understand when disciplining.
- Parents provide opportunities for the child to learn about others' perspectives and feelings.
- Parents involve children in family decision making and thinking about moral decisions.
- Parents model moral behaviors and thinking themselves and provide their children with opportunities to engage in such moral behaviors and thinking.

The Wider Social World   The family is one social context in which children's development occurs. But the broader culture, the child's peer relations, school influences, and the quality of the neighborhood in which the child lives also are important (Bronfenbrenner, 2000; Harkness & Super, 2002).

Today, psychologists are especially interested in improving the lives of children who live in impoverished neighborhoods and attend ineffective schools (Blyth, 2000; Booth & Crouter, 2000). They also are increasingly interested in studying children from ethnic minority groups. Although many ethnic minority families are not poor, poverty contributes to the stressful life experiences of many minority children, creating a double disadvantage for them (McLoyd, 1999, 2000): prejudice, discrimination, and bias because of their ethnic minority background; and the stressful effects of poverty.

Children's development is influenced not only by their family experiences but also by their experiences with peers, in the neighborhood, at school, and in the culture. A special concern is the effects of poverty on children's development. Poverty is especially high in ethnic minority families.

Developmental psychologists also are intrigued by cultural comparisons of children in the United States and other countries. For example, parents in the United States tend to rear their children to be more independent than their counterparts in Japan and other Asian countries (Matsumoto, 2000). Such cross-cultural variations reflect the nurture part of the nature versus nurture issue.

mhhe com/ santrockp7 *Cultural differences in child-rearing practices have been the subject of a number of research studies, including a study of solitary vs. group play. (Around the Globe)*

Moral Development Moral development involves changes with age in thoughts, feelings, and behaviors regarding the principles and values that guide what people should do. Moral development has both an intrapersonal dimension (a person's basic values and sense of self) and an interpersonal dimension (what people should do in their interactions with other people; Nucci, 2001; Turiel, 1983; Walker & Pitts, 1998).

Psychologists have studied how people reason and think about moral matters, how they feel about them, and how they actually behave. Their greatest interest in recent years has been moral reasoning and thinking. Much of their work has revolved around Lawrence Kohlberg's theory of moral development and reactions to it.

Kohlberg's Theory Kohlberg (1958) began his study of moral thinking by creating eleven stories and asking children, adolescents, and adults questions about the stories. One of the stories (set in Europe) goes like this:

> A woman was near death from a special kind of cancer. There was one drug that the doctors thought might save her. It was a form of radium that a druggist in the same town had recently discovered. The drug was expensive to make, but the druggist was charging ten times what the drug cost him to make. He paid $200 for the radium and charged $2,000 for a small dose of the drug. The sick woman's husband, Heinz, went to everyone he knew to borrow the money, but he could get together only $1,000. He told the druggist that his wife was dying and asked him to sell it cheaper or let him pay later. But the druggist said, "No. I discovered the drug, and I am going to make money from it." Desperate, Heinz broke into the man's store to steal the drug for his wife (Kohlberg, 1969).

After reading the story, the interviewee was asked a series of questions about the moral dilemma. Should Heinz have stolen the drug? Was stealing it right or wrong? Why? Is it a husband's duty to steal a lifesaving drug for his wife if he can get it in no other way? Would a good husband do it? Did the druggist have the right to charge so much in the absence of a law setting a limit on the price? Why or why not? Based on the answers that people gave to the questions about this and other moral dilemmas, Kohlberg constructed a theory.

Lawrence Kohlberg, who created a provocative theory of moral development. In his view, "Moral development consists of a sequence of qualitative changes in the way an individual thinks."

LEVEL 1
Preconventional Level
No Internalization

Stage 1
Heteronomous Morality

Individuals pursue their own interests but let others do the same. What is right involves equal exchange.

Stage 2
Individualism, Purpose, and Exchange

Children obey because adults tell them to obey. People base their moral decisions on fear of punishment.

LEVEL 2
Conventional Level
Intermediate Internalization

Stage 3
Mutual Interpersonal Expectations, Relationships, and Interpersonal Conformity

Individuals value trust, caring, and loyalty to others as a basis for moral judgments.

Stage 4
Social System Morality

Moral judgments are based on understanding and the social order, law, justice, and duty.

LEVEL 3
Postconventional Level
Full Internalization

Stage 5
Social Contract or Utility and Individual Rights

Individuals reason that values, rights, and principles undergird or transcend the law.

Stage 6
Universal Ethical Principles

The person has developed moral judgments that are based on universal human rights. When faced with a dilemma between law and conscience, a personal, individualized conscience is followed.

FIGURE 4.18 **Kohlberg's Three Levels and Six Stages of Moral Development**

Kohlberg (1986) proposed that moral development consists of three levels with two stages at each level (see figure 4.18).

1. The *preconventional level* is based primarily on punishments (stage 1) or rewards (stage 2) that come from the external world. In regard to the Heinz story, at stage 1 an individual might say that Heinz should not steal the drug because he might get caught and sent to jail. At stage 2, the person might say he should not steal the drug because the druggist needs to make a profit on the drug.
2. At the *conventional level,* the individual abides by standards, such as those learned from parents (stage 3) or society's laws (stage 4). At stage 3, an individual might say that Heinz should steal the drug for his wife because that is what people expect a good husband would do. At stage 4, the person might say that it is natural for Heinz to want to save his wife but that the law says it still is always wrong to steal.
3. At the *postconventional level,* the individual recognizes alternative moral courses, explores the options, and then develops a personal moral code. The code reflects the principles generally accepted by the community (stage 5) or it reflects more abstract principles for all of humanity (stage 6). At stage 5, a person might say that the law was not set up for these circumstances, so Heinz can steal the drug. It is not really right, but he is justified in doing it. At stage 6, the individual evaluates alternatives but recognizes that Heinz's wife's life is more important than a law.

Kohlberg believed that these levels and stages develop in a sequence and are age-related. Some evidence for the sequence of Kohlberg's stages has been found, although few people reach stage 6 (Colby & others, 1983). Children are often in stages 1 and 2, although in the later elementary school years they may be in stage 3. Most adolescents are at stage 3 or 4.

Kohlberg also believed that advances in moral development take place because of the maturation of thought (especially in concert with Piaget's stages), opportunities for role taking, and opportunities to discuss moral issues with a person who reasons at a stage just above one's own. In Kohlberg's view, parents contribute little to children's moral thinking because parent-child relationships are often too power-oriented.

Evaluating Kohlberg's Theory Kohlberg's ideas stimulated considerable interest in the field of moral development. His provocative view continues to promote considerable research about how people think about moral issues.

At the same time, his theory has numerous critics. One criticism is that moral *reasoning* does not necessarily mean moral *behavior*. When people are asked about their moral reasoning, what they say might fit into Kohlberg's advanced stages, but their actual behavior might be filled with cheating, lying, and stealing. The cheaters, liars, and thieves might know what is right and what is wrong but still do what is wrong.

Another major criticism is that Kohlberg's view does not adequately reflect interpersonal relationships and concerns for others, that it focuses too much on the intrapersonal dimension of moral development. Kohlberg's theory is thus a *justice perspective* concerned with the rights of "the individual," who stands alone and independently makes moral decisions. In contrast, the *care perspective*, which lies at the heart of Carol Gilligan's (1982) theory of moral development, views people in terms of their connectedness with others and focuses on interpersonal communication, relationships, and concern for others. Gilligan faults Kohlberg for greatly underplaying the care perspective in moral development. She believes he may have done so because he is a male, because most of his research was with males rather than females, and because he used male responses as a model for his theory. However, not everyone adopts Gilligan's view either, and even she argues that at the highest level of moral development the individual and relationship aspects of moral reasoning are likely to be integrated.

Carol Gilligan, who argues that Kohlberg's view does not give adequate attention to relationships. In Gilligan's view, "Many girls seem to fear, most of all, being alone—without friends, family, and relationships."

Gender Development Carol Gilligan's view of moral development points up another important aspect of socioemotional development in childhood: gender. Recall from chapter 1 that *gender* refers to the social and psychological aspects of being female and male. Gilligan's view of moral development provides some good examples of the differences between girls' and boys' experiences as they grow up and the potential lasting effects of those experiences. For instance, Gilligan (1996, 1998) says that at the edge of adolescence—at about 11 to 12 years of age—girls become aware that their intense interest in intimacy is not prized by the male-dominated culture, even though society values females as caring and altruistic. The dilemma, says Gilligan, is that girls are presented with a choice that makes them appear either selfish (if they become independent and self-sufficient) or selfless (if they remain responsive to others), neither of which may be desirable. As young adolescent girls experience this dilemma, Gilligan says, they increasingly "silence" their distinctive voices. They become less confident and more tentative in offering their opinions, behavior that may persist into adulthood. Some researchers believe this self-doubt and ambivalence may translate into depression and eating disorders among adolescent girls (Piran, 2002).

Gilligan's work is only one aspect of psychology's intense interest in gender development. Other avenues of research include how strongly biology shapes gender, how strongly social experiences with parents and others influence the way girls and boys behave, and how gender and cognition are linked.

Biology and Gender Development Not until the 1920s did researchers confirm the existence of human sex chromosomes, the genetic material that determines our sex. Anatomical differences were obvious, of course, but not the underlying biological elements that differentiate the sexes. Humans normally have 46 chromosomes arranged in pairs. The 23rd pair may have two X-shaped chromosomes, which produces a female, or it may have both an X-shaped and a Y-shaped chromosome, which produces a male (see figure 4.19).

However, in the first few weeks after conception, male and female embryos look alike. When the Y chromosome in the male embryo triggers the secretion of **androgens,** the main class of male sex hormones, male sex organs start to differentiate from female sex organs. (As noted in chapter 3, hormones are powerful chemical substances secreted by the endocrine glands and carried by the blood throughout the

androgens The main class of male sex hormones.

FIGURE 4.19 The Genetic Difference Between Males and Females The chromosome structures of a male (*left*) and female (*right*). The 23rd pair is shown at bottom right. Notice that the male's Y chromosome is smaller than his X chromosome. To obtain pictures of chromosomes, a cell is removed from a person's body, usually from inside the mouth, and the chromosomes are photographed under magnification.

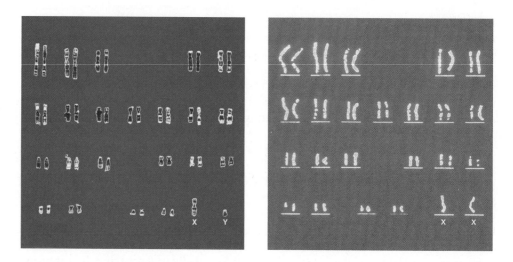

body.) Low levels of androgen in a female embryo allow the normal development of female sex organs. Not until about the 7th week after conception can the developing genitals be observed externally. Long after conception, hormones can still play a powerful role in shaping sex characteristics and possibly in influencing gender-related behaviors (Tobach, 2002). You will soon read about the hormonal changes that take place in androgens and **estrogens,** the main class of female sex hormones, during puberty and adulthood.

In rare instances, an imbalance in the secretion of hormones occurs during prenatal development. Insufficient androgens in the male embryo or an excess of androgens in the female embryo creates a hermaphrodite: an individual with both male and female sex organs. When genetically female (XX chromosomes) infants are born with masculine-looking genitals, surgery can achieve a genital-genetic match. Prior to puberty these females often behave in more aggressive, "tomboyish" ways than most girls (Berenbaum & Hines, 1992; Ehrhardt, 1987).

Is the gender behavior of these surgically corrected girls due to their prenatal hormones or is it the result of their social experience? Experiments with different animal species reveal that, when male hormones are injected into female embryos, the females develop masculine physical traits and behave more aggressively (Hines, 1982). However, as we move from animals to humans, hormones exert less control over behavior. Perhaps because these girls looked more masculine, they were treated more like boys and so adopted their tomboyish ways. Thus, as with other aspects of development, in gender behavior both biology and experience likely are at work.

Evolutionary psychologists emphasize the importance of biology, however (as you may recall from chapter 1). In the evolutionary psychology view of gender, differences in gender behavior are the product of gradual genetic adaptations (Buss, 1995, 2000). Evolutionary psychologists argue that women and men have faced different pressures throughout human evolution (Bjorklund, Yunger, & Pellegrini, 2002; Mealey, 2000). They stress that the sexes' different status in reproduction is the key to understanding how this evolution took place (Mealey, 2000).

In this view, male competition led to a reproductive advantage for dominant males. Men adopted short-term mating practices because this allowed them to increase their reproductive advantage by fathering more children. In contrast, women devoted more effort to parenting and chose mates who could provide their offspring with resources for protection. Because men competed with other men for access to women, men have evolved dispositions that favor violence and risk taking. Women have developed a preference for long-term mates who can support a family. Men strive to acquire more resources than other men in order to attract more women, and women seek to attract successful, ambitious men who can provide these resources.

Critics of evolutionary psychology theory argue that humans have the decision-making ability to change their gender behavior and thus are not locked into

estrogens The main class of female sex hormones.

cathy®   **by Cathy Guisewite**

their evolutionary past. They cite extensive cross-cultural variation in gender behavior and mate preference as proof that social experience affects gender behavior (Wood, 2001). For instance, in Alice Eagly's (1997, 2000, 2001) *social roles* view of gender, it is indeed social experiences that have caused differences in gender behavior. She stresses that as women were forced to adapt to roles with less power and less status in society, they showed more cooperative and less dominant profiles than men. Following are some ways in which social experiences might influence gender behavior.

Social Experience and Gender Development   As children grow up, they adopt **gender roles,** which involve expectations for how females and males should think, act, and feel (Crawford & Unger, 2000).

Some cultures emphasize that children should be reared to adopt traditional gender roles (Best, 2001). Boys are reared to be "masculine" (powerful, aggressive, and independent, for example) and girls brought up to be "feminine" (sensitive to others, good at relationships, and less assertive, for example). Other cultures, especially in recent times, have placed more emphasis on rearing boys and girls to be more similar—girls being raised to be just as assertive as boys and boys being raised to be just as caring toward others as girls, for example. Egypt and China are two of the countries in which traditional gender roles continue to dominate, but the United States is moving toward more diversity in gender roles. Still, much socialization in our culture is gender based (Lott & Maluso, 2001).

In a gendered society, parents often apply the "pink" and "blue" treatment to infants. Boys are dressed in blue, girls in pink. Boys are given trucks to play with, girls are given dolls. Parents let boys be more aggressive and require girls to be more reserved. These social experiences inevitably influence the behavior of these individuals when they get older.

Peers also play an important role in gender development. Especially during middle and late childhood (6 to 10 or 11 years of age or until puberty begins), peer groups are often highly segregated into boy groups and girl groups. After observing children on many elementary school playgrounds, two gender researchers described the observations as like "going to gender school" (Luria & Herzog, 1985). Peers are stricter than most parents in rewarding what is considered gender-appropriate behavior in the culture and punishing gender-inappropriate behavior.

Interestingly, tolerance of gender-inappropriate behavior is itself gendered. Americans tend to disapprove more of boys engaging in feminine behavior (playing with dolls and crying, for example) than of girls displaying masculine behavior (being a tomboy and being assertive, for example). In other words, female gender roles are somewhat more flexible than male gender roles.

First imagine that this is a photograph of a baby girl. *What expectations would you have for her?* Then imagine that this is a photograph of a baby boy. *What expectations would you have for him?*

gender role Expectations for how females and males should think, act, and feel.

Cognition and Gender How do children learn what girls and boys are supposed to be like? And do girls and boys actually think differently? Both of these questions link cognitive development to gender development.

Recall from our discussion of Piaget's theory earlier in the chapter that a schema is a mental framework that organizes and guides an individual's thoughts. A recent theory proposes that children develop a gender schema based on what is considered appropriate behavior for females and males in their culture (Martin, 2000; Martin & Dinella, 2001). Their gender schema then serves as a cognitive framework for interpreting further experiences related to gender. As their gender schema develops, children knit together all sorts of things with gender, such as "girls are expected to be nurturant," "boys are expected to be independent," and so on.

The research that has focused on how similar or different the cognitive skills of boys and girls are has mainly examined math skills, visuospatial skills, and verbal skills (Halpern, 2001). In math and visuospatial skills—the kinds of skills an architect needs to design a building's angles and dimensions—boys tend to perform better than girls, although the differences are usually small (Hyde & Plant, 1995). In the National Assessment of Educational Progress (1997), boys were better at math than girls in the fourth grade, but in the eighth and twelfth grades boys and girls achieved essentially equal scores. In the area of verbal skills, 20 years ago, researchers found that girls often had better verbal ability (such as a better vocabulary) than boys, but in most verbal areas that difference has not held up over the years (Hyde & Mezulis, 2001; National Assessment of Educational Progress, 2001). However, girls do have better reading skills than boys, and this gap widened from 1998 to 2000 (National Assessment of Educational Progress, 2001).

In other parts of this book, you will learn more about gender. It is one of the most frequently examined factors in psychological research. For example, chapter 16 ("Social Psychology") examines gender in relationships, gender in aggression, and gender in altruism.

Positive Psychology and Children's Development

We cannot fully understand children's development without examining their competence and adaptive capabilities. The concept of resilient children highlights this competence and adaptability.

Resilient Children Despite hardship, time and time again, resilient children grow up to be capable adults, just as Alice Walker did. But why does one person who is subjected to poverty or racism or the divorce of parents remain mired in lifelong misfortune whereas another rises above those obstacles to succeed in business, the community, or family life?

Researchers have found that resilient children have one or more advantages that help them to overcome their disadvantages (Masten, 2001; Masten & Coatsworth, 1998). These advantages include individual factors (such as good intellectual functioning), family factors (such as a close, caring relationship with at least one parent), and extrafamilial factors (such as bonds to supportive, competent adults outside the family; see figure 4.20). Not all of them need to be present to help a child develop successfully. If a child does not have responsible, caring parents, then high self-esteem and a bond to a caring adult outside the home could make the child resilient enough to overcome negative family factors.

The study of resilient children raises questions about what optimal functioning in children is like and which factors contribute to

Source	Characteristic
Individual	Good intellectual functioning
	Appealing, sociable, easygoing disposition
	Self-confidence, high self-esteem
	Talents
	Faith
Family	Close relationship to caring parent figure
	Authoritative parenting: warmth, structure, high expectations
	Socioeconomic advantages
	Connections to extended supportive family networks
Extrafamilial Context	Bonds to caring adults outside the family
	Connections to positive organizations
	Attending effective schools

FIGURE 4.20 Characteristics of Resilient Children and Their Contexts

positive development. The same characteristics that show up in resilient children are those that appear in competent children who don't face adverse circumstances.

Improving the Lives of Children   Unfortunately, however, many children living in at-risk circumstances—characterized by such factors as poverty, lack of quality parenting, inadequate schools, and high-crime neighborhoods—are not resilient. There are a lot of them: Almost 20 percent of all children and more than 50 percent of ethnic minority children in the United States live in poverty today (Children's Defense Fund, 2000). These children desperately need prevention and intervention programs that give them an opportunity to become competent—for example, health education and help in developing both cognitive and socioemotional skills, including self-control, stress management, and communication (Compas & others, 2001; Powell, 2001). Competence enhancement programs for children living in poverty are increasingly two-generational: They help parents find good jobs and obtain quality health care, in addition to helping the child (McLoyd, 2000; Weissberg & Greenberg, 1998).

At the beginning of the twenty-first century, the well-being of children is one of America's foremost challenges. Children who do not reach their potential, who are unable to contribute to society, and who do not take their place as productive adults diminish the vitality of society's future.

Children learn to love when they are loved

Review and Sharpen Your Thinking

2   *Describe children's development from conception to adolescence.*

- Identify the stages of prenatal development and describe the risks associated with this period.
- Summarize the physical changes after birth that make possible rapid cognitive and socioemotional growth in childhood.
- Explain Piaget's theory of cognitive development and the key criticisms of it.
- Discuss Erikson's theory of psychosocial development and other key research on specific factors believed to have an influence on children's socioemotional development.
- Describe the contributions of positive psychology to our understanding of children's development.

Is there a best way to parent? Explain.

mhhe●com/
santrockp7

For study tools related to this learning goal, see the Study Guide, the CD-ROM, and the Online Learning Center.

ADOLESCENCE 3

Positive Psychology and Adolescents

Cognitive Development in Adolescence

At-Risk Youth

Physical Development in Adolescence

Socioemotional Development in Adolescence

What are the most important physical, cognitive, and socioemotional changes in adolescence?

Adolescence is the developmental period of transition from childhood to adulthood. It begins around 10 to 12 years of age and ends at 18 to 21 years of age. In explor-

Adolescence is a time of evaluation, decision making, and commitment, as adolescents seek to find out who they are and carve out a place for themselves in the world.

ing adolescence, it is important to balance the positive side of adolescence with the negative side and to examine the search for an identity that every adolescent pursues.

Remember too that adolescents do not make up a homogeneous group (Santrock, 2003). Ethnic, cultural, historical, gender, socioeconomic, and lifestyle variations characterize their actual life trajectories. Our image of adolescents should take into account the particular adolescent or group of adolescents we are considering (Hirsch & others, 2000).

Positive Psychology and Adolescents

Too often adolescents have been stereotyped as abnormal and deviant. For example, Freud described adolescents as sexually driven and conflicted. Young people of every generation have seemed radical, unnerving, and different to adults—different in how they look, how they behave, and even the music they enjoy.

However, thinking of adolescence as a time of rebellion, crisis, pathology, and deviation does little good and can do considerable disservice to adolescents. It is far more accurate to view adolescence as a time of evaluation, a time of decision making, and a time of commitment as young people carve out their place in the world (Santrock, 2003). It is an enormous error to confuse the adolescent's enthusiasm for trying on new identities and enjoying moderate amounts of outrageous behavior with hostility toward parents and society. Searching for an identity is a time-honored way in which adolescents move toward accepting, rather than rejecting, parental and societal values.

How competent adolescents will eventually become often depends on their access to legitimate opportunities for growth, such as a quality education, community and societal support for achievement and involvement, and access to good jobs. Especially important in adolescents' development is long-term support from adults who deeply care about them (Larson, Brown, & Thortimer, 2002).

As evidence that the majority of adolescents develop more positively than is commonly believed, consider the research study conducted by Daniel Offer and his colleagues (1988). They sampled the self-images of adolescents around the world—in the United States, Australia, Bangladesh, Hungary, Israel, Italy, Japan, Taiwan, Turkey, and West Germany. About three of every four of these adolescents had healthy self-images. Most were happy, enjoyed life, and believed they had the ability to cope effectively with stress. They valued school and work.

From *Penguin Dreams and Stranger Things* by Berke Breathed. Copyright © 1985 by The Washington Post Company. By permission of Little, Brown and Company.

But what about the one in four adolescents who did not have positive self-images? What might be done to help them negotiate adolescence? Reed Larson (2000) argues that adolescents need more opportunities to develop the capacity for initiative, which he defined as becoming self-motivated and expending effort to reach challenging goals. Too often adolescents find themselves bored with life. To counter this boredom and help adolescents develop more initiative, Larson recommends structured voluntary activities such as sports, the arts, and participation in organizations.

Physical Development in Adolescence

The signature physical change in adolescence is **puberty,** a period of rapid skeletal and sexual maturation that occurs mainly in early adolescence. In general, we know when an individual is going through puberty, but we have a hard time pinpointing its beginning and its end. Except for menarche (girls' first menstrual cycle), no single marker defines it. For boys, the first whisker or first wet dream could mark its appearance, but both may go unnoticed.

Imagine a toddler displaying features of puberty: a 3-year-old girl with fully developed breasts or a boy of 4 with a deep voice. We would see such accelerated growth by 2250 if the age of puberty continued to decrease at its present pace. In the United States, the age at which menarche begins has declined on average from 14.2 years in 1900 to about 12.45 years today, a decline of about 4 months per decade for the past century. We are unlikely, though, to see pubescent toddlers in the future because what happened in the past was the result of increasingly higher levels of nutrition and health (Petersen, 1979).

In addition to menarche, a spurt in height and weight characterize pubertal change. This growth spurt occurs about 2 years earlier for girls than for boys (see figure 4.21). Today, in the United States, the mean beginning of the growth spurt is 9 years of age for girls and 11 years of age for boys. The peak of pubertal change occurs at an average age of 11½ for girls and 13½ for boys.

Hormonal changes lie at the core of pubertal development (Sarigiani & Petersen, 2000). The concentrations of certain hormones increase dramatically during puberty (Dorn & Chrousos, 1996). *Testosterone*, an androgen, is associated in boys with the development of genitals, an increase in height, and voice change. *Estradiol*, an estrogen, is associated in girls with breast, uterine, and skeletal development. In one study, testosterone levels doubled in girls but increased eighteenfold in boys during puberty; similarly, estradiol doubled in boys but increased eightfold in girls (Nottelmann & others, 1987).

Are concentrations of hormones and adolescents' behavior linked? Developmental psychologists believe that hormonal changes account for at least some of the emotional ups and downs of adolescence (Archibald, Graber, & Brooks-Gunn, in press).

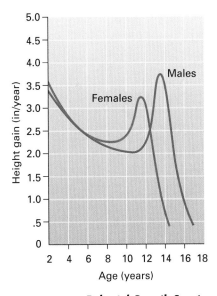

FIGURE 4.21 Pubertal Growth Spurt
On average, the pubertal growth spurt begins and peaks about 2 years earlier for girls (starts at 9, peaks at 11½) than for boys (starts at 11½, peaks at 13½).

puberty A period of rapid skeletal and sexual maturation that occurs mainly in early adolescence.

Researchers have found that higher levels of androgens, such as testosterone, are associated with violence and other problems in boys (van Goozen & others, 1998). There also is some indication that increased levels of estrogens, such as estradiol, are linked with depression in adolescent girls (Angold & others, 1998).

But hormones alone are not responsible for adolescent behavior. For example, in one study, social factors (such as stress, getting bad grades, and relationship problems) accounted for two to four times as much variance as hormonal factors in young girls' depression and anger (Brooks-Gunn & Warren, 1989). Keep in mind, too, that stress, eating patterns, sexual activity, and depression can either activate or suppress hormones (Alan Guttmacher Institute, 2000).

Cognitive Development in Adolescence

Adolescents undergo some significant cognitive changes. One is the advance to Piaget's stage of formal operational thinking, which was described earlier in the chapter. Another change has to do with adolescent egocentrism.

Piaget's Formal Operational Stage Piaget said that adolescents enter a fourth, most advanced stage of cognitive development, which he called the formal operational stage, at about 11 to 15 years of age. It is characterized by thought that is abstract, idealistic, and logical.

The abstract quality of thought at the formal operational level is evident in the adolescent's new verbal problem-solving ability. The concrete operational thinker would need to see the concrete elements, A, B, and C, to be able to make the logical inference that if A = B = C, then A = C. But the formal operational thinker can solve this problem merely through verbal presentation.

Another indication of the abstract quality of adolescents' thought is their increased tendency to think about thought itself. One adolescent commented, "I began thinking about why I was thinking what I was. Then I began thinking about why I was thinking about why I was thinking about what I was." If this sounds abstract, it is.

Formal operational thought is also full of idealism and possibilities. Children often think in concrete ways or in terms of what is real and limited. Adolescents begin to engage in extended speculation about the qualities they desire in themselves and in others. In search of the ideal, adolescents' thoughts may take fantasy flights into future possibilities. It is not unusual for adolescents to become impatient with these newfound ideals, however, and become perplexed over which of many ideal standards to adopt.

At the same time at which adolescents begin to think more abstractly and idealistically, they begin to think more logically about problems and possible solutions. This hypothetical-deductive reasoning, as Piaget called it, refers to the ability to develop hypotheses, or best hunches, about ways to solve problems, and then to deduce or conclude the best way to solve the problem.

In actuality, not all adolescents engage in formal operational thought, especially in hypothetical-deductive reasoning (Flavell, Miller, & Miller, 2002). Some adolescents and adults remain at Piaget's concrete operational stage. Others may be overwhelmed at times by their idealistic thinking and may not reason very logically.

Adolescent Egocentrism Especially in early adolescence, adolescent thought is egocentric. *Adolescent egocentrism* involves the belief that others are as preoccupied with the adolescent as he or she is, the belief that one is unique, and the belief that one is invincible (Elkind, 1978). Notice that adolescent egocentrism does not mean feeling "conceited" or necessarily superior to others.

Adolescent egocentrism does mean that adolescents perceive others to be noticing and watching them more than actually is the case. Imagine the eighth-grade boy who senses that everyone else has noticed the small pimple on his face. Another example of the adolescent's sense of uniqueness is the adolescent girl who says, "My mother has no idea about how much pain I'm going through. She has never been hurt like I have. Why did he break up with me?"

The aspect of adolescent egocentrism that can produce the most harm is a sense of invincibility, which may lead to drag racing down a city street, to drug use, to suicide attempts, or to sexually transmitted diseases or adolescent pregnancy. Imagine that an adolescent girl hears that a friend of hers has become pregnant. She may exclaim, "I won't ever let that happen to me," and then goes out and has unprotected sex the next week. Her sense of invincibility causes her to behave in a high-risk manner. On a positive note, the adolescent's sense of invincibility may also lead to courageous efforts to save people's lives in hazardous circumstances, as when someone is drowning or is trapped in a burning car.

"Do you have any idea who I am?"

Socioemotional Development in Adolescence

The increase in abstract and idealistic thought during adolescence serves as a foundation for exploring one's identity. Many aspects of socioemotional development—such as relationships with parents, peer interaction and friendships, and cultural and ethnic values—contribute to an adolescent's identity development. Erikson's theory addresses the manner in which adolescents seek their identities.

Erikson's Theory and Identity Development As you learned in the section on socioemotional development in children, Erik Erikson's life-span theory states that people go through eight psychosocial stages of development. Within the eight stages that Erikson (1968) proposed, his ideas about the formation of identity during adolescence are among his most important contributions to psychology. They changed the way we think about adolescence (Marcia, 2001). For example, Erikson encouraged us to look at adolescents, not just as hormone-driven beings, but as individuals finding out who they are and searching for their niche in the world.

Erikson's theory characterizes the main concern of the fifth stage of socioemotional development as **identity versus identity confusion.** In seeking an *identity,* adolescents face the challenges of finding out who they are, what they are all about, and where they are going in life. Adolescents are confronted with many new roles and adult statuses—from the vocational to the romantic. If they do not adequately explore their identities during this stage, they emerge with a sense of confusion about who they are. Therefore, Erikson argues, parents should allow adolescents to explore many different roles and paths within a particular role and not push an identity on them.

Erikson described adolescence as a moratorium, a temporal and psychological gap between the security of childhood and the autonomy of adulthood. Adolescents who use the moratorium to explore alternatives can reach some resolution of the identity crisis and emerge with a new sense of self that is both refreshing and acceptable; those who do not successfully resolve the crisis become confused, suffering what Erikson calls *identity confusion.* This confusion is expressed in one of two ways: Either individuals withdraw, isolating themselves from peers and family, or they lose themselves in the crowd.

Erikson noted that in the American culture, adolescents want to decide freely for themselves such matters as what careers they will pursue, whether they will go to college, and whether they will marry. In other words, they want to free themselves from the control of their parents and other adults and make their own choices. At the same time, many deeply fear making the wrong decisions and failing. In some cases the problem may be simply that adolescents have not yet realized their own growing cognitive abilities. One strength that equips them to effectively pursue their identities is that their thoughts have become more abstract and logical, and they are able to reason in increasingly sophisticated ways.

identity versus identity confusion Erikson's fifth psychological stage in which adolescents face the challenge of finding out who they are, what they are all about, and where they are going in life.

FIGURE 4.22 Marcia's Four Statuses of Identity

Position on Occupation and Ideology	Identity Status			
	Identity moratorium	Identity foreclosure	Identity diffusion	Identity achievement
Crisis	Present	Absent	Absent	Present
Commitment	Absent	Present	Absent	Present

Identity Status Building on Erikson's ideas, James Marcia (1980) proposed the concept of *identity status* to describe a person's position in the development of an identity. In his view, two dimensions of identity are important. *Exploration* refers to a person's exploring various options for a career and for personal values. *Commitment* involves making a decision about which identity path to follow and making a personal investment in attaining that identity.

Various combinations of exploration and commitment give rise to one of four identity statuses (see figure 4.22):

- *Identity diffusion.* A person has not yet explored meaningful alternatives and also has not made a commitment. Many young adolescents have a diffuse identity status. They have not yet begun to explore different career options and personal values.
- *Identity foreclosure.* A person makes a commitment to an identity before adequately exploring various options. For example, an adolescent might say that she wants to be a doctor because that is what her parents want her to be, rather than exploring career options and then deciding on her own to be a doctor.
- *Identity moratorium.* A person is exploring alternative paths but has not yet made a commitment. Many college students are in a moratorium status with regard to a major field of study or a career.
- *Identity achievement.* A person has explored alternative paths and made a commitment. For example, an individual might have examined a number of careers over an extended period of time and finally decided to pursue one wholeheartedly.

Ethnic Identity Developing an identity in adolescence can be especially challenging for individuals from ethnic minority groups (Phinney, 2000; Spencer, 2000). As they mature cognitively, many adolescents become acutely aware of the evaluation of their ethnic group by the majority culture. In addition, an increasing number of minority adolescents face the challenge of biculturalism—identifying in some ways with their ethnic minority group, in other ways with the majority culture.

In one study, a researcher examined the development of ethnic identity in Asian American, African American, Latino, and White 10th-grade students in Los Angeles (Phinney, 1989). Adolescents from each of the three ethnic minority groups faced a similar need to deal with their ethnic-group identity in a predominately White, Anglo-American culture. But the three groups faced different challenges. For Asian American adolescents, the pressure to achieve academically was an important identity concern. Female African American adolescents were concerned that White standards of beauty (especially hair and skin color) did not apply to them. Male African American adolescents were concerned with possible job discrimination and the need to distinguish themselves from a negative societal image. For Latino adolescents, prejudice was a recurrent theme, as was the conflict in values between their cultural heritage and the majority culture.

For both minority and majority adolescents, however, developing a positive identity is an important life theme. To further explore your development of a positive identity, see the Psychology and Life box.

Michelle Chin, age 16, reflecting on her identity, commented, "Parents do not understand that teenagers need to find out who they are, which means a lot of experimenting, a lot of mood swings, a lot of emotions and awkwardness. Like any teenager, I am facing an identity crisis. I am still trying to figure out whether I am a Chinese American or an American with Asian eyes."

Developing a Positive Identity

Following are some helpful attitudes for developing a positive identity:

- *Be aware that your identity is complex and takes a long time to develop.* Your identity has many components. One of your main identity tasks is to integrate all of these parts into a meaningful whole. Your identity does not spring forth in a sudden burst of insight. It is achieved in bits and pieces over your lifetime. What are some of the bits and pieces of your identity development?
- *Make the most of your college years.* For many people, the college years are an important time for identity development. College by its very nature encourages exploration and exposure to a wide variety of ideas and values. Your views likely will be challenged by instructors and classmates, which may motivate you to change some aspects of your identity.
- *Examine whether your identity is your own or your parents'.* Some college students have foreclosed on an identity without adequately considering alternatives. Identity foreclosure occurs especially when individuals accept their parents' views without deeply questioning whether they want to be just like their parents. Individuals might come to an identity similar to that of their parents, but while evaluating different paths, a more suitable identity may be discovered. Have you adequately developed an identity that is your own?
- *Expect your identity to change.* Even people who think they have achieved the identity they want could find it changing in the future. Your world will change and you will change, especially if you explore new opportunities and face new challenges. What do you expect your identity to be like after you finish college? Different from what it is now? The same?

At-Risk Youth

Although adolescence is best viewed positively as a time of decision making and commitment rather than a time of crisis and pathology, for a large subset of adolescents it is a time of risk. This risk limits the likelihood that they will become productive adults.

Four key aspects of risk are delinquency, substance abuse, unprotected sex and adolescent pregnancy, and school-related problems (Dryfoos, 1990). Estimates are that as many as 25 percent of adolescents have three or more of these problems. Drug use and juvenile delinquency are briefly explored here.

Given the far-reaching effects of at-risk behavior by adolescents, a number of programs for helping individuals navigate adolescence have been established. Some are more effective than others. In her analysis, Joy Dryfoos (1990) found that the greatest success has come from individualized attention and community-wide programs.

In successful individualized programs, at-risk youths are paired with responsible adults who pay attention to the adolescents' specific needs. For example, in substance abuse programs, a student-assistance counselor might be available full time for individual counseling. In delinquency prevention, a family worker might give intensive support to a predelinquent and the family so that they will make the necessary changes to avoid repeated delinquent acts.

School counselors can play an important role in detecting which students need individualized psychological services and intervention. Armando Ronquillo is a high school counselor at Pueblo High School in Tucson, Arizona. He has been especially successful at counseling students on the merits of staying in school and on the life-long opportunities provided by a college education. He also works with parents when adolescents at his school have problems. Because of his caring and his success at turning around students' lives, Ronquillo was named Arizona's counselor of the year in 2000.

The basic concept of community-wide programs is that improving the lives of at-risk youth requires a number of interrelated programs and services (O'Donnell & others, 1999). For example, a substance abuse program might feature community-wide health promotion through local media and community events in conjunction with a

Armando Ronquillo counseling a Latina high school student about coping with problems and the importance of a college education.

substance abuse prevention curriculum in the schools. Delinquency problems might be addressed by a neighborhood development program in which local residents work with schools, police, courts, gang leaders, and the media. The goal, as with individualized attention, is to ensure that the minority of adolescents who do experience a rocky youth have a better chance of developing into successful, productive adults.

mhhe.com/
santrockp7

For study tools related to this learning goal, see the Study Guide, the CD-ROM, and the Online Learning Center.

Review and Sharpen Your Thinking

3 *Identify the most important changes that occur in adolescence.*

- Explore the contribution of positive psychology to our thinking about adolescent development.
- Discuss the nature of puberty.
- Describe the key aspects of cognitive development during adolescence.
- Explain these aspects of adolescent socioemotional development: identity development and risk factors for youths.

Are Marcia's identity statuses useful to you in thinking about your own identity development? To explore this question, return to table 4.2 and evaluate your levels of exploration and commitment in regard to career and personal values. Into which identity status would you place yourself?

4 ADULT DEVELOPMENT AND AGING

Physical Development in Adulthood

Socioemotional Development in Adulthood

Cognitive Development in Adulthood

Positive Psychology and Aging

What are the main physical, cognitive, and socioemotional changes in adults?
Development does not end with adolescence. It continues throughout the roughly 50 (and often more) years of adulthood. Developmental psychologists identify three approximate periods in adult development: early adulthood (20s and 30s), middle adulthood (40s and 50s), and late adulthood (60s until death). Each phase features some distinctive physical, cognitive, and socioemotional changes.

Physical Development in Adulthood

Singer-actress Bette Midler said that after 30 a body has a mind of its own. Comedian Bob Hope once remarked that middle age is when your age starts to show around your middle. How do we age physically as we go through the adult years?

Physical Changes in Early Adulthood Most adults reach their peak physical development during their 20s and also are the healthiest then. For athletes—not only at the Olympic level but also the average athlete—performance peaks in the 20s, especially for strength and speed events such as weight lifting and the 100-meter dash (Schultz & Curnow, 1988). The main exceptions are female gymnasts (like Zhang Liyin, whose story started this chapter) and swimmers, who often peak in adolescence, and marathon runners, who tend to peak in their late 30s.

Unfortunately, early adulthood also is when many skills begin to decline. The decline in strength and speed often is noticeable in the 30s.

Perhaps because of their robust physical skills and overall health, young adults rarely recognize that bad eating habits, heavy drinking, and smoking in early adulthood can impair their health as they age. Despite warnings on packages and in advertisements that cigarettes are hazardous to health, individuals actually increase their use of cigarettes as they enter early adulthood (Johnston, Bachman, & O'Malley, 1989). They also increase their use of alcohol, marijuana, amphetamines, barbiturates, and hallucinogens.

A special concern is heavy drinking by college students. In one recent study of 14,000 college students, approximately 40 percent said they had engaged in binge drinking (drinking five or more drinks in a row for men and four or more in a row for women) at least once a week in the 2 weeks before they were surveyed (Wechsler and others, 2000). Heavy drinking can take a toll on college students and threaten their futures. In one study at 140 colleges, binge drinking was associated with class absences, physical injuries, troubles with police, and unprotected sex (Wechsler & others, 1994).

Fortunately, by the time individuals reach their mid-20s, many have reduced their use of alcohol and drugs, according to a study of 33,000 individuals from high school through the mid-20s (Bachman, 1997). Other findings in this study were that

- College students drank more than their counterparts who ended their education after high school.
- Those who did not go to college were more likely to smoke.
- Single adults used marijuana more than married adults.
- Drinking was heaviest among single and divorced adults. Becoming engaged, married, or remarried quickly reduced alcohol use.

As you can see, living arrangements and marital status are key factors in alcohol and drug use rates during a person's 20s.

Physical Changes in Middle Adulthood One of the most visible physical changes in middle adulthood is appearance. By the 40s or 50s, the skin begins to wrinkle and sag because of a loss of fat and collagen in underlying tissues. Small, localized areas of pigmentation in the skin produce age spots, especially in areas exposed to sunlight, such as the hands and face. Hair becomes thinner and grayer due to a lower replacement rate and a decline in melanin production.

Individuals actually begin to lose height in middle age, and many gain weight. Adults lose about ½ inch of height per decade beginning in their 40s (Memmler & others, 1995). Fat generally accounts for about 10 percent of body weight in adolescence but for 20 percent or more in middle age.

Perhaps because the signs of aging are all too visible to us, we become more acutely concerned about our health in our 40s. In fact, we do experience a general decline in physical fitness throughout middle adulthood and some deterioration in health. The three greatest health concerns at this age are heart disease, cancer, and weight. Cancer related to smoking often surfaces in middle adulthood.

Because the U.S. culture values a youthful appearance, the physical deterioration that takes place in middle adulthood—graying hair, wrinkling skin, and a sagging body—can be difficult to handle. Many middle-aged adults dye their hair and join weight reduction programs; some even undergo cosmetic surgery to look young.

For women, entering middle age also means that menopause will soon occur. Usually in the late 40s or early 50s, a woman's menstrual periods cease completely. The average age at which women have their last period is 52, but 10 percent of women undergo menopause before age 40.

What are some physical changes that women go through as they age?

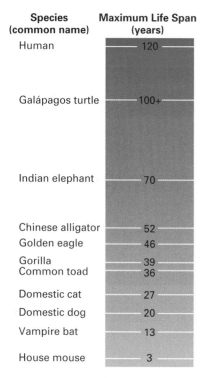

FIGURE 4.23 **Maximum Recorded Life Spans of Various Species**

Species (common name)	Maximum Life Span (years)
Human	120
Galápagos turtle	100+
Indian elephant	70
Chinese alligator	52
Golden eagle	46
Gorilla	39
Common toad	36
Domestic cat	27
Domestic dog	20
Vampire bat	13
House mouse	3

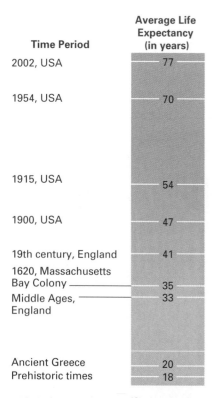

FIGURE 4.24 **Human Life Expectancy at Birth from Prehistoric to Contemporary Times**

Time Period	Average Life Expectancy (in years)
2002, USA	77
1954, USA	70
1915, USA	54
1900, USA	47
19th century, England	41
1620, Massachusetts Bay Colony	35
Middle Ages, England	33
Ancient Greece	20
Prehistoric times	18

With menopause comes a dramatic decline in the production of estrogen by the ovaries. Estrogen decline produces some uncomfortable symptoms in some menopausal women, such as hot flashes (sudden brief flushing of the skin and a feeling of elevated body temperature), nausea, fatigue, and rapid heartbeat. Some menopausal women report depression and irritability, but in some instances these feelings are related to other circumstances in the women's lives, such as becoming divorced, losing a job, or caring for a sick parent (Dickson, 1990). Research reveals that menopause does not produce psychological or physical problems for most women (McKinlay & McKinlay, 1984).

Although menopause is not the negative experience for most women that it was once thought to be, the loss of fertility is an important marker for women: Its approach means that they have to make final decisions about having children (Sommer, 2002). Women in their 30s who have never had children sometimes speak about being "up against the biological clock" because they cannot postpone the decision much longer.

Estrogen replacement therapy is recommended increasingly for women in the transition to menopause (Stefanick, 1999). According to the American Geriatrics Society's most recent recommendations (Bidikov & Meier, 1997),

• Middle-aged women should consider estrogen replacement therapy because it can reduce the risk of osteoporosis (loss of bone mass), coronary disease, and menopausal symptoms such as hot flashes and sweating. However, the risk of estrogen replacement therapy can outweigh its benefits for women who are at risk for breast cancer.

• Women should actively participate in decision making about using estrogen replacement therapy.

Do men go through anything like the menopause that women experience? Men do experience sex-related hormone declines in their 50s and 60s, but they are usually not as precipitous as women's estrogen decline (Crooks & Bauer, 2002).

Physical Changes in Late Adulthood   The concept of a period called "late adulthood" is a recent one: Until the twentieth century, most individuals died before they were 65. Many societies around the world have become less youthful, however, and so need to develop a better understanding of the later years of life (Birren, 2000; Masoro & Austad, 2001).

Developmentalists distinguish between life span and life expectancy. The term *life span* is used to describe the upper boundary of a species' life, the maximum number of years an individual can expect to live. The maximum number of years human beings can live is about 120. As can be seen in figure 4.23, *Homo sapiens* is believed to have one of the longest life spans, if not the longest.

The term *life expectancy* is used to describe the number of years that will probably be lived by the average person born in a particular year. Improvements in medicine, nutrition, exercise, and lifestyle have increased our life expectancy an average of 30 additional years since 1900 (see figure 4.24). The life expectancy of individuals born today in the United States is 77 years (80 for women, 73 for men). One in three women born today is expected to live to be 100 or more. The world's population of individuals 65 years and older doubled from 1950 to 1990, and the fastest growing segment of the population is 85 years and older.

Although life expectancy has increased dramatically, life span does not seem to have increased since the beginning of recorded history. Even if we are remarkably healthy through our adult lives, we begin to age at some point.

Biological Theories of Aging   Many biological theories of aging have been proposed, but two that especially merit attention are the cellular-clock theory and the free-radical theory. Both of these theories look within the body's cells for causes of aging. The cellular-clock theory is Leonard Hayflick's (1977) view that cells can divide a

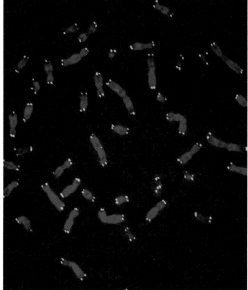

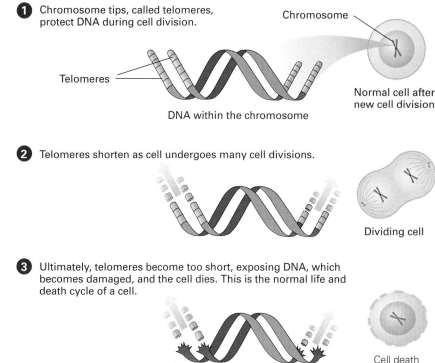

1. Chromosome tips, called telomeres, protect DNA during cell division.

Chromosome

Telomeres

DNA within the chromosome

Normal cell after new cell division

2. Telomeres shorten as cell undergoes many cell divisions.

Dividing cell

3. Ultimately, telomeres become too short, exposing DNA, which becomes damaged, and the cell dies. This is the normal life and death cycle of a cell.

Cell death

FIGURE 4.25 **Telomeres and Aging** The above photograph shows telomeres lighting up the tips of chromosomes.

maximum of about 100 times and that, as we age, our cells become less capable of dividing. Hayflick found that cells extracted from adults in their 50s to 70s had divided fewer than 100 times. The total number of cell divisions was roughly related to the age of the individual. Based on the way cells divide, Hayflick places the upper limit of the human life span at about 120 years.

In the past decade, scientists have tried to explain why cells lose their ability to divide (Shay & Wright, 2000). The answer may lie at the tips of chromosomes. Each time a cell divides, the *telomeres* that protect the ends of chromosomes become shorter and shorter (see figure 4.25). After about 100 replications, the telomeres are dramatically reduced, and the cell no longer can reproduce. In one recent study, age-related telomere erosion was linked with an inability to recover from stress and an increase in cancer (Rudolf & others, 1999).

Another biological theory of aging is *free-radical theory*, which states that people age because inside their cells unstable oxygen molecules known as "free radicals" are produced. These molecules ricochet around in the cells, damaging DNA and other cellular structures (Knight, 2000). The damage done by free radicals may lead to a range of disorders, including cancer and arthritis.

Physical Changes and Health Even without the development of disease, the aging process produces many physical changes. Changes in physical appearance become more pronounced in older adults, including wrinkles and aging spots. Whereas weight often increases in middle age, it frequently declines after 60 because of muscle loss. Blood pressure often rises in older adults but can be treated by exercise and/or drugs.

Normal aging involves some bone tissue loss from the skeleton, and in some instances the loss can be severe, as in osteoporosis (Whitbourne, 2000). Almost two-thirds of women over 60 are affected to some degree by osteoporosis. Estrogen replacement therapy can reduce bone loss for women, and a program of weight lifting can help (Nelson & others, 1994).

Chronic diseases—characterized by a slow onset and long duration—are rare in early adulthood, increase in middle adulthood, and become more common in late

Frenchwoman Jeanne Louise Calumet pushed the upper boundary of the human life span, dying in 1997 at the age of 122. Asked on her 120th birthday about the kind of future she expected, Calumet replied, "A very short one." Greater ages have been claimed, but scientists say that the human life span is approximately 120 years of age. However, as genetic engineering continues to make progress, the possibility of altering cellular functioning to increase the human life span is raised. Some biologists even have brought up the possibility that in the future humans might live 400 years! *What kinds of ethical issues are involved in genetically engineering cellular functioning to increase the human life span?*

Eighty-five-year-old Sadie Halperin doubled her strength in exercise after just 11 months. Before developing an exercise routine, she felt wobbly and often had to hold on to a wall when she walked. Now she walks down the middle of hallways and says she feels wonderful.

How do you know when you're old? It may depend on cultural factors. (Around the Globe) mhhe.com/santrockp7

Former president Ronald Reagan was diagnosed with Alzheimer's at the age of 83.

adulthood. The most common chronic disorder in late adulthood is arthritis; the second most common is hypertension (high blood pressure).

This list of physical deteriorations may sound rather dismal. However, a substantial portion of individuals even over the age of 85 are still robust and active. Consider 85-year-old Sadie Halperin, who has been working out for 11 months at a rehabilitation center for the aged in Boston. She lifts weights and rides a stationary bicycle. She says that before she started working out, almost everything she did—shopping, cooking, walking—was a major struggle. She felt wobbly and had to hold on to a wall when she walked. Now she walks down the center of the hallways and reports that she feels great. Sadie's exercise routine has increased her muscle strength and helped her to battle osteoporosis by slowing the calcium loss in her bones (Ubell, 1992). Researchers continue to document how effective exercise is in slowing the aging process and helping older adults function in society (Burke & others, 2001).

Another important factor in the health of older adults is their sense of control over their lives. In a classic experimental study, Judith Rodin and Ellen Langer (1977) found that the sense of control, a cognitive factor, was linked not only with the health of nursing home residents but even with their survival. The researchers encouraged one group of elderly nursing home residents to make more day-to-day choices and thus to feel more responsible and have more control over their lives. They were allowed to decide on such matters as what they ate, when visitors could come, what movies to see, and who could come to their rooms. A similar group in the same nursing home was told by the administrator how caring the nursing home was and how much the staff wanted to help. However, they were given no opportunities to be responsible and make their own decisions. Eighteen months later, the nursing home residents who were given responsibility and control were more alert, active, and happier, and they were likelier to still be alive than residents who were encouraged to be dependent on the nursing staff. Perceived control and responsibility for oneself, then, may be literally a matter of life or death. Researchers continue to document the importance of perceived control over one's world in the health and well-being of older adults (Clark-Plaskie & Lachman, 1999; DeVellis & DeVellis, 2001).

The Brain and Alzheimer's Disease · Just as the aging body has been found to have a greater capacity for renewal than previously believed, so has the aging brain (Taub, 2001). For decades, scientists believed that no new brain cells are generated past the early childhood years. However, as mentioned in chapter 3, researchers recently discovered that adults can grow new brain cells throughout their lives (Gould & others, 1999). In one study, the growth of dendrites (the receiving, branching part of the neuron or nerve cell) continued through the 70s, although no new dendritic growth was discovered in people in their 90s (Coleman, 1986).

Even in late adulthood, the brain has remarkable repair capability. Stanley Rapaport (1994), chief of the neurosciences laboratory at the National Institute of Aging, compared the brains of younger and older adults when they were engaged in the same tasks. The older adults' brains literally rewired themselves to compensate for losses. If one neuron was not up to the job, neighboring neurons helped to pick up the slack. Rapaport concluded that as brains age, they can actually shift responsibilities for a given task from one region to another.

Alzheimer's disease—a progressive, irreversible brain disorder that is characterized by gradual deterioration of memory, reasoning, language, and eventually physical functioning—does not present such encouraging prospects (Santacruz & Swagerty, 2001). Approximately 2.5 million people over the age of 65 in the United States have Alzheimer's disease; the percentage of people who have it doubles for every 5 years beyond age 65.

As Alzheimer's disease progresses, the brain deteriorates and shrinks (Salmon, 2000). Figure 4.26 strikingly contrasts the brain of a normal aging individual with the brain of an individual who has Alzheimer's disease. Among the main character-

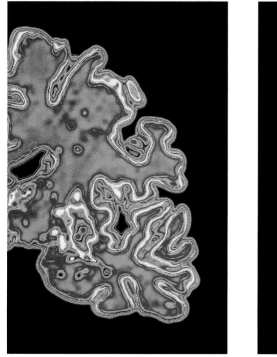
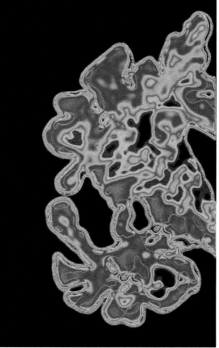

FIGURE 4.26 **Two Brains: Normal Aging and Alzheimer's Disease**
(*Left*) A slice of a normally aging brain. (*Right*) A slice of a brain ravaged by Alzheimer's disease. Notice the deterioration and shrinking in the Alzheimer's diseased brain.

istics of Alzheimer's disease are the increasing number of tangles (tied bundles of proteins that impair the function of neurons) and plaques (deposits that accumulate in the brain's blood vessels). The formation of tangles and plaques is a normal part of aging, but it is far more pronounced in Alzheimer's disease.

Alzheimer's disease also involves a deficiency in the important brain messenger chemical acetylcholine, which you read about in chapter 3 (Hodges, 2000). This neurotransmitter plays an important role in memory. The main drug currently used to treat Alzheimer's disease is Aricept, which works by blocking chemicals that ordinarily cut acetylcholine apart. However, such drugs do not prevent the brain from continuing to deteriorate in Alzheimer's patients.

Research on the aging brain does give cause for hope. An intriguing ongoing study involves nearly 700 nuns in a convent in Mankato, Minnesota (Snowden, 1995, 1997, 2001; see figure 4.27). The nuns are the largest group of brain donors in the world. By examining the nuns' donated brains, as well as others, neuroscientists have documented the remarkable ability of the aging brain to grow and change. Even the oldest Mankato nuns lead intellectually challenging lives, and neuroscientists believe that stimulating mental activities increase dendritic branching. The researchers are also intrigued to find that the nuns are showing almost no signs of Alzheimer's disease. Indeed, researchers have consistently found support for the "use it or lose it" concept: The cognitive skills of older adults benefit considerably when they engage in challenging intellectual activities (Schaie & Willis, 2001).

Cognitive Development in Adulthood

Earlier in the chapter, you learned that considerable changes take place in children's cognitive development. What kind of cognitive changes occur in adults?

Cognition in Early Adulthood   Piaget believed that formal operational thought is the highest level of thinking, and he argued that no new qualitative changes in cognition take place in adulthood. He didn't believe that a person with a Ph.D. in physics thinks any differently than a young adolescent who has reached the stage of formal operational thought. The only difference is that the physicist has more knowledge in

FIGURE 4.27 **The Brains of the Mankato Nuns**   At 90 years old, nun study participant Sister Rosella Kreuzer, SSND, remains an active, contributing member of her community of sisters. Sister Rosella designed the nun study logo, *That You May Have Life to the Full. Inset:* A neuroscientist holds a brain donated by one of the Mankato nun study participants.

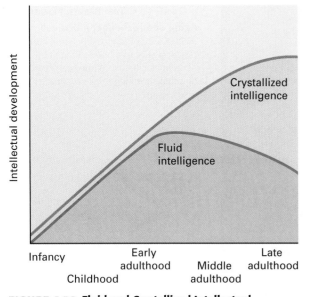

a specific scientific domain. The physicist and the young adolescent both use logical thought to develop alternatives for solving a problem and to deduce a solution from the options.

Piaget was right about some adolescents and some adults—but not about all of them. As you learned earlier, some adolescents are not formal operational thinkers, and many adults never reach that stage either.

Yet some experts on cognitive development argue that the typical idealism of Piaget's formal operational stage is replaced in young adulthood by more realistic, pragmatic thinking (Labouvie-Vief, 1986). Also, adolescents tend to think in absolute terms—things are either all this way or that way. As they go through the college years, individuals often begin to think in more relative and reflective ways (Kitchener & King, 1981). In sum, for the most part, intellectual skills are strong in early adulthood (Berg, 2000). Do they begin to decline in middle age?

Cognition in Middle Adulthood John Horn's view is that some intellectual abilities begin to decline in middle age, whereas others increase (Horn & Donaldson, 1980). He believes that **crystallized intelligence,** an individual's accumulated information and verbal skills, increases in middle adulthood. By contrast, **fluid intelligence,** one's ability to reason abstractly, begins to decline in middle adulthood (see figure 4.28).

Horn's view is based on data he collected in a *cross-sectional study,* which assesses a number of people all at one point in time. A cross-sectional study, for example, might assess the intelligence of six hundred 40-, 50-, and 60-year-olds in a single evaluation in September 2002. In a cross-sectional study, differences on intelligence tests might be due to *cohort effects,* the effects of living through a certain historical time in a certain culture, rather than to age. The 40-year-olds and the 60-year-olds were born in different eras, which offered different economic, educational, and health opportunities. For example, as the 60-year-olds grew up, they likely had fewer educational opportunities than the 40-year-olds had, which may influence their performance on intelligence tests.

In contrast, a *longitudinal study* assesses the same participants over a lengthy period. A longitudinal study of intelligence in middle adulthood might consist of giving the same intelligence test to the same individuals over a 20-year time span, when they are 40, 50, and 60 years of age. As is discussed next, whether data on intelligence are collected cross-sectionally or longitudinally can make a difference in the results.

K. Warner Schaie (1983, 1996) is conducting an extensive longitudinal study of intellectual abilities in adulthood. Five hundred individuals initially were tested in 1956. New waves of participants are added periodically. The main abilities tested by Schaie are

- Vocabulary (ability to encode and understand ideas expressed in words)
- Verbal memory (ability to encode and recall meaningful language units, such as a list of words)
- Number (ability to perform simple mathematical computations such as addition, subtraction, and multiplication)
- Spatial orientation (ability to visualize and mentally rotate stimuli in two- and three-dimensional space)
- Inductive reasoning (ability to recognize and understand patterns and relationships in a problem and use this understanding to solve other instances of the problem)
- Perceptual speed (ability to quickly and accurately make simple discriminations in visual stimuli)

crystallized intelligence An individual's accumulated information and verbal skills.

fluid intelligence One's ability to reason abstractly.

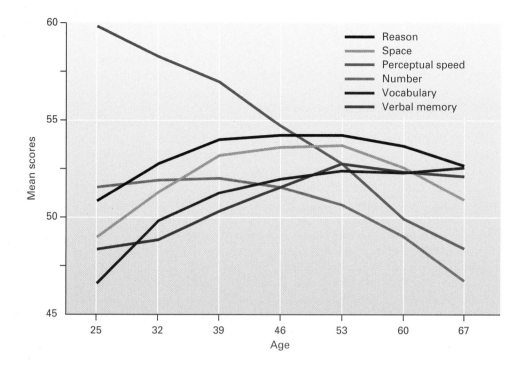

As shown in figure 4.29, the highest level of functioning for four of the six intellectual abilities—vocabulary, verbal memory, inductive reasoning, and spatial orientation—occurred in middle adulthood (Schaie & Willis, 2001; Willis & Schaie, 1999). Only two of the six abilities—numerical ability and perceptual speed—declined in middle age. Perceptual speed showed the earliest decline, beginning in early adulthood.

Those are encouraging results, but should we accept them uncritically? When Schaie (1994) assessed intellectual skills both cross-sectionally and longitudinally, he found more decline in middle age in the cross-sectional assessment. For example, as shown in figure 4.30, when he assessed inductive reasoning longitudinally, it increased until the end of middle adulthood, at which point it began a slight decline. By contrast, when he assessed it cross-sectionally, inductive reasoning already was declining at the beginning of middle adulthood.

Interestingly, Schaie found middle adulthood to be a time of peak performance for some aspects of both crystallized intelligence (vocabulary) and fluid intelligence (spatial orientation and inductive reasoning). John Horn, as you may recall, found that fluid intelligence peaks in early adulthood and crystallized intelligence in middle age. Schaie concluded, based on the longitudinal data he has collected so far, that middle adulthood, not early adulthood, is when many people reach their peak for many intellectual skills.

Cognition in Late Adulthood At age 70, medical researcher John Rock introduced the birth control pill. At age 76, Anna Mary Robertson, better known as Grandma Moses, took up painting and became internationally famous. When Pablo Casals reached 95 years of age, a reporter called him the greatest cellist who ever lived but wondered why he still practiced 6 hours a day. Casals replied, "Because I feel like I am making progress."

Claims about intellectual functioning through the late adult years are provocative. Many contemporary psychologists believe that, as with middle adulthood, some dimensions of intelligence decline in late adulthood, whereas others are maintained or may even increase.

One of the most consistent findings is that, when speed of processing information is involved, older adults do more poorly than their younger counterparts (figure 4.31;

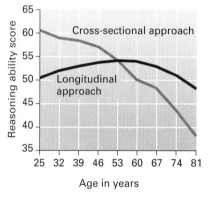

FIGURE 4.30 **Cross-Sectional and Longitudinal Comparisons of Reasoning Ability Across the Adulthood Years** In Schaie's most recent research, the cross-sectional approach revealed declining scores with age; the longitudinal approach showed a slight rise of scores in middle adulthood and only a slight decline beginning in the early part of late adulthood.

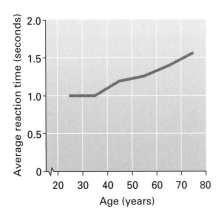

FIGURE 4.31 The Relation of Age to Reaction Time In one study, the average reaction time began to slow in the 40s and this decline accelerated in the 60s and 70s (Salthouse, 1984). The task used to assess reaction time required individuals to match numbers with symbols on a computer screen.

Older adults might not be as quick with their thoughts as younger adults, but wisdom may be an entirely different matter. This woman shares the wisdom of her experiences with a classroom of children.

wisdom Expert knowledge about the practical aspects of life.

Craik & Salthouse, 2000; Madden, 2001). This decline in speed of processing is apparent in middle-aged adults and becomes more pronounced in older adults.

Older adults also tend to do more poorly than younger adults in most areas of memory (Backman, Small, & Wahlin, 2001; Light, 2000). Older adults do not remember the "where" and "when" of life's happenings as well as younger adults (Tulving, 2000). For example, older adults don't remember their high school classmates or the names of their teachers as well as younger adults do. In the area of memory involving knowledge of the world (for instance, the capital of Peru or the chemical formula for water), older adults usually take longer than younger adults to retrieve the information, but they often are able to retrieve it. And in the important area of memory in which individuals manipulate and assemble information to solve problems and make decisions, decline occurs in older adults (Light, 2000; Salthouse, 2000).

However, some aspects of cognition might actually improve with age. One candidate is **wisdom,** expert knowledge about the practical aspects of life. Wisdom may increase with age because of the buildup of life experiences we have. However, not every older person has wisdom (Baltes, Lindenberger, & Staudinger, 1998). Individual variations characterize all aspects of our cognitive lives (Belsky, 1999).

Do we all face the prospect, then, of gradually becoming less competent intellectually? Not necessarily, as the study of the Mankato nuns suggests. Even for those aspects of cognitive aging that decline, such as memory, educating and training older adults can improve their cognitive skills (Park, Nisbett, & Hedden, 1999; Schaie & Willis, 2001). Researchers have demonstrated that training older adults to use certain strategies can even improve their memories (Baltes, 1993; Willis & Schaie, 1994). However, many experts on aging believe that older adults are less able to change and adapt than younger adults and thus are limited in how much they can improve their cognitive skills (Baltes, 2000).

Socioemotional Development in Adulthood

As both Sigmund Freud and the nineteenth-century Russian novelist Leo Tolstoy observed, adulthood's two most important themes are work and love. The study of socioemotional development in the adult years largely bears them out. Psychologists have proposed different theories about adult socioemotional development. Most theories address themes of work and love, career and intimacy. But before examining what psychologists have learned about these themes, let's return to Erikson's stage theory of life-span development.

Erikson's Adult Stages Recall that Erikson's eight stages of the human life span include one stage for early adulthood, one for middle adulthood, and one for late adulthood. Erikson (1968) said that individuals enter his sixth stage of *intimacy versus isolation* during early adulthood. At this time, people face the developmental task of either forming intimate relationships with others or becoming socially isolated. Erikson describes intimacy as both finding oneself and losing oneself in another. If the young adult develops healthy friendships and an intimate close relationship with a partner, intimacy will likely be achieved.

Generativity versus stagnation, Erikson's seventh stage, occurs in middle adulthood. A main concern in middle adulthood is to assist and guide the younger generation in developing and leading useful lives—this is what Erikson means by *generativity* (Pratt & others, 2001). The feeling of having done nothing to help the next generation is *stagnation.*

Integrity versus despair, Erikson's eighth stage, occurs in late adulthood. In the later years of life, we look back and evaluate what we have done with our lives. If the older adult has resolved many of the earlier stages negatively, looking back likely will produce doubt or gloom—the *despair* Erikson speaks of. But if the older adult has successfully negotiated most or all of the previous stages of development, the looking

rewarding relationships. They may deliberately withdraw from social contact with individuals on the fringes of their lives. This narrowing of social interaction maximizes positive emotional experiences and minimizes emotional risks as individuals become older. Researchers have found support for this theory (Lang & Carstensen, 1994; Lee & Markides, 1990).

Researchers also have found that the emotional lives of older adults are more positive than previously believed (Ryan & LaGuardia, 2000). In one study of everyday emotions in individuals from early through late adulthood, researchers gave participants electronic pagers to carry for 1 week (Carstensen, Pasupathi, & Mayr, 1998). The participants were paged at random 35 times, and they recorded their emotions at each paging. Positive emotions (such as joy) were reported about equally across the adult years. Negative emotions (such as anger) were highest in young adults and lowest in older adults. In another study, the percentage of emotional material that individuals recalled increased with age (see figure 4.34).

Positive Psychology and Aging

Until fairly recently, middle-aged and older adults were perceived as enduring a long decline in physical, cognitive, and socioemotional functioning, and the positive dimensions of aging were ignored (Antonucci and others, 2000; Rowe & Kahn, 1997). Throughout this section, however, you have seen examples and evidence of successful aging. The earlier stereotypes of aging are being overturned as researchers discover that being a middle-aged or older adult has many positive aspects.

Once developmentalists began focusing on the positive aspects of aging, they discovered that far more robust, healthy middle-aged and older adults are among us than they previously envisioned. A longitudinal study of aging documented some of the ways that positive aging can be attained (Vaillant, 2002). Individuals were assessed at age 50 and then again at 75 to 80 years of age. As shown in figure 4.35, when individuals at 50 years of age were not heavy smokers, did not abuse alcohol, had a stable marriage, engaged in exercise, maintained a normal weight, and had good coping skills, they were more likely to be alive and happy at 75 to 80 years of age.

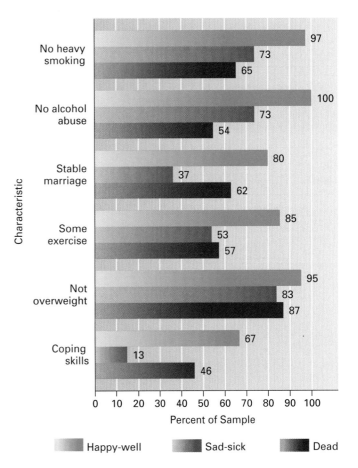

FIGURE 4.35 Linkage Between Characteristics at Age 50 and Health and Happiness at Age 75 to 80 In a longitudinal study, the characteristics shown at age 50 were related to whether individuals were happy-well, sad-sick, or dead at age 75 to 80 (Vaillant, 2002).

Review and Sharpen Your Thinking

4 *Discuss adult development and the positive dimensions of aging.*

- Describe physical development throughout adulthood.
- Identify major changes in cognitive development in adulthood.
- Discuss the main aspects of socioemotional development in adulthood.
- Summarize the positive view of aging that now exists.

For study tools related to this learning goal, see the Study Guide, the CD-ROM, and the Online Learning Center.

Suppose that you wanted to construct a test for "wisdom" that would be fair to adults of all ages. Write down two or three questions or items that you would want to include in your test.

Human Development

1 EXPLORING HUMAN DEVELOPMENT

What Is Development?

Do Early Experiences Rule Us for Life?

How Do Nature and Nurture Influence Development?

2 CHILD DEVELOPMENT

Prenatal Development

Cognitive Development in Childhood

Positive Psychology and Children's Development

Physical Development in Childhood

Socioemotional Development in Childhood

3 ADOLESCENCE

Positive Psychology and Adolescents

Cognitive Development in Adolescence

At-Risk Youth

Physical Development in Adolescence

Socioemotional Development in Adolescence

4 ADULT DEVELOPMENT AND AGING

Physical Development in Adulthood

Socioemotional Development in Adulthood

Cognitive Development in Adulthood

Positive Psychology and Aging

1 Explain how psychologists think about development.

- Development refers to the pattern of change in human capabilities that begins at conception and continues throughout the life span. Important developmental processes are biological (the person's physical nature), cognitive (thought, intelligence, and language), and socioemotional (relationships, emotion, and personality).

- Developmental psychologists debate the extent to which early experience (as in infancy or early childhood) is more important than later experience in development. Most agree that both early and later experiences influence development.

- Both nature (biological inheritance) and nurture (environmental experience) influence development extensively. However, people are at the mercy of neither their genes nor their environment when they actively construct optimal experiences.

2 Describe children's development from conception to adolescence.

- Prenatal development progresses through the germinal, embryonic, and fetal periods. Certain drugs, such as alcohol, can have an adverse effect on the fetus. Preterm birth is another potential problem, especially if the infant is very small or grows up in an adverse environment.

- The newborn comes into the world with several genetically "wired" reflexes, including grasping and sucking. The infant's physical development is dramatic in the first year, and a number of motor milestones are reached in infancy. Motor behaviors are assembled for perceiving and acting, drawing on the infant's physical abilities, perceptual skills, and factors in the environment. Extensive changes in the brain, including denser connections between synapses, take place in infancy and childhood.

- In Piaget's view, children use schemas to actively construct their world, either assimilating new information into existing schemas or adjusting schemas to accommodate it. Piaget also said that people go through four stages of cognitive development: (1) the sensorimotor stage (birth to 2 years of age), (2) the preoperational stage (2 to 7 years of age), (3) the concrete operational stage (7 to 11 years of age), and (4) the formal operational stage (11 to 15 years of age through adulthood). Piaget opened up new ways of looking at how children's minds develop, and he gave us the model of a child as an active, constructivist thinker. However, critics believe that Piaget's stages are too rigid and do not adequately take into account the influence of culture and education on cognitive development.

- Erikson presented a major, eight-stage psychosocial view of life-span development; its first four stages occur in childhood. In each stage, the individual seeks to resolve a particular socioemotional conflict. Other researchers have focused on specific aspects of socioemotional development in childhood. For instance, Bowlby and Ainsworth theorized that the first year of life is crucial for the formation of a secure attachment between infant and caregiver. Development also depends on temperament, an individual's behavioral style or characteristic way of responding. Among the important aspects of parenting are parenting style, divorce, and positive parenting. The family is an important context for children's development, but other social contexts such as peers, schools, neighborhood quality, and culture are also important. Kohlberg proposed a major cognitive-developmental theory of moral development with three levels (preconventional, conventional, and postconventional) and two stages at each level. Gilligan presented an alternative view of moral development that emphasizes interpersonal relationships more heavily than Kohlberg's theory does. Finally, gender development includes biology, social experience, and cognitive factors.

- Positive psychology emphasizes children's resiliency and focuses on improving children's lives.

3 Identify the most important changes that occur in adolescence.

- Positive psychology views adolescence as a time of evaluation, decision making, and commitment. Adolescents are not all alike, but the majority of them develop competently.

- Puberty is a period of rapid skeletal and sexual maturation that occurs mainly in early adolescence. It occurs about two years earlier in girls than in boys. Hormonal changes lie at the core of pubertal development.

- According to Piaget, cognitive development in adolescence is characterized by the appearance of formal operational thought, the final stage in his theory. He believed that children enter this stage between 11 and 15 years of age. This stage involves abstract, idealistic, and logical thought. Hypothetical-deductive reasoning is Piaget's term for adolescents' logical thought. Another key feature of cognitive development, especially in early adolescence, is egocentric thought.

- One of the most important aspects of socioemotional development in adolescence is identity. Erikson's fifth stage of psychosocial development is identity versus identity confusion. Marcia proposed four statuses of identity based on crisis and commitment. A special concern is the development of ethnic identity. Successful programs for intervening in adolescent problems involve individual attention and community-wide interventions.

4 ## Discuss adult development and the positive dimensions of aging.

- Most adults reach their peak physical performance during their 20s and also are the healthiest then. However, physical skills begin to decline during the 30s. Changes in physical appearance are among the most visible signs of aging in middle adulthood. Menopause, which also takes place during middle adulthood, has been stereotyped as more negative than it actually is. The cellular-clock and free-radical theories are two important cellular theories of aging. Alzheimer's disease is a special concern. Even in late adulthood, the brain has remarkable repair capacity and plasticity.

- Piaget argued that no new cognitive changes occur in adulthood. However, some psychologists have proposed that the idealistic thinking of adolescents is replaced by the more realistic, pragmatic thinking of young adults. Horn argued that crystallized intelligence increases in middle age, whereas fluid intelligence declines. Schaie conducted a longitudinal study of intelligence and found that many cognitive skills reach their peak in middle age. Overall, older adults do not do as well on memory and other cognitive tasks and are slower to process information than younger adults. But older adults may have greater wisdom than younger adults.

- Erikson's three stages of socioemotional development in adulthood are intimacy versus isolation (early adulthood), generativity versus stagnation (middle adulthood), and integrity versus despair (late adulthood). Career and work become central themes in the life of young adults. Lifestyles, marriage, and commitment also become important aspects of adult life for most people. In middle adulthood, people begin to realize the limits of their ideals and dreams. Levinson proposed that a majority of people experience midlife crises as a result, but researchers have found that only a small percentage of middle-aged adults experience such a crisis. Nevertheless, a special concern, beginning in the 50s, is understanding the meaning of life. Researchers have found that remaining active increases the likelihood that older adults will be happier and healthier. They also have found that older adults often reduce their general social affiliations. Instead, they are motivated to spend more time with close friends and family members.

- The positive dimensions of aging were largely ignored until recently. Developmentalists now recognize that many adults can sustain or even improve their functioning as they age.

Key Terms

development, p. 119
genotype, p. 121
phenotype, p. 121
nature, p. 122
nurture, p. 122
schema, p. 128
assimilation, p. 128
accommodation, p. 129
sensorimotor stage, p. 129

preoperational stage, p. 130
concrete operational stage, p. 131
formal operational stage, p. 133
attachment, p. 136
imprinting, p. 137
secure attachment, p. 137
temperament, p. 138

authoritarian parenting, p. 139
authoritative parenting, p. 139
neglectful parenting, p. 139
indulgent parenting, p. 139
androgens, p. 145
estrogens, p. 146

gender role, p. 147
puberty, p. 151
identity versus identity confusion, p. 153
crystallized intelligence, p. 162
fluid intelligence, p. 162
wisdom, p. 164

Apply Your Knowledge

1. The possibility of human cloning has received extensive media coverage. If you could clone yourself, your clone would have the same genetic makeup as you have. Take a quick survey of some of your friends to ask whether they would clone themselves if they were given the opportunity. Ask them to explain their answers and critically examine their reasons, keeping in mind the lessons on nature and nurture in the text. Do you think the phenotype of your clone would most resemble you physically, cognitively, or socioemotionally?

2. Find a copy of a popular child-rearing book. Read a few pages and comment on how the perspective on children's development in the popular book relates to the scientific perspectives on children's development in the text. Are all perspectives represented, or does one view dominate?

3. The text discusses development during childhood, adolescence, and adulthood. How are the boundaries across these periods defined, and how would you decide which phase of development best describes you?

4. Visit the website of the National Center for Health Statistics maintained by the Centers for Disease Control and Prevention (http://www.cdc.gov/nchs/about/otheract/aging/trendsoverview.htm) and examine one or more of the aging trends described. How well do these trends correspond to your perception of what happens as we age?

5. Recent genetic advances have offered the possibility of expanding the human life span. Consider the physical, cognitive, and socioemotional changes of adulthood described in the text, and discuss what might happen to these psychological functions if the human life span increases significantly.

Connections

For extra help in mastering the material in this chapter, see the review sections and practice quizzes in the Student Study Guide, the CD-ROM, and the Online Learning Center.

5 Sensation and Perception

Chapter Outline

Learning Goals

HOW WE SENSE AND PERCEIVE THE WORLD　**1**

Detecting, Processing, and Interpreting Experiences
▼
Sensory Receptors and the Brain
▼
Thresholds
▼
Signal Detection Theory
▼
Perceiving Sensory Stimuli
▼
Sensory Adaptation

Discuss basic principles of sensation and perception.

THE VISUAL SYSTEM　**2**

The Visual Stimulus and the Eye
▼
Visual Processing in the Brain
▼
Color Vision
▼
Perceiving Shape, Depth, Motion, and Constancy
▼
Illusions

Explain how the visual system enables us to see and, by communicating with the brain, to perceive the world.

THE AUDITORY SYSTEM　**3**

The Nature of Sound and How We Experience It
▼
Structures and Functions of the Ear
▼
Theories of Hearing
▼
Auditory Processing in the Brain
▼
Localizing Sound
▼
Noise Pollution

Understand how the auditory system registers sound and how it connects with the brain to perceive it.

OTHER SENSES　**4**

The Skin Senses
▼
The Chemical Senses
▼
The Kinesthetic and Vestibular Senses

Know how the skin, chemical, and kinesthetic and vestibular senses work.

PERCEPTION AND HUMAN FACTORS PSYCHOLOGY　**5**

Describe what human factors psychologists do.

Blind people sometimes achieve greatness through the medium of sound. In 1950, the newly born Steveland Morris was placed in an incubator in which he was given too much oxygen. The result was permanent blindness. In 1962, as 12-year-old singer and musician Stevie Wonder, he began a performing and recording career that has included such hits as "My Cherie Amour" and "Signed, Sealed, Delivered." At the beginning of the twenty-first century, his music is still perceived by many as "wondrous."

At age 12, Andrea Bocelli lost his sight in a soccer mishap. Today, now in his 40s and after a career as a lawyer, Andrea has taken the music world by storm with his magnificent, classically trained voice. Although Bocelli's and Stevie Wonder's accomplishments are great, it is extremely difficult for an individual lacking either vision or hearing to do all of the things that a hearing, sighted person can do. Yet people who lose one channel of sensation—such as vision—often adapt and compensate for the loss by enhancing their sensory skills in another area—such as hearing or touch. For example, researchers have found that blind individuals are more accurate at locating a sound source and have greater sensitivity to touch than sighted individuals (Levanen & Hamdorf, 2001; Lessard & others, 1998). Other studies indicate that the auditory cortex of deaf individuals becomes more responsive to touch than does this area of the brain in normal hearing individuals (Levanen & others, 1998).

These changes illustrate an important point made in chapter 3: how *adaptive* the brain is.

In this chapter, I explore the processes of sensation and perception. A general introduction to basic concepts of sensation and perception leads to a detailed discussion of vision, the sense that scientists know the most about. Then I examine hearing, the skin senses, taste and smell, and the kinesthetic and vestibular senses. Finally, I touch on the area of human factors to see how it applies information about sensation and perception to designing equipment and machines that are more compatible with human capabilities.

Two "sensations": Stevie Wonder and Andrea Bocelli. *How have they adapted to life without sight?*

1 HOW WE SENSE AND PERCEIVE THE WORLD

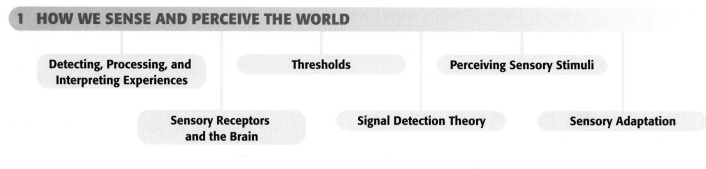

Detecting, Processing, and Interpreting Experiences

Thresholds

Perceiving Sensory Stimuli

Sensory Receptors and the Brain

Signal Detection Theory

Sensory Adaptation

How do we detect and perceive the world around us?

When Stevie Wonder's hands touch the keys of a piano, his brain recognizes the sensation and directs his fingers to press one or more of the keys, and he begins to play. The brain automatically interprets the information it receives from the fingers as they feel the piano keys and responds to its sensation. What may seem like the simple act of playing one note on the piano, however, is really the outcome of two complex, virtually inseparable processes: sensation and perception.

Detecting, Processing, and Interpreting Experiences

sensation The process of receiving stimulus energies from the environment.

Sensation is the process of receiving stimulus energies from the external environment. Stimuli consist of physical energy—light, sound, and heat, for example. A stimulus is detected by specialized receptor cells in the sense organs—eyes, ears, skin, nose, and tongue. When the receptor cells have registered a stimulus, the energy is converted to an electrochemical impulse. The process of transforming physical energy into electrochemical energy is called **transduction.** Transduction produces an action potential that relays information about the stimulus through the nervous system to the brain. When it reaches the brain, the information travels to the appropriate area of the cerebral cortex (Sekular & Blake, 2002).

The brain gives meaning to sensation through perception. **Perception** is the process of organizing and interpreting sensory information to give it meaning. Receptor cells in our eyes record a silver object in the sky, but they do not "see" a jet plane; receptor cells in the ear vibrate in a particular way, but they do not "hear" a symphony. Finding meaningful patterns in sensory information is perception. Sensing and perceiving give us three-dimensional views of the setting sun, the sounds of a scintillating rock concert, the touch of soft caresses, the taste of sweets, and the smells of flowers and peppermint.

Bottom-Up and Top-Down Processing Psychologists distinguish between bottom-up and top-down processing in sensation and perception. In **bottom-up processing,** sensory receptors register information about the external environment and send it up to the brain for analysis and interpretation. Bottom-up processing is initiated by stimulus input (Sun, 2002; Sussman & others, 2001). **Top-down processing** starts out with cognitive processing at the higher levels of the brain (Miyashita & Hayashi, 2000). These cognitive processes include knowledge, beliefs, and expectations. Thus top-down processing does not start with the detection of a stimulus, as bottom-up processing does.

When Stevie Wonder's hands touch the keys of a piano and he hears a sound resulting from the pressure he places on the keys, bottom-up processing is taking place. When he listens to a recording of one of his songs and modifies the song based on his past music experience, top-down processing is occurring. Clearly, both bottom-up and top-down processing take place in sensing and perceiving the world. By themselves, our ears provide only incoming information about sound in the environment. Only when we consider both what the ears hear (bottom-up processing) and what the brain interprets (top-down processing) can we fully understand how we perceive sounds in our world.

Let's look at another example in which bottom-up and top-down processing might be involved: a jigsaw puzzle (Friedrich, 2001). If you have ever tried to put together a jigsaw puzzle without the puzzle's original box, you understand how difficult it is to finish the puzzle without knowing what the finished picture looks like. Basically, you have to proceed on the basis of the shapes and colors of the pieces to determine how they fit together. That is essentially bottom-up processing. However, if you have a picture of the finished product, you can select a particular area to work on. For example, if you know that there will be a castle on the right side of the puzzle, you can go through the pieces and pick out in advance those that look like they are part of a castle. That makes your task of fitting the pieces together much easier—you have fewer to work with and have a general idea of how they should look once they are put together. Your selection process based on prior knowledge is an example of top-down processing.

In everyday life, the two processes of sensation and perception are virtually inseparable. The brain automatically perceives the information it receives from the sense organs. For this reason, most psychologists refer to sensation and perception as a unified information processing system (Goldstein, 2002).

The Purpose of Perception Important insights about perception can be gained by asking the simple question What is its purpose? According to a leading expert in this field, David Marr (1982), the purpose of perception is to represent information from the outside world internally. For example, the purpose of vision is to create a three-dimensional representation or map of the world in the brain.

transduction The process of transforming physical energy into electrochemical energy.

perception The brain's process of organizing and interpreting sensory information to give it meaning.

bottom-up processing Processing that begins with sensory receptors registering environmental information and sending it to the brain for integration and cognitive processing.

top-down processing Processing of perceptual information that starts out with cognitive processing at the higher levels of the brain.

Anableps microlepis, a fish with four eyes. Two eyes allow it to observe the world above water, two the world below water, as it swims just at the surface of the water. *Why was this evolutionary adaptation developed?*

From an evolutionary perspective, the purpose of sensation and perception is adaptation that improves a species' chances for survival. An organism must be able to sense and respond quickly and accurately to events in the immediate environment, such as the approach of a predator, the presence of prey, or the appearance of a potential mate. Thus it is not surprising that most animals—from goldfish to elephants to humans—have eyes and ears, as well as sensitivities to touch and chemicals (smell and taste). However, a close comparison of sensory systems in animals reveals that each species is exquisitely adapted to the habitat in which it evolved.

A marvelous example of evolutionary accomplishment appears in a fish called *Anableps microlepis,* which has four eyes! To survive, *Anableps microlepis* swims just at the surface of the water, with two aerial eyes monitoring the visual field above the water and two aquatic eyes monitoring the visual field underwater. This remarkable adaptation enables *Anableps microlepis* to search for food while watching for predators.

Sensory Receptors and the Brain

All sensation begins with sensory receptors. **Sensory receptors** are specialized cells that detect and transmit stimulus information to sensory (afferent) nerves and the brain (Lewis, 2001). Sensory receptors are the openings through which the brain and nervous system experience the world. Figure 5.1 shows the types of sensory receptors for each of the five senses in humans.

The sensory receptors of every animal species have evolved to fit their environments. For example, the sensory receptors that a bat uses to find food are very different from but no more specialized than those that an eagle uses. Bats use sound to locate prey at night, whereas eagles hunt with their eyes from great heights to avoid detection from potential prey.

Figure 5.2 depicts the general flow of information from the environment to the brain. Sensory receptors trigger action potentials in sensory neurons, which carry that information to the central nervous system. Recall from chapter 3 that an action potential is the brief wave of electrical charge that sweeps down the axon of a neuron for possible transmission to another neuron. The action potentials of all sensory nerves are alike, which raises an intriguing question: How can an animal distinguish sight, sound, odor, taste, and touch? The answer is that sensory receptors are selective and

sensory receptors Specialized cells that detect and transmit stimulus information to sensory neurons and the brain.

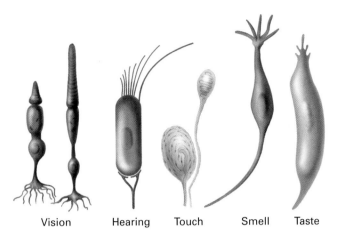

Vision   Hearing   Touch   Smell   Taste

have different neural pathways. They are specialized to absorb a particular type of energy—light energy, mechanical energy (such as sound vibrations), or chemical energy, for example—and transduce (convert) it into the electrochemical energy of an action potential.

Humans have multiple receptors that provide a rich tapestry of sensations (Lewis, 2001). Your skin, for example, contains 4 million pain receptors, 500,000 pressure receptors, 150,000 receptors for cold, and 16,000 receptors for heat. Specialized receptors in the joints, ligaments, and muscles produce information that is combined with information from other sensory receptors, such as those in the eyes and ears, to give us a sense of where certain body parts are in relation to other body parts. Thus—although vision, hearing, touch, taste, and smell are the five most commonly described senses—the nervous system blends these into a wider spectrum of sensations.

The sense organs and sensory receptors fall into several main classes based on the type of energy that is transmitted. These include

- *Photoreception* (detection of light, perceived as sight)
- *Mechanoreception* (detection of pressure, vibration, and movement perceived as touch, hearing, and equilibrium)
- *Chemoreception* (detection of chemical stimuli detected as smell and taste)

Thus, when Andrea Bocelli hears the audience applauding one of his performances, sensory receptors in his ears pick up the sound in the form of mechanical energy and transduce it into electrochemical energy, which the brain perceives as applause.

FIGURE 5.2 **Information Flow in Senses** The diagram shows a general flow of sensory information from energy stimulus to sensory receptor cells to sensory neuron to sensation and perception.

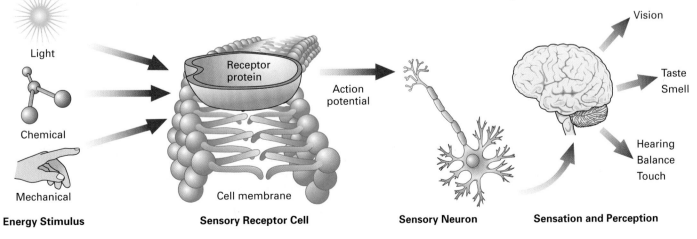

Light

Chemical

Mechanical

Energy Stimulus

Receptor protein

Action potential

Cell membrane

Sensory Receptor Cell

Sensory Neuron

Vision

Taste
Smell

Hearing
Balance
Touch

Sensation and Perception

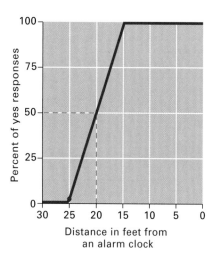

FIGURE 5.3 Measuring Absolute Threshold Absolute threshold is the minimum amount of energy we can detect. To measure absolute threshold, psychologists have arbitrarily decided to use the criterion of detecting the stimulus 50 percent of the time. In this graph, the person's absolute threshold for detecting the ticking clock is at a distance of 20 feet.

psychophysics The field that studies links between the physical properties of stimuli and a person's experience of them.

absolute threshold The minimum amount of stimulus energy that people can detect.

In the brain, nearly all sensory signals go through the thalamus. Recall from chapter 3 that the thalamus is the brain's great relay station. From the thalamus, the signals go to the sensory areas of the cerebral cortex, where they are modified and distributed throughout a vast network of neurons.

Also recall from chapter 3 that certain areas of the cerebral cortex are specialized to handle different sensory functions. Visual information is processed mainly in the occipital lobes, hearing in the temporal lobes, and pain, touch, and temperature in the parietal lobes. Keep in mind, however, that the interactions and pathways of sensory information are complex, and the brain often must coordinate extensive information and interpret it (Sejnowski, 2001). Vision and the other senses evolved to help animals solve important problems, such as knowing when to flee and understanding how to build a shelter. Large numbers of sensory neurons make this behavior possible. As they do so, they allow us to perceive the world in a unified way.

An important part of perception is figuring out what the sensory messages mean (Pines, 2001). Many top-down factors determine this meaning, including signals from different parts of the brain, prior learning, the person's goals, and how aroused the person is. Moving in the opposite direction, bottom-up signals from a sensory area may help other parts of the brain maintain arousal, form an image of where the body is in space, or regulate movement.

Thresholds

How close does an approaching bumblebee have to be before you can hear its buzzing? How far away from a brewing coffeepot can you be and still detect the smell of coffee? How different does the percentage of fat in the "low-fat" and "regular" versions of your favorite ice cream have to be for you to taste a difference?

Questions like these are answered by **psychophysics,** the field that studies links between the physical properties of stimuli and a person's experience of them. (For example, an experiment in psychophysics might examine the relation between the rate at which a light flashes and a participant's ability to see individual flashes.)

Absolute Threshold Any sensory system must have the ability to detect varying degrees of energy in the environment. This energy can take the form of light, sound, chemical, or mechanical stimulation. How much of a stimulus is necessary for you to see, hear, taste, smell, or feel something? One way to address this question is to assume that there is an **absolute threshold,** or minimum amount of energy that a person can detect. When the energy of a stimulus falls below this absolute threshold, we cannot detect its presence; when the energy of the stimulus rises above the absolute threshold, we can detect the stimulus. An experiment with a clock will help you understand the principle of absolute threshold. Find a clock that ticks; put it on a table and walk far enough across the room so that you no longer hear it ticking. Then gradually move toward the clock. At some point you will begin to hear it ticking. Hold your position and notice that occasionally the ticking fades, and you may have to move forward to reach the threshold; at other times it may become loud, and you can move backward.

In this experiment, if you measure your absolute threshold several times, you likely will record several different distances for detecting the stimulus. For example, the first time you try it, you might hear the ticking at 25 feet from the clock. But you probably won't hear it every time at 25 feet. Maybe you hear it only 38 percent of the time at this distance, but you hear it 50 percent of the time at 20 feet away and 65 percent of the time at 15 feet. Also, people have different thresholds, because some people have better hearing than others and some people have better vision than others. Figure 5.3 shows one person's measured absolute threshold for detecting a clock's ticking sound. Psychologists have arbitrarily decided that absolute threshold is the point at which the individual detects the stimulus 50 percent of the time—in this case 20 feet away. Using the same clock, another person might have a measured

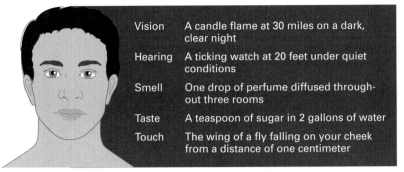

Vision	A candle flame at 30 miles on a dark, clear night
Hearing	A ticking watch at 20 feet under quiet conditions
Smell	One drop of perfume diffused throughout three rooms
Taste	A teaspoon of sugar in 2 gallons of water
Touch	The wing of a fly falling on your cheek from a distance of one centimeter

FIGURE 5.4 **Approximate Absolute Thresholds for Five Senses**

absolute threshold of 26 feet, and yet another, 18 feet. The approximate absolute thresholds of five different senses are listed in figure 5.4.

Under ideal circumstances, our senses have very low absolute thresholds, and so we can be remarkably good at detecting small amounts of stimulus energy. You can demonstrate this to yourself by using a sharp pencil point to carefully lift a single hair on your forearm. Most people can easily detect this tiny bit of pressure on the skin. You might be surprised to learn that the human eye can see a candle flame at 30 miles on a dark, clear night. But our environment seldom gives us ideal conditions to detect stimuli. If the night is cloudy or the air is polluted, for example, you would have to be much closer to see the flicker of a candle flame. And other lights on the horizon—car or house lights—would hinder your ability to detect the candle's flame. **Noise** is the term given to irrelevant and competing stimuli. For example, suppose someone speaks to you from the doorway of the room in which you are sitting. You might fail to respond because your roommate is talking on the phone and a CD player is blaring out your favorite song. We usually think of noise as being auditory, but the psychological meaning of *noise* also involves other senses. Air pollution, cloudiness, car lights, and house lights are forms of visual noise that hamper your ability to see a candle flame from a great distance.

Subliminal Perception   Is it possible to experience sensations at levels below your absolute threshold without being aware of them? **Subliminal perception**—the ability to detect information below the level of conscious awareness—fascinates us. In one of the bizarre moments in the year 2000 presidential campaign, someone took a close look at a Republican TV commercial criticizing then Vice President Al Gore's Medicare proposal. The word "RATS" flashed for $\frac{1}{30}$ of a second across the phrase "The Gore prescription plan: Bureaucrats decide." Presidential candidate George W. Bush's campaign team did its best to make light of the situation, but, clearly, someone in the Bush campaign had intended to broadcast an unflattering subliminal label for the Democratic candidate.

Also, when Tiger Woods was a young boy, he played subliminal motivational tapes while he was asleep at night in the hope that they would improve his golf game. Just how effective are such strategies?

An experiment by Carol Fowler and her colleagues (1981) provides some evidence that people can process information beneath their awareness. In this study, words were shown on a screen so rapidly that the participants could not tell what they were seeing. Subsequently, they were shown two words (such as *hotel* and *book*) and asked which was most like the subliminally presented word (*lodge*). Somewhat amazingly, the participants answered most questions correctly. These results suggest that subliminal perception is possible. More recent research has verified that people's performance is affected by stimuli that are too faint to be recognized at a conscious level (Allen, Kraus, & Bradlow, 2000; Greenwald & others, 1996; Monahan, Murphy, & Zajonc, 2000).

noise Irrelevant and competing stimuli.

subliminal perception The ability to detect information below the level of conscious awareness

Mötley Crüe's *Shout at the Devil* album has been a target of groups who believe that backward messages are embedded in songs. The protesters say that this album has the phrase *Backward mask where are you, oh. Lost in error, Satan.* However, researchers have been unable to find any evidence whatsoever that these and other satanic messages are encoded in the music or that, if they are, they can influence behavior.

A controversial application of subliminal perception research involves the purported insertion of subliminal messages in recordings of rock music. Some people claim that the records and tapes of some rock groups, when played backward, contain messages from Satan. In theory, when the record is played normally (forward), the messages cannot be consciously perceived, but they influence our behavior in a subliminal way. Researchers have been unable to find any evidence whatsoever that such messages exist or, if they do, that they influence our behavior (McIver, 1988). Even if we were to take a very clearly recorded sentence and play it backward, no one could tell what it said. Investigators have found that people's perceptions of whether or not these messages exist is largely a function of what they expect to hear. In one experiment, when told beforehand that a message of a satanic nature would influence them, participants were likely to hear the message. With no such expectation, participants did not hear the message (Vokey & Read, 1985). In another study, individuals failed to perceive any information in subliminal self-help auditory tapes (Moore, 1995).

What can we make of the claims of subliminal perception enthusiasts and of the research conducted by experimental psychologists? First, weak sensory stimuli can be registered by sensory receptors and is possibly encoded in the brain at a level beneath conscious awareness. Second, no evidence supports the claims of advertisers and rock music critics that such sensory registry and neural encoding have any influence on our thoughts and behavior. Rather, evidence suggests that we are influenced extensively by those sounds and views we are consciously aware of and can attend to efficiently (Smith & Rogers, 1994).

Difference Threshold In addition to studying how much energy is required for a stimulus to be detected, psychologists investigate the degree of *difference* that must exist between two stimuli before the difference is detected. This is the **difference threshold,** or *just noticeable difference.* An artist might detect the difference between two similar shades of color. A tailor might determine a difference in the texture of two fabrics. How different must the colors and textures be to determine the difference? Just as the absolute threshold is determined by a 50 percent detection rate, the difference threshold is the smallest difference in stimulation required to discriminate one stimulus from another 50 percent of the time.

difference threshold Also called *just noticeable difference,* this concept refers to the smallest difference in stimulation required to discriminate one stimulus from another 50 percent of the time.

An important aspect of difference thresholds is that the threshold increases with the magnitude of the stimulus. When music is playing softly, you may notice when your roommate increases the volume by even a small amount. But if he or she turns the volume up an equal amount when the music is playing very loudly, you may not notice. More than 150 years ago, E. H. Weber, a German psychologist, noticed that, regardless of their magnitude, two stimuli must differ by a constant proportion to be detected. **Weber's law** is the principle that two stimuli must differ by a constant minimum percentage, rather than a constant amount, to be perceived as different. Weber's law generally holds true. For example, we add 1 candle to 60 candles and notice a difference in the brightness of the candles; we add 1 candle to 120 candles and do not notice a difference. We discover, though, that adding 2 candles to 120 candles does produce a difference in brightness. Adding 2 candles to 120 candles is the same proportionately as adding 1 candle to 60 candles. The exact proportion varies with the stimulus involved. For example, a change of 3 percent in a tone's pitch can be detected, but a 20 percent change is required for a person to detect a difference in taste, and a 25 percent change in smell is required.

Signal Detection Theory

Nearly all reasoning and decision making takes place with some degree of uncertainty. One theory about perception—**signal detection theory**—focuses on decision making about stimuli in the presence of uncertainty. In signal detection theory, detection of sensory stimuli depends on a variety of factors besides the physical intensity of the stimulus and the sensory abilities of the observer. These factors include individual and contextual variations such as fatigue, expectancy, and the urgency of the moment (Kiernan & others, 2001; Phillips, Saks, & Peterson, 2001).

Consider the case of two air traffic controllers with exactly the same sensory ability to detect blips on a radar screen. One is monitoring the radar screen while working overtime late into the night and feeling fatigued. The other is watching the screen in the morning after having a good night's sleep. The fatigued radar operator fails to see a blip indicating that a small private plane is flying too close to a large passenger jet, and the two collide. However, in a similar situation, the well-rested controller detects a private plane intruding in the air space of a large passenger jet and contacts the small private plane's pilot, who then changes course. Consider also the circumstance of two individuals at a dentist's office. One begins to "feel" pain the instant the drill touches the tooth's surface; the other doesn't "feel" pain until the dentist drills deep into a cavity.

Signal detection theory provides a precise language and graphic representation for analyzing decision making in the presence of uncertainty. To see how signal detection theory works, consider the following medical context (Heeger, 1997). A radiologist is scanning an image of the brain created by magnetic resonance imaging (MRI) to determine if a tumor is present. Either there is a tumor (signal present) or there is not (signal absent). Either the radiologist sees the tumor (responding "yes") or does not (responding "no"). This leads to four possible outcomes: (1) hit (tumor present and doctor says, "Yes, I see it"), (2) miss (tumor present and doctor says, "No, I don't see it"), (3) false alarm (tumor absent and doctor says, "Yes, I see it"), and (4) correct rejection (tumor absent and doctor says, "No, I don't see it"; see figure 5.5).

There are two main components to the decision-making process in signal detection theory: information acquisition and criterion. In terms of *information acquisition,* the question is What information is in the image produced by the brain scan? For example, a healthy brain has a characteristic shape. The presence of a tumor might distort that shape. Tumors might have different image characteristics, such as brightness or darkness or a difference in texture.

The *criterion* component of signal detection theory is the basis for making a judgment about the information that is available. That is, responses depend on the criterion that decision makers set for determining whether a stimulus is present or not.

What is the nature of signal detection theory? How might signal detection theory be applied to a physician's decision making?

Weber's law The principle that two stimuli must differ by a constant minimum percentage (rather than a constant amount) to be perceived as different.

signal detection theory Focuses on decision making about stimuli in the presence of uncertainty; detection depends on a variety of factors besides the physical intensity of the stimulus and the sensory abilities of the observer.

	Observer's Response	
	"Yes, I see it"	*"No, I don't see it"*
Signal Present	Hit (correct)	Miss (mistake)
Signal Absent	False alarm (mistake)	Correct rejection (correct)

FIGURE 5.5 **Four Outcomes in Signal Detection**

The criterion depends on more than the information provided by the environmental stimuli. For example, in addition to relying on technology or testing to provide information, doctors also make judgments about the information. They may feel that different types of errors are not equal. For example, a doctor may believe that missing an opportunity for early diagnosis may mean the difference between life and death, whereas a false alarm may simply result in a routine biopsy operation. This type of doctor may err on the side of "yes" (tumor present) decisions. However, other doctors may believe that unnecessary surgeries, even routine biopsies, should not be done because of the expense, the stress, and so on. This type of doctor may tend to be more conservative and say "no" (tumor absent) more often. This doctor may miss more tumors but will reduce unnecessary surgeries. The conservative doctor also may believe that if a tumor is present, it will be detected in time on the next checkup.

Perceiving Sensory Stimuli

As we just saw, the perception of stimuli is influenced by more than the characteristics of the environmental stimuli themselves. Important factors in perceiving sensory stimuli are attention and perceptual set.

Attention   The world holds a lot of information to perceive. Right now you are perceiving the letters and words that make up this sentence. Now look around you and pick out something other than this book to look at. Afterward curl up the toes on your right foot. In each of these circumstances, you engaged in **selective attention,** which involves focusing on a specific aspect of experience while ignoring others. A familiar example of selective attention is the ability to focus on one voice among many in a crowded room or a noisy restaurant. Psychologists call this common occurrence the "cocktail party effect."

Research suggests that people's daily lifestyle influences how they perceive visual details. (Around the Globe)

mhhe com/ **santrockp7**

Not only is attention selective, but it also is *shiftable.* For example, if someone calls your name in a crowded room, you can shift your attention to that person. Or if you go to an art museum, you look at one painting, then another, then others, moving your attention from one painting to the next. And as you look at each painting, you shift your vision from one part of the painting to another, seeking to understand it better. The fact that we can attend selectively to one thing and shift it readily to something else indicates that we must be monitoring many things at once.

Why do we pay attention to some aspects of our experience and block out others? What you attend to is influenced by your motivation and interests. Art is one of my interests, so I will be more likely to attend to an advertisement for an art show than someone who has no interest in art. A person who is interested in sports is more likely to attend to an announcement that a basketball game will be on TV tonight than someone who is not interested in sports. Certain features of stimuli also cause people to attend to them. Novel stimuli (those that are new, different, or unusual) often attract our attention. If a Ferrari convertible whizzes by, you are more likely to notice it than you would a Ford. Size, color, and movement also influence our attention. Objects that are large, vividly colored, or moving are more likely to grab our attention than objects that are small, dull-colored, or stationary.

Highly practiced and familiar stimuli, such as your own name or hometown, often are perceived so automatically that it is almost impossible to ignore them. The *Stroop effect* is an example of an automatic perception whereby it is difficult to name the colors in which words are printed when the words name different colors (Monsell, Taylor, & Murphy, 2001). To experience the Stroop effect, see figure 5.6. Most of the time, the highly practiced and almost automatic perception of word meaning makes reading easier. However, this same automaticity makes it hard to ignore the meaning

selective attention Focusing on a specific aspect of experience while ignoring others.

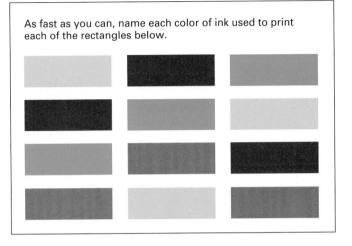

As fast as you can, name each color of ink used to print each of the rectangles below.

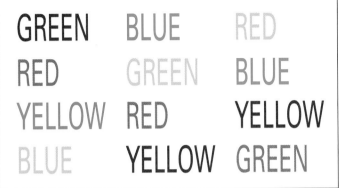

Now, as fast as you can, name the color of ink used to print each word shown below, ignoring what each word says.

GREEN   BLUE   RED

RED   GREEN   BLUE

YELLOW   RED   YELLOW

BLUE   YELLOW   GREEN

of the words for colors (such as blue) when they are printed in a different color (such as orange). Thus the Stroop effect represents a failure of selective attention.

Psychologists also are interested in the top-down and bottom-up processing aspects of attention (Pashler, Johnston, & Ruthruff, 2001). For example, the Stroop effect is an example not only of selective attention but also of *bottom-up processing,* in which attention is stimulus driven (Monahan, 2001). However, attention also involves *top-down processing,* in which attention is not stimulus driven but rather is due to decisions people make to initiate attention. Thus you can make a decision to look at your watch to see how much more time you have to study this book today.

Perceptual Set   Place your hand over the playing cards on the right in the illustration below and look at the playing cards on the left. As quickly as you can, count how many aces of spades you see. Then place your hand over the cards on the left and count the number of aces of spades among the cards on the right.

FIGURE 5.6 The Stroop Effect
Before reading further, read the instructions above and complete the tasks. Now, you probably had little or no difficulty naming the colors of the rectangles in the set on the left. However, you likely stumbled more when you were asked to name the color of ink used to print each word in the set on the right. This demonstration of automaticity in perception is the Stroop effect.

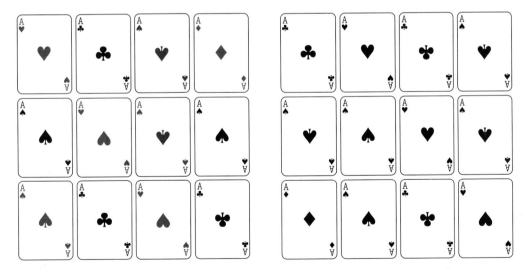

Most people report that they see two or three aces of spades in the set of 12 cards on the left. However, if you look closely, you'll see that there are five. Two of the aces of spades are black and three are red. When people look at the set of 12 cards on the right, they are more likely to count five aces of spades. Why do we perceive the two sets of cards differently? We expect the ace of spades to be black because it is always black in a regular deck of cards. We don't expect it to be red, so we skip right over the red ones. Our expectations influence our perceptions.

Psychologists refer to a predisposition or readiness to perceive something in a particular way as a **perceptual set.** Perceptual sets act as a "psychological" filter in

perceptual set A predisposition or readiness to perceive something in a particular way.

processing information about the environment. Interpretation is another consequence of a perceptual set. Interpretation can occur even before a stimulus or signal appears, as in the case of a runner waiting for a starting signal.

Interestingly, young children are more accurate at the task involving the ace of spades than adults are. Why? Because they have not built up the perceptual set that aces of spades are black. The underestimation of aces of spades in the left set of 12 cards reflects the concept of top-down processing.

Sensory Adaptation

Turning out the lights in your bedroom at night, you stumble across the room to your bed, completely blind to the objects around you. Gradually, the objects in your room reappear and become clearer. The ability of the visual system to adjust to a darkened room is an example of **sensory adaptation**—a change in the responsiveness of the sensory system based on the average level of surrounding stimulation (Durgin, 2000). You have experienced sensory adaptation countless times in your life—adapting to the temperature of a shower, to the water in an initially "freezing" swimming pool, or to the smell of the Thanksgiving dinner that is wonderful to the arriving guests but almost undetectable to the cook who spent all day over it. Although all senses adapt to prolonged stimulation, I use vision as an example to illustrate this topic.

I used the example of adapting to the dark. When you turn out the lights, everything is black. Conversely, when you step out into the bright sunshine after spending some time in a dark basement, your eyes are flooded with light and everything appears light. An important function of the eye is to get a good picture of the world. Good pictures have sharp contrasts between dark and light parts. The pupil of the eye adjusts the amount of light that gets into the eye and therefore helps to preserve the contrast between dark and light areas in our picture. Additionally, structures throughout the visual system adapt. You may have noticed that the change in the size of the pupil as you dim or brighten the lights happens very quickly. You also may have noticed that when you turn out the lights in your bedroom, the contrast between dark and light continues to improve for nearly 45 minutes. The reason is that the sensory receptors in your visual system adapt or adjust their response rates on the basis of the average light level of the surrounding room. This adaptation takes longer than it does for the pupil to adjust. All of these mechanisms allow the visual system to preserve contrast over an extremely large range of background illumination conditions. The price we pay for our ability to adapt to the mean light level is *time*. Driving out of a dark tunnel under a mountain into the glistening and blinding reflection of the sun off the snow reminds us of this trade-off.

mhhe com/ santrockp7

For study tools related to this learning goal, see the Study Guide, the CD-ROM, and the Online Learning Center.

sensory adaptation A change in the responsiveness of the sensory system based on the average level of surrounding stimulation.

Review and Sharpen Your Thinking

1 *Discuss basic principles of sensation and perception.*

- Explain what sensation and perception mean.
- Outline the sensory reception process and define three types of sensory reception.
- Distinguish between absolute threshold and difference threshold, and evaluate subliminal perception.
- Understand how signal detection theory accounts for the effect of uncertainty on perception.
- Discuss these aspects of perception: attention and perceptual set.
- Describe sensory adaptation.

Try the absolute threshold experiment described on p. 180. Discuss your results with others in your class who tried the experiment.

| The Visual Stimulus and the Eye | Color Vision | Illusions |
| Visual Processing in the Brain | Perceiving Shape, Depth, Motion, and Constancy | |

How do we see the world and know what we are seeing?

Dr. P. was a distinguished musician who also taught music. However, he began having difficulty in visually perceiving his world. Sometimes he would fail to recognize his students, whom he had taught for many years, until they spoke. Dr. P. knew who they were by their voices. Aware that there was something wrong with the way he was seeing his world, Dr. P. went to see an opthalmologist. Dr. P. was told that there was nothing wrong with his eyes but that he should see a neurologist. Dr. P. was referred to neurologist Oliver Sacks (1985), who wrote about him in *The Man Who Mistook His Wife for a Hat.* By the time he saw Sacks, nothing was familiar to Dr. P. He actually did confuse his wife with a hat. When shown a glove, Dr. P. said it was a container of some sort, maybe a change purse. Visually, he was lost in a world of lifeless abstractions. In Dr. P.'s case, damage to his brain interfered with his ability to integrate into meaningful wholes what his eyes saw. That is, his eyes detected visual information in the world, but his brain failed to accurately interpret the sensory information. Only when we consider what the eyes see and the brain interprets can we fully understand how people visually perceive the world. The next section explores the physical foundations of the visual system.

The Visual Stimulus and the Eye

Our ability to detect visual stimuli depends on the sensitivity of our eyes to differences in light. This section covers some basic facts about light energy and the complex structure of the eye.

Light *Light* is a form of electromagnetic energy that can be described in terms of wavelengths. Like ocean waves moving toward the beach, light travels through space in waves. The *wavelength* of light is the distance from the peak of one wave to the peak of the next. Wavelengths of visible light range from about 400 to 700 nanometers (a nanometer is 1-billionth of a meter and is abbreviated nm). Outside the range of visible light are longer radio and infrared radiation waves and shorter ultraviolet and X rays (see figure 5.7). These other forms of electromagnetic energy continually bombard us, but we do not see them. Why do we see only the narrow band of electromagnetic energy with wavelengths between 400 and 700 nanometers? The likeliest answer is that our visual system evolved in the sun's light. Thus our visual system is able to perceive the range of energy emitted by the sun. By the time sunlight reaches the earth's surface, it is strongest in the 400 to 700 nanometer range. The wavelength of light that is reflected by a visual stimulus determines its *hue,* or color.

Two other characteristics of light waves are amplitude and purity. *Amplitude* refers to the height of a wave, and it is linked with the brightness of a visual stimulus (see figure 5.8). *Purity,* the mixture of wavelengths in light, is related to the perceived saturation or richness of a visual stimulus. The color tree shown in figure 5.9 can help you to understand saturation. Colors that are very pure have no white light in them. They are located on the outside of the color tree. Notice how the saturation of a color changes toward the interior of the color tree. The closer we get to the center, the more white light has been added to the single wavelength of a particular color. In other words, the deep colors at the edge fade into pastel colors toward the center.

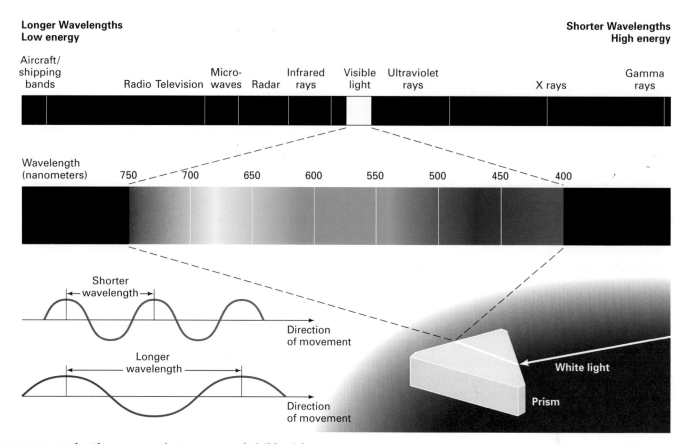

FIGURE 5.7 The Electromagnetic Spectrum and Visible Light (*Top*) Visible light is only a narrow band in the electromagnetic spectrum. Visible light wavelengths range from about 400–700 nm. X rays are much shorter, radio waves much longer. (*Bottom*) The two graphs show how waves vary in length between successive peaks. Shorter wavelengths are higher in frequency, as reflected in blue colors; longer wavelengths are lower in frequency, as reflected in red colors.

Light waves of greater amplitude make up brighter light.

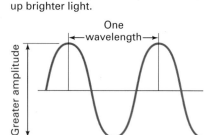

Light waves of smaller amplitude make up dimmer light.

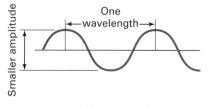

FIGURE 5.8 Light Waves of Varying Amplitude

The Structure of the Eye   The eye, not unlike a camera, is constructed to get the best possible "picture" of the world. Let's see how the eye performs this task.

Getting the Best "Picture" of the World   A good picture is in focus, is not too dark or too light, and has good contrast between the dark and light parts. Each of several structures in the eye plays an important role in this process. If you look closely at your eyes in the mirror, you will notice three parts—the sclera, iris, and pupil (figure 5.10). The *sclera* is the white outer part of the eye that helps to maintain the shape of the eye and to protect it from injury. The *iris* is the colored part of the eye, which might be light blue in one individual and dark brown in another. The *pupil,* which appears black, is the opening in the center of the iris. The iris contains muscles that control the size of the pupil and, hence, the amount of light that gets into the eye. This allows the eye to function optimally under different conditions of illumination, which can range in the course of a normal day from the darkest moonless night to the brightest summer sunshine. To get a good picture of the world, the eye needs to be able to adjust the amount of light that enters. In this sense, the pupil acts like the aperture of a camera, opening to let in more light when it is needed and closing to let in less light when there is too much.

You can demonstrate changes in the size of the pupil by looking at your eyes in the mirror and turning the room lights up and down. (You need to try this experiment in a room with sufficient light to be able to see your eyes even when the lights are turned all the way down.) As you dim the light, your pupils will begin to enlarge to let in more light; as you turn the room lights back up, the pupil opening will shrink to let in less light.

If the eye acts like a camera, then, in addition to having the right amount of light, the image has to be in focus at the back of the eye. Two structures serve this purpose: the *cornea*, which is a clear membrane just in front of the eye, and the *lens* of the eye, which is a transparent and somewhat flexible disklike entity filled with a gelatinous material. The function of both of these structures is to bend the light falling on the surface of the eye just enough to focus it at the back of the eye. The curved surface of the cornea does most of this bending, while the lens fine-tunes the focus. When you are looking at faraway objects, the lens has a relatively flat shape, because the light reaching the eye from faraway objects is parallel and the bending power of the cornea is sufficient to keep things in focus. However, the light reaching the eye from objects that are close is more scattered, and so more bending of the light is required to achieve focus.

Without this ability of the lens to change its curvature, the eye would have a tough time focusing on objects that are close to us, like needlework or reading. As we get older, the lens of our eye begins to lose its flexibility and, hence, its ability to change from its normal flattened shape to the rounder shape needed to bring close objects into focus. This is the reason that many people whose vision is normal throughout their young adult lives will require reading glasses when they get older.

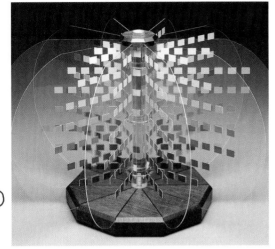

FIGURE 5.9 **A Color Tree Showing Color's Three Dimensions: Hue, Saturation, and Brightness**
Hue is represented around the color tree, saturation horizontally, and brightness vertically.

Recording Images on the Retina   The parts of the eye that have been discussed so far work together to get the best possible picture of the world. All of this effort, however, would be for naught without a method for keeping or "recording" the images we take of the world (De Valois, 2000). In a camera, film serves just such a purpose. Film is made of a material that responds to light. At the back of the eye, the multi-layered **retina** is the light-sensitive surface that records what we see and converts it to neural impulses for processing in the brain.

Making an analogy between the film of a camera and the retina, however, vastly underestimates the complexity and elegance of the retina's design. The retina is, in fact, the primary mechanism of sight, but even after decades of intense study, the full marvel of this structure is far from understood (Masland & Raviola, 2000).

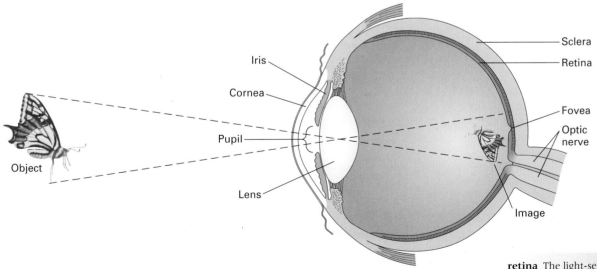

FIGURE 5.10 **Parts of the Eye**
Note that the image of the butterfly on the retina is upside down. The brain allows us to see the image right side up.

retina The light-sensitive surface in the back of the eye that houses light receptors called rods and cones.

FIGURE 5.11 **Rods and Cones**

Because the retina is so important to vision, we need to study its makeup in some detail. Earlier in this chapter, I discussed transduction, the conversion of one form of energy into another. In sensation, stimulus energy is transduced into neural impulses (Reid, 2000). How does transduction occur in vision?

The human retina has approximately 126 million receptor cells. They turn the electromagnetic energy of light into a form of energy that can be processed by the nervous system. There are two kinds of visual receptor cells: rods and cones. Rods and cones are involved in different aspects of vision, and they differ both in how they respond to light and in their patterns of distribution on the surface of the retina (Blake, 2000). **Rods** are the receptors in the retina that are sensitive to light, but they are not very useful for color vision. Thus they function well under low illumination; as you might expect, they are hard at work at night. Humans have about 120 million rods. **Cones** are the receptors that we use for color perception. Like the rods, cones are light sensitive. However, they require a larger amount of light than the rods do to respond, and so they operate best in daylight or under high illumination. There are about 6 million cone cells in human eyes. Figure 5.11 shows what rods and cones look like.

The most important part of the retina is the *fovea*, a minute area in the center of the retina at which vision is at its best (see figure 5.10). The fovea contains only cones and is vitally important to many visual tasks (try reading out of the corner of your eye!). Rods are found almost everywhere on the retina except in the fovea. Because rods require little light, they work best under conditions of low illumination. This light sensitivity and the rods' location on the retina give us the ability to detect fainter spots of light on the peripheral retina than at the fovea. Thus, if you want to see a very faint star, you should gaze slightly away from the star.

Figure 5.12 shows how the rods and cones at the back of the retina transduce light into electrochemical impulses (Sandell, 2000). The signal is transmitted to the *bipolar cells* and then moves on to another layer of specialized cells called *ganglion cells*.

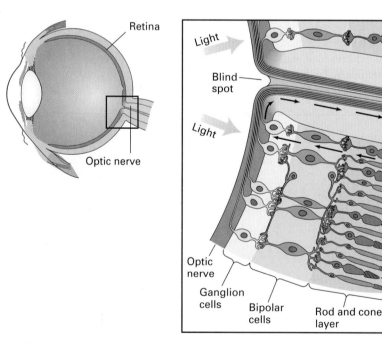

rods The receptors in the retina that are sensitive to light but are not very useful in color vision.

cones The receptors in the retina that process information about color.

FIGURE 5.12 **Direction of Light in the Retina** After light passes through the cornea, pupil, and lens, it falls on the retina. Three layers of specialized cells in the retina convert the image into a neural signal that can be transmitted to the brain. First, light triggers a reaction in the rods and cones at the back of the retina, transducing light energy into electrochemical neural impulses. The neural impulses activate the bipolar cells, which in turn activate the ganglion cells. Then light information is transmitted to the optic nerve, which conveys it to the brain. The arrows indicate the sequence in which light information moves in the retina.

FIGURE 5.13 **The Eye's Blind Spot** There is a normal blind spot in your eye, a small area where the optic nerve leads to the brain. To find your blind spot, hold this book at arm's length, cover your left eye, and stare at the red pepper on the left with your right eye. Move the book slowly toward you until the yellow pepper disappears. To find the blind spot in your left eye, cover your right eye, stare at the yellow pepper, and adjust the book until the red pepper disappears.

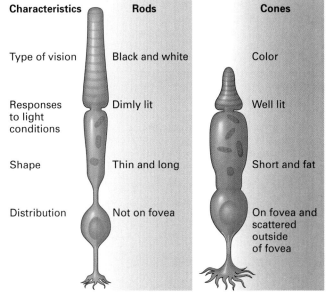

Characteristics	Rods	Cones
Type of vision	Black and white	Color
Responses to light conditions	Dimly lit	Well lit
Shape	Thin and long	Short and fat
Distribution	Not on fovea	On fovea and scattered outside of fovea

FIGURE 5.14 **Characteristics of Rods and Cones**

The axons of the ganglion cells make up the optic nerve that carries the visual information to the brain for further processing.

There is one place on the retina that contains neither rods nor cones. Not surprisingly, this area is called the *blind spot;* it is the place on the retina where the optic nerve leaves the eye on its way to the brain (see figure 5.12). We cannot see anything that reaches only this part of the retina. To prove to yourself that you have a blind spot, see figure 5.13. A summary of the characteristics of rods and cones is presented in figure 5.14.

Visual Processing in the Brain

Recall the case of Dr. P., the musician who lost the ability to recognize familiar people and objects on sight. The eyes are just the beginning of visual perception. The next step occurs when neural impulses generated in the retina are dispatched to the brain for analysis and integration.

The optic nerve leaves the eye, carrying information about light toward the brain. Light travels in a straight line; therefore, stimuli in the left visual field are registered in the right half of the retina in both eyes, and stimuli in the right visual field are registered in the left half of the retina in both eyes (see figure 5.15). In the brain, at a point called the *optic chiasm,* the optic nerve fibers divide, and approximately half of the nerve fibers cross over the midline of the brain. As a result, the visual information originating in the right halves of the two retinas is transmitted to the left side of the occipital lobe in the cerebral cortex, and the visual information coming from the left halves of the retinas is transmitted to the right side of the occipital lobe. What these crossings mean is that what we see in the left side of our visual field is registered in the right side of the brain, and what we see in the right visual field is registered in the left side of the brain (see figure 5.15). Then this information is processed and combined into a recognizable object or scene in the visual cortex.

The Visual Cortex The *visual cortex,* located in the occipital lobe of the brain, is the part of the cerebral cortex that functions in vision. Most visual information travels to the primary visual cortex, where it is processed, before moving to other visual areas for further analysis (Zeki, 2001).

FIGURE 5.15 Visual Pathways to and Through the Brain Light from each side of the visual field falls on the opposite side of each eye's retina. Visual information then travels along the optic nerve to the optic chiasm, where most of the visual information crosses over to the other side of the brain. From there, visual information goes to the occipital lobe at the rear of the brain. All these crossings mean that what we see in the left side of our visual field (here, the woman) is registered in the right side of our brain, and what we see in the right visual field (the man) is registered in the left side of our brain.

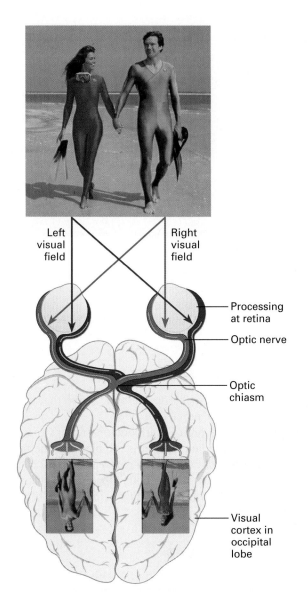

Left visual field

Right visual field

Processing at retina

Optic nerve

Optic chiasm

Visual cortex in occipital lobe

An important aspect of visual information processing is the specialization of neurons. Like the cells in the retina, many cells in the primary visual cortex are highly specialized. **Feature detectors** are neurons in the brain's visual system that respond to particular features of a stimulus. David Hubel and Torsten Wiesel (1965) won a Nobel Prize for their research on feature detectors. By recording the activity of a *single* neuron in a cat while it looked at patterns that varied in size, shape, color, and movement, the researchers found that the visual cortex has neurons that are individually sensitive to different types of lines and angles. One neuron might show a sudden burst of activity when stimulated by lines of a particular angle; another neuron might fire only when moving stimuli appear; yet another neuron might be stimulated when the object in the visual field has a combination of certain angles, sizes, and shapes.

Parallel Processing *What?* and *Where?* are two basic questions that need to be answered in visual perception. Not only must people realize what they are looking at, but they also need to know where it is in order to respond appropriately (Gazzaniga, Ivry, & Magnum, 2001). The elegantly organized brain has two pathways—dubbed "what" and "where"—to handle these important vision tasks (see figure 5.16; Ungerleider & Mishkin, 1982).

feature detectors Neurons in the brain's visual system that respond to particular lines or other features of a stimulus.

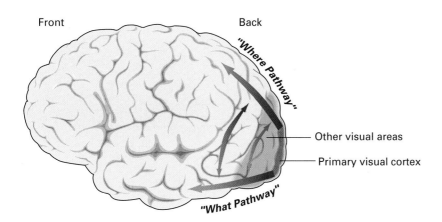

Front   Back

"Where Pathway"

Other visual areas

Primary visual cortex

"What Pathway"

FIGURE 5.16 The What and Where Pathways for Visual Information These parallel neural pathways process information about an object's characteristics ("what") and location ("where"). Note the interconnecting arrows between the pathways. As the what and where pathways carry information to other areas of the cerebral cortex, they are not completely isolated: Connections between them contribute to the integration of "what" and "where" information.

The *what pathway* in the temporal lobe processes information about what the object is, including its color, form, and texture. For instance, there is an area along the what pathway in the temporal lobe that is activated when we try to recognize someone's face. In rare cases in which these areas are damaged, individuals have difficulty recognizing the person whose face they are seeing, even though they know they're seeing a face.

The *where pathway* processes information on an object's location, including information about movement and the depth of the object. This pathway is located in the parietal lobe. In a rare case, a woman with damage in an area of the parietal lobe that is activated by movement has great difficulty crossing the street because she cannot distinguish approaching cars from parked cars (Zeki, 1991).

The what and where pathways are examples of **parallel processing,** the simultaneous distribution of information across different neural pathways. Parallel processing helps sensory information travel rapidly through the brain. A sensory system designed to process information about sensory qualities serially or consecutively (such as the shapes of images, their colors, their movements, their locations, and so on) would be too slow to keep us current with a rapidly changing world. There is some evidence suggesting that parallel processing also occurs for sensations of touch and hearing (Bloom, Nelson, & Lazerson, 2001).

Binding   Although the what and where pathways work in parallel, connections between them serve to unify sensory information into a complete picture of the what and where of all we see. For instance, if you were to look at a parrot, visual information about the parrot would enter the visual system through the portal of your eyes as a complete object. However, as we have seen, the sensory system breaks down this visual information and transmits it in distributed pathways and to specific neurons. Seeing the whole parrot requires reassembling the information (Crick & Koch, 1998).

One of the most exciting topics in visual perception today is what neuroscientists call **binding,** the bringing together and integration of what is processed by different pathways or cells (Zeki, 2001). Binding involves the coupling of the activity of various cells and pathways. Thus, through binding, you can integrate information about the parrot's shape, size, location, color, motion, and so on into a complete image of the parrot in the cerebral cortex. Exactly how binding occurs is not completely known at this time, but the process is a major focus of research in the neuroscience of visual perception today.

Researchers have found that all the neurons throughout pathways that are activated by a visual object vibrate together at the same frequency (Engel & Singer, 2001; Singer & Gray, 1995). Within the vast network of cells in the cerebral cortex, this set of neurons appears to *bind* together all the features of the objects into a unified perception.

parallel processing The simultaneous distribution of information across different neural pathways.

binding The bringing together and integration of what is processed through different pathways or cells.

FIGURE 5.17 **Examples of Stimuli Used to Test for Color Blindness**
People with normal vision see the number 16 in the left circle and the number 8 in the right circle. People with red-green color blindness may see just the 16, just the 8, or neither. A complete color blindness assessment involves the use of fifteen stimuli.

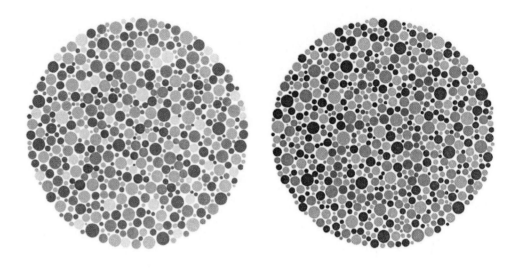

Color Vision

Imagine how dull a world without color would be. Our art museums are filled with paintings that are remarkable for their use of color, and flowers would lose much of their beauty for us if we could not see their rich colors. The ability to see color evolved because it provides many advantages to animals, including the ability to detect and discriminate various objects (Sekuler & Blake, 2002). For example, the edibility of foods depends on ripeness, which is reflected in color.

Color is a pattern of neural responses, not the wavelengths of light themselves, that generate color vision (Shevell, 2000). The study of human color vision using psychological methods has a long and distinguished history. A full century before the methods existed to study the anatomical and neurophysiological bases of color perception, psychological studies had discovered many of the basic principles of our color vision system. These studies produced two main theories: trichromatic theory and opponent-process theory. Both turned out to be correct.

The **trichromatic theory** states that color perception is produced by three types of receptors (cone cells in the retina) that are particularly sensitive to different, but overlapping, ranges of wavelengths. The trichromatic theory of color vision was proposed by Thomas Young in 1802 and extended by Hermann von Helmholtz in 1852. The theory is based on the results of experiments on human color-matching abilities, which show that a person with normal vision can match any color in the spectrum by combining three other wavelengths. In this type of experiment, individuals are given a light of a single wavelength and are asked to combine three other single-wavelength lights to match the first light. They can do this by changing the relative intensities of the three lights until the color of the combination light is indistinguishable from the color of the first light. Young and Helmholtz reasoned that if the combination of any three wavelengths of different intensities is indistinguishable from any single pure wavelength, the visual system must base its perception of color on the relative responses of three receptor systems.

Further support for the trichromatic theory is found in the study of defective color vision, or what is commonly referred to as color blindness (see figure 5.17). The term *color blind* is somewhat misleading because it suggests that a color-blind person cannot see color at all. Complete color blindness is rare; most people who are color blind, the vast majority of whom are men, can see some colors but not others. The nature of color blindness depends on which of the three kinds of cones is inoperative (Shevell, 2000). The three cone systems are green, red, and blue. In the most common form of color blindness, the green cone system malfunctions in some way, rendering green indistinguishable from certain combinations of blue and

trichromatic theory Color perception is based on the existence of three types of receptors that are maximally sensitive to different, but overlapping, ranges of wavelengths.

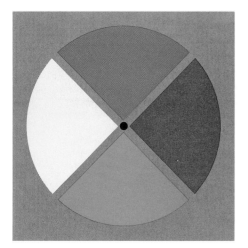

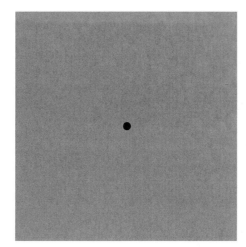

FIGURE 5.18 Negative Afterimage—Complementary Colors If you gaze steadily at the dot in the colored panel on the left for a few moments, then shift your gaze to the gray box on the right, you will see the original hues' complementary colors. The blue appears as yellow, the red as green, the green as red, and the yellow as blue. This pairing of colors has to do with the fact that color receptors in the eye are apparently sensitive as pairs: When one color is turned off (when you stop staring at the panel), the other color in the receptor is briefly turned on. The afterimage effect is especially noticeable with bright colors.

red. Color-matching experiments performed by people with this form of color blindness show that they need only two other colors to match a pure color and hence have dichromatic color perception. *Dichromats* are people with only two kinds of cones. *Trichromats* have three kinds of cone receptors and normal color vision.

In 1878, the German physiologist Ewald Hering observed that some colors cannot exist together, whereas others can. For example, it is easy to imagine a greenish blue or a reddish yellow, but nearly impossible to imagine a reddish green or a bluish yellow. Hering also noticed that trichromatic theory could not adequately explain *afterimages,* sensations that remain after a stimulus is removed (see figure 5.18 to experience an afterimage). Color afterimages are common and involve complementary colors. One example of afterimages occurs after prolonged exposure to a computer terminal screen with green lettering, such as those used in many businesses. Working with a computer like this all day can cause white objects and walls to appear reddish. Conversely, if you look at red long enough, eventually a green afterimage will appear. And, if you look at yellow long enough, eventually a blue afterimage will appear. Such afterimages are examples of bottom-up processing.

Hering's observations led him to propose that the visual system treats colors as complementary pairs: red-green and blue-yellow. Hering's view is called **opponent-process theory,** which states that cells in the visual system respond to red-green and blue-yellow colors; a given cell might be excited by red and inhibited by green, whereas another cell might be excited by yellow and inhibited by blue. Researchers have found that opponent-process theory does indeed explain afterimages (Hurvich & Jameson, 1969; Jameson & Hurvich, 1989). If you stare at red, for instance, your red-green system seems to "tire," and when you look away, it rebounds and gives you a green afterimage. Also, if you mix equal amounts of opponent colors, such as blue and yellow, you see gray; figure 5.19 illustrates this principle.

If the trichromatic theory of color perception is correct and we do in fact have three kinds of cone receptors like those predicted by Young and Helmholtz, then how can the opponent-process theory also be correct? The answer is that the red, blue, and green cones in the retina are connected to retinal ganglion cells in such a way

THE FAR SIDE   By GARY LARSON

© 1991 FarWorks, Inc./Dist. by Universal Press Syndicate

" . . . And please let Mom, Dad, Rex, Ginger, Tucker, me and all the rest of the family see color."

opponent-process theory Cells in the visual system respond to red-green and blue-yellow colors; a given cell might be excited by red and inhibited by green, whereas another might be excited by yellow and inhibited by blue.

FIGURE 5.19 **Color Wheel** Colors opposite each other produce the neutral gray in the center when they are mixed.

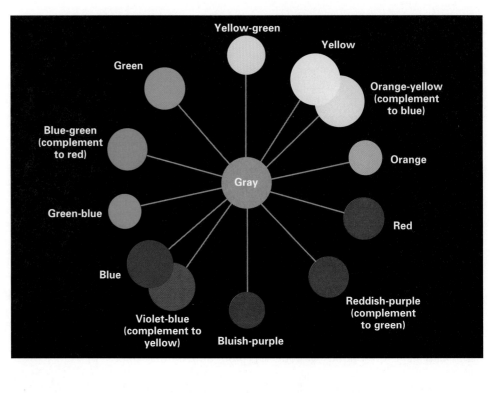

FIGURE 5.20 **Trichromatic and Opponent-Process Theories: Transmission of Color Information in the Retina** Cones responsive to green, blue, or red light form a trichromatic receptor system in the retina. As information is transmitted to the retina's ganglion cells, opponent-process cells are activated. As shown here, a retinal ganglion cell is inhibited by a green cone (−) and excited by a red cone (+), producing red-green color information.

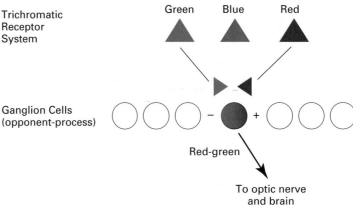

that the three-color code is immediately translated into the opponent-process code (see figure 5.20). For example, a green cone might inhibit and a red cone might excite a particular ganglion cell. Thus, *both* the trichromatic and opponent-process theories are correct—the eye and the brain use both methods to code colors.

This discussion of theories of color vision illustrates an important feature of psychology described in chapter 1: Science often progresses when conflicting ideas are posed and investigated. In many instances, as with color vision, seemingly conflicting ideas or systems may actually work, and even work best, together.

Perceiving Shape, Depth, Motion, and Constancy

Perceiving visual stimuli means organizing and interpreting the fragments of information that the eye sends to the visual cortex. Information about the dimensions of what we are seeing is critical to this process. Among these dimensions are shape, depth, motion, and constancy.

Think about the visible world and its shapes—buildings against the sky, boats on the horizon, letters on this page. We see these shapes because they are marked off from the rest of what see by *contour*, a location at which a sudden change of brightness

FIGURE 5.21 **Reversible Figure-Ground Pattern** *Do you see the silhouette of a goblet or a pair of faces in profile?*

FIGURE 5.22 Sophisticated Use of the Figure-Ground Relationship in Escher's Woodcut *Relativity* **(1938)**

occurs (Kerston, 2002). Now think about the letters on this page. As you look at the page, you see letters, which are shapes, in a field or background—the white page. The **figure-ground relationship** is the principle by which we organize the perceptual field into stimuli that stand out (*figure*) and those that are left over (*background*). Generally, this principle works well for us, but some figure-ground relationships are highly ambiguous, and it may be difficult to tell what is figure and what is ground. A well-known ambiguous figure-ground relationship is shown in figure 5.21. As you look at the figure, your perception is likely to shift from seeing two faces to seeing a single goblet. The work of artist M. C. Escher, which does not provide spatial location and depth cues, also illustrates figure-ground ambiguity (see figure 5.22).

One school of psychology has been especially intrigued by how we perceive shapes. According to **gestalt psychology,** people naturally organize their perceptions according to certain patterns (*gestalt* is German for "configuration" or "form"). One of gestalt psychology's main principles is that the whole is different from the sum of its parts. For example, when you watch a movie, the "motion" you see in the film cannot be found in the film itself; if you examine it, you see only separate frames. When you watch the film, the frames move past a light source at a rate of many per second, and you perceive a whole that is very different from the separate frames that are the film's parts. Thus, also, thousands of tiny dots (parts) make up an image (whole) in a newspaper or on the computer screen.

The figure-ground relationship is also a gestalt principle. Three other gestalt principles are closure, proximity, and similarity. The principle of *closure* states that when individuals see a disconnected or incomplete figure, they fill in the spaces and see it

figure-ground relationship People organize the perceptual field into stimuli that stand out (figure) and those that are left over (background).

gestalt psychology People naturally organize their perceptions according to certain patterns.

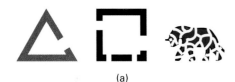

(a)

(b)   (c)

FIGURE 5.23 Gestalt Principles of Closure, Proximity, and Similarity
(*a*) *Closure:* When we see disconnected or incomplete figures, we fill in the spaces and see them as complete figures. (*b*) *Proximity:* When we see objects that are near each other, they tend to be seen as a unit. You are likely to perceive the grouping as 4 columns of 4 squares, not 1 set of 16 squares. (*c*) *Similarity:* When we see objects that are similar to each other, they tend to be seen as a unit. Here, you are likely to see vertical columns of circles and squares in the left box but horizontal rows of circles and squares in the right box.

as a complete figure (see figure 5.23a). The principle of *proximity* states that when individuals see objects close to each other, they tend to group them together (see figure 5.23b). The principle of *similarity* states that when objects are similar, individuals tend to group them together (see figure 5.23c).

Depth Perception Images appear on our retinas in two-dimensional form, yet remarkably we see a three-dimensional world. **Depth perception** is the ability to perceive objects three dimensionally. Look around you. You don't see your surroundings as flat. You see some objects farther away, some closer. Some objects overlap each other. The scene and objects that you are looking at have depth. How do you see depth? To see a world of depth, we use two kinds of information, or cues—binocular and monocular.

Because we have two eyes, we get two views of the world, one from each eye. **Binocular cues** are depth cues that depend on the combination of the images in the left and right eyes and on the way the two eyes work together. The pictures are slightly different because the eyes are in slightly different positions. Try holding your hand about 10 inches from your face. Alternately close and open your left and right eyes, so that only one eye is open at a time. The image of your hand will appear to jump back and forth because the image of your hand is in a slightly different place on the left and right retinas. The *disparity,* or difference between the images in the two eyes, is the binocular cue the brain uses to determine the depth or distance of an object. The combination of the two images in the brain, and the disparity between them in the eyes, gives us information about the three-dimensionality of the world (Cummings & DeAngelis, 2000; Landy, 2002).

The perception of depth from disparity can be demonstrated with figure 5.24, based on a principle for presenting stereoscopic information from a single two-dimensional image (Tyler, 1983). These kinds of displays have become extremely popular in recent years and can now be found in art books, on greeting cards, and on posters in specialty shops. In the late nineteenth century, stereograms were similarly popular when stereoviewers became easily available.

In addition to using binocular cues to get an idea of the depth of objects, we use a number of **monocular cues,** or depth cues, available from the image in one eye, either right or left. These are powerful cues and under normal circumstances can provide a very compelling impression of depth. Try closing one eye—your perception of the world still retains many of its three-dimensional qualities. Some examples of monocular cues are as follows:

1. *Familiar size.* This cue to the depth and distance of objects is based on what we have learned from experience about the standard sizes of objects. We know how large oranges tend to be, so we can tell something about how far away an orange is likely to be by the size of its image on the retina.
2. *Height in the field of view.* All other things being equal, objects positioned higher in a picture are seen as farther away.
3. *Linear perspective.* Objects that are farther away take up less space on the retina. As shown in figure 5.25 on page 200, as an object recedes into the distance, parallel lines in the scene appear to converge.

depth perception The ability to perceive objects three dimensionally.

binocular cues Depth cues that are based on the combination of the images on the left and right eyes and on the way the two eyes work together.

monocular cues Depth cues that can be extracted from the images in either eye.

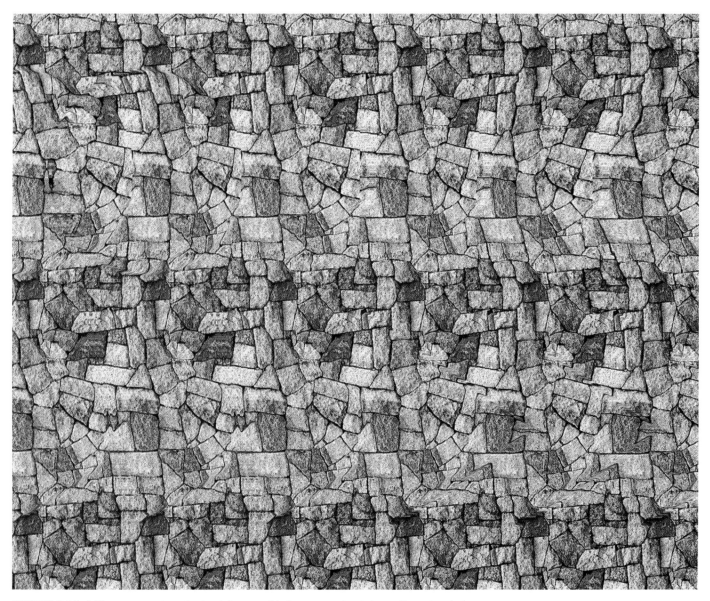

FIGURE 5.24 A Stereogram Seen in the right way, this figure contains 3 three-dimensional objects: a sphere in the top left, a pyramid in the top right, and a curved pointed conical figure in the center at the bottom. It may take a moment or two to see them, but when you do, they will be astoundingly clear. There are two ways to see the three-dimensional objects in this figure. *Technique 1:* Cross your eyes by holding your finger up between your face and the figure. Look at the tip of your finger, and then slowly move your finger back and forth, toward and away from the figure, being careful to maintain focus on your finger. When the correct distance is reached, the three-dimensional objects will pop out at you. *Technique 2:* Put your face very close to the figure, so that it is difficult to focus or converge your eyes. Wait a moment, and begin to pull your face very slowly back from the figure. The picture should appear blurred for a bit, but when the right distance is reached should snap into three dimensionality. Regardless of the technique you try, be patient! You may have to try one or both of these techniques a few times. The difficulty is that your eyes will try to converge at the distance of the page (very sensible of them!)—so you must trick them into converging elsewhere, such as in front of the page, as in technique 1, or into staying perfectly parallel and unconverged, as in technique 2. *Note:* Some people will not be able to see the three dimensionality in these figures at all, for one of several reasons. First, some of us have eyes too well adapted to the real world to be convinced to converge in the "wrong place," given the image data appearing on the retinas. Second, some very common visual deficits that can yield appreciable differences between the quality of the image on the left and right retinas can affect the development of normal binocular vision. The brain requires comparable image quality from the two eyes in the first few years of life to develop a high degree of stereoacuity. When this fails to happen, the development of binocular neural mechanisms, which need to compare information in the two eyes, can be affected and can pose problems in processing *pure* stereoscopic information, as in this figure. The information here is purely stereoscopic because other, monocular, kinds of cues to depth, such as shading and perspective, are not available.

FIGURE 5.25 An Artist's Use of the Monocular Cue of Linear Perspective

Famous landscape artist J. M. W. Turner used linear perspective to give the perception of depth in *Rain, Steam, and Speed.*

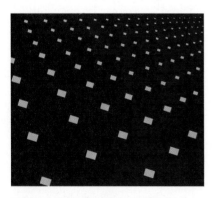

FIGURE 5.26 Texture Gradient The gradients of texture create an impression of depth on a flat surface.

4. *Overlap.* An object that partially conceals or overlaps another object is perceived as closer.
5. *Shading.* This cue involves changes in perception due to the position of the light and the position of the viewer. Consider an egg under a desk lamp. If you walk around the desk, you will see different shading patterns on the egg.
6. *Texture gradient.* Texture becomes denser and finer the farther away it is from the viewer (see figure 5.26).

Depth perception is especially intriguing to artists, who have to paint a three-dimensional world on a two-dimensional canvas. Artists often use monocular cues to give the feeling of depth to their paintings. Indeed, monocular cues have become so widely used by artists that they also are called *pictorial cues.*

Motion Perception Motion perception plays an important role in the lives of many species (Pines, 2001). Indeed, in some animals motion perception is critical for survival. Both predators and their prey depend on being able to quickly detect motion. Frogs and some other simple vertebrates may not even see an object unless it is moving. For example, if a dead fly is dangled motionlessly in front of a frog, the frog cannot sense its winged meal. The "bug detecting" cells in the frog's retinas are wired only to sense movement.

Whereas the retinas of frogs can detect movement, the retinas of humans and other primates cannot. According to one neuroscientist, "the dumber the animal, the 'smarter' the retina" (Baylor, 2001). In humans, the brain takes over the job of analyzing motion through highly specialized pathways. Recall from our discussion of the brain pathways in vision that the where pathway is involved in motion detection. How do humans perceive motion? First, we have neurons that are specialized to detect motion. Second, feedback from our body tells us whether we are moving or whether someone or an object is moving. For example, you move your eye muscles as you watch a ball coming toward you. Third, the environment we see is rich in cues that give us information about movement (Landy, 2001; Royden, 2000). For example, when we run, what's around us appears to be moving.

Psychologists are interested in both real movement and **apparent movement,** which occurs when an object is stationary, but we perceive it as moving. An example of apparent movement can be experienced at Disneyland. Bell Telephone mounted nine cameras on an airplane to obtain nine different perspectives on a number of sights around the United States; the films are shown at a Disneyland attraction. The motion pictures are shown on nine screens that surround the viewers, who stand in the middle of the room, a position that simulates the view from an airplane. Viewers are warned to hold the handrail because perceived movement is so realistic that they might fall.

Two forms of apparent motion are stroboscopic motion and movement aftereffects. *Stroboscopic motion* is the illusion of movement created when a rapid stimulation of different parts of the retina occurs. Motion pictures are a form of stroboscopic motion. *Movement aftereffects* happen when we watch continuous movement and then look at another surface, which then appears to move in the opposite direction. Figure 5.27 provides an opportunity to experience movement aftereffects.

Perceptual Constancy Retinal images are constantly changing. Yet, even though the stimuli that fall on the retinas of our eyes change as we move closer or farther away from objects or look at objects from different orientations and in light or dark settings, our perception of them remains stable. **Perceptual constancy** is the recognition that objects are constant and unchanging even though sensory input about them is changing.

We experience three types of perceptual constancy: size constancy, shape constancy, and brightness constancy. *Size constancy* is the recognition that an object remains the same size even though the retinal image of the object changes (see figure 5.28). *Shape constancy* is the recognition that an object retains the same shape even though its orientation to us changes. Look around. You probably see objects of various shapes—chairs and tables, for example. If you walk around the room, you will see these objects from different sides and angles. Even though the retinal image of the object changes as you walk, you still perceive the objects as having the same shape (see figure 5.29). *Brightness constancy* is the recognition that an object retains the same degree of brightness even though different amounts of light fall on it. For example, regardless of whether you are reading this book indoors or outdoors, the

FIGURE 5.27 **Movement Aftereffects** This is an example of a geometric pattern that produces afterimages in which motion can be perceived. Stare at the center of the pattern for about 10 seconds, then look at a white sheet of paper. You should perceive rotary motion on the paper.

FIGURE 5.28 **Size Constancy** Even though our retinal images of the hot air balloons vary, we still realize the balloons are approximately the same size. This illustrates the principle of size constancy.

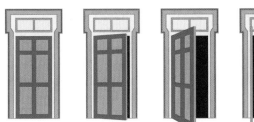

FIGURE 5.29 **Shape Constancy** The various projected images from an opening door are quite different, yet you perceive a rectangular door.

apparent movement The perception that a stationary object is moving.

perceptual constancy Recognition that objects are constant and unchanging even through sensory input about them is changing.

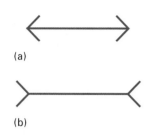

(a)

(b)

FIGURE 5.30 Müller-Lyer Illusion
The two lines are exactly the same length, although (b) looks longer than (a). This illusion was created by Franz Müller-Lyer in the late nineteenth century.

FIGURE 5.31 The Horizontal-Vertical Illusion The vertical line looks longer than the horizontal line, but they are the same length.

FIGURE 5.32 Ponzo Illusion The top line looks much longer than the bottom line, but they are the same length.

white pages and the black print do not look any different to you in terms of their whiteness or blackness.

How are we able to resolve the discrepancy between a retinal image of an object and its actual size, shape, and brightness? Experience is important. For example, no matter how far away you are from your car, you know how large it is. Not only is familiarity important in size constancy, but so are binocular and monocular distance cues. Even if we have never seen an object before, these cues provide us with information about an object's size. Many visual illusions are influenced by our perception of size constancy.

Illusions

Our perceptual interpretations are usually correct. For example, on the basis of differences in color or texture, we can conclude that a dog is on the rug. On the basis of a continuous increase in size, we conclude that a train is coming toward us. Sometimes, though, the interpretations or inferences are wrong, with the result being an illusion.

A **visual illusion** occurs when there is a discrepancy or incongruency between reality and the perceptual representation of it. Illusions are incorrect, but they are not abnormal. They can provide insight into how our perceptual processes work (Gregory, 2000). More than 200 different types of illusions have been discovered. Following are six of them.

One of the most famous visual illusions is the Müller-Lyer illusion, illustrated in figure 5.30. The two horizontal lines are exactly the same length, although (b) looks longer than (a). Another illusion is the horizontal-vertical illusion, in which a vertical line looks longer than a horizontal line even though the two are equal (see figure 5.31). In the Ponzo illusion, the top line looks much longer than the bottom line (see figure 5.32).

Why do these illusions trick us? One reason is that we mistakenly use certain cues for maintaining size constancy. For example, in the Ponzo illusion we see the upper line as being farther away (remember that objects higher in a picture are perceived as being farther away). The Müller-Lyer illusion, though, is not so easily explained. We might make judgments about the lines by comparing incorrect parts of the figures. For example, when the wings are a different color than the horizontal lines in the Müller-Lyer illusion, the illusion is less pronounced (Coren & Girus, 1972).

Another well-known illusion is the moon illusion (see figure 5.33). The moon is 2,000 miles in diameter and 289,000 miles away. Because both the moon's size and its distance from us are beyond our own experience, we have difficulty judging just how far away it really is. When the moon is high in the sky, directly above us, little information is present to help us judge its distance—no texture gradients or stereoscopic cues exist, for example. But when the moon is on the horizon, we can judge its distance in relation to familiar objects—trees and buildings, for example—which

© Sidney Harris

visual illusion A discrepancy or incongruency between reality and the perceptual representation of it.

FIGURE 5.33 **Moon Illusion** When the moon is on the horizon, it looks much larger than when it is high in the sky, directly above us. *Why does the moon look so much larger on the horizon?*

FIGURE 5.34 **Devil's Tuning Fork**
An example of a two-dimensional representation of an impossible three-dimensional figure.

FIGURE 5.35 **Why Does This Famous Face Look So Different When You Turn the Book Upside Down?**

make it appear farther away. The result is that we estimate the size of the moon as much larger when it is on the horizon than when it is overhead.

The devil's tuning fork is another fascinating illusion. Look at figure 5.34 for about 30 seconds, then close the book. Now try to draw the tuning fork. You undoubtedly found this a difficult, if not impossible, task. Why? Look carefully at the figure again. You'll see that the figure's depth cues are ambiguous.

In our final example of an illusion, a "doctored" face seen upside down goes unnoticed. Look at figure 5.35—you probably recognize this famous face as President George W. Bush. In what seems to be an ordinary portrait, however, the mouth and eyes have been cut out from the original and pasted back on upside down. If you turn this book upside down, the horrific look is easily seen. The "Bush" illusion may take place because the mouth is so far out of alignment that we simply cannot respond to its expression; it is still a fearsome face, but we do not see that, and we may have a difficult time telling what really is the top of the mouth in the picture.

mhhe com/
santrockp7

For study tools related to this learning goal, see the Study Guide, the CD-ROM, and the Online Learning Center.

Review and Sharpen Your Thinking

2 *Explain how the visual system enables us to see and, by communicating with the brain, to perceive the world.*

- Explain the nature of light and how it is detected and transduced into neural impulses in the human eye.
- Describe how neural impulses are processed in the brain and reassembled into a single image.
- Discuss the trichromatic and opponent-process theories of color vision.
- State how shape, depth, motion, and perceptual constancy enable us to transform flat images into three-dimensional objects and scenes.
- Give an explanation for visual illusions and cite examples.

Try to think of at least one perceptual illusion involving a sense other than vision.

3 THE AUDITORY SYSTEM

| **The Nature of Sound and How We Experience It** | **Theories of Hearing** | **Localizing Sound** |
| **Structures and Functions of the Ear** | **Auditory Processing in the Brain** | **Noise Pollution** |

What is the auditory system and how does it process sound so that the brain can hear it?

Luis Weiss is a 17-year-old senior honor student in high school: He speaks English, French, and Spanish; scored 700 on the math SAT; and wants to be an aeronautical engineer (Arana-Ward, 1997). Fourteen years ago, Luis had a cochlear implant inserted into his ear. Before the procedure, Luis was deaf. When he received the cochlear implant at age 3, there was a sensory rush of sound that took time for him to sort through and understand.

Just as light provides us with information about the environment, so does sound. What would Luis' life have been like without music, the rushing sound of ocean waves, or the voices of his parents and friends? Sounds tell us about the approach of a person behind us, an oncoming car, the force of the wind outside, or the mischief of a 2-year-old; perhaps most important, sounds enable us to communicate through language and song.

The Nature of Sound and How We Experience It

At a rock concert you may have felt the throbbing pulse of the music or sensed that the air around you was vibrating. Bass instruments are especially effective at creating mechanical pulsations, even causing the floor to vibrate. When the bass is played loudly, we can sense air molecules being pushed forward in waves from the speaker. How does sound generate these sensations?

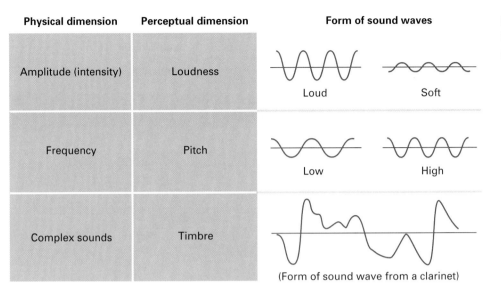

Sounds, or sound waves, are vibrations in the air that are processed by the auditory (or hearing) system. Remember that we described light waves as being much like the waves in the ocean moving toward the beach. Sound waves are similar. Sound waves also vary in wavelength. Wavelength determines the *frequency* of the sound wave, or the number of cycles (full wavelengths) that pass through a point in a given time. *Pitch* is the perceptual interpretation of the frequency of a sound. High-frequency sounds are perceived as having a high pitch, low-frequency sounds as having a low pitch. A soprano voice sounds high pitched. A bass voice has a low pitch. As with the wavelengths of light, human sensitivity is limited to a range of sound frequencies. It is common knowledge that dogs, for example, can hear higher frequencies than can humans.

Sound waves vary not only in frequency but also in amplitude (see figure 5.8). *Amplitude* of a sound wave, measured in decibels (dB), is the amount of pressure produced by a sound wave relative to a standard. The typical standard—zero decibels—is the weakest sound the human ear can detect. *Loudness* is the perception of the sound wave's amplitude. In general, the higher the amplitude of the sound wave, or the higher the decibel level, the louder the sound is perceived to be. In the world of amplitude, this means that the air is pressing more forcibly against you and your ears during loud sounds and more gently during quiet sounds.

So far I have been describing a single sound wave with just one frequency. A single sound wave is similar to the single wavelength of pure colored light I discussed in the context of color matching. Most sounds, including those of speech and music, are *complex sounds,* those in which numerous frequencies of sound blend together. *Timbre* is the tone saturation or the perceptual quality of a sound. Timbre is responsible for the perceptual difference between a trumpet and a trombone playing the same note and for the quality differences we hear in human voices. Figure 5.36 illustrates the physical differences in sound waves that produce the different qualities of sounds.

Structures and Functions of the Ear

What happens to sound waves once they reach your ear? How do various structures of the ear transform sound waves into signals that the brain will recognize as sound? Functionally, the ear is analogous to the eye. The ear serves the purpose of transmitting a high-fidelity version of sounds in the world to the brain for analysis and interpretation. Just as an image needs to be in focus and sufficiently bright for the brain to interpret it, a sound needs to be transmitted in a way that preserves information

FIGURE 5.37 The Outer, Middle, and Inner Ear On entering the outer ear, sound waves travel through the auditory canal, where they generate vibrations in the eardrum. These vibrations are transferred via the hammer, anvil, and stirrup to the fluid-filled cochlea in the inner ear. There the mechanical vibrations are converted to an electrochemical signal that the brain will recognize as sound.

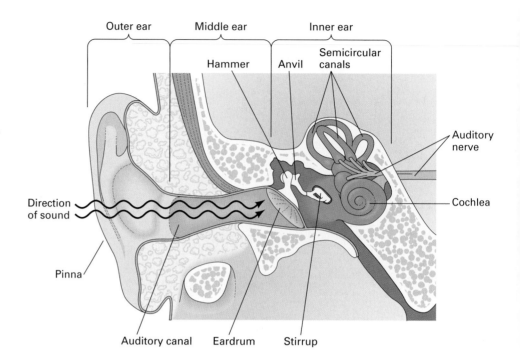

about its location, its frequency—which helps us distinguish the voice of a child from that of an adult—and its timbre, which allows us to identify the voice of a friend on the telephone.

The ear is divided into three parts: *outer ear, middle ear,* and *inner ear* (see figure 5.37).

Outer Ear   The **outer ear** consists of the pinna and the external auditory canal. The funnel-shaped *pinna* (plural, *pinnae*) is the outer visible part of the ear. (Elephants have very large pinnae). The pinna collects sounds and channels them into the interior of the ear. The pinnae of many animals, such as cats, are movable and serve a more important role in sound localization than do the pinnae of humans. Cats turn their ears in the direction of a faint and interesting sound.

Middle Ear   After passing the pinna, sound waves move through the auditory canal to the middle ear. The **middle ear** channels the sound through the eardrum, hammer, anvil, and stirrup to the inner ear. The *eardrum* is a membrane that vibrates in response to sound. It is the first structure that sound touches in the middle ear. The *hammer, anvil,* and *stirrup* are a connected chain of the three smallest bones in the human body. When they vibrate, they transmit sound waves to the fluid-filled inner ear.

If you are a swimmer, you know that sound travels far more easily in air than in water. Sound waves entering the ear travel in air until they reach the inner ear. At this border between air and fluid, sound meets the same kind of resistance encountered by shouts directed at an underwater swimmer when they hit the surface of the water. To compensate, the hammer, anvil, and stirrup also amplify the sound waves.

Inner Ear   The function of the **inner ear,** which includes the oval window, cochlea, and basilar membrane, is to transduce sound waves into neural impulses and send them on to the brain (Zwislocki, 2002). The stirrup is connected to the membranous *oval window,* which transmits sound waves to the cochlea. The *cochlea* is a tubular fluid-filled structure that is coiled up like a snail (see figure 5.38). The *basilar membrane* lines the inner wall of the cochlea and runs its entire length. It is narrow and rigid at the base of the cochlea but widens and becomes more flexible at the top. The variation in width and flexibility allows different areas of the basilar membrane to

outer ear Consists of the pinna and the external auditory canal.

middle ear Consists of eardrum, hammer, anvil, and stirrup.

inner ear Consists of oval window, cochlea, and basilar membrane.

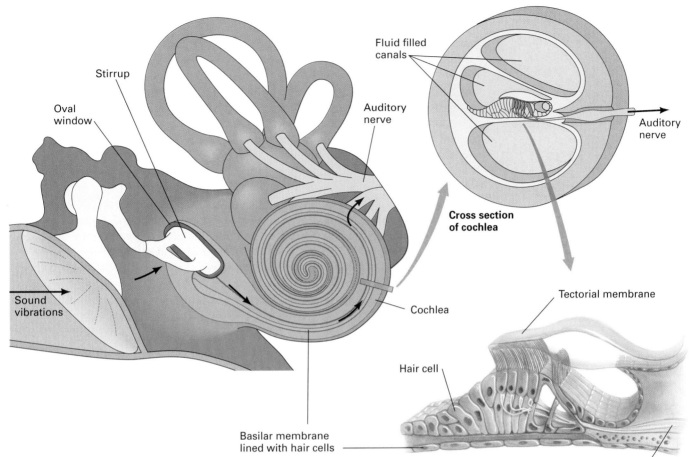

Stirrup

Oval window

Fluid filled canals

Auditory nerve

Cross section of cochlea

Auditory nerve

Sound vibrations

Cochlea

Tectorial membrane

Hair cell

Basilar membrane lined with hair cells

Auditory nerve

FIGURE 5.38 **The Cochlea**
The cochlea is a spiral structure consisting of fluid-filled canals. When the stirrup vibrates against the oval window, the fluid in the canals vibrates. Vibrations along portions of the basilar membrane correspond to different sound frequencies. The vibrations exert pressure on the hair cells (between the basilar and tectorial membranes); the hair cells in turn push against the tectorial membrane, which bends the hairs. This triggers an action potential in the auditory nerve.

vibrate more intensely when exposed to different sound frequencies. For example, the high-pitched tinkle of a bell stimulates the narrow region of the basilar membrane at the base of the cochlea, whereas the low-pitched tones of a tugboat whistle stimulate the wide end.

In humans and other mammals, hair cells line the basilar membrane (see figure 5.38). These *hair cells* are the sensory receptors of the ear. They are called hair cells because of the tufts of fine bristles, or cilia, that sprout from the top of them. The movement of the hair cells against the *tectorial membrane,* a jelly-like flap above them, generates resulting impulses that are interpreted as sound by the brain.

Theories of Hearing

One of the auditory system's mysteries is how the inner ear registers the frequency of sound. Two theories have been proposed to explain this mystery: place theory and frequency theory. **Place theory** states that each frequency produces vibrations at a particular spot on the basilar membrane. Georg von Békésy (1960) studied the effects of vibration applied at the oval window on the basilar membrane of human cadavers. Through a microscope, he saw that this stimulation produced a traveling wave on the basilar membrane. A traveling wave is like the ripples that appear in a pond when you throw in a stone. However, because the cochlea is a long tube, the ripples can travel in only one direction, from the oval window at one end of the cochlea to the far tip of the cochlea. High-frequency vibrations create traveling waves that maximally displace, or move, the area of the basilar membrane next to the oval window; low-frequency vibrations maximally displace areas of the membrane closer to the tip of the cochlea. Békésy won a Nobel Prize in 1961 for his research on the basilar membrane.

place theory A theory of hearing that states that each frequency produces vibrations at a particular spot on the basilar membrane

Place theory adequately explains high-frequency sounds but not low-frequency sounds. A high-frequency sound stimulates a very precise area on the basilar membrane. By contrast, a low-frequency sound causes such a large part of the basilar membrane to be displaced that it is hard to localize the maximal displacement. Because humans can hear low-frequency sounds better than can be predicted by looking at the basilar membrane's response to these sounds, some other factors must be involved. **Frequency theory** addresses this problem by stating that the perception of a sound's frequency depends on how often the auditory nerve fires. Higher frequency sounds cause the auditory nerve to fire more often than do lower frequency sounds. One limitation of frequency theory is that a single neuron has a maximum firing rate of about 1,000 times per second. Therefore, frequency theory cannot be applied to tones with frequencies that would require a neuron to fire more rapidly.

To deal with this limitation, a modification of frequency theory called the **volley principle** states that a cluster of nerve cells can fire neural impulses in rapid succession, producing a volley of impulses. Individual neurons cannot fire faster than 1,000 times per second. But if the neurons team up and alternate their neural firing, they can attain a combined frequency above that rate. Thus frequency theory better explains the perception of sounds below 1,000 times per second, whereas a combination of frequency and place theory is needed for those above 1,000 times per second.

Auditory Processing in the Brain

As you saw in the discussion of the visual system, once energy from the environment is picked up by our receptors, it must be transmitted to the brain for processing and interpretation. An image on the retina does not a Picasso make—likewise, a pattern of receptor responses in the cochlea does not a symphony make. In the retina, we saw that the responses of the rod and cone receptors feed into ganglion cells in the retina and leave the eye via the optic nerve. In the auditory system, information about sound moves from the hair cells of the inner ear to the **auditory nerve,** which carries neural impulses to the brain's auditory areas. Remember that it is the movement of the hair cells that transforms the physical stimulation of sound waves into the action potential of neural impulses.

Auditory information moves up the auditory pathway via electrochemical transmission in a more complex manner than does visual information in the visual pathway. Many synapses occur in the ascending auditory pathway, with most fibers crossing over the midline between the hemispheres of the cerebral cortex, although some proceed directly to the hemisphere on the same side as the ear of reception. This means that most of the auditory information from the left ear goes to the right side of the brain, but some also goes to the left side of the brain. The auditory nerve extends from the cochlea to the brain stem, with some fibers crossing over the midline. The cortical destination of most of these fibers is the temporal lobes of the brain (beneath the temples of the head). As in the case of visual information, researchers have found that features are extracted from auditory information and transmitted along parallel what and where pathways in the brain (Feng & Ratnam, 2000; Rubel & Fritzsch, 2002).

Localizing Sound

When you hear the siren of a fire engine or the bark of a dog, how do you know where the sound is coming from? The basilar membrane gives us information about the frequency, pitch, and complexity of a sound, but it doesn't tell us where a sound is located.

Earlier in the chapter, I indicated that because our two eyes see slightly different images, we can determine how near or far away an object is. Similarly, having two ears helps us to localize a sound because they receive somewhat different stimuli from

frequency theory Perception of a sound's frequency is due to how often the auditory nerve fires

volley principle A cluster of nerve cells can fire neural impulses in rapid succession, producing a volley of impulses.

auditory nerve Carries neural impulses to the brain's auditory area

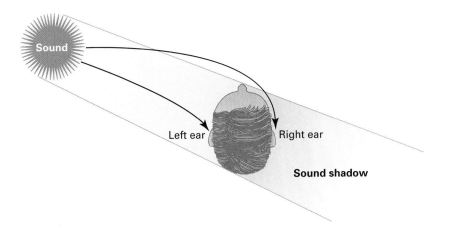

FIGURE 5.39 **The Sound Shadow**
The sound shadow is caused by the listener's head, which forms a barrier that reduces the sound's intensity. Here the sound is to the person's left, so the sound shadow will reduce the intensity of the sound that reaches the right ear.

the sound source. A sound coming from the left has to travel different distances to the two ears. So if a barking dog is to your left, your left ear receives the sound sooner than your right ear. Also, your left ear will receive a slightly more intense sound than your right ear in this case. The sound reaching one ear is more intense than the sound reaching the other ear for two reasons: (1) it has traveled less distance and (2) the other ear is in what is called the *sound shadow* of the listener's head, which provides a barrier that reduces the sound's intensity (see figure 5.39). The sound shadow is one means that blind individuals such as Stevie Wonder and Andrea Bocelli use for orientation.

Thus differences in both the *timing* of the sound and the *intensity* of the sound help us to localize a sound. Humans often have difficulty localizing a sound that is coming from a source that is directly in front of them because it reaches both ears simultaneously. The same is true for sounds directly above your head or directly behind you.

Compared with some animals, humans aren't very accurate at locating sounds (Matlin, 1988). For example, bats are able to hunt insects at night because of their exquisitely developed sensitivity to their own echoes. They emit sounds and then listen to the echoes coming back. Using this system—called *echolocation*—bats can fly through their environment at high speeds, avoid predators, and find prey. Why has evolution provided bats with such exquisite hearing? The answer is simple. Vision requires light, and bats are nocturnal animals. Any method of building internal representations of the environment that requires light would not be an effective perceptual system for the bat.

Humans do not need the bat's echolocation ability because we do not hunt bugs at night. Rather, we use our eyes to pursue food by day. Nonetheless, humans are fairly accurate at localizing sounds.

Noise Pollution

Earlier in the chapter, I discussed the effect of noise on the absolute threshold. It is also important to think about noise as a significant environmental influence on behavior. Usually auditory noise has little effect on us when it is at low volume or when we are doing simple, routine tasks. However, under some conditions noise can annoy us and disrupt our behavior (Passchier & others, 2001; Razdan & Sidhu, 2001).

Noise rated at 80 decibels or higher, if heard for prolonged periods of time, can cause permanent hearing loss. However, there are other consequences of constant, or even intermittent, noise at lower decibels. In a quiet library the noise level is about 40 decibels. The sound of a car horn is about 90 decibels, a rock band at close range 120 decibels, and a rocket launching 180 decibels. The decibel levels of various sounds are shown in figure 5.40 on page 211. Because noise levels in the environment have risen in recent years, noise pollution is a concern for an increasing number of people.

Love Your Ears

H.E.A.R. (Hearing Education and Awareness for Rockers) was founded by rock musicians whose hearing had been damaged by their exposure to high volumes of rock music. Such hearing loss is common among rock musicians and limits what they are able to do later in their lives.

Other noisy environments such as production factories and aviation grounds may pose threats to your hearing.

To determine how well you protect your hearing, answer the following questions:

- Do you work in a noisy environment? If so, ask your employer to inform you about the level of noise and company policy on protecting your hearing.
- If you use power equipment, are you using earmuffs or earplugs to protect your ears?
- Do you listen to music on headphones? If you listen to loud music often, go to a hearing specialist, get your hearing tested, and listen to the specialist's advice.
- Do you go to rock concerts? According to H.E.A.R., the sound levels at a rock concert can be as high as 140 dB in front of the speakers, which can damage hearing, and above 100 dB behind the speakers, still very loud and potentially dangerous.

Lars Ulrich of Metallica says, "Three of the four members of Metallica wear earplugs. Some people think earplugs are for wimps. But if you don't want to hear records in 5 or 10 years, that's your decision."

Noise is especially bothersome when we cannot do anything to control it, and too often in today's urban environments we do not have control over noise. This was the case for some children living in a New York City high-rise apartment building right next to a busy highway (Cohen, Glass, & Singer, 1973): Children who lived on the bottom floors (who were exposed to a high level of noise) did considerably worse on reading tests than children living on the upper floors (who were exposed to a much lower level of noise). In another study, children who lived in the corridor of the Los Angeles International Airport were compared with children living in a quieter neighborhood away from the air corridor (Cohen & others, 1981). Every day, more than 300 jets roared over the children in the air corridor. The children in the high-noise corridor had higher blood pressure and were more easily distracted on tasks than their counterparts who lived in the low-noise neighborhood.

Loud music is another modern development that can be physically harmful. The damage begins with the hair cells in the inner ear, which develop blister-like bulges that eventually pop. The tissue beneath the hair cells swells and softens until the hair cells, and sometimes the neurons leaving the cochlea, become scarred and degenerate (Lewis, 2001).

Following are some symptoms of possible hearing loss that could be caused by loud noise or music:

- Ringing or buzzing in ears
- Slight muffling of sounds
- Difficulty in understanding speech—hearing the words but not understanding them
- Problems hearing conversations in groups of people when there is background noise or in rooms with poor acoustics

To find out how well you protect your hearing, see the Psychology and Life box.

How do bats navigate through their environment?

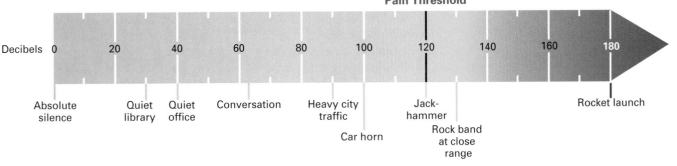

Pain Threshold

| Decibels | 0 | 20 | 40 | 60 | 80 | 100 | 120 | 140 | 160 | 180 |

Absolute silence — Quiet library — Quiet office — Conversation — Heavy city traffic — Car horn — Jack-hammer — Rock band at close range — Rocket launch

FIGURE 5.40 Sounds Around Us Shown here are the decibel (dB) levels of a number of sounds in our world. Every increase of 6 dB doubles a sound's intensity. For example, a 40-dB sound is twice as intense as a 34-dB sound. Noise rated at 80 dB or higher, if heard for prolonged periods of time, can cause permanent hearing loss. According to one comment, "The human ear was not made to handle the racket of modern civilization." By one estimate, machinery is making the Western world noisier by about 1 dB a year.

Review and Sharpen Your Thinking

3 ***Understand how the auditory system registers sound and how it connects with the brain to perceive it.***

- Describe the nature of sound and how it is experienced.
- Identify the structures of the ear and their functions.
- Discuss three theories of hearing.
- Explain how auditory signals are transmitted to the brain for processing.
- Describe sound localization.
- Discuss the effects of noise pollution on behavior.

Suppose you were in an accident and, in order to survive, had to sacrifice either your vision or hearing. Which sense would you preserve? Why?

mhhe●com/
santrockp7

For study tools related to this learning goal, see the Study Guide, the CD-ROM, and the Online Learning Center.

OTHER SENSES 4

The Skin Senses   **The Chemical Senses**   **The Kinesthetic and Vestibular Senses**

How do the skin, chemical, kinesthetic, and vestibular senses work?
Now that the visual and auditory systems have been described in some detail, let's take a look at our other sensory systems. You are familiar with the skin senses and the chemical senses (smell and taste). The lesser known kinesthetic and vestibular senses enable us to stay upright and to coordinate our movements.

Some people also claim to have another "sense" that enables them to read other people's minds, for example, or foresee the future. Such claims have not held up under scientific scrutiny, but many people continue to believe in so-called psychic powers. To learn about one man's efforts to expose fraudulent psychics, see the Critical Controversy box.

The Skin Senses

You know when a friend has a fever by putting your hand to her head; you know how to find your way to the light switch in a darkened room by groping along the wall; and you know whether or not a pair of shoes is too tight by the way the shoes touch different parts of your feet when you walk. Many of us think of our skin as a canvas rather than a sense. We color it with cosmetics, dyes, and tattoos. But the skin is our largest sensory system, draped over the body with receptors for touch, temperature, and pain. These three kinds of receptors form the *cutaneous senses*. A large variety of important information comes to us through our ability to detect touch.

Touch   Touch is one of the senses that we most often take for granted. Yet our ability to respond to touch is astounding.

Processing Information About Touch   What do we detect when we feel "touch"? What kind of energy does our sense of touch pick up from our external environment? In vision, we detect light energy. In audition, we detect the vibrations of air or sound waves pressing against our eardrums. In touch, we detect mechanical energy, or pressure against the skin. The lifting of a single hair causes pressure on the skin around the shaft of hair. This tiny bit of mechanical pressure at the base of the hair is sufficient for us to detect the touch of a pencil point. More commonly, we detect the mechanical energy of the pressure of a car seat against our buttocks or the pressure of a pencil in our hands. Is this kind of energy so different from the kind of energy we detect in vision or audition? Sometimes the only difference is one of intensity—the sound of a rock band playing softly is an auditory stimulus, but at the high volumes that make a concert hall reverberate, this auditory stimulus is also *felt* as mechanical energy pressing against our skin.

How does information about touch travel from the skin through the nervous system? Sensory fibers arising from receptors in the skin enter the spinal cord. From there the information travels to the brain stem, at which point most fibers from each side of the body cross over to the opposite side of the brain. Then the information about touch moves on to the thalamus, which serves as a relay station. The thalamus then projects the map of the body's surface onto the somatosensory areas of the parietal lobes in the cerebral cortex (Anderson, 2002).

As in the visual and auditory systems, both feature detection and parallel processing occur when information about touch is processed. Some cells in the somatosensory cortex respond to specific aspects of touch, such as movement across the skin. Also, such features of tactile (touch) sensation as pressure, temperature, and movement may be recombined in the somatosensory cortex through reassembly in the same manner as in vision (Bloom, Nelson, & Lazerson, 2001).

Just as the visual system is more sensitive to images on the fovea than to images in the peripheral retina, our sensitivity to touch is not equally good across all areas of the skin. As you might expect, human toolmakers need to have excellent touch discrimination in their hands, but they require much less touch discrimination in other parts of the body, such as the torso or legs. Because of this, the brain devotes more space to analyzing touch signals coming from the hands than from the legs.

Exploring Touch in Life   Psychologists Susan Lederman and Roberta Klatsky (1998) are working with engineers to determine whether touch input is important for such jobs as operating robots from afar or performing microsurgery. This research focuses mainly on the hands because the fingertips contain the highest densities of tactile

Should We Believe the Claims of Psychics?

A woman reports that she has power over the goldfish in a 50-gallon tank. She claims that she can will them to swim to either end of the tank.

Under the careful scrutiny of James Randi, this woman's account turned out to be just another fish story. The woman had written Randi, a professional magician who has a standing offer of $1,000,000 to anyone whose psychic claims withstand his analysis. In the case of the woman and her goldfish, Randi received a letter from her priest validating her extraordinary power. Randi talked with the priest, who told him that the woman would put her hands in front of her body and then run to one end of the tank. The fish soon swam to that end of the tank. Since the fish could see out of the tank just as we could see into it, Randi suggested that the woman put opaque brown wrapping paper over one end of the tank and then try her powers. The woman did and called Randi to tell him that she had discovered something new about her powers: Her mind could not penetrate brown paper. The woman, believing she had magical powers, completely misunderstood why Randi had asked her to place the brown paper over the fish tank.

To date, no one has met Randi's $1,000,000 challenge, but he has investigated hundreds of reports of supernatural and occult powers. Recently he has evaluated *cold-reading*, a popular technique among psychics (people who claim to have extrasensory perception). When cold-reading, the psychic tells the person nothing but makes guesses, puts out suggestions, and asks questions. For example, if the "reader" says, "I am visualizing an older woman," the person usually gives some reaction. It may be just a nod, somebody's name, or even identification of a sister, aunt, mother, or grandmother. The important thing is that this information is supplied by the person, not the reader. Of course, almost everyone will show some reaction to such a general statement, giving the reader new information to incorporate into subsequent comments or questions. Alternatively, the reader may say, "Mary? Do you recognize this person?" If there is a Mary, the person will give more helpful information

Magician James Randi (right) has investigated a large number of psychics' claims. No one has yet won Randi's standing offer of $1,000,000 to anyone whose psychic claims withstand his analysis.

to the reader. If no Mary is immediately recognized, the reader moves on. If "Mary" is remembered later, she is incorporated into the reader's comments. The reader can try many names, confident that the person will likely remember only suggested names that are meaningful to him or her. In this way, the person may well end up volunteering what he or she wants to hear.

According to Randi, cold-readers often interview people while they are waiting to get into the show. Then, when the show begins, they can choose to work with people they have already talked to. Suppose a person approaches the reader before the show and says he has a question about his deceased wife. That person can later be selected during the show and be asked, "Is your question about your dead wife?" To other people who are not aware of the previous conversation, the reader's question can seem miraculous.

Randi also says that when cold readers are not allowed to speak to anyone in advance, or to be asked or told anything in advance, and people are allowed to answer only "yes" or "no" when asked direct questions, they fail miserably. In general, according to Randi, cold readers have a way of leading people to believe that they knew something they didn't.

Randi (1997) makes a distinction between the tricks of magicians, such as himself, and the work of psychics and others who claim extraordinary ESP powers. He says that magic is done for entertainment, the other for swindling. Read more about the Amazing Randi's skeptical approach to supernatural phenomena at his website, www.randi.org.

What do you think?

- Do you think the Amazing Randi's $1,000,000 prize will ever be claimed? Why or why not?
- Why do you think people continue to believe in psychic phenomena when confronted with contradictory evidence produced by Randi and others?
- What kind of research would be necessary to establish that a particular psychic phenomenon is genuine?

---

receptors. In one study, they tested individuals' ability to perform several tasks with and without feedback to their index fingers (Lederman & Klatsky, 1998). They measured people's ability to feel vibrations, to sense whether they could feel two distinct objects or just one, and to detect the presence of a thin nylon hair. They also tested perceptual abilities, such as the ability to judge how rough a surface was and to compare the roughness of the two surfaces. To simulate a no-feedback situation, they covered participants' fingertips with a fiberglass sheath. The sheath had a dramatic

Warm water   Cold water

FIGURE 5.41 A "Hot" Experience
When two pipes, one containing cold water and the other warm water, are braided together, a person touching the pipes feels a sensation of "hot." The perceived heat coming from the pipes is so intense that a person cannot touch them for longer than a couple of seconds.

thermoreceptors Located under the skin, they respond to increases and decreases in temperature.

pain The sensation that warns us that damage to our bodies is occurring.

impact on the participants' perceptual judgments. For example, their ability to sense the thin hair declined 73 percent, and their skill in detecting two objects as opposed to one dropped 32 percent.

Another important aspect of touch is its role in infant development. Can newborns feel your caress when you touch them? Yes, they can. Indeed, they can feel touch better than they can see, hear, or even taste (Eliot, 2001). Newborn girls are more sensitive to touch than their male counterparts, a gender difference that remains throughout life. Psychologists believe that the sense of touch is especially helpful to infants, as it helps them detect and explore the physical world and is also important for health and emotional well-being. As was shown in chapter 4, touch is a key aspect of attachment to a caregiver, and massage therapy has been effective in helping preterm infants become healthier.

Temperature   Beyond the need to sense physical pressure on the skin, we need to detect temperature, even in the absence of direct contact with the skin. **Thermoreceptors,** which are located under the skin, respond to increases and decreases in temperature at or near the skin and also provide input to keep the body's temperature at 98.6 degrees Fahrenheit. There are two types of thermoreceptors: warm and cold (warm thermoreceptors respond to the warming of the skin, and cold thermoreceptors respond to the cooling of the skin).

Somewhat surprisingly, when warm and cold receptors that are close to each other in the skin are stimulated simultaneously, we experience the sensation of hotness. Figure 5.41 illustrates this "hot" experience.

Pain   When contact with the skin takes the form of a sharp pinch, our sensation of mechanical pressure changes from touch to pain. When a pot handle is so hot that it burns your hand, your sensation of temperature becomes one of pain. Many kinds of stimuli can cause pain. Intense stimulation of any one of the senses can produce pain—too much light, very loud sounds, or very spicy food, for example. Our ability to sense pain is vital for our survival as a species. **Pain** is the sensation that warns us of damage to our bodies. It functions as a quick-acting system that tells the motor systems of the brain that they must act to minimize or eliminate this damage. A hand touching a hot stove must be pulled away; ears should be covered up when one walks by a loud pavement drill; chili should be buffered with some crackers.

Pathways of Pain   Pain receptors are dispersed widely throughout the body—in the skin, in the sheath tissue surrounding muscles, in internal organs, and in the membranes around bone (Beatty, 1995). Although all pain receptors are anatomically similar, they differ in the type of physical stimuli to which they most readily respond. Mechanical pain receptors respond mainly to pressure, such as when a sharp object is encountered. Heat pain receptors respond primarily to strong heat that is capable of burning the tissue in which the receptors are embedded. Other pain receptors have a mixed function, responding to both types of painful stimuli. Many pain receptors are chemically sensitive and respond to a range of pain-producing substances.

Pain receptors have a much higher threshold for firing than receptors for temperature and touch (Bloom & others, 2001). Pain receptors react mainly to physical stimuli that distort them or to chemical stimuli that "irritate" them into action. Inflamed joints or sore, torn muscles produce *prostaglandins,* which stimulate the receptors and cause the experience of pain. Drugs such as aspirin likely reduce the feeling of pain by reducing the body's production of prostaglandins.

Two different neural pathways transmit pain messages to the brain: a fast pathway and a slow pathway (Bloom & others, 2001). In the *fast pathway,* fibers connect directly with the thalamus, then to the motor and sensory areas of the cerebral cortex. This pathway transmits information about sharp, localized pain, as when you cut your skin. The fast pathway may serve as a warning system, providing immediate information about an injury—it takes less than a second for the information in this

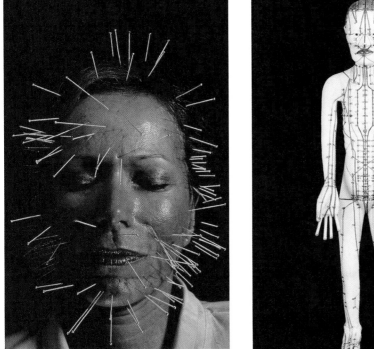

FIGURE 5.42 Acupuncture
(*Left*) This woman is being treated for pain by an acupuncturist. (*Right*) Acupuncture points are carefully noted on this nineteenth-century Japanese papier-mâché figure. In their adaptation of the Chinese methodology, the Japanese identified 660 points.

pathway to reach the cerebral cortex. In the *slow pathway,* pain information travels through the limbic system, a detour that delays the arrival of information at the cerebral cortex by seconds. The unpleasant, nagging pain that characterizes the slow pathway may function to remind the brain that an injury has occurred, that normal activity needs to be restricted, and that the pain needs to be monitored.

In the 1960s, Ronald Melzack and Patricia Wall (1965) proposed the **gate-control theory of pain,** which states that the spinal column contains a neural gate that can be opened (allowing the perception of pain) or closed (blocking the perception of pain). The brain can send signals downward to the spinal cord to close the gate and thus suppress the sensation of pain. The gate-control theory was proposed as an explanation for the effects of *acupuncture,* a technique in which thin needles are inserted at specific points in the body to produce various effects, such as local anesthesia (see figure 5.42). The gate-control theory assumes that the presence of acupuncture needles somehow manages to shut the pain gate, inhibiting the experience of pain. More recently, Wall and Melzack (1999) revised the gate-control theory. Although they still believe that some pain originates in signals coming through the spinal cord gate, they have now concluded that ultimately the brain generates the experience of pain.

Although the original conception of gate-control theory has been abandoned, there is evidence that turning pain signals on and turning them off is a chemical process that probably involves *endorphins,* which were discussed in chapter 3. Recall that endorphins are neurotransmitters that function as natural opiates in producing pleasure and pain. Endorphins are believed to be released mainly in the synapses of the slow pathway (Bloom & others, 2001).

Perception of pain is complex and often varies from one person to the next. Some people rarely feel pain; others seem to be in great pain if they experience a minor bump or bruise. To some degree these individual variations may be physiological. A person who experiences considerable pain even with a minor injury may have a neurotransmitter system that is deficient in endorphin production.

However, perception of pain goes beyond physiology. Although it is true that all sensations are affected by factors such as motivation, expectation, and other related

gate-control theory of pain The spinal column contains a neural gate that can be open (allowing the perception of pain) or closed (blocking the perception of pain).

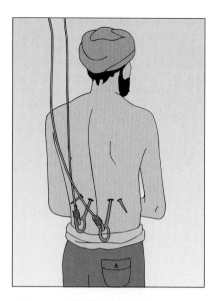

FIGURE 5.43 Hook-Swinging Ceremony (*Top*) Two steel hooks are shown hanging from the back of an Asian Indian participating in a hook-swinging ceremony. (*Bottom*) The man hangs on to ropes as a cart takes him from village to village. After he blesses each child and farm field in the village, he swings freely, suspended by the hooks in his back (after Kosambi, 1967).

decision factors, the perception of pain is especially susceptible to these factors (Philips & Rachman, 1996). Cultural and ethnic contexts, also, can greatly determine the degree to which an individual experiences pain. For example, one pain researcher described a ritual performed in India in which a chosen person travels from town to town delivering blessings to the children and the crops while suspended from metal hooks embedded in his back (Melzak, 1973). The chosen person apparently reports no sensation of pain and appears to be in ecstasy (see figure 5.43).

Nowhere is cultural variation more pronounced than in the perception of pain in childbirth. In some cultures, women do not expect childbirth to be painful. They may have their babies and in a matter of hours go back to performing their normal daily activities. However, in the United States and most other Western cultures, women expect childbirth to involve considerable pain. The Lamaze method of childbirth (natural childbirth) seeks to reduce this fear of pain by training women's muscle tone and breathing patterns. Women who use the Lamaze method experience reduced perception of pain in childbirth.

Pain Control and Treatment Most acute pain decreases over time with avoidance of activity or with analgesic medication. Treatment of chronic pain is often more complex. Often the most successful treatment of pain involves a combination of physical and psychological techniques (Watkins & Maier, 2000). A pain clinic may select one or more of the following techniques to treat an individual's pain: surgery, drugs, acupuncture, electrical stimulation, massage, exercise, hypnosis, relaxation, and thought distraction (Ezzo & others, 2001; Haythronthwaite, Lawrence, & Fauerbach, 2001). Hypnosis is discussed further in chapter 6 and relaxation techniques in chapter 15.

Let's further explore several strategies for reducing acute pain:

- *Distraction.* When you get an injection, do you focus on the needle as it is about to plunge into your flesh, or do you avert your eyes and concentrate on something else? Distraction is usually the best way to reduce pain, because attention to the sensation can magnify it. You might focus your attention on something pleasant that you plan to do this weekend, for example.
- *Focused breathing.* The next time you stub your toe, try panting—short, fast breaths (similar to the breathing practiced in Lamaze childbirth). Focused breathing may successfully close the pain gate and diminish your agony.
- *Counterstimulation.* If you pinch your cheek in the aftermath of a bad cut, it likely will mute your pain. This may close the pain gate. Applying ice to a sprained or swollen area not only reduces the pain but also can keep the swelling down.

The Chemical Senses

The information impinging on our senses comes in many diverse forms: electromagnetic energy in vision, sound waves in audition, and mechanical pressure and temperature in the cutaneous senses. The two senses presented in this section are responsible for processing chemicals in our environment (Doty, 2001). With the sense of smell we detect airborne chemicals, and with taste we detect chemicals that have been dissolved in saliva. Taste and smell are frequently stimulated simultaneously. We sometimes realize the strong links between the two senses only when a nasty cold and nasal congestion seem to take the pleasure out of eating. Our favorite foods become "tasteless" without the smells that characterize them. Despite this link, taste and smell are indeed two distinct systems.

Taste What would life be with no sense of taste? For anyone who has tried to diet, "not worth living" is a common response. The thought of giving up a favorite taste, such as chocolate or butter, can be very depressing. We use our sense of taste to select food and to regulate food intake. Although it is not so easy to see or smell mold on a blueberry, a small taste is enough to prompt you to sense that the fruit is no longer

Many animals have a stronger sense of smell than humans do. Dogs especially have a powerful olfactory sense. Watson, a Labrador retriever, reliably paws his owner 45 minutes before her epileptic seizures begin, giving her time to move to a safe place. How does Watson do this? The best hypothesis is that the dog smells the chemical changes known to precede epileptic seizures.

fit for consumption. Beyond that, the pleasure associated with the taste of food depends on many aspects of our body's need for a particular food (Bartoshuk & Beauchamp, 1994). The taste of devil's food cake can be very pleasurable when we are hungry but downright revolting after eating a banana split.

It is not the prettiest sight you've ever seen, but try this anyway. Take a drink of milk and allow it to coat your tongue. Then go to a mirror, stick out your tongue, and look carefully at its surface. You should be able to see rounded bumps above the surface of your tongue. Those bumps, called **papillae,** contain taste buds, which are the receptors for taste. About 10,000 of these taste buds are located on your tongue. As with all of the other sensory systems discussed in this chapter, the information picked up by these receptors is transmitted to the brain for analysis and, when necessary, response (spitting something out, for example).

The taste qualities we respond to can be categorized as sweet, sour, bitter, and salty (Scott, 2000). Though all areas of the tongue can detect each of the four tastes, different regions of the tongue are more sensitive to some tastes than others. The tip of the tongue is the most sensitive to sweet and salty substances, the sides to sour, and the rear to bitter (see figure 5.44; Bloom & others, 2001).

Today, many neuroscientists believe that the breakdown of taste into four independent, elementary categories is overdrawn (Cauller, 2001). The taste fibers leading from a taste bud to the brain often respond strongly to a range of chemicals that span multiple taste elements, such as salty and sour (Smith & Margolskee, 2001). The brain processes these somewhat ambiguous incoming signals and integrates them into a perception of taste.

Although people still often categorize taste sensations along the four dimensions of sweet, bitter, salty, and sour, our tasting ability goes far beyond them. Most of us pride ourselves on being able to distinguish different brands of ice cream; caffeinated and decaffeinated soda, coffee, and tea; and the many variations of product substitutes that are supposed to be better for us than the standard high-cholesterol, high-sugar, and high-fat culinary pleasures. Think of the remarkable range of tastes that you have that are generated by variations and combinations of sweet, sour, bitter, and salty.

Smell A good way to begin the discussion of smell is to consider the many functions it serves. It is often easier to understand the importance of smell when we think about animals with more sophisticated senses of smell than our own. A dog, for exam-

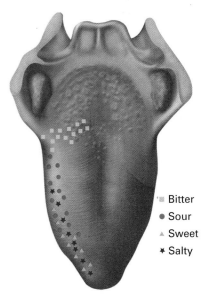

■ Bitter
● Sour
▲ Sweet
✻ Salty

FIGURE 5.44 Location on the Tongue of Sensitivity to Sweet, Salty, Sour, and Bitter Substances

papillae Bumps on the tongue that contain taste buds, the receptors for taste.

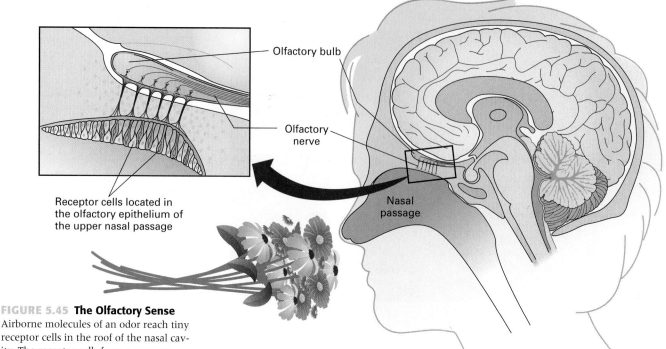

Olfactory bulb

Olfactory nerve

Nasal passage

Receptor cells located in the olfactory epithelium of the upper nasal passage

FIGURE 5.45 The Olfactory Sense
Airborne molecules of an odor reach tiny receptor cells in the roof of the nasal cavity. The receptor cells form a mucous-covered membrane called the olfactory epithelium. Then the olfactory nerve carries information about the odor to the brain for further processing.

olfactory epithelium Located in the roof of the nasal cavity, a sheet of receptor cells for smell.

ple, can use its sense of smell to find its way back from a lone stroll, to distinguish friend from foe, or even (with practice) to detect illegal drugs concealed in a suitcase. In fact, dogs can detect odors in concentrations 100 times lower than those detectable by humans. Given the nasal feats of the average dog, we might be tempted to believe that the sense of smell has outlived its usefulness in humans. What do we use smell for? For one thing, humans need the sense of smell to decide what to eat. We can distinguish rotten food from fresh food and remember (all too well) which foods have made us ill in the past. The smell of a food that has previously made us ill is often, by itself, enough to make us feel nauseous. Second, although tracking is a function of smell that we often associate only with animals, humans are competent odor trackers. We can follow the smell of gas to a leak, the smell of smoke to a fire, or the smell of a hot apple pie to a windowsill.

What physical equipment do we use to process odor information? Just as the eyes scan the visual field for objects of interest and the pinnae prick up to direct attention to sounds of interest, the nose is not a passive instrument. We actively sniff when we are trying to track down the source of a fire or of a burned-out fluorescent light. The **olfactory epithelium,** lining the roof of the nasal cavity, contains a sheet of receptor cells for smell (see figure 5.45), so sniffing has the effect of maximizing the chances of detecting an odor (Doty & Muller-Schwarze, 1992). The receptor cells are covered with millions of minute hairlike antennae that project through the mucus in the top of the nasal cavity and make contact with air on its way to the throat and lungs (Laurent & others, 2001; Yau, 2002). Interestingly, unlike the neurons of most sensory systems, the neurons in the olfactory epithelium tend to replace themselves after injury (Doty, 2001).

What is the neural pathway for information about smell? Although all other sensory pathways pass through the thalamus, the pathway for smell does not. In smell, the neural pathway first goes to the olfactory areas of the cerebral cortex in the temporal lobes and then projects to various brain regions, especially the limbic system, which is involved in emotion and memory. For many people, smells have a way of generating memories—often emotion-laden ones—undoubtedly because of the neural pathways that smell takes through the limbic system (Bloom & others, 2001).

The Kinesthetic and Vestibular Senses

You know the difference between walking and running and between lying down and sitting up. To perform even the simplest acts of motor coordination, such as reaching out to take a book off a library shelf or getting up out of a chair, the brain must be constantly receiving and coordinating information from every part of the body. Your body has two kinds of senses that provide information about your movement and orientation in space, as well as helping to maintain balance. The **kinesthetic senses** provide information about movement, posture, and orientation. The **vestibular sense** provides information about balance and movement.

No specific organ contains the kinesthetic senses. Instead, they are embedded in muscle fibers and joints. As we stretch and move, these receptors signal the state of the muscle. Kinesthesia is a sense that you often do not even notice until it is gone. Try walking when your leg is "asleep," or smiling (never mind talking) when you've just come from a dentist's office and you are still under the effects of novocaine. Perhaps the sophistication of kinesthesis can be best appreciated when we think in terms of memory. Even a mediocre typist can bang out 20 words per minute—but how many of us could write down the order of the letters on a keyboard without looking? Typing is a skill that relies on very coordinated sensitivity to the orientation, position, and movements of our fingers. We say that our fingers remember the positions of the keys. Likewise, the complicated movements a pitcher uses to throw a ball cannot be written down or communicated easily using language. They involve nearly every muscle and joint in the body. Most information about the kinesthetic sense is transmitted from the joints and muscles along the same pathways to the brain as information about touch.

The vestibular sense tells us whether our head (and hence usually our body) is tilted, moving, slowing down, or speeding up. It works in concert with the kinesthetic senses to coordinate our *proprioceptive feedback,* which is information about the position of our limbs and body parts in relation to other body parts. Consider the combination of sensory abilities involved in the motion of an ice hockey player skating down the ice cradling the puck and pushing it forward with the hockey stick. The hockey player is responding simultaneously to a multitude of sensations, including those produced by the slickness of the ice, the position of the puck, the speed and momentum of the forward progression, and the requirements of the play to turn and to track the other players on the ice.

The **semicircular canals,** located in the inner ear, contain the sensory receptors that detect head motion caused when we tilt or move our heads and/or bodies (see figure 5.46). These canals consist of three fluid-filled circular tubes that lie in the three planes of the body—right-left, front-back, and up-down. We can picture these as three intersecting hula hoops. As you move your head, the fluid of the semicircular canals flows in different directions and at different speeds (depending on the force of the head movement). Our perception of head movement and position is determined by the movements of these receptor cells. This ingenious system of using the motion of fluid in tubes to sense head position is not unlike the auditory system found in the inner ear. However, the fluid movement in the cochlea is caused by the pressure sound exerts on the oval window, whereas the movements in the semicircular canals reflect physical movements of the head and body. Vestibular sacs in the semicircular canals contain hair cells embedded in a gelatin-like mass, and, just as the hair cells in the cochlea trigger hearing impulses in the brain, the hair cells in the semicircular canals are involved in transmitting information about balance and movement.

The brain pathways for the vestibular sense begin in the auditory nerve, which contains both the cochlear nerve (with information about sound) and the vestibular nerve (which has information about balance and movement). Most of the axons of the vestibular nerve connect with the medulla, although some go directly to the cerebellum. There also appear to be vestibular projections to the temporal cortex,

FIGURE 5.46 **The Semicircular Canals and Vestibular Sense**
The semicircular canals provide feedback to the gymnast's brain as her head and body tilt in different directions. Any angle of head rotation is registered by hair cells in one or more semicircular canals in both ears. (*Inset*) The semicircular canals.

kinesthetic senses Provide information about movement, posture, and orientation.

vestibular sense Provides information about balance and movement.

semicircular canals Located in the inner ear; contain the sensory receptors that detect head motion.

© King Features. Reprinted with special permission of King Features Syndicate.

although their specific pathways have not been fully charted. Most neuroscientists believe that the projections to the cerebral cortex are responsible for dizziness, whereas the connections to the lower brain stem produce the nausea and vomiting that accompany motion sickness (Carlson, 2001).

The combination of kinesthetic and vestibular senses is supplemented by information from vision. This simple principle has made many an amusement park and large-screen movie theater profitable. When films are shown on screens that are large enough to fill our visual field, such as those found in many theme parks, the motion you perceive on the screen can make you feel like you are moving. This is the same principle that causes a motorist to slam on the brakes in his tiny sports car when the big truck next to him starts to move forward. When everything in our visual field appears to be moving, it is generally because we are moving.

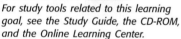

For study tools related to this learning goal, see the Study Guide, the CD-ROM, and the Online Learning Center.

Review and Sharpen Your Thinking

4 *Know how the skin, chemical, kinesthetic, and vestibular senses work.*

- Explain how the skin monitors touch, temperature, and pain
- Discuss the chemical senses of taste and smell
- Describe how the kinesthetic and vestibular senses function

Why can some individuals stand more pain than others?

5 PERCEPTION AND HUMAN FACTORS PSYCHOLOGY

What are some applications of research in perception?

In our discussion of touch, we described the research of Susan Lederman and Roberta Klatsky (1998), who have studied various aspects of touch input for jobs such as operating robots and performing microsurgery. This research falls into the area of psychology known as "human factors"; a number of perception psychologists conduct this type of research. *Human factors psychology* involves designing equipment and arranging environments in which humans function to improve them in various ways, such as making them safer and more efficient (O'Neil & Andrews, 2000; Wise & Hopkins, 2000). Human factors psychology is often associated with the field of industrial and organizational psychology. Human factors psychologists make the dials and controls on the instrument panel of your car easier to read, easier to handle, and minimally distracting. They also help to design computer interface software and devices to make them more "user friendly."

Human factors psychologists spend considerable time designing displays (Payne, Lang, & Blackwell, 1995). One of the initial decisions they have to make is which

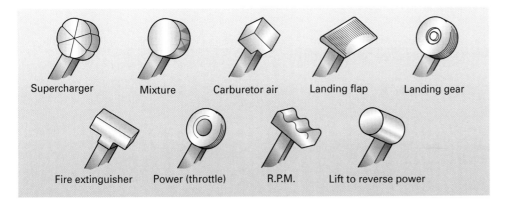

Supercharger   Mixture   Carburetor air   Landing flap   Landing gear

Fire extinguisher   Power (throttle)   R.P.M.   Lift to reverse power

FIGURE 5.47 **Shape-Coded Controls**
Controls need to be clearly coded to assure their correct and rapid identification. One way to accomplish this is to shape code the controls. Each knob on a console might be a recognizably different shape, which allows for rapid visual identification of the correct control. It also allows tactual identification in the dark or when the operator's eyes must focus somewhere else. An effective way of shape coding controls is to design the control so that its shape represents or symbolizes its function.

sensory modality to use. Typically, displays are visual. However, depending on the situation and the information that needs to be monitored, auditory and tactile displays might be used. Conside the routine operation of a car. You get visual feedback about the speed at which you are driving, the temperature of the engine, and the oil pressure. You might hear a beeping sound if a door is not completely closed. You might forget to latch your seatbelt and then hear a buzzer that signals you to latch it. Or consider airplane design. The landing flap controls on many airplanes are shaped like the landing flaps themselves, so that pilots can manage the controls without looking at them. The general idea is to provide information without interfering with the task (see figure 5.47).

Robert McCann is a human factors psychologist who works for NASA. He currently is working on a project to retrofit space shuttle cockpits with liquid crystal displays that provide much more flexibility in displaying information in the cockpit than current displays provide (McCann, 2001). He hopes the new displays will increase the safety of space shuttle missions by providing astronauts with better awareness of information that takes less mental effort.

Visual illusions are another concern of human factors psychologists. The view of an airplane pilot through the cockpit window varies considerably due to weather conditions and the amount of glare and degree of brightness (Hawkins, 1987). These changing factors can sometimes cause hazardous perceptual illusions. Illusions of apparent motion also can be a hazard as pilots wait for or initiate a takeoff. Human factors psychologists seek to find ways to minimize these illusions.

Human factors psychologists also study other aspects of commercial flying. For example, in the cockpit, they assess pilot fatigue and sources of error, such as miscommunication among the flight crew (Hancock & Desmond, 2000). In the passenger cabin, they might examine influences on the anxiety level, safety, and behavior of passengers.

Robert McCann, a human factors psychologist, at work at NASA.

Review and Sharpen Your Thinking

5 *Describe what human factors psychologists do.*

- Define human factors psychology and discuss some of its benefits.

Try to come up with some aspects of life other than those described in the text in which human factors research might improve functioning.

mhhe com/
santrockp7

For study tools related to this learning goal, see the Study Guide, the CD-ROM, and the Online Learning Center.

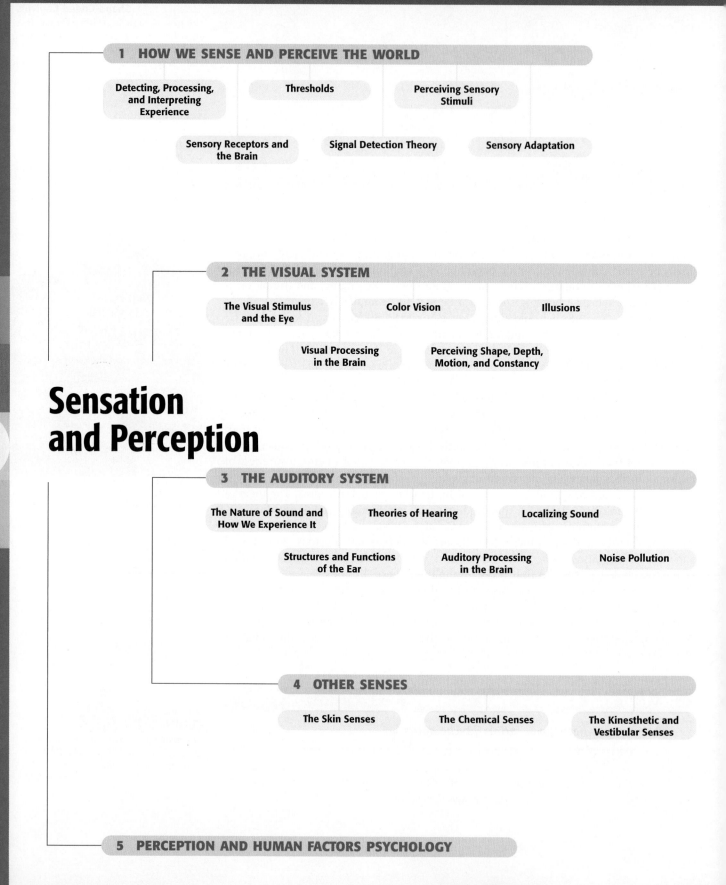

1 HOW WE SENSE AND PERCEIVE THE WORLD

Detecting, Processing, and Interpreting Experience

Thresholds

Perceiving Sensory Stimuli

Sensory Receptors and the Brain

Signal Detection Theory

Sensory Adaptation

2 THE VISUAL SYSTEM

The Visual Stimulus and the Eye

Color Vision

Illusions

Visual Processing in the Brain

Perceiving Shape, Depth, Motion, and Constancy

Sensation and Perception

3 THE AUDITORY SYSTEM

The Nature of Sound and How We Experience It

Theories of Hearing

Localizing Sound

Structures and Functions of the Ear

Auditory Processing in the Brain

Noise Pollution

4 OTHER SENSES

The Skin Senses

The Chemical Senses

The Kinesthetic and Vestibular Senses

5 PERCEPTION AND HUMAN FACTORS PSYCHOLOGY

1 Discuss basic principles of sensation and perception.

- Sensation is the process of receiving stimulus energies from the environment. Perception is the process of organizing and interpreting sensory information to give it meaning. Sensation and perception are integrated. Perceiving the world involves both bottom-up and top-down processing.
- All sensation begins with sensory receptors, which are specialized cells that detect and transmit information about a stimulus to sensory neurons and the brain. Sensory receptors are selective and have different neural pathways. The three main classes of sense organs and receptors are photoreception, mechanoreception, and chemoreception.
- Psychophysics, the field that studies links between the physical properties of stimuli and a person's experience of them, defines absolute threshold as the minimum amount of energy that people can detect. There is no evidence that subliminal perception—the ability to detect information below the level of conscious awareness—has any substantial influence on our thoughts and behavior. The difference threshold, or just noticeable difference, is the smallest difference in stimulation required to discriminate one stimulus from another 50 percent of the time. Weber's law holds that two stimuli must differ by a constant minimum percentage to be perceived as different.
- Signal detection theory focuses on decision making about stimuli in the presence of uncertainty. In this theory, detection of sensory stimuli depends on many other factors than the physical properties of the stimuli, and differences in these other factors may lead different people to make different decisions about identical stimuli.
- What we perceive depends in part on which stimuli engage our attention and on a tendency to perceive things according to our beliefs and expectations. Selective attention involves focusing on a specific aspect of experience while ignoring others. Attention may involve bottom-up or top-down processing. A perceptual set is a collection of experiences and expectations that influence perception.
- Sensory adaptation is a change in the responsiveness of the sensory system based on the average level of surrounding stimulation.

2 Explain how the visual system enables us to see and, by communicating with the brain, to perceive the world.

- Light is a form of electromagnetic energy that can be described in terms of wavelengths. Three characteristics of light are hue, amplitude, and purity. The eye responds to light within a narrow range of wavelengths (400–700 nm). Light passes through the cornea and lens to the retina, a light-sensitive surface in the back of the eye that houses light receptors called rods (which function in low illumination) and cones (which react to color). The fovea of the retina contains only cones and serves to sharpen detail in an image. Ganglion cells interpret incoming visual information and send it to the brain.
- The optic nerve transmits neural impulses to the brain. There it diverges at the optic chiasm, so that what we see in the left visual field is registered in the right side of the brain and vice versa. In the occipital lobes of the cerebral cortex, the information is integrated. Visual information processing involves feature detection, parallel processing, and binding.
- The trichromatic theory of color perception stipulates that three types of color receptors in the retina allow us to perceive three colors (green, red, and blue). The opponent-process theory states that cells in the visual system respond to red-green and blue-yellow colors. Both theories are probably correct—the eye and the brain use both methods to code colors.
- Shape perception is the ability to distinguish objects from their background. This figure-ground relationship is a principle of gestalt psychology, which emphasizes that people naturally organize their perceptions according to patterns. Depth perception is the ability to perceive objects three-dimensionally. Depth perception depends on binocular cues and monocular cues. Motion perception by humans depends on specialized neurons, feedback from the body, and environmental cues. Psychologists are interested in both real and apparent movement. Perceptual constancy is the recognition that objects are stable despite changes in the way we see them. Three types of perceptual constancy are size constancy, shape constancy, and brightness constancy.
- A visual illusion is the result of a discrepancy between reality and the perceptual representation of it. Examples are the Müller-Lyer illusion, the moon illusion, the horizontal-vertical illusion, the Ponzo illusion, and the devil's tuning fork.

Understand how the auditory system registers sound and how it connects with the brain to perceive it.

- Sounds, or sound waves, are vibrations in the air that are processed by the auditory system. Sound waves vary in wavelength. Wavelength determines frequency. Pitch is the perceptual interpretation of frequency. Amplitude, measured in decibels, is perceived as loudness. Complex sounds involve a blending of frequencies. Timbre is the tone saturation or perceptual quality of a sound.
- The outer ear consists of the pinna and external auditory canal and acts to funnel sound to the middle ear. In the middle ear, the eardrum, hammer, anvil, and stirrup vibrate in response to sound and transfer the vibrations to the inner ear. Important parts of the fluid-filled inner ear are the oval window, cochlea, and basilar membrane. The movement of hair cells between the basilar membrane and the tectorial membrane generates nerve impulses.
- Place theory states that each frequency produces vibrations at a particular spot on the basilar membrane. Place theory adequately explains high-frequency sounds but not low-frequency sounds. Frequency theory states that the perception of a sound's frequency depends on how often the auditory nerve fires. A modification of frequency theory, the volley principle, states that a cluster of neurons can fire impulses in rapid succession, producing a volley of impulses.
- Information about sound moves from the hair cells to the auditory nerve, which carries information to the brain's auditory areas. The cortical destination of most fibers is the temporal lobes of the cerebral cortex.
- Localizing sound involves both the timing of the sound and the intensity of the sound arriving at each ear.
- Noise pollution is a special concern, because it can have a negative effect on behavior. Noise at 80 decibels or higher, if heard for prolonged periods of time, can damage hearing.

Know how the skin, chemical, kinesthetic, and vestibular senses work.

- Touch is the detection of mechanical energy, or pressure, against the skin. Touch information travels through the spinal cord, brain stem, and thalamus, and on to the somatosensory areas of the parietal lobes. Psychologists are studying the role of touch in various jobs and in infant development. Thermoreceptors under the skin respond to increases and decreases in temperature. Pain is the sensation that warns us about damage to our bodies. Two different neural pathways transmit information about pain: a fast pathway and a slow pathway. One theory of pain is gate-control theory. Many physical and psychological techniques are used to control pain.
- Taste and smell enable us to detect and process chemicals in the environment. Papillae are bumps on the tongue that contain taste buds, the receptors for taste. The taste qualities we respond to are categorized as sweet, sour, bitter, and salty, although our tasting ability goes beyond these four qualities. The olfactory epithelium contains a sheet of receptor cells for smell in the roof of the nose.
- The kinesthetic sense provides information about movement, posture, and orientation. The vestibular sense provides information about balance and movement. Receptors for the kinesthetic sense are embedded in muscle fibers and joints. The semicircular canals in the inner ear contain the sensory receptors that detect head motion.

Describe what human factors psychologists study.

- Human factors psychologists design equipment and arrange environments in which humans function in order to improve those environments, for example, by designing displays to make them safer and more efficient.

Key Terms

sensation, p. 176	difference threshold, p. 182	opponent-process theory, p. 195	place theory, p. 207
transduction, p. 177	Weber's law, p. 183	figure-ground relationship, p. 197	frequency theory, p. 208
perception, p. 177	signal detection theory, p. 183	gestalt psychology, p. 197	volley principle, p. 208
bottom-up processing, p. 177	selective attention, p. 184	depth perception, p. 198	auditory nerve, p. 208
top-down processing, p. 177	perceptual set, p. 185	binocular cues, p. 198	thermoreceptors, p. 214
sensory receptors, p. 178	sensory adaptation, p. 186	monocular cues, p. 198	pain, p. 214
psychophysics, p. 180	retina, p. 189	apparent movement, p. 201	gate-control theory of pain, p. 214
absolute threshold, p. 180	rods, p. 190	perceptual constancy, p. 201	papillae, p. 217
noise, p. 181	cones, p. 190	visual illusion, p. 202	olfactory epithelium, p. 218
subliminal perception, p. 181	feature detectors, p. 192	outer ear, p. 206	kinesthetic senses, p. 219
	parallel processing, p. 193	middle ear, p. 206	vestibular sense, p. 219
	binding, p. 193	inner ear, p. 206	semicircular canals, p. 219
	trichromatic theory, p. 194		

Apply Your Knowledge

1. Find a partner and test your absolute detection threshold for sugar. Have your partner set up the following sugar-and-water mixtures. Mix 2 teaspoons of sugar in 4 cups of water. Label this solution ("solution X," for example). Take 2 cups of "solution X," add 2 cups of water, and give this solution a second label ("solution D," for example). Then, take 2 cups of "solution D," add 2 cups of water, and give this a third label ("solution Q"). Continue taking 2 cups from each successive solution until there is a total of 8 solutions, making sure to keep track of which solution is which. When you're done, the concentration of the solutions should be equivalent to 1 teaspoon in each of the following amounts of water: 1 pint (2 cups), 1 quart, 1 half-gallon, 1 gallon, 2 gallons, 4 gallons, and 8 gallons. Your partner should place a sample of one of the solutions in a cup and a sample of plain water in another, identical cup. You should taste the solution in each cup and decide which one is the sugar solution. Do this with all of the solutions until you can decide what your absolute detection threshold is according to the definition in the text. Do you think your detection threshold would vary depending on what you have recently eaten? Why or why not?

2. Imagine that you have two sets of dominoes. Each set contains 100 dominoes. With the first set, you make a straight line of 100. With the second set, you make an arrangement in which tipping a single domino causes five separate lines of dominoes to fall down simultaneously. Which set of dominoes will fall the fastest? How is this set of dominoes similar to the way we process visual information?

3. Compare and contrast the consequences of losing vision in one eye versus losing hearing in one ear.

4. You smell a delicious aroma coming from the kitchen, so you head that way, but you manage to stub your toe on your roommate's backpack and then hit your head on the table as you bend down to rub your toe. Your roommate hands you what looks like a brownie; it smells pretty good, so you take a big bite. First it tastes good; then, suddenly, your mouth feels as if it is on fire, so you grab the glass of ice water sitting on the table and take a big gulp of it. Describe the different kinds of sensory signals that your brain has processed during this episode and the different kinds of receptors you have used to make sense of what's happened.

5. Many websites are easy to use and navigate, but some would benefit from some design help from human factors psychologists. Browse the Web and find some sites that have good human factors designs and others that have bad human factors designs. Can you identify aspects of the good designs that are missing in the bad designs (or vice versa)?

Connections

mhhe.com/santrockp7

For extra help in mastering the material in this chapter, see the review sections and practice quizzes in the Student Study Guide, the CD-ROM, and the Online Learning Center.

6 States of Consciousness

Chapter Outline

Learning Goals

THE NATURE OF CONSCIOUSNESS   **1**

Levels of Awareness
▼
Consciousness and the Brain

Discuss the nature of consciousness.

SLEEP AND DREAMS   **2**

Biological Rhythms and Sleep
▼
Why Do We Need Sleep?
▼
Sleep Stages
▼
Sleep and Disease
▼
Sleep Disorders
▼
Dreams

Explain the nature of sleep and dreams.

HYPNOSIS   **3**

The Nature of Hypnosis
▼
Explaining Hypnosis
▼
Applications of Hypnosis

Describe hypnosis.

PSYCHOACTIVE DRUGS   **4**

Uses of Psychoactive Drugs
▼
Types of Psychoactive Drugs
▼
Addiction

Evaluate the uses and types of psychoactive drugs.

Frank Offner was a twentieth-century American electrical engineer and inventor. A highly creative individual, he developed electrical controls that eventually made jet planes possible. He also invented numerous medical devices. His invention of medical instrumentation made possible the electrocardiogram (ECG) for measuring cardiovascular functioning and the electroencephalogram (EEG) for measuring brain activity.

What was the nature of Offner's creative thought processes? He said that unique ideas for inventions would come to him in the middle of the night, somehow turning around in his brain. When Offner was trying to figure out the topic for his Ph.D. dissertation, the idea of a new formula for explaining how nerve excitation works came to him while he was taking a shower. Many creative ideas emerge while people are relaxed and are not focusing attention on a particular problem or project. In other words, taking a break from consciously trying to generate ideas may allow them to develop spontaneously (Csikszentmihalyi, 1995).

Sleep and relaxation represent different levels of awareness, or consciousness. In this chapter I discuss several states of consciousness that differ in a number of ways from a waking state. First, I explore the nature of consciousness itself, one of modern psychology's most intriguing topics. Second, I delve into the realm of sleep and dreams, in which most of us spend a great deal of time. The third topic is the mysterious and controversial topic of hypnosis. Fourth, I discuss the altered state of consciousness produced by psychoactive drugs and some of the reasons that people become addicted to them.

1 THE NATURE OF CONSCIOUSNESS

Levels of Awareness   **Consciousness and the Brain**

What is consciousness?

In the late nineteenth and early twentieth centuries, psychology pioneers such as Sigmund Freud and William James took great interest in the study of the conscious and unconscious mind. However, for much of the twentieth century, psychologists shunned the slippery, subjective trappings of consciousness and unconsciousness. Instead, they focused on behaviors and the rewards and punishments that determined those behaviors (Skinner, 1938; Watson, 1913). In the past decade, though, the study of consciousness has gained widespread respectability in psychology (Baars, 1999). And, for the first time in many decades, psychologists from many different fields are interested in consciousness, including its relation to subconsciousness (Hebb, 2002; Lehar, 2002; Schacter, 1999).

You process information at different levels of awareness. You are aware of some of the processing, unaware of other processing. Although there still is disagreement about how consciousness should be defined, here I define **consciousness** as the awareness of external events and internal sensations, including awareness of the self and thoughts about your experiences. Externally, you might be aware that your best friend just cracked a joke about his latest body piercing, that the car in front of you just swerved to miss a dog, and that your sunglasses fell off your nose as you leapt back to the curb. Internally, you might be aware that your headache just returned, that you are breathing too fast, that your stomach is rumbling because you missed breakfast, and that you are relieved that the weekend is almost here.

The contents of our awareness change from moment to moment. Information moves rapidly in and out of consciousness. William James (1890/1950) described the mind as a **stream of consciousness**—a continuous flow of changing sensations, images, thoughts, and feelings. Our minds can race from one topic to the next—from thinking about the person approaching us to how well we feel to what we are going to do tomorrow to where we are going to lunch and so on.

consciousness Awareness of external events and internal sensations, including awareness of the self and thoughts about one's experiences.

stream of consciousness James' concept that the mind is a continuous flow of sensations, images, thoughts, and feelings.

Level of Awareness	Description		
Higher Level Consciousness	Involves controlled processing, in which individuals actively focus their efforts on attaining a goal; the most alert state of consciousness.		This student is using controlled processes that require focused concentration.
Lower Level Consciousness	Includes automatic processing that requires little attention, as well as daydreaming.		This woman is an experienced computer operator. Her maneuvers with the keyboard are automatic, requiring minimal awareness.
Altered States of Awareness	Can be produced by drugs, trauma, fatigue, possibly hypnosis, and sensory deprivation.		These people, who are drinking alcohol, are in an altered state of consciousness.
Subconsciousness	Subconscious awareness can occur when people are awake, as well as when they are sleeping and dreaming.		All of us dream while we sleep, but some of us dream more than others.
No Awareness	Freud's belief that some unconscious thoughts are too laden with anxiety and other negative emotions for consciousness to admit them.		The woman on the couch is undergoing psychoanalytic therapy to reveal her unconscious thoughts.

FIGURE 6.1 **Levels of Awareness**

Levels of Awareness

The flow of sensations, images, thoughts, and feelings that James spoke of can occur at different levels of awareness. I discuss five levels of awareness here: higher level consciousness, lower level consciousness, altered states of consciousness, subconscious awareness, and no awareness (see figure 6.1).

Higher Level Consciousness **Controlled processes** represent the most alert states of human consciousness, in which individuals actively focus their efforts toward a goal (Cooper & others, 2002; Monsell & Driver, 2000). Watch Maria as she struggles to master the unfamiliar buttons on her new ten-function cell phone. She doesn't hear you humming to yourself or notice the intriguing shadow on the wall. Her state of focused awareness is what is meant by controlled processes.

In the previous chapter, I discussed the role of attention in perception. Controlled processes require selective attention, the ability to focus on a specific aspect of experience while ignoring others (Pashler, Johnston, & Ruthruff, 2001).

Lower Level Awareness Beneath the level of controlled processes are other levels of conscious awareness. Lower levels of awareness include automatic processes and the familiar state of daydreaming.

Automatic Processes A few weeks after acquiring her cell phone, Maria flips it open and places a call in the middle of a conversation with you. Her fingers fly almost automatically across the buttons. She doesn't have to concentrate on dialing now and hardly seems aware of the gadget against her cheek as she continues to talk on it while finishing her lunch. For her, cell phone dialing has reached the point of automatic

controlled processes The most alert states of consciousness.

"If you ask me, all three of us are in different states of awareness."
© The New Yorker Collection 1983 Edward Frascino from cartoonbank.com.
All Rights Reserved.

processing. **Automatic processes** are states of consciousness that require minimal attention and do not interfere with other ongoing activities. Automatic processes require less conscious effort than controlled processes (Trainor, McDonald, & Alpin, 2002). When we are awake, our automatic behaviors occur at a lower level of awareness than controlled processes, but they are still conscious behaviors. Maria pushed the right buttons, so she apparently was aware of what she was doing at some level.

Daydreaming Another state of consciousness that involves a low level of conscious effort, *daydreaming* lies somewhere between active consciousness and dreaming while we are asleep. It is a little like dreaming while we are awake. Daydreams usually begin spontaneously when we are doing something that requires less than our full attention.

Mind wandering is probably the most obvious type of daydreaming. We regularly take brief side trips into our own private kingdoms of imagery and memory while reading, listening, or working. When we daydream, we drift into a world of fantasy. We imagine ourselves on dates, at parties, on television, in faraway places, at another time in our lives, and so on. Sometimes our daydreams are about ordinary, everyday events, such as paying the rent, getting our hair done, or dealing with somebody at work.

The semiautomatic flow of daydreaming can be useful. As you daydream while you shave, iron a pair of pants, or walk to the store, you may make plans, solve a problem, or come up with a creative idea. Daydreams can remind us of important things ahead. Daydreaming keeps our minds active while helping us to cope, create, and fantasize (Klinger, 2000).

Altered States of Awareness *Altered states of consciousness or awareness* are mental states that are noticeably different from normal awareness. They can be produced by drugs, trauma, fatigue, possibly hypnosis, and sensory deprivation. In some cases, drug use may create a higher level of awareness. The popularity of coffee and other beverages that contain caffeine, a stimulant drug, provides evidence of the widespread belief that caffeine increases alertness. Awareness also may be altered to a lower level. Alcohol has this effect. Later in the chapter, I discuss drugs, as well as hypnosis, which some psychologists believe involves an altered state of consciousness.

Subconscious Awareness In chapter 5, you learned that a great deal of brain activity is going on beneath the level of conscious awareness. Psychologists are increasingly interested in subconscious processing of information, which can take place while we are awake or while we are asleep (Damasio, 2001).

Waking Subconscious Awareness According to creativity expert Mihaly Csikszentmihalyi (1995), insights such as those developed by inventor Frank Offner likely occurred when a subconscious connection between ideas was so strong that it was forced to "pop out" into awareness, somewhat like the way a cork held underwater bobs to the surface as soon as it is released. Csikszentmihalyi believes that creative ideas often "incubate" for some time below the threshold of conscious awareness before they emerge.

When an idea is incubating, our minds may be processing information even though we are not aware of it. Perhaps, in the absence of conscious connections, ideas simply combine more or less randomly beneath the level of awareness.

automatic processes States of consciousness that require little attention and do not interfere with other ongoing activities.

Evidence that we are not always aware of the processing of information in our brains also comes from studies of individuals with certain neurological disorders. In one case, a woman who suffered neurological damage was unable to describe or report the shape or size of objects in her visual field, although she was capable of describing other physical perceptions that she had (Milner & Goodale, 1995). Yet when she reached for an object she could accurately adjust the size of her grip to allow her to grasp the object. Thus she did possess some subconscious knowledge of the size and shape of objects, even though she had no awareness of this knowledge.

Subconscious information processing can occur simultaneously in a distributed manner along many parallel tracks. (Recall the discussion of parallel processing of visual information in chapter 5.) For example, when you look at a dog running down the street, you are consciously aware of the event but not of the subconscious processing of the object's identity (a dog), its color (black), its movement (fast), and so on. In contrast, conscious processing is *serial*. That is, it occurs in sequence and is slower than much subconscious processing.

Sleep and Dreams   When we sleep and dream, our level of awareness is lower than when we daydream, but sleep and dreams are not best regarded as the absence of consciousness. Rather, they should be viewed as low levels of consciousness.

Consider the German chemist August Kekulé, who in 1865 developed the insight that the benzene molecule might be shaped like a ring after he fell asleep while watching sparks in the fireplace make circles in the air. If he had remained awake, Kekulé presumably would have rejected as ridiculous the idea that there might be a link between the sparks and the shape of the benzene molecule. However, in his subconscious mind rational thought could not censor the connection, so when Kekulé woke up he could not ignore its possibility. It may be that irrelevant connections fade away and disappear but that those that are robust survive long enough to eventually emerge into consciousness (Csikszentmihalyi, 1995).

Researchers have found that when people are asleep they still remain aware of external stimuli to some degree. For example, in sleep laboratories, when people are clearly asleep (as determined by physiological monitoring devices), they are able to respond to faint tones by pressing a handheld button (Ogilvie & Wilkinson, 1988). In another study, the presentation of pure auditory tones to sleeping individuals activated auditory processing regions of the brain, whereas participants' names activated language areas, the amygdala, and the prefrontal cortex (Stickgold, 2001). Sleep and dreams are covered more thoroughly in the next section.

No Awareness   The term *unconscious* is generally applied to someone who has been knocked out by a blow, anesthetized, or fallen into a deep, prolonged unconscious state. However, Sigmund Freud (1917) used the term *unconscious* in a very different way. At about the same time that William James was charting the shifting nature of our stream of consciousness, Freud concluded that most of our thoughts are unconscious. **Unconscious thought,** said Freud, is a reservoir of unacceptable wishes, feelings, and thoughts that are beyond conscious awareness.

According to Freud, unconscious thoughts are too laden with anxiety and other negative emotions for consciousness to admit them. For example, if a young man is nervous around women and breaks into a cold sweat when a woman approaches him, he might be unconscious that his fear of women springs from the cold, punitive way his mother treated him when he was a child. Freud believed that one of psychotherapy's main goals was to bring unconscious thoughts into conscious awareness so they could be addressed and treated.

Freud's concept of the unconscious mind, especially its pervasiveness, is controversial. Whether or not we accept his view of the unconscious mind, we owe a debt to Freud for recognizing the complexity of consciousness.

Among those who practice altered states of consciousness in the world's religions are (*top*) Zen monks who explore the Buddha-nature at the center of their beings and (*bottom*) Muslims in Pakistan who fast from dawn to dusk during the month of Ramadan as the fourth pillar of Islam. *What are some other ways in which altered states of consciousness might be involved in religion?*

unconscious thought Freud's concept of a reservoir of unacceptable wishes, feelings, and thoughts that are beyond conscious awareness.

Consciousness and the Brain

One of the great unanswered questions about consciousness involves its location. Does consciousness stand alone (located in what might be called *mind*), separate in some way from the brain, or is it an intrinsic aspect of the brain's functioning? If consciousness is in the brain, is there a particular location that is the seat of consciousness, or is consciousness distributed across different areas of the brain?

Most neuroscientists do not believe that a specific location in the brain takes incoming information from one's body and the world and converts it into the conscious world we are aware of and can report on. Rather, it seems likely that a number of separate distributed processing systems connect to produce consciousness. Depending on what a person is aware of at a particular point in time, different areas of the brain "light up," or are activated (Alkire, Haier, & James, 1998; Kosslyn, 1994).

One view is that neural networks or assemblies shrink or swell more or less on demand as the consciousness of the situation demands (Greenfield, 1996). A number of neuroscientists believe that the cerebral cortex, especially its association areas and frontal lobes, are the key to understanding consciousness (Hobson, Pace-Schott, & Stickgold, 2000). It may be that the integration of information from the senses, along with information about emotions and memories in the association areas, creates consciousness (Bloom, Nelson, & Lazerson, 2001).

mhhe com/
santrockp7

For study tools related to this learning goal, see the Study Guide, the CD-ROM, and the Online Learning Center.

Review and Sharpen Your Thinking

1   *Discuss the nature of consciousness.*

- Define consciousness and describe five levels of awareness.
- Explain the brain's role in consciousness.

How many different states of awareness have you experienced? In one or two sentences each, describe the nature of your experience in each state.

2   SLEEP AND DREAMS

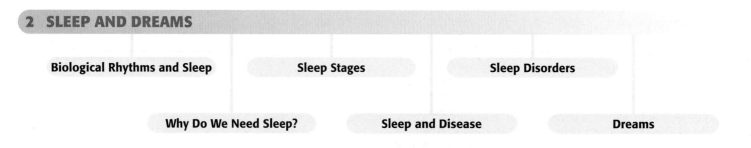

Biological Rhythms and Sleep	Sleep Stages	Sleep Disorders
Why Do We Need Sleep?	Sleep and Disease	Dreams

What is the nature of sleep and dreams?

Sleep claims about one-third of the time in our lives, more than any other pursuit. But it is possible that many of us are not getting enough sleep to function optimally. What is sleep and why is it so important? This section explores the answers to these questions, as well as the fascinating world of dreams. First, let's see how sleep is linked to our internal biological rhythms.

Biological Rhythms and Sleep

Biological rhythms are periodic physiological fluctuations in the body. We are unaware of most biological rhythms, such as the rise and fall of hormones in the bloodstream, accelerated and decelerated cycles of brain activity, and highs and lows in body temperature, but they can influence our behavior. These rhythms are controlled by biological clocks, which include

biological rhythms Periodic physiological fluctuations in the body.

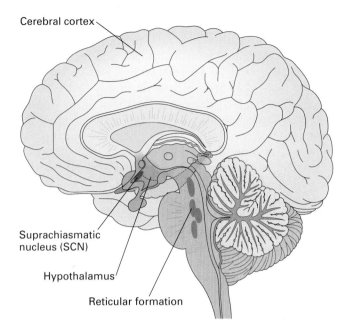

FIGURE 6.2 Suprachiasmatic Nucleus The suprachiasmatic nucleus plays an important role in keeping our biological clock running on time. The SCN is located in the hypothalamus. It receives information from the retina about light, which is the external stimulus that synchronizes the SCN. Output from the SCN is distributed to the rest of the hypothalamus and to the reticular formation.

- *Annual or seasonal cycles,* such the migration of birds, the hibernation of bears, and the seasonal fluctuations of humans' eating habits
- *Twenty-eight day cycles,* such as the female menstrual cycle that averages 28 days
- *Twenty-four hour cycles,* such as the sleep/wake cycle and temperature changes in the body

Let's further explore the 24-hour cycles.

Circadian Rhythms   A **circadian rhythm** is a daily behavioral or physiological cycle. Daily circadian rhythms involve the sleep/wake cycle, body temperature, blood pressure, and blood sugar level. The term *circadian* comes from the Latin words *circa,* meaning "about," and *dies,* meaning "day." For example, body temperature fluctuates about 3° Fahrenheit in a 24-hour day, peaking in the afternoon and reaching its lowest point between 2 A.M. and 5 A.M.

Researchers have discovered that the change from day to night is monitored by the **suprachiasmatic nucleus (SCN),** a small structure in the brain that synchronizes its own rhythm with the daily cycle of light and dark based on input from the retina (Zisapel, 2001). Output from the SCN allows the hypothalamus to regulate daily rhythms such as temperature and hunger and the reticular formation to regulate daily rhythms of sleep and wakefulness (see figure 6.2). Although a number of biological clocks or pacemakers seem to be involved in regulating circadian rhythms, researchers have found that the SCN is the most important one (Lavie, 2001; Ruby & others, 2002).

Many individuals who are totally blind experience lifelong sleeping problems because their retinas are unable to detect light. These people have a kind of permanent jet lag and periodic insomnia because their circadian rhythms often do not follow a 24-hour cycle (National Institute of Neurological Disorders and Stroke, 2001).

Desynchronizing the Biological Clock   Biological clocks can become desynchronized, or thrown off their regular schedules. Among the circumstances of modern life that can introduce irregularities in our sleep are jet travel, changing work shifts, and insomnia (Albrecht, 2002). What effects might such irregularities have on circadian rhythms?

circadian rhythms Daily behavioral or physiological cycles, such as the sleep/wake cycle.

suprachiasmatic nucleus (SCN) A small structure in the hypothalamus that registers changes in light.

What are the effects of jet travel across a number of time zones and working night shifts on individuals' biological clocks?

If you fly from Los Angeles to New York and then go to bed at 11 P.M. Eastern Standard Time, you may have trouble falling asleep because your body is still on Pacific time. Even if you sleep for 8 hours that night, you may have a hard time waking up at 7 A.M. Eastern time, because your body thinks it is 4 A.M. If you stay in New York for several days, your body will adjust to this new schedule.

The jet lag you experienced when you flew from Los Angeles to New York occurred because your body time was out of phase, or synchronization, with clock time. Jet lag is the result of two or more body rhythms being out of sync. You usually go to bed when your body temperature begins to drop, but, in your new location, you might be trying to go to sleep when it is rising. In the morning, your adrenal glands release large doses of the hormone *cortisol* to help you wake up. In your new geographical time zone, the glands may be releasing this chemical just as you are getting ready for bed at night.

Circadian rhythms may also become desynchronized when shift workers change their work hours (Ahasan & others, 2001). A number of near accidents in air travel have been associated with pilots who have not yet become synchronized to their new shifts and are not working as efficiently as usual. Shift rotation also may have been one of the causes of the nuclear accident at Three Mile Island in 1979 (Moore-Ede, Sulzman, & Fuller, 1982). The team of workers monitoring the nuclear plant when the accident took place had been placed on the night shift just after a 6-week period of constant shift rotation.

Shift-work problems most often affect night-shift workers who never fully adjust to sleeping in the daytime after their work shifts, may fall asleep at work, and are at increased risk for heart disease and gastrointestinal disorders (Quinlin, Mayhew, & Bohle, 2001). Not all shift workers are affected equally, though (Monk, 1993). A small portion actually prefer shift work. Individuals older than 50, those who require more than 9 hours of sleep a night, and those with a tendency to be "morning types" (get up early, go to bed early) are the most adversely affected by shift work.

Intrigued by the role of biological clocks in circadian rhythms, researchers naturally became curious about what happens when an individual is completely isolated from clocks, calendars, night, the moon, the sun, and all indices of time. A number of experiments have focused on such isolation experiences (Kales, 1970; Siffre, 1975). For example, French scientist Michael Siffre entered Midnight Cave near Del Rio, Texas, on February 14, 1972. A small nylon tent deep within the cave was Siffre's home for 6 months. Because Siffre could not see or sense the sun rising and setting while he was in the cave, he began to live by biological cycles instead of by days. When Siffre wanted to go to sleep, he called the support crew outside and told them to turn the lights off in the cave. Just before he went to sleep, he attached electrodes to his scalp so that his sleep cycles could be monitored. When he woke up, he called the support crew and asked them to turn on the cave's lights.

Siffre referred to each of his sleep/wake cycles as a day. He and other individuals who have been isolated judge a day to be about 25 hours. However, in recently conducted studies that exercised better control of the light participants experience, a day was judged to vary from 24 hours by only a few minutes (Lavie, 2001).

Resetting the Biological Clock If your biological clock for sleeping and waking becomes desynchronized, how can you reset it? With regard to jet lag, if you take a transoceanic flight and arrive at your destination during the day, it is a good idea to spend as much time outside in the daylight as possible. Bright light during the day, especially in the morning, increases wakefulness, whereas bright light at night delays sleep (Oren & Terman, 1998).

Melatonin, a hormone that increases at night in humans, also is being studied for its possible effects in reducing jet lag (Sharkey & Eastman, 2002). A number of recent studies have shown that a small dosage of melatonin can reduce jet lag by advancing the

Find out what happens to a person's sleep cycle in Antarctica during the summer, when the sun doesn't set. (Around the Globe)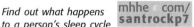

circadian clock, which makes it useful for eastward jet lag but not westward jet lag (Herxheimer & Petrie, 2001; Suhner & others, 2001). Note that although melatonin is available over the counter, the quality of the drug may vary. Further, the potential side effects of melatonin are still largely unknown, and negative long-term effects have not yet been adequately studied (National Institute of Neurological Disorders and Stroke, 2001).

Strategies for shift workers who need to reset their biological clocks include splitting sleep between after-work morning naps and before-work late-afternoon naps to increase the number of hours of sleep, brighter light in the workplace, and sleeping in complete darkness. Sedatives do not affect circadian realignment, and their long-term use is inadvisable for shift workers.

Why Do We Need Sleep?

Everyone sleeps, and when we do not get enough sleep, we often do not function well, physically and mentally. The important benefits of sleep include restoration, adaptation, growth, and memory.

Because all animals require sleep, it seems that sleep is a fundamental mechanism for survival. Examining the evolutionary basis for sleep, scientists have proposed that sleep restores, replenishes, and rebuilds our brains and bodies, which can become worn out or used up by the day's waking activities. This idea fits with the feeling of being "worn out" or tired before we go to sleep and "restored" when we wake up.

In support of the restorative function of sleep, many of the body's cells show increased production and reduced breakdown of proteins during deep sleep (National Institute of Neurological Disorders and Stroke, 2001). Protein molecules are the building blocks needed for cell growth and for repair of damages from factors such as stress. Also, some neuroscientists believe that sleep gives neurons that are used while we are awake a chance to shut down and repair themselves (National Institute of Neurological Disorders and Stroke, 2001). Without sleep, neurons might become so depleted in energy or so polluted by the by-products of cellular activity that they begin to malfunction.

In addition to having a restorative function, sleep also has had an adaptive evolutionary function. Sleep may have developed because animals needed to protect themselves. For example, for some animals the search for food and water is easier and safer when the sun is up. When it is dark, it is adaptive for these animals to save energy, avoid getting eaten, and avoid falling off a cliff that they cannot see. In general, animals that serve as food for other animals sleep the least. Figure 6.3 portrays the average amount of sleep per day of different animals.

Sleep also may be beneficial to physical growth and increased brain development in infants and children. For example, deep sleep coincides with the release of growth hormone in children (National Institute of Neurological Disorders and Stroke, 2001).

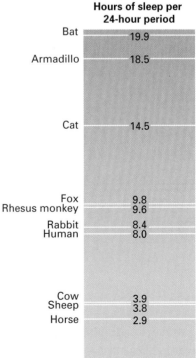

FIGURE 6.3 **From Bats to Horses: The Wide Range of Sleep in Animals**

	Hours of sleep per 24-hour period
Bat	19.9
Armadillo	18.5
Cat	14.5
Fox	9.8
Rhesus monkey	9.6
Rabbit	8.4
Human	8.0
Cow	3.9
Sheep	3.8
Horse	2.9

Sleep researchers record Randy Gardner's (he's the person doing push-ups) behavior during his 264-hour period of sleep deprivation. Most people who try to stay up even one night have difficulty remaining awake from 3 A.M. to 6 A.M. *Why shouldn't you follow Gardner's sleep deprivation example?*

REM sleep Rapid-eye-movement sleep; stage 5 of sleep, in which most dreaming occurs.

Sleep also is now thought to play an important role in the storage and maintenance of long-term memory. In one recent study, the stage of sleep called **REM sleep** (rapid-eye-movement sleep) was linked with the formation of emotional memories in humans (Wagner, Gais, & Born, 2001). One possible explanation is that during sleep the cerebral cortex is not busy with processing sensory input, active awareness, and motor functions. Therefore, it is free to conduct activities that strengthen memory associations so that memories formed during recent waking hours can be integrated into long-term memory storage.

Are you thinking about studying all night for the next test in one of your classes? You might want to think again. In one recent study, a good night's sleep helped the brain to store the memory of what had been learned during the day (Stickgold & Hobson, 2000). In the study, the memory of individuals who stayed up all night on one of the nights during the study was inferior to the memory of individuals who got a good night's sleep every night during the study. The conclusion: Lost sleep often results in lost memories.

The Effects of Chronic Sleep Deprivation Testing the limits of his capacity to function without sleep, one 17-year-old high school student, Randy Gardner, went without sleep for 264 hours (about 11 days), the longest observed period of total sleep deprivation. He did it as part of a science fair project (Dement, 1978). Randy, who was carefully monitored by sleep researchers, did suffer some hallucinations, as well as speech and movement problems. However, on the last night, Gardner played arcade games with sleep researcher William Dement and consistently beat him. Randy recovered fully, as well as could be detected, after a 14-hour, 40-minute restorative sleep. Randy's story is exceptional in that he was able to maintain a high level of physical activity and in that he received national TV coverage, which helped him to stay awake. Even so, he almost fell asleep several times, but his observers would not let him close his eyes. In more normal circumstances, individuals have far more difficulty staying awake all night, especially between 3 A.M. and 6 A.M.

Although Randy Gardner was able to go about 11 days without sleep, the following discussion should convince you that even getting 60 to 90 minutes less sleep than you need at night can harm your ability to perform optimally the next day. As you also will see, it does not take very long for sleep deprivation to play havoc with our lives.

In a recent national survey of more than 1,000 American adults conducted by the National Sleep Foundation (2001), 63 percent said that they get less than 8 hours of sleep a night, and 31 percent said that they get less than 7 hours of sleep a night. Many said they try to catch up on their sleep on the weekend, but they still reported getting less than 8 hours on weekend nights. Forty percent of those surveyed said that they become so sleepy during the day that their work suffers at least a few days per month, and 22 percent said their work suffers a few days each week. Seven percent said sleepiness on the job is a daily problem for them.

In the view of sleep expert James Maas (1998), at least 50 percent of the American population is sleep deprived. He argues that the quality of our lives, if not life itself, is jeopardized by sleep deprivation. Maas and others believe that people need to deposit at least 8 hours of sleep in their nightly sleep account to stay fully functional and optimize their performance the next day (Dement, 1999). A sleep debt can build quickly, not unlike finance charges on an unpaid credit card balance, when you are burning the candle at both ends. Consider a medical technician who tried to get by on 4 hours of sleep a night—ironically, while working at a sleep-disorders center—so she could take care of her infant daughter during the day. Before long, she developed heart palpitations, dizziness, a fear of driving, and wide mood swings from being awake 20 hours a day.

An increasing number of research studies underscore that optimal performance is enhanced by sleeping more than 8 hours a night and reduced by sleeping less. At one sleep-disorders research center, the alertness of 8-hour sleepers who claimed to be well rested increased when they added 2 more hours to their nightly sleep total (Roehrs & Roth, 1998). In a recent study, brain scans revealed that sleep deprivation decreased brain activity in the thalamus and the prefrontal cortex (Thomas & others, 2001). Alertness and cognitive performance declined, along with brain activity. In another study, sleep deprivation was linked with an inability to sustain attention (Doran, Van Dongen, & Dinges, 2001). In yet another recent study, EEGs of individuals who experienced total sleep deprivation for 24 hours revealed a decline in the complexity of brain activity (Jeong & others, 2001).

Sleep deprivation also can affect decision making. A recent review of studies on this topic concluded that the following aspects of decision making are affected especially adversely by sleep deprivation: dealing with the unexpected, innovation, revising plans, and effective communication (Harrison & Horne, 2000).

Why are Americans getting too little sleep? Work pressures, school pressures, family obligations, and social obligations often lead to long hours of wakefulness and irregular sleep/wake schedules. Not having enough hours to do all we want to do in a day, we cheat on our sleep. Most people need to get 60 to 90 minutes more sleep each night than they presently get.

Sleep Deprivation in Adolescents and Older Adults There recently has been a surge of interest in adolescent sleep patterns. This interest focuses on the belief that many adolescents are not getting enough sleep, that there are physiological underpinnings to adolescents' desires to stay up later at night and sleep longer in the morning, and that these findings have implications for understanding when adolescents learn most effectively in school (Eliasson & others, 2002).

Mary Carskadon and her colleagues (Carskadon, Acebo, & Seifer, 2001; Carskadon & others, 1998; Carskadon & others, 1999) have conducted a number of research studies on adolescent sleep patterns. They have found that adolescents sleep an average of 9 hours and 25 minutes when given the opportunity to sleep as long as they like. Most adolescents get considerably less sleep than this, especially during the week. The result is a sleep debt, which adolescents often try to make up for on the weekend. The researchers found that older adolescents (16–18 years old) are often sleepier during the day than younger adolescents (13–15 years old) are. Carskadon believes this developmental change is not due to factors such as academic work and social pressures. Rather, her research suggests that adolescents' biological clocks undergo a hormonal shift as they get older that pushes the time of wakefulness to an hour later than when they were younger adolescents. In her research, Carskadon found that this shift was caused by a delay in the nightly release of melatonin. Melatonin is secreted at about 9:30 P.M. in younger adolescents, but it is produced about 10:30 P.M. in older adolescents, delaying the onset of sleep.

Carskadon determined that early school starting times can result in grogginess and lack of attention in class and poor performance on tests. Based on this research, in 1997, schools in Edina, Minnesota, made the decision to start classes at 8:40 A.M. instead of the former starting time of 7:15 A.M. Under this later starting time, there have been fewer referrals for discipline problems and fewer illnesses. Test scores have also improved among high school students, but not middle school students, an outcome that supports Carskadon's conclusion that earlier school starting times are more detrimental to older adolescents than to younger adolescents.

Sleep patterns also change as people age through the middle-adult (40s and 50s) and late-adult (60s and older) years. Many adults go to bed earlier at night and wake up earlier in the morning. Thus, a clear reversal occurs in the time at which individuals go to bed—later to bed as adolescents, earlier to bed in middle age. Beginning in the 40s, individuals report that they are less likely to sleep through the entire night than when they were younger (Katchadourian, 1987). Middle-aged adults also spend less time in the deepest sleep stage than when they were younger. And almost one-half of individuals in late adulthood report that they experience some degree of insomnia.

What are some developmental changes in sleep patterns during adolescence? How might this influence alertness at school?

An individual being monitored by an EEG in a sleep experiment.

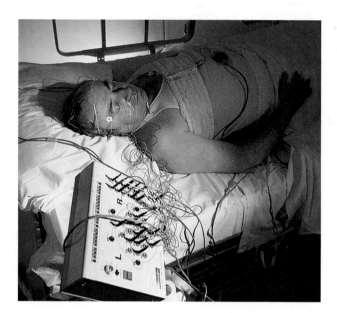

Sleep Stages

Have you ever been awakened from your sleep and been totally disoriented? Have you ever awakened in the middle of a dream and gone right back into the dream as if it were a movie that is running just under the surface of your consciousness? These two circumstances reflect two distinct stages in the sleep cycle.

Stages of sleep correspond to massive electrophysiological changes that occur throughout the brain as the fast, irregular, and low amplitude electrical activity of wakefulness is replaced by the slow, regular, high amplitude waves of deep sleep. Using the electroencephalograph (EEG) to monitor the brain's electrical activity during waking and sleep states, scientists have discovered five distinct stages of sleep and two stages of wakefulness.

When people are awake, their EEG patterns exhibit two types of waves: beta and alpha. *Beta waves* reflect wakefulness. These waves are the highest in frequency and lowest in amplitude. They also are more *desynchronous* than other waves. Desynchronous waves do not form a very consistent pattern. Inconsistent patterning makes sense given the extensive variation in sensory input and activities we experience when we are awake. When we are relaxed but still awake, our brain waves slow down, increase in amplitude, and become more *synchronous,* or regular. These waves are called *alpha waves.*

The five stages of sleep are differentiated by the types of wave patterns detected with an EEG. The depth of sleep varies from one stage to another.

Stages 1–4   *Stage 1 sleep* is characterized by *theta waves,* which are even slower in frequency and greater in amplitude than alpha waves. The difference between just being relaxed and stage 1 sleep is gradual. Figure 6.4 shows the EEG pattern of stage 1 sleep, along with the EEG patterns for the other four sleep stages and beta and alpha waves.

In *stage 2 sleep,* theta waves continue but are interspersed with a defining characteristic of stage 2 sleep: *sleep spindles.* These involve a sudden increase in wave frequency (Gottselig, Bassetti, & Achermann, 2002). Stages 1 and 2 are both relatively light stages of sleep, and if people awaken during one of these stages, they often report not having been asleep at all.

Stage 3 and *stage 4 sleep* are characterized by *delta waves,* the slowest and highest amplitude brain waves during sleep. These two stages are often referred to as *delta sleep.* Distinguishing between stage 3 and stage 4 is difficult, although typically stage 3 is characterized by delta waves occurring less than 50 percent of the time and stage 4 by delta waves occurring more than 50 percent of the time. Delta sleep is our deepest

"MY PROBLEM HAS ALWAYS BEEN AN OVERABUNDANCE OF ALPHA WAVES"

© 1990 by Sidney Harris.

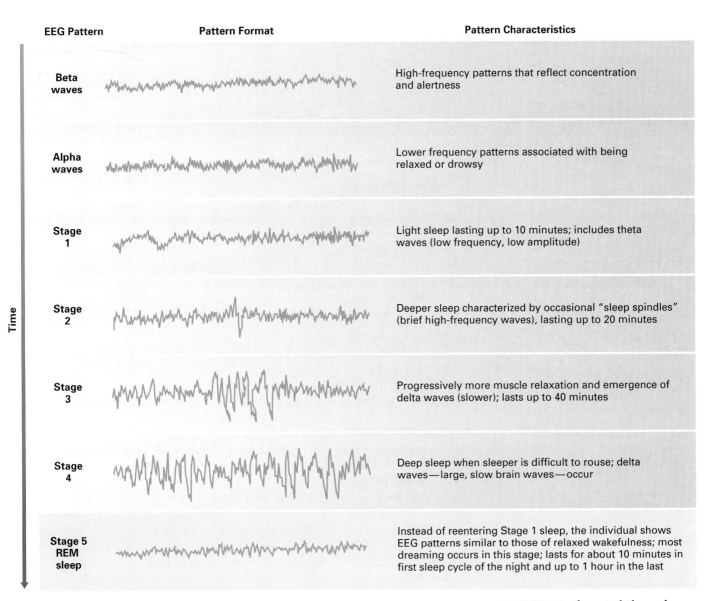

EEG Pattern	Pattern Format	Pattern Characteristics
Beta waves		High-frequency patterns that reflect concentration and alertness
Alpha waves		Lower frequency patterns associated with being relaxed or drowsy
Stage 1		Light sleep lasting up to 10 minutes; includes theta waves (low frequency, low amplitude)
Stage 2		Deeper sleep characterized by occasional "sleep spindles" (brief high-frequency waves), lasting up to 20 minutes
Stage 3		Progressively more muscle relaxation and emergence of delta waves (slower); lasts up to 40 minutes
Stage 4		Deep sleep when sleeper is difficult to rouse; delta waves—large, slow brain waves—occur
Stage 5 REM sleep		Instead of reentering Stage 1 sleep, the individual shows EEG patterns similar to those of relaxed wakefulness; most dreaming occurs in this stage; lasts for about 10 minutes in first sleep cycle of the night and up to 1 hour in the last

Time

FIGURE 6.4 Characteristics and Formats of EEG Recordings During Stages of Sleep

sleep, the time when our brain waves are least like waking brain waves. It is during delta sleep that it is the most difficult to wake sleepers. When they are awakened during this stage, they usually are confused and disoriented.

REM Sleep After going through stages 1 through 4, sleepers drift up through the sleep stages toward wakefulness. But, instead of reentering stage 1, they enter *stage 5*, a different form of sleep called *REM (rapid-eye-movement) sleep*. REM sleep is an active stage of sleep during which dreaming occurs. During REM sleep, the EEG pattern shows fast waves similar to those of relaxed wakefulness, and the sleeper's eyeballs move up and down and from left to right (see figure 6.5). Stages 1–4 are referred to as *non-REM sleep*. Non-REM sleep is characterized by a lack of rapid eye movement and little dreaming. A person who is awakened during REM sleep is more likely to report having dreamed than when awakened at any other stage. Even people who claim they rarely dream frequently report dreaming when they are awakened during REM sleep. The longer the period of REM sleep, the more likely it is that the person will report dreaming. Dreams also occur during slow-wave or non-REM sleep, but the frequency of dreams in these stages is relatively low (Takeuchi & others, 2001). Reports of dreaming by individuals awakened from REM sleep are typically longer, more vivid, more motorically animated, more emotionally charged, and less

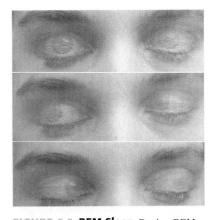

FIGURE 6.5 REM Sleep During REM sleep, your eyes move rapidly, as if following the images moving in your dreams.

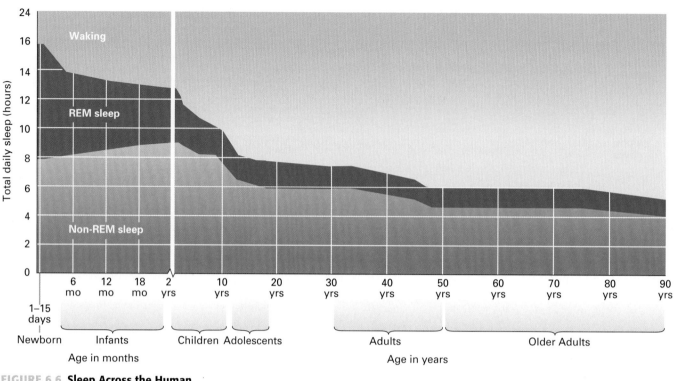

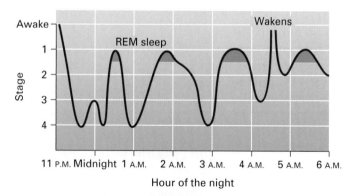

FIGURE 6.6 Sleep Across the Human Life Span

related to waking life than reports by those awakened from non-REM sleep (Hobson, Pace-Schott, & Stickgold, 2000).

The amount of time we spend in REM sleep changes over the life span. As shown in figure 6.6, the percentage of total sleep during a 24-hour period that consists of REM sleep is especially large during early infancy (almost 8 hours). Older adults engage in less than 1 hour of REM sleep per 24-hour period. Figure 6.6 also reveals how the total amount of sleep changes from approximately 16 hours per 24-hour period for young infants to less than 6 hours for older adults.

These dramatic developmental changes in sleep, especially REM sleep, raise questions about the function of sleep. For young infants, REM sleep may play a role in stimulating the brain and contributing to its growth. Because such a large percentage of an infant's life is spent in sleep, REM sleep may be nature's way of stimulating the brain.

REM sleep also likely contributes to memory. Researchers have presented individuals with unique phrases before they go to bed (Empson & Clarke, 1970). When they are awakened just before they begin REM sleep, they remember less the next morning than when they are awakened during the other sleep stages.

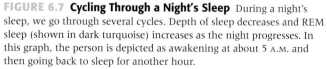

FIGURE 6.7 Cycling Through a Night's Sleep During a night's sleep, we go through several cycles. Depth of sleep decreases and REM sleep (shown in dark turquoise) increases as the night progresses. In this graph, the person is depicted as awakening at about 5 A.M. and then going back to sleep for another hour.

Sleep Cycling Through the Night The five stages of sleep described here make up a normal cycle of sleep. As shown in figure 6.7, one of these cycles lasts about 90 to 100 minutes and recurs several times during the night. The amount of deep sleep (stages 3 and 4) is much greater in the first half of a night's sleep than in the second half. Most REM sleep takes place toward the end of a night's sleep, when the REM stage becomes progressively longer. The night's first REM stage might last for only 10 minutes, and the final REM stage might continue for as long as an hour. During a normal night of sleep, individuals will spend about 60 percent of sleep in light sleep (stages 1 and 2), 20 percent in delta or deep sleep, and 20 percent in REM sleep (Webb, 2000).

Sleep and the Brain   The five sleep stages are associated with distinct patterns of neurotransmitter activity initiated in the reticular formation, the core of the brain stem. In all vertebrates, the reticular formation plays a crucial role in sleep and arousal (see figure 6.2). Damage to the reticular formation can result in coma and death.

Three important neurotransmitters involved in sleep are serotonin, epinephrine, and acetylcholine. As sleep begins, the levels of neurotransmitters sent to the forebrain from the reticular formation start dropping, and they continue to fall until they reach their lowest levels during the deepest sleep stage—stage 4. REM sleep (stage 5) is initiated by a rise in acetylcholine, which activates the cerebral cortex while the rest of the brain remains relatively inactive. REM sleep is terminated by a rise in serotonin and norepinephrine, which increase the level of forebrain activity nearly to the awakened state. You are most likely to wake up just after a REM period. If you don't wake up then, the level of the neurotransmitters begins to fall again, and you enter another sleep cycle.

Sleep and Disease

Sleep plays a role in a large number of diseases and disorders (National Institute of Neurological Disorders and Stroke, 2001). For example, stroke and asthma attacks are more common during the night and in the early morning, probably because of changes in hormones, heart rate, and other characteristics associated with sleep.

Neurons that control sleep interact closely with the immune system (Pollmacher & others, 2000). As anyone who has had the flu knows, infectious diseases make us sleepy. The probable reason is that chemicals called *cytokines*, produced by the body's cells while we are fighting an infection, are powerful sleep-inducing chemicals. Sleep may help the body conserve energy and other resources that the body needs to overcome infection.

Sleep problems afflict most people who have mental disorders, including those with depression (Blais & others, 2001). Individuals with depression often awaken in the early hours of the morning and cannot get back to sleep, and they often spend less time in delta wave or deep sleep than do nondepressed individuals (Armitage & others, 2001).

Sleep problems are common in many other disorders as well, including Alzheimer's disease, stroke, and cancer. In some cases, however, these problems may be due not to the disease itself but to the drugs used to treat the disease (Larsen & Tandberg, 2001).

Sleep Disorders

Each year, at least 40 million Americans suffer from chronic, long-term sleep disorders, and an additional 20 million experience occasional sleep problems (National Institute of Neurological Disorders and Stroke, 2001). Many people suffer from undiagnosed and untreated sleep disorders that leave them to struggle through the day feeling unmotivated and exhausted (National Commission on Sleep Disorders Research, 1993). Some of the major sleep problems are insomnia, sleepwalking and sleep talking, nightmares and night terrors, narcolepsy, and sleep apnea. To determine whether you are having sleep problems, see the Psychology and Life box.

Insomnia   A common sleep problem is *insomnia*, the inability to sleep. Insomnia can involve a problem in falling asleep, waking up during the night, or waking up too early (Harvey, 2001; Mahendran, 2001). As many as one in five Americans has insomnia. It is more common among women and older adults, as well as people who are thin, stressed, or depressed (Devries, 1998).

Do You Get Enough Sleep?

Many college students do not get enough sleep. In a survey of more than 200,000 first-year students, more than 80 percent said they stayed up all night at least once during the year (Sax & others, 1995). To evaluate whether you are sleep deprived, answer the following questions.

Yes	No	
_____	_____	I need an alarm clock to wake up at the appropriate time.
_____	_____	It's a struggle for me to get out of bed in the morning.
_____	_____	I feel tired, irritable, and stressed out during the week.
_____	_____	I have trouble concentrating.
_____	_____	I have trouble remembering.
_____	_____	I feel slow with critical thinking, problem solving, and being creative.
_____	_____	I often fall asleep watching TV.
_____	_____	I often fall asleep in boring meetings or lectures in warm rooms.
_____	_____	I often fall asleep after heavy meals or after low doses of alcohol.
_____	_____	I often fall asleep within five minutes of getting into bed.
_____	_____	I often feel drowsy while driving.
_____	_____	I often sleep extra hours on weekend mornings.
_____	_____	I often need a nap to get through the day.
_____	_____	I have dark circles around my eyes.

According to sleep expert James Maas (1998), who developed this quiz, if you responded "yes" to three or more of these items, you probably are not getting enough sleep.

If you are not getting enough sleep, the following behavioral strategies might help you:

1. Reduce stress as much as possible.
2. Exercise regularly, but not just before you go to bed.
3. Keep mentally stimulated during the day.
4. Become a good time manager.
5. Eat a proper diet.
6. Stop smoking.
7. Reduce caffeine intake.
8. Avoid alcohol, especially near bedtime.
9. Take a warm bath before bed.
10. Maintain a relaxing atmosphere in the bedroom.
11. Clear your mind at bedtime.
12. Before going to bed, engage in a relaxation technique such as listening to a tape designed for relaxation.
13. Learn to value sleep.
14. If necessary, contact the health service at your college or university for advice about your sleeping problem.

For short-term insomnia, most physicians prescribe sleeping pills (Ramesh & Roberts, 2002). However, most sleeping pills stop working after several weeks of nightly use, and their long-term use can actually interfere with good sleep. Mild insomnia often can be reduced by simply practicing good sleep habits. In more serious cases of insomnia, researchers are experimenting with light therapy, melatonin supplements, and other ways to alter circadian cycles (Cohen, 2002; Kennaway & Wright, 2002). Also, in one recent study, behavioral changes helped insomniacs to increase their sleep time, as well as to awaken less frequently in the middle of the night (Edinger & others, 2001). In this study, insomniacs were restricted from taking a nap during the day, even if they were exhausted, and they were required to set an alarm and to force themselves to get out of bed in the morning. Thus the longer the insomniacs stayed awake during the day, the better they were able to sleep at night.

Sleepwalking and Sleep Talking *Somnambulism* is the formal term for sleepwalking, which occurs during the deepest stages of sleep. For many years, experts believed that somnambulists were just acting out their dreams. But somnambulism occurs during stages 3 and 4, usually early in the night, at the time when a person is unlikely to be dreaming (Stein & Ferber, 2001). There is nothing really abnormal about sleepwalking. Despite superstition, it is safe to awaken sleepwalkers; in fact, they probably should be awakened, as they may harm themselves wandering around in the dark (Swanson, 1999).

Another quirky night behavior is sleep talking (Hublin & others, 2001). If you interrogate sleep talkers, can you find out what they did, for instance, last Thursday night? Probably not. Although sleep talkers will talk with you and make fairly coherent statements, they are soundly asleep. So even if a sleep talker mumbles a response to your question, don't count on its accuracy.

Nightmares and Night Terrors   A *nightmare* is a frightening dream that awakens a dreamer from REM sleep. The nightmare's content invariably involves danger—the dreamer is chased, robbed, raped, murdered, or thrown off a cliff. Nightmares are common. Most of us have had them, especially when we were young children. Nightmares peak at 3 to 6 years of age and then decline, although the average college student experiences 4 to 8 nightmares a year (Hartmann, 1993). Reported increases in nightmares or worsening nightmares are often associated with an increase in stress in people's lives, such as loss of a relative, conflict, or some type of negative event.

A *night terror* is characterized by sudden arousal from sleep and intense fear. Night terrors are accompanied by a number of physiological reactions, such as rapid heart rate and breathing, loud screams, heavy perspiration, and movement (Thiedke, 2001). Night terrors are less common than nightmares. Unlike nightmares, night terrors occur during slow-wave, non-REM sleep. Night terrors peak at 5 to 7 years of age and decline thereafter.

Narcolepsy   The overpowering urge to sleep is called *narcolepsy.* The urge is so strong that the person may fall asleep while talking or standing up. Narcoleptics immediately enter REM sleep rather than progressing through the first four sleep stages (Mignot, 2001; Mignot & Thorsby, 2001). Researchers suspect that narcolepsy is inherited. Treatment usually involves counseling to discover potential causes of the excessive sleepiness.

Sleep Apnea   *Sleep apnea* is a sleep disorder in which individuals stop breathing because the windpipe fails to open or because brain processes involved in respiration fail to work properly. People with sleep apnea experience numerous brief awakenings during the night so that they can breathe better, although they usually are not aware of their awakened state. During the day these people may feel sleepy because they were deprived of sleep at night.

Sleep apnea affects approximately 12 million Americans (American Sleep Apnea Association, 2001). Sleep apnea is most common among infants and adults over the age of 65. Sleep apnea also occurs more frequently among obese individuals (Davidson & Callery, 2001). Untreated, sleep apnea can cause high blood pressure, strokes, and impotence. In addition, the daytime sleepiness it causes can result in accidents, lost productivity, and relationship problems (Billmann & Ware, 2002).

Dreams

Ever since the dawn of language, dreams have been imbued with historical, personal, and religious significance. As early as 5000 B.C., Babylonians recorded and interpreted their dreams on clay tablets. Egyptians built temples in honor of Serapis, the god of dreams. People occasionally slept in these temples in the hope that Serapis would appear in their dreams and either heal them or tell them what to do to be healed. Dreams are described at length in more than 70 passages in the Bible.

Many people in modern societies, such as in the United States, view dreams as separate from reality and usually as having little importance to their waking lives. However, in primitive societies dreams are often thought of as an extension of reality. For example, in one account, an African chief dreamed that he had visited England. On awakening, he ordered a wardrobe of European clothes. As he walked through the village in his new wardrobe, he was congratulated for having made the trip. Similarly, Cherokee Indians who dreamed of being bitten by snakes were treated for the snakebite. Also, the Inuit people who live in the Arctic region of North America believe that dreams provide a vehicle for entering the spiritual world.

In terms of dream content, small traditional societies show a higher percentage of animal characters in their dreams, and variations exist from culture to culture in the percentage of aggressive actions in dreams (Domhoff, 1999). For example, in one study, Palestinian children living under the threat of violence reported more themes of persecution and aggression in their dreams than did Finnish or Palestinian children living in more peaceful surroundings (Punamaki & Joustie, 1998). In the Colombian village of Arimatima, many dreams are thought to symbolize the deaths of relatives (Paquin, 2000).

Not only are there cultural variations in dreaming, but there also are differences in the dreams of men and women (Kolchakian & Hill, 2002). Men are more likely than women to dream about aggression, torso anatomy, sexuality, and their own success (Domhoff & Schneider, 1998). The dream content of women is more likely to include friends and victimization.

Why do we dream? Many theorists and researchers have attempted to explain dreaming. But because dreams are written in the mind with little or no conscious participation, it is indeed difficult to unravel their mysteries. The most prominent theories of dreams are derived from Freud's theory, cognitive theory, and activation- synthesis theory.

Dreams as Wish Fulfillment Sigmund Freud (1900/1953) thought that the reason we dream is **wish fulfillment,** an unconscious attempt to fulfill needs (especially for sex and aggression) that cannot be expressed or that go ungratified during waking hours. In this view, for example, people who are sexually inhibited while awake would likely have dreams with erotic content. Those who have strong aggressive tendencies but suppress anger while awake would be inclined to have dreams filled with violence and hostility.

Freud also stressed that dreams often contain memories of infant and child experiences, especially events associated with parents. Additionally, he believed that our dreams frequently contain information from a day or two preceding the dream. In his view, many of our dreams reflect combinations of distant early experiences with our parents and more recent daily events. Freud said that the task of dream interpretation is a difficult one because we successfully disguise wish fulfillment when we dream. Note that the term *wish fulfillment* does not mean that dreams reflect only hopes; some reflect fears.

Freud distinguished between a dream's manifest content and its latent content. **Manifest content** is the dream's surface content, which contains dream symbols that distort and disguise the dream's true meaning. **Latent content** is the dream's hidden content, its unconscious meaning. For example, if a person had a dream that included snakes and neckties, the snakes and neckties would be the dream's manifest content. Another person might dream about a king or a president. Freud believed that such dreams symbolize underlying latent content. In these examples, the snakes and neckties symbolize a male's genitals and the king or president symbolizes a father or the therapist. Freud thought that once the therapist understood a client's symbolism, the nature of the dream could be interpreted (Scalzone & Zontini, 2001). As shown in figure 6.8, artists have sometimes incorporated the symbolic world of dreaming in their paintings.

A final point about Freud's dream theory involves its scientific merit. Although symbolic interpretation can be fascinating, researchers have found it very difficult to devise appropriate methods to even attempt to verify his dream theory. His theory has largely given way to newer theories of dreams.

Subconscious Cognitive Processing The **cognitive theory of dreaming** proposes that dreaming can be understood by relying on the same cognitive concepts that are used in studying the waking mind. That is, dreaming involves processing information, memory, and problem solving. In the cognitive theory of dreaming there

wish fulfillment Freud's concept of dreaming as an unconscious attempt to fulfill needs (especially for sex and aggression) that cannot be expressed, or that go ungratified, while awake.

manifest content In Freud's view, the dream's surface content, which contains symbols that distort and disguise the dream's true meaning.

latent content In Freud's view, the dream's hidden content; its unconscious meaning.

cognitive theory of dreaming Proposes that dreaming can be understood by relying on the same cognitive processes that are used in studying the waking mind.

FIGURE 6.8 Artists' Portrayals of Dreams Through the centuries, artists have been adept at capturing the enchanting or nightmarish characteristics of our dreams. (*Left*) Dutch painter Hieronymus Bosch (1450–1516) captured both the enchanting and frightening world of dreams in *Garden of Earthly Delights*. (*Right*) Marc Chagall painted a world of dreams in *I and the Village*.

is little or no search for the hidden, symbolic content of dreams that Freud sought (Foulkes, 1993, 1999).

Rather than being an arena for playing out our unsatisfied needs, dreams might be a mental realm in which we can solve problems and think creatively. For example, the Scots author Robert Louis Stevenson (1850–1894) claimed that he got the idea for Dr. Jekyll and Mr. Hyde in a dream. Elias Howe, attempting to invent a machine that sewed, reportedly dreamed that he was captured by savages carrying spears with holes in their tips. On waking, he realized that he should place the hole for the thread at the end of the needle, not in the middle. Dreams may spark such gifts of inspiration because, in unique and creative ways, they weave together current experiences with the past.

Criticisms of the cognitive theory of dreaming focus on skepticism about the ability to resolve problems during sleep and the lack of attention to the roles of brain structures and activity in dreaming, the main emphasis of the activation-synthesis theory of dreams.

Finding Logic in Random Brain Activity **Activation-synthesis theory** states that dreaming occurs when the cerebral cortex synthesizes neural signals generated from activity in the lower part of the brain. In this view, dreams reflect the brain's efforts to make sense out of neural activity that takes place during sleep (Hobson, 1999).

When we are awake and alert, the contents of our conscious experience tend to be driven by external stimuli that result in specific motor behavior. During sleep,

activation-synthesis theory States that dreaming occurs when the cerebral cortex synthesizes neural signals emanating from activity in the lower part of the brain.

according to activation-synthesis theory, conscious experience is driven by internally generated stimuli that have no apparent behavioral consequence. A key source of this internal stimulation is spontaneous neural activity in the reticular formation of the limbic system (Hobson, 2000).

Recently, proponents of activation-synthesis theory have suggested that neural networks in other areas of the forebrain play a key role in dreaming (Hobson & others, 2000). Specifically, they believe that the same regions of the forebrain that are involved in certain waking behaviors also function in particular aspects of dreaming. Thus the primary motor and sensory areas of the forebrain would be activated in the sensorimotor aspects of the dream; the parietal lobe would be activated in the spatial organization of the dream; the visual aspects of the dream in the visual association cortex; the amygdala, hippocampus, and frontal lobe would be activated in the emotional aspects of a dream, and so on.

The sudden, uncoordinated eye movements of REM sleep make the dream world move in odd ways. For instance, a dream might include magic carpets flying over an undulating landscape. Dreams tend to truncate, dissolve, or shift suddenly in midstream. Freud explained this phenomenon as the dreamer's attempt to elude the unpleasant and the taboo. Activation-synthesis theorists say that this shifting is due to normal cycles of neural activation (Hobson, 2000). As levels of neurotransmitters rise and fall during the stages of sleep, some neural networks are activated, and others shut down. As a new cycle is activated, a new dream landscape emerges. In sum, in the activation-synthesis view, dreams are merely a glitzy sideshow, not the main event (Hooper & Teresi, 1993).

Like all dream theories, activation-synthesis theory has its critics. Among their criticisms are the belief that the brain stem is not the only starting point for neural activity in dreaming and that life experiences stimulate and shape dreaming more than activation-synthesis theory acknowledges (Domhoff, 2001; Solms, 1997).

mhhe●com/
santrockp7

For study tools related to this learning goal, see the Study Guide, the CD-ROM, and the Online Learning Center.

Review and Sharpen Your Thinking

2 *Explain the nature of sleep.*

- Know about the relationship between biological rhythms and sleep.
- Summarize the benefits of sleep and the effects of sleep deprivation.
- Describe the five stages of sleep and changes in the level of activity in the brain during sleep.
- Explain the links between sleep and disease.
- Name and describe five types of sleep disorders.
- Understand the nature of dreams, including theories of why people dream.

Do you know someone who might have a diagnosed or undiagnosed sleep disorder? What might he or she be able to do about it?

3 HYPNOSIS

The Nature of Hypnosis   **Explaining Hypnosis**   **Applications of Hypnosis**

Is hypnosis an altered state of consciousness?

A young cancer patient is about to undergo a painful bone marrow transplant. His doctor directs the boy's attention, asking him to breathe and listen carefully. Soon the boy is absorbed in a pleasant fantasy in which he is riding a motorcycle over a huge pizza, dodging anchovies, and maneuvering around blobs of melted mozzarella. Minutes later the procedure is over. The boy is relaxed and feels good about his self-control. The doctor successfully used hypnosis as a technique to help the patient control pain by reducing his perception of it.

Hypnosis is defined as a psychological state or possibly altered attention and awareness in which the individual is unusually receptive to suggestions. Basic hypnotic techniques have been used since the beginning of recorded history in association with religious ceremonies, magic, the supernatural, and many erroneous theories.

In the late nineteenth century, the Austrian physician Friedrich Anton Mesmer cured patients of various problems by passing magnets over their bodies. Mesmer said the problems were cured by "animal magnetism," an intangible force that passes from therapist to patient. In reality, the cures were due to some form of hypnotic suggestion. A committee was appointed by the French Academy of Science to investigate Mesmer's claims. The committee agreed that his treatment was effective. However, they disputed his theory about animal magnetism and prohibited him from practicing in Paris. Mesmer's theory was called "mesmerism," and even today we use the term *mesmerized* to mean hypnotized or enthralled.

Today, hypnosis is recognized as a legitimate process in psychology and medicine, although we still have much to learn about how it works. In addition, as is discussed shortly, there still is debate about whether or not hypnosis truly is an altered state of consciousness (Chaves, 2000).

The brain activity of a hypnotized individual is being monitored. *How is hypnosis different from sleep?*

The Nature of Hypnosis

In the discussion of sleep, I described the five different stages of sleep and the distinctive brain waves associated with each stage. A common misconception is that the hypnotic state is much like a sleep state. However, unlike sleepers, hypnotized individuals are aware of what is happening and remember the experience later unless they are instructed to forget what happened. Evidence from recent EEG studies documents that during hypnosis individuals show different patterns of brain activity than they do when they are not under hypnosis (Isotani & others, 2001; Jensen & others, 2001). Researchers have found that individuals in a hypnotic state showed a predominance of alpha and beta waves, characteristic of persons in a waking state, when monitored by an EEG (De Benedittis & Sironi, 1985; Williams & Gruzelier, 2001). In another study, hypnotized individuals' EEGs resembled those of a person in a relaxed waking state (Graffin, Ray, & Lundy, 1995).

The Four Steps in Hypnosis Successful hypnosis involves four steps:

1. Distractions are minimized; the person to be hypnotized is made comfortable.
2. The hypnotist tells the person to concentrate on something specific, such as an imagined scene or the ticking of a watch.
3. The hypnotist tells the person what to expect in the hypnotic state, such as relaxation or a pleasant floating sensation.
4. The hypnotist suggests certain events or feelings he or she knows will occur or observes occurring, such as "Your eyes are getting tired." When the suggested effects occur, the person interprets them as being caused by the hypnotist's suggestions and accepts them as an indication that something is happening. This increase in the person's expectations that the hypnotist will make things happen in the future makes the person even more suggestible.

Individual Variations in Hypnosis Do you think that you could be hypnotized? For as long as hypnosis has been studied (about 200 years), some people have been found to be more easily hypnotized than others. About 10 to 20 percent of the population is very susceptible to hypnosis, 10 percent or less cannot be hypnotized at all, and the remainder fall somewhere in between (Hilgard, 1965).

hypnosis A psychological state or possibly altered attention and awareness in which the individual is unusually responsive to suggestions.

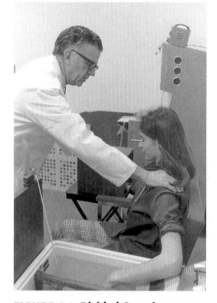

FIGURE 6.9 Divided Consciousness
Ernest Hilgard tests a participant in the study in which he had individuals place one arm in ice-cold water. *Why did Hilgard believe this study demonstrated the presence of divided consciousness?*

There is no simple way to tell beforehand who can be hypnotized. But if you have the capacity to immerse yourself in imaginative activities—listening to a favorite piece of music or reading a novel, for example—you are a likely candidate. People susceptible to hypnosis become completely absorbed in what they are doing, removing the boundaries between themselves and what they are experiencing in their environment. Nonetheless, such absorption is best described as a weak rather than a strong predictor of a person's likelihood of being hypnotized (Nash, 2001; Nash & Nadon, 1997).

Hypnosis and Will If you are in a hypnotic state, can the hypnotist make you do something against your will? Individuals being hypnotized abdicate their responsibility to the hypnotist and follow the hypnotist's suggestions. However, they are unlikely to do anything in a hypnotic state that violates their morals or that is dangerous.

Explaining Hypnosis

Ever since Anton Mesmer proposed his theory of animal magnetism, psychologists have been trying to figure out why hypnosis works. Contemporary theorists are divided on their answers to the question Is hypnosis a divided state of consciousness or is it simply a form of learned social behavior?

A Divided State of Consciousness Ernest Hilgard (1977, 1992) proposed that hypnosis involves a special divided state of consciousness, a sort of splitting of consciousness into separate components. One component follows the hypnotist's commands, while another component acts as a "hidden observer."

In one situation, Hilgard placed one arm of hypnotized individuals in a bucket of ice-cold water and told them that they would not feel any pain but that another part of their minds—the hidden part that is aware of what is going on—could signal any true pain by pressing a key with the hand that was not submerged (see figure 6.9). The individuals under hypnosis reported afterward that they did not experience any pain, but, while their arms were submerged in the ice-cold water, they had indeed pressed the key with their nonsubmerged hands, and they pressed it more frequently the longer their arms were in the cold water. Thus, in Hilgard's view, in hypnosis, consciousness has a hidden part that stays in contact with reality and feels pain while another part of consciousness feels no pain.

Social Cognitive Behavior Some experts are skeptical that hypnosis is truly an altered state of consciousness (Chaves, 2000). In the **social cognitive behavior view of hypnosis,** hypnosis is a normal state in which the hypnotized person behaves the way he or she believes a hypnotized person should behave. In this view, the important questions about hypnosis focus on cognitive factors—the attitudes, expectations, and beliefs of good hypnotic participants—and on the social context in which hypnosis occurs (Barber, 1969; Spanos & Chaves, 1989).

Applications of Hypnosis

Hypnosis is widely used in psychotherapy, medicine, and dentistry, in criminal investigations, and in sports. Hypnosis has been used in psychotherapy to treat alcoholism, somnambulism, suicidal tendencies, overeating, and smoking (Eimer, 2000; Yapko, 2001). Among the least effective, but most common, applications of hypnosis are those intended to help people stop overeating or quit smoking. Hypnotists direct individuals to stop these behaviors, but dramatic results rarely are achieved unless the individuals are already motivated to change. Hypnosis is most effective when combined with psychotherapy (Borckardt, 2002).

A long history of research and practice clearly has demonstrated that hypnosis can reduce the experience of pain (Crasilneck, 1995; De Pascalis & others, 2001;

social cognitive behavior view of hypnosis Views hypnosis as a result of social factors associated with the hypnotic context, coupled with cognitive events involved in the efforts of the hypnotized person to immerse himself or herself in the role of the hypnotized person.

Etzel Cardena is a hypnotherapist, professor of psychology at the University of Texas at Pan American, and has been president of Division 30 (Hypnosis) of the American Psychological Association. He is shown here hypnotizing an adolescent. Cardena's first experiences with hypnosis were at his father's hypnosis workshops in Mexico. He moved to the United States to pursue a doctoral degree in psychology with an emphasis on altered states of consciousness. Cardena is especially interested in hypnosis as a dissociated state of consciousness and its use in helping people who have experienced trauma and various mental disorders.

Langenfeld, Cipani, & Borckardt, 2002). However, not everyone is hypnotizable enough to benefit from this effect. Moreover, there is no evidence that hypnosis increases muscular strength and endurance, or sensory thresholds (Druckman & Bjork, 1994).

Hypnosis has sometimes been used in attempts to enhance people's ability to accurately recall forgotten events (Coleman, Stevens, & Reeder, 2001). For example, police departments sometimes arrange to have eyewitnesses to crimes hypnotized in the hope that this will significantly improve their recall of the crime. To read about the research on this topic and the issues involved in whether hypnosis is a window to forgotten events, see the Critical Controversy box on p. 250.

Review and Sharpen Your Thinking

3 Describe hypnosis.

- Explain what hypnosis is.
- Discuss two theoretical explanations of hypnosis.
- Identify some applications of hypnosis.

Do you think you are a good candidate for hypnosis? Why or why not?

mhhe com/
santrockp7

For study tools related to this learning goal, see the Study Guide, the CD-ROM, and the Online Learning Center.

PSYCHOACTIVE DRUGS 4

Uses of Psychoactive Drugs   Types of Psychoactive Drugs   Addiction

What are psychoactive drugs and how do they affect behavior?

During one phase of his career, Sigmund Freud experimented with therapeutic uses of cocaine. He was searching for possible medical applications, such as a painkiller for eye surgery. He soon found that the drug induced ecstasy. Writing to his fiancée, he told her how just a small dose of cocaine produced wonderful, lofty sensations. As it became apparent that cocaine produced considerable risk to its users, and after several died from overdoses, Freud quit using the drug. Cocaine is just one of many drugs taken to alter consciousness.

Is Hypnosis a Window to Forgotten Events?

In 1977, two nurses were accused of poisoning nine patients at a Veterans Administration Hospital in Ann Arbor, Michigan. Two of the patients died. At first no clear evidence was found to link the nurses to the crime. In an attempt to prove their case, FBI agents hypnotized the surviving victims and several staff members. Under hypnosis, one victim gradually began to remember the presence of one of the two nurses in his room. Were the memories of this witness accurate? How do we know whether events recalled under hypnosis actually happened as people recall them? While this critical testimony resulted in a conviction, a judge ordered a new trial and the prosecution chose to not retry the case (Loftus, 1979).

Hypnosis is sometimes used to enhance people's ability to recall forgotten events (Barnier, Bryant, & Brisco, 2001; Nash, 2001; Stafford & Lynn, 2002). Police departments use hypnosis occasionally to help eyewitnesses remember forgotten crime scene details. In 1976, for example, a school bus carrying twenty-six schoolchildren from Chowchilla, California disappeared. It turns out that three armed men kidnapped the bus driver and the children, and buried them alive in a trailer in a gravel quarry some distance away. After 16 hours underground, they were rescued. When the school bus driver was hypnotized, he recalled all but one digit of the license plate on the vehicle driven by the kidnappers. This memory proved critical in tracking down the suspects (Loftus, 1979).

Therapists sometimes use hypnosis to age-regress patients back to an earlier stage in life in order to help them work through long-forgotten, painful experiences. However, research suggests that improvements in memory due to hypnosis may often be more apparent than real. In one study, participants watched a videotape of a mock armed robbery and then recalled specific crime details six times: twice immediately after seeing the videotape, twice 1 week after seeing the videotape, once during hypnosis, and once after hypnosis (Nadon, Laurence & Perry, 1991). High-hypnotizability participants, in fact, remembered more specific crime details under hypnosis than they did just before hypnosis, while low-hypnotizability participants did not. At the same time, however, high-hypnotizability participants misremembered more false crime details than did low-hypnotizability participants. In other words, when people are hypnotized, they may remember more correct and incorrect information. One explanation of this result is that hypnosis may make participants more willing than normal to report whatever comes into their mind (Klatzky & Erdelyi, 1985).

Unfortunately for police and therapists, in most real-life circumstances it may be impossible to discriminate between correct and incorrect memories. In the Chowchilla case mentioned above, corroborating evidence confirmed the accuracy of the bus driver's hypnotic recall. In the Ann Arbor case, with no corroborating evidence, it was impossible to confirm or disconfirm the accuracy of the victim's recovered memory.

This uncertainty about the accuracy of memories recalled under hypnosis is magnified by the tendency of hypnotized participants to be influenced by leading questions. For example, after viewing a photo, hypnotized individuals might be asked, "What color was that person's mustache?" The individuals then often create an image of the person they saw and supply the person with a mustache, even though the photo did not show a mustache. Later they might recall, with confidence, the person as having a mustache. A number of studies have shown that hypnotized witnesses are more confident about the inaccurate aspects of their recall or about misidentifications than are non-hypnotized witnesses (Orne, 1959). In a court of law, hypnotized witnesses have so much confidence in their pseudomemories—false memories that are confidently believed to be real—that they are effectively immune against cross-examination (Orne, 1959). Jane Dywan (1995) has proposed that increased confidence in memories recovered under hypnosis is due to an illusion of familiarity that hypnosis helps to produce.

Because of its questionable reliability, hypnotic testimony is banned in some states. If hypnotic testimony is allowed in court, extreme caution must be exercised to obtain corroborating evidence and to minimize the risk of implanting pseudomemories when questioning victims and witnesses under hypnosis. Similarly, clinical psychologists must be careful when using hypnosis with their clients to minimize the risk of accidentally implanting highly emotional pseudomemories (Green, Lynn, & Malinoski, 1998).

There is some evidence that it may not be necessary to hypnotize eyewitnesses to help them remember more details about a crime. In one study, although individuals sometimes recalled new information following a hypnotic interview, they also sometimes recalled new information when motivated by non-hypnotic instructions (Frischoltz, 1995). However, even non-hypnotic methods of improving memory are vulnerable to the same problems, leading to the same concerns about the accuracy of recovered memories (Loftus, 1979).

What do you think?

- Why should extreme caution be exercised when evaluating memories generated by hypnotic testimony?
- Might age regression be a valuable therapeutic technique regardless of the risk of generating pseudomemories?
- Why might hypnosis cause someone to report recalled events inaccurately?

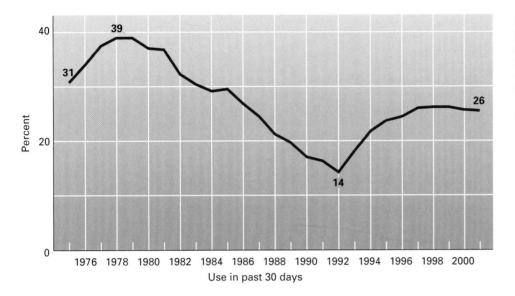

FIGURE 6.10 **Trends in Drug Use by U.S. High School Seniors** This graph shows the percentage of high school seniors who say they have taken an illicit drug in the previous 30 days. Notice the increased use in the latter half of the 1970s, the decrease in the 1980s, and the increase in the 1990s.

Illicit drug use is a global problem. More than 200 million people worldwide abuse drugs (UNDCP, 2001). The images span all segments of society: the urban professional snorting cocaine in a downtown nightclub, the farmer addicted to the opium poppy he grows, the teenage Ecstasy user in a comfortable suburban home.

Overall drug use among U.S. adolescents increased in the 1970s, as shown in figure 6.10, then decreased in the 1980s, but rose once again in the 1990s (Johnston, O'Malley, & Bachman, 2001). Later, in the discussion of specific drugs, I describe trends in adolescents' use of specific drugs.

Uses of Psychoactive Drugs

Psychoactive drugs are substances that act on the nervous system to alter states of consciousness, modify perceptions, and change moods. People are attracted to psychoactive substances because they help them adapt to an ever-changing environment. Drinking, smoking, and taking drugs reduce tension, relieve boredom and fatigue, and in some cases help people to escape from the harsh realities of the world. Some people take drugs because they are curious about their effects. Others may take drugs for social reasons, for example, to feel more at ease and happier in interacting with others.

The use of psychoactive drugs for personal gratification and temporary adaptation can carry a high price tag: drug dependence, personal disarray, and a predisposition to serious, sometimes fatal, diseases (Goldberg, 2003). What was initially intended to be pleasurable and adaptive can eventually turn to sorrow and maladaptation. For example, drinking alcohol may initially help people relax and forget about their worries. But if they turn more and more to alcohol to escape reality, they may develop a dependence that can destroy relationships, careers, and their bodies.

Continued use of psychoactive drugs leads to **tolerance,** which is the need to take increasing amounts of a drug to get the same effect. For example, the first time someone takes 5 milligrams of the tranquilizer Valium, the drug will make them feel very relaxed. However, after taking the pill every day for 6 months, the person may need to take 10 milligrams to achieve the same calming effect.

Continuing drug use can also result in **physical dependence,** the physiological need for a drug that causes unpleasant *withdrawal* symptoms, such as physical pain and a craving for the drug, when it is discontinued. **Psychological dependence** is the strong desire to repeat the use of a drug for emotional reasons, such as a feeling of well-being and reduction of stress. Experts on drug abuse use the term *addiction* to describe either a physical or psychological dependence, or both, on the

psychoactive drugs Drugs that act on the nervous system to alter consciousness, modify perceptions, and change moods.

tolerance The need to take increasing amounts of the drug to produce the same effect.

physical dependence The physical need for a drug, accompanied by unpleasant withdrawal symptoms when the drug is discontinued.

psychological dependence The strong desire and craving to repeat the use of the drug for emotional reasons.

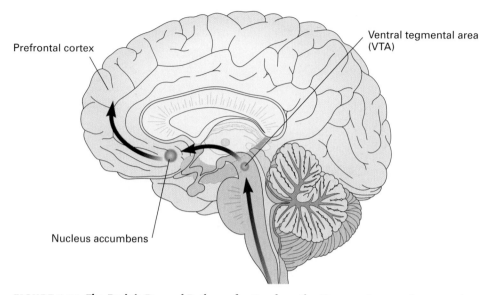

FIGURE 6.11 **The Brain's Reward Pathway for Psychoactive Drugs** The ventral tegmental area (VTA) and nucleus accumbens are important locations in the reward pathway for psychoactive drugs. Information travels from the VTA to the nucleus accumbens and then up to the prefrontal cortex. The VTA is located in the midbrain just above the pons, and the nucleus accumbens is located in the forebrain, just beneath the prefrontal cortex.

drug (Carroll, 2003). Both physical and psychological dependence mean that the psychoactive drug is exerting a powerful influence over the person's behavior.

From a neurobiological perspective, psychoactive drugs increase dopamine levels in the brain's reward pathways (National Institute on Drug Abuse [NIDA], 2001). This reward pathway is located in the *ventral tegmental area (VTA)* and *nucleus accumbens* (see figure 6.11). Only the limbic and prefrontal areas of the brain are directly activated by dopamine, which comes from the VTA (Kandel, Schwartz, & Jessell, 2003). Although different drugs have different mechanisms of action, each drug increases the activity of the reward pathway by increasing dopamine transmission. Recall from chapter 3 that when a drug mimics a particular neurotransmitter or blocks its reuptake, it is referred to as an *agonist*. Thus drugs that increase dopamine levels in the brain are agonists. In contrast, when a drug blocks a neurotransmitter or diminishes its release, it is called an *antagonist*.

Types of Psychoactive Drugs

Three main categories of psychoactive drugs are depressants, stimulants, and hallucinogens. All of them have the potential to cause health or behavior problems or both. To evaluate whether you abuse drugs, see figure 6.12.

Depressants **Depressants** are psychoactive drugs that slow down mental and physical activity. Among the most widely used depressants are alcohol, barbiturates, tranquilizers, and opiates.

Alcohol We do not always think of alcohol as a drug, but it is a powerful one. Alcohol acts on the body primarily as a depressant and slows down the brain's activities. This might seem surprising, as people who normally tend to be inhibited may begin to talk, dance, and socialize after a few drinks. However, people "loosen up" after a few drinks because the areas of the brain involved in inhibition and judgment slow down. As people drink more, their inhibitions become even further reduced, and their judgment becomes increasingly impaired. Activities that require intellectual functioning

depressants Psychoactive drugs that slow down mental and physical activity.

FIGURE 6.12 **Do You Abuse Drugs?**

Respond yes or no to the following items:

Yes	No	
_____	_____	I have gotten into problems because of using drugs.
_____	_____	Using alcohol or other drugs has made my college life unhappy at times.
_____	_____	Drinking alcohol or taking other drugs has been a factor in my losing a job.
_____	_____	Drinking alcohol or taking other drugs has interfered with my studying for exams.
_____	_____	Drinking alcohol or taking drugs has jeopardized my academic performance.
_____	_____	My ambition is not as strong since I've been drinking a lot or taking drugs.
_____	_____	Drinking or taking drugs has caused me to have difficulty sleeping.
_____	_____	I have felt remorse after drinking or taking drugs.
_____	_____	I crave a drink or other drugs at a definite time of the day.
_____	_____	I want a drink or other drug in the morning.
_____	_____	I have had a complete or partial loss of memory as a result of drinking or using other drugs.
_____	_____	Drinking or using other drugs is affecting my reputation.
_____	_____	I have been in the hospital or another institution because of my drinking or taking drugs.

College students who responded yes to items similar to these on the Rutgers Collegiate Abuse Screening Test were more likely to be substance abusers than those who answered no. If you responded yes to just 1 of the 13 items on this screening test, consider going to your college health or counseling center for further screening.

and motor skills, such as driving, become increasingly impaired as more alcohol is consumed. Eventually the drinker becomes drowsy and falls asleep. With extreme intoxication, a person may lapse into a coma and die. Each of these effects varies with the way the person's body metabolizes alcohol, body weight, the amount of alcohol consumed, and whether previous drinking has led to tolerance (Gotz & others, 2001).

How does alcohol affect the brain? Like other psychoactive drugs, alcohol goes to the ventral tegmental area (VTA) and the nucleus accumbens (NIDA, 2001). Alcohol also increases the concentration of the neurotransmitter gamma aminobutyric acid (GABA), which is widely distributed in many areas of the brain, including the cerebral cortex, cerebellum, hippocampus, amygdala, and nucleus accumbens (Melis & others, 2002). Researchers believe that the frontal cortex, which is involved in decision making and memory, holds a memory of the pleasure involved in prior alcohol use (relaxation, lowered stress, less inhibition) and contributes to continued drinking. Alcohol use also may affect the areas of the frontal cortex involved in judgment and impulse control (Mantere & others, 2002). It is further believed that the basal ganglia, which are involved in compulsive behaviors, may lead to a greater demand for alcohol, regardless of reason and consequences (Brink, 2001).

After caffeine, alcohol is the most widely used drug in America. Surveys indicate that as many as two-thirds of American adults drink beer, wine, or liquor at least occasionally, and in one recent survey approximately 10 percent reported that they drink excessively (National Center for Health Statistics, 2001). Drinking excessively in this survey was defined as consuming five or more drinks on one occasion at least 12 times in the past year.

Approximately 14 million people in the United States are alcoholics (Brink, 2001). Alcoholism is the third leading killer in the United States. Approximately 20,000 people are killed and 1.5 million injured by drunk drivers each year. More than 60 percent of homicides involve the use of alcohol by either the offender or the

FIGURE 6.13 Consequences of Binge Drinking

The Troubles Frequent Binge Drinkers Create for . . .

Themselves[1]		and Others[2]	
(% of those surveyed who admitted having had the problem)		(% of those surveyed who had been affected)	
Missed class	61	Had study or sleep interrupted	68
Forgot where they were or what they did	54	Had to care for drunken student	54
Engaged in unplanned sex	41	Were insulted or humiliated	34
Got hurt	23	Experienced unwanted sexual advances	26
Had unprotected sex	22	Had serious argument	20
Damaged property	22	Had property damaged	15
Got into trouble with campus or local police	11	Were pushed or assaulted	13
Had five or more alcohol-related problems in school year	47	Had at least one of the above problems	87

[1] Frequent binge drinkers were defined as those who had at least four or five drinks at one time on at least three occasions in the previous two weeks.
[2] These figures are from colleges where at least 50% of students are binge drinkers.

victim, and 65 percent of aggressive sexual acts against women involve the use of alcohol by the offender.

A special concern is the high rate of alcohol use by high school and college students in the United States. In a recent national survey of more than 17,000 high school seniors in the United States, 80 percent had tried alcohol, and about half had done so by the eighth grade (Johnston & others, 2001). In this survey, 62 percent of the twelfth graders and 25 percent of the eighth graders reported having been drunk at least once in their lives. Binge drinking (defined as having five or more drinks in a row at least once in the previous 2 weeks) had been engaged in by 33 percent of the high school seniors at least once in the previous month.

Heavy, binge drinking often increases during the first 2 years of college, and it can take its toll on students (Schulenberg, 1999). Chronic binge drinking is more common among male college students than among females and among students living away from home, especially males living in fraternity houses (Schulenberg & others, 2000). In one recent national survey of drinking patterns on college campuses, almost half of the binge drinkers reported problems that included missed classes, injuries, trouble with police, and unprotected sex (see figure 6.13; Wechsler & others, 2000). Binge-drinking college students were 11 times more likely to fall behind in school, 10 times more likely to drive after drinking, and twice as likely to have unprotected sex as college students who did not binge drink. Many young people decrease their use of alcohol as they move into adult roles, such as a permanent job, marriage or cohabitation, and parenthood.

Around the world, there are differences in alcohol use by religion and gender (Koenig, 2001; Lieber, 1997; Melinder & Anderson, 2001). Catholics, Reform Jews, and liberal Protestants all consume alcohol at a fairly high level. Males drink alcohol more than females.

Europeans, especially the French, drink alcohol at high rates. Estimates are that about 30 percent of French adults have health problems related to high alcohol consumption. Alcohol use also is high in Russia, but its use in China is low. In some religions, such as the Muslim religion, use of alcohol is forbidden.

alcoholism A disorder that involves long-term, repeated, uncontrolled, compulsive, and excessive use of alcoholic beverages and that impairs the drinker's health and work and social relationships.

Alcoholism is a disorder that involves long-term, repeated, uncontrolled, compulsive, and excessive use of alcoholic beverages and that impairs the drinker's health and social relationships. One in nine individuals who drink continues the path to alcoholism. Those who do are disproportionately related to alcoholics. Family studies consistently find a high frequency of alcoholism in the first-degree relatives of alcoholics (Hannigan & others, 1999). Indeed, researchers have found that heredity likely plays a role in alcoholism, although the precise hereditary mechanism has not been found

(Crabbe, 2001, 2002; Wall & others, 2001). An estimated 50 to 60 percent of those who become alcoholics are believed to have a genetic predisposition for it.

One possible explanation is that the brains of people genetically predisposed to alcoholism may be unable to produce adequate dopamine, a neurotransmitter that can make us feel pleasure. For these individuals, alcohol may increase dopamine concentration and resulting pleasure to the point at which it leads to addiction.

Although studies reveal a genetic influence on alcoholism, they also show that environmental factors play a role (Heath & others, 2002). For example, family studies indicate that many alcoholics do not have close relatives who are alcoholics (Sher, 1993). The large cultural variations in alcohol use mentioned earlier also underscore the environment's role in alcoholism.

About one-third of alcoholics recover, whether they are in a treatment program or not. This finding came from a long-term study of 700 individuals over 50 years (Vaillant, 1983, 1992) and has consistently been found by other researchers as well. George Vaillant formulated the one-third rule for alcoholism: By age 65, one-third are dead or in terrible shape; one-third are still trying to beat their addiction; and one-third are abstinent or drinking only socially. In his extensive research, Vaillant found that a positive outcome and recovery from alcoholism was predicted by (1) a strong negative experience with drinking, such as a serious medical emergency or condition, (2) finding a substitute dependency to compete with alcohol abuse, such as meditation, exercise, or overeating (which has its own adverse health effects), (3) developing new, positive relationships (such as a concerned, helpful employer or a new marriage), and (4) joining a support group, such as a religious organization, Alcoholics Anonymous, or Rational Recovery.

I have presented an extensive discussion of alcohol use and its effects because it is so widely used and abused. Now I consider several other depressant drugs, beginning with barbiturates.

Barbiturates **Barbiturates,** such as Nembutal and Seconal, are depressant drugs that are used to decrease central nervous system activity. They were once widely prescribed as sleep aids. In heavy dosages, they can lead to impaired memory and decision making. When combined with alcohol (for example, sleeping pills taken after a night of binge drinking), barbiturates can be lethal. Heavy doses of barbiturates by themselves can cause death. For this reason, barbiturates are the drug most often used in suicide attempts. Abrupt withdrawal from barbiturates can produce seizures. Because of the addictive potential and relative ease of toxic overdose, barbiturates have been largely replaced by tranquilizers in the treatment of insomnia.

Tranquilizers **Tranquilizers,** such as Valium and Xanax, are depressant drugs that reduce anxiety and induce relaxation. Unlike barbiturates, which often are given to induce sleep, tranquilizers are usually given to calm an anxious, nervous individual (Rosenbloom, 2002). Tranquilizers are among the most widely prescribed drugs in the United States. They can produce withdrawal symptoms when use is stopped.

Opiates Narcotics, or **opiates,** consist of opium and its derivatives and depress the central nervous system's activity. The most common opiate drugs—morphine and heroin—affect synapses in the brain that use endorphins as their neurotransmitter. When these drugs leave the brain, the affected synapses become understimulated. For several hours after taking an opiate, the person feels euphoric and pain free and has an increased appetite for food and sex. The opiates are highly addictive drugs, leading to craving and painful withdrawal when the drug becomes unavailable.

Another hazardous consequence of opiate addiction is the risk of exposure to the virus that causes acquired immunodeficiency syndrome (AIDS). Most heroin addicts inject the drug intravenously. When they share needles without sterilizing them, one infected addict can transmit the virus to others.

barbiturates Depressant drugs that decrease the activity of the central nervous system.

tranquilizers Depressant drugs that reduce anxiety and induce relaxation.

opiates Opium and its derivatives; they depress the central nervous system's activity.

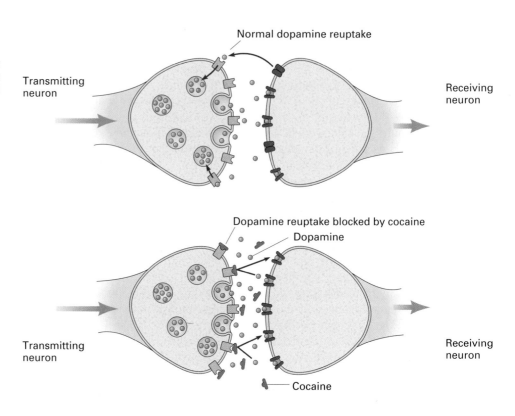

FIGURE 6.14 Cocaine and Neuro-transmitters Cocaine concentrates in areas of the brain that are rich in dopamine synapses, such as the VTA and the nucleus accumbens. (*Top*) What happens in normal reuptake. The transmitting neuron releases dopamine that stimulates the receiving neuron by binding to its receptor sites. After binding occurs, dopamine is carried back into the transmitting neuron for later release. (*Bottom*) What happens when cocaine is present in the synapse. Cocaine binds to the uptake pumps and prevents them from removing dopamine from the synapse. This results in more dopamine in the synapse, and more dopamine receptors are activated.

Stimulants   **Stimulants** are psychoactive drugs that increase the central nervous system's activity. The most widely used stimulants are amphetamines, cocaine, MDMA (Ecstasy), caffeine, and nicotine.

Amphetamines   *Amphetamines* are stimulant drugs that are used to boost energy, stay awake, or lose weight. They sometimes are called "pep pills" or "uppers." Amphetamines often are prescribed in the form of diet pills. These drugs increase the release of dopamine, which enhances the user's activity level and pleasurable feelings.

Cocaine   Cocaine is an illegal drug that comes from the coca plant, native to Bolivia and Peru. For centuries, Bolivians and Peruvians have chewed the leaves of the plant to increase their stamina. Generally, however, cocaine is either snorted or injected in the form of crystals or powder. Used this way, cocaine can trigger a heart attack, stroke, or brain seizure.

When animals and humans chew coca leaves, small amounts of cocaine gradually enter the bloodstream, without any apparent adverse effects. However, when extracted cocaine is sniffed or injected, it enters the bloodstream very rapidly, producing a rush of euphoric feelings that lasts for about 15 to 30 minutes. Because the rush depletes the supply of the neurotransmitters dopamine, serotonin, and norepinephrine in the brain, an agitated, depressed mood usually follows as the drug's effects decline. Figure 6.14 shows how cocaine affects dopamine levels in the brain.

Crack is a potent form of cocaine, consisting of chips of pure cocaine that are usually smoked. Crack is believed to be one of the most addictive substances known, being more addictive than heroin, barbiturates, or alcohol.

Treatment of cocaine addiction has not been very successful. Cocaine's addictive properties are so strong that 6 months after treatment more than 50 percent of cocaine abusers return to the drug. Experts on drug abuse argue that prevention is the best approach to reducing cocaine use.

MDMA (Ecstasy)   MDMA is an illegal synthetic drug with both stimulant and hallucinogenic properties. Street names for MDMA include Ecstasy, XTC, hug, beans, and

stimulants Psychoactive drugs that increase the central nervous system's activity.

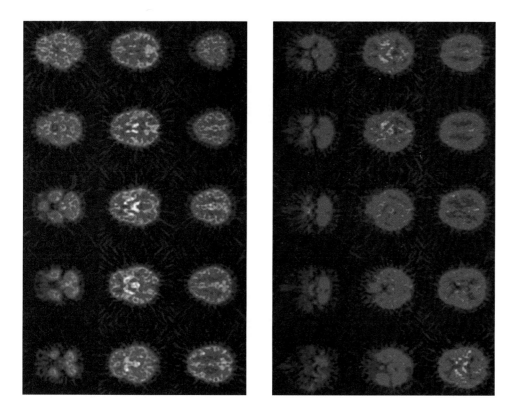

FIGURE 6.15 MDMA (Ecstasy) and the Brain (*Left*) Brain scans from individuals who have never taken MDMA. (*Right*) Brain scans from individuals who have taken MDMA regularly. Notice the prevalence of yellow in the brain scans on the left, which is indicative of healthy brain neuron connections, and its absence in the brain scans of the MDMA users on the right.

love drug. A special concern is the use of MDMA by secondary school students, which continued to increase in the year 2000 among eighth, tenth, and twelfth graders (Johnston & others, 2001).

Brain imaging studies show that MDMA can cause brain damage, especially to neurons that use serotonin to communicate with other neurons (see figure 6.15). Use for just 4 days can cause brain damage that is still evident 6 to 7 years later (NIDA, 2001).

Caffeine Often overlooked as a drug, caffeine is the most widely used psychoactive drug in the world. Caffeine is a stimulant and a natural component of the plants that are the sources of coffee, tea, and cola drinks. Caffeine also is present in chocolate and in many nonprescribed medications. The stimulating effects of caffeine are often perceived to be beneficial for boosting energy and alertness, but some people experience unpleasant side effects.

Caffeinism is the term given to overindulgence of caffeine. It is characterized by mood changes, anxiety, and sleep disruption. Caffeinism often develops in people who drink five or more cups of coffee (at least 500 milligrams) each day. Common symptoms of caffeinism are insomnia, irritability, headaches, ringing in the ears, dry mouth, increased blood pressure, and digestive problems (Hogan, Hornick, & Bonchoux, 2002).

Caffeine affects the brain's pleasure centers, so it is not surprising that it is difficult to kick the caffeine habit. When individuals who regularly consume caffeinated beverages remove caffeine from their diet, they typically experience headaches, lethargy, apathy, and concentration difficulties. These symptoms of withdrawal are usually mild and subside after several days.

Nicotine *Nicotine* is the main psychoactive ingredient in all forms of smoking and smokeless tobacco. Even with all the publicity given to the enormous health risks posed by tobacco, we sometimes overlook the highly addictive nature of nicotine.

In the brain, nicotine stimulates the reward centers by raising dopamine levels. Behavioral effects of nicotine include improved attention and alertness, reduced anger and anxiety, and pain relief (Rezvani & Levin, 2001).

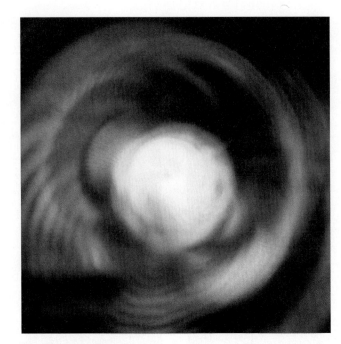

FIGURE 6.16 LSD-Induced Hallucination Under the influence of hallucinogenic drugs, such as LSD, several users have reported seeing tunnel-like images.

Tolerance develops for nicotine both in the long run and on a daily basis, so that cigarettes smoked later in the day have less effect than those smoked earlier in the day. Withdrawal from nicotine often quickly produces strong, unpleasant symptoms such as irritability, craving, inability to focus, sleep disturbance, and increased appetite. Withdrawal symptoms can persist for months or longer.

Despite the positive short-term effects of nicotine (such as increased energy and alertness), most smokers recognize the serious health risks of smoking and wish they could quit. Chapter 15 further explores the difficulty in quitting smoking and strategies that can be used to quit.

Hallucinogens **Hallucinogens** are psychoactive drugs that modify a person's perceptual experiences and produce visual images that are not real. Hallucinogens are also called psychedelic (meaning "mind-altering") drugs. Marijuana has a mild hallucinogenic effect, LSD a stronger one (see figure 6.16).

Marijuana Marijuana is the dried leaves and flowers of the hemp plant *Cannabis sativa,* which originated in central Asia but is now grown in most parts of the world. The plant's dried resin is known as hashish. The active ingredient in marijuana is THC (delta-9-tetrahydrocannabinol). Unlike other psychoactive drugs, THC does not affect a specific neurotransmitter. Rather, marijuana disrupts the membranes of neurons and affects the functioning of a variety of neurotransmitters and hormones.

The physical effects of marijuana include increases in pulse rate and blood pressure, reddening of the eyes, coughing, and dryness of the mouth. Psychological effects include a mixture of excitatory, depressive, and mildly hallucinatory characteristics that make it difficult to classify the drug. Marijuana can trigger spontaneous unrelated ideas; distorted perceptions of time and place; increased sensitivity to sounds, tastes, smells, and colors; and erratic verbal behavior. Marijuana can also impair attention and memory. When used daily in large amounts, marijuana also can alter sperm count and change hormonal cycles (Close, Roberts, & Berger, 1990). It may be involved in some birth defects. On a positive note, researchers have found some

hallucinogens Psychoactive drugs that modify a person's perceptual experiences and produce visual images that are not real.

Robert Chapman is coordinator of the alcohol and other drug program at La Salle University in Philadelphia. He coordinates the addictions counseling concentration in the master's degree program in clinical-counseling psychology. Robert recommends that students interested in becoming drug counselors should go to some open recovery-group sessions, such as Alcoholic Anonymous meetings. In his words, "You can read and study and learn all about addictions, but there is something about listening to recovering people talk about life that provides a perspective that can't be captured in books or films."

medical uses for marijuana, such as treating glaucoma, chemotherapy-caused vomiting, and AIDS-related weight loss.

Marijuana is the illegal drug most widely used by high school students. More than one-third of high school seniors in the United States say that they have used marijuana in the past year (Johnston & others, 2001).

LSD   LSD (lysergic acid diethylamide) is a hallucinogen that even in low doses produces striking perceptual changes. Objects change their shapes and glow. Colors become kaleidoscopic, and fabulous images unfold. Designs swirl, colors shimmer, and bizarre scenes appear. LSD-induced images are sometimes pleasurable and sometimes grotesque. Figure 6.16 shows one kind of perceptual experience that a number of LSD users have reported. LSD can also influence a user's sense of time. Time seems to slow down dramatically, so that brief glances at objects are experienced as deep, penetrating, and lengthy examinations, and minutes seem to be hours or even days. A bad LSD trip can trigger extreme anxiety, paranoia, and suicidal or homicidal impulses.

LSD's effects on the body can include dizziness, nausea, and tremors. LSD primarily acts on the neurotransmitter serotonin in the brain, though it also can affect dopamine (Nichols & Sanders-Bush, 2002). Emotional and cognitive effects may include rapid mood swings or impaired attention and memory. LSD is one psychoactive drug that has no beneficial effects. Its effects are summarized in figure 6.17, along with the characteristics of the other types of drugs that have been discussed.

The use of LSD reached a peak in the 1960s and 1970s but its popularity declined after its unpredictable effects became publicized. However, in the 1990s, use of LSD by high school students increased, although not to the level of use in the 1960s and 1970s (Johnston & others, 2001).

Drug Classification	Medical Uses	Short-Term Effects	Overdose Effects	Health Risks	Risk of Physical/ Psychological Dependence
Depressants					
Alcohol	Pain relief	Relaxation, depressed brain activity, slowed behavior, reduced inhibitions	Disorientation, loss of consciousness, even death at high blood-alcohol levels	Accidents, brain damage, liver disease, heart disease, ulcers, birth defects	Physical: moderate Psychological: moderate
Barbiturates	Sleeping pill	Relaxation, sleep	Breathing difficulty, coma, possible death	Accidents, coma, possible death	Physical and psychological: moderate to high
Tranquilizers	Anxiety reduction	Relaxation, slowed behavior	Breathing difficulty, coma, possible death	Accidents, coma, possible death	Physical: low to moderate Psychological: moderate to high
Opiates (narcotics)	Pain relief	Euphoric feelings, drowsiness, nausea	Convulsions, coma, possible death	Accidents, infectious diseases such as AIDS	Physical: high Psychological: moderate to high
Stimulants					
Amphetamines	Weight control	Increased alertness, excitability; decreased fatigue, irritability	Extreme irritability, feelings of persecution, convulsions	Insomnia, hypertension, malnutrition, possible death	Physical: possible Psychological: moderate to high
Cocaine	Local anesthetic	Increased alertness, excitability, euphoric feelings; decreased fatigue, irritability	Extreme irritability, feelings of persecution, convulsions, cardiac arrest, possible death	Insomnia, hypertension, malnutrition, possible death	Physical: possible Psychological: moderate (oral) to very high (injected or smoked)
MDMA (Ecstasy)	None	Mild amphetamine and hallucinogenic effects; high body temperature and dehydration; sense of well-being and social connectedness	Brain damage, especially memory and thinking	Cardiovascular problems; death	Physical: possible Psychological: moderate
Caffeine	None	Alertness and sense of well-being followed by fatigue	Nervousness, anxiety, disturbed sleep	Possible cardio-vascular problems	Physical: moderate Psychological: moderate
Nicotine	None	Stimulation, stress reduction, followed by fatigue, anger	Nervousness, disturbed sleep	Cancer and cardio-vascular disease	Physical: high Psychological: high
Hallucinogens					
LSD	None	Strong hallucinations, distorted time perception	Severe mental disturbance, loss of contact with reality	Accidents	Physical: none Psychological: low
Marijuana	Treatment of the eye disorder glaucoma	Euphoric feelings, relaxation, mild hallucinations, time distortion, attention and memory impairment	Fatigue, disoriented behavior	Accidents, respiratory disease	Physical: very low Psychological: moderate

FIGURE 6.17 Categories of Psychoactive Drugs: Depressants, Stimulants, and Hallucinogens

Addiction

Addiction is a pattern of behavior characterized by an overwhelming need to use the drug and to secure its supply. Addiction can occur despite adverse consequences of drug use. There is a strong tendency to relapse after quitting or withdrawal. Withdrawal symptoms consist of significant changes in physical functioning and behavior. Depending on the drug, these symptoms might include insomnia, tremors, nausea, vomiting, cramps, elevation of heart rate and blood pressure, convulsions, anxiety, and depression.

Controversy continues about whether addictions are diseases (Davidson & Neale, 2001). The **disease model of addiction** describes addictions as biologically based, lifelong diseases that involve a loss of control over behavior and require medical and/or spiritual treatment for recovery. In the disease model, addiction is believed to be either inherited or bred into the person early in life (Enoch & Goldman, 2002). In this view, current or recent problems or relationships are not thought to be causes of the disease. It is believed that an addict can never fully overcome the disease. This model has been strongly promoted and supported by the medical profession and Alcoholics Anonymous.

Critics of the disease model argue that (Grabowski, 1999)

- The biological origins of addiction have not been adequately identified.
- Treating addiction as a disease keeps people from pursuing and developing self-control.
- Addiction is not necessarily lifelong.

Many critics prefer to characterize addiction not as a disease but rather as a habitual response and source of gratification or security that has developed in the context of social relationships and experiences.

Review and Sharpen Your Thinking

4 *Evaluate the uses and types of psychoactive drugs.*
- Describe the effects of psychoactive drugs.
- Know the characteristics of the three main types of psychoactive drugs: depressants, stimulants, and hallucinogens.
- Explain what addiction is and evaluate the disease model of addiction.

Do you know someone who has a drug problem? If so, describe the nature of the problem. Is he or she willing to admit to having a problem?

mhhe com/
santrockp7

For study tools related to this learning goal, see the Study Guide, the CD-ROM, and the Online Learning Center.

addiction A pattern of behavior characterized by an overwhelming need to use the drug and to secure its supply.

disease model of addiction Describes addictions as biologically based, lifelong diseases that involve a loss of control over behavior and require medical and/or spiritual treatment for recovery.

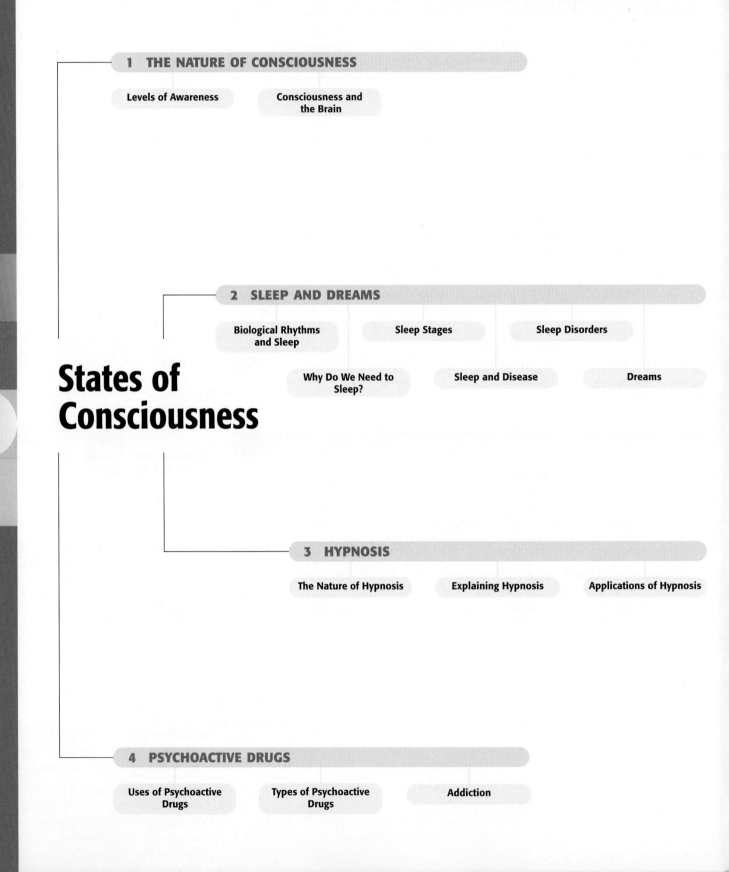

States of Consciousness

1 THE NATURE OF CONSCIOUSNESS

Levels of Awareness

Consciousness and the Brain

2 SLEEP AND DREAMS

Biological Rhythms and Sleep

Sleep Stages

Sleep Disorders

Why Do We Need to Sleep?

Sleep and Disease

Dreams

3 HYPNOSIS

The Nature of Hypnosis

Explaining Hypnosis

Applications of Hypnosis

4 PSYCHOACTIVE DRUGS

Uses of Psychoactive Drugs

Types of Psychoactive Drugs

Addiction

1 Discuss the nature of consciousness.

- Consciousness is the awareness of external events and internal sensations, including awareness of the self and thoughts about experiences. William James described the mind as a stream of consciousness. Consciousness occurs at different levels of awareness that include higher level awareness (controlled processes and selective attention), lower level awareness (automatic processes and daydreaming), altered states of consciousness or awareness (produced by drugs, trauma, fatigue, and other factors), subconscious awareness (waking subconscious awareness, sleep and dreams), and no awareness (Freud's concept of unconscious thought).

- One of the great unanswered questions about consciousness is its location—in the mind, in the brain—and, if in the brain, whether there is a seat of consciousness or rather a distribution across different areas of the brain. Most experts agree that consciousness is likely distributed across the brain, although the association areas and prefrontal lobes are believed to play important roles in consciousness.

2 Explain the nature of sleep and dreams.

- Biological rhythms are periodic physiological fluctuations. The biological rhythm that regulates the daily sleep/wake cycle is a circadian rhythm. The part of the brain that keeps our biological clocks synchronized is the suprachiasmatic nucleus, a small structure in the hypothalamus that registers light. Biological clocks can become desynchronized by such things as jet travel and work shifts. Some strategies are available for resetting the biological clock.

- We need sleep for physical restoration, adaptation, growth, and memory. An increasing number of research studies reveal that people do not function optimally when they are sleep deprived. There currently is a great deal of concern that Americans generally, and adolescents and aging adults in particular, are not getting enough sleep.

- Stages of sleep correspond to massive electrophysiological changes that occur in the brain and that can be assessed by an EEG. Humans go through four stages of non-REM sleep and one stage of REM sleep, or rapid-eye-movement sleep. Most dreaming occurs during REM sleep. The amount of REM sleep changes over the life span. A sleep cycle of five stages lasts about 90 to 100 minutes and recurs several times during the night. The REM stage lasts longer toward the end of a night's sleep. The sleep stages are associated with distinct patterns of neurotransmitter activity. Levels of the neurotransmitters serotonin, norepinephrine, and acetylcholine de-

crease as the sleep cycle progresses from stage 1 through stage 4. Stage 5, REM sleep, begins when the reticular formation raises the level of acetylcholine.

- Sleep plays a role in a large number of diseases and disorders. Neurons that control sleep interact closely with the immune system, and when our bodies are fighting infection our cells produce a substance that makes us sleepy. Individuals with depression often have sleep problems.

- Many Americans suffer from chronic, long-term sleep disorders, which can impair normal daily functioning. These disorders include insomnia, sleepwalking and sleep talking, nightmares and night terrors, narcolepsy, and sleep apnea.

- There are cultural and gender variations in dreaming. People in primitive cultures more often tie dreaming to reality or to the spiritual than do people in modern cultures. Males dream more about aggression, females more about friends. In Freud's view, the reason people dream is wish fulfillment. He distinguished between a dream's manifest (symbolic) and latent (unconscious) content. The cognitive theory of dreaming attempts to explain dreaming in terms of the same cognitive concepts that are used in studying the waking mind. In this view, dreams might be an arena for solving problems and thinking creatively. According to activation-synthesis theory, dreaming occurs when the cerebral cortex synthesizes neural signals emanating from activity in the lower part of the brain. In this view, the rising level of acetylcholine during REM sleep plays a role in neural activity in the reticular formation of the limbic system that the cerebral cortex tries to make sense of.

3 Describe hypnosis.

- Hypnosis can be defined as a psychological state or possibly altered attention and awareness in which the individual is unusually receptive to suggestions. The hypnotic state is different from a sleep state, as confirmed by EEG recordings. Inducing hypnosis involves four basic steps, beginning with minimizing distractions and making the person feel comfortable and ending with the hypnotist suggesting certain events or feelings that he or she knows will occur or observes occurring. There are substantial individual variations in people's susceptibility to hypnosis. People in a hypnotic state are unlikely to do anything that violates their morals or that involves a real danger.

- Two theories have been proposed to explain hypnosis. In Hilgard's divided consciousness view, hypnosis involves a divided state of consciousness, a splitting of consciousness into separate components. One component follows the hypnotist's commands, the other acts as a "hidden observer." In the social cognitive behavior view, the hypnotized individual behaves the way he or she believes a hypnotized individual is expected to behave.

- Hypnosis is widely used in psychotherapy, medicine, and dentistry, in criminal investigations, and in sports.

4 ***Evaluate the uses and types of psychoactive drugs.***

- Psychoactive drugs act on the nervous system to alter states of consciousness, modify perceptions, and change moods. Humans are attracted to these types of drugs because they help them adapt to change. Continued use of psychoactive drugs can lead to tolerance and physical or psychological addiction. Addictive drugs activate the reward system of the brain by increasing dopamine concentration. The reward pathway involves the ventral tegmental area (VTA) and nucleus accumbens.
- Depressants, including alcohol, barbiturates, tranquilizers, and opiates, slow down mental and physical activity. Among the most widely used depressants are alcohol,

barbiturates, tranquilizers, and opiates. After caffeine, alcohol is the most widely used drug in America. The high rate of alcohol abuse by high school and college students is especially alarming. Alcoholism is a disorder that involves long-term, repeated, uncontrolled, compulsive, and excessive use of alcoholic beverages that impairs the drinker's health and work and social relationships. Stimulants increase the central nervous system's activity and include caffeine, nicotine, amphetamines, cocaine, and MDMA (Ecstasy). Hallucinogens modify a person's perceptual experiences and produce visual images that are not real. Marijuana has a mild hallucinogenic effect. LSD has a strong one.

- Addiction is a pattern of behavior characterized by a preoccupation with use of a drug and with securing its supply. In the disease model of addiction, addictions are lifelong diseases that involve a loss of control over behavior and that require medical and/or spiritual treatment for recovery. Critics of the disease approach argue that it places too much emphasis on biology and not enough on social and cognitive factors.

Key Terms

consciousness, p. 228
stream of consciousness
    p. 228
controlled processes, p. 229
automatic processes, p. 230
unconscious thought,
    p. 231
biological rhythms, p. 232
circadian rhythms, p. 233

suprachiasmatic nucleus
    (SCN), p. 233
REM sleep, p. 236
wish fulfillment, p. 244
manifest content, p. 244
latent content, p. 244
cognitive theory of
    dreaming, p. 244
activation-synthesis
    theory, p. 245

hypnosis, p. 247
social cognitive behavior
    view of hypnosis, p. 248
psychoactive drugs, p. 251
tolerance, p. 251
physical dependence,
    p. 251
psychological
    dependence, p. 251
depressants, p. 252

alcoholism, p. 254
barbiturates, p. 255
tranquilizers, p. 255
opiates, p. 255
stimulants, p. 256
hallucinogens, p. 258
addiction, p. 261
disease model
    of addiction, p. 261

Apply Your Knowledge

1. As noted in the chapter, we process information at many levels of consciousness. Try to bring as much sensory information into the controlled process level of consciousness as you can; pay attention to every sensation available to you (Are your socks touching your ankles? How many sounds can you hear? What is available to your visual system? Is your stomach growling?) How long can you keep track of all of this sensory information, and what would happen if something important abruptly required all of your attention? What does this tell you about which levels of consciousness normally process all this information?

2. Keep a sleep journal for several nights. Compare your sleep patterns with those described in the text. Do you have a sleep debt? If so, which stages of sleep are you likely missing most? Does a good night's sleep affect your behavior? Keep a record of your mood and energy levels after a short night's sleep and then after you've had at least 8 hours sleep in one night. What changes do you notice, and how do they compare with the changes predicted by research on sleep deprivation described in the chapter?

3. A quick Web search reveals sites that offer "subliminal tapes for self-hypnosis" to help you do anything from losing

weight to getting a great new job. Based on the discussion of subliminal perception in chapter 5 and on hypnosis in this chapter, explain how a scientist would regard these tapes.

4. The website of the National Institute on Drug Abuse maintains a series of reports on current scientific knowledge about many commonly abused drugs. Visit the site (http:// www.nida.nih.gov/ResearchReports/ResearchIndex.html) and pick one of the listed reports. Using the report's information, compare the psychological effects and the risks associated with use of this drug with the psychological effects and risks of one of the psychoactive compounds described in the chapter.

Connections

For extra help in mastering the material in this chapter, see the review sections and practice quizzes in the Student Study Guide, the CD-ROM, and the Online Learning Center.

7 Learning

Chapter Outline

Learning Goals

Much of what we do results from what we have *learned*. If you had grown up in another part of the world, you would speak a different language, like different foods, and behave in ways characteristic of that culture. Why? Because the content of your *learning experiences* in that culture would have been different.

One way we learn is by watching what other people do and say. This kind of learning is called *observational learning*. Observational learning has changed dramatically in the twentieth and twenty-first centuries because of the introduction and pervasive use of television, which has touched virtually every American's life. Television has been accused of interfering with children's learning; critics say television lures children from schoolwork and books and makes them passive learners. But television can also contribute to children's learning. For example, *Sesame Street* was specifically designed to improve children's cognitive and social skills (Wright & others, 2001). Almost half of America's 2- to 5-year-olds watch it regularly.

Highly successful at teaching kids, *Sesame Street* uses fast-paced action, sound effects, music, and humorous characters to grab the attention of its young audience. While their eyes are glued to the screen, young children learn basic academic skills such as letter and number recognition. Researchers have found that when regular *Sesame Street* viewers from low-income families enter the first grade, they are rated as better prepared to learn in school than their counterparts who do not watch the program regularly (Bogatz & Ball, 1972; Cole, Richman, & Brown, 2001; Fisch & Truglio, 2001; Wright & others, 2001).

When *Sesame Street* first appeared in 1969, its creators had no idea that this "street" would lead to locations as distant as Kuwait, Israel, Latin America, and the Philippines. Since *Sesame Street* first aired in the United States, it has been televised in 84 countries, and 13 foreign-language versions have been pro-

Pino (big blue bird) from the Netherlands and Big Bird from *Sesame Street* in the U.S.

duced. *Barrio Sesamo* is shown in 17 South and Central American countries, as well as in Puerto Rico. It emphasizes learning about the diversity of cultures and lifestyles in South America. *Rechov Sumsum*, shown in Israel, especially encourages children to learn how people from different ethnic and religious backgrounds can live in harmony. When children in the Netherlands watch *Sesamstraat*, they learn about the concept of school and a 7-foot-tall blue bird named Pino who is always eager to learn.

Observational learning is a common way that people learn in educational and other settings. As is discussed in this chapter, learning applies to many areas of acquiring new behaviors, skills, and knowledge. The focus is on three types of learning: classical conditioning, operant conditioning, and observational learning. I also discuss the role of cognitive or mental processes in learning, as well as biological and cultural factors.

1 TYPES OF LEARNING

What is learning?

In learning the alphabet, you made some mistakes along the way, but at some point you learned all of your letters. You changed from someone who did not know the alphabet to someone who did. Learning anything new involves change. Once you learned the alphabet, it did not leave you. Once you learn how to drive a car, you do not have to go through the process again at a later time. If you ever decide to try out for the X-Games, you may break a few bones along the way, but at some point you probably will learn a trick or two, changing from a novice to someone who can at least stay on top of a skateboard. Learning involves a relatively permanent influence on behavior. You learned the alphabet through experience with the letters—

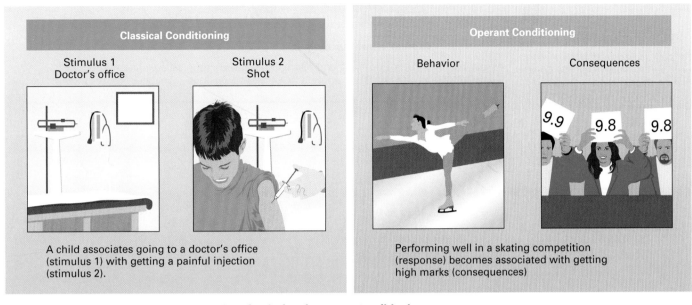

FIGURE 7.1 Associative Learning: Comparing Classical and Operant Conditioning
(*Left*) In this example of classical conditioning, a child associates a doctor's office (stimulus 1) with getting a painful injection (stimulus 2). (*Right*) In this example of operant conditioning, performing well in a skating competition (behavior) becomes associated with getting high marks (consequences).

some of you may have learned it by watching *Sesame Street.* Through experience, you also learned that you have to study to do well on a test, that there usually is an opening act at a rock concert, and that a field goal in American football adds 3 points to the score. Putting these pieces together, we arrive at a definition of **learning:** a relatively permanent change in behavior that occurs through experience.

Psychologists explain our many experiences with a few basic learning processes (Frieman, 2002). The opening story about *Sesame Street* focused on the type of learning called *observational learning,* in which organisms learn by watching what others do. A second type of learning is **associative learning,** in which a connection or association is made between two events (Kazdin, 2000; Pearce & Bouton, 2001). *Conditioning* is the process of learning associations. There are two types of conditioning: classical and operant. In *classical conditioning,* organisms learn the association between two stimuli. As a result of this association, organisms learn to anticipate events. For example, lightning is associated with thunder and regularly precedes it (Purdy & others, 2001). Thus, when you see lightning, you anticipate that you will hear thunder soon afterward. In *operant conditioning,* organisms learn the association between a behavior and a consequence. As a result of this association, organisms learn to increase behaviors that are followed by rewards and to decrease behaviors that are followed by punishment. For example, children are likely to repeat their good manners if their parents reward them with candy after they have shown good manners. Also, if children's bad manners are followed by a few nasty words and glances by parents, the children are less likely to repeat the bad manners. Figure 7.1 compares classical and operant conditioning.

Learning is not only extremely important in the lives of humans, but it is vital also to lower animals. To survive and function in their world, animals such as rats and rabbits have to learn and adapt just as humans do. Much learning research has been done with lower animals, largely because of the extensive control that researchers can exercise in studies on lower animals. A century of research on learning in lower animals and in humans suggests that many of the principles generated initially in research on lower animals also apply to humans (Barker, 2001; Leahy & Harris, 2001).

learning A relatively permanent change in behavior that occurs through experience.

associative learning In which a connection is made between two events.

Review and Sharpen Your Thinking

1 **Explain what learning is.**

- Define learning and distinguish between observational and associative learning.

How do you learn? Think of a behavior you engage in and describe how you learned it.

2 CLASSICAL CONDITIONING

Pavlov's Studies

Classical Conditioning in Humans

What is classical conditioning?

It is a nice spring day. A father takes his baby out for a walk. The baby reaches over to touch a pink flower and is stung by the bumblebee sitting on the petals. The next day, the baby's mother brings home some pink flowers. She removes a flower from the arrangement and takes it over for her baby to smell. The baby cries loudly as soon as she sees the pink flower. The baby's panic at the sight of the pink flower illustrates the learning process of **classical conditioning,** in which a neutral stimulus (the flower) becomes associated with a meaningful stimulus (the pain of a bee sting) and acquires the capacity to elicit a similar response (fear).

Pavlov's Studies

In the early 1900s, the Russian physiologist Ivan Pavlov was interested in the way the body digests food. In his experiments, he routinely placed meat powder in a dog's mouth, causing the dog to salivate. Pavlov noticed that the meat powder was not the only stimulus that caused the dog to salivate. The dog salivated in response to a number of stimuli associated with the food, such as the sight of the food dish, the sight of the individual who brought the food into the room, and the sound of the door closing when the food arrived. Pavlov recognized that the dog's association of these sights and sounds with the food was an important type of learning, which came to be called *classical conditioning.*

Pavlov (the white-bearded gentleman in the center) is shown demonstrating the nature of classical conditioning to students at the Military Medical Academy in Russia.

classical conditioning Learning by which a neutral stimulus becomes associated with a meaningful stimulus and acquires the capacity to elicit a similar response.

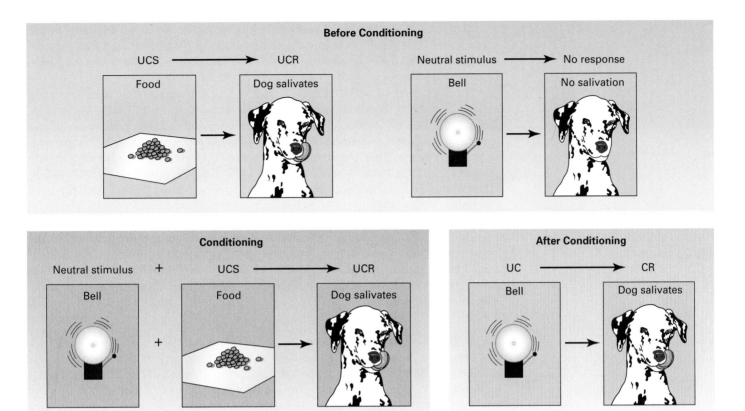

Before Conditioning

| UCS | ⟶ | UCR | | Neutral stimulus | ⟶ | No response |
| Food | | Dog salivates | | Bell | | No salivation |

Conditioning

Neutral stimulus	+	UCS	⟶	UCR
Bell		Food		Dog salivates
	+			

After Conditioning

| UC | ⟶ | CR |
| Bell | | Dog salivates |

FIGURE 7.2 **Pavlov's Classical Conditioning** In one experiment, Pavlov presented a neutral stimulus (bell) just before an unconditioned stimulus (food). The neutral stimulus became a conditioned stimulus by being paired with the unconditioned stimulus. Subsequently, the conditioned stimulus (bell) by itself was able to elicit the dog's salivation.

Pavlov wanted to know *why* the dog salivated to various sights and sounds before eating the meat powder. He observed that the dog's behavior included both learned and unlearned components. The unlearned part of classical conditioning is based on the fact that some stimuli automatically produce certain responses apart from any prior learning; in other words, they are inborn or innate. *Reflexes* are automatic stimulus-response connections. They include salivation in response to food, nausea in response to spoiled food, shivering in response to low temperature, coughing in response to the throat being clogged, pupil constriction in response to light, and withdrawal in response to blows or burns. An **unconditioned stimulus (UCS)** is a stimulus that produces a response without prior learning; food was the UCS in Pavlov's experiments. An **unconditioned response (UCR)** is an unlearned response that is automatically elicited by the UCS. In Pavlov's experiment, the saliva that flowed from the dog's mouth in response to food was the UCR.

In the case of the baby and the flower, the baby's learning and experience did not cause her to cry when the bee stung her. Her crying was unlearned and occurred automatically. The bee's sting was the UCS, and the crying was the UCR.

In classical conditioning, the **conditioned stimulus (CS)** is a previously neutral stimulus that eventually elicits the conditioned response after being associated with the unconditioned stimulus. The **conditioned response (CR)** is the learned response to the conditioned stimulus that occurs after CS-UCS pairing (Pavlov, 1927). In studying a dog's response to various stimuli associated with meat powder, Pavlov rang a bell before giving meat powder to the dog. Until then, ringing the bell did not have a particular effect on the dog, except perhaps to wake the dog from a nap. The bell was a neutral stimulus. But the dog began to associate the sound of the bell with the food and salivated when it heard the bell. The bell had become a conditioned (learned) stimulus (CS) and salivation was now a conditioned response (CR). For the unhappy baby, the flower was the "bell," or CS, and crying was the CR after the sting (UCS) and the flower (CS) were paired. A summary of how classical conditioning works is shown in figure 7.2.

unconditioned stimulus (UCS) A stimulus that produces a response without prior learning.

unconditioned response (UCR) An unlearned response that is automatically elicited by the UCS.

conditioned stimulus (CS) A previously neutral stimulus that eventually elicits the conditioned response after being associated with the unconditioned stimulus.

conditioned response (CR) The learned response to the conditioned stimulus that occurs after the CS-UCS pairing.

Acquisition **Acquisition** in classical conditioning is the initial learning of the stimulus-response link. This involves a neutral stimulus being associated with the UCS and becoming the conditioned stimulus (CS) that elicits the CR. Two important aspects of acquisition are timing and contingency/predictability.

The time interval between the CS and the UCS is one of the most important aspects of classical conditioning (Katani, Kawahara, & Kirino, 2002; Weidemann, Georgilas, & Kehoe, 1999). It defines the *contiguity*, or connectedness in time and space, of the stimuli. Conditioned responses develop when the CS and UCS are contiguous, occurring close together. Often, optimal spacing is a fraction of a second (Kimble, 1961). In Pavlov's work, if the bell had rung 20 minutes after the presentation of the food, the dog probably would not have associated the bell with the food.

Robert Rescorla (1966, 1988) believes that, for classical conditioning to take place, it is important to have not only a brief time interval in the CS-UCS connection but also contingency. *Contingency* in classical conditioning means the predictability of the occurrence of one stimulus from the presence of another. For example, as we mentioned earlier, a flash of lightning usually is followed by the sound of thunder. Thus, if you see lightning, you might put your hands over your ears or lean away in anticipation of the thunder.

Generalization and Discrimination Pavlov found that the dog salivated in response not only to the tone of the bell but also to other sounds, such as a whistle. Pavlov did not pair these sounds with the unconditioned stimulus of the food. He discovered that the more similar the noise was to the original sound of the bell, the stronger was the dog's salivary flow. **Generalization** in classical conditioning is the tendency of a new stimulus that is similar to the original conditioned stimulus to elicit a response that is similar to the conditioned response (Jones, Kemenes, & Benjamin, 2001). Generalization has value in preventing learning from being tied to specific stimuli. For example, we do not have to learn to drive all over again when we change cars or drive down a different road.

Stimulus generalization is not always beneficial. For example, the cat who generalizes from a minnow to a piranha has a major problem; therefore it is important to also discriminate between stimuli. **Discrimination** in classical conditioning is the process of learning to respond to certain stimuli and not to respond to others (Murphy, Baker, & Fouquet, 2001). To produce discrimination, Pavlov gave food to the dog only after ringing the bell and not after any other sounds. In this way, the dog learned to distinguish between the bell and other sounds.

Many multiple-choice tests place a premium on making careful discriminations among items. Professors often deliberately include similar items that require you to select the one correct answer from three or four possibilities.

Extinction and Spontaneous Recovery After conditioning the dog to salivate at the sound of a bell, Pavlov rang the bell repeatedly in a single session and did not give the dog any food. Eventually the dog stopped salivating. This result is **extinction,** which, in classical conditioning, is the weakening of the conditioned response in the absence of the unconditioned stimulus. Without continued association with the unconditioned stimulus (UCS), the conditioned stimulus (CS) loses its power to elicit the conditioned response (CR).

Extinction is not always the end of a conditioned response (Brooks, 2000). The day after Pavlov extinguished the conditioned salivation to the sound of a bell, he took the dog to the laboratory and rang the bell, still not giving the dog any meat powder. The dog salivated, indicating that an extinguished response can spontaneously recur. **Spontaneous recovery** is the process in classical conditioning by which a conditioned response can recur after a time delay without further conditioning. Consider an example of spontaneous recovery you may have had: You thought that you had totally forgotten about (extinguished) an old "love" you once

acquisition (in classical conditioning) The initial learning of the stimulus-response link, which involves a neutral stimulus being associated with a UCS and becoming a conditioned stimulus (CS) that elicits the CR.

generalization (in classical conditioning) The tendency of a new stimulus that is similar to the original stimulus to elicit a response that is similar to the conditioned response.

discrimination (in classical conditioning) The process of learning to respond to certain stimuli and not to others.

extinction (in classical conditioning) The weakening of the conditioned response in the absence of the unconditioned stimulus.

spontaneous recovery The process in classical conditioning by which a conditioned response can recur after a time delay without further conditioning.

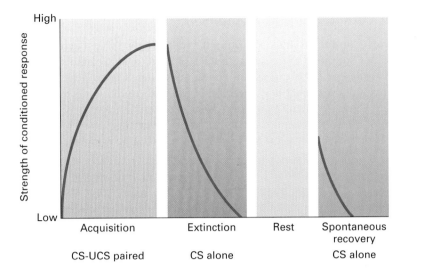

FIGURE 7.3 **The Strength of a Classically Conditioned Response During Acquisition, Extinction, and Spontaneous Recovery**
During acquisition the conditioned stimulus and unconditioned stimulus are associated. As seen in the graph, when this occurs, the strength of the conditioned response increases. During extinction the conditioned stimulus is presented alone, and, as can be seen, this results in a decrease of the conditioned response. After a rest period, spontaneous recovery appears, although the strength of the conditioned response is not nearly as great at this point as it was after a number of CS-UCS pairings. When the CS is presented alone again, after spontaneous recovery, the response is extinguished rapidly.

had. Then, all of a sudden, you are in a particular context and get a mental image of the person along with an emotional reaction to him or her from the past (spontaneous recovery).

Figure 7.3 shows the sequence of acquisition, extinction, and spontaneous recovery. Spontaneous recovery can occur several times, but as long as the conditioned stimulus is presented alone, spontaneous recovery becomes weaker and eventually ceases to occur.

Here is one more example to help you understand acquisition, generalization, discrimination, and extinction in classical conditioning.

- *Acquisition.* A young child learns to fear (CR) going to a dentist's office by associating it with the unlearned emotional response (UCR) to the pain of having a tooth cavity filled (UCS).
- *Generalization.* The child fears all dentists' offices and places similar to them, including doctors' offices and adults in them who wear white medical clothing, as well as the smells and sounds in them.
- *Discrimination.* The child goes with his mother to her doctor's office and learns that it is not associated with the pain of the UCS.
- *Extinction.* The child subsequently goes to the dentist on a number of occasions and does not have a painful experience, so the child's fear of dentists' offices goes away, at least for a while, until the child has another painful experience with a cavity being filled.

Researchers have found that the majority of dental fears originate in childhood, likely through classical conditioning, and that these fears can keep individuals from obtaining dental treatment as adults (Ost, 1991).

Interestingly, there are cultural variations in children's dental fear. Children in the United States have the most fear (20 percent have a high level of fear), and children in Norway and Sweden have the least fear (only 3 to 4 percent have a high level of fear; Milgram, Vigehesa, & Weinstein, 1992; Neverlien & Johnsen, 1991). This cultural difference likely is due to dental care being part of a free, universal health care system in Norway and Sweden. Consequently, children there go to the dentist on a regular basis, regardless of whether they have a dental problem or not. By contrast, the United States does not have a universal health care system, and children often go to the dentist only when they have a problem, thus experiencing dental treatment as painful and something to be avoided. Possibly, then, differences in cultural experience influence the occurrence of conditioned emotional responses.

Classical Conditioning in Humans

Since Pavlov conducted his experiments, individuals have been conditioned to respond to the sound of a buzzer, a glimpse of light, a puff of air, or the touch of a hand (Woodruff-Pak, 1999). Classical conditioning has a great deal of survival value for the individual (Vernoy, 1995). Because of classical conditioning, we jerk our hands away before they are burned by fire. Classical conditioning also is at work when a description of a tranquil scene, such as an empty beach with waves lapping the sand, causes a harried executive to relax as if she were actually lying on that beach.

Explaining and Eliminating Fears   A *phobia* is an irrational fear. Classical conditioning provides an explanation of these and other fears. John Watson and Rosalie Rayner (1920) demonstrated classical conditioning's role in phobias with an infant named Albert. They showed Albert a white laboratory rat to see if he was afraid of it. He was not. As Albert played with the rat, a loud noise was sounded behind his head. As you might imagine, the noise caused little Albert to cry. After only seven pairings of the loud noise with the white rat, Albert began to fear the rat even when the noise was not sounded. Albert's fear was generalized to a rabbit, a dog, and a sealskin coat.

Today, Watson and Rayner's (1920) study would violate the ethical guidelines of the American Psychological Association. Especially noteworthy is the fact that they did not reverse Albert's fear of furry objects, so presumably this phobia remained with him after the experiment. In the early part of the twentieth century, when the experiment with little Albert was conducted, there was less concern about the ethical aspects of research. As we saw in chapter 2, today, research psychologists must adhere to strict ethical guidelines.

Watson was right in concluding that many of our fears can be learned through classical conditioning. We might develop a fear of the dentist because of a painful experience, fear of driving after having been in an automobile accident, and fear of dogs after having been bitten by one.

If we can produce fears through classical conditioning, then we should be able to eliminate them using conditioning procedures. **Counterconditioning** is a classical conditioning procedure for weakening a CR by associating the fear-provoking stimulus with a new response that is incompatible with the fear. Though Watson did not eliminate little Albert's fear of white rats, an associate of Watson's, Mary Cover Jones (1924), did eliminate the fears of a 3-year-old boy named Peter. Peter had many of the same fears as Albert; however, Peter's fears were not produced by Jones. Among Peter's fears were white rats, fur coats, frogs, fish, and mechanical toys. To eliminate these fears, Jones brought a rabbit into Peter's view but kept it far enough away that it would not upset him. At the same time that the rabbit was brought into view, Peter was fed crackers and milk. On each successive day the rabbit was moved closer to Peter as he ate crackers and milk. Eventually Peter reached the point at which he would eat the food with one hand and pet the rabbit with the other. The feeling of pleasure produced by the crackers and milk was incompatible with the fear produced by the rabbit, and Peter's fear was extinguished through counterconditioning.

Explaining Pleasant Emotions   Classical conditioning is not restricted to unpleasant emotions, such as fear. Among the things in our lives that produce pleasure because they have become conditioned might be the sight of a rainbow, a sunny day, or a favorite song. If you have a positive romantic experience, the location in which that experience took place can become a conditioned stimulus. This is the result of the pairing of a place (CS) with the event (UCS). Stimuli that are often associated with sex, such as mood music, seductive clothing, a romantic restaurant, and so on, likely become conditioned stimuli that produce sexual arousal.

Sometimes, though, classical conditioning involves an experience that is both pleasant and deviant from the norm. Consider a fetishist who becomes sexually aroused by the sight and touch of certain clothing, such as undergarments or shoes.

In 1920, Watson and Rayner conditioned 11-month-old Albert to fear a white rat by pairing the rat with a loud noise. When little Albert was subsequently presented with other stimuli similar to the white rat, such as the rabbit shown here with little Albert, he was afraid of them, too. This illustrates the principle of stimulus generalization in classical conditioning. *What are some other examples of generalization in classical conditioning?*

counterconditioning A classical conditioning procedure for weakening a CR by associating the fear-provoking stimulus with a new response that is incompatible with the fear.

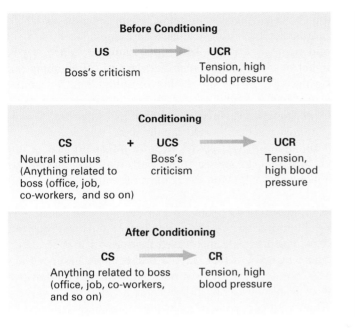

Before Conditioning

US → UCR

Boss's criticism → Tension, high blood pressure

Conditioning

CS + UCS → UCR

Neutral stimulus (Anything related to boss (office, job, co-workers, and so on) + Boss's criticism → Tension, high blood pressure

After Conditioning

CS → CR

Anything related to boss (office, job, co-workers, and so on) → Tension, high blood pressure

FIGURE 7.4 **Classical Conditioning: Boss's Criticism and High Blood Pressure**

The fetish may have developed when the fetish object (undergarment, shoe) was associated with sexual arousal, especially when the individual was young. The fetish object becomes a conditioned stimulus that can produce sexual arousal by itself (Chance, 2003).

Explaining Health Problems Some of the behaviors we associate with health problems or mental disorders can be attributed to classical conditioning. Certain physical complaints—asthma, headaches, ulcers, and high blood pressure, for example— can be partly the products of classical conditioning. We usually say that such health problems are caused by stress, but often what happens is that certain stimuli, such as a boss's critical attitude or a wife's threat of divorce, are conditioned stimuli for physiological responses. Over time, the frequent presence of the physiological responses may produce a health problem or disorder. A boss's persistent criticism may cause an employee to develop muscle tension, headaches, or high blood pressure. Anything associated with the boss, such as work itself, can then trigger stress in the employee (see figure 7.4).

Classical conditioning also can be involved in certain aspects of drug use. Pavlov realized that conditioned reflexes are important in digestion. He said that the digestive process begins as soon as food is seen or smelled. The body actually starts the digestive process before the food arrives. This reaction is similar to the response that occurs in the body before a drug arrives. When drugs are administered in particular circumstances—at a particular time of day, in a particular location, or in a particular ritual—the body reacts in anticipation of receiving the drug.

This aspect of drug use, which involves classical conditioning, can play a role in deaths caused by drug overdoses. How might this work? A user usually takes a drug in a particular setting, such as a bathroom, and acquires a conditioned response to this location (Siegel, 1988). Because of classical conditioning, as soon as the drug user walks into the bathroom, his or her body begins to prepare for and anticipate the drug dose in order to lessen the effect of the insult of the drug. However, if the user takes a drug in a location other than the usual one, such as at a rock concert, the effect of the drug is greater because no conditioned responses have built up in the new setting (Siegel, 2001) and therefore the body is not prepared for the drug. In cases in which heroin causes death, researchers often have found that the individuals took the drug under unusual circumstances or at a different time or different place from that at which they usually took the drug (Marlow, 1999).

Classical conditioning also can be involved in immune system functioning, which is important for producing antibodies to ward off disease and illness, such as AIDS and the flu. Robert Ader and Nicholas Cohen (Ader, 2000; Ader & Cohen, 1975, 2000) have conducted a number of studies that reveal that classical conditioning can produce *immunosuppression* (a decrease in the production of antibodies). The initial discovery of this link between classical conditioning and immunosuppression came as a surprise. In the course of studying Pavlovian conditioning, Ader (1974) was examining how long a conditioned response would last in some laboratory rats. A conditioned stimulus (saccharin solution) was paired with an unconditioned stimulus, a drug called Cytoxan, which induces nausea. Afterward, while giving the rats saccharin-laced water without the accompanying Cytoxan, Ader watched to see how long it would take the rats to forget the association between the two.

Unexpectedly, in the second month of the study, the rats developed a disease and began to die off. In analyzing the unforeseen result, Ader checked out the properties of the nausea-inducing drug he had used. He discovered that one of its side effects was immunosuppression. Thus it turned out that the rats had been classically conditioned to associate sweet water not only with nausea but also with the shutdown of the immune system. The sweet water apparently had become a CS for immunosuppression. Researchers have found that conditioned immune responses also may occur in humans (Ader, 2000; Voudouris, Peck, & Coleman, 1985).

Applying Classical Conditioning: Consumer Psychology *Consumer psychology* is the study of how consumers think, feel, reason, and select between different alternatives, such as brands and products. Many contemporary advertisers use classical conditioning in some way (Perner, 2001). Consider this sequence:

- Beautiful woman (UCS) → emotional arousal (UCR) in males
- Beautiful woman (UCS) paired with an automobile (not yet a CS) many times
- Automobile (CS) → emotional arousal (CR)

Recent research has shown that if the conditioned stimulus is encountered outside of ads, it doesn't predict the UCS (Bettman, 2001). Thus classical conditioning may work best for infrequently encountered products and cases in which the UCS is associated with only one brand. Also, classical conditioning usually works best when the CS precedes the UCS in ads.

Not all commercials involve classical conditioning. Some just give information about the product. The next time you watch TV, observe which ads are relying on classical conditioning to get their message across. Note what the UCS, UCR, CS, and CR are in the ads.

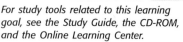

mhhe com/ santrockp7

For study tools related to this learning goal, see the Study Guide, the CD-ROM, and the Online Learning Center.

Review and Sharpen Your Thinking

2 *Describe classical conditioning.*

- Summarize the classical conditioning process. Include in your description the following terms: unconditioned stimulus (UCS), conditioned stimulus (CS), unconditioned response (UCR), and conditioned response (CR), as well as acquisition, generalization, discrimination, and extinction/spontaneous recovery.
- Discuss the role of classical conditioning in human phobias and specify other types of behavior that involve classical conditioning.

Think about an attachment that you or someone you know has for a certain object or environment. Explain how classical conditioning might account for the pleasant association.

Definition of Operant Conditioning	Skinner's Approach to Operant Conditioning	Principles of Reinforcement

Thorndike's Law of Effect	Shaping	Applications of Operant Conditioning

What is operant conditioning?

Classical conditioning helps us to learn about our environment, but we learn about our world in other ways, too. Classical conditioning describes an organism's *response* to the environment, a view that fails to capture the active nature of the organism and its influence on the environment. Another major form of learning—operant conditioning—places more emphasis on the organism's *activity* in the environment (Hergenhahn & Olson, 2001).

Definition of Operant Conditioning

Recall from the beginning of the chapter that classical conditioning and operant conditioning are forms of associative learning, which involves learning that two events are connected. In classical conditioning, organisms learn the association between two stimuli (UCS and CS). Classical conditioning is a form of *respondent behavior,* behavior that occurs in automatic response to a stimulus, such as a nausea-producing drug, and later to a conditioned stimulus, such as sweet water, that was paired with the drug. Classical conditioning excels at explaining how neutral stimuli become associated with unlearned, *involuntary responses,* but it is not as effective in explaining *voluntary behaviors,* such as studying hard for a test, playing slot machines in Las Vegas, or a pigeon playing ping-pong. Operant conditioning is usually much better at explaining such voluntary behaviors.

The concept of operant conditioning was developed by the American psychologist B. F. Skinner (1938). **Operant conditioning** (or instrumental conditioning) is a form of associative learning in which the consequences of behavior produce changes in the probability of a behavior's occurrence. Skinner chose the term *operant* to describe the behavior of the organism—the behavior operates on the environment, and the environment in turn operates on the behavior. As an example, in operant conditioning, performing a great skating routine in competition (behavior) is likely to result in a high score from the judges (consequences), which in turn encourages the skater to continue training and competing. Thus, whereas classical conditioning involves respondent behavior, operant conditioning consists of *operant behavior,* voluntary behavior that acts or operates on the environment and produces rewarding or punishing stimuli.

Recall that earlier we said *contingency* is an important aspect of classical conditioning in which the occurrence of one stimulus can be predicted from the presence of another one. Contingency is important in operant conditioning also. For example, when a rat pushes a lever (behavior) that delivers food, the delivery of food (consequence) is *contingent* on that behavior.

Thorndike's Law of Effect

Although Skinner emerged as the primary figure in operant conditioning, the experiments of E. L. Thorndike established the power of consequences in determining voluntary behavior. At about the same time that Pavlov was conducting classical conditioning experiments with salivating dogs, Thorndike, an American psychologist,

operant conditioning Also called instrumental conditioning; a form of learning in which the consequences of behavior change the probability of the behavior's occurrence.

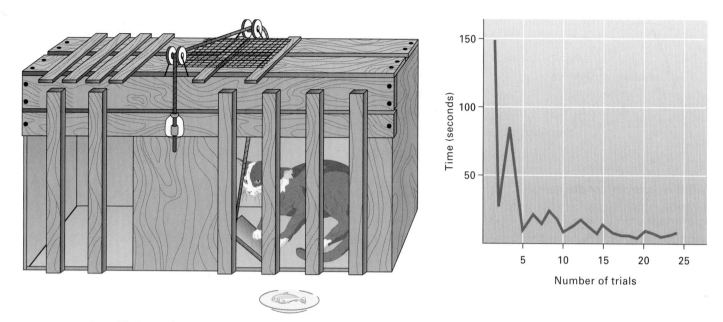

FIGURE 7.5 Thorndike's Puzzle Box and the Law of Effect (*Left*) A box typical of the puzzle boxes Thorndike used in his experiments with cats to study the law of effect. Stepping on the treadle released the door bolt; a weight attached to the door then pulled the door open and allowed the cat to escape. After accidentally pressing the treadle as it tried to get to the food, the cat learned to press the treadle when it wanted to escape the box. (*Right*) One cat's learning curve over 24 separate trials. Notice that the cat escaped much more quickly after about 5 trials. It had learned the consequences of its behavior.

was studying cats in puzzle boxes. Thorndike put a hungry cat inside a box and a piece of fish outside. To escape from the box and obtain the food, the cat had to learn how to open the latch inside the box. At first the cat made a number of ineffective responses. It clawed or bit at the bars and thrust its paw through the openings. Eventually the cat accidentally stepped on the treadle that released the door bolt. When the cat returned to the box, it went through the same random activity until it stepped on the treadle once more. On subsequent trials, the cat made fewer and fewer random movements, until finally it immediately stepped on the treadle to open the door (see figure 7.5). The **law of effect,** developed by Thorndike, states that behaviors followed by positive outcomes are strengthened, whereas behaviors followed by negative outcomes are weakened.

The key question for Thorndike was how the correct stimulus-response bond strengthens and eventually dominates incorrect stimulus-response bonds. According to Thorndike, the correct stimulus-response (S-R) association strengthens and the incorrect association weakens because of the *consequences* of the organism's actions. Thorndike's view is called *S-R theory* because the organism's behavior is due to a connection between a stimulus and a response. As the next section explains, Skinner's operant conditioning approach expanded Thorndike's basic ideas.

Skinner's Approach to Operant Conditioning

Skinner strongly believed that the mechanisms of learning are the same for all species. This conviction led him to study animals in the hope that he could discover the basic mechanisms of learning with organisms simpler than humans. During World War II, Skinner carried out an unusual study that involved a pigeon-guided missile. A pigeon in the warhead of the missile operated the flaps on the missile and guided it home by pecking at an image of a target. How could this possibly work? When the missile was in flight, the pigeon pecked the moving image on a screen, being rewarded with food to keep the designated target in the center of the screen. This produced corrective signals to keep the missile on its course. The pigeons did their job well in trial runs, but top Navy officials just could not accept pigeons piloting their missiles in a war. Skinner, however, congratulated himself on the degree of control he was able to exercise over the pigeons (see figure 7.6).

Following the pigeon experiment, Skinner (1948) wrote *Walden Two,* a novel in which he presented his ideas about building a scientifically managed society. Skinner envisioned a utopian society that could be engineered through operant conditioning.

law of effect Thorndike's concept that behaviors followed by positive outcomes are strengthened, whereas behaviors followed by negative outcomes are weakened.

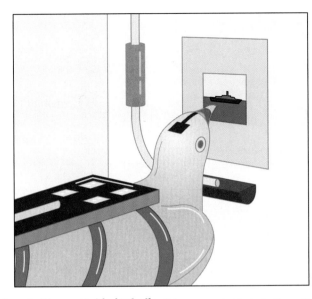

FIGURE 7.6 Skinner's Pigeon-Guided Missile Skinner wanted to help the military during World War II by using pigeons' tracking behavior. A gold electrode covered the tip of the pigeons' beaks. Contact with the screen on which the image of the target was projected sent a signal informing the missile's control mechanism of the target's location. A few grains of food occasionally given to the pigeons maintained their tracking behavior.

Skinner viewed existing societies as poorly managed because people believe in the myth of free will. He pointed out that humans are no more free than pigeons are; denying that our behavior is controlled by environmental forces is to ignore science and reality, he argued. Skinner believed that in the long run we would be much happier when we recognized such truths, especially his concept that operant conditioning would provide us with prosperous lives.

Skinner, and other behaviorists, made every effort to study organisms under precisely controlled conditions so that the connection between the operant and the specific consequences could be examined in minute detail (Klein, 2002). One of his creations in the 1930s to control experimental conditions was the Skinner box (see figure 7.7). A device in the box would deliver food pellets into a tray at random. After a rat became accustomed to the box, Skinner installed a lever and observed the rat's behavior. As the hungry rat explored the box, it occasionally pressed the lever, and a food pellet would be dispensed. Soon the rat learned that the consequences of pressing the lever were positive: It would be fed. Further control was achieved by soundproofing the box to ensure that the experimenter was the only influence on the organism. In many of the experiments, the responses were mechanically recorded, and the food (the stimulus) was dispensed automatically. Such precautions were designed to avoid human error.

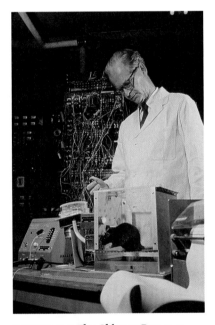

FIGURE 7.7 The Skinner Box B. F. Skinner conducting an operant conditioning study in his behavioral laboratory. The rat being studied is in a Skinner box.

Shaping

When a behavior takes time to occur, the learning process in operant conditioning can be shortened by rewarding an *approximation* of the desired behavior (Silverstein, Menditto, & Stuve, 2001). **Shaping** is the process of rewarding approximations of desired behavior. In one situation, parents used shaping to toilet train their 2-year-old son. The parents knew all too well that the grunting sound the child made signaled he was about to fill his diaper. In the first week they gave him candy if they heard the sound within 20 feet of the bathroom. The second week he was given candy only if he grunted within 10 feet of the bathroom, the third week only if he was in the bathroom, and the fourth week, he had to use the toilet to get the candy (Fischer & Gochros, 1975). It worked!

shaping The process of rewarding approximations of desired behavior.

Animal trainers coax some amazing behaviors from their star performers. *What type of operant conditioning is often used by animal trainers?*

"Once it became clear to me that, by responding correctly to certain stimuli, I could get all the bananas I wanted, getting this job was a pushover." ©1999 Jack Ziegler from cartoonbank.com. All Rights Reserved.

Shaping is extensively used in training animals. For example, shaping can be used to train a rat to press a bar to obtain food. When a rat is first placed in a Skinner box, it rarely presses the bar. Thus the experimenter may start off by giving the rat a food pellet if it is in the same half of the cage as the bar. Then the rat's behavior might be rewarded only when it is within 2 inches of the bar, then only when it touches the bar, and finally only when it presses the bar.

Shaping is also used to train animals to perform tricks. A dolphin that jumps through a hoop held high above the water has been trained to perform this behavior through shaping. You can use shaping to teach a dog tricks. For example, say that you want to teach a dog to "shake hands" with you. You first speak the command to "shake" and then wait until the dog moves one of its forepaws a little bit (operant behavior). Following this behavior, you give your dog a food treat (consequence). After requiring increasingly closer approximations to shaking your hand, the dog finally performs the desired behavior to the verbal command "shake."

Shaping can be used effectively in educational classrooms (Santrock, 2001). Suppose a teacher has a student who has never completed more than 50 percent of her math assignments. The teacher sets the target behavior at 100 percent but rewards her for successive approximations to the target. The teacher initially might provide a reward (some type of privilege, for example) when she completes 70 percent, then 80, then 90, and finally 100 percent. Shaping can be especially helpful for learning tasks that require time and persistence to complete.

Principles of Reinforcement

reinforcement The process by which a stimulus or event strengthens or increases the probability of an event that it follows.

Reinforcement is the process by which a stimulus or event strengthens or increases the probability of a behavior or an event that it follows. Behavioral psychologists have developed a number of principles of reinforcement, including a distinction between positive and negative reinforcement.

Positive Reinforcement

Behavior	Rewarding Stimulus Provided	Future Behavior
You turn in homework on time	Teacher praises your performance	You increasingly turn in homework on time
You wax your skis	The skis go faster	You wax your skis the next time you go skiing
You randomly press a button on the dashboard of a friend's car	Great music begins to play	You deliberately press the button again the next time you get into the car

Negative Reinforcement

Behavior	Unpleasant Stimulus Removed	Future Behavior
You turn in homework on time	Teacher stops criticizing late homework	You increasingly turn in homework on time
You wax your skis	People stop zooming by you on the slope	You wax your skis the next time
You randomly press a button on the dashboard of a friend's car	An annoying song shuts off	You deliberately press the button again the next time the annoying song is on

FIGURE 7.8 Positive and Negative Reinforcement

Positive and Negative Reinforcement In **positive reinforcement,** the frequency of a behavior increases because it is followed by a rewarding stimulus. For example, if someone you meet smiles at you after you say, "Hello, how are you?" and you keep talking, the smile has reinforced your talking. The same principle of positive reinforcement is at work when you teach a dog to "shake hands" by giving it a piece of food when it lifts its paw.

Conversely, in **negative reinforcement,** the frequency of a behavior increases because it is followed by the removal of an aversive (unpleasant) stimulus. For example, if your father nagged you to clean out the garage and kept nagging until you cleaned out the garage, your response (cleaning out the garage) removed the unpleasant stimulus (nagging). Taking an aspirin when you have a headache works the same way. A reduction of pain reinforces the act of taking an aspirin.

To understand the distinction between positive and negative reinforcement, remember that "positive" and "negative" do not have anything to do with "good" and "bad." Just remember that they are processes in which something is given (positive reinforcement) or something is removed (negative reinforcement). Figure 7.8 provides some other examples to further help you understand the distinction between positive and negative reinforcement.

Primary and Secondary Reinforcement Positive reinforcement can be classified as primary reinforcement or secondary reinforcement, based on whether the behavior is inborn and unlearned or learned. **Primary reinforcement** involves the use of reinforcers that are innately satisfying; that is, they do not take any learning on the organism's part to make them pleasurable. Food, water, and sexual satisfaction are primary reinforcers.

Secondary reinforcement acquires its positive value through experience; secondary reinforcers are learned or conditioned reinforcers. We encounter hundreds of secondary reinforcers in our lives, such as getting a pat on the back, praise, and eye contact. One popular story in psychology focuses on the use of eye contact as a secondary reinforcer to shape the behavior of a famous university professor, an expert on operant conditioning. Some students decided to train the professor to lecture from one corner of the classroom. They used eye contact as a reinforcer and began reinforcing successive approximations to the desired response. Each time the professor

positive reinforcement The frequency of a behavior increases because it is followed by a rewarding stimulus.

negative reinforcement The frequency of a behavior increases because it is followed by the removal of an aversive (unpleasant) stimulus.

primary reinforcement The use of reinforcers that are innately satisfying.

secondary reinforcement Acquires its positive value through experience.

Slot machines are on a variable-ratio schedule of reinforcement. *Why?*

moved toward the appropriate corner, the students would look at him. If he moved in another direction, they looked away. By gradually rewarding successive approximations to the desired response, the students were able to get the professor to deliver his lecture from just one corner of the classroom. The professor denies that this shaping ever took place. Whether it did or not, the story provides an excellent example of how secondary reinforcers can be used to shape behavior in real life (Chance, 1999).

Another example helps to illustrate the importance of secondary reinforcement in our everyday lives. When a student is given $25 for an A on her report card, the $25 is a secondary reinforcer. It is not innate, and it increases the likelihood that the student will work to get another A in the future. When an object can be exchanged for some other reinforcer, the object may have reinforcing value itself, so it is called a *token reinforcer*. Money, gift certificates, and poker chips are often referred to as token reinforcers.

Schedules of Reinforcement   Most of the examples of reinforcement we have discussed so far have involved *continuous reinforcement,* in which a behavior is reinforced every time it occurs. When continuous reinforcement occurs, organisms learn rapidly. However, when reinforcement stops, extinction also takes place quickly. If a pay telephone we often use starts "eating" our coins and not giving us a dial tone, we quickly stop putting in more coins. However, several weeks later, we might try it again, hoping it now works properly (this behavior illustrates spontaneous recovery).

Partial reinforcement follows a behavior only a portion of the time (Sangha & others, 2002). Most of life's experiences involve partial reinforcement. A golfer does not win every tournament she enters; a chess whiz does not win every match he plays; a student is not patted on the back each time she solves a problem. **Schedules of reinforcement** are "timetables" that determine when a behavior will be reinforced. The four main schedules of reinforcement are fixed ratio, variable ratio, fixed interval, and variable interval.

A *fixed-ratio schedule* reinforces a behavior after a set number of behaviors. For example, if you are playing the slot machines in Atlantic City and if the machines are on a fixed-ratio schedule, you might get $5 back every 20th times you put money in the machine. It wouldn't take long to figure out that if you watched someone else play the machine 18 or 19 times, not get any money back, and then walk away, you should step up, insert your coin, and get back $5. Fixed-ratio schedules often are used in business to increase production. For example, a salesperson might be required to sell a specific number of items to get a commission. One characteristic of fixed-ratio schedules is that performance often drops off just after reinforcement.

Consequently, slot machines are on a *variable-ratio schedule*, a timetable in which behaviors are rewarded an average number of times but on an unpredictable basis. For example, a slot machine might pay off at an average of every 20th time, but the gambler does not know when this payoff will be. The slot machine might pay off twice in a row and then not again until after 58 coins have been inserted. This averages out to a reward for every 20 behavioral acts, but when the reward will be given is unpredictable. Variable-ratio schedules produce high, steady rates of behavior that are more resistant to extinction than the other three schedules.

The interval reinforcement schedules are determined by *time elapsed* since the last behavior was rewarded. A *fixed-interval schedule* reinforces the first appropriate behavior after a fixed amount of time has elapsed. For example, you might get a reward the first time you put money in a slot machine after every 10-minute period has elapsed. The behavior of politicians campaigning for reelection often reflects a fixed-interval schedule of reinforcement. After they have been elected, they reduce their campaigning and then do not pick it up again heavily until just before the next election (which can be 2 to 4 years later). On a fixed-interval schedule, few behaviors

schedules of reinforcement
"Timetables" that determine when a behavior will be reinforced.

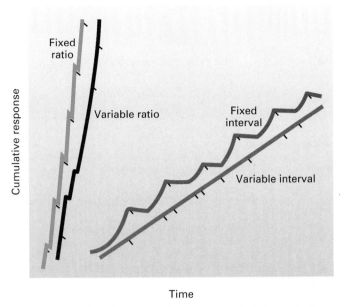

FIGURE 7.9 Schedules of Reinforcement and Different Patterns of Responding In this figure, each hash mark indicates the delivery of reinforcement. Notice on the fixed-ratio schedule the dropoff in responding after each response; on the variable-ratio schedule the high, steady rate of responding; on the fixed-interval schedule the immediate dropoff in responding after reinforcement and the increase in responding just before reinforcement (resulting in a scalloped curve); and on the variable-interval schedule the slow, steady rate of responding.

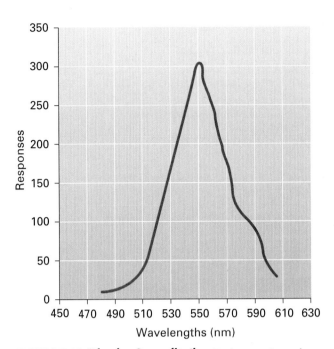

FIGURE 7.10 Stimulus Generalization In the experiment by Guttman and Kalish (1956), pigeons initially pecked a disk of a particular color (in this graph, a color with a wavelength of 550 nm) after they had been reinforced for this wavelength. Subsequently, when the pigeons were presented disks of colors with varying wavelengths, they were likelier to peck disks that were similar to the original disk.

are enacted until the time approaches when the behavior (such as getting reelected) likely will be reinforced and at that time the rate of behavior picks up rapidly.

A *variable-interval schedule* is a timetable in which a behavior is reinforced after a variable amount of time has elapsed (Staddon, Chelaru, & Higa, 2002). On this schedule, the slot machines might reward you after 10 minutes, then after 2 minutes, then after 18 minutes, and so on. Pop quizzes are on a variable-interval schedule. So is fishing—you don't know if the fish will bite in the next minute, in a half hour, in an hour, or at all. Because it is difficult to predict when a reward will come, behavior is slow and consistent on a variable-interval schedule (Staddon, Chelaru, & Higa, 2002).

Figure 7.9 shows how the different schedules of reinforcement result in different rates of responding.

Generalization, Discrimination, and Extinction Remember that generalization, discrimination, and extinction are important classical conditioning principles. They also are important principles in operant conditioning, but they are defined somewhat differently.

Generalization In operant conditioning, **generalization** means giving the same response to similar stimuli. For example, in one study pigeons were reinforced for pecking at a disk of a particular color (Guttman & Kalish, 1956). To assess stimulus generalization, researchers presented the pigeons with disks of varying colors. As shown in figure 7.10, the pigeons were most likely to peck at the disk closest in color to the original. An example from everyday life involves a student who has great success in dating people who dress neatly and not such good results with people who dress sloppily. The student subsequently seeks dates with people who dress neatly, the neater the better, and avoids dating sloppy dressers, especially the sloppiest.

generalization (in operant conditioning) Giving the same response to similar stimuli.

Punishment

Behavior	Aversive Stimulus Presented	Future Behavior
You take medication to cure a headache	You have a bad allergic reaction	You avoid that medication in the future
You show off to a friend by speeding past a police car	You get a $200 ticket	You stop speeding

Negative Reinforcement

Behavior	Aversive Stimulus Removed	Future Behavior
You take medication to cure a headache	The headache goes away	You take more medication in the future
You show off to a friend by speeding past a police car	The officer pays no attention to you although officers have ticketed you in the past	You continue to show off by speeding past police cars

FIGURE 7.11 **Punishment versus Negative Reinforcement**

Discrimination   In operant conditioning, **discrimination** means responding to stimuli that signal that a behavior will or will not be reinforced (Spector & Kopka, 2002). For example, you might look at two street signs, both made of metal, both the same color, and both with words on them. However, one sign says "Enter at your own risk" and the other says "Please walk this way." The words serve as discriminative stimuli because the sign that says "Please walk this way" indicates that you will be rewarded for doing so. However, the sign that says "Enter at your own risk" suggests that the consequences may not be positive. As another example, consider that football players are far likelier to tackle people in a football stadium than in a church. Further, they tackle people in a uniform with certain colors (the opposing team's rather than their own). They also don't tackle certain other people in uniforms, such as cheerleaders and referees.

Extinction   In operant conditioning, **extinction** occurs when a previously reinforced behavior is no longer reinforced and there is a decreased tendency to perform the behavior (Conklin & Tiffany, 2002). For example, a factory worker gets a monthly bonus for producing more than her quota. Then, as a part of economic tightening, the company decides that it can no longer afford the bonuses. When bonuses were given, the worker's productivity was above quota every month; once the bonus was removed, performance decreased. Spontaneous recovery also characterizes the operant form of extinction.

Punishment   From the discussion of positive and negative reinforcement, you learned that a behavior is strengthened by both types of reinforcement. In contrast, the effect of punishment is usually to weaken or extinguish a behavior. Let's explore the concept of punishment in the operant conditioning context and learn why psychologists generally disapprove of punishment.

What Is Punishment?   **Punishment** refers to a consequence that decreases the likelihood that a behavior will occur. For example, a child plays with an attractive matchbox and gets burned when one of the matches is lit. In the future, the child is less likely to play with matches. Or if a student interrupts the teacher and the teacher verbally reprimands the student, the student stops interrupting the teacher.

Punishment differs from reinforcement in that, in punishment, a behavior is weakened; in reinforcement, a behavior is strengthened. So punishment is not the

discrimination (in operant conditioning) The tendency to only respond to stimuli that signal whether a behavior will or will not be reinforced.

extinction (in operant conditioning) A previously reinforced behavior is no longer reinforced, and there is a decreased tendency to perform the behavior.

punishment A consequence that decreases the likelihood a behavior will occur.

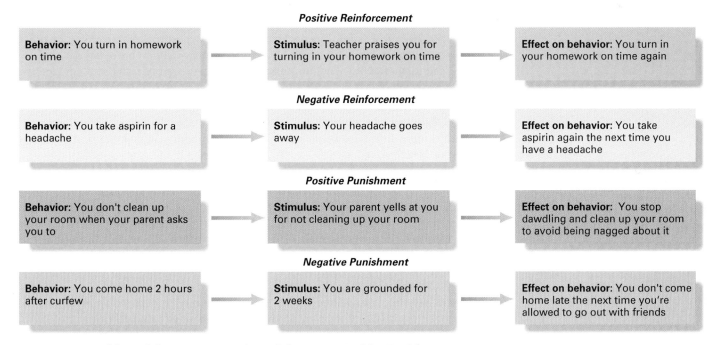

FIGURE 7.12 Positive Reinforcement, Negative Reinforcement, Positive Punishment, and Negative Punishment

same as negative reinforcement. Also, in punishment, a response decreases because of its consequences; in negative reinforcement, a response increases because of its consequences. Figure 7.11 provides additional examples of the distinction between negative reinforcement and punishment.

Here's another example to help you distinguish between negative reinforcement and punishment. When an alcoholic consumes liquor to alleviate uncomfortable withdrawal symptoms, the probability that the person will use alcohol in the future increases. The reduction of the withdrawal symptoms was a negative reinforcer for drinking. But if an inebriated alcoholic is seriously injured in a car wreck and subsequently drinks less, the incident served as punishment because a behavior (drinking) was subsequently decreased.

The positive negative distinction also can be applied to punishment, although it is not used as widely as in reinforcement. In **positive punishment,** a behavior decreases when it is followed by an unpleasant stimulus. In **negative punishment,** a behavior decreases when a positive stimulus is removed from it.

Time-out is a form of negative punishment in which a child is removed from a positive reinforcement. It generally is recommended over presenting an aversive stimulus (positive reinforcement), as typically is done when punishment is administered. If a child is behaving in disruptive ways in the classroom, the teacher might put the child in a chair in the corner of the room facing away from the class or take the child to a time-out room. Figure 7.12 compares positive reinforcement, negative reinforcement, positive punishment, and negative punishment.

Evaluating the Use of Punishment with Children Many people associate punishment wit yelling at children or spanking them. All too often, though, aversive stimuli do not do what they are intended to do—namely, decrease an unwanted behavior (Edwards, 1999). Some people turn too quickly to aversive stimuli when trying to change a child's behavior. They might do this for several reasons: because they were harshly disciplined when they were growing up and they are just repeating how their parents dealt with them; because they have developed a style of handling stress by

positive punishment A behavior decreases when it is followed by an unpleasant stimulus.

negative punishment A behavior decreases when a positive stimulus is removed from it.

yelling or screaming; because they feel they can effectively exercise power over their smaller charges; or because they are unaware of how positive reinforcement or other techniques, such as a time-out, can be used to improve children's behavior.

To read further about whether punishing children is an effective strategy, see the Critical Controversy box.

Timing, Reinforcement, and Punishment   How does the timing of reinforcement and punishment influence behavior? And does it matter whether the reinforcement is small or large?

Immediate Reinforcement and Delayed Reinforcement   As is the case with classical conditioning, learning is more efficient in operant conditioning when the interval between a behavior and its reinforcement is a few seconds rather than minutes or hours, especially in lower animals (Church & Kirkpatrick, 2001). If a food reward is delayed for more than 30 seconds after a rat presses a bar, it is virtually ineffective as reinforcement. However, humans have the ability to respond to delayed reinforcers (Holland, 1996).

Sometimes important life decisions involve whether to obtain a small immediate reinforcer or to wait for a delayed but more highly valued reinforcer (Martin & Pear, 2002). For example, you can spend your money now on clothes, trinkets, parties, and the like or save your money and buy a house and car later. Or, you might play around now and enjoy yourself in return for immediate small reinforcers, or you can study hard over the long haul for delayed stronger reinforcers, such as good grades, a scholarship to graduate school, and a better job.

Immediate Punishment and Delayed Punishment   As with reinforcement, in most instances of research with lower animals, immediate punishment is more effective than delayed punishment in decreasing the occurrence of a behavior. However, also as with reinforcement, delayed punishment can have an effect on human behavior.

Why do so many of us postpone such activities as going to the dentist, scheduling minor surgery, or paying campus parking fines (Martin & Pear, 2002)? If we act immediately, we experience a weak punisher—it hurts to have our teeth drilled, it is painful to have minor surgery, and it is not pleasurable to pay a campus parking fine. However, the delayed consequences can be more punishing—our teeth might fall out, we may need major surgery, and our car might be towed away or we might be thrown in jail if we delay paying a campus parking fine.

Immediate and Delayed Reinforcement and Punishment   How does receiving immediate small reinforcement versus delayed strong punishment affect human behavior (Martin & Pear, 2002)? One reason that obesity is such a major health problem is that eating is a behavior with immediate positive consequences—food tastes great and quickly provides a pleasurable feeling. Although the potential delayed consequences of overeating are negative (obesity and other possible health risks), immediate consequences are difficult to override. When the delayed consequences of behavior are punishing and the immediate consequences are reinforcing, the immediate consequences usually win, even when the immediate consequences are minor reinforcers and the delayed consequences are major punishers. Smoking and drinking follow a similar pattern. The immediate consequences of smoking are reinforcing for most smokers—the powerful combination of positive reinforcement (tension relief, energy boost) and negative reinforcement (removal of craving). The punishing aspects of smoking are primarily long term, such as shortness of breath, a sore throat, coughing, emphysema, heart disease, and cancer. Likewise, the immediate pleasurable consequences of drinking override the delayed consequences of a hangover or even alcoholism.

Will Sparing the Rod Spoil the Child?

For centuries, corporal (physical) punishments such as spanking have been considered a necessary and even desirable method for disciplining children (Greven, 1991). Use of corporal punishment is legal in every state in America, and it is estimated that 70 to 90 percent of American parents have spanked their children (Straus, 1991).

Despite the widespread use of corporal punishment, there have been surprisingly few research studies on physical punishment, and those that have been conducted are correlational. Clearly, it would be highly unethical to randomly assign parents to either spank or not spank their children in an experimental study. But, recall that cause and effect cannot be determined in a correlational study.

In one correlational study, spanking by parents was linked with children's antisocial behavior, such as cheating, telling lies, being mean to others, bullying, getting into fights, and being disobedient (Strauss, Sugarman, & Giles-Sims, 1997). In a national sample of 807 mothers of children 6 to 9 years old, 44 percent of the mothers spanked their children. The mothers reported that the week prior to being interviewed, they spanked their children an average of 2.1 times. The more the children were spanked, the likelier they were to engage in antisocial behavior 2 years later.

However, some studies of positive punishment suggest that it can be effective in getting children to comply, at least over the short term (Day & Roberts, 1993). Further, animal studies reveal that punishment is often effective in reducing undesired behaviors (Dinsmoor, 1998).

What are some of the reasons that spanking or other forms of intense punishment with children should be avoided? The reasons include

- When intense punishment such as yelling, screaming, or spanking is used, the adult is presenting children with an out-of-control model for handling stressful situations. The children might imitate this aggressive model.
- Punishment can instill fear, rage, or avoidance in children. Skinner's biggest concern was that punishment teaches organisms to avoid something. For example, spanking a child might cause the child to avoid and fear the parent.
- Punishment tells people what not to do rather than what to do. When making a punishing statement, such as "No, that's not right," always accompany it with positive feedback, such as "But why don't you try this."
- Punishment can be abusive. When parents discipline their children, they might not intend to be abusive but become so aroused when they are punishing the child that they do become abusive (Adams, 1998).
- What is intended as punishing can turn out to be reinforcing. In school, a child might learn that misbehaving will not only attract the teacher's attention but will also get the attention of classmates.

This second-grade student has been placed in "time-out" for misbehaving. *What is the nature of time out?*

For reasons such as these, a law was passed in Sweden in 1979 forbidding parents to physically punish (spank or slap, for example) when disciplining their children. The law still is in effect, and since it was enacted youth rates of juvenile delinquency, alcohol abuse, rape, and suicide have dropped (Durrant, 2000). The improved picture for Swedish youth could have occurred for other reasons, such as changing societal attitudes and opportunities for youth. Nonetheless, the Swedish experience suggests that physical punishment of children may be unnecessary to improve the well-being of youth. Joining Sweden in forbidding parents to physically punish their children, these countries also have passed antispanking laws: Finland (1984), Denmark (1986), Norway (1987), Austria (1989), Cyprus (1994), Latvia (1998), Croatia (1999), Germany (2000), and Israel (2000).

A recent cross-cultural comparison found that individuals in the United States and Canada had among the most favorable attitudes toward corporal punishment and remembered it being used by their parents (Curran & others, 2001). People in Sweden especially had an unfavorable attitude toward corporal punishment and were less likely than people in the other countries to remember it being used by their parents.

When asked why they use corporal punishment with their children, parents often respond that their children need such strong discipline to learn how to behave. They also sometimes say that their parents punished them and they turned out okay, so there must not be that much wrong with it.

What do you think?

- Should physical punishment of children be outlawed in the United States?
- Did your parents spank you when you were a child? What effect do you think it had on your behavior?
- Might negative reinforcement, such as using time-outs, be more effective than positive punishment, such as spanking? Explain.

How might timing, reinforcement, and punishment be involved in overeating, drinking excessively, and smoking? How might behavior modification be able to help people change these behaviors?

Now think about the following situations. Why are some us so reluctant to take up a new sport, try a new dance step, go to a social gathering, or do almost anything different? One reason is that learning new skills often involves minor punishing consequences, such as initially looking and feeling stupid, not knowing what to do, having to put up with sarcastic comments from onlookers, and so on. In these circumstances, reinforcing consequences are often delayed. For example, it may take a long time to become a good enough golfer or a good enough dancer to enjoy these activities.

Applications of Operant Conditioning

A preschool child repeatedly throws his glasses and breaks them. A high school student and her parents have intense arguments. A college student is deeply depressed. An elderly woman is incontinent. Operant conditioning procedures have helped people such as these to adapt more successfully and cope more effectively with their problems (Sussman, 2001).

Applied behavior analysis, or **behavior modification,** is the application of operant conditioning principles to change human behavior. Consequences for behavior are established to ensure that more adaptive actions are reinforced and less adaptive ones are not (Baldwin & Baldwin, 1999; Kohlenberg, Tsai, & Kohlenberg, 1996; Powell & Symbaluk, 2002). Advocates of behavior modification believe that many emotional and behavior problems are caused by inadequate, or inappropriate, response consequences (Alberto & Troutman, 1999; Petry & others, 2001). The child who throws down his glasses and breaks them may be receiving too much attention from his teacher and peers for his behavior; they unwittingly reinforce an unacceptable behavior. In this instance, the parents and teachers would be instructed to divert attention from the destructive behavior and transfer it to a more constructive behavior, such as working quietly or playing cooperatively with peers (Harris, Wolf, & Baer, 1964).

Mental and Physical Health   Consider the following situation. Barbara and her parents were on a collision course. Things got so bad that her parents decided to see a clinical psychologist. The psychologist, who had a behavioral orientation, talked with each family member, trying to get them to pinpoint the problem. The psychologist got the family to sign a behavioral contract that spelled out what everyone needed to do to reduce the conflict. Barbara agreed to (1) be home before 11 P.M. on weeknights; (2) look for a part-time job so she could begin to pay for some of her activities; and (3) refrain from calling her parents insulting names. Her parents agreed to (1) talk to Barbara in a low tone of voice rather than yell if they were angry; (2) refrain from criticizing teenagers, especially Barbara's friends; and (3) give Barbara a small sum of money each week for gas, makeup, and socializing, but only until she found a job.

applied behavior analysis (behavior modification) The application of operant conditioning principles to change human behavior

Also consider Sam, a 19-year-old college student, who has been deeply depressed lately. His girlfriend broke off their relationship of 2 years, and his grades have been dropping. He decides to go to a psychologist who has a behavioral orientation. The psychologist enrolls him in the Coping with Depression course developed by Peter Lewinsohn (1987). Sam learns to monitor his daily moods and increase his ratio of positive to negative life events. The psychologist trains Sam to develop more efficient coping skills and gets Sam to agree to a behavioral contract, just as the psychologist did with Barbara and her parents.

Mary is an elderly woman who lives in a nursing home. In recent months she has become incontinent and is increasingly dependent on the staff for help with her daily activities. The behavioral treatment designed for Mary's problem involves teaching her to monitor her behavior and schedule going to the toilet. She is also required to do pelvic exercises. The program for decreasing Mary's dependence requires that the staff attend more to her independent behavior when it occurs and remove attention from dependent behavior whenever possible. Such strategies have been effective in reducing incontinence and dependence in older adults.

Behavior modification can be used to help people improve their self-control in many aspects of mental and physical health (Kazdin, 2001; Miltenberger, 2001; Watson & Tharp, 2002). Following are five steps to better self-control (see figure 7.13; Martin & Pear, 2002):

- *Step 1. Define the behavior to be changed in specific, concrete terms.* For Al, this is easy—he is overweight and wants to lose 30 pounds. Stated even more precisely, he wants to consume about 1,000 fewer calories per day to achieve a weight loss of about 2 pounds per week. Some problems are more difficult to specify, such as "wasting time," "having a bad attitude toward school," "having a poor relationship with ——," or "being too nervous and worrying a lot." These types of problems have been called "fuzzies" because of their abstract nature (Mager, 1972). It is important to "unfuzzify" abstract problems and make them specific and concrete. Problems can be made precise by writing out a goal and listing the things that would give clear evidence of having reached the goal.
- *Step 2. Make a commitment to change.* Both a commitment to change and a knowledge of change techniques have been shown to help college students become more effective self-managers of their smoking, eating, studying, and relationship problems (Alterman, Gariti, & Mulvaney, 2001; Perkins & others, 2001). Building a commitment to change requires doing things that increase the likelihood that you will stick to your project. First, tell others about your commitment to change—they will remind you to stick to your program. Second, rearrange your environment to provide frequent reminders of your goal, making sure the reminders are associated with the positive benefits of reaching your goal. Third, put a lot of time and energy into planning your project. Make a list of statements about your project, such as "I've put a lot of time into this project; I am certainly not going to waste all of this effort now." Fourth, because you will invariably face temptations to backslide or quit your project, plan ahead for ways you can deal with temptation, tailoring these plans to your problem.
- *Step 3. Collect data about your behavior.* This is especially important in decreasing excessive behaviors such as overeating and frequent smoking. One of the reasons for tracking your behavior is that it provides a reference point for evaluating your progress. When recording the frequency of a behavior during initial observations, you should examine the immediate circumstances that could be maintaining the problem (Martin & Pear, 2002).
- *Step 4. Design a self-control program.* Many good self-control programs involve setting long-term and short-term goals and developing a plan for reaching the

1. Define the problem
2. Commit to change
3. Collect data about yourself
4. Design a self-control program
5. Make the program last—maintenance

FIGURE 7.13 **Five Steps in Developing a Self-Control Program**

goals. Good self-control programs also usually include some type of self-talk, self-instruction, or self-reinforcement. For example, a person whose goal is to jog 30 minutes a day 5 days a week might say, "I'll never make it. It just won't work." This person can benefit by saying something like "I know it's going to be tough, but I can make it." Also, individuals can engage in self-reinforcing statements or treat themselves. This might involve saying something like "Way to go. You are up to 30 minutes three times a week. You are on your way." Or they might treat themselves to something, such as a movie, a new piece of clothing, or a new CD.

- *Step 5. Make the program last—maintenance.* One strategy is to establish specific dates for postchecks and to plan a course of action if your postchecks are not favorable. For instance, if your self-control program involves weight reduction, you might want to weigh yourself once a week. If your weight increases to a certain level, then you immediately go back on your self-control program. Another strategy is to establish a buddy system by finding a friend or someone with a similar problem. The two of you set mutual maintenance goals. Once a month, get together and check each other's behavior. If your goals have been maintained, get together and celebrate in an agreed-on way.

For other ideas on how to establish an effective self-control program tailored to your needs, you might want to contact the counseling center at your college or university. You also might consider consulting a good book on behavior modification or self-control, such as *Behavior Modification* (Martin & Pear, 2002).

Education   Not only is behavior modification effective in improving mental and physical health, but it has also been applied in classrooms to improve the education of children (Charles, 2002; Evertson, Emmer, & Worsham, 2003; Kaufmann & others, 2002). Many of the concepts already discussed, including positive reinforcement, shaping, time-out, contracting, and developing self-control, have been applied to learning in the classroom. Here are some other educational applications.

Teaching Machines and Computer Instruction   Some years ago, Skinner developed a machine to help teachers instruct students. The teaching machine engaged the student in a learning activity, paced the material at the student's rate, tested the student's knowledge of the material, and provided immediate feedback about correct and incorrect answers. Skinner hoped that the machine would revolutionize learning in schools, but the revolution never took place.

Today the idea behind Skinner's teaching machine is applied to computers. Research comparisons of computer-assisted instruction with traditional teacher-based instruction suggest that, in some areas, such as drill and practice on math problems, computer-assisted instruction can produce superior results (Kulik, Kulik, & Bangert-Drowns, 1985).

Choosing Effective Reinforcers   Not all reinforcers are the same for every child. Teachers can explore what reinforcers work best with which children—that is, individualize the use of particular reinforcers. For one child, it might be praise, for another it might be getting to spend more time participating in a favorite activity, for another it might be getting to be hall monitor for a week, and for another it might be getting to surf the Internet. Natural reinforcers such as praise and privileges are generally recommended over material reinforcers such as stars and candy (Hall & Hall, 1998).

Activities are some of the most common reinforcers used by teachers. Named after psychologist David Premack, the *Premack principle* states that a high-probability activity can be used to reinforce a low-probability activity. The term "probability" here means likelihood of occurrence. For many children, playing a game on a computer has a higher likelihood of occurrence than doing a writing assignment. Thus, a teacher might tell a child, "When you complete your writing assignment, you can play a game on the computer." The Premack principle also can be used with an entire classroom of children. For example, a teacher might say, "If all of the class gets their homework done by Friday, we will take a field trip next week."

Review and Sharpen Your Thinking

3   *Discuss operant conditioning.*

- Define operant conditioning and distinguish it from classical conditioning.
- Describe Thorndike's law of effect.
- Understand Skinner's operant conditioning.
- Discuss shaping.
- Identify the principles of reinforcement and explain how they affect behavior.
- Know how behavior modification works.

Describe a behavior (yours or someone else's) that you would like to change through behavior modification. Outline the plan. If you enacted this plan, do you think it would work? Why or why not? Would you consider the enactment of this plan to be too manipulative? Why or why not?

mhhe ● com/
santrockp7

For further review, go to the CD Study Questions for this chapter.

OBSERVATIONAL LEARNING   4

How does observational learning occur?

Would it make sense to teach a 15-year-old boy how to drive by either classical conditioning or operant conditioning procedures? Driving a car is a voluntary behavior, so classical conditioning does not really apply. In terms of operant conditioning, we could ask him to drive down the road and then reward his positive behaviors. Not many of us would want to be on the road, though, when he makes mistakes. Albert Bandura (1986, 2000) believes that if we learned only in such a trial-and-error fashion, learning would be exceedingly tedious and at times hazardous. Instead, he says, many of our complex behaviors are the result of exposure to competent models who display appropriate behavior in solving problems and coping (Striefel, 1998). By observing other people, we can acquire knowledge, skills, rules, strategies, beliefs, and attitudes (Schunk, 2000).

You initially encountered Bandura's ideas in chapter 1, in which his social cognitive theory was introduced. This section discusses his view of observational learning further.

Observational learning, also called *imitation* or *modeling,* is learning that occurs when a person observes and imitates someone's behavior. The capacity to learn behavior patterns by observation eliminates trial-and-error learning. In many instances observational learning takes less time than operant conditioning.

Bandura (1986) described four main processes that are involved in observational learning: attention, retention, motor reproduction, and reinforcement. For observational learning to take place, the first process that has to occur is *attention* (which was initially discussed in chapter 5 due to its important role in perception). In order to reproduce a model's actions, you must attend to what the model is saying or doing. You might not hear what a friend says if the stereo is blaring, or you might miss the teacher's analysis of a problem if you are admiring someone sitting in the next row. Imagine that you decide to take a class to improve your artistic skills. You need to attend to the instructor's words and hand movements. Attention to the model is influenced by a host of characteristics. For example, warm, powerful, atypical people command more attention than do cold, weak, typical people.

observational learning Also called *imitation* or *modeling;* learning that occurs when a person observes and imitates another's behavior.

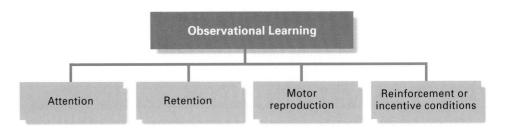

Observational Learning
- Attention
- Retention
- Motor reproduction
- Reinforcement or incentive conditions

FIGURE 7.14 Bandura's Model of Observational Learning In terms of Bandura's model, if you are learning to ski, you need to attend to the instructor's words and demonstrations. You need to remember what the instructor did and her tips for avoiding disasters. You also need the motor abilities to reproduce what the instructor has shown you. And praise from the instructor after you have completed a few moves on the slopes should improve your motivation to continue skiing.

Retention is the second process needed for observational learning to occur. To reproduce a model's actions, you must code the information and keep it in memory so that it can be retrieved. A simple verbal description or a vivid image of what the model did assists retention. (Memory is such an important cognitive process that chapter 8 is devoted exclusively to it.) In the example of taking a class to improve your art skills, you will need to remember what the instructor said and did in modeling good drawing skills.

Production is the process of imitating the model's actions. People might attend to a model and code in memory what they have seen, but limitations in motor development might make it difficult for them to reproduce the model's action. Thirteen-year-olds might see Michael Jordan do a reverse two-handed dunk but be unable to reproduce the pro's actions. In an art class, also, you will need good motor reproduction skills to follow the instructor's example.

Reinforcement, or incentive conditions, is the final component of observational learning. On many occasions we may attend to what a model says or does, retain the information in memory, and possess the motor capabilities to perform the action, but we might fail to repeat the behavior because of inadequate reinforcement. The importance of this step was demonstrated in one of Bandura's (1965) studies in which children who had seen a model punished for aggression reproduced the model's aggression only when they were offered an incentive to do so. In art class, if the instructor chooses one of your drawings for display, the reinforcement encourages you to keep drawing and to take another art skills class.

A summary of Bandura's model of observational learning is shown in figure 7.14. To think about the models and mentors in your life, see the Psychology and Life box.

mhhe com/
santrockp7

For study tools related to this learning goal, see the Study Guide, the CD-ROM, and the Online Learning Center.

Review and Sharpen Your Thinking

4 Understand observational learning.
- Define observational learning and outline the four steps in Bandura's model.

Who have been the most important models in your life? What have you learned from them?

5 COGNITIVE FACTORS IN LEARNING

Purposive Behavior **Insight Learning**

What role does cognition play in learning?

In discussing learning, I have said little about cognitive processes, except as they apply in observational learning. Skinner's operant conditioning approach and Pavlov's classical conditioning approach both ignore the possibility that cognitive factors such as memory, thinking, planning, or expectations might be important in learning. Skinnerian

Models and Mentors in My Life

Having positive role models and mentors to observe and learn from can make important contributions to whether individuals develop optimally and reach their full potential. A mentor is someone you look up to and respect, who serves as a competent model, and who is willing to work with you to help you achieve your goals.

In the Quantum Opportunities program, students from low-income backgrounds benefited significantly from having a mentor over a 4-year period from the 9th through the 12th grade (Carnegie Council on Adolescent Development, 1995). These mentors modeled appropriate behavior and strategies, gave sustained support, and provided guidance. Compared with a nonmentored control group, 63 percent of the mentored group graduated from high school, but only 42 percent of the control group did; 42 percent of the mentored students enrolled in college, but only 17 percent of the control group did.

Role models and mentors can be parents, teachers, an older peer, someone in the community. Spend a few minutes and think about the role models and mentors you have had in your life, including now. Do you remember any specific instances in which you watched them do or say something that had a lasting impact on you and that you later modeled? List the most important role models and mentors in your life and then describe what you learned from them and how they helped your learning.

A mentor can be very beneficial to students. If you currently don't have a mentor, think about the people at your college or university, or people in the community, whom you respect and look up to. Consider asking one of these people to be a mentor for you.

Role Models and Mentors	What I Learned from Them and How They Helped My Learning
1. _____	_____
	_____
	_____
	_____
2. _____	_____
	_____
	_____
	_____
3. _____	_____
	_____
	_____
	_____
4. _____	_____
	_____
	_____
	_____

Or you might want to become a mentor yourself. Do you have a particular skill or knowledge that you might be able to teach children or adolescents? Mentoring a child or an adolescent and serving as a positive model in observational learning can be an extremely rewarding experience.

behaviorists point out that they do not deny the existence of thinking processes, but, because such processes cannot be observed, they may interfere with the discovery of important environmental conditions that govern behavior.

Many contemporary psychologists, including behavioral revisionists who recognize the importance of cognition, believe learning involves more than environment-behavior connections (Bandura, 1986, 2000). Let's look at E. C. Tolman's contributions to the role of cognition in learning.

Purposive Behavior

E. C. Tolman (1932) emphasized the *purposiveness* of behavior. In other words, he believed that much of behavior is goal directed. Tolman believed it is necessary to study entire behavioral sequences in order to understand why people engage in particular actions. For example, high school students whose goal is to attend a leading college or university study hard in their classes. If we focus only on their studying, we would miss the purpose of their behavior. The students don't always study hard because they have been reinforced for studying in the past. Rather, studying is a means to intermediate goals (learning, high grades), which, in turn, improve their likelihood of getting into the college or university of their choice (Schunk, 2000).

Tolman's legacy can be seen today in the extensive interest in the role of goal setting in human behavior (Dweck, 1996; Zimmerman, 2000). Researchers are especially

"You will note that their ability to comprehend, assess and process information increases dramatically when Professor Podhertz throws in the cat."
© Leo Cullum

interested in how people engage in self-regulation and self-monitoring of their behavior to reach a goal (Pintrich, 2000; Pressley, 1995; Schunk & Ertmer, 2000; Winne & Perry, 2000). In every chapter of this book, I have set learning goals and asked you to monitor your studying so that you can reach these goals.

Expectancy Learning and Information In studying the purposiveness of behavior, Tolman went beyond the stimuli and responses of Pavlov and Skinner to focus on cognitive mechanisms. He said that when classical and operant conditioning occur, the organism acquires certain expectations. In classical conditioning, the young boy fears the rabbit because he expects it will hurt him. In operant conditioning, a woman works hard all week because she expects to be paid on Friday. Expectancies are acquired from experiences with environment.

Tolman (1932) emphasized that the information value of the CS is important as a signal or expectation that a UCS will follow. Tolman's belief that the information that the CS provides is the key to understanding classical conditioning anticipated contemporary thinking.

One contemporary view of classical conditioning describes an organism as an information seeker, using logical and perceptual relations among events, along with preconceptions, to form a representation of the world (Rescorla, 1988, 1996, 2001). A classic experiment conducted by Leon Kamin (1968) illustrates the importance of an organism's history and the information provided by a conditioned stimulus in classical conditioning. A rat was conditioned by repeatedly pairing a tone (CS) and a shock (UCS), until the tone alone produced fear (CR). Then, the tone continued to be paired with the shock, but a light (a second CS) was turned on each time the tone was sounded. Even though the light (CS) and the shock (UCS) were repeatedly paired, the rat showed no conditioning to the light (the light by itself produced no CR). Conditioning to the light was blocked, almost as if the rat had not paid attention. The rat apparently used the tone as a signal to predict that a shock would be forthcoming; information about the light's pairing with the shock was redundant with the information already learned about the tone's pairing with the shock. In this experiment, conditioning was governed not by the contiguity of the CS and UCS but, rather, by the rat's history and the information it received. Contemporary classical conditioning researchers are exploring further the role of information in an organism's learning (Domjan, 1996; Fanselow, DeCola, & Young, 1993).

One type of expectancy involves cognitive maps. Tolman (1948) believed that organisms form cognitive maps that are made up of expectancies about which actions are needed to attain a goal. A *cognitive map* is an organism's mental representation of the structure of physical space. His experiments with rats in a maze led Tolman to conclude that rats developed mental awareness of physical space and the elements in it. They used these cognitive maps to find the food at the end of the maze, their goal.

Tolman's idea of cognitive maps is alive and well today. As we move around in our environment, we develop a cognitive map of where things are located, on both small and large scales. We have a cognitive map of the locations of rooms in our houses or apartments, and we have a cognitive map of our location in the United States, for example. A popular exercise is to draw a cognitive map reflecting our perception of the city or state in which we live, relative to the rest of the United States. Texans, for example, usually make the state of Texas about three-fourths the size of the entire United States. People living in New York City often draw it to be about nine-tenths the size of the United States. Of course, such cognitive maps deliberately distort the physical world, reflecting the perceivers' egocentric interest in their city or state.

FIGURE 7.15 **Insight Learning** Sultan, one of Köhler's brightest chimps, is faced with the problem of reaching a cluster of bananas overhead. He solves the problem by stacking boxes on top of one another to reach the bananas. Köhler called this type of problem solving insight learning.

Latent Learning Other evidence to support the role of cognitive maps in learning was obtained in experiments on latent learning. **Latent learning** is unreinforced learning that is not immediately reflected in behavior. In one study, two groups of hungry rats were placed in a maze and required to find their way from a starting point to an end point (Tolman & Honzik, 1930). The first group found food (a reinforcer) at the end point; the second group found nothing there. In the operant conditioning view, the first group should learn the maze better than the second group, which is exactly what happened. However, when Tolman subsequently took some of the rats from the nonreinforced group and gave them food at the end point of the maze, they began to run the maze as effectively as the reinforced group. The nonreinforced rats apparently had learned a great deal about the maze as they roamed around and explored it. But their learning was *latent,* stored cognitively in their memories but not yet expressed behaviorally. When these rats were given a good reason (reinforcement with food) to run the maze speedily, they called on their latent learning to help them reach the end of the maze more quickly.

Outside of a laboratory, latent learning is evident in an animal's exploration of its surroundings. Learning the layout of its environment may bring the animal no immediate benefits, but it can prove critical in the future when fleeing a predator or searching for food.

Insight Learning

Tolman was not the only psychologist in the first half of the twentieth century who believed that cognitive factors play an important role in learning. So did gestalt psychologist Wolfgang Köhler. Köhler, a German psychologist, spent 4 months in the Canary Islands during World War I observing the behavior of apes. There he conducted two fascinating experiments. One is called the "stick problem," the other the "box problem." Though these two experiments are basically the same, the solutions to the problems are different. In both situations, the ape discovers that it cannot reach an alluring piece of fruit, either because the fruit is too high or because it is outside of the ape's cage and beyond reach. To solve the stick problem, the ape has to insert a small stick inside a larger stick to reach the fruit. To master the box problem, the ape must stack several boxes to reach the fruit (see figure 7.15).

latent learning Unreinforced learning that is not immediately reflected in behavior.

According to Köhler (1925), solving these problems does not involve trial and error or simple connections between stimuli and responses. Rather, when the ape realizes that his customary actions are not going to help him get the fruit, he often sits for a period of time and appears to ponder how to solve the problem. Then he quickly gets up, as if he had a sudden flash of insight, piles the boxes on top of one another, and gets the fruit. **Insight learning** is a form of problem solving in which the organism develops a sudden insight or understanding of a problem's solution.

For study tools related to this learning goal, see the Study Guide, the CD-ROM, and the Online Learning Center.

Review and Sharpen Your Thinking

5 *Know about the role of cognition in learning.*
- Discuss the role of expectations, latent learning, and cognitive maps in learning.
- Explain insight learning.

What are your career expectations? How might these expectations influence your behavior this term?

6 BIOLOGICAL AND CULTURAL FACTORS IN LEARNING

Biological Constraints   **Cultural Constraints**

How do biology and culture affect learning?

Albert Einstein had many special talents. He combined enormous creativity with great analytic ability to develop some of the twentieth century's most important insights about the nature of matter and the universe. Genes obviously endowed Einstein with extraordinary intellectual skills that enabled him to think and reason on a very high plane, but cultural factors also undoubtedly contributed to Einstein's genius. Einstein received an excellent, rigorous European education, and later in the United States he experienced the freedom and support believed to be important in creative exploration. Would Einstein have been able to fully develop his intellectual skills and make such brilliant insights if he had grown up in a developing country, such as Bolivia? Unlikely. Quite clearly both biological *and* cultural factors contribute to learning.

Biological Constraints

We can't breathe under water, fish can't play table tennis, and cows can't solve math problems. The structure of an organism's body permits certain kinds of learning and inhibits others (Chance, 2003; Morgan, 2002). For example, chimpanzees cannot learn to speak English because they lack the necessary vocal equipment. Some of us cannot solve difficult calculus problems, others of us can, and the differences do not all seem to be the result of experiences.

Instinctive Drift An example of biological influences on learning is **instinctive drift,** the tendency of animals to revert to instinctive behavior that interferes with learning. Consider the situation of Keller and Marion Breland (1961), students of B. F. Skinner, who used operant conditioning to train animals to perform at fairs, conventions, and in television advertisements. They used Skinner's techniques to teach pigs to cart large wooden nickels to a piggy bank and deposit them. They also trained raccoons to pick up a coin and place it in a metal tray. Although the pigs and raccoons, as well as chickens and other animals, performed well at most of the tasks

insight learning A form of problem solving in which the organism develops a sudden insight or understanding of the problem's solution.

instinctive drift The tendency of animals to revert to instinctive behavior that interferes with learning.

FIGURE 7.16 **Instinctive Drift** This raccoon's skill in using its hands made it an excellent basketball player, but because of instinctive drift, the raccoon had a much more difficult time dropping coins in a tray.

(raccoons became adept basketball players, for example—see figure 7.16), some of the animals began acting strangely. Instead of picking up the large wooden nickels and carrying them to the piggy bank, the pigs would drop the nickels on the ground, shove them with their snouts, toss them in the air, and then repeat these actions. The raccoons began to hold on to their coins rather than dropping them into the metal tray. When two coins were introduced, the raccoons rubbed them together in a miserly fashion. Somehow these behaviors overwhelmed the strength of the reinforcement. Why were the pigs and the raccoons misbehaving? The pigs were rooting, an instinct which is used to uncover edible roots. The raccoons were engaging in an instinctive food-washing response. Their instinctive drift interfered with learning.

Preparedness and Taste Aversion   Some animals learn readily in one situation but have difficulty learning in slightly different circumstances. The difficulty might result not from some aspect of the learning situation but from the organism's biological predisposition (Seligman, 1970). **Preparedness** is the species-specific biological predisposition to learn in certain ways but not others.

Much of the evidence for preparedness comes from research on taste aversion (Garcia, 1989). Consider this situation: A psychologist went to dinner with his wife and ordered filet mignon with béarnaise sauce, his favorite dish. Afterward they went to the opera. Several hours later, he became very ill with stomach pains and nausea. Several weeks later, he tried to eat béarnaise sauce but couldn't bear it. The psychologist's experience involves *taste aversion,* another biological constraint on learning (Yamamoto, Frequet, & Sandner, 2002).

If an organism ingests a substance that poisons but does not kill it, the organism often develops considerable distaste for that substance. Rats that experience low levels of radiation after eating show a strong aversion to the food they were eating when the radiation made them ill. This aversion has been shown to last for as long as 32 days. Such long-term effects cannot be accounted for by classical conditioning, which would argue that a single pairing of the conditioned and unconditioned stimuli would not last that long (Garcia, Ervin, & Koelling, 1966). Radiation and chemical treatment

preparedness The species-specific biological predisposition to learn in certain ways.

In Balinese culture many children are taught to be skilled dancers by the age 6, whereas other cultures value learning in other areas.

of cancer often produce nausea in patients, and the resulting pattern of aversions often resembles those shown by laboratory animals.

Knowledge about taste aversion has been used to discourage animals from preying on certain species. For example, the livestock of ranchers may be threatened by wolves or coyotes. Instead of killing the pests or predators, the ranchers feed them poisoned meat of their prey (cattle, sheep). The wolves and coyotes, poisoned but not killed, develop a taste aversion for cattle or sheep and, hence, are less of a threat to the ranchers and their livestock. In this way, ranchers, cattle, sheep, wolves, and coyotes can live in a semblance of ecological balance.

Cultural Constraints

Traditionally, the influence of culture on learning has received little or no attention. The behavioral orientation that dominated American psychology for much of the twentieth century does focus on the cultural contexts of learning, but the organisms in those contexts have often been animals. There has been limited interest in the cultural context of human learning.

How does culture influence learning? Most psychologists agree that the principles of classical conditioning, operant conditioning, and observational learning are universal and are powerful learning processes in every culture. However, culture can influence the *degree* to which these learning processes are used, and it often determines the *content* of learning. For example, punishment is a universal learning process, but, as is discussed next, its use and type show considerable sociocultural variation.

When behaviorism began its influential reign in the United States between 1910 and 1930, child-rearing experts regarded the infant as capable of being shaped into almost any type of child. Desirable social behavior could be achieved if the child's antisocial behaviors were always punished and never indulged and if positive behaviors were carefully conditioned and rewarded in a highly controlled and structured child-rearing regimen. John Watson (1928) authored a publication, *Psychological Care of the Infant and Child,* that was the official government booklet for parents. This booklet advocated never letting children suck their thumbs and, if necessary, restraining the child by tying her hands to the crib at night and painting her fingers with foul-tasting liquids. Parents were advised to let infants "cry themselves out" rather than reinforce this unacceptable behavior by picking them up to rock and soothe them.

From the 1930s to the 1960s, a more permissive attitude prevailed, and parents were advised to be concerned with the feelings and capacities of the child. Since the 1960s there has been a continued emphasis on the role of parental love in children's socialization, but experts now advise parents to play a less permissive and more active role in shaping children's behavior. Experts stress that parents should set limits and make authoritative decisions in areas in which the child is not capable of reasonable judgment. However, they should listen and adapt to the child's point of view, should explain their restrictions and discipline, and should not discipline the child in a hostile, punitive manner.

The content of learning is also influenced by culture (Cole & Cole, 2000). We cannot learn about something we do not experience. The 4-year-old who grows up among the Bushmen of the Kalahari Desert is unlikely to learn about taking baths or pouring water from one glass into another. Similarly, a child growing up in Chicago is unlikely to be skilled at tracking animals or finding water-bearing roots in the desert. Learning often requires practice, and certain behaviors are practiced more often in some cultures than in others. In Bali many children are skilled dancers by the age of 6, whereas Norwegian children are much likelier to be good skiers and skaters by that age. Children growing up in a Mexican village famous for its pottery may work with clay day after day, whereas children in a nearby village famous for woven rugs and sweaters rarely become experts at making clay pots.

mhhe com/ santrockp7 *Does learning about a foreign culture while learning the language of that culture have a positive or negative effect on learning? (Around the Globe)*

Review and Sharpen Your Thinking

6 **_Identify biological and cultural factors in learning._**

- Discuss these biological constraints on learning: instinctive drift, preparedness, and taste aversion.
- Explain how culture can influence learning.

Think about the various types of dogs, cats, or another species of domesticated animal with which you are familiar. What evidence do they present that every organism is biologically influenced to permit certain kinds of learning and inhibit others?

mhhe com/ santrockp7

For study tools related to this learning goal, see the Study Guide, the CD-ROM, and the Online Learning Center.

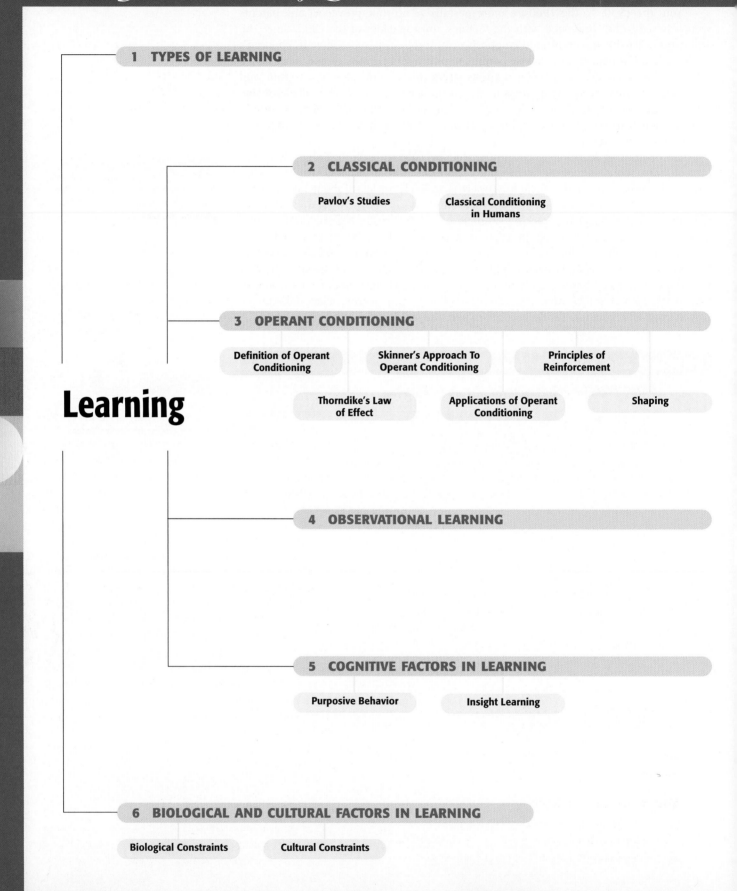

Learning

1 TYPES OF LEARNING

2 CLASSICAL CONDITIONING

Pavlov's Studies

Classical Conditioning
in Humans

3 OPERANT CONDITIONING

Definition of Operant
Conditioning

Skinner's Approach To
Operant Conditioning

Principles of
Reinforcement

Thorndike's Law
of Effect

Applications of Operant
Conditioning

Shaping

4 OBSERVATIONAL LEARNING

5 COGNITIVE FACTORS IN LEARNING

Purposive Behavior

Insight Learning

6 BIOLOGICAL AND CULTURAL FACTORS IN LEARNING

Biological Constraints

Cultural Constraints

1 Explain what learning is.

- Learning is a relatively permanent change in behavior that occurs through experience. Observational learning is learning by watching what other people do. In associative learning, a connection is made between two events. Conditioning is the process by which associative learning occurs. In classical conditioning, organisms learn the association between two stimuli and, in operant conditioning, they learn the association between behavior and a consequence.

2 Describe classical conditioning.

- Classical conditioning occurs when a neutral stimulus becomes associated with a meaningful stimulus and comes to elicit a similar response. Pavlov discovered that an organism learns the association between an unconditioned stimulus (UCS) and a conditioned stimulus (CS). The UCS automatically produces the unconditioned response (UCR). After conditioning (CS-UCS pairing), the CS elicits the conditioned response (CR) by itself. Acquisition in classical conditioning is the initial linking of stimuli and responses, which involves a neutral stimulus being associated with the UCS so that the CS comes to elicit the CR. Two important aspects of acquisition are contiguity and contingency/predictability. Generalization in classical conditioning is the tendency of a new stimulus that is similar to the original conditioned stimulus to elicit a response that is similar to the conditioned response. Discrimination in classical conditioning is the process of learning to respond to certain stimuli and not to others. Extinction in classical conditioning is the weakening of the CR in the absence of the UCS. Spontaneous recovery is the recurrence of a CR after a time delay without further conditioning.
- In humans, classical conditioning has been applied to explaining and eliminating fears. Counterconditioning, a classical conditioning procedure for weakening the CR by associating the fear-provoking stimulus with a new response that is incompatible with the fear, has been successful in eliminating fears. Classical conditioning also can explain pleasant emotions. Some of the behaviors we associate with health problems and mental disorders, including certain aspects of drug use and immune system functioning, can involve classical conditioning. Classical conditioning also has been applied to consumer behavior.

3 Discuss operant conditioning.

- Operant conditioning is a form of learning in which the consequences of behavior produce changes in the probability of the behavior's occurrence. B. F. Skinner described the behavior of the organism as operant: the behavior operates on the environment, and the environment in turn operates on the organism. Whereas classical conditioning involves respondent behavior, operant conditioning involves operant behavior. In most instances, operant conditioning is better at explaining voluntary behavior than classical conditioning is.
- Thorndike's law of effect states that behaviors followed by positive outcomes are strengthened, whereas behaviors followed by negative outcomes are weakened. Thorndike's view that the organism's behavior is due to a connection between a stimulus and a response was called S-R theory.
- Skinner believed that the mechanisms of learning are the same for all species. This led him to study lower animals extensively in the hope that the basic mechanisms of learning could be more easily understood in organisms simpler than humans. Like Skinner, contemporary behaviorists study organisms under precisely controlled conditions so that the connection between the operant behavior and the specific consequences can be examined in minute detail.
- Shaping is the process of rewarding approximations of desired behavior in order to shorten the learning process.
- Principles of reinforcement include the distinction between positive reinforcement (the frequency of a behavior increases because it is followed by a rewarding stimulus) and negative reinforcement (the frequency of behavior increases because it is followed by the removal of an aversive, or unpleasant, stimulus). Positive reinforcement can be classified as primary reinforcement (using reinforcers that are innately satisfying) and secondary reinforcement (using reinforcers that acquire positive value through experience). Reinforcement can also be continuous (a behavior is reinforced every time) or partial (a behavior is reinforced only a portion of the time). Schedules of reinforcement—fixed ratio, variable ratio, fixed interval, and variable interval—are timetables that determine when a behavior will be reinforced. Operant conditioning involves generalization (giving the same response to similar stimuli), discrimination (responding to stimuli that signal that a behavior will or will not be reinforced), and extinction (a decreasing tendency to perform a previously reinforced behavior when reinforcement is stopped). Punishment refers to a consequence that decreases the likelihood a behavior will occur. Punishment, through which a behavior is weakened, is different from negative reinforcement, through which a behavior is strengthened. In positive punishment, a behavior decreases when it is followed by an unpleasant stimulus. In negative punishment, a behavior decreases when a positive stimulus is removed from it. Time-out is

a form of negative punishment. Most psychologists recommend that positive punishment not be used with children. Operant conditioning is more efficient, especially in lower animals, when the interval between behavior and its reinforcement or punishment is very brief. However, in humans, delayed reinforcement and punishment can have significant effects on behavior. Connections between the timing of reinforcement and punishment (whether they are immediate or delayed) has implications for understanding health problems, such as obesity and substance abuse.

- Behavior modification is the application of operant conditioning principles to change human behavior. It involves establishing consequences for behavior to reinforce more adaptive actions. Operant conditioning has been applied to mental and physical health, as well as to education.

4 Understand observational learning.

- Observational learning occurs when a person observes and imitates someone's behavior. Bandura said that observational learning includes attention, retention, production, and reinforcement.

5 Know about the role of cognitive factors in learning.

- E. C. Tolman emphasized the purposiveness of behavior. The purposive aspect of Tolman's view refers to his belief that much of behavior is goal directed. There is considerable interest in goal-directed behavior today. In studying the purposiveness of behavior, Tolman went beyond stimuli and responses to discuss cognitive mechanisms. Tolman believed that expectancies, acquired through experiences with the environment, are an important cognitive mechanism in learning. Cognitive maps, an organism's mental representations of physical space, involve expectancies about which actions are needed to reach a goal.

- Evidence to support the role of cognitive maps was obtained in experiments on latent learning, uninforced learning that is not immediately reflected in behavior.

- Köhler developed the concept of insight learning, a form of problem solving in which the organism develops a sudden insight or understanding of a problem's solution.

6 Identify biological and cognitive factors in learning.

- Biological constraints restrict what an organism can learn from experience. These constraints include instinctive drift (the tendency of animals to revert to instinctive behavior that interferes with learned behavior), preparedness (the species-specific biological predisposition to learn in certain ways but not in others), and taste aversion (the biological predisposition to avoid foods that have caused sickness in the past).

- Although most psychologists agree that the principles of classical conditioning, operant conditioning, and observational learning are universal, cultural customs can influence the degree to which these learning processes are used, and culture also often determines the content of learning.

Key Terms

learning, p. 269
associative learning, p. 269
classical conditioning, p. 270
unconditioned stimulus (UCS), p. 271
unconditioned response (UCR), p. 271
conditioned stimulus (CS), p. 271
conditioned response (CR), p. 271
acquisition (classical conditioning), p. 272

generalization (classical conditioning), p. 272
discrimination (classical conditioning), p. 272
extinction (classical conditioning), p. 272
spontaneous recovery, p. 272
counterconditioning, p. 274
operant conditioning, p. 277
law of effect, p. 278
shaping, p. 279
reinforcement, p. 280

positive reinforcement, p. 281
negative reinforcement, p. 281
primary reinforcement, p. 281
secondary reinforcement, p. 281
schedules of reinforcement, p. 282
generalization (operant conditioning), p. 283
discrimination (operant conditioning), p. 284

extinction (operant conditioning), p. 284
punishment, p. 284
positive punishment, p. 284
negative punishment, p. 284
applied behavior analysis (behavior modification) p. 288
observational learning, p. 291
latent learning, p. 295
insight learning, p. 296
instinctive drift, p. 296
preparedness, p. 297

Apply Your Knowledge

1. One common association that people have is called a *conditioned taste aversion,* which occurs when you eat or drink something and then get sick. A conditioned taste aversion is most likely to occur when the food or drink is something that is relatively unfamiliar. Suppose that you have acquired a conditioned taste aversion to tequila. Identify what the unconditioned stimulus, unconditioned response, conditioned stimulus, and conditioned response are in this example.

2. Positive and negative reinforcement are often difficult concepts to understand. On the following website, examples and a practice exercise may help you figure out the distinction more easily:

   http://psych.athabascau.ca/html/prtut/reinpair.htm

Connections

For extra help in mastering the material in this chapter, see the review sections and practice quizzes in the Student Study Guide, the CD-ROM, and the Online Learning Center.

3. Think of all of the things you have learned in the past several days. Write down an example involving each of the following types of learning: classical conditioning, operant conditioning, observational learning, latent learning, and insight learning. Which kind of learning do you use most frequently? Which seems to be the least common for you? Are there types of learning you've done that don't seem to fit any category? If so, what aspects of those types exclude them from these categories?

Memory

<table>
<tr><td><h2>Chapter Outline</h2></td><td></td><td><h2>Learning Goals</h2></td></tr>
<tr><td>THE NATURE OF MEMORY</td><td>1</td><td>Identify three domains of memory.</td></tr>
<tr><td>MEMORY ENCODING</td><td>2</td><td>Explain how memories are encoded.</td></tr>
<tr><td>Attention
▼
Levels of Processing
▼
Elaboration
▼
Imagery</td><td></td><td></td></tr>
<tr><td>MEMORY STORAGE</td><td>3</td><td>Discuss how memories are stored.</td></tr>
<tr><td>Sensory Memory
▼
Short-Term Memory
▼
Long-Term Memory</td><td></td><td></td></tr>
<tr><td>MEMORY RETRIEVAL</td><td>4</td><td>Summarize how memories are retrieved.</td></tr>
<tr><td>Serial Position Effect
▼
Retrieval Cues and the Retrieval Task
▼
Retrieval of Autobiographical Memories
▼
Retrieval of Emotional Memories
▼
Eyewitness Testimony</td><td></td><td></td></tr>
<tr><td>FORGETTING</td><td>5</td><td>Describe how encoding and retrieval failure are involved in forgetting.</td></tr>
<tr><td>Encoding Failure
▼
Retrieval Failure</td><td></td><td></td></tr>
<tr><td>MEMORY AND STUDY STRATEGIES</td><td>6</td><td>Evaluate study strategies based on an understanding of memory.</td></tr>
<tr><td>Encoding Strategies
▼
Storage Strategies
▼
Retrieval Strategies</td><td></td><td></td></tr>
</table>

Unlike the other reporters, when S. listened to his editor making detailed assignments, he never took notes. Feeling exasperated by what he perceived as a lack of attention, his editor challenged S.'s professionalism. The editor was startled when S. reported not just the details of his own assignment but the details of others' assignments as well. S. was surprised himself. He thought everyone's memory operated in the same way and until this point had never thought of himself as different or special.

Psychologist Alexander Luria (1968) chronicled the life of S., whose unique visual imagination allowed him to remember an extraordinary amount of detail. Luria had become acquainted with S. in the 1920s in Russia. Luria began with some simple research to test S.'s memory. For example, he asked S. to recall a series of words or numbers, a standard method of testing memory skills. Luria concluded that S. had no apparent limits to his ability to recall. In such tests, people remember at most 5 to 9 numbers. Not only could S. remember as many as 70 numbers, but he could also recall them accurately in reverse order. S. also could report the sequence flawlessly with no warning or practice even as long as 15 years after his initial exposure to the sequence. In addition, after the 15-year interval, S. could describe what Luria had been wearing and where he had been sitting when S. learned the list. Similar feats of recall included accurately reproducing passages from languages he did not know after hearing the passage only once.

How could S. manage such tasks? As long as each number or word was spoken slowly, S. could represent it as a visual image that was meaningful to him. These images were durable—S. easily remembered the image he created for each sequence long after he learned the sequence.

Although you might think it would be wonderful to possess S.'s remarkable ability to remember, S. often found that it was a serious liability. He moved from job to job, often feeling overwhelmed by the amount of detail he automatically included in his everyday work tasks. His propensity to create visual images interfered with his normal processing of information. He had trouble comprehending whole passages of a text because he became bogged down in the details. To a casual observer, S. appeared to be disorganized and rather dim-witted—a person who talked too much and derailed social conversations by reporting the images that filled his mind.

Ironically, S. had a very poor memory for faces, finding them too flexible and changeable to recall. Worse, he experienced himself as being two people. He described himself as "I" when he felt in control of his memory and as "he" when his imagery ran away with him. Luria concluded that S. had difficulty knowing which aspect of his life was more real: "the world of imagination in which he lived, or the world of reality in which he was merely a temporary guest" (p. 159).

S.'s memory, although extraordinary, helps us to understand how ordinary memory is organized and how it works, which is the subject of this chapter. As you will see, memory is a complex interaction of brain function, emotion, and individual circumstances. As psychologists learn more about this complex system and develop models to explain it, we benefit: The practical implications of psychology research are helping people overcome memory problems, and they are helping students study more effectively.

1 THE NATURE OF MEMORY

What are the three domains of memory?

Memory is the retention of information over time through encoding, storage, and retrieval. That is, for memory to work, we have to take information in, store it or represent it in some manner, and then retrieve it for some purpose later. The next three sections of the chapter focus on the domains of memory: encoding, storage, and retrieval. Although memory is very complex, thinking about it in terms of these three domains should help you to understand it better (see figure 8.1).

Except for the annoying moments when memory fails or someone we know is afflicted with memory loss, most of us don't think about how much everything we do or say depends on how smoothly our memory systems operate (Schacter, 1996, 1999, 2001). Think about how important memory is in carrying out the simple task of meeting a friend at a restaurant. To begin with, you have to remember your friend's

memory The retention of information over time through encoding, storage, and retrieval.

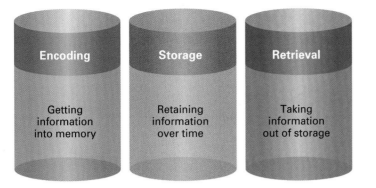

FIGURE 8.1 Processing Information in Memory As you read about the many aspects of memory in this chapter, think about the organization of memory in terms of these three main activities.

name and phone number. You have to bring to mind all of the information needed to execute the phone call. You have to use your memory of voices to determine whether the person answering the phone is your friend. To carry on the phone conversation with your friend, you have to access a vast dictionary of words, sounds, meanings, and syntax stored in your memory. At some point, you will have to sort through your memory of visits to restaurants or recommendations of new ones to decide where to meet. You have to recall details of how to get to the restaurant. You also have to remember what else is going on in your life so that you don't plan to meet your friend when you have something else scheduled.

We rely on our memory systems to carry out similar plans every day of our lives. Human memory systems truly are remarkable when you think of how much information we put into our memories and how much we must retrieve to perform all of life's activities.

Human memory also has its imperfections, as we have all experienced. It is not unusual for two people to argue about whether something did or didn't happen, each intensely confident that his or her memory is accurate and the other person's is inaccurate. Each of us also has had the frustrating experience of trying to remember the name of someone or some place but not quite being able to retrieve it.

Among the other imperfections of memory that surface are the stunning, high-profile disagreements in our nation's courtrooms and political arenas. The trials of O. J. Simpson, Timothy McVeigh, and others showed how common it is for one person to remember events one way while someone else remembers them another way. The main players in scandals such as Watergate, the Iran-Contra affair, and alleged sexual misconduct by President Bill Clinton often paint different portraits of events and circumstances from their memories.

Clearly, people do not just coldly store and retrieve bits of data in a computer-like fashion (Schacter, 1996, 1999, 2001). In the early scientific study of memory, the subjective nature of memory was considered inappropriate subject matter for psychology. However, today, many scientists who study memory recognize its subjective nature and investigate how people reconstruct their own versions of the past. Scientists recognize that the mind can distort, invent, and forget. And they know that emotions color memories. Thus we do not store judgment-free impressions of reality. In sum, psychologists today study memory's phenomenal abilities, as well as its numerous limitations.

Review and Sharpen Your Thinking

1 *Identify the three domains of memory.*

- Define memory and briefly profile the three domains of memory.

How important is memory in your life? What would your life be like without memory?

mhhe.com/
santrockp7

For study tools related to this learning goal, see the Study Guide, the CD-ROM, and the Online Learning Center.

2 MEMORY ENCODING

Attention	Elaboration

Levels of Processing	Imagery

FIGURE 8.2 Encoding Memories
Look at these three pictures for a few seconds; then look away and state what you remember about them.

encoding The way in which information gets into memory storage.

How are memories encoded?

Encoding is the way in which information is processed for storage in memory. When you are listening to a lecture, watching a movie, listening to music, or talking with a friend, you are encoding information into memory. In everyday experiences, encoding has much in common with learning.

Some information gets into memory virtually automatically, whereas getting other information in takes effort. Let's examine some of the encoding processes that require effort. The issues that interest psychologists include how effectively we attend to information, how deeply we process it, how extensively we elaborate it with details, and how much we use mental imagery to encode it.

Attention

Look at the pictures of the three individuals in figure 8.2 for a few seconds. Then, before reading further, look away from them and state what you remember about the pictures.

These actually are faces of famous people—George Washington, Mona Lisa, and George H. W. Bush—with Elvis Presley's hair grafted onto their images. You likely did not recognize these famous individuals because of the prominent hair. When we remember a face, we usually attend to only a few key features and ignore the others. Therefore, in these pictures, you may have focused more on the hair than on the facial features.

To begin the process of memory encoding, we have to attend to information (Mangels, Picton & Craik, 2001). Recall that in chapter 5 I discussed the role of attention in perception. Specifically, I highlighted the importance of *selective attention*, which involves focusing on a specific aspect of experience while ignoring others. Attention is selective by nature because the brain's resources are limited. Although our brains are remarkably efficient, they cannot attend to everything. Limitations mean that we have to selectively attend to some things in our environment and ignore others (O'Donnell, 2002; Macaluso, Frith & Driver, 2002).

Divided attention also affects memory encoding. It occurs when a person must attend to several things simultaneously (Brouwer & others, 2002). In studies of divided attention, researchers often have participants remember a set of materials, such as a list of words or a story (Schacter, 2001). At the same time that they are trying to encode this information, participants are required to perform an additional task that draws their attention away from the initial task. For example, participants might be asked to monitor a series of tones and report when they hear a low- or high-pitched tone, at the same time that they are trying to memorize the list of words or story. In a number of such studies, individuals who are allowed to give their full attention to information they are asked to remember do much better on subsequent memory tests of the information than do their counterparts who experienced divided attention (Pomplum, Reingold, & Shen, 2001; Reinitz & others, 1994).

Levels of Processing

Simple attention to a stimulus does not completely explain the encoding process. For example, if you paid attention to the word *boat,* you might process the word at three different levels. At the shallowest level, you might notice the shapes of the letters; at

Shallow Processing	Physical and perceptual features are analyzed.	The lines, angles, and contour that make up the physical appearance of an object, such as a car, are detected.
Intermediate Processing	Stimulus is recognized and labeled.	The object is recognized as a car.
Deep Processing	Semantic, meaningful, symbolic characteristics are used.	Associations connected with *car* are brought to mind—you think about the Porsche or Ferrari you hope to buy or the fun you and friends had on spring break when you drove a car to the beach.

(left axis) Depth of Processing

FIGURE 8.3 Depth of Processing
According to the levels of processing theory of memory, deeper processing of stimuli produces better memory of them.

an intermediate level, you might think of characteristics of the word (such as that it rhymes with *coat*); and, at the deepest level, you might think about the kind of boat you would like to own and the last time you went fishing.

This model of the encoding process was proposed by Fergus Craik and Robert Lockhart (1972). Their **levels of processing theory** states that encoding is on a continuum from shallow to deep, with deeper processing producing better memory (see figure 8.3):

- *Shallow level.* The sensory or physical features of stimuli are analyzed. For instance, we might detect the lines, angles, and contours of a printed word's letters or detect a sound's frequency, duration, and loudness (recall the discussion of feature detection in chapter 5).
- *Intermediate level.* The stimulus is recognized and given a label. For example, we identify a four-legged, barking object as a dog.
- *Deepest level.* Information is processed semantically, in terms of its meaning. At this deepest level, we make associations. For example, we might associate the barking dog with a warning of danger or with good times such as playing fetch with a pet. The more associations, the deeper the processing (Lee, Cheung, & Wurm, 2000; Otten, Henson, & Rugg, 2001).

A number of studies have shown that people's memories improve when they make associations to stimuli and use deep processing, as opposed to attending only to the physical aspects of the stimuli and using shallow processing (Baddeley, 1998). For example, researchers have found that if you encode something meaningful about a face and make associations with it, you are more likely to remember it (Harris & Kay, 1995). You might attach meaning to the face of a person in your introductory psychology class by noting that she reminds you of someone you have seen on TV, and you might associate her face with your psychology class.

Elaboration

Cognitive psychologists have recognized that good encoding of a memory depends on more than just depth of processing. Within deep processing, the more extensive the processing, the better the memory (Craik & Tulving, 1975). **Elaboration** is the extensiveness of processing at any given level. For example, rather than memorizing the definition of *memory*, you would do better to learn the concept of memory by coming up with some examples of how information enters your mind, how it is stored, and how you can retrieve it. Thinking of examples of a concept is a good way to understand it. Self-reference is another effective way to elaborate information (Czienskowski & Gilojohann, 2002) (see figure 8.4). For example, if the word *win* is on a list of words to remember, you might think of the last time you won a bicycle race; or if the word *cook* appears, you might imagine the last time you cooked dinner. In general, deep elaboration—elaborate processing of meaningful information—is an excellent way to remember.

The more that you elaborate about an event, the better your memory of the event will be. For example, if you were at an open-air rock concert and you encoded information about how large the crowd was, who accompanied you, which songs you heard, how powerful the performances were, what the weather was like, and other vivid sights, sounds, and smells, you probably will remember the concert clearly.

levels of processing theory States that memory is on a continuum from shallow to deep, with deeper processing producing better memory.

elaboration The extensiveness of processing at any given level of memory.

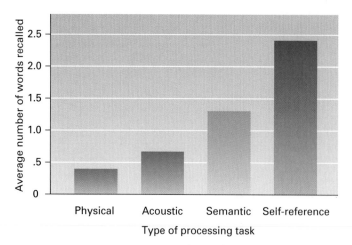

FIGURE 8.4 Memory Improves When Self-Referencing Is Used
In one study, researchers asked participants to remember lists of words according to the words' physical, acoustic (sound), semantic (meaning), or self-referent characteristics. As can be seen, when individuals generated self-references for the words, they remembered them better.

One reason elaboration produces good memory is that it adds to the *distinctiveness* of the "memory codes" (Ellis, 1987). To remember a piece of information, such as a name, an experience, or a fact about geography, you need to search for the code that contains this information among the mass of codes contained in long-term memory. The search process is easier if the memory code is somehow unique (Hunt & Kelly, 1996). The situation is not unlike searching for a friend at a crowded airport. A friend who is 6 feet tall and has flaming red hair will be easier to find in a crowd than a friend who is 5 feet, 9 inches tall with brown hair. Similarly, highly distinctive memory codes can be more easily differentiated.

Also, as encoding becomes more elaborate, more information is stored. And as more information is stored, the likelier it is that the code will be distinctive—that is, easy to differentiate from other memory codes. For example, if you witness a bank robbery and observe that the getaway car is a red 1987 or 1988 Pontiac with tinted windows and spinners on the wheels, your memory of the car is more distinctive than the memory of a person who notices only that the getaway car is red.

Neuroscience research has shown a link between elaboration during encoding and brain activity. In one study, individuals were placed in magnetic resonance imaging (MRI) machines (which were discussed in chapter 3), and one word was flashed every 2 seconds on a screen inside (Wagner & others, 1998). Initially, the individuals simply noted whether the words were in uppercase or lowercase letters. As the study progressed, they were asked to determine whether each word was concrete, such as *chair* or *book*, or abstract, such as *love* or *democracy*. In this study, the participants showed more neural activity and better memory during the "concrete/abstract" word task than they did when they were asked merely to state whether the words were uppercase or lowercase. The researchers' conclusions: Greater elaboration of information is linked with neural activity, especially in the brain's left frontal lobe, and with improved memory.

Imagery

Recall from the beginning of the chapter the story of S.'s phenomenal memory. Imagery helped S. remember complicated lists of items and information. For example, S. once was asked to remember the following formula:

$$N \cdot \sqrt{d^2 \cdot \frac{85}{VX}} \cdot 3\sqrt{\frac{276^2 \cdot 86x}{n^2 V \cdot \pi 264}} \, n^2 b$$
$$= sv \, \frac{1624}{32^2} \cdot r^2 s$$

S. studied the formula for 7 minutes and then reported how he memorized it. Notice in his account of this process, which follows, how he used imagery:

Neiman *(N)* came out and jabbed at the ground with his cane (·). He looked up at a tall tree, which resembled the square-root sign (√), and thought to himself: "No wonder this tree has withered and begun to expose its roots. After all, it was here when I built these two houses" (*d²*). Once again he poked his cane (·). Then he said: "The houses are old, I'll have to get rid of them; the sale will bring in far more money." He had originally invested 85,000 in them (85) . . . (Luria, 1968)

S.'s complete story was four times this length. But the imagery in the story he created must have been powerful, because S. remembered the formula perfectly 15 years later without any advance notice!

You may not be capable of this feat, but you still are likely to use imagery to encode information. Here's a demonstration: How many windows are in your apartment or house? If you live in a dorm room with only one or two windows, this question might be too easy. If so, how many windows are in your parents' home? Few of us have ever set out to memorize this information, but many of us can come up with a good answer, especially if we use imagery to "reconstruct" each room. We take a mental walk through the house, counting windows as we go.

For many years psychologists ignored the role of imagery in memory because behaviorists believed it to be too "mentalistic." But the studies of Allan Paivio (1971, 1986) documented how imagery can improve memory. Paivio argued that memory is stored in one of two ways: as a verbal code (a word or a label) or as an image code. Paivio thinks that the image code, which is highly detailed and distinctive, produces better memory. His *dual-code hypothesis* claims that memory for images is better than memory for words because the memory for the image is stored both as an image code *and* as a verbal code. Thus we have two potential avenues by which information can be retrieved.

Although imagery is widely accepted as an important aspect of memory, psychologists still debate whether we have separate codes for words and images. Nonetheless, imagery has been found helpful in many memory tasks. It is especially useful in remembering associations. Imagery techniques also have helped students learn a foreign language. More about imagery appears later in the chapter, in the discussion of strategies for improving memory. For now, just keep in mind that if you need to remember a list of things, forming mental images will help (Shepard, 1996).

Review and Sharpen Your Thinking

2 **Explain how memories are encoded.**
- Summarize how attention is involved in memory.
- Describe the levels of processing involved in memory.
- Discuss elaboration.
- Know about the role of imagery in memory.

Think of a common object or location that you see every day (for example, your alarm clock or the place where you live) but that is not currently in your sight. Draw the object or location, or write a detailed description of it. Then compare your results with the real thing. What differences do you notice? Does what you learned about encoding help to explain the differences?

mhhe.com/santrockp7

For study tools related to this learning goal, see the Study Guide, the CD-ROM, and the Online Learning Center.

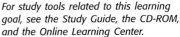

MEMORY STORAGE 3

Sensory Memory　　**Short-Term Memory**　　**Long-Term Memory**

What are the main features of the three systems of memory storage?

The quality of encoding is not the only thing that determines the quality of memory. The memory also needs to be stored properly after it is encoded. **Storage** encompasses how information is retained over time and how it is represented in memory.

We remember some information for less than a second, some for half a minute, and some for minutes, hours, years, even a lifetime. Richard Atkinson and Richard Shiffrin (1968) formulated an early popular theory of memory that acknowledged the varying life span of memories (see figure 8.5). The **Atkinson-Shiffrin theory** states that memory storage involves a system characterized by time frames:

storage Ways in which information is retained over time and how it is represented in memory.

Atkinson-Shiffrin theory The view that memory involves a sequence of three stages: sensory memory, short-term memory, and long-term memory.

FIGURE 8.5 **Atkinson and Shiffrin's Theory of Memory** In this model, sensory input goes into sensory memory. Through the process of attention, information moves into short-term memory, where it remains for 30 seconds or less, unless it is rehearsed. When the information goes into long-term memory storage, it can be retrieved over the lifetime.

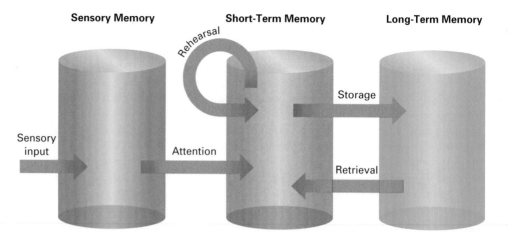

Type of sensory register	
Auditory	Visual
Up to several seconds	About ¼ second

FIGURE 8.6 **Auditory and Visual Sensory Memory** If you hear this bird's call while walking through the woods, your auditory sensory memory holds the information for several seconds. If you see the bird, your visual sensory memory holds the information for only about ¼ of a second.

sensory memory Holds information from the world in its original form only for an instant, not much longer than the brief time it is exposed to the visual, auditory, and other senses.

- *Sensory memory:* time frames of a fraction of a second to several seconds
- *Short-term memory:* time frames up to 30 seconds
- *Long-term memory:* time frames up to a lifetime

As you read about these three memory storage systems, you will find that time frame is not the only thing that makes them different from one another. Each type of memory operates in a distinctive way and has a special purpose.

Sensory Memory

Sensory memory holds information from the world in its original sensory form for only an instant, not much longer than the brief time it is exposed to the visual, auditory, and other senses (Rainer & Miller, 2002). Sensory memory is very rich and detailed, but the information in it is very quickly lost unless certain processes are engaged in that transfer it into short-term or long-term memory.

Think about all the sights and sounds you encounter as you walk to class on a typical morning. Literally thousands of stimuli come into your fields of vision and hearing—cracks in the sidewalk, chirping birds, a noisy motorcycle, the blue sky, faces of hundreds of people. We do not process all of these stimuli, but we do process a number of them. In general, you process many more stimuli at the sensory level than you consciously notice. Sensory memory retains this information from your senses, including a large portion of what you think you ignore.

But sensory memory does not retain the information very long (Grau & others, 2001). *Echoic memory* (from the word "echo") is the name given to auditory sensory memory, which is retained for up to several seconds. *Iconic memory* (from the word *icon,* which means "image") is the name given to visual sensory memory, which is retained only for about one-fourth of a second (see figure 8.6). The sensory memory for other senses, such as smell and touch, has received little attention.

The first scientific research on sensory memory focused on iconic memory. In George Sperling's (1960) classic study, participants were presented with patterns of stimuli such as those in figure 8.7. As you look at the letters, you have no trouble recognizing them. But Sperling flashed the letters on a screen for very brief intervals, about one-twentieth of a second. After a pattern was flashed on the screen, the participants could report only four or five letters. With such short exposure, reporting all nine letters was impossible.

Some of the participants in Sperling's study reported feeling that, for an instant, they could *see* all nine letters within a briefly flashed pattern. But they ran into trouble when they tried to *name* all the letters they had initially *seen.* One hypothesis to explain this experience is that all nine letters were initially processed as far as the iconic sensory memory level. This is why all nine letters were *seen.* However, forgetting was so rapid that the participants could name only a handful of letters before the others were lost from sensory memory.

Sperling reasoned that if all nine letters were actually processed in sensory memory, they should all be available for a brief time. To test this possibility, Sperling sounded a low, medium, or high tone just after a pattern of letters was shown. The participants were told that the tone was a signal to report only the letters from the bottom, middle, or top row, respectively. Under these conditions, the participants performed much better, suggesting a brief memory for most or all of the letters in the display.

FIGURE 8.7 Sperling's Sensory Memory Experiment This array of stimuli is similar to those flashed for about ¹/₂₀ of a second to the participants in Sperling's study.

Short-Term Memory

Much information goes no further than the stage of sensory memory of sounds and sights. This information is retained for only a brief instant. However, some of the information, especially that to which we pay attention, is transferred to short-term memory. **Short-term memory** is a limited-capacity memory system in which information is usually retained for only as long as 30 seconds unless strategies are used to retain it longer. Compared with sensory memory, short-term memory is limited in capacity, but it can store information for a longer time.

The limited capacity of short-term memory was examined by George Miller (1956) in a classic paper with a catchy title, "The Magical Number Seven, Plus or Minus Two." Miller pointed out that on many tasks individuals are limited in how much information they can keep track of without external aids. Usually the limit is in the range of 7 ± 2 items. The most widely cited example of the 7 ± 2 phenomenon involves *memory span*, which is the number of digits an individual can report back in order after a single presentation of them. Most college students can remember lists of 8 or 9 digits without making errors. Longer lists, however, pose problems because they exceed short-term memory capacity. If you rely on simple short-term memory to retain longer lists of items, you probably will make errors.

Chunking and Rehearsal Two ways to improve short-term memory are chunking and rehearsal. *Chunking* involves grouping or "packing" information that exceeds the 7 ± 2 memory span into higher order units that can be remembered as single units. In essence, chunking is a form of memory encoding: specifically, elaboration. It works by making large amounts of information more manageable.

For an example of how chunking works, consider this simple list of words: *hot, city, book, forget, tomorrow,* and *smile.* Try to hold these words in memory for a moment, then write them down. If you recalled the words, you succeeded in holding 34 letters, grouped into seven chunks, in your memory. Now try another example of how chunking works. Hold the following in memory and then write it down:

O LDH ARO LDAN DYO UNGB EN

How did you do? Don't feel bad if you did poorly. This string of letters is very difficult to remember, even though it is arranged in chunks. However, if you chunk the letters to form the meaningful words, "Old Harold and Young Ben," they become much easier to remember. Recall that this sort of deep, semantic processing during encoding helps with memory tasks.

Another way to improve short-term memory involves *rehearsal,* the conscious repetition of information. Information stored in short-term memory lasts half a minute or less without rehearsal. However, if rehearsal is not interrupted, information can be retained indefinitely. Rehearsal is often verbal, giving the impression of an inner voice, but it can also be visual or spatial, giving the impression of a private inner eye. One way to use your visualization skills is to maintain the appearance of an object or scene for a period of time after you have viewed it. People who are unusually good at this task are said to have *eidetic imagery,* or a photographic memory. All of us can do this to some degree, but a small number of individuals may be

short-term memory A limited-capacity memory system in which information is retained for only as long as 30 seconds unless strategies are used to retain it longer.

Working Memory

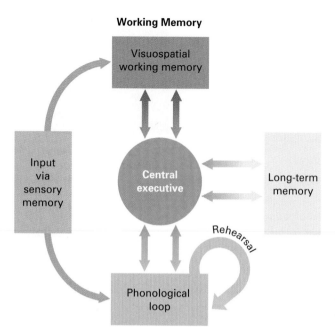

FIGURE 8.8 **Working Memory** In Baddeley's working memory model, working memory is like a mental workbench where a great deal of information processing is carried out. Working memory consists of three main components: The phonological loop and visuospatial working memory serve as assistants, helping the central executive do its work. Input from sensory memory goes to the phonological loop, where information about speech is stored and rehearsal takes place, and visuospatial working memory, where visual and spatial information, including imagery, are stored. Working memory is a limited-capacity system, and information is stored there for only a brief time. Working memory interacts with long-term memory, using information from long-term memory in its work and transmitting information to long-term memory for longer storage.

working memory A three-part system that temporarily holds information. Working memory is a kind of mental workbench on which information is manipulated and assembled to perform other cognitive tasks.

so good at maintaining an image that they literally "see" the page of a textbook as they try to remember information during a test. However, eidetic imagery is so rare it has been difficult to study; some psychologists even doubt its existence (Gray & Gummerman, 1975).

Rehearsal works best when we need to briefly remember a list of numbers or items. When we have to remember information for longer periods of time, as when we are studying for a test coming up next week, tomorrow, or even an hour from now, other strategies usually work better. A main reason rehearsal does not work well for retaining information over the long term is that rehearsal often involves just rotely repeating information without imparting any meaning to it. Remembering information over the long term works better when we add meaning to it, which is again an example of the importance of deep, semantic processing.

Working Memory Some contemporary experts on memory believe that Atkinson and Shiffrin's theory of the three time-linked memory systems is too simplistic (Baddeley, 1998, 2001; Bartlett, 2001). They believe that memory does not always work in a neatly packaged three-stage sequence such as Atkinson and Shiffrin proposed; and they think that both short-term and long-term memory are far more complex and dynamic. For example, some experts believe that short-term memory uses long-term memory's contents in more flexible ways than simply retrieving information from it (Murdock, 1999). And they believe that short-term memory involves far more than rehearsal and passive storage of information. I now examine the working-memory view of short-term memory.

British psychologist Alan Baddeley (1993, 1998, 2000, 2001) proposed the concept of **working memory,** a three-part system that temporarily holds information as people perform cognitive tasks. Working memory is a kind of mental "workbench" on which information is manipulated and assembled to help us comprehend written and spoken language, make decisions, and solve problems. Notice that working memory is not like a passive storehouse with shelves to store information until it moves to long-term memory. Rather it is an active memory system (Nyberg & others, 2002).

Figure 8.8 shows Baddeley's view of the three components of working memory. Think of them as an executive (the central executive) who has two assistants (the phonological loop and visuospatial working memory) to help do the work.

1. The *phonological loop* is specialized to briefly store speech-based information about the sounds of language. The phonological loop contains two separate components: an acoustic code, which decays in a few seconds, and rehearsal, which allows individuals to repeat the words in the phonological store.
2. *Visuospatial working memory* stores visual and spatial information, including visual imagery (Logie, 1995). Visuospatial working memory also has been called the *visuospatial scratch pad.* As in the case of the phonological loop, the capacity of visuospatial working memory is limited. For example, if you try to put too many items in visuospatial working memory, you can't represent them accurately enough to successfully retrieve them. The phonological loop and visuospatial memory function independently (Reed, 2000). You could rehearse numbers in the phonological loop while making spatial arrangements of letters in visuospatial working memory (Baddeley & Hitch, 1974).

3. The *central executive* integrates information not only from the phonological loop and visuospatial working memory but also from long-term memory. In Baddeley's (2000, 2001) view, the central executive plays important roles in attention, planning, and organizing. The central executive acts much like a supervisor who monitors which information and issues deserve attention and which should be ignored. It also selects which strategies to use to process information and solve problems. As with the other two components of working memory— phonological loop and visuospatial working memory—the central executive has a limited capacity.

The concept of working memory can help us understand how brain damage influences cognitive skills (LaBar & others, 2002). For example, some types of amnesiacs perform well on working memory tasks, but not on long-term memory tasks. Another group of patients have normal long-term memory abilities yet do very poorly on working memory tasks. One such patient has good long-term memory despite having a memory span of only two digits (Baddeley, 1992). The phonological loop was the source of this patient's memory problem. Because he could not maintain verbal codes in the loop, his memory span suffered. He also had difficulty learning new associations between words and nonsense sounds. Working memory deficits also are involved in Alzheimer's disease—a progressive, irreversible brain disorder in older adults that was discussed in chapter 4. Baddeley (1998) believes the central executive of the working memory model is the culprit—Alzheimer's patients have great difficulty coordinating different mental activities, one of the central executive's functions.

Let's examine another aspect of life in which working memory is involved. In one recent study, verbal working memory was impaired by negative emotion (Gray, 2001). Recall from chapter 2 that writing about emotionally traumatic experiences was linked with improvement in college students' health (Pennebaker, 1997, 2001). Might writing about negative events also produce improvement in working memory? In one recent study, college students who wrote about a negative emotional event showed sizable improvement in working memory compared with students who wrote about a positive event and those in a control group who wrote about their daily schedule (Klein & Boals, 2001). The expressive-writing effect on working memory occurred only when students had fewer intrusive and avoidant thoughts. In the study, improvement in working memory was associated with higher grade point averages. An important implication of this study is its demonstration that working memory is malleable and can be affected by an experience, such as expressive writing (Miyake, 2001). For example, students with math anxiety often experience working memory deficits when doing math problems because of intrusive thoughts and worry about performance (Ashcraft & Kirk, 2001). Such students might benefit from writing about their math anxiety.

Long-Term Memory

Long-term memory is a relatively permanent type of memory that stores huge amounts of information for a long time. The capacity of long-term memory is indeed staggering. John von Neumann, a distinguished computer scientist, put the size at 2.8×10^{20} (280 quintillion) bits, which in practical terms means that our storage capacity is virtually unlimited. Von Neumann assumed that we never forget anything, but even considering that we do forget things, we can hold several billion times more information than a large computer.

Long-term memory is complex, as figure 8.9 shows. At the top level, it is divided into substructures of explicit memory and implicit memory. Explicit memory can be further subdivided into episodic and semantic memory. Implicit memory includes the systems involved in procedural memory, priming, and classical conditioning.

In simple terms, explicit memory has to do with remembering who, what, where, when, and why; implicit memory has to do with remembering how. To explore the

long-term memory A relatively permanent type of memory that holds huge amounts of information for a long period of time.

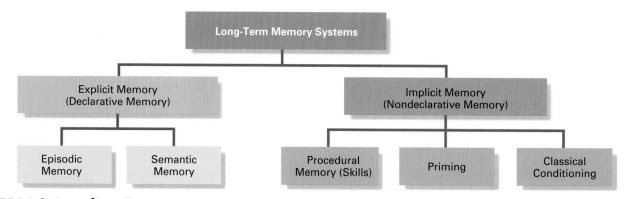

FIGURE 8.9 Systems of Long-Term Memory

distinction, let's look at a person known as H. M. He had a severe case of epilepsy and underwent surgery in 1953 that involved removing the hippocampus and a portion of the temporal lobes of both hemispheres in his brain. (The location and functions of these areas of the brain were discussed in chapter 3.) His epilepsy improved, but something devastating happened to his memory. The most dramatic problem he developed was an inability to form new memories that outlive working memory. H. M.'s memory time frame is only a few minutes at most, so he lives, as he has done since 1953, in a perpetual present and cannot remember past events (explicit memory). In contrast, his memory of how to do things (implicit memory) was less affected. For example, he can learn new physical tasks. In one such task, H. M. was asked to trace the outline of a star-shaped figure while he was able to view the figure and his hand only through a mirror. This is a task that most people find difficult in the beginning. Over 3 days of training, H. M. learned this task as effectively and rapidly as normal individuals. On the 2nd and 3rd days, he began at the level he had achieved the previous day (a success in implicit memory), even though he was completely unaware that he had previously practiced the task (a failure in explicit memory). H. M.'s situation clearly demonstrates a distinction between explicit memory, which was dramatically impaired in his case, and implicit memory, which in his case was less influenced by his surgery.

Let's now explore the subsystems of explicit and implicit memory. After you read about these basic structures, you will learn about the theories developed to explain how they are organized. You will also read about recent discoveries in neuroscience that shed light on where in the brain memory is stored.

Explicit Memory **Explicit memory** (or **declarative memory**) is the conscious recollection of information, such as specific facts or events and, at least in humans, information that can be verbally communicated (Tulving, 1989, 2000). Examples of explicit, or declarative, memory include recounting the events of a movie you have seen and describing a basic principle of psychology to someone. However, you do not need to be talking to be using explicit memory. Simply sitting and consciously reflecting about Einstein's theory of relativity or the date you had last weekend involves explicit memory.

Episodic and Semantic Memory Canadian cognitive psychologist Endel Tulving (1972, 1989, 2000) has been the foremost advocate of distinguishing between two subtypes of explicit memory: episodic and semantic. **Episodic memory** is the retention of information about the where and when of life's happenings (Fortin, Agster & Eichenbaum, 2002). It is autobiographical. For example, episodic memory includes the details of what it was like when your younger brother or sister was born, what happened on your first date, what you were doing when you heard of the terrorist attacks in New York City and Washington, D.C., and what you had for breakfast this morning.

Semantic memory is a person's knowledge about the world. It includes your fields of expertise, general knowledge of the sort you learned in school, and everyday

explicit memory (declarative memory) The conscious recollection of information, such as specific facts or events and, at least in humans, information that can be verbally communicated.

episodic memory The retention of information about the where and when of life's happenings.

semantic memory A person's knowledge about the world.

Characteristic	Episodic Memory	Semantic Memory
Units	Events, episodes	Facts, ideas, concepts
Organization	Time	Concepts
Emotion	More important	Less important
Retrieval process	Deliberate (effortful)	Automatic
Retrieval report	"I remember"	"I know"
Education	Irrelevant	Relevant
Intelligence	Irrelevant	Relevant
Legal testimony	Admissible in court	Inadmissible in court

FIGURE 8.10 Some Differences Between Episodic and Semantic Memory The above characteristics have been proposed as the main ways to differentiate episodic and semantic memory.

knowledge about meanings of words, famous individuals, important places, and common things. For example, semantic memory is involved in a person's knowledge of chess, of geometry, and of who Nelson Mandela and Mahatma Gandhi are. An important aspect of semantic memory is that it appears to be independent of an individual's personal identity with the past. You can access a fact—such as that Lima is the capital of Peru—and not have the foggiest notion of when and where you learned it.

Several examples help to clarify the distinction between episodic and semantic memory. Your memory of your first day on campus involves episodic memory. If you take a history class, your memory of the information you need to know to do well on the next test involves semantic memory.

Consider also that in a certain type of amnesiac state, a person might forget entirely who she is—her name, family, career, and all other information about herself—yet she can talk and demonstrate general knowledge about the world. Her episodic memory is impaired, but her semantic memory is functioning. Endel Tulving (1989) reported an especially dramatic case of this type, a young man named K. C. After suffering a motorcycle accident, K. C. lost virtually all use of his episodic memory. The loss was so profound that he was unable to consciously recollect a single thing that had ever happened to him. At the same time, K. C.'s semantic memory was sufficiently preserved that he could learn about his past as a set of facts, just as he would learn about another person's life. He could report, for example, that the saddest day of his life was when his brother died of drowning about 10 years before. But further questioning revealed that K. C. had no conscious memory of the event. He simply knew about the drowning because he was able to recall—apparently through use of his semantic memory—what he had been told about his brother by other members of his family.

Some aspects of the episodic/semantic distinction are summarized in figure 8.10. Although the distinctions listed have attracted considerable attention, they remain controversial. One criticism is that many cases of explicit, declarative memory are neither purely episodic nor purely semantic but fall in a gray area in between. Consider your memory for what you studied last night. You probably added knowledge to your semantic memory—that was, after all, the reason you were studying. You probably remember where you were studying, as well as about when you started and when you stopped. You probably also can remember some minor occurrences, such as a burst of loud laughter from the room next door or the coffee you spilled on the desk. Is episodic or semantic memory involved here? Tulving (1983, 2000) argues that semantic and episodic systems often work together in forming new memories. In such cases, the memory that ultimately is formed might consist of an autobiographical episode *and* semantic information.

Prospective Memory   Currently a hot topic in episodic memory research is *prospective memory* (Burgess, Quayle, & Frith, 2001; McDaniel & Einstein, 2000; Kliegel & others,

2001). The main focus of this chapter is **retrospective memory,** which is remembering the past. **Prospective memory** involves remembering information about doing something in the future; it includes memory for intentions. Many of us have somewhat embarrassing or difficult experiences when prospective memory fails. For example, we might forget to buy a food item at the store, miss an appointment, or forget that a homework assignment is due. Prospective memory includes both *timing*—when to do something—and *content*—what it is we have to do.

A distinction can be made between time-based and event-based prospective memory. *Time-based* prospective memory is your intention to engage in a given behavior after a specified amount of time has gone by (such as an intention to make a phone call to someone in one hour). In *event-based* prospective memory, you engage in the intended behavior when it is elicited by some external event or cue (such as giving a message to a roommate when you see him or her). Researchers have found that the cues available in event-based prospective memory make it more effective than time-based prospective memory (Einstein & McDaniel, 1996; McDaniel & Einstein, 1993).

Some failures in prospective memory are referred to as "absentmindedness." We become more absentminded when we become preoccupied with something else, are distracted by something, or are under a lot of time pressures (Matlin, 2001). Absentmindedness often involves a breakdown between attention and memory storage (Schacter, 2001). Absentmindedness may especially be a problem when we have too little time or are too distracted to elaboratively encode something we need to remember. We spend a great deal of our lives on autopilot, which helps us to perform routine tasks effectively but also makes us vulnerable to absentminded errors.

Continuing research on prospective memory is providing new clues that will help people improve their memories (d'Ydewalle, Bouckaert, & Brunfaut, 2001). In one recent study, individuals were given 4 minutes to recall what they did yesterday, last week, or last year (retrospective memories) and 4 minutes to recall what they intended to do tomorrow, next week, or next year (prospective memories; Maylor, Chater, & Brown, 2001). More prospective memories were recalled than retrospective memories. Researchers also have found that older adults perform worse on prospective memory tasks than younger adults do (Cherry & LeCompte, 1999; Einstein & others, 2000).

Implicit (Nondeclarative Memory)   In addition to explicit memory, there is a type of long-term memory that is related to nonconsciously remembering skills and sensory perceptions rather than consciously remembering facts. **Implicit memory (or nondeclarative memory)** is memory in which behavior is affected by prior experience without that experience being consciously recollected. Examples of implicit memory include the skills of playing tennis, riding a bicycle, and typing. Another example of implicit memory is the repetition in your mind of a song you heard playing in the supermarket, even though you did not consciously attend to what music was playing.

Three subsystems of implicit memory are procedural memory, priming, and classical conditioning. All instances of these subsystems consist of memories that you are not aware of, although they predispose you to behave in certain ways (Schacter, 2000).

Procedural memory involves memory for skills. For example, as I am typing the letters in this sentence, I'm not conscious of where the keys are for the various letters, yet my well-learned, nonconscious skill of typing allows me to hit the right keys. Once you have learned to drive a car, you remember how to do it: You do not have to consciously remember how to drive the car as you put the key in the ignition, turn the steering wheel, push on the gas pedal, hit the brakes, and so on.

To illustrate the distinction between explicit memory and procedural memory, imagine you are at Wimbledon. Venus Williams moves gracefully for a wide forehand, finishes her follow-through, runs quickly back to the center of the court, pushes off

retrospective memory Remembering the past.

prospective memory Remembering information about doing something in the future.

implicit memory (nondeclarative memory) Memory in which behavior is affected by prior experience without that experience being consciously recollected.

procedural memory Memory for skills

FRANK AND ERNEST   by Bob Thaves

FRANK & ERNEST reprinted by permission of Newspaper Enterprise Association, Inc.

for a short ball, and volleys the ball for a winner. If we asked her about this rapid sequence of movements, she probably would have difficulty explaining each move. In contrast, if we asked her who her toughest opponent is, she might quickly respond, "my sister." In the first instance, she was unable to verbally describe exactly what she had done because her actions had been based on procedural memory. In the second, she had no problem answering our question because it was based on explicit memory.

Priming is the activation of information that people already have in storage to help them remember new information better and faster (Badgaiyan, Schacter, & Alpert, 2001; Huber & others, 2001). In a common demonstration of priming, individuals study a list of words (such as *hope, walk,* and *cake*). Then they are given a standard recognition task to assess explicit memory. They must select all of the words that appeared on the first list—for example, "Did you see the word *hope*? Did you see the word *form*?" Then participants are given a "stem-completion" task, which assesses implicit memory. In this task, they are shown a list of incomplete words (for example, *ho__, wa__, ca__*), called word stems, and are told to fill in the blanks with whatever word comes to mind. The results show that individuals fill in the blanks with words they had previously studied more often than would be expected if they were filling them in randomly. For example, they are more likely to complete the stem *ho__* with *hope* than with *hole.* This is so even when individuals did not recognize the words on the earlier recognition task. Because priming occurs even when explicit memory for previous information is not required, it is assumed to be an involuntary and nonconscious process (Hauptmann & Karni, 2002).

Another type of implicit memory is found in *classical conditioning,* a form of learning discussed in chapter 7. Recall that classical conditioning involves the automatic learning of associations between stimuli. For instance, a person who is constantly criticized may develop high blood pressure or other physical problems. Classically conditioned associations such as this involve nonconscious, implicit memory.

How Memory Is Organized Cognitive psychologists have been successful in classifying the types of long-term memory. But explaining what forms long-term memory does not address the question of how the different types of memory are organized for storage. The word *organized* is important: Memories are not haphazardly stored but are instead carefully sorted.

Here's a demonstration. Recall the 12 months of the year as quickly as you can. How long did it take you? What was the order of your recall? Chances are you listed them within a few seconds in "natural," chronological order (January, February, March, and so on). Now try to remember the months in alphabetical order. Did you make any errors? How long did it take you? It should be obvious that your memory for the months of the year is organized in a particular way. Indeed, one of memory's most distinctive features is its organization. Researchers have found that if people are encouraged to simply organize material, their memories of the material improve, even

priming A type of implicit memory; information that people already have in storage is activated to help them remember new information better and faster.

FIGURE 8.11 Semantic Networks in the Organization of Long-Term Memory Originally, the theory of semantic networks envisioned long-term memory as a hierarchy of concepts with nodes (branching points) at different levels of abstraction. Notice how the information becomes more detailed and specific as you move through the levels of the hierarchy in this model. Some psychologists have challenged this representation as too "clean" to portray the true complexity of our representation processes.

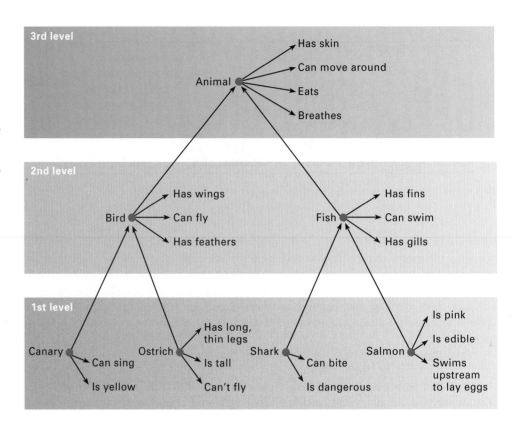

if no warning is given that their memories will be tested (Mandler, 1980). Psychologists have developed four main theories of how long-term memory is organized: hierarchies, semantic networks, schemas, and connectionist networks.

Hierarchies In many instances we remember facts better when we organize them hierarchically (Bruning, Schraw, & Ronning, 1999). A *hierarchy* is a system in which items are organized from general to specific classes. One common example is the organization chart showing the relationship of units in a business or a school, with the CEO or president at the top, the vice presidents or deans at the next level, and the managers or professors at a third level. This textbook also is organized hierarchically—with four levels of headings—to help you understand how the various bits of information in the book are related; the table of contents provides a visual representation of the hierarchy of the top two levels of headings.

In an early research study, Gordon Bower and his colleagues (1969) showed the importance of hierarchical organization in memory. Participants who were given the words in hierarchies remembered them better than those who were given the words in random groupings.

Semantic Networks We often use semantic networks to organize material in episodic memory (a form of explicit memory). One of the first network theories claimed that our memories can be envisioned as a complex network of nodes that stand for labels or concepts (see figure 8.11). The network was assumed to be hierarchically arranged, with more concrete concepts (canary, for example) nested under more abstract concepts (bird).

More recently, cognitive psychologists realized that such hierarchical networks are too simple to describe the way human cognition actually works (Shanks, 1991). For example, people take longer to answer the true-or-false statement "An ostrich is a bird" than they do to answer the statement "A canary is a bird." Memory researchers now see the semantic network as more irregular and distorted: a typical bird, such as a canary, is closer to the node or center of the category *bird* than is the atypical

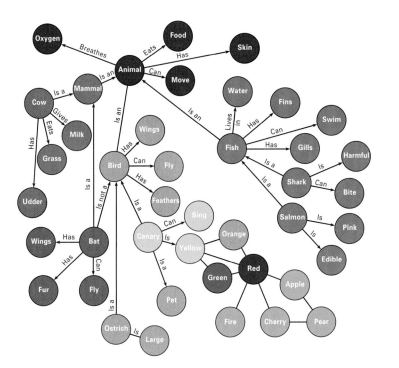

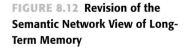

FIGURE 8.12 **Revision of the Semantic Network View of Long-Term Memory**

ostrich. Figure 8.12 shows an example of the revised model, which allows us to show how typical information is while still illustrating how it is linked together.

We add new material to a semantic network by placing it in the middle of the appropriate region of memory. The new material is gradually tied in to related nodes in the surrounding network. This model reveals why, if you cram for a test, you will not remember the information over the long term. The new material is not woven into the long-term web. In contrast, discussing the material or incorporating it into a research paper interweaves it and connects it to other knowledge you have. These multiple connections increase the probability that you will be able to retrieve the information many months or even years later. The concept of multiple connections fits with the description of the importance of elaboration in memory given earlier in the chapter.

Schemas Imagine that you overhear the following conversation between two college students living in a dorm:

Manuel: Did you order it?
Jordan: Yeah, it will be here in about 45 minutes.
Manuel: Well, I have to leave before then but save me a couple of slices, okay?

Do you know what these two students are talking about? You likely guessed that they were talking about pizza, but how did you know this? The word *pizza* was never mentioned. But you knew what they were talking about because you activated your concept of "pizza" or "ordering pizza for delivery" and used that concept to comprehend the situation.

When we store information in memory, we often fit it into the collection of information that already exists, as you did in comprehending the pizza delivery situation. A **schema** is a preexisting mental concept or framework that helps people to organize and interpret information. Schemas from prior encounters with the environment influence the way we encode, make inferences about, and retrieve information (Jou, Shanteau, & Harris, 1996).

Semantic network theories assume that memory involves specific facts with clear links from one to another. In contrast, schema theory claims that long-term memory is not very exact. We seldom find precisely the memory that we want, or at least not

schema A preexisting mental concept or framework that helps people to organize and interpret information.

Shown here are representative scripts from a Japanese tea ceremony, a Western dinner, and an Ethiopian meal. *With which script do you feel most comfortable? least comfortable?*

One night two young men from Egulac went down to the river to hunt seals, and while they were there it became foggy and calm. Then they heard war cries, and they thought: "Maybe this is a war party." They escaped to the shore, and hid behind a log. Now canoes came up, and they heard the noise of paddles, and they saw one canoe coming up to them. There were five men in the canoe and they said:

"What do you think? We wish to take you along. We are going up the river to make war on the people."

One of the young men said: "I have no arrows."

"Arrows are in the canoe," they said.

"I will not go along, I might be killed. My relatives do not know where I have gone. But you," he said, turning to the other, "may go with them."

So one of the young men went, but the other returned home.

And the warriors went up the river to a town on the other side of Kalama. The people came down to the water, and they began to fight, and many were killed. But presently the young man heard one of the warriors say: "Quick, let us go home: that Indian has been hit." Now he thought: "Oh, they are ghosts." He did not feel sick, but they said he had been shot.

So the canoes went back to Egulac and the young man went ashore to his house, and made a fire. And he told everybody and said: "Behold I accompanied the ghosts, and we went to fight. Many of our fellows were killed, and many of those who attacked us were killed. They said I was hit, and I did not feel sick."

He told it all, and then he became quiet. When the sun rose he fell down. Something black came out of his mouth. His face became contorted. The people jumped up and cried.

He was dead.

FIGURE 8.13 The War of the Ghosts
When Sir Frederick Bartlett (1932) asked individuals to recall this story, they tended to change details.

script A schema for an event.

all of what we want; hence, we have to reconstruct the rest. Our schemas support the reconstruction process, helping us fill in gaps between our fragmented memories.

The schema theory of memory began with Sir Frederick Bartlett's (1932) studies of how people remember stories. Bartlett was concerned with how people's backgrounds determine what they encode, store, and recall. Bartlett chose stories that sounded strange and were difficult to understand. He reasoned that a person's background, which is encoded in schemas, would reveal itself in the person's reconstruction (modification and distortion) of the story's content. One of Bartlett's stories was called "War of the Ghosts," an English translation of an American Indian folktale (see figure 8.13). The story tells of events that were completely foreign to the experiences of Bartlett's middle- and upper-income British research participants. They read the story twice and then, after 15 minutes, wrote down the tale the best they could remember it.

What interested Bartlett was how differently the participants might reconstruct this and other stories from the original versions. The British participants used both their general schemas for daily experiences and their specific schemas for adventurous ghost stories to reconstruct "War of the Ghosts." Familiar details from the story that fit into the participants' schemas were successfully recalled. But details that departed from the person's schemas were often extensively distorted. For example, the "something black" that came out of the Indian's mouth became blood in one reconstruction and condensed air in another. For one individual the two young men were hunting beavers rather than seals. Another person said the death at the end was due to a fever (this wasn't in the story).

We have schemas not only for stories but also for scenes or spatial layouts (a beach, a bathroom), as well as for common events (going to a restaurant, playing football, writing a term paper). A **script** is a schema for an event (Schank & Abelson, 1977). Scripts often have information about physical features, people, and typical occurrences. This kind of information is helpful when people need to figure out what is happening around them. For example, if you are enjoying your after-dinner coffee in a restaurant and a man in a tuxedo comes over and puts a piece of paper

	Theory		
	Semantic Network	**Schema**	**Connectionist**
Nature of memory units	Abstract concepts ("bird")	Large knowledge structures ("going to a restaurant")	Small units, connections among neurons
Number of units	Tens of thousands	Unknown	Tens of millions
Formation of new memories	Form new nodes	Form new schemas or modify old ones	Increased strength of excitatory connections among neurons
Attention to brain structure	Little	Little	Extensive

FIGURE 8.14 Key Features of Semantic-Network, Schema, and Connectionist Theories

on the table, your script tells you that the man probably is a waiter who has just given you the check. Thus scripts help to organize our storage of memories about events.

Connectionist Networks   Theories of semantic networks and schemas have little or nothing to say about the role of the physical brain in memory. Thus a new theory based on brain research has generated a wave of excitement among psychologists. **Connectionism,** or **parallel distributed processing (PDP),** is the theory that memory is stored throughout the brain in connections between neurons, several of which may work together to process a single memory (Dehaene & Naccache, 2001; Humphreys & others, 2000). Recall that the concept of neural networks was initially discussed in chapter 3 and the concept of parallel processing pathways in chapter 5. This section expands on those discussions and applies these concepts to memory.

In the connectionist view, memories are neither abstract concepts (as in semantic network theories) nor large knowledge structures (as in schema theories). Instead, memories are more like electrical impulses, organized only to the extent that neurons, the connections between them, and their activity are organized. Any piece of knowledge—such as the name of your dog, *Fido*—is embedded in the strengths of hundreds or thousands of connections between neurons and is not limited to a single location. Figure 8.14 compares the semantic-network, schema, and connectionist-network theories of memories.

How does the connectionist process work? A neural activity involving memory, such as remembering the name of your dog, Fido, is distributed across a number of areas of the cerebral cortex. The locations of neural activity, called *nodes,* are interconnected. When a node reaches a critical level of activation, it can affect another node, either by exciting it or inhibiting it, across synapses. We know that the human cerebral cortex contains millions of neurons that are richly interconnected through hundreds of millions of synapses. Because of these synaptic connections, the activity of one neuron can be influenced by many other neurons. For example, if there is an excitatory connection between neurons A and B, activity in neuron A will tend to increase activity in neuron B. If the connection is inhibitory, activity in neuron A will tend to reduce the activity in neuron B. Because of these simple reactions, the connectionist view argues that changes in the strength of synaptic connections are the fundamental bases of memory (O'Brien & Opie, 1999).

Part of the appeal of the connectionist view is that it is consistent with what we know about the way the brain functions. Another part of its appeal is that when programmed on a computer, the connectionist view has been successful in predicting the results of some memory experiments (Marcus, 2001; McClelland & Rumelhart, 1986).

"Why? You cross the road because it's in the script—that's why!"

connectionism (parallel distributed processing) The theory that memory is stored throughout the brain in connections between neurons, several of which may work together to process a single memory.

Its insights into the organization of memory also support brain research undertaken to determine where memories are stored in the brain.

So far I have discussed the time frames of storage, the differentiated systems for storage, and how information is represented in storage. The brain is a key aspect of the connectionist, PDP view of how memory is represented in storage. The next section further examines where memories are stored.

Where Memories Are Stored Karl Lashley (1950) spent a lifetime looking for a location in the brain in which memories are stored. He trained rats to discover the correct pathway in a maze and then cut out various portions of the animals' brains and retested their memory of the maze pathway. After experimenting with thousands of rats, Lashley found that the loss of various cortical areas did not affect rats' ability to remember the pathway. Lashley concluded that memories are not stored in a specific location in the brain. Other researchers, continuing Lashley's quest, would agree that memory storage is diffuse but have developed some new insights. Canadian psychologist Donald Hebb (1949, 1980) suggested that assemblies of cells, distributed over large areas of the cerebral cortex, work together to represent information. Hebb's idea of distributed memory was farsighted.

Neurons and Memory Today, many neuroscientists believe that memory is located in specific sets or circuits of neurons. Brain researcher Larry Squire (1990), for example, says that most memories are probably clustered in groups of about 1,000 neurons. Single neurons, of course, are at work in memory. Researchers who measure the electrical activity of single cells have found that some respond to faces, others to eye or hair color, for example. But, for you to recognize your Uncle Albert, individual neurons that provide information about hair color, size, and other characteristics act together.

Researchers also believe that brain chemicals may be the ink with which memories are written. Ironically, some of the answers to complex questions about neural mechanics of memory come from studies on a very simple experimental animal—the inelegant sea slug. Eric Kandel and James Schwartz (1982) chose this large snail-without-a-shell because of the simple architecture of its nervous system, which consists of only about 10,000 neurons. The sea slug can hardly be called a quick learner or an animal with a good memory, but it is equipped with a reliable reflex. When anything touches the gill on its back, it quickly withdraws it. First the researchers accustomed the sea slug to having its gill prodded. After a while, the animal ignored the prod and stopped withdrawing its gill. Next the researchers applied an electric shock to its tail when they touched the gill. After many rounds of the shock-accompanied prod, the sea slug violently withdrew its gill at the slightest touch. The researchers found that the sea slug remembered this message for hours or even weeks. They also found that shocking the sea slug's gill releases the neurotransmitter serotonin at the synapses of its nervous system, and this chemical release basically provides a reminder that the gill was shocked. This "memory" informs the nerve cell to send out chemical commands to retract the gill the next time it is touched. If nature builds complexity out of simplicity, then the mechanism used by the sea slug may work in the human brain as well.

One concept that has been proposed to understand how memory functions at the neuronal level is *long-term potentiation*. In line with connectionist theory, this concept states that if two neurons are activated at the same time, the connection between them—and thus the memory—may be strengthened (Squire & Kandel, 2000). Long-term potentiation has been demonstrated experimentally by administering a drug that increases the flow of information from one neuron to another across the synapse (Shakesby, Anwyl, & Rowan, 2002). In one study, rats given the drug learned a maze with far fewer mistakes along the way than those not given the drug (Service, 1994). In another study, the genes of mice were altered to increase long-term potentiation in the hippocampus and other areas of the brain (Tang & others, 1999; Tsien, 2000). The mice with the enhanced genes were able to remember information better than mice whose genes had not been altered. These studies raise the possibility of some-

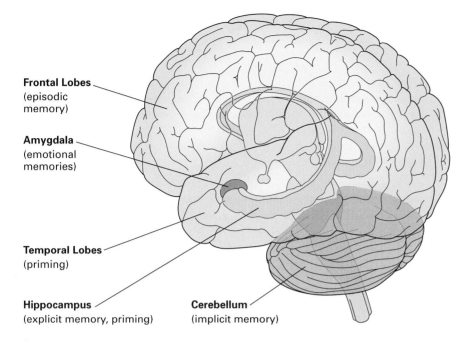

Frontal Lobes
(episodic memory)

Amygdala
(emotional memories)

Temporal Lobes
(priming)

Hippocampus
(explicit memory, priming)

Cerebellum
(implicit memory)

day improving memory through drugs or even gene enhancement to increase neural connections (Schacter, 2001).

Brain Structures and Memory Functions While some neuroscientists are unveiling the cellular basis of memory, others are examining its broadscale architecture in the brain. Larry Squire (1998) believes that memory is distributed throughout the brain and that no specific memory center exists. Many parts of the brain and nervous system participate in the memory of a particular event. Yet memory is localized in the sense that a limited number of brain systems and pathways are involved, and each probably contributes in different ways (Lynch, 1990).

Figure 8.15 shows the location of brain structures involved in different types of long-term memory. For instance, explicit and implicit memory take place in separate areas of the brain.

- *Explicit memory.* Neuroscientists have found that the hippocampus, the temporal lobes in the cerebral cortex, and other areas of the limbic system are involved in explicit memory (Gomez Beldarrain & others, 2002; Zola & Squire, 2001). In many aspects of explicit memory, information is transmitted from the hippocampus to the frontal lobes, which are involved in both retrospective and prospective memory (Burgess & others, 2001). The left frontal lobe is especially active when we encode new information into memory; the right frontal lobe is more active when we subsequently retrieve it (Otten, Henson, & Rugg, 2001). The amygdala, part of the limbic system, is involved in emotional memories (Siegle & others, 2002).
- *Implicit memory.* The cerebellum is involved in the implicit memory required to perform skills (Krupa, Thompson, & Thompson, 1993). Various areas of the cerebral cortex, such as the temporal lobes and hippocampus, function in priming (Jernigan, Ostergaard, & Fennema-Notestine, 2001; Yasuno & others, 2000).

Neuroscientists studying memory have benefited greatly from the use of MRI scans, which allow the tracking of neural activity during cognitive tasks (Pegna & others, 2002). In one research study, participants were shown color photographs of indoor and outdoor scenes while in an MRI machine (Brewer & others, 1998). They were not told that they would be given a memory test about the scenes. After the MRI scans, they were asked which pictures they remembered well, vaguely, or not at all. Their memories were compared with the brain scans. The longer that both prefrontal lobes and a particular region of the hippocampus remained lit up on the MRI scans, the better the participants remembered the scenes. Pictures paired with weak brain activity in these areas were forgotten.

As neuroscientists identify memory circuits in the brain, might the psychological study of memory become unimportant? That's unlikely. First, we are far from working out all of the complexities of neurochemical activity underpinning human memory. And, second, even if we were successful in unraveling the neurochemical mystery of memory, each person will always have a private kingdom of memories influencing her or his thoughts and actions.

mhhe.com/
santrockp7

For study tools related to this learning goal, see the Study Guide, the CD-ROM, and the Online Learning Center.

Review and Sharpen Your Thinking

3 **Discuss how memories are stored.**
- Explain sensory memory.
- Summarize how short-term memory works.
- Describe how long-term memory functions and the role of the brain in memory storage.

How might semantic network theory explain why cramming for a test is not a good way to acquire long-term memory?

4 MEMORY RETRIEVAL

Serial Position Effect

Retrieval of Autobiographical Memories

Eyewitness Testimony

Retrieval Cues and the Retrieval Task

Retrieval of Emotional Memories

How are memories retrieved?

Long-term memory has been compared to a library. Your memory stores information just as a library stores books. We retrieve information in a fashion similar to the process we use to locate and check out a book. To retrieve something from your mental data bank, you search your store of memory to find the relevant information. Memory **retrieval** takes place when information is taken out of storage.

The efficiency with which we retrieve information from memory is impressive. It usually takes only a moment to search through a vast storehouse to find the information we want. When were you born? Who discovered America? What was the name of your first date? Who developed the first psychology laboratory? You can, of course, answer these questions instantly.

But the process of retrieving information from long-term memory is not as precise as the library analogy suggests. When we search through our long-term memory storehouse we don't always find the exact "book" we want. Our memories are affected by a number of things, including the pattern of facts we remember, the situations we associate with memories, and the personal or emotional context. Or we might find the book we want but discover that only several pages are intact. We have to reconstruct the rest. There has been a flurry of interest in *reconstructive memory*, especially in the way people recall stories, remember their past, recall conversations, and give eyewitness testimony (Greene, 1999). Now let's take a closer look at some of these memory quirks and glitches.

retrieval The memory process of taking information out of storage.

Serial Position Effect

Understanding how retrieval works also requires knowledge of the **serial position effect**—the tendency for items at the beginning and at the end of a list to be recalled more readily. If someone gave you the directions "left on Mockingbird, right on Central, right on Stemmons, left on Balboa, and right on Parkside" you probably would remember "left on Mockingbird" and "right on Parkside" more easily than the turns and streets in the middle. The *primacy effect* refers to better recall for items at the beginning of a list. The *recency effect* refers to better recall for items at the end of the list. Together with the relatively low recall of items from the middle of the list, this pattern makes up the *serial position effect* (Howard & Kahana, 1999; Surprenant, 2001). See figure 8.16 for a typical serial position effect that shows a weaker primacy effect and a stronger recency effect. One application of primacy and recency effects is the advice to job candidates to try to be the first or last candidate interviewed.

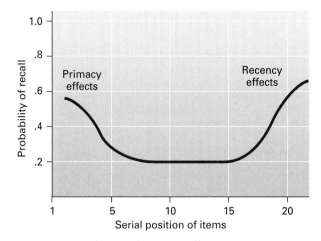

FIGURE 8.16 The Serial Position Effect When a person is asked to memorize a list of words, the words memorized last usually are recalled best, those at the beginning next best, and those in the middle least efficiently.

How can primacy and recency effects be explained? As for the primacy effect, the first few items in the list are easily remembered because they are rehearsed more often than later items (Atkinson & Shiffrin, 1968). Working memory is relatively empty when they enter, so there is little competition for rehearsal time. And, because they get more rehearsal, they stay in working memory longer and are more likely to be successfully encoded into long-term memory. In contrast, many items from the middle of the list drop out of working memory before being encoded into long-term memory.

As for the recency effect, the last several items are remembered for different reasons. First, at the time these items are recalled, they might still be in working memory. Second, even if these items are not in working memory, their relative recency, compared with other list items, makes them easier to recall. For example, if you are a sports fan, try remembering a football or baseball game you have seen at the end of the season. You probably will find that the more recent games are easier to remember than earlier games. This example of the recency effect extends far beyond the time span of working memory.

Retrieval Cues and the Retrieval Task

Two other factors involved in retrieval are (1) the nature of the cues that can prompt your memory and (2) the retrieval task that you set for yourself. If effective cues for what you are trying to remember do not seem to be available, you need to create them—a process that takes place in working memory. For example, if you have a block about remembering a new friend's name, you might go through the alphabet, generating names that begin with each letter. If you manage to stumble across the right name, you'll probably recognize it.

We can learn to generate retrieval cues (Allan & others, 2001; Halpern, 1996). One good strategy is to use different subcategories as retrieval cues. For example, write down the names of as many of your classmates from middle or junior high school as you can remember. When you run out of names, think about the activities you were involved in during those school years, such as math class, student council, eating lunch, drill team, and so on. Did this set of cues help you to remember more of your classmates?

Although cues help, your success in retrieving information also depends on the task you set for yourself. For instance, if you're simply trying to decide if something seems familiar, retrieval is probably a snap. Let's say you see a short, dark-haired woman walking toward you. You quickly decide she's someone who lives in the next dorm. But remembering her name or a precise detail, such as when you met her, can

serial position effect The tendency for items at the beginning and at the end of a list to be recalled more readily.

FIGURE 8.17 Remembering Faces
(*Left*) The FBI artist's sketch of Ted Kaczynski. (*Right*) A photograph of Kaczynski. The FBI widely circulated the artist's sketch, which was based on bits and pieces of observations people had made of the infamous Unabomber, in the hope that someone would recognize him. Would you have been able to recognize Kaczynski from the artist's sketch? Probably not. Although most people say they are good at remembering faces, they usually are not as good as they think they are.

be harder. Such distinctions have implications for police investigations: A witness might be certain she has previously seen a face, yet she might have a hard time deciding if it was at the scene of the crime or in a mug shot.

Recall and Recognition The presence or absence of good cues and the retrieval task required are factors in an important memory distinction: recall versus recognition (Nobel & Shiffrin, 2001). *Recall* is a memory task in which the individual has to retrieve previously learned information, as on essay tests. *Recognition* is a memory task in which the individual only has to identify (recognize) learned items, as on multiple-choice tests. Wouldn't you agree that multiple-choice tests are easier than essay tests or fill-in-the-blank tests? Recall tests, such as essay tests, have poor retrieval cues. You are told to try to recall a certain class of information ("Discuss the factors that caused World War II"). In recognition tests, such as multiple-choice tests, you merely judge whether a stimulus is familiar (whether it matches something you experienced in the past).

You probably have heard some people say that they are terrible at remembering names but that they never forget a face. What they likely are really saying is that they are better at recognition (realizing that they have seen a face before) than at recall (mentally reconstructing a person's facial features). If you have made that claim yourself, try to actually recall a face. It's not easy, as law enforcement officers know. In some cases they bring in an artist to draw the suspect's face from witnesses' descriptions (see figure 8.17). But recalling faces is difficult, and artists' sketches of suspects are frequently not detailed or accurate enough to result in apprehension.

Encoding Specificity Another consideration in understanding retrieval is the *encoding specificity principle,* which states that information present at the time of encoding or learning tends to be effective as a retrieval cue (Hanna & Remington, 2001; Hannon & Craik, 2001; Tulving & Thomson, 1973). For example, imagine that you have met someone who is a professional tennis player. If you encode that information, along with observations such as "the person looks fit and has long arms," this might help you to remember the person's occupation when you encounter him again.

Encoding specificity is compatible with our earlier discussion of elaboration. Recall that the more elaboration you use in encoding information, the better your memory of the information will be. Encoding specificity and elaboration reveal how interdependent encoding and retrieval are.

Priming Retrieval also benefits from *priming,* which was discussed earlier in the chapter. Recall that priming means that people remember information better and faster when it is preceded by similar information. Priming is a form of implicit memory that is nonconscious in nature (Goddard, Dritschel, & Burton, 2001).

In everyday life, priming likely is involved in unintentional acts of plagiarism (Schacter, 1996). For example, you propose an idea to a friend, who seems unimpressed by it or even rejects it outright. Weeks or months later, the friend excitedly describes your idea as if she had just come up with it herself. Her memory of having the idea has been primed by your explanation of the idea. When you call your friend's attention to the fact that her idea is really your idea, you likely will face either heated denial or a sheepish apology born of a sudden dose of explicit memory.

A practical example of priming involves those times when you are wandering the grocery store unable to remember one of the items you were supposed to buy. As you walk down an aisle you hear two people talking about fruit, which triggers your memory that you were supposed to buy raspberries. That is, hearing "fruit" primes your memory for raspberries.

Tip-of-the-Tongue Phenomenon One glitch in retrieving information that we're all familiar with is the *tip-of-the-tongue phenomenon,* or *TOT state.* It is a type of "effortful retrieval" that occurs when people are confident that they know something but they can't quite pull it out of memory (Kikyo, Ohki, & Sekihara, 2001; Schwartz, 2002). People in a TOT state usually can successfully retrieve characteristics of the word, such as the first letter and the number of syllables, but not retrieve the word itself.

In one study of the TOT state, participants were shown photographs of famous people and asked to say their names (Yarmey, 1973). The researcher found that people tended to use two strategies to try to retrieve the name of a person they thought they knew. One strategy was to pinpoint the person's profession. For example, one participant correctly identified the famous person as an artist, but the artist's name, Picasso, remained elusive. Another retrieval strategy was to repeat initial letters or syllables—such as *Monetti, Mona, Magett, Spaghetti,* and *Bogette* in the attempt to identify Liza Minnelli.

The TOT state arises because a person can retrieve some of the desired information but not all of it (Maril, Wagner, & Schacter, 2001; Schacter, 1996, 2001). For example, imagine that you are at a college social event and spot two people standing together. You easily recall that one of them is Barbara. You know that you've seen the other person before and are sure his name begins with a B (a good retrieval cue). You are sure that you know his name, although you can't remember it at the moment. But maybe you didn't pay enough attention to his name when you were introduced to remember more than the first letter. Your confidence in the retrieval cue can induce a strong—sometimes spurious—feeling of knowing other information (in this case the name) that you actually haven't stored in memory.

Context and State at Encoding and Retrieval In many instances, people remember better when they attempt to recall information in the same context in which they learned it, a process referred to as *context-dependent memory.* This is believed to occur because they have encoded features of the context in which they learned the information along with the information. Such features can later act as retrieval cues (Kimbrough, Wright, & Shea, 2001; Smith & Vela, 2001).

In one study, scuba divers learned information on land and under water (Godden & Baddeley, 1975). Later they were asked to recall the information when they either were on land or under water. The divers' recall was much better when the encoding and retrieval contexts were the same (both on land or both under water).

Level	Label	Description
Level 1	Life time periods	Long segments of time measured in years and even decades
Level 2	General events	Extended composite episodes measured in days, weeks, or months
Level 3	Event-specific knowledge	Individual episodes measured in seconds, minutes or hours

FIGURE 8.18 **The Three-Level Hierarchical Structure of Autobiographical Memory**

Just as external contexts can influence memory, so can internal states (Duka, Weissenborn, & Dienes, 2001; Weissenborn & Duka 2000). People tend to remember information better when their psychological state or mood is similar at encoding and retrieval, a process referred to as *state-dependent memory.* For example, when people are in sad moods, they are more likely to remember negative experiences, such as failure and rejection. When they are in happy moods, they are inclined to remember positive experiences, such as success and acceptance (Mineka & Nugent, 1995). Unfortunately, when people who are depressed recall negative experiences, it tends to perpetuate their depression.

Retrieval of Autobiographical Memories

The various quirks of memory related to retrieval cues and tasks are at play in many different facets of memory. Consider personal memories. *Autobiographical memory,* a form of episodic memory (discussed earlier in the chapter), is a person's recollections of his or her life experiences.

Autobiographical memories are complex and seem to contain unending strings of stories and snapshots, but researchers have found that they can be categorized (Schacter, 1996). For example, based on their research, Martin Conway and David Rubin (1993) sketch a structure of autobiographical memory that has three levels (see figure 8.18). The most abstract level consists of *life time periods;* for example, you might remember something about your life in high school. The middle level in the hierarchy is made up of *general events,* such as a trip you took with your friends after you graduated from high school. The most concrete level in the hierarchy is composed of *event-specific knowledge;* for example, from your postgraduation trip, you might remember the exhilarating time you had when you took your first bungee jump. When people tell their life stories, all three levels of information are usually present and intertwined.

Most autobiographical memories include some reality and some myth. Dan McAdams (1993) argues that autobiographical memories are in fact less about facts and more about meanings. They provide a reconstructed, embellished telling of the past that connects the past to the present. According to McAdams, autobiographical memories form the core of our personal identity.

Retrieval of Emotional Memories

When we remember our life experiences, the memories are often wrapped in emotion. Keep in mind that emotion affects the encoding and storage of memories and thus shapes the details that are retrieved. Today, the effects of emotion on memory are of considerable interest to researchers and have echoes in public life. Let's first examine flashbulb memories.

Flashbulb Memories *Flashbulb memories* are memories of emotionally significant events that people often recall with more accuracy and vivid imagery than everyday events (Davidson & Glisky, 2002). Perhaps you can remember where you were when you first heard of the terrorist attacks on New York City and Washington, D.C., on September 11, 2001. An intriguing dimension of flashbulb memories is that several decades later people often remember where they were and what was going on in their lives at the time of such an event. These memories seem to be part of an adaptive system that fixes in memory the details that accompany important events so that they can be interpreted at a later time.

The vast majority of flashbulb memories are of a personal nature rather than of nationally prominent events or circumstances. In one study, college students were asked to report the three most vivid memories in their lives (Rubin & Kozin, 1984). Virtually all of these memories were of a personal nature. They tended to center around an injury or accident, sports, members of the opposite sex, animals, deaths, the first week of college, and vacations. Students also answered questions about the types of events that were most likely to produce flashbulb memories. Figure 8.19 shows which types of events more than 50 percent of the students said were of flashbulb quality.

Most people are confident about the accuracy of their flashbulb memories. However, most flashbulb memories probably are not as accurately etched in our brains as we think. For example, many flashbulb memories deteriorate over time (Schmolck, Buffalo, & Squire, 2000). Still, flashbulb memories are far more durable and accurate than memories of day-to-day happenings (Schacter, 1996). One reason is that flashbulb memories are often discussed and thought about in the days, weeks, and even years following an event. That has certainly been the case with the 2001 terrorist attacks. However, it is not just the discussion and rehearsal of information that make flashbulb memories so long lasting. The emotions triggered by flashbulb events also are involved in their durability. The emotional arousal you experienced when you heard about the terrorist attacks also likely contributed to the vividness of your memory.

Some flashbulb memories involve emotionally uplifting experiences, such as the positive experience of high school graduation night. Other flashbulb memories are at the opposite end of the emotional spectrum and involve personal trauma.

Personal Trauma In 1890, William James said that an experience can be so arousing emotionally as to almost leave a scar on the brain's tissue. Personal traumas are candidates for the type of emotionally arousing experience James was referring to.

Some psychologists argue that memories of emotionally traumatic events are accurately retained, possibly forever, in considerable detail (Langer, 1991). There is good evidence that memory for traumatic events is usually more accurate than memory for ordinary events (Schacter, 1996). Consider the traumatic experience of the children who were kidnapped at gunpoint on a school bus in Chowchilla, California, in 1983, then buried underground for 16 hours before escaping. The children had the classic signs of traumatic memory: detailed and vivid recollections.

However, when a child psychiatrist interviewed the children 4 to 5 years after the chilling episode, she noted some striking errors and distortions in the memories of half of them (Terr, 1988). How can a traumatic memory be so vivid and detailed, yet at the same time have inaccuracies? A number of factors can be involved. Some children might have made perceptual errors while encoding information because the episode was so shocking. Others might have distorted the information and recalled the episode as being less traumatic than it actually was in order to reduce their anxiety about what happened. Others, in discussing the traumatic event with other people, might have incorporated bits and pieces of these persons' recollections of what happened into their own version of the event.

Event	Percent
A car accident you were in or witnessed	85
When you first met your first college roommate	82
The night of your high school graduation	81
The night of your senior prom (if you went or not)	78
An early romantic experience	77
A time you had to speak in front of an audience	72
When you got your admissions letter	65
Your first date—the moment you met him/her	57

FIGURE 8.19 College Students' Flashbulb Memories
The numbers refer to the percent of college students who said these events triggered memories of flashbulb quality.

Do you have a flashbulb memory of the terrorist attack on the World Trade Center in New York City, September 11, 2001?

Recovered Memories or False Memories?

George Franklin, a California man, spent 6 years in prison for the 1969 murder of a young woman. His own daughter's testimony, based on her memory of the attack, was at the heart of the prosecution's case against him. What made this case unusual is that the daughter's memories were allegedly recovered in adulthood as a part of her own ongoing therapy (Loftus & Ketcham, 1994). In fact, Franklin became the first person in the United States to be convicted on the basis of repressed memory evidence. During the 1990s, memories allegedly recovered during therapy also served as the basis for many charges of physical and sexual abuse. George Franklin's conviction was eventually overturned when it came out that his daughter might have lied about having been hypnotized before the trial.

The idea that childhood abuse, and in particular sexual abuse, could be completely repressed yet nevertheless lead to psychological disorders in adulthood was first expressed in Sigmund Freud's seduction theory. In this vein, some therapists today continue to believe that adult disorders such as depression, thoughts of suicide, eating disorders, low self-esteem, sexual dysfunction, and trouble maintaining relationships may stem from sexual abuse in childhood. Treatment usually involves bringing these long-repressed childhood traumas back into consciousness, thus freeing the client from their unconscious effects.

Methods used to recover repressed childhood memories have included hypnotic age regression, guided imagery, keeping a journal of fragments of childhood memories, and even the administration of truth drugs. In cases in which memories have been recovered, clients have often been encouraged to confront the alleged perpetrator, usually a parent. In many cases, charges have been filed as a part of the therapeutic process (Pezdek & Banks, 1996).

Almost all accused parents vehemently deny having ever abused their offspring in childhood. In 1992, the False Memory Syndrome (FMS) Foundation was formed as a parents' support group. The very name of this group expresses the conviction that their children's memories were not recovered but were somehow falsely implanted, perhaps as a result of the therapeutic process itself. Interestingly, almost 100 years earlier, Sigmund Freud himself had rejected his seduction theory in favor of the view that his patient's "memories" of childhood abuse were based on their own repressed sexual desires. What has complicated matters is the growing awareness that childhood sexual abuse is much more common than Freud was aware of and continues to be a serious problem today. Many therapists have wondered if Freud was afraid to face the implications of his seduction theory and instead ended up betraying his patients by claiming that their memories were just fantasies.

It was against this bitter backdrop that experimental psychology entered the fray. Led by the research of memory expert Elizabeth Loftus (Loftus & Ketcham, 1994), study after study found that it is easy to create false memories, especially by using hypnosis. All that is required is to hypnotize someone and to suggest that he or she has had an experience. After hypnosis, that person may well "remember" the experience as vividly real. In one recent study, Loftus and Jacquie Pickrell (2001) persuaded people that they had met Bugs Bunny at Disneyland, even though Bugs is a Warner Bros. character who would never appear at a Disney theme park. Their procedure was quite sim-

Usually, memories of real-life traumas are more accurate and longer lasting than those of everyday events. Although memories of traumas are subject to some deterioration and distortion, the central part of the memory is almost always effectively remembered. Where distortion often arises is in the details of the traumatic episode.

Some cases of memory of personal trauma involve a mental disorder called *post-traumatic stress disorder,* which includes severe anxiety symptoms whose onset can immediately follow the trauma or can be delayed by months or even years (North & others, 2002). The symptoms can include flashbacks in which the individual relives the traumatic event in nightmares or in an awake but distracted state. Individuals also can have difficulties with memory and concentration. Post-traumatic stress disorder can emerge after exposure to several kinds of traumatic events, such as war, severe abuse (such as rape), and accidental disasters (such as a plane crash). Post-traumatic stress disorder is discussed further in chapter 13.

Stress-related hormones likely play a role in memories that involve personal trauma. The release of stress-related hormones, signaled by the amygdala (see figure 8.15), likely accounts for some of the extraordinary durability and vividness of traumatic memories (Schacter, 1996).

Repressed Memories The emotional blows of personal trauma can produce distortions of memory or vivid reenactments of the event in memory. Personal trauma can also result in *repression,* in which all memory of the occurrence is pushed into

ple. Four groups of participants read ads and then answered questionnaires about a trip to Disneyland. One group saw an ad that mentioned no cartoon characters, the second read the same ad and also saw a four-foot-tall cardboard figure of Bugs Bunny, the third read a fake ad for Disneyland with Bugs Bunny in it, and the fourth saw the same fake ad along with the cardboard bunny. Although less than 10 percent of the first two groups later reported having actually met Bugs Bunny on a trip to Disneyland, approximately 30 to 40 percent of the third and fourth groups reported remembering meeting Bugs at Disneyland.

Research such as this has led to the concern that therapists who are convinced that their patients suffered sexual abuse as children may inadvertently implant false memories that are later "recovered" by the client. The end result may be false memories, which tear apart families and cause more harm than good. This research has led courts to be skeptical of recovered-memory testimony—and directly resulted in the reversal of George Franklin's murder conviction. Unfortunately, nothing can compensate him for the loss of 6 years of his life and the destruction of his family life. At the same time, rejecting all claims by adults that they were victims of childhood sexual abuse is also inappropriate.

Current consensus is well represented by the American Psychological Association's (1994) interim report of the working group investigating memories of childhood abuse, which offers these tentative conclusions: (1) Controversies regarding adult recollections should not be allowed to obscure the fact that child sexual abuse is a complex and pervasive problem in America that has historically gone unacknowledged; (2) most people who were sexually abused as children remember all or part of what happened to them; (3) it is possible for memories of abuse that have been forgotten for a long time to be remembered, although the mechanism by which such delayed recall occurs is not currently well understood; (4) it is also possible to construct convincing false memories for events that never occurred, although the mechanism by which these false memories occur is not currently well understood; (5) there are gaps in our knowledge about the processes that lead to accurate and inaccurate recollections of childhood abuse.

What do you think?

- How should courts of law deal with the recovered memory versus false memory problem?
- Suppose that you meet someone who reports recovered memories of childhood abuse. How can you tell whether you should believe him or her? What should your attitude be toward that person?
- Does the likelihood that some reports of childhood sexual abuse are in fact false memories entitle us to conclude that childhood sexual abuse rarely, if ever, occurs? If we cannot trust the testimony of adult survivors of childhood sexual abuse, how can we determine the likelihood of its occurrence today?

some inaccessible part of the unconscious mind. At some later point, the memory might emerge in consciousness, as in the case of post-traumatic stress disorder.

Psychodynamic theory, which was initially discussed in chapter 1, contends that repression's main function is to protect the individual from threatening information. Repression does not erase a memory, but it makes conscious remembering extremely difficult (Anderson & Green, 2001). Just how extensively repression occurs is a controversial issue.

Repressed memories are further discussed in chapters 12 and 14. To think about the accuracy of reconstructed memories of childhood abuse, see the Critical Controversy box.

Eyewitness Testimony

By now you should realize that memory is not a perfect reflection of reality. Understanding the distortions of memory is especially important when people are called on to report what they saw or heard in relation to a crime. Eyewitness testimonies, like other sorts of memories, may contain errors (Schacter, 1996, 2001). But faulty memory in criminal matters has especially serious consequences. When eyewitness testimony is inaccurate, the wrong person may go to jail or even be put to death, or the person who committed the crime might not be prosecuted. Estimates are that between

O. J. Simpson's white Bronco grabbed the country's attention when it was televised moving slowly along a Los Angeles freeway as he threatened suicide. During the trial, witnesses gave varying testimony about whether the Bronco had ever moved from its spot during the evening when Nicole Brown Simpson had been murdered. Possibly someone was lying, but it also is possible that witnesses reconstructed their memories differently but honestly.

Identification of individuals from police lineups or photographs is not always reliable. Also, people from one ethnic group often have difficulty recognizing differences among people of another ethnic group.

2,000 and 10,000 people are wrongfully convicted each year in the United States because of faulty eyewitness testimony (Cutler & Penrod, 1995).

In the high-profile O. J. Simpson murder trial, many people were puzzled when Simpson's housekeeper testified that his infamous white Bronco had not moved from its spot all evening. Yet Simpson's limousine driver testified that he did not remember seeing the car when he arrived late that evening. This was only one of many discrepancies in eyewitness testimony that occurred in the Simpson trial. They regularly occur in other trials as well.

Much of the interest in eyewitness testimony focuses on distortion, bias, and inaccuracy in memory (Loftus, 1993a). One reason for distortion is that memory fades over time. For that reason the amount of time that has passed between an incident and a person's recollection of it is a critical factor in eyewitness testimony. In one study, people were able to identify pictures with 100 percent accuracy after a 2-hour time lapse. However, 4 months later they achieved an accuracy of only 57 percent; chance alone accounts for 50 percent accuracy (Shepard, 1967).

Unlike a videotape, memory can be altered by new information. In one study, students were shown a film of an automobile accident (Loftus, 1975). Students were asked how fast the white sports car was going when it passed a barn. In fact, there was no barn in the film. However, 17 percent of the students who were asked the question mentioned the barn in their answer.

Bias is also a factor in faulty memory. Studies have shown that people of one ethnic group are less likely to recognize individual differences among people of another ethnic group (Behrman & Davey, 2001). Latino eyewitnesses, for example, may have trouble distinguishing among several Asian suspects. In one experiment, a mugging was shown on a television news program (Loftus, 1993a). Immediately after, a lineup of six suspects was broadcast, and viewers were asked to phone in and identify which of the six individuals they thought committed the robbery. Of the 2,000 callers, more than 1,800 identified the wrong person. In addition, even though the robber was White, one-third of the viewers identified an African American or Latino suspect as the criminal.

To get an idea of just how much eyewitness testimony should be trusted, researchers asked 64 psychologists who had either conducted eyewitness research or testified as expert witnesses to evaluate the accuracy of 30 statements regarding eyewitness testimony (Kassin & others, 2001). Figure 8.20 lists the statements that 90 percent or more of the experts agreed with and the statements that 50 percent or fewer disagreed with. As you can see, the experts had the most confidence in the statements related to the wording of questions and lineup instructions and the least confidence in statements related to long-term repression of memories. In sum, like other memories, eyewitness memories are constructions that do not always match what really happened.

Statements Rated as Reliable by 80 Percent or More of the Experts

Category	Statement	Percent
Wording of questions	An eyewitness's testimony about an event can be affected by how the questions put to the witness are worded.	98
Lineup instructions	Police instructions can affect an eyewitness's willingness to make an identification.	98
Confidence malleability	An eyewitness's confidence can be influenced by factors that are unrelated to identification accuracy.	95
Mug-shot induced bias	Exposure to mug shots of a suspect increases the likelihood that the witness will later select that suspect in the lineup.	95
Postevent information	Eyewitness testimony about an event often reflects not only what the witness saw but also information the witness obtained later on.	94
Child suggestibility	Young children are more vulnerable than adults to interviewer suggestion, peer pressures, and other social influences.	94
Attitudes and expectations	An eyewitness's perception of and memory for an event can be affected by his or her attitudes and expectations.	92
Hypnotic suggestibility	Hypnosis increases suggestibility to leading and misleading questions.	91
Alcoholic intoxication	Alcoholic intoxication impairs an eyewitness's later ability to recall persons and events.	91
Cross-race bias	Eyewitnesses are more accurate when identifying members of their own race than members of other races.	90

Statements Rated as Unreliable by 50 Percent or Less of the Experts

Category	Statement	Percent
Elderly witness	Elderly witnesses are less accurate than are younger adults.	50
Hypnotic accuracy	Hypnosis increases the accuracy of the eyewitness's reported memory.	45
Identification speed	The more quickly a witness makes an identification upon seeing the lineup, the more accurate he or she is likely to be.	40
Trained observers	Police officers and other trained observers are no more accurate as eyewitnesses than the average person.	39
Event violence	Eyewitnesses have more difficulty remembering violent than nonviolent events.	37
Discriminability	It is possible to reliably differentiate between true and false memories.	32
Long-term repression	Traumatic experiences can be repressed for many years and then be recovered.	22

FIGURE 8.20 **Expert's Judgments of Statements Regarding Eyewitness Testimony**

Review and Sharpen Your Thinking

4 *Summarize how memories are retrieved.*

- Describe the serial position effect.
- Explain the role of retrieval cues and the retrieval task.
- Define autobiographical memory.
- Discuss three types of emotional memories and complications in their retrieval.
- Evaluate eyewitness testimony.

Do you think that, on the whole, negative emotional events are likely to be more memorable than positive ones? How would you go about studying whether negative events are more memorable than positive ones?

mhhe.com/
santrockp7

For study tools related to this learning goal, see the Study Guide, the CD-ROM, and the Online Learning Center.

5 FORGETTING

Encoding Failure

Retrieval Failure

HERMANN EBBINGHAUS (1850–1909)
The first psychologist to conduct scientific research on forgetting. *What was the nature of this research?*

How does forgetting involve encoding and retrieval failures?

Missed appointments, misplaced eyeglasses, failures to recall the names of familiar faces, and not being able to remember your password for Internet access are common examples of forgetting. Why do we forget?

One of psychology's pioneers, Hermann Ebbinghaus (1850–1909), was the first person to conduct scientific research on forgetting. In 1885, he made up and memorized a list of thirteen nonsense syllables and then assessed how many of them he could remember as time passed. (*Nonsense syllables* are meaningless combinations of letters that are unlikely to have been learned already, such as *zeq, xid, lek, vut,* and *riy.*) Even just an hour later, Ebbinghaus could recall only a few of the nonsense syllables he had memorized. Figure 8.21 shows Ebbinghaus' learning curve for nonsense syllables. Based on his research, Ebbinghaus concluded that the most forgetting takes place soon after we learn something.

If we forget so quickly, why put effort into learning something? Fortunately, researchers have demonstrated that forgetting is not as extensive as Ebbinghaus envisioned (Baddeley, 1992). Ebbinghaus studied meaningless nonsense syllables. When we memorize more meaningful material, such as poetry, history, or the type of material in this text, forgetting is neither so rapid nor so extensive. Following are some of the factors that influence how well we can retrieve information from long-term memory.

Encoding Failure

Sometimes when people say they have forgotten something, they have not really forgotten it; they never encoded the information in the first place. *Encoding failure* is when the information was never entered into long-term memory.

As an example of encoding failure, think about what the U.S. penny looks like. In one study, researchers showed 15 versions of the penny to participants and asked them which was correct (Nickerson & Adams, 1979). Look at the pennies in figure 8.22 (but don't look at the caption yet!) and see if you can tell which one is the real penny. Most people do not do well on this task. Unless you are a coin collector, you likely have not encoded a lot of specific details about pennies. You may have encoded just enough information to distinguish them from other coins (pennies are copper colored, dimes and nickels are silver colored; pennies fall between the sizes of dimes and quarters).

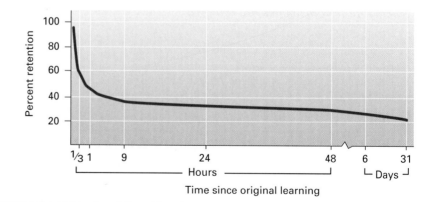

FIGURE 8.21 Ebbinghaus' Forgetting Curve

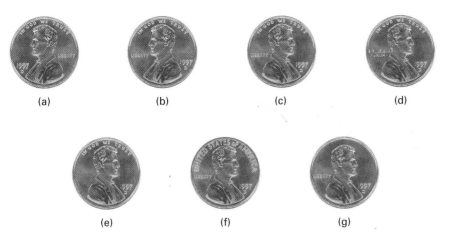

(a)   (b)   (c)   (d)

(e)   (f)   (g)

FIGURE 8.22 Which Is a Real U.S. Penny? In the original experiment, 15 versions of pennies were shown to participants; only 1 was an actual U.S. penny. We have included only 7 of the 15 versions, and, as you likely can tell, this still is a very difficult task. *Why?*
By the way, the actual U.S. penny is (*c*).

The penny exercise illustrates that we encode and enter into long-term memory only a small portion of the experiences we have in life. In a sense, then, encoding failures really are not cases of forgetting; they are cases of not remembering.

Retrieval Failure

Problems in retrieving information from memory are clearly examples of forgetting (Williams & Zacks, 2001). Psychologists have theorized that the causes of retrieval failure include problems with the information in storage, the effects of time, personal reasons for remembering or forgetting, and the brain's condition.

Interference   Interference has been proposed as one reason that people forget. **Interference theory** states that people forget not because memories are actually lost from storage but because other information gets in the way of what they want to remember (Altmann & Gray, 2002).

There are two kinds of interference: proactive and retroactive. **Proactive interference** occurs when material that was learned earlier disrupts the recall of material learned later (Humphreys, 2001). Remember that *pro-* means "forward in time." For example, suppose you had a good friend 10 years ago named *Prudence* and that last night you met someone named *Patience*. You might find yourself calling your new friend *Prudence* because the old information (*Prudence*) interferes with retrieval of new information (*Patience*). **Retroactive interference** occurs when material learned later disrupts the retrieval of information learned earlier. Remember that *retro-* means "backward in time." Suppose you have lately become friends with *Ralph*. In sending a note to your old friend *Raul,* you might mistakenly address it to *Ralph* because the new information (*Ralph*) interferes with the old information (*Raul*). Figure 8.23 depicts another example of proactive and retroactive interference.

Proactive and retroactive interference might both be explained as problems with retrieval cues. The reason *Prudence* interferes with *Patience* and *Ralph* interferes with *Raul* might be that the cue you are using to remember the one name does not distinguish between the two memories. For example, if the cue you were using was "my good friend," it might evoke both names. The result could be retrieving the wrong name or a kind of blocking in which each name interferes with the other and neither comes to mind. Retrieval cues (like "friend" in our example) can become overloaded, and when that happens we are likely to forget or to retrieve incorrectly.

Decay and Transience   Another possible reason for forgetting is the passage of time. **Decay theory** states that when something new is learned, a neurochemical "memory trace" is formed, but over time this trace tends to disintegrate. Decay theory suggests that the passage of time always increases forgetting.

interference theory States that people forget not because memories are actually lost from storage but because other information gets in the way of what we want to remember.

proactive interference Occurs when material that was learned earlier disrupts the recall of material learned later.

retroactive interference Occurs when material learned later disrupts the retrieval of information learned earlier.

decay theory States that when something new is learned, a neurochemical memory trace is formed, but over time this trace tends to disintegrate.

FIGURE 8.23 Proactive and Retroactive Interference *Pro-* means "forward"; in proactive interference, old information has a forward influence by getting in the way of new material learned. *Retro-* means "backward"; in retroactive interference, new information has a backward influence by getting in the way of material learned earlier.

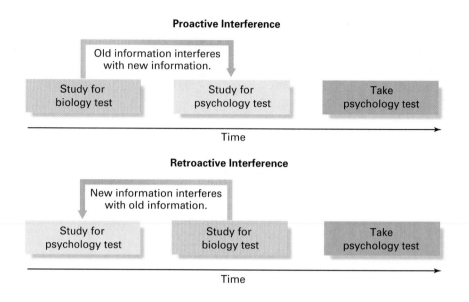

FIGURE 8.23 Proactive and Retroactive Interference *Pro-* means "forward"; in proactive interference, old information has a forward influence by getting in the way of new material learned. *Retro-* means "backward"; in retroactive interference, new information has a backward influence by getting in the way of material learned earlier.

Memory researcher Daniel Schacter (2001) refers to the forgetting that occurs with the passage of time as *transience.* As an example of transience, recall that on October 3, 1995, the most sensational criminal trial in recent times reached a dramatic conclusion: A jury acquitted O. J. Simpson. The Simpson verdict seemed like just the kind of "flashbulb" memory that most of us would remember vividly for years to come. How well can you remember finding out about the Simpson verdict? In one research study, undergraduate students provided detailed accounts of how they learned about the Simpson verdict (Schmolck & others, 2000). However, 15 months later, only half remembered the details, and nearly 3 years after the verdict, less than 30 percent of the students' memories were accurate.

Memories often do fade with the passage of time, but decay or transience alone cannot explain forgetting. For example, under the right retrieval conditions, memories that seem to have been forgotten can be retrieved. You might have forgotten the face or name of someone in your high school class, but when you return to the setting in which you knew the person, you may remember.

Motivated Forgetting *Motivated forgetting* occurs when people forget something because it is so painful or anxiety laden that remembering is intolerable. This type of forgetting may be a consequence of the emotional blows of personal trauma that occur in victims of rape or physical abuse, in war veterans, or in survivors of earthquakes, plane crashes, and other terrifying events. These emotional traumas may haunt people for many years unless they can put the details out of their minds. Even when people have not experienced trauma, they may use motivated forgetting to protect themselves from memories of painful, stressful, unpleasant circumstances.

One form of motivated forgetting is *repression,* which was described earlier in the discussion of difficulties that some people have in retrieving emotional memories. In the psychodynamic view, unpleasant memories are repressed into our unconscious minds, and we no longer are aware of them.

Amnesia Recall the case of H. M. in the discussion of explicit and implicit memory. In H. M.'s surgery, the part of his brain that was responsible for laying down new memories was damaged beyond repair, which resulted in **amnesia,** the loss of memory. Although some types of amnesia clear up over time, H. M.'s amnesia endured.

H. M. suffered from **anterograde amnesia,** a memory disorder that affects the retention of new information and events (*antero-* indicates amnesia that moves forward in time). What he learned before the surgery and the resulting onset of amnesia was not affected. For example, H. M. could identify his friends, recall their names, and even tell stories about them—but only if he had known them before surgery. People who

amnesia The loss of memory.

anterograde amnesia A memory disorder that affects the retention of new information or events.

Alabama businesswoman Patsy Cannon was in a car crash in 1986. Her injury was so severe that it left her with retrograde amnesia, and she had to relearn virtually everything she used to know. Cannon didn't even recognize her own daughter. (*Left*) Cannon in 1986 just prior to the car crash. (*Right*) Today Patsy works as an advocate for individuals with brain injury.

met H. M. after surgery remained strangers, even if they spent thousands of hours with him. H. M.'s postsurgical experiences were rarely encoded in his long-term memory.

Amnesia also occurs in a form known as **retrograde amnesia,** which involves memory loss for a segment of the past but not for new events (*retro-* indicates amnesia that moves back in time) (Dutton & others, 2002). Retrograde amnesia is much more common than anterograde amnesia and frequently occurs when the brain is assaulted by an electrical shock or a physical blow—such as a head injury to a football player. In contrast to anterograde amnesia, in retrograde amnesia the forgotten information is *old*—prior to the event that caused the amnesia—and the ability to acquire new memories is not affected. Sometimes, individuals have both anterograde and retrograde amnesia.

Review and Sharpen Your Thinking

5 **Describe how encoding and retrieval failure are involved in forgetting.**
- Define encoding failure.
- Discuss four reasons for retrieval failure.

Think about three or four instances recently in which you were unable to remember something. What principle of forgetting do you think best explains your failure to remember in each case?

mhhe ● com/
santrockp7

For study tools related to this learning goal, see the Study Guide, the CD-ROM, and the Online Learning Center.

MEMORY AND STUDY STRATEGIES 6

Encoding Strategies   **Storage Strategies**   **Retrieval Strategies**

How can you apply what you have learned about memory to your academic studies?

Most of us face memory problems far less serious than amnesia or repression. The simple memory strategies that follow can help you to encode, store, and retrieve information more effectively. In fact, using the right memory strategies to study can help you improve your academic performance.

retrograde amnesia A memory disorder that involves memory loss for a segment of the past but not for new events.

Keep in mind that even under the best circumstances memory is not perfect. And for students who engage in ill-advised habits, such as not getting enough sleep, taking drugs, and not going to class regularly, the remembering that is necessary to do well on an exam may be further impaired.

Encoding Strategies

The first step in improving your academic performance is to make sure the information you're studying is processed effectively so it will be stored in long-term memory. Although some types of information are encoded automatically, the academic learning process usually requires considerable effort. Recall that encoding involves paying attention, processing information at an appropriate level, elaborating, and using imagery.

Be a Good Time Manager and Planner Managing your time effectively and planning to allow the necessary time to study will give you the hours you need to do well academically. As suggested in the discussion of study habits in chapter 1, to-do lists are an effective way of planning and managing time (see figure 1.5). To make high grades, you need to set aside at least 2 or 3 study hours for each hour you spend in class (Santrock & Halonen, 2002). Thus, if you are in class 15 hours, you should be studying 30 to 45 hours outside of class each week.

Another aspect of good planning is having the right resources to draw on and allowing enough time for the task. When you're studying for a test, make sure you have your textbook and class notes on hand. If you are writing a paper, plan enough time to write a first draft and revise it one or more times.

Pay Attention and Minimize Distraction Once you have made a commitment to spending the time needed on your studies, you have to make sure you aren't distracted by other things during that time. If you want to remember something, you have to give it your undivided attention.

Monitor how well you are paying attention. If you find yourself getting distracted, say to yourself a cue word or phrase such as "focus" or "zero in" to increase your attention.

Understand the Material Rather Than Rotely Memorize It You are more likely to remember information over the long term if you understand it rather than just rotely rehearse and memorize it. Rehearsal works well for information in short-term memory, but when you need to encode, store, and then retrieve information from long-term memory, it is much less efficient. So, for most information, understand it, give it meaning, elaborate on it, and personalize it.

One technique you can use to make sure you understand the material is *cognitive monitoring,* which involves taking stock of your progress in an activity such as reading or studying. For example, you might make sure that you understand the material by summarizing what you have read and restudying those parts of the material that were unclear.

Ask Yourself Questions A self-questioning strategy can help you to remember. As you read, periodically stop and ask yourself questions, such as "What is the meaning of what I just read?" "Why is this important?" and "What is an example of the concept I just read about?" When you have made a concerted effort to ask yourself questions about what you have read or about an activity in class, you will expand the number of associations you make with the information you will need to retrieve later.

Take Good Notes Taking good notes while listening to a lecture or reading a textbook also benefits your memory. But don't try to write down everything: It is distracting, and it can prevent you from getting the big picture of what the instructor or textbook author is communicating.

Good note-taking strategies include the following:

- *Summarizing.* Listen or read for a few minutes and then write down the main idea that the instructor or author is trying to get across in that time frame. Then listen or read for several more minutes and write down another idea, and so on.
- *Outlining.* Create an outline of what the instructor is saying, using a hierarchy to show which ideas are related and how general or specific they are. Model your system after the one used to organize textbook chapters, with "A"-level heads being the main topics, "B"-level heads the subtopics under the "A" heads, and "C"-level heads the subtopics under the "B" heads.
- *Concept maps.* If outlines don't seem to capture your thought processes, try drawing concept maps of what the instructor is saying or what you are reading. Concept maps are similar to outlines, but they visually display information in a chart or diagram format.
- *The Cornell method.* Divide a sheet of paper into two columns by drawing a line down the page about one-fourth to one-third of the way from the left edge. Write your notes on the right two-thirds to three-fourths of the page. When you review your notes, you can then add comments about the notes on the left side, which personalizes them for better understanding and later retrieval.
- *Note reviews.* Get into the habit of reviewing your notes periodically rather than waiting to study them at the last minute before a test. If possible, take a few minutes to review your notes just after a lecture or a reading section. You will be able to fill in information you might have missed that is still in your memory. This strategy also helps you to consolidate your learning.

Use Mnemonic Strategies   *Mnemonics* are specific visual and/or verbal memory aids. Following are three types of mnemonic devices:

- *Method of loci.* You develop an image of items to be remembered and then store them mentally in familiar locations (which is what "loci" means). Rooms of houses or stores on a street are common locations used in this memory strategy. For example, if you need to remember a list of brain structures, you can mentally place them in the rooms of a house you are familiar with, such as the entry hall, the living room, the dining room, the kitchen, and so on. Then, when you need to retrieve the information, you imagine the house, mentally go through the rooms, and retrieve the concepts.
- *Keyword method.* You attach vivid imagery to important words. For example, recall from chapter 3 that the limbic system consists of two main regions: amygdala and hippocampus. To remember these three brain areas, you might imagine two legs (limbs) (limbic system) → ambling (amygdala) like a hippo (hippocampus).
- *Acronyms.* Create a word from the first letters of items to be remembered. For example, *HOMES* can be used to remember the Great Lakes: *H*uron, *O*ntario, *M*ichigan, *E*rie, and *S*uperior. An acronym commonly used to remember the sequence of colors in the light spectrum is the name of an imaginary man named *ROY G. BIV: R*ed, *O*range, *Y*ellow, *G*reen, *B*lue, *I*ndigo, and *V*iolet.

Many experts on memory and study skills recommend that mnemonics be used mainly when you need to memorize a list of items or specific facts. However, in most cases, techniques that promote memory by understanding the material are better than rote memorization.

"You simply associate each number with a word, such as 'lipoprotein' and 3,467,009." © Sidney Harris

Storage Strategies

Perhaps the best way to promote effective memory storage is to make sure that your brain is able to function at maximum capacity. For most of us, that means being well rested, well nourished, and free of mind-altering substances. In addition, you can try the following strategies.

Organize Your Memory You will remember information better if you consciously organize it while trying to absorb it. Arrange information, rework material, and give it a structure that will help you to remember it. One organizational technique is a hierarchy, like an outline. You might use a concept map, which draws on semantic-network theory, or create analogies (such as the earlier comparison of retrieval from long-term memory to a finding a book in the library) that take advantage of your preexisting schemas.

Spread Out and Consolidate Your Learning To help move information from working memory to long-term memory, regularly review what you learn. You will also benefit by distributing your learning over a longer period rather than cramming for a test at the last minute. Cramming tends to produce short-term memory that is processed in a shallow rather than a deep manner. Then you can do a final, concentrated tune-up before the test instead of struggling to learn everything at the last minute (Santrock & Halonen, 2002).

Retrieval Strategies

Assuming you have encoded and stored the desired information effectively, you should have a relatively easy time retrieving it when you participate in a class discussion, take a test, or write a paper. Following are several good strategies for retrieving information more easily and making sure it is as accurate as possible.

Use Good Retrieval Cues Tatiana Cooley was the U.S. National Memory Champion in 1999, beating out many other contestants in memorizing thousands of numbers and words, pages of faces and names, and lengthy poems (Schacter, 2001). Tatiana relied on elaborative encoding strategies, creating visual images, stories, and associations that linked new information with what she already knew.

Memory and Study Strategies

Candidly respond to the following items about your own memory and study strategies. Rate yourself 1 = never, 2 = some, and 3 = moderate, 4 = almost always, and 5 = always. Then total your points.

1. I'm a good time manager and planner.
2. I'm good at focusing my attention and minimizing distractions.
3. I try to understand material rather than rotely memorizing it.
4. I ask myself questions about what I have read or about class activities.
5. I take good notes in class and from textbooks.
6. I regularly review my notes.
7. I use mnemonic strategies.
8. I'm very organized in the way I encode information.
9. I spread out my studying and consolidate my learning.
10. I use good retrieval cues.
11. I use the PQ4R or a similar study system.

If you scored 50 to 55 points, you likely use good memory and study strategies. If you scored 45 to 49 points, you likely have some reasonably good memory and study strategies. If you scored below 45, spend some time working on improving your memory and study strategies. Most colleges and universities have a study skills center where specialists can help you.

The reason Tatiana is mentioned here, though, is that, in her everyday life, she says that she is incredibly absentminded. Fearing that she will forget to do many daily task (running errands, keeping appointments, and so on), she relies on to-do lists and notes scribbled on sticky pads as reminders. As Tatiana says, "I live by Post-Its." Like Tatiana, you can help your prospective memory by using good retrieval cues, as well as focused attention and elaboration at encoding.

Use the PQ4R Method Various systems have been developed to help students remember information that they are studying. One of them is called *PQ4R,* which is an acronym for a six-step process (*P, Q,* and four *R*s):

1. Preview
2. Question
3. Read
4. Reflect
5. Recite
6. Review

This system can benefit you by getting you to meaningfully organize information, ask questions about it, reflect on and think about it, and review it. All of these steps together make it easier to retrieve information when you need it, as well as to encode the information effectively.

To think further about your study strategies, see the Psychology and Life box.

Review and Sharpen Your Thinking

6 *Evaluate study strategies based on an understanding of memory.*

- Describe some effective encoding strategies.
- Summarize some good storage strategies.
- Discuss some efficient retrieval strategies.

Get together with three or four students in this class and compare your note-taking and study strategies for the class. How are your strategies similar to or different from those of the other students? What did you learn from the comparison and this chapter about how to study more effectively?

mhhe com/
santrockp7

For study tools related to this learning goal, see the Study Guide, the CD-ROM, and the Online Learning Center.

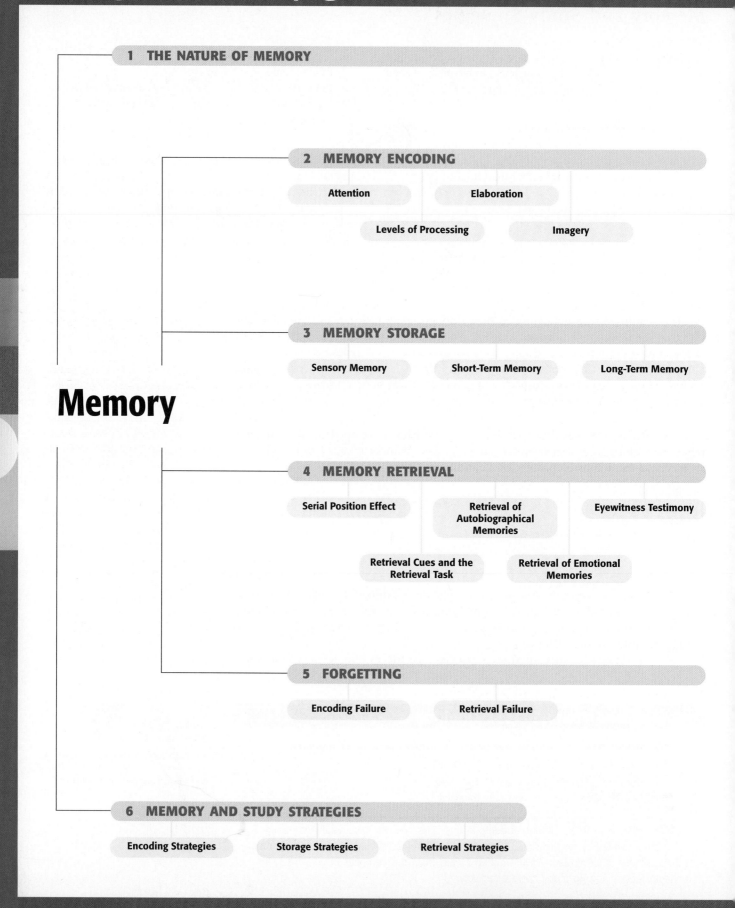

1 THE NATURE OF MEMORY

2 MEMORY ENCODING

Attention

Elaboration

Levels of Processing

Imagery

3 MEMORY STORAGE

Sensory Memory

Short-Term Memory

Long-Term Memory

Memory

4 MEMORY RETRIEVAL

Serial Position Effect

Retrieval of Autobiographical Memories

Eyewitness Testimony

Retrieval Cues and the Retrieval Task

Retrieval of Emotional Memories

5 FORGETTING

Encoding Failure

Retrieval Failure

6 MEMORY AND STUDY STRATEGIES

Encoding Strategies

Storage Strategies

Retrieval Strategies

1 Identify three domains of memory.

- Memory is the retention of information over time through encoding, storage, and retrieval—which are the three domains of memory. Encoding involves getting information into storage, storage consists of retaining information over time, and retrieval involves taking information out of storage.

2 Explain how memories are encoded.

- To begin the process of memory encoding, we have to attend to information. Selective attention is a necessary part of encoding. Memory is often negatively influenced by divided attention.
- Levels of processing theory states that information is processed on a continuum from shallow (sensory or physical features are encoded) to intermediate (labels are attached to stimuli) to deep (the meanings of stimuli and their associations with other stimuli are processed). Deeper processing produces better memory.
- Elaboration, the extensiveness of processing at any given level of memory, improves memory.
- Using imagery, or mental pictures, as a context for information can improve memory.

3 Discuss how memories are stored.

- The Atkinson-Shiffrin theory describes memory as a three-stage process: sensory memory, short-term memory, and long-term memory. Sensory memory holds perceptions of the world for only an instant, not much longer than the brief time the person is exposed to visual, auditory, and other sensory input. Visual sensory memory (iconic memory) retains information about one-fourth of a second, auditory sensory memory (echoic memory) for several seconds.
- Short-term memory is a limited-capacity memory system in which information is usually retained for as long as 30 seconds. Short-term memory's limitation is 7 ± 2 bits of information. Chunking and rehearsal can benefit short-term memory. Baddeley's concept of working memory characterizes short-term memory as more active and complex than Atkinson and Shiffrin proposed. Baddeley's model of working memory has three components: a central executive and two assistants (phonological loop and visuospatial working memory).
- Long-term memory is a relatively permanent type of memory that holds huge amounts of information for a long period of time. Long-term memory can be divided into two main subtypes. Explicit memory is the conscious recollection of information, such as specific facts or events. Implicit memory affects behavior through prior experiences that are not consciously recollected. Explicit

memory has two dimensions. One dimension includes episodic memory and semantic memory. The other dimension includes retrospective memory and prospective memory. Implicit memory is multidimensional, too. It includes systems for procedural memory, priming, and classical conditioning.

Several models have been developed to describe organization of long-term memory. The simplest theory recognizes that we store information better when we represent it in an organized, hierarchical manner. Another theory recognizes that we often use semantic networks (based on labels and meaning) to organize material. Schema theory claims that long-term memory is not exact; we construct our past by fitting new information into a preexisting mental framework. Scripts are schemas for events. Connectionist theory states that memory is organized as a wide range of connections between neurons, many of which operate simultaneously to store memory. Single neurons are involved in memory, but some neuroscientists believe that many memories are stored in circuits of about 1,000 neurons. There is no specific memory center in the brain, but some brain structures are more involved in certain aspects of memory than others. The hippocampus and nearby areas of the temporal lobes in the cerebral cortex, along with other areas of the limbic system, are involved in explicit memory. In many aspects of memory, information is transmitted from the hippocampus to the frontal lobes. The cerebellum is involved in implicit memory. Various areas of the cerebral cortex, such as the temporal lobes and the hippocampus, are involved in priming. The amygdala is at work in emotional memories.

4 Summarize how memories are retrieved.

- The serial position effect is the tendency for items at the beginning and the end of a list to be remembered better than items in the middle of a list. The primacy effect refers to better recall for items at the beginning of the list. The recency effect refers to better memory for items at the end of a list.
- Memory retrieval is easier when effective cues are present. Another factor in effective retrieval is the nature of the retrieval task. Simple recognition of previously remembered information in the presence of cues is generally easier than recall of the information. The encoding specificity principle states that information present at the time of encoding or learning tends to be effective as a retrieval cue. Retrieval also benefits from priming, which activates particular connections or associations in memory. The tip-of-the-tongue phenomenon occurs when we cannot quite pull something out of memory. In many

instances, people recall information better when they attempt to recall information in the same context or internal state in which they learned the information. These processes are referred to as context-dependent and state-dependent memory, respectively.

- Autobiographical memory is a person's recollections of his or her life experiences. Autobiographical memory has three levels: (1) life time periods, (2) general events, and (3) event-specific knowledge. Biographies of the self connect the past and the present to form our identity.
- Flashbulb memories are memories of emotionally significant events that people often recall with more accuracy and vivid imagery than they do everyday events. Although flashbulb memories typically are more vivid and durable than everyday memories, they are subject to some deterioration and change. Memory for personal trauma also is usually more accurate than memory for ordinary events, but it too is subject to some distortion and inaccuracy. People tend to remember the core information about a personal trauma but might distort some of the details. Some cases of personal trauma result in post-traumatic stress disorder. The release of stress hormones, which is signaled by the amygdala, likely accounts for some of the extraordinary longevity and vividness of memories of emotional or traumatic experiences. Personal trauma can cause individuals to repress emotionally laden information so that it is not accessible to consciousness. Repression does not erase a memory; it just makes it far more difficult to retrieve.
- Eyewitness testimony may contain errors due to memory decay or bias. Wording of questions and lineup instructions are examples of circumstances that influence eyewitness testimony.

5 *Describe how encoding and retrieval failure are involved in forgetting.*

- Encoding failure is forgetting information that was never entered into long-term memory.
- Retrieval failure can occur for at least four reasons: Interference theory states that we forget not because memories are lost from storage but because other information gets in the way of what we want to remember. Interference can be proactive or retroactive. Decay theory states that when something new is learned, a neurochemical memory trace is formed, but over time this chemical trail tends to disintegrate; the term for the phenomenon of memories fading with the passage of time is transience. Motivated forgetting, which occurs when people want to forget something, is common when a memory becomes painful or anxiety laden, as in the case of emotional traumas such as rape or physical abuse. Amnesia, the physiologically based loss of memory, can be anterograde, affecting the retention of new information or events; retrograde, affecting memories of the past but not new events; or both.

6 *Evaluate study strategies based on an understanding of memory.*

- Effective encoding strategies when studying include being a good time manager and planner, paying attention and minimizing distraction, understanding the material rather than rotely memorizing it, asking yourself questions, taking good notes, and using mnemonic strategies.
- Effective storage strategies when studying include organizing your memory and spreading out and consolidating your learning.
- Effective retrieval strategies when studying include using good retrieval cues and using the PQ4R method.

Key Terms

Apply Your Knowledge

1. Try the following exercise: Take the key terms in a chapter of this text that you have not yet read. Spend 20–30 minutes trying to learn half of the words in an environment filled with distractions (such as the cafeteria at lunchtime or a crowded coffeehouse). Then spend the same amount of time trying to learn the other half of the words in a distraction-free environment. Test yourself later on your memory for the words. Which list was easier to remember? Are there distractions in your current study environment, and how do you think eliminating them would affect your memory?

2. Some people believe that they have memories from past lives stored in their brains. Consider each of the ways the brain may store memory. Are any of these compatible with memories from past lives?

3. It is sometimes difficult to believe that our memories are not as accurate as we think they are. To test your ability to be a good eyewitness, visit one of the following websites:

   http://www.pbs.org/wgbh/pages/frontline/shows/dna/
   http://www.vuw.ac.nz/psyc/assefiEWT/homepage.html
   http://abcnews.go.com/sections/us/dailynews/
   eyewitness testimony.html

Did these exercises change your opinion of the accuracy of eyewitness testimony? What about eyewitness accounts of UFO sightings or other paranormal events? Are these likely to be more accurate than memories for other events?

4. Think about the serial position effect. What does it suggest about how you should organize your study time? When should you study information you think is most important?

5. For several days, keep a list of times when you failed to remember something. Take a look at the list and identify whether they were instances of encoding failure or one of the types of retrieval failure. Is there one kind of forgetting that seems to be most problematic for you? Can you think of any strategies to help you with this kind of forgetting?

Connections

For extra help in mastering the material in this chapter, see the review sections and practice quizzes in the Student Study Guide, the CD-ROM, and the Online Learning Center.

9 Thinking and Language

Chapter Outline

THE COGNITIVE REVOLUTION IN PSYCHOLOGY   **1**

CONCEPT FORMATION   **2**

Functions of Concepts
▼
Structure of Concepts

PROBLEM SOLVING   **3**

Steps in Problem Solving
▼
Obstacles to Solving Problems
▼
Expertise

CRITICAL THINKING, REASONING, AND DECISION MAKING   **4**

Critical Thinking
▼
Reasoning
▼
Decision Making

LANGUAGE AND THOUGHT   **5**

The Structure of Language
▼
The Link Between Language and Cognition
▼
Animal Language

LANGUAGE ACQUISITION AND DEVELOPMENT   **6**

Biological Influences
▼
Environmental Influences
▼
Early Development of Language
▼
Language and Education

Learning Goals

1 Characterize the "cognitive revolution" in psychology.

2 Explain concept formation.

3 Describe the requirements for solving problems.

4 Discuss the main factors in thinking critically, reasoning, and making decisions.

5 Identify the possible connections between language and thought.

6 Summarize how language is acquired and develops.

When she was 18 years old, Wendy Verougstraete felt that she was on the road to becoming a professional author. "You are looking at a professional author," she said. "My books will be filled with drama, action, and excitement. And everyone will want to read them. I am going to write books, page after page, stack after stack."

Overhearing her remarks, you might have been impressed not only by Wendy's optimism and determination but also by her expressive verbal skills. In fact, at a young age, Wendy showed a flair for writing and telling stories. And now, at age 25, Wendy has a rich vocabulary, creates lyrics for love songs, and enjoys telling stories. You probably would not be able to immediately guess that she has an IQ of only 49 and cannot tie her shoes, cross the street by herself, read or print words beyond the first-grade level, or do even simple arithmetic.

Wendy Verougstraete has *Williams syndrome*, a genetic birth disorder that was first described in 1961 and that affects about 1 in 20,000 births. The most noticeable features of the syndrome include a unique combination of expressive verbal skills, extremely low IQ, and limited spatial and motor control (Bohning, Campbell, & Karmiloff-Smith, 2002; Osborne & Pober, 2001; Vicari, Bellucci, & Carlesimo, 2001). Figure 9.1 shows the great disparity in the verbal and motor skills of one person with Williams syndrome. Individuals with Williams syndrome often have good musical skills and interpersonal skills. The syndrome also includes a number of physical characteristics as well, such as heart defects and a pixie-like facial appearance. Despite having excellent verbal skills and competent interpersonal skills, most individuals with Williams syndrome cannot live independent lives (American Academy of Pediatrics, 2001). For example, Wendy Verougstraete lives in a group home for adults who are mentally retarded.

The verbal abilities of individuals with Williams syndrome are very distinct from those shown by individuals with Down syndrome, a type of mental retardation that is discussed in chapter 10 (Bellugi & Wang, 1996). On vocabulary tests, children with Williams syndrome show a liking for unusual words. When asked to name as many animals as they can think of in 1 minute, Williams children come up with creatures such as ibex, chihuahua, saber-toothed tiger, weasel, crane, and newt. Children with Down syndrome give simple examples such as dog, cat, and mouse. When children with Williams syndrome tell stories, their voices come alive with drama and emotion, punctuating the dialogue with attention grabbers such as "gadzooks" or "lo and behold!" In contrast, children with Down syndrome tell very simple stories with little emotion.

Aside from being an interesting genetic disorder, Williams syndrome offers insights into the normal development of thinking and language. In our society, verbal ability is generally associated with high intelligence. But Williams syndrome raises the possibility that thinking and language might not be so closely related. Williams disorder is due to a defective gene that seems to protect expressive verbal ability but not reading and many other cognitive skills (Schultz, Grelotti, & Pober, 2001). Thus cases such as Wendy Verougstraete's cast some doubt on the general categorization of intelligence as verbal ability and prompts the question What is the relation between thinking and language? This question is addressed later in the chapter.

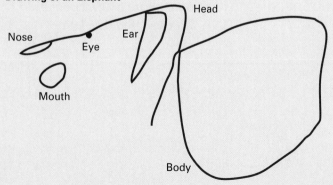

Drawing of an Elephant

Verbal Description of an Elephant

And what an elephant is, it is one of the animals. And what the elephant does, it lives in the jungle. It can also live in the zoo. And what it has, it has long gray ears, fan ears, ears that can blow in the wind. It has a long trunk that can pick up grass, or pick up hay. . . . If they're in a bad mood it can be terrible. . . . If the elephant gets mad it could stomp; it could charge. Sometimes elephants can charge. They have big long tusks. They can damage a car. . . . It could be dangerous. When they're in a pinch, when they're in a bad mood it can be terrible. You don't want an elephant as a pet. You want a cat or a dog or a bird. . . .

FIGURE 9.1 Disparity in the Verbal and Motor Skills of an Individual with Williams Syndrome

What is the "cognitive revolution" in psychology?

Behaviorism was a dominant force in psychology until the late 1950s and 1960s, when many psychologists began to realize that they could not understand or explain human behavior without referring to mental processes (Gardner, 1985; Reed, 2001). The term *cognitive psychology* became a label for approaches that sought to explain observable behavior by investigating mental processes and structures that cannot be directly observed (Sternberg, 2003; Willingham, 2001). Cognitive psychologists are fascinated by cases such as Wendy Verougstraete's because of their interest in language, problem solving, reasoning, and decision making. Cognitive psychologists also are interested in how people process memories in adapting to their world. Basically, cognitive psychologists study **cognition**—how information is processed and manipulated in remembering, thinking, and knowing.

One example of what cognitive psychologists do is provided by Mary Czerwinski, who works at Microsoft. She conducts research on attention and perception in three-dimensional environments. She believes that her psychology background has been invaluable in helping her to explore the best coupling between the computer user and various technologies.

It is no surprise that Czerwinski, with her degree in cognitive psychology, ended up at a computer company. Of all the factors that stimulated the growth of cognitive psychology, probably none was more important than the development of computers. The first modern computer, developed by John von Neumann in the late 1940s, showed that machines could perform logical operations. In the 1950s, researchers speculated that some mental operations might be modeled by computers, possibly telling us something about the way the human mind works (Marcus, 2001).

Cognitive psychologists often use the computer as an analogy to help explain the relation between cognition and the brain (Levine, 2000). The physical brain is described as the computer's hardware, cognition as its software. Herbert Simon (1969) was among the pioneers in comparing the human mind to computer processing systems. In this analogy, the sensory and perceptual systems provide an "input channel," similar to the way data are entered into the computer (see figure 9.2). As input

Mary Czerwinski, cognitive psychologist, at her Microsoft office.

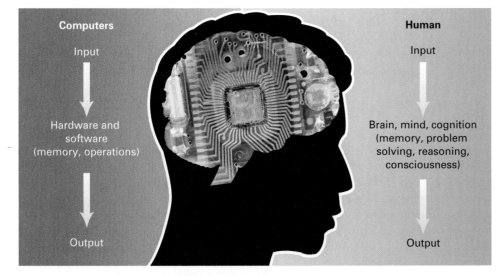

FIGURE 9.2 Computers and Human Cognition An analogy is commonly drawn between human cognition and the way computers work. The physical brain is analogous to a computer's hardware, and cognition is analogous to a computer's software.

cognition The way in which information is processed and manipulated in remembering, thinking, and knowing.

Artificial intelligence systems have been used to assist in medical diagnosis and treatment. *What are some other ways they can be used?*

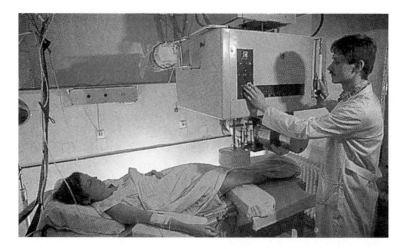

(information) comes into the mind, mental processes, or operations, act on it, just as the computer's software acts on the data. The transformed input generates information that remains in memory much in the way a computer stores what it has worked on. Finally, the information is retrieved from memory and "printed out" or "displayed" (so to speak) as an overt, observable response.

Computers provide a logical and concrete model of how information is processed in the mind, but the model is perhaps oversimplified. Although the development of computers played an important role in psychology's cognitive revolution, inanimate computers and human brains function quite differently in some respects (Auyang, 2001; Restak, 1988). For example, each brain cell, or neuron, is alive and can respond to information, often ambiguous, transmitted through the sensory receptors described in chapter 5, such as the eyes and ears. In contrast, most computers receive information from a human who has already coded the information and removed much of the ambiguity.

Computers can do some things better than humans. Computers can perform complex numerical calculations much faster and more accurately than humans could ever hope to (Bringsjord & Ferrucci, 2000). Computers can also apply and follow rules more consistently and with fewer errors than humans and represent complex mathematical patterns better than humans can.

But the brain's extraordinary capabilities will probably not be mimicked completely by computers any time in the near future. Attempts to use computers to process visual information or spoken language have achieved only limited success in highly specific situations. The human brain also has incredible ability to learn new rules, relationships, concepts, and patterns that it can generalize to novel situations. In comparison, computers are quite limited in their ability to learn and generalize. Although a computer can improve its ability to recognize patterns or use rules of thumb to make decisions, it does not have the means to develop new learning goals. Furthermore, the human mind is aware of itself; the computer is not. Indeed, no computer is likely to approach the richness of human consciousness (Favconnier & Turner, 2002).

Nonetheless, the computer's role in cognitive psychology continues to increase, giving rise in recent years to a field called **artificial intelligence (AI),** the science of creating machines capable of performing activities that require intelligence when they are done by people. AI is especially helpful in tasks requiring speed, persistence, and a vast memory (Hancock, 1999; Simon, 2000). AI systems also have been designed to assist in diagnosing medical illnesses and prescribing treatment, examining equipment failures, evaluating loan applicants, and advising students about which courses to take (Hatzakis & Tsoukas, 2002; Lisboa, 2002).

Artificial intelligence systems attempt to mimic the way humans think. But are their capabilities the same as thinking? What exactly is thinking? The next three

artificial intelligence (AI) The science of creating machines capable of performing activities that require intelligence when they are done by people.

sections explore this question. **Thinking** involves manipulating information, as when we form concepts, solve problems, think critically, reason, and make decisions. You will see that some of the processes you learned about in previous chapters, such as how people perceive information (chapter 5) and how information is encoded, stored, and retrieved (chapter 8) play a part in thinking.

Review and Sharpen Your Thinking

1 **_Characterize the "cognitive revolution" in psychology._**

  • Define cognition and discuss the cognitive revolution in psychology.

What can your mind do that a computer cannot do? What can a computer do that your mind cannot? Do you think you might have to answer these questions differently 40 to 50 years from now? Explain.

mhhe com/
santrockp7

For study tools related to this learning goal, see the Study Guide, the CD-ROM, and the Online Learning Center.

CONCEPT FORMATION 2

Functions of Concepts   **Structures of Concepts**

How are concepts formed?

Regardless of the kind of thinking we engage in, our thinking is fueled by concepts. **Concepts** are mental categories that are used to group objects, events, and characteristics. Humans have a special ability for creating categories to help us make sense of information in our world (Hahn & Ramscar, 2001; Zacks & Tversky, 2001). We know that apples and oranges are both fruits, although they have different tastes and colors. We know that Porsches and Ford Escorts are both automobiles, although they differ in cost, speed, and prestige. How do we know these things? The answer lies in our ability to group them on the basis of their features. For example, Porsches and Ford Escorts both have an engine, four wheels, and a steering wheel, and both provide transportation. By such features we know that they are both automobiles. In other words, we have a *concept* of what an automobile is.

Functions of Concepts

Concepts are important for several reasons:

1. Concepts allow us to generalize. If we did not have concepts, each object and event in our world would be unique to us.
2. Concepts allow us to associate experiences and objects. Basketball, ice hockey, and track are sports. The concept of *sport* gives us a way to compare these activities. Neoclassicism, impressionism, and expressionism are all schools of art. The concept *schools of art* lets us compare paintings by artists from these different schools (see figure 9.3).
3. Concepts grease the wheels of memory, making it more efficient so that we don't have to "reinvent the wheel" each time we come across a piece of information. For example, we don't have to relearn what the Dow Jones Industrial Average is each time we pick up a newspaper. We already have the concept.
4. Concepts also provide clues about how to react to a particular object or experience. For example, if we see a bowl of pretzels, our concept of food lets us know it is okay to eat them.

© The New Yorker Collection 1986 Edward Koren from cartoonbank.com. All Rights Reserved.

thinking Manipulating information, as when we form concepts, solve problems, think critically, reason, and make decisions.

concepts Mental categories that are used to group objects, events, and characteristics.

FIGURE 9.3 **The Concept of Schools of Art** The concept of schools of art lets us compare paintings by different artists. How do other neoclassicist paintings compare to the one by Michelangelo? How do other impressionist paintings compare to the one by Monet? How do other expressionist paintings compare to the one by Klee?

Monet's *Palazzo Da Mula, Venice*

Michelangelo's *Libyan Sibyl,* Sistine Chapel

Klee's *Dance You Monster to My Soft Song*

Forming a concept can be a complicated process. Suppose you are an avid tennis player but think you are losing too many matches because your serve is weak. Despite hours of practice, your serve just isn't getting any better. You decide that your problem might be that you have only a vague concept of what a "killer" serve is. Based on your observations, you develop a hypothesis about the mechanics of an excellent serve. For example, you decide that the ball must be tossed high so the server has to stretch to reach it and that the server needs to swing the racket the way a baseball pitcher throws an overhand pitch. You might want to scrutinize the serves of more highly skilled players to see if they confirm your hypothesis. You'll also want to test the hypothesis in your own game to see if it improves your serve.

Even though your concept formation is on track and your tennis serve improves, you might still be somewhat dissatisfied. With a difficult concept (such as the mechanics of a good serve), you might need an expert—a professional tennis coach—to help you. The pro's concept is likely to include many more features than the ones you discovered, as well as complex rules related to those features. For example, the pro might tell you that tossing the ball high helps, but that it works much better if you rotate the grip on your racket counterclockwise. In general, concepts with more features and more complicated rules are more difficult to learn. Part of being an expert in any field is grasping the complicated rules of difficult concepts.

Structure of Concepts

Three models of how people structure concepts have been proposed: (1) the classical model, (2) the prototype model, and (3) the exemplar model (Medin, Proffitt, & Schwartz, 2000). In the **classical model,** all instances of a concept share defining properties. For example, the concept of triangle requires that a geometric form have three sides and interior angles that equal 180.

Although the classical model describes concepts that involve geometric forms reasonably well, challenges to it have been raised. If a concept depends on its defining characteristics, then specifying these characteristics should be straightforward. However, it can be difficult to define the characteristics of even frequently used concepts. For example, "can fly" might seem to be an appropriate defining characteristic of the concept of "bird." However, ostriches and penguins are birds that do not fly. Another criticism of the classical model is that it cannot explain how people are able to judge some instances of a concept as being more typical than others. For example, robins are considered to be more typical of the concept of bird than penguins are.

The **prototype model** emphasizes that people decide whether an item reflects a concept by comparing it with the most typical item(s) in that category. To continue with the concept of bird, birds generally fly, sing, and build nests, but there are exceptions to these properties. Thus Eleanor Rosch (1973) argues that membership in a concept can be graded, rather than all or none. In her view, the better members of the concept (such as robins for the concept of bird) have more characteristics than the poorer members of the category (such as penguins). The prototype model maintains that characteristic properties are used to create a representation of the average or ideal member, prototype, for each concept. Potential members of the concept are then compared to this prototype. Thus the prototype model is able to explain typical effects (Minda & Smith, 2001).

Each of these models accounts for some but not all of the findings regarding the structure of concepts, and thus each has its proponents (Medin, Lynch, & Solomon, 2000). Although research continues to be carried out on the categorization aspects of concepts, current research also focuses on other aspects of concepts. For example, some researchers have found that the way we use concepts affects a concept's structure and organization (Ross, 2000). Other researchers are studying people's concepts of events (Zacks & Tversky, 2001). And, yet others are focusing on how people combine concepts to express new ideas or to refer to new situations (Wisniewski, 2000). Interest in the combination of concepts includes language use. For example, most of

classical model States that all instances of a concept share defining properties.

prototype model People decide whether an item reflects a concept by comparing it with the most typical item(s) of that concept that they know about.

the sentences you have ever read or heard, including this one, correspond to a novel combination of concepts. One contemporary research interest is on novel noun-noun and adjective-noun combinations, such as "ostrich steak" and "space shuttle." The creation of such combinations is an important mechanism that speakers use to expand their language.

mhhe com/
santrockp7

For study tools related to this learning goal, see the Study Guide, the CD-ROM, and the Online Learning Center.

Review and Sharpen Your Thinking

2 *Explain concept formation.*

- Discuss the functions of concepts.
- Describe two models of concept structure.

Write down seven concepts that come to your mind. Then create a diagram to show meaningful connections among them. Add more categories if you need them to link everything together. Compare your diagram with someone else's in the class. What does this exercise suggest about the simplicity or complexity of concepts?

3 PROBLEM SOLVING

| Steps in Problem Solving | Obstacles to Solving Problems | Expertise |

In the nineteenth century, New York City began to experience traffic jams. The horse-drawn vehicles were making street traffic dangerous. *How did William Eno solve this problem?*

What are the requirements for solving problems?

Concepts are basic to another cognitive skill: problem solving. It is impossible to solve problems without concepts. Think about driving. Signs and traffic signals tell us to stop, yield, or proceed or not to pass or park. Most of the symbols that keep traffic moving so smoothly are the brainchild of William Eno, the "father of traffic safety." Eno, born in New York City in 1858, became concerned about the city's horrendous traffic jams. Horse-drawn vehicles were making street traffic dangerous. Eno published a paper about the urgency of street traffic reform. His proposed solutions to the problem created new concepts, such as the concepts "stop signs," "one-way streets," and "pedestrian islands," which continue to be important to traffic safety today (Bransford & Stein, 1993).

Like William Eno, we face many problems in the course of our everyday lives. These include trying to figure out the fastest way to get across town, planning how to get enough money to buy a sound system, working a jigsaw puzzle, or estimating how much financial aid we need for school. **Problem solving** is an attempt to find an appropriate way of attaining a goal when the goal is not readily available. Among the methods for doing so are following the steps required for problem solving, overcoming mental obstacles, and developing expertise.

Steps in Problem Solving

Given the importance of solving problems in our everyday lives—and the importance of solving some extraordinarily difficult problems—psychologists have gone to great effort to specify the thinking process that individuals go through to effectively solve problems. Psychological research points to four steps in the process: (1) find and frame problems, (2) develop good problem-solving strategies, (3) evaluate solutions, and (4) rethink and redefine problems and solutions over time.

problem solving An attempt to find an appropriate way of attaining a goal when the goal is not readily available.

Find and Frame the Problem Before a problem can be solved, it has to be recognized (Mayer, 2000). Unfortunately, our society all too often discourages people from identifying problems. Many businesses, government agencies, and schools reprimand or fire employees who identify problems in the workplace. For example, increased incidences of cancer from asbestos might have been avoided if problems identified by employees had been acknowledged and acted on by people in authority. The pressure to ignore problems is so strong that Congress finally passed a bill that provides protection for employees who are brave enough to persist in their fight to have the problems they identify recognized. It became known as the Whistle-Blower Protection Act.

Finding and framing problems often involves asking questions in creative ways (Goleman, Kaufman, & Ray, 1993). Bill Bowerman (inventor of Nike shoes) asked, "What happens if I pour rubber over a waffle iron?" Fred Smith (founder of Federal Express) asked, "Why can't there be reliable overnight mail service?" Godfrey Hounsfield (inventor of the CAT scan) asked, "Why can't we see in three dimensions what is inside the human body without cutting it open?" Masaru Ibuka (honorary chairman of Sony) asked, "Why don't we remove the recording function and speaker from the portable music player and put the headphones directly on the player?"

Many of these questions were ridiculed at first. Other shoe companies thought Bowerman's waffle shoe was a "really stupid idea." Fred Smith proposed the idea of Federal Express during his days as a student at Yale and got a C on the paper. Godfrey Hounsfield was told that the CAT scan was impractical. And Masaru Ibuka was told that the Walkman would never sell: "A player without speakers—you must be crazy!"

In the past, students were taught to solve problems through exercises involving well-defined problems with well-defined steps for solving them. However, students can't really learn how to solve problems unless they have opportunities to identify problems as well. Many real-world problems are ill defined or vague and have no clearly defined solutions. Consider a common problem situation for students: You have to write a paper for your psychology course. This is an overly general, ill-defined problem that you will have to narrow down in order to proceed. You will need to define a more specific problem, such as deciding on the area of psychology (neuroscience, cognitive psychology, abnormal psychology, and so on) you will write about. Once you decide on an area of psychology, you will need to narrow your focus further to find a specific problem within that area to write about. This type of exercise—finding and framing problems—is an important aspect of problem solving.

Develop Good Problem-Solving Strategies Once you find a problem and clearly define it, you need to develop strategies for solving it. Among the effective strategies are subgoals, algorithms, and heuristics.

Subgoaling involves setting intermediate goals or defining intermediate problems that put you in a better position for reaching the final goal or solution. Let's return to the problem of writing a paper for a psychology course. What might be some subgoaling strategies? One might be locating the right books and research journals on the problem you have decided to study. At the same time that you are searching for the right books and journals, you will likely benefit from establishing some subgoals within the time frame you have for completing the project. If the paper is due in 2 months, you might set a subgoal of a first draft of the paper 2 weeks before it is due, another subgoal of completing reading for the paper 1 month before it is due, and yet another subgoal of starting library research tomorrow.

Notice that in establishing the subgoals for meeting the deadline, we worked backward. Working backward in establishing subgoals is a good strategy. You first create the subgoal that is closest to the final goal and then work backward to the subgoal that is closest to the beginning of the problem-solving effort.

Algorithms are strategies that guarantee a solution to a problem. Algorithms come in different forms, such as formulas, instructions, or trying out all possible solutions (Alexander & others, 2002). We often use algorithms in cooking (by following a recipe) and driving (by following directions to an address).

subgoaling Involves setting intermediate goals or defining intermediate problems that put you in a better position to reach the final goal or solution.

algorithms Strategies that guarantee a solution to a problem.

In some cases an algorithmic strategy might take a long time. Consider a person who is working a crossword puzzle. She comes across c_nt_ _ker_ _ _ and looks to see what hint is given. It says, "Ill-tempered and quarrelsome." An algorithm for finding the correct word exists. She could try every possible alphabet combination in the six blank spaces and then check through a dictionary to see which one is correct. However, not many people would want to go through the more than 1 million steps in this algorithmic effort. Clearly, the algorithmic strategy of trying out all possible solutions should be applied to problems with a small number of possible solutions.

So, instead of using an algorithm to solve this type of problem, most crossword-puzzle enthusiasts use **heuristics,** which are strategies or guidelines that suggest a solution to a problem but do not guarantee an answer (Oaksford, Roberts, & Chater, 2002). Crossword enthusiasts know that certain combinations of letters are likelier to work than others. For example, c_nt_ _ker_ _ _ is likely to require a vowel between *c* and *n*, so *b, q,* and a lot of other letters won't work. We also know that combinations of letters such as *an* are acceptable between *t* and *k*. We also know that it helps to sound out some words at this point. We come up with "contank" and "cantank." Then we get it: *cantankerous.*

In the real world, the types of problems we face are likelier to be solved by heuristics than by algorithms. Heuristics help us narrow down the possible solutions to find the one that works (Hall, 2002; Snook, Canter, & Bennell, 2002; Stanovich & West, 2000; Todd & Gigerenzer, 2001).

Evaluate Solutions   Once we think we have solved a problem, we really won't know how effective our solution is until we find out if it actually works. It helps to have in mind a clear criterion for the effectiveness of the solution.

For example, what will your criterion be for judging the effectiveness of your solution to the psychology assignment, your psychology paper? Will you judge your solution effective if you simply get it completed? If you receive positive feedback on the paper? If you get an A? If the instructor says that it is one of the best papers ever turned in on the topic?

Rethink and Redefine Problems and Solutions Over Time   An important final step in problem solving is to continually rethink and redefine problems (Bereiter & Scardamalia, 1993). People who are good at problem solving tend to be more motivated than the average person to improve on their past performances and to make original contributions.

Thus you can examine your psychology paper after it is returned by your instructor and use the feedback to think about ways to improve it. Sony continues to try to improve its Walkman, striving to make it lighter, smaller, and better sounding.

Obstacles to Solving Problems

Psychologists have not only sought to understand how problems can be solved; they have also studied the obstacles that often prevent people from solving problems effectively. The obstacles include becoming fixated and not being adequately motivated or not controlling emotions.

Becoming Fixated   It is easy to fall into the trap of becoming fixated on a particular strategy for solving a problem. **Fixation** involves using a prior strategy and failing to look at a problem from a fresh, new perspective. Psychologists have identified several kinds of fixation.

One type is **functional fixedness,** in which individuals fail to solve a problem because they are fixated on a thing's usual functions. If you have ever used a shoe to hammer a nail, you have overcome functional fixedness to solve a problem.

heuristics Strategies or guidelines that suggest, but do not guarantee, a solution to a problem.

fixation Involves using a prior problem-solving strategy and failing to look at a problem from a new perspective.

functional fixedness A type of fixation in which individuals fail to solve a problem because they are fixated on a thing's usual functions.

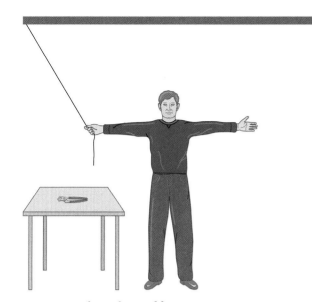

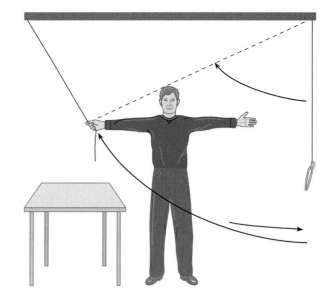

FIGURE 9.4 **Maier String Problem** How can you tie the two strings together if you cannot reach them both at the same time?

FIGURE 9.5 **Solution to the Maier String Problem** Use the pliers as a weight to create a pendulum motion that brings the second string closer.

An example of a problem that requires overcoming functional fixedness is the Maier String Problem, which is depicted in figure 9.4 (Maier, 1931). The problem is to figure out how to tie two strings together when you must stand in one spot and cannot reach both at the same time. It seems as though you are stuck, but there is a pair of pliers on a table. Can you solve the problem?

The solution is to use the pliers as a weight, tying them to the end of one string (see figure 9.5). Swing this string back and forth like a pendulum and grasp the stationary string. Your past experience with pliers and fixation on their usual function makes this a difficult problem to solve. To solve the problem, you need to find an unusual use for the pliers, in this case as a weight to create a pendulum.

Effective problem solving may also be blocked by a **mental set,** a type of fixation in which an individual tries to solve a problem in a particular way that has worked in the past. Each of us occasionally gets in the mental rut of trying to solve problems with a well-worn strategy.

I had a mental set about using a typewriter rather than a computer to write my books. I felt comfortable with a typewriter and never lost any sections I had written. It took a long time to break out of this mental set. Once I did, though, the problem goal of finishing a book became much easier. You might feel the same about some aspects of technology. A good strategy is to keep an open mind and monitor whether your mental set is keeping you from trying something new.

Figure 9.6 invites you to explore how fixation might be involved in your own problem-solving efforts.

Motivation and Emotion Individuals might have great problem-solving skills and know all the steps for solving problems, but it hardly matters what talents they have if they are not motivated to use them (Sternberg & Spear-Swerling, 1996). It is especially important to be internally motivated to solve a problem and to persist with the effort at finding a solution. Some people give up too easily.

Emotion can also facilitate or inhibit problem solving. As well as being highly motivated, good problem solvers are often able to control their emotions and concentrate on a solution to a problem (Barron & Harackiewicz, 2001). Individuals who are competent at solving problems also are usually not afraid of making mistakes (Shewchuk, Johnson, & Elliott, 1999; Slavin, 2000).

mental set A type of fixation in which an individual tries to solve a problem in a particular way that has worked in the past.

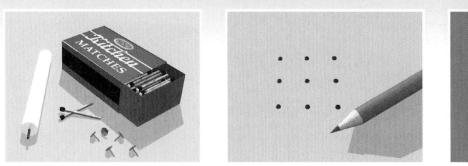

The Candle Problem
How would you mount a candle on a wall so that it won't drip wax on a table or a floor while it is burning?

The Nine-Dot Problem
Take out a piece of paper and copy the arrangement of dots shown below. Without lifting your pencil, connect the dots using only four straight lines.

The Six-Matchstick Problem
Arrange six matchsticks of equal length to make four equilateral triangles, the sides of which are one matchstick long.

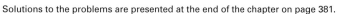

Solutions to the problems are presented at the end of the chapter on page 381.

FIGURE 9.6 Examples of How Fixation Impedes Problem Solving

Stephen J. Hawking is a world-renowned expert in physics. Hawking authored the best-selling books *A Brief History of Time* and *The Universe in a Nutshell*. Hawking has a neurological disorder that prevents him from walking or talking. He communicates with the aid of a voice-equipped computer. *What might be some differences in the ways Hawking solves physics problems and the ways novices solve them?*

Expertise

Researchers are very interested in how experts and novices differ in the way they think and solve problems (Prietula, Feltovich, & Marchak, 2000). Researchers have studied experts and novices in such diverse areas as chess, physics, mathematics, electronics, squash, and history (Abernethy & others, 2001). They have found that experts have acquired extensive knowledge that affects what they pay attention to and how they organize, represent, and interpret information. The way they encode and store information, in turn, influences their ability to remember, reason, and solve problems (National Research Council, 1999).

Experts solve problems differently than novices do because they are better than novices in four specific ways:

- *Knowledge base*. Experts have broad and highly organized knowledge about their fields, which often allows them to solve a problem from memory without going through a tedious problem-solving effort (Wilding & Valentine, 1996). In the expert's mind, knowledge is organized hierarchically. Specific details are grouped into chunks, which in turn are grouped into more general topics, which in turn come under the heading of more general topics, and so on as described in chapter 8. Figure 9.7a shows the hierarchical arrangement one physicist used to organize the knowledge that was needed to solve a physics problem. The dotted lines connecting the smaller branches of the "concept tree" are *pointers*, associations made by experience that possibly produce shortcuts in solving the problem. An example of how a novice might try to solve the same problem is shown in Figure 9.7b. Notice the absence of pointers and the smaller number of levels and interconnections. Experts usually have far more interconnections in their storehouse of knowledge, and these interconnections are organized in ways that reflect a deep understanding of their subject matter (National Research Council, 1999).
- *Domain memory*. Experts are usually better than novices at remembering information in their domain of expertise (Chase & Simon, 1973). It is not that their general memory skills are better; it is just that they use their vast storehouse of knowledge to organize and chunk information in ways that make it more memorable. Good memory for relevant information in a problem can often improve your ability to solve it.
- *Strategies*. Experts often have more effective strategies to solve a problem than novices. Experts are more likely to have effective strategies at their command

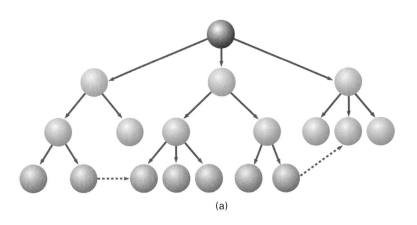

(a)

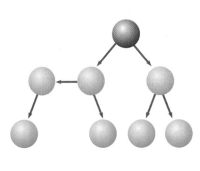

(b)

FIGURE 9.7 An Example of How Information Is Organized in the Minds of an Expert and a Novice (*a*) An expert's knowledge is based on years of experience in which small bits of information have been linked with many others, which together are placed in a general category. This category is in turn placed in a more general category of knowledge. The dotted lines, *pointers*, show associations between specific elements of knowledge that connect the lower branches and provide mental shortcuts in the expert's mind. (*b*) A novice's knowledge shows far fewer connections, levels, and shortcuts than an expert's knowledge.

before they start to solve the problem and are more flexible in reorganizing or modifying them as the problem solving progresses.

- *Deliberate practice*. Becoming an expert in a particular field is not accomplished overnight. It usually takes years of experience and a conscious effort to practice, whether the field is cardiology, commodities trading, chemical engineering, law, or even gardening (Ericsson & others, 1993). In deliberate practice, individuals expend extensive effort and time motivated by the goal of improving their skill.

We can all appreciate and admire expertise but need to remember that the ability to solve specific kinds of problems effectively is often limited to a particular field. For example, being an expert at chess does not make you an expert at gardening or chemical engineering. Being an expert at playing sports or music or acting does not make you an expert at policy making or running a business—just as being an expert politician or entrepreneur does not make you an expert athlete or entertainer.

Review and Sharpen Your Thinking

3   *Describe the requirements for solving problems.*
- Define problem solving and identify four steps in solving problems.
- Evaluate obstacles to solving problems.
- Discuss the role of expertise in solving problems.

Think of a problem that you have not been able to solve or would like to solve. How might following the steps in problem solving and avoiding obstacles in problem solving help you solve this problem? Explain.

mhhe com/
santrockp7

For study tools related to this learning goal, see the Study Guide, the CD-ROM, and the Online Learning Center.

CRITICAL THINKING, REASONING, AND DECISION MAKING   4

Critical Thinking   Reasoning   Decision Making

What are the main factors in thinking critically, reasoning, and making decisions?
In addition to forming concepts and solving problems, thinking includes three types of higher-order mental processing: critical thinking, reasoning, and decision making. All require rich connections among neurons and the ability to apply judgment. The end result of this type of thinking is an evaluation, conclusion, or decision.

"For God's sake, think! Why is he being so nice to you?"

The New Yorker Collection © 1998 Sam Gross from cartoonbank.com. All Rights Reserved.

Critical Thinking

In chapter 1, I defined *critical thinking* as thinking reflectively and productively and evaluating the evidence. People who think critically grasp the deeper meaning of ideas, keep an open mind about different approaches and perspectives, and decide for themselves what to believe or do (Halpern, 2002; Kamin & others, 2001).

Critical thinking is currently of considerable interest to both psychologists and educators. However, critical thinking is not an entirely new idea. Educator John Dewey (1933) was working with a similar idea when he advocated teaching students to "think reflectively." Today, educators at all levels embrace the idea that an important outcome of education is to develop students' ability to think critically.

Yet few schools teach students to think critically and to develop a deep understanding of concepts (Brooks & Brooks, 2001). For example, many high school students read *Hamlet* but are not asked to think about how its notions of power, greed, and conflicting relationships apply to their lives or the wider world. They rarely are stimulated to rethink their prior ideas about these matters.

Instead, schools spend too much time on getting students to give a single correct answer in an imitative way rather than encouraging students to come up with new ideas (Brooks & Brooks, 2001). Too often teachers ask students to recite, define, describe, state, and list rather than to analyze, infer, connect, synthesize, criticize, create, evaluate, think, and rethink. Too often we are inclined to stay on the surface of problems rather than to stretch our minds.

One attempt to encourage critical thinking in schools is the Fostering a Community of Learners (FCL) program, created by Ann Brown and Joseph Campione (1996; Brown, 1997; Campione, 2001). Currently, FCL is running in inner-city elementary schools for 6- to 12-year-old children. Reflection and discussion are key dimensions of the program. Questioning, making constructive comments, and critiquing are the mode rather than the exception. These skills are modeled for the children by visiting experts and classroom teachers. The adults ask students to justify their opinions and to support them with evidence, to think of counterexamples, and so on. Research evaluation of the FCL program revealed that it improved participants' achievement in reading, writing, and problem solving (Brown, 1997; Campione,

The "Fostering a Community of Learners" approach is used in this science classroom at Compton-Drew High School in St. Louis. *What are some of the main themes in this approach?*

2001). Programs such as this have helped us to identify two important characteristics of critical thinkers: mindfulness and open-mindedness.

Mindfulness   Mindfulness is a characteristic of critical thinkers, according to Ellen Langer (1989, 1997, 2000; Langer & Moldoveanu, 2000). She studies mindless behavior and encourages people to be more mindful. One of her favorite examples of mindless behavior involves the time she used a new credit card in a department store. The clerk noticed that she had not signed the card and handed it to her to sign on the back. After passing the credit card through the machine, the clerk handed her a receipt to sign. Then the clerk held up the receipt Langer had signed and compared the signatures.

Langer's concept of mindfulness is similar to the description of critical thinking. She says that a mindful person continues to create new ideas, is open to new information, and is aware of more than one perspective. In contrast, a mindless person is entrapped in old ideas, engages in automatic behavior, and operates from a single perspective. Langer believes that asking good questions is an important ingredient of mindful thinking.

Open-Mindedness   Note that, in Langer's view, mindful people are aware of more than one perspective. Too often, we take one side of an issue without really evaluating the issue or examining it from different perspectives. However, critical thinking means being open to the possibility of other ways of looking at things.

People often don't know that there even is another side to an issue or evidence contrary to what they believe (Slife & Yanchar, 2000). Simple openness to other viewpoints can help to keep people from jumping to conclusions. As Socrates once said, such caution in thinking—that is, knowing what it is you don't know—is sometimes the first step to true wisdom.

In chapter 1, I urged you to think critically about controversies in psychology. Psychology has advanced as a field because psychologists have thought deeply about controversial issues, conducted extensive research on them, examined the evidence, and kept open minds about interpreting the results. I hope the critical controversy boxes that appear in each chapter challenge you to think about issues in less biased, more flexible, more reflective ways. In doing so, you will become a better critical thinker. To evaluate the extent to which you use critical thinking strategies, see the Psychology and Life box.

Reasoning

Reasoning is the mental activity of transforming information to reach conclusions. It is a skill closely tied to critical thinking (Hunt, 2002; Markman & Gentner, 2001). Reasoning can be either inductive or deductive (see figure 9.8).

Inductive Reasoning   **Inductive reasoning** involves reasoning from the specific to the general (Rips, 2002). That is, it consists of drawing conclusions (forming concepts) about all members of a category based on observing only some members. For example, in a literature class after reading a few of Shakespeare's plays, you might draw some likely conclusions about his general ways of using language. Psychological research is often inductive as well, studying a sample of participants in order to draw conclusions about the population from which the sample is drawn.

Notice that an inductive conclusion is never entirely certain—that is, it may be inconclusive. And, although an inductive conclusion may be likely, there is always a chance that it is wrong, perhaps because the sample does not perfectly represent its population (Johnson-Laird, 2000).

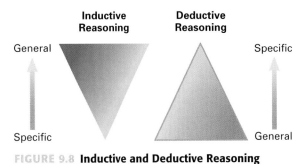

FIGURE 9.8 Inductive and Deductive Reasoning
(*Left*) The upside-down pyramid represents inductive reasoning—going from specific to general. (*Right*) The right-side-up pyramid represents deductive reasoning—going from general to specific.

reasoning The mental activity of transforming information to reach conclusions.

inductive reasoning Reasoning from the specific to the general.

Sharpening the Saw

Critical thinkers ask good questions (Santrock & Halonen, 2002). Some college students feel discouraged about asking questions, possibly because they acquired passive learning habits in elementary and secondary school. They also may fear being embarrassed by asking a question. However, critical thinkers get their curiosity out in the open, and developing an enthusiasm for asking questions can make college more interesting and enjoyable.

Sometimes you can spot people who have studied psychology just by the questions they ask about behavior. Just as carpenters keep their tools well honed, psychological thinkers use questions as tools to help them make good judgments about behavior. Consider the following questions:

- *What exactly do you mean by that?*
  Once you have examined behavior carefully, you recognize that it is important to precisely *describe* it. Starting with precise descriptions can help you interpret behavior or make good predictions about behavior. For example, a fuzzy description is "He is a nervous person." A more precise description might be "His anxious behavior is characterized by feelings of helplessness, trembling, and sweating, which intensify when he takes tests."
- *I wonder why that happens.*
  Thinking like a psychologist involves trying to *explain* behavior. Showing curiosity about what motivates people to do what they do is a hallmark of people interested in psychology. For example, you might wonder why some people ask good questions and others don't.

- *What is the evidence to back up your claims?*
  When an explanation about the causes of behavior is at issue, personal testimony is not sufficient. When you think like a psychologist, you need to see the data that back up claims before you believe them. For example, if someone claims that the vast majority of Americans believe in vouchers for schools, ask to see the evidence: One newscaster who made this claim based the statement on a survey in which 51 percent believed in vouchers for schools, hardly an overwhelming majority.
- *Is there another way to explain the behavior?*
  When you don't have data to support an explanation, you may be able to generate other ideas. Coming up with alternative explanations for the cause of a behavior is a skill that psychologists value highly. For example, you might originally hypothesize that the reason someone is behaving in a particular way is because he or she is a firstborn child. However, further inquiry might suggest other possible explanations, such as current stressful circumstances and growing up in impoverished conditions.
- *Is that a label or an explanation of behavior?*
  If Trudy has problems sleeping through the night, her behavior is labeled "insomnia." When asked why she has trouble sleeping, she says, "Because I have insomnia." However, insomnia is not an explanation; it is not the *cause* of her inability to sleep, it is simply the *fact* that she is unable to sleep. The *cause* of her insomnia might be drinking too much coffee at night, stress in her life, or sleeping too much during the day.

Inductive reasoning is basic to analogies (Chen, 2002). An *analogy* is a type of formal reasoning that involves four parts, with the relation between the first two parts being the same as the relation between the last two. For example, solve this analogy: Beethoven is to music as Picasso is to _____. To answer correctly ("art"), you had to induce the relation between Beethoven and music (the former created the latter) and apply this relationship to Picasso (what did he create?).

Analogies can be helpful in solving problems, especially when they are visually represented (Mumford & Porter, 1999). Benjamin Franklin noticed that a pointed object drew a stronger spark than a blunt object when both were in the vicinity of an electrified body. Originally he believed this was an unimportant observation, but then he realized that a pointed rod could be used to attract lightning (analogous to the spark), thus deflecting it from buildings and ships.

Deductive Reasoning In contrast to inductive reasoning, **deductive reasoning** is reasoning from the general to the specific (Knauff & others, 2002). The fictional British detective Sherlock Holmes was a master at deductive reasoning. When solving a case, he sorted through a number of clues to zero in on the one correct solution to a crime.

When you solve puzzles or riddles, you are engaging in deductive reasoning. When you learn a general rule and then understand how it applies in some situations but not in others, you are engaging in deductive reasoning. When psychologists and other scientists use theories and intuitions to make predictions and then

deductive reasoning Reasoning from the general to the specific.

evaluate their predictions by making further observations, deductive reasoning is at work.

Deductive reasoning is always certain in the sense that if the initial rules or assumptions are true, then the conclusion will follow directly as a matter of logic. For example, if you know the general rules that dogs bark and cats meow (and if they are always true), you can deduce whether your neighbor's strange-looking pet is a dog or a cat on the basis of the specific sound it makes. When psychologists develop a hypothesis from a theory, they are using a form of deductive reasoning, because the hypothesis is a specific, logical extension of the general theory. And if the theory is true, then the hypothesis will be true as well.

Decision Making

Think of all the decisions you have to make in your life. Should I major in biology, psychology, or business? Should I go to graduate school right after college or get a job first? Should I establish myself in a career before settling down to have a family? Should I buy a house or rent? **Decision making** involves evaluating alternatives and making choices among them (Galotti, 2002).

In inductive reasoning, people use established rules to draw conclusions. In contrast, when we make decisions, such rules are not established, and we don't know the consequences of the decisions (Gigenrenzer & Selton, 2001; Tversky & Fox, 1995). Some of the information might be missing, and we might not trust all of the information we have (Matlin, 2001).

In one type of decision-making research, investigators study how people weigh the costs and benefits of various outcomes. They have found that people choose the outcome with the highest expected value (Smyth & others, 1994). For example, in choosing a college, you might have listed the pluses and minuses of going to different colleges (related to such factors as cost, quality of education, social life, and so on) and then made a decision based on how the colleges rated on these criteria. In making your decision, you might have weighed some of these factors more heavily than others (e.g., giving cost 3 points, quality of education 2 points, and social life 1 point).

Another fruitful subject of decision-making research is the biases and flawed heuristics (rules of thumb) that affect the quality of decisions. In many cases, our decision-making strategies are well adapted to deal with a variety of problems (Nisbett & Ross, 1980). However, we are prone to make a number of mistakes in our thinking (Stanovich, 1999, 2001).

Confirmation Bias **Confirmation bias** is the tendency to search for and use information that supports our ideas rather than refutes them (Betch & others, 2001). Let's say that I have an initial hypothesis that something is going to work to solve a problem. I test the hypothesis and find that it is right some of the time. I conclude that my hypothesis was right rather than exploring possible reasons it did not work all of the time. Our decisions can also become further biased because we tend to seek out and listen to people whose views confirm our own and tend to avoid those who have dissenting views.

It is easy to detect the confirmation bias in the way that many people think. Consider politicians. They often accept news that supports their views and dismiss evidence that runs counter to their views. Consider also physicians who misdiagnose a patient because one or two symptoms fit with previous successful diagnoses they have made. In their desire to confirm their diagnosis, they ignore symptoms that do not fit their diagnosis.

In one study, Deanna Kuhn and her colleagues (Kuhn, Weinstock, & Flaton, 1994) had participants listen to an audiotaped reenactment of an actual murder trial.

"You take all the time you need, Larry—this certainly is a big decision."

decision making Involves evaluating alternatives and making choices among them.

confirmation bias The tendency to search for and use information that supports, rather than refutes, our ideas.

FIGURE 9.9 Belief Perseverance
Belief perseverance is a common bias that infiltrates our judgments. *How is belief perseverance involved in thinking it improbable that Madonna would have become a mother?*

belief perseverance The tendency to hold on to a belief in the face of contradictory evidence.

overconfidence bias The tendency to have more confidence in judgments and decisions than we should based on probability or past occurrence.

hindsight bias The tendency to falsely report, after the fact, that we accurately predicted an event.

Then they were asked what their verdict would be and why. Rather than considering and weighing possibilities drawing on all the evidence, many participants hurriedly composed a story that drew only from evidence that supported their views of what happened. These participants showed a confirmation bias by ignoring evidence that ran counter to their version of events.

Belief Perseverance Closely related to confirmation bias, **belief perseverance** is the tendency to hold on to a belief in the face of contradictory evidence. People have a difficult time letting go of an idea or strategy once they have embraced it. Consider Madonna (see figure 9.9). We have a hard time thinking of her in a maternal role because of the belief perseverance that she is a wild, fun-loving rock star.

Another example of belief perseverance gives some students trouble in the first year of college. They may have gotten good grades in high school by using the strategy of cramming for tests the night before. The ones who don't adopt a new strategy—spacing their study sessions more evenly through the term—often do poorly in college.

Overconfidence Bias **Overconfidence bias** is the tendency to have more confidence in judgments and decisions than we should based on probability or past experience. People are overconfident about how long people with a fatal disease will live, which businesses will go bankrupt, which psychiatric inpatients have serious mental disorders, whether a defendant is guilty in a court trial, and which students will do well in graduate school (Kahneman & Tversky, 1995). People consistently have more faith in their judgments than predictions based on statistically objective measures indicate they should (Flannelly, 2001).

In one study, college students were asked to make predictions about themselves in the coming academic year (Vallone & others, 1990). They were asked to predict whether they would drop any courses, vote in an election, and break up with their girlfriend or boyfriend. Then they were asked to rate how confident they were in their predictions. At the end of the year, the accuracy of their predictions was examined. The results: They were more likely to drop a class, not vote in an election, and break up with a girlfriend or a boyfriend than they had predicted.

Overconfidence can have serious consequences for people's lives (Matlin, 2001). For instance, in 1988, Captain Will Rogers was in charge of the USS *Vincennes* in the Persian Gulf. The ship's radar detected an unknown aircraft. Rogers had to make a decision about whether the aircraft was a civilian plane or an enemy plane attacking the USS *Vincennes*. His decision: Launch two missiles at the airplane. Both Rogers and the world soon learned that it was a civilian airplane. All 290 passengers on board were killed when it was shot down. A panel of decision-making experts concluded that Rogers had been overconfident about his original decision and had failed to verify critical factors in the situation (Bales, 1988).

Hindsight Bias People not only are overconfident about what they predict will happen in the future but they also tend to be overconfident about circumstances that already have happened (Bonds-Raacke & others, 2001; Louie, Curren, & Harich, 2000) **Hindsight bias** is our tendency to falsely report, after the fact, that we accurately predicted an event.

As I write this chapter, baseball season is just beginning. Lots of people in different cities are predicting that their teams are going to make it to the World Series. Come October, after almost all of the teams have fallen by the wayside, many of the same people will say, "I told you our team wasn't going to have a good season."

In one study of introductory psychology students, a professor had students make either preverdict predictions regarding the outcome of the O. J. Simpson trial or postverdict predictions about what they would have predicted the outcome to be (Demakis, 1997). Students who estimated their prediction of the trial postverdict were more accurate than students who predicted the outcome preverdict, illustrating the principle of hindsight bias.

Availability Heuristic   Earlier in the chapter we described heuristics as rules of thumb that suggest a solution but do not ensure that it will work. One heuristic that can produce flawed thinking is the **availability heuristic,** a prediction about the probability of an event based on the frequency of the event's past occurrences. When an event has recently occurred, we especially tend to overestimate its future occurrence (McKelvie & Drumheller, 2001).

How likely do you think you are to be a victim of a crime, for instance? The fear of crime tends to go up when the media go through a phase of highlighting murder or covering a sensational murder story. Because of the excess information about crime, we are likely to estimate that crime is more prevalent than it really is. The media contribute to this prediction error every time they expose us to a rash of vivid stories about tornadoes, murders, diseases, accidents, or terrorist attacks.

Representativeness Heuristic   The **representativeness heuristic** suggests that we sometimes make faulty decisions based on how well something matches a prototype—that is, the most common or representative example—rather than its relevance to a particular situation. Consider the following description of an individual's dinner companion: skilled at carpentry, proficient at wrestling, owns a pet snake, knows how to repair motorcycles, and has a police record. What is the probability that this person is a male? Most likely the description fits your prototype of a male more than a female, so you might estimate that there is a 9 in 10 chance that the dinner companion is a male.

In this example, your prototype served you well, because there are far more men than women in the population who fit the description. Sometimes, however, our prototypes do not take into account the frequency of events in the entire population. For example, would you say that the dinner companion is more likely to be a member of a motorcycle gang or a salesman? You would probably say there is a much greater chance that he is a member of a motorcycle gang, in which case you would be wrong. Why? Although only a small percentage of the millions of salesmen fit the description of this dinner companion, the total number is greater than the total number of motorcycle gang members who fit the description. Let's assume that there are 10,000 members of motorcycle gangs in the world versus 100 million salesmen. Even if 1 of every 100 motorcycle gang members (1 percent) fits our description, there would be only 100 of them. If just 1 of every 100,000 salesmen fits our description (.01 percent), their number would total 1,000. So the probability is 10 times greater that the dinner companion is a salesman than a member of a motorcycle gang.

Our lives involve many such instances in which we judge probabilities based on representativeness and fail to consider the population from which a sample is drawn. If we are to make better decisions, we have to try to avoid this logical error, along with the others mentioned here.

Review and Sharpen Your Thinking

4   *Discuss the main factors in thinking critically, reasoning, and making decisions.*

- Describe what critical thinking is and discuss its role in schools, along with mindfulness and open-mindedness.
- Define reasoning and explain the distinction between inductive and deductive reasoning.
- Summarize how people make decisions and the biases and flawed heuristics that can develop.

Do you ever rely on the availability heuristic or the representativeness heuristic? Give examples.

availability heuristic A prediction about the probability of an event based on the frequency of the event's past occurrences.

representativeness heuristic Making faulty decisions based on how well something matches a prototype—the common or representative example—rather than on its relevance to the particular situation.

5 LANGUAGE AND THOUGHT

The Structure of Language **The Link Between Language and Cognition** **Animal Language**

How are language and thought connected?

Language is a form of communication, whether spoken, written, or signed, that is based on a system of symbols. Think how important language is in our everyday lives. We need language to speak with others, listen to others, read, and write (de Boysson-Bardies, 2001). Our language enables us to describe past events in detail and to plan for the future. Without language, much of our thinking would be focused on the here and now. Language also lets us pass down information from one generation to the next and create a rich cultural heritage, which in turn affects not only the language that we use but the way that we think about the world. Before exploring the links between language and cognition more closely, let's examine the way language is structured.

The Structure of Language

All human languages possess **infinite generativity,** the ability to produce an endless number of meaningful sentences, making language a highly creative enterprise. The beauty of language is that this superb flexibility comes from a relatively limited set of rules (Camrie, 2002). In fact, all human languages are characterized by four main rule systems:

- **Phonology:** a language's sound system. Language is made up of basic sounds, or phonemes. Phonological rules ensure that certain sound sequences occur (for example, *sp, ba,* or *ar*) and others do not (for example, *zx* or *qp*; Mattys & Jusczyk, 2001). A good example of a phoneme in the English language is /k/, the sound represented by the letter *k* in the word *ski* and the letter *c* in the word *cat*. Although the /k/ sound is slightly different in these two words, the /k/ sound is described as a single phoneme in English. In some languages, though, such as Arabic, this kind of variation is represented by separate phonemes.

- **Morphology:** a language's rules for word formation. Every word in the English language is made up of one or more morphemes. A morpheme is the smallest unit of language that carries meaning. Some words consist of a single morpheme: for example, *help*. Others are made up of more than one: for example, *helper* has two morphemes, *help + er*. The morpheme *-er* means "one who," in this case "one who helps." As you can see, not all morphemes are words: for example, *pre-, -tion,* and *-ing*. Just as the rules that govern phonemes ensure that certain sound sequences occur, the rules that govern morphemes ensure that certain strings of sounds occur in particular sequences.

- **Syntax:** a language's rules for combining words to form acceptable phrases and sentences (DuBois, 2002). If someone says to you, "Bob slugged Tom" or "Bob was slugged by Tom," you know who did the slugging and who was slugged in each case because you share that person's same syntactic understanding of sentence structure. You also understand that the sentence, "You didn't stay, did you?" is a grammatical sentence but that "You didn't stay, didn't you?" is unacceptable and ambiguous. Recall the opening story about individuals with Williams syndrome. Their language is syntactically impeccable and grammatically complex.

- **Semantics:** the meaning of words and sentences in a particular language. Every word has a unique set of semantic features (Bloom, 2000). *Girl* and *woman*, for example, share many of the same semantic features (for example, both signify female human beings), but they differ semantically in regard to age. Words have

language A form of communication, whether spoken, written, or signed, that is based on a system of symbols.

infinite generativity The ability to produce an infinite number of sentences using a finite set of words and rules.

phonology A language's sound system.

morphology A language's rules for word formation.

syntax A language's rules for the way words are combined to form acceptable phrases and sentences.

semantics The meaning of words and sentences in a particular language.

Frank & Ernest reprinted by permission of Newspaper Enterprize Association, Inc.

semantic restrictions on how they can be used in sentences. The sentence *The bicycle talked the boy into buying a candy bar* is syntactically correct but semantically incorrect. The sentence violates our semantic knowledge that bicycles do not talk. Recall from the chapter opening story that the semantic quality of the language of individuals with Williams syndrome is rich but unusual.

Now that you have a basic understanding of what language is and how it is structured, you can examine some connections between language and cognition.

The Link Between Language and Cognition

Because language is virtually an unbounded symbol system, it is capable of expressing most thoughts. At the same time, language is the way we humans communicate most of our thoughts to each other. We do not always think in words, but our thinking would be greatly impoverished without words. This connection between language and thought has been a topic of considerable interest to psychologists. Some psychologists have argued that we cannot think without language, a proposition that has produced heated controversy. Is thought dependent on language, or is language dependent on thought?

Language's Role in Cognition What role does language play in important cognitive activities? For one thing, memory is stored not only in the form of sounds and images but also in words. Language helps us think, make inferences, tackle difficult decisions, and solve problems (Amsel & Byrnes, 2001). Language can be thought of as a tool for representing ideas (Gentner & Lowenstein, 2001).

Today, most psychologists would accept these points. However, linguist Benjamin Whorf (1956) went a step further. He argued that language actually determines the way we think. Whorf and his student Edward Sapir were specialists in Native American languages, and they were fascinated by the possibility that people might view the world differently as the result of the different languages they speak. The Inuit in Alaska, for instance, have a dozen or more words to describe the various textures, colors, and physical states of snow. But English has relatively few words to describe snow, and, thus, according to Whorf's view, English speakers cannot as easily talk or even think about it. The Hopi Indian language has no words for past or future, and so Whorf would argue that traditional Hopis focus mainly on the present.

Our cultural experiences for a particular concept shape a catalog of names that can be either rich or poor. An example of a name-rich concept in America is "automobile" (we use terms such as *coupe, convertible, minivan, station wagon,* and many others, not to mention various makes and models). The *automobile* part of your mental library of names is the product of many years of experience with automobiles. You probably will see and think about them in finer gradations than people who live in a jungle in South America or on an isolated island in the Pacific Ocean. In this way, language acts as a window that filters the amount and nature of information that is passed on for further processing.

Whorf's view is that our cultural experiences with a particular concept shape a catalog of names that can be either rich or poor. Consider how rich your mental library of names for camel might be if you had extensive experience with camels in a desert world and how poor your mental library of names for snow might be if you lived in a tropical world of palm trees and parrots. Despite its intriguing appeal, Whorf's view is controversial, and many psychologists do not believe it plays a pivotal role in shaping thought.

Critics of Whorf's view say that words merely reflect, rather than cause, the way we think. The Inuits' adaptability and livelihood in Alaska depend on their capacity to recognize various conditions of snow and ice. A skier or snowboarder, who is not Inuit, might also know numerous words for snow, far more than the average person; and a person who doesn't know the words for the different types of snow might still be able to perceive these differences.

A study by Eleanor Rosch (1973) found that a lack of words for a concept does not reflect a lack of ability to perceive and think about it. She studied the effect of language on color perception among the Dani in New Guinea. The Dani have only two words for color—one that approximately means "white" and one that approximately means "black." If the linguistic relativity hypothesis were correct, the Dani would lack the ability to tell the difference between colors such as green, blue, red, yellow, and purple. But Rosch found that the Dani perceived colors just as we perceive them. As we know, color perception is biologically determined by receptors in the retinas in the eyes. Even though Whorf's view appears to have missed the mark—language does not determine thought—researchers agree that language can influence thought.

Cognition's Role in Language   Researchers also are studying the possibility that cognition is an important foundation for language (Gupta & Dell, 1999; Zwaan, Stanfield, & Yaxley, 2002). If language is a reflection of cognition in general, we would expect to find a close link between language ability and general intellectual ability. In particular, we would expect to find that problems in one domain (cognition) are paralleled by problems in the other domain (language). For example, we would anticipate that general mental retardation is accompanied by lowered language abilities. That is often, but not always, the case.

Researchers have found that mental retardation is not always accompanied by poor language skills. Consider the discussion of Williams syndrome earlier in the chapter. Individuals with Williams syndrome have a general intelligence that places them in the category of mentally retarded. However, their language abilities, especially syntax and semantics, are well within the normal range, as is their ability to use language for communicative purposes. The nature of Williams syndrome suggests a mind composed of separate, biologically prepared thinking and language abilities rather than a single, all-purpose cognitive ability that includes language (Flavell, Miller, & Miller, 2002; Pinker, 1994).

Other evidence that cognition is separate from language comes from studies of deaf children. On a variety of thinking and problem-solving tasks, deaf children perform at the same level as children of the same age who have no hearing problems. Some of the deaf children in these studies do not even have command of written or sign language (Furth, 1971).

In sum, although thought likely can influence language, and language likely can influence thought, there is increasing evidence that language and thought are not part of a single, automated cognitive system. Instead, they seem to have evolved as separate, modular, biologically prepared components of the mind.

Animal Language

The desire to figure out the link between language and thought has generated a great deal of research interest in animal language (Fouts & Waters, 2001; Rilling & Seligman, 2002). Do animals use language in the same way that humans do? What cognitive abilities are linked to their use of language?

"Remember, don't talk sex, politics, or religion."
Reprinted courtesy of Omni Magazine © 1982.

Many animal species do have complex and ingenious ways to signal danger and to communicate about basic needs such as food and sex. For example, in one species of firefly, the female has learned to imitate the flashing signal of another species to lure them into her territory. Then she eats them. But is this language in the human sense? Most psychologists agree that it is not.

But what about the language abilities of animals with more brain power—specifically, our closest relatives, the great apes? Chimpanzees and *Homo sapiens* have 98 percent of their genetic material in common. Chimpanzee behavior includes many things that human beings do, such as hunting, toolmaking, embracing, back patting, kissing, and holding hands.

Some researchers believe apes can learn human language. One celebrity in this field is a chimp named Washoe, who was adopted when she was about 10 months old (Gardner & Gardner, 1971). Because apes do not have the vocal apparatus to speak, the researchers taught Washoe American Sign Language, which is one of the sign languages of the deaf. Washoe used sign language during everyday activities, such as meals, play, and car rides. In 2 years, Washoe learned 38 different signs, and by the age of 5 she had a vocabulary of 160 signs. Washoe learned how to put signs together in novel ways, such as *You drink* and *You me tickle*. A number of other efforts to teach language to chimps have had similar results (Premack, 1986).

The debate about chimpanzees' ability to use language focuses on two key issues: Can apes understand the meaning of symbols—that is, can they comprehend that one thing stands for another? And can apes learn syntax—that is, can they learn the kinds of mechanics and rules that give human language its creative productivity? The first of

In the wild, chimps communicate through calls, gestures, and expressions, which evolutionary psychologists believe might be the roots of true language.

FIGURE 9.10 **Chimps and Symbols** Sue Savage-Rumbaugh and her colleagues at the Yerkes Primate Center and Georgia State University have studied the basic question of whether chimps understand symbols. Their research suggests that the answer is yes.

these issues may have been settled by Sue Savage-Rumbaugh and her colleagues (1993). These researchers found strong evidence that the chimps Sherman and Austin can understand symbols. For example, if either Sherman or Austin is sitting in a room, and a symbol for an object is displayed on a screen, he will go into another room, find the object, and bring it back. If the object is not there, he will come back empty-handed (Cowley, 1988). Austin and Sherman play a game in which one chimp points to a symbol for food (such as M&Ms), the other chimp selects the food from a tray, and then they both eat it. These observations are clear evidence that chimps can understand symbols (see figure 9.10).

Recent evidence concerning chimps' syntactic ability has come from study of rare pygmy chimpanzees (*Pan paniscus*), also known as bonobos. These chimps are friendlier and brighter than their cousins, and show some remarkable language abilities. For example, star pupil Kanzi is very good at understanding spoken English and has been shown to comprehend over 600 sentences, such as *Can you make the bunny eat the sweet potato?* (Savage-Rumbaugh, Shanker, & Taylor, 1998). Kanzi also produces fairly complex sentences using a response board hooked to a speech synthesizer.

The debate over whether animals can use language to express thoughts is far from resolved. Researchers agree that animals can communicate with each other and that some can manipulate language-like symbols with syntax that resembles that of young children. At the same time, research has not yet proved that any animals can use language to express as many ideas as adult humans can or can use language as complexly as adult humans do.

Review and Sharpen Your Thinking

5 *Identify the possible connections between language and thought.*
  - Define language and describe the structure of language.
  - Summarize the possible links between language and thought.
  - Evaluate whether animals have language.

When a pet, such as a dog or cat, barks or meows, is that language in the human sense? Explain.

For study tools related to this learning goal, see the Study Guide, the CD-ROM, and the Online Learning Center.

6 LANGUAGE ACQUISITION AND DEVELOPMENT

Biological Influences

Early Development of Language

Environmental Influences

Language and Education

How is language acquired and how does it develop?

In 1799, a nude boy was observed running through the woods in France. The boy was captured when he was 11 years old. He was called the Wild Boy of Aveyron and was believed to have lived alone in the woods for 6 years (Lane, 1976). When found, he made no effort to communicate. Even after a number of years, he failed to learn to communicate effectively. This "wild child" case raises questions about how people acquire language. Is the ability to generate rules for language and then use them to create an infinite number of words the product of biological factors and evolution? Or is language learned and influenced by the environment? Precisely when and how does language ability develop? As you will see, the answers to their questions are complex and are still a focus of research inquiry.

Biological Influences

Estimates vary, but scientists believe that humans acquired language about 100,000 years ago. In evolutionary time, then, language is a very recent human ability. However, a number of experts believe biological evolution that took place long before language emerged undeniably shaped humans into linguistic creatures (Chomsky, 1975). The brain, nervous system, and vocal apparatus of our predecessors changed over hundreds of thousands of years. Physically equipped to do so, *Homo sapiens* went beyond grunting and shrieking to develop abstract speech. This sophisticated language ability gave humans an enormous edge over other animals and increased their chances of survival (Lieberman, 2002; Pinker, 1994).

Language Universals The famous linguist Noam Chomsky (1975) is one of those who argues that humans are biologically prewired to learn language at a certain time and in a certain way. According to Chomsky and many other language experts, the strongest evidence for language's biological basis is the fact that children all over the world reach language milestones at about the same time developmentally and in about the same order, despite vast variations in the language input they receive from their environments. For example, in some cultures adults never talk to infants under 1 year of age, yet these infants still acquire language. Also, there is no convincing way other than biological factors to explain how quickly children learn language (Locke, 1999; Maratsos, 1999).

MIT linguist Noam Chomsky was one of the early architects of the view that children's language development cannot be explained by environmental input. In Chomsky's view, language has strong biological underpinnings, with children biologically prewired to learn language at a certain time and in a certain way.

In Chomsky's view, children cannot possibly learn the full rules and structure of languages by only imitating what they hear. Rather, nature must provide children with a biological prewired universal grammar, allowing them to understand the basic rules of all languages and apply these rules to the speech they hear. They learn language without awareness of the underlying logic involved.

Language and the Brain   There is strong evidence to back up those who believe language has a biological foundation. Neuroscience research has shown that the brain contains particular regions that are predisposed to be used for language (Banich & Mack, 2002; Grodzinsky, 2001). As discussed in chapter 3, accumulating evidence further suggests that language processing mainly occurs in the brain's left hemisphere (Gazzaniga & others, 2001). Also recall from chapter 3 the importance of these two areas of the brain in language: *Broca's area*, which contributes to speech production, and *Wernicke's area*, which is involved in language comprehension. Neuroscience research also has shown that the left hemisphere comprehends syntax and grammar, which the right hemisphere does not.

Using brain imaging techniques, such as PET scans, researchers have found that when an infant is about 9 months old, the part of the brain that stores and indexes many kinds of memory becomes fully functional (Bloom, Nelson, & Lazerson, 2001). This is also the time at which infants appear to be able to attach meaning to words, suggesting a link between language, cognition, and the development of the brain.

Environmental Influences

Contradicting those who believe that language is biologically determined, behaviorists have advocated the view that language is primarily determined by environmental influences. For example, the famous behaviorist B. F. Skinner (1957) said that language is just another behavior, like sitting, walking, or running. He argued that all behaviors, including language, are learned through reinforcement. Albert Bandura (1977) later emphasized that language is learned through imitation.

However, virtually all language experts today agree that reinforcement and imitation cannot explain children's language development. Many of children's sentences are novel in the sense that the children have not previously heard them. A child might hear the sentence, "The plate fell on the floor," but then be able to say, "My mirror fell on the blanket." Reinforcement imitation (modeling of words and syntax) simply cannot explain this utterance.

Roger Brown (1973) spent long hours observing parents and their young children, searching for evidence that children learn the rules of language through their parents' reinforcement (smiles, hugs, pats on the back, corrective feedback). He found that parents sometimes smiled and praised their children for sentences they liked but that they reinforced ungrammatical sentences as well. Brown concluded that no evidence exists that reinforcement is responsible for the development of children's language rule systems.

Although reinforcement and imitation are not responsible for children's development of language rule systems, it is important that children interact with language-skilled people (Snow, 1999). The Wild Boy of Aveyron was not around such people when he was a young child, and it clearly harmed his language development.

In one study of more typical language learning, researchers observed the language environments of children from two different backgrounds: middle-income professional families and welfare families (Hart & Risley, 1995). Then they examined the children's language development. All of the children developed normally in terms of learning to talk and acquiring all of the basic rules of English and a basic vocabulary. However, the researchers found enormous differences in the sheer amount of language the children were exposed to and the level of the children's language development. For example, in a typical hour, the middle-income professional parents spent almost twice as much time communicating with their children as the welfare parents did. The children from the middle-income professional families heard about 2,100 words an hour, their child counterparts in welfare families only 600 words an hour. The researchers estimated that by 4 years of age, the average welfare-family child would have 13 million fewer words of cumulative language experience than the child in the average middle-income professional family. Amazingly, some of the 3-year-old children from middle-class professional families had a recorded vocabulary that exceeded the recorded vocabulary of some of the welfare parents.

In another study, researchers carefully assessed the level of maternal speech to infants (Huttenlocher & others, 1991). As indicated in figure 9.11, mothers who regularly used a higher level of language when interacting with their infants had infants with markedly higher vocabularies. By the second birthday, vocabulary differences were substantial.

What are some good strategies for parents in talking to their babies? They include (Baron, 1992)

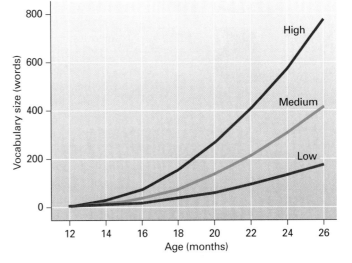

FIGURE 9.11 **Level of Maternal Speech and Infant Vocabulary**

- *Be an active conversational partner.* Initiate conversation with the infant. If the infant is in a day-long childcare program, ensure that he or she gets adequate language stimulation from adults.
- *Talk as if the infant understands what you are saying.* Adults can generate positive self-fulfilling prophecies by addressing their young children as if they understand what is being said. The process may take 4 to 5 years, but children gradually rise to match the language model presented them.
- *Use a language style with which you feel comfortable.* Don't worry about how you sound to other adults when you talk with an infant. The mood and feeling you convey, not the content, is more important when talking with an infant. Use whatever type of baby talk you feel comfortable with in the first years of the child's life.

Research findings about environmental influences on language learning complicate the understanding of its foundations. In the real world of language learning, children appear to be neither exclusively biologically programmed linguists nor exclusively socially driven language experts (Ratner, 1993). As with all areas of psychology we have studied, we have to look at how biology and environment interact when children learn language. That is, children are biologically prepared to learn language but benefit enormously from being bathed in a competent language environment from an early age (Pan & Snow, 1999).

Early Development of Language

One of the most interesting things about the development of language is that the child's linguistic interactions with parents and others obey certain rules (MacWhinney, 1999). Although children are learning vocabulary and concepts from an early age, they are also learning how their language is stitched together. In a classic study of this aspect of language learning, Jean Berko (1958) presented preschool and first-grade children with cards like the one shown in figure 9.12. The children were asked to look at the card while the experimenter read the words on it aloud. Then the children were asked to supply the missing word. *Wugs* is the correct response for the card shown. Coming up with "wugs" might seem easy, but it requires an understanding of morphological rules (in this case, the proper word ending for plurals). Although the children's responses were not always completely accurate, they were much better than chance. What makes Berko's study so impressive is that the words were fictional, created solely for the

It is unquestionably good for parents to begin talking to their babies right at the start. The best language teaching occurs when talking is begun before the infant becomes capable of its first intelligible speech.

This is a wug.

Now there is another one.
There are two of them.
There are two _____.

FIGURE 9.12 Stimuli in Berko's Classic Study of Children's Understanding of Morphological Rules In Jean Berko's study, young children were presented cards such as this one with a "wug" on it. Then the children were asked to supply the missing word and say it correctly.

GENIE

What were Genie's experiences like? What implications do they have for language acquisition?

purpose of the study. Thus the children could not have based their answers on remembering past instances of hearing the words. Instead, they were forced to rely on rules.

The "Critical Period" Some language researchers have focused on the question of whether language must be learned by a certain time in development. A *critical period* is a span of time when the individual is ready to learn; beyond this period learning is difficult or impossible. This is basically a biological view of language acquisition, which is controversial.

In the 1960s, Eric Lenneberg (1967) proposed that there is a critical period between about 18 months of age and puberty during which a first language must be acquired. Lenneberg provided support for his critical period concept from studies of children and adults with damage in the left hemisphere of the brain, deaf children, children with mental retardation, and other people who had not been able to learn language in the typical way (Tager-Flusberg, 1994, 1999). Lenneberg found that the children he studied were able to recover their language skills, but the adults were not. Lenneberg believed that the difference was that the children's brains had plasticity. Once the brain structures matured and became more rigid, the brain could reassign language skills to undamaged areas. However, because the adults had already passed the critical period, they did not have the neurological capability to relearn language skills.

The stunted language development of a modern "wild child," similar to the Wild Boy of Aveyron, also supports the idea of a critical period for language acquisition. In 1970, a California social worker made a routine visit to the home of a partially blind woman who had applied for public assistance. The social worker discovered that the woman and her husband kept their 13-year-old daughter, Genie, locked away from the world. Kept in almost total isolation during her childhood, Genie could not speak or stand erect. She was forced to sit naked all day on a child's potty seat, restrained by a harness her father had made—she could move only her hands and feet. At night she was placed in a kind of straitjacket and caged in a crib with wire mesh sides and a cover. Whenever Genie made a noise, her father beat her. He never communicated with her in words but growled and barked at her.

Genie spent a number of years in extensive rehabilitation programs, such as speech and physical therapy (Curtiss, 1977; Rymer, 1993). She eventually learned to walk upright with a jerky motion and to use the toilet. Genie also learned to recognize many words and to speak in rudimentary sentences. At first she spoke in one-word utterances. Later she was able to string together two-word combinations such as "big teeth," "little marble," and "two hand." Consistent with the language development of most children, three-word combinations followed—for example, "small two cup." Unlike normal children, however, Genie did not learn how to ask questions, and she does not understand grammar. Genie is not able to distinguish between pronouns or between passive and active verbs. Four years after she began stringing words together, her speech still sounded like a garbled telegram. And as an adult she speaks in short, mangled sentences, such as "Father hit leg," "Big wood," and "Genie hurt." Her unfortunate story supports the idea that people have to learn language rules during childhood or miss the chance to become fully proficient.

Language Milestones Most people do develop a clear understanding of their language's structure during childhood, as well as a large vocabulary. Most adults in the United States have acquired a vocabulary of nearly 50,000 words. Researchers have taken a great interest in the process by which these aspects of language develop. Through many studies, we now have an understanding of the important milestones of language development (see figure 9.13).

Before babies ever say their first words, they babble. Babbling—endlessly repeating sounds and syllables such as *bababa or dadada*—begins at the age of 3 to 6 months and is determined by biological readiness, not by the amount of reinforcement or the

FIGURE 9.13 **Language Milestones**

0–6 Months	Cooing Discrimination of vowels Babbling present by 6 months
6–12 Months	Babbling expands to include sounds of spoken language Gestures used to communicate about objects First words spoken 10–13 months
12–18 Months	Understands 50+ words on average
18–24 Months	Vocabulary increases to an average of 200 words Two-word combinations
2 Years	Vocabulary rapidly increases Correct use of plurals Use of past tense Use of some prepositions
3–4 Years	Mean length of utterances increases to 3–4 morphemes in a sentence Use of "yes" and "no" questions, wh- questions Use of negatives and imperatives Increased awareness of pragmatics
5–6 Years	Vocabulary reaches an average of about 10,000 words Coordination of simple sentences
6–8 Years	Vocabulary continues to increases rapidly More skilled use of syntactical rules Conversational skills improve
9–11 Years	Word definitions include synonyms Conversational strategies continue to improve
11–14 Years	Vocabulary increases with addition of more abstract words Understanding of complex grammar forms Increased understanding of function a word plays in a sentence Understands metaphor and satire
15–20 Years	Understands adult literary works

Note: This list is meant not to be exhaustive but rather to highlight some of the main language milestones. Also keep in mind that there is a great deal of variation in the ages at which children can reach these milestones and still be considered within the normal range of language development.

ability to hear (Locke, 1993). Even deaf babies babble for a time (Lenneberg, Rebelsky, & Nichols, 1965). Babbling probably allows the baby to exercise its vocal cords and helps develop the ability to articulate different sounds.

Patricia Kuhl's (1993, 2000) research reveals that long before they actually begin to learn words, infants can sort through a number of spoken sounds in search of the ones that have meaning. Kuhl argues that from birth to about 6 months of age, children are "universal linguists" who are capable of distinguishing each of the sounds that make up human speech. But, by about 6 months of age, they have started to specialize in the speech sounds of their native language.

An important language task for infants is to fish out individual words from the nonstop stream of sound that makes up ordinary speech (Brownlee, 1998). But, to do so, they have to find the boundaries between words, which is very difficult for infants because adults don't pause between words when they speak. Still, researchers have found that infants begin to detect word boundaries by 8 months of age. For example, in one study, 8-month-old infants listened at home to recorded stories that

Around the world, young children learn to speak in two-word utterances at 18 to 24 months of age. *What implications does this have for the biological basis of language?*

contained unusual words, such as *hornbill* and *python* (Jusczyk & Hohne, 1997). Two weeks later, the researchers tested the infants with two lists of words, one made up of words they had already heard in the stories and the other of new, unusual words that had not appeared in the stories. The infants listened to the familiar words for a second longer, on average, than to new words.

A child's first words, uttered at the age of 10 to 13 months, name important people (*dada*), familiar animals (*kitty*), vehicles (*car*), toys (*ball*), food (*milk*), body parts (*eye*), clothes (*hat*), household items (*clock*), and greetings (*bye*). These were babies' first words 50 years ago, and they are babies' first words today (Clark, 1983).

By the time children reach the age of 18 to 24 months, they usually utter two-word statements. They quickly grasp the importance of expressing concepts and the role that language plays in communicating with others (Schafer, 1999). To convey meaning in two-word statements, the child relies heavily on gesture, tone, and context. Still, children can communicate a wealth of meaning with two words: for instance (Slobin, 1972),

Identification: See doggie.
Location: Book there.
Repetition: More milk.
Nonexistence: Allgone thing.
Negation: Not wolf.
Possession: My candy.
Attribution: Big car.
Agent-action: Mama walk.
Action-direct-object: Hit you.
Action-indirect-object: Give papa.
Action-instrument: Cut knife.
Question: Where ball?

These examples are from children whose first languages were English, German, Russian, Finnish, Turkish, and Samoan. Although these two-word sentences omit many parts of speech, they are remarkably succinct in conveying many messages. When we send a telegram, we try to be short and precise, excluding any unnecessary words. As a result, we usually omit articles, auxiliary verbs, and other connectives. In every language, a child's first combination of words has this economical quality. *Telegraphic speech*—the use of short and precise words to communicate—characterizes young children's two- and three-word combinations.

Of course, telegraphic speech is not limited to two-word phrases. "Mommy give ice cream" or "Mommy give Tommy ice cream" also are examples of telegraphic speech. As children leave the two-word stage, they move rather quickly into three-, four-, and five-word combinations.

Language and Education

The early development of language skills through informal interaction with parents and other people in the family's social circle is an essential part of language acquisition. However, formal education in schools is also important. There children learn more sophisticated rules of language structure, increase their vocabularies, and apply language skills to learn about a wide variety of concepts. In fact, one of the main purposes of schooling is to increase language skills. The ways that schools go about this is controversial, however. One controversy is how to teach the dominant language in this country, English, to children who have first learned a different language. Another controversy is how children best learn to read.

Bilingualism As many as 10 million children in the United States come from homes in which English is not the primary language. One major concern regarding such children is to find the best way for them to succeed in a culture in which English

Is Bilingual Education a Good Thing?

Bilingual education, which has been the preferred strategy of schools for the past two decades, aims to teach academic subjects to immigrant children in their native languages (most often Spanish) while slowly and simultaneously teaching them English (Garcia & others, 2002; Lessow-Hurley, 2000; Peregoy & Boyle, 2001). Bilingual education continues to be controversial.

Some states have passed laws declaring English to be their official language, eliminating the obligation of schools to teach minority children in languages other than English. In California, voters repealed bilingual education altogether.

Critics of bilingual education argue that it harms immigrant children by failing to instruct them in English quickly enough, which can handicap their ability to interact with people from the dominant culture and leave them behind in the workplace. Some critics stress that bilingualism is a divisive force. They say that the United States must remain an English-speaking nation to be united as one people, whereas bilingual education advocates believe that bilingualism is a natural aspect of a multicultural society. Critics of bilingualism also argue that it impedes academic skills, but bilingual education supporters argue that it improves cognitive skills. Proponents of bilingual education also argue that teaching immigrants in their native language respects their family and community culture and increases their self-esteem, thus making their future academic success likelier.

It is difficult to arrive at a firm conclusion from research on the effectiveness of bilingual education because bilingual programs vary considerably in their labeling, content, length (some last for less than 1 year, others for 4 to 5 years), and quality of teaching. One analysis of 10 studies concluded that English immersion is superior to bilingual education (Rossell & Baker, 1996), but, on closer inspection, 6 of the 10 studies actually showed stronger characteristics of bilingualism than English immersion (Krashen, 1996). Also, some supporters of immersion report that many immigrants do well in school without bilingualism. In such reports, often, the participants came to the United States with a good education in their own country, making instruction in English more effective.

Consider also the following claim by the Westminster School District in New York: After 18 months of English-only instruction, immigrant students made better academic progress and learned more English than students who were taught in their native languages. But gains were modest, and no comparisons were made with previous programs. In fact, Westminster actually increased the amount of first-language support for immigrant students during the time frame of the study, which could have caused the modest gains.

Let's examine the evidence on one dimension of the bilingual education debate: Does bilingualism help or hinder cognitive skills? Researchers have found that bilingual children in a number of countries (such as Canada, Israel, Singapore, and Switzerland) do better than monolingual children on tests of intelligence (Bialystok, 2001; Lambert & others, 1993). Based on these findings, a Canadian program was developed to immerse English-speaking children in French for much of their early elementary school education in Quebec. Their English does not appear to have been harmed, and their math scores and aptitude scores—not to mention their appreciation of French culture—appear to have benefited. On the basis of such results, some educators favor teaching second languages to all U.S. students.

Another important question regarding bilingual education is How long does it take language-minority students to learn English? Kenji Hakuta and his colleagues (2000) collected data on children in four different school districts to determine how long it takes language-minority students to speak and read English effectively. Speaking proficiency took 3 to 5 years, and reading proficiency took 4 to 7 years. However, many schools assume that language-minority students will learn English effectively in 1 year or less, which may be unrealistic.

What do you think?

- How important is it for new immigrants to America to learn to speak fluent English as soon as possible? Explain.
- Is bilingual education likely to be divisive to the United States? Why or why not?
- Are you monolingual or bilingual? If you are monolingual, do you wish that you had learned one or more other languages in addition to your native language? Explain. If you are bilingual or multilingual, what positive or negative effects do you think this has had on your development? Explain.

is dominant, in school and beyond (Hurley & Tinajero, 2001). For example, Octavio's parents moved to the United States before he was born. They do not speak English fluently and always have spoken to Octavio in Spanish. At age 6, Octavio has just entered the first grade. He speaks no English. What is the best way to teach Octavio? Should he be immersed in an all-English classroom to speed up his learning of English? Or should he be placed in a bilingual program so he can more easily keep up with what his English-speaking peers are learning in school? Bilingual education has been a controversial approach in American classrooms, as the Critical Controversy box explains.

Regardless of the way in which children learn English as a second language, we need to be sensitive to the implications of asking them to communicate in some language other than the one they learned at home. Following are some recommendations for working with linguistically and culturally diverse children (NAEYC, 1996):

- Recognize that all children are cognitively, linguistically, and emotionally connected to the language and culture of their homes.
- Understand that second-language learning can be difficult. It takes time to become linguistically competent in any language. Although verbal proficiency in a second language can be attained in 2 to 3 years, the skills needed to understand academic content through reading and writing can take 4 or more years. Children who do not become proficient in their second language after 2 or 3 years usually are not proficient in their first language, either.
- Recognize that children can and will acquire the use of English even when their home language is respected.

One question is when to offer second-language classes. Typically, they are offered in high school, which may not be the best time. Although adolescents and adults can become competent at a second language, learning it as a child is a much easier task. Recall our earlier discussion of critical period (Birdsong, 1999). Also, although adults make faster initial progress in learning a second language, their eventual success is not as great as children's. In one study, Chinese and Korean adults who immigrated to the United States at different ages were given a test of grammatical knowledge (Johnson & Newport, 1989). Those who began learning English from 3 to 7 years of age scored as well as native speakers on the test, but those who arrived in the United States, and therefore started learning English, later in childhood or in adolescence had lower test scores. Children's ability to pronounce a second language with the correct accent also decreases with age, with an especially sharp decline occurring after age 10 to 12 (Asher & Garcia, 1969).

The United States is one of the few countries in the world in which most students graduate from high school knowing only their own language. For example, in Russia, schools have 10 grades, called forms, which roughly correspond to the 12 grades in American schools. Children begin school at age 7 in Russia and begin learning English in the third form. Because of this emphasis on teaching English, most Russian citizens under the age of 40 today are bilingual, able to speak at least some English in addition to their native language. That ability gives them an edge in conducting business or pursuing studies in the global arena.

Reading Another important school-related aspect of language involves the best way to teach children to read (Meyer, 2002; Morris & Slavin, 2003). As with the debate between those in favor of bilingual education and those in favor of English immersion, the reading debate focuses on two very different approaches to learning to read. Recall from the chapter opening story that individuals with Williams syndrome find learning to read very difficult, even though they have exceptional ability to express themselves verbally. They do better at word identification and spelling than at reading comprehension, which requires more abstract reasoning and the ability to go from the parts to a whole. These are two types of language skills around which major reading approaches have been developed.

The **basic skills-and-phonetics approach** is the method for teaching reading that stresses the basic rules for translating written patterns into sounds (Fox & Hull, 2002). It emphasizes that early reading instruction should involve simplified materials. Only after they have learned phonological rules (how letters represent sounds) should children be given complex reading materials such as stories and poems.

In contrast, the **whole-language approach** stresses that reading instruction parallel children's natural language learning. In early reading instruction, children should be presented with materials in their complete form, such as stories and poems. Reading also is integrated with other skills (such as listening and writing), subjects (such

basic skills-and-phonetics approach Stresses that reading instruction should emphasize the basic rules for translating written patterns into sounds.

whole-language approach Stresses that reading instruction should parallel a child's natural language learning; so reading materials should be whole and meaningful.

as science and social studies), and real-world activities. A class might read newspapers, magazines, or books and then write about them and discuss them. In this way, say the whole-language advocates, children learn to understand language's communicative function.

Which approach is best? Researchers have not been able to consistently document that either approach is better than the other. A national panel of 17 reading experts concluded that a combination of the two approaches is the best strategy (Snow, 1998). The panel recommended that beginning readers be taught to sound out letters as the main way to identify unfamiliar words, the cornerstone of the basic skills-and-phonetics approach. But the panel also endorsed several aspects of the whole-language approach: encourage children, as they begin to recognize words, to predict what might happen in a story, draw inferences about stories, and write their own stories. The combination approach helps children learn the full range of language rules: phonology, morphology, syntax, and semantics (Combs, 2002).

Review and Sharpen Your Thinking

6   *Summarize how language is acquired and develops.*

- Discuss the biological foundations of language.
- Identify the environmental influences on language.
- Describe the relevance of a critical period in learning language and the major milestones in early language development.
- Explain the opposing views of how schools should approach teaching a second language and reading.

How did you learn to read? Was it an effective approach? Explain.

mhhe.com/
santrockp7

For study tools related to this learning goal, see the Study Guide, the CD-ROM, and the Online Learning Center.

The Candle Problem

The solution requires a unique perception of the function of the box in which the matches came. It can become a candleholder when tacked to the wall.

The Nine-Dot Problem

Most people have difficulty with this problem because they try to draw the lines within the boundaries of the dots. Notice that by extending the lines beyond the dots, the problem can be solved.

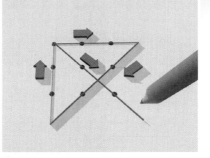

The Six-Matchstick Problem

Nothing in the instructions said that the solution had to be two-dimensional.

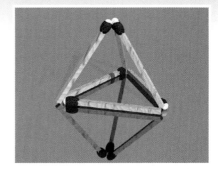

Solutions to problems from Figure 9.6.

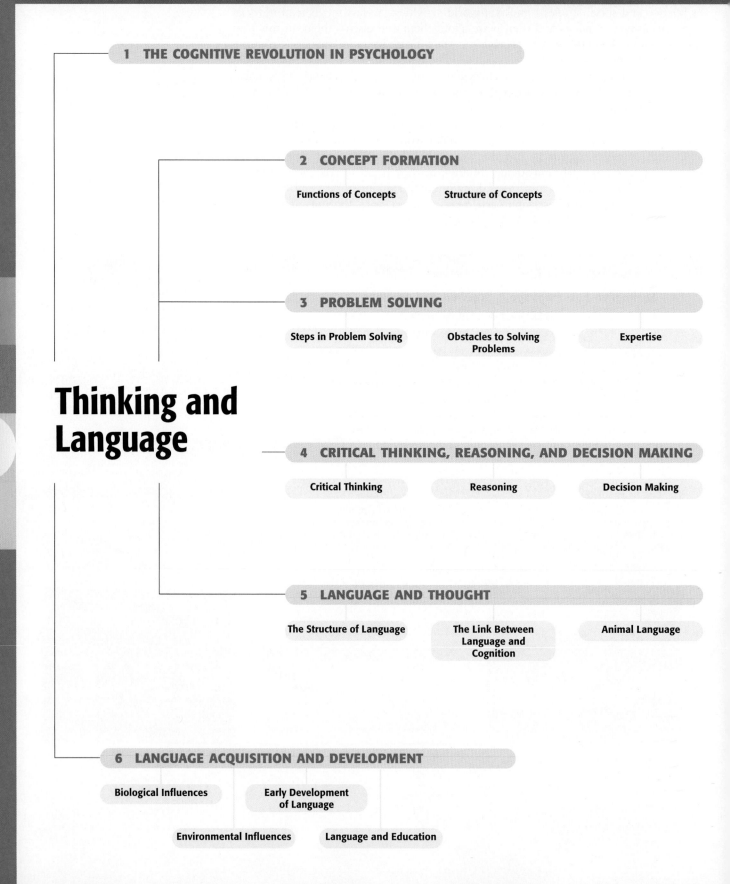

Thinking and Language

1 THE COGNITIVE REVOLUTION IN PSYCHOLOGY

2 CONCEPT FORMATION

Functions of Concepts   Structure of Concepts

3 PROBLEM SOLVING

Steps in Problem Solving   Obstacles to Solving   Expertise
                             Problems

4 CRITICAL THINKING, REASONING, AND DECISION MAKING

Critical Thinking   Reasoning   Decision Making

5 LANGUAGE AND THOUGHT

The Structure of Language   The Link Between   Animal Language
                             Language and
                             Cognition

6 LANGUAGE ACQUISITION AND DEVELOPMENT

Biological Influences   Early Development
                             of Language

     Environmental Influences   Language and Education

1 Characterize the "cognitive revolution" in psychology.

- Cognition is the way in which information is processed and manipulated in remembering, thinking, and knowing. The cognitive revolution, which has occurred over the past 50 years, is an interest in the way the mind works to process and to manipulate information. The computer has played an important role in this revolution, stimulating the model of the mind as an information-processing system. A by-product of the cognitive revolution, artificial intelligence (AI) is the science of creating machines capable of performing activities that require intelligence when they are done by people.

2 Explain concept formation.

- Concepts are mental categories that are used to group objects, events, and characteristics. Concepts are important because they help us to generalize, improve our memories, and keep us from constantly having to learn.
- Two models of concept structure are classical (all instances of a concept share defining properties) and prototypical (people decide whether an item reflects a concept by comparing it with the most typical item(s) of the concept).

3 Describe the requirements for solving problems.

- Problem solving is an attempt to find an appropriate way of attaining a goal when the goal is not readily available. Four main steps in problem solving are (1) find and frame the problem, (2) develop good problem-solving strategies, (3) evaluate solutions, and (4) rethink and redefine problems and solutions over time. Finding and framing problems is an often-overlooked dimension of problem solving. Among effective strategies for solving problems are subgoaling (setting intermediate goals that put you in a better position to reach your goal), using algorithms (strategies that guarantee a solution), and using heuristics (strategies or guidelines that suggest, but do not guarantee, a solution to a problem).
- Obstacles to problem solving include being fixated, as well as not being adequately motivated and not controlling emotions. Being fixated means focusing on prior strategies and failing to look at a problem from a new perspective. Functional fixedness is being fixated on the usual functions of a thing. A mental set is a type of fixation in which an individual tries to solve a problem in a particular way that has worked in the past.
- There is considerable interest in the role of expertise in problem solving. Compared with novices, experts have a superior knowledge base, are better at remembering information in the domain in which they are experts, use better problem-solving strategies, and engage in deliberate practice to a far greater extent.

4 Discuss the main factors in critical thinking, reasoning, and making decisions.

- Critical thinking involves thinking reflectively and productively and evaluating the evidence. Some critics argue that schools do not do a good job of guiding students to think critically, especially in coming up with new ideas and revising earlier conclusions. One obstacle to critical thinking is engaging in mindless behavior. People can become more mindful by creating new ideas, being open to new information, and being aware of more than one perspective. Open-mindedness is another good strategy for improving critical thinking. Too often we take one side of the issue without thinking in depth about the issue and evaluating it from different perspectives.
- Reasoning is the mental activity of transforming information to reach conclusions. It is closely tied to critical thinking. Inductive reasoning is reasoning from the specific to the general. Analogies draw on inductive reasoning. Deductive reasoning is reasoning from the general to the specific.
- Decision making involves evaluating alternatives and making choices among them. One type of decision making research studies how people weigh costs and benefits of various outcomes. Another type studies people's biases and the flawed heuristics they use in making decisions. These biases and flaws include confirmation bias, belief perseverance, overconfidence bias, hindsight bias, availability heuristics, and representativeness heuristics.

5 Identify the possible connections between language and thought.

- Language is a form of communication, whether spoken, written, or signed, that is based on a system of symbols. All human languages have some common characteristics, including infinite generativity and organizational rules about structure. Language has four sets of structural rules: phonology, the sound system of a language; morphology, the rules for combining morphemes, meaningful strings of sounds that contain no smaller meaningful parts; syntax, the ways words are combined to form acceptable phrases and sentences; and semantics, the meaning of words and sentences.
- Thoughts and ideas are associated with words. Language does not completely determine thought but does influence it. For instance, different languages promote different

ways of thinking. Language is also important in the cognitive activities, such as memory. Cognitive activities also can influence language. Although language and thought influence each other, there is increasing evidence that they are not part of a single, automated cognitive system but rather evolved as separate, modular, biologically prepared components of the mind.

- Animals clearly can communicate but few have language skills that approach those of adult humans. Chimps have been taught to use symbols, and some pygmy chimps demonstrate an understanding of syntax. Whether animals have the same language abilities as humans continues to be debated.

6 *Summarize how language is acquired and develops.*

- Evolution shaped humans into linguistic creatures. Linguist Noam Chomsky said that humans are biologically prewired to learn language at a certain time and in a certain way. Chomsky and other experts believe that the strongest evidence for the biological foundations of language resides in the fact that children all over the world reach language milestones at about the same age and in the same order, despite vast variations in the language input they receive from the environment. In addition, there is strong evidence that particular regions in the brain, such as Broca's area and Wernicke's area, are predisposed to be used for language.
- Behaviorists, such as B. F. Skinner and Albert Bandura, have advocated that language is primarily determined by environmental influences, especially reinforcement and imitation. However, evidence suggests that reinforcement and imitation are not responsible for children's ac-

quisition of language's rule systems. Nonetheless, it is important for children to interact with language-skilled people. Evidence for the influence of the environment on language acquisition comes from studies comparing children in language-impoverished and language-enriched environments. Children are biologically prepared to learn language but benefit enormously from being in a competent language environment from early in development.

- Language learning, especially learning a language's structure, may be linked to a critical period, which is a time span in which there is learning readiness. Beyond this period, learning is difficult or impossible. The stunted language development of wild children such as Genie supports the notion that a critical period exists. However, this concept is still controversial. Far less controversial is the understanding of the milestones in early language development. Before babies say their first words, they babble. At about 8 months, they discover boundaries between words. At 10 to 13 months, they utter their first word. Infants' early speech is telegraphic.
- The issue of how to teach children whose first language is not English revolves around two approaches: Bilingual education focuses on teaching students the subject matter in their native language with secondary attention to learning English; the monolingual approach immerses these children in English by placing them in regular academic classes from the beginning. The reading debate focuses on the basic skills-and-phonetics approach and the whole-language approach. A national panel of experts concluded that the best reading instruction consists of a combination of these two approaches.

Key Terms

cognition, p. 351
artificial intelligence
  (AI), p. 352
thinking, p. 353
concepts, p. 353
classical model, p. 355
prototype model, p. 355
problem solving, p. 356
subgoaling, p. 357

algorithms, p. 357
heuristics, p. 358
fixation, p. 358
functional fixedness, p. 358
mental set, p. 359
reasoning, p. 363
inductive reasoning, p. 363
deductive reasoning, p. 364
decision making, p. 365

confirmation bias, p. 365
belief perseverance, p. 366
overconfidence bias, p. 366
hindsight bias, p. 366
availability heuristic, p. 367
representativeness
  heuristic, p. 367
language, p. 368
infinite generativity, p. 368

phonology, p. 368
morphology, p. 368
syntax, p. 368
semantics, p. 368
basic skills-and-phonetics
  approach, p. 380
whole-language
  approach, p. 380

Apply Your Knowledge

1. Due to the cognitive revolution, the computer is currently the dominant model psychologists use to think about how our brains process information. Could this model contribute to functional fixedness among psychologists? How? Can you think of a model other than the computer to describe how the brain works? Think back to how the brain actually works—in what ways might it be similar to a computer, and in what ways does it differ?

2. Currently, you should be trying to form a concept that we could call "cognitive psychology." What kinds of things would fit into this concept? What would make it easier to define your "cognitive psychology" concept? Compare this to a concept that you're already familiar with. What are the differences between the familiar concept and the new concept? How do you think your "cognitive psychology" concept differs from your instructor's "cognitive psychology" concept?

3. Think about two or three courses you are currently taking or have taken recently. Based on the definitions of critical thinking, mindfulness, and open-mindedness discussed in this chapter, which courses most required or best encouraged these practices? How did they do this? Which was the worst course from this perspective? How might this course be improved? Should all courses encourage critical thinking, or are there some for which this should not be a goal?

4. Think critically about the characteristics of language that have been applied to determining whether animals other than humans are capable of language. Now, listen to communication sounds that have been recorded from species not described in the text. Are these sounds language? How would we know? Websites offering to some such sounds include

   http://www.findsounds.com/types.html
   http://cmave.usda.ufl.edu/~rmankin/soundlibrary.html
   http://www.ent.iastate.edu/list/insect_sounds.html
   http://buzz.ifas.ufl.edu/index.htm
   http://www.bekkoame.ne.jp/~sibutaka/nature/html/
   insects/insectsounds_e.html

Connections

For extra help in mastering the material in this chapter, see the review sections and practice quizzes in the Student Study Guide, the CD-ROM, and the Online Learning Center.

Intelligence

Learning Goals

1   Describe what intelligence is.

2   Explain how intelligence is measured and what the limitations of intelligence tests are.

3   Identify four neuroscience approaches to intelligence.

4   Evaluate theories of multiple intelligences.

5   Discuss characteristics of mental retardation, giftedness, and creativity.

6   Analyze the contributions of heredity and environment to intelligence.

His cartoons include cows, aliens, nerds, nature, and improbable science. Although he retired in the mid-1990s you still see his cartoons everywhere. The artist is Gary Larson, who finished college but not in any blaze of glory. His most impressive job before his cartoons began to support him was as an investigator for the local Humane Society (Larson claims that on his way to the job interview, he actually ran over a dog).

Look at Larson's cartoons themselves. Is this cartoonist just totally wacko? The success of *The Far Side* cartoons and books suggests that Larson is anything but. Many people, including scientists all over the world, consider his work creative and intelligent. Larson has even had a louse and a butterfly named after him.

Should Larson's highly creative talent be considered a part of intelligence? Traditionally, they have not been. However, an increasing number of psychologists believe that creativity is a component of intelligence. In this chapter, the discussion of cognition continues with an examination of the nature of intelligence. Controversy exists over both how intelligence should be conceptualized and how it should be measured. Creativity is discussed both as a component of intelligence and as a separate process. Other topics covered are the extremes of intelligence—mental retardation and giftedness—as well as the contributions of heredity and environment to intelligence.

THE FAR SIDE By GARY LARSON

© 1985 FarWorks, Inc./Dist. by Universal Press Syndicate

11-7

"The picture's pretty bleak, gentlemen. ... The world's climates are changing, the mammals are taking over, and we all have a brain about the size of a walnut."

Source: © 1985 FAR WORKS, Universal Press Syndicate.

Gary Larson in front of some of his *The Far Side* cartoons.

1 THE NATURE OF INTELLIGENCE

What is intelligence?

What does the term *intelligence* mean to psychologists? Some experts describe intelligence as the ability to solve problems. Others describe it as the capacity to adapt and learn from experience. Still others argue that defining intelligence in these cognitive terms ignores other dimensions of intelligence, such as creativity and practical and interpersonal intelligence.

The problem with intelligence is that, unlike height, weight, and age, intelligence cannot be directly seen or measured. We can't peel back a person's scalp and see how much intelligence he or she has. We can evaluate intelligence only *indirectly* by studying and comparing the intelligent acts that people perform.

The primary components of intelligence are similar to those of the cognitive processes—problem solving, thinking, and memory—that were discussed in chapter 9. The differences in how these cognitive processes were described there and how intelligence is discussed here lie in the concepts of individual differences and assessment. *Individual differences* are the stable, consistent ways in which people are different from one another. Intelligence and personality, the subject of chapter 12, are the two areas of psychology in which individual differences have mainly been emphasized. Individual differences in intelligence generally have been measured by tests designed to tell us whether a person can reason better than others who have taken the test. As you will see later in the chapter, though, the use of conventional intelligence tests to assess intelligence is controversial. However, temporarily I set aside the contentions of psychologists over the measurement of intelligence and fall back on the definition of **intelligence** as the ability to solve problems and to adapt and learn from experience.

Review and Sharpen Your Thinking

1 Describe what intelligence is.

- Define intelligence and explain how it is linked to the concepts of individual differences and assessment.

Given the definition of intelligence proposed here, do you think that humans are the only intelligent species on earth? Explain.

mhhe.com/
santrockp7

For study tools related to this learning goal, see the Study Guide, the CD-ROM, and the Online Learning Center.

INTELLIGENCE TESTING 2

Approaches to Testing

Cultural Bias in Testing

Criteria of a Good Test of Intelligence

The Use and Misuse of Intelligence Tests

How is intelligence measured?

If you took the SAT exam before entering college, you might understand psychologist Robert Sternberg's (1997) childhood anxieties about intelligence tests. Because he got so stressed out about taking the tests, he did very poorly on them. Fortunately, a fourth-grade teacher worked with Robert and helped instill the confidence in him to overcome his anxieties. He not only began performing better on the tests but, also, when he was 13, he devised his own intelligence test and began using it to assess classmates—until the school principal found out and scolded him. Sternberg became so fascinated by intelligence that he made its study a lifelong pursuit. His approach to intelligence is discussed later in the chapter.

Approaches to Testing

Early psychologists completely ignored the "higher mental processes," such as thinking and problem solving, that we equate with intelligence today. They believed that simple sensory, perceptual, and motor processes were the key dimensions of intelligence.

intelligence Problem-solving skills and the ability to adapt to and learn from life's everyday experiences.

ALFRED BINET (1857–1911)
Alfred Binet constructed the first intelligence test after being asked to create a measure to determine which children would benefit from instruction in France's schools.

Sir Frances Galton, an English psychologist who is considered the father of mental tests, shared this point of view. However, in the late nineteenth century, he set out to demonstrate that there are systematic individual differences in these processes. Although his research provided few conclusive results, Galton raised many important questions about intelligence—how it should be measured, what its components are, and the degree to which it is inherited—that we continue to study today.

The Binet Tests   In 1904 the French Ministry of Education asked psychologist Alfred Binet to devise a method that would determine which students did not benefit from regular classroom instruction. School officials wanted to reduce overcrowding by placing those who did not benefit in special schools. Binet and his student Theophile Simon developed an intelligence test to meet this request. The test consisted of 30 items ranging from the ability to touch one's nose or ear when asked to the ability to draw designs from memory and to define abstract concepts.

Binet developed the concept of **mental age (MA),** which is an individual's level of mental development relative to that of others. Binet reasoned that a mentally retarded child would perform like a normal child of a younger age. He developed norms for intelligence by testing 50 nonretarded children from the ages of 3 to 11. Children suspected of mental retardation were given the test, and their performances were compared with those of children of the same chronological age in the normal sample. Average mental age (MA) corresponds to chronological age (CA), which is age from birth. A bright child has an MA considerably above CA; a dull child has an MA considerably below CA.

The term **intelligence quotient (IQ)** was devised in 1912 by William Stern. IQ consists of an individual's mental age divided by chronological age multiplied by 100:

$$IQ = \frac{MA}{CA} \times 100$$

If mental age is the same as chronological age, then the individual's IQ is 100 (average); if mental age is above chronological age, the IQ is more than 100 (above average); if mental age is below chronological age, the IQ is less than 100 (below average). For example, a 6-year-old child with a mental age of 8 would have an IQ of 133, whereas a 6-year-old child with a mental age of 5 would have an IQ of 83.

The Binet scales represented a major advance over earlier efforts to measure intelligence. Binet stressed that the core of intelligence consists of complex cognitive processes, such as memory, imagery, comprehension, and judgment. In addition, he believed that a developmental approach was crucial for understanding the concept of intelligence. His developmental interest was underscored by the emphasis on the child's mental age compared with chronological age.

The Binet test has been revised many times to incorporate advances in the understanding of intelligence and intelligence testing (Caruso, 2001). Many of the revisions were carried out by Lewis Terman, who applied Stern's IQ concept to the test, developed extensive norms, and provided detailed, clear instructions for each problem on the test. In 1985, the test, now called the Stanford-Binet (the revisions were done at Stanford University), was revised to analyze an individual's responses in four content areas: verbal reasoning, quantitative reasoning, abstract/visual reasoning, and short-term memory. A general composite score also is obtained to reflect overall intelligence.

The current Stanford-Binet is given to individuals from the age of 2 through adulthood. It includes a wide variety of items, some requiring verbal responses, others nonverbal responses. For example, items that characterize a 6-year-old's performance on the test include the verbal ability to define at least six words, such as *orange* and *envelope,* and the nonverbal ability to trace a path through a maze. Items that reflect the average adult's intelligence include defining such words as *disproportionate* and *regard,* explaining a proverb, and comparing idleness and laziness.

mental age (MA) An individual's level of mental development relative to that of others.

intelligent quotient (IQ) Consists of an individual's mental age divided by chronological age multiplied by 100.

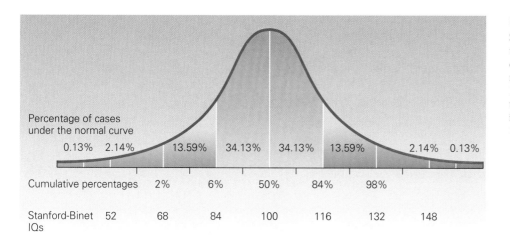

FIGURE 10.1   **The Normal Curve and Stanford-Binet IQ Scores** The distribution of IQ scores approximates a normal curve. Most of the population falls in the middle range of scores, between 84 and 116. Notice that extremely high and extremely low scores are rare. Only about 1 in 50 individuals has an IQ of more than 132 or less than 68.

Over the years, the Binet test has been given to thousands of children and adults of different ages selected at random from different parts of the United States. By administering the test to large numbers of individuals and recording the results, it has been found that intelligence measured by the Binet approximates a normal distribution (see figure 10.1). A **normal distribution** is a symmetrical, bell-shaped curve with a majority of the scores falling in the middle of the possible range and few scores appearing toward the extremes of the range. The Stanford-Binet continues to be one of the most widely used individual tests of intelligence.

The Wechsler Scales   Besides the Stanford-Binet, the most widely used intelligence tests are the Wechsler scales, developed by David Wechsler. In 1939, Wechsler introduced the first of his scales, designed for use with adults (Wechsler, 1939). Now in its third edition, the Wechsler Adult Intelligence Scale—III (WAIS-III), was followed by the Wechsler Intelligence Scale for Children—III (WISC-III), for children between the ages of 6 and 16, and the Wechsler Preschool and Primary Scale of Intelligence (WPPSI) for children from the ages of 4 to 6½.

The Wechsler scales not only provide an overall IQ score but also yield scores on six verbal and five nonverbal measures. This allows the examiner to separate verbal and nonverbal IQ scores and to see quickly the areas of mental performance in which the individual is below average, average, or above average. The inclusion of a number of nonverbal subscales makes the Wechsler test more representative of verbal and nonverbal intelligence; the Binet test includes some nonverbal items, but not as many as the Wechsler scales. Several of the Wechsler subscales are shown in figure 10.2.

Group Tests of Intelligence   The Stanford-Binet and Wechsler tests are individually administered intelligence tests. A psychologist approaches the testing situation as a structured interaction between the psychologist and the individual being tested. This provides an opportunity to sample the individual's behavior. During testing the psychologist observes the ease with which rapport is established, the level of energy and enthusiasm the individual expresses, and the degree of frustration tolerance and persistence the individual shows in performing difficult tasks. Each of these observations helps the psychologist understand the individual.

On some occasions, though, it is more convenient and economical to administer group intelligence tests than individual tests. For example, when World War I began, Binet's test was already popular, and the idea of using tests to measure intelligence was generally accepted. The armed services thought it would be beneficial to know the intellectual abilities of its thousands of recruits; but, clearly, not all of them could be tested individually. The result was the publication of the Army Alpha Test in 1917 to measure the intelligence of this large number of individuals on a group basis. In

normal distribution A symmetrical, bell-shaped curve with a majority of the scores falling in the middle of the possible range and few scores appearing toward the extremes of the range.

VERBAL SUBSCALES

Similarities

An individual must think logically and abstractly to answer a number of questions about how things might be similar.

Example: "In what ways are boats and trains the same?"

Comprehension

This subscale is designed to measure an individual's judgment and common sense.

Example: "Why do individuals buy automobile insurance?"

NONVERBAL SUBSCALES

Picture Arrangement

A series of pictures out of sequence is shown to an individual, who is asked to place them in their proper order to tell an appropriate story. This subscale evaluates how individuals integrate information to make it logical and meaningful.

Example: "The pictures below need to be placed in an appropriate order to tell a story."

Block Design

An individual must assemble a set of multicolored blocks to match designs that the examiner shows. Visual-motor coordination, perceptual organization, and the ability to visualize spatially are assessed.

Example: "Use the four blocks on the left to make the pattern at the right."

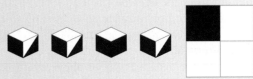

FIGURE 10.2 **Sample Subscales of the Wechsler Adult Intelligence Scale—Revised** The Wechsler includes 11 subscales, 6 verbal and 5 nonverbal. Examples from four of the subscales are shown here. Wechsler Adult Intelligence Scale, Third Edition, Copyright © 1997 by the Psychological Corporation, a Harcourt Assessment Company. Reproduced by permission. All rights reserved. "Wechsler Adult Intelligence Scale" and "WAIS" are trademarks of the Psychological Corporation, a Harcourt Assessment Company, registered in the United States of America and/or other jurisdictions.

the same year, the Army Beta Test, mainly a performance test given orally, was designed for individuals who could not read the Army Alpha Test.

Though economical and convenient, group tests have some significant disadvantages. When a test is given to a large group, the examiner cannot establish rapport, determine the level of anxiety, and so on. Most testing experts recommend that, when important decisions are to be made about an individual, a group intelligence test should be supplemented by other information about the individual's abilities. For example, many children take ability tests at school in a large group. If a decision is to be made about placing a child in a special education class, it is a legal requirement that the decision not be based on a group intelligence test. A psychologist must administer an individual intelligence test, such as the Stanford-Binet or Wechsler, and obtain extensive additional information about the child's abilities outside the testing situation.

The Scholastic Assessment Test (SAT), a group test taken each year by more than 1 million high school seniors, measures some of the same abilities as intelligence tests.

However, it does not yield an overall IQ score; rather, the SAT provides separate scores for verbal and mathematical ability. The SAT is similar to the original Binet test in that it was developed to predict success in school.

The SAT is used widely as a predictor of success in college, but it is only one of many pieces of information that determine whether a college admits a student. High school grades, the quality of the student's high school, letters of recommendation, individual interviews with the student, and special circumstances in the student's life that might have impeded academic ability are taken into account, along with the SAT scores.

In recent years, a debate has developed over whether private coaching can raise a student's SAT scores. The student's verbal and mathematical abilities, which the SAT assesses, have been built over years of experience and instruction. Research shows that private coaching on a short-term basis does not raise SAT scores substantially. Researchers have found that, on the average, SAT preparation courses raise a student's scores only 15 points on the SAT's 200- to 800-point scale (Kulik, Bangert-Drowns, & Kulik, 1984).

Another debate focuses on possible gender bias in the SAT. In 2000, males outscored females by 42 points on the average—35 points higher in the math section and 8 points in the verbal section (College Board, 2001). This represents a 4-point increase in the SAT gender gap from 1999, and only a slight narrowing of the gap since the early 1990s. Educational Testing Service claims that the SAT is supposed to predict college success, especially in terms of 1st-year grades. However, females make better grades than males in their 1st year of college, so it would appear that the SAT underpredicts the 1st-year success of females and overpredicts the 1st-year success of males.

Aptitude and Achievement Tests   Psychologists distinguish between aptitude tests and achievement tests. **Aptitude tests** predict an individual's ability to learn a skill or what the individual can accomplish with training. **Achievement tests** measure what a person has learned or the skills the person has mastered. Because the SAT is used to predict college success, it usually is referred to as an aptitude test. The tests you take in this and other college courses that assess what you have learned are achievement tests. Aptitude tests typically measure future performance; achievement tests assess current performance.

In many cases the distinction between aptitude and achievement tests becomes blurred. Although the SAT is used along with other information to predict college success (which makes it an aptitude test), it also examines what you have learned and the skills that you have mastered, such as math and vocabulary skills (characteristics of an achievement test). Indeed, the name of the SAT recently was changed from Scholastic Aptitude Test to Scholastic Assessment Test to acknowledge that the test measures both aptitude and achievement.

Criteria of a Good Test of Intelligence

Measurement and testing have been components of human decision making for centuries. The Chinese first developed formal oral tests of knowledge as early as 2200 B.C., when the Chinese emperor Ta Yü conducted a 3-year cycle of "competency testing" of government officials. After three examinations, the officials were either promoted or fired (Sax, 1997). In today's world, tests have become commonplace as psychologists have sought more precise measurement of psychology's concepts (Aiken, 2003; Haladyna, 2002).

Psychometrists specialize in psychological testing, possibly creating tests, administering them, or interpreting them. Most psychometrists have at least a minimum of a master's degree in psychology and have completed extensive coursework in psychological testing. Psychometrists work in education, business, and clinical fields. A school psychometrist might test children who are having difficulties in school to determine

aptitude tests Tests that predict an individual's ability to learn.

achievement tests Tests that measure what a person has learned or the skills that a person has mastered.

Frances Berger, a psychometrist, works for Psychometrics, Inc. She helps the company answer questions such as Which staff members might be good at computer programming? Among her jobs is to get subject matter experts together to write test items on the topic at hand. She also is involved in developing tests herself and administering them. Berger has created customized tests for many large corporations and government organizations, such as AT&T, GTE, Federal Express, and the Air Force.

validity The extent to which a test measures what it is intended to measure.

reliability The extent to which a test yields a consistent, reproducible measure of performance.

standardization Involves developing uniform procedures for administering and scoring a test, as well as creating norms for the test.

their weaknesses, as well as their strengths. A psychometrist who works for a corporation might test job candidates to determine which are most likely to succeed in a job. Yet another psychometrist might work in a mental health clinic or hospital giving psychological tests to determine an individual's mental health profile. In any of these settings, psychometrists might use a test of intelligence to determine an individual's intellectual strengths and weaknesses.

Psychometrists are generally quite knowledgeable about the tests they administer. They know that a good test must meet three criteria: validity, reliability, and standardization.

Validity **Validity** is the extent to which a test measures what it is intended to measure. If a test is supposed to measure intelligence, then it should measure intelligence, not some other characteristic of the person, such as anxiety.

A test's validity can be established in a number of ways. One is making sure that the test samples a broad range of the content that is to be measured. For example, a final exam in this class, if it is to cover the entire book, should sample items from each of the chapters rather than just two or three chapters. If an intelligence test purports to measure both verbal ability and problem-solving ability, the items should include a liberal sampling of items that reflect both of these domains; it should not test mostly vocabulary items with few items that require logical reasoning in solving problems.

One of the most important measures of validity is the degree to which it predicts an individual's performance when assessed by other measures, or criteria, of the attribute. For example, a psychologist might validate an intelligence test by asking the employers of the individuals who took the intelligence test how intelligent they are at work. The employers' perceptions would be another criterion for measuring intelligence. It is not unusual for the validation of an intelligence test to be another intelligence test. When the scores on the two measures overlap substantially, we say the test has high *criterion validity*. Of course, we may use more than one other measure to establish criterion validity. We might give the individuals a second intelligence test, get their employers' perceptions of their intelligence, and observe their behavior in real-life, problem-solving situations ourselves.

Reliability A test that is stable and consistent should not fluctuate significantly because of chance factors, such as how much sleep the test taker gets the night before the test, who the examiner is, the temperature in the room where the test is given, and so on. **Reliability** is the extent to which a test yields a consistent, reproducible measure of performance. Ideally, a test should yield the same measure of performance when an individual is given the test on two different occasions. Thus, if we gave an intelligence test to a group of high school students today and then gave them the same test in 6 months, the test would be considered reliable if those who scored high on the test today generally score high on the test in 6 months. However, individuals sometimes do better the second time they take the test because they are familiar with it (McMillan, 2001). Giving alternate forms of the same test on two different occasions is a way of dealing with this problem. The test items on the two forms of the test are similar but not identical. This strategy eliminates the chance of individuals performing better due to familiarity with the items, but it does not eliminate an individual's familiarity with the procedures and strategies involved in the testing. Also, it is difficult to create two truly parallel alternate forms of the test in which the items are similar but not identical.

In considering reliability and validity, a test that is valid is reliable, but a test that is reliable is not necessarily valid. People can respond consistently on a test, but the test might not be measuring what it purports to measure (Carey, 2001).

Standardization Good tests are not only reliable and valid but are also standardized (Impara & Plake, 2001). **Standardization** involves developing uniform procedures for administering and scoring a test, as well as creating *norms* or performance standards for the test. Uniform testing procedures require that the testing environment be as similar as possible for all individuals. The test directions and the amount of time allowed to complete the test should be the same, for example. Without standardization, it is difficult to compare scores across individuals. If some individuals take the SAT in a room in which loud music is playing, they are at a disadvantage compared with others who take the test in a quiet room.

Norms are created by giving the test to a large group of individuals representative of the population for whom the test is intended. This allows the test constructor to determine the distribution of test scores. Norms inform us which scores are considered high, low, or average. For example, suppose you receive a score of 120 on an intelligence test; that number alone has little meaning. The score takes on meaning when we compare it with the other scores. If only 20 percent of the standardized group scored above 120, then we can interpret your score as high rather than low or average. Many tests of intelligence are designed for individuals from diverse groups. So that the tests are applicable to such different groups, many of them have norms for individuals of different ages, socioeconomic statuses, and ethnic groups (Popham, 2002). Figure 10.3 summarizes the criteria for test construction and evaluation.

Cultural Bias in Testing

Many of the early intelligence tests were culturally biased, favoring people who were from urban rather than rural environments, of middle socioeconomic status rather than low socioeconomic status, and White rather than African American (Miller-Jones, 1989; Provenzo, 2002; Watras, 2002). For example, a question on an early test asked what one should do if one finds a 3-year-old child in the street. The correct answer was "call the police." But children from inner-city families who perceive the police as adversaries are unlikely to choose this answer. Similarly, children from rural areas might not choose this answer if there is no police force nearby. Such questions clearly do not measure the knowledge necessary to adapt to one's environment or to be "intelligent" in an inner-city or rural neighborhood (Scarr, 1984). Also, members of minority groups often do not speak English or may speak nonstandard English. Consequently, they may be at a disadvantage in trying to understand verbal questions that are framed in standard English, even if the content of the test is appropriate (Banks, 2002; Gibbs & Huang, 1989).

A specific case illustrating how cultural bias in intelligence tests can affect people is that of Gregory Ochoa. When Gregory was a high school student, he and his classmates took an IQ test. When Gregory looked at the test questions, he understood only a few words because he did not speak English very well and spoke Spanish at home. Several weeks later, Gregory was placed in a special class for mentally retarded students. Many of the students in the class, it turns out, had last names such as Ramirez and Gonzales. Gregory lost interest in school, dropped out, and eventually joined the Navy where he took high school courses and earned enough credits to attend college later. He graduated from San Jose City College as an honor student, continued his education, and became a professor of social work at the University of Washington in Seattle.

As a result of such cases as Gregory Ochoa's, researchers have tried to develop tests that accurately reflect a person's intelligence. **Culture-fair tests** are intelligence tests that are intended to be culturally unbiased. Two types of culture-fair tests have been developed. The first includes questions that are familiar to people from all socioeconomic and ethnic backgrounds. For example, a child might be asked how a bird and a dog are different, on the assumption that virtually all children are familiar with birds and dogs. The second type of culture-fair test contains no verbal questions. Figure 10.4 shows a sample question from the Raven Progressive Matrices Test. Even though tests such as the Raven Progressive Matrices are designed to be culture-fair, people with more education still score higher than those with less education do.

Validity

Does the test measure what it purports to measure?

Reliability

Is test performance consistent?

Standardization

Are uniform procedures for administering and scoring the test used?

FIGURE 10.3 **Test Construction and Evaluation**

culture-fair tests Intelligence tests that are intended to be culturally unbiased.

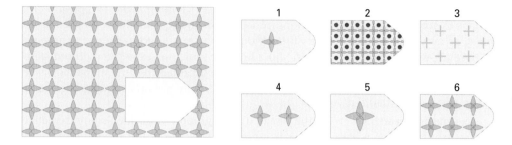

"How are her scores?"

One test that takes into account the socioeconomic background of children is the SOMPA, which stands for System of Multicultural Pluralistic Assessment (Mercer & Lewis, 1978). This test can be given to children from 5 to 11 years of age and was especially designed for children from low-income families. Instead of relying on a single test, SOMPA is based on information from four different areas of a child's life: (1) verbal and nonverbal intelligence, assessed by the WISC-III; (2) social and economic background, obtained through a 1-hour parent interview; (3) social adjustment to school, determined through a questionnaire that parents complete; and (4) physical health, assessed by a medical examination.

Why is it so hard to create culture-fair tests? Most tests tend to reflect what is important to the dominant culture. If tests have time limits, the test will be biased against groups not concerned with time. If languages differ, the same words might have different meanings for different language groups. Even pictures can produce bias, because some cultures have less experience with drawings and photographs (Anastasi & Urbina, 1996). Within the same culture, different groups can have different attitudes, values, and motivation, and this could affect their performance on intelligence tests. Items that ask why buildings should be made of brick are biased against children who have little or no experience with brick houses. Questions about railroads, furnaces, seasons of the year, distances between cities, and so on can be biased against groups who have less experience than others with these contexts.

The Use and Misuse of Intelligence Tests

Psychological tests are tools. Like all tools, their effectiveness depends on the knowledge, skill, and integrity of the user. A hammer can be used to build a beautiful kitchen cabinet, or it can be used as a weapon of assault. Like a hammer, psychological tests can be used for positive purposes, or they can be abused. It is important for both the test constructor and the test examiner to be familiar with the current state of scientific knowledge about intelligence and intelligence tests. Even though they have limitations, tests of intelligence are among psychology's most widely used tools. To be effective, they should be used in conjunction with other information about an individual, not relied on as the sole indicator of intelligence. For example, an intelligence test alone should not determine whether a child is placed in a special education or gifted class. The child's developmental history, medical background, performance in school, social competencies, and family experiences should be taken into account too.

The single number provided by many IQ tests can easily lead to stereotypes and expectations about an individual (Rosnow & Rosenthal, 1996). Many people do not know how to interpret the results of intelligence tests, and sweeping generalizations are too often made on the basis of an IQ score. For example, imagine that you are a teacher in the teacher's lounge the day after school has started in the fall. You mention a student—Johnny Jones—and a fellow teacher remarks that she had Johnny in class last year; she comments that he was a real dunce and points out that his IQ is 78. You cannot help but remember this information, and it might lead to thoughts that Johnny Jones is not very bright, so it is useless to spend much time teaching him. In this way, IQ scores are misused, and stereotypes are formed (Rosenthal & Jacobsen, 1968).

Ability tests can help a teacher group together children who function at roughly the same level in math or reading so they can be taught the same concepts together. However, extreme caution is necessary when test scores are used to place children in tracks such as "advanced," "intermediate," and "low." Periodic assessment of the groups, especially the "low" group, is required. Ability tests measure *current* performance, and maturational changes or enriched environmental experiences may advance a child's intelligence, indicating that she should be moved to a higher level group.

Despite their limitations, when used judiciously by a competent examiner, intelligence tests provide valuable information about individuals (Kaufman & Lichtenberger, 2002). There are not many alternatives to these tests. Subjective judgments about individuals simply reintroduce the bias that the tests were designed to eliminate.

Review and Sharpen Your Thinking

2 ***Explain how intelligence is measured and what the limitations of intelligence tests are.***

- Distinguish among these aspects of testing: early approaches, the Stanford-Binet tests, the Wechsler scales, group tests, and aptitude and achievement tests.
- Identify the criteria for a good test of intelligence.
- Evaluate cultural bias in testing.
- Describe the use and misuse of intelligence tests.

mhhe com/ santrockp7

For study tools related to this learning goal, see the Study Guide, the CD-ROM, and the Online Learning Center.

A CD-ROM is being sold to parents for testing their child's IQ and how the child is performing in relation to his or her grade in school. The company that makes the CD-ROM says that it helps to get parents involved in their child's education. What might be some problems with parents giving their children an IQ test and interpreting the results?

NEUROSCIENCE AND INTELLIGENCE 3

Head and Brain Size   **Electrical Activity in the Brain**

Information Processing Speed   **Energy Consumption in the Brain**

What can neuroscience tell us about intelligence?

The use of intelligence tests such as the Stanford-Binet and the Wechsler scales is one way to examine individual differences in intelligence. Might it be possible to also examine people's brains to reveal individual variations in their intelligence? For neuroscientists, intelligence is a research area that has opened up only recently, as advances in technology have made it possible to study the living brain at work. Most neuroscience studies have focused on the correlation of head and brain size with intelligence or on individual differences in brain activity, such as information-processing speed, brain electrical activity, and brain energy consumption (Vernon, 2000). Results

HERMAN®   by Jim Unger

"You did very well on your IQ test!"
Copyright 1980 Universal Press Syndicate.
Reprinted with permission. All rights reserved.

to date do not suggest that physical characteristics or measures of brain activity provide an assessment alternative to the standard type of intelligence tests.

Head and Brain Size

Does having a big head or brain have anything to do with intelligence? Early studies used external measures such as head size as a substitute for brain size or measured the brain sizes of deceased individuals. Modern brain imaging technology such as magnetic resonance imaging (MRI) now enables neuroscientists to routinely estimate brain size in living persons.

In general, researchers have found that a larger head size and a larger brain size are associated with higher intelligence, brain size more so than head size (Tisserand & others, 2001). However, the magnitude of this correlation is not very large, and it has not been determined whether the correlation is due to larger brains having more neurons, greater myelination of neurons, or some other reason. Also, because these studies are correlational, it's not certain whether a larger brain size causes greater intelligence or whether behaving intelligently causes a larger brain size.

Information Processing Speed

A number of studies have identified a possible connection between intelligence and the speed with which individuals can process information (Fry & Hale, 2000; Roberts & Pallier, 2001). The main focus of these studies has been on reaction time. One measure of reaction time is the speed with which individuals press a button on a console when they see a light appear. Using such measures, researchers have found significant correlations of reaction time with scores on traditional intelligence tests such as the Stanford-Binet, with higher IQ scores being associated with faster, or shorter, reaction times (Rijsdijk, Vernon, & Boomsma, 1998; Schretlen & others, 2000). Based on these studies, some experts on intelligence have concluded that the speed with which individuals can process information is an important aspect of intelligence (Vernon, 2000).

Others, however, say that the link between intelligence and processing speed is more complex. Some researchers have found that individuals who do well on intelligence tests actually take more time to decide on the type of reasoning needed to solve a problem, which enables them to respond more quickly with the correct answer (Marr & Sternberg, 1987; Sternberg, 1997a). Thus speed of processing by itself does not determine intelligence.

Electrical Activity in the Brain

Given the association of information processing speed and intelligence found in some studies, researchers began to explore the possibility that actual neural transmission might be linked with intelligence (Jausovec & Jausovec, 2001; Rijsdijk & Boomsma, 1997). Neuroscientists have sought to discover a link between brain activity and intelligence by measuring nerve conduction velocity and evoked potential.

Nerve conduction velocity (NCV) is the speed with which electrical impulses are transmitted along nerve fibers and across synapses. Research on NCV has focused on peripheral nerves. There has been less consistency in the results involving a relation between NCV and intelligence (Vernon, 2000).

Evoked potential refers to an electrical activity in the sensory areas of the brain that is caused by some external stimulus, such as a visual stimulus (a flash of light) or an auditory stimulus (a beep or a click). Researchers have found that individuals who register such stimuli more quickly score higher on intelligence tests than perceptually slower counterparts (Jausovec & Jausovec, 2000). Remember, though, that these are correlational studies, so we cannot conclude that faster brain activity in the evoked potential studies causes higher intelligence—it is just related to it.

Energy Consumption in the Brain

Like any physical organ, the brain consumes energy. Thus, when people engage in a task that requires cognitive activity, one index of the extent to which their brain is "working" is the rate at which it breaks down glucose to compensate for the energy it uses (Vernon, 2000). The rate at which the brain uses glucose can be measured by positron emission tomography (PET) scans.

The results of a number of PET scan studies reveal that when individuals are at rest and can engage in any cognitive activity they choose, those with higher intelligence demonstrate increased brain activity and their brains use more glucose (Hu & others, 2000; Wu & others, 2000). However, when individuals perform an assigned cognitive task, those with higher intelligence successfully complete the task using less energy. This possibly means that individuals with higher intelligence have higher levels of brain activity at their disposal and can use it more efficiently than less intelligent individuals (Vernon, 2000).

In sum, the overall results of using biological measures to assess intelligence have not been very robust. As technology progresses, better biological measures of intelligence may be found.

Review and Sharpen Your Thinking

3 *Identify four neuroscience approaches to the study of intelligence.*
- Describe the relation of head size and brain size to intelligence.
- Discuss the possibility of a connection between information processing speed and intelligence.
- Explain what the brain's electrical activity reveals about intelligence.
- Relate the brain's energy consumption to intelligence.

Nonhuman primates often have faster processing speeds in terms of reaction time than humans. Does that make them more intelligent than humans? Explain.

THEORIES OF MULTIPLE INTELLIGENCES   4

Factor Analysis, Two-Factor Theory, and Multiple-Factor Theory

Sternberg's Triarchic Theory

Evaluating the Multiple-Intelligences Approach

Gardner's Theory of Eight Intelligences

Emotional Intelligence

Do we have a single intelligence or multiple intelligences?

The concept of mental age and IQ is based on the idea that intelligence is a general ability. So, although the early Binet tests assessed some different cognitive skills (such as memory and comprehension), performance measures of these skills were combined to describe an individual's general intellectual ability. The Wechsler scales provide scores on a number of different intellectual skills, as well as an indication of a person's general intelligence.

Wechsler was not the first psychologist to break down intelligence into a number of abilities. Nor was he the last. A number of contemporary psychologists continue to search for specific components that make up intelligence. Unlike Wechsler and other intelligence theorists, however, they do not rely on traditional intelligence tests in their conceptualization of intelligence. Following are several key alternative conceptions of intelligence, beginning with that of Charles Spearman.

Ludwig van Beethoven, a musical genius, did not do well in math or English. *What are the implications of such inconsistencies for the concept of intelligence?*

Factor Analysis, Two-Factor Theory, and Multiple-Factor Theory

Some time before Wechsler analyzed intelligence in terms of general and specific abilities, Charles Spearman (1927) proposed that intelligence has two factors. His **two-factor theory** states that individuals have both general intelligence, which he called *g*, and a number of specific abilities, or *s*. Spearman believed that these two factors accounted for a person's performance on an intelligence test.

Spearman developed his theory by applying a technique called **factor analysis** to a number of intelligence tests. Factor analysis is a statistical procedure that correlates test scores to identify clusters, or factors, that measure a specific ability, such as verbal or mathematical reasoning.

L. L. Thurstone (1938) also used factor analysis in analyzing a number of intelligence tests, but he concluded that the tests measure only specific factors, not general intelligence. Thurstone's **multiple-factor theory** states that intelligence consists of seven primary mental abilities: verbal comprehension, number ability, word fluency, spatial visualization, associative memory, reasoning, and perceptual speed.

Gardner's Theory of Eight Intelligences

Imagine someone who has great musical skills but does not do well in math or English. Just such a person was the famous musical composer, Ludwig van Beethoven. Would you call Beethoven "unintelligent?" Unlikely! Recently, Howard Gardner has considerably expanded the components of intelligence to include even musical skills.

From Verbal Intelligence to Naturalist Intelligence Gardner (1983, 1993, 2001, 2002) believes there are eight types of intelligence. They are described below, along with examples of the occupations in which they are reflected as strengths (Campbell, Campbell, & Dickinson, 1999):

- *Verbal skills:* The ability to think in words and to use language to express meaning.
  Occupations: Authors, journalists, speakers.
- *Mathematical skills:* The ability to carry out mathematical operations.
  Occupations: Scientists, engineers, accountants.
- *Spatial skills:* The ability to think three-dimensionally.
  Occupations: Architects, artists, sailors.
- *Bodily-kinesthetic skills:* The ability to manipulate objects and be physically adept.
  Occupations: Surgeons, craftspeople, dancers, athletes.
- *Musical skills:* A sensitivity to pitch, melody, rhythm, and tone.
  Occupations: Composers, musicians, and sensitive listeners.
- *Interpersonal skills:* The ability to understand and effectively interact with others.
  Occupations: Teachers, mental health professionals.
- *Intrapersonal skills:* The ability to understand oneself.
  Occupations: Theologians, psychologists.
- *Naturalist skills:* The ability to observe patterns in nature and understand natural and human-made systems.
  Occupations: Farmers, botanists, ecologists, landscapers.

Naturalist skills are Gardner's (1999) latest addition to his multiple-intelligences list. Cartoonist Gary Larson excels in naturalist skills. Larson has had a strong interest in science and nature since he was a young boy, but, rather than pursing a career in these areas, he incorporated them as themes in many of his cartoons. Recall that his naturalist skills were recognized by biologists, who have named species of animals after him.

Gardner believes that each of the eight intelligences can be destroyed by brain damage, that each involves unique cognitive skills, and that each shows up in exag-

two-factor theory Spearman's theory that individuals have both general intelligence (*g*) and a number of specific abilities (*s*).

factor analysis A statistical procedure that examines various items or measures and identifies factors that are correlated with each other.

multiple-factor theory Thurstone's theory that intelligence consists of seven primary mental abilities: verbal comprehension, number ability, word fluency, spatial visualization, associative memory, reasoning, and perceptual speed.

gerated fashion in both the gifted and individuals who have mental retardation or autism (a psychological disorder marked by deficits in social interaction and interests). Dustin Hoffman portrayed an individual with autism who had a remarkable computing ability in the movie *Rain Man.* In one scene, Hoffman's character helped his brother successfully gamble in Las Vegas by keeping track of all the cards that had been played.

Multiple Intelligences in the Classroom Currently there is considerable interest in applying Gardner's theory of multiple intelligences to children's education. One experimental program, Project Spectrum, begins with the idea that every student has the potential to develop strengths in one or more areas (Gardner, 1993).

What is a Spectrum classroom like? The classroom has rich and engaging materials that can stimulate a range of intelligences. Teachers do not try to evoke intelligences directly by using materials that are labeled *spatial* or *verbal*. Rather, materials that relate to a combination of intelligence domains are used. For example, a naturalist corner has biological specimens that students can explore and compare. This area stimulates students' sensory capacities and logical thinking skills. In a storytelling area, students create imaginative tales with stimulating props and design their own storyboards. This area encourages children to use their linguistic, dramatic, and imaginative skills. In a building corner, students can construct a model of their classroom and arrange small-scale photographs of the students and the teachers in their class using spatial and personal skills. In all, the Spectrum classroom has 12 areas that are designed to bring out students' multiple intelligences.

The Spectrum classroom can identify skills that typically are not tapped in a regular classroom. In one first-grade class, a boy who was a product of a highly conflicted broken home was at risk for school failure. However, when Project Spectrum was introduced, the boy was identified as especially skilled in one area: He was the best student in the class at taking apart and putting together common objects, such as a doorknob and a food grinder. His teacher became encouraged when she found that he possessed this skill, and his overall school performance began to improve.

In addition to identifying unexpected strengths in students, Project Spectrum also can pinpoint undetected weaknesses. Gregory, who was especially skilled in math computation and conceptual knowledge, was doing very well in the first grade. However,

In *Rain Man,* Dustin Hoffman portrayed a man with autism and cognitive deficits who accomplished remarkable feats of counting and mathematics. Such skills are described as *savant skills.* They support the idea that intelligence can be expressed in multiple abilities.

A student in the naturalist corner of a Spectrum classroom. *What combinations of materials might you expect to find in other corners of a Spectrum classroom?*

"You're wise, but you lack tree smarts."

he performed poorly in a number of Spectrum areas. Gregory did well only in the areas in which he needed to give the correct answer and when a person in authority gave it to him. As a result of the Spectrum Project, Gregory's teacher began to search for ways to encourage him to take risks on more open-ended tasks, to try different ways of doing things, and to realize that it is okay to make mistakes.

Sternberg's Triarchic Theory

At the beginning of the chapter, I profiled cartoonist Gary Larson's creative talents and asked whether his creativity should be considered a part of the concept of intelligence. Gardner does not have a category for creativity in his intelligence theory, but Robert J. Sternberg does. In his **triarchic theory,** Sternberg (1986, 2002) proposes that there are three main types of intelligence: analytical, creative, and practical. Recall from earlier in the chapter that Sternberg had some very stressful experiences when he had to take traditional intelligence tests as a child. As an adult, he concluded that those intelligence tests did not adequately assess several important dimensions of intelligence.

Analytical, Creative, and Practical Intelligence   Let's explore further what analytical, creative, and practical intelligence mean and look at examples of people who reflect these types of intelligence.

Analytical Intelligence   Consider Latisha, who scores high on traditional intelligence tests such as the Stanford-Binet and is a star analytical thinker. Sternberg calls Latisha's analytical thinking and abstract reasoning *analytical intelligence*. It is the closest to what has traditionally been called intelligence and what is commonly assessed by intelligence tests.

In Sternberg's view of analytical intelligence, the basic unit in intelligence is a component simply defined as a basic unit of information processing. Sternberg believes such components include the ability to acquire or store information; to retain or retrieve information; to transfer information; to plan, make decisions, and solve problems; and to translate our thoughts into performance.

Creative Intelligence   Todd does not have the best test scores but has an insightful and creative mind. Sternberg called the type of thinking at which Todd excels *creative intelligence*. According to Sternberg, creative people such as Todd have the ability to solve new problems quickly, but they also learn how to solve familiar problems in an automatic, rote way so that their minds are free to handle other problems that require insight and creativity.

Practical Intelligence   Consider Emanuel, a street-smart person who learned to deal in practical ways with his world, although his scores on traditional IQ tests are low. Emanuel's street smarts and practical know-how indicate that he has what Sternberg calls *practical intelligence*, which includes the ability to get out of trouble, an aptitude for replacing a fuse, and a knack for getting along with people. Sternberg describes practical intelligence as all of the important information about getting along in the world that you are not taught in school. He believes practical intelligence is sometimes more important than analytical intelligence, the book knowledge that is taught in school.

Triarchic Intelligence in the Classroom   Sternberg (1997a) says that students with different triarchic patterns look different in school. Students with high analytic ability tend to be favored in conventional schools. They often do well in direct

triarchic theory Sternberg's theory that there are three main types of intelligence: analytical, creative, and practical.

instruction classes in which the teacher lectures and gives objective tests. They often are considered smart students, typically get good grades, do well on traditional IQ tests and the SAT, and later gain admission to competitive colleges. Students who are high in creative intelligence often are not in the top rung of their class. Sternberg says that many teachers have expectations about how assignments should be done, to which creatively intelligent students might not conform. Instead of giving expected answers, they give unconventional, although correct, answers—for which they might get reprimanded or marked down. Like students high in creative intelligence, students who are practically intelligent often do not relate well to the demands of school. However, these students frequently do well outside of the classroom's walls. They often have excellent social skills and good common sense. As adults, they may become successful managers, entrepreneurs, or politicians, despite undistinguished school records.

Sternberg (1999) believes that few tasks are purely analytic, creative, or practical. Most tasks require some combination of these skills. For example, when students write a book report, they might (1) analyze the book's main themes, (2) generate new ideas about how the book could have been written better, and (3) think about how the book's themes can be applied to people's lives. Sternberg argues that it is important to balance classroom instruction with respect to all three types of intelligence. That is, students should be given opportunities to learn through analytical, creative, and practical thinking, in addition to conventional memorization.

Emotional Intelligence

Both Gardner's and Sternberg's theories include one or more categories of social intelligence. In Gardner's theory, the categories are interpersonal intelligence and intrapersonal intelligence. In Sternberg's theory, the category is practical intelligence. Another theory that captures the importance of the interpersonal, intrapersonal, and practical aspects of intelligence has generated a great deal of interest (Lam & Kirby, 2002). It is **emotional intelligence,** defined by Peter Salovy and John Mayer (1990) as the ability to monitor one's own and other's feelings and emotions, to discriminate among them, and to use this information to guide one's thinking and actions.

The concept of emotional intelligence has been popularized by Daniel Goleman (1995). Goleman believes that when it comes to predicting a person's competence, IQ as measured by traditional intelligence tests matters less than emotional intelligence. In Goleman's view, emotional intelligence involves these four areas:

- *Developing emotional awareness* (such as the ability to separate feelings from actions)
- *Managing emotions* (such as being able to control anger)
- *Reading emotions* (such as taking the perspective of others)
- *Handling relationships* (such as the ability to solve relationship problems)

Evaluating the Multiple-Intelligences Approach

The multiple-intelligence theories have much to offer. They have stimulated us to think more broadly about what makes up people's intelligence and competence. And they have motivated educators to develop programs that instruct students in different domains.

Figure 10.5 on page 405 provides a comparison of Gardner's, Sternberg's, and Salovy/Mayer/ Goleman's views. Notice that Gardner includes a number of types of intelligence that are not addressed by the other views and that Sternberg is unique in emphasizing creative intelligence.

Some critics say that Gardner's classification of such domains as musical skills as a type of intelligence is off base. They ask whether there might not be other skills domains that Gardner has left out. For example, there are outstanding chess players, prizefighters, writers, politicians, lawyers, ministers, and poets. Yet we don't refer to

emotional intelligence The ability to monitor one's own and others' emotions and feelings, to discriminate among them, and to use this information to guide one's thinking and actions.

Do People Have a General Intelligence?

Charles Spearman (1927) believed that people have both a general intelligence (*g*) and specific intelligences (*s*). With all of the interest in the multiple intelligences proposed by Gardner (2001) and Sternberg (1999), it might seem that the concept of a general intelligence is outdated. Contemporary experts on general intelligence disagree. They argue that individuals do have a general intelligence and that it includes abstract reasoning or thinking, the capacity to acquire knowledge, and problem-solving ability (Brody, 2000; Carroll, 1993). In addition, they maintain, it has real-world applications as a predictor of school and job success (Brody, 2000). For example, scores on tests of general intelligence are substantially correlated with academic achievement and moderately correlated with work performance (Lubinski, 2000). Individuals with higher scores on tests of general intelligence tend to get higher-paying, more prestigious jobs (Wagner, 1997).

However, general IQ tests predict only about one-fourth of the variation in job success, with the majority of job success linked to such other factors as motivation and education (Wagner & Sternberg, 1986). Further, the correlations between IQ and achievement decrease the longer people work at a job, presumably because as they gain more experience they perform better (Hunt, 1995).

Like Spearman, some experts on intelligence believe that people have both a general intelligence and specific intelligences. For example, in one study, John Carroll (1993) extensively assessed intellectual abilities and concluded that, although all intellectual abilities are related to each other (which supports the concept of general intelligence), there are many specialized abilities as well. Beyond general intelligence, Carroll found an intermediate level of intellectual abilities, reflected in such abilities as memory and speed of processing information to make decisions, and a narrower level, reflected in such abilities as the skill to code sounds.

There is a further wrinkle in the general intelligence issue. Researchers have found that the higher individuals' general IQ scores are, the more their scores on subtests of intellectual abilities vary (Hunt, 1995). For example, some bright individuals might score high on vocabulary and low on perceiving geometric patterns, and the reverse might be true for other bright individuals. However, researchers have found that individuals who score low on intelligence tests tend not to do well on any of the subtests (Hunt, 1995). These findings suggest that general intelligence might be a more appropriate concept for individuals with low intellectual ability than for individuals with high intellectual ability.

In sum, there continues to be controversy about whether people have a general intelligence. There also continues to be controversy about what the specific intelligences are.

What do you think?

- Do you have a general intelligence? If so, how would you describe it?
- Are there some specialized intellectual abilities, such as spatial abilities and mechanical abilities, that should be included or emphasized more in school curriculums?
- Do you have any specialized intellectual abilities that would not be reflected in a traditional intelligence test, the kind that measures general intelligence? If so, what are they?

chess intelligence, prizefighter intelligence, and so on. Other critics say that the research base to support either the eight intelligences of Gardner, the three intelligences of Sternberg, or the emotional intelligence of Salovy/Mayer/Goleman as the best way to characterize intelligence has not yet been developed.

Gardner (1999)—the ultimate multiple-intelligences advocate—has even criticized the emotional-intelligence advocates as going too far in including emotions in the concept of intelligence. He also believes that creativity should not be included. Although he believes that understanding emotions and being creative are important aspects of human competence and functioning, Gardner thinks that emotional understanding and creativity are not factors of intelligence.

There also are a number of psychologists who still support Spearman's concept of *g* (general intelligence), and many of them believe that the multiple-intelligences views have taken the concept of *s* (specific intelligences) too far. For example, one expert on intelligence, Nathan Brody (2000), argues that people who excel at one type of intellectual task are likely to excel at other intellectual tasks. Thus individuals who do well at memorizing lists of digits are also likely to be good at solving verbal and spatial layout problems. To learn more about the continuing debate over general intelligence versus multiple intelligences, see the Critical Controversy box.

Gardner	Sternberg	Salovy/Mayer/Goleman
Verbal Mathematical	Analytical	
Spatial Movement Musical	Creative	
Interpersonal Intrapersonal	Practical	Emotional
Naturalistic		

FIGURE 10.5 Comparing Gardner's, Sternberg's, and Salovy/Mayer/Goleman's Intelligences

Review and Sharpen Your Thinking

4 *Evaluate theories of multiple intelligence.*

- Explain the role of factor analysis in the development of two-factor theory and multiple-factor theory.
- Discuss Gardner's theory of eight intelligences.
- Describe Sternberg's triarchic theory.
- Summarize what emotional intelligence is.
- Evaluate the multiple-intelligences approach.

Apply Gardner's and Sternberg's multiple intelligences to yourself (or someone else you know well). Write a narrative description of yourself based on each of these theorists' views.

THE EXTREMES OF INTELLIGENCE AND CREATIVITY 5

Mental Retardation	Giftedness	Creativity

What are the characteristics of mental retardation, giftedness, and creativity?

Mental retardation and intellectual giftedness are the extremes of intelligence. Often, intelligence tests are used to identify exceptional individuals. Keeping in mind that an intelligence test should not be used as the sole basis for decisions about intelligence, let's first consider the nature of mental retardation and giftedness, then discuss how creativity differs from intelligence.

Mental Retardation

The most distinctive feature of mental retardation is inadequate intellectual functioning. Long before formal tests were developed to assess intelligence, individuals with mental retardation were identified by a lack of age-appropriate skills in learning and caring for themselves. Once intelligence tests were developed, numbers were assigned to indicate degrees of mental retardation. It is not unusual to find that, of two individuals with mental retardation who have the same low IQ, one is married, employed, and involved in the community and the other requires constant supervision in an institution. Such differences in social competence led psychologists to include deficits in adaptive behavior in their definition of mental retardation (Hallahan & Kauffman, 2003).

Type of Mental Retardation	IQ Range	Percentage
Mild	55–70	89
Moderate	40–54	6
Severe	25–39	4
Profound	Below 25	1

FIGURE 10.6 Classification of Mental Retardation Based on IQ

A child with Down syndrome. *What causes Down syndrome?*

mental retardation A condition of limited mental ability in which the individual has a low IQ, usually below 70, has difficulty adapting to everyday life, and has an onset of these characteristics in the so-called developmental period

gifted Individuals who have an IQ of 120 or higher and/or superior talent in a particular domain.

Mental retardation is a condition of limited mental ability in which an individual has a low IQ, usually below 70 on a traditional intelligence test, and has difficulty adapting to everyday life; he or she first exhibited these characteristics during the so-called developmental period—by age 18. The reason for including developmental period in the definition of mental retardation is that we do not usually think of a college student who suffers massive brain damage in a car accident, resulting in an IQ of 60, as "mentally retarded." Low IQ and low adaptiveness are evident in childhood, not following a long period of normal functioning that is interrupted by an insult of some form. About 5 million Americans fit this definition of mental retardation.

There are several classifications of mental retardation (Hallahan & Kaufmann, 2000). As indicated in figure 10.6, mental retardation may be mild, moderate, severe, or profound. Note that a large majority of individuals diagnosed with mental retardation fit into the mild category. Most school systems still use these classifications. However, because these categories are based on IQ ranges, they are not perfect predictors of functioning. The American Association on Mental Retardation (1992) developed a different classification based on the degree of support required for a person with mental retardation to function at the highest level. As shown in figure 10.7, these categories of support are intermittment, limited, extensive, and pervasive.

Mental retardation may have an organic cause, or it may be social and cultural in origin. *Organic retardation* is mental retardation caused by a genetic disorder or by brain damage; "organic" refers to the tissues or organs of the body, so there is some physical damage in organic retardation. Down syndrome, one form of organic mental retardation, occurs when an extra chromosome is present in the individual's genetic makeup. It is not known why the extra chromosome is present, but it may involve the health or age of the female ovum or male sperm.

Other types of organic retardation include Williams syndrome, which was discussed in chapter 9; fragile X syndrome, caused by an abnormality in the X chromosome that is more common in males than females; prenatal malformation; metabolic disorders; and diseases that affect the brain (Das, 2000). Most people who suffer from organic retardation have IQs between 0 and 50.

Cultural-familial retardation is a mental deficit in which no evidence of organic brain damage can be found. Individuals with this type of retardation have IQs between 55 and 70. Psychologists suspect that such mental deficits result at least in part from growing up in a below-average intellectual environment. As children, those who are familially retarded can be identified in school, where they often fail, need tangible rewards (candy rather than praise), and are highly sensitive to what others—both peers and adults—expect of them (Vaughn, Bos, & Schumm, 2003). However, as adults, the familially retarded are usually invisible, perhaps because adult settings don't tax their cognitive skills as sorely. It may also be that the familially retarded increase their intelligence as they move toward adulthood.

Giftedness

There have always been people whose abilities and accomplishments outshine those of others—the whiz kid in class, the star athlete, the natural musician. People who are **gifted** have high intelligence (an IQ of 120 or higher) and/or superior talent for something. When it comes to programs for the gifted, most school systems select children who have intellectual superiority and academic aptitude. Children who are talented in the visual and performing arts (arts, drama, dance) or in athletics or who have other special aptitudes tend to be overlooked.

Until recently, giftedness and emotional distress were thought to go hand in hand. English novelist Virginia Woolf suffered from severe depression, for example, and eventually committed suicide. And Sir Isaac Newton, Vincent van Gogh, Anne Sexton, Socrates, and Sylvia Plath all had emotional problems. However, these individuals are

Intermittent	Supports are provided "as needed." The individual may need episodic or short-term support during life-span transitions (such as job loss or acute medical crisis). Intermittent supports may be low or high intensity when provided.
Limited	Supports are intense and relatively consistent over time. They are time-limited but not intermittent. Require fewer staff members and cost less than more intense supports. These supports likely will be needed for adaptation to the changes involved in the school-to-adult period.
Extensive	Supports are characterized by regular involvement (e.g., daily) in at least some setting (such as home or work) and are not time-limited (for example, extended home-living support).
Pervasive	Supports are constant, very intense, and are provided across settings. They may be of a life-sustaining nature. These supports typically involve more staff members and intrusiveness than the other support categories.

FIGURE 10.7 Classification of Mental Retardation Based on Levels of Support Needed

the exception rather than the rule; in general, no relation between giftedness and mental disorder has been found. Recent studies support the conclusion that gifted people tend to be more mature and have fewer emotional problems than others and to have grown up in a positive family climate (Feldhusen, 1999; Feldman, 1997).

Lewis Terman (1925) conducted a study of 1,500 children whose Stanford-Binet IQs averaged 150. A popular myth is that gifted children are maladjusted, but Terman found in his study that they were not only academically gifted but also socially well adjusted. Many of these gifted children went on to become successful doctors, lawyers, professors, and scientists.

Ellen Winner (1996) recently described three criteria that characterize gifted children, whether in art, music, or academic domains:

1. *Precocity.* In most instances, gifted children are precocious because they have an inborn high ability in a particular domain or domains. They begin to master an area earlier than their peers. Learning in their domain is more effortless for them than for ordinary children.
2. *Marching to their own drummer.* Gifted children learn in a qualitatively different way than ordinary children do. For one thing, they need minimal help, or scaffolding, from adults to learn. In many cases, they resist any kind of explicit instruction. They also often make discoveries on their own and solve problems in unusual ways.
3. *A passion to master.* Gifted children are driven to understand the domain in which they have high ability. They display an intense, obsessive interest and an ability to focus. They are not children who need to be pushed by their parents. They motivate themselves.

As a 10-year-old, Alexandra Nechita was described as a child prodigy. She paints quickly and impulsively on large canvases, some as large as 5 feet by 9 feet. It is not unusual for her to complete several of these large paintings in a week's time. Her paintings—in the modernist tradition—sell for up to $80,000 apiece. When she was only 2 years of age, Alexandra colored in coloring books for hours. She had no interest in dolls or friends. Once she started school, she would start painting as soon as she got home. And she continues to paint—relentlessly and passionately. It is, she says, what she loves to do.

Is giftedness such as Alexandra Nechita's artistic talent a product of heredity or environment? Likely both. Experts who study giftedness point out that gifted individuals recall that they had signs of high ability in a particular area at a very young age, prior to or at the beginning of formal training (Howe & others, 1995). This suggests the importance of innate ability in giftedness. However, researchers also have found that the individuals who enjoy world-class status in the arts, mathematics, science, and

Art prodigy Alexandra Nechita. *What are some characteristics of gifted children?*

"What do you mean 'What is it?' It's the spontaneous, unfettered expression of a young mind not yet bound by the restraints of narrative or pictorial representation."
© Sidney Harris

sports all report strong family support and years of training and practice (Bloom, 1985). Recall the distinction between experts and novices made in chapter 9, that deliberate practice is an important characteristic of individuals who become experts in a particular domain. For example, in one study, the best musicians engaged in twice as much deliberate practice over their lives as the least successful ones did (Ericsson, Krampe, & Tesch-Roemer, 1993).

Do gifted children become gifted and highly creative adults? In Terman's research, gifted children typically did become experts in a well-established domain, such as medicine, law, or business. However, although they may have been creative in coming up with innovative ideas in these well-established domains, Ellen Winner (2000) points out that they did not become major creators. That is, they did not create a new domain or revolutionize an old domain.

Thus, although giftedness in childhood and in adulthood are linked, only a fraction of gifted children eventually become revolutionary adult creators. Those who do must make a difficult transition from child prodigy (learning rapidly and effortlessly in an established domain) to adult creator (disrupting and ultimately remaking a domain or creating a new one).

One reason that some gifted children do not become gifted adults or even adult creators is that they have been pushed so hard by overzealous parents and teachers that they lose their intrinsic (internal) motivation (Winner, 1996). As adolescents, they may ask themselves, "Who am I doing this for?" If the answer is not for one's self, they may not want to do it anymore.

I have brought up the term *creative* on several occasions in discussing giftedness. The next section explores the topic of creativity in greater depth.

Creativity

What does it mean to be creative? **Creativity** is the ability to think about something in novel and unusual ways and to come up with unconventional solutions to problems. Gary Larson's bizarre cartoons certainly reflect the ability to think in novel and unusual ways. Science and nature are two areas in which Larson's creative thinking skills clearly emerge in his cartoons.

Intelligence and creativity are not the same thing (Michael, 1999). Sternberg (2000, 2001), who included creativity in his triarchic theory of intelligence, says that many highly intelligent people produce large numbers of products, but the products are not necessarily novel. He also believes that highly creative people defy the crowd, whereas people who are highly intelligent but not creative often try to simply please the crowd.

Creative people tend to be divergent thinkers (Guilford, 1967). **Divergent thinking** produces many answers to the same question. In contrast, the kind of thinking required on conventional intelligence tests is **convergent thinking.** For example, a typical item on an intelligence test is "How many quarters will you get in return for 60 dimes?" There is only one correct answer to this question. However, the following question has many possible answers: What image comes to mind when you hear the phrase "sitting alone in a dark room"?

Thinking further about intelligence and creativity, most creative people are quite intelligent, but the reverse is not necessarily true. Many highly intelligent people (as measured by high scores on conventional tests of intelligence) are not very creative (Sternberg & O'Hara, 2000).

Steps in the Creative Process The creative process has often been described as a five-step sequence:

1. *Preparation.* You become immersed in a problem or an issue that interests you and arouses your curiosity.

creativity The ability to think about something in novel and unusual ways and come up with unconventional solutions to problems.

divergent thinking Thinking that produces many answers to the same question; characteristic of creativity.

convergent thinking Thinking that produces one correct answer; characteristic of the type of thinking required on traditional intelligence tests.

Paul MacCready is one of America's most prolific inventors. His best-known invention is the Gossamer Condor, the first human-powered plane to travel a mile. MacCready's task was to design something stable and very light that would fly. It had to be different from any other airplane. MacCready's accomplishment won him $100,000 and a place in the Smithsonian Institution next to the Wright brothers' plane. MacCready says that asking the right questions and seeing things in a fresh way are critical for creativity.

2. *Incubation.* You churn ideas around in your head. This is the point at which you are likely to make some unusual connections in your thinking.
3. *Insight.* At this point, you experience the "Aha!" moment when all the pieces of the puzzle seem to fit together.
4. *Evaluation.* Now you must decide whether the idea is valuable and worth pursuing. Is the idea really novel, or is it obvious?
5. *Elaboration.* This final step often covers the longest span of time and the hardest work. This is what the famous twentieth-century American inventor Thomas Edison was talking about when he said that creativity is 1 percent inspiration and 99 percent perspiration. Elaboration may require a great deal of perspiration.

Mihaly Csikszentmihalyi (1996) believes that this five-step sequence provides a helpful framework for thinking about how creative ideas are formed and developed. However, he argues that creative people don't always go through the steps in a linear sequence. For example, elaboration is often interrupted by periods of incubation. Fresh insights also may appear during incubation, evaluation, and elaboration. And, in terms of a time frame, insight might last for years or it might take only a few hours. Sometimes the creative idea consists of one deep insight and other times a series of small ones.

Characteristics of Creative Thinkers Creative thinkers tend to have the following characteristics (Perkins, 1994):

- *Flexibility and playful thinking.* Creative thinkers are flexible and play with problems, which gives rise to a paradox. Although creativity takes hard work, the work goes more smoothly if it is taken lightly. In a way, humor greases the wheels of creativity (Goleman, Kaufman, & Ray, 1993). When you are joking around, you are more likely to consider any possibility. Having fun helps to disarm the inner censor that can condemn your ideas as off base. *Brainstorming* is a technique in which members of a group are encouraged to come up with as many ideas as possible, play off each other's ideas, and say practically whatever comes to mind. Individuals usually avoid criticizing others' ideas until the end of the session.
- *Inner motivation.* Creative people often are motivated by the joy of creating. They tend to be less inspired by grades, money, or favorable feedback from others. Thus creative people are motivated more internally than externally. (Motivation is discussed more thoroughly in chapter 11.)
- *Willingness to risk.* Creative people make more mistakes than their less imaginative counterparts. It's not that they are less proficient but that they come up with more ideas, more possibilities. They win some, they lose some. For example, the twentieth-century Spanish artist Pablo Picasso created more than 20,000 paintings. Not all of them were masterpieces. Creative thinkers learn to cope with unsuccessful projects and see failure as an opportunity to learn.

Mark Strand, former U.S. poet laureate, says that in his most creative moments he loses a sense of time and becomes absorbed in what he is doing. In this state, he feels he is dismantling meaning and remaking it. Strand comments that he can't stay in this absorbed frame of mind for an entire day. It comes and goes: His attention coils and uncoils; his focus sharpens and softens. When an idea clicks, he focuses intensely, transforming the idea into a vivid verbal image that will communicate its essence to the reader.

Nina Holton, a leading contemporary sculptor, turns playfully wild germs of ideas into stunning sculptures. She says that sculpture is a combination of wonderful, unique ideas and a lot of hard work. She comments that when she is introduced to people they often say, "It must be so exciting and wonderful being a sculptor." Holton loves her work but says that most people see only its creative side, not the hard work.

Jonas Salk, who invented the polio vaccine, says his best ideas come to him when he suddenly wakes up. After a few minutes of visualizing problems he had thought about the day before, he begins to see an unfolding, as if a painting or story is taking form. Salk also believes that many creative ideas are generated in conversations with others who have open, curious minds and positive attitudes. Salk's penchant for seeing emergent possibilities often brought him in conflict with people who had orthodox opinions.

- *Objective evaluation of work.* Despite the stereotype that creative people are eccentric and highly subjective, most creative thinkers strive to evaluate their work objectively. They may use an established set of criteria to make judgments or rely on the judgments of respected, trusted others. In this manner, they can determine whether further creative thinking will improve their work.

Living a More Creative Life Csikszentmihalyi (1996) interviewed 90 leading figures in art, business, government, education, and science to learn how creativity works. He discovered that creative people regularly engage in challenges that absorb them. Based on his interviews with some of the most creative people in the world, he concluded that the first step toward a more creative life is to cultivate your curiosity and interest. Here are his recommendations for doing this:

- *Try to be surprised by something every day.* Maybe it is something you see, hear, or read about. Become absorbed in a lecture or a book. Be open to what the world is telling you. Life is a stream of experiences. Swim widely and deeply in it, and your life will be richer.
- *Try to surprise at least one person every day.* In a lot of things you do, you have to be predictable and patterned. Do something different. Ask a question you normally would not ask. Invite someone to go to a show or a museum you have never visited.
- *Write down each day what surprised you and how you surprised others.* Most creative people keep a diary, notes, or lab records to ensure that experiences are not fleeting or forgotten. Start with a specific task. Each evening record the most surprising event that occurred that day and your most surprising action. After

How Creative Is Your Thinking?

Rate each of the following items as they apply to you on a scale from 1 = not like me at all, 2 = somewhat unlike me, 3 = somewhat like me, to 4 = very much like me.

	1	2	3	4
1. I am good at coming up with lots of new and unique ideas.				
2. I like to brainstorm with others to creatively find solutions to problems.				
3. I tend to be internally motivated.				
4. I'm a flexible person and like to play with my thinking.				
5. I like to be around creative people and I learn from how they think.				
6. I like to be surprised by something every day and surprise others.				
7. I wake up in the morning with a mission.				
8. I search for alternative solutions to problems rather than giving a pat answer.				
9. I know which settings stimulate me to be creative and I try to spend time in those settings.				

Total your scores for all 9 items. Your creativity score is _____. If you scored 32–36 points, you likely are a creative thinker. If you scored 27–31 points, you are inclined to be creative but could benefit from thinking about some ways to get more creativity in your life. If you scored 26 or below, seriously think about ways to become more creative. Read again the suggestions in the text for becoming a more creative person.

a few days, reread your notes and reflect on your past experiences. After a few weeks, you might see a pattern of interest emerging in your notes, one that might suggest an area you can explore in greater depth.

- *When something sparks your interest, follow it.* Usually when something captures your attention, it is short-lived—an idea, a song, a flower. Too often we don't explore the idea, song, or flower further. Or we think these areas are not our business because we are not experts about them. Yet the world is our business. We can't know which parts are most interesting until we make a serious effort to learn as much about as many aspects of it as possible.
- *Wake up in the morning with a specific goal to look forward to.* Creative people wake up eager to start the day. Why? Not necessarily because they are cheerful, enthusiastic types but because they know that there is something meaningful to accomplish each day, and they can't wait to get started.
- *Take charge of your schedule.* Figure out which time of the day is your most creative time. Some of us are more creative late at night, others early in the morning. Carve out time for yourself when your creative energy is at its best.
- *Spend time in settings that stimulate your creativity.* In Csikszentmihalyi's (1996) research, he gave people an electronic pager and beeped them randomly at different times of the day. When he asked them how they felt, they reported the highest levels of creativity when walking, driving, or swimming. I do my most creative thinking when I'm jogging. These activities are semiautomatic in that they take only a certain amount of attention while leaving some free to make connections among ideas. Highly creative people also report coming up with novel ideas in the deeply relaxed state we are in when we are half-asleep, half-awake.

To evaluate the extent to which you engage in creative thinking, see the Psychology and Life box.

For study tools related to this learning goal, see the Study Guide, the CD-ROM, and the Online Learning Center.

Review and Sharpen Your Thinking

5 *Describe the characteristics of mental retardation, giftedness, and creativity.*

- Define mental retardation and discuss its causes.
- Explain what makes people gifted.
- Identify the characteristics associated with creativity.

How many of the tips in the section on Living a More Creative Life do you currently practice? How might you benefit from these suggestions, in addition to becoming more creative?

6 THE INFLUENCE OF HEREDITY AND ENVIRONMENT

Genetic Influences   **Environmental Influences**   **Group Influences**

What do heredity and environment contribute to intelligence?

One of the hottest areas in the study of intelligence centers on the extent to which intelligence is influenced by genetics and the extent to which it is influenced by environment. In chapter 3, I indicated how difficult it is to tease apart these influences, but the difficulty has not kept psychologists from trying.

Genetic Influences

There is no doubt that genes influence intelligence. Researchers recently have found genetic markers (unique genetic locations) for intelligence on chromosomes 4, 6, and 22 (Plomin, 1999; Plomin & Craig, 2001). In fact, the genetic marker on chromosome 6 was shown to be carried by approximately one-third of children with high IQs but by only one-sixth of children with average IQs (Chorney & others, 1998). As research on the human genome continues, it is expected that more markers will be found and identified. So the issue with respect to genetics and intelligence is the degree to which our genes make us smart.

On one side of the debate, Arthur Jensen (1969) claims that intelligence is primarily inherited and that environment and culture play only a minimal role in intelligence. Jensen reviewed the research on intelligence, much of which involved comparisons of identical and fraternal twins. Identical twins have the same genetic makeup. If intelligence is genetically determined, Jensen reasoned, identical twins' IQs should be similar. Fraternal twins and ordinary siblings are less similar genetically, so their IQs should be less similar. Jensen found support for his argument.

The studies on intelligence in identical twins that Jensen examined showed an average correlation of .82, a very high positive association. Investigations of fraternal twins, however, produced an average correlation of .50, a moderately high positive correlation. A difference of .32 is substantial; however, in one research review, the difference in intelligence between identical and fraternal twins was .15, considerably less (see figure 10.8; Grigorenko, 2000).

To demonstrate that genetic factors are more important than environmental factors, Jensen compared identical twins reared together with those reared apart. The correlation for those reared together was .89—and for those reared apart it was .78—a difference of .11. Jensen argued that if environmental factors were more important than genetic factors, siblings reared apart, in different environments, should have IQs that differed more than .11.

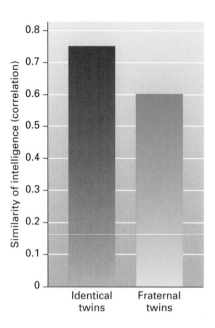

FIGURE 10.8 Correlation Between Intelligence Test Scores and Twin Status The graph represents a summary of research findings that have compared the intelligence test scores of identical and fraternal twins. An approximate .15 difference has been found, with a higher correlation (.75) for identical twins and a lower correlation (.60) for fraternal twins.

Adoption studies have been inconclusive about the relative importance of heredity in intelligence. In most *adoption studies,* researchers determine whether the behavior of adopted children is more like that of their biological parents or that of their adoptive parents. In one study, the educational levels attained by biological parents were better predictors of children's IQ scores than were the IQs of the children's adoptive parents (Scarr & Weinberg, 1983). Because of the genetic link between the adopted children and their biological parents, the implication is that heredity is more important than environment. But environmental effects also have been found in adoption studies. For example, moving children into families with better environments than the children had had in the past increased the children's IQs by an average of 12 points (Lucurto, 1990).

How strong is the correlation between parental IQ and children's IQ? The concept of **heritability**, the fraction of the variance in IQ in a population that is attributed to genetics, is used to sort out the effects of heredity and environment. The *heritability index* is computed using correlational statistical techniques. Thus the highest degree of heritability is 1.00, and correlations of .70 and above suggest a strong genetic influence. A committee of respected researchers convened by the American Psychological Association concluded that by late adolescence, the heritability of intelligence is about .75, which reflects a strong genetic influence (Neisser & others, 1996).

Interestingly, researchers have found that the heritability of intelligence increases from childhood to adulthood (from as low as 35 percent in childhood to as high as 75 percent in adulthood; McGue & others, 1993). Why might hereditary influences on intelligence increase with age? Possibly as we grow older, our interactions with the environment are shaped less by the influence of others and the environment on us and more by our ability to choose environments that allow the expression of genetic tendencies we have inherited (Neisser & others, 1996). For example, sometimes, children's parents push them into environments that are not compatible with their genetic inheritance (wanting them to be doctors or engineers, for example), but as adults these individuals may choose to select their own career and intellectual interests (being sculptors or hardware store owners).

An important point to keep in mind about heritability is that it applies to groups (populations), not to individuals (Okagaki, 2000). Researchers rely on the concept of heritability to describe why people differ, not to explain why a single individual, like yourself, has intelligence that is influenced by heredity to a certain degree.

The heritability index is by no means flawless in computing the contribution of heredity to intelligence (Dickens & Flynn, 2001). It is only as good as the data that are entered into its analysis and the interpretations made from it. One problem with the data is that they are virtually all from traditional IQ tests, which some experts believe are not always the best indicator of intelligence (Gardner, 2002; Sternberg, 2000). Also, the heritability index assumes that we can treat genetic and environmental influences as quantitatively separate factors, with each part contributing a distinct amount of influence. Many experts on intelligence believe that heredity and environment are so interconnected that any independent influence is almost impossible to determine.

Environmental Influences

Today, most researchers agree that heredity does not determine intelligence to the extent that Jensen claimed (Ceci, 1996; Grigorenko, 2000). For most people, this means that modifications in environment can change their IQ scores considerably (Campbell & Ramey, 1993). It also means that programs designed to enrich an environment can have considerable effects, improving school achievement and fostering acquisition of skills needed for employment. Although genetic endowment may always influence a person's intellectual ability, the environmental influences and opportunities that children and adults experience do make a difference.

heritability The fraction of the variance in IQ in a population that is attributed to genetics.

In one study (described in the discussion of environmental influences on language in chapter 9), researchers went into homes and observed how extensively parents from welfare and middle-income professional families talked and communicated with their young children (Hart & Risley, 1995). They found that middle-income professional parents were much likelier to talk and communicate with their young children than welfare parents were. And how much the parents talked and communicated with their children in the first 3 years of their lives was correlated with the children's Stanford-Binet IQ scores at age 3: The more they talked and communicated with their children, the higher the children's IQs were. Others studies also have found substantial socioeconomic status differences in intelligence (Seifer, 2001).

Researchers are increasingly interested in manipulating the early environment of children who are at risk for impoverished intelligence (Blair & Ramey, 1996; Ramey, Ramey, & Lanzi, 2001; Sternberg & Grigorenko, 2001). The emphasis is on prevention rather than remediation. Many low-income parents have difficulty providing an intellectually stimulating environment for their children. Programs that educate parents to be more sensitive caregivers and that train them to be better teachers can make a difference in a child's intellectual development, as can support services, such as high quality childcare programs.

In one study, Craig Ramey and his colleagues (Ramey & Campbell, 1984; Ramey & Ramey, 1998) randomly assigned 111 young children from low-income, poorly educated families to either an intervention group, which received full-time, year-round day care along with medical and social work services, or a control group, which received medical and social benefits but no day care. The day-care program included gamelike learning activities aimed at improving language, motor, social, and cognitive skills. The success of the program in improving IQ was evident by the time the children were 3 years of age. At that age, the experimental group showed IQs averaging 101, a 17-point advantage over the control group. Recent follow-up results suggest that the effects are long-lasting. More than a decade later, at age 15, children from the intervention group still maintained an IQ advantage of 5 points (97.7 to 92.6) over the control-group children (Campbell & others, 2001; Ramey & others, 2001). They also did better on standardized tests of reading and math and were less likely to be held back a year in school. Also, the greatest IQ gains were by the children whose mothers had especially low IQs—below 70. At age 15, these children showed a 10-point IQ advantage over children whose mothers had IQs below 70 but who did not experience the day-care intervention.

Studies of schooling also reveal effects on intelligence (Ceci & Gilstrap, 2000; Christian, Bachnan, & Morrison, 2001). The biggest effects have been found in cases in which large groups of children have been deprived of formal education for an extended period of time, resulting in lower intelligence. One study investigated the intellectual functioning of Indian children in South Africa whose schooling was delayed for 4 years because of the unavailability of teachers (Ramphal, 1962). Compared with children in nearby villages who had teachers, the Indian children whose schooling was delayed experienced a decrement of 5 IQ points for every year of delay.

Another possible effect of education on intelligence can be seen in rapidly increasing IQ test scores around the world (Flynn, 1999). Scores on these tests have been increasing so fast that a high percentage of people regarded as having average intelligence at the turn of century would be regarded as having below average intelligence today (see figure 10.9; Howard, 2001). If a representative sample of people today took the Stanford-Binet test used in 1932, about one-fourth would be defined as having very superior intelligence, a label usually accorded to fewer than 3 percent of the population (Horton, 2001). Because the increase has taken place in a relatively short period of time, it cannot be due to heredity but rather may be due to increasing levels of education attained by a much greater percentage of the world's population or to other environmental factors, such as the explosion of information to which people

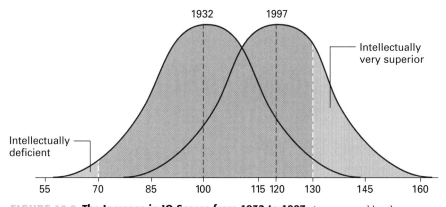

FIGURE 10.9 **The Increase in IQ Scores from 1932 to 1997** As measured by the Stanford-Binet intelligence test, American children seem to be getting smarter. Scores of a group tested in 1932 fell along a bell-shaped curve with half below 100 and half above. Studies show that if children took that same test today, using the 1932 scale, half would score above 120. Few of them would score in the "intellectually deficient" range and about one-fourth would rank in the "very superior" range.

are exposed. This worldwide increase in intelligence test scores occurring over a short time frame has been called the *Flynn effect,* after the researcher who discovered it, James Flynn.

Keep in mind that environmental influences are complex (Neisser & others, 1996; Sternberg, 2001). Growing up with all the advantages, for example, does not necessarily guarantee success. Children from wealthy families may have easy access to excellent schools, books, travel, and tutoring, but they may take such opportunities for granted and not be motivated to learn and to achieve. And, alternatively, poor or disadvantaged children may be highly motivated and successful.

Group Influences

Among the ways that group influences can be linked to intelligence are comparisons of cultures, ethnic groups, and males and females.

Cross-Cultural Comparisons Cultures vary in the way they define intelligence (Rogoff, 1990; Serpell, 2000). Most European Americans, for example, think of intelligence in terms of reasoning and thinking skills, but people in Kenya consider responsible participation in family and social life an integral part of intelligence. An intelligent person in Uganda is someone who knows what to do and then follows through with appropriate action. Intelligence to the Iatmul people of Papua, New Guinea, involves the ability to remember the names of 10,000 to 20,000 clans. And the residents of the widely dispersed Caroline Islands incorporate the talent of navigating by the stars into their definition of intelligence (see figure 10.10). In a cross-cultural context, then, intelligence depends a great deal on environment.

Ethnic Comparisons In the United States, children from African American and Latino families score below children from White families on standardized intelligence tests. On the average, African American schoolchildren score 10 to 15 points lower on standardized intelligence tests than White American schoolchildren do (Brody, 2000; Lynn, 1996). We are talking about average scores, though. Estimates also indicate that 15 to 25 percent of all African American schoolchildren score higher than 50 percent of all White schoolchildren do, and many Whites score lower than most African Americans. The reason is that the distribution of scores for African Americans and Whites overlap.

The intelligence of the Iatmul people of Papua, New Guinea, involves the ability to remember the names of many clans.

FIGURE 10.10 Iatmul and Caroline Islander Intelligence

On the 680 Caroline Islands in the Pacific Ocean east of the Philippines, the intelligence of their inhabitants includes the ability to navigate by the stars.

"You can't build a hut, you don't know how to find edible roots and you know nothing about predicting the weather. In other words, you do *terribly* on our I.Q. test."
© by Sidney Harris.

How extensively are ethnic differences in intelligence influenced by heredity and environment? In one of his most provocative statements, Arthur Jensen (1969) claimed that genetics accounts for clear-cut differences in average intelligence between races, nationalities, and socioeconomic groups. When Jensen published an article in the *Harvard Educational Review* stating that lower intelligence probably was the reason that African Americans do not perform as well in school as Whites, he was called naive and racist. He received hate mail by the bushel, and police had to escort him to his classes at the University of California at Berkeley.

A more recent uproar about the heredity and intelligence controversy focuses on *The Bell Curve: Intelligence and Class Structure in American Life* (1994) by Richard Herrnstein and Charles Murray. The authors argued that America is rapidly evolving a huge underclass that consists of intellectually deprived individuals whose cognitive abilities will never match the future needs of most employers. They believe that this underclass, a large proportion of which is African American, may be doomed by their shortcomings to welfare dependency, poverty, crime, and lives devoid of any hope of ever reaching the American dream.

Why do Herrnstein and Murray call their book *The Bell Curve*? Recall that a bell curve is the shape of a normal distribution graph (see figure 10.1) and that a normal distribution graph is used to represent large numbers of people who are sorted according to some shared characteristic, such as weight, exposure to asbestos, taste in clothes, or IQ.

Herrnstein and Murray often refer to bell curves to make a point: that predictions about any individual based exclusively on the person's IQ are basically useless. Weak correlations between intelligence and job success have predictive value only when applied to large groups of people. Within such large groups, say Herrnstein and Murray, the pervasive influence of IQ on human society becomes apparent. Significant criticisms have been leveled at *The Bell Curve,* as well as at Jensen's work. Experts on intelligence generally agree that African Americans score lower than Whites on IQ tests. However, many of these experts raise serious questions about the ability of IQ tests to accurately measure a person's intelligence. For instance, we saw earlier in this chapter that the tests are culturally biased toward European Americans. In 1971, the Supreme Court endorsed such criticism and ruled that tests of general intelligence, in contrast to tests that solely measure fitness for a particular job, are discriminatory and cannot be administered as a condition of employment. Cognitive psychologist Robert J. Sternberg (1994) said that using one index—IQ—for a basis of policy judgment is not only irresponsible but also dangerous. Another criticism is that most research on heredity and environment does not include environments that differ radically. Thus it is not surprising that many genetic studies show environment to be a fairly weak influence on intelligence (Fraser, 1995).

As African Americans have gained social, economic, and educational opportunities, the gap between African Americans and Whites on standardized intelligence tests has begun to narrow (Ogbu & Stern, 2001; Onwuegbuzi & Daley, 2001). This gap especially narrows in college, where African American and White students often experience more similar educational environments than they did in elementary and high school (Myerson & others, 1998). Also, when children from disadvantaged African American families are adopted into more advantaged middle socioeconomic status families, their scores on intelligence tests more closely resemble national averages for middle socioeconomic status children than for lower socioeconomic status children (Scarr & Weinberg, 1983).

Gender Comparisons The average scores of males and females do not differ on intelligence tests, but their scores' variability does differ (Brody, 2000). For example, males are more likely than females to have extremely high or extremely low scores. There also are gender differences in specific intellectual abilities (Brody, 2000). Males score better than females in some nonverbal areas, such as spatial reasoning, and females score better than males in some verbal areas, such as the ability to find synonyms for words. However, as discussed in chapter 4, there often is extensive overlap in the scores of females and males in these areas, and debate continues about how strong such differences are (Eagly, 2001; Hyde & Mezulis, 2001).

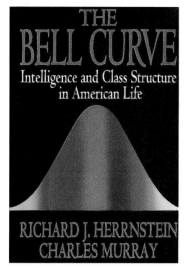

Herrnstein and Murray's *The Bell Curve,* advocates a strong role for heredity in intelligence and claims that a large portion of underclass individuals, especially African Americans, are doomed because of their heredity. *What are some of the criticisms that have been leveled at Herrnstein and Murray's claims?*

Review and Sharpen Your Thinking

6 *Analyze the contributions of heredity and environment to intelligence.*

- Discuss the ways in which heredity influences intelligence.
- Identify several ways in which changes in environment can produce gains in intelligence.
- Explain how cultural, ethnic, and gender differences are linked with intelligence.

Someone tells you that he or she has analyzed his or her genetic background and environmental experiences and reached the conclusion that environment definitely has had little influence on his or her intelligence. What would you say to this person about his or her ability to make this self-diagnosed conclusion?

mhhe.com/
santrockp7

For study tools related to this learning goal, see the Study Guide, the CD-ROM, and the Online Learning Center.

Reach Your Learning Goals

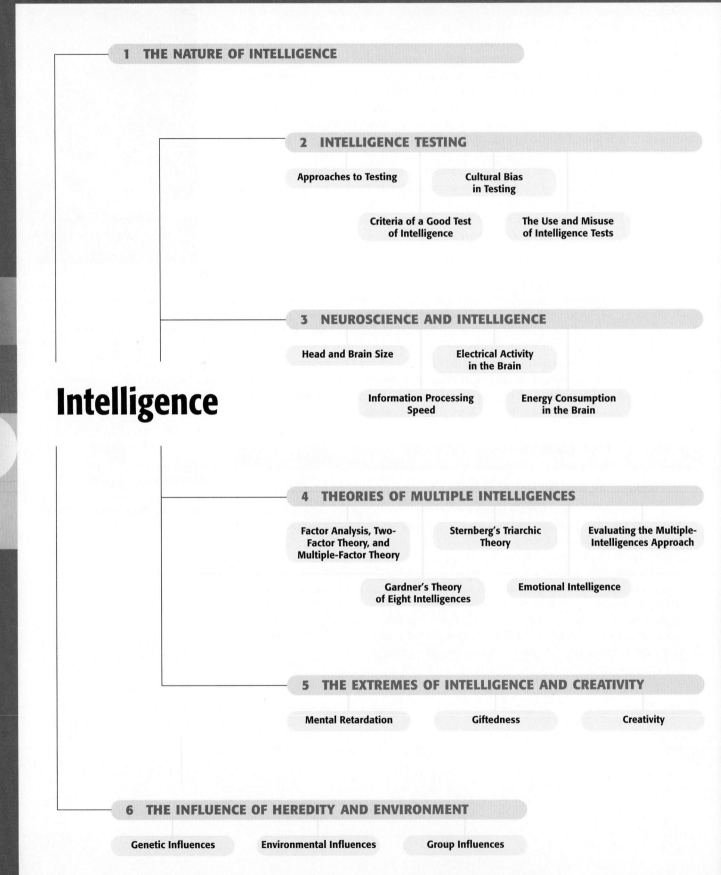

Intelligence

1 THE NATURE OF INTELLIGENCE

2 INTELLIGENCE TESTING

Approaches to Testing

Cultural Bias in Testing

Criteria of a Good Test of Intelligence

The Use and Misuse of Intelligence Tests

3 NEUROSCIENCE AND INTELLIGENCE

Head and Brain Size

Electrical Activity in the Brain

Information Processing Speed

Energy Consumption in the Brain

4 THEORIES OF MULTIPLE INTELLIGENCES

Factor Analysis, Two-Factor Theory, and Multiple-Factor Theory

Sternberg's Triarchic Theory

Evaluating the Multiple-Intelligences Approach

Gardner's Theory of Eight Intelligences

Emotional Intelligence

5 THE EXTREMES OF INTELLIGENCE AND CREATIVITY

Mental Retardation

Giftedness

Creativity

6 THE INFLUENCE OF HEREDITY AND ENVIRONMENT

Genetic Influences

Environmental Influences

Group Influences

1 ***Describe what intelligence is.***

- Intelligence consists of the ability to solve problems and to adapt and learn from everyday experiences. A key aspect of intelligence involves individual variations. Traditionally, intelligence has been measured by tests designed to compare people's performance on cognitive tasks.

2 ***Explain how intelligence is measured and what the limitations of intelligence tests are.***

- Sir Frances Galton is the father of mental tests. Alfred Binet developed the first intelligence test and created the concept of mental age. William Stern developed the concept of IQ for use with the Binet test. Revisions of the Binet test are called the Stanford-Binet. The test scores on the Stanford-Binet approximate a normal distribution. The Wechsler scales, created by David Wechsler, are the other main intelligence-assessment tool. These tests provide an overall IQ, verbal and performance IQs, and information from 11 subtests. Group intelligence tests are convenient and economical, but they do not allow an examiner to closely monitor the testing. The SAT is a group test used in conjunction with information about a high school student's performance to predict academic success in college. Aptitude tests predict an individual's ability to learn a skill or future performance. Achievement tests assess what a person already knows. The distinction between these two types of tests is sometimes blurred.
- A good test of intelligence meets three criteria: validity, reliability, and standardization. Validity can be assessed in terms of content validity and criterion validity. Criterion validity involves either concurrent or predictive validity. Reliability means how consistently an individual performs on a test. Validity is the extent to which a test measures what it is intended to measure. Standardization focuses on uniform procedures for administering and scoring a test; it also involves norms.
- Early intelligence tests favored White, middle socioeconomic status, urban individuals. Culture-fair tests are intelligence tests that are intended to be culturally unbiased. Many psychologists believe that such culture-fair tests cannot replace traditional intelligence tests.
- When used by a judicious examiner, tests can be valuable tools for determining individual differences in intelligence. Test scores should be used with other types of information to evaluate an individual. IQ scores can produce unfortunate stereotypes and expectations. Ability tests can help divide children into homogeneous groups, but periodic testing should be done to ensure that the groupings are appropriate.

3 ***Identify four neuroscience approaches to intelligence.***

- In general, researchers have found that a larger head size and a larger brain size, especially larger brain size, are associated with higher intelligence. However, because these findings are correlational, it's not certain whether a large head or brain size causes greater intelligence or vice versa.
- There is a correlation between information processing speed, often measured as reaction time, and IQ scores. Higher scores are linked with faster, or shorter, reaction times. However, the relation of processing speed to intelligence is complex, and processing speed by itself does not determine intelligence.
- Efforts to link electrical activity in the brain and intelligence have focused on measures of nerve conduction velocity and evoked potential. Studies of nerve conduction velocity have yielded inconsistent results, but studies of evoked potential show more robust correlation with intelligence.
- Individuals with higher intelligence test scores demonstrate increased brain activity (increased use of glucose) when they are engaged in a cognitive activity of their own choosing. However, individuals with higher intelligence successfully complete an assigned task using less energy. This finding may mean that individuals with high intelligence have more active brains than those with less intelligence and use them more efficiently.

4 ***Evaluate theories of multiple intelligence.***

- Factor analysis is a statistical procedure that compares various items or measures and identifies factors that are correlated with each other. Spearman (two-factor theory of *g* and *s*) and Thurstone (multiple-factor theory) used factor analysis in developing their views of intelligence.
- Gardner believes there are eight types of intelligence: verbal skills, mathematical skills, spatial skills, bodily-kinesthetic skills, musical skills, interpersonal skills, intrapersonal skills, and naturalist skills. Project Spectrum applies Gardner's view to educating children.
- Sternberg's triarchic theory states there are three main types of intelligence: analytical, creative, and practical.
- Emotional intelligence is the ability to monitor one's own and others' feelings and emotions, to discriminate among them, and to use this information to guide one's thinking and actions. Goleman popularized emotional intelligence.
- The multiple-intelligences approaches have broadened the definition of intelligence and motivated educators to develop programs that instruct students in different domains. Critics maintain that the multiple-intelligences

theories include factors that really are not part of intelligence, such as musical skills and creativity. Critics also say that there is not enough research to support the concept of multiple intelligences.

5 ***Discuss characteristics of mental retardation, giftedness, and creativity.***

- Mental retardation is a condition of limited mental ability in which the individual has a low IQ, usually below 70; has difficulty adapting to everyday life; and has an onset of these characteristics during the so-called developmental period. Most affected individuals have IQs in the 55 to 70 range (mild retardation). Mental retardation can have an organic cause (called organic retardation) or can be social and cultural in origin (called cultural-familial retardation).

- People who are gifted have high intelligence (IQs of 120 or higher) and/or superior talent for a particular domain. Three characteristics of gifted children are precocity, marching to one's own drummer, and a passion to master. Giftedness is likely a consequence of both heredity and environment.

- Creativity is the ability to think about something in novel and unusual ways and come up with unconventional solutions to problems. The difference between intelligence and creativity is the ability to produce something original or unique. Creative people tend to be divergent thinkers who can see more than one possible answer to a question. Traditional intelligence test questions have only one correct answer and thus measure convergent thinking. Creativity has often been described as occurring in a five-step process: preparation, incubation, insight, evaluation, and elaboration. Characteristics of creative thinkers include flexibility and playful thinking, inner motivation, willingness to risk, and objective evaluation of work. Csikszentmihalyi believes that cultivating curiosity and interest is the first step toward a more creative life.

6 ***Analyze the contributions of heredity and environment to intelligence.***

- Recently, researchers have found genetic markers for intelligence on specific chromosomes. Genetic similarity might explain why identical twins show stronger correlations on intelligence tests than fraternal twins do. Some studies indicate that the IQs of adopted children are more similar to the IQs of their biological parents than to those of their adoptive parents. Many studies show that intelligence has a reasonably strong heritability component, although criticisms of the heritability concept have been made.

- Environmental influences on intelligence have been demonstrated in studies of the effects of parenting, intervention programs for children at risk for having low IQs and dropping out of school, and sociohistorical changes. Researchers have found that how much parents talk with their children in the first 3 years of life is correlated with the children's IQs. Ramey's research revealed the positive effects of educational child care on intelligence. Intelligence test scores have risen considerably around the world in recent decades—called the Flynn effect—which supports the role of environment in intelligence.

- Among the ways that group influences can be linked with intelligence are comparisons of cultures, ethnic groups, and males and females. Cultures vary in the way they define intelligence. In the United States, children from African American and Latino families score below children from White families on standardized intelligence tests; the extent to which such differences are caused by heredity or environment is controversial. The average scores of males and females do not differ on intelligence tests, but variability in their scores does differ. For example, males are more likely than females to have extremely high or extremely low scores. There also are gender differences in specific intellectual abilities.

Key Terms

intelligence, p. 389
mental age (MA), p. 390
intelligence quotient (IQ), p. 390
normal distribution, p. 391
aptitude tests, p. 393

achievement tests, p. 393
validity, p. 394
reliability, p. 394
standardization, p. 394
culture-fair tests, p. 395
two-factor theory, p. 400

factor analysis, p. 400
multiple-factor theory, p. 400
triarchic theory, p. 402
emotional intelligence, p. 404

mental retardation, p. 406
gifted, p. 406
creativity, p. 408
divergent thinking, p. 408
convergent thinking, p. 408
heritability, p. 413

Apply Your Knowledge

1. There are many different intelligence tests available on-line. Do a web search for intelligence tests, and take one. How reliable is the test you took, and how do you know if it's reliable? How well standardized is the test, and on what evidence did you base your answer? How valid is the test, and how do you know what its validity is?

2. Think about the tests used to assess intelligence. Now consider the ways in which neuroscientists have tried to determine the neural basis of intelligence. Do the tasks that have been assessed by neuroscientists match those used in other intelligence tests? How might this contribute to the kinds of answers neuroscientists have gotten?

3. What is, or should be, the purpose of intelligence testing? To determine who will do well in school? To determine what career someone should pursue? To keep psychologists occupied? Or? Given what you think the purpose should be, which definition of intelligence is most useful?

4. Consider the characteristics of gifted people and creative people. Which would you rather be? Why? If you had children, which would you rather have, gifted children or creative children? Why? (Of course, I am assuming that you would not choose to be mentally retarded, but, if this would be your choice, justify it.)

5. One controversial theory about intelligence suggests a relationship between birth order and intelligence: The IQs of children born first are higher than those of children born second, and so on. Imagine this is true. What would this tell you about the role of environment and heredity on intelligence? What does it say about large families? Now imagine it's not true. What factors might have influenced researchers to make this conclusion erroneously?

Connections mhhe.com/ santrockp7

For extra help in mastering the material in this chapter, see the review sections and practice quizzes in the Student Study Guide, the CD-ROM, and the Online Learning Center.

11 Motivation and Emotion

Chapter Outline

APPROACHES TO MOTIVATION

The Evolutionary Approach
▼
Drive Reduction Theory
▼
Optimum Arousal Theory
▼
The Cognitive Approach
▼
Maslow's Hierarchy of Human Needs
▼
Issues in Motivation

HUNGER

The Biology of Hunger
▼
Obesity and Eating Behavior
▼
Dieting
▼
Eating Disorders

SEXUALITY

The Biology of Sex
▼
Cognitive and Sensory/Perceptual Factors
▼
Cultural Factors
▼
Psychosexual Dysfunctions
▼
Sexual Behavior and Orientation

SOCIAL COGNITIVE MOTIVES

Achievement
▼
Affiliation
▼
Well-Being

EMOTION

The Biology of Emotion
▼
Cognitive Factors
▼
Behavioral Factors
▼
Sociocultural Factors
▼
Classifying Emotions

Learning Goals

1 *Describe psychological approaches to motivation.*

2 *Explain the physiological basis of hunger and the nature of eating behavior.*

3 *Discuss the motivation for sex.*

4 *Characterize the social cognitive motives and how they influence behavior.*

5 *Summarize views of emotion.*

The 3-week, 2,287-mile Tour de France, the world's premier bicycle race, is one of the great tests of human motivation in sports. American Lance Armstrong won the Tour de France cycling event not just once, but three times—in 1999, 2000, and 2001. This was a remarkable accomplishment, as Lance was diagnosed with testicular cancer in 1996. Chances of his recovery were estimated at less than 50 percent when he began chemotherapy.

After the cancer was diagnosed, Lance said that the first thing he thought was, "Oh, no! My career's in jeopardy! Then, they kept finding new problems and I forgot about my career—I was more worried about getting to my next birthday. I had the same emotions when I was sick as I have as a competitive athlete. At first I was angry, then I felt motivated and driven to get better. And then when I knew I was getting better, I knew I was winning."

Lance's experience with cancer motivated him to think about his priorities in life. He says that the experience ultimately made him a happier and better person. He became a spokesperson for cancer and established the Lance Armstrong Foundation, which supports cancer awareness and research. He married and became a father.

When you are motivated, you do something. The way you feel—your emotions—can either strengthen or weaken your motivation. For Lance Armstrong, motivation and emotion played a significant role in his recovery and accomplishments:

- *Motivation.* The intense motivation required to make it through grueling practices, day after day; the motivation to battle cancer and defeat it; the motivation to set a goal of winning the Tour de France and then winning it; the motivation to improve his personal life by getting married and starting a family; and the motivation to donate his time and effort to promoting cancer research and awareness.

- *Emotion.* The anger that emerged when he found out that he had cancer; the fear that he would die; the happiness of getting married and starting a family; and the elation and joy of winning the Tour de France.

Hunger, sex, achievement, affiliation, and well-being are five important motives in our lives. Hunger is usually described as a biological motive, sex is categorized as a bridge between biological and social cognitive motives, and achievement, affiliation, and well-being are portrayed as social cognitive motives. Each of these areas of motivation is examined in greater depth in the chapter.

Motivations differ not only in kind, such as an individual being motivated to eat rather than have sex, but also in intensity. We can speak of an individual as being more or less hungry or more or less motivated to have sex. The first section looks at different approaches to motivation.

Armstrong among a throng of admirers after winning the Tour de France in 2001.

The Evolutionary Approach	**Optimum Arousal Theory**	**Maslow's Hierarchy of Human Needs**
Drive Reduction Theory	**The Cognitive Approach**	**Issues in Motivation**

How do psychologists think about motivation?

We are all motivated, but some of us are motivated to do different things. Thus some students are motivated to watch television, others to study for an exam. **Motivation** moves people to behave, think, and feel the way they do. Motivated behavior is energized, directed, and sustained.

There is no shortage of theories about why organisms are motivated to do what they do. This section explores the main approaches to motivation, beginning with the evolutionary approach, which emphasizes the biological basis of motivation.

The Evolutionary Approach

Early in psychology's history, the evolutionary approach emphasized the role of instincts in motivation. Ethology also has described motivation from an evolutionary perspective.

An **instinct** is an innate (unlearned), biological pattern of behavior that is assumed to be universal throughout a species. A student of Darwin's evolutionary theory, American psychologist William McDougall (1908) argued that all behavior involves instincts. In particular, he said that we have instincts for acquisitiveness, curiosity, pugnacity, gregariousness, and self-assertion. At about the same time, Sigmund Freud (1917) argued that behavior is based on instinct. Freud believed that sex and aggression were especially powerful instincts.

It was not long before a number of psychologists had crafted laundry lists of instincts, some lists running to thousands of items. However, it soon became apparent that what the early instinct theorists were doing was naming a behavior rather than explaining it. If we say that people have an instinct for sex or for curiosity or for acquisitiveness, we are merely naming these behaviors, not explaining them.

Although the approach of merely labeling behaviors as instincts landed in psychology's trash heap many years ago, the idea that some motivation is unlearned is still alive and well today. It is widely accepted that instinctive behavior is common in nonhuman species, and in chapter 4 you learned that human infants come into the world equipped with some unlearned instincts such as sucking. Most attachment theorists also believe that infants have an unlearned instinct for orienting toward a caregiver.

Recently, evolutionary psychology, which was discussed in chapters 1 and 3, has rekindled interest in the evolutionary basis of motivation. According to evolutionary psychologists, the motivation for sex, aggression, achievement, and other behaviors is rooted in our evolutionary past (Buss, 2000; Cosmides & others, 2003). Thus, if a species is highly competitive, it is because such competitiveness improved the chance for survival and was passed down through the genes from generation to generation.

Drive Reduction Theory

If you do not have an instinct for sex, maybe you have a drive or a need for it. A **drive** is an aroused state that occurs because of a physiological need. A **need** is a

motivation Why people behave, think, and feel the way they do. Motivated behavior is energized, directed, and sustained.

instinct An innate (unlearned), biological pattern of behavior that is assumed to be universal throughout a species.

drive An aroused state that occurs because of a physiological need.

need A deprivation that energizes the drive to eliminate or reduce the deprivation.

deprivation that energizes the drive to eliminate or reduce the deprivation. You might have a need for water, for food, or for sex. The body's need for food, for example, arouses your hunger drive. Hunger motivates you to do something—to go out for a hamburger, for example—to reduce the drive and satisfy the need. *Drive reduction theory* explains that, as a drive becomes stronger, we are motivated to reduce it.

Usually, but not always, needs and drives are closely associated in time. For example, when your body needs food, your hunger drive will probably be aroused. An hour after you have eaten a hamburger, you might still be hungry (thus you need food), but your hunger drive might have subsided. From this example you can sense that drive pertains to a psychological state; need involves a physiological state.

The goal of drive reduction is **homeostasis,** the body's tendency to maintain an equilibrium, or steady state. Literally hundreds of biological states in our bodies must be maintained within a certain range: temperature, blood sugar level, potassium and sodium levels, oxygen, and so on. When you dive into an icy swimming pool, your body uses energy to maintain its normal temperature. When you walk out of an air-conditioned room into the heat of a summer day, your body releases excess heat by sweating. These physiological changes occur automatically to keep your body in an optimal state of functioning.

An analogy for homeostasis is the thermostat that keeps the temperature constant in a house. For example, assume that the thermostat in your house is set at 68° during the winter. The furnace heats the house to 68°, and then the furnace shuts off. Without a source of heat, the temperature in the house eventually falls below 68°—if the outside temperature is below 68°. The thermostat detects this change and turns the furnace back on again. The cycle is repeated so that the temperature is maintained within narrow limits. Today, homeostasis is used to explain both physiological and psychological imbalances.

Most psychologists believe that drive reduction theory does not provide a comprehensive framework for understanding motivation because people often behave in ways that increase rather than reduce a drive. For example, they might skip meals in an effort to lose weight, which can increase their hunger drive rather than reduce it. Consider also people who seek stimulation and thrills, say, by bungee jumping or riding a roller coaster. Instead of reducing a drive, they appear to be increasing their level of stimulation.

Optimum Arousal Theory

The circumstance just described—seeking stimulation and thrills—suggests that individuals seek arousal (a state of alertness or activation) in their lives. Is there an optimum level of arousal that motivates behavior? Early in this century, two psychologists described what optimum arousal might be. Their formulation, now known as the **Yerkes-Dodson law,** states that performance is best under conditions of moderate arousal than either low or high arousal. At the low end of arousal, you might be too lethargic to perform tasks well; at the high end, you may not be able to concentrate. Think about how aroused you were the last time you took a test. If your arousal was too high, your performance probably suffered. If it was too low, you may not have worked fast enough to finish the test. Also, think about performance in sports. Being too aroused usually harms athletes' performance. For example, a thumping heart and rapid breathing have accompanied many golfers' missed putts and basketball players' failed free-throw attempts. However, if athletes' arousal is too low, they may not concentrate well on the task at hand.

Moderate arousal often serves us best in tackling life's tasks, but there are times when low or high arousal produces optimal performance. For well-learned or simple tasks (signing your name, pushing a button on request), optimal arousal may be quite high. In contrast, when learning a task or doing something complex (solving an alge-

homeostasis The body's tendency to maintain an equilibrium, or steady state.

Yerkes-Dodson law States that performance is best under conditions of moderate arousal than under those of low or high arousal.

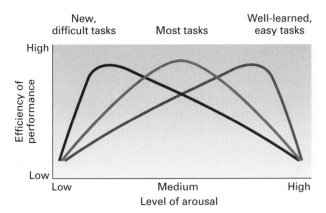

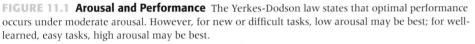

FIGURE 11.1 Arousal and Performance The Yerkes-Dodson law states that optimal performance occurs under moderate arousal. However, for new or difficult tasks, low arousal may be best; for well-learned, easy tasks, high arousal may be best.

braic equation), much lower arousal is preferred. Figure 11.1 projects how arousal might influence easy, moderate, and difficult tasks. As tasks become more difficult, the ability to be alert and attentive but relaxed is critical to optimal performance.

As mentioned earlier, some people seek a great deal of stimulation in their lives and enjoy the thrill of engaging in risky behavior. *Sensation seeking* is the motivation to experience varied, novel, complex, and intense sensations and experiences. It also involves the willingness to take risks just for the sake of such an experience.

Zuckerman and colleagues (1994, 2000; Zuckerman & others, 1993) have found that high sensation seekers are more likely than low sensation seekers to

- Be motivated to engage in sports such as mountain climbing, parachuting, hang gliding, scuba diving, car and motorcycle racing, and downhill skiing
- Be attracted to vocations involving exciting experiences, such as firefighting, emergency-room work, and air traffic control (When confined to monotonous desk jobs, they report high job dissatisfaction.)
- Drink heavily, smoke, and use illicit drugs
- Have a short-term hedonistic attitude toward intimate relationships (High sensation seekers also tend to engage in more varied sexual activities with more partners.)

The Cognitive Approach

The contemporary view of motivation emphasizes cognitive factors (Zimmerman & Schunk, 2001). Consider your motivation to do well in this class. Your confidence in your ability to do well and your expectation for success may help you to relax, concentrate better, and study more effectively. If you think too much about not doing well in the class and fear that you will fail, you can become too anxious and not perform as well. Your ability to consciously control your behavior and resist the temptation to party too much and avoid studying will improve your achievement, as will your ability to use your information processing abilities of attention, memory, and problem solving as you study for and take tests.

Psychologists continue to debate the role of conscious versus unconscious thought in understanding motivation. Freud's legacy to contemporary psychodynamic theory is the belief that we are largely unaware of why we behave the way we do. Psychodynamic theorists argue that few of us know why we love someone, why we eat so much, why we are so aggressive, or why we are so shy. Although some cognitive psychologists have begun to study the role of the unconscious mind, for the most part, they emphasize that human beings are rational and aware of their motivation.

Humanistic theorists also stress our ability to examine our lives and become aware of what motivates us.

Intrinsic and Extrinsic Motivation Intrinsic motivation is another important aspect of the cognitive approach to motivation. **Intrinsic motivation** is based on internal factors such as self-determination, curiosity, challenge, and effort. **Extrinsic motivation** involves external incentives such as rewards and punishments. Some students study hard because they are internally motivated to put forth considerable effort and achieve high quality in their work (intrinsic motivation). Other students study hard because they want to make good grades or avoid parental disapproval (extrinsic motivation).

Almost every boss, parent, or teacher has wondered whether to offer a reward to someone who does well (extrinsic motivation) or whether to let the results of the individual's self-determined efforts be the reward (intrinsic motivation). If someone is producing shoddy work, seems bored, or has a negative attitude, offering incentives may improve motivation. But there are times when external rewards can diminish achievement motivation. One study showed that, among students who already had a strong interest in art, those who did not expect a reward spent more time drawing than did their counterparts who knew they would be rewarded for drawing (Lepper, Greene, & Nisbett, 1973). The problem with using a reward as an incentive is that individuals may perceive that the reward rather than their own motivation to be competent caused their achievement behavior.

Many psychologists believe intrinsic motivation has more positive outcomes than extrinsic motivation (Deci & Ryan, 1994; Ryan & Deci, 2000, 2001). They argue that intrinsic motivation is more likely to produce competent behavior and mastery. Indeed, research comparisons often reveal that people whose motivation is intrinsic show more interest, excitement, and confidence in what they are doing than those whose motivation is extrinsic. Intrinsic motivation often results in improved performance, persistence, creativity, and self-esteem (Deci & Ryan, 1995; Ryan & Deci, 2000, 2001; Sheldon & others, 1997).

Especially important to these psychologists is the idea that self-determination (which is intrinsic) produces a sense of personal control that benefits the individual. In this view, individuals do something because of their own will, not because of external success or rewards (deCharms, 1984; Deci & Ryan, 1994; Ryan & Deci, 2000, 2001). Researchers have found, for instance, that students' internal motivation and intrinsic interest in school tasks increases when they have some choice and some opportunities to take responsibility for their learning (Stipek, 1996, 2001).

Some psychologists stress that many highly successful individuals are both intrinsically motivated (have a high personal standard of achievement and emphasize personal effort) and extrinsically motivated (are highly competitive). Lance Armstrong is a good example. Armstrong had an incredible amount of intrinsic motivation to come back from testicular cancer to win the Tour de France. However, the extrinsic motivation of winning the Tour de France trophy and the millions of dollars in endorsement contracts also likely played a role in his motivation. For the most part, though, psychologists believe that intrinsic motivation is the key to achievement. Lance Armstrong, like many other athletic champions, decided early on that he was training and racing for himself, not for his parents, coaches, or the medals.

The Importance of Self-Generated Goals Currently, there is considerable interest in studying people's self-generated goals (Eccles & Wigfield, 2002). Some examples of these goals are personal projects, life tasks, and personal strivings. Personal projects can range from trivial pursuits (such as letting a bad haircut grow out) to life goals (such as becoming a good parent). Life tasks are problems individuals currently are working on. They usually focus on normal life transitions such as going to college, getting married, and entering an occupation. Many college students say that

intrinsic motivation Based on internal factors, such as self-determination, curiosity, challenge, and effort.

extrinsic motivation Involves external incentives, such as rewards and punishments.

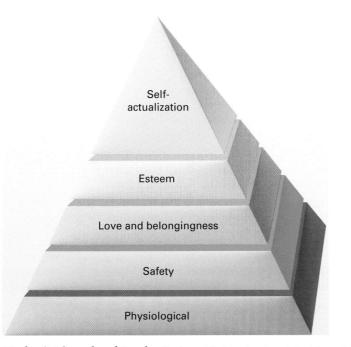

FIGURE 11.2 **Maslow's Hierarchy of Needs** Abraham Maslow developed the hierarchy of human needs to show that we have to satisfy basic physiological needs before we can satisfy other, higher needs.

their life tasks revolve around academic achievement and social concerns (Cantor & Langston, 1989). Personal strivings represent what a person is typically trying to do. For example, someone might say that she typically tries to do well in school. Later, in discussing achievement, I explore goal setting in greater detail.

Maslow's Hierarchy of Human Needs

Is getting an A in this class more important than eating? If the person of your dreams told you that you were marvelous, would that motivate you to throw yourself in front of a car for the person's safety? According to the humanistic theorist Abraham Maslow (1954, 1971), our basic needs must be satisfied before our higher needs can be. Maslow's **hierarchy of needs** states that individuals' main needs are satisfied in the following sequence: physiological, safety, love and belongingness, esteem, and self-actualization (see figure 11.2). According to this hierarchy, people are motivated to satisfy their need for food first, and their need for safety must be satisfied before their need for love.

Self-actualization, the highest and most elusive of Maslow's needs, is the motivation to develop one's full potential as a human being. According to Maslow, self-actualization is possible only after the other needs in the hierarchy are met. Maslow cautions that most people stop maturing after they have developed a high level of esteem and thus do not become self-actualized. Many of Maslow's writings focus on how people can reach this elusive motivational state. Self-actualization is discussed further in chapter 12.

The idea that human motives are hierarchically arranged is an appealing one. Maslow's theory stimulates us to think about the ordering of motives in our own lives. However, the ordering of the needs is somewhat subjective. Some people might seek greatness in a career to achieve self-esteem, while putting on hold their needs for love and belongingness.

hierarchy of needs Maslow's view that individuals' main needs are satisfied in the following sequence: physiological, safety, love and belongingness, esteem, and self-actualization.

self-actualization The highest and most elusive of Maslow's needs; the motivation to develop one's full potential as a human being.

Issues in Motivation

What motivates people to lie? Do people in different cultures lie for the same reasons? (Around the Globe)

mhhe com/
santrockp7

In the discussion of dimensions of motivation, three important issues were discussed: (1) To what degree are we motivated by innate, unlearned, biological factors as opposed to learned, experientially based factors? (2) To what degree are we aware of what motivates us—that is, to what extent is our motivation conscious? (3) To what degree are we internally or externally motivated? These are issues that researchers continue to wrangle with and debate.

Keep in mind that, although I separated the biological, cognitive, and behavioral/social/cultural underpinnings of motivation for the purpose of organization and clarification, in reality they are often interrelated. For example, in the study of social cognition, psychologists call attention to how contextual/social factors interact with thinking to determine our motivation. Thus a person's achievement motivation might be influenced by both the person's optimistic outlook (cognitive) and his or her relationship with an outstanding mentor (social).

mhhe com/
santrockp7

For study tools related to this learning goal, see the Study Guide, the CD-ROM, and the Online Learning Center.

Review and Sharpen Your Thinking

1 Describe psychological approaches to motivation.
- Define motivation and instinct and explain the evolutionary approach to motivation.
- Summarize drive reduction theory.
- Discuss optimum arousal theory.
- Identify the cognitive factors involved in emotion.
- Characterize Maslow's hierarchy of human needs.
- List three main issues in motivation research.

Advertisers often draw on Maslow's hierarchy of human needs to sell their products. Look through some magazine advertisements for evidence of Maslow's hierarchy.

2 HUNGER

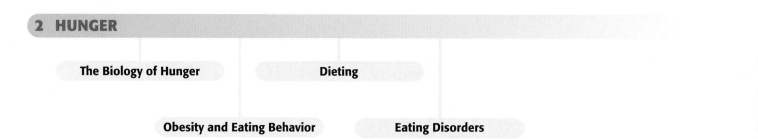

The Biology of Hunger

Dieting

Obesity and Eating Behavior

Eating Disorders

What is the physiological basis of hunger and the nature of eating behavior?
As Maslow's hierarchy indicates, hunger is a very basic human need and a powerful motivator. Food is an important aspect of life in all cultures. Whether we have very little or large amounts of food available to us, hunger influences our behavior. We have to eat to stay alive. What mechanisms cause us to feel hungry?

The Biology of Hunger

You are sitting in class and it is 2 P.M. You were so busy today that you skipped lunch. As the professor lectures, your stomach starts to growl. What role, if any, do such gastric signals play in hunger?

Gastric Signals In 1912, Walter Cannon and A. L. Washburn conducted an experiment that revealed a close association between stomach contractions and hunger (see figure 11.3). As part of the procedure, a partially inflated balloon was passed through a tube inserted in Washburn's mouth and pushed down into his stomach. A machine that measures air pressure was connected to the balloon to monitor Washburn's stomach contractions. Every time Washburn reported hunger pangs, his stomach was also contracting. This finding, which was confirmed in subsequent experiments with other volunteers, led the two researchers to believe that gastric activity was *the* basis for hunger.

Stomach signals are not the only factors that affect hunger, however. People whose stomachs have been surgically removed still get hunger pangs. And, the stomach may contract to signal hunger, but the stomach also can send signals that stop hunger. We all know that a full stomach can decrease our appetite. In fact, the stomach actually tells the brain not only how full it is but also how much nutrient is present. That is why rich food stops your hunger faster than the same amount of water. The hormone *cholecystokinin* (CCK) helps start the digestion of food, travels to the brain through the bloodstream, and signals you to stop eating (Naslund, Hellstrom, and Kral, 2002). As explained in the following sections, there is a lot more involved in hunger than an empty stomach.

Blood Chemistry   Three important chemical substances are involved in hunger, eating, and satiety (the sense of being filled and not wanting to eat more): glucose, insulin, and leptin.

Glucose (blood sugar) is an important factor in hunger, probably because the brain is critically dependent on sugar for energy. One set of sugar receptors, located in the brain itself, triggers hunger when sugar levels fall too low. Another set of sugar receptors is in the liver, which stores excess sugar and releases it into the blood when needed. The sugar receptors in the liver signal the brain when its sugar supply falls, and this signal also can make you hungry.

Another important factor in blood sugar control is the hormone *insulin*, which causes excess sugar in the blood to be stored in cells as fats and carbohydrates (Laboure & others, 2002). Insulin injections cause profound hunger because they lower blood sugar drastically. Psychologist Judith Rodin (1984) has investigated the role of insulin and glucose in hunger and eating behavior. She has pointed out that when we eat complex carbohydrates such as cereals, bread, and pasta, insulin levels go up but then fall off gradually. When we consume simple sugars such as candy bars and Cokes, insulin levels rise and then fall off sharply—the all-too-familiar "sugar low." Glucose levels in the blood are affected by complex carbohydrates and simple sugars in similar ways. The consequence is that we are more likely to eat within the next several hours after eating simple sugars than after eating complex carbohydrates. And the food we eat at one meal often influences how much we will eat at our next meal. So consuming doughnuts and candy bars, which provide no nutritional value, sets up an ongoing sequence of what and how much we probably will crave the next time we eat.

Another chemical substance, called *leptin* (from the Greek word *leptos*, which means "thin"), is involved in satiety. Leptin, a protein that is released by fat cells, decreases food intake and increases energy expenditure (Oberbauer & others, 2001). The role of leptin in long-term satiety was discovered in a strain of *ob mice*, genetically obese mice (Campfield & others, 1995; Carlson, 2001). The ob mouse has a low metabolism, overeats, and gets extremely fat. A particular gene called *ob* normally produces leptin. However, because of a genetic mutation, the fat cells of ob mice cannot produce leptin. Leptin strongly affects metabolism and eating, acting as an antiobesity hormone (Misra & others, 2001). If ob mice are given daily injections of leptin, their metabolic rate increases, they become more active, and they eat less.

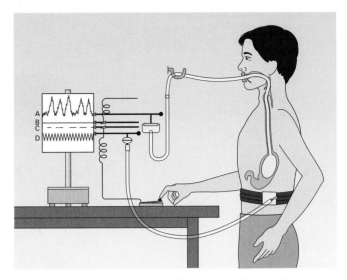

FIGURE 11.3 **Cannon and Washburn's Classic Experiment on Hunger** In this experiment, the researchers demonstrated that stomach contractions, which were detected by the stomach balloon, accompany a person's hunger feelings, which were indicated by pressing the key. Line A in the chart records increases and decreases in the volume of the balloon in the participant's stomach. Line B records the passage of time. Line C records the participant's manual signals of feelings of hunger. Line D records a reading from the belt around the participant's waist to detect movements of the abdominal wall and ensure that such movements are not the cause of changes in stomach volume.

FIGURE 11.4 Leptin and Obesity
The ob mouse on the left is untreated; the one on the right has been given injections of leptin.

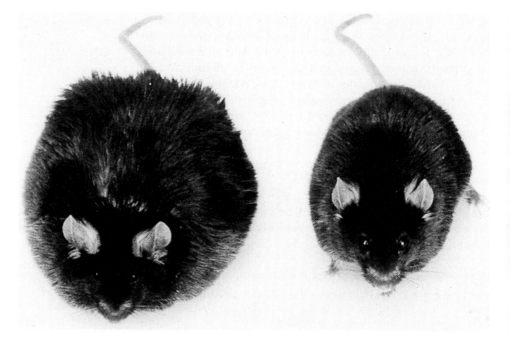

Consequently, their weight falls to a normal level. Figure 11.4 shows an untreated ob mouse and an ob mouse that has received injections of leptin.

In humans, leptin concentrations have been linked with weight, percentage of body fat, weight loss in a single diet episode, and cumulative percentage of weight loss in all diet episodes (Benini & others, 2001; Van Dielen & others, 2002). Today, scientists are interested in the possibility that leptin might help obese individuals lose weight (Wauters & others, 2001).

Brain Processes Chapter 3 described the central role of the hypothalamus in regulating important body functions, including hunger. More specifically, activity in two areas of the hypothalamus contributes to our understanding of hunger. The *lateral hypothalamus* is involved in stimulating eating. When it is electrically stimulated in a well-fed animal, the animal begins to eat. And if this area of the hypothalamus is destroyed, even a starving animal will show no interest in food. The *ventromedial hypothalamus* is involved in reducing hunger and restricting eating. When this area of an animal's brain is stimulated, the animal stops eating. When the area is destroyed, the animal eats profusely and quickly becomes obese.

Today, neuroscientists believe that, although the lateral and ventromedial hypothalamus play roles in hunger, there is much more to the brain's role in determining hunger than these on/off centers in the hypothalamus. They are exploring how neurotransmitters (the chemical messengers that convey information from neuron to neuron) and neural circuits (clusters of neurons that often involve different parts of the brain) function in hunger.

Leptin influences eating by inhibiting the production of a neuropeptide neurotransmitter in the hypothalamus that induces eating (Cowley & others, 2001; Sorenson & others, 2002). The neurotransmitter serotonin is partly responsible for the satiating effect of CCK, and serotonin antagonists have been used to treat obesity in humans (Halford & Blundell, 2000; Thrybom, Rooth, & Lindstrom, 2001). Neural circuits involved in the action of such drugs may be in the brain stem, as well as the hypothalamus (Carlson, 2001). The neural circuitry also extends to the cerebral cortex, where humans make decisions about whether to eat or not to eat.

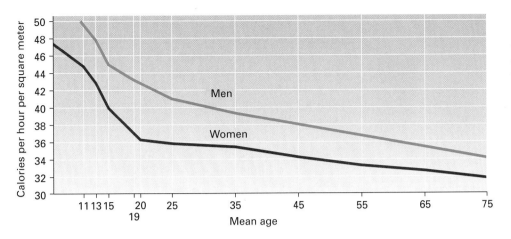

FIGURE 11.5 **Changes in Basal Metabolism Rate with Age** BMR varies with age and sex. Rates are usually higher for males and decline proportionately with age for both sexes.

Obesity and Eating Behavior

Approximately one-third of the American population is overweight enough to be at increased risk for health problems such as hypertension, cardiovascular disease, and diabetes. The health care costs linked to obesity are estimated to be $46 billion per year in the United States alone. And the rate of obesity is increasing: During the 1990s, the prevalence of obesity in the United States rose 8 percent (Friedman & Brownell, 1998). Obesity often becomes more common with increased age, especially among women. Thus, as baby boomers age, the number of obese individuals is likely to increase.

Why do so many Americans overeat to the point of being obese? As is the case with much behavior, biological, cognitive, and sociocultural factors interact in diverse ways in different individuals, making it difficult to point to a specific cause. Let's look at some of the factors that are known to contribute to overeating, beginning with the biological causes.

The Biology of Overeating Until recently, the genetic component of obesity was underestimated. As discussed earlier, scientists discovered an ob gene in mice that controls the production of leptin. In the 1990s, a similar gene was found in humans.

Some individuals do inherit a tendency to be overweight (Yanovski & Yanovski, 2002). Only 10 percent of children who do not have obese parents become obese themselves, whereas 40 percent of children who have one obese parent become obese, and 70 percent of children who have two obese parents become obese. Researchers also have documented that animals can be inbred to have a propensity for obesity (Blundell, 1984). Further, identical human twins have similar weights, even when they are reared apart. Estimates of the degree to which heredity can explain obesity range from 25 to 70 percent.

Another factor in weight is **basal metabolism rate (BMR),** the minimal amount of energy an individual uses in a resting state (Marra & others, 2002). BMR varies with age and sex. It declines precipitously during adolescence and then more gradually in adulthood; it is slightly higher for males than for females (see figure 11.5). Many people gradually increase their weight over many years. To some degree, this weight gain can be due to a declining basal metabolism rate.

Set point, the weight maintained when no effort is made to gain or lose weight, is determined in part by the amount of stored fat in the body. Fat is stored in *adipose cells,* or fat cells. When these cells are filled, you do not get hungry. When people gain weight—because of genetic predisposition, childhood eating patterns, or adult overeating—the number of their fat cells increases, and they might not be able to get rid of extra ones. A normal-weight individual has 30 to 40 billion fat cells. An obese individual has 80 to 120 billion fat cells. Consequently, an obese individual has to eat

basal metabolism rate (BMR) The minimal amount of energy an individual uses in a resting state.

set point The weight maintained when no effort is made to gain or lose weight.

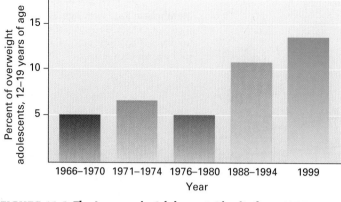

FIGURE 11.6 The Increase in Adolescent Obesity from 1966 to 1999 in the United States

more to feel satisfied. Some scientists have proposed that fat cells may shrink but might not go away.

Researchers have found that a high-fat diet may raise a person's set point for body weight (Frederich & others, 1995). They also have found that exercise can lower the body's set point for weight and contribute to weight loss (Rosenbaum, Leibel, & Hirsch, 1997).

Cognitive and Sociocultural Factors in Hunger and Obesity   Not too long ago, we believed that obesity was caused by such factors as unhappiness or responding to external food cues. But according to Judith Rodin (1984), a number of biological, cognitive, and social factors are more important than emotional state and external stimuli. We already discussed some biological factors, including heredity, chemical substances, and brain processes. In regard to external cues, Rodin says that, although obese persons are more responsive to external food cues than normal-weight persons are, there are individuals at all weight levels who respond more to external than to internal stimuli. Many persons who respond to external cues also have the conscious ability to control their behavior and keep environmental food cues from controlling their eating patterns.

Time and place do affect our eating. Learned associations of food with a particular place and time are characteristic of organisms (Bloom, Nelson, & Lazerson, 2001). For example, when it is noon we are likely to feel hungry even if we have had a big breakfast and snacked at midmorning. We also associate eating with certain places. Many people link watching television with eating and feel uncomfortable if they aren't eating something while they are watching TV.

The human gustatory system and taste preferences developed at a time when reliable food sources were scarce. Our earliest ancestors probably developed a preference for sweets, because ripe fruit, which is a concentrated source of sugar (and calories), was so accessible. Today many people still have a "sweet tooth," but, unlike our ancestors' ripe fruit that contained sugar *plus* vitamins and minerals, the soft drinks and candy bars we snack on today often fill us with nutrient-free calories.

Strong evidence of the environment's influence on weight is the doubling of the rate of obesity in the United States since 1900. Also, as shown in figure 11.6, obesity among adolescents in the United States has increased significantly since the late 1960s (National Center for Health Statistics, 2000). This dramatic increase likely is due to greater availability of food (especially food high in fat), energy-saving devices, and declining physical activity. Obesity is six times more prevalent among women with low incomes than among women with high incomes. Also, Americans are more obese than Europeans and people in many other areas of the world.

The American culture provides substantial opportunities and encouragement for overeating. Food is everywhere you go, and it is easily accessed—in vending machines, fast-food restaurants, at work. Nowhere else in the world will you find as many fast-food restaurants as in the United States. Also, both portion size and the quantity of food that people eat at mealtime in the United States have grown. Fast-food restaurants capitalize on this by giving you the opportunity to "super-size" your meal at a relatively low additional cost. Also, a higher percentage of our food is made up of fat content than in the past. And, although we hear a lot about exercise in the media and although people talk about exercising, there is good evidence that Americans overall are getting less exercise than they did in the past (National Center for Health Statistics, 2000).

In sum, an abundance of food in a culture that encourages food consumption, an increase in the amount of food eaten, a higher percentage of fat content in the food we eat, and a decrease in exercise add up to a population that has a serious number of overweight and obese individuals.

Judith Rodin (*center*) has had a distinguished research and teaching career in psychology, and she became the first female president of an Ivy League university—the University of Pennsylvania—in 1993. As an undergraduate student at the University of Pennsylvania, she says, "I fell in love with the field of psychology." In her book, *Body Traps* (1993), Rodin argued that our society has constructed a number of psychological traps for women, such as the dieting rituals trap, which involves unrealistic expectations. She believes that too often women fall into the body trap of using goods and being thin as the measure of their self-worth.

Dieting

Ironically, even as obesity is on the rise, dieting has become an obsession with many Americans. This section explores a number of factors in dieting, beginning with restrained eating.

Restrained Eaters   Many people spend their lives on one long diet, interrupted by occasional hot fudge sundaes or chocolate chip cookies. They are *restrained eaters,* individuals who chronically restrict their food intake to control their weight (Drobes & others, 2001). Restrained eaters are often on diets, are very conscious of what they eat, and tend to feel guilty after splurging on sweets (Mulvihill, Davies, & Rogers, 2002). An interesting characteristic of restrained eaters is that when they stop dieting, they tend to binge eat—that is, to eat large quantities of food in a short time (McFarlane, Polivy, & Herman, 1998).

The Use and Misuse of Diets   The topic of dieting is of great interest to many diverse groups in the United States, including the public, health professionals, policy makers, the media, and the powerful diet and food industries. On one side are the societal norms that promote a lean, aesthetic body. This ideal is supported by $30 billion a year in sales of diet books, programs, videos, foods, and pills. On the other side are health professionals and a growing minority of the press, who, although they recognize that the rate of obesity is alarming, are frustrated by high relapse rates and the widespread obsession with excessive thinness that can lead to chronic dieting and serious health risks (Tavris, 2002, in press).

Although many Americans regularly embark on diets, few are successful in keeping weight off in the long run. Some critics argue that all diets fail (Wooley & Garner, 1991). However, studies show that some individuals do lose weight and maintain the loss (Brownell & Cohen, 1995). How often this occurs and whether some diet programs work better than others are still open questions.

What we do know about losing weight is that the most effective programs include an exercise component (Sothern & others, 2002). Exercise not only burns calories but also continues to elevate the person's metabolic rate for several hours *after* the exercise. Also, as indicated earlier, exercise may lower a person's set point for weight, which makes it easier to maintain a lower weight (Bennett & Gurin, 1982).

Dieting is a pervasive concern of many Americans, but the population is not uniform, and many people who are on diets should not be. A 10 percent reduction in body weight might produce striking benefits for an older, obese, hypertensive man yet be unhealthy for a female college student who is not overweight. The pressure to be thin, and thus to diet, is greatest among young women, yet they do not have the highest risk of obesity.

Even when diets produce healthy weight loss, they can place the dieter at risk for health problems. One main concern focuses on weight cycling (commonly called "yo-yo dieting"), in which the person is in a recurring cycle of dieting and weight gain (Wadden & others, 1996). Researchers have found a link between frequent changes in weight and chronic disease (Brownell & Rodin, 1994). Also, liquid diets and other very low calorie strategies are related to gall bladder damage.

With these problems in mind, when overweight people diet and maintain their weight loss, they do become less depressed and reduce their risk for a number of health-impairing disorders (Christensen, 1996). The next section explores problems that occur at the other end of the weight spectrum—people who become so thin that it impairs their health.

Eating Disorders

This section examines two major eating problems, anorexia nervosa and bulimia nervosa, both of which are more common in young women than in any other gender/age segment of the population.

Anorexia Nervosa   **Anorexia nervosa** is an eating disorder that involves the relentless pursuit of thinness through starvation. Anorexia nervosa can eventually lead to death. The main characteristics of anorexia nervosa are (Davison & Neale, 2001)

- Weighing less than 85 percent of what is considered normal for age and height
- Having an intense fear of gaining weight that does not decrease with weight loss
- Having a distorted body image (Dohm & others, 2001). (Even when individuals with anorexia nervosa are extremely thin, they see themselves as fat, especially in the abdomen, buttocks, and thighs. They never think they are thin enough: They weigh themselves frequently, often take their body measurements, and gaze critically at themselves in mirrors.)

Anorexia nervosa typically begins in the teenage years, often following an episode of dieting and the occurrence of some type of life stress (Lewinsohn, Striegel-Moore, & Seeley, 2000). About 10 times more females than males have anorexia nervosa. Although most U.S. adolescent girls go on diets at some point, less than 1 percent develop anorexia nervosa (Walters & Kendler, 1994). When anorexia nervosa does occur in males, its symptoms and other characteristics (including family conflict) are usually similar to those reported by females who have the eating disorder (Olivardia & others, 1995).

Most anorexics are White adolescent or young adult females from well-educated, middle- and upper-income families that are competitive and high achieving. Females who become anorexic often set high standards for themselves and become stressed about not being able to reach them; they are intensely concerned about how others perceive them (Striegel-Moore, Silberstein, & Rodin, 1993). Unable to meet their own high expectations, they turn to something they can control: their weight.

anorexia nervosa An eating disorder that involves the relentless pursuit of thinness through starvation.

The fashion image in the American culture that emphasizes that "thin is beautiful" contributes to the incidence of anorexia nervosa (Simpson, 2002). This image is reflected in the saying "You never can be too rich or too thin." The media portrays thin as beautiful in their choice of models, whom many females want to emulate.

About 70 percent of individuals with anorexia nervosa eventually recover. Recovery often takes 6 to 7 years, and relapses are common before a stable pattern of eating and weight maintenance are achieved (Strober, Freeman, & Morrell, 1997).

Bulimia Nervosa   **Bulimia nervosa** is an eating disorder in which the individual consistently follows a binge-and-purge eating pattern. The bulimic goes on an eating binge and then purges by self-induced vomiting or using a laxative. As with anorexics, most bulimics are preoccupied with food, have a strong fear of becoming overweight, and are depressed or anxious (Byrne & Mclean, 2002; Cooley & Toray, 2001). Unlike anorexia nervosa, the binge-and-purge pattern in bulimia nervosa occurs within a normal weight range, which means that it is often difficult to detect (Mizes & Miller, 2000).

Bulimia nervosa typically begins in late adolescence or early adulthood (Levine, 2002). About 90 percent of the cases are females. Approximately 1 to 2 percent of females are estimated to develop bulimia nervosa (Gotesdam & Agras, 1995). Many females who develop bulimia nervosa were somewhat overweight before the onset of the disorder, and the binge eating often began during an episode of dieting. As with anorexia nervosa, about 70 percent of individuals with bulimia nervosa eventually recover from it (Keel & others, 1999). Chapter 15 further explores eating patterns and proper nutrition.

Might the current fashion image of "thin is beautiful" contribute to anorexia nervosa?

Review and Sharpen Your Thinking

2 **Explain the physiological basis of hunger and the nature of eating behavior.**

- Discuss the biology of hunger.
- Describe the biological, cognitive, and sociocultural factors involved in overeating and obesity.
- Evaluate the benefits and risks of dieting.
- Distinguish between anorexia nervosa and bulimia nervosa.

The "freshman 15" refers to the approximately 15 pounds that many students gain in their first year of college. What factors might explain this weight increase?

For study tools related to this learning goal, see the Study Guide, the CD-ROM, and the Online Learning Center.

SEXUALITY 3

The Biology of Sex   **Cultural Factors**   **Sexual Behavior and Orientation**

Cognitive and Sensory/Perceptual Factors   **Psychosexual Dysfunctions**

What factors motivate our sexual behavior?
We do not need sex for everyday survival, the way we need food and water, but we do need it for the survival of the species. Like hunger, sex has a strong physiological basis, as well as cognitive and sociocultural components.

bulimia nervosa An eating disorder in which the individual consistently follows a binge-and-purge eating pattern.

The Biology of Sex

What brain areas are involved in sex? What role do hormones play in sexual motivation? What is nature of the human sexual response pattern?

The Hypothalamus, Cerebral Cortex, and Limbic System Motivation for sexual behavior is centered in the hypothalamus (Carter, 1998). However, like many other areas of motivation, brain functioning related to sex radiates outward to connect with a wide range of other brain areas in both the limbic system and the cerebral cortex.

The importance of the hypothalamus in sexual activity has been shown by electrically stimulating or surgically removing it. Electrical stimulation of certain hypothalamic areas increases sexual behavior; surgical removal of some hypothalamic areas produces sexual inhibition. Electrical stimulation of the hypothalamus in a male can lead to as many as 20 ejaculations in 1 hour. The limbic system, which runs through the hypothalamus, also seems to be involved in sexual behavior. Its electrical stimulation can produce penile erection in males and orgasm in females.

In humans, the temporal lobes of the neocortex play an important role in moderating sexual arousal and directing it to an appropriate goal object (Cheasty, Condren, & Cooney, 2002). Temporal lobe damage in male cats has been shown to impair the animals' ability to select an appropriate partner. Male cats with temporal lobe damage try to copulate with everything in sight: teddy bears, chairs, even researchers. Temporal lobe damage in humans also has been associated with changes in sexual activity (Mendez & others, 2002).

The brain tissues that produce sexual feelings and behaviors are activated by various neurotransmitters in conjunction with various sex hormones. Sexual motivation also is characterized by a basic urge-reward-relief neural circuit. The motivation for sex is generated by excitatory neurotransmitters. The intense reward of orgasm is caused by a massive rush of dopamine, and the deep feeling of relaxation that follows is linked with a hormone called oxytocin.

Sex Hormones Sex hormones are powerful chemicals that are controlled by the master gland in the brain, the pituitary. The two main classes of sex hormones are estrogens and androgens. **Estrogens,** the class of sex hormones that predominate in females, are produced mainly by the ovaries. **Androgens,** the class of sex hormones that predominate in males, are produced by the testes in males and by the adrenal glands in both males and females. Testosterone is an androgen. Estrogens and androgens can influence sexual motivation in both sexes.

The secretion of sex hormones is regulated by a feedback system. The pituitary gland, regulated by the hypothalamus, monitors hormone levels. The pituitary gland signals the testes or ovaries to manufacture the hormone. Then the pituitary gland, through interaction with the hypothalamus, detects the point at which an optimal hormone level is reached and stops production of the hormone.

The role of hormones in motivating human sexual behavior, especially for females, is not clear (Crooks & Bauer, 2002). For human males, higher androgen levels are associated with sexual motivation and orgasm frequency (Booth, Johnson, & Granger, 1999; Thiessen, 2002). Nonetheless, sexual behavior is so individualized in humans that it is difficult to specify the effects of hormones.

The Human Sexual Response Pattern What physiological changes do humans experience during sexual activity? To answer this question, gynecologist William Masters and his colleague Virginia Johnson (1966) carefully observed and measured the physiological responses of 382 female and 312 male volunteers as they masturbated or had sexual intercourse. The **human sexual response pattern** consists of four phases—excitement, plateau, orgasm, and resolution—as identified by Masters and Johnson (see figure 11.7).

estrogens The class of sex hormones that predominate in females.

androgens The class of sex hormones that predominate in males.

human sexual response pattern Identified by Masters and Johnson; consists of four phases—excitement, plateau, orgasm, and resolution

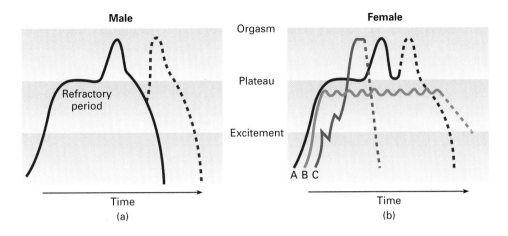

Male

Female

Orgasm

Plateau

Excitement

Refractory period

Time

(a)

A B C

Time

(b)

FIGURE 11.7 **Male and Female Sexual Response Patterns Identified by Masters and Johnson** (*a*) The excitement, plateau, orgasm, and resolution phases of the human male sexual response pattern. Notice that males enter a refractory period, which lasts from several minutes up to a day, in which they cannot have another orgasm. (*b*) The excitement, plateau, orgasm, and resolution phases of the human female sexual response pattern. Notice that female sexual responses follow one of three basic patterns: Pattern A somewhat resembles the male pattern, except it includes the possibility of multiple orgasm (the second peak in pattern A) without falling below the plateau level. Pattern B represents nonorgasmic arousal. Pattern C represents intense female orgasm, which resembles the male pattern in its intensity and rapid resolution.

The *excitement phase* begins erotic responsiveness; it lasts from several minutes to several hours depending on the nature of the sex play involved. Engorgement of blood vessels and increased blood flow in genital areas and muscle tension characterize the excitement phase. The most obvious signs of response in this phase are lubrication of the vagina and partial erection of the penis.

The second phase of the human sexual response, called the *plateau phase,* is a continuation and heightening of the arousal begun in the excitement phase. The increases in breathing, pulse rate, and blood pressure that occurred during the excitement phase become more intense, penile erection and vaginal lubrication are more complete, and orgasm is closer.

The third phase of the human sexual response cycle is *orgasm.* How long does orgasm last? Some individuals sense that time is standing still when it takes place, but orgasm lasts for only about 3 to 15 seconds. Orgasm involves an explosive discharge of neuromuscular tension and an intense pleasurable feeling. However, orgasms are not all alike. For example, females show three different patterns in the orgasm phase: multiple orgasms; no orgasm; and excitement rapidly leading to orgasm, bypassing the plateau phase (this pattern most clearly corresponds to the male pattern in intensity and resolution; see figure 11.7).

Following orgasm, the individual enters the *resolution phase,* in which blood vessels return to their normal state. One difference between males and females in this phase is that females may be stimulated to orgasm again without delay. Males enter a *refractory period,* lasting anywhere from several minutes to a day, in which they cannot have another orgasm. The length of the refractory period increases as men age.

Cognitive and Sensory/Perceptual Factors

From experience, we know that our cognitive world plays an important role in our sexuality (Crooks & Bauer, 2002). We might be sexually attracted to someone but understand that it is important to inhibit our sexual urges until the relationship has time to develop and we get to know the person better. We have the cognitive capacity to think about the importance of not raping or inflicting sexual harm on others. We also have the cognitive capacity to generate sexual images. For example, some individuals become sexually aroused by generating erotic images and even reach orgasm while they are having fantasy images of sex (Whipple, Ogden, & Komisaruk, 1992).

Sexual motivation is influenced by *sexual scripts,* stereotyped patterns of expectancies for how people should behave sexually (recall from the discussion of memory in chapter 9 that *scripts* are schemas for events). We carry these scripts with us in our memories. Two well-known sexual scripts are the traditional religious script and the romantic script. In the *traditional religious script,* sex is accepted only within marriage.

Extramarital sex is taboo, especially for women. Sex means reproduction and sometimes affection. In the *romantic script,* sex is equated with love. In this script, if we develop a relationship with someone and fall in love, it is acceptable to have sex with the person whether we are married or not.

Typically, men and women have different sexual scripts. Females tend to link sexual intercourse with love more than males do, and males are more likely to emphasize sexual conquest. Some sexual scripts involve a double standard: For example, it is okay for male adolescents to have sex, but not for females; and women are held solely to blame if they become pregnant.

Cognitive interpretation of sexual activity also involves our perception of the individual with whom we are having sex and his or her perception of us. We imbue our sexual acts with such perceptual questions as Is he loyal to me? What is our future relationship going to be like? How important is sex to her? What if she gets pregnant? Amid the wash of hormones in sexual activity is the cognitive ability to control, reason about, and try to make sense of the activity.

Along with cognitive factors, sensory/perceptual factors are involved in sexual behavior. The sensory system of touch usually predominates during sexual intimacy, but vision also plays an important role for some individuals (Brown, Steele, & Walsh-Childers, 2002).

Men and women differ in how much touch and visual stimulation motivate them sexually. In general, women are more aroused by touch, men by what they see. This might explain why erotic magazines and movies are directed more toward males than toward females (Money, 1986). Women are more aroused by tender, loving touches that are coupled with verbal expressions of love than men are. Moreover, men are likely to become sexually aroused quickly, whereas women's sexual arousal tends to build gradually.

Might smell also be involved in sexual interest between women and men? **Pheromones** are scented substances that are powerful attractants in some animals (Beckman, 2002; Savic, 2000). Pheromones in the urine of ovulating female guinea pigs attract male guinea pigs. All the male cats in a neighborhood know that a female cat is in heat when they pick up the scent of pheromones. Several years ago, Jovan developed a fragrance the company claimed would attract men to women who wore it. The company advertised that the perfume contained a pheromone derived from human sweat. It was designed to lure human males, just as pheromones attract male guinea pigs and cats. The fragrance was not the smashing success the perfumery anticipated, indicating that there is far more to sexual attraction in humans than smell.

Various foods and other substances also have been proposed as dramatically increasing sexual arousal. *Aphrodisiacs* are substances that supposedly arouse a person's sexual desire and increase their capacity for sexual activity. Recall from chapter 1 that I urged you to be skeptical about claims that eating ground-up tiger's penis will increase the male's sexual potency. Some foods, such as oysters, bananas, celery, tomatoes, and potatoes, are touted as aphrodisiacs. Be wary of such claims. These foods do not influence sexual behavior. A substance referred to as "Spanish fly" also has been promoted as a powerful aphrodisiac. Not only is Spanish fly not an effective sexual stimulant, but it can cause genital inflammation, tissue damage, and even death.

Cultural Factors

Sexual motivation also is influenced by cultural factors. The range of sexual values across cultures is substantial. Some cultures consider sexual pleasures to be "normal" or "desirable," other cultures view sexual pleasures as "weird" or "abnormal." We would consider the people who live on the small island of Ines Beag off the coast of Ireland to be among the most sexually repressed people in the world. They know nothing about tongue kissing or hand stimulation of the penis, and they detest nudity. For both females and males, premarital sex is out of the question. Men avoid most

pheromones Odorous substances released by animals that are powerful attractants.

Sexual behavior has its magnificent moments throughout the animal kingdom. Insects mate in midair, peacocks display their plumage, and male elephant seals have prolific sex lives. Experience plays a more important role in human sexual behavior. We can talk about sex with each other, read about it in magazines, and watch it on television and the movie screen.

sexual experiences because they believe that sexual intercourse reduces their energy level and is bad for their health. Under these repressive conditions, sexual intercourse occurs only at night and takes place as quickly as possible as the husband opens his nightclothes under the covers and the wife raises her nightgown. As you might suspect, female orgasm is rare in this culture (Messinger, 1971).

In contrast, the Mangaian culture in the South Pacific seems promiscuous to us. In Mangaia, young boys are taught about masturbation and are encouraged to engage in it as much as they like. At age 13, the boys undergo a ritual that initiates them into sexual manhood. First, their elders instruct them about sexual strategies, including how to aid their female partner in having orgasms. Then, 2 weeks later, the boy has intercourse with an experienced woman who helps him hold back ejaculation until she can achieve orgasm with him. By the end of adolescence, Mangaians have sex pretty much every day. Mangaian women report a high frequency of orgasm.

Psychosexual Dysfunctions

Myths about females and males would have us believe that many women are uninterested in sexual pleasure and that most men can hardly get enough. Although men do think about sex more than women do, most men and women have desires for sexual pleasure, and both sexes can experience psychological problems that interfere with the attainment of sexual pleasure. *Psychosexual dysfunctions* are disorders that involve impairments in the sexual response pattern, either in the desire for gratification or in the inability to achieve it.

In disorders associated with the desire phase, both men and women show little or no sexual drive or interest. In disorders associated with the excitement phase, men may not be able to maintain an erection (Becker & others, 2002; McKinlay, 1999). In disorders associated with the orgasmic phase, both women and men reach orgasm either too quickly or not at all. Premature ejaculation in men occurs when the time between the beginning of sexual stimulation and ejaculation is unsatisfactorily brief. Many women do not routinely experience orgasm in sexual intercourse. Inhibited male orgasm does occur, but it is much less common than inhibited female orgasm.

The treatment of psychosexual dysfunctions has undergone nothing short of a revolution in recent years. Once thought of as extremely difficult therapeutic challenges, most cases of psychosexual dysfunction now yield to techniques tailored to improve sexual functioning (Bhugra & de Silva, 1998; Crooks & Bauer, 2002).

Attempts to treat psychosexual dysfunctions through traditional forms of psychotherapy, as if the dysfunctions were personality disorders, have not been very successful; however, new treatments that focus directly on each sexual dysfunction have reached success rates of 90 percent or more (McConaghy, 1993). For example, the success rate of a treatment that encourages women to enjoy their bodies and engage in self-stimulation to orgasm, with a vibrator if necessary, approaches 100 percent (Anderson, 1983). Some of these women subsequently transfer their newly developed sexual responsiveness to interactions with partners.

Recently, attention in helping males with sexual dysfunction has focused on Viagra, a drug designed to conquer impotence (Nehra & others, 2002; Seidman, 2002). Its success rate is in the range of 60 to 80 percent, and its prescription rate has outpaced such popular drugs as Prozac (antidepressant) and Rogaine (baldness remedy) in first-year comparisons (Padma-Nathan, 1999). Viagra also is being taken by some women to improve their sexual satisfaction. However, Viagra is not an aphrodisiac; it won't work in the absence of desire. The downside of Viagra includes headaches in 1 of 10 men, seeing blue (because the eyes contain an enzyme similar to the one on which Viagra works in the penis, about 3 percent of users develop temporary vision problems ranging from blurred vision to a blue or green halo effect), and blackouts (Viagra can trigger a sudden drop in blood pressure; Steers & others, 2001). Also, scientists do not yet know the long-term effects of taking the drug, although in short-term trials it appears to be relatively safe.

Sexual Behavior and Orientation

Earlier we contrasted the sexual values and behaviors of two remote cultures—Ines Beag and Mangaia. Few cultures are as isolated and homogeneous as these two. In the United States, sexual behaviors and attitudes reflect its diverse, multicultural population, placing Americans somewhere in the middle of a continuum going from repressive to liberal. We are more conservative in our sexual habits than once thought but somewhat more open-minded regarding sexual orientation than a century ago.

Sexual Attitudes and Practices Describing sexual practices in America has always been challenging (Dunne, 2002; Wiederman & Whitley, 2002). In 1948, Alfred Kinsey and his colleagues shocked the nation by reporting that his survey of American's sexual practices revealed that, among other observations, half of American men had engaged in extramarital affairs. However, Kinsey's results were not representative, because he recruited volunteers wherever he could find them, including hitchhikers who passed through town, fraternity men, and even mental patients. Despite the study's flaws, the Kinsey data were widely circulated, and many people felt that they must be leading more conservative sexual lives than others.

Subsequent large-scale magazine surveys confirmed the trend toward permissive sexuality (e.g., a *Playboy* magazine poll of its readers; Hunt, 1974). In these surveys, Americans were portrayed as engaging in virtually unending copulation. However,

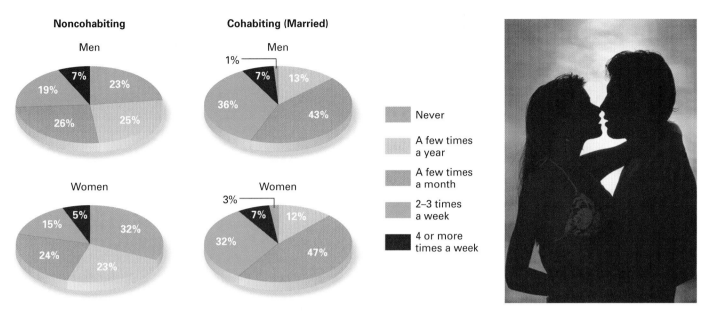

Noncohabiting

Men

7% | 23% | 25% | 26% | 19%

Women

5% | 32% | 23% | 24% | 15%

Cohabiting (Married)

Men

1% | 7% | 13% | 43% | 36%

Women

3% | 7% | 12% | 47% | 32%

Never

A few times a year

A few times a month

2–3 times a week

4 or more times a week

FIGURE 11.8 **The 1994 *Sex in America* Survey** Percentages show noncohabiting and cohabiting (married) males' and females' responses to the question "How often have you had sex in the past year?"

most magazine polls are skewed because of the background of the readers who complete the surveys. For example, surveys in *Playboy* and *Cosmopolitan* might appeal to subscribers who want to use the survey to brag about their sexual exploits.

Not until 1994 were more accurate data obtained from a well-designed, comprehensive study of American's sexual patterns. Robert Michael and his colleagues (1994) interviewed nearly 3,500 people from 18 to 50 years of age who were randomly selected, a sharp contrast from earlier samples that were based on unrepresentative groups of volunteers. Here are some of the key findings from that survey:

• Americans tend to fall into three categories: One-third have sex twice a week or more, one-third a few times a month, and one-third a few times a year or not at all.

• Married couples have sex most often and also are the most likely to have orgasms when they do. Figure 11.8 portrays the frequency of sex for married and noncohabitating individuals in the year before the survey was taken.

• Most Americans do not engage in kinky sexual acts. When asked about their favorite sexual acts, the vast majority (96 percent) said that vaginal sex was "very" or "somewhat" appealing. Oral sex was in third place, after an activity that many might not even label a sexual act—watching a partner undress.

• Adultery is clearly the exception rather than the rule. Nearly 75 percent of the married men and 85 percent of the married women indicated that they have never been unfaithful.

• Men think about sex far more often than women do—54 percent of the men said they think about it every day or several times a day, whereas 67 percent of the women said they think about it only a few times a week or a few times a month.

In sum, one of the most powerful messages in the 1994 survey was that Americans' sexual lives are more conservative than previously believed. Although 17 percent of the men and 3 percent of the women said they have had sex with at least 21 partners, the overall impression from the survey was that sexual behavior is ruled by marriage and monogamy for most Americans.

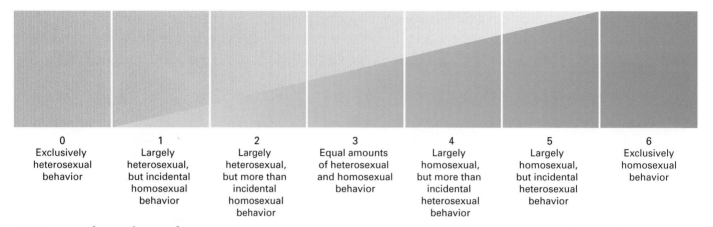

0	1	2	3	4	5	6
Exclusively heterosexual behavior	Largely heterosexual, but incidental homosexual behavior	Largely heterosexual, but more than incidental homosexual behavior	Equal amounts of heterosexual and homosexual behavior	Largely homosexual, but more than incidental heterosexual behavior	Largely homosexual, but incidental heterosexual behavior	Exclusively homosexual behavior

FIGURE 11.9 **The Continuum of Sexual Orientation** The continuum ranges from exclusive heterosexuality, which Kinsey and associates (1948) labeled 0, to exclusive homosexuality, 6. People who are about equally attracted to both sexes, 2 to 4, are bisexual.

According to sexuality expert Bernie Zilbergeld (1992), dramatic changes in the sexual landscape have taken place in the past several decades—from changing expectations of women to new definitions of masculinity, from the fear of disease to the renewed focus on long-term relationships. Sexuality's many myths have led to unrealistic expectations for our sexual lives. One man commented that he had learned so much misinformation about scx as a child that it was taking him thc rest of his life to unlearn it. In middle age, he still cannot believe how much stress he caused himself when he was younger and wishes he could apologize to the women who knew him in his earlier years. Among sexual myths, according to Zilbergeld (1992), are that men need a large penis to satisfy a woman; that male and female orgasm are absolutely necessary for sexual satisfaction; that intercourse is the only real sexual act; that good sex has to be spontaneous (without planning or talking); and that for men to have questions, doubts, or problems in sex is virtually a crime.

Too often people think of sex as a performance skill, like race car driving or swimming. However, sex is best conceptualized as a form of communication within a relationship. Indeed, caring couples with good communication skills can usually survive most sexual problems, although uncaring couples with poor communication skills often do not have lasting relationships even if their sexual experiences are adequate or even good.

Although the majority of us manage to develop a mature sexuality, most individuals experience some periods of vulnerability and confusion along the way. Many individuals have an almost insatiable curiosity about sexuality. Some wonder and worry about their sexual attractiveness, their ability to satisfy their sexual partner, and whether they will experience their ultimate sexual fantasy. Often our worries about our sexuality are fueled by media stereotypes about sexual potency and superhuman sexual exploits.

Sexual Orientation Until the end of the nineteenth century, it was generally believed that people were either heterosexual or homosexual. Today, it is more accepted to view sexual orientation along a continuum, from exclusive heterosexuality to exclusive homosexuality, rather than as an either/or proposition. Kinsey, Pomeroy, and Martin (1948) described this continuum on a scale ranging from 0 (exclusive heterosexuality) to 6 (signifying exclusive homosexuality; see figure 11.9). Also, some individuals are *bisexual*, being sexually attracted to people of both sexes. In Kinsey's research, approximately 1 percent of individuals reported being bisexual (1.2 percent of males and 0.7 percent of females) and about 2 to 5 percent of individuals reported being homosexual (4.7 percent of males and 1.8 percent of females). In the 1994 *Sex in America* survey, only 2.7 percent of the men and 1.3 percent of the women reported that they had had homosexual sex in the past year (Michael & others, 1994).

An individual's sexual preference is most likely determined by a combination of genetic, hormonal, cognitive, and environmental factors.

Why are some individuals homosexual and others heterosexual? Speculation about this question has been extensive, but no firm answers are available. Homosexuals and heterosexuals have similar physiological responses during sexual arousal and seem to be aroused by the same types of tactile stimulation. Investigators find no differences between homosexuals and heterosexuals in a wide range of attitudes, behaviors, and adjustments (Bell, Weinberg, & Mammersmith, 1981). Homosexuality once was classified as a mental disorder, but both the American Psychiatric Association and the American Psychological Association discontinued this classification in the 1970s.

More recently, researchers have explored the possible biological basis of homosexuality (Gladue, 1994). The results of hormone studies have been inconsistent. If male homosexuals are given male sex hormones (androgens), their sexual orientation doesn't change; their sexual desire merely increases. A very early prenatal critical period might influence sexual orientation. In the 2nd to 5th months after conception, exposure of the fetus to hormone levels characteristic of females might cause the individual (whether male or female) to become attracted to males (Ellis & Ames, 1987). If this critical period hypothesis turns out to be correct, it would explain why clinicians have found that sexual orientation is difficult, if not impossible, to modify.

With regard to anatomical structures, neuroscientist Simon LeVay (1991) found that an area of the hypothalamus that governs sexual behavior is twice as large (about the size of a grain of sand) in heterosexual males as in homosexual males. This area was found to be about the same size in homosexual males and heterosexual females. Critics of this research point out that many of the homosexuals in the study had AIDS and suggest that their brains could have been altered by the disease.

An individual's sexual orientation—homosexual, heterosexual, or bisexual—is most likely determined by a combination of genetic, hormonal, cognitive, and environmental factors (Baldwin & Baldwin, 1998; Garnets, 2002). Most experts on homosexuality believe that no one factor alone causes homosexuality and that the relative weight of each factor can vary from one individual to the next. In effect, no one knows exactly why some individuals are homosexual. Scientists have a clearer picture of what does *not* cause homosexuality: For example, children raised by gay or lesbian parents or couples are no more likely to be homosexual than are children raised by heterosexual parents (Patterson, 1995, 2000). There also is no evidence that male homosexuality is caused by a dominant mother or a weak father, or that female homosexuality is caused by girls choosing male role models.

How do gays and lesbians adapt to a world in which they are a minority? According to psychologist Laura Brown (1989), gays and lesbians experience life as a minority in a dominant, majority culture. For lesbian women and gay men, developing a *bicultural identity* creates new ways of defining themselves. Brown believes that gays and lesbians adapt best when they do not define themselves in polarities— for instance, either by trying to live in a completely gay or lesbian world divorced from the majority culture or by completely accepting the dictates and biases of the majority culture. Balancing the demands and seeking the benefits of the two cultures—the minority gay/lesbian culture and the majority heterosexual culture—can often lead to more effective coping for homosexuals, says Brown.

For study tools related to this learning goal, see the Study Guide, the CD-ROM, and the Online Learning Center.

Review and Sharpen Your Thinking

3 ***Discuss the motivations for sexual behavior.***
- Describe the biology of sex.
- Identify cognitive and sensory/perceptual factors that affect sexual behavior.
- Summarize the importance of culture in sexual motivation.
- Explain the nature and treatment of psychosexual dysfunctions.
- Characterize sexual behavior and orientation in the United States.

A substance called "Spanish fly" has been promoted as a powerful aphrodisiac. As mentioned, it is not an effective sexual stimulant and can cause severe side effects. Could the placebo effect (discussed in chapter 2) explain people's faith in this and other aphrodisiacs? How?

4 SOCIAL COGNITIVE MOTIVES

| Achievement | Affiliation | Well-Being |

What are some important social cognitive motives and how do they influence behavior?

The previous discussions of hunger and sexual motivation focused to a large degree on physiological factors and on the involvement of the hypothalamus and other brain structures. Although there is a significant cognitive component to sexual behavior, it does not always predominate. This section presents three motives that have strong social cognitive foundations: achievement, affiliation, and well-being.

Achievement

Some people are highly motivated to succeed and spend considerable effort striving to excel—like Lance Armstrong, whose remarkable recovery from cancer was capped by winning the Tour de France, the world's premier bicycle race. But individuals differ in their achievement motivation. Others are not as motivated to succeed and don't work as hard to achieve.

Calvin and Hobbes   by Bill Watterson

Need for Achievement   **Need for achievement** is the desire to accomplish something, to reach a standard of excellence, and to expend effort to excel. Borrowing from Henry Murray's (1938) theory and measurement of personality, psychologist David McClelland (1955) assessed achievement by showing individuals ambiguous pictures that were likely to stimulate achievement-related responses. The individuals were asked to tell stories about the pictures, and their comments were scored according to how strongly they reflected achievement. Researchers have found that individuals whose stories reflect high achievement motivation have a stronger hope for success than fear of failure, are moderate rather than high or low risk takers, and persist with effort when tasks become difficult (Atkinson & Raynor, 1974).

McClelland (1978) also wondered if achievement behavior could be increased by increasing achievement motivation. To find out, he trained the businessmen in a village in India to be more achievement oriented, encouraging them to increase their hope for success, reduce their fear of failure, take moderate risks, and try harder in the face of difficulty. Compared with businessmen in a nearby village, the businessmen that McClelland trained started more new businesses and employed more new people in the 2 years after the training.

Cognitive Factors   Chapter 1 discussed Albert Bandura's social cognitive theory. You might recall that Bandura (1997, 2000, 2001) believes that cognitive factors are an important aspect of understanding behavior. Earlier in this chapter, I highlighted a key cognitive factor in motivation: intrinsic motivation. Intrinsic motivation, which is based on such internal factors as self-determination, curiosity, challenge, and effort, contrasts with extrinsic motivation, which involves external incentives such as rewards and punishments. The following section on attribution shows that intrinsic and extrinsic motivation are often one set of causes that individuals look at as they attempt to explain their behavior.

Attribution   **Attribution theory** states that individuals are motivated to discover the underlying causes of behavior in an effort to make sense out of the behavior. In a way, say attribution theorists, people are like intuitive scientists, seeking the cause behind what happens. Attribution is also discussed in context of social thinking in chapter 16.

The reasons individuals behave the way they do can be classified in a number of ways, but one basic distinction stands out above all others—the distinction between internal causes, such as personality traits or motives, and external causes, which are environmental, situational factors, such as rewards or task difficulty (Heider, 1958). If college students do not do well on a test, do they attribute it to the teacher's plotting

need for achievement The desire to accomplish something, to reach a standard of excellence, and to expend effort to excel.

attribution theory States that individuals are motivated to discover the underlying causes of behavior as part of their effort to make sense of it.

How Goal-Directed Are You?

To evaluate how goal-directed you are, consider how much each of the following statements is like you or not like you.

- I set long-term and short-term goals.
- I set challenging goals that are neither too easy nor beyond my reach.
- I am good at managing my time and setting priorities to make sure I get the most important things done.
- I regularly make "to do" lists and successfully get most items done.
- I set deadlines and consistently meet them.
- I regularly monitor how well I'm progressing toward my goals and make changes in my behavior if necessary.
- When I am under pressure, I still plan my days and weeks in a clear, logical manner.
- I set task-involved, mastery goals rather than ego-involved or work-avoidant goals.

If most of these descriptions characterize you, then you likely are a goal-directed individual. If these statements do not characterize you, then consider ways that you can become more goal-directed.

against them and making the test too difficult (external cause) or to not studying hard enough (internal cause)? The answer to such a question influences how people feel about themselves. If students believe that their performance is the teacher's fault, they will not feel as bad when they do poorly as they will if they believe they did not spend enough time studying.

An extremely important aspect of internal cause for achievement is *effort.* Unlike many causes of success, effort is under a person's control and amenable to change. The importance of effort in achievement is recognized even by children. In one study, third- to sixth-grade students felt that effort was the most effective strategy for good school performance (Skinner, Wellborn, & Connell, 1990).

Goal Setting, Planning, and Monitoring In the discussion of cognitive factors earlier in the chapter, the importance of self-generated goals was emphasized. Goal setting, planning, and self-monitoring are critical aspects of achievement (Pintrich & Schunk, 2002). Goals help individuals to reach their dreams, increase their self-discipline, and maintain interest. Goal setting and planning often work in concert.

Researchers have found that individuals' achievement improves when they set goals that are specific, short term, and challenging (Bandura, 1997; Schunk, 2000). A fuzzy, nonspecific goal is "I want to be successful." A concrete, specific goal is "I want to have a 3.5 average at the end of the semester." You can set both long-term (distal) and short-term (proximal) goals. It is okay to set long-term goals, such as "I want to be a clinical psychologist," but, if you do, make sure that you also create short-term goals as steps along the way, such as "I want to get an A on the next psychology test" or "I will do all of my studying for this class by 4 P.M. Sunday." David McNally (1990), author of *Even Eagles Need a Push,* advises that when individuals set goals and plan how to reach them, they should remind themselves to live their lives one day at a time. Make commitments in bite-size chunks. A house is built one brick at a time; an artist paints one stroke at a time. You also should work in small increments.

Another good strategy is to set challenging goals. A challenging goal is a commitment to self-improvement. Strong interest and involvement in activities are sparked by challenges. Goals that are easy to reach generate little interest or effort. However, unrealistically high goals can bring failure and diminish self-confidence.

Achievement motivation researcher John Nicholls and his colleagues (1979; Nicholls & others, 1990) distinguish among ego-involved goals, task-involved goals, and work-avoidant goals. Individuals with ego-involved goals strive to maximize favorable evaluations and minimize unfavorable ones. Thus ego-involved individuals focus on how smart they will look and on their ability to outperform others. In contrast, individuals with task-involved goals focus more on mastering tasks. They concentrate on how well they can do the task and what they can learn. Individuals with work-avoidant goals try to exert as little effort as possible on a task. A good achievement strategy is to develop task-involved mastery goals rather than ego-involved or work-avoidant goals.

Planning how to reach a goal and monitoring progress toward the goal are critical aspects of achievement (Eccles, Wigfield, & Schiefele, 1998). Researchers have found that high-achieving individuals monitor their own learning and systematically evaluate their progress toward their goals more than low-achieving individuals do (Zimmerman, 2001; Zimmerman & Schunk, 2001). To evaluate how goal directed you are, see the Psychology and Life box.

Sociocultural Factors   In addition to cognitive factors such as attribution, intrinsic motivation, and self-generation of goals, the sociocultural contexts in which we live contribute to our motivation to achieve (Wigfield & Eccles, 2002). This section focuses on comparisons across cultures and ethnicities.

Cross-Cultural Comparisons   People in the United States tend to be more achievement oriented than people in many other countries. One study of 104 societies revealed that parents in nonindustrialized countries placed a lower value on their children's achievement and independence and a higher value on obedience and cooperation than did the parents in industrialized countries (Barry, Child, & Bacon, 1959). In comparisons of Anglo-American children with Mexican and Latino children, the Anglo-American children were more competitive and less cooperative. For example, one study found that Anglo-American children were likelier to keep other children from achieving a goal when they could not achieve the goal themselves (Kagan & Madsen, 1972). Another study showed that Mexican children were more family oriented than Anglo-American children, who tended to be more concerned about themselves (Holtzmann, 1982).

Another series of studies focused on the poor performance of American students on tests of mathematics and science in comparison to students in other countries. In one such study, American eighth- and twelfth-grade students were below the overall national average of 20 countries in math problem solving, geometry, algebra, and calculus (McKnight & others, 1987). In the eighth grade, Japanese students had the highest average scores of all students, and, in the twelfth grade, Chinese students in Hong Kong had the highest scores, followed by Japanese students. In another comparison that focused on 9- and 13-year-olds in 16 countries, Korean and Taiwanese students placed first and second in math achievement (Educational Testing Service, 1992). In this study, U.S. students finished 15th in math and 13th in science (out of 15 countries studied). In more recent cross-cultural comparisons, U.S. students fared a little better, falling in the average range of eighth-grade students in math and science from 45 countries (Atkin & Black, 1997). In this study, Korean, Singapore, and Japanese students scored the highest.

Harold Stevenson and his colleagues (1992, 1995, 1997, 2000) have completed five cross-cultural studies of students in the United States, China, Taiwan, and Japan. In these studies, Asian students consistently outperform American students. And the longer they are in school, the wider the gap between Asian and American students becomes—the lowest difference is in the first grade, the highest in eleventh grade (the highest grade studied). To learn more about the reasons for these large cross-cultural differences, Stevenson and his colleagues spent thousands of hours observing in classrooms, as well as interviewing and surveying teachers, students, and parents. They found that Asian teachers spent more time teaching math than American teachers did: For example, more than one-fourth of total classroom time in the first grade was spent on math instruction in Japan, compared with only one-tenth of the time in U.S. first-grade classrooms. Also, Asian students were in school an average of 240 days a year compared to 178 days in the United States.

Differences in Asian and American parents were also found. American parents had much lower expectations for their children's education and achievement than Asian parents did. Also, American parents were likelier to believe that their children's math achievement is due to innate ability, whereas Asian parents were likelier to say that their children's math achievement is the consequence of effort and training (see figure 11.10). Asian students were likelier than American students to do math homework, and Asian parents were far likelier to help their children with their math homework than American parents were (Chen & Stevenson, 1989).

In another cross-cultural comparison of math education, researchers analyzed videotapes of eighth-grade teachers' instruction in the United States, Japan, and Germany (Stigler & Hiebert, 1997). Differences included these: (1) Japanese students spent less time solving routine math problems and more time inventing, analyzing, and proving than American or German students; (2) Japanese teachers engaged in

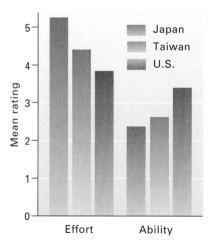

FIGURE 11.10 Mothers' Beliefs About the Factors Responsible for Children's Math Achievement in Three Countries In one study, mothers in Japan and Taiwan were likelier to believe that their children's math achievement was due to effort rather than to innate ability, whereas U.S. mothers were likelier to believe their children's math achievement was due to innate ability (Stevenson, Lee, & Stigler, 1986).

Asian students score considerably higher than U.S. students on math achievement tests. *What are some possible explanations for these findings?*

more direct lecturing than American or German teachers; and (3) Japanese teachers were likelier to emphasize math thinking, whereas American and German teachers were likelier to stress math skills (solving a specific problem or using a specific formula). Also noticeable was how much emphasis there is on collaborative planning with other teachers in Japanese math education.

An important conclusion from these cross-cultural studies is that learning and achievement take time. The more time students spend learning, the likelier they are to learn the material and achieve high standards.

Ethnic Comparisons Until recently, researchers studying achievement focused almost exclusively on White males, and any studies of achievement in ethnic minorities measured them against standards of achievements for White males. As a result, many researchers unfortunately concluded that ethnic minorities were somehow deficient in achievement (Gibbs & Huang, 1989).

In addition, most studies on ethnic minorities do not take into account socioeconomic status. Socioeconomic status (SES) is determined by a combination of occupation, education, and income. When both ethnicity and socioeconomic status are taken into account in the same study, socioeconomic status tends to be a far better predictor of achievement than is ethnicity (Graham, 1986, 2001). For example, middle-SES individuals, regardless of their ethnic background, have higher aspirations and expectations than low-SES individuals do. Sandra Graham (1986) has found that middle-SES African American children do not fit the stereotypes of either deviant or special populations. They, like middle-SES White children, have high expectations for their own achievement and understand that failure is often due to lack of effort rather than to luck.

Achievement Applications Findings about achievement can be applied to many different aspects of life. On a personal level, attribution, intrinsic motivation, goal setting, planning, and monitoring can be used to reach educational, career, and financial goals, even to find fulfillment. In the workplace, managers apply techniques based on achievement research to motivate employees.

The Workplace Work is what most of us will do at least half of our waking hours for more than 40 years of our lives. *Industrial/organizational (I/O) psychology* is the branch of psychology that focuses on the workplace—both the workers and the organization that employs them—to make work more enjoyable and productive.

The workplace is characterized by both intrinsic and extrinsic motivation. An important I/O task is to select employees who will be intrinsically motivated to do the job required. Another important task is to figure out how to extrinsically motivate employees to do their best work possible. Among possible reinforcements or incentives are bonuses, awards, time off, promotions, and praise. For example, an I/O psychologist might recommend that the company initiate an "Employee of the Month" program.

UCLA psychologist Sandra Graham talking with a group of young boys about motivation. Dr. Graham has conducted research showing that middle-class African American children—like their White counterparts—have high achievement expectations and attribute their failures to lack of effort, rather than to lack of luck.

Good leaders know how to motivate employees. The contemporary view of effective leadership in the workplace involves creating a vision for others to follow, establishing values and ethics, and transforming the way an organization does business to improve its effectiveness and efficiency (Nickels, McHugh, & McHugh, 2002).

The workplace is changing from a context in which a few people dictate what others do to a context in which all employees work together to reach common goals. Participating in an organization's decision making gives employees a sense of intrinsic motivation and self-determination that is lacking when they are simply told what to do by superiors.

Goal setting, planning, and monitoring are seen as important aspects of motivation in the workplace (Ilgen, 2000). I/O psychologists advise companies to guide employees in setting goals, planning how to achieve them, and monitoring their progress toward goals.

I/O psychologists attempt to influence the motivation of employees through *job design*. In this case, the goal is to design jobs so that employees will believe that their needs are met in a way that also meets the organization's goals. Recent emphasis in job design has focused on modifying jobs so that they will allow employees to have more control, autonomy, feedback, and opportunity for involvement in their work (Ilgen, 2001).

Another aspect of motivation that interests I/O psychologists is whether workers are more productive and happier when they work individually or in groups. Historically, Americans have worked individually. Employees in many Eastern countries, such as China, Japan, and Korea, have traditionally worked as teams. In recent years, many American companies have increasingly emphasized working in teams and groups.

Sports Athletes tend to be achievement-oriented individuals, at least in their sports domain. Some athletes turn to sport psychologists for help in achieving their full potential. For example, in his amazing rise to the world's best golfer, Tiger Woods benefited from the advice of a team of advisors and coaches, including sport psychologist Jay Brunza. *Sport psychology* is a relatively new field that applies psychological principles to improving sports performance and the enjoyment of sports.

Many sport psychology techniques come from the cognitive and behavioral perspectives. Five techniques that many sport psychologists use to improve the motivation and performance of athletes are

- *Emphasize the process rather than the outcome.* Legendary Green Bay Packers football coach Vince Lombardi once said, "Winning isn't everything; it is the only thing." Today, however, sport psychologists advise against this type of thinking because it can actually take the athlete's focus away from immediate performance. Sport psychologists encourage athletes to immerse themselves in what they are doing and not worry about the outcome. Focusing on the achievement process and the task at hand has been described as *mastery motivation,* in contrast with focusing on achievement outcome and winning, described as *performance motivation* (Henderson & Dweck, 1990; Treasure & Roberts, 2001).
- *Use cognitive restructuring and positive self-talk.* Often athletes in a slump think and say negative things about themselves. A sport psychologist might get them to cognitively restructure their thoughts and words more positively. For example, if a baseball player has been in a hitting slump for 3 weeks, a sport psychologist would encourage the player to think more about his overall successful batting average for the entire year to help rebuild his confidence.
- *Overcome adversity.* Adverse, difficult circumstances crop up for athletes, not just in sports but in life as well. Consider Lance Armstrong's tremendous struggle with life-threatening cancer. His ability to cope and overcome this adversity strengthened his motivation. Former Wimbledon tennis champion Chuck McKinley said on a number of occasions, "In becoming a champion, you learn a lot more from your losses than from your wins." Setbacks become an opportunity for learning, opening the way for growth and improvement.
- *Use deep breathing and muscle relaxation.* Some athletes get nervous as the competition is about to begin. Deep breathing and muscle relaxation can help them calm down and concentrate better. Deep breathing and muscle relaxation are discussed further in chapter 15.
- *Use visualization.* In visualization, athletes imagine how they will perform. The sport psychologist might work with a golfer to visualize the golf ball going in the hole after it is putted or with a tennis player to visualize clean, fluid strokes. Sport psychologists sometime review video clips of the athlete's performance, select the best performance, and have the athlete watch those clips as part of developing positive imagery. Psychologist Richard Suinn caught the interest of athletes when he worked with the U.S. Olympic ski team. He divided the team into two groups of equally matched ability, one group using visual imagery, the other group not using it. The group using visual imagery improved so much that the coach called off the experiment and insisted that all the skiers use visual imagery (Suinn, 1976). In the 2000 Olympics, more than 20 sport psychologists worked with U.S. athletes and coaches.

Achievement is an important social cognitive motive. But people not only have varying degrees of need for achievement, they also vary in the extent to which they are motivated to be with other people.

Affiliation

Are you the kind of person who likes to be around people a lot? Or would you rather stay home and read a book? The **need for affiliation** is the motive to be with other people. This involves establishing, maintaining, and restoring warm, close, personal relationships. Our need for affiliation is reflected in the importance of parents' nurturance in children's development, the intimate moments of sharing private thoughts in friendship, the uncomfortable feelings we have when we are lonely, and the powerful attraction we have for someone else when we are in love.

need for affiliation The motive to be with other people.

Although each of us has a need for affiliation or relatedness, some people have a stronger need than others. Some of us are motivated to be surrounded by lots of friends and feel as if something is drastically missing from our lives if we are not in love with someone and they with us. Others of us don't have such a strong need for relatedness. We don't fall apart if we don't have friends around us all of the time, and we don't sit around all day in an anxious state because we don't have someone in love with us.

Cultures vary in how strongly they promote the need for relatedness. Many Western cultures—such as the United States, Canada, and Western European countries—emphasize individual achievement, independence, and self-reliance. Many Eastern cultures—such as China, Japan, and Korea—emphasize affiliation, cooperation, and interdependence (Triandis, 2000). Affiliation and relatedness are believed to be an important dimension of well-being.

Well-Being

Are you motivated to live the good life? What constitutes living the good life and well-being? What do you think? What would your list of items be for living the good life and well-being? Might it include happiness? Being able to spend time with the people you love? And what about intelligence and wisdom? Might they be important dimensions of the good life and well-being? Some people might value happiness more than intelligence and wisdom; others might value intelligence and wisdom more than happiness (King & Pennebaker, 1998).

Well-being is subjective. Indeed, when researchers study well-being, they often refer to it as *subjective well-being*. Richard Ryan and Edward Deci (2000) recently proposed that three factors need to be present for well-being:

- *Competence.* This sense of mastery entails the motivation to do whatever you attempt well. It involves using your intelligence and skills effectively.
- *Autonomy.* This consists of doing things independently. It involves intrinsic motivation, self-initiation, and self-determination.
- *Affiliation.* As we have seen, affiliation has to do with the need to be with other people.

In Ryan and Deci's view, when the needs for competence, autonomy, and affiliation are satisfied, the result is enhanced well-being. When these needs are thwarted, the result is diminished well-being. They believe that excessive control by others, non-optimal challenges, and lack of connectedness result in a lack of initiative and responsibility and, in some cases, produce distress and psychological problems.

Some critics argue, though, that you can have too much autonomy (Schwartz, 2000). In this view, autonomy, freedom, and self-determination can become excessive, and when that happens people have an imbalance in their lives that may undermine their competence and affiliation. Thus living the good life and attaining well-being may involve a balance of the three components of competence, autonomy, and affiliation.

As was mentioned previously, cultures often vary in the extent to which they emphasize autonomy or affiliation. Thus what individuals believe constitutes the good life and well-being in some cultures might include a stronger emphasis on autonomy (for example, the United States), in others a stronger emphasis on affiliation (for example, Japan).

Carol Ryff and Burton Singer (1998) have conducted research on well-being for a number of decades. Based on their research, they concluded that living the good life and experiencing well-being involves both positive physical health and positive psychological health. Furthermore, they argued that positive psychological health is most likely to be achieved by leading a life of purpose (a sense of doing something meaningful), having quality connections with others (affiliation and relatedness), having positive self-regard (self-esteem), and having mastery (a sense of competence and doing things effectively).

Let's examine Lance Armstrong's well-being and see how these dimensions are involved.

- *Physical well-being.* Lance was a great athlete before his cancer. However, the cancer threatened his physical well-being. Rather than dwelling on this major physical setback, he turned the situation into a positive life experience by challenging himself to become physically stronger than he was before the cancer and to focus on his psychological well-being as well.
- *Psychological well-being.* Lance is extremely competent in his profession; indeed, the very best in the world. Becoming a great cyclist required considerable autonomy, self-determination, and intrinsic motivation. He may have focused too much on developing those attributes, though. During his bout with cancer, he realized that his psychological well-being required more than autonomy. He recognized that he needed to develop better relationships with others. This change in motivation resulted in his marriage and the birth of a son, which he says has greatly increased his happiness.

mhhe com/
santrockp7

For study tools related to this learning goal, see the Study Guide, the CD-ROM, and the Online Learning Center.

Review and Sharpen Your Thinking

4   ***Characterize the social cognitive motives and how they influence behavior.***

- Discuss the need for achievement and the factors that motivate people to excel.
- Describe the concept of affiliation.
- Identify the components of well-being.

Make a list of five factors that you believe are the most important aspects of your well-being. How well do they match up with the factors discussed in the chapter?

5   EMOTION

The Biology of Emotion   **Behavioral Factors**   **Classifying Emotions**

Cognitive Factors   **Sociocultural Factors**

What are some views of emotion?

As Lance Armstrong rode onto the Champs-Elysseé at the end of the Tour de France, he felt a swell of emotion. He was about to win cycling's most storied race. With joy etched across his face, in front of thousands of happy fans, Lance was awarded the Tour de France trophy. His third trophy was no less thrilling than his first.

As was mentioned at the beginning of the chapter, motivation and emotion are closely linked. Think about sex, which often is associated with joy; about aggression, which usually is associated with anger; and about achievement, which is associated with pride, joy, and anxiety. The terms *motivation* and *emotion* both come from the Latin word *movere*, which means "to move." Both motivation and emotion spur us into action.

Just as there are different kinds and intensities of motivation, so it is with emotions. A person can be more motivated to eat than to have sex and at different times can be more or less hungry or more or less interested in having sex. Similarly, a person can be happy—and be fairly happy to ecstatic—or angry—and be annoyed to fuming.

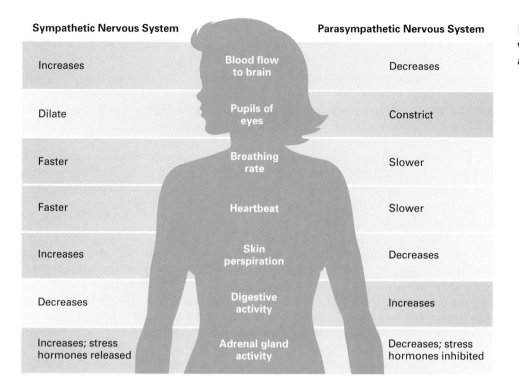

Sympathetic Nervous System		Parasympathetic Nervous System
Increases	Blood flow to brain	Decreases
Dilate	Pupils of eyes	Constrict
Faster	Breathing rate	Slower
Faster	Heartbeat	Slower
Increases	Skin perspiration	Decreases
Decreases	Digestive activity	Increases
Increases; stress hormones released	Adrenal gland activity	Decreases; stress hormones inhibited

FIGURE 11.11 **The Autonomic Nervous System and Its Role in Arousing and Calming the Body**

Defining emotion is difficult because it is not easy to tell when a person is in an emotional state. Are you in an emotional state when your heart beats fast, your palms sweat, and your stomach churns? Or are you in an emotional state when you think about how much you are in love with someone? Or when you smile or grimace? The body, the mind, and the face play important roles in emotion, although psychologists debate which of these components is the most important aspect of emotion and how they mix to produce emotional experiences (Davidson, Scherer, & Goldsmith, 2002). For our purposes, **emotion** is defined as feeling, or affect, that can involve physiological arousal (a fast heartbeat, for example), conscious experience (thinking about being in love with someone, for example), and behavioral expression (a smile or grimace, for example).

The Biology of Emotion

As you drive down the highway, the fog thickens. Suddenly you see a pile of cars in front of you. Your mind temporarily freezes, your muscles tighten, your stomach becomes queasy, and your heart feels like it is going to pound out of your chest. You immediately slam on the brakes and try to veer away from the pile of cars. Tires screech, windshield glass flies, and metal smashes. Then all is quiet. After a few short seconds, you realize that you are alive. You find that you can climb out of the car. Your fear turns to joy, as you sense your luck in not being hurt. In a couple of seconds, the joy turns to anger. You loudly ask, "Who caused this accident?" As you moved through the emotions of fear, joy, and anger, your body changed.

Arousal Recall from chapter 3 that the *autonomic nervous system (ANS)* takes messages to and from the body's internal organs, monitoring such processes as breathing, heart rate, and digestion. The ANS is divided into the sympathetic and the parasympathetic nervous systems (see figure 11.11). The *sympathetic nervous system (SNS)* is involved in the body's arousal; it is responsible for a rapid reaction to a stressor, sometimes is referred to as the fight-or-flight response. The SNS immediately causes an increase in blood pressure, a faster heart rate, more rapid breathing for greater oxygen intake, and more efficient blood flow to the brain and major muscle

emotion Feeling, or affect, that can involve physiological arousal, conscious experience, and behavioral expression.

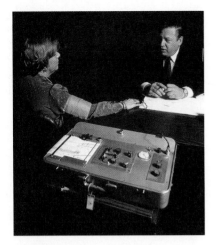

Examiners use a polygraph to tell if someone is lying. A polygraph monitors changes in the body believed to be influenced by emotional states. Controversy has swirled about the polygraph's use because it is unreliable.

groups. All of these changes prepare us for action. At the same time the body stops digesting food, because it is not necessary for immediate action (which could explain why just before an exam, students usually are not hungry).

The *parasympathetic nervous system (PNS)* calms the body. Whereas the sympathetic nervous system prepares the individual for fighting or running away, the parasympathetic nervous system promotes relaxation and healing. When the PNS is activated, heart rate and blood pressure drop, stomach activity and food digestion increase, and breathing slows.

The sympathetic and parasympathetic nervous systems evolved to improve the human species' likelihood for survival, but it does not take a life-threatening situation to activate them. Emotions such as anger are associated with elevated SNS activity as exemplified in heightened blood pressure and heart rate. But states of happiness and contentment also activate the SNS to a lesser extent.

Measuring Arousal Because arousal includes a physiological response, researchers have been intrigued by how to accurately measure it. One aspect of emotional arousal is *galvanic skin response (GSR),* which involves an increase in the skin's electrical conductivity when sweat gland activity increases. Measurement of this electrical activity provides an index of arousal that has been used in a number of studies of emotion.

Another measure of arousal is the **polygraph,** a machine used by examiners to try to determine if someone is lying; it monitors changes in the body—heart rate, breathing, and electrodermal response (an index detecting skin resistance to passage of a weak electric current)—thought to be influenced by emotional states.

In a typical polygraph test, an individual is asked a number of neutral questions and several key, less neutral questions. If the individual's heart rate, breathing, and electrodermal responses increase substantially when the key questions are asked, the individual is assumed to be lying.

How accurate is the lie detector at doing its job? Although the degree of arousal to a series of questions is measured through simple physiological changes, no one has found a unique physiological response to deception (Lykken, 1987, 2001). Heart rate and breathing can increase for reasons other than lying, making it difficult to interpret the physiological indicators of arousal.

Accurately identifying truth or deception is linked with the skill of the examiner and the skill of the individual being examined. Body movements and the presence of certain drugs in the person's system can interfere with the polygraph's accuracy. Sometimes the mere presence of the polygraph and the individual's belief that it is accurate in detecting deception triggers a confession of guilt. Police may use the polygraph in this way to get a suspect to confess. However, in too many instances it has been misused and misrepresented. Experts argue that the polygraph errs just under 50 percent of the time, especially as it cannot distinguish between such feelings as anxiety and guilt (Iacono & Lykken, 1997).

The Employee Polygraph Protection Act of 1988 restricts polygraph testing outside government agencies, and most courts do not accept the results of polygraph testing. However, some psychologists defend the polygraph's use, saying that polygraph results are as sound as other, admissible forms of evidence, such as hair fiber analysis (Honts, 1998). The majority of psychologists, though, argue against the polygraph's use because of its inability to tell who is lying and who is not (Saxe, 1988).

polygraph A machine that monitors physiological changes thought to be influenced by emotional states; it is used by examiners to try to determine if someone is lying.

James-Lange theory States that emotion results from physiological states triggered by stimuli in the environment.

James-Lange and Cannon-Bard Theories Imagine that you and your date are enjoying a picnic in the country. Suddenly, a bull runs across the field toward you. Why are you afraid? Two well-known theories of emotion that involve physiological processes provide answers to this question.

Common sense tells you that you are trembling and running away from the bull because you are afraid. But William James (1890/1950) and Carl Lange (1922) said emotion works in the opposite way. The **James-Lange theory** states that emotion results from physiological states triggered by stimuli in the environment: Emotion occurs *after* physiological reactions. Moreover, each emotion, from anger to rapture,

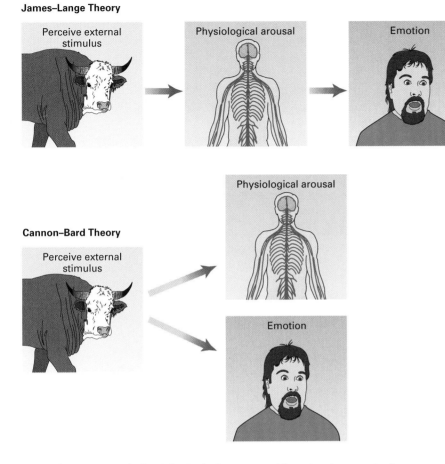

James–Lange Theory

Perceive external stimulus

Physiological arousal

Emotion

Cannon–Bard Theory

Perceive external stimulus

Physiological arousal

Emotion

FIGURE 11.12 **James-Lange and Cannon-Bard Theories**

has a distinct set of physiological changes, evident in changes in heart rate, breathing patterns, sweating, and other responses. Essentially, the James-Lange theory proposes that after the initial perception, the experience of the emotion results from the perception of one's own physiological changes.

Let's see how the James-Lange theory would explain fear in the situation with the bull. You see the bull scratching his hoof on the ground, and you begin to run away. Your aroused body then sends sensory messages to your brain, at which point emotion is perceived. According to this theory, you do not run away because you are afraid; rather, you are afraid because you are running away. In other words, you perceive a stimulus in the environment, your body responds, and you interpret the body's reaction as emotion. In one of James' own examples, you perceive you have lost your fortune, you cry, and then interpret the crying as feeling sad. This goes against the commonsense sequence of losing your fortune, feeling sorry, and then crying.

Walter Cannon (1927) objected to the assumption in the James-Lange theory that each emotional experience has its own particular set of physiological changes. He argued that different emotions could not be associated with specific physiological changes because autonomic nervous system responses are too diffuse and slow to account for rapid and differentiated emotional responses.

To understand Cannon's view, imagine the bull and the picnic once again. Seeing the bull scratching its hoof causes the thalamus of your brain to do two things simultaneously: First, it stimulates your autonomic nervous system to produce the physiological changes involved in emotion (increased heart rate, rapid breathing); second, it sends messages to your cerebral cortex, where the experience of emotion is perceived. Philip Bard (1934) supported this theory, and so the theory became known as the **Cannon-Bard theory,** the theory that emotion and physiological reactions occur simultaneously. In the Cannon-Bard theory, the body plays a less important role than in the James-Lange theory. Figure 11.12 shows how the James-Lange and Cannon-Bard theories differ.

Cannon-Bard theory States that emotion and physiological states occur simultaneously.

FIGURE 11.13 Direct and Indirect Brain Pathways in the Emotion of Fear Information about fear can follow two pathways in the brain when an individual sees a snake. The direct pathway (*broken arrow*) conveys information rapidly from the thalamus to the amygdala. The indirect pathway (*solid arrows*) transmits information more slowly from the thalamus to the sensory cortex (here, the visual cortex), then to the amygdala.

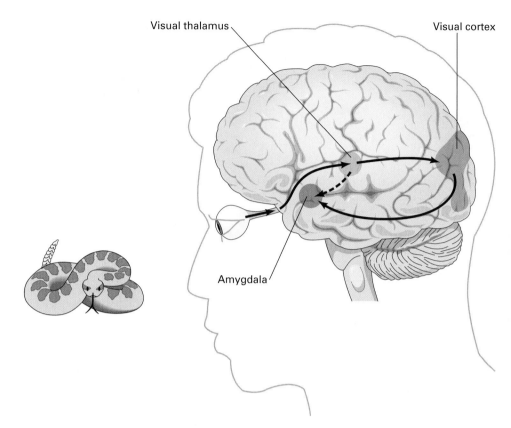

The question of whether or not emotions involve discrete autonomic nervous system responses continues to be debated (Keltner & Ekman, 2000). Recent studies have documented some emotion-specific autonomic nervous system responses (Lang, Davis, & Ohman, 2000). For example, fear, anger, and sadness are associated with increased heart rate, but disgust is not. Also, anger is linked with increased blood flow to the hands, an effect that is not triggered by fear.

Neural Circuits and Neurotransmitters Contemporary researchers are more interested in charting the neural circuitry of emotions and discovering the role of neurotransmitters in emotion than was the case in the early twentieth century. The focus of much of their work has been on the amygdala, the almond-shaped structure in the limbic system discussed in chapter 3. The amygdala houses circuits that are activated when we experience negative emotions.

Joseph LeDoux (1996, 2000, 2001, 2002; LaBar & LeDoux, 2002) has conducted a number of research studies that focus on the neural circuitry of one emotion: fear. The amygdala plays a central role in fear. When the amygdala determines that danger is present, it shifts into high gear, marshaling the resources of the brain in an effort to protect the organism from harm. This fear system was designed by evolution to detect and respond to predators and other types of natural dangers that threaten survival or territory.

The amygdala receives neurons from all of the senses: sight, hearing, smell, touch. If a danger is communicated by any of these neurons, the amygdala is activated and immediately sends out messages to bodily organs that respond in ways to prevent harm to the organism.

The brain circuitry that involves the emotion of fear can follow two pathways: a direct pathway from the thalamus to the amygdala or an indirect pathway from the thalamus through the sensory cortex to the amygdala (see figure 11.13). The direct pathway does not convey detailed information about the stimulus, but it has the advantage of speed. And speed clearly is an important characteristic of information available to an organism facing a threat to its survival. The indirect pathway carries nerve impulses from the sensory organs (eye, ear, for example) to the thalamus (recall that the thalamus is a relay station for incoming sensory stimuli); from the thalamus, the nerve impulses travel to the sensory cortex, which then sends appropriate signals to the amygdala.

Recall from chapter 9 that the amygdala is linked with emotional memories. LeDoux (2000, 2001) says that the amygdala hardly ever forgets. This quality is useful because, once we learn that something is dangerous, we don't have to relearn it. However, we pay a penalty for this ability. Many people carry fears and anxieties around with them that they would like to get rid of but cannot seem to shake. Part of the reason for this dilemma is that the amygdala is well connected to the cerebral cortex, in which thinking and decision making primarily occur (McGaugh & Cahill, 2002). The amygdala is in a much better position to influence the cerebral cortex than the other way around, because it sends more connections to the cerebral cortex than it gets back. This may explain why it is so hard to control our emotions, and why, once fear is learned, it is so hard to erase.

LeDoux (2000, 2002) says that it is unlikely that the amygdala mediates all emotions. There is some evidence that the amygdala participates in positive emotions, but that role is not yet well understood (Lane & others, 1997; Park & others, 2001; Zalla & others, 2000).

Researchers are also finding that the brain's cerebral hemispheres may be involved in understanding emotion. Richard Davidson and his colleagues (2000; Davidson, Shackman, & Pizzagalli, 2002; Reuter-Lorenz & Davidson, 1981) have shown that the cerebral hemispheres work differently in approach- and withdrawal-related emotions. Approach-related emotions, such as happiness, are linked more strongly with left hemisphere brain activity, whereas withdrawal-related emotions, such as disgust, show stronger activity in the brain's right hemisphere.

In addition to charting the main brain structures involved in neural pathways of emotions, researchers are intrigued by the roles that neurotransmitters play in these pathways. Endorphins and dopamine might be involved in positive emotions such as happiness, and norepinephrine might function in regulating arousal (Berridge & O'Neil, 2001; Panskepp, 1993; Robbins, 2000).

Cognitive Factors

Does emotion depend on the tides of the mind? Are we happy only when we think we are happy? Cognitive theories of emotion center on the premise that emotion always has a cognitive component (Derryberry & Reed, 2002; Ellsworth, 2002). Thinking is said to be responsible for feelings of love and hate, joy and sadness. Cognitive theorists also recognize the role of the brain and body in emotion, but they give cognitive processes the main credit for emotion.

The Two-Factor Theory of Emotion   In the **two-factor theory of emotion** developed by Stanley Schachter and Jerome Singer (1962), emotion is determined by two factors: physiological arousal and cognitive labeling (see figure 11.14). They argued that we look to the external world for an explanation of why we are aroused. We interpret external cues and label the emotion. For example, if you feel good after someone has made a pleasant comment to you, you might label the emotion "happy." If you feel bad after you have done something wrong, you may label the feeling "guilty."

To test their theory of emotion, Schachter and Singer (1962) injected volunteer participants with epinephrine, a drug that produces high arousal. After participants were given the drug, they observed someone else behave in either a euphoric way (shooting papers at a wastebasket) or an angry way (stomping out of the room). As predicted, the euphoric and angry behavior influenced the participants' cognitive interpretation of their own arousal. When they were with a happy person, they rated

two-factor theory of emotion
Schachter and Singer's theory that emotion is determined by two main factors: physiological arousal and cognitive labeling.

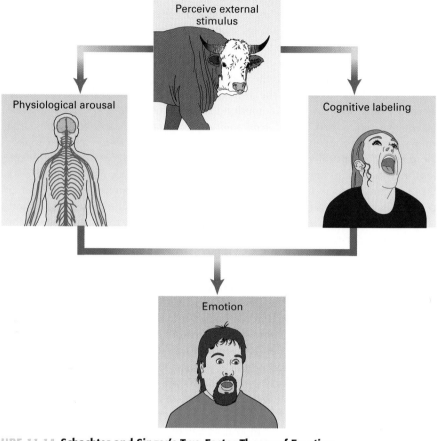

FIGURE 11.14 **Schachter and Singer's Two-Factor Theory of Emotion**

FIGURE 11.15 **Capilano River Bridge Experiment: Misinterpreted Arousal Intensifies Emotional Experiences**
(*Top*) The precarious Capilano River Bridge in British Columbia. (*Bottom*) The experiment in progress. An attractive woman approached men while they were crossing the bridge; she asked them to make up a story to help her with a creativity project. She also made the same request on a lower, much safer bridge. The men on the Capilano River Bridge told sexier stories, probably because they were aroused by the fear or excitement of being up so high on a swaying bridge and interpreted their arousal as sexual attraction for the female interviewer.

themselves as happy; when they were with an angry person, they said they were angry. But this effect occurred only when the participants were not told about the true effects of the injection. When they were told that the drug would increase their heart rate and make them jittery, they said the reason for their own arousal was the drug, not the other person's behavior.

Psychologists have had difficulty replicating the Schachter and Singer experiment, but, in general, research supports the belief that misinterpreted arousal intensifies emotional experiences (Leventhal & Tomarken, 1986). An intriguing study by Dutton and Aron (1974), substantiates this conclusion. In the study, an attractive woman approached men while they were walking across the Capilano River Bridge in British Columbia. Only those without a female companion were approached. The woman asked the men to make up a brief story for a project she was doing on creativity. The Capilano River Bridge sways precariously more than 200 feet above rapids and rocks (see figure 11.15). The female interviewer made the same request of other men crossing a much safer, lower bridge. The men on the Capilano River Bridge told more sexually oriented stories and rated the female interviewer more attractive than did men on the lower, less frightening bridge.

The Primacy Debate: Cognition or Emotion? Richard Lazarus (1991) believes cognitive activity is a precondition for emotion. He says that we cognitively appraise ourselves and our social circumstances. These appraisals, which include values, goals, commitments, beliefs, and expectations, determine our emotions. People may feel happy because they have a deep religious commitment, angry because they did not get the raise they anticipated, or fearful because they expect to fail an exam.

Robert Zajonc (1984) disagrees with Lazarus. Emotions are primary, he says, and our thoughts are a result of them. Who is right? Both likely are correct. Lazarus refers

Does Extrinsic Motivation Undermine Intrinsic Motivation?

The distinction between intrinsic and extrinsic motivation is well established in psychology. The basic idea is that we can be motivated by internal (intrinsic) factors, like self-generated goals, or external (extrinsic) factors, like praise or a monetary reward. It is commonly argued that intrinsic motivation is preferable to extrinsic motivation because it leads to more positive outcomes (Deci, 2001). Also, extrinsic motivation is thought to reduce intrinsic motivation (Lepper, Greene, & Nisbett, 1973). A wide variety of social (extrinsic) events, such as deadlines, surveillance (Enzle & Anderson, 1993) and coercive rewards (Enzle, Roggeveen, & Look, 1991), can reduce the enjoyment (intrinsic motivation) associated with work, play, and study. These ideas have exerted a broad influence in educational and occupational settings, where teachers and employers seek to increase the intrinsic motivation of their students and employees, respectively (Stipek, 2002; Wigfield & Eccles, 2002).

Recently, however, two reviews of studies on intrinsic and extrinsic motivation (Deci & others, 1999; Cameron & others, 2001) reached opposite conclusions. Edward Deci and his colleagues (1999) analyzed 128 studies and concluded that the main negative effect of external rewards was to restrict self-determination and interfere with intrinsic motivation. In contrast, an analysis of 145 studies by Judy Cameron and her colleagues (2001) yielded mixed results. Cameron's group found that extrinsic rewards sometimes produced the expected negative effects on intrinsic motivation, but that sometimes they had a positive effect or no effect at all. The true state of affairs, they suggest, is that extrinsic motivation has no overall effect on intrinsic motivation.

For example, some psychologists argue that tangible reinforcers, such as money or prizes, often undermine intrinsic motivation, while verbal reinforcers, such as praise, can actually enhance intrinsic motivation (Carton, 1996). Thus, paying a beginning reader money to read books may undermine that child's interest in reading, but praising that child for good reading may increase the child's interest. Similarly, Cameron (2001) believes that extrinsic motivation undermines intrinsic motivation when intrinsic motivation is high but can be very helpful when intrinsic motivation is low. Thus, many beginning readers are motivated to read and may actually lose interest if they are reinforced for reading. In contrast, children who are not internally motivated to read may benefit from reinforcement and encouragement until their intrinsic motivation increases.

The problem, according to Cameron (2001), lies in the rigid acceptance of general statements about motivation, such as "extrinsic motivation reduces internal motivation." In the case of beginning readers, using this statement as a guiding principle may not damage the intrinsic motivation of motivated readers, but it may also leave poorly motivated beginning readers with little reason to practice their reading. Cameron argues that people often do things that are not intrinsically motivating (such as mowing the lawn or studying mathematics) and that without external rewards, we may simply lose interest in doing them. In such cases, extrinsic motivation may help foster intrinsic motivation in an activity. For example, a creative mathematics teacher might use rewards, such as extra credit, math games, and verbal praise, as a way to instill a life-long love of mathematics.

Cameron (2001) suggests that we need a better understanding of extrinsic rewards and intrinsic motivation, to distinguish between the effects of verbal and material reinforcement, for example, and between weak and strong intrinsic motivation. A richer understanding of intrinsic and extrinsic motivation might make it possible to better predict when extrinsic motivation will reduce, increase, or not affect intrinsic motivation. We might then be able to help more employees and students develop the deep intrinsic motivation that most of us agree is indispensable to well-being.

What do you think?
- Can you think of examples from your own life where your intrinsic motivation was reduced by external rewards? Increased by external rewards?
- What are some other factors that might determine whether extrinsic motivation influences intrinsic motivation?
- If you were a classroom teacher and a child in your class was not motivated to learn, how would you use intrinsic and/or extrinsic motivation to help the child become more motivated to learn?

mainly to a cluster of related events that occur over a period of time, whereas Zajonc describes single events or a simple preference for one stimulus over another. Lazarus speaks about love over the course of months and years, a sense of value to the community, and plans for retirement; Zajonc talks about a car accident, an encounter with a snake, and liking ice cream better than spinach. Some of our emotional reactions are virtually instantaneous and probably do not involve cognitive appraisal, such as shrieking on detecting a snake. Other emotional circumstances, especially those that occur over a long period of time, such as a depressed mood or anger toward a friend, are likelier to involve cognitive appraisal. Indeed, the direct and indirect brain pathways described earlier support the idea that some of our emotional reactions do not involve deliberate thinking, whereas others do (LeDoux, 2000, 2001).

Behavioral Factors

Remember that our definition of emotion includes not only physiological and cognitive components but also a behavioral component. The behavioral component can be verbal or nonverbal. Verbally, a person might show love for someone by professing it verbally or might display anger by saying some nasty things. Nonverbally, a person might smile, frown, show a fearful expression, look down, or slouch.

The most interest in the behavioral dimension of emotion has focused on the nonverbal behavior of facial expressions. Emotion researchers have been intrigued by people's ability to detect emotion from a person's facial expression. In a typical research study, participants, shown photographs like those in figure 11.16, are usually able to identify these six emotions: happiness, anger, sadness, surprise, disgust, and fear (Ekman & O'Sullivan, 1991).

Might our facial expressions not only reflect our emotions but also influence them? The **facial feedback hypothesis** states that facial expressions can influence emotions, as well as reflect them. In this view, facial muscles send signals to the brain, which help individuals to recognize the emotion they are experiencing (Keillor & others, 2002). For example, we feel happier when we smile and sadder when we frown.

Support for the facial feedback hypothesis comes from an experiment by Ekman and his colleagues (1983). In this study, professional actors moved their facial muscles in very precise ways, such as raising their eyebrows and pulling them together, raising their upper eyelids, and stretching their lips horizontally back to their ears (you might want to try this out yourself). They were asked to hold their expression for 10 seconds, during which time the researchers measured their heart rate and body temperature. When they moved facial muscles in the ways described, they showed a rise in heart rate and a steady body temperature, physiological reactions that characterize fear. When the actors made an angry expression with their faces (eyes have a penetrating stare, brows are drawn together and downward, and lips are pressed together or opened and pushed forward), their heart rate and body temperature both increased. The concept involved in the facial feedback hypothesis might sound familiar. It provides support for the James-Lange theory of emotion discussed earlier—namely, that emotional experiences can be generated by changes in and awareness of our own bodily states.

Sociocultural Factors

Are the facial expressions that are associated with different emotions largely innate, or do they vary across cultures? Are there gender variations in emotion?

Culture and the Expression of Emotion In *The Expression of the Emotions in Man and Animals,* Charles Darwin (1872/1965) stated that the facial expressions of human beings are innate, not learned; are the same in all cultures around the world; and

facial feedback hypothesis States that facial expressions can influence emotions, as well as reflect them.

FIGURE 11.16 **Recognizing Emotions in Facial Expressions** Look at the six photographs and determine the emotion reflected in each of the six faces. (*Top*) happiness, anger, sadness (*Bottom*) surprise, disgust, fear

evolved from the emotions of animals. Darwin compared the similarity of human snarls of anger with the growls of dogs and the hisses of cats. He compared the giggling of chimpanzees when they are tickled under their arms with human laughter.

Today psychologists still believe that emotions, especially facial expressions of emotion, have strong biological ties (Goldsmith, 2002). For example, children who are blind from birth and have never observed the smile or frown on another person's face smile or frown in the same way that children with normal vision do. If emotions and facial expressions that go with them are unlearned, then they should be the same the world over.

The universality of facial expressions and the ability of people from different cultures to accurately label the emotion that lies behind the facial expression has been researched extensively. Psychologist Paul Ekman's (1980, 1996) careful observations reveal that the many faces of emotion do not differ significantly from one culture to another. For example, Ekman and his colleague photographed people expressing emotions such as happiness, fear, surprise, disgust, and grief. They found that when they showed the photographs to other people from the United States, Chile, Japan, Brazil, and Borneo (an Indonesian island in the western Pacific Ocean), all tended to label the same faces with the same emotions (Ekman & Friesen, 1968). Another study focused on the way the Fore tribe, an isolated Stone Age culture in New Guinea, matched descriptions of emotions with facial expressions (Ekman & Friesen, 1971). Before Ekman's visit, most of the Fore had never seen a Caucasian face. Ekman showed them photographs of American faces expressing emotions such as fear, happiness, anger, and surprise. Then he read stories about people in emotional situations. The Fore were able to match the descriptions of emotions with the facial expressions in the photographs. The similarity of facial expressions of emotions by persons in New Guinea and the United States is shown in figure 11.17.

FIGURE 11.17 Emotional Expressions in the United States and New Guinea (*Left*) Two women from the United States. (*Right*) Two men from the Fore tribe in New Guinea. Notice the similarity in their expressions of disgust and happiness. Psychologists believe that the facial expression of emotion is virtually the same in all cultures.

In the Middle Eastern country of Yemen, male-to-male kissing is commonplace, but in the United States it is uncommon.

display rules Sociocultural standards that determine when, where, and how emotions should be expressed.

Whereas facial expressions of basic emotions appear to be universal across cultures, display rules for emotion are not culturally universal. **Display rules** are sociocultural standards that determine when, where, and how emotions should be expressed. For example, although happiness is a universally expressed emotion, when, where, and how it is displayed may vary from one culture to another. The same is true for other emotions, such as fear, sadness, and anger. For example, members of the Utku culture in Alaska discourage anger by cultivating acceptance and by dissociating themselves from any display of anger. If a trip is hampered by an unexpected snowstorm, the Utku do not become frustrated but accept the presence of the snowstorm and build an igloo. Most of us would not act as mildly in the face of subzero weather and barriers to our travel.

Just as facial expressions are, some other nonverbal signals appear to be universal indicators of certain emotions. For example, when people are depressed, it shows not only in their sad facial expressions but also in their slow body movements, downturned heads, and slumped posture.

Many nonverbal signals of emotion, though, vary from one culture to another (Cohen & Borsoi, 1996; Mesquita, 2002). For example, male-to-male kissing is commonplace in Yemen but uncommon in the United States. And the "thumbs up" sign, which in most cultures means either everything is okay or the desire to hitch a ride, is an insult in Greece, similar to a raised third finger in the United States.

Gender Influences Unless you've been isolated on a mountaintop, away from people, television, magazines, and newspapers, you probably know the stereotype about gender and emotion: She is emotional, he is not. This stereotype is a powerful and pervasive image in our culture (Shields, 1991).

Is this stereotype supported by research on the nature of emotional experiences in females and males? Researchers have found that females and males are often more alike in the way they experience emotion than the stereotype would lead us to believe. Females and males often use the same facial expressions, adopt the same language, and describe their emotional experiences similarly when they keep diaries about their life experiences. Thus the stereotype that females are emotional and males are not is simply that—a stereotype. For many emotional experiences, researchers do not find differences between females and males—both sexes are equally likely to experience love, jealousy, anxiety in new social situations, anger when they are insulted, grief when close relationships end, and embarrassment when they make mistakes in public (Tavris & Wade, 1984).

When we go beyond stereotype and consider some specific emotional experiences, contexts in which emotion is displayed, and certain beliefs about emotion, gender does matter in understanding emotion (Brannon, 1999; Shields, 1991).

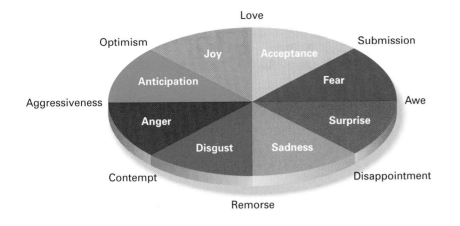

FIGURE 11.18 **Plutchik's Classification of Emotions** Plutchik theorized that people experience the eight basic emotions represented in the colored sections of the drawing, well as combinations of these emotions, shown outside the wheel.

Consider anger. Men are more likely to show anger toward strangers, especially other men, when they feel they have been challenged, and men are more likely to turn their anger into aggressive action than women are.

Differences between females and males regarding emotion are more likely to occur in contexts that highlight social roles and relationships. For example, females are more likely than males to give accounts of emotion that include interpersonal relationships. And females are more likely to express fear and sadness than males are, especially when communicating with their friends and family.

Classifying Emotions

There are more than 200 words for emotions in the English language, indicating the complexity and variety of emotions. Not surprisingly, psychologists have created ways to classify emotions. One of these schemes is the wheel model. Another is a two-dimensional model.

The Wheel Model A number of psychologists have classified the emotions we experience by placing them on a wheel. One such model was proposed by Robert Plutchik (1980; see figure 11.18). He believes emotions have four dimensions: (1) They are positive or negative, (2) they are primary or mixed, (3) many are polar opposites, and (4) they vary in intensity. Ecstasy and enthusiasm are positive emotions; grief and anger are negative emotions. For example, think about your ecstasy when you get an unexpected A on a test or your enthusiasm about the football game this weekend—these are positive emotions. In contrast, think about negative emotions, such as grief when someone close to you dies or anger when someone verbally attacks you. Positive emotions enhance our self-esteem; negative emotions lower our self-esteem. Positive emotions improve our relationships with others; negative emotions depress the quality of those relationships.

Plutchik believes that emotions are like colors. Every color of the spectrum can be produced by mixing the primary colors. Possibly some emotions are primary, and, if mixed together, they combine to form all other emotions. Happiness, disgust, surprise, sadness, anger, and fear are candidates for primary emotions. For example, combining sadness and surprise gives disappointment. Jealousy is composed of love and anger. Plutchik developed the emotion wheel to show how primary emotions work. Mixtures of primary emotions adjacent to each other produce other emotions. Some emotions are opposites—love and remorse, optimism and disappointment.

Another wheel-like model of emotion was proposed by Sylvan Tompkins (1962, 1981). He believes that the basic emotions are fear, anger, joy, distress, disgust, interest, surprise, contempt, and shame. Figure 11.19 shows that there is some consensus between Plutchik and Tompkins.

Plutchik	Tompkins
Fear	Fear
Anger	Anger
Joy	Joy
Sadness	Distress
Acceptance	Interest
Surprise	Surprise
Disgust	Contempt
Anticipation	Shame

FIGURE 11.19 **Comparison of Plutchik's and Tompkins' Classifications of Basic Emotions**

Theorists such as Plutchik and Tompkins view emotions as essentially innate reactions that require little cognitive interpretation. As such, their views reflect an evolutionary perspective on emotion. In this perspective, the basic emotions evolved and were retained because of their adaptive survival value.

The Two-Dimensional Approach The two-dimensional approach to classifying emotions argues that there are two broad dimensions of emotional experiences: positive affectivity and negative affectivity. *Positive affectivity (PA)* refers to positive emotions, such as joy, happiness, love, and interest. *Negative affectivity (NA)* refers to negative emotions, such as anxiety, anger, guilt, and sadness.

Positive emotions facilitate approach behavior (Cacioppo & Gardner, 1999; Davidson, 1993; Watson, 2001; Watson & others, 1999). In other words, positive affect increases the likelihood that individuals will interact with their environment and engage in activities, many of which are adaptive for the individual, its species, or both. Positive emotions can also broaden people's horizons and build their personal resources. For example, joy broadens by creating the urge to play, push the limits, and be creative. Interest broadens by creating the motivation to explore, absorb new information and experiences, and expand the self (Csikzentmihalyi, 1990; Ryan & Deci, 2000).

Negative emotions, such as fear, carry direct and immediate adaptive benefits in situations that threaten survival. However, whereas positive emotions tend to broaden a person's attention, negative emotions—such as anxiety and depression—often narrow attention (Basso & others, 1996). So to speak, negative emotions may cause a person to miss the forest (or the suspect's style of dress or gun) for the trees.

There is increasing interest in the role that positive affectivity might play in well-being. For example, positive emotions can serve as markers of well-being (Frederickson, 2001). When people's lives are characterized by joy, happiness, love, and interest, it is likely that these override negative emotions such as sadness, anger, and despair (Diener, 1999).

Positive emotions can improve coping. In one study, individuals who experienced more positive emotions than others developed broader-based coping strategies, such as thinking about different ways to deal with a problem and stepping back from the situation and being more objective (Frederickson & Joiner, 2000, 2002).

In some cases, positive emotions can undo lingering negative emotions (Frederickson, 2001). For example, mild joy and contentment have been found to undo the lingering cardiovascular effects of negative emotions, such as sadness (Frederickson & Levenson, 1998). In sum, positive emotions likely serve important functions in an individual's adaptation, growth, and social connection. By building personal and social resources, positive emotions improve people's well-being.

A Negative Emotion: Anger Anger is a powerful emotion. It has strong effects not only on social relationships but also on the person experiencing the emotion. We can easily recount obvious examples of anger that causes such harm—unrestrained and recurrent violence toward others, verbal and physical abuse of children, perpetual bitterness, the tendency to carry a "chip on the shoulder" in which a person over-interprets others' actions as demeaning, and the inability to inhibit the expression of anger.

What makes people angry? People often get angry when they feel they are not being treated fairly or when their expectations are violated. One researcher asked people to remember or keep records of their anger experiences (Averill, 1983). Most of the people said they became at least mildly angry several times a week; some said they became mildly angry several times a day. In many instances, people said they got angry because they perceived that a friend or a loved one performed a misdeed. They especially got angry when they perceived the other person's behavior as unjustified, avoidable, and willful (Zillman, 1998).

Catharsis is the release of anger or aggressive energy by directly or vicariously engaging in anger or aggression; the *catharsis hypothesis* states that behaving angrily or watching others behave angrily reduces subsequent anger. Psychodynamic theory promotes catharsis as an important way to reduce anger, arguing that people have a natural, biological tendency to display anger. From this perspective, taking out your anger on a friend or a loved one should reduce your subsequent tendency to display anger; so should heavy doses of anger on television and the anger we see in professional sports and other aspects of our culture. Why? Because such experiences release pent-up anger.

Social cognitive theory argues strongly against this view. This theory states that by acting angrily, people often are rewarded for their anger, and that by watching others display anger, people learn how to be angry themselves. Which view is right? Research on catharsis suggests that acting angrily does not have any long-term power to reduce anger. If the catharsis hypothesis were correct, war should have a cathartic effect in reducing anger and aggression, but a study of wars in 110 countries since 1900 showed that warfare actually stimulated domestic violence (Archer & McDaniel, 1995; Archer & Gartner, 1976). Compared with nations that remained at peace, postwar nations saw an increase in homicide rates. As psychologist Carol Tavris (1989) says in her book *Anger: The Misunderstood Emotion*, one of the main results of the ventilation approach to anger is to raise the noise level of our society, not to reduce anger or solve our problems. Individuals who are the most prone to anger get angrier, not less angry. Ventilating anger often follows a cycle of a precipitating event, an angry outburst, shouted recriminations, screaming or crying, a furious peak (sometimes accompanied by physical assault), exhaustion, and a sullen apology or just sullenness.

Every person gets angry at one time or another. How can we control our anger so it does not become destructive? Mark Twain once remarked, "When angry, count four; when very angry, swear." Tavris (1989) would agree with Twain's first rule, if not the second. She makes the following recommendations:

1. When your anger starts to boil and your body is getting aroused, work on lowering the arousal by waiting. Emotional arousal will usually decrease if you just wait long enough.
2. Cope with the anger in ways that involve neither being chronically angry over every little annoyance nor passively sulking, which simply rehearses your reasons for being angry.
3. Form a self-help group with others who have been through similar experiences with anger. The other people will likely know what you are feeling, and together you might come up with some good solutions to anger problems.
4. Take action to help others, which can put your own miseries in perspective, as exemplified by the actions of the women who organized Mothers Against Drunk Driving or any number of people who work to change conditions so that others will not suffer as they did.
5. Seek ways of breaking out of your usual perspective. Some people have been rehearsing their "story" for years, repeating over and over the reasons for their anger. Retelling the story from other participants' points of view often helps people to find routes to empathy.

A Positive Emotion: Happiness   Earlier in the chapter we discussed well-being and raised the question of whether happiness is an important aspect of well-being. Indeed, some psychologists equate happiness with subjective well-being, although it was not until 1973 that *Psychological Abstracts*, the major source of psychological research summaries, included *happiness* as an index term.

Psychologists' interest in happiness focuses on positive ways we experience life, including cognitive judgments of our well-being (Diener, Lucas, & Oishi, 2001; Locke,

catharsis The release of anger or aggressive energy by directly or vicariously engaging in anger or aggression; the *catharsis hypothesis* states that behaving angrily or watching others behave angrily reduces subsequent anger.

FIGURE 11.20 **Religious Attendance and Happiness** In surveys of more than 34,000 Americans from 1972 to 1996, the more often American adults attended religious services the more likely they were to say that they were "very happy."

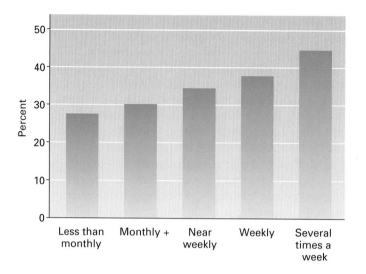

2002). That is, psychologists want to know what makes you happy and how you perceive your happiness.

Many years ago, the French philosopher Jean-Jacques Rousseau described the subjective nature of happiness this way: "Happiness is a good bank account, a good cook, and a good digestion." In a review of research on happiness, having a good cook and a good digestion were not on the list of factors that contribute to our happiness, but the following were (Diener & Seligman, 2002; Diener and others, 2001; Diener & others, 1999):

*   Psychological and personality characteristics: high levels of self-esteem, optimism, extraversion, and personal control
*   A supportive network of close relationships
*   A culture that offers positive interpretations of most daily events
*   Being engaged by work and leisure
*   A faith that embodies social support, purpose, hope, and religious attendance (see figure 11.20)

Some factors that many people believe are involved in happiness, such as age and gender, are not.

But what about Rousseau's "good bank account"? Can we buy happiness? One study tried to find out if lottery winners are happier than people who have not received a landslide of money (Brickman, Coates, & Janoff-Bulman, 1978). Twenty-two major lottery winners were compared with 22 other people living in the same area of the city. The general happiness of the two groups did not differ when they were asked about the past, the present, and the future. The people who hadn't won a lottery actually were happier doing mundane things, such as watching television, buying clothes, and talking with a friend.

Winning a lottery does not appear to be the key to happiness. What is important, though, is having enough money to buy life's necessities. Extremely wealthy people are not happier than people who can purchase what they need. The message is clear: If you believe money buys happiness, think again (Diener, 1984).

Psychologist Ed Diener (1984) agrees that intense positive emotions—such as winning a lottery or getting a date with the person of your dreams—do not add much to a person's general sense of well-being, in part because they are rare and in part because they can decrease the positive emotions and increase the negative emotions we feel in later circumstances. According to Diener, happiness boils down to the frequency of positive emotions and the infrequency of negative emotions. Diener's

How might winning the lottery affect your happiness?

view flies in the face of common sense; you would think that frequent, intense positive emotions and minimal nonintense negative emotions produce the most happiness. But the commonsense view fails to consider that intense positive moments can diminish the sensation of future positive events. For example, if you shoot par in a round of golf, you will be overwhelmed with happiness at the time, but if you play golf a week later and do well but not as well, the previous emotional high can diminish your positive emotion this time. It is the rare human being, if such a person exists, who experiences intense positive emotions and infrequent negative emotions week after week after week.

Evolutionary psychologist David Buss (2000) believes that humans possess evolved mechanisms that can produce a deep sense of happiness. These include mating bonds, friendship, close kinship, and cooperative relationships. However, he cautions that some evolved mechanisms impede happiness. These include the distress created by jealousy and anger and the competition that benefits one person at the expense of another.

"My life is O.K., but it's no jeans ad."
Richard Cline © 1988 from The New Yorker Collection. All Rights Reserved.

Review and Sharpen Your Thinking

5 *Summarize views of emotion.*

- Define emotion and explain the biology of emotion in terms of arousal and neural activity.
- Discuss the two-factor theory and the primacy debate over cognition and emotion.
- Describe behavioral expressions of emotion.
- Identify sociocultural similarities and differences in the expression of emotion.
- Compare the wheel model and the two-dimensional model of classifying emotions, and discuss the role of emotions in well-being.

Think about the last time you became angry. Compare how you handled your anger with the strategies recommended in the chapter. What strategies can you use to better control your anger? Is catharsis a good way to handle your anger? Explain.

mhhe com/
santrockp7

For study tools related to this learning goal, see the Study Guide, the CD-ROM, and the Online Learning Center.

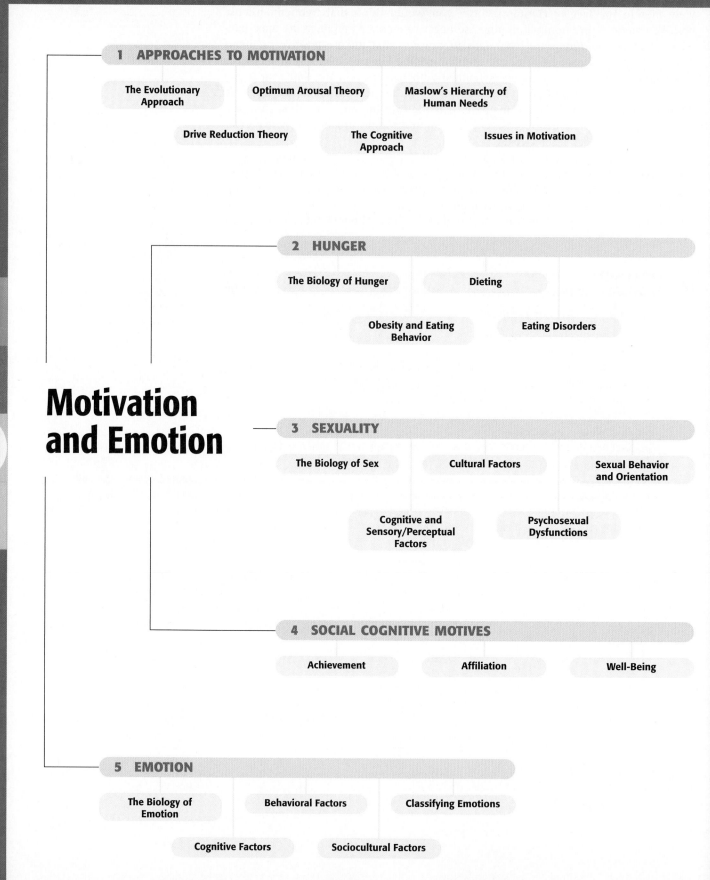

Motivation and Emotion

1   APPROACHES TO MOTIVATION

The Evolutionary Approach

Optimum Arousal Theory

Maslow's Hierarchy of Human Needs

Drive Reduction Theory

The Cognitive Approach

Issues in Motivation

2   HUNGER

The Biology of Hunger

Dieting

Obesity and Eating Behavior

Eating Disorders

3   SEXUALITY

The Biology of Sex

Cultural Factors

Sexual Behavior and Orientation

Cognitive and Sensory/Perceptual Factors

Psychosexual Dysfunctions

4   SOCIAL COGNITIVE MOTIVES

Achievement

Affiliation

Well-Being

5   EMOTION

The Biology of Emotion

Behavioral Factors

Classifying Emotions

Cognitive Factors

Sociocultural Factors

1   *Describe psychological approaches to emotion.*

- Motivation gives our behavior, thoughts, and feelings a purpose. Motivated behavior is energized, directed, and sustained. Early evolutionary theorists considered motivation to be based on instinct, the innate biological pattern of behavior that is assumed to be universal throughout a species. The idea that some of our motivation is unlearned and involves physiological factors is still present today. The evolutionary psychology view emphasizes that various aspects of motivation that provided evolutionary advantages were passed down through the genes from generation to generation.

- A drive is an aroused state that occurs because of a physiological need. A need is a deprivation that energizes the drive to eliminate or reduce the deprivation. Drive reduction theory was proposed as an explanation of motivation, with the goal of drive reduction being homeostasis, the body's tendency to maintain an equilibrium.

- Optimum arousal theory focuses on the Yerkes-Dodson law, which states that performance is best under conditions of moderate rather than low or high arousal. Moderate arousal often serves us best when we tackle life's tasks, but there are times when low or high arousal is linked with better performance. Sensation seeking is one aspect of the motivation for high arousal that psychologists study.

- The contemporary view of motivation emphasizes cognitive factors, including such information processing abilities as attention, memory, and problem solving. Psychologists debate how extensively motivation is influenced by conscious versus unconscious thought. Intrinsic motivation, based on internal factors such as self-determination, curiosity, challenge, and effort, is one of the most widely studied aspects of achievement motivation. Extrinsic motivation is based on external incentives such as rewards and punishments. Most psychologists believe that intrinsic motivation is more positively related to achievement than extrinsic motivation is.

- According to Maslow's hierarchy of needs, our main needs are satisfied in this sequence: physiological, safety, love and belongingness, esteem, and self-actualization. Maslow gave the most attention to self-actualization, the motivation to develop to one's full potential.

- Three important issues in motivation are whether motivation is based on innate, unlearned, biological factors or learned, sociocultural, experiential factors; to what degree we are aware of what motivates us; and to what degree we are internally or externally motivated.

2   *Explain the physiological basis of hunger and the nature of eating behavior.*

- Interest in the stomach's role was stimulated by Cannon's classic research, but stomach signals are not the only factors that affect hunger. Glucose (blood sugar) is an important factor in hunger, probably because the brain is critically dependent on sugar for energy. Rodin's work helped clarify the role of insulin and glucose in hunger. Leptin, a protein secreted by fat cells, decreases food intake and increases energy expenditure. The hypothalamus plays an important role in regulating hunger. The lateral hypothalamus is involved in stimulating eating, the ventromedial hypothalamus in restricting eating. Today, neuroscientists are exploring the roles that neurotransmitters and neural circuits play in hunger.

- Obesity is a serious and pervasive problem in the United States. Heredity, basal metabolism, set point, and fat cells are biological factors involved in obesity. Obese persons are more responsive to external cues than normal-weight persons are; although, there are individuals at all weight levels who respond more to external than to internal stimuli. Self-control is an important cognitive factor in eating behavior. Time and place affect eating, as does the type of food available. Our early ancestors ate natural fruits to satisfy nutritional needs, but today we fill up on the empty calories in candy and soda. The dramatic increase in obesity in the late twentieth century underscores the significance of environmental factors in obesity as increasing numbers of people eat high-fat foods and lead sedentary lives.

- Dieting for weight loss and restrained eating for weight control are common in American society. Most diets don't work, although some people do lose weight when they diet and maintain the loss. Exercise is an important component of a successful weight-loss program. Many people, especially in their teens and 20s, diet even if they don't need to lose weight. The pressure to be thin can be harmful for people who are not overweight. However, when overweight people diet and maintain their weight loss, they reap health benefits.

- Anorexia nervosa is an eating disorder that involves the relentless pursuit of thinness through starvation. Bulimia nervosa is an eating disorder that consists of a binge-and-purge pattern. Both disorders are most common among adolescent and young adult females.

3   *Discuss the motivation for sex.*

- Motivation for sexual behavior involves the hypothalamus. The pituitary gland controls the secretion of two classes of sex hormones: estrogens, which predominate in females, and androgens, which have stronger concentrations in males. The role of sex hormones in human sexual behavior, especially in women, is not clear. Masters and Johnson mapped out the human sexual response pattern, which consists of four physiological phases: excitement, plateau, orgasm, and resolution.

- Thoughts and images are central in the sexual lives of humans. Sexual scripts influence sexual behavior, as do sensory/perceptual factors. Females tend to be more sexually aroused by touch, males by visual stimulation. Pheromones are sexual attractants for many nonhuman animals, but their role in human sexual behavior has not been documented. Many aphrodisiacs allegedly act as sexual stimulants, but there is no clear evidence that what we eat, drink, or inject has aphrodisiac qualities.

- Sexual values vary extensively across cultures. These values exert a significant effect on sexual behavior.

- Psychosexual dysfunctions involve impairments in the sexual response pattern. Significant advances have been made in treating these dysfunctions in recent years.

- Describing sexual practices in America has always been challenging due to the difficulty of surveying a representative sample of the population. The 1994 *Sex in America* survey was a major improvement over earlier surveys by Kinsey and Hunt. The 1994 survey revealed that Americans' sex lives are more conservative than earlier surveys had indicated. Sexual orientation—heterosexual, homosexual, or bisexual—is most likely determined by a combination of genetic, hormonal, cognitive, and environmental factors.

4 Characterize the social cognitive motives and how they influence behavior.

- Early interest in achievement focused on need for achievement. Cognitive factors in achievement focus on intrinsic motivation, attribution, and goal setting, planning, and monitoring. Attribution theory states that people are motivated to discover the underlying causes of behavior in an effort to make sense out of the behavior. The main emphasis in attribution theory has focused on internal causes, especially effort, and external causes. High achievers often set specific, proximal, and challenging goals. Individuals in the United States are often more achievement oriented than individuals in other countries, although recent comparisons with Asian countries reveal higher achievement in those countries. A special concern is the achievement of individuals in ethnic minority groups. When both ethnicity and socioeconomic status (SES) are considered in the same study, SES usually is a better predictor of achievement than ethnicity.

Strategies based on achievement research are used in the workplace and in sports to motivate individuals to do their best.

- The need for affiliation (relatedness) is the motive to be with other people. It is a powerful motive in many people's lives. Cultures vary in how strongly they promote affiliation.

- Psychologists are increasingly interested in what constitutes the good life and well-being. One proposal is that well-being involves competence, autonomy, and affiliation.

5 Summarize views of emotion.

- Emotion is feeling, or affect, that has three components: physiological arousal, conscious experience, and behavioral expression. The biology of emotion focuses on physiological arousal involving the autonomic nervous system and its two subsystems. The galvanic skin response and the polygraph have been used to measure emotional arousal. The polygraph is considered unreliable for use as a lie detector. The James-Lange theory states that emotion results from physiological states triggered by environmental stimuli: Emotion follows physiological reactions. The Cannon-Bard theory states that emotion and physiological reactions occur simultaneously. Contemporary biological views of emotion increasingly highlight neural circuitry and neurotransmitters. LeDoux has charted the neural circuitry of fear, which focuses on the amygdala and consists of two pathways, one direct and the other indirect. It is likely that positive and negative emotions use different neural circuitry and neurotransmitters.

- Schachter and Singer's two-factor theory states that emotion is the result of both physiological arousal and cognitive labeling. Lazarus believes that cognition always directs emotion, but Zajonc argues that emotion directs cognition. Both probably are right.

- Research on the behavioral component of emotion focuses on facial expressions. The facial feedback hypothesis states that facial expressions can influence emotions, as well as reflect them.

- Most psychologists believe that facial expressions of basic emotions are the same across cultures. However, display rules, which involve nonverbal signals of body movement, posture, and gesture, vary across cultures. The stereotype that women are emotional and men are not is just a stereotype. However, there are many contextual influences on the expression of emotion by males and females.

- Classifications of emotions have included wheel models and the two-dimensional approach. Plutchik's wheel model portrays emotions in terms of four dimensions:

positive or negative, primary or mixed, polar opposites, and intensity. Both Plutchik's and Tompkins' lists of basic emotions reflect an evolutionary perspective. The two-dimensional approach to classifying emotions argues that there are just two broad dimensions of emotional experi-

ences: positive affectivity and negative affectivity. Positive emotions likely play an important role in well-being through adaptation, growth, social connection, and building personal and social resources.

Key Terms

motivation, p. 425
instinct, p. 425
drive, p. 425
need, p. 425
homeostasis, p. 426
Yerkes-Dodson law, p. 426
intrinsic motivation, p. 428
extrinsic motivation, p. 428
hierarchy of needs, p. 429

self-actualization, p. 429
basal metabolism rate
    (BMR), p. 433
set point, p. 433
anorexia nervosa, p. 436
bulimia nervosa, p. 437
estrogens, p. 437
androgens, p. 438

human sexual response
    pattern, p. 438
pheromones, p. 440
need for achievement,
    p. 447
attribution theory, p. 447
need for affiliation, p. 452
emotion, p. 455
polygraph, p. 456

James-Lange theory, p. 456
Cannon-Bard theory, p. 457
two-factor theory of
    emotion, p. 459
facial feedback
    hypothesis, p. 462
display rules, p. 464
catharsis, p. 467

Apply Your Knowledge

1. Ask your friends to define the word *motivation*. Think about the way your friends define motivation and the way psychologists approach motivation. What are the similarities? What are the differences? Are your friends likelier to say they have too much motivation or not enough? Why might that be?

2. Do a web search for the word *hunger*. What kinds of sites are listed first? How do the topics that these sites cover compare with the discussion of hunger in the text? Do the sites give you any insight into the role of environment in hunger?

3. Imagine that someone offered you a pill that would double the size of your lateral hypothalamus but make your androgen levels go down to half their current level. How might this pill affect your eating and sexual behavior? Would you take the pill?

4. How much of our interpretation of emotions depends on verbal or nonverbal cues? Try the following exercise: Watch a movie that you're not familiar with and find a scene with a number of people in it. First watch the scene with the sound off and try to guess what emotions are being experienced by each person; describe the nonverbal cues that led you to your conclusions. Find a different scene, and listen to it without watching to guess what emotions are being experienced; describe the verbal cues that you used. Then, watch both scenes with the sound on. Were verbal or nonverbal cues more useful?

Connections

For extra help in mastering the material in this chapter, see the review sections and practice quizzes in the Student Study Guide, the CD-ROM, and the Online Learning Center.

12 Personality

Learning Goals

1 *Define personality and identify the major issues in the study of personality.*

2 *Summarize the psychodynamic perspectives.*

3 *Explain the behavioral and social cognitive perspectives.*

4 *Describe the humanistic perspectives.*

5 *Discuss the trait perspectives.*

6 *Characterize the main methods of personality assessment.*

What makes a U.S. president great? Do certain personality traits characterize successful candidates? In one recent research study, Steve Rubenzer and his colleagues (2000) asked more than 100 history experts to rate presidents on their personality characteristics for the 5 years before they became president. The researchers did not ask the historians to assess a president's personality while in office because the researchers believed that the pressure might alter his personality.

Rubenzer and his colleagues then correlated each president's personality traits with his degree of presidential greatness as determined by referencing generally accepted lists of America's great presidents. In order, Abraham Lincoln, Franklin Roosevelt, George Washington, Thomas Jefferson, Theodore Roosevelt, Woodrow Wilson, Harry Truman, Andrew Jackson, Dwight Eisenhower, and James Madison have been ranked by expert historians as the 10 greatest U.S. presidents.

The personality trait of openness to experience showed the highest correlation with greatness as a president. The researchers concluded that openness to experience may be at the top of the list partially because individuals with higher cognitive abilities have more open minds. However, they had no available data on the cognitive ability of presidents to test this idea.

In addition to openness to experience, great presidents were rated as attentive to their emotions, willing to question traditional values and try new ways of doing things, imaginative, and more interested in art and beauty than less successful presidents. Successful presidents also have tended to be *assertive:* to be stubborn and stand up for their ideas.

The researchers also found that most presidents are extraverts, although earlier presidents were less extraverted than more recent ones. The increasing extraversion of U.S. presidents has coincided with the increased exposure of presidents in the media.

The personality of presidents is interesting, but what about your own personality? Think about your own characteristics, and write down seven or eight personality traits that you think best describe you. Do people who know you well describe you as serious or wild? Shy or outgoing? Self-confident or uncertain? Friendly or hostile?

In compiling this list, you likely chose personality characteristics that you believe are an enduring part of your makeup as a person. For example, if you said that you are an outgoing person, wouldn't you also say that you were outgoing a year ago and that you will probably be an outgoing person 1 year, 5 years, and 10 years from now? The concept of personality involves the notion that each of us has some unified and enduring core characteristics. We are not just a random collection of traits that change from day to day. Each of us has a more or less persistent style of thinking and behaving. Personality theories, which are the topic of this chapter, seek to describe such patterns and their underlying causes (Pervin & John, 2001).

How might the personalities of presidential candidates influence the outcome of a presidential election? Do you think the personalities of George W. Bush and Al Gore influenced the 2000 presidential election? How? How are the personalities of Bush and Gore similar to or different from those of great presidents such as Abraham Lincoln?

What is personality? What are the major issues in the study of personality?

Personality is one of those concepts that is familiar to everyone but difficult to define. In this chapter, **personality** is defined as a pattern of enduring, distinctive thoughts, emotions, and behaviors that characterize the way an individual adapts to the world.

Personality theorists and researchers ask why individuals react to the same situation in different ways, and they come up with different answers. For example, why is Sam so talkative and gregarious and Al so shy and quiet when meeting someone for the first time? Why is Gretchen so confident and Mary so insecure about upcoming job interviews? Some theorists believe that biological and genetic factors are responsible; others argue that life experiences are more important factors. Some theorists claim that the way we think about ourselves is the key to understanding personality, whereas others stress that the way we behave toward each other is. This chapter presents four broad theoretical perspectives on personality—psychodynamic, behavioral and social cognitive, humanistic, and trait—and you will see how different the answers can be.

As you read about these perspectives on personality, you will notice that they address three important questions:

1. *Is personality innate or learned?* Is personality due more to heredity and biological factors or more to learning and environmental experiences? For example, are individuals conceited and self-centered because they inherited the tendency to be conceited and self-centered from their parents, or did they learn to be that way through experiences with other conceited, self-centered individuals? As you will see, psychodynamic perspectives have a strong biogenetic foundation, although some theorists who adopt this approach believe that environmental experiences and culture play a role in determining personality. Behaviorial and social cognitive perspectives, along with humanistic perspectives, endorse environment as a powerful determinant of personality, Skinner being the strongest advocate of environment's influence. However, humanistic theorists do believe that people have the innate ability to reach their full potential. Trait perspectives vary in their emphasis on heredity and environment.

2. *Is personality conscious or unconscious?* How aware are individuals that they are, say, conceited and self-centered? How aware are they of the reasons they became conceited and self-centered? Psychodynamic theorists have been the strongest advocates of the unconscious mind's role in personality. Most argue that we are largely unaware of how our individual personalities developed. Behaviorists argue that neither unconscious nor conscious thought is important in determining personality, whereas social cognitive theorists stress that conscious thought affects the way the environment influences personality. Humanists stress the conscious aspects of personality, especially in the form of self-perception. Trait theorists pay little attention to the conscious/unconscious issue.

3. *Is personality influenced by internal or external factors?* Is the way personality is expressed in any given situation due more to an inner disposition or to the situation itself? Are individuals conceited and self-centered because of something inside themselves, a characteristic they have and carry around with them, or are they conceited and self-centered because of the situations they are in and the way they are influenced by people around them? Psychodynamic, humanistic, and trait theorists emphasize the internal dimensions of personality. Behaviorists emphasize personality's external, situational determinants. Social cognitive theorists examine both external and internal determinants.

You will learn more about how the four theoretical perspectives address these issues in the rest of the chapter. The diversity of theories makes understanding

personality A pattern of enduring, distinctive thoughts, emotions, and behaviors that characterize the way an individual adapts to the world.

SIGMUND FREUD (1856–1939)
The architect of psychoanalytic theory.

personality a challenging undertaking. Just when you think one theory has correctly explained personality, another theory will crop up and make you rethink that conclusion. To keep from getting frustrated, remember that personality is a complex, multifaceted topic. And, remember, much of the information from various theories is complementary rather than contradictory. Each theory has contributed an important piece or pieces to the personality puzzle. Together they let us see the total landscape of personality in all its richness (Funder, 2001).

Review and Sharpen Your Thinking

1 Define personality and identify the major issues in the study of personality.

- Define the concept of personality and summarize three issues addressed by the major personality perspectives.

Earlier we asked you to list your main personality characteristics. Go over the list and evaluate whether you think you inherited these traits or learned them, how conscious you are of these traits, and the extent to which they are internally or externally determined.

2 PSYCHODYNAMIC PERSPECTIVES

Freud's Psychoanalytic Theory   **Psychodynamic Dissenters and Revisionists**   **Evaluating Psychodynamic Perspectives**

What are the main themes of psychodynamic perspectives?

Psychodynamic perspectives view personality as being primarily unconscious (that is, beyond awareness) and as developing in stages. Most psychodynamic perspectives emphasize that early experiences with parents play an important role in sculpting the individual's personality. Psychodynamic theorists believe that behavior is merely a surface characteristic and that to truly understand someone's personality we have to explore the symbolic meanings of behavior and the deep inner workings of the mind (Feist & Feist, 2002). These characteristics were sketched by the architect of psychoanalytic theory—Sigmund Freud. As you learned in chapter 1, the psychodynamic theorists who took issue with and who followed Freud have diverged from his original theory but still embrace his core ideas about personality.

Freud's Psychoanalytic Theory

Sigmund Freud (1917), one of the most influential thinkers of the twentieth century, was born in Austria in 1856 and died in London at the age of 83. Freud spent most of his life in Vienna, but he left the city near the end of his career to escape the Holocaust. Freud was a medical doctor who specialized in neurology. He developed his ideas about psychoanalytic theory from his work with psychiatric patients.

As a child, Freud was regarded as a genius by his younger brothers and sisters and doted on by his mother. One aspect of Freud's theory emphasizes a young boy's sexual attraction for his mother; it is possible that this aspect of his theory derived from his own romantic attachment to his mother, who was beautiful and some 20 years younger than Freud's father.

psychodynamic perspectives View personality as primarily unconscious (that is, beyond awareness) and as occurring in stages. Most psychoanalytic perspectives emphasize that early experiences with parents play a role in sculpting personality.

For Freud, the unconscious mind holds the key to understanding behavior. Our lives are filled with tension and conflict; to reduce them we keep troubling information locked in our unconscious mind. Freud believed that even trivial behaviors have special significance when the unconscious forces behind them are revealed. A twitch, a doodle, a joke, a smile, each may have an unconscious reason for appearing. They often slip into our lives without our awareness. For example, Barbara is kissing and hugging Tom, whom she is to marry in several weeks. She says, "Oh, *Jeff*, I love you so much." Tom pushes her away and says, "Why did you call me Jeff? I thought you didn't think about him anymore. We need to have a talk!" You probably can think of times when these so-called *Freudian slips* (misstatements that perhaps reveal unconscious thoughts) have tumbled out of your own mouth.

Freud also believed that dreams hold important clues to our behavior (Blum, 2001). He said dreams are unconscious representations of the conflict and tension in our everyday lives that are too painful to handle consciously. Much of the dream content is disguised in symbolism and requires extensive analysis and probing to be understood.

Remember that Freud considered the unconscious mind to be the key to understanding personality (Gedo, 2002). He likened personality to an iceberg, existing mostly below the level of awareness, just as the massive part of an iceberg is beneath the surface of the water. Figure 12.1 illustrates this analogy and how extensive the unconscious part of our mind is in Freud's view.

Personality's Structures Notice that figure 12.1 shows the iceberg divided into three segments. Freud (1917) believed that personality has three structures: the id, the ego, and the superego.

The **id** consists of instincts and is the individual's reservoir of psychic energy. In Freud's view, the id is unconscious; it has no contact with reality. The id works according to the *pleasure principle,* the Freudian concept that the id always seeks pleasure and avoids pain.

It would be a dangerous and scary world, however, if our personalities were all id. As young children mature, they learn they cannot slug other children in the face. They also learn that they have to use the toilet instead of their diaper. As children experience the demands and constraints of reality, a new structure of personality is formed—the **ego,** the Freudian structure of personality that deals with the demands of reality. According to Freud, the ego abides by the *reality principle*. It tries to bring the individual pleasure within the norms of society. Most of us accept the obstacles to satisfaction that exist in our world. We recognize that our sexual and aggressive impulses cannot go unrestrained. Few of us are voracious gluttons, sexual wantons, or cold-blooded killers. The ego helps us to test reality, to see how far we can go without getting into trouble and hurting ourselves. Whereas the id is completely unconscious, the ego is partly conscious. It houses our higher mental functions—reasoning, problem solving, and decision making, for example. For this reason, the ego is referred to as the executive branch of the personality; like an executive in a company, it makes the rational decisions that help the company succeed.

"Good morning beheaded—uh, I mean beloved."

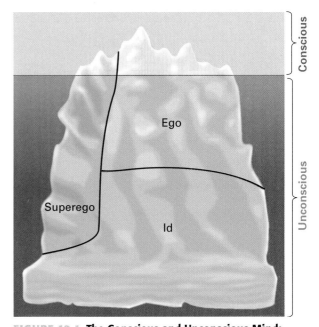

FIGURE 12.1 The Conscious and Unconscious Mind: The Iceberg Analogy The analogy of the conscious and unconscious mind to an iceberg is often used to illustrate how much of the mind is unconscious in Freud's theory. The conscious mind is the part of the iceberg above water, the unconscious mind the part below water. Notice that the id is totally unconscious, while the ego and superego can operate at either the conscious or the unconscious level.

id The Freudian structure of personality that consists of instincts, which are the individual's reservoir of psychic energy.

ego The Freudian structure of personality that deals with the demands of reality.

Defense Mechanism	How It Works	Example
Repression	The master defense mechanism; the ego pushes unacceptable impulses out of awareness, back into the unconscious mind.	A young girl was sexually abused by her uncle. As an adult, she can't remember anything about the traumatic experience.
Rationalization	The ego replaces a less acceptable motive with a more acceptable one.	A college student does not get into the fraternity of his choice. He says that if he had tried harder he could have gotten in.
Displacement	The ego shifts feelings toward an unacceptable object to another, more acceptable object.	A woman can't take her anger out on her boss so she goes home and takes it out on her husband.
Sublimation	The ego replaces an unacceptable impulse with a socially acceptable one.	A man with strong sexual urges becomes an artist who paints nudes.
Projection	The ego attributes personal shortcomings, problems, and faults to others.	A man who has a strong desire to have an extramarital affair accuses his wife of flirting with other men.
Reaction Formation	The ego transforms an unacceptable motive into its opposite.	A woman who fears her sexual urges becomes a religious zealot.
Denial	The ego refuses to acknowledge anxiety-producing realities.	A man won't acknowledge that he has cancer even though a team of doctors has diagnosed his cancer.
Regression	The ego seeks the security of an earlier developmental period in the face of stress.	A woman returns home to mother every time she and her husband have a big argument.

FIGURE 12.2 Defense Mechanisms
Defense mechanisms reduce anxiety in various ways, in all instances by distorting reality.

superego The Freudian structure of personality that deals with morality.

defense mechanisms The ego's protective methods for reducing anxiety by unconsciously distorting reality.

The id and ego have no morality. They do not consider whether something is right or wrong. The **superego** is the Freudian structure that is the moral branch of personality. It is what we often refer to as our "conscience." Like the id, the superego does not consider reality; it only considers whether the id's sexual and aggressive impulses can be satisfied in moral terms.

Both the id and the superego make life rough for the ego. Your ego might say, "I will have sex only occasionally and be sure to use an effective form of birth control." But your id is saying, "I want to be satisfied; sex feels so good." And your superego says, "I feel guilty about having sex at all."

Defense Mechanisms The ego calls on a number of strategies to resolve the conflict between its demands for reality, the wishes of the id, and the constraints of the superego. These **defense mechanisms** reduce anxiety by unconsciously distorting reality. For example, when the ego blocks the pleasurable pursuits of the id, a person feels anxiety, which the ego resolves by means of defense mechanisms. Figure 12.2 describes several of Freud's defense mechanisms and gives an example of each. All of them work to protect the ego and reduce anxiety.

Repression is the most powerful and pervasive defense mechanism, according to Freud; it pushes unacceptable id impulses out of awareness and back into the unconscious mind. Repression is the foundation for all of the psychological defense mechanisms, the goal of which is to push, or *repress*, threatening impulses out of awareness. Freud said that our early childhood experiences, many of which he believed were sexually laden, are too threatening and stressful for us to deal with consciously; so, we reduce the anxiety of childhood conflict through repression.

Two final points about defense mechanisms need to be understood. First, they are unconscious; we are not aware that we are calling on them. Second, when used in moderation or on a temporary basis, defense mechanisms are not necessarily unhealthy. For example, the defense mechanism of *denial* can help a person cope with impending death. For the most part, though, we should not let defense mechanisms dominate our behavior and prevent us from facing life's demands.

Personality Development As Freud listened to, probed, and analyzed his patients, he became convinced that their personalities were the result of experiences early in life. Freud believed that we go through five stages of personality development and that at each stage of development we experience pleasure in one part of the body more than in others. *Erogenous zones,* according to Freud, are parts of the body that have especially strong pleasure-giving qualities at particular stages of development. Freud thought that our adult personality is determined by the way we resolve conflicts between these early sources of pleasure—the mouth, the anus, and then the genitals—and the demands of reality.

- *Oral stage* (first 18 months of age). The infant's pleasure centers on the mouth. Chewing, sucking, and biting are chief sources of pleasure that reduce tension in the infant.
- *Anal stage* (18 to 36 months of age). The child's greatest pleasure involves the anus or the eliminative functions associated with it. In Freud's view, the exercise of anal muscles reduces tension.
- *Phallic stage* (3 to 6 years of age). The name of Freud's third stage comes from the Latin word *phallus,* which means "penis." Pleasure focuses on the genitals as the child discovers that self-stimulation is enjoyable. In Freud's view the phallic stage has a special importance in personality development because it triggers the Oedipus complex. This name comes from Greek mythology, in which Oedipus unwittingly killed his father and married his mother. The **Oedipus complex** is the young child's development of an intense desire to replace the parent of the same sex and enjoy the affections of the opposite-sex parent. At about 5 to 6 years of age, children recognize that their same-sex parent might punish them for their incestuous wishes. To reduce this conflict, the child identifies with the same-sex parent, striving to be like him or her. If the conflict is not resolved, though, the individual may become fixated at the phallic stage.
- *Latency stage* (6 years of age to puberty). The child represses all interest in sexuality and develops social and intellectual skills. This activity channels much of the child's energy into emotionally safe areas and aids the child in forgetting the highly stressful conflicts of the phallic stage.
- *Genital stage* (adolescence and adulthood). The genital stage is the time of sexual reawakening; the source of sexual pleasure now becomes someone outside of the family. Freud believed that unresolved conflicts with parents reemerged during adolescence. But once resolved, the individual becomes capable of developing a mature love relationship and functioning independently as an adult.

Freud believed that the individual may become fixated at any of these stages of development if the underlying conflict is not resolved. *Fixation* is the psychoanalytic defense mechanism that occurs when the individual remains locked in an earlier developmental stage because needs are under- or overgratified. For example, a parent might wean a child too early, be too strict in toilet training, punish the child for masturbation, or "smother" the child with too much attention. Figure 12.3 illustrates

Oedipus complex In Freud's theory, the young child's development of an intense desire to replace the same-sex parent and enjoy the affections of the opposite-sex parent.

Stage	Adult Extensions (Fixations)	Sublimations	Reaction Formations
Oral	Smoking, eating, kissing, oral hygiene, drinking, chewing gum	Seeking knowledge, humor, wit, sarcasm, being a food or wine expert	Speech purist, food faddist, prohibitionist, dislike of milk
Anal	Notable interest in one's bowel movements, love of bathroom humor, extreme messiness	Interest in painting or sculpture, being overly giving, great interest in statistics	Extreme disgust with feces, fear of dirt, prudishness, irritability
Phallic	Heavy reliance on masturbation, flirtatiousness, expressions of virility	Interest in poetry, love of love, interest in acting, striving for success	Puritanical attitude toward sex, excessive modesty

FIGURE 12.3 **Defense Mechanisms and Freudian Stages**

some possible links between adult personality characteristics and fixation at oral, anal, and phallic stages.

Psychodynamic Dissenters and Revisionists

Because Freud was among the first theorists to explore personality, over time some of his ideas have needed to be updated, others revised, and some tossed out altogether. In particular, Freud's critics have said that his ideas about sexuality, early experience, social factors, and the unconscious mind were misguided (Adler, 1927; Erikson, 1968; Fromm, 1947; Horney, 1945; Jung, 1917; Kohut, 1977; Rapaport, 1967; Sullivan, 1953). His critics stress the following points:

- Sexuality is not the pervasive force behind personality that Freud believed it to be. Nor was the Oedipus complex as universal as Freud believed. Freud's concepts were heavily influenced by the setting in which he lived and worked—turn-of-the-century Vienna, a society that was, compared with contemporary society, sexually repressed and paternalistic.
- The first 5 years of life are not as powerful in shaping adult personality as Freud thought; later experiences deserve more attention.
- The ego and conscious thought processes play more dominant roles in our personality than Freud gave them credit for; he claimed that we are forever in thrall to the instinctual, unconscious clutches of the id. Also, the ego has a separate line of development from the id, so achievement, thinking, and reasoning are not always tied to sexual impulses.
- Sociocultural factors are much more important than Freud believed. In stressing the id's dominance, Freud placed more emphasis on the biological basis of personality.

The theories of three dissenters and revisionists—Horney, Jung, and Adler—have been especially influential in the development of psychodynamic theories, the successors to Freud's psychoanalytic theory.

Horney's Sociocultural Approach   Karen Horney (1885–1952) rejected the classical psychoanalytic concept that "anatomy is destiny" and cautioned that some of Freud's most popular ideas were only hypotheses. She insisted that these hypotheses be supported with observable data before being accepted as fact and that sociocultural influences on personality development be considered.

Take Freud's concept of "penis envy": He attributed some of the behavior of his female patients to their repressed desire to have a penis. Horney pointed out that previous research about how women function was limited by the fact that those who described women, who influenced and represented the culture, and who determined the standards for suitable growth and development were men. She countered the notion of penis envy with the hypothesis that both sexes envy the attributes of the other, with men coveting women's reproductive capacities. She also argued that

KAREN HORNEY (1885–1952)
Developed the first feminist criticism of Freud's theory. Horney's view emphasizes women's positive qualities and self-evaluation.

women who feel penis envy are desirous only of the status that men have in most societies (Gilman, 2001).

Horney also believed that the need for security, not for sex or aggression, was the prime motive in human existence. Horney reasoned that an individual whose needs for security are met should be able to develop his or her capacities to the fullest extent.

She also suggested that people usually develop one of three strategies in their effort to cope with anxiety. First, individuals might *move toward* people, seeking love and support. Second, individuals might *move away* from people, becoming more independent. And, third, individuals might *move against* people, becoming competitive and domineering. The secure individual uses these three ways of coping in moderation and balance, whereas the insecure individual often uses one or more of these strategies in an exaggerated fashion, becoming too dependent, too independent, or too aggressive.

Psychologists are still revamping psychoanalytic theory in the sociocultural direction that Horney pointed. Nancy Chodorow's (1978, 1989) feminist revision of psychoanalytic theory, for example, emphasizes that many more women than men define themselves in terms of their relationships and that emotions tend to be more important in women's lives. In short, personality is not simply a matter of biology; social experiences and culture also shape personality.

Jung's Analytical Theory   Freud's contemporary Carl Jung (1875–1961) had a different complaint about psychoanalytic theory. Jung shared Freud's interest in the unconscious, but he believed that Freud underplayed the unconscious mind's role in personality. In fact, Jung believed that the roots of personality go back to the dawn of human existence. The **collective unconscious** is the impersonal, deepest layer of the unconscious mind, shared by all human beings because of their common ancestral past. The experiences of a common past have made a deep, permanent impression on the human mind (Mayer, 2002).

The collective unconscious is expressed through what Jung called **archetypes,** emotionally laden ideas and images that have rich and symbolic meaning for all people. Jung believed that these archetypes emerge in art, religion, and dreams. He used archetypes to help people understand themselves (Knox, 2001; McDowell, 2001).

Two common archetypes are anima (woman) and animus (man). Jung believed each of us has a passive "feminine" side and an assertive "masculine" side. Another archetype, the mandala, a figure within a circle, has been used so often in art that Jung took it to represent the self (see figure 12.4). Another archetype is the shadow, our darker self. The shadow, which is evil and immoral, is represented by many fictitional characters, such as Dracula, Mr. Hyde (of Jekyll and Hyde), and Darth Vader in the *Star Wars* films (see figure 12.5; Peterson, 1988).

CARL JUNG (1875–1961)
Swiss psychoanalytic theorist Carl Jung developed the concepts of the collective unconscious and archetypes.

FIGURE 12.4 **The Mandala as an Archetype of the Self** In his exploration of mythology, Carl Jung found that the self is often symbolized by a mandala, from the Sanskrit word for "circle." Jung believed that the mandala represents the self's unity.

collective unconscious Jung's term for the impersonal, deepest layer of the unconscious mind, shared by all human beings because of their common ancestral past.

archetypes The name Jung gave to the emotionally laden ideas and images in the collective unconscious that have rich and symbolic meaning.

FIGURE 12.5 *Star Wars* Characters as Archetypes of Good and Evil
In *Star Wars,* Ben Kenobi (*left*) represented the archetype of good and Darth Vader (*right*) the archetype of evil.

Adler's Individual Psychology   Alfred Adler (1870–1937) was another of Freud's contemporaries. In Adler's **individual psychology,** people are motivated by purposes and goals. They are creators of their own lives. Unlike Freud, who believed in the overwhelming power of the unconscious mind, Adler argued that people have the ability to consciously monitor their lives. He also believed that social factors are more important than sexual motivation in shaping personality (Silverman & Corsini, 1984).

Adler thought that everyone strives for superiority, seeking to adapt, improve, and master the environment. Striving for superiority is our response to the uncomfortable feelings of inferiority that we all experience as infants and young children when we interact with people who are bigger and more powerful. *Compensation* is Adler's term for the individual's attempt to overcome imagined or real inferiorities or weaknesses by developing one's own abilities. Adler believed that compensation was normal, and he said that we often make up for a weakness in one ability by excelling in a different ability. For example, one person may be a mediocre student but compensate by excelling in athletics.

Overcompensation is Adler's term for the individual's attempt to deny rather than acknowledge a real situation or for the exaggerated effort to conceal a weakness. Adler described two patterns of overcompensation: *Inferiority complex* is his term for exaggerated feelings of inadequacy; *superiority complex* is his term for exaggerated self-importance invoked to mask feelings of inferiority.

Evaluating the Psychodynamic Perspectives

Although psychodynamic theories have diverged from Freud's original psychoanalytic version, they do share some core principles:

- Personality is determined both by current experiences and, as the original psychoanalytic theory proposed, by those from early in life.
- Personality can be better understood by examining it developmentally, as a series of stages that unfold with the individual's physical, cognitive, and socioemotional development.
- We mentally transform our experiences, giving them meaning that shapes our personality.

individual psychology The term for Adler's approach, which views people as motivated by purposes and goals, being creators of their own lives.

- The mind is not all consciousness; unconscious motives lie behind some of our puzzling behavior.
- The individual's inner world often conflicts with the outer demands of reality, creating anxiety that is not easy to resolve.
- Personality and adjustment—not just the experimental laboratory topics of sensation, perception, and learning—are rightful and important topics of psychological inquiry.

One persistent criticism of the psychodynamic perspective is that its main concepts have been difficult to test; they are largely matters of inference and interpretation. Researchers have not, for example, successfully investigated such key concepts as repression in the laboratory.

Thus much of the data used to support psychodynamic perspectives have come from clinicians' subjective evaluations of clients; clinicians can easily see evidence of theories they hold. Other data come from patients' recollections of the distant past (especially those from early childhood) and are of unknown accuracy.

Others object that psychodynamic perspectives have too negative and pessimistic a view of the person. For example, these perspectives place too much weight on early experiences within the family and their influence on personality and do not acknowledge that we retain the capacity for change and adaptation throughout our lives. Some psychologists believe that Freud and Jung placed too much faith in the unconscious mind's ability to control behavior. Others object that Freud overemphasized the importance of sexuality in understanding personality; we are not born into the world with only a bundle of sexual and aggressive instincts. The demands of reality do not always conflict with our biological needs.

Finally, some critics have noted that many psychodynamic perspectives, especially Freud's, have a male, Western bias. Although Horney's theory helped to correct this bias, psychodynamic theory continues to be revised today by psychologists studying female personality development, as well as personality development in various ethnicities and cultures (Callan, 2002).

Review and Sharpen Your Thinking

2 **Summarize the psychodynamic perspectives.**
- Describe the main tenets of the psychodynamic perspectives.
- Explain the key concepts in Freud's psychoanalytic theory.
- Discuss how the ideas of three psychodynamic dissenters and revisionists differed from Freud's.
- Identify the pros and cons of the psychodynamic perspectives.

What psychodynamic ideas may apply to all human beings? Which ones may not apply to everyone?

mhhe com/
santrockp7

For study tools related to this learning goal, see the Study Guide, the CD-ROM, and the Online Learning Center.

BEHAVIORAL AND SOCIAL COGNITIVE PERSPECTIVES 3

| Skinner's Behaviorism | Bandura's Social Cognitive Theory | Evaluating the Behavioral and Social Cognitive Perspectives |

What are the main features of the behavioral and social cognitive perspectives?
Tom is engaged to marry Ann. Both have warm, friendly personalities, and they enjoy being with each other. Psychodynamic theorists would say that their personalities derive from long-standing relationships with their parents, especially from their early

childhood experiences. They also would say that the reason for their attraction is unconscious, that they are unaware of how their biological heritage and early life experiences have been carried forward to influence their adult personalities.

But behaviorists and social cognitive theorists would observe Tom and Ann and see something quite different. They would examine the two people's experiences, especially their most recent ones, to understand the reason for Tom and Ann's attraction to each another. Tom might be described as rewarding Ann's behavior, and vice versa. Behaviorists and social cognitive theorists would make no reference to unconscious thoughts, the Oedipus complex, defense mechanisms, and so on.

The behavioral and social cognitive perspectives, introduced in chapter 1, emphasize the importance of environmental experiences and people's observable behavior to understand their personalities. Within that broad framework, behaviorists focus on behavior; social cognitive theorists also examine cognitive factors in personality.

Skinner's Behaviorism

At about the same time at which Freud was interpreting his patients' unconscious minds through recollections of their childhood experiences, John B. Watson and Ivan Pavlov were conducting detailed observations of behavior under controlled laboratory conditions. Recall from chapter 7 that Pavlov believed organisms learn through classical conditioning.

Chapter 7 also described B. F. Skinner's approach to learning, called operant conditioning. Skinner concluded that personality is the individual's observed, overt behavior, which is determined by the external environment; personality does not include internal traits and thoughts. Skinner believed we do not have to understand biological or cognitive processes to explain personality (behavior). Some psychologists say that including Skinner among personality theorists is like inviting a wolf to a party of lambs because he took the "person" out of personality (Phares, 1984).

Behaviorists counter that you cannot pinpoint where personality is or how it is determined; you can only observe what people do. For example, observations of Sam might reveal his shy, achievement-oriented, and caring behaviors. According to Skinner, these behaviors *are* his personality. Furthermore, Sam is this way because rewards and punishments in his environment shaped him into a shy, achievement-oriented, and caring person. Because of interactions with family members, friends, teachers, and others, Sam has *learned* to behave in this fashion.

Skinner stressed that our behavior always has the capacity for change if new experiences are encountered. Thus Sam's shy, achievement-oriented, and caring behavior may not be consistent and enduring. For example, Sam may be uninhibited on Saturday night with friends at a bar, unmotivated to excel in English class, and occasionally nasty to his sister. Skinnerians believe that consistency in behavior comes only from consistency in environmental experiences. If Sam's shy, achievement-oriented, and caring behavior is consistently rewarded, his pattern of behavior likely will be consistent. The issue of consistency in personality is an important one, and it will be discussed often throughout this chapter.

Because behaviorists believe that personality is learned and often changes according to environmental experiences and situations, it follows that, by rearranging experiences and situations, the individual's personality can be changed. For the behaviorist, shy behavior can be changed into outgoing behavior; aggressive behavior can be shaped into docile behavior; and lethargic, bored behavior can be shaped into enthusiastic, interested behavior.

Bandura's Social Cognitive Theory

Some psychologists believe the behaviorists are right when they say that personality is learned and influenced strongly by environmental experiences. But they think

Skinner went too far in declaring that characteristics of the person are irrelevant in understanding personality. **Social cognitive theory** states that behavior, environment, and cognitive factors are important in understanding personality. Like the behavioral approach of Skinner, the social cognitive view relies on empirical research in studying personality. But this research has focused not just on observable behavior but also on the cognitive factors that influence what we are like as people. Albert Bandura (1986, 1997, 2000, 2001) and Walter Mischel (1973, 1995; Idson & Mischel, 2001; Mischel & Shoda, 2001) are the main architects of social cognitive theory's contemporary version, which initially was labeled *cognitive social learning theory* by Mischel (1973). Bandura, Mischel, and others are actively developing this perspective today.

Reciprocal Determinism   Bandura coined the term *reciprocal determinism* to describe the way behavior, environment, and person/cognitive factors interact to create personality (see figure 12.6). The environment can determine a person's behavior (which matches up with Skinner's view), but, also, the person can act to change the environment. And, person/cognitive factors can influence behavior and can be influenced by behavior.

Observational Learning   Remember from chapter 7 that Bandura believes observational learning is a key aspect of how we learn. Through observational learning we form ideas about the behavior of others and then possibly adopt this behavior ourselves. For example, a young boy might observe his father's aggressive outbursts and hostile exchanges with people; when the boy is with his peers, he interacts in a highly aggressive way, showing the same characteristics that his father's behavior does. Or a young executive adopts the dominant and sarcastic style of her boss. When interacting with one of her subordinates, she says, "I need this work immediately if not sooner; you are so far behind you think you are ahead!" Social cognitive theorists believe that we acquire a wide range of behaviors, thoughts, and feelings through observing others' behavior; these observations form an important part of our personalities.

Personal Control   Social cognitive theorists also differ from the behavioral view of Skinner by emphasizing that we can regulate and control our own behavior, despite our changing environment (Metcalfe & Mischel, 1999; Mischel & Shoda, 2001; Mischel, Shoda, & Mendoza-Denton, 2002). For example, another young executive who observes her boss behave in a dominant and sarcastic manner may find the behavior distasteful and go out of her way to be encouraging and supportive of her subordinates. Or imagine that someone tries to persuade you to join a particular social club on campus and makes you an enticing offer. You reflect on the offer, consider your interests and beliefs, and make the decision not to join. Your *cognition* (your thoughts) leads you to control your behavior and resist environmental influence in this instance.

Bandura (2001) and other social cognitive theorists and researchers emphasize that psychological health—being well-adjusted—can be measured by people's beliefs in their capacity to exercise some control over their own functioning and over environmental events. Three aspects of personal control that these theorists are exploring are delay of gratification, self-efficacy, and locus of control.

Delay of Gratification   One process that Walter Mischel (Mischel, Cantor, & Feldman, 1996; Mischel & Moore, 1980) believes is important in understanding an individual's personality is the ability to delay gratification. Those who can defer immediate satisfaction for a desirable future outcome are demonstrating the importance of person/cognitive factors in determining their own behavior. For example, when you are in school you resist the temptation to slack off and have a good time now so you will be rewarded with good grades later. Again, the point is that we are capable of controlling our behavior rather than being influenced by others.

Albert Bandura (*above*) and Walter Mischel are the architects of contemporary social cognitive theory.

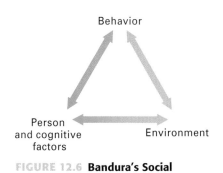

FIGURE 12.6 Bandura's Social Cognitive Theory Bandura's social cognitive theory emphasizes reciprocal influences of behavior, environment, and person/cognitive factors.

social cognitive theory States that behavior, environment, and person/cognitive factors are important in understanding personality.

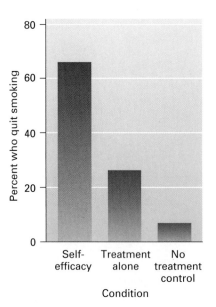

FIGURE 12.7 Self-Efficacy and Smoking Cessation In one study, smokers were randomly assigned to one of three conditions. In the self-efficacy condition, individuals were told they had been chosen for the study because they had great potential to quit smoking. Then, they participated in a 14-week program on smoking cessation. In the treatment-alone condition, individuals participated in the 14-week smoking cessation program but were told that they had been randomly selected for it. In the no-treatment control condition, individuals did not participate in the smoking cessation program. At the conclusion of the 14-week program, individuals in the self-efficacy condition were likelier to have quit smoking than their counterparts in the other two conditions.

self-efficacy The belief that one can master a situation and produce positive outcomes.

locus of control Individuals' beliefs about whether the outcomes of their actions depend on what they do (internal control) or on events outside of their personal control (external control).

Self-Efficacy **Self-efficacy** is the belief that one can master a situation and produce positive outcomes. Bandura (1997, 2000, 2001) and others have shown that self-efficacy is related to a number of positive developments in people's lives, including solving problems, becoming more sociable, initiating a diet or exercise program and maintaining it, and quitting smoking (see figure 12.7; Borelli & others, 2002; Fletcher & Banasik, 2001; Warnecke & others, 2001). Self-efficacy influences whether people even try to develop healthy habits, as well as how much effort they expend in coping with stress, how long they persist in the face of obstacles, and how much stress they experience (Clark & Dodge, 1999). Self-efficacy is related to whether people initiate psychotherapy to deal with their problems and whether it succeeds or not (Kavanaugh & Wilson, 1989; Longo, Lent, & Brown, 1992). Researchers also have found that self-efficacy is linked with successful job performance (Judge & Bono, 2001).

Self-efficacy helps people in unsatisfactory situations by encouraging them to believe that they can succeed (Rose & others, 2002). Overweight individuals will likely have more success with their diets if they believe they have the self-control to restrict their eating. Smokers who believe they will not be able to break their habit probably won't even try to quit smoking, even though they know that smoking is likely to cause poor health and shorten their lives.

How can you increase your self-efficacy? The following strategies can help (Watson & Tharp, 2002):

- Select something you expect to be able to do, not something you expect to fail at accomplishing. As you develop self-efficacy, you can tackle more daunting projects.
- Distinguish between past performance and your present project. You might come to expect from past failures that you cannot do certain things. However, remind yourself that your past failures are in the past and that you now have a new sense of confidence and accomplishment.
- Pay close attention to your successes. Some individuals have a tendency to remember their failures, but not their successes.
- Keep written records so that you will be concretely aware of your successes. A student who sticks to a study schedule for 4 days and then fails to stick to it on the 5th day should not think, "I'm a failure. I can't do this." This statement ignores the fact that the student was successful 80 percent of the time (keeping to the schedule 4 out of 5 days).
- Make a list of the specific kinds of situations in which you expect to have the most difficulty and the least difficulty. Begin with the easier tasks and cope with the harder ones after you have experienced some success.

Locus of Control Much of psychology's current interest in intrinsic motivation, self-determination, and self-responsibility (discussed in chapter 11) grew out of the concept of **locus of control.** This concept refers to individuals' beliefs about whether the outcomes of their actions depend on what they do (internal control) or on events outside of their personal control (external control; Rotter, 1966). Internally controlled people assume that their own behaviors and actions are responsible for the consequences that happen to them. In contrast, externally controlled people believe that, regardless of how they behave, they are subject to the whims of fate, luck, or other people.

Locus of control has especially been studied in regard to physical and mental health. Individuals with internal locus of control know more about the conditions that lead to good physical and psychological health and are likelier to take positive steps to improve their health, such as quitting smoking, avoiding substance abuse, and exercising regularly (Lindquist & Aberg, 2002; Powell, 1992).

Individuals with external locus of control are likelier to conform and not question authority (Singh, 1984). They often use defensive strategies in problem solving and coping instead of actively pursuing solutions; thus they more often fail (Lester,

1992). A wealth of research has documented that having an internal locus of control is associated with positive functioning and adjustment (Engler, 1999).

Optimism Another factor that is often related to positive functioning and adjustment is being optimistic (Catford, 2002; Kubansky & others, 2002). Interest in the concept of optimism in the field of psychology has especially been fueled by Martin Seligman's (1990) theory and research on optimism. Seligman views optimism as a matter of how a person explains the causes of bad events. Optimists explain the causes of bad events as due to external, unstable, and specific causes. Pessimists explain bad events as due to internal, stable, and global causes.

To illustrate the power of optimism, Seligman (1990) recalled the situation of 45-year-old Bob Dell, who had a wife, two children, and a mortgage. After working 25 years in a meat-packing plant, he suddenly was fired from his job. With no immediate job prospects and only a high school education, his situation looked grim. He was approached by an insurance agent who wanted to sell him a policy. Bob informed the agent that he was unemployed and could not afford anything. The agent told Bob that his insurance company currently was hiring new sales representatives and suggested that he apply for a position. Bob had never sold anything, but, being an optimist, he decided to give it a try.

Seligman was a consultant for the insurance company at the time. He had persuaded the company to hire salespeople who did not meet all of their qualifications but were high in optimism. Dell was one of 130 applicants who were identified as "optimists" on a measure Seligman had developed, which was included in the measures that job applicants had to complete.

In less than 1 year, Bob went from sausage-stuffer to super-salesman, earning twice what he had at the meat-packing plant. When Bob learned from a magazine article about the experimental program that he had participated in, with characteristic optimism, he called Seligman, introduced himself, and sold him a retirement policy!

Seligman's interest in optimism stemmed from his work on *learned helplessness,* which initially focused on animals who learned to become helpless (passive and unresponsive) after they experienced uncontrollable negative events (1975). In his view, pessimism is much like learned helplessness and belief in external locus of control. Optimism is much like belief in self-efficacy and internal locus of control.

Other researchers have defined optimism as the expectancy that good things are more likely, and bad things less likely, to occur in the future (Carver & Scheier, 2001; Scheier & Carver, 1992). This view focuses on how people pursue their goals and values. In the face of adversity, optimists still believe that their goals and values can be attained. Their optimism keeps them working to attain their goals, whereas pessimism results in people giving up.

Numerous research studies reveal that optimists generally function more effectively and are physically and mentally healthier than pessimists:

- *Physical health.* In one rather remarkable finding, people who were classified as optimistic at age 25 were healthier at ages 45 to 60 than those who had been classified as pessimistic (Peterson, Seligman, & Vaillant, 1988). In another study, pessimism was linked with less effective immune system functioning and poor health (Brennan & Charnetski, 2000). Optimists also have been found to have lower blood pressure than pessimists (Raikkonen & others, 1999).
- *Mental health.* In one study, optimism was a better predictor than self-efficacy of the person's ability to avoid depression over time (Shnek & others, 2001). In another study, optimism was related to better mental health in cancer patients (Cohen, de Moor, & Amato, 2001). In yet another study, optimism was linked with better mental health and lower perceptions of pain in older adults (Achat & others, 2000).

Optimism is not all good, however. It can have costs if it is too unrealistic (Clarke & others, 2000; Peterson, 2000; Schneider, 2001). But being optimistic is a good strategy when you have some chance of affecting the future through an optimistic outlook. Thinking optimistically is discussed further in chapter 15.

Martin Seligman went from pessimist to optimist and believes that you can, too. Seligman (1990) provided the details in his book *Learned Optimism.* Recall Seligman's interest in changing psychology from a discipline that focuses mainly on the negative aspects of life to one that spends more time charting the positive aspects of life.

Evaluating the Behavioral and Social Cognitive Perspectives

The behavioral and social cognitive theories both focus on the influence of environment on personality. They have fostered a scientific climate for understanding personality that highlights the observation of behavior. In addition, social cognitive theory emphasizes the influence of cognitive processes in explaining personality and suggests that people have the ability to control their environment.

Critics of both the behavioral and social cognitive perspectives take issue with one or more of these points:

- The behavioral view is criticized for ignoring the importance of cognition in personality and giving too much importance to the role of environmental experiences.
- Both approaches have been described as too concerned with change and situational influences on personality and not paying adequate tribute to the enduring qualities of personality.
- Both views are said to ignore the role biology plays in personality.
- Both are labeled reductionistic, which means they try to explain the complex concept of personality in terms of one or two factors.
- Both the behavioral and social cognitive views are criticized for being too mechanical, missing the most exciting, richest dimensions of personality.

This latter criticism—that the creative, spontaneous, human dimensions of personality are missing from the behavioral and social cognitive perspectives—has been made on numerous occasions by humanists, whose perspective is considered next.

Review and Sharpen Your Thinking

3 *Explain the behavioral and social cognitive perspectives.*
- Define the behavioral and social cognitive perspectives.
- Summarize Skinner's behaviorism.
- Discuss social cognitive theory.
- Evaluate the behavioral and social cognitive perspectives.

Are you an optimist or a pessimist? Explain how your style of thinking about bad events has helped you or hindered you as a student.

4 HUMANISTIC PERSPECTIVES

Rogers' Approach

Self-Esteem

Maslow's Approach

Evaluating Humanistic Perspectives

What are the main themes of the humanistic perspectives?

Remember the example of the engaged couple, Tom and Ann, who were described as having warm, friendly personalities? Humanistic psychologists would say that Tom's and Ann's warm, friendly personalities are a reflection of their inner selves. They would emphasize that a key to understanding the attraction between Tom and Ann is their positive perception of each other. Tom and Ann are not trying to control each other. Rather, they have determined their own courses of action, and each has freely chosen to marry. According to the humanistic perspectives, neither raw biological instincts nor unconscious thoughts are reasons for their attraction.

The **humanistic perspectives** stress a person's capacity for personal growth, freedom to choose one's own destiny, and positive human qualities. Humanistic psychologists believe that each of us has the ability to cope with stress, to control our lives, and to achieve what we desire (Cain, 2001; O'Hara & Taylor, 2000; Smith, 2001). Each of us has the ability to break through and understand ourselves and our world; we can burst the cocoon and become a butterfly, say the humanists.

You probably sense that the humanistic perspectives provide clear contrasts to the psychodynamic perspectives, which often seem to be based on conflict, destructive drives, and a pessimistic view of human nature. The humanistic perspectives also seem to contrast with the behavioral perspective, which, at its extreme, reduces human beings to mere puppets on the strings of rewards and punishments. It does have some similarities with the social cognitive perspective, though, especially with those theories that emphasize the role of personal control and optimism in personality.

Carl Rogers and Abraham Maslow were the leading architects of the humanistic perspectives. Their work has provided the foundation for more contemporary studies of self-esteem.

CARL ROGERS (1902–1987)
Carl Rogers was a pioneer in the development of the humanistic perspective.

Rogers' Approach

Like Freud, Carl Rogers (1902–1987) began his inquiry about human nature with people who were troubled. In the knotted, anxious, defensive verbal stream of his clients, Rogers (1961) noted the things that seemed to be keeping them from having positive self-concepts and reaching their full potential as human beings.

Rogers believed that most people have considerable difficulty accepting their own true, innately positive, feelings. As we grow up, people who are central to our lives condition us to move away from these positive feelings. Too often we hear our parents, siblings, teachers, and peers say things like "Don't do that," "You didn't do that right," and "How can you be so stupid?" When we don't do something right, we often get punished. Parents may even threaten to withhold their love unless we conform to their standards. The result is lower self-esteem.

These constraints and negative feedback continue during our adult lives. The result tends to be either that our relationships carry the dark cloud of conflict or that we conform to what others want. As we struggle to live up to society's standards, we distort and devalue our true selves. And we might even completely lose our sense of self by mirroring what others want.

The Self   Through the individual's experiences with the world, a self emerges—the "I" or "me" of our existence. Rogers did not believe that all aspects of the self are conscious, but he did believe they are all accessible to consciousness. The self is a whole, consisting of one's self-perceptions (how attractive I am, how well I get along with others, how good an athlete I am) and the values we attach to these perceptions (good/bad, worthy/unworthy).

Self-concept, a central theme in Rogers' and other humanists' views, refers to individuals' overall perceptions and assessments of their abilities, behavior, and personalities. In Rogers' view, a person who has an inaccurate self-concept is likely to be maladjusted.

In discussing self-concept, Rogers distinguished between the real self, which is the self resulting from our experiences, and the ideal self, which is the self we would like to be. The greater the discrepancy between the real self and the ideal self, said Rogers, the more maladjusted we will be. To improve our adjustment, we can develop more positive perceptions of our real self, not worry as much about what others want, and increase our positive experiences in the world.

humanistic perspectives Stress the person's capacity for personal growth, freedom to choose a destiny, and positive qualities.

self-concept A central theme in Rogers' and other humanists' views; self-concept refers to individuals' overall perceptions of their abilities, behavior, and personalities.

Unconditional Positive Regard, Empathy, and Genuineness Rogers proposed three methods to help a person develop a more positive self-concept: *unconditional positive regard, empathy,* and *genuineness.*

Rogers said that we need to be accepted by others, regardless of what we do. **Unconditional positive regard** is his term for accepting, valuing, and being positive toward another person regardless of the person's behavior. When a person's behavior is inappropriate, obnoxious, or unacceptable, the person still needs the respect, comfort, and love of others. Rogers strongly believed that unconditional positive regard elevates the person's self-worth. However, Rogers (1974) distinguished between unconditional positive regard directed at the individual as a person of worth and dignity and directed at the individual's behavior. For example, a therapist who adopts Rogers' view might say, "I don't like your behavior, but I accept you, value you, and care about you as a person."

Rogers also said that we can help other people develop a more positive self-concept if we are *empathic* and *genuine.* Being empathic means being a sensitive listener and understanding another's true feelings. Being genuine means being open with our feelings and dropping our pretenses and facades.

For Rogers, unconditional positive regard, empathy, and genuineness are three key ingredients of human relations. We can use these techniques to help other people feel good about themselves and to help us get along better with others (Bozarth, Zimring, & Tausch, 2001; LaVigna and others, 2002).

The Fully Functioning Person Rogers (1980) stressed the importance of becoming a fully functioning person—someone who is open to experience, is not overly defensive, is aware of and sensitive to the self and the external world, and for the most part has a harmonious relationship with others. Rogers believed that we are highly resilient and capable of being fully functioning persons—whether we experience a discrepancy between our real selves and our ideal selves, whether we encounter others who may try to control us, or whether we receive too little unconditional positive regard.

Humans' self-actualizing tendencies, which were discussed in chapter 11, are reflected in Rogers' comparison of a person with a plant he once observed on the northern California coastline. As Rogers looked out at the waves furiously beating against the jagged rocks and shooting mountains of ocean spray into the air, he noticed the waves were also pounding against a palm tree 2 or 3 feet tall. The waves bent its slender trunk and whipped its leaves in a torrent of spray. Yet the moment each wave passed, the tree stood erect once again. The tree took this incessant pounding hour after hour, week after week, possibly even year after year, all the time nourishing itself, maintaining its position, and growing. In this persevering tree, Rogers saw the tenacity of the human spirit and the ability of a living thing to push into a hostile environment and not only hold its own, but adapt, develop, and become itself.

Rogers believed that a person's basic tendencies are to actualize, maintain, and enhance life. He thought that the tendency for fulfillment—toward actualizing one's essential nature and attaining potential—is inborn in every person.

Maslow's Approach

Recall from chapter 11 that another psychologist, Abraham Maslow (1908–1970), believed that self-actualization is the highest form of motivation. He also believed that it is an important aspect of personality. Maslow was one of the most powerful figures in psychology's humanistic movement. He called the humanistic approach the "third force" in psychology—that is, an important alternative to the psychodynamic and behavioral forces. Maslow argued that psychodynamic theories place too much emphasis on disturbed individuals and their conflicts. Behaviorists ignore the person altogether, he said.

unconditional positive regard
Rogers' term for accepting, valuing, and being positive toward another person regardless of the person's behavior.

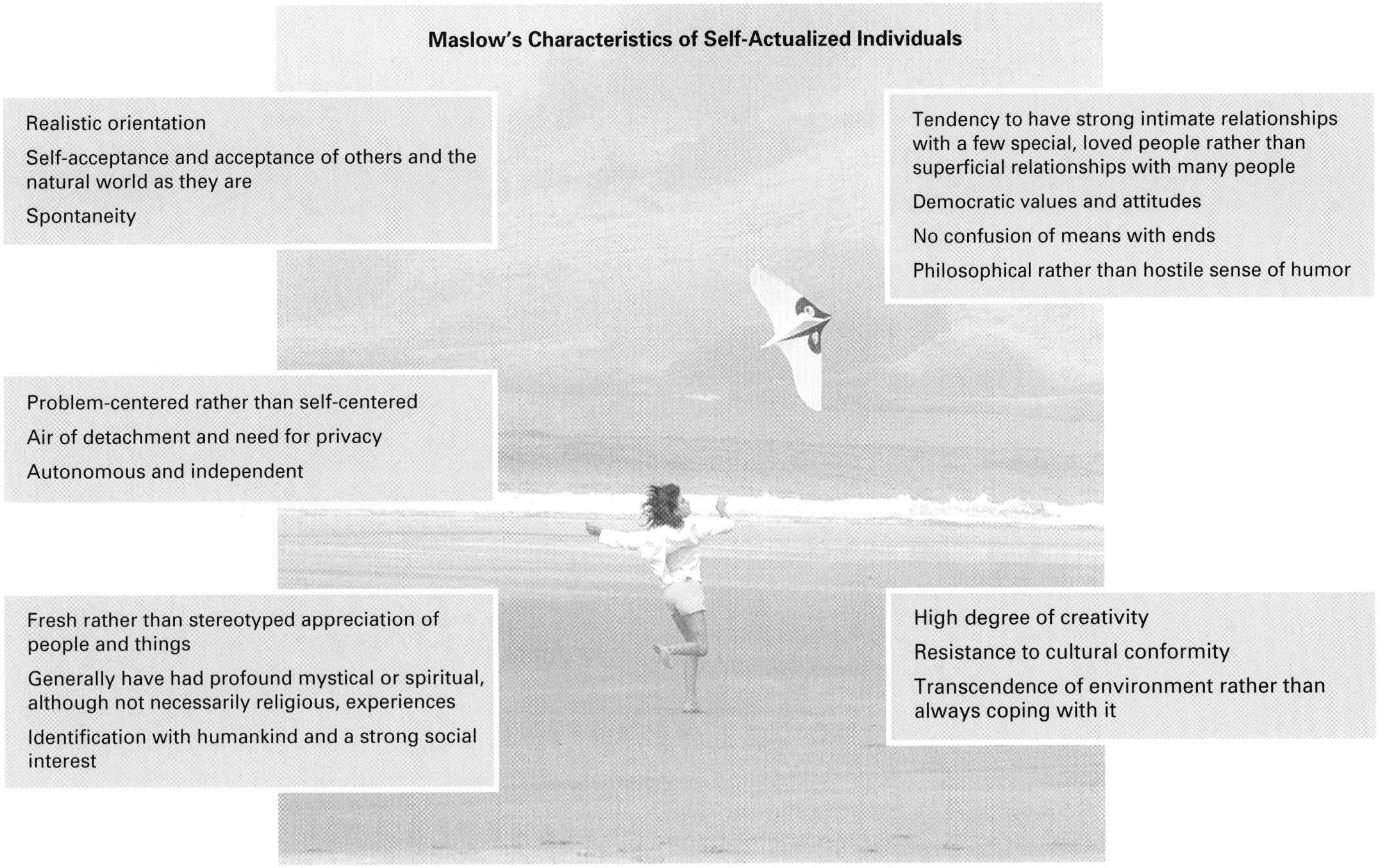

Maslow's Characteristics of Self-Actualized Individuals

Realistic orientation

Self-acceptance and acceptance of others and the natural world as they are

Spontaneity

Tendency to have strong intimate relationships with a few special, loved people rather than superficial relationships with many people

Democratic values and attitudes

No confusion of means with ends

Philosophical rather than hostile sense of humor

Problem-centered rather than self-centered

Air of detachment and need for privacy

Autonomous and independent

Fresh rather than stereotyped appreciation of people and things

Generally have had profound mystical or spiritual, although not necessarily religious, experiences

Identification with humankind and a strong social interest

High degree of creativity

Resistance to cultural conformity

Transcendence of environment rather than always coping with it

FIGURE 12.8 Maslow's Characteristics of Self-Actualized Individuals

According to Maslow's (1954, 1971) hierarchy of needs, self-actualization is the highest level human need. The motivation to develop one's full potential as a human being is what Maslow primarily focused on. Figure 12.8 describes the main characteristics that Maslow attributes to a self-actualized individual.

Although Maslow believed that most people have difficulty reaching this level, he identified the following individuals as among the self-actualized: Pablo Casals (cellist), Albert Einstein (physicist), Ralph Waldo Emerson (writer), William James (psychologist), Thomas Jefferson (politician), Abraham Lincoln (politician), Eleanor Roosevelt (humanitarian, diplomat), and Albert Schweitzer (humanitarian).

Maslow made up his list over three decades ago. Not all of his examples of self-actualized individuals were included here, but he did name considerably more men than women on the complete list. Most of the individuals also were from Western cultures. With Maslow's description of self-actualization in mind (including the characteristics listed in figure 12.8), think of others you would add to Maslow's list of self-actualized persons. For starters, consider Mother Teresa (spiritual leader) and Martin Luther King (clergyman, civil rights activist; Endler, 1995).

Self-Esteem

Rogers' and Maslow's interest in the self led to the belief that self-esteem is an important aspect of personality. **Self-esteem** is a person's overall evaluation of his or her self-worth or self-image.

Psychologists have shown considerable interest in self-esteem and how it is developed and maintained (Hewitt, 2001; Scarpa & Luscher, 2002). Following are some of the research issues and findings on self-esteem (Baumeister, 1997):

self-esteem The person's overall evaluation of self-worth or self-image.

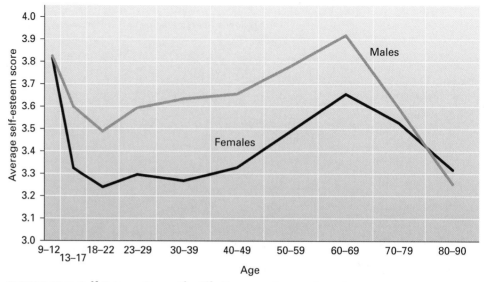

FIGURE 12.9 Self-Esteem Across the Life Span One large-scale study asked more than 300,000 individuals to rate the extent to which they have high self-esteem on a 5-point scale, 5 being "Strongly Agree" and 1 being "Strongly Disagree." Self-esteem dropped in adolescence and late adulthood. Self-esteem of females was lower than self-esteem of males through most of the life span and was especially low for females during adolescence.

- *Does self-esteem fluctuate from day to day or remain stable?* Most research studies have found it to be stable at least across a month or so (Baumeister, 1991). Self-esteem can change, however, especially in response to transitions in life (such as graduating from high school or going to college) and to life events (such as getting or losing a job). One recent study found that self-esteem is high in childhood, declines in adolescence, and increases through adulthood until late adulthood, at which time it declines again (see figure 12.9; Robins & others, in press). In this study, the self-esteem of males was higher than that of females through most of the life span. During adolescence, the self-esteem of girls declined more than that of boys.

- *Is self-esteem something very general or does it consist of a number of independent self-evaluations in different areas?* That is, is it more appropriate to think of people having high or low self-esteem overall or as having high or low self-esteem in specific areas of their lives, such as high in social self-esteem and low in cognitive (academic) self-esteem? Current thinking about this issue has evolved toward the conclusion that people do have a general level of self-esteem but still can have fluctuating levels of self-esteem in particular domains of their lives (Fleming & Courtney, 1984).

- *How does the lack of self-esteem affect the individual's ability to cope with the demands of life?* Researchers have found that low self-esteem is linked with depression (Harter, 1998). The failure to live up to one's own standards is especially implicated in the connection between low self-esteem and depression.

- *Are there sometimes costs associated with seeking high self-esteem?* The pursuit of self-esteem has become a preoccupation in America. Self-help books advise how to achieve high self-esteem, child-rearing guides tell parents how to raise children with high self-esteem, and many people avoid certain activities, situations, and people to protect and enhance their self-esteem (Miller, 2001). Might there be some costs in this pursuit? In one recent study of more than 600 college freshmen, the costs occurred when individuals sought high self-esteem for external reasons, especially appearance, to get positive feedback from others (Crocker, 2001). In this study, seeking high self-esteem because of a motivation to look physically attractive to others was linked with stress, drug and alcohol use, and disordered eating.

An important point needs to be made about much of the research on self-esteem: It is correlational rather than experimental. Remember from the discussion in chapter 2, that correlation does not equal causation. Thus, if a correlational study finds an association between low self-esteem and depression, depression could cause low self-esteem as much as low self-esteem causes depression.

A topic of considerable interest among clinical and educational psychologists is what can be done to increase the self-esteem of individuals with low self-esteem. Researchers have found that four main strategies help to improve self-esteem (Bednar, Wells, & Peterson, 1995; Harter, 1998):

- Identifying the causes of low self-esteem
- Experiencing emotional support and approval
- Achieving
- Coping

The strategy of experiencing emotional support and approval meshes with Carl Rogers' concept of unconditional positive regard. But some psychologists argue that the most effective ways to improve self-esteem are to improve the person's achievement and coping skills. Rogers himself believed that when a person's achievement and coping skills improve, the individual's self-esteem is likely to follow suit. Coping skills are further discussed in chapter 15.

Evaluating Humanistic Perspectives

The humanistic perspectives made psychologists aware that the way we perceive ourselves and the world around us are key elements of personality. Humanistic psychologists also reminded us that we need to consider the whole person and the positive bent of human nature (Bohart & Greening, 2001). Their emphasis on conscious experience has given us the view that personality contains a well of potential that can be developed to its fullest (Hill, 2000).

A weakness of the humanistic perspective is that it is difficult to test. Self-actualization, for example, is not even clearly defined, much less easy to observe. Psychologists are not certain how to study this concept empirically. Complicating matters is the fact that some humanists scorn the experimental approach, preferring clinical interpretation as a database. Indeed, verification of humanistic concepts has come mainly from clinical experiences rather than from controlled, experimental studies.

Some critics also believe that humanistic psychologists are too optimistic about human nature, overestimating the freedom and rationality of humans. And some critics say the humanists may encourage excessive self-love and narcissism by encouraging people to think so positively about themselves.

Review and Sharpen Your Thinking

4   *Describe the humanistic perspectives.*

- Define the main themes of the humanistic perspectives.
- Explain the key elements in Rogers' theory.
- Summarize Maslow's theory.
- Discuss the importance of self-esteem to individuals.
- Evaluate the humanistic perspectives.

What is the level of your self-esteem? That is, on the whole, are you satisfied with yourself? Or do you wish that you could have a more positive attitude toward yourself? Is your self-esteem higher in some areas of your life than others? If so, which ones? If your self-esteem is low, what do you think it would take to get it higher?

mhhe com/
santrockp7

For study tools related to this learning goal, see the Study Guide, the CD-ROM, and the Online Learning Center.

5 TRAIT PERSPECTIVES

Trait Theories

Trait-Situation Interaction

The Big Five Personality Factors

Evaluating Trait Perspectives

What are the main ideas of the trait perspectives?

Through the ages we have described ourselves and one another in terms of basic traits. A **trait** is an enduring personality characteristic that tends to lead to certain behaviors. Around 400 B.C., Hippocrates, the "father of medicine," described human beings as having one of four basic personalities, determined by their physical makeup: choleric (quick-tempered), phlegmatic (placid), sanguine (optimistic), or melancholic (pessimistic). Others have proposed different sets of traits, but some descriptions of personality have remained remarkably constant. More than 2,000 years ago, for example, Theophrastus described the basic traits of the "stingy man," the "liar," and the "flatterer." A magazine article takes a modern swipe at the stingy man:

> Could a miser be lurking beneath the sensuous flesh and persuasive charm? Well, don't expect sapphires from him, if he
>
> - itemizes who owes what when you're out Dutch-treat rather than splitting the bill
> - washes plastic party cups to reuse them
> - steams uncanceled stamps from letters
> - reshapes bent paper clips
> - has a dozen recipes for chicken wings
> - cuts his own hair
> - wants rolls and butter included in his doggie bag. (*Cosmopolitan*, September 1976, p. 148)

Think about how you would quickly describe yourself and your friends. You might say that you're outgoing and sociable and that, in contrast, one of your friends is shy and quiet. You might refer to yourself as emotionally stable and describe one of your other friends as a bit skittish. Part of our everyday existence involves describing ourselves and others in terms of traits.

Trait Theories

Trait theories state that personality consists of broad, enduring dispositions that tend to lead to characteristic responses. In other words, people can be described in terms of the basic ways they behave, such as whether they are outgoing and friendly or whether they are dominant and assertive. People who have a strong tendency to behave in certain ways are described as high on the traits; those who have a weak tendency to behave in these ways are described as low on the traits. Although trait theorists sometimes differ on which traits make up personality, they all agree that traits are the fundamental building blocks of personality (Larson & Buss, 2002; Matthews & Dreary, 1998).

Allport's View of Traits Gordon Allport (1897–1967) believed that each individual has a unique set of personality traits. He argued that if we can determine a person's traits, we can predict the individual's behavior in various circumstances.

In going through an unabridged dictionary, Allport (1937) identified more than 4,500 personality traits. To impose some organization on the vast number of terms that might be used to describe an individual's personality, Allport grouped personality traits into three main categories:

trait An enduring personality characteristic that tends to lead to certain behaviors.

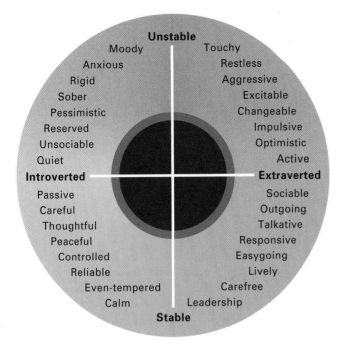

FIGURE 12.10 Eysenck's Dimensions of Personality Eysenck believed that for people without a psychological disorder, personality consists of two basic dimensions: introversion-extraversion and stability-instability. He thought that a third dimension—psychoticism—was needed to describe the personality of individuals with a psychological disorder.

- *Cardinal traits* are the most powerful and pervasive. When they are present, they dominate an individual's personality. However, according to Allport, few people actually possess cardinal traits. We might think of some famous individuals as having these (Hitler's craving for power, Mother Teresa's altruism). But most people aren't characterized by just one or two traits (unlike the way we think about Hitler or Mother Teresa).
- *Central traits* are limited in number. Allport believed that most people have about 6 to 12 central traits that are usually adequate to describe personalities. For an example, an individual's personality might be described as friendly, calm, kind, humorous, messy, and nostalgic.
- *Secondary traits* are limited in frequency and least important in understanding an individual's personality. They include particular attitudes and preferences, such as the type of food or music a person likes.

Eysenck's Dimensions of Personality   Hans Eysenck (1967) also tackled the task of determining the basic traits of personality. He gave personality tests to large numbers of people and analyzed each person's responses. Eysenck said that three main dimensions were needed to explain personality:

- *Introversion-extraversion.* An introverted person is quiet, unsociable, passive, and careful; an extraverted person is active, optimistic, sociable, and outgoing (Thorne, 2001).
- *Stable-unstable* (known as the *neuroticism* dimension). A stable person is calm, even-tempered, carefree, and capable of leadership; an unstable person is moody, anxious, restless, and touchy.
- *Psychoticism.* This dimension reflects the degree to which people are in contact with reality, control their impulses, and are cruel or caring toward others.

Figure 12.10 shows the interaction of what Eysenck considered to be the two basic dimensions of personality: introversion/extraversion and stable/unstable. Eysenck believed that various combinations of these dimensions result in certain personality traits. For example, a person who is extraverted and unstable is likely to be impulsive. To evaluate the extent to which you are introverted or extraverted, see the Psychology and Life box.

Are You Extraverted or Introverted?

To determine how extraverted or introverted you are, read each of the following 20 questions and answer either *yes* (if it is generally true for you) or *no* (if it is not generally true for you).

	Yes	No
1. Do you often long for excitement?		
2. Are you usually carefree?		
3. Do you stop and think things over before doing anything?		
4. Would you do almost anything on a dare?		
5. Do you often do things on the spur of the moment?		
6. Generally, do you prefer reading to meeting people?		
7. Do you prefer to have few but special friends?		
8. When people shout at you, do you shout back?		
9. Do other people think of you as very lively?		
10. Are you mostly quiet when you are with people?		
11. If there is something you want to know about, would you rather look it up in a book than talk to someone about it?		
12. Do you like the kind of work that you need to pay close attention to?		
13. Do you hate being with a crowd who plays jokes on one another?		
14. Do you like doing things in which you have to act quickly?		
15. Are you slow and unhurried in the way you move?		

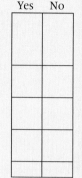

	Yes	No
16. Do you like talking to people so much that you never miss a chance of talking to a stranger?		
17. Would you be unhappy if you could not see lots of people most of the time?		
18. Do you find it hard to enjoy yourself at a lively party?		
19. Would you say that you were fairly self-confident?		
20. Do you like playing pranks on others?		

To arrive at your score for extraversion, give one point for each of the following items answered *yes:* 1, 2, 4, 5, 8, 9, 14, 16, 17, 19, and 20. Then give yourself one point for each of the following items answered *no:* 3, 6, 7, 10, 11, 12, 13, 15, 18. Add up all the points to arrive at a total score.

Your total score should be between 0 and 20. If your scores are very high (15–20), you are the "life of the party." You clearly prefer being with others to being alone. If your scores are very low (0–5), you are a loner. You find greater pleasure in solitary activities. If you are somewhere in between (6–14), you are flexible in how you prefer to spend your time. You take pleasure in the company of others (especially if your score is in the higher range) but still also appreciate solitude.

The Big Five Personality Factors

Psychologists still take considerable interest in determining what the key factors of personality really are. A rash of research studies point toward a handful of factors as being the most important dimensions of personality (Costa & McCrae, 1995, 1998; Hogan, 1987; McCrae & Costa, 2001; McCrae & Allik, 2002). The **big five factors of personality,** the "supertraits" that are thought to describe the main dimensions of personality, are openness, conscientiousness, extraversion, agreeableness, and neuroticism (emotional stability; see figure 12.11). (Notice that if you create an acronym from these trait names, you get the word OCEAN.) Recall, from the beginning of the chapter, the description of the personality traits of great presidents. One trait that characterized great presidents was openness to experience and, in recent years, extraversion also has characterized great presidents.

Research on the big five factors includes the extent to which the factors appear in personality profiles in different cultures, how stable the factors are over time, and

big five factors of personality Are openness to experience, conscientiousness, extraversion, agreeableness, and neuroticism (emotional stability).

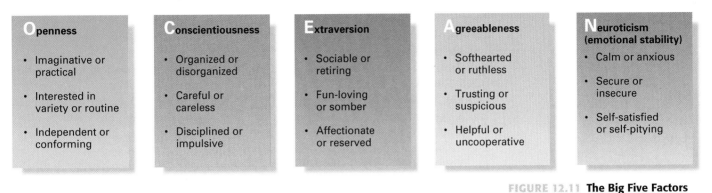

the role the factors might play in predicting physical and mental health (Lingjaerde, Foreland, & Engvik, 2001; Pukrop, Sass, & Steinmeyer, 2000). The more universal, stable, and predictive the big five factors prove to be, the more confidence we can have that they truly describe a person's fundamental traits.

Do the five factors show up in the assessment of personality in cultures around the world? There is increasing evidence that they do (Ozer & Riese, 1994; McCrae & Allik, 2002). Researchers have found that some version of the five factors appears in people in countries as diverse as Canada, Finland, Poland, China, and Japan (Paunonen & others, 1992).

What about the stability of these particular traits? Using a five-factor personality test that they devised, Paul Costa and Robert McCrae (1995) studied approximately 1,000 college-educated men and women ages 20 to 96, assessing the same individuals over many years. Data collection began in the 1950s to the mid-1960s and is ongoing. Costa and McCrae have so far concluded that the five personality factors—openness, conscientiousness, extraversion, agreeableness, and neuroticism (emotional stability)—are reasonably stable. For instance, individuals high on agreeableness tend to remain so throughout the years.

Can the big five factors help us to understand how personality is linked to physical and mental health? The notion that personality characteristics might influence health continues to attract widespread research attention. Much of this research, though, has been conducted using a hodgepodge of traits. The big five trait structure offers the potential of a unified, coherent framework for understanding which types of people are likely to stay healthy and to recover quickly from illness.

Research has generally supported the concept of the big five "general" traits, but some personality researchers believe they might not end up being the final list of broad supertraits and that more specific traits are better predictors of behavior (Saucier, 2001). For example, some support has been found for two additional personality dimensions: excellent-ordinary and evil-decent. The big five could become the big seven (Almagor, Tellegen, & Waller, 1995; Benet & Waller, 1995).

Trait-Situation Interaction

Today, most psychologists in the field of personality are interactionists. They believe that both trait (person) and situation need to be taken into account to understand personality (Ackerman, Kyllonen, & Roberts, 1999; Block, 2002; Edwards & Rothbard, 1999; Mischel, Shoda, & Mendoza-Denton, 2002). They also agree that consistency in personality depends on the kind of persons, situations, and behaviors sampled (Pervin, 2000; Mischel, 1995; Swartz-Kulstad & Martin, 2000).

Suppose you want to assess the happiness of Bob, an introvert, and of Jane, an extravert. According to trait-situation interaction theory, we cannot predict who will be happier unless we know something about the situations they are in. Imagine you get the opportunity to observe them in two situations, at a party and in a library. Do you think Bob or Jane will feel more comfortable at the party? Which one will be more content at the library? The extravert, Jane, is likelier to enjoy the party; and the introvert, Bob, is likelier to enjoy the library.

Trait-situation studies are clarifying the link between traits and situations (Martin & Swartz-Kulstad, 2000; Walsh, 1995). For example, researchers have found that (1) the narrower and more limited a trait is, the likelier it will predict behavior; (2) some people are consistent on some traits and other people are consistent on other traits; and (3) personality traits exert a stronger influence on an individual's behavior when situational influences are less powerful.

Cross-cultural psychologists go several steps further. They believe that both the immediate setting *and* the broader cultural context are important (Kitayama, 2002; Oyserman, Coon, & Kemmelmeier, 2002; Triandis & Suh, 2002). For example, if they were investigating certain aspects of personality and religion, they might observe a person's behavior in a chapel (the immediate setting) and put it in the context of social conventions regarding who should be in church, when, and with whom and how the person is expected to behave (cultural characteristics).

Evaluating Trait Perspectives

Studying people in terms of their personality traits has practical value. Identifying a person's traits allows us to know the person better. Also, the traits that we have influence our health, the way we think, how well we do in a career, and how well we get along with others (Larson & Buss, 2002; McCrae & Costa, 2001).

However, viewing people only in terms of their traits may provide only a partial view of personality. In his landmark book *Personality and Assessment,* Walter Mischel (1968) criticized the trait view of personality, which emphasizes the internal organization of personality. Rather than viewing personality as consisting of broad, internal traits that are consistent across situations and time, Mischel said that personality often changes according to a given situation. This view is consistent with Mischel's social cognitive perspective.

Mischel went beyond theoretical criticism, however. He reviewed an array of studies and concluded that trait measures by themselves often do a poor job of predicting actual behavior. For example, let's say Anne is described as an aggressive person. But when we observe her behavior we find that she is more or less aggressive depending on the situation—she might be aggressive with her boyfriend but almost submissive with her new boss. Mischel's view was called *situationism,* which means that personality often varies considerably from one context to another. Many trait psychologists were not willing to abandon altogether the idea of consistent, enduring personality characteristics, and Mischel's situationism helped to pave the way for viewing personality in terms of trait-situation interaction.

mhhe com/
santrockp7

For study tools related to this learning goal, see the Study Guide, the CD-ROM, and the Online Learning Center.

Review and Sharpen Your Thinking

5 **Discuss the trait perspectives.**

- Define traits and describe the views of Allport and Eysenck.
- Identify the big five factors in personality.
- Explain trait-situation interaction.
- Evaluate the trait perspectives.

To what extent do you believe the big five factors capture your personality? Look at the characteristics of the five factors listed in figure 12.11 and decide how you line up on each one. Then choose one of the factors, such as extraversion or openness to experience, and give an example of how situation might influence expression of this trait in your life.

Projective Tests	Behavioral and Cognitive Assessment
Self-Report Tests	Assessment in the Selection of Employees

What are the main methods of personality assessment?

"This line running this way indicates that you are a gregarious person, someone who really enjoys being around people. This division over here suggests that you are a risk taker; I bet you like to do things that are adventurous sometimes." These are words you might hear from a palmist. Palmistry purports to "read" an individual's personality by interpreting the irregularities and folds in the skin of the palm. Each of these signs is interpreted in a precise manner. For example, a large mound of Saturn, the portion of the palm directly below the third joint of the middle finger, is said to relate to wisdom, good fortune, and prudence.

Although palmists claim to provide a complete assessment of personality through reading lines on the palm, researchers debunk palmistry as quackery. Researchers argue that palmists give no reasonable explanation for their inferences about personality and point out that the palm's characteristics can change through age and even exercise.

Even so, palmists manage to stay in business. They do so, in part, because they are keen observers—they respond to such cues as voice, general demeanor, and dress, which are more relevant signs of personality than the lines and folds on a person's palm. Palmists also are experts at offering general, trivial statements such as "Although you usually are affectionate with others, sometimes you don't get along with people." This statement falls into the category of the *Barnum effect:* If you make your predictions broad enough, any person can fit the description. The effect was named after circus owner P. T. Barnum.

In contrast to palmists, psychologists use a number of scientifically developed methods to evaluate personality (Kraik, 2000; Walsh & Betz, 1995). And they assess personality for different reasons. Clinical and school psychologists assess personality to better understand an individual's psychological problems; they hope the assessment will improve their diagnosis and treatment of the individual. Industrial psychologists and vocational counselors assess personality to aid the individual's selection of a career. And research psychologists assess personality to investigate the theories and dimensions of personality we have discussed so far in this chapter. For example, if a psychologist wants to investigate self-concept, some measure of self-concept is needed.

Before we describe some specific personality tests, two more important points need to be made about the nature of personality assessment. First, the kinds of tests chosen by psychologists frequently depend on the psychologist's theoretical bent. And, second, most personality tests are designed to assess stable, enduring characteristics, free of situational influence (Hy & Loevinger, 1996; Ozer, 2001).

Projective Tests

A **projective test** presents individuals with an ambiguous stimulus and then asks them to describe it or tell a story about it—in other words, to *project* their own meaning onto the stimulus. Projective tests are based on the assumption that the ambiguity of the stimulus allows individuals to invest it with their feelings, desires, needs, and attitudes. The test is especially designed to elicit the individual's unconscious feelings

projective test Personality assessment tool that presents individuals with an ambiguous stimulus and then asks them to describe it or tell a story about it; based on the assumption that the ambiguity of the stimulus allows individuals to project their personalities onto it.

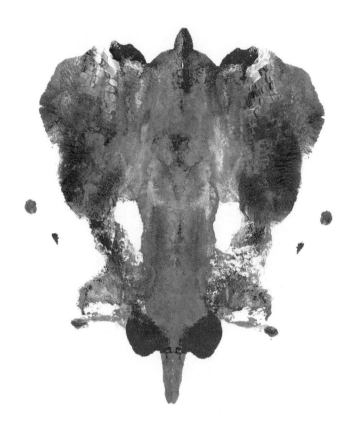

FIGURE 12.12 **Type of Stimulus Used in the Rorschach Inkblot Test**

and conflicts, providing an assessment that goes deeper than the surface of personality (Blatt, 2000; Handler, 1999). Projective tests attempt to get inside of your mind to discover how you really feel and think, going beyond the way you overtly present yourself. Projective tests are theoretically aligned with the psychodynamic perspectives on personality, which give more weight than the other perspectives to the unconscious.

Rorschach Inkblot Test The **Rorschach inkblot test,** developed in 1921 by the Swiss psychiatrist Hermann Rorschach, is a widely used projective test; it uses an individual's perception of the inkblots to determine his or her personality. The test consists of 10 cards, half in black and white and half in color, which are shown to the individual one at a time (see figure 12.12). The person taking the Rorschach test is asked to describe what he or she sees in each of the inkblots. For example, an individual may say, "That looks like two people fighting." After the individual has responded to all 10 inkblots, the examiner presents each of the inkblots again and inquires about the individual's earlier response. For example, the examiner might ask, "*Where* did you see the two people fighting?" and "*What* about the inkblot made the two people look like they were fighting?" Besides recording the responses, the examiner notes the individual's mannerisms, gestures, and attitudes.

How useful is the Rorschach in assessing personality? The answer depends on one's perspective. From a scientific perspective, researchers are skeptical about the Rorschach (Feshbach & Weiner, 1996; Garb & others, 2001). Their disenchantment stems from the failure of the Rorschach to meet the criteria of reliability and validity. If the Rorschach were reliable, two different scorers should agree on the personality characteristics of the individual being tested. If the Rorschach were valid, it should be able to predict behavior outside of the testing situation; that is, it should

Rorschach inkblot test A widely used projective test; it uses an individual's perception of inkblots to determine his or her personality.

predict whether an individual will attempt suicide, become severely depressed, cope successfully with stress, or get along well with others. Conclusions based on research evidence suggest that the Rorschach does not meet these criteria of reliability and validity (Lilienfeld, Wood, & Garb, 2000). Thus many psychologists have serious reservations about the Rorschach's use in diagnosis and clinical practice.

Yet the Rorschach continues to enjoy widespread use in clinical circles; some clinicians swear by the Rorschach, saying it is better than any other measure at getting at the true, underlying core of the individual's personality (Ephraim, 2000; Meyer, 2001; Sloan & others, 1996). They are not especially bothered by the Rorschach's low reliability and validity, pointing out that the test encourages extensive freedom of response. This freedom of response is what makes the Rorschach such a rich clinical tool, say its advocates. In one survey, Rorschach-based testimony was legally challenged in only 6 of nearly 8,000 court cases (Weiner, Exner, & Sciara, 1996).

The Rorschach controversy continues (Garb & others, 2001; Meyer & Archey, 2001; Murstein & Mathes, 1996; Viglione & Hilsenroth, 2001). And it probably will not subside in the near future. Research psychologists will continue to criticize the low reliability and validity of the Rorschach; many clinicians will continue to claim that the Rorschach is a valuable clinical tool, providing insights about the unconscious mind that no other personality test can provide (Hilsenroth, 2000).

"Rorschach! What's to become of you?"
© Sidney Harris

Other Projective Tests The **Thematic Apperception Test (TAT),** which was developed by Henry Murray and Christina Morgan in the 1930s, is designed to elicit stories that reveal something about an individual's personality. The TAT consists of a series of pictures like the one in figure 12.13, each on an individual card. The person taking the TAT is asked to tell a story about each of the pictures, including events leading up to the situation described, the characters' thoughts and feelings, and the way the situation turns out. The tester assumes that the person projects his or her own unconscious feelings and thoughts into the story (Herzberg, 2000). In addition to being used as a projective test in clinical practice, the TAT is used in research on people's need for achievement (Cramer, 1999; Cramer & Brilliant, 2001). Several of the TAT cards stimulate the telling of achievement-related stories (McClelland & others, 1953).

Many other projective tests are used in clinical assessment. One test asks the individual to complete a sentence (for example, "I often feel . . . ," "I would like to . . . "); another test asks the individual to draw a person; and another test presents a word, such as *fear* or *happy,* and asks the individual to say the first thing that comes to mind. Like the Rorschach, these projective tests have their detractors and advocates; the detractors often criticize the tests' low reliability and validity, and the advocates describe the tests' abilities to reveal the underlying nature of the individual's personality better than more straightforward tests can (Holaday, Smith, & Sherry, 2000; Lilienfeld & others, 2000).

Another controversial projective measure is *graphology,* the use of handwriting analysis to determine an individual's personality. Examine the writing in figure 12.14 to see the kinds of interpretations graphologists make. At one time, many firms in the United States—and even more in Israel, Japan, and Europe—used graphology as part of their employee-selection process (Levy, 1979). But the growing research literature on graphology is almost universally negative (Furnham, 1988; King & Koehler, 2000; Lindeman, 1998; Nevo, 1986).

One investigation typifies these negative results (Ben-Shakhar & others, 1986). Three professional graphologists agreed to rate handwriting samples from 52 bank employees. The graphologists were asked to assess the employees' competence at their

FIGURE 12.13 **Picture from the Thematic Apperception Test (TAT)**

Thematic Apperception Test (TAT)
An ambiguous projective test designed to elicit stories that reveal something about an individual's personality.

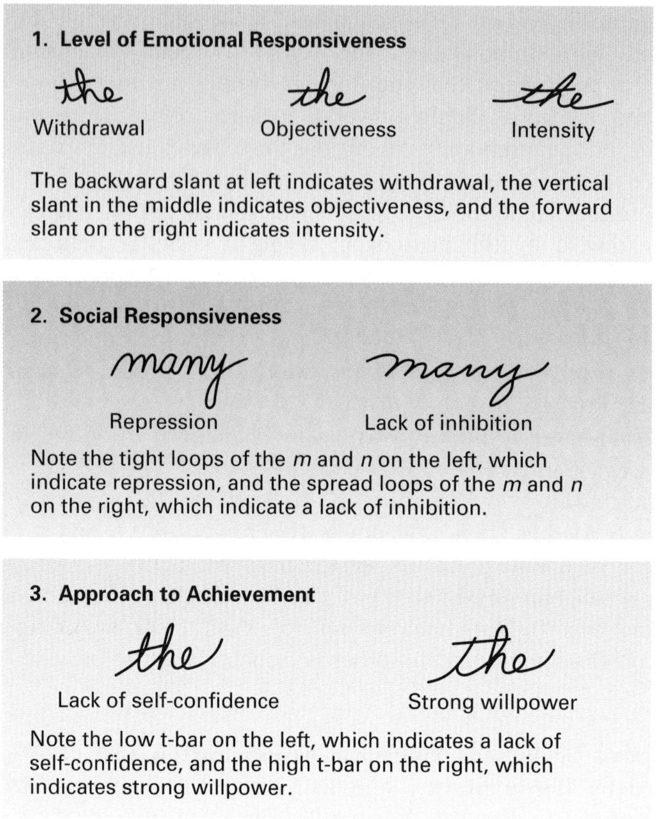

1. Level of Emotional Responsiveness

the
Withdrawal

the
Objectiveness

the
Intensity

The backward slant at left indicates withdrawal, the vertical slant in the middle indicates objectiveness, and the forward slant on the right indicates intensity.

2. Social Responsiveness

many
Repression

many
Lack of inhibition

Note the tight loops of the *m* and *n* on the left, which indicate repression, and the spread loops of the *m* and *n* on the right, which indicate a lack of inhibition.

3. Approach to Achievement

the
Lack of self-confidence

the
Strong willpower

Note the low t-bar on the left, which indicates a lack of self-confidence, and the high t-bar on the right, which indicates strong willpower.

FIGURE 12.14 **Some Graphological Interpretations**   Graphology is a highly controversial assessment technique, unsupported by empirical research.

jobs and the nature of their relationships with co-workers. The samples consisted of brief autobiographical essays and responses to a short biographical questionnaire. At the same time, the researchers used information from the samples, such as the employees' ages and job interests, the quality of their essays, and the attractiveness of their handwriting to make assessments about the employees' competence. The researchers' predictions and the graphologists' ratings were compared with ratings by the employees' supervisors. The graphologists did no better than the researchers at matching the supervisors' ratings. A battery of personality tests were better at matching the supervisors' ratings. In a second study, five graphologists did no better than chance when asked to predict the occupations of 40 successful professional men based on several pages of their handwriting.

If the research results are so negative, why is graphology still used and accepted? To some degree, it is because graphologists' predictions, like those of palmists and astrologers, are usually so general they're difficult to prove or disprove. However, all projective tests are difficult to validate scientifically, which has led some to suggest that projective tests do little more than show the biases of the testers. See the Critical Controversy box for further information about this dispute.

Self-Report Tests

self-report tests Also called *objective tests* or *inventories,* they directly ask people whether items (usually true/false or agree/disagree) describe their personality traits or not.

Unlike projective techniques, self-report tests do not attempt to assess an individual's hidden, unconscious personality. Rather, **self-report tests,** also called *objective tests* or *inventories,* directly ask people whether items describe their personality traits or not. For example, self-report personality tests include items such as

Who Is Projecting What?

The Rorschach inkblot test has been said to be "simultaneously, the most cherished and the most reviled of all psychological assessment instruments" (Hunsley & Bailey, 1999). How can this be?

With millions of tests administered every year, the Rorschach is one of the most frequently used projective tests. According to one survey, 82 percent of clinical psychologists occasionally administer the Rorschach and 43 percent often use the test (Watkins & others, 1995). Yet the Rorschach has long been attacked as unreliable and lacking in validity (Lilienfeld, Wood, & Garb, 2001).

A psychological assessment is judged to be reliable if it yields consistent results over repeated use. If different scorers can interpret the same individual's test differently, the test does not meet the reliability criterion. To understand how different clinicians might reach different conclusions about an individual from answers to a Rorschach series, consider whether a description should be scored as food-related if someone identifies the whole inkblot as a hamburger. What if the person identifies only one small portion of the inkblot as food? What if other, non-edible, objects are identified in the same inkblot? What if the individual sees another person eating? What if the color of the inkblot played (or did not play) a role in the description? And what would any of this tell you about the person's state of mind?

Some psychologists believe that many of the ways in which the Rorschach is scored are not reliable enough to be clinically useful (Lilienfeld, Wood, & Garb, 2001). What would it mean, for example, if two clinical psychologists administered the Rorschach to the same person and came up with diametrically opposed interpretations? It could mean that the two clinicians are projecting their own personalities onto their patient's Rorschach responses. In other words, the test interpretation might depend more on the interpretations of the clinicians than on any characteristic of the test taker. Because the results of a clinical assessment may determine the course of treatment or even the outcome of a court case, the stakes can be very high.

A psychological assessment is considered valid if it measures what it is intended to measure. One use of the Rorschach has been to diagnose psychological disorders, such as schizophrenia and depression (Weiner, 1997, 2001). Therefore, one way to test the diagnostic validity of the Rorschach would be to administer the test to two groups: a known group of normal people and a known group of people with a disorder such as schizophrenia. If the Rorschach is valid for diagnosing schizophrenia, then the responses of the two groups should differ. Otherwise, as said above, a diagnosis might well depend on the interpretations of clinicians. And, indeed, research evidence suggests that the Rohrschach has little validity as a diagnostic tool (Lilienfeld, Wood, & Garb, 2001).

So why would clinical psychologists continue to use a test with known problems of reliability and validity? Some clinicians swear by the Rorschach, saying it is better than any other measure at getting at the true, underlying core of the individual's personality (Hilsenroth, 2000; Ephraim, 2000; Sloan & others, 1996). They are not especially bothered by the Rorschach's low reliability and validity, pointing out that the test encourages extensive freedom of response. This freedom of response is what makes the Rorschach such a rich clinical tool, say its advocates. In one survey, Rorschach-based testimony was legally challenged in only 6 of nearly 8,000 court cases (Weiner, Exner, & Sciara, 1996).

Additionally, when coupled with information from structured interviews and other personality assessment tools, the results from projective tests like the Rorschach provide extra information the insightful clinician can use to better understand an individual (Meyer & Archer, 2001). Even critics caution that projective tests like the Rorschach should not be rejected as inherently unreliable and/or invalid (Lilenfield, Wood, & Garb, 2001). Instead they urge continuing efforts to construct better projective tests.

Attempts have been made to improve reliability by standardizing scoring systems (Exner, 1974). As a result, responses are typically scored for

Location: Does the person respond to the whole inkblot or specific parts?
Quality: Does the person respond to the color, shape, or perceived movement?
Content: Does the person perceive animals, humans, or objects?
Conventionality: How do the responses compare with average responses?

The goals of such systems include standardizing the test procedure itself as well as improving the reliability and validity of the test interpretation.

What do you think?

- What role should evidence based on projective tests like the Rorschach play in courts of law?
- If you took an actual Rorschach test, what would you make of the results as they were explained to you by a clinical psychologist?
- Spend some time looking at the inkblot in Fig 12.12. Write down everything you see there. Ask some friends to do the same. Discuss your interpretations of your responses. If you do not agree, how could you settle the matter?

- I am easily embarrassed.
- I love to go to parties.
- I like to watch cartoons on TV.

Self-report tests include a large number of statements or questions such as these. The respondent has a limited number of answers to choose from (yes or no, true or false, agree or disagree).

Adherents of the trait perspectives on personality have strong faith in self-report tests. They point out that self-report tests have produced a better understanding of an individual's personality traits than can be derived from, for example, projective tests. However, some critics (especially psychodynamic theorists) believe that the self-report measures do not get at the underlying core of personality and its unconscious determinants. Other critics (especially behaviorists and social cognitive theorists) believe that the self-report measures do not adequately capture the situational variation in personality and the way personality changes as the individual interacts with the environment.

Supporters of self-report tests do concede, however, that they have room for improvement. Many of the early personality tests were based on *face validity,* which is an assumption that the content of the test items is a good indicator of the individual's personality. For example, if I develop a test item that asks you to respond whether or not you are introverted, and you answer positively to "I enjoy being with people," I accept your response as a straightforward indication that you are not introverted. Tests based on face validity assume that you are responding honestly and nondefensively, giving the examiner an accurate portrayal of your personality.

But not everyone is honest, especially when it concerns one's own personality. Even if the individual is basically honest, he or she may be giving socially desirable answers. When motivated by *social desirability,* individuals say what they think the interviewer wants to hear or what they think will make them look better. For example, if I am basically a lazy person, I may try to present myself in a more positive way; therefore, I would respond negatively to the following item: "I fritter away time too much."

Because of such responses, psychologists developed empirically keyed tests. An **empirically keyed test** relies on its items to predict some criterion. Unlike tests based on face validity, in which the content of the items is supposed to be a good indicator of what the individual's personality is like, empirically keyed tests make no assumptions about the nature of the items (Segal & Coolidge, 2000). Imagine that we want to develop a test that will determine whether or not applicants for a position as police officer are likely to be competent at the job. We might ask a large number of questions of police officers, some of whom have excellent job records and others who have not performed as well. We would then use the questions that differentiate between competent and incompetent police officers on our test to screen job applicants. If the item "I enjoy reading poetry" predicts success as a police officer, then we would include it on the test even though it seems unrelated to police work.

Minnesota Multiphasic Personality Inventory (MMPI) The most widely used and researched empirically keyed self-report personality test is the **Minnesota Multiphasic Personality Inventory (MMPI).** The MMPI was initially constructed in the 1940s to assess "abnormal" personality tendencies and to improve the diagnosis of individuals with mental disorders. One thousand statements were given to both mental patients and apparently normal people. How often individuals agreed with each item was calculated; only the items that clearly differentiated the psychiatric patients from the normal individuals were retained. A statement might be included on the Depression scale of the MMPI if patients diagnosed with a depressive disorder agreed with the statement significantly more than did normal individuals. For example, the statement "I sometimes tease animals" seems to have little to do with depression—

empirically keyed test Relies on items to predict some criterion that discriminates between groups individually.

Minnesota Multiphasic Personality Inventory (MMPI) The most widely used and researched self-report personality test.

Clinical Scales	Sample Items
Hypochondriasis (Hs). (Abnormal concern with bodily functions)	"At times I get strong cramps in my intestines."
Depression (D). (Pessimism, hopelessness, slowing of action and thought)	"I am often very tense on the job."
Conversion Hysteria (Hy). (Unconscious use of physical and mental problems to avoid conflicts or responsibility)	"Sometimes there is a feeling like something is pressing in on my head."
Psychopathic Deviate (Pd). (Disregard of social custom, shallow emotions, inability to profit from experience)	"I wish I could do over some of the things I have done."
Masculinity-Femininity (Mf). (Items differentiating between men and women)	"I used to like to do the dances in gym class."
Paranoia (Pa). (Abnormal suspiciousness, delusions of grandeur or persecution)	"It distresses me that people have the wrong ideas about me."
Psychasthenia (Pt). (Obsessions, compulsiveness, fears, guilt, indecisiveness)	"The things that run through my head sometimes are horrible."
Schizophrenia (Sc). (Bizarre, unusual thoughts or behavior, withdrawal, hallucinations, delusions)	"There are those out there who want to get me."
Hypomania (Ma). (Emotional excitement, flight of ideas, overactivity)	"Sometimes I think so fast I can't keep up."
Social Introversion (Si). (Shyness, disinterest in others, insecurity)	"I give up too easily when discussing things with others."

FIGURE 12.15 Clinical Scales of the MMPI and Sample Items
The MMPI is the most widely used self-report personality test. This figure shows the 10 clinical scales and a sample item for each scale. Answering each sample item "true" would reflect the direction of the scales.

that is, it has little face validity—but it might still be included on the depression scale of the MMPI.

The MMPI eventually was streamlined to 550 items, each of which can be answered "true," "false," or "cannot say." The items vary widely in content and include such statements as

- I like to read magazines.
- I never have trouble falling asleep.
- People are out to get me.

A person's answers are grouped according to 10 clinical categories, or scales, that measure problems such as depression, psychopathic deviation, schizophrenia, and social introversion. Figure 12.15 shows the 10 clinical scales of the MMPI and sample items for each scale.

The MMPI includes 4 validity scales in addition to the 10 clinical scales. The validity scales were designed to indicate whether an individual is lying, careless, defensive, or evasive when answering the test items. For example, if the individual responds "false" repeatedly to certain items, such as "I get angry sometimes," she might be trying to make herself look better than she really is. The rationale for the lie scale is that each of us gets angry at least some of the time, so the individual who responds "false" to such items may be faking her response to other items.

The MMPI was revised for the first time in 1989. The revision, called the MMPI-2, has a number of new items (for a total of 567 items), but the 10 clinical scales were retained, as were several of the validity scales (such as the lie scale). New content scales were added to the MMPI-2. These include substance abuse, eating disorders, anger, self-esteem, family problems, and inability to function in a job.

The MMPI-2 continues to be widely used around the world to assess personality and predict outcomes (Archer & others, 2001; Butcher, 1999; Handel & Ben-Porath, 2000). It has been so popular that it has been translated into more than 20 languages. Not only is it used by clinical psychologists to assess a person's mental health, but it also is used to predict which individuals will make the best job candidates or which career an individual should pursue. Another important trend is the increased use of computers to score the MMPI-2 (Iverson & Barton, 1999). However, some critics argue that too often the availability of computer scoring has tempted untrained individuals to use the test in ways for which it has not been validated.

Assessments of the Big Five Factors   Paul Costa and Robert McCrae (1992) constructed a test, the *Neuroticism Extraversion Openness Personality Inventory—Revised* (or *NEO-PI-R,* for short), to assess the big five factors: openness, conscientiousness, extraversion, agreeableness, and neuroticism (emotional stability). The test also evaluates six subdimensions that make up the five main factors. Costa and McCrae believe that the test can improve the diagnosis of personality disorders and help therapists understand how therapy might influence different types of clients. For instance, individuals who score high on the extraversion factor might prefer group over individual psychotherapy, whereas introverts might do better in individual psychotherapy.

The NEO-PI-R is used in many research studies of personality as well. For instance, it was the test used to analyze the personality traits of great presidents in the example at the beginning of the chapter.

Another measure that is used to assess the big five factors is the Hogan Personality Inventory (HPI) created by Robert Hogan (1986). One way in which the HPI is used, as is the NEO-PI-R, is to attempt to predict job success. Researchers have found that the HPI effectively predicts such job performance criteria as supervisor ratings and training course success (Wiggins & Trapnell, 1997).

Behavioral and Cognitive Assessment

Unlike either projective tests or self-report tests, behavioral assessment of personality is based on observing the individual's behavior directly. Instead of removing situational influence, as projective tests and self-report measures do, behavioral assessment assumes that personality cannot be evaluated apart from the environment.

Behavioral assessment of personality emerged from the tradition of behavior modification, which you learned about in chapter 7. Recall that often the first step in the process of changing an individual's maladaptive behavior is to make baseline observations of its frequency. The therapist then modifies some aspect of the environment, such as getting the parents and the child's teacher to stop giving the child attention when he or she engages in aggressive behavior. After a specified period of time, the therapist will observe the child again to determine if the changes in the environment were effective in reducing the child's maladaptive behavior.

What does a psychologist with a behavioral orientation do to assess personality? Direct observation may be desirable, but it is not always possible. When it is not, the psychologist might ask individuals to make their own assessments of behavior, encouraging them to be sensitive to the circumstances that produced the behavior and the outcomes or consequences of the behavior. For example, a therapist might want to know the course of marital conflict in the everyday experiences of a couple. Figure 12.16 shows a Spouse Observation Checklist that couples can use to record their partner's behavior.

The influence of social cognitive theory has increased the use of cognitive assessment in personality evaluation. The strategy is to discover what thoughts underlie the individual's behavior; that is, how do individuals think about their problems? What kinds of thoughts precede maladaptive behavior, occur during its manifestation, and follow it? Cognitive processes such as expectations, planning, and memory are assessed, possibly by interviewing the individual or asking him or her to complete a questionnaire. An interview might include questions that address whether the individual overexaggerates his faults and condemns himself more than is warranted. A questionnaire might ask a person what her thoughts are after an upsetting event, or it might assess the way she thinks during tension-filled moments.

Type of Behavior	Item
Shared activities	We sat and read together. We took a walk.
Pleasing interactive events	My spouse asked how my day was. We talked about personal feelings. My spouse showed interest in what I said by agreeing or asking relevant questions.
Displeasing interactive events	My spouse commanded me to do something. My spouse complained about something I did. My spouse interrupted me.
Pleasing affectionate behavior	We held each other. My spouse hugged and kissed me.
Displeasing affectionate behavior	My spouse rushed into intercourse without taking time for foreplay. My spouse rejected my sexual advances.
Pleasing events	My spouse did the dishes. My spouse picked up around the house.
Displeasing events	My spouse talked too much about work. My spouse yelled at the children.

FIGURE 12.16 Items from the Spouse Observation Checklist Couples are instructed to complete an extensive checklist for 15 consecutive evenings. Spouses record their partner's behavior and make daily ratings of their overall satisfaction with the spouse's behavior. The Spouse Observation Checklist is a behavioral assessment instrument.

Locus of control, a key concept in the social cognitive perspectives, is most often assessed with Julian Rotter's (1966) I-E Scale, in which I stands for *internal* and E for *external*. Following are examples of the types of items used on the I-E Scale:

I More Strongly Believe That	*Or*
Promotions are earned through hard work and persistence.	Making a lot of money is largely a matter of getting the right breaks.
When I am right I can convince others.	It is silly to think that one can really change another person's basic attitudes.
I believe there is a direct connection between how hard I study and the grades I get.	Many times the reactions of teachers seem haphazard to me.
I am the master of my fate.	A great deal that happens to me is probably due to chance.
The number of divorces suggests that more and more people are not trying to make their marriages work.	Marriage is largely a gamble.

If you more strongly believed that the items in the left column are like you, you likely have a stronger internal locus of control. If you more more strongly believed that the items in the right column are like you, you likely have a stronger external locus of control.

The I-E Scale has been used in a wide range of research studies (Al-Mashaan, 2001; Wallston, 2001). Generally, those studies have found that individuals with internal loci of control are more perceptive than those who have external loci of control and are readier to learn about their surroundings. People with internal loci of control ask more questions and show better problem-solving skills.

PERSONALITY PERSPECTIVES

	Psychodynamic Perspectives	Behavioral and Social Cognitive Perspectives	Humanistic Perspectives	Trait Perspectives
Preferred Personality Assessment Techniques	Clinical interviews, unstructured personality tests, psychohistorical analysis of clients' lives	Observation, especially laboratory observation	Self-report tests, interviews. For many humanists, clinical judgment is more important than scientific measurement.	Self-report tests, such as MMPI-2
Theoretical Issues				
Is personality innate or learned?	Freud strongly favored biological foundations. Horney, Jung, and Adler gave social experiences and culture more weight.	Skinner said personality is behavior, which is environmentally determined. Social cognitive theorists, such as Bandura, also emphasize environmental experiences.	Rogers, Maslow, and other humanistic psychologists believe personality is influenced by experience and can be changed.	Eysenck stresses personality's biological basis. Allport and other trait theorists consider both heredity and environment.
Is personality conscious or unconscious?	Psychodynamic theorists, especially Freud and Jung, place a strong emphasis on unconscious thought.	Skinner didn't think conscious or unconscious thought was important. Bandura and Mischel emphasize the cognitive process.	Humanistic psychologists stress the conscious aspects of personality, especially self-concept and self-perception.	Trait theorists pay little attention to this issue.
Is personality determined internally or externally?	Psychodynamic theorists emphasize internal determinants and internal personality structures.	Behaviorists emphasize external, situational determinants. Social cognitive theorists emphasize both internal and external determinants but especially self-control.	Humanistic theorists emphasize internal determinants such as self-concept and self-actualization.	Trait theorists stress internal, personal variables.

FIGURE 12.17 Comparing Perspectives on Personality

Mary Tenopyr became an industrial/organizational (I/O) psychologist by accident. After being rejected for a job because she was a woman, she was leaving the interviewer's office almost in tears. The interviewer called her back and asked what she had been doing on her last job. She said that she had been writing items for job knowledge tests. Tenopyr was hired to supervise personnel testing for the company. Currently, Tenopyr is an executive in the human resources department of AT&T.

Assessment in the Selection of Employees

Personality assessments are used in clinical psychology for diagnosis and therapy and are sometimes used in educational settings. But another important use is in the workplace. Industrial psychologists use many different selection tools to pick the right person for the right job (Gatewood, Perloff, & Perloff, 1998; Roberts & Hogan, 2001). Among the most widely used personnel selection tools are application forms, psychological tests, interviews, and work sample tests.

Interviews are often given special weight in hiring decisions (Barber & others, 1994), and they can be especially helpful in evaluating a candidate's interpersonal and communication skills. Interviews that are structured and specific often are the most successful at selecting employees who eventually perform well on the job. Indeed, unstructured interviews have shown little success in predicting job performance (Huffcutt & others, 2001).

Psychological tests are also useful predictors of job performance. The tests used by industrial psychologists include general aptitude tests (such as IQ tests), specific aptitude tests (such as those designed to assess mechanical ability, clerical ability, or spatial relations), personality tests (such as the MMPI), and vocational inventories (such as the Strong Interest Inventory; Reynolds, 2001). Currently, researchers are interested in whether psychological tests based on the big five personality factors can predict job success.

Whether personality assessments are being used by industrial psychologists, clinical psychologists, or psychological researchers, the choice of instrument depends to a great extent on the psychologist's theoretical perspective. Figure 12.17 summarizes which methods are advocated by different types of theorists. The figure also summarizes the positions of the main personality perspectives on the three issues mentioned earlier in the chapter: whether personality is innate or learned, whether it is conscious or unconscious, and whether it is determined internally or externally. Although the diversity of perspectives—psychodynamic, behavioral and social cognitive, humanistic, and trait—may seem overwhelming, remember that together they give us a more complete picture of human complexity.

Review and Sharpen Your Thinking

6 **Characterize the main methods of personality assessment.**
- Describe the reasons psychologists use personality assessment.
- Discuss projective techniques.
- Explain self-report tests.
- Summarize behavioral and cognitive assessment.
- Identify assessment in the selection of employees.

Which of the assessment tools that we discussed do you think would likely provide the most accurate picture of your personality? Explain.

For study tools related to this learning goal, see the Study Guide, the CD-ROM, and the Online Learning Center.

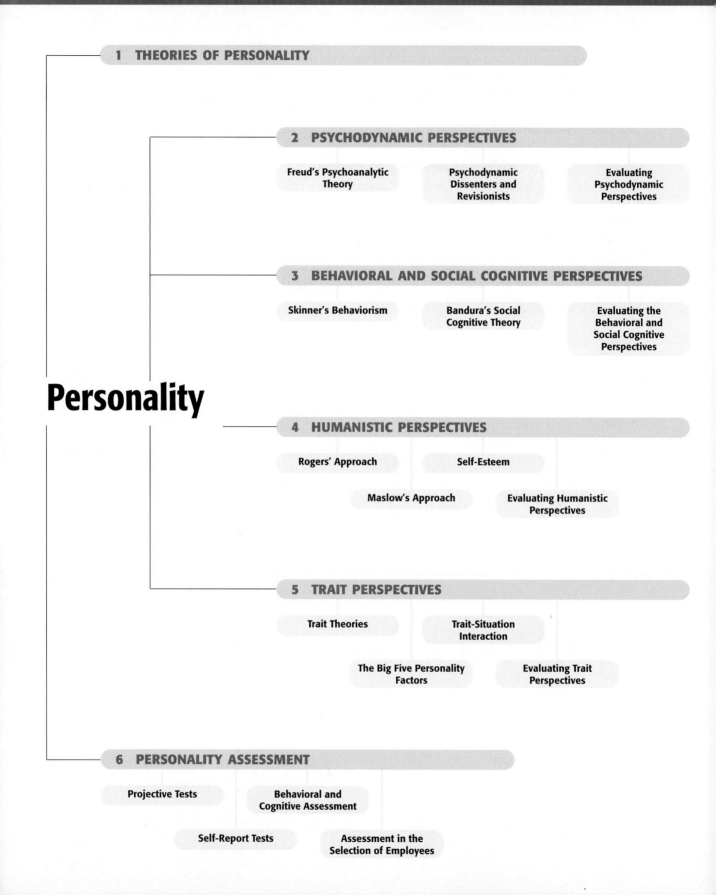

Personality

1 THEORIES OF PERSONALITY

2 PSYCHODYNAMIC PERSPECTIVES

Freud's Psychoanalytic Theory

Psychodynamic Dissenters and Revisionists

Evaluating Psychodynamic Perspectives

3 BEHAVIORAL AND SOCIAL COGNITIVE PERSPECTIVES

Skinner's Behaviorism

Bandura's Social Cognitive Theory

Evaluating the Behavioral and Social Cognitive Perspectives

4 HUMANISTIC PERSPECTIVES

Rogers' Approach

Self-Esteem

Maslow's Approach

Evaluating Humanistic Perspectives

5 TRAIT PERSPECTIVES

Trait Theories

Trait-Situation Interaction

The Big Five Personality Factors

Evaluating Trait Perspectives

6 PERSONALITY ASSESSMENT

Projective Tests

Behavioral and Cognitive Assessment

Self-Report Tests

Assessment in the Selection of Employees

1 Define personality and identify the major issues in the study of personality.

- Personality involves our enduring thoughts, emotions, and behaviors that characterize the way we adapt to the world. A key question is why different individuals respond to the same situation in different ways.

2 Summarize the psychodynamic perspectives.

- The psychodynamic perspectives view personality as primarily unconscious and as occurring in stages. Most psychodynamic perspectives emphasize the importance of early experience with parents in sculpting personality.

- Freud believed that most of the mind is unconscious, and his psychoanalytic theory stated that personality has three structures: id, ego, and superego. The conflicting demands of these personality structures produce anxiety. Defense mechanisms protect the ego and reduce this anxiety. Freud was convinced that problems develop because of early childhood experiences. He said that we go through five psychosexual stages: oral, anal, phallic, latency, and genital. During the phallic stage, which occurs in early childhood, the Oedipus complex is a major source of conflict.

- A number of psychodynamic theorists criticized Freud for placing too much emphasis on sexuality and the first 5 years of life. They argued that Freud gave too little credit to the ego, conscious thought, and sociocultural factors. Horney said that the need for security, not sex or aggression, is our most important need. Jung thought Freud underplayed the unconscious mind's role. He developed the concept of the collective unconscious and placed special emphasis on archetypes. Adler's theory, called individual psychology, stresses that people are striving toward a positive being and that they create their own goals. Adler placed more emphasis on social motivation than Freud did.

- Strengths of the psychodynamic perspectives include emphases on the individual's past experiences, on personality's developmental course, on mental representation of the environment, on the unconscious mind, and on conflict as an influence on personality. These perspectives have also had a substantial influence on psychology as a discipline. Weaknesses of the psychodynamic perspectives include overreliance on reports from the past, too much emphasis on sexuality and the unconscious mind, a negative view of human nature, too much attention to early experience, and a male, Western bias.

3 Explain the behavioral and social cognitive perspectives.

- The behavioral and social cognitive perspectives emphasize the importance of environmental experience in understanding the person's personality. Within that broad framework, behaviorists focus on people's observable behavior; social cognitive theorists also examine cognitive factors in personality.

- Skinner's behaviorism emphasizes that cognition is unimportant in personality; personality is observable behavior, which is influenced by rewards and punishments in the environment. In the behavioral view, personality often varies according to the situation.

- Social cognitive theory, created by Albert Bandura and Walter Mischel, states that behavior, environment, and person/cognitive factors are important in understanding personality. In Bandura's view, these factors reciprocally interact. Three important concepts in social cognitive theory are self-efficacy, locus of control, and optimism. Self-efficacy is the belief that one can master a situation and produce positive outcomes. Locus of control refers to individuals' beliefs about whether the outcomes of their actions depend on what they do (internal) or on events outside of their control (external). Seligman defines optimism as an individual's explanatory style, especially how a person explains the causes of bad events. Optimists explain bad events as being caused by external, unstable, and specific circumstances. Pessimists explain bad events as being caused by internal, stable, and global factors. Another view of optimism involves the expectancy that good things are more likely, and bad things less likely, to occur in the future. Numerous research studies reveal that individuals characterized by self-efficacy, internal locus of control, and optimism generally show positive functioning and adjustment.

- Strengths of the behavioral and social cognitive perspectives include their emphases on environmental determinants and on a scientific climate for investigating personality. An additional strength of social cognitive theory is its focus on cognitive processes and self-control. The behavioral view has been criticized for taking the "person" out of personality and for ignoring cognition. These approaches also have not given adequate attention to enduring individual differences, to biological factors, and to personality as a whole.

4 *Describe the humanistic perspectives.*

- The humanistic perspectives stress the person's capacity for personal growth and freedom, ability to choose a destiny, and positive qualities.
- In Rogers' approach, each of us has a need for unconditional positive regard. The result is that the real self is not valued unless it meets the standards of other people. The self is the core of personality; it includes both the real and ideal selves. Rogers said that we can help others develop more positive self-concept in three ways: unconditional positive regard, empathy, and genuineness. Rogers also stressed that each of us has the innate, inner capacity to become a fully functioning person.
- Maslow called the humanistic movement the "third force" in psychology. Maslow developed the hierarchy of needs concept, with self-actualization being the highest human need.
- Self-esteem is the person's overall evaluation of self-worth or self-image. Four main strategies for increasing a person's self-esteem are to identify the causes of low self-esteem, provide emotional support and approval, help the person achieve valued goals, and help the person learn to cope successfully with challenges.
- The humanistic perspectives sensitized us to the importance of subjective experience, of consciousness, of self-conception, of considering the whole person, and of our innate, positive nature. Its weaknesses are a tendency to avoid empirical research, a tendency to be too optimistic, and an inclination to encourage excessive self-love.

5 *Discuss the trait perspectives.*

- A trait is an enduring personality characteristic that tends to lead to certain behaviors. Trait theories emphasize that personality consists of broad, enduring dispositions that lead to characteristic responses. Trait theorists also are interested in how traits are organized within the individual. Traits are assumed to be essentially stable over time and across situations. Allport believed that each individual has a unique set of personality traits, grouped into three main categories: cardinal, central, and secondary. Eysenck's basic dimensions of personality are introversion-extraversion, stability-instability (neuroticism), and psychoticism.
- There is much current interest in the big five factors in personality, which are considered to be "supertraits": openness to experience, conscientiousness, extraversion, agreeableness, and neuroticism (emotional stability).

- Today, most personality psychologists are interactionists. They believe that personality is determined by a combination of traits, or person factors, and the situation, or environmental factors.
- Studying people in terms of their traits has practical value. Identifying a person's traits allows us to know the person better. Understanding a person's traits also may help us better predict the person's health, thinking, job success, and interpersonal skills. Mischel's (1968) *Personality and Assessment* ushered in an attack on trait theory, basically arguing that personality varies across situations more than trait theorists acknowledged.

6 *Characterize the main methods of personality assessment.*

- Psychologists use a wide variety of tests and measures to assess personality. These measures often are tied to psychologists' theoretical orientations. Personality tests were designed to measure stable, enduring aspects of personality.
- Projective tests, designed to assess the unconscious aspects of personality, present individuals with an ambiguous stimulus and then ask them to describe it or tell a story about it. Projective tests are based on the assumption that the ambiguity of the stimuli allows individuals to project their personalities onto them. The Rorschach inkblot test is a widely used projective test; its effectiveness is controversial. The Thematic Apperception Test (TAT) is another projective test.
- Self-report tests assess personality traits by asking test takers questions about their preferences and behaviors. Even though a self-report test may have face validity, it may still elicit invalid responses when people try to answer in a socially desirable way. Empirically keyed tests, which rely on items that are indirect questions about some criterion, were developed to overcome the problem of face validity. The Minnesota Multiphasic Personality Inventory (MMPI) is the most widely used and researched self-report personality test; it has 10 clinical scales to assist therapists in diagnosing psychological problems and also contains validity scales. Tests also have been created to assess the big five personality factors. Two of the most popular are the Neuroticism Extraversion Openness Personality Inventory (NEO-PI-R) and the Hogan Personality Inventory (HPI).
- Behavioral assessment seeks to obtain objective information about personality through observation of be-

havior and its environmental ties. Cognitive assessment seeks to discover individual differences in processing and acting on information through interviews and questionnaires.

- Industrial psychologists use many different selection tools to pick the right person for the right job. Among the most widely used personnel selection tools are application forms, psychological tests, interviews, and work sample tests.

Key Terms

personality, p. 477
psychodynamic perspectives, p. 478
id, p. 479
ego, p. 479
superego, p. 480
defense mechanisms, p. 480
Oedipus complex, p. 481
collective unconscious, p. 483

archetype, p. 483
individual psychology, p. 484
behavioral and social cognitive perspectives, p. 486
social cognitive theory, p. 487
self-efficacy, p. 488
locus of control, p. 488

humanistic perspectives, p. 491
self-concept, p. 491
unconditional positive regard, p. 492
self-esteem, p. 493
trait, p. 496
big five factors of personality, p. 498
projective test, p. 501

Rorschach inkblot test, p. 502
Thematic Apperception Test (TAT), p. 503
self-report tests, p. 504
empirically keyed test, p. 506
Minnesota Multiphasic Personality Inventory (MMPI), p. 506

Apply Your Knowledge

1. Consider a facet of your personality that you might want to change. From the perspective of Freud's psychoanalytic theory, could you change this aspect of your personality? How? From the perspective of the psychodynamic revisionists, would it be possible to make the desired change? How?

2. Try the following exercise: The next time you are in a situation in which the outcome is unknown (for example, you have a test coming up, or you're thinking about an upcoming date), pay attention to how you respond to the situation in terms of the three important concepts of social cognitive theory described in this chapter. Now try to approach the situation using the characteristic opposite to whatever you would normally do. How easy or hard is this? Did it have an effect on the outcome? How would you know?

3. Think about the big five (or big seven) factors in personality and their relationship to various situations. Which factors

can be assessed in the individual, and which are measures of interactions between people? Based on your answers, which factors would you expect to vary more depending on the situation?

4. Type "personality test" into an on-line search engine, and take two or more of the tests available on-line. Now look at the results—which perspective do the results seem to reflect most? How might the structure of the test have affected the outcome?

5. Think about the three major issues in the study of psychology described in the text. In many cases, questions posed as "either/or" turn out to be best answered by "some of both." After reading about all of the theories in the chapter, how might you rephrase the personality questions if you were interested in answering them scientifically?

Connections

For extra help in mastering the material in this chapter, see the review sections and practice quizzes in the Student Study Guide, the CD-ROM, and the Online Learning Center.

Psychological Disorders

Chapter Outline

Learning Goals

UNDERSTANDING PSYCHOLOGICAL DISORDERS   **1**

Defining Abnormal Behavior
▼
Theoretical Approaches to Psychological Disorders
▼
Classifying Abnormal Behavior

Discuss the characteristics and classifications of abnormal behavior.

ANXIETY DISORDERS   **2**

Generalized Anxiety Disorder
▼
Panic Disorder
▼
Phobic Disorders
▼
Obsessive-Compulsive Disorder
▼
Post-Traumatic Stress Disorder

Distinguish among the various anxiety disorders.

DISSOCIATIVE DISORDERS   **3**

Dissociative Amnesia and Fugue
▼
Dissociative Identity Disorder

Describe the dissociative disorders.

MOOD DISORDERS   **4**

Depressive Disorders
▼
Bipolar Disorder
▼
Causes of Mood Disorders
▼
Suicide

Compare the mood disorders and specify risk factors for depression and suicide.

SCHIZOPHRENIA   **5**

Types of Schizophrenia
▼
Causes of Schizophrenia

Characterize schizophrenia.

PERSONALITY DISORDERS   **6**

Odd/Eccentric Cluster
▼
Dramatic/Emotionally Problematic Cluster
▼
Chronic-Fearfulness/Avoidant Cluster

Identify the behavior patterns typical of personality disorders.

Kay Redfield Jamison is a psychologist and a leading expert on serious mood disorders. For years, Jamison harbored a secret. She herself had a serious psychological disorder: bipolar disorder, in which moods alternate between mania (an overexcited, unrealistically optimistic state) and depression. In her memoir, Jamison (1995) tells of her battle with the disorder, of the joy of manic highs and the terrifying depressions that led her to want to die:

> There is a particular kind of pain, elation, loneliness, and terror involved in this kind of madness. When you're high it's tremendous. The ideas and feelings are fast and frequent like shooting stars, and you follow them until you find better and brighter ones. Shyness goes, the right words and gestures are suddenly there, the power to captivate others a felt certainty. There are interests found in uninteresting people. Sensuality is pervasive and the desire to seduce and be seduced irresistible. Feelings of ease, intensity, power, well-being, financial omnipotence, and euphoria pervade one's marrow. But, somewhere this changes. The fast ideas are too fast, and there are far too many, overwhelming confusion replaces clarity. Memory goes. Everything previously moving with the grain is now against you. . . . You are irritable, angry, frightened, uncontrollable, and submerged totally in the blackest caves of the mind.

Kay Redfield Jamison, a psychologist who has waged her own personal battle with bipolar disorder.

Jamison eventually, through strong support from friends and colleagues, excellent mental health care, medication, and her own acceptance of the disorder, has been able to reach a point at which her mood swings have become dampened. Today, she continues to be a leading expert on psychological disorders as a professor of psychology at Johns Hopkins School of Medicine.

1   UNDERSTANDING PSYCHOLOGICAL DISORDERS

| Defining Abnormal Behavior | Theoretical Approaches to Psychological Disorders | Classifying Abnormal Behavior |

What are the characteristics of abnormal behavior and how is it categorized?

An estimated 44 million Americans each year suffer from some kind of psychological disorder (National Institute of Mental Health [NIMH], 2001a). In one study, nearly 20,000 randomly selected individuals from five different regions of the United States were asked whether they had experienced any item on a list of psychological disorders in their lifetimes and whether they currently were suffering from one (Robins & Regier, 1991). Almost one-third (32 percent) of the respondents said that they had experienced one or more psychological disorders in their lifetimes, and 20 percent said they currently had an active disorder.

You might be surprised that so many individuals acknowledge having a psychological disorder. However, the figures from the study include both individuals in institutions and in the community. They also include individuals with a substance abuse disorder (alcohol or other drugs, 17 percent). Surprisingly, only one-third of the individuals in this study who said they currently had a psychological disorder had received treatment for it in the previous 6 months.

Defining Abnormal Behavior

To understand psychological disorders, we need to examine what is meant by abnormal behavior. In thinking about how to define abnormal behavior, consider the following three individuals:

- Thirty-year-old Ruth has a long-standing feeling of contamination that compels her to carry out numerous cleansing activities each day (Leon, 1990). She becomes intensely uncomfortable when she notices any dirt on herself or in her immediate environment. Whenever she detects the presence of even the smallest bit of dirt, she thoroughly washes her hands and arms. If she finds any dirt in her apartment, she feels compelled to scrub it from top to bottom, then shower in a rigidly specific manner. She also feels contaminated after using the bathroom, doing housework, or cooking, again feeling compelled to wash herself after these activities. Currently, she is washing her hands at least three to four times an hour, showering six to seven times a day, and thoroughly cleaning her apartment at least twice a day. She reports that her life is very restricted because most of the time she feels driven to carry out these cleansing activities.

- Thirty-year-old Janet has been divorced for about a year. She is raising her three children and recently resumed her college education on a part-time basis (Oltmanns, Neale, & Davison, 1986). Her return to college didn't last long, however. One of her children, 2-year-old Adam, was having sleep-related problems, so Janet began spending considerable time with him. Janet's mood had become depressed when her husband asked for a divorce because he had fallen in love with a younger woman. She felt sad, discouraged, and lonely. The feeling became more severe just prior to her withdrawal from college. She has bouts of crying, in some cases for long periods of time. Nothing seems to cheer her up, she doesn't have any interest in her friends, and she sees her children as more burdensome than ever. In her current situation, the future looks bleak.

- Twenty-seven-year-old Jim is an unemployed, single man who says that what really bothers him is that he has a special power (Gorenstein, 1997). He says he can influence other people, even endanger them, with the way he breathes. He believes he has to go to great lengths to avoid people so that he won't put them in jeopardy. He currently has isolated himself from others by secluding himself in a room at his parents' house. Jim doesn't like avoiding the world but feels he has no other choice. Jim explains it is like having God's power, but with none of the desire or wisdom to use it. He comes out of his room only for occasional meals, bathroom visits, and church services. He doesn't want his power to fall into malevolent hands, which he sees as another reason for not appearing in public.

Would you agree that the behavior of all three of these individuals is abnormal? If so, what would you base your judgment on?

There are a number of myths and misconceptions about abnormal behavior. These are some of the most common:

Myth: Abnormal behavior is always bizarre.
Fact: The behavior of many people who are diagnosed as having a mental disorder often cannot be distinguished from that of normal people. In Jim's case, belief in the power of his breath is bizarre. However, Janet's behavior would not be considered bizarre.
Myth: Normal and abnormal behavior are different in kind.
Fact: Few, if any, types of behavior displayed by people with a mental disorder are unique to them. Abnormal behavior consists of a poor fit between the behavior and the situation in which it is enacted.
Myth: Once people have a mental disorder, they will always have it.
Fact: Most people, like Kay Redfield Jamison, can be successfully treated for a mental disorder.

On January 16, 1996, multimillionaire John Dupont (*above*), a 58-year-old heir to the Dupont chemical fortune, pulled out a gun and killed Olympic Gold Medal wrestler David Schultz, who lived in a home on Dupont's estate and was one of several wrestlers training at Dupont's state-of-the art wrestling facility. No one disputes that Dupont killed Schultz, but Dupont's lawyers, using the so-called insanity defense, argued that he was so incapacitated by schizophrenia that he could not be held accountable for the murder. Prosecutors claimed he was an eccentric man driven by envy and anger who knew exactly what he was doing. After a week's deliberation, the jury concluded that Dupont had a psychological disorder but found him guilty of third-degree murder.

abnormal behavior Behavior that is deviant, maladaptive, or personally distressful.

medical model A biological approach that describes psychological disorders as medical diseases with a biological origin.

Abnormal behavior is one of those concepts that is not easy to define. The definition varies across academic disciplines and across social, medical, and legal institutions. For example, the federal courts define *insanity*—a legal term, not a psychological term—as the inability to appreciate the nature and quality or wrongfulness of one's acts (Pikona-Sapir, Melamed, & Elizur, 2001). The American Psychiatric Association (2001) defines *abnormal behavior* in medical terms: a mental illness that affects or is manifested in a person's brain and can affect the way a person thinks, behaves, and interacts with people.

Keeping in mind that the line between what is normal and what is abnormal is not always clear-cut, we can use three criteria to help distinguish normal from abnormal behavior. **Abnormal behavior** is behavior that is deviant, maladaptive, or personally distressful. Only one of the three criteria listed needs to be met for the behavior to be classified as abnormal, but two or all three may be present.

Let's take a closer look at what each of the three criteria of abnormal behavior entails. First, abnormal behavior is *deviant*. One way that abnormal behavior has been described is as being *atypical*. However, people such as Albert Einstein and Barbara Walters are atypical, but we do not usually categorize them as abnormal, because of their extraordinary intellectual power and interviewing skills, respectively. However, when atypical behavior deviates from what is acceptable in a culture, it often is considered abnormal. Ruth's compulsive behavior deviates from acceptable norms. People do not normally wash their hands three to four times an hour, take seven showers a day, and clean their apartments at least twice a day.

Second, abnormal behavior is *maladaptive*. Maladaptive behavior interferes with a person's ability to function effectively in the world. Jim's belief that his breath has powerful, even harmful, effects on others keeps him isolated from society and prevents him from functioning in the everyday world.

Third, abnormal behavior involves *personal distress*. Ruth is distressed about how driven she is to stay clean and keep her immediate environment clean. Janet also is distressed about her life and sees her future as extremely bleak.

Theoretical Approaches to Psychological Disorders

What causes people to develop a psychological disorder? To behave in deviant, maladaptive, and personally distressful ways? We can look to the biological, psychological, and sociocultural perspectives for theoretical explanations and also consider the possibility that a combination of factors might contribute to an individual's maladaptive behavior.

The Biological Approach The biological approach to psychological disorders attributes them to organic, internal causes. Scientists who adopt a biological approach to psychological disorders often focus on brain and genetic factors as the sources of abnormal behavior. In the biological approach, drug therapy is frequently used to treat abnormal behavior.

The biological approach is evident in the **medical model,** which describes psychological disorders as medical diseases with a biological origin. From the perspective of the medical model, abnormalities are called mental *illnesses*, the individuals afflicted are *patients*, and they are treated by *doctors*.

Biological views on psychological disorders fall into three main categories (Nolen-Hoeksema, 2001):

- *Structural views*. Abnormalities in the brain's structure cause mental disorders.
- *Biochemical views*. Imbalances in neurotransmitters or hormones cause mental disorders.
- *Genetic views*. Disordered genes cause mental disorders.

These biological factors are discussed as appropriate later in the chapter.

The Psychological Approach Chapter 12 described the psychodynamic, behavioral and social cognitive, and humanistic perspectives on personality. These perspectives serve as a foundation for understanding the psychological factors involved in psychological disorders:

- *Psychodynamic perspectives.* Psychological disorders arise from unconscious conflicts that produce anxiety and result in maladaptive behavior. Ineffective early relationships with parents are believed to be the origin of psychological disorders. Recall that these ideas stem from Freud's psychoanalytic theory but that some contemporary proponents of this approach place less emphasis on unconscious thought and sexuality.
- *Behavioral and social cognitive perspectives.* In the behavioral perspective, the focus is on the rewards and punishments in the environment that determine abnormal behavior. Social cognitive theory accepts that environmental experiences are important determinants of psychological disorders but adds that a number of social cognitive factors also are involved. In this way, observational learning, expectancies, self-efficacy, self-control, beliefs about oneself and the world, and many other cognitive processes are key to psychological disorders.
- *Humanistic perspectives.* These perspectives emphasize a capacity for growth, freedom to choose one's own destiny, and positive personal qualities. A psychological disorder reflects an inability to fulfill one's potential, likely arising from pressures of society to conform to others' expectations and values. A person with a psychological disorder is likely to have a low self-concept because he or she has experienced excessive criticism and negative circumstances.

The psychological perspectives focus mainly on the individual. Chapter 14 extensively examines how theories of personality—psychodynamic, behavioral and social cognitive, and humanistic—influence the treatment of psychological disorders.

The Sociocultural Approach Although the psychological approach mainly attributes psychological problems to unconscious conflicts, negative cognitions, low self-concept, and other factors within the individual, they still give environmental experiences a role in creating psychological disorders (Nolen-Hoeksema, 2001). The sociocultural approach places more emphasis on the larger social contexts in which a person lives—including the individual's marriage or family, neighborhood, socioeconomic status, ethnicity, gender, or culture—than do the other approaches. For example, marital conflict might be the cause of mental disorder in one individual. In this view, when a member of a family has a psychological problem, it may not be due to something within the individual but rather to ineffective family functioning (Atwood, 2001). Any number of psychological problems can develop because of power struggles in a family: sibling conflicts, one child being favored over another, marital conflict, and so on.

Individuals from low-income, minority neighborhoods have the highest rates of mental disorders. In studies of the role of socioeconomic status and ethnicity in psychological disorders, socioeconomic status plays a much stronger role than does ethnicity: The living conditions of poverty create stressful circumstances that can contribute to the development of a mental disorder (Elliott, Beattie, & Kaitfors, 2001; Schultz & others, 2000; Weich, Lewis, & Jenkins, 2001).

Gender, another sociocultural factor, is associated with the presence of certain psychological disorders (Greenglass, 1998; Nolen-Hoeksema, 2001; Wood, 2001). Women tend to be diagnosed as having internalized disorders. In particular, women are likelier than men to suffer from anxiety disorders and depression, which have symptoms that are turned inward (internalized). Conversely, men are socialized to direct their energy toward the external world (to externalize their feelings) and they more often have externalized disorders that involve aggression and substance abuse. Gender differences are discussed more fully later in the chapter.

FIGURE 13.1 Some Culture-Related Disorders

Disorder	Culture	Description/Characteristics
Amok	Malaysia, Philippines, Africa	This disorder involves sudden, uncontrolled outbursts of anger in which the person may injure or kill someone. Amok is often found in males who are emotionally withdrawn before the onset of the disorder. After the attack on someone, the individual feels exhausted and depressed and does not remember the rage and attack.
Anorexia Nervosa	Western cultures, especially the United States	This eating disorder involves a relentless pursuit of thinness through starvation, and can eventually lead to death.
Windigo	Algonquin Indian hunters	This disorder involves a fear of being bewitched. The hunter becomes anxious and agitated, worrying he will be turned into a cannibal with a craving for human flesh.

Most experts on abnormal behavior agree that many psychological disorders are universal (Al-Issa, 1982). However, the frequency and intensity of psychological disorders varies across cultures and depends on social, economic, technological, and religious aspects of cultures (Cueller & Paniagua, 2000; Draguns, 1990; Lopez & Guarnaccia, 2000; Tanaka-Matsumi, 2001). Some disorders, though, are culture-related, as indicated in figure 13.1 (Marsella, 2000).

An Interactionist Approach: Biopsychosocial Normal and abnormal behavior alike may involve biological, psychological, and sociocultural factors alone or in combination with other factors. Abnormal behavior can be influenced by biological factors (such as brain processes and heredity), psychological factors (such as distorted thoughts or low self-esteem), and sociocultural factors (such as ineffective family functioning or poverty). These factors can interact to produce abnormal behavior. Sometimes this interactionist approach is called *biopsychosocial* (Evans, 1999).

Classifying Abnormal Behavior

Ever since human history began, people have suffered from diseases, sadness, and bizarre behavior. And, for almost as long, healers have tried to treat and cure them. The classification of psychological disorders goes back to the ancient Egyptians and Greeks and has its roots in biology and medicine. To this day, the classification of psychological disorders follows a medical model.

Classifying psychological disorders is a difficult undertaking and one that provokes criticism not only from mental health professionals but also from many other segments of society. However, the benefits of a classification system far outweigh the disadvantages. For one thing, a classification system gives mental health professionals a common basis for communicating with one another. For example, if one psychologist says in a case review that her client has a panic disorder and another psychologist says that his client has schizophrenia, the two psychologists understand that the clients have exhibited certain behavior that led to their diagnoses. In addition, a classification system can help clinicians make predictions about disorders; it provides information about the likelihood that a disorder will occur, about which individuals are most susceptible to the disorder, about the progress of the disorder once it has appeared, and about the prognosis for effective treatment (Meehl, 1996; Rogers, 2001).

The DSM-IV Classification System In 1952, the American Psychiatric Association published the first major classification of psychological disorders in the United

States. **DSM-IV** (*Diagnostic and Statistical Manual of Mental Disorders*, 4th edition; American Psychiatric Association [APA], 1994) is the current edition of the APA's guidelines; it contains 17 major classifications and describes more than 200 specific disorders.

Continuing changes in the *DSM* reflect advancements in knowledge about the classification of psychological disorders (First & Pincus, 2002; Widiger, 2000). On the basis of research and clinical experience, the *DSM-IV* added, dropped, or revised categories, sometimes generating controversy among the diagnosticians who rely on the classification system.

A key feature of the *DSM-IV* is its *multiaxial system*, which classifies individuals on the basis of five dimensions, or axes, that take into account the individual's history and highest level of functioning in the previous year. This system ensures that the individual is not merely assigned to a psychological disorder category but instead is characterized in terms of a number of clinical factors (Gelder, Mayou, & Geddes, 1999).

The five axes of *DSM-IV* are

Axis I: All diagnostic categories except personality disorders and
mental retardation
Axis II: Personality disorders and mental retardation
Axis III: General medical conditions
Axis IV: Psychosocial and environmental problems
Axis V: Current level of functioning

Axes I and II comprise the classification of psychological disorders (Davison & Neale, 2001). Figure 13.2 describes the major categories of these psychological disorders. Axes III through V may not be needed to diagnose a psychological disorder, but they are included so that the person's overall life situation is considered. Thus a person might have a heart condition (Axis III), which has important implications for treatment because some antidepressant drugs can worsen heart conditions. Axis IV includes occupational problems, economic problems, and family problems. On Axis V, the clinician makes a diagnosis about the highest level of adaptive functioning the person has attained in the preceding year in social, occupational, or school activities. This diagnosis ranges from a rating of 100 (superior functioning in a wide range of activities) to 10 (persistent danger of severely hurting self or others), with eight other ratings at 10-point increments. For example, a rating of 50 indicates serious symptoms or impairment in social, occupational, or school functioning.

The more than 200 mental health professionals who contributed to the development of the *DSM-IV* were a much more diverse group than their predecessors, who were mainly White male psychiatrists. More women, ethnic minorities, and nonpsychiatrists, such as clinical psychologists, were involved in the construction of the *DSM-IV*, and greater attention was given to gender- and ethnicity-related diagnoses. For example, the *DSM-IV* contains an appendix titled "Guidelines for Cultural Formation and Glossary of Culture-Related Syndromes" (Nathan, 1994). Also, the *DSM-IV* is accompanied by a number of sourcebooks that present the empirical base of the *DSM-IV*. In previous versions of the *DSM*, the reasons for diagnostic changes were not always explicit, so the evidence that led to their formulation was never available for public evaluation.

The most controversial aspect of the *DSM-IV* is an issue that has existed since the publication of the *DSM-I* in 1952. Although more nonpsychiatrists than ever were responsible for drafting the *DSM-IV*, it still classifies individuals based on their symptoms and uses medical terminology in the psychiatric tradition of thinking about mental disorders in terms of illness and disease. (Clark, Watson, & Reynolds, 1995; Nathan & Langenbucher, 1999; Oltmanns & Emory, 2001). This strategy implies an internal cause that is more or less independent of external or environmental factors (Adams & Cassidy, 1993). Thus, even though researchers have begun to shed light on the complex interaction of genetic, neurobiological, cognitive, and environmental factors in the *DSM* disorders, the *DSM-IV* continues to

DSM-IV *Diagnostic and Statistical Manual of Mental Disorders,* fourth edition; the APA's major classification of psychological disorders.

Major Categories of Psychological Disorders	Description
Axis I Disorders	
Disorders usually first diagnosed in infancy, childhood, or adolescence and communication disorders	Include disorders that appear before adolescence, such as attention-deficit hyperactivity disorder, autism, learning disorders (stuttering, for example).
Anxiety disorders	Characterized by motor tension, hyperactivity, and apprehensive expectations/thoughts. Includes generalized anxiety disorder, panic disorder, phobic disorder, obsessive-compulsive disorder, and post-traumatic stress disorder.
Somatoform disorders	Occur when psychological symptoms take a physical form even though no physical causes can be found. Includes hypochondriasis and conversion disorder.
Factitious disorders	The person deliberately fabricates symptoms of a medical or mental disorder, but not for external gain (such as a disability claim).
Dissociative disorders	Involve a sudden loss of memory or change of identity. Includes the disorders of dissociative amnesia, dissociative fugue, and dissociative identity disorder.
Delirium, dementia, amnestic, and other cognitive disorders	Consist of mental disorders involving problems in consciousness and cognition, such as substance-induced delirium or dementia involving Alzheimer's disease.
Mood disorders	Disorders in which there is a primary disturbance in mood; includes depressive disorders and bipolar disorder (which involves wide mood swings from deep depression to extreme euphoria and agitation).
Schizophrenia and other psychotic disorders	Disorders characterized by distorted thoughts and perceptions, odd communication, inappropriate emotion, and other unusual behaviors.
Substance-related disorders	Include alcohol-related disorders, cocaine-related disorders, hallucinogen-related disorders, and other drug-related disorders.
Sexual and gender identity disorders	Consist of three main types of disorders: gender-identity disorders (person is not comfortable with identity as a female or male), (person has a preference for unusual sexual acts to stimulate sexual arousal), and sexual dysfunctions (impairments in sexual functioning; see chapter 11).
Eating disorders	Include anorexia nervosa and bulimia nervosa, (see chapter 11).
Sleep disorders	Consist of primary sleep disorders, such as insomnia and narcolepsy, (see chapter 6), and sleep disorder due to a general medical condition.
Impulse control disorders not elsewhere classified	Include kleptomania, pyromania, and compulsive gambling.
Adjustment disorders	Characterized by distressing emotional or behavioral symptoms in response to an identifiable stressor.
Axis II Disorders	
Mental retardation	Low intellectual functioning and an inability to adapt to everyday life, (see chapter 10).
Personality disorders	Develop when personality traits become inflexible and maladaptive.
Other conditions that may be a focus of clinical attention.	Include relational problems (with a partner, sibling, and so on), problems related to abuse or neglect (physical abuse of a child, for example), or additional conditions (such as bereavement, academic problems, religious or spiritual problems).

FIGURE 13.2 **Main Categories of Psychological Disorders in *DSM-IV***

espouse the medical/disease model of psychological disorders (Sarbin & Keen, 1998).

A new edition of the *DSM* will not be published until 2006, but the American Psychiatric Association revised the text of *DSM-IV* to include new research information conducted since its publication in 1994. The revision, *DSM-IV-TR* (Text Revision; APA, 2000) includes changes in the criteria for several disorders. For example, paraphilias (sexual disorders such as exhibitionism and voyeurism) can now be diagnosed if they are acted on, even though they may not cause the person whose behavior is in question distress or impaired functioning as a result.

The Issue of Labeling   The *DSM-IV* is also controversial because it labels as psychological disorders what are often thought of as everyday problems. For example, under learning or academic skills disorders, the *DSM-IV* includes the categories of reading disorder, mathematics disorder, and disorder of written expression. Under substance-related disorders, the *DSM-IV* includes the category of caffeine-use disorders. We don't usually think of these everyday problems as mental disorders, but including them implies that these "normal" behaviors should be treated as such. The developers of the *DSM* system argue that mental health providers have been treating many problems not included in earlier editions of *DSM* and that the classification system should be more comprehensive. One practical reason for including everyday problems in living in the *DSM-IV* is to help more individuals get their health insurance companies to pay for professional help. Most health insurance companies reimburse their clients only for disorders listed in the *DSM-IV* system.

Another criticism of the *DSM-IV*, and indeed of this type of classification system in general, is that the system focuses strictly on pathology and problems, with a bias toward finding something wrong with anyone who becomes the object of diagnostic study (Allen, 1998). Because labels can become self-fulfilling prophecies, emphasizing strengths as well as weaknesses might help to destigmatize labels such as *paranoid schizophrenic* or *ex-mental patient*. It would also help to provide clues to treatments that promote mental competence rather than working only to reduce mental distress.

In a classic and controversial study that illustrated the problem of labeling a person with a psychological disorder, David Rosenhan (1973) recruited eight college students, none with a psychological disorder, to see a psychiatrist at a hospital. They were instructed to act in a normal way except to complain about hearing voices that said such things as "empty" and "thud." All eight expressed an interest in leaving the hospital and behaved in a cooperative manner. Nonetheless, they were labeled with schizophrenia, a severe psychological disorder, and kept in the hospital from 3 to 52 days.

Labels can be damaging to a person when they draw attention to one aspect of a person and ignore others (Sarason & Sarason, 2002). For example, the label of "mental patient" or of any disorder, such as anxiety disorder, often has negative connotations, such as incompetent, dangerous, and socially unacceptable. Negative labels can reduce a person's self-esteem and cause the person to be discriminated against. Also, when people feel they might be stigmatized, they may be reluctant to seek help because they don't want to be labeled "mentally ill" or "crazy." Further, even when a person who has had a psychological disorder improves, the label may nevertheless stay with the person. As detailed in the Critical Controversy box, some individuals have gone so far as to argue that psychological disorders are a myth.

Although psychologists usually go along with the *DSM-IV*, psychiatrists are more satisfied with it because of its medical approach. Even though the *DSM-IV* has its critics, it is still the most comprehensive classification system available.

Are Psychological Disorders a Myth?

When he published *The Myth of Mental Illness* in 1961, psychiatrist Thomas Szasz set off a bitter debate, which still rages today. He made the surprising claim that there is no such thing as "mental illness." Szasz begins his argument with a distinction between diseases of the brain and diseases of the mind. Although he accepts that there are diseases of the brain, such as epilepsy, he suggests that psychological disorders are not "illnesses" and are better labeled "problems of living." Imagine someone, for example, who believes that his body is already dead. That person may behave in strange ways but may exhibit no physical defects or diseases. In this case, according to Szasz, the person certainly holds some maladaptive beliefs but does not have a psychological disorder.

For Szasz this is not just a question of semantics. Suppose someone's "problems of living" stem from interacting with other people? In such instances, Szasz says it is inconsistent to refer to that person's social problems as "mental illness" and treat them through a medical model that prescribes drugs. If the person who believes that his body is already dead does nothing more than offend or frighten other people with his bizarre belief, then what right do mental health professionals have to label him "mentally ill" and administer drugs to him?

A poignant example of dealing with "problems of living" can be found in the origins of dissociative identity disorder (having two or more distinct personalities or selves; Braun, 1985). Children whose parents have dissociative identity disorder may develop signs of the disorder as a learned behavior. This tragedy may be compounded by diagnosing such children as having a psychological disorder and treating them with drugs. For Szasz, the treatment of such children should be sociocultural in nature (such as removing them from unhealthy environments and placing them in healthy ones) and may involve behavioral techniques.

Szasz's critique extends to suggesting that the insanity defense be abolished. He says that finding people not guilty of a crime by reason of insanity means that they have a psychological disorder, which he disputes; otherwise, they are misbehaving by committing a crime, in which case they should be held responsible. Stripping them of responsibility and yet depriving them of liberty for a longer period than they would have served for a criminal conviction is doing them no favor.

Szasz's critics reply that there is sound evidence that biological factors are implicated in psychological disorders, including the mood disorders and schizophrenia. They also argue that many psychological disorders are now successfully treated using drug therapies that were unavailable when Szasz first published his arguments. When it comes to the insanity defense, critics argue that imprisoning someone suffering from a psychological disorder for a crime is much less humane than providing him or her with treatment aimed at curing the disorder.

This issue continues to attract attention, as in this commentary: "There is a heightened awareness of the dangers inherent in labeling somebody with a disease category like schizophrenia, and many people are beginning to realize that there is no such entity" (Masson, 1998, p. 2). Szasz's supporters argue that defining an individual's problems as illness only encourages them to lose hope.

If any resolution to this controversy is in sight, it is that everyone agrees on the need for further research to clarify what "depression" and "schizophrenia" really are. Nobody wants to inappropriately label, misdiagnose, or mistreat people who are already suffering.

What do you think?

- When do you think it is appropriate to label someone as having a psychological disorder?
- When do you think medical interventions for mental disorders are appropriate?
- Under what circumstances, if any, is the insanity defense an acceptable legal alternative? Why?

For study tools related to this learning goal, see the Study Guide, the CD-ROM, and the Online Learning Center.

mhhe.com/santrockp7

Review and Sharpen Your Thinking

1 ***Discuss the characteristics and classification of abnormal behaviors.***

- Define abnormal behavior.
- Summarize the biological, psychological, and sociocultural approaches to psychological disorders.
- Describe the classification of psychological disorders and evaluate its advantages and disadvantages.

Ed Gein, a serial killer from Wisconsin, admitted to murdering two women in the 1950s and to robbing bodies from graves. He made corpse parts into ornaments and clothes that he wore to replicate the image of his dead mother. Gein was acquitted by reason of insanity and committed to a mental institution. He was the inspiration for *Psycho* and *Silence of the Lambs*. Do you think Gein should have been acquitted? What do you think about the insanity defense?

Generalized Anxiety Disorder		**Phobic Disorders**		**Post-Traumatic Stress Disorder**
	Panic Disorder		**Obsessive-Compulsive Disorder**	

What are the characteristics of the various anxiety disorders?

Anxiety is a diffuse, vague, highly unpleasant feeling of fear and apprehension. People with high levels of anxiety worry a lot, but their anxiety does not necessarily impair their ability to function in the world. **Anxiety disorders** are psychological disorders that feature motor tension (jumpiness, trembling, inability to relax); hyperactivity (dizziness, a racing heart, or possibly perspiration); and apprehensive expectations and thoughts. Approximately 19.1 million American adults from 18 to 54 years of age, or about 13.3 percent of people in this age group, are diagnosed with an anxiety disorder in any given year (NIMH, 2001b). The five types of anxiety disorders are generalized anxiety disorder, panic disorder, phobic disorders, obsessive-compulsive disorder, and post-traumatic stress disorder.

Generalized Anxiety Disorder

Anna, who is 27 years old, has just arrived for her visit with the psychologist. She was very nervous, wringing her hands, crossing and uncrossing her legs, and playing nervously with strands of her hair. She said her stomach felt like it was in knots, that her hands were cold, and that her neck muscles were so tight they hurt. She said that lately arguments with her husband had escalated. In recent weeks, Anna indicated that she felt more and more nervous throughout the day as if something bad were about to happen. If the doorbell sounded or the phone rang, her heart beat rapidly and her breathing quickened. When she was around people, she had a difficult time speaking. She began to isolate herself. Her husband became impatient with Anna, so she decided to see a psychologist. (Goodstein & Calhoun, 1982)

Anna has a **generalized anxiety disorder,** an anxiety disorder that consists of persistent anxiety for a period of at least 1 month; the individual with generalized anxiety disorder is unable to specify the reasons for the anxiety (Coupland, 2002; Rickels & Rynn, 2001). People with generalized anxiety disorder are nervous most of the time. They may worry about their work, their relationships, their health. They also may worry about minor things in life, such as being late for an appointment or whether their clothes fit just right. Their anxiety often shifts from one aspect of life to another. Approximately 4 million Americans from 18 to 54 years of age, or about 2.8 percent of people in this age group, have generalized anxiety disorder in any given year (NIMH, 2001b).

What is the etiology of generalized anxiety disorder? (The term *etiology* here means investigating the causes or significant antecedents of a mental disorder). Among the biological factors involved in generalized anxiety disorder are a genetic predisposition and a deficiency in the neurotransmitter GABA (Nutt, 2001). Among the psychological and sociocultural factors are having harsh self-standards that are virtually impossible to achieve or maintain, having parents who were overly strict and critical (which can produce low self-esteem and excessive self-criticism), automatic negative thoughts in the face of stress, and a history of uncontrollable stressors or traumas, such as an abusive parent.

anxiety disorders Psychological disorders that include these features: motor tension, hyperactivity, and apprehensive expectations and thoughts.

generalized anxiety disorder An anxiety disorder that consists of persistent anxiety over at least 1 month; the individual with this disorder cannot specify the reasons for the anxiety.

Edvard Munch's *The Scream.* Many experts interpret Munch's painting as an expression of the terror brought on by a panic attack.

Panic Disorder

Panic disorder is an anxiety disorder marked by the recurrent sudden onset of intense apprehension or terror. The individual often has a feeling of impending doom but may not feel anxious all the time. Panic attacks often strike without warning and produce severe palpitations, extreme shortness of breath, chest pains, trembling, sweating, dizziness, and a feeling of helplessness. Victims are seized by fear that they will die, go crazy, or do something they cannot control. Approximately 2.4 million Americans from 18 to 54 years of age, or about 1.7 percent of the people in this age group, have panic disorder in any given year (NIMH, 2001b).

In many instances, a stressful life event occurred in the 6 months prior to the onset of panic disorder, most often a threatened or actual separation from a loved one or a change in job. Biological factors in panic disorder also have been explored (Battaglia, 2002; Otte & others, 2002). For example, a panic attack is associated with an overreaction to lactic acid (which is produced by the body when it is under stress).

In *DSM-IV*, panic disorder can be classified as with or without **agoraphobia,** a cluster of fears centered on public places and an inability to escape or find help should one become incapacitated (Fava & others, 2001; Yardley & others, 2001). Crowded public places; traveling away from home, especially by public transportation; feeling confined or trapped; and being separated from a place or person all can produce agoraphobia, which causes some people to remain housebound. It usually first appears in early adulthood, with 2.5 percent of individuals in the United States classified as having the disorder. Females are likelier than males to have panic disorder. The following individual was classified as having panic disorder with agoraphobia:

Mrs. Reiss is a 48-year-old woman who is afraid to go out alone, a fear that she has had for six years but which has intensified in the last two years. The first signs of her fear appeared after an argument with her husband. After the argument, she went to the mailbox

panic disorder An anxiety disorder marked by the recurrent sudden onset of intense apprehension or terror.

agoraphobia A cluster of fears centered around public places and being unable to escape or to find help should one become incapacitated.

to get the mail and began to feel very anxious and dizzy. It was a struggle for her to get back to the house. Her fear lessened for several years, but reappeared even more intensely after she learned that her sister had cancer. Her fear continued to escalate after arguments with her husband. She became increasingly apprehensive about going outside alone. When she did try to leave, her heart would pound, she would perspire, and she would begin to tremble. After being outside only briefly, she would quickly go back into her house. (Greenberg, Szmulker, & Tantum, 1986)

What is the etiology of panic disorder? In terms of biological factors, individuals may have a predisposition for the disorder, which runs in families and occurs more often in identical than in fraternal twins (Goldstein & others, 1997; Torgerson, 1986). One biological view is that individuals who experience panic disorder may have an autonomic nervous system that is predisposed to be overly active (Barlow, 1988). Another biological view is that panic disorder may be caused by problems involving either or both of two neurotransmitters: norepinephrine and GABA (Sand & others, 2001; Versiani & others, 1999, 2002). In yet another biological link, panic attacks involve hyperventilation or overbreathing (Abelson & others, 2001; Nardi & others, 2001).

In terms of psychological factors, one view focuses on panic disorder with agoraphobia. It is called the *fear-of-fear hypothesis,* which means that agoraphobia may not represent a fear of public places per se but rather a fear of having a panic attack in public places.

In terms of sociocultural factors, U.S. women are twice as likely as men to have panic attacks with or without agoraphobia (Fodor & Epstein, 2002). However, in India, men are far likelier to have panic disorders, probably because in India and other Eastern and Middle Eastern countries, women rarely leave home alone (McNally, 1994). Reasons for U.S. women having higher incidence than men of panic disorder with or without agoraphobia include gender socialization (boys are encouraged to be more independent, girls are protected more) and traumatic experiences (rape and child sexual abuse occur more often in the backgrounds of women than men; Fodor & Epstein, 2002).

Phobic Disorders

A **phobic disorder,** commonly called *phobia,* is an anxiety disorder in which the individual has an irrational, overwhelming, persistent fear of a particular object or situation. Individuals with generalized anxiety disorder cannot pinpoint the cause of their nervous feelings; individuals with phobias can (Barlow, 2001). A fear becomes a phobia when a situation is so dreaded that an individual goes to almost any length to avoid it. Some phobias are more debilitating than others. An individual with a fear of automobiles has a more difficult time functioning in our society than a person with a fear of snakes, for example. Approximately 6.3 million Americans from 18 to 54 years of age, or about 4.4 percent of the people in this age group, have a phobic disorder in any given year (NIMH, 2001b).

Phobias come in many forms. Some of the most common phobias involve social situations, dogs, height, dirt, flying, and snakes. Figure 13.3 labels and describes a number of phobias. Let's look at one person with a phobic disorder.

Agnes is an unmarried 30-year-old who has been unable to go higher than the second floor of any building for more than a year. When she tried to overcome her fear of heights by going up to the third, fourth, and fifth floor, she became overwhelmed by anxiety. She remembers how it all began. One evening she was working alone and was seized by an urge to jump out of an eighth-story window. She was so frightened by her impulse that she hid behind a file cabinet for more than 2 hours until she calmed down enough to gather her belongings and go home. As she reached the first floor of the building, her heart was pounding and she was perspiring heavily. After several months, she gave up her position and became a lower-paid salesperson so she could work on the bottom floor of the building (Cameron, 1963).

Acrophobia	Fear of high places
Aerophobia	Fear of flying
Ailurophobia	Fear of cats
Algophobia	Fear of pain
Amaxophobia	Fear of vehicles, driving
Arachnophobia	Fear of spiders
Astrapophobia	Fear of lightning
Cynophobia	Fear of dogs
Gamophobia	Fear of marriage
Hydrophobia	Fear of water
Melissophobia	Fear of bees
Mysophobia	Fear of dirt
Nyctophobia	Fear of darkness
Ophidiophobia	Fear of nonpoisonous snakes
Thanatophobia	Fear of death
Xenophobia	Fear of strangers

FIGURE 13.3 Phobias
This is only a partial listing.

phobic disorder Commonly called *phobia,* an anxiety disorder in which the individual has an irrational, overwhelming, persistent fear of a particular object or situation.

Popular professional football announcer John Madden has a fear of flying. Because of this phobia, Madden crisscrosses the United States from week to week during football season in his "Madden-cruiser" bus.

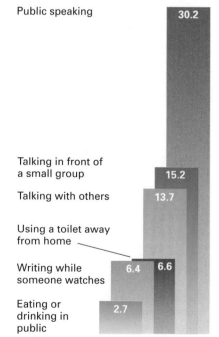

Social Phobias	Percent Who Experience This Phobia in Their Lifetime
Public speaking	30.2
Talking in front of a small group	15.2
Talking with others	13.7
Using a toilet away from home	6.6
Writing while someone watches	6.4
Eating or drinking in public	2.7

 FIGURE 13.4 Social Phobias in the United States In a national survey, the most common social phobia was public speaking.

Let's examine another phobia. *Social phobia* is an intense fear of being humiliated or embarrassed in social situations. Individuals with this phobia are afraid that they will say or do the wrong thing. As a consequence, they might avoid speaking up in a conversation, giving a speech, going out to eat, or attending a party. Their intense fear of such contexts can severely restrict their social life and increase their loneliness (Erwin & others, 2002; McLean & Wood, 2001). Figure 13.4 shows the percentage of people in the United States who say they have experienced a social phobia in their lifetimes (Kessler, Steini & Bergland, 1998).

What is the etiology of phobic disorders? In terms of biological factors, identical twins reared apart sometimes develop the same phobias; one pair independently became claustrophobic, for example (Eckert, Heston, & Bouchard, 1981). About 16 percent of first-degree relatives of individuals with social phobia have an increased risk of developing the phobia, compared with only 5 percent of the relatives of people without social phobia (Kessler, Olfson, & Bergland, 1998). A neural circuit has been proposed for social phobia that includes the thalamus, amygdala, and cerebral cortex (Li, Chokka, & Tibbo, 2001). Also, a number of neurotransmitters may be involved in social phobia, especially serotonin (Van Ameringen & others, 2000).

In terms of psychological factors, different theoretical perspectives provide different explanations (Coupland, 2001; Kendler, Myers, & Prescott, 2002). Psychodynamic theorists, for example, say phobias develop as defense mechanisms to ward off threatening or unacceptable impulses—Agnes hid behind a file cabinet because she feared she would jump out of an eighth-story window. Learning theorists, however, explain phobias differently; they say phobias are learned fears. In Agnes' case, she may have fallen from a high place when she was a little girl. As a result, she associates falling with pain and now fears high places (a classical conditioning explanation). Or she may have heard about or seen other people who were afraid of high places (an observational-learning explanation).

Obsessive-Compulsive Disorder

Earlier, you read about 30-year-old Ruth, who has an obsessive-compulsive disorder. Twenty-seven-year-old Bob also has this disorder. As a young adult, he found himself ensnared in an exacting ritual in which he would remove his clothes in a prearranged sequence, then scrub every inch of his body from head to toe. He dresses himself in an order precisely the opposite to that in which he takes off his clothes. If he deviates from this order, he feels compelled to start the sequence all over again. Sometimes Bob performs the cleansing ritual four or five times a day, and even though he is aware that the ritual is absurd, he simply cannot stop performing it (Meyer & Osborne, 1982).

Obsessive-compulsive disorder (OCD) is an anxiety disorder in which the individual has anxiety-provoking thoughts that will not go away (obsession) and/or urges to perform repetitive, ritualistic behaviors to prevent or produce some future situation (compulsion). Individuals with OCD repeat and rehearse normal doubts and daily routines, sometimes hundreds of times a day (Frost & Steketee, 1998). Approximately 3.3 million Americans from 18 to 54 years of age, or about 2.3 percent of the people in this age group, have obsessive-compulsive disorder in any given year (NIMH, 2001b).

"He always times '60 Minutes.'" © The New Yorker Collection 1983 Mischa Richter from cartoonbank.com. All Rights Reserved.

The most common compulsions are excessive checking, cleansing, and counting. For example, a young man feels he has to check his apartment for gas leaks and make sure the windows are locked. His behavior is not compulsive if he does this once, but if he goes back to check five or six times and then constantly worries that he might not have checked carefully enough once he has left the house, his behavior is compulsive. Most individuals do not enjoy their ritualistic behavior but feel anxious when they do not carry it out.

What is the etiology of obsessive-compulsive disorder? In terms of biological factors, there seems to be a genetic component, because OCD runs in families (Bellodi & others, 2001). Also, researchers using positron emission tomography (PET) and other brain-imaging techniques have found neurological links for OCD (Cavedini & others, 2002). One interpretation of these data is that the frontal cortex or basal ganglia are so active in OCD that numerous impulses reach the thalamus, generating obsessive thoughts or compulsive actions (see Figure 13.5; Rappaport, 1989). Depletion of the neurotransmitter serotonin likely is involved in the neural circuit linked with OCD (Jenike, 2001; Saxena & others, 1998).

Jack Nicholson portrayed an individual with obsessive-compulsive disorder in the movie, *As Good As It Gets.*

NORMAL CONTROL

OBSESSIVE COMPULSIVE

52.0
49.6
47.2
44.9
42.5
40.2
37.8
35.4
33.1
30.7
28.3
26.0
23.6
21.3
18.9
16.5
14.2
11.8
9.5
7.1
4.7

FIGURE 13.5 Pet Scans of Individuals with Obsessive-Compulsive Disorder
(*Top*) Brain images of normal individuals. (*Bottom*) Brain images of individuals with obsessive-compulsive disorder (OCD). The brain images of the individuals with OCD show more activity in the frontal cortex, basal ganglia, and thalamus than the brain images of normal individuals.

obsessive-compulsive disorder (OCD) An anxiety disorder; the individual has anxiety-provoking thoughts that will not go away (obsession) and/or urges to perform repetitive, ritualistic behaviors to prevent or produce some future situation (compulsion).

In terms of psychological factors, OCD often occurs during a period of life stress, such as childbirth, a change in occupational status, or a change in marital status (Stanley, 2000). According to the cognitive perspective, what differentiates individuals with OCD from those who do not have it is the ability to turn off negative, intrusive thoughts by ignoring or dismissing them (Salkovskis & others, 1997). Onset of the disorder frequently occurs in late adolescence or early adulthood, although it can also emerge in young children.

Post-Traumatic Stress Disorder

Post-traumatic stress disorder (PTSD) is a psychological disorder that develops through exposure to a traumatic event, such as war; severely oppressive situations, such as the Holocaust; severe abuse, as in rape; natural disasters, such as floods and tornados; and unnatural disasters, such as plane crashes (Wilson, Friedman, & Lindy, 2001). Approximately 5.2 million Americans between the ages of 18 and 54, or about 3.6 percent of people in this age group, have PTSD in any given year (NIMH, 2001c).

PTSD Symptoms The symptoms of PTSD vary but can include the following:

- Flashbacks, in which the individual relives the event
- Constricted ability to feel emotions, often reported as feeling numb, resulting in an inability to experience happiness, sexual desire, or enjoyable interpersonal relationships
- Excessive arousal, resulting in an exaggerated startle response, or inability to sleep
- Difficulties with memory and concentration
- Feelings of apprehension, including nervous tremors
- Impulsive outbursts of behavior, such as aggressiveness, or sudden changes in lifestyle

Not every individual exposed to the same event develops post-traumatic stress disorder, which overloads the individual's usual coping abilities (Clark, 2001; Livanou & others, 2002; Norris & others, 2001). For example, it is estimated that 15 to 20 percent of Vietnam veterans experienced PTSD. Vietnam veterans who had some autonomy and decision-making authority, such as Green Berets, were less likely to develop the disorder than soldiers who had no control over where they would be sent or when and who had no option but to follow orders. Preparation for a trauma also makes a difference in whether an individual will develop the disorder. For example, emergency workers who are trained to cope with traumatic circumstances usually do not develop PTSD. Some experts consider sexual abuse and assault victims to be the single largest group of post-traumatic stress disorder sufferers (Koss & Boeschen, 1998).

Developmental Course of PTSD PTSD is characterized by anxiety symptoms that may either immediately follow the trauma or be delayed by months or even years (Ford, 1999). Most people who are exposed to a traumatic, stressful event experience some of the symptoms in the days and weeks following exposure (National Center for PTSD, 2001). Overall, approximately 8 percent of men and 20 percent of women go on to develop PTSD, and about 30 percent of these individuals develop a chronic form that persists through their lifetimes.

The course of PTSD typically involves periods of symptom increase followed by remission or decrease, although for some individuals the symptoms may be unremitting and severe. Ordinary events can serve as reminders of the trauma and trigger flashbacks or intrusive images.

A flashback can make the person lose touch with reality and reenact the event for a period of seconds, hours or, very rarely, days. A person having a flashback, which can come in the form of images, sounds, smells, and/or feelings, usually believes that the traumatic event is happening all over again.

post-traumatic stress disorder (PTSD) An anxiety disorder that develops through exposure to a traumatic event, severely oppressive situations, severe abuse, and natural and unnatural disasters.

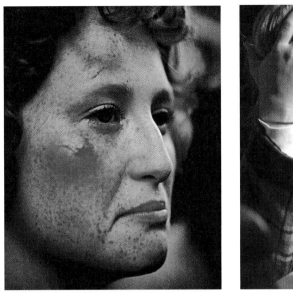

Post-traumatic stress disorder (PTSD) can be caused by a variety of traumatic events, including war (PTSD has been a common disorder in Vietnam veterans), abuse (such as spousal abuse or rape), unnatural disasters (such as terrorist attacks), and natural disasters (such as hurricanes).

Combat and War-Related Traumas   Much of what is known about PTSD comes from individuals who have developed the disorder because of combat and war-related traumas (Freeman & Roca, 2001). The Holocaust produced many individuals who developed PTSD. In one study of 124 survivors of the Holocaust, almost half were still suffering from PTSD 40 years after experiencing this traumatic event (Kuch & Cox, 1982). In another study, 10 percent of Vietnamese, Hmong, Laotian, and Cambodian refugees who left their war-torn countries to live in California had PTSD (Gong-Guy, 1986). A study of Bosnian refugees just after they had come to the United States indicated that 65 percent had PTSD (Weine & others, 1995). This figure may be so high because many of these Bosnian refugees had experienced numerous atrocities, organized mass rapes, and murders of relatives and neighbors.

Rather than waiting years for the effects of the stress of combat to take its toll on those who have served in the military, branches of the U.S. armed forces now use military psychologists—those who specialize in research and application to military problems—and other mental health professionals in preventive efforts in combat zones around the world (Rabasca, 2000). The mental health units typically have a psychologist, social worker, and several mental health technicians. Units also might have a psychiatrist, psychiatric nurses, and occupational therapists. The frontline teams take a rapid, short-term, on-site approach. Treatment is prompt—beginning as soon as possible after a service member shows symptoms such as tremors, nightmares, or headaches. How effective is this new approach? The military believes that it is much more effective than the old practice of sending troubled individuals to the rear. Their data indicate that 70 to 90 percent of service members return to active duty within several days when they are treated at the front (Rabasca, 2000).

Abuse Abuse can come in many forms, including abuse of a spouse, the sexual abuse of rape or incest, and emotional abuse (as when parents harshly criticize and belittle their children; Hanson & others, 2001: Trowell & others, 2002). Researchers have found that approximately 95 percent of rape survivors experience PTSD symptoms in the first 2 weeks following the traumatic event. About 50 percent still have symptoms 3 months later, and as many as 25 percent have symptoms 4 to 5 years after the rape (Foa & Riggs, 1995). Consider the following case (NIMH, 2001c):

> I started having flashbacks. They kind of came over me like a splash of water. I would be terrified. Suddenly I was reliving the rape. Every instant was startling. I felt like my entire head was moving a bit, shaking, but that wasn't so at all. I would get flushed or a very dry mouth and my breathing changed. . . . And it was scary. Having a flashback can wring you out. You're really shaken.

Natural and Unnatural Disasters Natural disasters such as tornados, hurricanes, earthquakes, and fires can cause the individuals involved in these traumatic events to develop PTSD (Auger & others, 2000; Goenjian & others, 2001). In one study of children who lived through Hurricane Andrew, in 1992, 20 percent still had PTSD 1 year later (La Greca & others, 1996). Fourteen years after a flood destroyed the community of Buffalo Creek in West Virginia, 25 percent of the survivors were still suffering from PTSD (Green & others, 1992).

Unnatural disasters such as plane crashes and terrorist attacks can cause individuals to develop post-traumatic stress syndrome. The September 11, 2001, terrorist attacks on New York City and Washington, D.C., are expected to produce post-traumatic stress syndrome in many of the survivors of the attacks (Norris & others, 2001).

mhhe.com/santrockp7

For study tools related to this learning goal, see the Study Guide, the CD-ROM, and the Online Learning Center.

Review and Sharpen Your Thinking

2 *Distinguish among the various anxiety disorders.*

- Define anxiety disorders and characterize generalized anxiety disorder.
- State the key features of panic disorder.
- Identify the sources of anxiety in phobic disorders.
- Explain obsessive-compulsive disorder.
- Describe post-traumatic stress disorder.

Family members and friends of individuals with obsessive-compulsive disorder frequently tell them to stop their obsessions and compulsions. However, just telling someone to stop these obsessions and compulsions usually does not work. If you had a friend with this disorder, what would you try to do about it?

Dissociative Amnesia and Fugue	Dissociative Identity Disorder

What are the dissociative disorders?

Dissociative disorders are psychological disorders that involve a sudden loss of memory or change in identity. Under extreme stress or shock, the individual's conscious awareness becomes dissociated (separated or split) from previous memories and thoughts (Gast & others, 2001; Simeon & others, 2002).

Recall that, in Chapter 7, we discussed Ernest Hilgard's (1986) *hidden observer* concept, which he used to explain hypnosis. In Hilgard's view, people can develop a special divided state of consciousness, a sort of splitting of consciousness into separate components. One component is *active* and includes conscious awareness; the other is *passive*, registering and storing information in memory without being aware that the information has been processed, as if a hidden observer is watching and recording events in people's lives without their awareness.

For most of us, the active and passive dimensions of consciousness connect our experiences so effectively that we don't detect any division between them (Nolen-Hoeksema, 2001). However, individuals who develop dissociative disorders may have problems integrating the active and passive dimensions of consciousness (Dell, 2002; Hilgard, 1992; Kihlstrom, 1992). That is, in some individuals, dimensions of the conscious mind remain split and function independently of each other.

Three kinds of dissociative disorders are dissociative amnesia, dissociative fugue, and dissociative identity.

Dissociative Amnesia and Fugue

Amnesia is the inability to recall important events (LaBar & others, 2002). Amnesia can be caused by a blow to the head, causing trauma to the brain. But **dissociative amnesia** is a dissociative disorder characterized by extreme memory loss that is caused by extensive psychological stress. For example, an individual showed up at a hospital and said he did not know who he was. After several days in the hospital, he awoke one morning and demanded to be released. Eventually he remembered that he had been involved in an automobile accident in which a pedestrian had been killed. The extreme stress of the accident and the fear that he might be held responsible triggered the amnesia.

Dissociative fugue (*fugue* means "flight") is a dissociative disorder in which the individual not only develops amnesia but also unexpectedly travels away from home and assumes a new identity. Consider the following example of this disorder:

> One day a woman named Barbara vanished without a trace. Two weeks later, looking more like a teenager—with her hair in a ponytail and wearing bobby socks—than a 31-year-old woman, Barbara was picked up by police in a nearby city. When her husband came to see her, Barbara asked, "Who are you?" She could not remember anything about the last 2 weeks of her life. During psychotherapy, she gradually began to recall her past. She had left home with enough money to buy a bus ticket to the town where she grew up as a child. She spent days walking the streets and standing near a building where her father had worked. Later she went to the motel with a man. According to the motel manager, she entertained a series of men there over a three-day period. (Goldstein & Palmer, 1975)

Dissociative Identity Disorder

Dissociative identity disorder (DID), formerly called *multiple personality disorder,* is the most dramatic but least common dissociative disorder; individuals suffering from this disorder have two or more distinct personalities or selves, like the fictional Dr.

dissociative disorders Psychological disorders that involve a sudden loss of memory or change in identity.

dissociative amnesia A dissociative disorder involving extreme memory loss caused by extensive psychological stress.

dissociative fugue A dissociative disorder in which the individual not only develops amnesia but also unexpectedly travels away from home and establishes a new identity.

dissociative identity disorder (DID) Formerly called *multiple personality disorder,* this is the most dramatic but least common dissociative disorder; individuals suffering from this disorder have two or more distinct personalities.

FIGURE 13.6 **The Three Faces of Eve**
Chris Sizemore, the subject of *The Three Faces of Eve*, is shown here with a work she painted, titled *Three Faces in One*.

Jekyll and Mr. Hyde of Robert Louis Stevenson's short story. Each personality has its own memories, behaviors, and relationships; one personality dominates the individual at one time, and another personality will take over at another time. The shift from one personality to the other usually occurs under distress (Dell, 2002; Gleaves, May, & Cardena, 2001).

One of the most famous cases of dissociative identity disorder involves the "three faces of Eve" (see figure 13.6; Thigpen & Cleckley, 1957):

> Eve White was the original dominant personality. She had no knowledge of her second personality, Eve Black, although Eve Black had been alternating with Eve White for a number of years. Eve White was bland, quiet, and serious—a rather dull personality. By contrast, Eve Black was carefree, mischievous, and uninhibited. She would "come out" at the most inappropriate times, leaving Eve White with hangovers, bills, and a reputation in local bars that she could not explain. During treatment, a third personality, Jane, emerged. More mature than the other two, Jane seemed to have developed as a result of therapy.

In some cases, therapists have been ascribed responsibility for creating a second or third personality. At one point, Eve said that her therapist had created one of her personalities.

A summary of research on dissociative identity disorder suggests that the disorder is characterized by an inordinately high rate of sexual or physical abuse during early childhood (McAllister, 2000; Stafford & Lynn, 2002). Sexual abuse occurred in 56 percent of reported cases of the disorder. Note, though, that the majority of individuals who have been sexually abused do not develop dissociative identity disorder. Mothers of individuals who develop this disorder tend to be rejecting and depressed; fathers distant, alcoholic, and abusive. The vast majority of individuals with dissociative identity disorder are adult females. When males develop the disorder, they show more aggression than females with the disorder (Ross & Norton, 1989). A genetic predisposition might exist, as the disorder tends to run in families (Dell & Eisenhower, 1990). Some research suggests that a person's different personalities have different EEG patterns (Allen & Movius, 2000; APA, 1994).

Fascinating as it is, dissociative identity disorder is rare. Until the 1980s, only about 300 cases had ever been reported (Suinn, 1984). In the past decade, hundreds more have been labeled "dissociative identity disorder," although some psychologists argue this increase represents a diagnostic fad. Others believe that it is not so rare but has been frequently misdiagnosed as schizophrenia. Improved techniques for assessing physiological changes that occur when individuals change personalities increase the likelihood that more accurate rates of occurrence can be determined.

Review and Sharpen Your Thinking

3 **Describe the dissociative disorders.**
- Define dissociative disorders.
- Explain dissociative amnesia and fugue.
- Discuss dissociative identity disorder.

Imagine that you are on a jury in which an individual who has been accused of killing someone claims that he suffers from dissociative identity disorder and doesn't remember committing the murder. How difficult would it be for you and the other jury members to determine if he really has this disorder? What questions would you want answered before making your decision about the individual?

mhhe com/
santrockp7

For study tools related to this learning goal, see the Study Guide, the CD-ROM, and the Online Learning Center.

MOOD DISORDERS 4

Depressive Disorders   **Causes of Mood Disorders**

Bipolar Disorder   **Suicide**

What are the symptoms and causes of mood disorders, and who is at risk for depression and suicide?

The **mood disorders** are psychological disorders in which there is a primary disturbance of mood (prolonged emotion that colors the individual's entire emotional state). The mood disturbance can include cognitive, behavioral, and somatic (physical) symptoms, as well as interpersonal difficulties (Coyne, 2000). Two main types of mood disorders are the depressive disorders and bipolar disorder. Depression can occur alone, as in the depressive disorders, or it can alternate with mania (an overexcited, unrealistically optimistic state), as in bipolar disorder. Recall Kay Redfield Jamison's description of her battle with bipolar disorder, at the beginning of the chapter, in which she oscillated between manic highs and terrifying depressions. Approximately 18.8 million Americans between the ages of 18 and 54, or about 9.5 percent of the people in this age group, have a mood disorder in any given year (NIMH, 2001b).

Depressive Disorders

The **depressive disorders** are mood disorders in which the individual suffers depression without ever experiencing mania. The severity of the depressive disorders varies. Some individuals experience what is classified as *major depressive disorder*, whereas others are given the diagnosis of *dysthymic disorder* (more chronic depression with fewer symptoms than major depression; Beckham, 2000).

Consider a person with a depressive disorder:

Peter had been depressed for several months. Nothing cheered him up. As he reflected, "My brain is like on time out. I just can't get anything done. I feel virtually exhausted all of the time. I try to study but I read the same pages over and over again and can't remember

mood disorders Psychological disorders in which there is a primary disturbance in mood (prolonged emotion that colors the individuals entire emotional state). Two main types are the depressive disorders and bipolar disorder.

depressive disorders Mood disorders in which the individual suffers depression without ever experiencing mania.

This painting by Vincent Van Gogh, *Portrait of Dr. Gachet*, reflects the extreme melancholy that characterizes the depressive disorders.

a thing I've read. I feel like the bottom is falling out of my life. It's so empty." Nothing cheered Peter up. His depression began when the girl he wanted to marry decided that marriage was not for her, at least not marriage to Peter. Peter's emotional state deteriorated to the point at which he didn't leave his room for days at a time, he kept his shades down and the room dark, and he could hardly get out of bed in the morning. When he managed to leave the room, he had trouble maintaining a conversation. By the time Peter contacted his college counseling center, he had gone from being mildly depressed to being in the grips of major depression.

Peter was diagnosed with **major depressive disorder,** in which the individual experiences a major depressive episode and depressed characteristics, such as lethargy and hopelessness, for at least 2 weeks. The individual's daily functioning becomes impaired. Approximately 9.9 million Americans from 18 to 54 years of age, or about 5 percent of the people in this age group, have major depressive disorder in any given year (NIMH, 2001b).

Nine symptoms define a major depressive episode (of which, at least five must be present during a 2-week period):

1. Depressed mood most of the day
2. Reduced interest or pleasure in all or most activities
3. Significant weight loss or gain, or significant decrease or interest in appetite
4. Trouble sleeping or sleeping too much
5. Psychomotor agitation or retardation
6. Fatigue or loss of energy
7. Feeling worthless or guilty in an excessive or inappropriate manner
8. Problems in thinking, concentrating, or making decisions
9. Recurrent thoughts of death and suicide

Dysthymic disorder is generally more chronic and has fewer symptoms than major depressive disorder (Dunner & others, 2002). The individual is in a depressed mood for most days for at least 2 years as an adult or at least 1 year as a child or adolescent. To be classified as having dysthymic disorder, a major depressive episode must not have occurred, and the 2-year period of depression must not have been broken by a normal mood lasting more than 2 months. Two or more of these six symptoms must be present: poor appetite or overeating, sleep problems, low energy or fatigue, low self-esteem, poor concentration or difficulty making decisions, and feelings of hopelessness (Munoz, 1998). Approximately 10.9 million people in the United States, or about 5.4 percent of the population, will have dysthymic disorder in their lifetimes (NIMH, 2001b).

Although most people do not spiral into major depression as Peter did, everyone feels "blue" sometimes. In our stress-filled world, people often use the term *depression* to describe brief bouts of normal sadness or discontent over life's problems. Perhaps you haven't done well in a class or things aren't working out in your love life. You feel down in the dumps and say you are depressed. In most instances, though, your depression won't last as long or be as intense as Peter's; after a few hours, days, or weeks, you snap out of your gloomy state and begin to cope more effectively with your problems. Nonetheless, depression is so widespread that it has been called the "common cold" of mental disorders; more than 250,000 individuals are hospitalized every year for the disorder. Students, professors, corporate executives, laborers—no one is immune to depression, not even F. Scott Fitzgerald, Ernest Hemingway, Virginia Woolf, Abraham Lincoln, or Winston Churchill—each of whom experienced depression. After years of depression, Hemingway eventually took his own life. Suicide is discussed later in this section.

The inadequate care that results from a lack of understanding or a misunderstanding of depression is tragic. Given the range of psychological and pharmacological treatments available today, those individuals who go untreated suffer needlessly. To evaluate whether you might be depressed, see the Psychology and Life box.

major depressive disorder Indicated by a major depressive episode and depressed characteristics, such as lethargy and hopelessness, lasting at least 2 weeks.

dysthymic disorder A depressive disorder that is generally more chronic and has fewer symptoms than major depressive disorder.

Are You Depressed?

Below is a list of the ways that you might have felt or behaved in the past week. Indicate what you felt by putting an X in the appropriate box for each item.

During the past week	Rarely or None of the Time (Less Than 1 Day)	Some or a Little of the Time (1–2 Days)	Occasionally or a Moderate Amount of the Time (3–4 Days)	Most or All of the Time (5–7 Days)
1. I was bothered by things that usually don't bother me.	☐	☐	☐	☐
2. I did not feel like eating; my appetite was poor.	☐	☐	☐	☐
3. I felt that I could not shake off the blues even with help from my family and friends.	☐	☐	☐	☐
4. I felt that I was just as good as other people.	☐	☐	☐	☐
5. I had trouble keeping my mind on what I was doing.	☐	☐	☐	☐
6. I felt depressed.	☐	☐	☐	☐
7. I felt that everything I did was an effort.	☐	☐	☐	☐
8. I felt hopeful about the future.	☐	☐	☐	☐
9. I thought my life had been a failure.	☐	☐	☐	☐
10. I felt fearful.	☐	☐	☐	☐
11. My sleep was restless.	☐	☐	☐	☐
12. I was happy.	☐	☐	☐	☐
13. I talked less than usual.	☐	☐	☐	☐
14. I felt lonely.	☐	☐	☐	☐
15. People were unfriendly.	☐	☐	☐	☐
16. I enjoyed life.	☐	☐	☐	☐
17. I had crying spells.	☐	☐	☐	☐
18. I felt sad.	☐	☐	☐	☐
19. I felt that people disliked me.	☐	☐	☐	☐
20. I could not get going.	☐	☐	☐	☐

For items 4, 8, 12, and 16, give yourself a 3 each time you checked Rarely or None, 2 each time you checked Some or a Little, 1 each time you checked Occasionally or Moderate, and a 0 each time you checked Most or All of the Time. For the remaining items, give yourself a 0 each time you checked Rarely or None, 1 each time you checked Some or a Little, 2 each time you checked Occasionally or Moderate, and 3 each time you checked Most or All of the Time. Total up your score for all 20 items.

If your score is around 7, then you are like the average male in terms of how much depression you have experienced in the past week. If your score is around 8 or 9 your score is similar to the average female's. Scores less than the average for either males or females indicate that depression probably has not been a problem for you during the past week. If your score is 16 or more and you are bothered by your feelings, you might benefit from professional help.

Keep in mind, though, that self-diagnosis is not always accurate and to adequately diagnose anyone, the professional judgment of a qualified clinician is required.

Bipolar Disorder

Although she had experienced extreme mood swings since she was a child, Mrs. M. was first admitted to a mental hospital at the age of 38. At 33, shortly before the birth of her first child, she became very depressed. One month after the baby was born, she became agitated and euphoric. Mrs. M. signed a year's lease on an apartment, bought furniture, piled up debts. Several years later other manic and depressive mood swings occurred. In one of her excitatory moods, Mrs. M. swore loudly and created a disturbance at a club where she was not a member. Several days later she began divorce proceedings. On the day prior to her admission to the mental hospital, she went on a spending spree and bought 57 hats. Several weeks later, she became despondent, saying, "I have no energy. My brain doesn't work right. I have let my family down. I don't have anything to live for." In a subsequent manic bout, Mrs. M. pursued a romantic relationship with a doctor. (Kolb, 1973)

Bipolar disorder is a mood disorder that is characterized by extreme mood swings that include one or more episodes of mania (an overexcited, unrealistically optimistic state; Brickman, LoPiccolo, & Johnson, 2002). *Bipolar* means that the person may experience both depression and mania. Most bipolar individuals experience multiple cycles of depression interspersed with mania. Less than 10 percent of bipolar individuals tend to experience manic-type episodes without depression. Approximately

bipolar disorder A mood disorder characterized by extreme mood swings that include one or more episodes of mania.

2.3 million Americans, or about 1.2 percent of the U.S. population 18 years and older, have bipolar disorder in any given year (NIMH, 2001b).

A manic episode is like the flip side of a depressive episode (Miklowitz, 2002). Instead of feeling depressed, the person feels euphoric and on top of the world. However, as the manic episode unfolds, the person can experience panic and eventually depression. Instead of feeling fatigued, as many depressed individuals do, when individuals experience mania they have tremendous energy and might sleep very little. There is often an impulsivity when individuals are in a manic state that can get them in trouble in business and legal transactions. For example, they might spend their life savings on a foolish business venture. By definition in the *DSM-IV* classification, manic episodes must last 1 week. They average 8 to 16 weeks. Individuals with bipolar disorder can have manic and depressive episodes that occur four or more times a year, but they usually are separated by 6 months to a year.

Bipolar disorder is much less common than depressive disorders (Mackinnon & others, 2002), but unlike depressive disorders (which are likelier to occur in females), bipolar disorder is equally common in females and males. About 1 or 2 in 100 people are estimated to experience bipolar disorder at some point in their lifetimes (Kessler & others, 1994).

Causes of Mood Disorders

Mood disorders, such as Peter's depression and Mrs. M.'s bipolar disorder, can involve biological, psychological, and sociocultural factors. I distinguish between depressive disorders and bipolar disorder as appropriate in discussing the causes of mood disorders.

Biological Factors   Biological explanations of mood disorders include heredity, neurophysiological abnormalities, neurotransmitter deregulation, and hormonal factors (Nolen-Hoeksema, 2001). The links between biology and mood disorders are well established.

Heredity   Depressive and bipolar disorders tend to run in families, although the family link is stronger for bipolar disorder than for depressive disorders (Bradbury, 2001). One of the greatest risks for developing a mood disorder is having a biological parent who suffers from a mood disorder. In bipolar disorder, the rate of the disorder in first-degree relatives (parents, siblings) is 10 to 20 times higher than in the general population (MacKinnon, Jamison, & DePaulo, 1997). An individual with an identical twin who has bipolar disorder has a more than 60 percent probability of also having the disorder, and a fraternal twin more than 10 percent, whereas the rate of bipolar disorder in the general population is 1 to 2 percent (see figure 13.7). Researchers are zeroing in on the specific genetic location of bipolar disorder—recent studies suggest that it may be on chromosome 22 (Kelsoe & others, 2001).

Neurobiological Abnormalities   One of the most consistent findings of neurobiological abnormalities in individuals with mood disorders is altered brain-wave activity during sleep. Depressed individuals experience less slow-wave sleep (which contributes to a feeling of being rested and restored) and go into rapid-eye-movement (REM) sleep earlier in the night than nondepressed individuals (Benca, 2001). These neurobiological abnormalities correspond to the reports of depressed individuals that they have difficulty going to sleep at night or remaining asleep, that they often wake up early in the morning and can't get back to sleep, and that they do not feel rested after they sleep (Cosgrave & others, 2000).

Neuroimaging studies also reveal decreased metabolic activity in the cerebral cortex of individuals with severe major depressive disorder (Buchsbaum & others, 1997). Figure 13.8 shows the metabolic activity of an individual cycling through depressive and manic phases of bipolar disorder. Notice the decrease in metabolic activity in the brain during depression and the increase in metabolic activity during mania (Baxter & others, 1995).

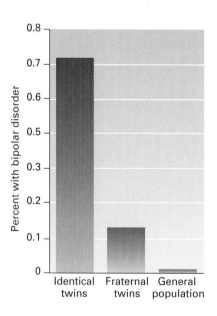

FIGURE 13.7 Risk of Bipolar Disorder in Identical Twins, Fraternal Twins, and the General Population
Notice how much stronger the incidence of bipolar disorder is in identical twins compared with fraternal twins and the general population; these statistics suggest a strong genetic role in the disorder.

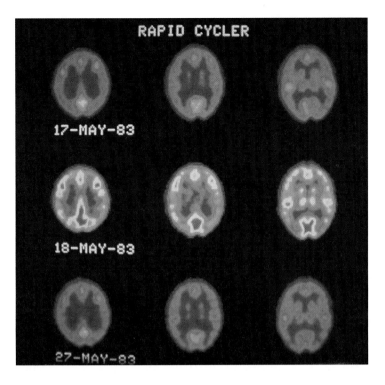

FIGURE 13.8 Brain Metabolism in Mania and Depression PET scans of an individual with bipolar disorder, who is described as a rapid-cycler because of how quickly severe mood changes occurred in the individual. (*Top, bottom*) The person's brain in a depressed state. (*Middle*) A manic state. The PET scans reveal how the brain's energy consumption falls in depression and rises in mania. The red areas in the middle row reflect rapid consumption of glucose.

Most areas of the brains of depressed individuals are underactive. For example, one section of the prefrontal cortex, which is involved in generating actions, is underactive in depressed individuals. However, certain brain areas are overactive. For example, recent studies using brain imaging techniques revealed that the amygdala is overactive in depression (Posner & Raichle, 1998; Van Elst, Ebert, & Trimble, 2001). Some of depression's symptoms may be explained by this change in brain activity in the amygdala, which helps to store and recall emotionally charged memories and sends information to the prefrontal cortex at the sight of something fearful. In turn, the prefrontal cortex should signal the amygdala to slow down when the source of the fear is gone. But, in depression, the prefrontal cortex may fail to send the all-clear signal. Thus the amygdala may continue sending signals that keep triggering extended rumination about sad events.

Another neurobiological abnormality in depression is neuron death or disability. Recent research studies revealed that depressive disorders are linked to both neuron death or disability (Manji, 2001; Manji, Drevets, & Charney, 2001). Individuals with depression seem to have fewer neurons in some parts of their brain, including the prefrontal cortex, which should be sending the slowdown signals to the amygdala (Drevets, 2001).

Neurotransmitter Deregulation Deregulation of a number of neurotransmitters is likely involved in depression (Stahl, 2002). Abnormalities in the monoamine neurotransmitters, such as norepinephrine, serotonin, and dopamine, have been implicated in mood disorders. An imbalance in the monoamine neurotransmitters in one direction is thought to be involved in depression, an imbalance in the other direction in mania. Researchers also have found abnormalities in the number of monoamine neurotransmitters in individuals with mood disorders (Wong & others, 2000). For example, individuals with major depressive disorder appear to have too few receptors for serotonin and norepinephrine. Recent studies also have revealed that changes in the neurotransmitter glutamate occur in bipolar disorder (Benes & others, 2000; Shaldubina, Agam, & Belmaker, 2001). Still other research suggests that regulation of a neurotransmitter called substance P is involved in depression (Pacher & others, 2001).

Hormones Depressed individuals show chronic hyperactivity in the neuroendocrine glandular system and an inability to return to normal functioning following a stressful experience (Young & Korzun, 1998). In turn, the excess hormones produced by the neuroendocrine glands (such as the pituitary gland and adrenal cortex) may be linked to the deregulation of the monoamine neurotransmitters just discussed.

Also in regard to the role of hormones in depression, it has been argued that women's increased vulnerability to depression is linked to their ovarian hormones, estrogen and progesterone. However, the evidence that women's moods are tied to their hormones is mixed at best (Nolen-Hoeksema, 2001). Some women do experience more depression during the postpartum period, menopause, and other times when their hormone levels are changing. Nonetheless, the extent to which hormonal changes in women account for their higher rate of depression in comparison with men is less clear.

Psychological Factors Psychodynamic, behavioral, and cognitive theories have all proposed explanations for depression. These ideas are significant for their influence on treatment of disorders, as discussed in Chapter 14.

Psychodynamic Explanations Psychodynamic theories emphasize that depression stems from individuals' childhood experiences that prevented them from developing a strong, positive sense of self (Nolen-Hoeksema, 2001). In this view, depressed individuals become overly dependent on the evaluations and approval of others for their self-esteem mainly because of inadequate nurturing by parents (Blatt & Zuroff, 1992).

Many modern psychodynamic theorists still rely on Freud's (1917) theory that depression is a turning inward of aggressive instincts. Freud theorized that a child's early attachment to a love object (usually the mother) contains a mixture of love and hate. When the child loses the love object or when his or her dependency needs are frustrated, feelings of loss coexist with anger. Because the child cannot openly accept such angry feelings toward the individual he or she loves, the hostility is turned inward and experienced as depression. The unresolved mixture of anger and love is carried forward to adolescence and adulthood, when loss can bring back these early feelings of abandonment.

Behavioral Explanations Peter Lewinsohn and his colleagues (Lewinsohn & Gottlib, 1995; Lewinsohn, Joiner, & Rohde, 2001) proposed that life's stresses can lead to depression by reducing the positive reinforcers in a person's life. The sequence goes like this: When people experience considerable stress in their lives, they may withdraw from the stress. The withdrawal produces a further reduction in positive reinforcers, which can lead to more withdrawal, which leads to even fewer positive reinforcers.

Another behavioral view of depression focuses on **learned helplessness,** which occurs when individuals are exposed to aversive stimulation, such as prolonged stress, over which they have no control. The inability to avoid such aversive stimulation produces an apathetic state of helplessness. Martin Seligman (1975) proposed that learned helplessness is one reason that some individuals become depressed. When individuals cannot control the stress they encounter, they eventually feel helpless and depressed.

Research on learned helplessness led Susan Nolen-Hoeksema (1995, 2000) to examine the ways that people cope when they are depressed. She found that some depressed individuals use a *ruminative coping style*, in which they focus intently on how they feel (their sadness and hopelessness) but do not try to do anything about the feelings: They just ruminate about their depression. In a series of research studies, Nolen-Hoeksema and her colleagues (Nolen-Hoeksema, Larson, & Grayson, 1999; Nolen-Hoeksema, Parker, & Larson, 1994; Nolen-Hoeksema & Morrow, 1991) have found that individuals with

learned helplessness Occurs when individuals are exposed to aversive stimulation, such as prolonged stress, over which they have no control. The inability to avoid such aversive stimulation can produce an apathetic state of helplessness.

All-or-nothing thinking	You see things in black-and-white categories. If your performance falls short of perfect, you see yourself as a total failure.
Overgeneralization	You see a single negative event as a never-ending pattern of defeat.
Mental filter	You pick out a single negative detail and dwell on it exclusively so that your vision of all reality becomes darkened, like the drop of ink that discolors the entire beaker of water.
Disqualifying the positive	You reject positive experiences by insisting they "don't count" for some reason or other. In this way you can maintain a negative belief that is contradicted by your everyday experiences.
Jumping to conclusions	You make a negative interpretation even though there are no definite facts that convincingly support your conclusion. (a) *Mind reading*. You arbitrarily conclude that someone is reacting negatively to you, and you don't bother to check this out. (b) *The Fortune Teller Error*. You anticipate that things will turn out badly, and you feel convinced that your prediction is an already-established fact.
Magnification (catastrophizing) or minimization	You exaggerate the importance of things (such as your goof-up or someone else's achievement), or you inappropriately shrink things until they appear tiny (your own desirable qualities or other fellow's imperfections). This is also called the "binocular trick."
Emotional reasoning	You assume that your negative emotions necessarily reflect the way things really are: "I feel it, therefore it must be true."
Should statements	You try to motivate yourself with shoulds and shouldn'ts, as if you had to be whipped and punished before you could be expected to do anything. "Musts" and "oughts" are also offenders. The emotional consequence is guilt. When you direct should statements toward others, you feel anger, frustration, and resentment.
Labeling and mislabeling	This is an extreme form of overgeneralization. Instead of describing your error, you attach a negative label to yourself: "I'm a *loser*." When someone else's behavior rubs you the wrong way, you attach a negative label to him: "He's a . . . louse." Mislabeling involves describing an event with language that is highly colored and emotionally loaded.
Personalization	You see yourself as the cause of some negative external event which in fact you were not primarily responsible for.

FIGURE 13.9 Cognitive Distortions That Can Contribute to Depression

depression remain depressed longer when they use a ruminative coping style rather than an action-oriented coping style. Women are more likely to ruminate when they are depressed than men are (Nolen-Hoeksema & others, 1999).

Cognitive Explanations   The cognitive approach provides another perspective on mood disorders (Newman & others, 2002). Individuals who are depressed rarely think positive thoughts. They interpret their lives in self-defeating ways and have negative expectations about the future (Gilbert, 2001). Psychologist Aaron Beck (1967) believes that such negative thoughts reflect schemas that shape the depressed individual's experiences. These habitual negative thoughts magnify and expand a depressed person's negative experiences (Teasdale & others, 1995). The depressed person might overgeneralize about a minor occurrence and think that he is worthless because a work assignment was turned in late, his son was arrested for shoplifting, or a friend made a negative comment about his hair. An individual might be given a work evaluation that shows a deficiency in one area and then magnify the significance of the evaluation. *Catastrophic thinking,* such as expecting to be fired and not being able to find another job, might ensue. The accumulation of such cognitive distortions can lead to depression. Figure 13.9 describes a number of cognitive distortions that can contribute to depression (Nolen-Hoeksema, 2000).

Another cognitive view of depression involves a cognitive reformulation of the hopelessness involved in learned helplessness (Joiner & others, 2001). It focuses on people's attributions, discussed in chapter 12. When people make attributions, they attempt to explain what caused something to happen. In this attributional view of depression, individuals who regularly explain negative events as being caused by internal ("It is my fault I failed the exam"), stable ("I'm going to fail again and again"), and global ("Failing this exam shows how I won't do well in any of my courses")

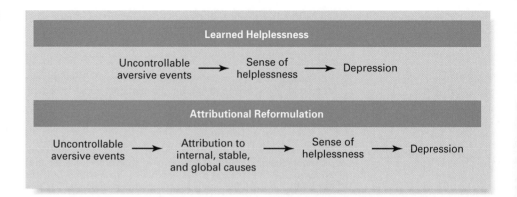

and global ("Failing this exam shows how I won't do well in any of my courses") causes blame themselves for these negative events, expect the negative events to recur in their lives in the future, and tend to experience negative events in many areas of their lives (see figure 13.10; Abramson, Seligman, & Teasdale, 1978).

Closely related to the attributional view of learned helplessness is a distinction between optimistic and pessimistic cognitive styles. Recall from chapter 12 that being either optimistic or pessimistic can have profound effects on a person's well-being, with optimistic individuals showing better physical and mental health. In one study, researchers interviewed 1st-year college students at two universities and distinguished those with an optimistic style from those with a pessimistic style (Alloy, Abramson, & Francis, 1999). They interviewed the students on a regular basis over the next 2½ years. In this time frame, among students with no prior history of depression, 17 percent of the students with a pessimistic style developed major depression, whereas only 1 percent of those with an optimistic style did. Also, among students with a prior history of depression, 27 percent of those who had a pessimistic style relapsed into depression over the 2½ years, but only 6 percent of those with the optimistic style did.

Another cognitive explanation of depression focuses on what is called *depressive realism* (McKendree-Smith & Scogin, 2000). Some people who are depressed may be seeing their world accurately and realistically. That is, there really are negative things going on in their lives that make them depressed. Researchers have found that when depressed individuals are asked to make judgments about how much control they have over situations that actually cannot be controlled, they are accurate in saying that they do not have control (Alloy & Abramson, 1979). In contrast, nondepressed individuals overestimate the amount of control they have in such situations. Thus nondepressed individuals often have an illusion of control over their world that depressed individuals do not. In this view, it may not be accurate, realistic thinking that prevents individuals from becoming depressed but optimism and a perceived sense of illusory control over one's world.

Sociocultural Factors Among the sociocultural factors involved in depression are relationships with other people, socioeconomic and ethnic variations, cultural variations, and gender.

Interpersonal Relationships One view of depression is that it may stem from problems that develop in relationships with other people (Segrin, 2001). Both proximal (recent) and distal (distant, earlier) interpersonal experiences might be involved in depression. In terms of a proximal factor, recent marital conflict might trigger depression. In terms of distal factors, possibly inadequate early relationships with parents are carried forward to influence the occurrence of depression later in a person's life. In support of the view that interpersonal relationships contribute to depression, one study of college students found that those with an anxious, insecure attachment style

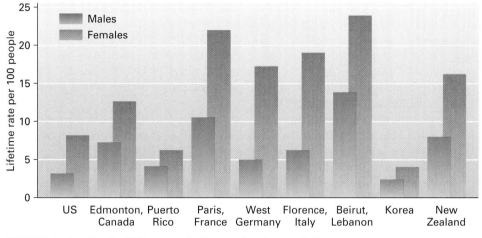

FIGURE 13.11 **Gender Differences in Depression Across Cultures** One study showed that women were more likely than men to have major depression in nine cultures.

were likelier to have depressive symptoms than their counterparts with secure attachment styles (Roberts, Gottlib, & Kassel, 1996).

The British psychiatrist John Bowlby (1989) suggested that both interpersonal relationships and cognitive factors can explain the development of depression. He believes a combination of an insecure attachment to the mother, a lack of love and affection as a child, and the actual loss of a parent during childhood gives rise to a negative cognitive set, or schema. The schema built up during childhood causes the individual to interpret later losses as yet other failures in one's effort to establish enduring and close positive relationships.

Socioeconomic and Ethnic Factors Individuals with a low socioeconomic status (SES), especially those living in poverty, are more likely to develop depression than their higher SES counterparts. In addition, in one study, Latinos in the United States had a higher incidence of depression than Whites (Blazer & others, 1994). The higher rate of depression among Latinos may be due to their higher incidence of poverty. Very high rates of depression also have been found in Native Americans, among whom poverty, hopelessness, and alcoholism are widespread (Manson & others, 1990).

Cultural Variations Martin Seligman (1989) believes that the reason so many young American adults are prone to depression is our society's emphasis on self, independence, and individualism, coupled with an erosion of connectedness to others, family, and religion. This phenomenon, Seligman says, has spawned a widespread sense of hopelessness.

Depressive disorders are found in virtually all cultures in the world, but their incidence, intensity, and components vary across cultures. The incidence of depressive disorders is lower in less industrialized, less modernized countries than in more industrialized, modernized countries (Cross-National Collaborative Group, 1992). This difference likely is due to the fast-paced, stressful lifestyles of individuals in industrialized, modernized countries and the stronger family, community orientation of people in less industrialized, less modernized countries. Also, one difference in depression between Western and many non-Western cultures is an absence of guilt and self-deprecation in the non-Western cultures (Draguns, 1990).

Gender Bipolar disorder occurs about equally among women and men, but women are about twice as likely as men to develop depression. This gender difference occurs in many countries (see figure 13.11; Weissman & Olfson, 1995).

Suicide tends to run in families. Five suicides occurred in different generations of the Hemingway family, including famous author Ernest (*top*) and his granddaughter Margaux (*bottom*).

Studies have shown that depression is especially high among single women who are the heads of households and among young married women who work at unsatisfying, dead-end jobs (Bernstein, 2001). Marriage often confers a greater protective buffer against stress for men than for women. In unhappy marriages, women are three times as likely as men to be depressed. Mothers of young children are especially vulnerable to stress and depression. Also, the more children in the household, the more depression women report.

As we saw earlier, poverty may be a pathway to depression, and three of every four people living in poverty in the United States are women and children. Minority women also are a high-risk group for depression.

Careful diagnosis of depression in women is critical (Kornstein & Clayton, 2002). According to the American Psychological Association's Task Force on Women and Depression, depression is misdiagnosed at least 30 to 50 percent of the time in women (McGrath & others, 1990). Approximately 70 percent of prescriptions for antidepressants are given to women, too often with improper diagnosis and monitoring.

Suicide

Severe depression and other psychological disorders can cause individuals to want to end their lives, as bipolar disorder did to Kay Redfield Jamison. Although attempting suicide is abnormal behavior, it is not uncommon for individuals to contemplate suicide at some point in their lives. For example, as many as 2 of every 3 college students have thought about suicide on at least one occasion.

Approximately 31,000 individuals commit suicide every year in the United States, and the number of attempted suicides is estimated at 600,000 (NIMH, 2000). The number of actual suicides reflects a three-fold increase since 1950.

After about the age of 15, the suicide rate begins to rise rapidly (Weissman & others, 1999). Sucide is the third leading cause (after automobile accidents and homicides) of death today among adolescents 13 through 19 years of age (National Center for Health Statistics, 2000).

Females are likelier than males to attempt suicide, but males are more likely to actually commit suicide. This difference may be due to the fact that males tend to use lethal means, such as guns, whereas females tend to cut their wrists or take overdoses of sleeping pills, both less likely to result in death (Maris, 1998).

Biological Factors   Genetic factors appear to play a role in suicide, which tends to run in families (Fu & others, 2002). One famous family that has been plagued by suicide is the Hemingway family. Five members of this family, spread across generations, committed suicide. The best-known of the five Hemingways are the writer Ernest Hemingway and his granddaughter Margaux (who committed suicide on the 35th anniversary of her father's suicide).

A number of studies have linked suicide with low levels of the neurotransmitter serotonin (Mann & Arango, 1999; van Pragg, 2000). Postmortem analyses of the brains of individuals who have committed suicide show abnormally low levels of this transmitter. Also, individuals who attempt suicide and who have low levels of serotonin are 10 times likelier to attempt suicide again than are those attempters who have high levels of serotonin (Roy, 1992).

Poor physical health, especially when it is long-standing and chronic, is another risk factor for suicide. For example, Ernest Hemingway had been in failing health for a number of years when he committed suicide.

Psychological Factors   Psychological factors that can contribute to suicide include mental disorders and traumas, such as sexual abuse. Approximately 90 percent of individuals who commit suicide are estimated to have a diagnosable mental disorder (NIMH, 2000). The most common mental disorder among individuals who commit suicide is depression (Fergusson & Woodward, 2002).

What to Do

1. Ask direct, straightforward questions in a calm manner. For example, "Are you thinking about hurting yourself?"

2. Be a good listener and be supportive. Emphasize that unbearable pain can be survived.

3. Take the suicide threat very seriously. Ask questions about the person's feelings, relationships, and thoughts about the type of method to be used. If a gun, pills, rope, or other means is mentioned and a specific plan has been developed, the situation is dangerous. Stay with the person until help arrives.

4. Encourage the person to get professional help and assist him or her in getting help. If the person is willing, take the person to a mental health facility or hospital.

What Not to Do

1. Don't ignore the warning signs.

2. Don't refuse to talk about suicide if the person wants to talk about it.

3. Don't react with horror, disapproval, or repulsion.

4. Don't offer false reassurances ("Everything will be all right") or make judgments ("You should be thankful for . . .").

5. Don't abandon the person after the crisis seems to have passed or after professional counseling has begun.

FIGURE 13.12 **What to Do and What Not to Do When Someone Is Threatening Suicide**

Immediate and highly stressful circumstances, such as the loss of a job, flunking out of school, or an unwanted pregnancy can lead people to threaten and/or commit suicide (Rudd, Joiner, & Rajab, 2001). Also, substance abuse is linked with suicide more today than it was in the past.

Sociocultural Factors   The loss of a loved one through death, divorce, or separation can lead to a suicide attempt (Heikkinen, Aro, & Loennqvist, 1992). There also is a link between suicide and a long-standing history of family instability and unhappiness. And chronic economic hardship can be a factor in suicide. In one study, 8.5 percent of people living below the poverty line, compared with 5.4 percent living above the line, said that they had contemplated suicide (Crosby, Cheltenham, & Sacks, 1999).

In the United States, Native Americans have the highest suicide rate of all demographic groups, followed by Whites (Hendin, 1995). Across cultures, Hungary, Germany, Austria, Denmark, and Japan have the highest suicide rates, and Egypt, Mexico, Greece, and Spain have the lowest rates (National Center for Health Statistics, 1994). Suicide rates for the United States and Canada fall between the rates in these countries. Among the reasons for the variations is the degree to which there are cultural and religious norms against suicide.

Psychologists cannot prevent suicidal impulses with certainty. However, psychologists believe that the most effective intervention comes from those who have had special training. Figure 13.12 provides some good advice on what to do and what not do when someone is threatening suicide.

Review and Sharpen Your Thinking

4 *Compare the mood disorders and specify risk factors for depression and suicide.*

- Define the mood disorders.
- Distinguish between depressive disorders and normal feelings of sadness.
- Describe the mood disturbances that characterize bipolar disorder.
- Discuss the causes of mood disorders.
- Explain the factors that can lead to suicide.

Do any of the theories about the causes of depression seem better at accounting for depression in college students? Explain.

5 SCHIZOPHRENIA

Types of Schizophrenia   **Causes of Schizophrenia**

What is the nature of schizophrenia and its different forms?

> One day, while I was in the principal's office, suddenly the room became enormous, illuminated by a dreadful electric light that cast false shadows. Everything was exact, smooth, artificial, extremely tense; the chairs and tables seemed models placed here and there. Pupils and teachers were puppets revolving without cause, without objective. I recognized nothing, nobody. It was as though reality, attenuated, had slipped away from all these things and these people. Profound dread overwhelmed me, and as though lost, I looked around desperately for help. I heard people talking, but I did not grasp the meaning of their words. The voices were metallic, without warmth or color. From time to time, a word detached itself from the rest. It repeated itself over and over in my head, absurd, as though cut off by a knife. (Sechehaye, 1951, p. 22)

This passage was written by a person with **schizophrenia,** a severe psychological disorder that is characterized by highly disordered thought processes. Individuals with schizophrenia may show odd communication, inappropriate emotion, abnormal motor behavior, and social withdrawal (Heinrichs, 2001). The term *schizophrenia* comes from the Latin words *schizo*, meaning "split," and *phrenia*, meaning "mind." It signifies that the individual's mind is split from reality and that personality disintegrates. Schizophrenia is not the same as multiple personality, which sometimes is called "split personality." Schizophrenia involves the split of an individual's personality from reality, not the coexistence of several personalities within one individual. Approximately 2.2 million adults in the United States, or about 1.1 percent of the population 18 years and older, have schizophrenia in any given year (NIMH, 2001b).

Schizophrenia is a serious, debilitating mental disorder. About one-half of the patients in mental hospitals are individuals with schizophrenia. More often now than in the past, individuals with schizophrenia live in society and return to mental hospitals periodically for treatment. Drug therapy is primarily responsible for fewer individuals with schizophrenia being hospitalized. The "rule of fourths" characterizes outcomes for individuals with schizophrenia: One-fourth get well and stay well; one-fourth go on medication, do relatively well, and are able to live independently; another one-fourth are well enough to live in a group home; and one-fourth do poorly and are usually institutionalized.

Schizophrenia produces a bizarre set of symptoms and wreaks havoc on the individual's personality (VandenBos, 2000). At the core of these symptoms are highly disordered thought processes. For example, individuals with schizophrenia have *delusions*, or false beliefs. One individual might think he is Jesus Christ, another Napoléon. The delusions are utterly implausible. One individual might think her thoughts are being broadcast over the radio, another might think that a double agent is controlling her every move. Individuals with schizophrenia also might hear, see, feel, smell, and taste things that are not there. These *hallucinations* often take the form of voices. An individual with schizophrenia might think that he hears two people talking about him. Or, on another occasion, he might say, "Hear that rumbling noise in the pipe. That is one of my men watching out for me."

Often individuals with schizophrenia do not make sense when they talk or write. For example, one individual with schizophrenia might say, "Well, Rocky, babe, help is out, happening, but where, when, up, top, side, over, you know, out of the way, that's it. Sign off." Such speech has no meaning. These incoherent, loose word associations are called *word salad*.

schizophrenia A severe psychological disorder that is characterized by highly disordered thought processes.

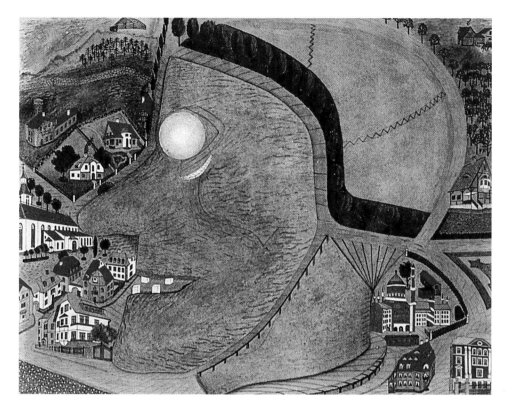

FIGURE 13.13 A Person with Catatonic Schizophrenia Unusual motor behaviors are prominent symptoms in catatonic schizophrenia. Individuals may cease to move altogether, sometimes holding bizarre postures.

The motor behavior of the individual with schizophrenia can be bizarre, sometimes taking the form of an odd appearance, pacing, statuelike postures, or strange mannerisms. Some individuals with schizophrenia withdraw from their social world, totally absorbed in their own thoughts.

Types of Schizophrenia

There are four main types of schizophrenia: disorganized, catatonic, paranoid, and undifferentiated. Their outward behavior patterns vary, but they have in common the characteristics of disordered thought processes.

Disorganized Schizophrenia In **disorganized schizophrenia,** an individual has delusions and hallucinations that have little or no recognizable meaning—hence, the label "disorganized." An individual with disorganized schizophrenia may withdraw from human contact and may regress to silly, childlike gestures and behavior. Many of these individuals were isolated or maladjusted during adolescence.

Catatonic Schizophrenia **Catatonic schizophrenia** is characterized by bizarre motor behavior, which sometimes takes the form of a completely immobile stupor (see figure 13.13). Even in this stupor, individuals with catatonic schizophrenia are completely conscious of what is happening around them. In a catatonic state, the individual sometimes shows *waxy flexibility*; for example, if the person's arm is raised and then allowed to fall, the arm stays in the new position. The following excerpt describes an individual with catatonic schizophrenia:

> Todd, a 16-year-old high school student, began to change for the worse. A few months ago, he began to take Tai Chi lessons and often stood for long periods of time in karate-like positions, oblivious to what was going on around him. When his parents tried to get him out of bed in the morning, he lay motionless. When he was taken to see a mental

disorganized schizophrenia A type of schizophrenia in which an individual has delusions and hallucinations that have little or no recognizable meaning.

catatonic schizophrenia A type of schizophrenia that is characterized by bizarre motor behavior, which sometimes takes the form of a completely immobile stupor.

health professional, Todd stood motionless in the center of the room with his head flexed forward and his hands at his sides. He seemed unresponsive to much of what was going on around him. When the mental health professional placed Todd's hands in an awkward position, he remained frozen in that position for several minutes. (Carson, Butcher, & Mineka, 2000).

Paranoid Schizophrenia   **Paranoid schizophrenia** is characterized by delusions of reference, grandeur, and persecution. The delusions usually form a complex, elaborate system based on a complete misinterpretation of actual events. It is not unusual for individuals with paranoid schizophrenia to develop all three delusions in the following order: First, they sense that they are special and have been singled out for attention (delusions of reference). Individuals with delusions of reference misinterpret chance events as being directly relevant to their own lives—a thunderstorm, for example, might be perceived as a personal message from God. Second, they believe that this special attention is the result of their admirable and special characteristics (delusions of grandeur). Individuals with delusions of grandeur think of themselves as exalted beings—the pope or the president, for example. Third, they think that others are so jealous and threatened by these characteristics that they spy and plot against them (delusions of persecution). Individuals with delusions of persecution often feel that they are the target of a conspiracy, as in Bob's case:

> Bob began to miss work. He spent his time watching his house from a rental car parked inconspicuously down the street and following his fellow employees as they left work to see where they went and what they were doing. He kept a little black book in which he scribbled cryptic notes. When he went to the water cooler at work, he pretended to drink but instead looked around the room to observe if anyone looked guilty or frightened. Bob's world seemed to be closing in on him. After an explosive scene at the office one day, he became very agitated. He left and never returned. By the time Bob arrived home, he was in a rage. He could not sleep that night and the next day he kept his children home from school. All day he kept the shades pulled on every window. The next night he maintained his vigil. At 4 A.M., he armed himself and burst out of the house, firing shots in the air while daring his enemies to come out. (McNeil, 1967)

Undifferentiated Schizophrenia   **Undifferentiated schizophrenia** is characterized by disorganized behavior, hallucinations, delusions, and incoherence. This diagnosis is used when an individual's symptoms either do not meet the criteria for one of the other types or meet the criteria for more than one of the other types.

Causes of Schizophrenia

Like the mood disorders, schizophrenia may have biological, psychological, and sociocultural causes. Schizophrenia is a heavily researched mental disorder, with recent research especially focusing on biological factors.

Biological Factors   There is strong research support for biological explanations of schizophrenia. Particularly compelling is the evidence for a genetic predisposition, but structural abnormalities and neurotransmitters also seem to be linked to this devastating disorder.

Heredity   If you have a relative with schizophrenia, what are the chances you will develop schizophrenia? It depends on how closely you are related. As genetic similarity increases, so does a person's risk of becoming schizophrenic (Tsuang, Stone, & Faraone, 2001). As shown in figure 13.14, an identical twin of an individual with schizophrenia has a 46 percent chance of developing the disorder, a fraternal twin 14

paranoid schizophrenia A type of schizophrenia that is characterized by delusions of reference, grandeur, and persecution.

undifferentiated schizophrenia A type of schizophrenia that is characterized by disorganized behavior, hallucinations, delusions, and incoherence.

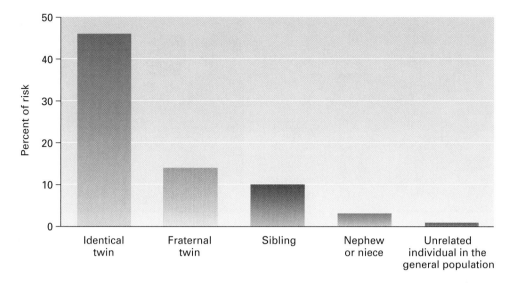

Lifetime Risk of Developing Schizophrenia, According to Genetic Relatedness As genetic relatedness to an individual with schizophrenia increases, so does the risk of developing schizophrenia.

percent, a sibling 10 percent, a nephew or niece 3 percent, and an unrelated individual in the general population 1 percent (Gottesman & Shields, 1982). Such data strongly suggest that genetic factors are involved in schizophrenia. Researchers are seeking to pinpoint the chromosomal location of genes involved in schizophrenia. They recently have found possible genetic markers for schizophrenia on chromosomes 10, 13, and 22 (Bassett & others, 2001; Kelsoe & others, 2001).

The role of heredity in schizophrenia may be illustrated through the story of the Genain quadruplets, who have been extensively studied at the National Institute of Mental Health (NIMH). Henry Genain had forgotten to buy his wife a birthday present, so she suggested that he give her a child for their third wedding anniversary instead. The wish came true, but there were four presents instead of one. Their birth in a midsize midwestern U.S. town was a celebrated occasion; one paper ran a contest to name the girls and received 12,000 entries. The family was given a rent-free house and a baby carriage for four, and a dairy company donated milk. Newspaper stories appeared from time to time about the quadruplets, portraying their similarities, especially their drama talent and a song-and-dance routine they had developed.

The quadruplets' problems emerged by the time they reached high school. It became clear then that the girls had serious mental problems. By the time they were in their twenties, each had been diagnosed with schizophrenia. A perceptive doctor recognized their symptoms and contacted NIMH. A research team led by David Rosenthal (1963) began extensive evaluation of the schizophrenic quadruplets.

About 20 years later, psychologist Alan Mirksy invited the quadruplets back to NIMH to determine how they might have changed. The scientists also wanted to know if recently developed techniques could discover something special about their biological makeup. PET scans revealed an unusually high rate of energy use in the rear portion of the quadruplets' brains (see figure 13.15). Their brains also showed much less alpha-wave activity than the brains of normal individuals. Remember that alpha-wave activity appears in individuals in a relaxed state; scientists speculate that the onset of hallucinations might possibly block alpha-wave activity.

Environmental experiences may have contributed to the Genain quadruplets' schizophrenia as well. Their father placed strict demands on his daughters, delighted in watching them undress, and would not let them play with friends or participate in school or church activities. He refused to let the quadruplets participate in social activities even as adults, and he followed them to their jobs and opened their mail.

What makes the Genain quadruplets so fascinating is their uniqueness—identical quadruplets occur once in every 16 million births, only half survive to adulthood, and only 1 in 100 develops schizophrenia. The chances of all of them surviving and

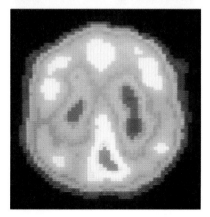

PET Scans of the Genain Quadruplets In a normal brain (*top*), the areas of high energy use are at the top, in the frontal lobes. The quadruplets all showed abnormal energy use in the visual areas (*red area, bottom*). *Are these hallucinations?*

The Genain quadruplets as children and as middle-aged adults. All four had been diagnosed with schizophrenia by the time they were in their 20s.

developing schizophrenia are one in tens of billions of births, a figure much greater than the current world population.

In a follow-up of the Genain quadruplets when they were 66 years of age, significant variations in the courses of their lives were apparent (Mirsky & others, 2000). Myra worked, married, and raised a family despite having schizophrenia. Hester never completed high school and has never been able to function independently outside a group home or institution. Nora and Iris fared somewhat better than Hester but have never married nor had substantial careers. The Genain quadruplets' thought processes remained stable or even improved somewhat as they got older, supporting the idea that schizophrenia is not a degenerative disorder, as many mental health professionals previously believed.

Structural Brain Abnormalities   Structural abnormalities in the brain have been found in individuals with schizophrenia. Imaging techniques, such as the PET scan, clearly show enlarged ventricles in the brains of these people (Puri & others, 1999, 2001). Ventricles are fluid-filled spaces in the brain, and enlargement of the ventricles indicates atrophy or deterioration in other brain tissue. Individuals with schizophrenia also have a small frontal cortex (the area in which thinking, planning, and decision making take place) and show less activity than is seen in individuals who do not have schizophrenia (Allen, Goldstein, & Weiner, 2001; Cotter & others, 2002). Among the questions raised by such findings are Do these deficits cause the disorder? Or are they simply symptoms of a disorder whose true origin lies deeper in the brain, in the genes, or in the environment?

Neurotransmitter Deregulation   An early biological explanation for schizophrenia stated that individuals with schizophrenia produce higher than normal levels of the neurotransmitter dopamine and that the excess dopamine causes schizophrenia. That theory is probably too simple, although there is good evidence that dopamine does play a role in schizophrenia (Bressan & others, 2001).

Psychological Factors   Although contemporary theorists do not propose psychological factors as stand-alone causes of schizophrenia, stress may be a contributing factor. The **diathesis-stress model** argues that a combination of biogenetic disposition and stress causes schizophrenia (Meehl, 1962). The term *diathesis* means physical vulnerability or predisposition to a particular disorder. A defective gene makeup might produce schizophrenia only when the individual lives in a stressful environment. Advocates of the diathesis-stress view emphasize the importance of stress reduction and family support in treating schizophrenia.

Sociocultural Factors   Disorders of thought and emotion are common to schizophrenia in all cultures, but the type and incidence of schizophrenic disorders may

diathesis-stress model A model of schizophrenia that proposes a combination of biogenetic disposition and stress as the cause of the disorder.

vary from culture to culture. Individuals living in poverty are likelier to have schizophrenia than people at higher socioeconomic levels. The link between schizophrenia and poverty is correlational, and contemporary theorists do not believe that poverty causes schizophrenia (Schiffman & Walker, 1998).

To learn how social change affected the percentage of individuals diagnosed with schizophrenia in Algeria, go to the Online Learning Center. (Around the Globe)

Review and Sharpen Your Thinking

5   *Characterize schizophrenia.*

- Describe the different types of schizophrenia.
- Explain the causes of schizophrenia.

Imagine that you are a clinical psychologist who has been given the opportunity to interview the Genain quadruplets. What questions would you want to ask them in an effort to sort through why the paths of their schizophrenia varied through their adult years?

For study tools related to this learning goal, see the Study Guide, the CD-ROM, and the Online Learning Center.

PERSONALITY DISORDERS 6

| Odd/Eccentric Cluster | Dramatic/Emotionally Problematic Cluster | Chronic-Fearfulness/ Avoidant Cluster |

What behavior patterns are typical of personality disorders?

Personality disorders are chronic, maladaptive cognitive-behavioral patterns that are thoroughly integrated into the individual's personality and that are troublesome to others or whose pleasure sources are either harmful or illegal (Livesly, 2001). The patterns are often recognizable by adolescence or earlier. Personality disorders usually are not as bizarre as schizophrenia, and they do not have the intense, diffuse feelings of fear and apprehension that characterize the anxiety disorders (Evans & others, 2002).

In the *DSM-IV*, the personality disorders are grouped into three clusters: odd/eccentric, dramatic/emotionally problematic, and chronic-fearfulness/avoidant.

Odd/Eccentric Cluster

The odd/eccentric cluster includes the paranoid, schizoid, and schizotypal disorders:

- *Paranoid.* These individuals have a lack of trust in others and are suspicious. They see themselves as morally correct yet vulnerable and envied.
- *Schizoid.* They do not form adequate social relationships. They show shy, withdrawn behavior and have difficulty expressing anger. Most are considered to be "cold" people.
- *Schizotypal.* They show odd thinking patterns that reflect eccentric beliefs, overt suspicion, and overt hostility. The following case describes an individual with schizotypal personality disorder.

Mr. S. was 35-year-old chronically unemployed man who was thought to have a vitamin deficiency. This was believed to have occurred because Mr. S. avoided any foods that could have been contaminated by a machine. He had started to develop alternative ideas about food and diet in his 20s. He left his family to study an eastern religion. As he said, "It opened my third eye, corruption is all about." Later, Mr. S. moved to live by himself on a small farm, attempting to grow his own food. He spent his days and evenings researching the mechanisms of food contamination. (Quality Assurance Project, 1990, p. 344)

Individuals with paranoid personality disorder show chronic and pervasive mistrust and suspicion of other people that is not warranted.

personality disorders Chronic, maladaptive cognitive-behavioral patterns that are thoroughly integrated into the individual's personality.

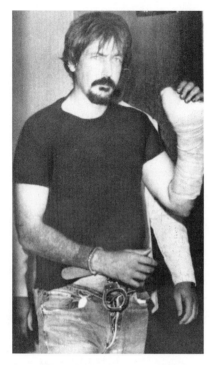

Gary Gilmore was a classic case of antisocial personality disorder. As a young adolescent, Gilmore had low grades, was often truant, and stole from classmates. At 14, he was placed in a juvenile detention center for stealing a car. He was arrested on numerous occasions in high school and at 20 was sent to the state penitentiary for burglary and robbery. Several years later, Gilmore was released, but it didn't take long for him to be put back in the penitentiary for other armed robberies. Released again, he moved in with a woman, but his drinking, carousing, and fighting caused her to kick him out. Later that year, he pulled into a gas station in Utah and ordered the attendant to hand over his cash, which the attendant did. Gilmore shot him twice in the head, anyway, killing him. The next morning, Gilmore walked into a hotel and shot the manager. Gilmore was caught and convicted of the two murders. He was executed in 1977.

As you can see, some personality disorders have names that are similar to other disorders described in other categories earlier in the chapter, such as schizotypal personality disorder and schizophrenic disorders. However, individuals with schizotypal disorder are not as clearly bizarre in their thinking and behavior as individuals with schizophrenia.

Dramatic/Emotionally Problematic Cluster

The dramatic and emotionally problematic cluster consists of the histrionic, narcissistic, borderline, and antisocial personality disorders.

- *Histrionic.* These individuals seek a lot of attention and tend to overreact. They respond more dramatically and intensely than is required by the situation, hence the term *histrionic.* The disorder is more common in women than men.
- *Narcissistic.* They have an unrealistic sense of self-importance, can't take criticism, manipulate people, and lack empathy. These characteristics lead to substantial problems in relationships.
- *Borderline.* These individuals are often emotionally unstable, impulsive, unpredictable, irritable, and anxious. They also are prone to boredom. Their behavior is similar to that of individuals with schizotypal personality disorder, but they are not as consistently withdrawn and bizarre.
- *Antisocial.* They are guiltless, law-breaking, exploitive, self-indulgent, irresponsible, and intrusive. They often resort to a life of crime and violence. This disorder is far more common in men than in women.

In the national study of the prevalence of psychological disorders, 2.6 percent of the individuals reported that they had at some time experienced an antisocial personality disorder (Robins & Regier, 1991). The following individual has an antisocial personality disorder (Carson, Butcher, & Mineka, 2000):

Mark, 22 years old, is awaiting trial for car theft and armed robbery. He has a long history of arrests beginning at 9 years of age, when he was arrested for vandalism. He was expelled from high school for truancy and disruptive behavior. He ran away from home on numerous occasions. He has not held a job for more than two days at a time, even though his charming manner enables him to obtain work rather easily. Mark is a loner with few friends and, although initially charming, he soon antagonizes the people he meets with his aggressive, self-oriented behavior. While Mark was awaiting trial, he skipped bail and left town.

People with antisocial personality disorder used to be called psychopaths or sociopaths. They regularly violate other people's rights. The disorder begins before the age of 15 and continues into adulthood. It is much more common in males than in females. These individuals represent a small percentage of the population but commit a disproportionately large percentage of violent and property crimes (Meyer, Wolverton, & Deitsch, 1998). The disorder is very difficult to treat. Also, most HMOs will not authorize treatment of antisocial personality disorder or any of the other personality disorders. (Managed care issues are discussed in the next chapter.)

Explanations for the causes of antisocial personality disorder include biological, psychological, and sociocultural factors. In terms of biological factors, a genetic predisposition for the disorder may be present (Goldstein, Prescott, & Kendler, 2001). For example, the disorder is likelier to appear in identical twins than in fraternal twins (Gottesman & Goldsmith, 1994). In terms of psychological factors, the impulsive and aggressive behavior that characterizes individuals with antisocial personality disorders suggests that they have not adequately learned how to delay gratification. In terms of sociocultural factors, inadequate socialization regularly appears in the history of individuals who develop antisocial personality disorder (Sutker & Allain, 1993). Parents of these children may be neglectful or inconsistent and punitive in their discipline. Individuals with this disorder are likelier to have at least one parent with antisocial personality traits than are their counterparts without the disorder. Thus children growing up in these families presumably have many opportunities to observe and imitate parents who behave in exploitive, immoral ways.

Chronic-Fearfulness/Avoidant Cluster

The chronic-fearfulness/avoidant cluster includes the avoidant, dependent, passive-aggressive, and obessesive-compulsive personality disorders:

- *Avoidant*. These individuals are shy and inhibited yet desire interpersonal relationships, which distinguishes them from the schizoid and schizotypal disorders. They often have low self-esteem and are extremely sensitive to rejection. This disorder is close to being an anxiety disorder but is not characterized by as much personal distress.
- *Dependent*. They lack self-confidence and do not express their own personalities. They have a pervasive need to cling to stronger personalities, whom they allow to make decisions for them. The disorder is far more common in women than in men.
- *Passive-Aggressive*. These individuals often pout and procrastinate; they are stubborn or are intentionally inefficient in an effort to frustrate others.
- *Obsessive-Compulsive*. This personality disorder is often confused with obsessive-compulsive anxiety disorder. However, an individual with obsessive-compulsive personality disorder rarely becomes obsessed about issues. In the personality disorder, the individual also engages in a specific behavior, such as persistent hand washing. And, in the personality disorder, the person does not become upset or distressed about his or her lifestyle. These individuals are obsessed with rules, are emotionally insensitive, and are oriented toward a lifestyle of productivity and efficiency.

Review and Sharpen Your Thinking

6   *Identify the behavior patterns typical of personality disorders.*

- Define personality disorders.
- Discuss the odd/eccentric cluster.
- Explain the dramatic/emotionally problematic cluster.
- Describe the chronic-fearfulness/avoidant cluster.

We described a possible psychological cause for antisocial personality disorder. Go down the list of other personality disorders and try to come up with psychological causes for them.

mhhe com/
santrockp7

For study tools related to this learning goal, see the Study Guide, the CD-ROM, and the Online Learning Center.

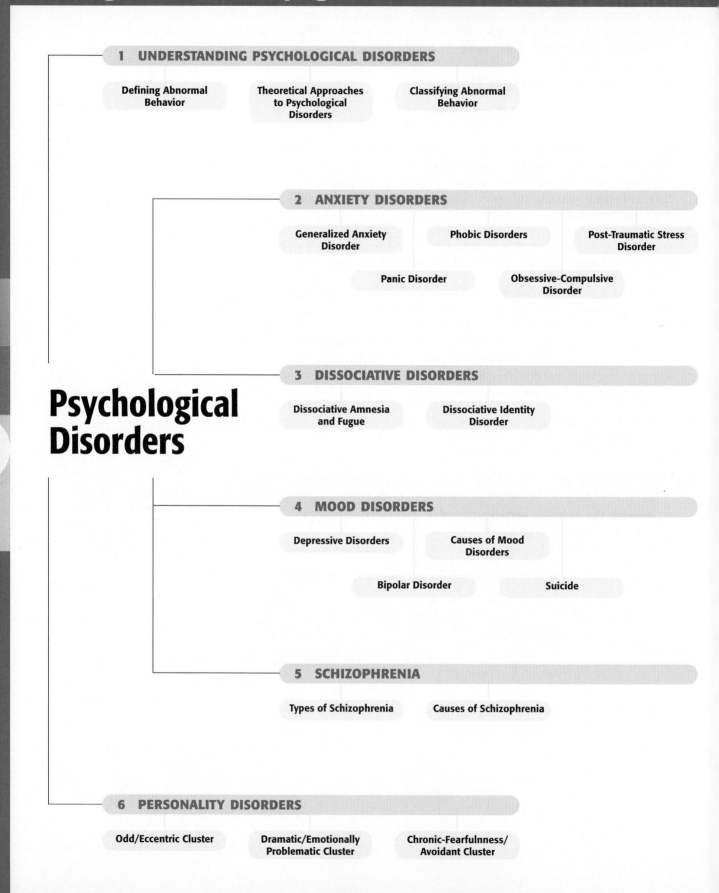

Psychological Disorders

1 UNDERSTANDING PSYCHOLOGICAL DISORDERS

Defining Abnormal Behavior

Theoretical Approaches to Psychological Disorders

Classifying Abnormal Behavior

2 ANXIETY DISORDERS

Generalized Anxiety Disorder

Phobic Disorders

Post-Traumatic Stress Disorder

Panic Disorder

Obsessive-Compulsive Disorder

3 DISSOCIATIVE DISORDERS

Dissociative Amnesia and Fugue

Dissociative Identity Disorder

4 MOOD DISORDERS

Depressive Disorders

Causes of Mood Disorders

Bipolar Disorder

Suicide

5 SCHIZOPHRENIA

Types of Schizophrenia

Causes of Schizophrenia

6 PERSONALITY DISORDERS

Odd/Eccentric Cluster

Dramatic/Emotionally Problematic Cluster

Chronic-Fearfulness/ Avoidant Cluster

1 Discuss the characteristics and classifications of psychological disorders.

- Psychologists define abnormal behavior as behavior that is deviant, maladaptive, or personally distressful. Only one of these criteria is necessary for the classification of abnormal behavior, but two or three can be present. There are a number of myths about abnormal behavior, and a thin line often exists between normal and abnormal behavior.

- Theoretical perspectives on the causes of psychological disorders include biological, psychological, and sociocultural approaches. In terms of biological factors, the medical model describes psychological disorders as diseases with a biological origin. Structural, biochemical, and genetic views also have been proposed. Psychological approaches include the psychodynamic perspective, the behavioral/social cognitive perspective, and the humanistic perspective. The sociocultural approach places more emphasis on the larger social context in which a person lives than on psychological factors. Sociocultural contexts include the individual's marriage or family, neighborhood, socioeconomic status, ethnicity, gender, and culture. The biopsychosocial approach is an interactionist approach to understanding psychological disorders.

- The classification of mental disorders gives mental health professionals a shorthand to use in their communications and allows clinicians to make predictions about disorders and determine what kind of treatment is appropriate. The *Diagnostic and Statistical Manual of Mental Disorders (DSM)*, published by the American Psychiatric Association, is the classification system used by clinicians to diagnose and treat psychological disorders. The *DSM-IV* features a multiaxial diagnostic system that enables clinicians to characterize an individual on the basis of five dimensions. Some psychologists contend that *DSM-IV* perpetuates the medical model of psychological disorders and labels some everyday problems that are not considered deviant or maladaptive as psychological disorders.

2 Distinguish among the various anxiety disorders.

- Anxiety is a diffuse, vague, highly unpleasant feeling of fear and apprehension. The main features of anxiety disorders are motor tension, hyperactivity, and apprehensive expectations and thoughts. Generalized anxiety disorder is defined as anxiety that persists for at least 1 month with no specific reason for the anxiety. Biological, psychological, and sociocultural factors may be involved.

- Recurrent panic attacks marked by the sudden onset of intense apprehension or terror characterize panic disorder. Panic disorder can occur with or without agorapho-

bia. Biological and psychological factors may contribute to the development of panic disorder.

- Phobic disorders involve an irrational, overwhelming fear of a particular object, such as snakes, or situation, such as flying. Biological and psychological factors have been proposed as causes of phobias.

- Obsessive-compulsive disorder (OCD) is an anxiety disorder in which the individual has anxiety-provoking thoughts that will not go away (obsession) and/or urges to perform repetitive, ritualistic behaviors to prevent or produce some future situation (compulsion). Biological and psychological factors are likely involved in OCD.

- Post-traumatic stress disorder (PTSD) is an anxiety disorder that develops through exposure to traumatic events, such as war; severely oppressive situations, such as the Holocaust; severe abuse, as in rape; natural disasters, such as floods and tornados; and unnatural disasters, such as plane crashes and terrorist attacks. Symptoms include flashbacks, which may appear immediately after the trauma or may be delayed.

3 Describe the dissociative disorders.

- Dissociative disorders are characterized by a sudden loss of memory or change in identity. Under extreme stress, conscious awareness becomes dissociated (separated or split) from previous memories and thoughts. Hilgard's hidden observer concept has been applied to understanding the dissociative disorders.

- Dissociative amnesia involves memory loss caused by extensive psychological stress. Dissociative fugue also involves a loss of memory, but individuals with this disorder also unexpectedly travel away from home or work, assume a new identity, and do not remember the old one.

- Dissociative identity disorder, formerly called multiple personality disorder, involves the presence of two or more distinct personalities in the same individual. This disorder is rare.

4 Compare the mood disorders and specify the risk factors for depression and suicide.

- Mood disorders are psychological disorders in which there is a primary disturbance of mood. The mood disturbance can include cognitive, behavioral, and somatic (physical) symptoms, as well as interpersonal difficulties. Two main types of mood disorders are depressive disorders and bipolar disorder. The depressive disorders are mood disorders in which the individual suffers depression without experiencing mania. In major depressive disorder, the individual experiences a major depressive episode and depressed characteristics, such as lethargy and hopelessness, for 2 weeks or longer. Dysthymic disorder is generally more chronic and has fewer symptoms than major depressive disorder.

- Bipolar disorder is characterized by extreme mood swings that include one or more episodes of mania (an overexcited, unrealistic, optimistic state). *Bipolar* means that the person may experience both depression and mania. Less than 10 percent of bipolar individuals experience mania without depression.

- Biological explanations of mood disorders focus on heredity, neurophysiological abnormalities, neurotransmitter deregulation, and hormonal factors. Psychological explanations include psychoanalytic, behavioral, and cognitive perspectives. Sociocultural explanations emphasize interpersonal relationships, socioeconomic and ethnic factors, cultural variations, and gender.

- Severe depression and other psychological disorders can cause individuals to want to end their lives. Biological, psychological, and sociocultural explanations of suicide have been proposed.

5 *Characterize schizophrenia.*

- Schizophrenia is a severe psychological disorder that is characterized by highly disordered thought processes. Individuals with schizophrenia may show odd communication, inappropriate emotion, abnormal motor behavior, and social withdrawal. There are four main types of schizophrenia: disorganized, catatonic, paranoid, and undifferentiated. In disorganized schizophrenia, an individual has delusions and hallucinations that have little

or no recognizable meaning. Catatonic schizophrenia is characterized by bizarre motor behavior, which may take the form of a completely immobile stupor. Paranoid schizophrenia is characterized by delusions of reference, grandeur, and persecution. Undifferentiated schizophrenia is characterized by disorganized behavior, hallucinations, delusions, and incoherence.

- Biological factors (heredity, structural brain abnormalities, and neurotransmitter deregulation), psychological factors (diathesis-stress view), and sociocultural factors may be involved in schizophrenia. Psychological and sociocultural factors are not viewed as stand-alone causes of schizophrenia.

6 *Identify the behavior patterns typical of personality disorders.*

- Personality disorders are chronic, maladaptive cognitive-behavioral patterns that are throughly integrated into the individual's personality. The three main clusters of personality disorders are odd/eccentric, dramatic/emotionally problematic, and chronic fearfulness/avoidant.

- The odd/eccentric cluster includes the paranoid, schizoid, and schizotypal personality disorders.

- The dramatic/emotionally problematic cluster consists of the histrionic, narcissistic, borderline, and antisocial personality disorders. Biological, psychological, and sociocultural explanations of antisocial personality disorder have been proposed.

- The chronic-fearfulness/avoidant cluster includes the avoidant, dependent, passive-aggressive, and obsessive-compulsive personality disorders.

Key Terms

abnormal behavior, p. 520
medical model, p. 520
DSM-IV, p. 523
anxiety disorders, p. 527
generalized anxiety disorder, p. 527
panic disorder, p. 528
agoraphobia, p. 528
phobic disorder, p. 529

obsessive-compulsive disorder (OCD), p. 531
post-traumatic stress disorder, p. 532
dissociative disorders, p. 535
dissociative amnesia, p. 535
dissociative fugue, p. 535
dissociative identity disorder (DID), p. 535

mood disorders, p. 537
depressive disorders, p. 537
major depressive disorder, p. 538
dysthymic disorder, p. 538
bipolar disorder, p. 539
learned helplessness, p. 542
schizophrenia, p. 548
disorganized schizophrenia, p. 549

catatonic schizophrenia, p. 549
paranoid schizophrenia, p. 550
undifferentiated schizophrenia, p. 550
diathesis-stress model p. 552
personality disorders p. 553

Apply Your Knowledge

1. Spend 15 to 20 minutes observing in an area with a large number of people (a mall, the cafeteria, etc.) and identify behaviors that you would classify as abnormal. How does your list of behaviors compare with the definition of abnormal in the text? What would change on the list if you were in a different setting (a church, a bar, a library)? What does this tell you about defining abnormal behavior?

2. Imagine the following events. For each event, describe the kind of anxiety or dissociative disorder that might be most likely to develop. Is it likelier that the person would or would not develop a disorder?
   a. Marcy was bitten by a dog as a young child.
   b. Alex is a firefighter in New York City called to the World Trade Center to aid in the rescue efforts.
   c. Andy was involved in a serious automobile accident.
   d. Sam's parents were always critical about her behavior and sometimes locked her in a room for several days at a time when she was growing up.

3. Take a quick survey of your friends and acquaintances and ask them whether they've ever experienced the symptoms of a common cold (e.g., runny nose, coughing, stuffy head). Then ask them if they've ever experienced symptoms of the "common cold of psychological disorders," as described in the text. How many indicated they've had colds, and how many indicated they've had a mood disorder? Are the numbers consistent with the numbers suggested in the book? Why might your numbers be different from those in the book?

4. The Internet provides a wealth of mental health information. Find a site (such as *mentalhealth.com*) that gives more information about personality disorders or schizophrenia. What information can you find that's not discussed in the text? Does it change your view of either disorder?

Connections

For extra help in mastering the material in this chapter, see the review sections and practice quizzes in the Student Study Guide, the CD-ROM, and the Online Learning Center.

Chapter Outline

Learning Goals

BIOLOGICAL THERAPIES   **1**

Drug Therapy

▼

Electroconvulsive Therapy

▼

Psychosurgery

Describe the biological therapies.

PSYCHOTHERAPIES   **2**

Psychodynamic Therapies

▼

Humanistic Therapies

▼

Behavior Therapies

▼

Cognitive Therapies

Define psychotherapy and characterize four types of psychotherapies.

SOCIOCULTURAL APPROACHES AND ISSUES IN TREATMENT   **3**

Group Therapy

▼

Family and Couples Therapy

▼

Self-Help Support Groups

▼

Community Mental Health

▼

Cultural Perspectives

Explain the sociocultural approaches and issues in treatment.

THE EFFECTIVENESS OF PSYCHOTHERAPY   **4**

Research on the Effectiveness of Psychotherapy

▼

Common Themes in Psychotherapy

▼

Therapy Integrations

▼

Funding and Finding Therapy

▼

Mental Health Professionals

▼

Guidelines for Seeking Professional Help

Evaluate the effectiveness of psychotherapy.

Steve M. has paranoid schizophrenia, which you read about in chapter 13. He hears voices all the time, telling him he has done something wrong, and feels that he is being constantly monitored by people he doesn't know. He is convinced that a transmitter has been placed in his head and that someone is transmitting messages to it.

Medications from the psychiatrist he sees on a regular basis have significantly reduced the frequency of the voices Steve hears. Several times he has stopped taking the medication, and each time he has had to be hospitalized for treatment. In between hospitalizations, he goes to a day treatment program and has taken some college classes. Steve still struggles with what is real and not real in his life. However, through psychotherapy, he has learned to trust certain people in his life, especially his stepmother, brother, and father.

In the clinic at the day program Steve attends, he has developed a long-term psychotherapy relationship with the psychologist he sees once a week (these sessions supplement periodic visits with a psychiatrist, who monitors his medication). The psychotherapist is helping Steve to set some short-term goals and improve his outlook on life. The day treatment program, including his sessions with the psychotherapist, are providing him with practice in coping with stress, interacting more effectively with people, and living an independent life. Steve says that he now understands the importance of taking the medication to ward off the intruding voices and the fear of being monitored. His mother and stepfather have joined a support group, which is helping them to better understand Steve's psychological disorder and what needs to be done to help him (Bernheim, 1997).

In this introductory story, Steve has benefited from several types of therapy—biological therapy, the use of medications to reduce the frequency of voices he heard and his fear that people he did not know were monitoring him; psychotherapy, to help him cope more effectively and adjust to daily living; and sociocultural therapy, support groups to help his parents understand his disorder better and help him with his adjustment to the disorder.

The discussion of personality and psychological disorders in chapters 12 and 13, respectively, provide a foundation for understanding the modes of treatment that are used to help people with their psychological problems. For example, in chapters 12 and 13, I discussed a number of theories—psychodynamic, behavioral and social cognitive, and humanistic—that attempt to explain the nature of personality and psychological disorders. Also, chapter 13 explored the biological, psychological, and sociocultural factors involved in anxiety disorders, mood disorders, schizophrenia, and personality disorders.

This chapter again focuses on biological, psychological, and sociocultural factors and on how they are used in therapy to improve the lives of people with psychological disorders. It begins with the biological therapies, which often involve the use of medication to treat psychological disorders. Later, the chapter examines the wide range of mental health professionals who provide therapy.

1 BIOLOGICAL THERAPIES

Drug Therapy   **Electroconvulsive Therapy**   **Psychosurgery**

biological therapies Treatments to reduce or eliminate the symptoms of psychological disorders by altering the way an individual's body functions.

psychotherapy The process used by mental health professionals to help individuals recognize, define, and overcome their psychological and interpersonal difficulties.

What are the biological therapies?

Biological therapies are treatments to reduce or eliminate the symptoms of psychological disorders by altering the way an individual's body functions. Drug therapy is the most common form of biomedical therapy. Much less widely used biomedical therapies are electroconvulsive therapy and psychosurgery. Recall from chapter 1 that psychiatrists, who are medical doctors, can administer drugs as part of therapy. However, psychologists, who are not trained as medical doctors, cannot administer drugs as part of therapy. Psychologists and other mental health professionals may provide **psychotherapy** to help individuals recognize and overcome their problems in conjunction with the biological therapy administered by psychiatrists and other medical doctors. Indeed, in many instances, a combination of psychotherapy and medication is a desirable course of treatment (Kay, 2002).

Drug Therapy

Although medicine and herbs have long been used to alleviate symptoms of emotional distress, it was not until the twentieth century that drug treatments began to revolutionize mental health care. Psychotherapeutic drugs are used mainly in three diagnostic categories: anxiety disorders, mood disorders, and schizophrenia. This section discusses the effectiveness of drugs in these areas, beginning with drugs to treat anxiety.

Antianxiety Drugs   **Antianxiety drugs** are commonly known as *tranquilizers.* These drugs reduce anxiety by making individuals calmer and less excitable. Benzodiazepines are the antianxiety drugs that most often offer the greatest relief for anxiety symptoms. They work by binding to the receptor sites of neurotransmitters that become overactive during anxiety. The most frequently prescribed benzodiazepines include Xanax, Valium, and Librium. A nonbenzodiazepine—buspirone, or BuSpar—is commonly used to treat generalized anxiety disorder.

Benzodiazepines are relatively fast-acting medications, taking effect even within hours. Buspirone must be taken daily for 2 to 3 weeks before it takes effect.

Benzodiazepines, like all drugs, have some side effects (Roy-Byrne & Cowley, 2002). They can be addicting. Also, drowsiness, loss of coordination, fatigue, and mental slowing can accompany their use. These effects can be hazardous when driving or operating some types of machinery, especially when the person first starts taking benzodiazepines. Benzodiazepines also have been linked to abnormalities in babies born to mothers who took them during pregnancy (Perault & others, 2000).

When benzodiazepines are combined with other medications, problems can result. When combined with alcohol, anesthetics, antihistamines, sedatives, muscle relaxants, and some prescription pain medications, benzodiazepines can lead to depression (Dalfen & Stewart, 2001; Gutierrez-Lobos & others, 2001).

Why are antianxiety drugs so widely used? Many individuals experience stress and/or anxiety. Family physicians or psychiatrists prescribe these drugs to improve people's ability to cope with their problems effectively. The relaxed feelings brought on by antianxiety drugs bring welcome relief from high levels of anxiety and stress. Antianxiety medications are best used only temporarily for symptomatic relief. Too often they are overused and, as mentioned earlier, can become addictive.

Antidepressant Drugs

> Linda has a good marriage and her second child, a healthy boy, was just born, so you would think that everything is likely great in her life. However, she describes her life as if it were an unbearable weight on her shoulders. Usually energetic and focused, Linda considers it a major accomplishment to get through the day. These feelings continue for several months and finally she decides to see a psychiatrist, who prescribes an antidepressant drug for treating her depression, along with psychotherapy. After several weeks of being on the medication and participating in psychotherapy, Linda begins to feel better. The dreary Midwest winter and the responsibility involved in caring for her young children no longer overwhelm her. (Nathan, Gorman, & Salkind, 1999)

Antidepressant drugs regulate mood. The three main classes of antidepressant drugs are tricyclics, such as Elavil; MAO inhibitors, such as Nardil; and SSRI drugs, such as Prozac (Gorman & Kent, 1999).

The *tricyclics,* so called because of their three-ringed molecular structure, are believed to work by increasing the level of certain neurotransmitters, especially norepinephrine and serotonin (Evans, 1999; Feighner, 1999). The tricyclics reduce the symptoms of depression in approximately 60 to 70 percent of cases. The tricyclics usually take 2 to 4 weeks to improve mood. They sometimes have adverse side effects, such as restlessness, faintness, trembling, sleepiness, and difficulty remembering.

The MAO (monoamine oxidase) inhibitors are not as widely used as the tricyclics because they are more toxic. However, some individuals who do not respond to the

antianxiety drugs Commonly known as *tranquilizers,* they reduce anxiety by making people calmer and less excitable.

antidepressant drugs Drugs that regulate mood.

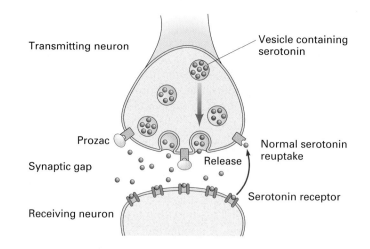

FIGURE 14.1 How the Antidepressant Prozac Works Serotonin is secreted by a transmitting neuron, moves across the synaptic gap, and then binds to receptors in a receiving neuron. Excess serotonin in the synaptic gap is normally reabsorbed by the transmitting neuron. However, Prozac blocks the reuptake of serotonin to the transmitting neuron, which leaves excess serotonin in the synaptic gap. The excess serotonin will be transmitted to the receiving neuron and circulated through the brain, thus reducing the serotonin deficit found in depressed individuals.

tricyclics do respond to the MAO inhibitors. The MAO inhibitors may be especially risky because of their potential interactions with certain foods and drugs. Cheese and other fermented foods, as well as some alcoholic beverages such as red wine, can interact with the MAOs to increase blood pressure and eventually cause a stroke.

Psychiatrists increasingly are prescribing a newer type of antidepressant drug called selective serotonin reuptake inhibitors (SSRIs). SSRI drugs work mainly by interfering with the reabsorption of serotonin in the brain (Rosenbaum, 2001). Figure 14.1 shows how this process works.

Three widely prescribed SSRI antidepressants are Prozac (fluoxetine), Paxil (paroxetine), and Zoloft (sertraline). Their increased prescription is based on their effectiveness in reducing the symptoms of depression with relatively fewer side effects than the other antidepressant drugs (Nemeroff & Schatzberg, 2002; Polsky & others, 2002). Nonetheless, they can have negative effects, including insomnia, anxiety, headache, and diarrhea. They also can impair sexual functioning and produce severe withdrawal symptoms if their use is ended too abruptly (Clayton & others, 2001).

Antidepressant drugs not only are used to treat mood disorders but also are often effective for a number of anxiety disorders, including generalized anxiety disorder, panic disorder, obsessive-compulsive disorder, social phobia, and post-traumatic stress disorder (Shelton & Hollon, 2000). In addition, eating disorders, especially bulimia nervosa, may be amenable to treatment with antidepressant drugs (Devlin & others, 2000).

Although antidepressant drugs, especially the SSRI drugs, have been effective in treating many cases of depression, at least 25 percent of individuals with major depressive disorder do not respond to any antidepressant drug (Shelton & Hollon, 2000). Several factors related to nonresponse include the presence of a personality disorder or psychotic symptoms.

Some antidepressant drugs are being developed to target not norepinephrine or serotonin but rather an amino acid, substance P. Preliminary studies reveal that drugs that affect substance P may reduce depression with few serious side effects (Argyropoulos & Nutt, 2000; Kramer & others, 1998; Stout, Owens, & Nemeroff, 2001).

The use of Prozac and other antidepressant drugs to treat depression is not without controversy. To read further about the use of antidepressant drugs, see the Critical Controversy box.

Lithium is widely used to treat bipolar disorder. The amount of lithium that circulates in the bloodstream must be carefully monitored because the effective dosage is precariously close to toxic levels. Kidney and thyroid gland complications can arise as a consequence of lithium therapy (Keck, McElroy, & Arnold, 2001).

lithium A drug that is widely used to treat bipolar disorder.

Should Depression Be Treated with Drugs?

The 1993 publication of Peter Kramer's *Listening to Prozac* led to a fierce controversy over the way drugs are used to treat depression. The argument started when Kramer reported that Prozac (generic name fluoxetine), an SSRI (selective serotonin reuptake inhibitor), did more than alleviate depression. Apparently, patients' personalities became instantly altered, and they believed Prozac gave them insight into their own psychological fragilities. In the end, they felt that Prozac allowed them to overcome their problems and limitations and become better adjusted. Kramer called this phenomenon "listening to Prozac." Partly as a result of the publication of the book, Prozac became one of the most widely prescribed drugs in history. People asked their doctors for Prozac for everything from poor appetites to a lack of competitiveness. Some even wanted to try Prozac just to find out what the fuss was all about.

In 1995, Peter Breggin and Ginger Ross Breggin published *Talking to Prozac: What Doctors Aren't Telling You About Today's Most Controversial Drug*, which criticized the then-rampant overprescription of Prozac. They raised the interesting question of how research on antidepressants establishes the usefulness of a particular drug. In a *clinical double-blind study*, the most common approach, the drug is administered to one group and a placebo to another, and both groups and the data collection team are kept in the dark about who is actually taking the medication. Under these conditions, if the drug produces better results than the placebo, it can be said to show promise. According to Breggin and Breggin (1995), some of the original studies of Prozac found that people taking a placebo actually became less depressed than those in the treatment group who were taking Prozac.

The general question of the effectiveness of Prozac and other depressants, as compared with placebos, has since been a focus of ongoing investigation. One meta-analysis included 19 clinical double-blind trials involving 2,318 patients randomly assigned to antidepressant or placebo conditions (Kirsch & Sapperstein, 1998). The results revealed that placebos produced 75 percent of the effectiveness of actual drugs and that drug and placebo effects were very highly correlated (+.90). Further, active drugs that were not antidepressants also produced strong effects. The conclusion of the researchers was that the effects of antidepressant drugs may be due to an active placebo effect (Kirsch & Sapperstein, 1998).

Although this conclusion is open to argument (Rehm, 1998), it does raise the questions of how a placebo might alleviate depression and just what depression is. Feeling down now and then is part of living and may be psychologically healthy in some cases. Immediately using drugs to treat such common despondent moods as a "disorder" may interrupt normal processes of grieving or self-evaluation, possibly blocking healthy development. Also, a diet rich in refined carbohydrates and alcohol may produce some depression. The choice, then, may not be between Prozac and other antidepressant medications but between drug and "natural" interventions such as dietary improvements and exercise. Another benefit: such natural interventions do not have the side effects that antidepressants do, such as a tendency toward increased violence in some people.

In the end, this controversy will likely lessen as researchers discover more about how different antidepressants exert their influence and, more important, learn more about depression itself. As mental health professionals develop better diagnostic techniques and learn to avoid overprescription, they may more confidently deliver antidepressant medication to people with otherwise untreatable biochemical imbalances while learning how to help many others cope naturally with the inevitable cases of the blues.

What do you think?

- Have antidepressants helped anyone you know? Were there any negative side effects you are aware of? Any positive side effects?
- What do you think of the tendency to first treat depression with medication?
- Do you think occasional bouts of depression might play a normal role in psychological development?

Antipsychotic Drugs   **Antipsychotic drugs** are powerful drugs that diminish agitated behavior, reduce tension, decrease hallucinations, improve social behavior, and produce better sleep patterns in individuals who have a severe psychological disorder, especially schizophrenia. Before antipsychotic drugs were developed in the 1950s, few, if any, interventions brought relief from the torment of psychotic symptoms. Once the effectiveness of these medications was apparent, the medical community significantly reduced more intrusive interventions, such as brain surgery, for schizophrenia (Grunberg, Klein, & Brown, 1998).

The *neuroleptics* are the most widely used class of antipsychotic drugs (Bradford, Stroup, & Lieberman, 2002). The most widely accepted explanation for the effectiveness of the neuroleptics is their ability to block the dopamine system's action in

antipsychotic drugs Powerful drugs that diminish agitated behavior, reduce tension, decrease hallucinations, improve social behavior, and produce better sleep patterns in people who have a severe psychological disorder, such as schizophrenia.

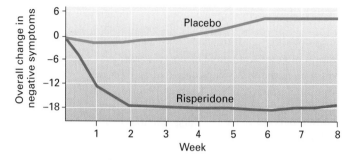

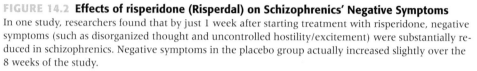

FIGURE 14.2 Effects of risperidone (Risperdal) on Schizophrenics' Negative Symptoms
In one study, researchers found that by just 1 week after starting treatment with risperidone, negative symptoms (such as disorganized thought and uncontrolled hostility/excitement) were substantially reduced in schizophrenics. Negative symptoms in the placebo group actually increased slightly over the 8 weeks of the study.

the brain (Rebec, 1996). Schizophrenics have too much of the neurochemical messenger dopamine. Numerous well-controlled investigations reveal that when used in sufficient doses, the neuroleptics reduce a variety of schizophrenic symptoms, at least in the short term (Friedman, Temporini, & Davis, 1999; Holcomb & others, 1996).

The neuroleptics do not cure schizophrenia; they only treat the symptoms of schizophrenia, not its causes. If an individual with schizophrenia stops taking the drug, the symptoms return. Neuroleptic drugs have substantially reduced the length of hospital stays for individuals with schizophrenia. However, although these individuals are able to return to the community because drug therapy keeps their symptoms from reappearing, most have difficulty coping with the demands of society, and most are chronically unemployed. Also, the neuroleptics can have severe side effects.

Tardive dyskinesia is a major side effect of neuroleptics; it is a neurological disorder characterized by grotesque, involuntary movements of the facial muscles and mouth, as well as extensive twitching of the neck, arms, and legs. As many as 20 percent of individuals with schizophrenia who take neuroleptics develop this disorder. Older women are especially vulnerable. Long-term neuroleptic therapy also is associated with increased depression and anxiety. Nonetheless, for the majority of schizophrenics, the benefits of neuroleptic treatment outweigh its risk and discomforts.

A group of medications called *atypical antipsychotic medications* was introduced in the 1990s. Like the SSRI drugs, atypical antipsychotic medications block the reuptake of the neurotransmitter serotonin. The two most widely used drugs in this group are clozapine (trade name Clozaril) and risperidone (Risperdal), which show promise for reducing schizophrenia's symptoms without the side effects of neuroleptics (Buckley & others, 2001). Figure 14.2 shows the substantial reduction in negative symptoms when schizophrenics take risperidone (Marder, Davis, & Chouinard, 1997).

Strategies to increase the effectiveness of the antipsychotic drugs involve administering small dosages over time, rather than a large initial dose, and combining drug therapy with psychotherapy. The fact that only a small percentage of schizophrenics are able to hold jobs suggests that drugs alone will not help them be contributing members of society. They also need training in vocational, family, and social skills.

A summary of the drugs used to treat various psychological disorders, the disorders for which they are used, their effectiveness, and their side effects are shown in figure 14.3. Notice that for some types of anxiety disorders, such as agoraphobia, MAO inhibitors (antidepressant drugs) might be used, rather than antianxiety drugs.

Electroconvulsive Therapy

electroconvulsive therapy (ECT)
Commonly called shock therapy, this treatment is used for severely depressed individuals; it causes a seizure to occur in the brain.

Electroconvulsive therapy (ECT), commonly called *shock therapy,* is used mainly to treat severely depressed individuals. The goal of ECT is to cause a seizure in the brain much like what happens spontaneously in some forms of epilepsy. A small electric

Psychological Disorder	Drug	Effectiveness	Side Effects
Everyday Anxiety and Anxiety Disorders			
Everyday anxiety	Antianxiety drugs; antidepressant drugs	Substantial improvement short-term	Antianxiety drugs: less powerful the longer people take them; may be addictive Antidepressant drugs: see below under depressive disorders
Generalized anxiety disorder	Antianxiety drugs	Not very effective	Less powerful the longer people take them; may be addictive
Panic disorder	Antianxiety drugs	About half show improvement	Less powerful the longer people take them; may be addictive
Agoraphobia	Tricyclic drugs and MAO inhibitors	Majority show improvement	Tricyclics: restlessness, fainting, and trembling MAO inhibitors: toxicity
Specific phobias	Antianxiety drugs	Not very effective	Less powerful the longer people take them; may be addictive
Mood Disorders			
Depressive disorders	Tricyclic drugs, MAO inhibitors, and SSRI drugs	Majority show moderate improvement	Tricylics: cardiac problems, mania, confusion, memory loss, fatigue MAO inhibitors: toxicity SSRI drugs: nausea, nervousness, insomnia, and in a
Bipolar disorder	Lithium	Large majority show substantial improvement	Toxicity
Schizophrenic Disorders			
Schizophrenia	Neuroleptics; atypical antipsychotic medications	Majority show partial improvement	Neuroleptics: irregular heartbeat, low blood pressure, uncontrolled fidgeting, tardive dyskinesia, and immobility of face Atypical antipsychotic medications: Less extensive side effects than with neuroleptics, but can have a toxic effect on white blood cells.

FIGURE 14.3 **Drug Therapy for Psychological Disorders**

current lasting for 1 second or less passes through two electrodes placed on the individual's head. The current excites neural tissue, stimulating a seizure that lasts for approximately 1 minute.

ECT has been used for more than 40 years. In earlier years it often was used indiscriminately, sometimes even to punish patients. ECT is still used with as many as 60,000 individuals a year, mainly to treat major depressive disorder. Today ECT is given mainly to individuals who have not responded to drug therapy or psychotherapy. You may think that ECT would entail intolerable pain, but the manner in which it is administered today involves little discomfort. The patient is given anesthesia and muscle relaxants before the current is applied; this allows the individual to sleep through the procedure, minimizes convulsions, and reduces the risk of physical injury. The individual awakens shortly afterward with no conscious memory of the treatment.

How effective is electroconvulsive therapy? In one analysis of studies of the use of electroconvulsive therapy, its effectiveness in treating depression was compared with cognitive therapy and antidepressant drugs (Seligman, 1994). ECT was as effective as cognitive therapy or drug therapy, with about 4 of 5 individuals showing marked improvement in all three therapies. However, as with the other therapies, the relapse rate for ECT is moderate to high.

Adverse side effects, such as memory loss and other cognitive impairments, are more severe than drug side effects. Cognitive therapy shows no side effects. A positive aspect of ECT is that its beneficial effects appear in a matter of days, whereas the

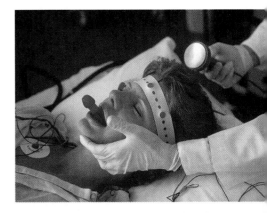

Electroconvulsive therapy (ECT), commonly called *shock therapy,* causes a seizure in the brain. ECT is still given to as many as 60,000 people a year, mainly to treat major depressive disorder.

beneficial effects of antidepressant drugs can take weeks, and those of cognitive therapy months, to appear (Dannon & others, 2002).

Psychosurgery

Psychosurgery is a biological therapy that involves removal or destruction of brain tissue to improve the individual's adjustment. The effects of psychosurgery are irreversible. In the 1930s, Portuguese physician Egas Moniz developed a procedure known as a *prefrontal lobotomy*. In this procedure, a surgical instrument is inserted into the brain and rotated, severing fibers that connect the frontal lobe, which is important in higher thought processes, and the thalamus, important in emotion. Moniz theorized that by severing the connections between these brain structures, the symptoms of severe mental disorders could be alleviated. Prefrontal lobotomies were conducted on thousands of patients from the 1930s through the 1950s. Moniz was awarded the Nobel Prize for his work. However, whereas some patients may have benefited from the lobotomies, many were left in a vegetable-like state because of the massive assaults on their brains.

These crude lobotomies are no longer performed. Since the 1960s, psychosurgery has become more precise. When psychosurgery is now performed, a small lesion is made in the amygdala or another part of the limbic system. Today, only several hundred patients who have severely debilitating conditions undergo psychosurgery each year. It is used only as a last resort and with extreme caution.

Review and Sharpen Your Thinking

1 *Describe the biological therapies.*

- Identify the types of drugs used to treat psychological disorders and evaluate their effects.
- Explain what electroconvulsive therapy is and when it is used.
- Discuss psychosurgery.

Before prescribing drug therapy for an individual, what might be some important factors for a psychiatrist or other medical doctor (such as a general practitioner) to consider?

---

2 PSYCHOTHERAPIES

| Psychodynamic Therapies | Behavior Therapies |

| Humanistic Therapies | Cognitive Therapies |

What is psychotherapy and what are the four main types of psychotherapy?

Psychotherapy is the process used by mental health professionals to help individuals recognize, define, and overcome their psychological and interpersonal difficulties and improve their adjustment. Psychotherapists use a number of strategies to accomplish these goals: talking, interpreting, listening, rewarding, and modeling, for example. Both psychologists and psychiatrists use psychotherapy in treating people who have psychological problems.

This section focuses on four main approaches to psychotherapy: psychodynamic, humanistic, behavioral, and cognitive. The term **insight therapy** characterizes both psychodynamic and humanistic therapies, because they encourage

psychosurgery A biological therapy that involves removal or destruction of brain tissue to improve an individual's adjustment.

insight therapy Encourages insight and self-awareness; includes the psychodynamic and humanistic therapies.

To encourage his patients to relax, Freud had them recline on this couch while he sat in the chair on the left, out of their view.

insight and self-awareness. The psychodynamic therapies are the oldest of these approaches.

Psychodynamic Therapies

The **psychodynamic therapies** stress the importance of the unconscious mind, extensive interpretation by the therapist, and the role of early-childhood experiences in the development of an individual's problems. The goal of the psychodynamic therapies is to help individuals recognize the maladaptive ways in which they have been coping with problems and the sources of their unconscious conflicts (Nolen-Hoeksema, 2001). Many psychodynamic approaches grew out of Freud's psychoanalytic theory of personality. Today some therapists with a psychodynamic perspective practice Freudian techniques, but others do not (Watkins & Guarnaccia, 1999).

Freud's Psychoanalysis Freud once said that if you give psychoanalysis your little finger, it will soon have your whole hand. As you read about the basic philosophy of psychoanalysis and its therapy techniques, you will see that Freud believed that the therapist acts like a psychological detective, sometimes taking the smallest clue and using it as a springboard for understanding the individual's major problems. The following shows how one analyst approached an individual's problems (Davison & Neale, 1994):

A 50-year old business executive came to therapy because he felt depressed and anxious and these feelings would not go away. Although he was perceived as being very successful by his family and business associates, he perceived himself to be weak and incompetent. Through many sessions, the psychoanalyst had begun to suspect that the man's feelings of failure stemmed from his childhood experiences with a critical and punitive father. The father never seemed satisfied with the son's efforts. Following is an exchange between the analyst and the businessman that occurred one year into therapy:
Client: "I don't really feel like talking today."
Analyst: Remains silent for several minutes, then says, "Perhaps you would like to talk about why you don't feel like talking."
Client: "There you go again, making demands on me, insisting I do what I just don't feel up to doing. (Pause) Do I always have to talk here, when I don't feel like it? (Voice becomes angry and petulant) Can't you just get off my back? You don't really care how I feel."
Analyst: "I wonder why you feel I don't care?"

psychodynamic therapies Stress the importance of the unconscious mind, extensive interpretation by the therapist, and the role of experiences in the early-childhood years. The goal of the psychodynamic therapies is to help individuals recognize their maladaptive ways of coping and the sources of their unconscious conflicts.

"Looking good!" © The New Yorker Collection 1994. Gahan Wilson from cartoonbank.com. All Rights Reserved.

psychoanalysis Freud's psychotherapeutic technique for analyzing an individual's unconscious thoughts. Freud believed that clients' current problems could be traced to childhood experiences, involving conflicts about sexuality.

free association The psychoanalytic technique of having individuals say aloud whatever comes into their minds.

catharsis The psychoanalytic term for people's release of emotional tension when they relive an emotionally charged and conflicting experience.

dream analysis The psychotherapeutic technique used by psychoanalysts to interpret a person's dream. Psychoanalysts believe dreams contain information about the individual's unconscious thoughts and conflicts.

transference The psychoanalytic term for the person's relating to the analyst in ways that reproduce or relive important relationships in the individual's life.

Client: "Because you're always pressuring me to do what I feel I can't do."
This exchange was interpreted by the analyst as an expression of resentment by the client of his father's pressures that were put on him and had little to do with the analyst himself. The transfer of the client's feelings from the father to the analyst was regarded as significant by the analyst and was used in subsequent sessions to help the client overcome his fear of expressing anger toward his father.

Psychoanalysis is Freud's therapeutic technique for analyzing an individual's unconscious thoughts. Freud believed that clients' current problems could be traced to childhood experiences, many of which involved conflicts about sexuality. He also recognized that the early experiences were not readily available to the individual's conscious mind. Only through extensive questioning, probing, and analyzing was Freud able to put the pieces of the person's personality together and help the individual become aware of how these early experiences were affecting present adult behavior.

To reach the shadowy world of the unconscious, psychoanalytic therapists often use the following therapeutic techniques: free association, catharsis, interpretation, dream analysis, analysis of transference, and analysis of resistance, each of which is discussed in turn.

Free association consists of encouraging individuals to say aloud whatever comes to mind no matter how trivial or embarrassing (Kris, 2002). When Freud detected a person resisting the spontaneous flow of thoughts, he probed further. He believed that the crux of the person's emotional problem probably lurked below this point of resistance. Encouraging people to talk freely, Freud thought, would help emotional feelings to emerge. **Catharsis** is the psychoanalytic term for the release of emotional tension a person experiences when reliving an emotionally charged and conflicting experience.

Interpretation plays an important role in psychoanalysis. As the therapist interprets free association and dreams, the person's statements and behavior are not taken at face value. To understand what is truly causing the person's conflicts, the therapist constantly searches for symbolic, hidden meanings in what the individual says and does. From time to time the therapist suggests possible meanings of the person's statements and behavior.

The following case study reveals how a psychoanalyst used interpretation to improve a woman's understanding of her problems (Langs, 1978):

Mrs. A. H. began her session with a psychoanalyst by describing how her husband, a businessman, had been caught in a financial squeeze and had anxiously gone to the bank to raise additional funds. She was in a state of panic, even though there was a good chance that her husband would be able to obtain a loan from the bank. The previous night she had diarrhea and had dreamed that her two sisters were discussing her mother, saying that she seldom did all that she promised to others. Mrs. A. H. then commented that her mother had been wealthy and could have provided all the money her husband needed. Her father could have too, she said, but he was hard to deal with. She went on to recall her mother's involvement with another man and the illness her mother had when Mrs. A. H. was an infant. Her sisters, who were considerably older, had taken care of their mother, but Mrs. A. H. wondered why they criticized her mother who had been briefly hospitalized. They tended to blame poor health habits for her illness. Mrs. A. H. also reviewed her adolescent years, during which her mother denied the impact of her absence. She thought her mother's attitude was rather strange.

The psychoanalytic session seemed to be prompted by her husband's financial crisis and the repercussions it had for Mrs. A. H.'s longings for her mother, who would rescue her and her husband; her rage at her mother for her absence and possible unfaithfulness; and some implied concerns regarding her husband's ability to handle the business situation. There was little in the session to suggest what unconscious thoughts were evoking the gastrointestinal symptoms.

However, this session is intriguing in the light of the next session that took place. In that session, Mrs. A. H. revealed that she inadvertently had forgotten to mention an incident that had occurred prior to the previous session. One of her girlfriends had seen her husband having a drink at a local restaurant with an attractive woman. In this context, the psychoanalyst was able to gain more insight into what Mrs. A. H. had said in the previous session. In fact, she had used the past to conceal the present. She had used her mother as a screen to hide her most active and meaningful conflicts and unconscious fantasies about her husband. In the second session, her free associations related to fears of finding out that her husband was having an affair, to her dread of confronting him, and to her anxiety that others would be talking about his having an affair. The associations revealed her rage, her wishes to humiliate him in public, and her death wishes toward him. The sister in the dream had also been suspected of having an affair. The bowel symptoms actually related to fantasies of defecating on and soiling her husband in an uncontrolled release of aggression, according to the analyst.

Dream analysis is the psychotherapeutic technique used by psychoanalysts to interpret a person's dream. Psychoanalysts believe dreams contain information about the individual's unconscious thoughts and conflicts. Freud distinguished between the dream's manifest and latent content. *Manifest content* is the psychoanalytic term for the conscious, remembered aspects of a dream. *Latent content* is the psychoanalytic term for the unconscious, unremembered, symbolic aspects of a dream. The psychoanalyst interprets the dream by analyzing the manifest content for disguised unconscious wishes and needs, especially those that are sexual and aggressive in nature. For some examples of the sexual symbols psychoanalysts use to interpret dreams, see figure 14.4. But even Freud cautioned against overinterpreting. As he once quipped, "Sometimes a cigar is just a cigar."

Freud believed transference was an inevitable and essential aspect of the analyst-patient relationship. **Transference** is the psychoanalytic term for the person's relating to the analyst in ways that reproduce or relive important relationships in the individual's life. A person might interact with an analyst as if the analyst were a parent or lover, for

Sexual Theme	Objects or Activities in Dreams That Symbolize Sexual Themes
Male genitals, especially penis	Umbrellas, knives, poles, swords, airplanes, guns, serpents, neckties, tree trunks, hoses
Female genitals, especially vagina	Boxes, caves, pockets, pouches, the mouth, jewel cases, ovens, closets
Sexual intercourse	Climbing, swimming, flying, riding (a horse, an elevator, a roller coaster)
Parents	Kings, queens, emperors, empresses
Siblings	Little animals

FIGURE 14.4 Freudian Interpretation of Sexual Symbolism in Dreams

example. When transference dominates therapy, the person's comments may become directed toward the analyst's personal life. Transference is often difficult to overcome in psychotherapy. However, transference can be used therapeutically as a model of how individuals relate to important people in their lives (Boyer, 1999; Marcus, 2002).

Resistance is the psychoanalytic term for the person's unconscious defense strategies that prevent the analyst from understanding the person's problems. Resistance occurs because it is painful to bring conflicts into conscious awareness. By resisting therapy, individuals do not have to face their problems. Showing up late or missing sessions, arguing with the psychoanalyst, or faking free associations are examples of resistance. Some people go on endlessly about a trivial matter to avoid facing their conflicts. A major goal of the analyst is to break through this resistance (Strean, 1996).

Contemporary Psychodynamic Therapies   Although the face of psychodynamic therapy has changed extensively since its inception almost a century ago, many contemporary psychodynamic therapists still probe a person's unconscious thoughts about early childhood experiences to obtain clues to the person's current problems (Comarow & Chescheir, 1999; Marcus, 2002; Sugarman & DePottel, 2002). Many contemporary psychodynamic therapists also try to help individuals gain insight into their emotionally laden, repressed conflicts (Horowitz, 1998; Sonnenberg & Ursano, 2002). They also accord more power to the conscious mind and to a person's current relationships (Orfanos, 2002). Today individuals rarely lie on a couch or see their therapist several times a week. Instead, weekly appointments are typical, and people sit in a comfortable chair facing the therapist.

Only a small percentage of contemporary therapists rigorously practice Freudian psychoanalysis. Those who do often see an individual frequently. Some contemporary psychodynamic therapies also can be intensive and extensive, lasting for years. However, in some cases, contemporary psychodynamic therapy is brief, lasting only a few months.

Contemporary psychodynamic approaches emphasize the development of the self in social contexts (Erikson, 1968; Horowitz, 1998; Kohut, 1977). In Heinz Kohut's view, early relationships with attachment figures, such as one's parents, are critical. As we develop we do not relinquish these attachments; we continue to need them. Kohut's prescription for therapy involves getting the person to identify and seek out appropriate relationships with others. He also wants individuals to develop more realistic appraisals of relationships. Kohut (1977) believes therapists need to interact with individuals in ways that are empathic and understanding. Empathy and understanding are absolute cornerstones for humanistic therapists, who encourage individuals to further their sense of self.

Humanistic Therapies

The underlying philosophy of humanistic therapies is captured by the metaphor of how an acorn, if provided with appropriate conditions, will grow in positive ways, pushing naturally toward its actualization as an oak (Corey, 1996; Schneider, 2002). In the **humanistic therapies,** people are encouraged to understand themselves and to grow personally. The humanistic therapies are unique in their emphasis on the person's self-healing capacities (Bohart, 1995). In contrast to the psychodynamic therapies, the humanistic therapies emphasize conscious rather than unconscious thoughts, the present rather than the past, and growth and self-fulfillment rather than illness.

Client-Centered Therapy

Therapist: Everything's lousy, huh? You feel lousy. [Silence of 39 seconds]
Want to come in Friday at 12 at the usual time?
Client: [Yawns and mutters something unintelligible. Silence of 48 seconds]

resistance The psychoanalytic term for the person's unconscious defense strategies that prevent the analyst from understanding the person's problems.

humanistic therapies Encourages people to understand themselves and to grow personally. The humanistic therapies are unique in their emphasis on self-healing capacities.

Therapist: Just kind of feel sunk way down deep in those lousy, lousy feelings, hm? Is that something like it?

Client: No.

Therapist: No? [Silence of 20 seconds]

Client: No. I'm just no good to anybody, never was, and never will be.

Therapist: Feeling that now, hm? That you're no good to yourself, no good to anybody. Just that you're completely worthless, huh? Those are really lousy feelings. Just feel that you're no good at all, hm?

This is an excerpt from a therapy session conducted by a client-centered therapist with a young man who was depressed. The therapist was Carl Rogers (Meador & Rogers, 1979). Notice how Rogers unconditionally accepted the client's feelings. **Client-centered therapy** is a form of humanistic therapy developed by Carl Rogers (1961, 1980), in which the therapist provides a warm, supportive atmosphere to improve the client's self-concept and encourage the client to gain insight about problems. Compared with psychodynamic therapies, which emphasize analysis and interpretation by the therapist, client-centered therapy places far more emphasis on the client's self-reflection (Hill, 2000).

The relationship between the therapist and the person is an important aspect of Rogers' therapy. The therapist must enter into an intensely personal relationship with the client, not as a physician diagnosing a disease but as one human being to another. Notice that Rogers referred to the "client" and then the "person" rather than the "patient."

You might recall from chapter 12 that Rogers believed each of us grows up in a world filled with *conditional positive regard*, the sense of worth we receive from others that has strings attached. We usually do not receive love and praise unless we conform to the standards and demands of others. This causes us to be unhappy and have low self-esteem. Rarely do we feel that we measure up to such standards or that we are as good as others expect us to be.

To free a person from worry about society's demands, the therapist engages in *unconditional positive regard*, in which the therapist creates a warm and caring environment, never disapproving of the client. Rogers believed this unconditional positive regard improves the person's self-esteem. The therapist's role is *nondirective*, that is, he or she does not lead the client to any particular revelation. The therapist is there to listen sympathetically to the client's problems and to encourage positive self-regard, independent self-appraisal, and decision making. Though client-centered therapists give approval of the person, they do not always approve of the person's behavior.

In addition to unconditional positive regard, Rogers advocated the use of these two techniques in client-centered therapy:

- *Genuineness* (also called *congruence*), which involves letting a client know the therapist's feelings and not hiding behind a facade.
- *Active listening*, which consists of giving total attention to what the person says and means. One way therapists improve active listening is to restate and support what the client has said and done.

Gestalt Therapy **Gestalt therapy** is a humanistic therapy developed by Fritz Perls (1893–1970), in which the therapist challenges clients to help them become more aware of their feelings and face their problems. Perls was trained in Europe as a Freudian psychoanalyst, but he developed his own ideas and eventually parted from some of Freud's teachings.

Perls (1969) agreed with Freud that psychological problems originate in unresolved past conflicts and that these conflicts need to be acknowledged and worked through. Also like Freud, Perls stressed that interpretation of dreams is an important aspect of therapy. But, in other ways, Perls and Freud were miles apart. Perls believed that unresolved conflicts should be brought to bear on the here and now of the individual's life.

client-centered therapy Rogers' humanistic therapy in which the therapist provides a warm, supportive atmosphere to improve the client's self-concept and encourage the client to gain insight about problems.

gestalt therapy Perls' humanistic therapy in which the therapist challenges clients to help them become more aware of their feelings and face their problems.

FREDERICK (FRITZ) PERLS (1893–1970)
The founder of gestalt therapy.

The therapist *pushes* clients into deciding whether they will continue to allow the past to control their future or whether they will choose right now what they want to be in the future. To this end, Perls both confronted individuals and encouraged them to actively control their lives and to be open about their feelings (Garza, 1999).

Gestalt therapists use a number of techniques to encourage individuals to be open about their feelings, to develop self-awareness, and to actively control their lives. The therapist sets examples, encourages congruence between verbal and nonverbal behavior, and uses role playing. To stimulate change, the therapist often openly confronts the client. To demonstrate an important point to a client, the Gestalt therapist might exaggerate a client's characteristics.

In the following excerpt from a gestalt therapy session, the therapist (in this case, gestalt therapy founder Fritz Perls) exaggerates a phrase the client uses:

Perls: Now talk to your Top Dog! Stop nagging.
Jane: [Loud, pained] Leave me alone.
Perls: Yah, again.
Jane: Leave me alone.
Perls: Again.
Jane: [Screaming it and crying] Leave me alone!
Perls: Again.
Jane: [She screams it, a real blast.] Leave me alone! I don't have to do what you say! [Still crying] I don't have to be in this chair! I don't have to. You make me. You make me come here! [Screams] Aarhh. You make me pick my face [crying], that's what you do. [Screams and cries] Aarhh! I'd like to kill you.
Perls: Say this again.
Jane: I'd like to kill you.
Perls: Again.
Jane: I'd like to kill you.

Another technique used in gestalt therapy is role playing, either by the client, the therapist, or both. For example, if an individual is bothered by conflict with her mother, the therapist might play the role of the mother and reopen the quarrel. The therapist might encourage the individual to act out her hostile feelings toward her mother by yelling, swearing, or kicking the couch, for example. In this way, gestalt therapists hope to help individuals better manage their feelings instead of letting their feelings control them.

As you probably noticed, the gestalt therapist is much more directive than the client-centered therapist. By being more directive, the gestalt therapist provides more interpretation and feedback (Zahm & Gold, 2002). Nonetheless, both of these humanistic therapies encourage individuals to take responsibility for their feelings and actions, to truly be themselves, to understand themselves, to develop a sense of freedom, and to look at what they are doing with their lives.

Behavior Therapies

Having explored the insight therapies—the psychodynamic and humanistic approaches—I turn to therapies that take a different approach to reducing people's problems and improving their adjustment: the behavior therapies. Behavior therapies offer action-oriented strategies to help people change what they are doing (Kazdin, 2002; Spiegler & Guevremont, 2003).

Behavior therapies use principles of learning to reduce or eliminate maladaptive behavior. Behavior therapies are based on the behavioral and social cognitive theories of learning and personality. Behavior therapists do not search for unconscious conflicts, as psychodynamic therapists do, or encourage individuals to develop accurate perceptions of their feelings and selves as humanistic therapists do. Insight and self-awareness are not the keys to helping individuals develop more adaptive behavior patterns, say the behavior therapists.

behavior therapy Uses principles of learning to reduce or eliminate maladaptive behavior.

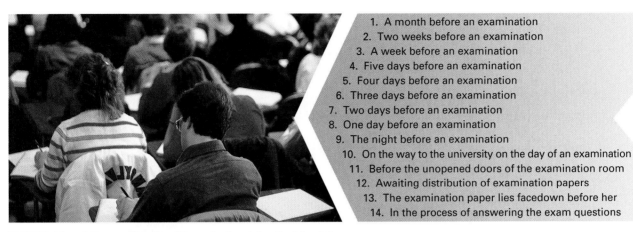

1. A month before an examination
2. Two weeks before an examination
3. A week before an examination
4. Five days before an examination
5. Four days before an examination
6. Three days before an examination
7. Two days before an examination
8. One day before an examination
9. The night before an examination
10. On the way to the university on the day of an examination
11. Before the unopened doors of the examination room
12. Awaiting distribution of examination papers
13. The examination paper lies facedown before her
14. In the process of answering the exam questions

FIGURE 14.5 A Desensitization Hierarchy Involving Test Anxiety
In the above hierarchy, the individual begins with their least feared circumstance (a month before the exam) and moves through each of the circumstances until reaching their most feared circumstance (being in the process of answering the exam questions). At each step of the way, the person replaces fear with deep relaxation and successful visualizations.

Behavior therapists assume that the overt maladaptive symptoms are the problem (Sloan & Mizes, 1999). Individuals can become aware of why they are depressed and still be depressed, say the behavior therapists. The behavior therapist tries to eliminate the depressed symptoms or behaviors themselves rather than trying to get individuals to gain insight or awareness of why they are depressed (Forsyth & Savsevitz, 2002; Lazarus, 1996).

The behavior therapies were initially based almost exclusively on the learning principles of classical and operant conditioning, but behavior therapies have become more diverse in recent years (McKay & Tryon, 2002). As social cognitive theory grew in popularity, behavior therapists increasingly included observational learning, cognitive factors, and self-instruction in their efforts to help people with their problems (Maultsby & Wirga, 1998; Tracy, Sherry, & Albright, 1999). In self-instruction, therapists try to get people to change what they say to themselves. Chapter 15 discusses self-instructional strategies in the context of coping with stress.

Techniques Based on Classical Conditioning Some behaviors, especially fears, can be acquired or learned through classical conditioning. If such fears can be learned, possibly they can be unlearned as well (Taylor, 2002). If an individual has learned to fear snakes or heights through classical conditioning, perhaps the individual can unlearn the fear through counterconditioning. Two types of counterconditioning involve systematic desensitization and aversive conditioning.

Systematic Desensitization **Systematic desensitization** is a method of behavior therapy based on classical conditioning that treats anxiety by getting the person to associate deep relaxation with increasingly intense anxiety-producing situations (Wolpe, 1963). Consider the common fear of taking an exam. Using systematic desensitization, the behavior therapist first asks the person which aspects of the feared situation—in this case, taking an exam—are the most and least frightening. Then the behavior therapist arranges these circumstances in order from most to least frightening. An example of this type of desensitization hierarchy is shown in figure 14.5.

The next step is to teach individuals to relax. Clients are taught to recognize the presence of muscular contractions or tensions in various parts of their bodies and then how to contract and relax different muscles. Once individuals are relaxed, the therapist asks them to imagine the least feared stimulus in the hierarchy. Subsequently, the therapist moves up the list of items, from least to most feared, while clients remain relaxed. Eventually, individuals are able to imagine the most fearsome circumstance without being afraid—in our example, being in the process of answering

systematic desensitization A method of behavior therapy based on classical conditioning that treats anxiety by getting the person to associate deep relaxation with increasingly intense anxiety-producing situations.

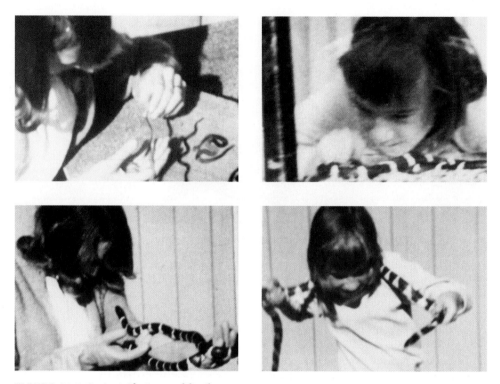

FIGURE 14.6 Systematic Desensitization Systematic desensitization is often used to help eliminate phobias. In this systematic desensitization treatment, the individual progresses from handling rubber snakes (*top left*), to peering at snakes in an aquarium (*top right*), to handling snakes with rubber gloves (*bottom left*), to handling live but harmless snakes (*bottom right*).

Systematic desensitization has a new format. Virtual reality technology is being used by some therapists to expose individuals to more vivid situations than their imagination might generate. Here, an individual with a fear of spiders is wearing a virtual reality headset and has become immersed in a vivid, three-dimensional world in which spiders appear very real.

exam questions. In this manner, individuals learn to relax while thinking about the exam instead of feeling anxious.

Researchers have found that systematic desensitization is often an effective treatment for a number of phobias, such as fear of giving a speech, fear of heights, fear of flying, fear of dogs, and fear of snakes (Barlow, 2001). If you were afraid of snakes, for instance, the therapist might initially have you watch someone handle a snake. Then the therapist would ask you to engage in increasingly more feared behaviors—you might first just go into the same room with the snake, next you would approach the snake, subsequently you'd touch the snake, and eventually you would play with the snake. Figure 14.6 shows a desensitization treatment with individuals who were afraid of snakes.

Desensitization involves exposing someone to a feared situation in a real or imagined way. A more intense form of exposure involves *flooding*, which consists of exposing individuals to feared stimuli or situations to an excessive degree while not allowing them to avoid the object or situation (Miller, 2002). The following case reveals how flooding works (Meyer & Osborne, 1982):

A 45-year-old divorced woman suffered from an obsessive-compulsive disorder that involved washing and cleansing rituals whenever she came into contact with objects she thought might be even remotely linked with death. For example, holding a newspaper article about someone she did not know who had been killed made her intensely anxious. The disorder first occurred when she was 15 years old, at the time of her mother's death.

When the woman sought treatment, she was to be remarried in two weeks. She did not believe that she could handle the marriage in her current condition of almost daily experiencing panic attacks related to her fear of contamination. The therapist used flooding to alleviate her problem. Most of the treatment took place in her home, although the first treatment was in a hospital mortuary. There the woman and the therapist became "contaminated" by handling a corpse, which produced intense anxiety. Later, the therapist gave her "contaminated" objects related to death, such as newspaper articles about death, photographs of funerals, dead animal meat, and so on, in her home during hour-long therapy sessions. After 12 days of flooding, the woman reported considerable progress and was married.

Aversive Conditioning The other behavior therapy technique involving classical conditioning is **aversive conditioning,** which consists of repeated pairings of the undesirable behavior with aversive stimuli to decrease the behavior's rewards. Aversive conditioning is used to teach people to avoid such behaviors as smoking, eating, and drinking. Electric shocks, nausea-inducing substances, and verbal insults are some of the noxious stimuli used in aversive conditioning. How could aversive conditioning be used to reduce a person's alcohol consumption? Every time a person drank an alcoholic beverage, he or she also would consume a mixture that induced nausea. In classical conditioning terminology, the alcoholic beverage is the conditioned stimulus and the nausea-inducing agent is the unconditioned stimulus. By repeatedly pairing alcohol with the nausea-inducing agent, alcohol becomes the conditioned stimulus that elicits nausea, the conditioned response. As a consequence, alcohol no longer is associated with something pleasant but rather something highly unpleasant. Figure 14.7 illustrates how classical conditioning is the backbone of aversive conditioning.

Operant Conditioning Approaches The basic philosophy of using operant conditioning as a therapy approach is that, because maladaptive behavior patterns are learned, they can be unlearned. Therapy involves conducting a careful analysis of the person's environment to determine what factors need to be modified. Especially important is changing the consequences of the person's behavior to ensure that behavioral responses are followed by positive reinforcement.

Operant therapy's techniques focus on **behavior modification,** the application of operant conditioning principles to change human behavior; its main goal is to replace unacceptable, maladaptive behaviors with acceptable, adaptive ones. Consequences for behavior are established to ensure that acceptable actions are reinforced and unacceptable ones are not (Kearney & Vecchio, 2002; Poling & Carr, 2002). Advocates of behavior modification believe that many emotional and behavioral problems are caused by inadequate (or inappropriate) response consequences (Stanley & Turner, 1995).

A behavior modification system in which behaviors are reinforced with tokens (such as poker chips) that later can be exchanged for desired rewards (such as candy, money, or going to a movie) is called a *token economy.* Token economies have been established in classrooms, institutions for the mentally retarded, homes for delinquents, and mental hospitals.

Behavior modification does not always work. One person may become so wedded to the tokens that when they are no longer given, the positive behavior associated with them may disappear. Yet, another person might continue the positive behavior without the tokens as rewards. Some critics object to behavior modification because they believe such extensive control of another person's behavior unethically infringes on the individual's rights. But, as in the case of the college student with an intense fear of exams, maladaptive responses can be turned into adaptive ones through behavior modification.

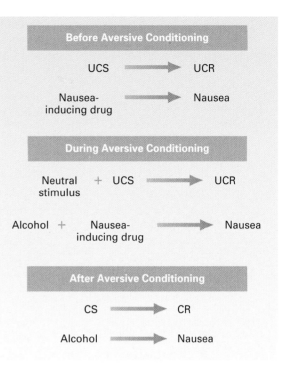

FIGURE 14.7 Classical Conditioning: The Backbone of Aversive Conditioning The above illustrates how classical conditioning can provide a conditional aversion to alcohol. After the association of the drug with alcohol, the alcohol becomes a conditioned stimulus for nausea. Recall these abbreviations: UCS (unconditioned stimulus), UCR (unconditioned response), CS (conditioned stimulus), and CR (conditioned response).

aversive conditioning A classical conditioning treatment which consists of repeated pairings of the undesirable behavior with aversive stimuli to decrease the behavior's rewards.

behavior modification The application of operant conditioning principles to change human behaviors, especially to replace unacceptable, maladaptive behaviors with acceptable, adaptive behaviors.

To end this discussion of behavior therapies, consider a case in which behavior modification helped an individual replace maladaptive responses with more adaptive ones to reduce his depression (Rosenfeld, 1985):

Henry Greene is a 36-year-old lawyer who wrestled with depression for months before finally seeking psychotherapy. His initial complaints were physical—fitful sleep, often ending at 3 A.M., lack of appetite, weight loss of 15 pounds, and a disinterest in sex. Henry began to move more slowly and his voice became monotonous. He reached the point where he could hardly bear to cope with life. Henry finally let his guard down and confessed that, although he looked successful on the outside, he felt like a failure on the inside. He said that he actually was a third-rate lawyer, husband, lover, and father. He felt that he was bound to remain that way.

How would a behaviorist treat Henry Greene? Peter Lewinsohn and his colleagues (1984) developed the "Coping with Depression Course" for such individuals. A basic principle of this approach is that feelings are caused by behaviors. Behavior therapists encourage people to increase the ratio of positive life events to negative life events to improve their mood. To accomplish the desired ratio, most individuals require a variety of skill exercises.

Henry Greene was first given the assignment of monitoring his moods. This task forced him to pay attention to his daily mood changes, and the information was used to determine which events are associated with which moods. Relaxation training followed, because relaxation skills improve an individual's sense of well-being.

The next step for Henry Greene was to determine how his moods are associated with pleasant and unpleasant events in his life. Henry was asked to fill out a "Pleasant Events Schedule" and an "Unpleasant Events Schedule." Each week, Henry completed a graph showing the number of pleasant and unpleasant events, as well as his mood, for each day. Henry was able to see a close relation between pleasant events and pleasant moods and between unpleasant events and unpleasant moods. The therapist then encouraged Henry to increase the amount of time he spends in pleasant activities with the hope that more positive moods would follow. The positive outcome was that Henry was able to gain control over his moods.

The final stage for Henry was maintenance planning. Henry was asked to identify the components of behavior therapy that were the most successful in changing his maladaptive behavior. Once Henry identified these, he was encouraged to continue their use. He also was required to develop emergency plans for those times when stress might overwhelm him. Henry continued to go to follow-up sessions for 6 months after his initial treatment.

Cognitive Therapies

D., a 21-year-old, single, undergraduate student, perceives himself as a failure in school and a failure to his parents. He is preoccupied with negative thoughts, dwells on his problems, and exaggerates his faults. Such thinking is common among depressed individuals and suggests that cognitive therapy might be a viable approach to treat D.'s depression. **Cognitive therapies** emphasize that individuals' cognitions or thoughts are the main source of abnormal behavior and psychological problems, and they attempt to change the individual's feelings and behaviors by changing cognitions. *Cognitive restructuring,* a general concept for changing a pattern of thought that is presumed to be causing maladaptive behavior or emotion, is central to cognitive therapies. Cognitive therapies differ from psychoanalytic therapies by focusing more on overt symptoms than on deep-seated unconscious thoughts, by providing more structure to the individual's thoughts, and by being less concerned about the origin of the problem. Unlike humanistic therapies, cognitive therapies provide more structure, more analysis, and more specific cognitive techniques.

Cognitive therapists guide individuals in identifying their irrational and self-defeating thoughts. Then they use various techniques to get clients to challenge these thoughts and consider different, more positive ways of thinking. These cognitive techniques often are implemented through a Socratic method of asking questions to help

cognitive therapies Emphasize that individuals' cognitions or thoughts are the main source of abnormal behavior and psychological problems.

clients gain self-understanding about their negative thinking. As part of this process, a cognitive therapist usually asks clients what the worst thing is that could happen to them. Then clients are asked to propose how they would cope with their ultimate worst situation. In this way, cognitive therapists help clients see that they will be able to cope even if the worst possible thing happens to them.

The two main forms of cognitive therapy are Albert Ellis' rational-emotive behavior therapy and Aaron Beck's cognitive therapy. Cognitive-behavior therapy uses a combination of cognitive and behavorial techniques.

Rational-Emotive Behavior Therapy **Rational-emotive behavior therapy (REBT)** is based on Albert Ellis' assertion that individuals develop a psychological disorder because of their beliefs, especially irrational and self-defeating beliefs. Ellis (1962, 1996, 2000, 2002) says that we usually talk to ourselves when we experience stress; too often the statements are irrational, making them more harmful than helpful.

Ellis (2000, 2002) believes that many individuals construct three basic demands: (1) I *absolutely must* perform well and win the approval of other people; (2) Other people *have to* treat me kindly and fairly; and (3) My life conditions *should not* be frustrating but rather *should be* enjoyable. Once people convert their important desires into demands, they often create dysfunctional, exaggerated beliefs, such as "Because I'm not performing well, as I *absolutely must*, I'm an inadequate person."

The goal of REBT is to get the person to eliminate self-defeating beliefs by rationally examining them. Clients are shown how to dispute their dysfunctional beliefs—especially their absolute musts—and change them to realistic and logical thoughts. Homework assignments provide them opportunities to engage in the new self-talk and experience the positive results of not viewing life in such a castastrophic way.

Beck's Cognitive Therapy Aaron Beck (1976, 1993) developed a somewhat different form of cognitive therapy to treat psychological problems, especially depression. A basic assumption Beck makes is that psychological problems such as depression result when people think illogically about themselves, the world they live in, and the future. Beck's approach shares with Ellis' the idea that the goal of therapy should be to help people to recognize and discard self-defeating cognitions.

In the initial phases of therapy, individuals are taught to make connections between their patterns of thinking and their emotional responses. The therapist helps them to identify their own automatic thoughts and to keep records of their thought content and emotional reactions. With the therapist's assistance, they learn about logical errors in their thinking and learn to challenge the accuracy of these automatic thoughts. Logical errors in thinking can lead an individual to the following erroneous beliefs (Carson, Butcher, & Mineka, 1996):

- Perceive the world as harmful while ignoring evidence to the contrary, for example, still feeling worthless even though a friend has just told her how much other people like her
- Overgeneralize on the basis of limited examples, such as seeing himself as worthless because one individual stopped dating him
- Magnify the importance of undesirable events, such as seeing the loss of a dating partner as the end of the world
- Engage in absolutist thinking, such as exaggerating the importance of someone's mildly critical comment and perceiving it as proof of total inadequacy.

Figure 14.8 describes some of the most widely used cognitive therapy techniques.

The following case study involves a cognitive therapist guiding a depressed 26-year-old graduate student to understand the connection between how she interprets her experiences and the way she feels and to begin seeing the inaccuracy of her interpretations (Beck & others, 1979, pp. 145–146):

rational-emotive behavior therapy (REBT) Based on Ellis' assertion that individuals develop a psychological disorder because of their beliefs, especially those that are irrational and self-defeating; the goal of REBT is to get the person to eliminate self-defeating beliefs by rationally examining them.

Cognitive Therapy Technique	Description	Example
Challenge idiosyncratic meanings	Explore personal meaning attached to the client's words and ask the client to consider alternatives.	When a client says he will be "devastated" by his spouse leaving, ask just how he would be devastated and ways he could avoid being devastated.
Question the evidence	Systematically examine the evidence for the client's beliefs or assertions.	When a client says she can't live without her spouse, explore how she lived without the spouse before she was married.
Reattribution	Help the client distribute responsibility for events appropriately.	When a client says that his son's failure in school must be his fault, explore other possibilities, such as the quality of the school.
Examine options and alternatives	Help the client generate alternative actions to maladaptive ones.	If a client considers leaving school, explore whether tutoring or going part-time to school are good alternatives.
Decatastrophize	Help the client evaluate whether he is overestimating the nature of a situation.	If a client states that failure in a course means she must give up the dream of medical school, question whether this is a necessary conclusion.
Fantasize consequences	Explore fantasies of a feared situation: If unrealistic, the client may recognize this; if realistic, work on effective coping strategies.	Help a client who fantasizes "falling apart" when asking the boss for a raise to role-play the situation and develop effective skills for making the request.
Examine advantages and disadvantages	Examine advantages and disadvantages of an issue, to instill a broader perspective.	If a client says he "was just born depressed and will always be that way," explore the advantages and disadvantages of holding that perspective versus other perspectives.
Turn adversity to advantage	Explore ways that difficult situations can be transformed to opportunities.	If a client has just been laid off, explore whether this is an opportunity for her to return to school.
Guided association	Help the client see connections between different thoughts or ideas.	Draw the connections between a client's anger at his wife for going on a business trip and his fear of being alone.
Scaling	Ask the client to rate her emotions or thoughts on scales to help gain perspective.	If a client says she was overwhelmed by an emotion, ask her to rate it on a scale from 0 (not at all present) to 100 (I fell down in a faint).
Thought stopping	Provide the client with ways of stopping a cascade of negative thoughts.	Teach an anxious client to picture a stop sign or hear a bell when anxious thoughts begin to snowball.
Distraction	Help the client find benign or positive distractions to take attention away from negative thoughts or emotions temporarily.	Have a client count to 200 by 13s when he feels himself becoming anxious.
Labeling of distortions	Provide labels for specific types of distorted thinking to help the client gain more distance and perspective.	Have a client keep a record of the number of times a day she engages in all-or-nothing thinking—seeing things as all bad or all good.

FIGURE 14.8 **Cognitive Therapy Techniques**

Student: I agree with the description of me but I guess I don't agree that the way I think makes me depressed.

Therapist: How do you understand it?

Student: I get depressed when things go wrong. Like when I fail a test.

Therapist: How can failing a test make you depressed.

Student: Well, if I fail I'll never get into law school.

Therapist: So failing the test means a lot to you. But if failing a test could drive people into clinical depression, wouldn't you expect everyone who failed the test to have depression? Did everyone who failed the test get depressed enough to require treatment?

Student: No, but it depends on how important the test was to the person.

Therapist: Right, and who decides the importance?

Student: I do.

Therapist: And so, what we have to examine is your way of viewing the test or the way that you think about the test and how it affects your chances of getting into law school. Do you agree?

Student: Right . . .

Therapist: Now what did failing mean?

Student: (Tearful) That I couldn't get into law school.

Therapist: And what does that mean to you?

Student: That I'm just not smart enough.

Therapist: Anything else?

Student: That I can never be happy.

Therapist: And how do these thoughts make you feel?

Student: Very unhappy.

Therapist: So it is the meaning of failing a test that makes you very unhappy. In fact, believing that you can never be happy is a powerful factor in producing unhappiness. So, you get yourself into a trap—by definition, failure to get into law school equals, "I can never be happy."

As we mentioned earlier, Beck's and Ellis' cognitive therapies have some similarities. However, there also are some differences: Rational-emotive behavior therapy is very directive, persuasive, and confrontational. In contrast, Beck's cognitive therapy involves more of an open-ended dialogue between the therapist and the individual. The aim of this dialogue in Beck's approach is to get individuals to reflect on personal issues and discover their own misconceptions. Beck also encourages individuals to gather information about themselves and to try out unbiased experiments that reveal the inaccuracies of their beliefs.

Cognitive-Behavior Therapy **Cognitive-behavior therapy** consists of a combination of cognitive therapy, with its emphasis on reducing self-defeating thoughts, and behavior therapy, with its emphasis on changing behavior (Epstein & Boucom, 2002; Roth, Eng, & Heimberg, 2002). An important aspect of cognitive-behavior therapy is *self-efficacy*, Albert Bandura's (1997, 2001) concept that one can master a situation and produce positive outcomes. Bandura believes that self-efficacy is the key to successful therapy. At each step of the therapy process, people need to bolster their confidence by telling themselves, "I'm going to master my problem," "I can do it," "I'm improving," "I'm getting better," and so on. As people gain confidence and engage in adaptive behavior, the successes become intrinsically motivating. Before long, individuals persist with considerable effort in their attempts to solve personal problems because of the positive outcomes that were set in motion by self-efficacy.

Self-instructional methods are cognitive-behavior techniques aimed at teaching individuals to modify their own behavior (Dowd, 2002; Meichenbaum, 1977). Using self-instructional methods, cognitive-behavior therapists try to get clients to change what they say to themselves. The therapist gives the client examples of constructive statements, known as "reinforcing self-statements," that the client can repeat in order to take positive steps to cope with stress or meet a goal. The therapist also will encourage the client to practice the statements through role playing and will strengthen the client's newly acquired skills through reinforcements. Following is a series of examples of self-instructional methods that individuals can use to cope with stressful situations (Meichenbaum, Turk, & Burstein, 1975):

Preparing for anxiety or stress:

What do I have to do?

I'm going to map out a plan to deal with it.

I'll just think about what I have to do.

I won't worry. Worry doesn't help anything.

cognitive-behavior therapy Consists of a combination of cognitive therapy and behavior therapy; self-efficacy is an important goal of cognitive-behavior therapy.

I have a lot of different strategies I can call on.
Confronting and handling the anxiety or stress:
I can meet the challenge.
I'll keep on taking one step at a time.
I can handle it. I'll just relax, breathe deeply, and use one of the strategies.
I won't think about the pain. I will think about what I have to do.
Coping with feelings at critical moments:
What is it I have to do?
I was supposed to expect the pain to increase. I just have to keep myself in control.
When the pain comes, I will just pause and keep focusing on what I have to do.
Reinforcing self-statements:
Good, I did it.
I handled it well.
I knew I could do it.
Wait until I tell other people how I did it!

Using Cognitive Therapy to Treat Psychological Disorders Cognitive therapy has been used effectively in the treatment of some anxiety disorders, mood disorders, schizophrenia, and personality disorders (Barlow, 2001; Beck, 2002). In many instances, cognitive therapy used conjointly with drug therapy is an effective treatment for psychological disorders (Barlow & others, 2000).

Among the anxiety disorders to which cognitive therapy has been applied is panic disorder (Stuart, Treat, & Wade, 2000). The central concept in the cognitive model of panic is that individuals catastrophically misinterpret relatively benign physical or psychological events. In cognitive therapy, the therapist encourages individuals to test the catastrophic misinterpretations by inducing an actual panic attack. The individuals then can test the notion that they will die or go crazy, which they find out is not the case. In one recent study, a combination of an SSRI drug and cognitive therapy was effective in treating panic disorder (Azhar, 2001). Cognitive therapy has shown considerable promise in the treatment of post-traumatic stress disorder, especially when individuals are encouraged to relive traumatic experiences in the service of coming to grips with the threatening cognitions precipitated by those experiences (Cohen, Mannarino, & Rogal, 2001). Cognitive therapy also has been successful in treating generalized anxiety disorder, certain phobias, and obsessive-compulsive disorder (Borkovec & Ruscio, 2001; Wells & Papageorgiou, 2001).

In one study, cognitive-behavior therapy was given to children (as well as their parents) who were highly anxious about going to school (Dadds & others, 1999). As shown in Figure 14.9, the therapy (provided over a 10-week period) was considerably more effective in reducing anxiety than no therapy at all, and the positive effects of the therapy were still present 2 years later.

One of the earliest applications of cognitive therapy was in the treatment of depression. A number of studies have shown that cognitive therapy can be just as successful as drug therapy in the treatment of depressive disorders (Dunner, 2001). Some studies also have shown that individuals treated with cognitive therapy are less likely to relapse into depression than individuals treated with drug therapy (Jarrett & others, 2001).

Considerable strides have been made in recent years in applying cognitive therapy to the treatment of schizophrenia.

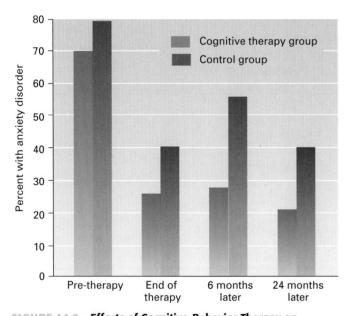

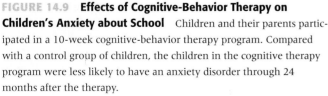

FIGURE 14.9 Effects of Cognitive-Behavior Therapy on Children's Anxiety about School Children and their parents participated in a 10-week cognitive-behavior therapy program. Compared with a control group of children, the children in the cognitive therapy program were less likely to have an anxiety disorder through 24 months after the therapy.

	Topic		
	Cause of Problem	**Therapy Emphasis**	**Nature of Therapy and Techniques**
Psychodynamic Therapies	Client's problems are symptoms of deep-seated, unresolved unconscious conflicts.	Discover underlying unconscious conflicts and work with client to develop insight.	Psychoanalysis, including free association, dream analysis, resistance, and transference: therapist interprets heavily. operant conditioning.
Humanistic Therapies	Client is not functioning at an optimal level of development.	Develop awareness of inherent potential for growth.	Person-centered therapy, including unconditional positive regard, genuineness, accurate empathy, and active listening; Gestalt therapy including confrontation to encourage honest expression of feelings; self-appreciation emphasized.
Behavior Therapies	Client has learned maladaptive behavior patterns.	Learn adaptive behavior patterns through changes in the environment or cognitive processes.	Observation of behavior and its controlling conditions; specific advice given about what should be done; therapies based on classical conditioning, operant conditioning.
Cognitive Therapies	Client has developed inappropriate thoughts.	Change feelings and behaviors by changing cognitions.	Conversation with client designed to get him or her to change irrational and self-deflating beliefs.

FIGURE 14.10 **Therapy Comparisons**

Although not a substitute for drug therapy in the treatment of schizophrenia, cognitive therapy has been effective in reducing the schizophrenic's belief in delusions and lowering the probability that the schizophrenic will act out in an impulsive fashion (Rector & Beck, 2001).

Cognitive therapy also has been used effectively in treating personality disorders. The focus is on using cognitive therapy to change individuals' core beliefs and to reduce their automatic negative thoughts.

So far in this chapter we have studied the biological therapies and psychotherapies. A comparison of the biological therapies and the four psychotherapies—psychodynamic, humanistic, behavioral, and cognitive—is presented in figure 14.10.

Review and Sharpen Your Thinking

2 *Define psychotherapy and characterize four types of psychotherapies.*

- Explain what psychotherapy is.
- Describe the psychodynamic therapies.
- Discuss the humanistic therapies.
- Summarize the classical conditioning and operant conditioning approaches to behavioral therapies.
- Distinguish among three cognitive therapies.

Imagine that you are a psychotherapist and that you diagnose an individual as having a depressive disorder. Which of the psychotherapies would you use to treat the individual? Explain your choice.

mhhe com/ santrockp7

For study tools related to this learning goal, see the Study Guide, the CD-ROM, and the Online Learning Center.

3 SOCIOCULTURAL APPROACHES AND ISSUES IN TREATMENT

| Group Therapy | Self-Help Support Groups | Cultural Perspectives |

| Family and Couples Therapy | Community Mental Health |

What treatment needs do the sociocultural approaches address?

In the treatment of psychological disorders, biological therapies change the person's body, behavioral therapies modify the person's behavior, and cognitive therapies alter the person's thinking. This section focuses on sociocultural approaches to the treatment of psychological disorders. These approaches view the individual as part of a social system of relationships, influenced by various social and cultural factors, and believe that these sociocultural aspects must be dealt with in the treatment of psychological disorders (Nolen-Hoeksema, 2001). The sociocultural approaches and issues include group therapy, family and couples therapy, self-help support groups, community mental health, and cultural perspectives on therapy.

Group Therapy

A major issue in therapy is how to structure it to reach more people at less cost. One way to address this problem is for the therapist to see clients in a group (MacKenzie, 2002).

Nine people make their way into a room, each looking tentatively at the others. Although each person has met the therapist during a diagnostic interview, no one knows any of the other clients. Some of the people seem reluctant, others enthusiastic. All are willing to follow the therapist's recommendation that group therapy might help each of them learn to cope better with their problems. As they sit down and wait for the session to begin, one thinks, "Will they really understand me?" Another thinks, "Do the others have problems like mine?" Yet another thinks, "How can I stick my neck out with these people?"

Individual therapy is often expensive and time-consuming. Freud believed that therapy is a long process and saw clients as often as three to five times a week for a number of years. Advocates of group therapy stress that individual therapy is limited because the client is seen outside the normal context of relationships, relationships that may hold the key to successful therapy (Gladding, 1999; Kline, 2003). Many psychological problems develop in the context of interpersonal relationships—within one's family, marriage, or peer group, for example. By taking into account the context of these important groups, therapy may be more successful (Capuzzi, 2003; Gazda, Horne, & Guiter, 2001).

Group therapy is diversified. Psychodynamic, humanistic, behavior, and cognitive therapy are all used in group therapy, in addition to approaches that are not based on the major psychotherapeutic perspectives. Six features make group therapy an attractive treatment format (Yalom, 1975, 1995):

Because many psychological problems develop in the context of interpersonal relationships and group experiences—within family, marriage, work or social group—group therapy can be an important context for learning how to cope more effectively with these problems.

1. *Information.* The individual receives information about his problem from either the group leader or other group members.
2. *Universality.* Many individuals develop the sense that no one else has frightening and unacceptable impulses. In the group, individuals observe that others feel anguish and suffering as well.

3. *Altruism.* Group members support one another with advice and sympathy and learn that they have something to offer others.
4. *Corrective recapitulation of the family group.* A therapy group often resembles a family (in family therapy the group *is* a family), with the leaders representing parents and the other members siblings. In this "new" family, old wounds may be healed and new, more positive "family" ties made.
5. *Development of social skills.* Corrective feedback from peers may correct flaws in the individual's interpersonal skills. A self-centered individual may see that he is self-centered if five other group members inform him about his self-centeredness; in individual therapy he might not believe the therapist.
6. *Interpersonal learning.* The group can serve as a training ground for practicing new behaviors and relationships. A hostile woman may learn that she can get along better with others by behaving less aggressively, for example.

Family and Couples Therapy

"A friend loves you for your intelligence, a mistress for your charm, but your family's love is unreasoning; you were born into it and are of its flesh and blood. Nevertheless, it can irritate you more than any group of people in the world," commented the French biographer André Maurois. As his statement suggests, the family may be the source of an individual's problems.

Family therapy is group therapy with family members. **Couples therapy** is group therapy with married or unmarried couples whose major problem is their relationship. These approaches stress that, although one person may have some abnormal symptoms, the symptoms are a function of the family or couple relationships (Capuzzi & Gross, 1999; Griffin, 2002). Psychodynamic, humanistic, and behavior therapies may be used in family and couples therapy.

Consider the following case study to gain an understanding of how family therapy works (Sheras & Worchel, 1979):

> Father: I just don't understand. We have had a happy family all along until Tommy started acting up. . . .
> Therapist: Have you ever had to hit Tommy?
> Father: Sure, a couple of times, but it didn't seem to do any good.
> Tommy (Son): Yeah, he hit me a lot, for no reason at all!
> Mother: Now, that's not true, Tommy. If you behaved yourself a little better, you wouldn't get hit. . . .
> Therapist: I get the feeling that people in this famly would like for things to be different. Bob, I can see how frustrating it must be for you to work so hard and not be able to relax when you get home. And Ginny, your job is not easy either. You have a lot to do at home and Bob can't be there to help a lot of the time. It must be hard for you, Tommy, to be catching so much flack these days.
>
> Therapist now looks at each person briefly and then says, "There seems to be a lot going on. What I would like to do is talk with you together a little longer, then see the parents alone and then Tommy alone, to hear the different sides of what is going on. I would like for each of you to think about how you would change the other family members so that you would be happier as a family."

Four of the most widely used family therapy techniques are

1. *Validation.* The therapist expresses an understanding and acceptance of each family member's feelings and beliefs and thus validates the person. When the therapist talks with each family member, she finds something positive to say.
2. *Reframing.* The therapist helps families reframe problems as family problems, not an individual's problems. A delinquent adolescent boy's problems are reframed in terms of how each family member contributed to the situation. The father's lack of attention to his son and marital conflict may be involved, for example.

Family therapy has become increasingly popular in recent years. In family therapy, the assumption is that psychological adjustment is related to patterns of interaction within the family unit.

family therapy Group therapy with family members.

couples therapy Therapy with married or unmarried couples whose major problem is within their relationship.

3. *Structural change.* The family systems therapist tries to restructure the coalitions in a family. In a mother-son coalition, the therapist might suggest that the father take a stronger disciplinarian role to relieve some of the burden from the mother. Restructuring might be as simple as suggesting that parents explore satisfying ways to be together; the therapist may recommend that once a week the parents go out for a quiet dinner together, for example.

4. *Detriangulation.* In some families, one member is the scapegoat for two other members who are in conflict but pretend not to be. For example, in the triangle of two parents and one child, the parents may insist that their marriage is fine but find themselves in subtle conflict over how to handle the child. The therapist tries to disentangle, or detriangulate, this situation by shifting attention away from the child to the conflict between the parents.

Couples therapy proceeds in much the same way as family therapy. Conflict in marriages and in relationships between unmarried individuals frequently involves poor communication. In some instances, communication has broken down entirely. The therapist tries to improve the communication between the partners. In some cases, she will focus on the roles partners play: one may be "strong," the other "weak"; one may be "responsible," the other "spoiled," for example. Couples therapy addresses diverse problems such as jealousy, sexual messages, delayed childbearing, infidelity, gender roles, two-career families, divorce, and remarriage (Sullivan & Christensen, 1998).

Self-Help Support Groups

Self-help support groups are voluntary organizations of individuals who get together on a regular basis to discuss topics of common interest. The groups are not conducted by a professional therapist but rather by a paraprofessional or a member of the common interest group. A paraprofessional is someone who has been taught by a professional to provide some mental health services but who does not have formal mental health training. The group leader and members provide support to help individuals with their problems. Self-help support groups play an important role in our nation's mental health, with as many as 10 million people participating in such groups each year. In addition to reaching so many people in need of help, these groups are important because they use community resources and are relatively inexpensive. They also serve people who are less likely to receive help otherwise, such as less educated adults, individuals living in low-income circumstances, and homemakers.

Self-help support groups provide members with a sympathetic audience for confession, sharing, and emotional release (Burlingame & Davies, 2002). The social support, role modeling, and sharing of concrete strategies for solving problems that unfolds in self-help groups adds to their effectiveness. A woman who has been raped might not believe a male therapist who tells her that, with time, she will be able to put back together the pieces of her shattered life and work through much of the psychological pain. But the same message from another rape survivor—someone who has had to work through the same feelings of rage, fear, and violation—might be more believable.

Alcoholics Anonymous (AA), founded in 1935 by a reformed alcoholic and a physician, is one of the best-known self-help groups. Mental health professionals often recommend AA for their alcoholic clients. Another self-help organization is Compeer, which matches community volunteers in supportive friendship relationships with children and adults receiving mental health treatment. In some cases, both partners in a Compeer relationship may have psychological disorders. There are myriad self-help groups, such as Parents Without Partners, lesbian and gay support groups, cocaine abuse support groups, Weight Watchers and TOPS (Take Off Pounds Sensibly), child abuse support groups, and many medical (heart disease, cancer) support groups. Figure 14.11 shows a sampling of the more than 200 self-help groups in Tulsa, Oklahoma, found in a local newspaper.

Social Concerns	
Tulsa Society for Depressed Women	Relocated Corporate Wives
Love Without Shame	Rebuilders: For Divorces
Gamblers Anonymous	Sex Addicts Anonymous
Phobia Society of Tulsa	Rap Group and Caring and Coping
	Partners of Vietnam Veterans

Eating/Weight Disorders	
Movers and Shapers	TOPS (Take Off Pounds Sensibly)
Overeaters Anonymous	

Alcohol/Substance Abuse	
Students Against Drugs and Alcohol	Alcoholics Anonymous
Alcoholics Victorious	Teen Awareness Group
How to Cope with a Dependent Person	Cocaine Anonymous
Adult Children of Alcoholic Parents	

Parenting	
Single Working Mothers	Happier Home Parents
Tulsa Adoptive Parents	Stepparents Group
Parents Without Partners	Sooner Parents of Twins
After Baby Comes	

Health	
Resolve of Tulsa (an infertility group)	SHHH (Self-Help for the Hard of Hearing)
Group for Alzheimer's Caregivers	Families of Children with Diabetes
AIDS Support Program	Indian Health Care Resource Center
ENCORE (for breast cancer patients)	Families of Nursing Home Residents
Mended Hearts (for those who have had open-heart surgery)	LITHIUM Group (for those with bipolar disorder)

FIGURE 14.11 Examples of Self-Help Groups A listing of self-help groups in a Tulsa, Oklahoma, Sunday newspaper included more than 200 entries. Among the wide variety of self-help groups were those listed here.

Self-help support groups have broad, though not universal, appeal (Gottlieb, 1998). For people who tend to cope by seeking information and affiliation with similar peers, such groups can reduce stress and promote adjustment. However, as with any group therapy, there is the possibility that negative emotions will spread through the group, especially if the members face circumstances that deteriorate over time, such as terminal cancer patients. Group leaders who are sensitive to the spread of negative emotions can minimize such effects.

Community Mental Health

The community mental health movement was born in the 1960s when it became apparent that the mental health care system was not reaching the poor and when the care of large numbers of individuals with psychological disorders was transferred from mental institutions to community-based facilities. This transfer (called *deinstitutionalization*) came about largely because of the development of new drugs for treating individuals with psychological disorders, especially schizophrenia.

The community mental health approach includes training teachers, ministers, family physicians, and others who directly interact with community members to offer lay counseling and workshops on such topics as coping with stress, reducing drug use, and assertiveness training. In the community mental health approach, it is believed that the best way to treat a psychological disorder is to prevent it from happening in the first place. Prevention takes one of three courses: primary, secondary, or tertiary.

In *primary prevention,* efforts are made to reduce the number of new cases of psychological disorders. In some instances, high-risk populations are targeted for prevention, such as children of alcoholics, children with chronic illnesses, and children in poverty.

In *secondary prevention,* screening for early detection of problems and early intervention may take place. Secondary prevention programs seek to reach large numbers of people. One way they do this is by educating *paraprofessionals,* individuals without formal mental health training, about preventing psychological problems and by having them work with psychologists. One type of early intervention involves screening schoolchildren to find those who show early signs of problems and provide them with psychological services.

In *tertiary prevention,* an effort is made to treat psychological disorders that were not prevented or arrested early in the course of the disorders. Tertiary programs are often geared toward people who once required long-term care or hospitalization but who now are living in the community. An example of a tertiary intervention is *halfway houses* (community residences for individuals who no longer require institutionalization but who still need support in readjusting to the community) for formerly hospitalized schizophrenics.

An explicit goal of community mental health is to help people who are disenfranchised from society, such as those living in poverty, to lead happier, more productive lives. A key concept involved in this effort is *empowerment,* which consists of assisting individuals to develop the skills they need to control their own lives.

Cultural Perspectives

The psychotherapies that were discussed earlier in the chapter—psychodynamic, humanistic, behavioral, and cognitive—focus mainly on the individual. This approach is compatible with the needs of many people in Western cultures, such as the United States, where the focus is on the individual rather than the group—family, community, ethnic group. However, these psychotherapies may not be as effective with people who live in cultures that place more importance on the group—called *collectivist* cultures. Some psychologists argue that family therapy is likely to be more effective with people in cultures that place a high value on the family, such as Latino and Asian cultures (Tharp, 1991).

Ethnicity Many ethnic-minority individuals prefer discussing problems with parents, friends, and relatives rather than mental health professionals (Atkinson, Morten, & Sue, 1999; Canino & Spurlock, 2000; Gibson & Mitchell, 1999; Sue, 2002). Might therapy progress best when the therapist and the client are from the same ethnic background? Researchers have found that when there is an ethnic match between the therapist and the client and when ethnic-specific services are provided, clients are less likely to drop out of therapy early and in many cases have better treatment outcomes (Jackson & Greene, 2000; Orlinksy, Grawe, & Parks, 1994). Ethnic-specific services include culturally appropriate greetings and arrangements (for example, serving tea rather than coffee to Chinese American clients), providing flexible hours for treatment, and employing a bicultural/bilingual staff (Nystul, 1999).

Nonetheless, therapy can be effective when the therapist and client are from different ethnic backgrounds if the therapist has excellent clinical skills and is culturally sensitive (Gibson & Mitchell, 2003; Pedersen & Carey, 2003). Culturally skilled psychotherapists have good knowledge of the cultural groups they work with, understand sociopolitical influences, and have skills in working with culturally diverse groups (Foulks, 2002; Jenkins, 2002).

Gender One by-product of changing gender roles for women and men is evaluation of the goals of psychotherapy (Nolen-Hoeksema, 2001; Vatcher & Bogo, 2001). Traditionally, the goal of psychotherapy has been autonomy or self-determination for the client. However, autonomy and self-determination are often more central characteristics of life for men than for women, whose lives generally are more characterized by relatedness and connection with others. Thus some psychologists believe that therapy goals should involve more emphasis on relatedness and connection with others, especially for women, or an emphasis on both autonomy/self-determination and relatedness/connection to others (Notman & Nadelson, 2002; Worrell & Robinson, 1993).

Stanley Sue is a professor of clinical psychology at UCLA and the director of the National Research Center on Asian American Health. Unlike psychologists who specialize in a technique or a theory, he specializes in a population. Much of his work focuses on Asian American clients with special needs, especially if they are immigrants. When he was thinking about a career, Sue told his father, who was a Chinese immigrant to the United States, that he wanted to be a clinical psychologist. His father told him that he didn't understand what a psychologist does and didn't think he could make a living at it. But Sue persisted and obtained a Ph.D. in clinical psychology. His three brothers are psychologists and one even married a psychologist! In his research, Sue has found that Asian Americans underutilize mental health services and that those who do use them often have very serious psychological problems. This means that many Asian Americans with more moderate psychological problems are not getting adequate therapy.

Because traditional therapy often has not adequately addressed the specific concerns of women in a sexist society, several nontraditional approaches have arisen. These nontraditional therapies emphasize the importance of helping people break free from traditional gender roles and stereotypes. Feminist therapists believe that traditional psychotherapy continues to carry considerable gender bias and that women clients cannot realize their full potential without becoming aware of society's sexism.

The goals of feminist therapists are no different from other therapists' goals, and feminist therapists make no effort to turn clients into feminists. However, they do want the female client to be fully aware of how the nature of the female role in American society can contribute to the development of a psychological disorder. Feminist therapists believe that women must become aware of the bias and discrimination in their own lives to achieve their mental health goals.

Review and Sharpen Your Thinking

3 **Explain the sociocultural approaches and issues in treatment.**
- Define group therapy.
- Decribe family and couples therapy.
- Discuss the features of self-help support groups.
- Explain the community mental health approach.
- Identify cultural perspectives that can affect the success of treatment.

Which therapy setting do you think you would benefit from the most—individual or group? Why?

mhhe com/
santrockp7

For study tools related to this learning goal, see the Study Guide, the CD-ROM, and the Online Learning Center.

THE EFFECTIVENESS OF PSYCHOTHERAPY 4

Research on the Effectiveness of Psychotherapy

Therapy Integrations

Mental Health Professionals

Common Themes in Psychotherapy

Funding and Finding Therapy

Guidelines for Seeking Professional Help

How effective is psychotherapy?

Do individuals who go through therapy get better? Are some approaches more effective than others? Or is the situation similar to that of the Dodo in *Alice's Adventures in Wonderland*? Dodo was asked to judge the winner of a race; he decided, "Everybody has won and all must have prizes." How would we evaluate the effectiveness of psychotherapy? Would we take the client's word? The therapist's word? What would be our criteria for effectiveness? Would it be "feeling good," "adaptive behavior," "improved interpersonal relationships," "autonomous decision making," or "more positive self-concept," for example? During the past several decades an extensive amount of thought and research has addressed these questions (Brems, 2001; Moras, 2002).

Research on the Effectiveness of Psychotherapy

Four decades ago, Hans Eysenck (1952) came to the shocking conclusion that psychotherapy is ineffective. Eysenck analyzed 24 studies of psychotherapy and found that approximately two-thirds of the individuals with neurotic symptoms improved. Sounds impressive so far. But Eysenck also found that a similar percentage of neurotic

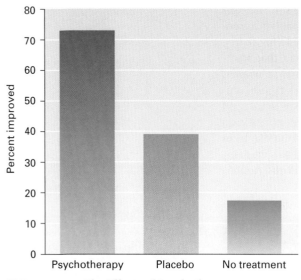

individuals on waiting lists to see a psychotherapist also showed marked improvement, even though they were not given any psychotherapy at all.

Eysenck's pronouncement prompted a flurry of research on psychotherapy's effectiveness (Lambert, 2001; Pilkonis, 1999; Orlinsky & Howard, 2000; Pilkonis & Krause, 1999). Hundreds of studies on the outcome of psychotherapy have now been conducted.

One strategy for analyzing these diverse studies is called **meta-analysis**, in which the researcher statistically combines the results of many different studies (Rosenthal & DiMatteo, 2001). In one meta-analysis of psychotherapy research, 475 studies were statistically combined (Smith, Glass, & Miller, 1980). Only those studies in which a therapy group had been compared with an untreated control group were used. The results showed greater psychotherapy effectiveness than Eysenck's earlier results: On 88 percent of the measures, individuals who received therapy improved more than those who did not. This meta-analysis and others (Lipsey & Wilson, 1993) document that psychotherapy is effective in general, but they do not inform us about the specific ways in which different therapies might be effective.

Figure 14.12 provides a summary of numerous studies and reviews of research in which clients were randomly assigned to a no-treatment control group, a placebo control group, or a psychotherapy treatment (Lambert, 2001; Lambert & Ogles, 2002). As can be seen, individuals who did not get treatment improved, probably because they sought help from friends, family, the clergy, or others. Individuals who were in a placebo control group fared better than nontreated individuals, probably because of having contact with a therapist, expectations of being helped, or the reassurance and support that they were given during the study. However, by far the best outcomes were for individuals who were given psychotherapy.

People who are thinking about seeing a psychotherapist want to know not only whether psychotherapy in general is effective but also especially which form of psychotherapy is most effective for their particular problem. Mary Lee Smith and her colleagues (1980) conducted a meta-analysis to compare types of psychotherapy. For example, behavior therapies were compared with insight therapies (psychodynamic and humanistic); both were found to be superior to no treatment at all, but they did not differ from each other in effectiveness.

Research that evaluates the effectiveness of a psychotherapy usually includes a comparison group—either a control group of individuals who do not experience the therapy or a group that receives a different type of psychotherapy (Alloy, Jacobson, & Acocella, 1999). When a control group is included, it often consists of individuals waiting to see a psychotherapist but who as yet have not been given therapy (this is called a *wait-list control group*). Why is it so important for psychotherapy research to include a control or comparison group? Because it gives us some idea of how many people in the study who experienced the targeted psychotherapy (such as cognitive therapy for depression) would have gotten better without the psychotherapy.

I present here one study that illustrates how control and comparison groups are used in psychotherapy research. The National Institute of Mental Health conducted an evaluation of three types of treatment for depression (cognitive therapy; interpersonal therapy, which emphasized improving the individual's social relationships; and drug therapy; Mervis, 1996). Two-hundred and forty individuals who were depressed were randomly assigned to one of the three psychotherapy conditions or to a control group who received a placebo medication along with supportive advice. After 16 weeks in treatment, just over 50 percent of the individuals in each of the three psychotherapy groups were no longer depressed. How did the people in the control group fare? After 16 weeks, 29 percent of them no longer were depressed, a significantly lower percentage than in the psychotherapy groups.

meta-analysis Statistical analysis that combines the results of many different studies.

Although no particular therapy was found to be best in this study, some therapies have been found to be more effective than others in treating some disorders (DeRubeis & Crits-Cristoph, 1998; Nathan & Gorman, 2002; Nathan, Stuart, & Dolan, 2000):

- Cognitive therapies and behavior therapies have been successful in treating anxiety disorders (Barlow, 2001; Bowers & Clum, 1988; Sanderson, 1995).
- Cognitive therapies and behavior therapies have been successful in treating depressive disorders (Butler & others, 1991; Clark & others, 1994; Craighead & Craighead, 2001).
- Relaxation therapy (discussed in chapter 15) also has been successful in treating anxiety disorders (Amitz & van den Hout, 1996; Hidalgo & Davidson, 2001).

Individuals who see a therapist also want to know how long it will take them to get better. In one study, individuals showed substantial improvement in therapy over the course of the first 6 months, with diminishing returns after that (Howard & others, 1996). In a recent study, individuals rated their symptoms, interpersonal relations, and quality of life on a weekly basis before each treatment session (Anderson & Lambert, 2001). Figure 14.13 shows that one-third of the individuals had improved outcomes by the 10th session, 50 percent by the 20th session, and 70 percent by the 45th session. In sum, therapy benefits most individuals with psychological problems at least through the first 6 months of therapy and possibly longer.

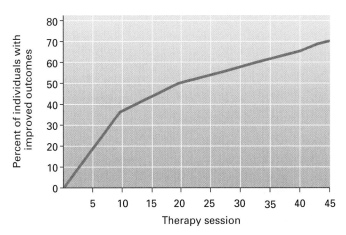

FIGURE 14.13 **Number of Therapy Sessions and Improvement** In one recent study, a large number of people undergoing therapy rated their well-being (based on symptoms, interpersonal relations, and quality of life) before each treatment session (Anderson & Lambert, 2001). The percentage of people who showed improved outcomes after each additional session of treatment indicated that about one-third of the individuals recovered by the 10th session, 50 percent by the 20th session, and 70 percent by the 45th session.

Common Themes in Psychotherapy

After carefully studying the nature of psychotherapy for more than 25 years, Jerome Frank (1982) concluded that effective psychotherapies have the common elements of expectations, mastery, and emotional arousal. By inspiring expectations of help, the therapist motivates the client to continue coming to therapy (Jennings & Skovholt, 1999). These expectations are powerful morale builders and symptom relievers in themselves (Arnkoff, Glass & Shapiro, 2002). The therapist also increases the client's sense of mastery and competence (Brammer & MacDonald, 1999; Hill & O'Brien, 1999). For example, clients begin to feel that they can cope effectively with their world. Therapy also arouses the individual's emotions, an essential motivator for behavior change, according to Frank.

The therapeutic relationship is another important element of successful psychotherapy (Norcross, 2002; Strupp, 1989, 1995). A relationship in which the client has confidence and trust in the therapist is essential to effective psychotherapy. In one study, the most common ingredient in the success of different psychotherapies was the therapist's supportiveness of the client (Wallerstein, 1989). The client and therapist engage in a "healing ritual," which requires the active participation of both the client and the therapist. As part of this ritual, the client gains hope and becomes less alienated.

Therapy Integrations

In the single-therapy approach, the therapist believes that one particular kind of therapy works best. However, approximately 30 to 50 percent of practicing therapists do not identify themselves as adhering to one particular approach but rather refer to themselves as "integrative" or "eclectic" (Garfield & Kurtz, 1976; Gold, 2002; Norcross & Kobayshi, 2000; Norcross & Prochaska, 1983, 1988). **Integrative therapy** is a combination of techniques from different therapies based on the therapist's judgment of which particular techniques will provide the greatest benefit for the client.

integrative therapy A combination of techniques from different therapies based on the therapist's judgment of which particular techniques will provide the greatest benefit for the client.

Integrative therapy is characterized by an openness to various ways of integrating diverse therapies. For example, a therapist might use a behavioral approach to treat an individual with panic disorder and a cognitive therapy approach to treat an individual with major depressive disorder. There is no single well-defined integrative therapy that ties all of the therapy approaches together. For that reason, the term *therapy integrations* probably best captures what is taking place in this field (Arkowitz, 1997).

In the past two decades, therapy integration has grown dramatically (Arkowitz, 1997). What has fostered the movement toward integrative therapy? The motivating factors include the proliferation of therapies, the inadequacy of a single therapy to be relevant to all clients and all problems, a lack of evidence that one therapy is better than others, and recognition that therapy commonalities play an important role in therapy outcomes (Norcross & Newman, 1992).

At their best, integrative therapies are effective, systematic uses of a variety of therapy approaches (Corey, 1996). However, one worry about integrative therapies is that their increased use will result in an unsystematic, haphazard eclecticism, which some therapists say would be no better than a narrow, dogmatic approach to therapy (Lazarus, Beutler, & Norcross, 1992).

With the increased diversity of client problems and populations, future therapy integration is likely to include more attention to ethnic and cultural factors in treating clients (Sue, 2000). This increased ethnic and cultural diversity also will require therapists to integrate spiritual concerns into their therapy approach (Pate & Bondi, 1992).

Integrative therapy also is at work when individuals are treated with both psychotherapy and drug therapy. For example, combined drug therapy and cognitive therapy have been effective in treating anxiety and depressive disorders (Dunner, 2001). And combined drug therapy and cognitive therapy hold promise in treating schizophrenia (Rector & Beck, 2001). This integrative therapy might be conducted by a mental health team that included a psychiatrist and a clinical psychologist.

Therapy integrations are conceptually compatible with the biopsychosocial model of abnormal behavior described in chapter 13. That is, many therapists believe that abnormal behavior involves biological, psychological, and social factors. Many single-therapy approaches focus on one aspect of the person more than others; for instance, drug therapies focus on biological factors, and cognitive therapies focus on psychological factors. Therapy integrations often taken a broader look at individuals' problems.

Funding and Finding Therapy

Psychotherapy can be expensive. Even though reduced fees and, in some cases, free services can be arranged in public hospitals and community mental health centers, many people who most need psychotherapy do not get it. Psychotherapists have been criticized for limiting their work to *y*oung, *a*ttractive, *v*erbal, *i*ntelligent, and *s*uccessful clients (*YAVIS*es) rather than *q*uiet, *u*gly, *o*ld, *i*nstitutionalized, and *d*ifferent clients (*QUOID*s). Mental health professionals have become increasingly sensitive to this problem, but it still has not been completely solved (Nielson, Johnson, & Ellis, 2001).

The challenge of paying for psychotherapy has led to substantial changes in mental health care delivery in recent years, especially the introduction of managed care. *Managed care* consists of strategies for controlling health care costs, including mental health treatment, and demand for accountability of treatment success. This goal typically is accomplished by interjecting a managed care organization between the mental health client and the providers of mental health services. Managed care providers attempt to offer services at lower costs by limiting traditional services, using stringent review procedures, and using lower cost brief-treatment options (Villani & Sharfstein, 1999). Managed care emerged in the early 1980s and has grown dramatically (Hoge, 1998).

Criticisms of managed care abound and include the following (Giles & Marafiote, 1998; Roback & others, 1999):

Professional Type	Degree	Education Beyond Bachelor's Degree	Nature of Training
Clinical psychologist	Ph.D. or Psy.D	5–7 years	Requires both clinical and research training. Includes a 1-year internship in a psychiatric hospital or mental health facility. Some universities have developed Psy.D. programs, which have a stronger clinical than research emphasis. The Psy.D. training program takes as long as the clinical psychology Ph.D. program and also requires the equivalent of a 1-year internship.
Psychiatrist	M.D.	7–9 years	Four years of medical school, plus an internship and residency in psychiatry are required. A psychiatry residency involves supervision in therapies, including psychotherapy and biomedical therapy.
Counseling psychologist	M.A., Ph.D., Psy.D., or Ed.D.	3–7 years	Similar to clinical psychologist but with emphasis on counseling and therapy. Some counseling psychologists specialize in vocational counseling. Some counselors complete master's degree training, others Ph.D. or Ed.D training, in graduate schools of psychology or education.
School psychologist	M.A., Ph.D., Psy.D., or Ed.D.	3–7 years	Training in graduate programs of education or psychology. Emphasis on psychological assessment and counseling practices involving students' school-related problems. Training is at the master's or doctoral level.
Social worker	M.S.W./D.S.W. or Ph.D.	2–5 years	Graduate work in a school of social work that includes specialized clinical training in mental health facilities.
Psychiatric nurse	R.N., M.A., or Ph.D.	0–5 years	Graduate work in a school of nursing with special emphasis on care of mentally disturbed individuals in hospital settings and mental health facilities.
Occupational therapist	B.S., M.A., or Ph.D.	0–5 years	Emphasis on occupational training with focus on physically or psychologically handicapped individuals. Stresses getting individuals back into the mainstream of work.
Pastoral counselor	None to Ph.D. or D.D. (Doctor of Divinity)	0–5 years	Requires ministerial background and training in psychology. An internship in a mental health facility as a chaplain is recommended.
Counselor	M.A. or M.Ed.	2 years	Graduate work in a department of psychology or department of education with specialized training in counseling techniques.

FIGURE 14.14 Main Types of Mental Health Professionals

- Managed care organizations are reluctant to provide for more than a few therapy sessions for a given patient.
- Long-term psychotherapy has been eliminated except for a relatively few wealthy clients who can pay their own way.
- Some managed care organizations are employing less well trained therapists who work at lower fees.

Mental Health Professionals

Psychotherapy is practiced by a variety of mental health professionals, including clinical psychologists, psychiatrists, and counselors. Recall that psychiatrists have a medical degree. Clinical psychologists, in contrast, are trained in graduate programs in psychology. Figure 14.14 lists the main types of mental health professionals, their degrees, the years of education required, and the nature of their training.

Licensing and certification are two ways in which society retains control over individuals who practice psychotherapy (Harmatz, 1997). Laws at the state level are used to license or certify such professionals. These laws vary in toughness from one state to another, but invariably they specify the training the mental health professional must have and provide for some assessment of the applicant's skill through formal examination. Licensing boards exist to protect the public from unscrupulous individuals who might use the title *psychologist* to offer treatment, and collect payment, without sufficient training to do so.

Licensing and certification require mental health practitioners to engage in ethical practices. Laws typically address the importance of doing no harm to clients, protecting the privacy of clients, and avoiding inappropriate relationships with clients. Violations of ethical codes can result in a loss of the license to practice psychotherapy (Wierzbicki, 1999).

Guidelines for Seeking Professional Help

Marcia felt anxious most of the time. But what caused her the greatest difficulty was that she became so anxious during exams in her classes that she would nearly freeze. Her mind would go blank, and she would begin to sweat and shake all over. It was such a problem that she was failing her classes. She told one of her professors that this was the problem with her grades. He told her that it sounded as if she had a serious case of test anxiety and that she should get some help. Marcia decided that she should take his advice and wanted to find a psychotherapist. How would she go about finding a therapist? Are certain professionals more qualified than others? How could she know that she was going to see someone who could help her as opposed to someone who would not be helpful, or perhaps even make things worse? These are only a few of the questions people commonly have when they want to find a therapist.

When trying to find a therapist, Marcia could consider a psychologist, psychiatrist, social worker, counselor, or any number of other helping professionals. Each of these mental health professionals is qualified to provide psychotherapeutic services. They all practice any one or a combination of the therapeutic orientations discussed in this chapter. They may also see people on an individual, one-to-one, basis or in small groups, as in group therapy. The critical question is, of course, how does someone go about selecting a therapist to help him or her? This is not as easy a question as it may appear at first glance. We may face many of the same problems when we try to find a "good" medical doctor, accountant, or dentist; however, the way that most people go about finding these other professional services may not be the best way of selecting a therapist. Asking a friend to recommend a good therapist ignores the fact that some approaches to therapy work better with some problems than others. Also, every therapeutic relationship is different, so one person's experience in therapy is not translatable to another person's. Following are some general suggestions when looking for a therapist.

Identify the Professional's Credentials Although all different types of mental health professionals may be competent, psychologists, psychiatrists, and social workers all differ in their approach to therapy based on differences in training: Psychologists tend to be focused on the person's emotions and behaviors; psychiatrists are trained as medical doctors, so their perspective is likely to involve physical aspects of psychological problems; and social workers are inclined to take a person's entire family and social situation into account. Regardless of the specific profession, some minimal credentials should be considered important. All states have licensing regulations for professionals who provide public services. Thus a therapist should be licensed or certified by a state in order to practice. In addition, in some cases it may be important for a professional to have some advanced, specialized training in a certain area. For example, if a person is seeking help with a specific problem, such as drug abuse, alcohol abuse, or a sexual problem, the therapist should have some training in that area. You should ask about the professional's credentials either before or during a first visit.

Give Therapy Some Time   Making changes is very difficult. Expecting too much too soon can result in premature dissatisfaction and disappointment. Because a large part of therapy involves the development of a relationship with the therapist, it may take several meetings to really know if things are going well. One suggestion is to give it between four and six weekly meetings. If it does not seem as if things are going the way you would like, it is a good idea to discuss your progress with the therapist and ask what you should expect with regard to making progress. Setting specific goals with specific time expectations can be helpful. If your goals are not being met, consider a new therapist.

Be a Thoughtful and Careful Consumer of Mental Health Services   Just as is true in seeking any services, the more informed you are about the services provided, the better decision you can make about whether or not they are the right services for you. Calling around and asking specific questions about approaches and specializations is one way to become informed about the services offered by therapists. Consider how important it may be that the therapist is of your or the opposite sex, whether it is important that he or she have experience with your specific difficulty, as well as other specific characteristics. You may also want to learn more about his or her theoretical orientation to therapy as described in this chapter. Another way to find out more about the therapist is to ask these kinds of questions during your first visit. Most professionals are quite comfortable talking about their background and training. Your confidence and trust in the professional is an important part of how well therapy will work for you.

Use these general guidelines when first looking for a therapist. Remember that people should continually evaluate their own progress throughout therapy and, when they are dissatisfied with how it is going, they should discuss this feeling with their therapists. Remember that therapy is like other services: When dissatisfied, you can always look for another therapist. Don't think that just because one therapist has not been helpful, none will be. All therapists and therapeutic relationships are different. Finding the right therapist is one of the most important factors in therapy success. See the Psychology and Life box to help evaluate whether you should see a therapist.

Evaluating Whether You Need A Therapist

There are no hard-and-fast rules about when people should go to a psychotherapist for help with their personal problems. However, to get a sense of whether you should see a psychotherapist, evaluate whether you have recently experienced the following:

- I feel sad or blue a lot.
- My self-esteem is really low.
- I feel like other people are always out to get me.
- I feel so anxious that it is hard for me to function.
- I have trouble concentrating on my academic work.
- I don't do anything social and spend much of my spare time alone.
- I have a tendency to alienate people when I don't really want to.
- I'm frightened by things that I know should not be fear-provoking.
- I hear voices that tell me what I should do.
- I know I have problems, but I just don't feel I can talk with anyone about them.

If any of these statements describe your life, consider talking over your concerns with a qualified therapist. Most colleges and universities have counseling or mental health services that are covered by your student fees. This is a good place to start in seeking mental health consultation.

Review and Sharpen Your Thinking

4   *Evaluate the effectiveness of psychotherapy.*

- Discuss research on psychotherapy effectiveness.
- Describe common themes in psychotherapy.
- Explain therapy integrations.
- List the kinds of health professionals who are qualified to provide mental health treatment and state the effects of managed care on mental health treatment.
- Summarize the guidelines for seeking professional help.

Explain why a control group is important in research on psychotherapy effectiveness.

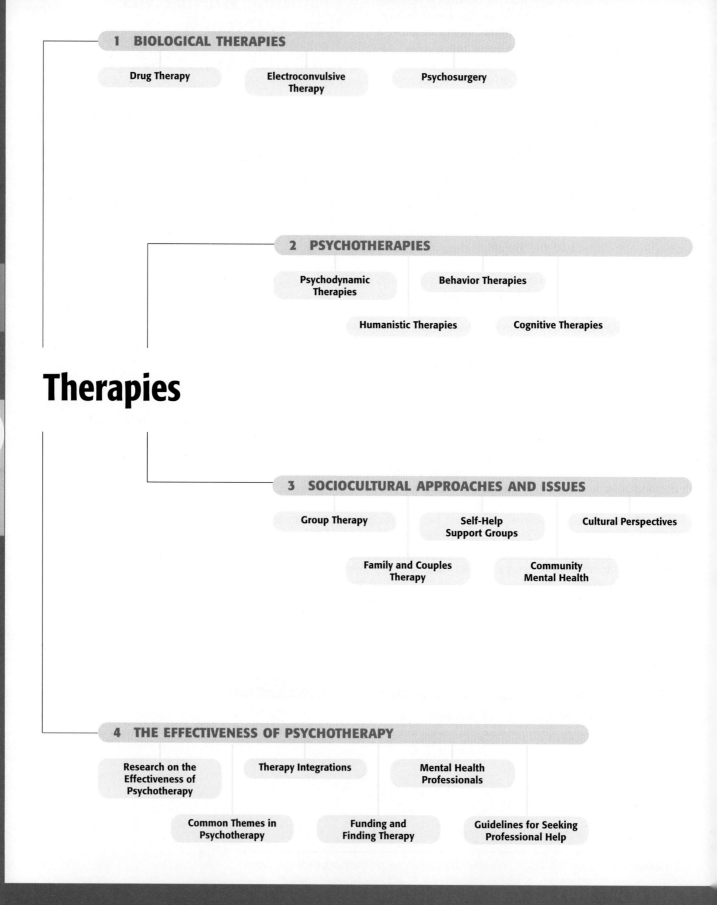

1 BIOLOGICAL THERAPIES

Drug Therapy

Electroconvulsive Therapy

Psychosurgery

2 PSYCHOTHERAPIES

Psychodynamic Therapies

Behavior Therapies

Humanistic Therapies

Cognitive Therapies

Therapies

3 SOCIOCULTURAL APPROACHES AND ISSUES

Group Therapy

Self-Help Support Groups

Cultural Perspectives

Family and Couples Therapy

Community Mental Health

4 THE EFFECTIVENESS OF PSYCHOTHERAPY

Research on the Effectiveness of Psychotherapy

Therapy Integrations

Mental Health Professionals

Common Themes in Psychotherapy

Funding and Finding Therapy

Guidelines for Seeking Professional Help

1 Describe the biological therapies.

- Psychotherapeutic drugs that are used to treat psychological disorders fall into three main categories: antianxiety drugs, antidepressant drugs, and antipsychotic drugs. Antianxiety drugs are commonly known as tranquilizers. Benzodiazepines are the most commonly used antianxiety drugs. Antidepressant drugs regulate mood; the three main classes are tricyclics, MAO inhibitors, and SSRI drugs. Lithium often is successful in treating bipolar disorder. The antidepressant drugs are increasingly being used to treat some anxiety disorders as well. Antipsychotic drugs are powerful drugs that are used to treat people with severe psychological disorders, especially schizophrenia. Psychotherapeutic drugs have varying effectiveness and side effects.
- Electroconvulsive therapy, commonly called *shock therapy*, is used to treat severe depression when other strategies have not worked.
- Psychosurgery is an irreversible procedure in which brain tissue is destroyed in an attempt to improve adjustment. Today, psychosurgery is rarely used but is more precise than the early prefrontal lobotomies.

2 Define psychotherapy and characterize four types of psychotherapy.

- Psychotherapy is the process used by mental health professionals to help individuals recognize, define, and overcome their psychological and interpersonal difficulties and improve their adjustment. Psychotherapists use a number of strategies to accomplish these goals: talking, interpreting, listening, rewarding, and modeling, for example. The insight therapies consist of the psychodynamic therapies and the humanistic therapies.
- Psychodynamic therapies stress the importance of the unconscious mind, early family experiences, and extensive interpretation by therapists. In Freudian psychoanalysis, psychological disorders are caused by unresolved unconscious conflicts, believed to originate in early family experiences. A therapist's interpretation of free association, dreams, transference, and resistance provide tools for understanding the client's unconscious conflicts. Although psychodynamic therapy has changed, many contemporary psychodynamic therapists still probe the unconscious mind for early family experiences that might provide clues to clients' current problems. The development of the self in social contexts is an important theme in Kohut's contemporary approach.
- In humanistic therapy, clients are encouraged to understand themselves and to grow personally. The humanistic therapies emphasize conscious thoughts, the present, and growth and fulfillment. Client-centered therapy was developed by Carl Rogers. In this therapy, the therapist provides a warm, supportive atmosphere to improve the client's self-concept and to enourage the client to gain insight into problems. Client-centered techniques include unconditional positive regard, genuineness, empathy, and active listening to raise the client's self-esteem. Fritz Perls developed gestalt therapy, in which therapists question and challenge clients to help them become more aware of their feelings and face their problems. Gestalt psychologists use such therapy techniques as setting examples and role playing. Gestalt therapy's techniques are more directive than Rogers' client-centered techniques.
- Behavior therapies use principles of learning to reduce or eliminate maladaptive behavior. They are based on the behavioral and social cognitive theories of personality. Behavior therapies seek to eliminate the symptoms of behaviors rather than to help individuals to gain insight into their problems. Behavior therapists increasingly use observational learning, cognitive factors, and self-instruction in their efforts to help people with their problems. Classical conditioning and operant conditioning techniques are used in behavior therapies. The two main therapy techniques based on classical conditioning are systematic desensitization and aversive conditioning. In systematic desensitization, anxiety is treated by getting the individual to associate deep relaxation with increasingly intense anxiety-producing situations. A concentrated form of desensitization is flooding. In aversive conditioning, pairings of the undesirable behavior with aversive stimuli are repeated to decrease the behavior's rewards. In operant conditioning approaches to therapy, a careful analysis of the person's environment is conducted to determine which factors need to be modified. Behavior modification is the application of operant conditioning to change human behavior. Its main goal is to replace unacceptable, maladaptive behaviors with acceptable, adaptive ones. A token economy is a behavior modification system in which behaviors are reinforced with tokens that later can be exchanged for desired rewards.
- Cognitive therapies emphasize that the individual's cognitions or thoughts are the main source of abnormal behavior. Cognitive therapies attempt to change the person's feelings and behaviors by changing cognitions. Three main forms of cognitive therapy are Ellis' rationale-motive behavior therapy, Beck's cognitive therapy, and cognitive-behavior therapy. Ellis' approach is based on the assertion that individuals develop psychological disorders because of their beliefs, especially those that are irrational and self-defeating.

Beck's cognitive therapy has been especially effective in treating depression. In Beck's therapy, the therapist assists the client in learning about logical errors in thinking and then guides the client in challenging these thinking errors. Ellis' approach is more directive, persuasive, and confrontational than Beck's. Cognitive-behavior therapy combines cognitive therapy and behavior therapy techniques. Self-efficacy and self-instructional methods are used in this approach. Cognitive therapy has been demonstrated to be effective in treating a number of psychological problems.

3 Explain the sociocultural approaches and issues in treatment.

- Group therapies emphasize that relationships can hold the key to successful therapy. Psychodynamic, humanistic, behavior, and cognitive therapies, as well as unique group approaches, are used in group therapy.
- Family therapy is group therapy with family members. Four widely used family therapy techniques are validation, reframing, structural change, and detriangulation. Couples therapy is group therapy with married or unmarried couples whose major problem is within their relationship.
- Self-help support groups are voluntary organizations of individuals who get together on a regular basis to discuss topics of common interest. They are conducted without a professional therapist.
- The community mental health movement was born out of the belief that the mental health care system was not adequately reaching people in poverty and who had been deinstitutionalized. Community mental health emphasizes primary, secondary, and tertiary prevention. Empowerment is often a goal of community mental health.
- Psychotherapies have mainly focused on the individual, which may work well in individualized cultures such as in the United States. However, these psychotherapies may not work as well in collectivist cultures. Many ethnic-minority individuals prefer to discuss problems with parents, friends, and relatives rather than with mental health professionals. Therapy is often more effective when there is an ethnic match between the therapist and the client, although culturally sensitive therapy can be provided by a therapist who is from a different ethnic background. The emphasis on autonomy in psychotherapies may produce a problem for many women, who place a strong emphasis on connectedness in relationships. Some feminist-based therapies have emerged.

4 Evaluate the effectiveness of psychotherapy.

- Psychotherapy is generally effective. Researchers have found, using meta-analysis, that the cognitive and behavior therapies are successful in treating anxiety and depressive disorders. Relaxation therapy also has been effective in treating anxiety disorders.
- Successful psychotherapy commonly includes positive expectations of help, increasing the client's sense of mastery, arousing the client's emotions, and developing the client's confidence and trust in the therapist.
- Approximately 30 to 50 percent of practicing therapists refer to themselves as "integrative" or "eclectic." Integrative therapy uses a combination of techniques from different therapies based on the therapist's judgment of which particular techniques will provide the greatest benefit for the client. In some instances, a combination of a particular type of psychotherapy and drug therapy is most effective in treating a psychological disorder.
- Psychotherapy is not always available to those who need it. Managed care has led to substantial changes in the delivery of mental health care and has been criticized for eliminating long-term treatment for all but the wealthy and for using less well trained therapists who accept low fees.
- Mental health professionals include clinical and counseling psychologists, psychiatrists, school psychologists, social workers, psychiatric nurses, occupational therapists, pastoral counselors, and counselors. These mental health professionals have different degrees, education, and training. Society retains control over individuals who practice psychotherapy through licensing and certification.
- Guidelines for seeking professional mental health care include identifying the professional's credentials, giving therapy some time before judging its usefulness, and being a thoughtful and careful consumer of mental health services.

Key Terms

biological therapies, p. 562	psychodynamic therapies, p. 569	client-centered therapy, p. 573	cognitive therapies, p. 578
psychotherapy, p. 562	psychoanalysis, p. 570	gestalt therapy, p. 573	rational-emotive behavior therapy, p. 579
antianxiety drugs, p. 563	free association, p. 570	behavior therapy, p. 574	cognitive-behavior therapy, p. 581
antidepressant drugs, p. 563	catharsis, p. 570	systematic desensitization, p. 575	family therapy, p. 585
lithium, p. 564	dream analysis, p. 570	aversive conditioning, p. 577	couples therapy, p. 585
antipsychotic drugs, p. 565	transference, p. 570	behavior modification, p. 577	meta-analysis, p. 590
electroconvulsive therapy (ECT), p. 566	resistance, p. 572		integrative therapy, p. 591
psychosurgery, p. 568	humanistic therapies, p. 572		
insight therapy, p. 568			

Apply Your Knowledge

1. The chapter describes some types of psychosurgery previously performed on patients. Use the Internet to research the kinds of problems that are currently treated with psychosurgery. Do you think psychosurgery should still be used?

2. Think critically about the use of antidepressant and antipsychotic drugs. Using your library, do some research for evidence that drug therapy works. If you were diagnosed with a psychological disorder, would you take a drug? Why or why not?

3. Behavioral and cognitive approaches may be helpful to change behaviors that wouldn't be considered abnormal but that you might want to change (for example, procrastinating, eating unhealthy food, or watching too much TV). Think about a behavior that you would like to do more, or

less, frequently; then think like a behavioral or cognitive therapist and describe the kinds of recommendations you might hear during a therapy session.

4. Think about the sociocultural approaches to therapy; for which kinds of problems would you be most likely to choose one of these approaches? Which approach would you choose? Do some research and see whether you can find a local group or therapist that would be helpful to someone with this kind of problem. What would you do if none were available in your area?

5. Imagine that a good friend confesses that he or she has been having some difficulties coping with some aspects of his or her life and asks you for advice in finding a psychotherapist. Based on the therapies and their effectiveness discussed in the text, what kind of advice would you give your friend?

Connections

For extra help in mastering the material in this chapter, see the review sections and practice quizzes in the Student Study Guide, the CD-ROM, and the Online Learning Center.

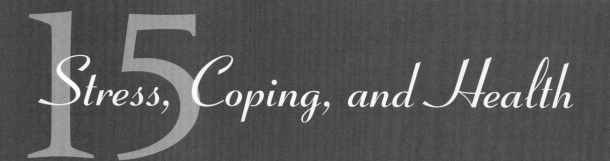

15 Stress, Coping, and Health

Chapter Outline

Learning Goals

HEALTH PSYCHOLOGY AND BEHAVIORAL MEDICINE   **1**

Describe the scope of health psychology and behavioral medicine.

STRESS AND ITS SOURCES   **2**

Define stress and identify its sources.

Personality Factors
▼
Environmental Factors
▼
Sociocultural Factors

STRESS RESPONSES   **3**

Explain how people respond to stress.

General Adaptation Syndrome
▼
Fight or Flight, Tend and Befriend
▼
Cognitive Appraisal

STRESS AND ILLNESS   **4**

Discuss links between stress and illness.

Stress and the Immune System
▼
Stress and Cardiovascular Disease
▼
Stress and Cancer
▼
Positive Emotions, Illness, and Health

COPING STRATEGIES   **5**

Outline strategies for coping with stress.

Problem-Focused and Emotion-Focused Coping
▼
Optimism and Positive Thinking
▼
Social Support
▼
Assertive Behavior
▼
Religion
▼
Stress Management Programs

HEALTHFUL LIVING   **6**

Summarize how to promote health.

Exercising Regularly
▼
Eating Healthily
▼
Quitting Smoking
▼
Making Sound Sexual Decisions

Mort, age 52, has worked as an air traffic controller for the past 15 years. An excitable person, he compares the job to being in a cage. During peak air traffic, the tension is almost unbearable. In these frenzied moments, Mort's emotions are a mixture of rage, fear, and anxiety. Unfortunately, the tension also spills over into his family life. In his own words, "When I go home, my nerves are still hopping. I tend to take it out on the nearest person." Two years ago, Mort's wife, Sally, told him that if he could not learn to calm his emotions and handle stress more effectively, she would leave him. She suggested that he change to a less-tension-filled job, but he ignored her advice, and she filed for divorce.

Last week the roof fell in on Mort. That Sunday evening, the computer that monitors air traffic temporarily went down, and Mort had a heart attack. Quadruple bypass surgery saved his life.

Yesterday his doctor talked with him about the stress in his life and what could be done to reduce it. Mort rarely gets enough sleep, weighs too much but frequently skips meals, never exercises, smokes two packs of cigarettes a day, and drinks two or three scotches every evening (more on weekends). He professes no religious interests. He rarely dates since his divorce and has no relatives living within 50 miles. He has only one friend and does not feel very close to him. Mort says that he never has enough time to do the things he wants to do and rarely has quiet time to himself during the day. He does something fun only about once every 2 weeks.

The doctor gave Mort a test, shown in figure 15.1, to reveal his vulnerability to stress. Mort scored 68, indicating he is seriously vulnerable to stress and close to the extremely vulnerable range. How do *you* fare on the stress test?

Rate yourself on each item, using a scale of 1–5:

1 = almost always   2 = often   3 = sometimes   4 = seldom   5 = never

_____ 1. I eat at least one hot, balanced meal a day.

_____ 2. I get 7 to 8 hours of sleep at least four nights a week.

_____ 3. I give and receive affection regularly.

_____ 4. I have at least one relative within 50 miles whom I can rely on.

_____ 5. I exercise to the point of perspiration at least twice a week.

_____ 6. I smoke less than half a pack of cigarettes a day.

_____ 7. I have fewer than five alcoholic drinks a week.

_____ 8. I am the appropriate weight for my height.

_____ 9. I have an income adequate to meet my basic expenses.

_____ 10. I get strength from my religious beliefs.

_____ 11. I regularly attend church.

_____ 12. I have a network of friends and acquaintances.

_____ 13. I have one or more friends to confide in about personal matters.

_____ 14. I am in good health (including eyesight, hearing, teeth).

_____ 15. I am able to speak openly about my feelings when angry or worried.

_____ 16. I have regular conversations with the people I live with about domestic problems (e.g., chores, money, and daily living issues).

_____ 17. I do something for fun at least once a week.

_____ 18. I am able to organize my time effectively.

_____ 19. I drink fewer than three cups of coffee (or tea or cola drinks) a day.

_____ 20. I take quiet time for myself during the day.

Total: _____

To get your total score, add your answers and subtract 20. Any number over 30 indicates a vulnerability to stress. You are seriously vulnerable if your score is between 50 and 75, extremely vulnerable if it is over 75.

FIGURE 15.1 **How Stressed Are You?**

What is the scope of health psychology and behavioral medicine?

Stress is inevitable in human lives, given the conflict between our needs and desires and the realities of our environment and relationships. Sometimes stress is useful, but extreme stress often leads to serious health problems, like Mort's. Thus human beings have long sought to understand what factors are involved in causing stress, in managing it effectively, and in maintaining a healthy lifestyle.

Asian physicians, around 2600 B.C., and Greek physicians, around 500 B.C., recognized that good habits are essential for good health. They did not blame the gods for illness and think that magic was a cure. They realized that people have some control over their health. The physician's role was as a guide, assisting the patient in restoring a natural and emotional balance. Except for these ancient Asian and Greek physicians, however, throughout most of history physical illness has been viewed purely in biological terms. That is, health has been thought to involve only bodily factors, not mental factors.

Today, we are returning to the ancient view that the ultimate responsibility for influencing health rests with the individuals themselves. In addition, the contemporary view is that body *and* mind can exert important influences on health, just as the ancient physicians believed. Indeed, a combination of biological, psychological, and social factors may be explored as possible causes of health or illness. The *biopsychosocial model* that we discussed in chapter 13 applies to health psychology as well.

Two relatively new fields of study—health psychology and behavioral medicine—reflect the belief that lifestyles and psychological states can play important roles in health. **Health psychology** emphasizes psychology's role in promoting and maintaining health and preventing and treating illness. **Behavioral medicine** is an interdisciplinary field that focuses on developing and integrating behavioral and biomedical knowledge to promote health and reduce illness. Behavioral medicine and health psychology are overlapping, and sometimes indistinguishable, fields. But, when distinctions are made, behavioral medicine is viewed as a broader field that focuses on both behavioral and biomedical factors, whereas health psychology tends to focus on cognitive and behavioral factors.

The interests of health psychologists and behavioral medicine researchers are broad (Baum, Revenson, & Singer, 2001; Boll & others, 2002; Nakao & others, 2001; Waldstein & others, 2001). They include examining how stress affects an individual's immune functioning, why we do or do not comply with medical advice, how effective media campaigns are in reducing smoking, what psychological factors play a part in losing weight, and how exercise helps in reducing stress (Wood, 2001).

Changing patterns of illness in developed countries have fueled the increased interest in health psychology and behavioral medicine. Just a century ago, the leading causes of death were infectious diseases such as influenza, tuberculosis, polio, typhoid fever, rubella, and smallpox. Today, none of these diseases are among the major causes of death in developed countries. Rather, 7 of the 10 leading causes of death in the United States today are related to personal habits and lifestyles. The major causes of death now are heart disease (36 percent), cancer (22 percent), and stroke (17 percent). Other chronic diseases such as diabetes are also major contributors to disability and death. Health behaviors often play key roles in these diseases, as they did in the heart attack suffered by Mort, the air traffic controller (Taylor, 2003).

Because of the increase in chronic disease, America's annual health care costs are soaring toward the $1 trillion mark. Health experts hope to make a dent in these costs by encouraging people to live healthier lives. Many corporations now recognize that health promotion for their employees is cost effective. They increasingly are creating smoke-free work environments, on-site exercise programs, bonuses for quitting smoking and losing weight, and company-sponsored athletic events.

(Top) Members of the Masai tribe in Kenya, Africa, can stay on a treadmill for a long time because of their active lives. Heart disease is extremely low in the Masai tribe, which also can be attributed to their energetic lifestyle. *(Bottom)* Americans are increasingly recognizing the health benefits of exercise and an active lifestyle. The role of exercise in health is one of health psychology's many interests.

health psychology Emphasizes psychology's role in promoting and maintaining health and in preventing and treating illness.

behavioral medicine An interdisciplinary field that focuses on developing and integrating behavioral and biomedical knowledge to promote health and reduce illness.

Health experts are also acknowledging that psychological and social factors are involved in many chronic diseases (Forshaw, 2002). In fact, the fields of health psychology and behavioral medicine evolved partly to examine these factors and to find ways to help people cope more effectively (Baum & Posluszny, 1999). One of the main areas of research in health psychology and behavioral medicine is the link between stress and illness (Dougall & Baum, 2001). Researchers are finding that our psychological and physical well-being are related to how much stress we face and how we cope with it. These topics are the focus of this chapter.

mhhe com/
santrockp7

For study tools related to this learning goal, see the Study Guide, the CD-ROM, and the Online Learning Center.

Review and Sharpen Your Thinking

1 *Describe the scope of health psychology and behavioral medicine.*

- Define health psychology and behavioral medicine and describe how they seek to promote health and reduce illness.

How high would you estimate your stress level to be? Do you think stress affects your health? What are the signs that it does?

2 STRESS AND ITS SOURCES

Personality Factors	**Environmental Factors**	**Sociocultural Factors**

What is stress and what are its sources?

According to the American Academy of Family Physicians, two-thirds of office visits to family doctors these days are for stress-related symptoms. Stress is believed to be a major contributor to coronary heart disease, cancer, lung problems, accidental injuries, cirrhosis of the liver, and suicide—six of the leading causes of death in the United States. Antianxiety drugs and ulcer medications are among the best-selling prescription drugs in the United States today.

Stress is a sign of the times. Everywhere you look, people are trying to reduce the effects of excessive tension by jogging, going to health clubs, and following special diets. Even corporations have developed elaborate stress management programs. No one really knows whether we experience more stress than our parents or grandparents did, but it seems as if we do.

Initially, the word *stress* was loosely borrowed from physics. Humans, it was thought, are in some ways similar to physical objects such as metals, which resist moderate outside forces but lose their resiliency under greater pressure. But, unlike metals, human beings can think and reason, and they experience a myriad of social and environmental circumstances that make defining stress more complex in psychology than in physics (Hobfoll, 1989). Thus, in psychological terms, we can define **stress** as the response of individuals to stressors, the circumstances and events that threaten them and tax their coping abilities.

To understand stress, we need to examine its sources. They include personality factors, environmental factors, and sociocultural factors.

Personality Factors

Do certain personality characteristics help people cope more effectively with stress and make them less vulnerable to illness? The answer to this question is yes and focuses on three aspects of personality that have been studied extensively in relation to stress: Type A/Type B behavior patterns, hardiness, and personal control.

"I think we can rule out stress."
© Sidney Harris.

stress The response of individuals to stressors, the circumstances and events that threaten and tax their coping abilities.

Type A/Type B Behavior Patterns In the late 1950s, a secretary for two California cardiologists, Meyer Friedman and Ray Rosenman, observed that the chairs in their waiting rooms were tattered and worn, but only on the front edges. The cardiologists had also noticed the impatience of their cardiac patients, who often arrived exactly on time for an appointment and were in a great hurry to leave. Intrigued by this consistency, they conducted a study of 3,000 healthy men between the ages of 35 and 59 over a period of 8 years to find out whether people with certain behavioral characteristics might be prone to heart problems (Friedman & Rosenman, 1974). During the 8 years, one group of men had twice as many heart attacks or other forms of heart disease as the other men. And autopsies of the men who died revealed that this same group had coronary arteries that were more obstructed than those of the other men.

Friedman and Rosenman described the common personality characteristics of the men who developed coronary disease as the **Type A behavior pattern.** They theorized that a cluster of characteristics—being excessively competitive, hard-driven, impatient, and hostile—is related to the incidence of heart disease. Rosenman and Friedman labeled the behavior of the healthier group, who were commonly relaxed and easygoing, the **Type B behavior pattern.**

Type **Z** behavior

Further research on the link between Type A behavior and coronary disease indicates that the association is not as strong as Friedman and Rosenman believed (Suls & Swain, 1998; Williams, 1995). However, researchers have found that certain components of Type A behavior are more precisely linked with coronary risk.

The Type A behavior component most consistently associated with coronary problems is hostility (Pickering, 2001; Markovitz, Jonas, & Davidson, 2001; Räikkönen & others, 1999). People who are hostile outwardly or who turn anger inward are more likely to develop heart disease than their less angry counterparts (Allan & Scheidt, 1996). Such people have been called "hot reactors" because of their intense physiological reactions to stress: Their hearts race, their breathing quickens, and their muscles tense up. Redford Williams (1995, 2001, 2002), a leading behavioral medicine researcher, believes that such people can reduce their risk for heart disease by learning to control their anger and developing more trust in others.

A hostile personality may also affect the course of such diseases as AIDS. One recent study of 140 HIV-positive individuals found that the immune systems of those with hostile personalities who confronted distressing events weakened more than the immune systems of their counterparts who did not have hostile personalities (Ironson, 2001). In another study, of 96 HIV-positive men who were assessed over a 9-year-period, those who experienced a lot of stress, had high levels of anger, and felt less satisfied with support from others developed AIDS most quickly (Lesserman & others, 2001).

Hardiness **Hardiness** is a personality style characterized by a sense of commitment (rather than alienation) and of control (rather than powerlessness) and a perception of problems as challenges (rather than threats). The links between hardiness, stress, and illness were the focus of the Chicago Stress Project (Kobasa, Maddi, & Kahn, 1982; Maddi, 1998). It studied male business managers 32 to 65 years of age over a 5-year period. During the 5 years, most of the managers experienced stressful events, such as divorce, job transfers, the death of a close friend, inferior performance evaluations at work, and working at a job with an unpleasant boss.

In one aspect of the Chicago study, managers who developed an illness (ranging from the flu to a heart attack) were compared with those who did not (Kobasa & others, 1982). Those who did not were likelier to have hardy personalities. In another

Type A behavior pattern A cluster of characteristics—being excessively competitive, hard-driven, and hostile—thought to be related to the incidence of heart disease.

Type B behavior pattern A relaxed and easygoing personality.

hardiness A personality style characterized by a sense of commitment (rather than alienation), control (rather than powerlessness), and a perception of problems as challenges (rather than threats).

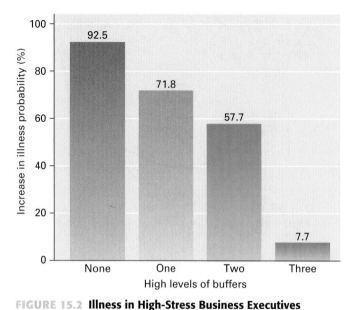

FIGURE 15.2 Illness in High-Stress Business Executives
In one study of high-stress business executives (all of whom were selected for this analysis because they were above the stress mean for the entire year of the study), a low level of all three buffers (hardiness, exercise, and social support) involved a high probability of at least one serious illness in that year. High levels of one, two, and all three buffers decreased the likelihood of at least one serious illness occurring in the year of the study.

aspect of the study, whether or not hardiness, along with exercise and social support, buffered stress and reduced illness in executives' lives was investigated (Kobasa & others, 1986). When all three factors were present in an executive's life, the level of illness dropped dramatically (see figure 15.2).

Other researchers also have found support for the role of hardiness in illness and health (Pengilly & Dowd, 2000; Waysman, Schwarzwald, & Solomon, 2001). The results of hardiness research suggest the power of multiple factors, rather than any single factor, in buffering stress and maintaining health (Maddi, 1998; Ouelette & DiPlacido, 2001).

Personal Control An important aspect of stress is the extent to which people can do something to control or reduce the stress, as well as their *perception* of a sense of control (Taylor, 2003; Thompson, 2001; Wallston, 2001). As discussed in chapter 13, perceived lack of control in the face of stress can produce learned helplessness (Seligman, 1975), which can lead to depression.

In contrast, having a general sense of control reduces stress and can lead to the development of problem-solving strategies to cope with the stress. A person with a good sense of personal control might say, "If I stop smoking now, I will not develop lung cancer," or "If I exercise regularly, I won't develop cardiovascular disease."

A sense of control is important for people experiencing stressful events (Taylor, 1999). It may be especially important for people who are vulnerable to health problems, such as medical patients (including people with cancer), children, and older adults. You might recall, from chapter 4, the study by Judith Rodin and Ellen Langer (1977), in which a group of elderly nursing home residents were given greater control over their environment. Not only was their overall health better than the health of their counterparts who remained dependent on nursing home staff, but the more independent residents were also less likely to die within the 18-month time frame of the study.

A sense of personal control may also help people avoid a risky lifestyle that involves health-compromising behaviors. Consider a study of East German migrants to West Germany who found themselves unemployed (Mittag & Schwarzer, 1993). They often turned to heavy drinking for solace unless they had a sense of personal control (as measured by such survey items as, "When I'm in trouble, I can rely on my ability to deal with the problem effectively"). Across a wide range of studies, a sense of personal control over the stressful events that go on around people has been related to emotional well-being, successful coping with a stressful event, behavior change that can promote good health, and good health (Decruyenaere & others, 2000; Pickering, 2001; Taylor, 1999; Thompson & Spacapan, 1991).

Environmental Factors

Many circumstances, large and small, can produce stress in our lives. In some instances, cataclysmic events, such as war, an automobile accident, a fire, or the death of a loved one, produce stress. But often the everyday pounding of being overloaded with work, dealing with a difficult situation, or being frustrated in an unhappy relationship produces stress.

Life Events and Daily Hassles Think about your own life. What events have created the most stress for you? Were they big problems like a change in financial status, getting fired, a divorce, the death of someone you loved, a personal injury? Or were they the everyday circumstances of your life, such as not having enough time

The events listed below commonly occur in the lives of college students. Check the space provided for the events that have occurred in your life during the past 12 months. When you have checked off all the events that have happened in the past 12 months, total the point values in parentheses for each checked item.

(100)	_____ Death of a close family member	(25)	_____ Problems with your boss or professor
(80)	_____ Jail term	(25)	_____ Outstanding personal achievement
(63)	_____ Final year or first year in college	(25)	_____ Failure in some course
(60)	_____ Pregnancy (yours or caused by you)	(20)	_____ Final exams
(53)	_____ Severe personal illness or injury	(20)	_____ Increased or decreased dating
(50)	_____ Marriage	(20)	_____ Change in working conditions
(45)	_____ Any interpersonal problems	(20)	_____ Change in your major
(40)	_____ Financial difficulties	(18)	_____ Change in your sleeping habits
(40)	_____ Death of a close friend	(15)	_____ Several-day vacation
(40)	_____ Arguments with your roommate (more than every other day)	(15)	_____ Change in eating habits
(40)	_____ Major disagreements with your family	(15)	_____ Family reunion
(30)	_____ Major change in personal habits	(15)	_____ Change in recreational activities
(30)	_____ Change of living environment	(15)	_____ Minor illness or injury
(30)	_____ Beginning or ending a job	(11)	_____ Minor violations of the law

Total Life Events Score _____

Your total may predict the frequency of serious illness you will experience in the coming year. If your life events score totals 300 points or more, you have an 80 percent chance of having a significant illness in the coming year. If your total score is 299 to 150, you have a 50 percent chance of having a significant illness. If your total score is 149 points or less, your risk of significant illness decreases to 30 percent.

Keep in mind, in interpreting your life events total score, that such events checklists don't take into account how you cope with such events. Some people who experience stressful life events cope and adjust well to them, and others do not.

FIGURE 15.3 **Impact of Life Events: Social Readjustment Scale**

to study, arguing with your girlfriend or boyfriend, not getting enough credit for the work you do at your job?

Some health psychologists have proposed that significant life events are the main environmental source of stress. Some of them have studied the effects of individual life events, such as a tornado or volcanic eruption; others have evaluated the effects of *clusters* of events. Thomas Holmes and Richard Rahe (1967) devised a scale to measure the possible cumulative effect of clusters of life events and their possible influence on illness. Their widely used Social Readjustment Rating Scale includes events ranging from the death of a spouse (100 stress points) to minor violations of the law (11 stress points). Figure 15.3 provides an opportunity for you to evaluate the stressfulness of life events you have experienced in the past year.

People who experience clusters of stressful life events are likelier to become ill than they normally would be (Maddi, 1996). However, the ability to predict illness from life events alone is modest. Total scores of life-events scales such as the Social Readjustment Rating Scale are frequently ineffective at predicting future health problems. A life-events checklist tells us nothing about a person's physiological makeup, constitutional strengths and weaknesses, ability to cope with stressful circumstances, support systems, or the nature of the social relationships involved—all of which are important in understanding how stress is related to illness. A divorce, for example, might be less stressful than a marriage filled with day-to-day tension. And the changes related to positive events in the Social Readjustment Scale, such as reconciling with a spouse and gaining a new family member, are not as difficult to cope with as the changes that result from negative events.

Because of these limitations, some health psychologists believe information about daily hassles and daily uplifts provide better clues than life events about the effects of stress (Crowther & others, 2001; DaCosta & others, 2000; Pillow, Zautra, & Sandler, 1996). Enduring a boring and tense job and living in poverty do not show up on scales of major life events. Yet the everyday tension involved in these living conditions creates a highly stressful life and, in some cases, psychological disorder or illness. In one study, people who experienced the most daily hassles had the most negative self-images (Tolan, Miller, & Thomas, 1988).

What are the biggest hassles for college students? One study showed that the most frequent daily hassles of college students were wasting time, being lonely, and worrying about meeting high achievement standards (Kanner & others, 1981). In fact, the fear of failing in our success-oriented world often plays a role in college students' depression. College students also found that the small things in life—having fun, laughing, going to movies, getting along well with friends, and completing a task—were their main sources of daily uplifts.

Critics of the daily-hassles approach argue that it faces some of the same problems as life-events scales (Dohrenwend & Shrout, 1985). For example, knowing about a person's daily irritations and problems tell us nothing about her or his physiological resilience to stress, coping ability or strategies, or perceptions of stress. Further, the daily-hassles and -uplifts scale has not been consistently related to objective measures of health and illness. Yet another criticism is that daily hassles can be conceived of as dependent measures rather than as causes. People who complain about things, who report being anxious and unhappy, and who see the bad side of everything are likely to see more problems in their daily lives than are people with an optimistic outlook. From this perspective, problems do not predict bad moods; bad moods predict problems. But supporters of the daily-hassles and -uplifts concept reply that information about daily events can be used in concert with information about a person's physiological reactions, coping, and perceptions of stress to provide a more complete picture of the causes and consequences of stress.

Conflict Stress researchers who are interested in the effects of daily environmental experiences have studied a number of specific types of environmental stimuli. One such stimulus is conflict, which occurs when we must decide between two or more incompatible options. There are three major types of conflict, which were initially investigated by Neal Miller (1959):

- **Approach/approach conflict:** Conflict in which the individual must choose between two attractive stimuli or circumstances. Should you go out with the attractive music lover or with the attractive sports lover? Do you buy a Corvette or a Porsche? The approach/approach conflict is the least stressful of the three types of conflict because either choice leads to a positive result.

- **Avoidance/avoidance conflict:** Conflict in which the individual must choose between two unattractive stimuli or circumstances. Do you go through the stress of giving an oral presentation in class or not show up and get a zero? You want to avoid both, but you must choose one or the other. Obviously, this conflict is more stressful than having the luxury of having two enticing choices. In many instances, we delay our decision about the avoidance/avoidance conflict until the last possible moment.

- **Approach/avoidance conflict:** Conflict involving a single stimulus or circumstance that has both positive and negative characteristics. Let's say you really like the person you are going with and are thinking about getting married. On the one hand, you are attracted by the steady affection and love that marriage might bring, but, on the other hand, marriage is a commitment you might not feel ready to make. On a more mundane level, you might look at a menu and face a dilemma—the double chocolate delight would be sumptuous, but is it worth the extra pound of weight? Our world is full of approach/avoidance conflicts, and they can be highly stressful. In these circumstances, we often vacillate before deciding.

Overload Daily hassles can also result in a stress reaction called *overload*. Sometimes stimuli become so intense that we can no longer cope with them. For example, persistent high levels of noise overload our adaptability to other stimuli.

approach/approach conflict A conflict in which the individual must choose between two attractive stimuli or circumstances.

avoidance/avoidance conflict A conflict in which the individual must choose between two unattractive stimuli or circumstances.

approach/avoidance conflict A conflict involving a single stimulus or circumstance that has both positive and negative characteristics.

Overload can occur with work as well. How often have you said to yourself, "There are not enough hours in the day to do all I have to do." In today's computer age, we are especially faced with information overload. It is easy to develop the uncomfortable feeling that we don't know as much about a topic as we should, even if we are a so-called expert.

Overload can lead to a state of physical and emotional exhaustion that includes a hopeless feeling, chronic fatigue, and low energy (Leiter & Maslach, 2001). **Burnout** usually occurs not because of one or two traumatic events but because of a gradual accumulation of everyday stresses (Demerouti & others, 2001; Leiter & Maslach, 1998). Burnout is likeliest to occur among individuals who deal with others in highly emotional situations (such as nurses and social workers) but who have only limited control over the behavior of their clients or patients or the results of the cases they handle (Alexander & Klein, 2001; DiGiacomo & Adamson, 2001).

Burnout affects a quarter of the students at some colleges. On a number of college campuses it is the most frequent reason students leave school before earning their degrees. Dropping out of college for a term or two used to be considered a sign of weakness. Now it is more accepted, and counselors may actually encourage some students who feel overwhelmed with stress to take a break from college. Before recommending "stopping out," though, most counselors first suggest that the student examine ways to reduce overload and explore possible coping strategies that would allow the student to remain in school. The simple strategy of taking a reduced or better balanced course load sometimes works, for example. Most college counseling services have professionals who can effectively work with students to alleviate the sense of being overloaded and overwhelmed by life.

Work-Related Stress American workers are working harder and longer than they have in past decades just to maintain their standard of living. In one generation, the number of hours Americans work each week has increased by 8 percent to a current average of 47. Twenty percent of Americans are working 49 hours or more per week (National Institute for Occupational Safety and Health [NIOSH], 2001). The predictable result is greater work-related stress and increased risk for psychological and physical health problems (McGuire, 1999; Nelson, Quick, & Simmons, 2001). Researchers have found that one-fourth to one-third of American workers have high job stress and are emotionally drained at the end of a work day (NIOSH, 2001). American workers' stress levels have also increased because economic dips and downsizing trends among corporations have made their jobs less secure.

The stress level of workers also increases when their jobs do not meet their expectations (Rabasca, 1999). When employees find their work personally rewarding, they are better able to handle the stress of the workplace. Americans want jobs that are secure, offer advancement, provide them with some control over the work they do, offer a sense of community among co-workers, and allow them to use their creative and problem-solving skills. However, many jobs do not match these expectations.

Earlier in the chapter, we indicated that perceptions of personal control influence stress. Work-related stress usually increases when job demands are high and the individual has little choice in deciding how to meet the demands (low autonomy, high external control). In one study of Swedish workers, men who held jobs that were demanding and low in autonomy reported high levels of exhaustion, depression, and insomnia, tranquilizer and sleeping pill use, and sick leave (Karacek, 1979).

In a more recent study, a combination of personal and job factors placed individuals at risk for getting sick (Schaubroeck, Jones, & Xie, 2001). Employees who perceived they had control over their job responsibilities but did not have confidence in their problem-solving abilities or who blamed themselves for bad outcomes were the likeliest to experience stress. These types of job situations placed these employees at risk for getting infections.

What creates stress for workers?

burnout A feeling of overload, including mental and physical exhaustion, that usually results from a gradual accumulation of everyday stresses.

This Chinese American family association has helped its members cope with acculturative stress. *What are some strategies for coping with acculturative stress?*

Recall from the beginning of the chapter that Mort, the air traffic controller, often took the stress of his job home with him. Psychologists and policy makers worry that work-related stress can carry over to influence well-being in other areas of a person's life, especially the family (European Agency for Safety and Health at Work, 2000). In one survey, 56 percent of workers said that they felt "some" or "a great deal" of interference between their jobs and their home lives (Canadian Mental Health Association, 1984). The interference affected family routines and events, child-rearing and household responsibilities, leisure activities, and social life.

Sociocultural Factors

The personality and environmental factors described so far are not the only sources of stress. Sociocultural factors help to determine which stressors individuals are likely to encounter, whether they are likely to perceive events as stressful or not, and how they believe stressors should be confronted (Kawachi & Kennedy, 2001). Sociocultural factors involved in stress include conflict between cultures and poverty.

Acculturative Stress Moving to a new place is a stressful experience in the best of circumstances. It is even more stressful when a person from one culture moves into a different culture. **Acculturative stress** refers to the negative consequences that result from contact between two distinctive cultural groups. Many individuals who have immigrated to the United States have experienced acculturative stress (Hovey, 2000; Uppaluri, Schumm, & Lauderdale, 2001).

South Florida middle school teacher Daniel Arnoux (1998) learned firsthand about acculturative stress when he called out a student's name in his class and asked her if she was Haitian. She was so embarrassed by his question that she slid under her seat and disappeared from his view. Later she told him, "You are not supposed to say you are Haitian around here!" That is when Arnoux realized how stressful school could be for many immigrant students, some of whom were beaten and harassed for being Haitian. He began developing lessons to help students gain empathy and tolerance for individuals from different ethnic and cultural backgrounds.

Canadian cross-cultural psychologist John Berry (1980) believes that when people like the young middle school girl experience cultural change, they can adapt in one of four main ways:

acculturative stress The negative consequences that result from contact between two distinctive cultural groups.

Vonnie McLoyd (*right*) has conducted a number of important investigations of the roles of poverty, ethnicity, and unemployment in children's and adolescents' development. She has found that economic stressors often diminish children's and adolescents' belief in the utility of education and their achievement strivings.

- *Assimilation* occurs when individuals relinquish their native cultural identity and adopt an identity that helps them blend into the larger society. If enough individuals follow this path, the nondominant group is absorbed into the established, mainstream society. Sometimes assimilation occurs when many groups merge to form a new society (what is often called a "melting pot").
- *Integration* implies that people move into the larger culture but, in contrast to assimilation, maintain many aspects of their distinctive cultural identity. In this circumstance, a number of ethnic groups all cooperate within a large social system (a "mosaic").
- *Separation* refers to self-imposed withdrawal from the larger culture. If imposed by the larger society, however, separation becomes *segregation*. People might maintain their traditional way of life because they desire an independent existence (as in separatist movements), or the dominant culture may exercise its power to exclude the other culture (as in slavery and apartheid).
- *Marginalization* refers to the process by which nondominant groups lose cultural and social contact with both their traditional society and the larger, dominant society. This option involves considerable confusion and anxiety because the essential features of one's culture are lost, but they are not replaced by those of the larger society. Thus marginalization involves feelings of alienation and a loss of identity. Marginalization does not mean that a group has no culture but does indicate that the culture may be disorganized and unsupportive of the acculturating individual.

As you can see, separation and marginalization, especially, are the least adaptive responses to acculturation. Although separation can have benefits under certain circumstances, it may be especially stressful for individuals who seek separation while most members of their group seek assimilation. Integration and assimilation are healthier adaptations to acculturative pressures. But assimilation means some cultural loss, so it may be more stressful than integration. For the most part, the person who can pick and choose the most useful features of the two cultural systems may cope best with the stresses of acculturation.

Poverty   Poverty can cause considerable stress for individuals and families (Landrine & Klonoff, 2001; McLoyd, 2000). Chronic conditions such as inadequate housing, dangerous neighborhoods, burdensome responsibilities, and economic uncertainties are potent stressors in the lives of the poor (Adler, 2001).

Ethnic-minority families are disproportionately among the poor, as are female-headed families. For example, Puerto Rican families headed by women are 15 times likelier to live in poverty than are families headed by White men, and families headed by African American women are 10 times likelier to live in poverty than are families headed by White men (National Advisory Council on Economic Opportunity, 1980). Many people who become poor during their lives remain so for only 1 or 2 years. However, African Americans and female heads of household are especially at risk for persistent poverty.

Poverty is also related to threatening and uncontrollable life events (Russo, 1990). For example, women living in poverty are likelier to experience crime and violence than are women with higher incomes. And poverty undermines sources of social support that help to buffer the effects of stress. Poverty is related to marital unhappiness and to having spouses who are unlikely to serve as confidants (Brown, Bhrolchain, & Harris, 1975). Further, poverty means having to depend on many overburdened and unresponsive bureaucratic systems for financial, housing, and health assistance, which may contribute to a poor person's perception of powerlessness—itself a factor in stress.

For study tools related to this learning goal, see the Study Guide, the CD-ROM, and the Online Learning Center.

Review and Sharpen Your Thinking

2 *Define stress and identify its sources.*

- Define stress.
- Explain the role of personality factors in stress.
- Identify environmental factors in stress.
- Evaluate the effects of sociocultural factors on stress.

What are the main sources of stress in your life? Would you classify them as personality factors, environmental factors, or sociocultural factors?

3 STRESS RESPONSES

General Adaptation Syndrome	Fight or Flight, Tend and Befriend	Cognitive Appraisal

How do people respond to stress?

When we experience stress, we may respond physiologically and cognitively. Physiological responses to stress are discussed first.

General Adaptation Syndrome

When we experience stress, our body readies itself to handle the assault of stress; a number of physiological changes take place. Those changes were the main interest of Hans Selye (1974, 1983), the Austrian-born founder of stress research. He defined stress as the wear and tear on the body due to the demands placed on it. After observing patients with different problems—the death of someone close, loss of income, arrest for embezzlement—Selye concluded that any number of environmental events or stimuli will produce the same stress response. Regardless of which problem the patient had, similar symptoms appeared: loss of appetite, muscular weakness, and decreased interest in the world.

General adaptation syndrome (GAS) is Selye's term for the common effects on the body when demands are placed on it. The GAS consists of three stages: alarm, resistance, and exhaustion (see figure 15.4). Selye's model is especially useful in helping us understand the link between stress and health.

general adaptation syndrome (GAS) Selye's term for the common effects on the body when demands are placed on it. The GAS consists of three stages: alarm, resistance, and exhaustion.

Alarm The body's first reaction to a stressor, in the *alarm stage*, is a temporary state of shock, a time at which resistance to illness and stress falls below normal limits. In trying to cope with the initial effects of stress, the body quickly releases hormones that, in a short time, adversely affect the immune system's functioning. It is during this time that the individual is prone to infections from illness and injury. Fortunately, the alarm stage passes rather quickly.

Scientists today are zeroing in on some more precise descriptions of the biological changes in the stress-body linkage that takes place during the alarm stage. Many scientists now agree that two main biological pathways between the brain and the endocrine system respond to stress (Anderson, 1998, 2000; Anderson, Kiecolt-Glaser, & Glaser, 1994; Sternberg & Gold, 1996): the neuroendocrine-immune pathway and the sympathetic nervous system pathway (see figure 15.5).

As shown in figure 15.5, the neuroendocrine-immune pathway (pathway 1) goes through the hypothalamus and pituitary gland to the adrenal glands, from which cortisol is released. Cortisol is a steroid that is good for the body over the short term because it causes cellular fuel—glucose—to move to muscles. But over the long term, high levels of cortisol can be bad for the body, suppressing the immune system and straining the brain's cellular functioning. Too much cortisol also increases appetite and can cause weight gain.

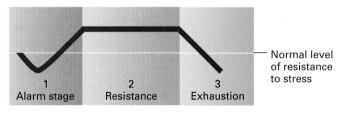

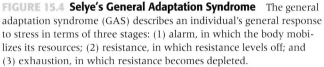

FIGURE 15.4 Selye's General Adaptation Syndrome The general adaptation syndrome (GAS) describes an individual's general response to stress in terms of three stages: (1) alarm, in which the body mobilizes its resources; (2) resistance, in which resistance levels off; and (3) exhaustion, in which resistance becomes depleted.

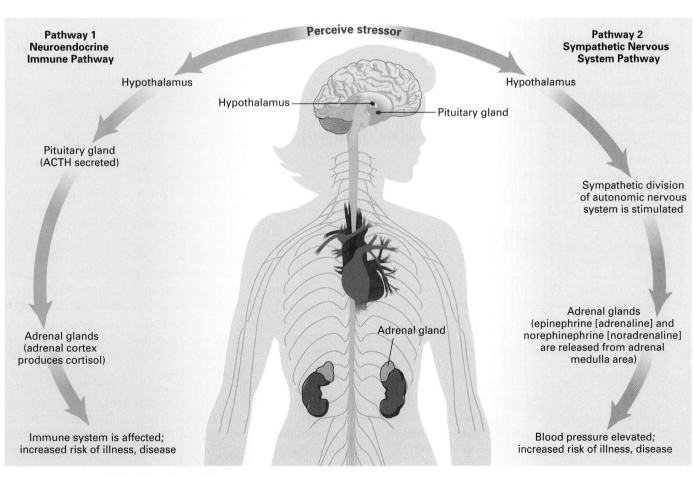

FIGURE 15.5 Two Biological Pathways in Stress

Shelly Taylor (2003), a leading expert in health psychology, believes that recent trends in medicine, psychology, and health care have combined to make health psychology an important area of psychology. These trends include the rise of chronic or lifestyle-related illnesses, the expanding role of health care in the economy, the realization that psychological and social factors are often important factors in health and illness, and the demonstrated importance of psychological interventions in improving people's health care. Taylor and her colleagues developed the tend-and-befriend model or reinterpretation of fight or flight that takes into account the motivation of females in threatening contexts.

Health psychologists such as Shelly Taylor usually have a doctoral degree in psychology. At the graduate level, many doctoral programs in clinical, counseling, social, or experimental psychology have a specialized track in some area of health psychology.

In the sympathetic nervous pathway (pathway 2), the route is through the hypothalamus and then the sympathetic nervous system (rather than the pituitary gland). When the signal reaches the adrenal glands, epinephrine and norepinephrine (but not cortisol) are released. Recall, from chapter 11, that the sympathetic nervous system is the subsystem of the autonomic nervous system that is responsible for the body's arousal. It produces a quick response to a stressor (often referred to as the "fight-or-flight" response). The release of the hormones epinephrine and norepinephrine causes a number of physiological changes, including elevation of blood pressure. Over time, high blood pressure can lead to increased risk of illness and disease, such as cardiovascular disease.

Resistance   In the *resistance stage* of Selye's general adaptation syndrome, a number of glands throughout the body begin to manufacture different hormones that protect the individual in many ways. Endocrine and sympathetic nervous system activity are not as high as in the alarm stage, although they still are elevated.

During the resistance stage, the body's immune system can fight off infection with remarkable efficiency. Similarly, hormones that reduce the inflammation normally associated with injury circulate at high levels.

Exhaustion   If the body's all-out effort to combat stress fails and the stress persists, the individual moves into the *exhaustion stage*. At this point, the wear and tear on the body takes its toll—the person might collapse in a state of exhaustion, and vulnerability to disease increases. Mort, the air traffic controller introduced at the beginning of the chapter, had reached this point in life. He was so overwhelmed with stress that his body broke down and he had a heart attack. Some type of serious, possibly irreversible damage to the body, or even death, may occur in the exhaustion stage.

One of the main criticisms of Selye's general adaptation syndrome is that human beings do not always react to stress in the uniform way he proposed (Seffge-Krenke, 1995). There is more to understanding stress in humans than knowing their physical reactions to it. We also need to know about their personalities, their physical makeup, their perceptions, and the contexts in which the stressors occurred.

Fight or Flight, Tend and Befriend

Selye's concept of alarm reaction—the first stage of the general adaptation syndrome—is essentially the same as the fight-or-flight response. The central notion of both concepts is that the body's physiological resources are mobilized quickly to prepare the organism to deal with threats to survival.

The fight-or-flight response was first observed by Walter Cannon (1929) when he studied the reaction of cats suddenly confronted by a dog. Cannon noted that the cats experienced such changes as more rapid blood circulation, muscular tension, and heavy breathing. He concluded that these changes were adaptive in preparing the organisms for survival. He called the entire reaction "fight or flight" because it prepared the animals for engaging in one of these two behaviors when confronted with a threatening situation.

Today, threats to survival are not the only situations that generate the fight-or-flight response. Virtually any threat to personally important motives that taxes an individual's coping abilities might trigger this response.

Recently, Shelley Taylor and her colleagues (2000) proposed that females are less likely to respond to stressful and threatening situations with a fight-or-flight response than males are. They argue that females are likelier to "tend and befriend." That is, females often respond to stressful situations by protecting themselves and their young through nurturing behaviors (the *tend* part of the model) and forming alliances with a larger social group, especially one populated by other women (the *befriend* part of the model).

Although females do show the same immediate hormonal and sympathetic nervous system response to acute stress that males do, other factors can intervene and make the fight-or-flight response less likely in females. In terms of the fight response, male aggression is regulated by androgen hormones, such as testosterone, and is linked to sympathetic nervous system reactivity and hostility. In contrast, female aggression appears to be more cerebral in nature, moderated more by social circumstances, learning, culture, and the situation. In terms of the flight response, fleeing too quickly at the first sign of danger can place offspring at risk and reduce reproductive success, which was a poor choice evolutionarily, especially for females.

Cognitive Appraisal

Most of us think of stressors as environmental events that place demands on our lives, such as losing one's notes from a class, being yelled at by a friend, failing a test, or being in a car wreck. But, although our bodies may have a similar response to stressors, not everyone perceives the same events as stressful. For example, one person may perceive an upcoming job interview as threatening, whereas another person may perceive it as merely challenging. One person may perceive a D on a paper as threatening; another person may perceive the same grade as an incentive to work harder. To some degree, then, what is stressful depends on how people cognitively appraise and interpret events. This view has been most clearly presented by Richard Lazarus (1993, 2000). **Cognitive appraisal** is Lazarus' term for individuals' interpretation of the events in their lives as harmful, threatening, or challenging and their determination of whether they have the resources to effectively cope with the events.

In Lazarus' view, events are appraised in two steps: primary appraisal and secondary appraisal (see figure 15.6). In *primary appraisal,* individuals interpret whether an event involves *harm* or loss that has already occurred, a *threat* of some future danger, or a *challenge* to be overcome. Lazarus believes that perceiving a stressor as a challenge to be overcome, rather than as a threat, is a good strategy for reducing stress. This strategy fits with the concept of hardiness, a personality factor involved in stress, discussed earlier.

To understand Lazarus' concept of primary appraisal, consider two students, each of whom has a failing grade in their psychology class at midterm. Student A is almost frozen by the stress of the low grade and looks at the rest of the term as a threatening circumstance. In contrast, student B does not become overwhelmed by the harm already done and the threat of future failures. She looks at the low grade as a challenge that she can address and overcome.

In *secondary appraisal,* individuals evaluate their resources and determine how effectively they can be used to cope with the event. This appraisal is *secondary* because it both comes after primary appraisal and depends on the degree to which the event was appraised as harmful, threatening, or challenging. For example, student A might have some helpful resources for coping with her low midterm grade, but she views the stressful circumstance as so harmful and threatening that she doesn't use her resources. Student B would instead evaluate the resources she can call on to improve her grade during the second half of the term. These include asking the instructor for suggestions about how to study better for the tests in the course, setting up a time management program to include more study hours, and asking several students who are doing well in the class about their strategies.

In many instances, viewing stress as a challenge during primary appraisal paves the way for finding effective coping resources during secondary appraisal. However, sometimes people do not have adequate resources for coping with an event they have defined as a challenge. For example, if student B is extremely shy, she might lack the courage and skills to talk to the instructor or to ask several students in the class about their strategies for doing well in the course.

Step 1:
Primary Appraisal
Do I perceive the event as
(a) harmful?
(b) threatening?
(c) challenging?

Step 2:
Secondary Appraisal
What coping resources do I have available?

FIGURE 15.6 Lazarus' Cognitive Appraisal View of Stress
Perceiving a stressor as harmful and/or threatening in step 1 and having few or no coping resources available in step 2 yields high stress. Perceiving a stressor as challenging in step 1 and having good coping resources available in step 2 reduces stress.

cognitive appraisal Lazarus' term for individuals' interpretation of events in their lives as threatening, harmful, or challenging and their determination of whether they have the resources to effectively cope with the events.

mhhe.com/
santrockp7

*For study tools related to this learning
goal, see the Study Guide, the CD-ROM,
and the Online Learning Center.*

Review and Sharpen Your Thinking

3 *Explain how people respond to stress.*

- Describe the general adaptation syndrome.
- Discuss the differences between the fight-or-flight response and the tend-and-befriend response.
- Explain the nature of cognitive appraisal.

How do your body and mind react when you face a stressful experience?

4 STRESS AND ILLNESS

- **Stress and the Immune System**
- **Stress and Cardiovascular Disease**
- **Stress and Cancer**
- **Positive Emotions, Illness, and Health**

How are stress and illness linked?

It has already been mentioned several times that stress makes the body more vulnerable to illness. This section examines what research has revealed about links between stress and specific types of illness. In particular, stress has been identified as a factor in weakened immune systems, cardiovascular disease, and cancer. The good news, which is also discussed, is that positive emotions have been shown to help in staving off illness and maintaining health.

Stress and the Immune System

Currently, researchers have considerable interest in links between the immune system and stress (Herberman, 2002; Kiecolt-Glaser & others, 2002a, 2002b; Marsland & others, 2001). Their theory and research have spawned a new field of scientific inquiry, **psychoneuroimmunology,** which explores connections among psychological factors (such as attitudes and emotions), the nervous system, and the immune system (Ader, 2000).

The immune system keeps us healthy by recognizing foreign materials such as bacteria, viruses, and tumors and then destroying them. Its machinery consists of billions of white blood cells located in the lymph system. The number of white blood cells and their effectiveness in killing foreign viruses or bacteria are related to stress levels. When a person is in the alarm or exhaustion stage, for example, the immune system functions poorly. During these stages, viruses and bacteria are likelier to multiply and cause disease.

The immune system and the central nervous system at first glance appear to be organized in different ways. The brain is usually regarded as a command center for the nervous system, sending and receiving electronic signals along fixed pathways, much like a telephone network. In contrast, the immune system is decentralized, with its organs (spleen, lymph nodes, thymus, and bone marrow) located throughout the body. The classical view is that the immune system communicates by releasing immune cells into the bloodstream, in which they float to new locations to deliver their messages.

However, scientists increasingly are recognizing that the central nervous system and immune system are in fact more similar than different in their modes of receiving,

psychoneuroimmunology The field that explores connections among psychological factors (such as attitudes and emotions), the nervous system, and the immune system.

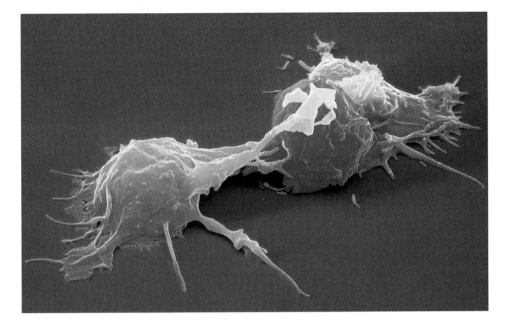

FIGURE 15.7 NK Cells and Cancer
Two natural killer (NK) cells (*yellow*) are shown attacking a leukemia cell (*red*). Notice the blisters that the leukemia cell developed to defend itself. Nonetheless, the NK cells are surrounding the leukemia cell and are about to destroy it.

recognizing, and integrating signals from the external environment (Sternberg & Gold, 1996). The central nervous system and the immune system both possess "sensory" elements, which receive information from the environment and other parts of the body, and "motor" elements, which carry out an appropriate response. Both systems also rely on chemical mediators for communication. A key hormone shared by the central nervous system and the immune system is corticotropin-releasing hormone (CRH), which is produced in the hypothalamus and unites the stress and immune responses.

Three lines of research provide support for the conclusion that the immune system and stress are linked (Anderson, 1998, 2000; Anderson, Golden-Kreutz, & DiLillo, 2001; Kiecolt-Glaser & others, 2002a, 2002b). This is what researchers have found:

- Acute stressors (sudden, one-time life events or stimuli) can produce immunological changes. For example, in relatively healthy HIV-infected individuals, as well as in individuals with cancer, acute stressors are associated with poorer immune system functioning (Roberts, Anderson, & Lubaroff, 1994).
- Chronic stressors (those that are long lasting) are associated with an increasing downturn in immune system responsiveness, rather than adaptation (Irwin, 2002; Kiecolt-Glaser & others, 2002a, 2002b). This effect has been documented in a number of circumstances that include living next to a damaged nuclear reactor, failures in close relationships (divorce, separation, and marital distress), and burdensome caregiving for a family member with progressive illness (Kiecolt-Glaser & others, 1991).
- Positive social circumstances and low stress are associated with increased ability to fight cancer. For example, having good social relationships and support is often linked with higher NK-cell levels (*NK* stands for "natural killer"), whereas a high degree of stress is often related to lower NK-cell levels (Levy & others, 1990). NK cells can attack tumor cells (see figure 15.7).

Psychoneuroimmunology is relatively young. Much of what we know needs to be clarified, explained, and verified further. Researchers hope to clarify the precise links among psychological factors, the brain, and the immune system (Redd, 1995). Some preliminary hypotheses about the interaction that causes vulnerability to disease include the following: (1) Stressful experiences lower the efficiency of immune systems, making individuals more susceptible to disease; (2) stress directly promotes disease-producing processes; and (3) stressful experiences may cause the activation of dormant viruses that diminish the individual's ability to cope with disease. These hypotheses may lead to clues for more successful treatments for some of the most baffling diseases—cancer and AIDS among them (Servaes & others, 1999).

In an example of research on psychoneuroimmunology conducted by Sheldon Cohen and his colleagues (1998), adults who faced interpersonal or work-related stress for at least 1 month were likelier than people who were less stressed to catch a cold after exposure to viruses. In the study, 276 adults were exposed to viruses, then quarantined for 5 days. The longer people had experienced major stress, the likelier they were to catch a cold. Individuals who reported high stress for the preceding 2 years tripled their risk of catching a cold. Those who experienced work-related stress for 1 month or longer were nearly five times likelier to develop colds than individuals without chronic stress. Those who experienced interpersonal stress for 1 month or more were twice as likely to catch a cold. Cohen concluded that stress-triggered changes in the immune system and hormones might create greater vulnerability to infection. The findings suggest that when we know we are under stress, we need to take better care of ourselves than usual, although often we do just the opposite (Cohen, 2002; Cohen, Miller, & Rabin, 2001). Cohen and his colleagues (1997) also found that positive social ties with friends and family provide a protective buffer that helps to prevent people from catching a cold when they are exposed to cold viruses.

Stress and Cardiovascular Disease

You may have heard someone say something like "It's no wonder she died of a heart attack with all of the stress he put her through." But is it true that emotional stress can cause a person to have a heart attack? A clear link has not been found, but there is evidence that chronic emotional stress is associated with high blood pressure, heart disease, and early death (Rozanski, Blumenthal, & Kaplan, 1999). Apparently, the surge in adrenaline caused by severe emotional stress causes the blood to clot more rapidly, and blood clotting is a major factor in heart attacks (Fogoros, 2001).

In one recent study of 103 couples, each with one mildly hypertensive (high blood pressure) spouse, the researchers found that a happy marriage was linked with lower blood pressure and an unhappy marriage was related to higher blood pressure (Baker, 2001). Over the 3-year time frame of the study, the blood pressure of the mildly hypertensive spouse in a happy marriage fell by 6 points on average, whereas the blood pressure of the mildly hypertensive spouse in an unhappy marriage rose by 6 points on average.

Emotional stress can contribute to cardiovascular disease in several other ways (Fogoros, 2001). For instance, people who have had major life changes (loss of a spouse or other close relative, loss of a job) have a higher incidence of cardiovascular disease and early death (Taylor, 1999). And, as discussed earlier in the chapter, people who are quick to anger or who display frequent hostility have an increased risk of cardiovascular disease (Williams, 2001).

The body's internal reactions to stress are not the only risk. People who live in a chronically stressed condition are likelier to take up smoking, start overeating, and avoid exercising. All of these stress-related behaviors are linked with the development of cardiovascular disease (Schneiderman & others, 2001).

Stress and Cancer

In addition to finding that stress is linked to immune system weaknesses and cardiovascular disease, researchers have found links between stress and cancer. Barbara Anderson (2000; Anderson & others, 2001) believes that the link between stress and cancer can best be understood by examining three factors:

- *Quality of life.* Although negative life events, such as finding out that one has cancer, do not always produce stress and lowered quality of life, a number of studies have documented acute stress at the time cancer is diagnosed (McKenna & others, 1999). Lengthy cancer treatments and the disruptions the disease creates in family, social, economic, and/or occupational functioning can cause chronic stress. As has been shown, these stressors can suppress the body's ability to fight off many types of disease, including cancer.

- *Behavioral factors.* An increase in negative health behaviors and/or a decrease in positive health behaviors can accompany cancer. For instance, in terms of negative health behaviors, individuals with cancer may become depressed or anxious and more likely to medicate with alcohol and other drugs. Also, individuals who are stressed by cancer may not begin or may abandon their previous positive health behaviors, such as participating in regular exercise. These health factors may in turn affect immunity. For example, substance abuse directly suppresses immunity and is associated with poor nutrition, which indirectly affects health (Anderson, 2000). Also, there is growing evidence that positive health behaviors such as exercise can have positive effects on both the immune and endocrine systems, even among individuals with chronic diseases (Phaneuf & Leeuwenburgh, 2001).

- *Biological pathways.* Stress sets in motion biological changes involving the autonomic, endocrine, and immune systems, as you already have seen. If the immune system is not compromised, it appears to help provide resistance to cancer and slow its progression (Anderson, 2000). But researchers have found that the physiological effects of stress inhibit a number of cellular immune responses (Anderson & others, 2001). Cancer patients have diminished NK-cell activity in the blood. Low NK-cell activity is linked with the development of further malignancies, and the length of survival for the cancer patient is related to NK-cell activity (McEwen, 1998).

Positive Emotions, Illness, and Health

Researchers have mainly focused on the role of negative factors, such as emotional stress and anger, in illness. However, the recent interest in positive psychology has sparked research on the role that positive emotions might play in reducing illness and promoting health (Salovey & others, 2000).

Although the data concerning the effects of negative states are more extensive, positive emotional states are thought to be associated with healthy patterns of physiological functioning in both the cardiovascular system and the immune system (Booth-Kewley & Friedman, 1987; Herbert & Cohen, 1993).

Positive emotions have been shown to be linked with the release of secretory immunoglobulin A (S-IgA), the antibody that is believed to be the first line of defense against the common cold (Stone & others, 1994). In one study, S-IgA levels increased after healthy college women watched a funny, happy video but dropped after watching a sad video (Labott & Martin, 1990). Indeed, levels of S-IgA are positively linked with frequent use of humor as a coping strategy (Dillon, Minchoff, & Baker, 1985/1986). In one study, increased frequency of desirable events predicts higher levels of immune response on subsequent days (Stone & others, 1994). Researchers also have found that when people can regain and maintain positive emotional states, they are less likely to get sick or to use medical services when faced with a stressful life experience (Goldman, Kraemer, & Salovey, 1996).

Moods also can influence people's beliefs regarding their ability to carry out health-promoting behaviors. For example, in one study, happy individuals were likelier to engage in health-promoting behaviors and had more confidence that these behaviors would relieve their illness than sad individuals (Salovey & Birnbaum, 1989).

Recall, from chapter 11, Barbara Frederickson's (2001) belief that the main function of positive emotions is to facilitate the ability to cope with problems. In one study, individuals who experienced more positive emotions (such as happiness) used broader coping strategies than those who experienced more negative emotions (such as sadness). For example, individuals who experienced positive emotions were likelier to think about ways to deal with the problem and to step back from the situation and be more objective than individuals who experienced negative emotions (Frederickson & Joiner, 2000).

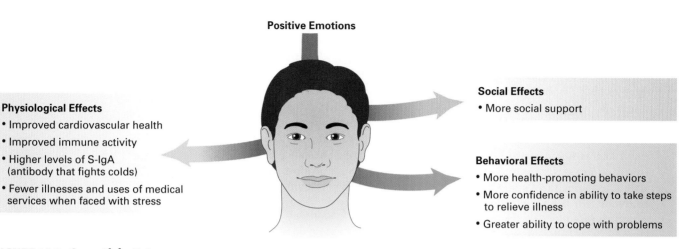

Positive Emotions

Physiological Effects
• Improved cardiovascular health
• Improved immune activity
• Higher levels of S-IgA (antibody that fights colds)
• Fewer illnesses and uses of medical services when faced with stress

Social Effects
• More social support

Behavioral Effects
• More health-promoting behaviors
• More confidence in ability to take steps to relieve illness
• Greater ability to cope with problems

FIGURE 15.8: Some Links Between Positive Emotions and Health

Social support, such as caring family and friends, is another important factor in stress and coping that is likely linked with positive emotions (Salovey & others, 2000). Emotional experience and social support are reciprocally linked: Not only does social support improve a person's emotional state, but a person's emotional state also influences the likelihood that the support will be provided. Researchers have found that positive emotions are correlated with people having more family members and friends they could count on in times of need (Cohen, 1988).

In sum, positive emotions do appear to be involved in helping to reduce illness and promote health (see figure 15.8). However, much more research needs to be carried out to determine the precise linkages. See the Critical Controversy box for more information.

mhhe com/ santrockp7

For study tools related to this learning goal, see the Study Guide, the CD-ROM, and the Online Learning Center.

Review and Sharpen Your Thinking

4 **Discuss the links between stress and health.**
• Outline the findings of psychoneuroimmunology.
• Evaluate the link between stress and cardiovascular disease.
• Explain the connection between stress and cancer.
• Describe how positive emotions, illness, and health are related.

Think about the last several times you were sick. Did you experience any stressful circumstances prior to getting sick? Might they have contributed to your illness?

5 COPING STRATEGIES

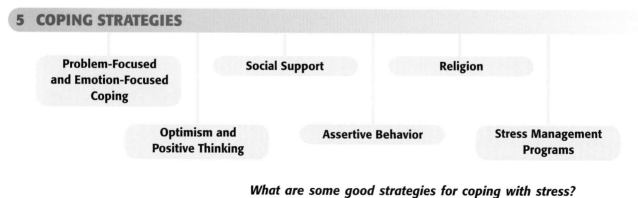

Problem-Focused and Emotion-Focused Coping

Social Support

Religion

Optimism and Positive Thinking

Assertive Behavior

Stress Management Programs

What are some good strategies for coping with stress?

A stressful circumstance is rendered considerably less stressful when a person successfully copes with it. Successful coping is associated with a number of factors, including a

Can Positive Thinking Make You Healthy?

If your best friend offered you a piece of candy when you had the flu and told you that it would make you better, would you believe it? What if the candy came from a famous medical doctor who told you the candy contained powerful medicine? If you ate the candy and your achiness and fever disappeared, the reason might simply be that the illness had run its course, and you would have felt better even if you hadn't eaten the candy. Or you might have experienced the placebo effect, a change believed to have been brought about by a medically inactive substance.

The word *placebo* stems from the Latin "I shall please" and commonly refers to a medication prescribed more for the mental or emotional relief of the patient than for any actual curative properties. The placebo effect has been known for centuries. In the second century, the Greek physician Galen noted, "He cures most successfully in whom the people have the most confidence." In the intervening centuries, doctors have been divided over whether to deliberately use the placebo effect to help their patients. Recently, the placebo effect has again become the focus of considerable controversy.

On the one hand, Asbjorn Hróbjartsson and Peter Gotzsche (2001) published a meta-analysis they claimed showed no support whatsoever for the use of placebos in clinical practice. In order to explore the existence of a placebo effect, they searched the medical literature to find studies that included both a placebo group and an untreated group (along, of course, with a treatment group). If the placebo effect was real, they suggested, then it should show up in comparisons of these two groups. Their meta-analysis included 114 studies, with 7,500 patients involving 40 different medical conditions. The results revealed that patients who received placebo treatment fared no better than those left untreated.

On the other hand, researchers from the University of British Columbia (de la Fuente-Fernandez & others, 2001) injected patients suffering from Parkinson's disease with either a drug (apomorphine) or a placebo (an inactive salt solution). Using PET scans, they showed that the drug produced improvement by initiating the release of the neurotransmitter dopamine in the brain. Surprisingly, PET scans revealed a similar release of dopamine in patients who were given the placebo injection. These patients apparently derived real benefit from the placebo effect.

It has also recently been argued that placebos work by helping people to adopt a positive attitude about their health, that placebo effects are a powerful part of healing, and that more effort should be made to use them (Brown, 1998). In this view, placebo effects are not just inactive "sugar pills" but affect patients' attitudes toward their own health outcomes. Seeking help, getting a diagnosis, beginning treatment, and looking forward to resuming a healthful life are all part of a positive attitude toward one's own health. Thus, while the placebo itself may be inactive, the positive attitude triggered by the placebo, and other interventions, may be life-saving.

There is evidence that positive thinking is important in promoting health. In one study, older men and women who expressed a positive outlook toward life were less likely to suffer heart attacks than those who expressed a negative outlook (Ostir & others, 2001). The effect of positive thinking can even be life-long. Analysis of brief autobiographies written more than 60 years ago by Catholic nuns when they were in their 20s suggests that those with a positive outlook lived longer than nuns who wrote about their lives in more neutral terms (Danner, Snowdon, & Friesen, 2001). Of course, it is possible that positive attitudes are merely a result of good health. It is also quite possible that adopting a more positive attitude generates health benefits.

What do you think?

- Have you ever been aware of a connection between a positive attitude in yourself and good health?
- How could you design an experiment to test whether positive thinking fosters better health or whether good health fosters positive thinking?
- A survey published in *Prevention* in February 1996, identified seven positive attitudes associated with an optimistic mindset: being very optimistic; having a strong belief in a higher power; thinking of the future, not the past; thinking people are good; being very trusting; thinking you control your life; and thinking you control your health. Is this list complete? What other attitudes might you add to the list? Why?

sense of personal control, a healthy immune system, personal resources, and positive emotions. What precisely is coping? **Coping** involves managing taxing circumstances, expending effort to solve life's problems, and seeking to master or reduce stress.

Keep in mind that multiple strategies often work better than a single strategy. People who have experienced a stressful life event or a cluster of life events (such as the death of a parent, a divorce, and a significant reduction in income) might adopt the following multiple-strategy plan for coping:

coping Managing taxing circumstances, expending effort to solve life's problems, and seeking to master or reduce stress.

- Engage in problem-focused coping
- Use positive self-talk
- Seek social support
- Practice relaxation

Problem-Focused and Emotion-Focused Coping

In the discussion of stress earlier in this chapter, I described Richard Lazarus' (1993, 2000) view that cognitive appraisal is critical to coping. Lazarus believes that people can make two general types of coping efforts: problem-focused coping and emotion-focused coping.

Problem-focused coping is Lazarus' term for the cognitive strategy of squarely facing one's troubles and trying to solve them. For example, if you are having trouble with a class, you might go to the study skills center at your college or university and enter a training program to learn how to study more effectively. Having done so, you have faced your problem and attempted to do something about it.

Emotion-focused coping is Lazarus' term for responding to stress in an emotional manner, especially by using defensive mechanisms. In emotion-focused coping, we might avoid something, rationalize what has happened to us, deny it is occurring, laugh it off, or call on our religious faith for support. If you use emotion-focused coping, you might avoid going to a class that is a problem for you. You might say the class doesn't matter, deny that you are having a problem, laugh and joke about it with your friends, or pray that you will do better. This is not necessarily a good way to face a problem. For example, in one study, depressed individuals used coping strategies to avoid facing their problems more than individuals who were not depressed (Ebata & Moos, 1989).

Sometimes emotion-focused coping is adaptive and helps us deal with problems. For example, denial is one of the main protective psychological mechanisms for dealing with the flood of feelings that occur when the reality of death or dying becomes too great. Denial can be used to avoid the destructive impact of shock by postponing the time when you have to deal with stress. In other circumstances, however, emotion-focused coping is maladaptive. Denying that the person you were dating doesn't love you anymore when that person has actually become engaged to someone else keeps you from getting on with your life.

Many individuals successfully use both problem-focused and emotion-focused coping when adjusting to a stressful circumstance. For example, in one study, individuals said they used both problem-focused and emotion-focused coping strategies in 98 percent of the stressful encounters they face (Folkman & Lazarus, 1980). Over the long term, though, problem-focused coping rather than emotion-focused coping is what usually works best (Heppner & Lee, 2001).

Optimism and Positive Thinking

Thinking positively and avoiding negative thoughts is generally a good coping strategy when trying to handle stress more effectively. A positive mood improves our ability to process information more efficiently, makes us more altruistic, and gives us higher self-esteem.

In addition, in most cases, an optimistic attitude is better than a pessimistic one because it gives us a sense that we are controlling our environment. In chapter 12, I discussed the positive benefits of being optimistic rather than pessimistic. Although some individuals at times use a strategy of defensive pessimism to improve their ability to cope with stress, overall a positive feeling of optimism is the best strategy.

Cognitive Restructuring and Positive Self-Talk Martin Seligman (1990, 2001) believes the best tools for overcoming chronic pessimism lie in cognitive therapy, one of the major psychotherapies discussed in chapter 14. In cognitive therapy, the client

problem-focused coping Lazarus' term for the cognitive strategy of squarely facing one's troubles and trying to solve them.

emotion-focused coping Lazarus' term for responding to stress in an emotional manner, especially using defensive appraisal.

is encouraged to think positively and talk back to negative thoughts in an optimistic style that limits self-blame and negative generalizations.

Many cognitive therapists believe the process of *cognitive restructuring*—modifying the thoughts, ideas, and beliefs that maintain an individual's problems—can also be used to get people to think more positively and optimistically. The process is often aided by changes in *self-talk* (also called *self-statements*), the soundless, mental speech that we use when we think about something, plan, or solve problems. Positive self-talk can foster the confidence that frees us to use our talents to the fullest. Because self-talk has a way of being self-fulfilling, uncountered negative thinking can spell trouble. That's why it's so important to monitor your self-talk.

Several strategies can help you to monitor your self-talk. First, at random times during the day, ask yourself, "What am I saying to myself right now?" Then, if you can, write down your thoughts along with a few notes about the situation you are in and how you're feeling. At the beginning, it is important to record your self-talk without any censorship. But your goal is to fine-tune your self-talk to make it as accurate and positive as possible.

You can also use uncomfortable emotions or moods—such as stress, depression, and anxiety—as cues for listening to your self-talk. When this happens, identify the feeling as accurately as possible. Then ask yourself, "What was I saying to myself right before I started feeling this way?" or "What have I been saying to myself since I've been feeling this way?"

Situations that you anticipate might be difficult for you also are excellent opportunities to assess your self-talk. Write down a description of the coming event. Then ask yourself, "What am I saying to myself about this event?" If your thoughts are negative, think how you can use your strengths to turn these disruptive feelings into more positive ones and help turn a potentially difficult experience into a success.

You also might compare your self-talk predictions (what you thought would or should happen in a given situation) with what actually took place. If the reality conflicts with your predictions—as it often does when your self-talk is in error—pinpoint how you can adjust your self-talk to fit reality.

You are likely to have a subjective view of your own thoughts. So you might try to enlist the assistance of a sympathetic but objective friend, partner, or therapist who is willing to listen, discuss your self-assessment with you, and help you to identify ways in which your self-talk is distorted and might be improved. Some examples of positive self-statements that might replace negative self-statements in coping with various stressful situations are presented in figure 15.9.

Positive Self-Illusion For a number of years, mental health professionals believed that seeing reality as accurately as possible was the best path to health. Recently, though, researchers have found increasing evidence that maintaining some positive illusions about oneself and the world is healthy. Happy people often have falsely high opinions of themselves, give self-serving explanations for events, and have exaggerated beliefs about their ability to control the world around them (Taylor, 1998; Taylor & Brown, 1994).

In some instances, developing positive self-illusions has been shown to have dramatic effects on performance. For example, sport psychologist Jim Loehr (1989) pieced together videotaped segments of 17-year-old Michael Chang's most outstanding tennis points in the past year. Chang periodically watched the videotape and always saw himself winning, never saw himself make mistakes, and always saw himself in a positive mood. Several months later Chang became the youngest male to win the French Open tennis championship.

Illusions, whether positive or negative, are related to one's sense of self-esteem. Having too grandiose an idea of yourself or thinking too negatively about yourself both have negative consequences. Rather, the ideal overall orientation may be to have either mildly inflated illusions or a reality orientation (see figure 15.10; Baumeister, 1989).

Situation	Negative Self-Statements	Positive Self-Statements
Having a long, difficult assignment due the next day	"I'll never get this work done by tomorrow."	"If I work real hard I may be able to get it all done by tomorrow." "This is going to be tough but it is still possible to do it." "Finishing this assignment by tomorrow will be a real challenge." "If I don't get it finished, I'll just have to ask the teacher for an extension."
Losing one's job	"I'll never get another job."	"I'll just have to look harder for another job." "There will be rough times ahead, but I've dealt with rough times before." "Hey, maybe my next job will be a better deal altogether." "There are agencies that can probably help me get some kind of job."
Moving away from friends and family	"My whole life is left behind."	"I'll miss everyone, but it doesn't mean we can't stay in touch." "Just think of all the new people I'm going to meet." "I guess it will be kind of exciting moving to a new home." "Now I'll have two places to call home."
Breaking up with a person you love	"I have nothing to live for. He/she was all I had."	"I really thought our relationship would work, but it's not the end of the world." "Maybe we can try again in the future." "I'll just have to try to keep myself busy and not let it bother me." "If I met him (her), there is no reason why I won't meet someone else someday."
Not getting into graduate school	"I guess I'm really dumb. I don't know what I'll do."	"I'll just have to reapply next year." "There are things I can do with my life other than going to grad school." "I guess a lot of good students get turned down. It's just so unbelievably competitive." "Perhaps there are a few other programs that I could apply to."
Having to participate in a class discussion	"Everyone else knows more than I do, so what's the use of saying anything."	"I have as much to say as anyone else in the class." "My ideas may be different, but they're still valid." "It's OK to be a bit nervous; I'll relax when I start talking." "I may as well say something; how bad could it sound?"

FIGURE 15.9 Replacing Negative Self-Statements with Positive Ones

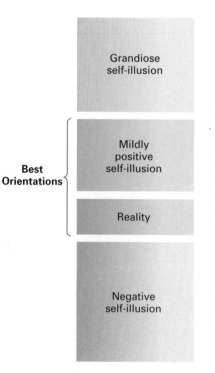

Grandiose self-illusion

Mildly positive self-illusion

Best Orientations

Reality

Negative self-illusion

Overstating the negative aspects of reality—what some people refer to as "just being realistic"—can be a problem. A negative outlook can increase our chances of getting angry, feeling guilty, and magnifying our mistakes. And, for some people, seeing things too accurately can lead to depression. Seeing one's suffering as meaningless and random may not help a person cope and move forward, even if the suffering is random and meaningless. An absence of illusions may also thwart individuals from undertaking the risky and ambitious projects that sometimes yield the greatest rewards (Baumeister, 1993).

In some cases, though, a strategy of defensive pessimism may actually work best in handling stress. By imagining negative outcomes, people can prepare for stressful circumstances (Norem & Cantor, 1986). Think about the honors student who is worried that she will flunk the next test or the nervous host who is afraid his lavish dinner party will fall apart. Thoughts of failure may not be paralyzing but instead may motivate them to do everything necessary to ensure that things go smoothly. By imagining potential problems, they may develop workable strategies for dealing with or preventing the problems. One study found that negative thinking spurred several constructive responses: evaluating negative possibilities, wondering what the future would hold, psyching up for future experiences so they would be positive, feeling

FIGURE 15.10 Reality and Self-Illusion Individuals often have self-illusions that are slightly above average. However, having too grandiose an opinion or thinking negatively can have negative consequences. For some individuals, seeing things too accurately can be depressing. Overall, in most contexts, a reality orientation or a mildly inflated self-illusion might be most effective.

good about being prepared to cope with the worst, and forming positive expectations (Showers, 1986).

Self-Efficacy Earlier, I indicated that perceived control is an important factor in stress. Closely linked with the concept of perceived control is **self-efficacy,** the belief that one can master a situation and produce positive outcomes. Self-efficacy can be an effective strategy in coping with stress and challenging circumstances.

As you read in chapter 11, Albert Bandura (1997, 2000, 2001) and others have shown that people's self-efficacy affects their behavior in a variety of circumstances, ranging from solving personal problems to going on diets. Self-efficacy influences whether people even try to develop healthy habits, how much effort they expend in coping with stress, how long they persist in the face of obstacles, and how much stress they experience (Clark & Dodge, 1999; Maddux, 2001).

Researchers have found that self-efficacy can improve individuals' ability to cope and be mentally healthy (Bandura, 2001). In one study, clients' self-efficacy was strongly linked to their motivation to come to psychotherapy sessions and overcome setbacks in the course of psychotherapy (Longo, Lent, & Brown, 1992). In another study, researchers examined a number of cognitive therapy techniques to determine their effectiveness (Kavanaugh & Wilson, 1989). Perceived self-efficacy to control dejecting thoughts was the best predictor of successful cognitive therapy.

Social Support

Our crowded, polluted, noisy, and achievement-oriented world can make us feel overwhelmed and isolated. Now more than ever, we may need support systems such as family members, friends, and co-workers to buffer stress. **Social support** is information and feedback from others that one is loved and cared for, esteemed and valued, and included in a network of communication and mutual obligation.

Social support has three types of benefits: tangible assistance, information, and emotional support (Taylor, 2003).

- *Tangible assistance.* Family and friends can provide actual goods and services in stressful circumstances. For example, gifts of food are often given after a death in the family occurs, so that bereaved family members won't have to cook for themselves and visiting relatives at a time when their energy and motivation is low.
- *Information.* Individuals who provide support can also recommend specific actions and plans to help the person under stress cope more effectively. Friends may notice that a co-worker is overloaded with work and suggest ways for him or her to manage time more efficiently or delegate tasks more effectively.
- *Emotional support.* In stressful situations, individuals often suffer emotionally and may develop depression, anxiety, and loss of self-esteem. Friends and family can reassure the person under stress that he or she is a valuable individual who is loved by others. Knowing that others care allows a person to approach stress and cope with stress with greater assurance.

Researchers consistently have found that social support helps individuals cope with stress (Taylor, 2001). For example, in one study, depressed persons had fewer and less supportive relationships with family members, friends, and co-workers than people who were not depressed (Billings, Cronkite, & Moos, 1983). In another study, the prognosticators of cancer, mental disorders, and suicide were linked with distance from one's parents and a negative attitude toward one's family (Thomas, 1983). Widows die at a rate that is 3 to 13 times higher than that of married women for every known cause of death.

self-efficacy The belief that one can master a situation and produce positive outcomes.

social support Information and feedback from others that one is loved and cared for, esteemed and valued, and included in a network of communication and mutual obligation.

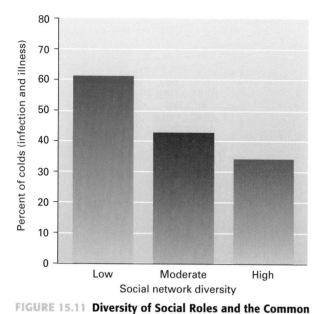

FIGURE 15.11 **Diversity of Social Roles and the Common Cold** In one study, the more social roles (diversity) involved in individuals' social networks, the less likely they were to develop a cold after being infected by a cold virus (Cohen & others, 1997). Note that low = 1 to 3 social roles; moderate = 4 to 5 social roles; and high = 6 or more social roles.

Having diverse social ties may be especially important in coping with stress. People who participate in more diverse social networks—for example, having a close relationship with a partner; interacting with family members, friends, neighbors, and fellow workers; and belonging to social and religious groups—live longer than people with fewer types of social relationships (Berkman & Syme, 1979; Vogt & others, 1992). One study investigated the effects of diverse social ties on susceptibility to getting a common cold (Cohen & others, 1997). Individuals reported the extent of their participation in 12 types of social ties. Then they were given nasal drops containing a cold virus and monitored for the appearance of a cold. Individuals with more diverse social ties were less likely to get a cold than their counterparts with less diverse social networks (see figure 15.11).

Keep in mind that the studies of social support are correlational. What does that mean about interpreting their results?

Assertive Behavior

We have just seen that social ties, especially diverse ties, play important roles in helping people cope more effectively with stress in their lives. Another aspect of social relationships that can affect coping is how we deal with conflict in these relationships. Assertive expression has become a communication ideal.

However, not everyone acts assertively. We can deal with conflict in our lives in four main ways: aggressively, manipulatively, passively, and assertively.

- *Acting aggressively.* People who respond aggressively to conflict run roughshod over others. They are demanding, abrasive, and hostile. Aggressive people are often insensitive to the rights of others.
- *Acting manipulatively.* Manipulative people try to get what they want by making other people feel sorry for them or feel guilty. They don't take responsibility for meeting their own needs. Instead, manipulative people play the role of the victim or martyr to get others to do things for them. They work indirectly to get their needs met.
- *Acting passively.* Passive people act in nonassertive, submissive ways. They let others run roughshod over them. Passive people don't express their feelings. They don't let others know what they want or need.
- *Acting assertively.* Assertive individuals express their feelings, ask for what they want, and say "no" to something they don't want. When individuals act assertively, they act in their own best interests and stand up for their legitimate rights. In the view of assertiveness experts Robert Alberti and Michael Emmons (1995), assertiveness builds equal relationships.

The Psychology and Life box, "Dealing with Conflict," gives you a chance to evaluate the styles that you use.

Following are some strategies for becoming more assertive (Bourne, 1995):

- *Set up a time for discussing what you want to discuss.* Talk with the other person to establish a mutually convenient time to talk. Omit this step when you need to be assertive on the spot.
- *State the problem in terms of its consequences for you.* Outline your point of view clearly to give the other person a better sense of your position. Describe the problem as objectively as you can without blaming or judging the other person. For example, you might tell a roommate or family member, "I'm having a problem with the loud music you are playing. I'm studying for a test tomorrow and the music is so loud I can't concentrate."

Dealing with Conflict

Think about the following situations one at a time. Check which response is most typical of the way you would behave in that situation.

	Assertive	Aggressive	Manipulative	Passive
You are being kept on the phone by a salesperson trying to sell you something you don't want.	___	___	___	___
You want to break off a relationship that is no longer working for you.	___	___	___	___
You are sitting in a movie and the people behind you are talking.	___	___	___	___
Your doctor keeps you waiting more than 20 minutes.	___	___	___	___
You are standing in line and someone moves in front of you.	___	___	___	___
Your friend has owed you money for a long time and it is money you could use.	___	___	___	___
You receive food at a restaurant that is over- or undercooked.	___	___	___	___
You want to ask a major favor of your friend, romantic partner, or roommate.	___	___	___	___
Your friends ask you to do something that you don't feel like doing.	___	___	___	___
You are in a large lecture hall. The instructor is speaking too softly and you know other students are having trouble hearing what is being said.	___	___	___	___
You want to start a conversation at a gathering, but you don't know anyone there.	___	___	___	___
You are sitting next to someone who is smoking, and the smoke bothers you.	___	___	___	___
You are talking to someone about something that is important to you, but they don't seem to be listening.	___	___	___	___
You are speaking and someone interrupts you.	___	___	___	___
You receive an unjust criticism from someone.	___	___	___	___

In most circumstances, being assertive is the best strategy. However, there may be some situations in which a different style of interaction is needed. Look at each situation again and determine if the assertive style is always the best strategy and whether there is any circumstance in which one of the other styles might work best.

- *Express your feelings.* Go ahead and express your feelings openly—but noncombatively. You need to let the other person know how important the issue is to you. Suppressing your feelings prolongs the problem.
- *Make your request.* A key part of being assertive is asking for what you want in a straightforward, direct way.

Religion

Might religion have an effect on a person's physical and mental health? Although people in some religious sects try to avoid using medical treatment or pain-relieving medications, individuals in the religious mainstream generally enjoy a positive link or neutral link between religion and physical health (Paloutzian, 2000). Researchers have found that religious commitment helps to moderate blood pressure and hypertension (Levin & Vanderpool, 1989). Also, a number of studies have confirmed that religious participation is related to a longer life (Gartner, Larson, & Allen, 1991; McCullough & others, 2000).

How might religion promote physical health? Part of the answer may be simply that some religious organizations provide some health-related services. Another possible explanation is that religious individuals have healthier life styles (for example, they use fewer drugs).

In general, various dimensions of religion can also help some people cope more effectively with the stress in their lives (Bergin & Richards, 2000; Koenig & Cohen, 2002).

Religious interest is widespread around the world. Of the world's 5.5 billion people, approximately two-thirds either are involved in a religion or have been affected by religion in important ways. (*Center*) Worshipers at the Makka (Mecca) mosque in Saudi Arabia. (*Top left*) A Jewish rabbi reading a prayer. (*Top right*) Temple of the Thousand Buddhas in Bangkok, Thailand. (*Lower left*) A congregation singing at an American Protestant church. (*Lower right*) Children at the San Fernando Catholic Christmas service in San Antonio, Texas. *How might religion be linked to physical and mental health?*

Religious thoughts can play a role in maintaining hope and stimulating motivation for recovery. Although the evidence is not clear, it also has been argued that prayer might be associated with positive health-related changes in the face of stress, such as decreased perception of pain and reduced muscle tension. A recent study found that some individuals with AIDS who lived much longer than expected had used religion as a coping strategy, participating in religious activities such as praying and attending church services (Ironson & others, 2001).

Yet another explanation for the link between religion and good health is that religious organizations sponsor social connections; it is well documented that socially connected individuals have fewer health problems (Hill & Butter, 1995). The social

tone (or in some cases, seeing a dot move up or down on a screen) as the individual learns to control muscle tension (Labbe, 1998).

Researchers have found that biofeedback can help people reduce the intensity of migraine headaches and chronic pain (Qualls & Sheehan, 1981; Scharff, Marcus, & Masek, 2002). But is biofeedback more effective than less expensive, simpler methods of relaxation? This issue has not been completely resolved, but several large-scale studies have found no distinct advantage of biofeedback over meditation and relaxation techniques (Labbe, 1998). Indeed, relaxation is believed to be a key aspect of how biofeedback works.

Review and Sharpen Your Thinking

5 *Outline strategies for coping with stress.*
- Evaluate problem-focused and emotion-focused coping.
- Understand the importance of optimism and positive thinking.
- Describe the role of social support in coping.
- Explain assertive behavior and its benefits.
- Discuss the link between religion and health.
- Summarize what stress management programs are like.

Think about a stressful circumstance that has occurred during the past year in your life. How effectively did you cope with it? Now that you have read about various coping strategies, would you have been better off if you had used one or more of them? Explain.

mhhe.com/
santrockp7

For study tools related to this learning goal, see the Study Guide, the CD-ROM, and the Online Learning Center.

HEALTHFUL LIVING 6

Exercising Regularly   Quitting Smoking

Eating Healthily   Making Sound Sexual Decisions

What are some ways to promote your own health?

Effectively coping with stress is essential for physical and mental health. But we can do a great deal more to promote better health. Healthful living—establishing healthy habits and evaluating and changing our behaviors that interfere with good health—helps avoid the damaging effects of stress (DiMatteo & Martin, 2002). Among the essential ingredients of a healthier lifestyle are regular exercise and good nutrition. Not smoking and sound sexual decision making are also important in improving the quality of our health.

Exercising Regularly

In 1961, President John F. Kennedy offered the following message: "We are under-exercised as a nation. We look instead of play. We ride instead of walk. Our existence deprives us of the minimum of physical activity essential for healthy living." Without question, people are jogging, cycling, and taking exercise classes more today than in 1961, but we are getting far less exercise in our daily lives. Too many of us ride instead of walk, take the elevator instead of climbing the stairs, and hire somebody else to do the little physical work that remains in our lives. Far too many of us spend most of our leisure time sitting in front of the TV or the computer screen.

FIGURE 15.12 **Moderate and
Vigorous Physical Activities**

Moderate	Vigorous
Walking, briskly (3–4 mph)	Walking, briskly uphill or with a load
Cycling for pleasure or transportation (≤10 mph)	Cycling, fast or racing (>10 mph)
Swimming, moderate effort	Swimming, fast treading crawl
Conditioning exercise, general calisthenics	Conditioning exercise, stair ergometer, ski machine
Racket sports, table tennis	Racket sports, singles tennis, racketball
Golf, pulling cart or carrying clubs	Golf, practice at driving range
Canoeing, leisurely (2.0–3.9 mph)	Canoeing, rapidly (≥4 mph)
Home care, general cleaning	Moving furniture
Mowing lawn, power mower	Mowing lawn, hand mower
Home repair, painting	Fix-up projects

One of the main reasons that health experts want us to exercise is that it helps to prevent heart disease (Billman, 2002; Williams, 2001). Although exercise designed to strengthen muscles and bones or to improve flexibility is important to fitness, many health experts stress aerobic exercise. **Aerobic exercise** is sustained activity—jogging, swimming, or cycling, for example—that stimulates heart and lung functioning. Elaborate studies of 17,000 male alumni of Harvard University found that those who exercised strenuously on a regular basis had a lower risk of heart disease and were likelier to still be alive in their middle adulthood years than their more sedentary counterparts (Lee, Hsieh, & Paffenbarger, 1995; Paffenbarger & others, 1986).

People in some occupations get more vigorous exercise than those in others. (Howley, 2001). For example, longshoremen who are on their feet all day and who lift, push, and carry heavy cargo have about half the risk of fatal heart attacks as such co-workers as crane drivers and clerks, who have physically less demanding jobs.

Some health experts conclude that, regardless of other risk factors (smoking, high blood pressure, overweight, heredity), if you exercise enough to burn more than 2,000 calories a week, you can cut your risk of heart attack by an impressive two-thirds (Sherwood, Light, & Blumenthal, 1989). But burning up 2,000 calories a week through exercise requires a lot of effort, far more than most of us are willing to expend. To burn 300 calories a day through exercise, you would have to do one of the following: swim or run for about 25 minutes, walk for 45 minutes at about 4 miles an hour, or participate in aerobic dancing for 30 minutes.

As a more realistic goal, many health experts recommend that adults engage in 30 minutes or more of moderate physical activity on most, preferably all, days of the week. Most recommend that you should try to raise your heart rate to at least 60 percent of your maximum heart rate. However, only about one-fifth of adults are active at these recommended levels of physical activity. Examples of the physical activities that qualify as moderate (and, for comparison, vigorous activities) are listed in figure 15.12.

Researchers have found that exercise benefits not only physical health but also mental health (Leith 1998; Pennix & others, 2002; Phillips, Kiernan, & King, 2001). In particular, exercise improves self-concept and reduces anxiety and depression. In one study, 109 nonexercising volunteers were randomly assigned to one of four conditions: high-intensity aerobic training, moderate-intensity aerobic training, low-intensity nonaerobic

aerobic exercise Sustained exercise that stimulates heart and lung activity.

Moderate or intense exercise benefits physical and mental health.

training, and waiting list (Moses & others, 1989). In the high-intensity aerobic group, participants engaged in a continuous walk-jog program that elevated their heart rate to between 70 and 75 percent of maximum. In the moderate-intensity aerobic group, participants engaged in walking or jogging that elevated their heart rate to 60 percent of maximum. In the low-intensity nonaerobic group, participants engaged in strength, mobility, and flexibility exercises in a slow, discontinuous manner for about 30 minutes. Those who were assigned to exercise programs worked out three to five times a week. Those who were on the waiting list did not exercise. The programs lasted for 10 weeks. As expected, the group assigned to the high-intensity aerobic program showed the greatest aerobic fitness on a 12-minute walk-run. Fitness also improved for those assigned to moderate- and low-exercise programs. However, only the people assigned to the moderate-intensity aerobic training programs showed psychological benefits. These benefits appeared immediately in the form of reduced tension and anxiety and, after 3 months, in the form of improved ability to cope with stress.

Why were the psychological benefits superior in the moderate-intensity aerobic condition? Perhaps the participants in the high-intensity program found the training too demanding, not so surprising as these individuals were nonexercisers prior to the study. The superiority of the moderate-intensity aerobic training program over the nonaerobic low-intensity exercise program suggests that a minimum level of aerobic conditioning may be required to obtain important psychological benefits.

Research on the benefits of exercise suggests that both moderate and intense activities may produce important physical and psychological gains (Thayer & others, 1996). Some people enjoy rigorous, intense exercise. Others enjoy moderate exercise routines. The enjoyment and pleasure we derive from exercise added to its aerobic benefits make exercise one of life's most important activities.

Following are some helpful strategies for building exercise into your life:

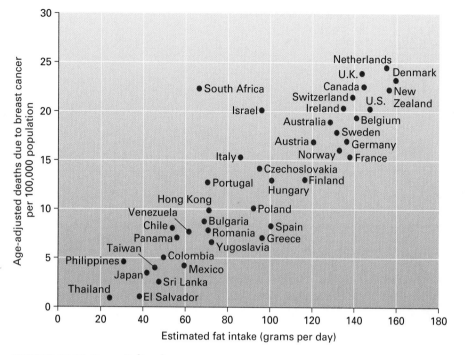

FIGURE 15.13 Cross-Cultural Comparisons of Diet and Breast Cancer Rates In countries in which individuals have a low daily intake of fat, the rate of breast cancer is low (in Thailand, for example). In countries in which individuals have a high daily intake of fat, the rate of breast cancer is high (the Netherlands, for example).

- *Reduce TV time.* Heavy TV viewing by college students is linked to their poor health (Astin, 1993). Replace some of your TV time with exercise time.
- *Chart your progress.* Systematically recording your exercise workouts will help you to chart your progress. This strategy is especially helpful in maintaining an exercise program over an extended period.
- *Get rid of excuses.* People make up all kinds of excuses for not exercising. A typical excuse is "I just don't have enough time." You probably do have the time to make exercise a priority.
- *Imagine the alternative.* Ask yourself whether you are too busy to take care of your own health. What will your life be like if your lose your health?
- *Learn more about exercise.* The more you know about exercise, the more you are likely to start an exercise program and continue it.

Eating Healthily

In chapter 11, I discussed many aspects of eating and weight. Obesity is a serious and pervasive health problem, with about one-third of the American population overweight enough to be at increased health risk. On the other hand, the pressure to be thin can lead to harmful effects for people who are not overweight. Researchers have found that the most effective component of weight loss programs is regular exercise.

Despite the growing variety of choices Americans can make in the grocery store, many of us are unhealthy eaters. We take in too much sugar and not enough foods high in vitamins, minerals, and fiber, such as fruits, vegetables, and grains. We eat too much fast food and too few well-balanced meals, choices that increase our fat and cholesterol intake, both of which are implicated in long-term health problems.

Evidence for the negative effects of poor nutritional choices comes from both animal and cross-cultural research. For example, mice fed a high-fat diet are likelier to develop breast cancer than are mice fed on a low-fat diet. And a cross-cultural study of women found a strong positive correlation between fat consumption and death rates from breast cancer (see figure 15.13; Cohen, 1987).

One of the most telling comparisons to link fat intake and cancer is between the United States and Japan. These countries have similar levels of industrialization and education, as well as similarly high medical standards. Although the overall cancer rates of the two countries are similar, cancers of the breast, colon, and prostate are common in the United States but rare in Japan. Yet, within two generations, descendants of Japanese immigrants to Hawaii and California have developed breast cancer rates that are significantly higher than those in Japan and that approach those of Americans. Many researchers believe that the high fat intake of Americans and the low fat intake of the Japanese are implicated in the countries' different cancer rates.

American nutritional standards have changed over time, adding to our confusion about which foods we should eat. Only a few decades ago, eggs and dairy foods were promoted as virtually ideal food sources. Now we are told that some dairy products, such as whole milk and butter, and eggs should generally be avoided.

Today, nutritionists believe that proper nutrition involves more than merely taking in an appropriate number of calories. It involves carefully selecting foods that provide appropriate nutrients along with their calories. A sound nutritional plan provides the right amounts of all the nutrients we need—fat, carbohydrates, proteins, vitamins, minerals, and water.

Several health goals can be accomplished through a sound nutritional plan. Not only does a well-balanced diet provide more energy but it also can lower blood pressure and lessen our risk of cancer and even tooth decay.

Quitting Smoking

A decade after the U.S. surgeon general warned that cigarettes are responsible for major health problems, the tobacco industry was besieged with lawsuits—from consumers whose health was impaired and from states that have had to foot much of the bill for smoking-related illness. Such massive litigation has prompted tobacco companies to begin negotiations with legal authorities to figure out a way to stem the tide of lawsuits and limit their liability for health-related damages.

Converging evidence from a number of studies underscores the dangers of smoking or being around those who smoke (Millis, 1998). For example, smoking is linked to 30 percent of cancer deaths, 21 percent of heart disease deaths, and 82 percent of chronic pulmonary disease deaths. Secondhand smoke is implicated in as many as 9,000 lung cancer deaths a year. Children of smokers are at special risk for respiratory and middle-ear diseases.

Fewer people smoke today than in the past, and almost half of the living adults who ever smoked have quit. The prevalence of smoking in men has dropped from over 50 percent in 1965 to about 28 percent today (National Center for Health Statistics, 2000). However, more than 50 million Americans still smoke cigarettes today. And cigar smoking and tobacco chewing, which have risk levels similar to those of cigarette smoking, have increased.

Most smokers would like to quit, but their addiction to nicotine often makes quitting a challenge. Nicotine, the active drug in cigarettes, is a stimulant that increases the smoker's energy and alertness, a pleasurable and reinforcing experience (Payne & others, 1996; Seidman, Rosecan, & Role, 1999). Nicotine also stimulates neurotransmitters that have a calming or pain-reducing effect. Smoking also works as a negative reinforcer by ending a smoker's painful craving for nicotine. The immediate gratification of smoking is hard to overcome even for those who recognize that smoking is "suicide in slow motion." Figure 15.14 shows that when individuals quit smoking, over time their risk of fatal lung cancer declines.

How can smokers quit? Five main methods are used to help smokers abandon their habit:

- *Using a substitute source of nicotine.* Nicotine gum, the nicotine patch, the nicotine inhaler, and nicotine spray

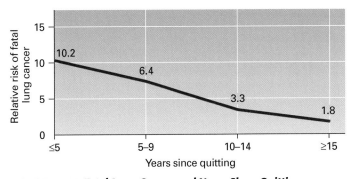

FIGURE 15.14 **Fatal Lung Cancer and Years Since Quitting Smoking** One study compared more than 43,000 former male smokers with almost 60,000 males who had never smoked (Enstrom, 1999). For comparison purposes, a zero level was assigned as the risk of fatal lung cancer for men who had never smoked. Over time, the relative risk for smokers who had quit declined, but even after 15 years it was still above that of nonsmokers.

work on the principle of supplying small amounts of nicotine to diminish the intensity of withdrawal (Eissenberg, Stitzer, & Henningfield, 1999). Nicotine gum, now available without a prescription, is a drug that smokers can take orally when they get the urge to smoke. The nicotine patch is a nonprescription adhesive pad that delivers a steady dose of nicotine to the individual. The dose is gradually reduced over an 8- to 12-week period. Success rates for nicotine substitutes have been encouraging. The percentage of study participants who are still not smoking after 5 months ranges from 18 percent for the nicotine patch to 30 percent for the nicotine spray (Centers for Disease Control and Prevention, 2001).

- *Taking an antidepressant.* Bupropion SR, an antidepressant sold as Zyban, helps smokers control their cravings while they ease off nicotine. Zyban works at the neurotransmitter level in the brain by inhibiting the uptake of dopamine, serotonin, and norepinephrine. In recent research, smokers using Zyban to quit have had a 30 percent average success rate after 5 months of taking the antidepressant (Centers for Disease Control and Prevention, 2001; Gonzales & others, 2001; Steele, 2000). Some deaths have been reported as a consequence of Zyban, however, which has led to screening for the seizures that may occur in some individuals (Bhattacharjee & others, 2001).
- *Controlling stimuli associated with smoking.* This behavior modification technique sensitizes the smoker to social cues associated with smoking. For example, the individual might associate a morning cup of coffee or a social drink with smoking. Stimulus control strategies help the smoker to avoid these cues or learn to substitute other behaviors for smoking. This approach has met with mixed results.
- *Undergoing aversive conditioning.* Chapter 14 discussed the behavioral therapy technique of aversive conditioning, which involves repeated pairings of an undesirable behavior with aversive stimuli to decrease the behavior's rewards. Imagine smoking as many cigarettes as possible until the ashtray overflows, the smell of stale cigarettes seems permanently embedded in your fingertips, your throat is dry and scratchy, and you feel nauseated. The concept behind aversive conditioning is to make smoking so unpleasant that you won't want to smoke anymore. Sometimes this technique works, sometimes it doesn't.
- *Going cold turkey.* Some people succeed by simply stopping smoking without making any major changes in their lifestyle. They decide they are going to quit and they do. Lighter smokers usually have more success with this approach than heavier smokers.

As you can see, no one method is foolproof for quitting smoking. Often a combination of these methods is the best approach. And, often, truly quitting requires more than one try.

Making Sound Sexual Decisions

Chapter 11 discussed sexual motivations and sexual orientations. This section focuses on the importance of making healthy decisions in your sex life.

Sexual Knowledge How much do we really know about sex? According to June Reinisch (1990), director of the Kinsey Institute, the United States is a nation whose citizens know more about how their automobiles function than about how their bodies function sexually. Reinisch directed a national assessment of approximately 2,000 adults' sexual knowledge. Almost two-thirds did not know that most erection problems arise from physical, not psychological, causes. Fifty percent did not know that some oil-based lubricants can make holes in condoms or diaphragms in less than a minute.

One conclusion we can draw from Reinisch's national survey is that there is a great deal we do not know. But what might be even more problematic are the

Read each of the following statements and check whether you think it is true or false.

	True	False		True	False
1. There is a right way and a wrong way to have sexual intercourse.	☐	☐	7. You can tell immediately if you have a sexually transmitted disease.	☐	☐
2. It is important for couples to have simultaneous orgasms.	☐	☐	8. Gonorrhea, syphilis, and AIDS can be contracted from toilet seats.	☐	☐
3. Individuals should not have sexual intercourse at any time during pregnancy.	☐	☐	9. Masturbation can cause mental disorders.	☐	☐
4. Once individuals are sterilized, their interest in sex diminishes.	☐	☐	10. Females rarely masturbate.	☐	☐
5. You can tell the size of a man's penis by the size of his hands and feet.	☐	☐	11. Only homosexual males and intravenous drug abusers are at risk for contracting AIDS.	☐	☐
6. If you contract a sexually transmitted disease and treat it effectively, you can't get it again.	☐	☐	12. Most sexual dysfunctions are due to physical problems.	☐	☐

Most people mark one or more of the above items true. However, according to experts on human sexuality, all of the above statements are myths (Crooks & Bauer, 1999; Greenberg, Bruess, & Mullen, 1992). Thus, although sexuality is an integral part of life, many people have misconceptions about it.

FIGURE 15.15 Sexual Myths and Realities

unfounded sexual myths that we believe. American adolescents especially encounter a distressing amount of misinformation about sex. There is a serious need to improve our sexual awareness and knowledge, which can help to reduce unwanted pregnancies and promote sexual self-awareness. For an assessment of your own sexual knowledge, see figure 15.15.

Contraception   Most couples in the United States want to control whether and when they will conceive a child. For them it is important to have accurate knowledge about contraception. But inadequate knowledge about contraception, coupled with inconsistent use of effective contraceptive methods, has given Americans the dubious distinction of having one of the highest adolescent pregnancy rates in the industrialized world (Alan Guttmacher Institute, 2000; Coleman, 1995; Wielandt, Bolden, & Knudsen, 2002). Adolescent pregnancy is linked with a host of problems for the mother, such as less future education and lower socioeconomic status, and for the offspring (Leadbeater & Way, 2001; Whitman & others, 2001).

Although the rate of contraceptive use among teenagers is improving, many still do not use contraception (Child Trends, 2000). A majority of adolescents do not use contraception during their first sexual intercourse experience (Hofferth, 1990): Seventy percent of females who become sexually active before the age of 15, and about 50 percent of those who become active around the age of 18 or 19, have unprotected first intercourse.

Age also influences the choice of contraceptive method. Older adolescents and young adults are likelier to rely on the pill or diaphragm; younger adolescents are likelier to use a condom or withdrawal, both of which are less reliable than other methods (Hofferth, 1990). Even adults in stable relationships sometimes do not use adequate contraception, perhaps feeling that some contraceptives, such as condoms, interrupt the spontaneity of sex. Or they might overestimate the effectiveness of some of the unreliable methods (Weisman & others, 2002).

No method of contraception is best for everyone (Hyde & DeLamater, 2003). When choosing a method of contraception, couples need to consider such factors as their physical and emotional concerns, the method's effectiveness, the nature of their relationship, their values and beliefs, and the method's convenience. Calculations of the effectiveness of a contraceptive method often are based on the failure rates during the 1st year of use. It is estimated that if no contraceptive method were used, about 90 percent of

Pat Hawkins is deputy director of the Whitman-Walker Clinic in Washington, D.C., helping HIV and AIDS patients. She came to the clinic as a volunteer in 1983, just after HIV/AIDS exploded into an epidemic.

Hawkins says that she would not do anything else but community work. "Nothing gets you engaged so fast as getting involved," she comments. "We often keep the academic world separate from the real world, and we desperately need psychologists' skills in the real world."

Why does she like working in a nonprofit organization? "I knew I wanted to treat people clinically, but I wanted a broader impact," she says. "In private clinical work, you might see 1,000 people in a whole lifetime. I wanted to do more than that."

Hawkins was a double major in psychology and sociology as an undergraduate and then went on to obtain her Ph.D. in community psychology.

sexually transmitted diseases (STDs) Diseases that are contracted primarily through sex—intercourse as well as oral-genital and anal-genital sex.

acquired immunodeficiency syndrome (AIDS) Caused by the human immunodeficiency virus (HIV), a sexually transmitted disease that destroys the body's immune system.

women would become pregnant in their 1st year of being heterosexually active (Hatcher & others, 1988).

Sexually Transmitted Diseases **Sexually transmitted diseases (STDs)** are diseases that are contracted primarily through sex—intercourse as well as oral-genital and anal-genital sex. STDs affect about one of every six adults (National Center for Health Statistics, 2001). The main STDs are often caused by bacterial infections, as in the case of gonorrhea and syphilis, or viruses, as in the case of genital herpes and AIDS.

No single STD has had a greater impact on sexual behavior, or created more fear, in the past decades than has AIDS. **Acquired immunodeficiency syndrome (AIDS)** is caused by the *human immunodeficiency virus (HIV)*, a sexually transmitted disease that destroys the body's immune system. A person who has contracted HIV is thus vulnerable to germs that a normal immune system could destroy. Once an individual is infected with HIV, the prognosis is likely illness. New drug "cocktails" and a healthy lifestyle can keep HIV in check for a time, but most individuals will eventually develop AIDS and will probably die of it.

Of the U.S. AIDS cases reported through the end of 1999, 82 percent were men, 18 percent were women (National Center for Health Statistics, 2001). Overall, 47 percent of the U.S. AIDS cases were injection drug users, 10 percent were persons infected heterosexually, and 2 percent were individuals infected through blood or blood products. In the 1990s, there were increasing rates of HIV/AIDS in women and in African Americans and Latinos.

Because of education and the development of more effective drug treatments, deaths due to AIDS have begun to decline in the United States (National Center for Health Statistics, 2001). However, the power of AIDS drugs to prolong life has increased the number of people in the United States who are living with HIV/AIDS to nearly 1 million (Fleming, 2002).

Although the incidence of HIV/AIDS is relatively low in the United States, the disease has reached epidemic proportions in sub-Saharan Africa (World Health Organization, 2000). Adolescent girls in these countries, who are often sexually exploited by adult men, are the population most vulnerable to HIV. In Kenya, 25 percent of 15- to 19-year-old girls are HIV-positive compared with only 4 percent of the boys in this age group. AIDS has become the leading cause of death in adolescents and young adults in sub-Saharan Africa (Centers for Disease Control and Prevention, 2001).

Remember that it is not who you are but what you do that puts you at risk for HIV. Experts (Kalichman, 1996) say that HIV can be transmitted only by

- sexual contact
- other direct contact of cuts or mucous membranes with blood and sexual fluids
- sharing hypodermic needles
- blood transfusions (which in the past few years have been tightly monitored)

Anyone who is sexually active or uses intravenous drugs is at risk. *No one* is immune. The only safe behavior is abstinence from sex, which is not perceived as an option by most individuals. Beyond abstinence, there is only safer behavior, such as sexual behavior without exchange of semen, vaginal fluids, or blood and sexual intercourse with a condom (Perloff, 2001).

Just asking a date about his or her previous sexual behavior does not guarantee protection from HIV and other sexually transmitted diseases. In one investigation, 655 college students were asked to answer questions about lying and sexual behavior (Cochran & Mays, 1990). Of the 422 respondents who said they were sexually active, 34 percent of the men and 10 percent of the women said they had lied so their partner would have sex with them. Much higher percentages—47 percent of the men and 60 percent of the women—said they had been lied to by a potential sexual partner. When asked what aspects of their pasts they would be likeliest to lie about, more than 40 percent of the men and women said they would understate the number of their sexual partners. Twenty percent of the men, but only 4 percent of the women, said they would lie about their results from an HIV blood test.

What are some good strategies for protecting against HIV and other sexually transmitted diseases? They include

- *Know your and your partner's risk status.* Anyone who has had previous sexual activity with another person might have contracted an STD without being aware of it. Spend time getting to know a prospective partner before you have sex. Use this time to inform the other person of your STD status and inquire about your partner's. Remember that many people lie about their STD status.
- *Obtain medical examinations.* Many experts recommend that couples who want to begin a sexual relationship have a medical checkup to rule out STDs before they engage in sex. If cost is an issue, contact your campus health service or a public health clinic.
- *Have protected, not unprotected, sex.* When correctly used, latex condoms help to prevent many STDs from being transmitted. Condoms are most effective in preventing gonorrhea, syphilis, chlamydia, and HIV. They are less effective against the spread of herpes.
- *Don't have sex with multiple partners.* One of the best predictors of getting STDs is having sex with multiple partners. Having more than one sex partner elevates the likelihood that you will encounter an infected partner.

Review and Sharpen Your Thinking

6   *Summarize how to promote health.*

- Explain why exercise is important to good health.
- Evaluate the role of nutrition in health.
- Describe why quitting smoking is important and how it might be accomplished.
- Discuss sound sexual decision making.

How good are you at maintaining a regular exercise program, eating nutritiously and healthily, not smoking, and engaging in sound sexual decision making? Has your lifestyle and behavior in these areas affected your health? Might they affect your health in the future? Explain.

mhhe.com/
santrockp7

For study tools related to this learning goal, see the Study Guide, the CD-ROM, and the Online Learning Center.

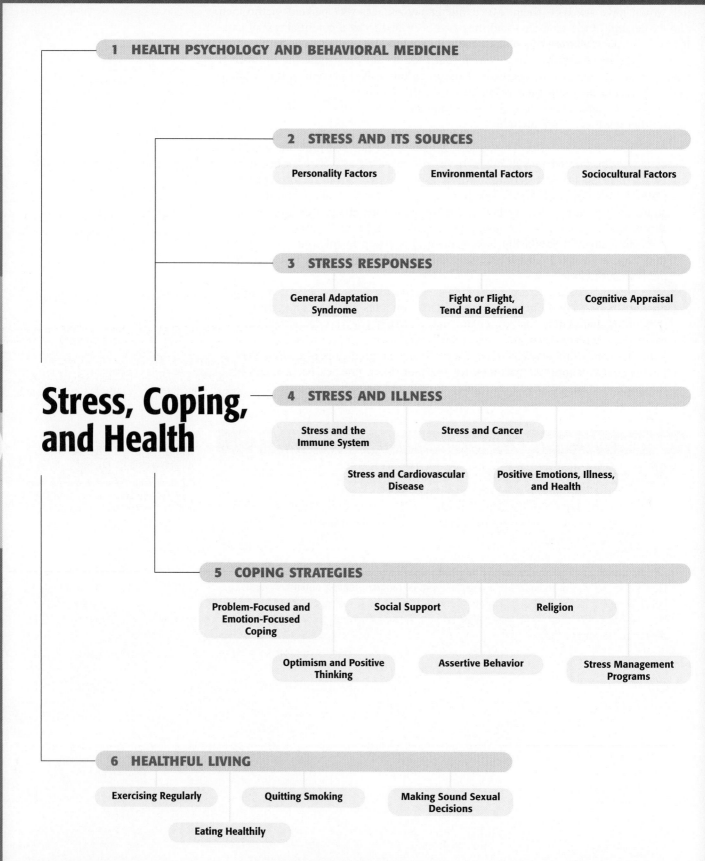

Stress, Coping, and Health

1 HEALTH PSYCHOLOGY AND BEHAVIORAL MEDICINE

2 STRESS AND ITS SOURCES

Personality Factors

Environmental Factors

Sociocultural Factors

3 STRESS RESPONSES

General Adaptation Syndrome

Fight or Flight, Tend and Befriend

Cognitive Appraisal

4 STRESS AND ILLNESS

Stress and the Immune System

Stress and Cancer

Stress and Cardiovascular Disease

Positive Emotions, Illness, and Health

5 COPING STRATEGIES

Problem-Focused and Emotion-Focused Coping

Social Support

Religion

Optimism and Positive Thinking

Assertive Behavior

Stress Management Programs

6 HEALTHFUL LIVING

Exercising Regularly

Quitting Smoking

Making Sound Sexual Decisions

Eating Healthily

1. Describe the scope of health psychology and behavioral medicine.

- Health psychology is a multidimensional approach to health that emphasizes psychological factors, lifestyle, and the nature of the health care delivery system. Closely aligned with health psychology is behavioral medicine, which combines medical and behavioral knowledge to reduce illness and promote health.
- Psychological and social factors are often involved in chronic diseases. A special interest is the link between stress and illness.

2. Define stress and identify its sources.

- Stress is the response of individuals to the circumstances and events, called stressors, that threaten them and tax their coping abilities.
- Personality factors involved in stress include the Type A/Type B behavior pattern, hardiness, and personal control. The Type A behavior pattern is a cluster of personality characteristics—such as being hostile, excessively competitive, impatient, and hard driven—that seem to be related to cardiovascular disease. The dimension of the Type A cluster most consistently related to heart disease is hostility. The Type B behavior pattern includes being relaxed and easygoing. Hardiness—which involves a sense of commitment, a sense of control, and a perception of problems as challenges rather than threats—is a stress buffer and is related to reduced illness. Another important aspect of stress is the extent to which people can control or reduce stress, as well as a related personality characteristic: their perception of control. Across a wide range of studies, a sense of personal control over stressful events has been related to emotional well-being, successful coping with a stressful event, and behavior change that can promote good health.
- Environmental factors involved in stress include life events, daily hassles, conflict, overload, and work-related stress. People who experience clusters of life events tend to become ill; daily hassles, ongoing daily annoyances, can also produce health-sapping stress. Everyday conflicts can be stressful. The three types of conflict are approach/approach (least stressful), avoidance/avoidance, and approach/avoidance. Daily hassles can result in overload, which can lead to burnout. The stress level of workers increases when their jobs do not meet their expectations, when job demands are high, and when workers have little choice in deciding how to meet the demands.
- Sociocultural sources of stress include acculturation and poverty. Acculturative stress refers to the negative consequences that result from contact between two distinctive cultural groups. People can adapt to cultural change in one of four ways: assimilation, integration, separation, and marginalization. Poverty can cause considerable stress for individuals and families and is related to threatening and uncontrollable life events.

3. Explain how people respond to stress.

- Selye proposed the general adaptation syndrome as a model of how the body responds to stress. It consists of three stages: alarm, resistance, and exhaustion. Many scientists now agree that two main biological pathways can be involved in the stress response: the neuroendocrine-immune pathway and the sympathetic nervous system pathway.
- A quick response to stress may take the form of a fight-or-flight response. The central notion of this concept is that the body's physiological resources are mobilized to prepare the organism to deal with threats to survival. However, females are less likely to respond to a threatening situation with a fight-or-flight response than males are. Rather, females responding to threatening circumstances are likelier to tend (protect themselves and their young through nurturing behaviors) and befriend (form alliances with a larger social group, especially one populated by women).
- Lazarus believes that how people respond to stress depends on the way in which they cognitively appraise events. Cognitive appraisal consists of primary appraisal (Is the stressful event harmful, threatening, or challenging?) and secondary appraisal (What resources do I have available to cope with the stressful event?).

4. Discuss links between stress and illness.

- Psychoneuroimmunology is the field that explores connections among psychological factors (such as attitudes and emotions), the nervous system, and the immune system. Researchers have found that acute stressors can produce immunological changes in healthy individuals. Chronic stressors are associated with a downturn in immune system functioning. Research with cancer patients shows that a good quality of life is associated with a healthier immune system.
- Emotional stress likely is an important factor contributing to cardiovascular disease. People who live in a chronically stressed condition are likelier to smoke, overeat, and not exercise. All of these stress-related behaviors are linked with cardiovascular disease.
- The link between stress and cancer can best be understood by considering connections between stress and quality of life, behavioral factors, and biological pathways.

- The recent interest in positive psychology has sparked research on the role that positive emotions might play in reducing illness and promoting health. In general, positive emotional states are thought to be associated with healthy patterns of physiological functioning in both the cardiovascular and the immune systems.

5 *Outline strategies for coping with stress.*

- Lazarus distinguished between problem-focused coping, which involves squarely facing stressors and trying to solve them, and emotion-focused coping, which consists of responding to stress in an emotional manner and usually takes the form of defensive appraisal. Problem-focused coping is usually the better coping strategy.
- Many cognitive therapists believe cognitive restructuring, including positive self-talk, can be used to get people to think more positively and optimistically. Positive self-talk is often helpful in cognitive restructuring. Individuals' ability to cope often benefits from mildly positive self-illusion, although some people cope best by facing reality. Grandiose self-illusion and negative self-illusion are generally not good coping strategies, although some people use defensive pessimism to prepare for stressful situations. Bandura has shown that self-efficacy, the belief that one can master a situation and produce positive outcomes, is an effective strategy in many domains of coping.
- Social support consists of information and feedback from others that one is loved and cared for, esteemed and valued, and included in a network of communication and mutual obligation. Three important benefits are tangible assistance, information, and emotional support. Researchers consistently find that social support, especially diverse social ties, helps people to cope with stress and to live healthier lives.
- People can deal with conflict aggressively, manipulatively, passively, or assertively. Assertive behavior has become the communication ideal.
- A positive link or no link has been found between religion and physical health. Various dimensions of religion can help people cope with stress in their lives.
- Stress management programs teach people how to appraise stressful events, to develop skills for coping with stress, and to put these skills into use in their everyday lives. These programs often are taught through workshops. Meditation, relaxation, and biofeedback are used in stress management. Meditation is a system of thought that incorporates exercises to attain bodily or mental control and well-being, as well as enlightenment. Researchers have found that meditation reduces body arousal and anxiety, but whether it is more effective than relaxation is debated. Biofeedback is the process in which individuals' muscular or visceral activities are monitored by instruments and the information from the instruments is fed back to the individuals so that they can learn to voluntarily control the activities. Biofeedback has been successful in reducing muscle tension and blood pressure.
- Multiple coping strategies often work better than a single coping strategy.

6 *Summarize how to promote health.*

- Both moderate and intense exercise produce important physical or psychological gains, such as lowered risk of heart disease and reduced anxiety.
- Too many people are unhealthy eaters, taking in too much sugar and not eating balanced meals. Healthy food selections can lower blood pressure, risk for cancer, and even tooth decay.
- Smoking is linked to 30 percent of cancer deaths, 21 percent of heart disease deaths, and 82 percent of chronic pulmonary disease deaths. Secondhand smoke is implicated in as many as 9,000 lung cancer deaths a year. Strategies for quitting smoking include nicotine substitutes, Zyban (an antidepressant), stimulus control, aversive conditioning, and going cold turkey. Combining strategies may have the best results.
- Inadequate knowledge about sex, especially contraception, and inconsistent use of effective methods, has resulted in the United States having one of the highest adolescent pregnancy rates in the industrialized world. Thus becoming knowledgeable about sex and planning contraception before having sex are both aspects of sound sexual decision making. Sexually transmitted diseases (STDs) are contracted primarily through sex—intercourse as well as oral-genital and anal-genital sex. The most devastating STD is HIV/AIDS. A special concern is the extremely high rate of HIV/AIDS in sub-Saharan African countries, especially among young females. Some good strategies for protecting against STDs are (1) know your and your partner's risk status, (2) obtain medical examinations, (3) have protected, not unprotected, sex, and (4) do not have sex with multiple partners.

Key Terms

health psychology, p. 603
behavioral medicine, p. 603
stress, p. 604
Type A behavior
    pattern, p. 605
Type B behavior pattern,
    p. 605
hardiness, p. 605
approach/approach
    conflict, p. 608

avoidance/avoidance
    conflict, p. 608
approach/avoidance
    conflict, p. 608
burnout, p. 609
acculturative stress, p. 610
general adaptation
    syndrome (GAS), p. 612
cognitive appraisal, p. 615
psychoneuroimmunology,
    p. 616

coping, p. 621
problem-focused coping,
    p. 622
emotion-focused coping,
    p. 622
self-efficacy, p. 625
social support, p. 625
stress management
    programs, p. 629
meditation, p. 629

transcendental meditation
    (TM), p. 629
biofeedback, p. 630
aerobic exercise, p. 632
sexually transmitted
    diseases (STDs), p. 638
acquired immune deficiency
    syndrome (AIDS), p. 638

Apply Your Knowledge

1. The text describes personality, environment, and sociocultural influences as three factors contributing to stress. What are the advantages and disadvantages of categorizing factors in this manner and considering them separately? Can you think of examples of stressors in which these factors clearly interact? Or in which these factors don't seem to play a role?

2. The text describes physiological stress responses in terms of the damage they cause to our health. If stress responses are so damaging, why do we have them? What purpose might physiological stress responses serve? Why might people differ in their physiological stress responses (for example, men and women)?

3. The links between stress and illness are currently based primarily on correlational studies. Take one of the specific examples described in the text and explain how you would test whether there is a causal link between stress and illness.

4. Do an Internet search on the topic of "stress management" or "coping with stress." Visit three or four sites and critically evaluate the suggestions made on the sites. How are they similar to the suggestions given in the text? How much information is available to evaluate the claims on the sites? Based on your critical evaluation, is the advice something you would follow or not?

5. One method that has helped to decrease unhealthy behaviors such as smoking is to make them more expensive. Currently, some people are calling for a tax on unhealthy foods. Why would such a tax be useful? Would you be in favor of such a tax, or opposed? Why?

Connections

For extra help in mastering the material in this chapter, see the review sections and practice quizzes in the Student Study Guide, the CD-ROM, and the Online Learning Center.

16 Social Psychology

Chapter Outline

SOCIAL THINKING   **1**

Attribution
▼
Social Perception
▼
Attitudes

SOCIAL INFLUENCE   **2**

Conformity and Obedience
▼
Group Influence
▼
Leadership

INTERGROUP RELATIONS   **3**

Group Identity: Us Versus Them
▼
Prejudice
▼
Ways to Improve Interethnic Relations

SOCIAL INTERACTION   **4**

Aggression
▼
Altruism

RELATIONSHIPS   **5**

Attraction
▼
Love
▼
Relationships and Gender
▼
Loneliness

Learning Goals

1 Describe how people think about the social world.

2 Identify how people are influenced in social settings.

3 Discuss intergroup relations.

4 Explain how aggression and altruism characterize social interaction.

5 Understand the nature of relationships.

The news from Vietnam during the 1960s was troubling enough. But then in 1968 came the My Lai massacre in which 500 women, children, babies, and old men were slaughtered by out-of-control U.S. ground troups. However, there was a grace note in the My Lai story.

Helicopter pilot Hugh Thompson was one of the Americans who had been given orders to join a search-and-destroy mission in the area of My Lai, which was suspected to be under the control of the enemy Viet Cong and local sympathizers. The target area consisted of six different communities with a population of 10,000 people, mostly civilians. Most of the Americans who participated in the mission interpreted the orders as, quite literally, a license to kill indiscriminately.

Instead of following the search-and-destroy orders, though, Thompson and his crew set their helicopter down in the midst of the massacre and risked their lives to save nine unarmed Vietnamese civilians from certain death. Thompson also got on the airwaves, loudly protesting the massacre to other American pilots and officers. His efforts brought about a cease-fire that stopped the massacre before it worsened.

Had it not been for Thompson resisting the impulse to conform with the commands of officers and the actions of other soldiers, many more Vietnamese civilians would have been killed. During the My Lai massacre trials that followed, despite pressure from fellow soldiers to be quiet, Thompson was a key witness for the prosecution (Angers, 1999).

Think about the times in your life when you have faced the pressure to conform to what peers or authority figures wanted

Hugh Thompson walks past a drainage ditch at the My Lai Memorial March 15, 1998 after a reunion with two villagers he rescued 30 years ago.

you to do. Did you go along to avoid conflict? Or did you have the courage of Hugh Thompson and resist their pressure? Was it easy? Probably not. What makes it so hard for human beings to follow their consciences? Later in the chapter, the factors that are related to the pressure to conform are examined.

But, more generally, this chapter is about **social psychology**—the study of how people think about, influence, and relate to other people. Social psychology differs from sociology in that social psychology focuses more on the individual as a social being, whereas sociology places more emphasis on society at large.

1 SOCIAL THINKING

Attribution   Social Perception   Attitudes

How do people think about the social world?

Among the many aspects of social life that engage people, one of the most intriguing is how people think about the social world. This area of social psychology, which is often referred to as *social cognition*, involves how people select, interpret, remember, and use social information. Each person may have a unique combination of expectations, memories, and attitudes based on his or her social history. Nevertheless, certain common principles apply to the way people process information in a social situation (Bordens & Horowitz, 2002; Forgas, 2001; Moskowitz, 2001). The most important of these principles focus on the way people attribute causes to behavior, the processes of social perception, and the link between attitudes and behavior.

social psychology The study of how people think about, influence, and relate to other people.

Attribution

Human beings are curious, seeking answers to all sorts of questions about their social world. We often try to figure out why something has happened or is happening. We might be curious about why someone is yelling at another person, why someone is in love with a particular person, or why someone joined a certain organization.

Finding causal explanations for these and many other social circumstances is a complex task. We can observe people's behavior and listen to what they say, but, to determine the underlying cause of their behavior, we often have to make inferences from these observations. For example, when we observe someone make a nasty remark to another person, do we infer that the person deserved to be talked to that way, or do we infer that the negative comment occurred because of the perpetrator's hostile personality?

Given the fact that determining the causes of behavior is a challenge, our desire to find causal explanations is a bit of a puzzle. Why is it so important to us? Attribution theorists argue that we want to know why people do the things they do because the knowledge will enable us to cope more effectively with the situations that confront us (Alderman, 1999). Recall from chapter 11 that **attribution theory** views people as motivated to discover the underlying causes of behavior as part of their effort to make sense of the behavior. Thus attributions are thoughts about why people behave the way they do. Attribution theorists say people are, in a way, a lot like detectives or scientists, seeking the reasons for human actions.

The Dimensions of Causality   The attributions people make vary along three dimensions (Jones, 1998):

- *Internal/external causes.* Chapter 11 explained that an important attribution people make is whether the cause of achievement is due to external causes or internal causes. *Internal attributions* include all causes internal to the person, such as personality traits, intelligence, attitudes, and health. *External attributions* include all causes external to the person, such as social pressure, aspects of the social situation, money, the weather, and luck. Fritz Heider (1958) argued that this internal/external dimension is the central issue in attribution.

  Consider the attributions we are likely to make in this situation: Jason and Ashley have been dating for several months when Ashley breaks off the relationship. When we speculate about the reasons (as human beings are apt to do), we might observe that Ashley says she is ending the relationship because of pressure from her parents, who want her to tone down her social life and study more (external cause). But, we might wonder, is that the true reason she is breaking off the relationship? Possibly the vivacious Ashley is dumping Jason because she has grown tired of his introverted personality (internal cause).

- *Stable/unstable causes.* Whether we perceive the cause to be stable or unstable is also involved in making attributions. Is the cause relatively enduring and permanent or is it temporary? If Ashley has inferred that Jason's introverted personality is not going to change, she perceives a stable cause of his behavior. Alternatively, if Ashley believes that Jason just isn't putting forth enough effort but has the capability of being more outgoing, she perceives an unstable cause. These are both internal causes. If Ashley's parents never like anybody she dates, that is an external stable cause. If they don't like Jason but will approve of someone else Ashley dates, that is an external unstable cause.

- *Controllable/uncontrollable causes.* Whether a cause is perceived as controllable or uncontrollable is another dimension of causality (Weiner, 1986). We perceive that we can control some causes but not others. This dimension can coexist with any combination of internal/external and stable/unstable dimensions. Consider these examples of causes that we can control and causes that we can't control: An internal unstable cause such as effort or mood is usually

attribution theory Views people as motivated to discover the underlying causes of behavior as part of their effort to make sense of the behavior.

FIGURE 16.1 The Fundamental Attribution Error In this situation, the female supervisor is the observer and the male employee is the actor. *If the employee has made an error in his work, how are the employee and his supervisor likely to differ in their explanations of his behavior, based on your knowledge of actor/observer differences and the fundamental attribution error?*

Actor

Tends to give external, situational explanations of own behavior

"I'm late with my report because other people keep asking me to help them with their projects."

Observer

Tends to give internal, trait explanations of actor's behavior

"He's late with his report because he can't concentrate on his own responsibilities."

thought of as controllable; an external unstable cause such as luck is generally seen as uncontrollable.

Bernard Weiner (1986) argues that the various types of attributions have different emotional and motivational implications. When we believe that we have succeeded because of our internal characteristics, our self-esteem is higher than it is when we believe that our success is due to external causes such as the ease of a task or luck. Weiner emphasizes that the attributions we make regarding controllability are of particular importance because personal responsibility is involved. Attributing to ourselves the ability to control the causes of personal failure opens us to such emotions as guilt, shame, and humiliation. In contrast, perceiving the causes of personal failure to be uncontrollable does not lead to self-criticism. We also might hold others responsible for failures attributed to controllable causes and might even feel angry toward them. Or, we might feel sympathy toward people whose failures are the result of circumstances beyond their control. For example, if a vase is accidentally knocked off a table and broken, we would feel more forgiving of a child and much less forgiving of a drunken adult.

Attributional Errors and Biases So far what I have said about attribution suggests that it is a logical, rational process. However, some common errors and biases infiltrate our attributions. The *fundamental attribution error* is important in understanding how people assign causes to their own behavior and the behavior they observe. The *self-serving bias* is people's tendency to be overly positive about their own behavior, characteristics, and beliefs.

The Fundamental Attribution Error In attribution theory, the person who acts or produces the behavior to be explained is called the *actor*. The onlooker, or the person who offers a causal explanation of the actor's behavior or experience, is called the *observer*. Attribution theorists have observed that actors often explain their own behavior in terms of external causes. In contrast, observers frequently explain the actor's behavior in terms of internal causes. The **fundamental attribution error** means that observers overestimate the importance of internal traits and underestimate the importance of external situations when they seek explanations of an actor's behavior (see figure 16.1).

The fundamental attribution error suggests that when most people encounter examples of social behavior, they have a tendency to explain the behavior in terms of the personalities of the people involved rather than of the situation the people are in (Aronson, Wilson, & Akert, 1997). For example, when we try to explain why people do repugnant or bizarre things, our tendency is to describe them as flawed human beings. In 1997, 38 people in the Heaven's Gate cult took their own lives in response

fundamental attribution error The tendency for observers to overestimate the importance of traits and underestimate the importance of situations when they seek explanations of a person's behavior.

to the appearance of the Hale-Bopp comet. Their leader, Marshall Herff Applewhite, is known to have believed that this mass suicide would guarantee his followers a type of immortality, taking them to the "level above human." Delusion on such a scale is hard to fathom, and it was easy to conclude that all involved were "kooks." But Applewhite was highly charismatic and exerted enormous pressure on his acolytes to go along. The public's emphasis on the traits of the actors, without considering how they may have been overpowered by the social forces of the situation, reflects the fundamental attribution error.

Self-Serving Bias   Behavior is determined by a number of factors, so it is not surprising that our lives are full of squabbling and arguing about its causes (Harvey, 1995). In addition, as you have just learned, actors and observers have different ideas about what causes behavior. What accounts for these differences in attributions is often bias (Krull, 2001). Our personal attitudes and experiences shape our perceptions of causes.

When explaining our own actions, our bias is usually self-serving. That is, we tend to be self-enhancing in the way that we attribute the causes of our behavior, and we often exaggerate positive beliefs about ourselves (Sedikides & others, 1998). We often believe that we are more trustworthy, moral, and physically attractive than other people are. We also tend to believe that we are above-average teachers, managers, and leaders. We maintain these exaggerated positive beliefs about ourselves through self-serving bias (Pittman, 1998).

Self-serving bias especially emerges when our self-esteem is threatened. We may attribute our successes to internal factors and our failures to external factors: That is, we tend to take credit for our successes and blame our failures on others or on the situation. In the case of Ashley breaking up with Jason, Jason might find it a lot easier to accept Ashley's external attribution—that she is doing it because of her parents—than the internal attribution—that he is too introverted. Jason's attribution helps to protect him from harsh self-criticism.

Social Perception

When we think about our social world and try to make sense of it, we not only make attributions but also engage in these social perceptions: We develop impressions of other people, gain self-knowledge by comparing ourselves with others, and present ourselves to others in such a way as to influence the way they perceive us.

Developing Impressions of Others   As we move through the world, we develop shortcuts for evaluating which people to seek out and which to avoid. Often we use broad, polar dimensions to categorize them—good or bad, happy or sad, introvert or extravert, for example. If someone asked for your impression of your psychology professor, you might respond, "She is great. She is dynamic and well organized." From this description we can infer that you have a positive impression of her.

Our first encounter with someone contributes to the impression we form. First impressions are often enduring. *Primacy effect* is the term used to describe the enduring quality of initial impressions. One reason for the primacy effect is that we pay more attention to what we first learn about a person and less attention to subsequent information (Anderson, 1965). The next time you want to impress someone, a wise strategy is to make sure that you put your best foot forward in your first encounter.

As we form impressions of others, we cognitively organize the information in two important ways:

- *We unify our impressions.* Traits, actions, appearance, and all of the other information we have obtained about a person are closely connected in memory even though the information may have been obtained in an interrupted or random fashion. We might obtain some information today, more next week,

Good-bad

Strong-weak

Active-passive

FIGURE 16.2 Developing Impressions of Others: Three Dimensions We Use to Categorize People Look at the individual running. What is your impression of her? You probably will categorize her as strong or weak, as active or passive, or possibly as good or bad.

some more in 2 months. During those 2 months, we interacted with many other people and developed impressions of them as well. Nonetheless, we usually perceive the information about a particular person as unified, as a continuous block of information (Brown, 1986).

- We integrate our impressions. We reach beyond the spotty information we may have about a person—adding to, manipulating, and modifying it—to form a whole impression (Asch, 1946). Solomon Asch's original work (1946) uncovered this principle. Participants in his study were asked to think of a short list of traits for an individual. Asch then asked the participants to write character sketches based on a brief list of traits. The sketches included many different combinations of the traits and went far beyond the original list, indicating the tendency to integrate impressions of the person.

When we integrate information about people, we follow certain rules. **Implicit personality theory** is the term given to the public's or a layperson's conception of which personality traits go together (Bruner & Tagiuri, 1954). One person might have an implicit personality theory that all extraverted people are optimistic. The integration of these traits might be based on a thought process similar to this: "Because most of my friends who are extraverted also are optimistic, I assume all extraverted people are optimistic."

Another rule shaping the integration of information about people is that we use some evaluative dimensions more than others. Norman Anderson (1974, 1989) thinks we use three dimensions more than any others to categorize people. The most common dimension is *good/bad*. Think for a moment about the people you know. Chances are you categorize each of them as either good or bad. Our tendency to categorize people as good or bad is so strong that Anderson calls this *the* evaluation dimension. Potency (*strong/weak*) and activity (*active/passive*) are two other dimensions we often use to categorize people (see figure 16.2).

Recall from the discussion in chapter 8 that a *schema* is a conceptual framework that we use to organize information. When we read a book, we do not remember every paragraph word for word; rather, we get the gist of what the author says and fit the information into the schemas in our mind. We "read" people in a similar way. We don't remember everything about what they are like and what they do, but we get the gist of their personality and behavior, and we fit the information about them into existing categories of memory.

We tend to simplify the task of understanding people by classifying them as members of groups or categories with which we are familiar. It takes more mental effort to consider a person's individual characteristics than it does to label her as a member of a particular group or category. Thus, when we categorize an individual, the categorization is often based on stereotypes. Imagine that you meet a sales representative. You develop an impression of him based on the "sales representative" schema in your mind. Without seeking any additional information, you might perceive that person as pushy, self-serving, and materialistic.

We do not always respond to others on the basis of categories, however. As you interact with the sales representative, you might discover that he is actually interesting, modest, bright, and altruistic. You would then have to revise your impression and perceive him differently. When we discover information that is inconsistent with a category, or when we simply become more personally involved with someone, we tend to take an individual approach rather than a category-based approach to impression formation.

implicit personality theory The term given to the public or layperson's conception of which personality traits go together in an individual.

Comparing Ourselves with Others How many times have you asked yourself questions such as "Am I as smart as Jill?" "Is Bob better looking than I am?" or "Is my taste as good as Carmen's?" We gain self-knowledge from our own behavior, of course; but we also gain it from others through *social comparison*, the process by which individuals evaluate their thoughts, feelings, behaviors, and abilities in relation to other people. Social comparison helps individuals to evaluate themselves, tells them what their distinctive characteristics are, and aids them in building an identity.

Some years ago, social psychologist Leon Festinger (1954) proposed a theory of social comparison. He stressed that when no objective means is available to evaluate our opinions and abilities, we compare ourselves with others. Festinger believed that we are likelier to compare ourselves with others who are similar to us than dissimilar to us. He reasoned that if we compare ourselves with someone who is very different from us, we will not be able to obtain an accurate appraisal of our own behavior and thoughts. We will develop more accurate self-perceptions if we compare ourselves, for example, with people in communities similar to where we live, with people who have similar family backgrounds, and with people of the same sex or sexual orientation. Social comparison theory has been extended and modified over the years and continues to provide an important rationale for why we affiliate with others and how we come to know ourselves (Michinov & Michinov, 2001).

Festinger studied social comparison with those who are similar to us; other researchers have focused on social comparison on with those whom we consider to be inferior to us. Individuals under threat (from negative feedback, low self-esteem, depression, and illness, for example) try to improve their mental well-being by comparing themselves with others who are less fortunate (Gibbons & McCoy, 1991). It can be comforting to tell ourselves, "Well, at least I'm not as bad off as that guy."

Presenting Ourselves to Others   At the same time that we are forming impressions of others, others are forming impressions of us. In most cases, of course, we want others to think the best of us. But how can we influence others to perceive us more positively? Is it better to try to act naturally and be ourselves, or should we deliberately change our behavior to get other people to have a more favorable impression? Two aspects of presenting ourselves to others are *impression management* and *self-monitoring*.

Impression Management   **Impression management (or self-presentation)** involves acting in a way that will present an image of you to others as a certain sort of person, which might or might not be who you really are. In most instances, we try to present ourselves to look better than we really are. We spend years and small fortunes rearranging our faces, bodies, minds, and social skills. We especially use impression management with people we are not familiar with and with people who interest us sexually (Leary & others, 1994).

Nonverbal cues are a key element of successful impression management. Certain facial expressions, patterns of eye contact, and body postures or movements are part of the reason we are liked or disliked. Although impression management is common among people in all cultures, the specific techniques that work in one cultural setting may not work in another. For example, Americans tend to believe that an open, friendly style makes a positive impression on others. But, in some places, people are more impressed by reserve. In particular, appreciation and flattery are often culture bound. For example, in some Eastern European countries, if one person expresses great admiration for another's watch, courtesy dictates that the watch should be given to the admirer. In the culture of the Sioux, it's considered courteous to open a conversation with a compliment.

One setting in which most of us especially want to make a good impression is a job interview, and a great deal has been written about how to do it. For example, to improve the likelihood that an interviewer will have a favorable impression of you, you are advised to use the right nonverbal cues: smile often, lean forward, maintain a high degree of eye contact, and frequently nod your head in agreement with what the interviewer says. In general, researchers have found that individuals who use these impression management techniques receive more favorable ratings than individuals who do not (Riggio, 1986). In one study, researchers observed that individuals who were selected for engineering apprenticeships were indeed the ones who had

"Randall, my old college nemesis, I was hoping I'd find you here."
Copyright © 1996, *USA Today*. Reprinted with permission.

impression management (self-presentation) Involves acting in a way to present an image of oneself as a certain type of person, which might or might not be who one really is.

These statements concern personal reactions to a number of situations. No two statements are exactly alike, so consider each statement carefully before answering. If a statement is true or mostly true as applied to you, check True. If a statement is false or not usually true as applied to you check False.

	True	False			True	False
1. I find it hard to imitate the behavior of other people.	☐	☐	6. In different situations and with different people, I often act like very different persons.		☐	☐
2. I guess I put on a show to impress or entertain people.	☐	☐	7. I can only argue for ideas I already believe.		☐	☐
3. I would probably make a good actor.	☐	☐	8. In order to get along and be liked, I tend to be what people expect me to be.		☐	☐
4. I sometimes appear to others to be experiencing deeper emotions than I actually am.	☐	☐	9. I may deceive people by being friendly when I really dislike them.		☐	☐
5. In a group of people, I am rarely the center of attention.	☐	☐	10. I m not always the person I appear to be.		☐	☐

Scoring: Give yourself one point for 1, 5, and 7 if you answered False. Give yourself one point for each of the remaining questions that you answered True. Add up your points. If you are a good judge of yourself and scored 7 or above, you are probably a high-self-monitoring individual; 3 or below, you are probably a low-self-monitoring individual.

FIGURE 16.3 **Self-Monitoring**

smiled more, maintained greater eye contact with the interviewer, and more often nodded their heads affirmatively during their interviews than rejected applicants did (Forbes & Jackson, 1980). Some people use nonverbal cues such as these more naturally than others. But even if you do not normally behave this way when you are interacting with someone, you can make a conscious effort to control your nonverbal behavior.

Three other techniques of impression management are conforming to situational norms (for example, adopting the same form of dress and the same type of language and etiquette as other people in that setting), showing appreciation of others, and behavioral matching (engaging in behavior that the other person displays, such as clasping one's hands together).

As with most forms of manipulation, impression management can become counterproductive. You overdo it if you use so many positive nonverbal cues that the other individual perceives you to be insincere. And remember that impression management goes only so far: One study found that the frequent use of nonverbal cues had favorable outcomes in a job interview only when the applicants also had competent qualifications to do the job (Rasmussen, 1984).

Self-Monitoring Some people are more concerned about and aware of the impressions they make than others are (Snyder & Stukas, 1999). **Self-monitoring** is paying attention to the impressions you make on others and the degree to which you fine-tune your performance to optimize the impressions you make. Lawyers and actors are among the best self-monitors; salespeople, con artists, and politicians are not far behind. A former mayor of New York City, Fiorello LaGuardia, was so good at self-monitoring that, by watching silent films of his campaign speeches, it was possible to tell which ethnic group he was courting for votes.

Individuals who are very skilled at self-monitoring seek information about appropriate ways to present themselves and invest considerable time in trying to "read" and understand others (Simpson, 1995). In and of itself, such behavior is neither good nor bad. Nobody can be a successful member of a family or a community without attention to the expectations and opinions of others. The danger is that the energy spent in self-monitoring might reduce the amount of energy we can devote to trying to understand ourselves. To get an idea of your skill at self-monitoring, see figure 16.3.

self-monitoring Individuals' attention to the impressions they make on others and the degree to which they fine-tune their performances accordingly.

Attitudes

Social thinking involves not only attributions and social perceptions but also attitudes. **Attitudes** are beliefs or opinions about people, objects, and ideas. We have attitudes about all sorts of things, such as "Most people are out for themselves," "Money is evil," and "Television has caused family members to talk less with one another." We also live in a world in which people try to influence others' attitudes, as when politicians try to get your vote and advertisers try to convince you that their product is the best. Social psychologists are interested not only in how attitudes are changed but also in whether changing an individual's attitude will actually have an effect on his or her behavior—or whether changing an individual's behavior will lead to an attitude change.

Can Attitudes Predict Behavior?   People sometimes say one thing but do another. For example, they might respond in a poll that they prefer one candidate and then actually vote for another. But, often, what people say is what they do. Studies over the course of the past half century indicate some of the conditions under which attitudes guide actions (Eagly & Chaikin, 1998; Smith & Fabrigar, 2000):

- *When the person's attitudes are strong* (Azjen, 2001; Petty & Krosnick, 1995). For example, senators whose attitudes toward President Bush are "highly favorable" are likelier to vote for his policies than are senators who have only "moderately favorable" attitudes toward him.
- *When the person shows a strong awareness of his or her attitudes and when the person rehearses and practices them* (Fazio & others, 1982). For example, we would expect a person who vigorously argues for a ban on snowmobiles in national parks to avoid driving one; a person with the same desire to protect national parks from snowmobiles but who hasn't had to put it into words or define it in public might be likelier to try riding a snowmobile.
- *When the attitudes are relevant to the behavior.* For example, one study found that general attitudes toward birth control were virtually unrelated to the use of birth control pills in the following 2 years; however, a specific attitude toward taking birth control pills showed a much higher correlation with actual use in the following 2 years (Davidson & Jacard, 1979). The more relevant the attitude is to the behavior, the better it will predict the behavior.

Can Behavior Predict Attitudes?   "The actions of men are the best interpreters of their thoughts," asserted seventeenth-century English philosopher John Locke. Does doing change believing? If you quit drinking, will you then have a negative attitude toward drinking? If you take up an exercise program, are you then likely to extol the benefits of cardiovascular fitness when someone asks about your attitude toward exercise?

Ample evidence exists that changes in behavior sometimes precede changes in attitudes (Bandura, 1989). Social psychologists offer two main explanations of why behavior influences attitudes. The first view is that we have a strong need for cognitive consistency; we change our attitudes to make them more consistent with our behavior (Carkenord & Bullington, 1995). The second view is that our attitudes are not completely clear even to us, so we observe our own behavior and make inferences about it to determine what our attitudes should be.

Cognitive Dissonance Theory   **Cognitive dissonance,** a concept developed by social psychologist Leon Festinger (1957), refers to an individual's motivation to reduce the discomfort (dissonance) caused by two inconsistent thoughts. According to the theory, we are likely to feel uneasy if we can't justify to ourselves the difference between what we believe and what we do.

We can reduce cognitive dissonance in one of two general ways: change our attitudes or change our behaviors. For example, most smokers believe that it is unhealthy

attitudes Beliefs or opinions about people, objects, and ideas.

cognitive dissonance A concept developed by Festinger that refers to an individual's motivation to reduce the discomfort (dissonance) caused by two inconsistent thoughts.

to smoke, yet they can't seem to resist lighting up. This discrepancy between attitude and behavior creates discomfort. To reduce the dissonance, the smoker must either stop smoking or decide that smoking really isn't so bad. "No one has proven smoking kills people" and "I'll have to die from something" are both dissonance-reducing attitudes.

Since Festinger's original work on cognitive dissonance, social psychologists have refined the theory. For instance, dissonance theory predicts that individuals will avoid information inconsistent with their views. Early attempts to document this selective exposure failed. However, more recently, researchers have found that people will avoid unpleasant information—but only if they think that they cannot refute the uncomfortable argument and if they are highly committed to their way of thinking or behaving. Perhaps you have a friend or relative who has strong political or religious opinions that are not only at odds with yours but that seem contrary to common sense. You may have tried and tried, to no avail, to introduce facts that would convince the other person to change his or her mind. These recent findings suggest that you are unlikely to succeed.

Researchers also have focused on the specific situations that are linked with dissonance. Sometimes cognitive dissonance causes us to justify things in our lives that are unpleasant (Aronson, 1995). As George Bernard Shaw said of his father's alcoholism, "If you cannot get rid of the family skeleton, you may as well make it dance." "Making the family skeleton dance" helped Shaw to reduce the tension between his attitude about his father's drinking problem and its actual occurrence.

We also try to justify the negative things we do ourselves. We need to convince ourselves that we are decent, reasonable human beings. For example, when we have had a bad argument with someone, we often develop a negative attitude toward that person, which justifies the nasty things we said.

We especially have a strong need to justify the effort we put forth in life—a process called *effort justification*. In general, goals that require considerable effort are the ones that we value most highly. If we put forth considerable effort, yet still do not reach the goal, we develop dissonance. We could reduce the dissonance by convincing ourselves that we did not work as hard as we actually did, or we could say that the goal was not all that important in the first place. Think of the person who goes to a lot of trouble to get a particular job but gets passed over. The person might justify the effort by saying that she should have followed up more diligently, or she might say that the job really wasn't a good match with her skills and career goals.

Our most intense justifications of our actions take place when our self-esteem is involved (Aronson, 2000; Aronson, Cohen, & Nails, 1999). If you do something cruel, then it follows that you have to perform some mental gymnastics to keep yourself from thinking you are a cruel person. The clearest results in the hundreds of research studies on cognitive dissonance occur when self-esteem is involved, and the most dissonance results when individuals with the highest self-esteem act in cruel ways. What about individuals with low self-esteem? They probably experience less dissonance because acting in a cruel way is consistent with their attitudes toward themselves—indicated by such self-labels as *loser, jerk, zero,* or *bad guy.* Put another way, individuals who think of themselves as bad might do bad things because it keeps dissonance at a minimum. The emphasis on self-esteem in understanding cognitive dissonance suggests that dissonance is not produced by a discrepancy between two cognitions (as Festinger believed) but rather by a discrepancy between a cognition about a particular behavior and the person's self-image (Aronson, 2000). Not all of our thoughts and behaviors are aimed at reducing dissonance, however. Some of us learn from our mistakes. We catch ourselves doing something we don't approve of, look in the mirror, and say, "You blew it. Now what can you do to prevent that from happening again?" Eliot Aronson (1995) offers these three suggestions for avoiding the treadmill of dissonance reduction—simply trying to justify the bad things in our lives and the bad things we do:

	Cognitive Dissonance Theory	Self-Perception Theory
Theorist	Festinger	Bem
Nature of theory	We are motivated toward consistency between attitude and behavior and away from inconsistency.	We make inferences about our attitudes by perceiving and examining our behavior and the context in which it occurs, which might involve inducements to behave in certain ways.
Example	"I hate my job. I need to develop a better attitude toward it or else quit."	"I am spending all of my time thinking about how much I hate my job. I really must not like it."

FIGURE 16.4 **Two Theories of the Connections Between Attitudes and Behavior**

- Know your defensive and dissonance-reducing tendencies. Be able to sense them before you get in over your head.
- Realize that behaving in stupid and cruel ways does not necessarily mean that you are a stupid and cruel person.
- Develop enough strengths and competencies to be able to tolerate your mistakes without having to rationalize them away.

Self-Perception Theory Not all social psychologists believe that the theory of cognitive dissonance explains the influence of behavior on attitudes. Daryl Bem (1967), for example, believes that the cognitive dissonance view relies too heavily on internal factors, which are difficult to measure. Bem argues that we should move away from such fuzzy and nebulous concepts as "cognitions" and "psychological discomfort" and replace them with more behavioral terminology. **Self-perception theory** is Bem's idea about the connection between attitudes and behavior; it stresses that individuals make inferences about their attitudes by perceiving their behavior. For example, consider the remark "I am spending all of my time thinking about the test I have next week. I must be anxious." Or "This is the third time I have gone to the student union in two days. I must be lonely." Bem believes we look to our own behavior when our attitudes are not completely clear. Figure 16.4 provides a comparison of cognitive dissonance theory and self-perception theory.

Which theory is right: cognitive dissonance or self-perception? The pattern of research on cognitive dissonance suggests that people do change their attitudes to avoid feeling cheap or stupid or guilty about their behavior. But, at the same time, Bem's self-perception theory is compelling. People who are not strongly committed to attitudes before acting on them do seem to analyze their behavior for hints about their true opinions (Aronson, Wilson, & Akert, 1997). Self-perception theory also has been more useful in explaining what happens to people's attitudes when they are offered an inducement to do something they would want to do anyway. In sum, cognitive dissonance theory and self-perception theory both have merit in explaining the connection between attitudes and behavior.

How Are People's Attitudes Changed? We spend many hours of our lives trying to persuade people to do certain things. You've probably tried to persuade your friends to go to a movie or to play the game that you are interested in. If you're a parent, you've probably tried to persuade your children to eat their peas or to go to bed early. At some point in your life, you also likely have tried to persuade someone to buy something from you.

self-perception theory Bem's theory about the connection between attitudes and behavior; stresses that individuals make inferences about their attitudes by perceiving their behavior.

Professional persuaders have similar goals, but they use more polished techniques based on extensive research on attitude change. What makes people decide to give up their original attitudes and to adopt new ones instead? What makes people decide to act on an attitude that they haven't acted on before? Teachers, lawyers, and sales representatives study techniques that will help them sway their audiences (children, juries, and buyers, respectively). Politicians have arsenals of speech writers and image consultants to ensure that their words are as persuasive as possible. Perhaps most skilled of all are advertisers, who combine the full array of techniques in an effort to sell cars, insurance policies, and cornflakes.

A full review of the factors involved in persuasion and attitude change could fill volumes. But here are a few of social psychologists' findings, organized around the main elements of the communication process: who conveys the message (the source), what the message is (the communication), how the message is conveyed (the medium), and who receives the message (the target, or audience).

The Communicator (Source)   Suppose you are running for president of the student body. You tell your fellow students that you are going to make life at your college better. Would they believe you? That likely would depend on some of your characteristics as a communicator. Whether or not we believe someone depends in large part on their *expertise* or *credibility*. If you have held other elective offices, students would be likelier to believe you have the expertise to be their president. Trustworthiness, power, attractiveness, likability, and similarity are all credibility characteristics that help a communicator change people's attitudes or convince them to act.

The Message   What kind of a message is persuasive? One line of research has focused on whether a rational or an emotional strategy is more effective. Is it better to use basic motivators such as love, sex, or fear to persuade someone? Or is it better to use facts or logic?

Emotional appeals are very powerful. How often have we seen politicians vow to run a clean political campaign, but as soon as the bell sounds come out swinging below the belt? In the 2000 presidential election, the Gore campaign consistently badgered the Bush campaign for their negative ads. Negative appeals play to the audience's emotions, whereas positive appeals are directed at the audience's logical, rational thinking. The less informed we are, the likelier it is that we will respond to an emotional appeal.

All other things being equal, the more frightened we are, the more we will change our attitudes. Advertisers sometimes take advantage of our fears to stimulate attitude change. You may have seen the Michelin tire ad that shows a baby playing near tires or the life insurance company ad that shows a widow and her young children moving out of their home because they did not have enough insurance.

Not all emotional appeals are negative, though. Music is widely used to make us feel good about a message. Think about how few television commercials you have seen without some form of music either in the background or as a prominent part of the message. When we watch such commercials, we may associate the pleasant feelings of the music with the product, even though the music itself provides us with no information about the product.

The less informed we are about the topic of the message, the likelier we are to respond to an emotional appeal. However, most people are persuaded only when rational and emotional appeals are used together. The emotional appeal arouses our interest, and the facts give us a logical reason for going along with the message. Consider an ad for a new cell phone. Our emotions might be aroused by images of people using the cell phone to call for help or to keep in touch with someone attractive. But then we are given the facts that make the cell phone an appealing purchase. Perhaps the cost is reasonable, it is engineered to reduce static and broken connections, or it combines in one device the capabilities of a phone and an Internet connection.

One model that has been proposed to explain the relation between emotional and rational appeals is the **elaboration likelihood model.** It proposes two ways to persuade: a central route and a peripheral route (Petty & Cacioppo, 1986; Petty, Wheeler, & Bizer, 2000). The central route to persuasion works by engaging someone thoughtfully. The peripheral route involves nonmessage factors, such as the source's credibility and attractiveness or emotional appeals. The peripheral route is effective when people are not paying close attention to what the communicator is saying. As you might guess, television commercials often involve the peripheral route to persuasion on the assumption that during the commercials you are probably not paying full attention to the screen. However, the central route is more persuasive when people have the ability, and are motivated, to pay attention to the facts (Lammers, 2000).

Another aspect of the message that has been of interest to social psychologists is the order in which arguments are presented. Should you wait until the end of your presentation to make your strongest points or put your best foot forward at the beginning? The *foot-in-the-door strategy* involves presenting a weaker point at the beginning or making a small request with which the listeners will probably comply, saving the strongest point until the end. In the words of social psychologist Robert Cialdini (1993), "Start small and build." For example, a sales pitch for a health spa might offer you 4 weeks' use of the facility for $10 and hope that, after the 4 weeks, you will pay $200 for a 1-year membership.

In contrast, the *door-in-the-face strategy* involves a communicator making the strongest point or demand in the beginning, which the listeners probably will reject. Then a weaker point or moderate "concessionary" demand is made toward the end. For example, the salesperson for the health spa might offer you the 1-year membership for $200, which you turn down, and then offer you a "bargain" 4-weeks-for-$10 package.

The Medium   Another persuasion factor is which medium or technology to use to get the message across. Consider the difference between watching a presidential debate on television and reading about it in the newspaper. Television lets us see how the candidates deliver their messages, what their appearance and mannerisms are like, and so on. Because it presents live images, television is often considered to be a more powerful medium for changing attitudes. In one study, the winners of various political primaries were predicted by the amount of media exposure they had (Grush, 1980).

The Target (Audience)   Age and attitude strength are two characteristics of the audience that determine whether a message will be effective. Younger people are likelier to change their attitudes than older ones. And, if the attitudes of the audience are weak, attitude change is likelier; if audience attitudes are strong, the communicator will have more difficulty changing them.

Review and Sharpen Your Thinking

1   *Describe how people think about the social world.*

- Explain attribution.
- Discuss the three main elements of social perception.
- Identify the relationship between attitudes and behavior.

Which television ads do you like the best? Have they persuaded you to buy the products that are being advertised? What is it about the ads that is persuasive?

mhhe com/
santrockp7

For study tools related to this learning goal, see the Study Guide, the CD-ROM, and the Online Learning Center.

elaboration likelihood model States that there are two ways to persuade—by a central route and by a peripheral route.

Conformity and Obedience   **Group Influence**   **Leadership**

How are people influenced in social settings?

Another topic that social psychologists are interested in is how our behavior is influenced by other people and groups (Cialdini, 2001). The section on social thinking discussed how we present ourselves to others to influence their perceptions of us and how we can change other people's attitudes and behavior. This section explores some other aspects of social influence: conformity and obedience, group influence, and cultural and ethnic influences.

Conformity and Obedience

Research on conformity and obedience started in earnest after World War II. Psychologists began to seek answers to the disturbing question of how ordinary people could be influenced to commit the sort of atrocities inflicted on Jews, Gypsies, and other minorities during the Holocaust. How extensively will people change their behavior to coincide more with what others are doing? How readily do people obey someone in authority? What factors influence whether people will resist such social influences? These questions are still relevant when we try to understand contemporary events such as vicious group attacks on ethnic minorities or gays. They also are relevant in trying to understand everyday human behavior.

Conformity   **Conformity** is a change in a person's behavior to coincide more closely with a group standard. Conformity comes in many forms and affects many aspects of people's lives. Conformity is at work when a person takes up mountain biking because everyone else is doing it. Conformity also is at work when an individual cuts her hair short one year because short hair is fashionable and then lets it grow long the next year because long hair has become the vogue.

Although conformity has some unpleasant or unattractive aspects, it is not entirely a negative thing. People's conformity to rules and regulations allows society to run more smoothly. Consider how chaotic it would be if most people did not conform to social norms such as stopping at red lights, driving on the correct side of the road, going to school regularly, and not punching others in the face. However, some of the most dramatic and insightful work on conformity has examined how we sometimes act against our better judgment in order to conform.

Asch's Conformity Experiment   Put yourself in this situation: You are taken into a room in which you see five other people seated around a table. A person in a white lab coat enters the room and announces that you are about to participate in an experiment on perceptual accuracy. The group is shown two cards, the first having only a single vertical line on it, the second card three vertical lines of varying length. You are told that the task is to determine which of the three lines on the second card is the same length as the line on the first card. You look at the cards and think, "What a snap. It's so obvious which is the same" (see figure 16.5).

What you do not know is that the other people in the room are actually in league with the experimenter; they've been hired to perform in ways the experimenter dictates. On the first several trials, everyone agrees about which line matches the standard. Then, on the fourth trial, each of the others picks an incorrect line. As the last person to make a choice, you have the dilemma of responding as your eyes tell you or conforming to what the others before you said. How do you think you would answer?

conformity Involves a change in a person's behavior to coincide more with a group standard.

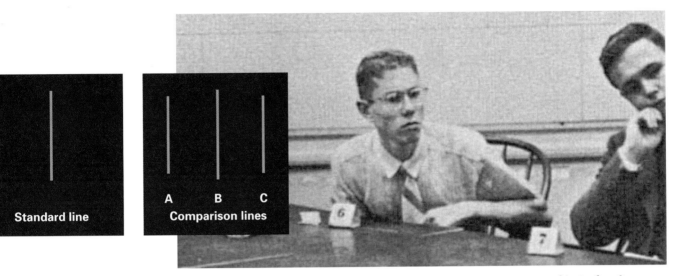

FIGURE 16.5 Asch's Conformity Experiment   The figures on the left show the stimulus materials for the Asch conformity experiment on group influence. The photograph shows the puzzlement of one subject after five confederates of the experimenter chose the incorrect line.

Solomon Asch conducted this classic experiment on conformity in 1951. He believed few of his volunteer participants would yield to group pressure. To test his hypothesis, Asch instructed the hired accomplices to give incorrect responses on 12 of the 18 trials. To his surprise, Asch (1951) found that the volunteer participants conformed to the incorrect answers 35 percent of the time.

In a more recent test of group pressure and conformity, college students watched the third George H. W. Bush–Bill Clinton presidential debate and then rated the candidates' performances (Fein & others, 1993). Students were randomly assigned to one of three groups: (1) a 30-student group that included 10 confederates of the experimenter who openly supported Bush and criticized Clinton, (2) a 30-student group that included 10 confederates who cheered Clinton and put down Bush, and (3) a 30-student group with no confederates of the experimenter. The effects of the group pressure exerted by the confederates were powerful; even Bush supporters rated Clinton's performance more favorably when their group included pro-Clinton confederates of the experimenter.

In sum, research has shown that the pressure to conform is strong (Pines & Maslach, 2002). Even when faced with clear-cut information such as the lines in the Asch experiment, we often conform to what others say and do. We do not want to be laughed at or make others angry at us.

Factors that Contribute to Conformity   Many factors influence whether an individual will conform or not (Cialdini & Trost, 1998). But in general people conform because of either normative social influence or informational social influence.

Normative social influence is the influence to conform that other people have on us because we seek their approval or seek to avoid their disapproval. So, if a group is important to us, we might wear a particular kind of clothing that people in the group wear, adopt a particular hairstyle, use the same slang words, and adopt a certain set of attitudes that characterize the group's members. This is true whether the group is an inner-city gang or members of a profession, such as the medical or legal profession.

Whereas normative social influence causes people to conform because they want to be liked, **informational social influence** causes people to conform because they want to be right (Taylor, Peplau, & Sears, 1997). The tendency to conform based on informational social influence depends especially on two factors: how confident we are in our own independent judgment and how well informed we perceive the group to be. Thus, if you don't know much about computers and three of your acquaintances who work in the computer industry tell you not to buy a particular brand of computer, you are likely to conform to their recommendation.

normative social influence The influence that other people have on us because we seek their approval or to avoid their disapproval.

informational social influence The influence other people have on us because we want to be right.

Researchers have found some other factors that are involved in conforming or not conforming:

- *Unanimity of the group.* In Asch's study with lines on cards, the group's opinion was unanimous. When the group's opinion is divided, individuals feel less pressure to conform.
- *Prior commitment.* If you do not have a prior commitment to an idea or action, you are likelier to be influenced by others. But if you have publicly committed to an idea or action, conformity to another idea or action is less likely.
- *Personal characteristics.* People with low self-esteem and doubts about their abilities are likelier to conform (Campbell, Tesser, & Fairey, 1986).
- *Group members' characteristics.* You are likelier to conform if the group members are experts, attractive to you, or similar to you in any way.
- *Cultural values.* In experiments conducted in 14 countries, conformity rates were lower in individualistic cultures (such as that of the United States), in which people tend to pursue their own interests, and higher in collectivistic cultures (such as that of China), in which people typically seek to contribute to the group's success (Bond & Smith, 1994).

Obedience   **Obedience** is behavior that complies with the explicit demands of the individual in authority. That is, we are obedient when an authority figure demands that we do something and we do it. How is obedience different from conformity? In conformity, people change their thinking or behavior so that it will be more like that of others. In contrast to obedience, there is no explicit demand to conform.

Obedient behavior sometimes can be distressingly cruel. The massacre of Vietnamese civilians at My Lai, described at the beginning of the chapter, and the Nazi crimes against Jews and others in World War II are examples of cruel obedience. A more recent example is the obedience of radical Islamics who are instructed to participate in suicide attacks and other acts of aggression against Israelis and Westerners. Acts like these seem obviously wrong, yet millions of people throughout history have obeyed commands to commit them.

A classic experiment by Stanley Milgram (1965, 1974) provides insight into such obedience. Imagine that, as part of an experiment in psychology, you are asked to deliver a series of painful electric shocks to another person. You are told that the purpose of the study is to determine the effects of punishment on memory. Your role is to be the "teacher" and punish the mistakes made by the "learner." Each time the learner makes a mistake, you are to increase the intensity of the shock by a certain amount.

You are introduced to the learner, a nice 50-year-old man who mumbles something about having a heart condition. He is strapped to a chair in the next room; he communicates with you through an intercom. The apparatus in front of you has thirty switches, ranging from 15 volts (light) to 450 volts (marked as dangerous, "severe shock XXX"). Before this part of the experiment began, you had been given a 75-volt shock to see how it felt.

As the trials proceed, the learner quickly runs into trouble and is unable to give the correct answers. Should you shock him? As you increase the intensity of the shock, the learner says he's in pain. At 150 volts, he demands to have the experiment stopped. At 180 volts, he cries out that he can't stand it anymore. At 300 volts, he yells about his heart condition and pleads to be released. But if you hesitate in shocking the learner, the experimenter tells you that you have no choice; the experiment must continue.

By the way, the 50-year-old man is in league with the experimenter. He is not being shocked at all. Of course the teachers are completely unaware that the learner is pretending to be shocked.

As you might imagine, the teachers in this experiment were uneasy about shocking the learner. At 240 volts, one teacher responded, "240 volts delivered; aw, no. You mean I've got to keep going with that scale? No sir, I'm not going to kill that

obedience Behavior that complies with the explicit demands of the individual in authority.

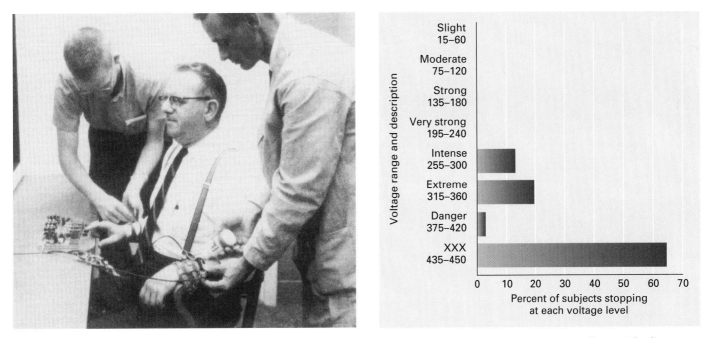

FIGURE 16.6 **Milgram Obedience Study** A 50-year-old man, the "learner," is strapped into a chair. The experimenter makes it look as if a shock generator is being connected to his body through several electrodes. The chart at the right shows the percentage of "teachers" who stopped shocking the learner at each voltage level.

man—I'm not going to give him 450 volts!" (Milgram, 1965). At the very strong voltage, the learner quit responding. When the teacher asked the experimenter what to do, the experimenter simply instructed the teacher to continue the experiment and told him that it was his obligation to complete the job.

Forty psychiatrists were asked how they thought individuals would respond to this situation. The psychiatrists predicted that most teachers would go no further than 150 volts, that fewer than 1 in 25 would go as far as 300 volts, and that only 1 in 1,000 would deliver the full 450 volts. The psychiatrists, it turns out, were way off the mark. The majority of the teachers obeyed the experimenter. In fact, almost two-thirds delivered the full 450 volts. Figure 16.6 shows the results of the Milgram study.

In subsequent studies, Milgram set up a storefront in Bridgeport, Connecticut, and recruited volunteers through newspaper ads. Milgram wanted to create a more natural environment for the experiment and to use a wider cross section of volunteers. In these additional studies, close to two-thirds of the individuals still selected the highest level of shock for the learner.

In variations of the experiment, Milgram discovered that more people would disobey in certain circumstances. Disobedience was more common when participants could see others disobey, when the authority figure was not perceived to be legitimate and was not close by, and when the victim was made to seem more human.

An important point has been raised about the Milgram experiments: How *ethical* were they? The volunteer teachers in Milgram's experiment clearly felt anguish, and some were very disturbed about "harming" another individual. After the experiment was completed, they were told that the learner was not actually shocked. But even though they were debriefed and told that they really had not shocked or harmed anyone, was the anguish imposed on them ethical?

Milgram argued that we have learned a great deal about human nature from the experiments. He claimed that they tell us how far individuals will go in their obedience, even if it means being cruel to someone. The volunteers were interviewed later, and more than four-fifths said that they were glad they had participated in the study; none said that they were sorry they participated.

When Milgram conducted his studies on obedience, the ethical guidelines for research were not as stringent as they are today. The current ethical guidelines of the American Psychological Association stress that researchers should obtain informed consent from their volunteers. Deception should be used only for very important pur-

In 1989, Chinese students led a massive demonstration against the government in Beijing. The students resisted the government's social influence by putting together resources to challenge the Chinese authorities; however, the government eventually eliminated the protests, massacring hundreds.

poses. Individuals are supposed to feel as good about themselves when the experiment is over as they did when it began. Under today's guidelines, it is unlikely that the Milgram experiment would be conducted.

Resistance to Social Influence "If a man does not keep pace with his companions, perhaps it is because he hears a different drummer. Let him step to the music which he hears, however measured or far away." Thoreau's words suggest that some of us resist social influence, just as helicopter pilot Hugh Thompson did in the My Lai massacre in Vietnam. Most of us would prefer to think of ourselves as stepping to our own music, maybe even setting the rhythms for others, rather than trying to keep pace with our companions. However, a certain degree of conformity is required if society is to function at all. As we go through our lives, we are both conformists and nonconformists. Sometimes we are overwhelmed by the persuasion and influence of others; in other circumstances we resist and gain personal control over our lives. It is important to remember that our relation to the social world is reciprocal. Individuals may be trying to control us, but we can exert personal control over our actions and influence others in turn (Bandura, 1986).

If you believe that someone in a position of authority is making an unjust request or ordering you to do something wrong, what choice of action do you have?

- You can comply.
- You can give the appearance of complying but secretly do otherwise.
- You can publicly dissent by showing doubts and disenchantment but still follow the request/order.
- You can openly disregard the order and refuse to comply.
- You can challenge or confront the authority.
- You can get higher authorities to intervene or organize a group of people who agree with you to show the strength of your view.

Resistance to authority can be difficult, but living with the knowledge that you compromised your own moral integrity may be more difficult in the long run.

Group Influence

A student joining a campus organization, a jury making a decision about a criminal case, a president of a company delegating authority, a prejudiced remark against a minority group, conflict among nations, and attempts to reach peace—all of these circumstances reflect our lives as members of groups. They range in size from *dyads*, which consist of two people, to immense groups of all the people linked by national identity, religion, ethnicity, or gender. Some groups we choose, others we do not. We choose to belong to a club, but we are all born into a particular family, for example.

Regardless of their size, groups serve a useful human purpose. They satisfy our personal needs, reward us, provide information, raise our self-esteem, and give us an identity. We might join a group because we think it will be enjoyable and exciting and satisfy our need for affiliation and companionship. We might join a group because we will receive rewards, either material or psychological. For example, by taking a job with a company, we not only get paid to work as part of a group but we also reap a portion of the company's prestige and recognition. Groups are also an important source of information. For example, as we listen to other members talk in a Weight Watchers group we learn about their strategies for losing weight.

Many of the groups of which we are members—family, college, company, ethnicity—also provide identities; when asked who we are, we often answer in terms of which groups we belong to.

Some of the important questions about group relations that interest social psychologists are these: What is the structure of groups? How does group performance compare with individual performance? How do people in groups interact and make decisions?

The Structure of Groups Any group to which you belong has certain things in common with all other groups. One is the existence of *norms*, or rules that are specific to that group and apply to all of its members. Norms can be formal or informal. An example of a formal norm is an employer's requirement that all of its workers wear socks or Mensa's requirement that all of its members demonstrate a high IQ. Informal norms are such things as the subtle pressure you face to sit in the same seat or the same area of a lecture hall every time you attend a certain class.

Another characteristic that all groups have in common is a set of *roles*, or expectations that govern certain positions in the group. Roles define how different people in the group behave. In a family, parent is one role, sibling is another role, and grandparent is yet another role. A parent isn't expected to behave the same way toward the children in a family that siblings or grandparents are expected to behave. On a football team, many different roles must be fulfilled: on offense alone, center, guard, tackle, end, quarterback, running back, and wide receiver; each member of the team has a different job to do to accomplish the group's goals.

Group Performance The very first experiment in social psychology examined the question of whether individuals perform better in a group or when alone. Norman Triplett (1898) found that bicyclists performed better when they raced against each other than when they raced alone against the clock. Triplett also built a "competition machine" made out of fishing reels. The machine allowed two individuals to turn the reels side by side. Observing 40 children, he discovered that those who reeled next to another child worked faster than those who reeled alone.

Since Triplett's work over a century ago, many investigations of group versus individual performance have been conducted. Some studies reveal that we do better in groups, others that we are more productive when we work alo,ne (Paulus, 1989). We can make sense out of these contradictory findings by looking more closely at the circumstances in which performance is being analyzed.

Social Facilitation **Social facilitation** occurs when an individual's performance improves because of the presence of others. Robert Zajonc (1965) argued that the presence of other individuals arouses us. The arousal produces energy and facilitates our performance in groups. If our arousal is too high, however, we won't be able to learn new or difficult tasks efficiently. Social facilitation, then, improves our performance on well-learned tasks. For new or difficult tasks, we might be best advised to work things out on our own before trying them in a group.

In one investigation, expert and poor pool players were observed in the student union at Virginia Polytechnic Institute (Michaels & others, 1982). When they were observed unobtrusively, the experts hit 71 percent of their shots, the poor players 36 percent. When four individuals walked up to observe their play, the experts improved, making 80 percent of their shots. The poor players got worse, however, making only 25 percent of their shots.

Social Loafing Another factor in group performance is how closely our behavior is monitored. **Social loafing** refers to each person's tendency to exert less effort in a group because of reduced accountability for individual effort. The effect of social loafing is lowered group performance (Latané, 1981). Social loafing is common when a group of students is assigned a school project. Also, the larger the group, the likelier it is that a person can loaf without being detected. Among the ways to decrease social loafing are to increase the identifiability and uniqueness of individual contributions, to make it easier to evaluate these contributions, and to make the task more attractive (Karau & Williams, 1993).

The tendency to socially loaf is linked to gender and culture. Men are likelier to loaf than women (Karau & Williams, 1993). Why might this be the case? Because women are more likely to care about the welfare of others in the group and the group's

Do you perform better as a member of a group or as an individual?

social facilitation Occurs when an individual's performance improves because of the presence of others.

social loafing Each person's tendency to exert less effort in a group because of reduced monitoring.

We can become deindividuated in groups. People can lose their individual identities in situations such as Mardi Gras (*top*) and national patriotic displays (*bottom*).

collective performance. In contrast, men tend to be more individualistic, focusing on their own needs and performances (Wood, 1987). The tendency to socially loaf is stronger in individualistic Western cultures such as in the United States than in collectivistic Eastern cultures such as in China and Japan (Karau & Williams, 1993).

Under certain conditions, working with others can increase, rather than decrease, individual effort (Levine, 2000). For example, a person who views the group's task as important and who does not expect other group members to contribute adequately to the group's performance is likely to work harder than usual.

Deindividuation Individuals in groups also can become deindividuated and thus behave much differently than they would on their own (Dodd, 1995). **Deindividuation** occurs when being part of a group reduces personal identity and erodes the sense of personal responsibility. As early as 1895, Gustav LeBon observed that being in a group can foster uninhibited behavior, ranging from wild celebrations to mob activity. Ku Klux Klan violence, Mardi Gras wild times, and spring break riots might be due to deindividuated behavior.

One explanation of deindividuation is that groups give us anonymity. We may act in a disinhibited way because we believe that authority figures and victims are unlikely to identify us as the culprits.

Group Interaction and Decision Making Many of the decisions we make take place in groups—juries, teams, families, clubs, school boards, the Senate, or a class vote, for example (Davis, 1996; Levine & Moreland, 1998). What happens when people put their minds to the task of making a group decision? How do they decide whether a criminal is guilty, whether a country should attack another, whether a family should stay home or go on vacation, or whether sex education should be part of a school curriculum? Three aspects of group decision making bear special mention: the *risky shift* and *group polarization*, *groupthink*, and *majority-minority influence*.

The Risky Shift and Group Polarization When we make decisions in a group, do we take risks and stick our necks out, or do we compromise our opinions and move toward the center? The evidence is mixed.

Some research indicates that many times group decisions are riskier than individual decisions. The **risky shift** is the tendency for a group decision to be riskier than the average decision made by the individual group members. In one investigation, fictitious dilemmas were presented, and participants were asked how much risk the characters in the dilemmas were willing to take (Stoner, 1961). When the individuals discussed the dilemmas as a group, they were more willing to respond that the characters would make risky decisions than when they were queried alone. Many studies have been conducted on this topic with similar results (Goethals & Demorest, 1995).

We do not always make riskier decisions in a group than when alone, however; hundreds of research studies show that being in a group moves us more strongly in the direction of the position we initially held (Moscovici, 1985). The **group polarization effect** is the solidification and further strengthening of a position as a consequence of a group discussion. For instance, imagine a "hawk" and a "dove" in the U.S. Senate who listen to the same endless hours of committee discussion about nuclear disarmament. Research indicates that neither is likely to be converted to a different point of view. After 2 years on the committee, each will be even more strongly committed to his or her position than before the deliberation began. Initially held views often become more polarized because of group discussion.

Group polarization may occur because people hear new, more persuasive arguments that strengthen their original position and they dismiss the arguments that do not support their position. Group polarization also might occur because of social comparison. We may find that our opinion is not as extreme as others' opinions and be influenced to take a stand at least as strong as the most extreme advocate's position.

deindividuation Occurs when being part of a group reduces personal identity and the sense of responsibility.

risky shift The tendency for a group decision to be riskier than the average decision made by individual group members.

group polarization effect The solidification and further strengthening of a position as a consequence of a group discussion.

Groupthink In 1961, when John F. Kennedy was president, the United States sent a group of Cuban exiles into Cuba on a mission to overthrow Communist dictator Fidel Castro. The plan failed miserably: The exiles were either captured or killed, Castro remained in power, and the United States looked rather foolish. How could the very intelligent men in the Kennedy administration have agreed to go through with such a fiasco as the Bay of Pigs?

According to social psychologist Irving Janis (1972), the answer is **groupthink,** which refers to group members' impaired decision making and avoidance of realistic appraisal in order to maintain group harmony. Groupthink evolves because members are motivated to boost each other's egos and increase each other's self-esteem in search of conformity, especially in the face of stress. Groupthink involves many heads, but only one group mind. This motivation for harmony and unanimity can result in disastrous decisions.

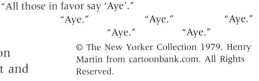

"All those in favor say 'Aye'."
"Aye." "Aye." "Aye."
"Aye." "Aye."

© The New Yorker Collection 1979. Henry Martin from cartoonbank.com. All Rights Reserved.

Following are some of the symptoms of groupthink and how they worked in the Kennedy administration's Bay of Pigs decision (Stolley, 2001):

- *Overestimation of the power and morality of the group*. The Kennedy decision makers believed that they could keep news of their involvement secret and that the world would think the Cuban dissidents were acting on their own. Although at least two group members had misgivings about the plan's morality, these were either not voiced or not evaluated in meetings, which reflects a symptom of groupthink: ignoring moral consequences.
- *Closed-mindedness*. After a group has selected a course of action, it is difficult for the group to change that course, even when the course of action is going badly. As they recommit to past decisions, group members collectively rationalize what they have decided to do, discounting warnings and other negative indications that might call previous policy decisions into question. The Kennedy group believed that Castro's forces would be easy to overcome, an example of such discounting. However, the Cuban Air Force shot down half of the U.S. planes sent to protect the invading exiles and bombed the invaders arriving on Cuban shores.
- *Pressures toward uniformity*. Members pressure those who momentarily express misgivings to conform with the plan supported by the majority. President Kennedy did not provide adequate time for discussion of dissidents' concerns and played down the criticisms of the one group member who had serious doubts about the Bay of Pigs invasion. Some members may act as "mindguards" to suppress dissenting views or information that conflicts with the group's decision. For instance, the Secretary of State kept the group from learning about the concerns raised by the director of the United States Information Agency. Group members also tend to suppress their own doubts.

Groupthink has been behind many disasters. Other examples in U.S. history are failure to prepare for the Japanese bombing of Pearl Harbor during World War II, escalation of the Vietnam War in the 1960s, the Watergate cover-up that led to President Richard Nixon's resignation in 1974, and the explosion of the space shuttle *Challenger* in 1986. In the case of the *Challenger*, NASA leaders went ahead with its launch despite engineers' warnings that freezing temperatures at the launch site might damage O-ring seals, which did fail during the launch, and cause the rocket's explosion—and the death of all aboard. Because of a string of successes in prior launches and the overconfidence of NASA leaders, the engineers' objections were ignored in a disastrous groupthink decision.

Here are some helpful strategies for avoiding groupthink:

- *Reduce isolation*. Invite people who are not part of the decision-making group to attend meetings. Encourage them to give their opinions and criticize plans without any retribution.

groupthink Involves impaired decision making and avoidance of realistic appraisal to maintain group harmony.

Certain individuals in the minority have played important roles in history. (*Top*) Martin Luther King, Jr., helped African Americans gain important rights. (*Bottom*) Corazon Aquino, who became president of the Philippines after defeating Ferdinand Marcos, toppled a corrupt political regime and reduced the suffering of many Philippine citizens.

- *Make leadership impartial.* To encourage a wide range of options, leaders should not state their own preferences and expectations up front.
- *Use outside experts.* They may put a different perspective on the issues at hand and can challenge core beliefs of the group.
- *Discuss with trusted subordinates.* Before final consensus, each member should report to the group what their own associates outside of the group have to say about the topic under consideration.
- *Hold second-chance meetings and review sessions.* After the "final" decision has been made, meet again to provide a second chance to object to the group decision before it is implemented.

Majority and Minority Influence In most groups—even when groupthink is not involved—the majority of the members tend to hold sway over the minority. Think about the groups in which you have been a member. The majority exerts both normative and informational pressure on the group: It sets the group's norm; those who do not go along may be ignored or even given the boot. The majority also has a greater opportunity to provide information that will influence decision making.

Although in most cases the majority wins, sometimes the minority has its day (Latané, 1996). The minority cannot win through normative pressure because it is outnumbered; so, it must do its work through informational pressure. If the minority presents its view consistently and confidently, then the majority is likelier to listen to the minority's views.

Certain individuals within the minority may play a crucial role. For instance, those who can command the attention of others have a better opportunity to shape and direct the group's decision making. To achieve such influence, individuals have to distinguish themselves in various ways from the rest of the group. They have to make themselves noticed by the opinions they express, the jokes they tell, or their nonverbal style. They might be the first ones to raise a new idea, to disagree with a prevailing point of view, or to propose a creative alternative solution to a problem. People who have a strong social influence often are willing to be different.

Individuals with a history of taking minority stands also have influence. They may trigger others to dissent by showing them that disagreement is possible and may indeed be the best course. Such is the basis of some of history's greatest moments. When Lincoln spoke out against slavery, racism dominated and tore at the country; when Corazon Aquino became a candidate for president of the Philippines, few people thought Ferdinand Marcos could be beaten.

The influence of the minority has been studied in jury room deliberations (Hastie, 2001). Researchers have found that the people on a jury with a minority view often convince the majority to change their minds. Is that a good thing or a bad thing? Although trials would proceed faster if the jury's initial majority vote determined the defendant's innocence or guilt, a number of social psychologists believe that the minority opinion is useful in the deliberation process (Aronson, Wilson, & Akert, 1997). First, forcing juries to reach a unanimous verdict with both majority and minority coming to an agreement makes everyone consider the evidence more carefully (Hastie, Penrod, & Pennington, 1983). Second, even if the minority seldom succeeds in convincing the majority to change their opinion about guilt or innocence, the minority often does change opinions about the degree of guilt. In criminal trials, juries often have some discretion about the type of guilty verdict, such as first-degree murder, second-degree murder, or manslaughter.

Leadership

What makes people leaders? What makes them so influential within a group that others willingly follow them into difficult or even dangerous endeavors? Is it a set of personality traits, the situations in which leaders emerge, or some combination of the two?

The *great-person theory* states that some individuals have certain traits that are best suited for leadership positions. Leaders are commonly thought to be assertive, cooperative, decisive, dominant, energetic, self-confident, tolerant of stress, willing to assume responsibility, diplomatic and tactful, and persuasive. "I am certainly not one of those who needs to be prodded," the British Prime Minister Winston Churchill once said of himself. "In fact, if anything, I am the prod." This is a classic statement of the great-person theory. However, although we can list traits and skills possessed by leaders, a large number of research studies conclude that we cannot predict who will become a leader solely from the individual's personality characteristics (Wilson, 2002).

Is it the situation, then, that produces leaders? The *situational view* of leadership argues that the needs of a group change from time to time. The individual who emerges as the leader in one particular circumstance will not necessarily be the individual who becomes the leader in another circumstance. But what determines which member of a group emerges as leader in a particular situation?

The *contingency model* of leadership states that both personality characteristics and situational influences determine who will become a leader. It views leadership as a complex undertaking in which leaders influence their followers and followers influence their leaders (Fielder, 1978). The contingency model notes that leaders have two basic styles: They direct their efforts either toward getting a task completed or toward helping group members get along. If a group is working under very favorable or very unfavorable conditions, a task-oriented leader is better, but if working conditions are moderate, a relationship-oriented leader is better. These ideas have not been fully tested by researchers, but the concept that leadership is a function of both personality characteristics and situational influences is an important one.

The idea of different leadership styles has been useful to social psychologists studying the increasing number of women in leadership roles that once were reserved for men. Reviews of research on gender and leadership conclude that men appear to be more directive and task-oriented leaders, whereas women are more democratic and interpersonally oriented (O'Leary & Flanagan, 2001). A man might just tell people what to do, whereas a woman might say, "Let's discuss how we should go about doing this and let's also get some more opinions."

By adopting a participative and collaborative style, women may be able to overcome others' resistance to their leadership, win their acceptance, gain self-confidence, and be effective (Lips, 2003). And, indeed, women have proved to be very effective leaders. In one recent study, ratings of 9,000 female and male managers by subordinates and peers indicated that women were perceived as more effective leaders than men were (Center for Leadership Studies, 2000). This outcome may reflect more than just preference for relationship-oriented leadership or the influence of gender roles. It may also reflect the tendency for women to have to meet a higher standard than men to attain leadership positions and then to have to maintain a higher standard of performance.

Review and Sharpen Your Thinking

2 *Identify how people are influenced in social settings.*

- Describe the factors that affect conformity and obedience.
- Discuss group performance.
- Summarize the factors that influence leadership.

How do you think you would have responded in the Asch conformity and Milgram obedience experiments? What makes you say so? Have you ever been in a situation in which social circumstances seemed to pressure you to do something against your values?

mhhe com/
santrockp7

For study tools related to this learning goal, see the Study Guide, the CD-ROM, and the Online Learning Center.

3 INTERGROUP RELATIONS

Group Identity:
Us Versus Them

Prejudice

Ways to Improve
Interethnic Relations

What affects relations between groups?

Conflicts between groups, especially ethnic and cultural groups, are rampant around the world today (Chirot & Seligman, 2001). Groups such as al-Qaida attack countries such as the United States that they perceive to be too secular and materialistic. And the United States retaliates. Israelis and Palestinians fight over territory in the Middle East, each claiming religious and historical rights to the disputed land. In countries across Africa, tribal chiefs try to craft a new social order favorable to their own rule. In Northern Ireland, clashes between Catholics and Protestants still break out. Prejudice, stereotyping, ethnocentrism, and other concepts introduced by social psychologists can help us understand the intensity of such cultural and ethnic conflicts and how to reduce the conflicts (Ellemers, Spears, & Doosje, 2002; Hewstone, Rubin, & Willis, 2002).

Group Identity: Us Versus Them

Think about the groups in which you are a member—possibly social organizations, your ethnicity, your nationality. When someone asks you to identify yourself, how often do you respond by mentioning these group memberships? And how much does it matter to you whether the people you associate with are members of the same groups?

Ethnicity and Religion

Asian American
Jewish
Southern Baptist
West Indian

Political Affiliation

Feminist
Republican
Environmentalist

Vocations and Avocations

Psychologist
Artist
Athlete
Military veteran

Relationships

Mother
Parent
Teenager
Widow

Stigmatized Identities

Person with AIDS
Homeless person
Overweight person
Alcoholic

FIGURE 16.7 **Types of Identity**

Social Identity   **Social identity** refers to the way we define ourselves in terms of our group membership (Deaux, 2002). In contrast to personal identity, which can be highly individualized, social identity assumes some commonalities with others. A person's social identity might include identifying with a religious group, a country, a social organization, and many others. To identify with a group does not necessarily mean that we know or interact with every other member of the group. However, it does mean that we believe that we share numerous features with other members of the group.

Many forms of social identity exist, reflecting the many ways in which people connect to other groups and social categories. Social psychologist Kay Deaux (2001) identified five distinct types of social identity: ethnic and religious, political, vocations and avocations, personal relationships, and stigmatized groups (see figure 16.7).

For many people, ethnic identity and religious identity are central aspects of their social identity (Eriksen, 2001). Social psychologist Henry Tajfel (1978), one of a small number of Jews who survived the Holocaust, wanted to explain the extreme violence and prejudice that his religious group experienced. Tajfel's **social identity theory** states that when individuals are assigned to a group, they invariably think of their group as an in-group. This occurs because they want to have a positive self-image.

Self-image consists of both a personal identity and many different social identities. Tajfel argues that individuals can improve their self-images by enhancing either their personal or their social identities, but he believes that social identity is especially important. Think about how you behave when you introduce yourself to a stranger. Are you more likely to say, "Hi, I'm an ambitious hard-working idealist"? Or are you more likely to say, "Hi, I'm a student at State U. and I'm a member of the debate team"? Chances are you are more likely to tell people about the groups with which you identify.

(*Left*) A Palestinian—Israeli clash in the Gaza Strip. (*Right*) An outbreak of violence in Northern Ireland. *How might a group's social identity be involved in such violence?*

We are continually comparing our groups (*in-groups*) with other groups (*out-groups*). In the process, we often focus more on the differences between the two groups than on their similarities. Imagine two fans of professional basketball teams, one a Los Angeles Lakers fan, the other a Philadelphia 76ers fan. As these two fans talk, they are less likely to discuss how much they both like basketball than to argue about the virtues of their teams. As they strive to promote their social identities, they soon lapse into self-congratulatory remarks about their own team and nasty comments about the opposing team. In short, the theme of the conversation has become "My team is good and I am good. Your team is bad and you are bad." And so it goes with the sexes, ethnic groups, nations, socioeconomic groups, religions, sororities, fraternities, and countless other groups. These comparisons often lead to competition and even discrimination against other groups. Thus, social identity theory helps explain prejudice and conflict between groups.

Tajfel (1978) showed how easy it is to lead people to think in terms of "we" and "they." In one experiment, he assigned those who overestimated the number of dots on a screen to one group and those who underestimated the number to another group. Once assigned to the two groups, the participants were asked to award money to the other participants. Invariably, individuals awarded money only to members of their own group. If we favor our own group on such trivial criteria, it is no wonder that we show intense in-group favoritism when differences are not so trivial (Jussim, Ashmore, & Wilder, 2001).

Ethnocentrism   At the beginning of the twenty-first century, group pride—especially group pride based on ethnicity and culture—has mushroomed. There's Black Pride and Gay Pride. The Scots grow more Scottish, the Brazilians more Brazilian, Americans more American. The tendency to favor one's own group over other groups is called **ethnocentrism.** Ethnocentrism's positive side is that it fosters a sense of pride in the group that fulfills the human urge to attain and maintain a positive self-image. Of course, the negative side of ethnocentrism is that it encourages in-group/out-group, we/they thinking.

There is something paradoxical, though, about ethnic pride. Most members of an ethnic group celebrate their own heritage and culture and set themselves apart from, and even above, others. But, still, they often attest that they do not discriminate against others. As African American activist Stokely Carmichael said in 1966, "I'm for the Negro. I'm not against anything." In reality, however, members of ethnic groups often stress differences with others rather than solely emphasizing pride in their own group.

In-group pride does not always reflect ethnocentrism. African Americans, Latinos, as well as members of other groups such as women, gays, and lesbians often assert in-group pride to counter the negative messages transmitted by society about their group (Crocker, Major, & Steele, 1998).

social identity Refers to the way we define ourselves in terms of group memberships.

social identity theory Tajfel's theory that when individuals are assigned to a group, they invariably think of it as an in-group.

ethnocentrism The tendency to favor one's own ethnic group over other groups.

Group members often show considerable pride in their group identity, as reflected in Mexican Americans' celebration of Cinco de Mayo, Native Americans' celebration of their heritage, Polish Americans' celebration of their cultural background, and African Americans' celebration of Martin Luther King Day.

prejudice An unjustified negative attitude toward an individual based on the individual's membership in a group.

Prejudice

Understanding the antagonism that develops between groups requires knowledge about prejudice and the stereotyping and discrimination that often accompany it (Fishbein, 2002; Schaller & Conway, 2001). Like most people, you probably do not consider yourself as prejudiced. But, in fact, each of us has prejudices. **Prejudice** is an unjustified negative attitude toward an individual based on the individual's membership in a group. The group can be made up of people of a particular race, sex, age, religion, or nationality or can share some other detectable difference from the prejudiced individual (Jones, 1997; Nelson, 2002).

Prejudice, as a worldwide phenomenon (Baker, 2001), has seen many eruptions of hatred in human history. The Taliban were so prejudiced against women that they tried to make them invisible. Serbs were so prejudiced against Bosnians that they pursued a policy of "ethnic cleansing." Hutus in Rwanda were so prejudiced against Tutsis that they went on a murderous rampage, hacking off their arms and legs with machetes. European Americans were so prejudiced against Native Americans that they systematically robbed them of their property and self-respect, killed them, and herded the survivors like animals onto reservations.

The most blatant instance of destructive prejudice in U.S. history is racial prejudice against African Americans. When Africans were brought to America as slaves, they were considered property and treated inhumanely. In the first half of the twentieth century, most African Americans still lived in the South and were still largely segregated from White society by law; restaurants, movie theaters, and buses had separate areas for Whites and African Americans. Even decades after legal segregation was abolished, much higher percentages of African Americans than Whites live in impoverished neighborhoods and lack access to good schools, jobs, and health care.

African Americans and Native Americans are not the only ethnic minority groups that have been subjected to prejudice in the United States. Historically, emigrants from Europe, Asia, and other parts of the world have struggled against the negative attitudes of those born in the United States. Many Latinos, Vietnamese, and others also live below the poverty line and may be limited in educational opportunities and to low-paying jobs. Lesbians and gays also have been subjected to considerable prejudice by the heterosexual majority. This prejudice has been so intense that most homosexuals stayed "in the closet" until recently, not revealing their sexual preferences for fear of jeopardizing other members of their community and losing their jobs or even their lives. In fact, virtually every social group has been the victim of prejudice at one time or another.

Why do people develop prejudice? Among the reasons given by social psychologists are the following (Monteith, 2000):

- *Individual personality.* Some years ago social psychologist Theodor Adorno and his colleagues (1950) described the *authoritarian personality:* strict adherence to conventional ways of behaving, aggression against people who violate conventional norms, rigid thinking, and exaggerated submission to authority. He believed that individuals with an authoritarian personality are likely to be prejudiced. However, not all individuals who harbor prejudice have an authoritarian personality.
- *Competition between groups over scarce resources.* Feelings of hostility and prejudice can develop when a society does not have enough jobs or land or power or status—or any of a number of other material and social resources—to go around. Given the historical distributions of resources in a particular society, certain groups may regularly be involved in competing with each other and thus be likeier to develop prejudice toward each other. For instance, immigrants often compete with established low-income members of a society for jobs, leading to persistent conflict between the two groups.
- *Motivation to enhance self-esteem.* As Henry Tajfel (1978) stated, individuals derive a sense of self-esteem through their identification as members of a particular group and, to the extent that their group is viewed more favorably than other groups, their self-esteem will be further enhanced. In this view, prejudice against other groups leads to a positive social identity and higher self-esteem.
- *Cognitive processes that contribute to a tendency to categorize and stereotype others.* Human beings are limited in their capacity for careful and thorough thought (Allport, 1954). The social environment is extremely complex and makes many demands on our limited information processing capacity, which can produce an unfortunate consequence: simplification of the social environment through categorization and stereotyping. Once stereotypes are in place, prejudice is often not far behind.
- *Cultural learning.* Families, friends, traditional norms, and institutionalized patterns of discrimination provide plenty of opportunities for individuals to be exposed to the prejudice of others. In this manner, others' prejudiced belief systems can be incorporated into one's own system. Children often show prejudice before they even have the cognitive abilities or social opportunities to develop their own attitudes.

Stereotyping At the very root of prejudice is a **stereotype,** a generalization about a group's characteristics that does not consider any variations from one individual to the next (Kite, 2001). Think about your image of a dedicated accountant. Most of us would probably describe such a person as quiet, boring, unsociable, and so on. Rarely would we come up with a mental image of this person as extraverted, the life of the party, or artistic. But characterizing all accountants as introverts is a clear example of a stereotype. Some accountants may be reserved, but at least some are likely to be sociable.

Researchers have found that we are less likely to detect variations among individuals who belong to "other" groups than among individuals who belong to "our" group. For example, studies of eyewitness identification have found that Whites tend to stereotype African Americans more than other Whites during eyewitness identification (Brigham, 1986). What might be occurring is the tendency to view members of one's own group as having heterogeneous and desirable qualities and to view the members of other groups as having homogeneous and undesirable qualities.

Although stereotyping can be harmful, we should keep in mind that all people stereotype. As was discussed in chapter 9, people use categories, or schemas, when thinking about groups and individuals from these groups (Fiske, 1998; Steele, 1996). Thus, we might engage in stereotyping without being aware of it (Greenwald & Banaji, 1995). The main problem is not that we use these categories but that we limit our perceptions of others to the rough outlines of the schema; we do not add specific information about an individual's characteristics. In addition, we may develop biases against whole groups of people.

Emotion also can be involved in stereotyping (Bodenhausen & others, 2001). Anger especially can intensify stereotyping by producing irrational and biased judgments about people.

Discrimination Having a stereotype does not mean that you have to act on it. But if you do act on your prejudices, you may be guilty of **discrimination,** an unjustified negative or harmful action toward a member of a group simply because the person belongs to that group. Discrimination results when negative emotional reactions combine with prejudiced beliefs and are translated into behavior.

Early research on discrimination focused on overt forms of discrimination in which the target (person or group), the action, and the intention of the actor were clear and identifiable. Overt discrimination is the outcome of old-fashioned racism or sexism. The actor tries to maintain self-esteem by using the power of being a member of a particular group to treat women or individuals from ethnic minority groups unfairly.

Overt discrimination is no longer acceptable in mainstream American society, however. Civil rights legislation and changing attitudes expressed widely in popular media have made it "politically incorrect" to publicly discriminate. But more subtle forms of racism have appeared, described by such terms as *symbolic racism, aversive racism, ambivalent racism,* and *modern racism* (Blair, 2001). They involve negative feelings about minority groups, but not traditional stereotypes. Symbolic racism assumes that, because discrimination is no longer acceptable, it must not exist; any difficulties that individuals in minority groups might face are their own fault. It encompasses the ideas that African Americans, for example, are pushing too hard and too fast for equality, are making unfair demands, and are getting undeserved special attention, such as favoritism in job hiring and college admissions (Taylor, Peplau, & Sears, 2003). This subtler form of racism is based on discrimination that is covert rather than overt, unconscious rather than conscious, and denied rather than acknowledged (Monteith & Voils, 2001).

Ways to Improve Interethnic Relations

Martin Luther King, Jr., once said, "I have a dream that my four little children will one day live in a nation where they will not be judged by the color of their skin but

stereotype A generalization about a group's characteristics that does not consider any variations from one individual to another.

discrimination An unjustified negative or harmful action toward a member of a group simply because he or she is a member of that group.

by the content of their character." How might we possibly reach the world King envisioned, a world without prejudice and discrimination? Researchers have consistently found that contact itself—attending the same school or living next door to each other or working in the same company—does not necessarily improve relations with people from other ethnic backgrounds (Brewer & Brown, 1998). They have found that more focused efforts, such as task-oriented cooperation and intimate contact, are needed to break down barriers based on prejudice.

Task-Oriented Cooperation   Decades ago, social psychologist Muzafer Sherif and his colleagues (1961) fueled "we/they" competition between two groups of 11-year-old boys at a summer camp called Robbers Cave in Oklahoma. In the 1st week, one group hardly knew the other group existed. One group became known as the Rattlers (a tough, cursing group whose shirts were emblazoned with a snake insignia), and the other was known as the Eagles.

Near the end of the 1st week each group learned of the other's existence. It took little time for "we/they" talk to surface ("They had better not be on our ball field." "Did you see the way one of them was sneaking around?"). Sherif, who disguised himself as a janitor so he could unobtrusively observe the Rattlers and Eagles, arranged for the two groups to compete in baseball, touch football, and tug-of-war. Counselors manipulated and judged events so the teams were close. Each team perceived the other to be competing unfairly. Raiding the other group's area, burning the other group's flag, and fighting resulted. The Rattlers and Eagles further derided one another, holding their noses in the air as they passed each other. Rattlers described all Rattlers as brave, tough, and friendly and called all Eagles sneaky and smart alecks. The Eagles reciprocated by calling the Rattlers crybabies.

After "we/they" conflict transformed the Rattlers and Eagles into opposing "armies," Sherif devised ways to reduce hatred between the groups. He tried noncompetitive contact, but that didn't work. Only when both groups were required to work cooperatively to solve a problem did the Rattlers and Eagles develop a positive relationship. Sherif created tasks that required the efforts of both groups: working together to repair the only water supply to the camp, pooling their money to rent a movie, and cooperating to pull the camp truck out of a ditch. Figure 16.8 shows how competitive and cooperative activities changed perceptions of the out-group.

Might Sherif's idea—creating cooperation between groups rather than competition—be applied to ethnic groups? When the schools in Austin, Texas, were desegregated through extensive busing, increased racial tension among African Americans, Mexican Americans, and Whites resulted in violence in the schools. The superintendent consulted Eliot Aronson, a prominent social psychologist, who was at the University of Texas at Austin at the time. Aronson (1986) thought it was more important to prevent ethnic hostility than to control it. He observed a number of elementary school classrooms in Austin and saw how fierce the competition was between children of unequal status.

Aronson stressed that the reward structure of the classrooms needed to be changed from a setting of unequal competition to one of cooperation among equals, without making any curriculum changes. To accomplish this, he put together the *jigsaw classroom*. The jigsaw classroom works by creating a situation in which all of the students have to pull together to get the "big picture." Let's say we have a class of 30 students, some White, some African American, and some Latino. The academic goal is to learn about the life of Joseph Pulitzer. The class might be broken up into five study groups of six students each, with the groups being as equal as possible in ethnic composition and academic achievement level. Learning about Pulitzer's life becomes a class project divided into

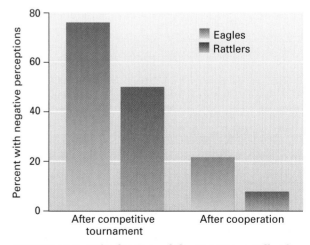

FIGURE 16.8 Attitudes Toward the Out-Group Following Competitive and Cooperative Activities   In Sherif's research, hostility peaked after an athletic tournament, as reflected in the high percentage of Eagles and Rattlers who perceived the other group unfavorably following this event. However, after the groups worked together to reach a goal, their unfavorable attitudes toward each other dropped considerably.

Eliot Aronson developed the concept of the jigsaw classroom to reduce ethnic conflict. *How does the jigsaw classroom work?*

six parts, with one part given to each member of the six-person group. The components might be paragraphs from Pulitzer's biography, such as how the Pulitzer family came to the United States, Pulitzer's childhood, his early work, and so on. The parts are like the pieces of a jigsaw puzzle: They have to be put together to form the complete puzzle.

Each student has an allotted time to study her or his part. Then the group meets, and each member tries to teach her or his part to the group. Each student must learn the entire lesson, so learning depends on the cooperation and effort of other members. After an hour or so each student is tested on the life of Pulitzer. Aronson believes that cooperatively working to reach a common goal increases students' interdependence.

The strategy of emphasizing cooperation rather than competition and the jigsaw approach have been widely used in classrooms in the United States (Johnson & Johnson, 1999, 2003). A number of studies reveal that this type of cooperative learning is associated with increased self-esteem, better academic performance, friendships among classmates, and improved interethnic perceptions (Slavin, 1989).

It is not easy to get groups who do not like each other to cooperate. The air of distrust and hostility is hard to overcome. Creating goals that require cooperation of both groups is one viable strategy, as shown in Sherif's and Aronson's work. Other strategies involve spreading positive information about the "other" and reducing the potential threat of each group.

Intimate Contact   I stated earlier that contact by itself does not improve interethnic relations. However, one form of contact—intimate contact—can (Brislin, 1993). Intimate contact in this context does not mean sexual relations; rather, it involves sharing one's personal worries, troubles, successes, failures, personal ambitions, and coping strategies. When people reveal personal information about themselves, they are likelier to be perceived as individuals than as members of a category. And the sharing of personal information often produces the discovery that others have many of the same feelings, hopes, and concerns that we have, which can help to break down in-group/out-group, "we/they" barriers. Intimate contact may be more effective, however, when the individuals involved are of relatively equal status (Devine, Evett, & Vasquez-Suson, 1996).

One of the initial investigations of interethnic contact focused on African American and White residents in an integrated housing project (Deutsch & Collins, 1951).

The residents lived in small apartments and shared facilities, such as laundry rooms and playgrounds for children. The residents discovered that it was more enjoyable to talk with each other than to stare at the walls while doing their laundry, and African American and White parents began to converse with each other as they watched their children play with each other without regard to skin color. Initially the conversations focused on such nonintimate matters as the quality of the washing machines and the weather, but eventually they moved on to more personal matters. Whites and African Americans discovered that they shared a number of similar concerns, such as jobs and work, schools for their children, taxes, and so on. The revelation that both groups shared many of the same concerns and problems helped to diminish in-group/out-group thoughts and feelings. Sharing intimate information and becoming friendly with someone from another ethnic group helped to make people more tolerant and less prejudiced toward the other ethnic group (Brewer & Gaertner, 2001; Pettigrew & Tropp, 2000).

Intimate personal contact that involves sharing doubts, hopes, problems, ambitions, and much more is one way to improve interethnic relations.

Review and Sharpen Your Thinking

3 *Discuss intergroup relations.*
   - Identify how group identity leads to "we/they" thinking.
   - Describe the relationships among prejudice, stereotyping, and discrimination.
   - Explain two effective strategies for improving interethnic relations.

What personal experiences have you had with prejudice, stereotyping, and discrimination? Explain why you think these occurred.

SOCIAL INTERACTION 4

Aggression   Altruism

How do aggression and altruism characterize social interaction?

Our social interactions can bring us experiences we would rather forget, moments that are charged with conflict and harm. They also can bring us warm and cherished acts of kindness. Let's explore these two faces of social interaction: the negative side—aggression—and the positive side—altruism.

Aggression

The danger of aggression was captured vividly by the wise Yoda in the movie *The Empire Strikes Back:* "Beware of the dark side. Anger, fear, aggression. Easily they flow. Once you start down the dark path, it will forever dominate your destiny and consume your will." Is this dark side biologically based or is it learned?

Biological Influences   There is nothing new about human aggression. The primate ancestors of human beings and the earliest humans are thought to have committed aggressive acts against others of their own kind. Ancient writings describe the violent ways of the Assyrian king Ashurbanipal, who delighted in beheading his enemies and blinding and mutilating his prisoners. The Russian czar Ivan the Terrible bludgeoned his own son to death and destroyed the second largest city in his empire, Novgorod, in the sixteenth century. In the 1970s, 4 million Cambodians were killed by their fellow Cambodians. Murders in the United States take place at the rate of 20,000 per year, assaults at the rate of 700,000 per year; there are at least 200,000 reports of rape per year in the United States. In the twentieth century, 80 to 100 million people were violently killed. Asked Shakespeare, "Is there any cause in nature that makes these hard hearts?" Is aggression an inborn characteristic of the human species?

Evolutionary Views Ethologists say that aggression is biologically based; certain stimuli release *innate* aggressive responses (Lorenz, 1965; Tinbergen, 1969). For example, a male robin will attack another male when it sees the red patch on the other bird's breast. When the patch is removed, however, no attack takes place.

Vigorous fighting does occur in the animal kingdom, but most hostile encounters do not escalate to killing or even severe harm. Much of the fighting is ritualistic and involves threat displays. For example, elephant seals show approximately 65 threat displays for every fight that actually takes place (LeBoeuf & Peterson, 1969). The type of threat display varies from one species to the next: a cat arches its back, bares its teeth, and hisses; a chimpanzee stares, stomps the ground, and screams.

Evolutionary theorists believe that human beings are not much different from other animals. A basic theme of their theory is the survival of the fittest. Thus they conclude that early in human evolution, the survivors were probably aggressive individuals. Hunters and food gatherers not only had to kill animals to eat but also had to compete for the best food territories if they were to survive.

Freud's Theory of the Aggression Instinct Freud (1917) also argued that aggression is biologically based. He said we have a self-destructive urge he called the *death instinct*. Because the death instinct comes in conflict with our self-preserving life instinct, the death instinct is redirected toward others in the form of aggression.

Most psychologists feel uneasy about the concept of instinct when discussing human behavior. But instinct theorists often support their belief that humans have an instinct for aggression by pointing out examples of how common aggression is. However, simply calling aggression an instinct does not prove that it is one.

Genetic Basis Even though a human instinct for aggression has not been proved, genes are important in understanding the biological basis of aggression. The selective breeding of animals provides the evidence. After a number of breedings among only aggressive animals and among only docile animals, vicious and timid strains of animals emerge. The vicious strains attack nearly anything in sight; the timid strains rarely fight, even when attacked.

The genetic basis for aggression is more difficult to demonstrate with humans (Brennan, Mednick, & Kandel, 1991). Nonetheless, in one investigation of 573 sets of adult twins, identical twins had more similar aggressive tendencies than did fraternal twins (Rushton & others, 1986).

Neurobiological Factors Rather than an instinct for aggression, what may have evolved is an aggressive capacity wired into the human neuromuscular system. Researchers point to the behavior of children born deaf and blind, who still show aggressive patterns—foot stomping, teeth clenching, and fist making—even though they have had no opportunity to observe these behaviors (Eibl-Eibesfeldt, 1977).

Studies by neuroscientists indicate how the brain is involved in the biological processes of aggression (Niehoff, 1999). In 1966 Charles Whitman climbed to the top of the campus tower at the University of Texas at Austin. As he looked down on students walking to and from class, he pulled the trigger of a high-powered rifle and killed 15 people. Then he took his own life. An autopsy revealed a tumor in the limbic system of Whitman's brain, an area associated with emotion. In another instance, an electrode was implanted in the amygdala (which is part of the limbic system) of a meek female mental patient. Immediately after electric current stimulated the amygdala, the mild-mannered woman became violent. She yelled, snarled, and flailed around the room (King, 1961). We do not appear to have a specific aggression center in the brain, but when the lower, more primitive areas of the brain (such as the

Aggression has been pervasive throughout the past. (*Top*) Russian czar Ivan the Terrible killed his own son. (*Bottom*) In the 1970s, 4 million Cambodians were killed by fellow Cambodians.

limbic system) are stimulated by electric currents, aggressive behavior often results (Herbert, 1988).

Neurotransmitters have also been linked to highly aggressive behavior (Filley & others, 2001). Individuals with depressive disorders who commit suicide by violent means (such as using a gun) have been found to have lower levels of the neurotransmitter serotonin than most people do (Van Winkle, 2000). In one study, young men whose serotonin levels were low relative to those of other men their age were far likelier to have committed a violent crime (Moffitt & others, 1998). Also, children who show high rates of aggression have lower levels of serotonin than children who display low rates of aggression (Holmes, Slaughter, & Kashani, 2000).

Alcohol, which acts on the brain to stifle our inhibitions, has been strongly linked to violence and aggression. Individuals under the influence of alcohol are more easily provoked than they would be when they are sober to unleash harsh words, throw a punch, or pull the trigger of a gun (Dougherty, Cherek, & Bennett, 1996). People under the influence of alcohol commit almost one-half of rapes and other violent crimes (Abbey, Ross, & McDuffie, 1993). Unfortunately, the people who are already prone to aggression are also the ones who are likely to drink and then become violent when they become intoxicated (Seto & Barbaree, 1995).

Hormones are another biological factor that may play a role in aggression (Susman & others, 1996). For example, Sam, a bull, was a terror. With hooves scratching, eyes glazed, and nostrils snorting, he roared across a field at an intruder. Barely escaping with his life, the intruder (who turned out to be a tractor salesman) filed a complaint against the bull's owner. The local sheriff convinced the owner it was time to do something about Sam. What was Sam's fate? He was castrated, which changed him from a simmering volcano into a docile ox. The castration reduced Sam's motivation to terrorize by acting on his male hormone system. However, a clear link between testosterone and aggressive behavior has not been found in humans (Brain & Susman, 1997).

Psychological Factors   Numerous psychological factors appear to be involved in aggression. They include individuals' responses to certain circumstances, cognitive and learning factors, and sociocultural factors.

Frustrating and Aversive Circumstances   Some years ago, John Dollard and his colleagues (1939) proposed that frustration, the blocking of an individual's attempts to reach a goal, triggers aggression. Their *frustration-aggression hypothesis* states that frustration always leads to aggression. Not much later, however, psychologists found that aggression is not the only possible response to frustration. Some individuals who experience frustration become passive, for example (Miller, 1941).

Psychologists later recognized that a broad range of aversive experiences besides frustration can cause aggression. They include physical pain, personal insults, and unpleasant events such as divorce. Aversive circumstances also include the physical environment. Environmental psychologists have demonstrated how such factors as noise, weather, and crowding can stimulate aggression. Murder, rape, and assault increase when temperatures are the hottest (during the third quarter of the year), as well as in the hottest years and in the hottest cities (Anderson, 1989; Anderson & Bushman, 2002). Our everyday encounters with other people also produce aversive experiences that can trigger aggressive responses (Schwartz, 1999). For example, when someone cuts into a line in front of us (such as at a ticket booth), we may respond aggressively toward that person (Milgram & others, 1986).

Cognitive Factors   Whether we respond aggressively to aversive situations is determined by our interpretation of the event (Baumeister, 1999; Berkowitz, 1990):

- *Expectations.* You expect to be jostled on a crowded bus, but you don't expect someone to run into you when there are only five or six people on the bus.

Thus you might respond more aggressively when you are bumped on a relatively empty bus than on a crowded one.

- *Equity*. If you perceive that an aversive experience is not fair, or justified, you might respond aggressively. For example, if you deserve a D in a class, you are less likely to say nasty things about the professor than if you perceive the grade to be unfair.
- *Intentions*. If you think someone has intentionally tripped you, you are more likely to respond aggressively than if you think the individual's feet accidentally became tangled with yours.
- *Responsibility*. When you perceive that other people are responsible for frustrating or aversive actions, you are more likely to behave aggressively toward them. For example, when are you more likely to respond aggressively: when an 8-year-old child runs into you with a shopping cart in a store, or when her assertive, healthy, 30-year-old mother does the same thing? You are likely to perceive that the mother is more responsible for her own behavior than the young girl is, so you would probably respond more aggressively toward the mother.

Reinforcement and Observational Learning   Behavioral and social cognitive theorists believe that aggression is learned through the processes of reinforcement and observational learning. Aggression is reinforced when it helps people attain money, attention, sex, power, or status. For example, a young adolescent who succeeds in getting the seat he wants by glowering at the schoolmate who is occupying it may try the same sort of aggressive tactic again. If he gets no such response, he begins to learn that aggression is not the key to success.

Aggression can also be learned by watching others engage in aggressive actions (Bandura, 1989). One of the most frequent opportunities people have to observe aggression in our culture is to watch violence on television, which is discussed further in the next section.

Sociocultural Factors   Aggression not only involves biological and cognitive factors but is also linked with factors in the wider social world. Among the sociocultural factors involved in aggression are variations across cultures and the extent to which people watch violence on TV.

Cross-Cultural Variations   The incidence of aggression and violence has varied throughout human history. We think of our own era as relatively violent, but, in the past, hunters and food gatherers had to be even more aggressive just to survive. However, as anthropologist Loren Eiseley commented, "The need is now for a gentler, a more tolerant people than those who won for us against the ice, the tiger, and the bear."

Even today, aggression and violence are more common in some cultures than others (Bellesiles, 1999). The U.S. homicide rate does not compare well to rates for other countries (United Nations, 1999; U.S. Bureau of Justice Statistics, 2001). The risk of being murdered in the United States is much higher than in many other countries—about three times as high as in Canada and six times as high as in Europe. South Africa, Colombia, Mexico, and the Philippines have very high homicide rates, much higher than the United States. Crime rates tend to be higher in countries with a considerable gap between the rich and the poor (Triandis, 1994).

Cultural differences in aggression and violence are related to the circumstances that people in a culture face. Imagine yourself on a barren mountainside away from civilization in the country of Uganda. For about 2,000 years, your ancestors lived as nomadic hunters, but, early in this century, the government of Uganda turned your hunting grounds into a national park. Hunting is forbidden in the park, so you now are forced to farm its steep, barren mountain areas. Famine, crowding, and drought have led to tremendous upheaval in families and moral values. You were sent out to live on your own at the age of 6 with no life supports; you fight and maim others to obtain food and water (Turnbull, 1972). This may seem like an exaggeration, but

Calvin and Hobbes   by Bill Watterson

it is a description of normal life for the Ik people for most of the twentieth century. The world of the Ik involved many frustrating and aversive circumstances that produced pain and hunger. If you were placed in the same circumstances, wouldn't you become more callous and aggressive?

Media Violence   Violence is pictured as a way of life throughout the popular media: on the news and on television shows, in movies, in video games, and in song lyrics. Evildoers kill and get killed; police and detectives violently uphold or even break society's laws; sports announcers glorify players, whether their behavior is sportsmanlike or contributes to their team's success. It is easy to get the message that aggression and violence are the norm—in fact, are the preferred mode of behavior—in American society.

Part of the reason that violence seems so glamorous is that it usually is portrayed unrealistically. Viewers rarely see its lasting effects, whether the violence is real or fictitious. In real life, an injured person may not recover for weeks, for months, or perhaps not at all, but on television recovery is either assumed or takes only 30 to 60 minutes.

The amount of aggression on television is a special problem for children. In the 1990s, children watched an average of 26 hours of television each week (National Center for Children Exposed to Violence, 2001). Almost every day of their lives, children watch someone being stabbed, maimed, or slaughtered. Does such pervasive exposure to violence merely stimulate children to go out and buy Star Wars ray guns, or can it trigger aggressive attacks on playmates and increase the likelihood that children will violently attack or murder someone when they grow up?

In one early study of the effects of TV violence, children were randomly assigned to one of two groups: One watched violent Saturday morning cartoon shows on 11 different days; the second group watched the same cartoon shows with the violence removed (Steur, Applefield, & Smith, 1971). The children were then observed during play at their preschool. The children who saw the TV cartoon shows with violence were likelier to kick, choke, and push their playmates than were the children who saw the cartoon shows with the violence removed.

What children watch on TV is related not only to their aggression but also to their cognitive skills and achievement. In one recent longitudinal study, viewing educational programs as preschoolers was associated with a host of desirable characteristics in adolescence: getting higher grades, reading more books, placing a higher value on achievement, being more creative, and acting less aggressively (Anderson & others, 2001). These associations were more consistent for boys than girls. However, girls who were more frequent viewers of violent TV programs in the preschool years had

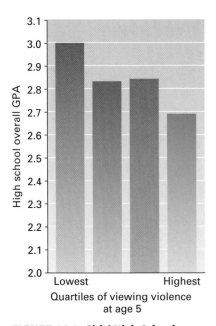

FIGURE 16.9 Girls' High School Grade Point Average by Quartiles of Violence Viewing at Age 5
Girls who watched the least TV violence at age 5 had a higher grade point average in high school than girls who watched more TV violence at age 5. The bar on the left represents the 25 percent of girls who watched the least violence at age 5, the second bar the next 25 percent of girls, and so on.

lower grades in adolescence than girls who infrequently watched violent TV programs in the preschool years (see figure 16.9).

Some critics have argued that research results do not warrant the conclusion that TV violence causes aggression (Freedman, 1984). But many experts insist that TV violence can cause aggressive or antisocial behavior in children (Bushman & Huesmann, 2001; Perse, 2001; Singer & Singer, 1998). Of course, television violence is not the *only* cause of aggression. There is no *one* cause of any social behavior. Aggression, like all other social behaviors, has multiple determinants (Donnerstein, 2002). Television violence does not affect adults in isolation from such other factors as aggressive tendencies, marital problems, and job stress. Likewise, the link between TV violence and aggression in children is influenced by children's aggressive tendencies, by their attitudes toward violence, and by the monitoring of children's exposure to it.

Another aspect of media violence involves whether watching pornography leads to violence against women. To read further about this topic, see the Critical Controversy box.

Aggression and Gender   Our stereotypes clearly tag boys and men as more aggressive than girls and women. In general, research has supported this view. As children, boys are more likely to engage in rough-and-tumble play and get in more fights in which they are physically aggressive toward each other. As adolescents, males are more likely to be members of gangs and to commit violent acts. Children and adolescents who are diagnosed with conduct disorder (a pattern of offensive behavior that violates the basic rights of others) are three times more likely to be boys than girls (Cohen & others, 1993). As adults, men are more likely to be chronically hostile and to murder or rape than women are (Barefoot & others, 1987).

In a classic analysis of research studies, the following conclusions were reached about aggression and gender (Maccoby & Jacklin, 1974):

- Males are more aggressive than females in all cultures.
- Males are more aggressive than females from early in life, with differences consistently appearing as early as 2 years of age.
- Aggression is more common among males than among females, in animals as well as humans.

These findings often have been interpreted as supporting the view that gender differences in aggression are biologically based.

However, environment and culture also contribute to gender differences in aggression (White, 2001). In one study, individuals in twelve countries were asked to write stories in response to conflicts presented to them (Archer & McDaniel, 1995). In all twelve countries, males wrote stories with more violent themes than females did, suggesting a biological interpretation of gender differences in aggression. However, the degree of violence used in the descriptions varied considerably across the cultures, suggesting an environmental or cultural interpretation.

Despite the strong evidence that gender is a factor in aggression, we need to remind ourselves of an important point about the conclusions drawn from psychological research. When we say that males are more aggressive than females, we cannot jump to the conclusion that all males are more aggressive than all females (Hyde & Mezulis, 2001). In any given culture, some females will be more aggressive than some males.

In addition, we need to consider the type of aggression. Researchers have found stronger gender differences in physical aggression than in verbal aggression (Eagly & Steffen, 1986). One longitudinal study found no gender differences in verbal aggression among 8-year-old children (Björkqvist, Österman, & Lagerspetz, 1994). However, at age 18, females displayed more verbal aggression than males.

Ways To Reduce Aggression   You might recall that chapter 11 explored the powerful, negative emotion of anger, which can generate aggression. Several strategies for reducing anger were examined that apply to our evaluation of aggression here. Among

Does Pornography Lead to Violence Against Women?

In 1999, there were 383,000 rapes, attempted rapes, and sexual assaults in the United States, according to the Justice Department's annual National Crime Victimization Survey. Statistics such as these fuel concerns that pornography contributes to a climate in which some men feel that sexual violence toward women is acceptable. Critics of pornography have repeatedly called for laws restricting access to pornography. Defenders, often citing the First Amendment guarantee of freedom of expression, argue against such laws on the grounds that no clear link has been demonstrated between pornography and sexual violence against women (Hawkins & Zimring, 1988). Psychologists have entered the fray to attempt to scientifically evaluate whether or not the consumption of pornography, in fact, can lead to violence against women.

The most widely accepted explanation of how pornography may affect men's behavior toward women comes from social cognitive theory (Bandura, 1977, 2000). Studies suggest that children who regularly watch violence on television may learn to become more violent. So perhaps men who watch pornography learn to become sexually violent toward women or at least become desensitized to sexual violence.

Based on several meta-analyses and on research of their own, Neil Malamuth and his colleagues (Malamuth, Addison, & Koss, 2000) concluded that pornography consumption does have a small effect on male sexual aggression, but they caution that it is only one of a number of factors that may lead to sexual violence against women. They stress that the nature of pornographic material, the characteristics of the men viewing pornography, and the surrounding culture all combine to produce an effect. In other words, no one factor (such as pornography) is likely to control a complex behavior (such as men's violence against women).

Adding to the complexity of the controversy over pornography is the absence of agreement on a definition of pornography. To some people, *pornography* means all sexually explicit materials. In contrast, the report of the Attorney General's Commission on Pornography (1986) distinguished between erotica and pornography: Erotica depicts nudity and explicit consensual sex, whereas pornography depicts the domination and humiliation of women, as well as explicit sexual violence toward women. When a further distinction is drawn between nonviolent and violent pornography, the consumption of erotica and even nonviolent pornography are not associated with increases in sexual violence toward women (Malamuth & others, 2000). Apparently, the most problematic materials are those that depict women enjoying being the victims of male sexual violence. Such violent pornography reinforces the rape myth, the false belief that women actually desire coercive sex.

Further, most men are not prone to sexual violence against women (Malamuth & others, 2000). Rather, men who score higher on self-report measures of attraction to sexual aggression, hostile masculinity, and/or low intelligence appear to be prone to sexual violence against women (Bogaert, Woodard, & Hafer, 1999). In addition, they come from backgrounds in which gender equality is deemphasized and education about sexuality limited. In other words, some men are vulnerable to believing in the rape myth that women desire rape and deserve sexual abuse. When such at-risk men are exposed to violent pornography, they are even more prone to become perpetrators of sexual violence against women (Donnerstein, 2001).

Cultural variables may also be important (Lips, 2003). For example, research conducted after the legalization of pornography in Denmark failed to find evidence of increased criminal sexual acts as a function of the wider availability of pornography (Kutchinsky, 1991). It seems that public attitudes toward pornography vary with the cultural environment. The Danes generally enjoy a more natural approach to sex. Public nudity, for example, is more common and more accepted in Denmark than in the United States. Perhaps their more relaxed attitudes make the Danes less vulnerable to the effects of pornography.

One of the most difficult aspects of interpreting research on the effects of pornography on sexual violence against women is distinguishing between correlation and causality. Consider the Danish experience. The relationship between the wider availability of pornography and a lower rate of reported sexual violence probably is not a causal relationship. More likely, broader changes in Danish society underlie both variables. Similarly, it may be that high-risk men need greater stimulation, which is not satisfied even by heavy exposure to pornography. If so, pornography use may be a symptom of an underlying compulsion. Alternatively, it may be that the use of pornography raises an already high level of sexual aggressiveness above a threshold necessary to elicit actual behavior. In this case, pornography would be a contributing cause. Further research is needed to determine whether one or both of these explanations is correct.

What do you think?

- Do you think the distinction between erotica, nonviolent pornography, and violent pornography is a helpful one?
- Do you think that the availability of sexually explicit materials should be restricted?
- How could you use experimental methods to investigate whether sexually explicit materials contribute to sexual violence against women?

"All I'm saying is, giving a little something to the arts might help our image." © The New Yorker Collection 1989. Peter Steiner from cartoonbank.com. All Rights Reserved.

them is *catharsis*, the release of anger by directly engaging in anger or aggression. According to psychodynamic and ethological theories, behaving angrily or watching others behave angrily reduces subsequent anger or aggression. But social cognitive theorists disagree strongly. They believe that by acting aggressively people often are rewarded for their aggression and that by watching others behave aggressively, people learn to be aggressive themselves. Researchers have found more support for the social cognitive view than for the psychoanalytic and ethological views on reducing aggression (Bandura, 1986, 1997). Thus good candidates for strategies that will reduce aggression are decreasing rewards for aggression and allowing people to observe fewer incidences of aggression.

Parents have been specially targeted to help children to reduce aggression. Because of their importance in children's lives, they often have considerable influence. Recommended parenting strategies include encouraging young children to develop empathy toward others and better monitoring of adolescents' activities. Gerald Patterson and his colleagues (1989) consistently have found that a lack of parental monitoring is related to juvenile delinquency.

Strategies for reducing aggression that are being tried in many schools are teaching conflict management skills to students and having students serve as peer counselors. The students discuss real and hypothetical problem situations and work together to develop positive, nonaggressive solutions. Children in these programs are taught to analyze their thoughts and consider alternatives to aggression.

Altruism

We know from experience that social interaction is not all a matter of aggression. We often hear or read about acts of generosity and courage, such as the rock concerts and fund-raisers to help the victims of the terrorist attacks on September 11, 2001, the police and firefighters who risked their lives to save the people in the World Trade Center towers, and the volunteers who rushed to the various scenes of the disaster to offer their services to victims and rescuers (Oliner, 2001). On a more mundane level, you may have placed some of your hard-earned cash in the palm of a homeless person or perhaps cared for a wounded cat. What all of these acts have in common is **altruism,** an unselfish interest in helping someone else.

Psychological and Sociocultural Foundations of Altruism How do psychologists account for such acts of human altruism? One key aspect is the concept of *reciprocity*, which encourages us to do unto others as we would have them do unto us. It is present in every widely practiced religion in the world—Judaism, Christianity, Buddhism, and Islam, for example. Complex human sentiments are involved in reciprocity: Trust in the people with whom we are interacting is probably the most important principle over the long run. But reciprocity can involve more negative sentiments, such as guilt, if we do not reciprocate a favor, and anger, if someone else does not reciprocate. One study found that college students were more likely to pledge to the charity of someone who had previously bought them candy (Webster & others, 1999). Altruistic reciprocity was more likely when the donor's name was made public to the recipient, but even when the recipient did not know who the donor was, altruistic reciprocity occurred, although at a lower level.

Not all altruism is motivated by reciprocity, but this view alerts us to the importance of considering interactions between oneself and others to understand altruism. And not all seemingly altruistic behavior is unselfish. Some psychologists even argue that true altruism has never been demonstrated. Others argue that a distinction between altruism and egoism in giving can be made (Cialdini & others, 1987).

altruism An unselfish interest in helping someone else.

(*Left*) An example of animal altruism—a baboon plucking bugs from another baboon. Most acts of animal altruism involve kin. (*Right*) A young woman assists a child with a disability.

Egoism involves giving to another person to ensure reciprocity, to gain self-esteem, to present oneself as powerful, competent, or caring, or to avoid social and self-censure for failing to live up to society's expectations. In contrast, altruism is giving to another person with the ultimate goal of benefiting that other person; any benefits that come to the giver are unintended.

Altruistic behavior is determined by the nature of both the person and the situation (Post & others, 2002; Sober, 2001). Describing individuals as having altruistic or egoistic motives implies that psychological variables—a person's ability to empathize with the needy or to feel a sense of responsibility for another person's welfare—are important in understanding altruistic behavior. The stronger these personality dispositions are, the less we would expect situational variables to influence whether giving, kindness, or helping occurs. But, as with any human behavior, characteristics of the situation influence the strength of altruistic motivation. Some of these characteristics include the degree of need shown by the other individual, the needy person's responsibility for his plight, the cost of assisting the needy person, and the extent to which reciprocity is expected (Batson, 1998, 2001, 2002).

The Biological Foundations of Altruism   Evolutionary psychologists look for biological explanations of altruism rather than psychological or situational ones. They emphasize that some types of altruism help to perpetuate our genes (Ruse, 2001, 2002; Simpson & Gangestad, 2001). An act in the biological realm is considered altruistic if it simply increases another organism's prospects for survival and opportunity to reproduce (Sober & Wilson, 1998).

Evolutionary psychologists believe that tremendous benefits can accrue to individuals who form cooperative, reciprocal relationships (Trivers, 1971). By being good to someone now, individuals increase the likelihood that they will receive a benefit from the other person in the future. Through this reciprocal process, both gain something beyond what they could have by acting alone.

Evolutionary psychologists also stress that those who carry our genes—our children—have a special place in the domain of altruism. Natural selection favors parents who care for their children and improve their probability of surviving. A parent feeding its young is performing a biologically altruistic act because the offspring's chance of survival is increased. So is a mother bird who tries to lure predators away from the fledglings in her nest. She is willing to sacrifice herself so that three or four of her young offspring will have the chance to survive, thus preserving her genes.

Human beings also often show more empathy toward relatives, who share their genes or have the potential to perpetuate their genes. In the case of a natural disaster, people's uppermost concern is their family. In one study involving a hypothetical decision to help in life-or-death situations, college students chose to aid close kin over distant kin, the young over the old, the healthy over the sick, the wealthy over

egoism Giving to another person to ensure reciprocity, to gain self-esteem, to present oneself as powerful, competent, or caring, or to avoid social and self-censure for failing to live up to normative expectations.

the poor, and premenopausal women over postmenopausal woman (Burnstein, Crandall, & Kitayama, 1994). In this same study, when an everyday favor rather than a life-or-death situation was involved, the college students gave less weight to kinship and chose to help either the very young or the very old over those of intermediate age, the sick over the healthy, and the poor over the wealthy.

The Bystander Effect   One of the most widely studied aspects of altruism is why one person will help a stranger in distress whereas another won't lift a finger. Social psychologists have found that it often depends on the circumstances.

More than 30 years ago a young woman named Kitty Genovese was brutally murdered. She was attacked at about 3 A.M. in a respectable area of New York City. The murderer left and returned three times; he finally put an end to Kitty's life as she crawled to her apartment and screamed for help. It took the slayer about 30 minutes to kill Kitty. Thirty-eight neighbors watched the gory scene and heard Kitty Genovese's screams. No one helped or even called the police. This incident prompted social psychologists to study the **bystander effect,** the tendency for individuals who observe an emergency to help less when other people are present than when the observers are alone. The bystander effect helps to explain the apparent cold-blooded indifference to Kitty Genovese's murder.

Social psychologists John Darley and Bibb Latané (1968) documented the bystander effect in a number of criminal and medical emergencies. Most of the bystander intervention studies show that, when alone, a person will help 75 percent of the time, but when another bystander is present, the figure drops to 50 percent. Apparently the difference is due to the diffusion of responsibility among witnesses and the tendency to look to the behavior of others for clues about what to do. We may think that someone else will call the police or that, because no one else is helping, possibly the person does not need help.

Many other aspects of the situation influence whether the individual will intervene and come to the aid of the person in distress. Bystander intervention is less likely to occur in the following situations (Shotland, 1985):

- The situation is not clear.
- The individuals struggling or fighting appear to be married or related.
- The victim is perceived to be intoxicated.
- The victim is thought to be from a different ethnic group.
- Intervention might lead to personal harm or retaliation by the criminal.
- Helping requires considerable time, such as days in court testifying.
- Bystanders have no prior history of victimization themselves, have seen few crimes and intervention efforts, or have not had training in first aid, rescue, or police tactics.

Trends in Altruistic Behavior   How altruistic are people today? Are they less altruistic than several decades ago? Over the past two decades, college students have shown an increased concern for personal well-being and a decreased concern for the well-being of others, especially the disadvantaged (Sax & others, 1998). And, as shown in figure 16.10, today's college freshmen are more strongly motivated to be well-off financially and less motivated to develop a meaningful philosophy of life than were their counterparts some 30 years ago (Sax & others, 2001).

However, today's college students show some signs of shifting toward a stronger interest in the welfare of our society. For example, between 1986 and 1998, there was a small increase in the percentage of college freshman who said they were strongly interested in participating in community action programs (19 percent in 1998 compared to 18 percent in 1986) and helping promote racial understanding (40 percent in 1998 compared with 27 percent in 1986; Sax & others, 1998). These trends are a good sign. For successful adjustment in adult life, it is important to seek self-fulfillment *and* to have a strong commitment to others.

bystander effect The concept that individuals who observe an emergency help less when someone else is present than when they are alone.

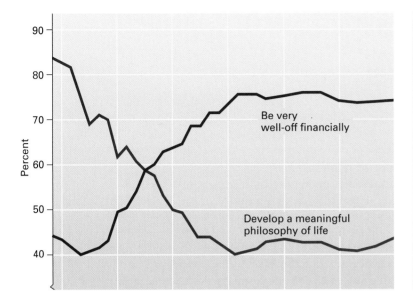

FIGURE 16.10 Changing Freshman Life Goals, 1968–2001 In the past three decades, a significant change has occurred in freshmen students' life goals. A far greater percentage of today's college freshmen state that a "very important" life goal is to be well-off financially; far fewer state that developing a meaningful philosophy of life is a "very important" life goal.

Altruism and Gender Who are more helping and caring, males or females? The stereotype is that females are. However, as in most domains, it is a good idea to think about gender in context.

Researchers have found that females are more likely than males to help when the context involves nurturing, as when volunteering time to help a child with a personal problem. However, males are more likely to help in situations in which a perceived danger is present and they feel competent to help (Eagly & Crowley, 1986). For example, males are more likely than females to help a person who is stranded by the roadside with a flat tire. An automobile problem is an area in which many males feel a sense of competence. Males also are more likely than females to give a ride to a hitchhiker, because of the perceived danger in this situation.

In terms of caring, females have a stronger orientation than males toward caregiving. However, in the few cultures in which both boys and girls are regularly placed in charge of caring for their younger siblings, girls and boys are similar in their tendencies to nurture (Whiting, 1989).

Review and Sharpen Your Thinking

4 *Explain how aggression and altruism characterize social interaction.*

- Discuss the influence of aggressive behavior.
- Describe what social psychologists know about altruism.

Analyze the acts of altruism surrounding the September 11, 2001, terrorist attacks. Can you determine which acts likely were altruistic and which acts likely were egoistic?

mhhe com/
santrockp7

For study tools related to this learning goal, see the Study Guide, the CD-ROM, and the Online Learning Center.

5 RELATIONSHIPS

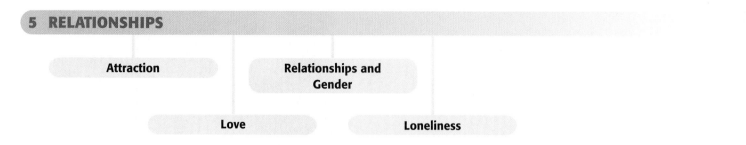

What is the nature of relationships?

Our close relationships are among the most important aspects of our lives. In some cases, these relationships are extremely positive, in others they can be highly conflicted (Harvey, 2001). Perhaps worst of all is the lack of relationships, which creates the deeply unsettling feeling of loneliness.

Social psychologists have explored several aspects of social relationships. Attraction, love, and intimacy are key dimensions (Baumeister & Bratslavsky, 1999). This section begins with a discussion on the formation of relationships.

Attraction

What attracts us to others and motivates us to spend more time with them? Does just being around someone increase the likelihood a relationship will develop? Or, are we likely to seek out and associate with those who are similar to us? How important is physical attraction in the initial stages of a relationship?

Familiarity and Similarity Familiarity breeds contempt, as the old saying goes, but social psychologists have found that familiarity is a necessary condition for a close relationship to develop. For the most part, friends and lovers are people who have been around each other for a long time; they may have grown up together, gone to high school or college together, worked together, or gone to the same social events (Brehm, 2002).

Once we have been exposed to someone for a while, what is it that creates friendship and even love? Another old saying, "Birds of a feather flock together," also helps to explain attraction. One of the most powerful lessons generated by the study of close relationships is that we like to associate with people who are similar to us (Berscheid, 2000). Our friends and lovers are much more like us than unlike us. We have similar attitudes, behavior patterns, and personal characteristics, as well as similar taste in clothes, intelligence, personality, other friends, values, lifestyle, physical attractiveness, and so on. In some limited cases and on some isolated characteristics, opposites may attract. An introvert may wish to be with an extravert, or someone with little money may wish to associate with someone who has a lot of money, for example. But overall we are attracted to individuals with similar rather than opposite characteristics. One study, for example, found that depressed college students preferred to meet unhappy others, whereas nondepressed college students preferred to meet happy others (Wenzlaff & Prohaska, 1989). The fact that individuals are attracted to each other on the basis of similar characteristics and attitudes is reflected in the questions that computer dating services ask their clients.

The concept of *consensual validation* explains why people are attracted to others who are similar to them. Our own attitudes and behavior are supported when someone else's attitudes and behavior are similar to ours—their attitudes and behavior validate ours. Another reason that similarity matters is that people tend to shy away from the unknown. We often prefer to be around people whose attitudes and behavior we can predict. And similarity implies that we will enjoy doing things with another person who likes the same things and has similar attitudes. In one study, this sort of similarity was shown to be especially important in successful marriages (Swann, De La Ronde, & Hixon, 1994).

DILBERT reprinted by permission of United Feature Syndicate, Inc.

Physical Attraction You may be thinking at this point that something is missing from our discussion of attraction. As important as familiarity and similarity may be, they do not explain the spark that often ignites a romantic relationship: physical attraction.

How important is physical attraction in a romantic relationship? Many advertising agencies would have us believe it is the most important factor in establishing and maintaining a relationship. Psychologists do not consider the link between physical beauty and attraction to be so clear-cut. For example, they have determined that heterosexual men and women differ on the importance of good looks when they seek an intimate partner. Women tend to rate as most important such traits as considerateness, honesty, dependability, kindness, and understanding; men prefer good looks, cooking skills, and frugality (Buss & Barnes, 1986).

Complicating research about the role of physical attraction in romantic relationships is changing standards of what is deemed attractive. The criteria for beauty can differ, not just *across* cultures, but over time *within* cultures as well (Lamb & others, 1993). In the 1940s, the ideal of female beauty in the United States was typified by the well-rounded figure of Marilyn Monroe. As a result of the American preoccupation with health, Monroe's 135-pound, 5-foot, 5-inch physique is regarded as overweight by today's standards. Today, the ideal physique for both men and women is neither pleasingly plump nor extremely slender.

Social psychologists have found that the force of similarity also operates at a physical level. We usually seek out someone at our own level of attractiveness in both physical characteristics and social attributes. Research validates the *matching hypothesis*—which states that, although we may prefer a more attractive person in the abstract, in the real world we end up choosing someone who is close to our own level (Kalick & Hamilton, 1986).

We should take some of these findings with a grain of salt. Much of the research on physical attraction has focused on initial or short-term encounters; researchers have not often evaluated attraction over the course of months and years. As relationships endure, physical attraction probably assumes less importance. Rocky Dennis, as portrayed in the movie *Mask*, is a case in point. His peers and even his mother initially wanted to avoid Rocky, whose face was severely distorted, but over the course of his childhood and adolescent years, the avoidance turned into attraction and love as people got to know him. As Rocky's story demonstrates, familiarity can overcome even severely negative initial reactions to a person.

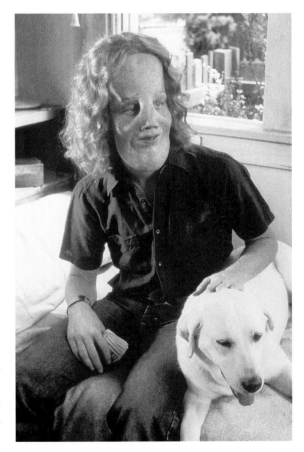

Eric Stoltz's portrayal of Rocky Dennis in the movie *Mask*. Rocky was unloved and unwanted as a young child because of his grotesque features. But, as his mother and peers got to know him, they became attracted to him.

Love

Some relationships never progress much beyond the attraction stage. But some relationships deepen to friendship and perhaps to love in one of its guises (Harvey & Weber, 2002). Three types of love that have been described by social psychologists are romantic love, affectionate love, and consummate love.

Romantic Love   **Romantic love** is also called *passionate love.* Poets, playwrights, and musicians through the ages have lauded the fiery passion of romantic love—and lamented the searing pain when it fails. Think for a moment about songs and books that hit the top of the charts. Chances are they are about love.

Romantic love has strong components of sexuality and infatuation, and it often predominates in the early part of a love relationship. Well-known love researcher Ellen Berscheid (1988) says that it is romantic love we mean when we say that we are "in love" with someone. It is romantic love she believes we need to understand if we are to learn what love is all about. Berscheid believes that sexual desire is the most important ingredient of romantic love.

In our culture, romantic love is the main reason we get married. In 1967, a famous study showed that most men maintained that they would not get married if they were not in love. Women either were undecided or said that they would get married even if they were not in love with their prospective husband (Kephart, 1967). In the 1980s, both women and men tended to agree that they would not get married unless they were in love. More than half of today's men and women say that not being in love is sufficient reason to dissolve a marriage (Berscheid, Snyder, & Omoto, 1989). Romantic love is especially important among college students. One study of unattached college men and women found that more than half identified a romantic partner, rather than a parent, sibling, or friend, as their closest relationship (Berscheid & others, 1989).

Romantic love includes a complex intermingling of different emotions—fear, anger, sexual desire, joy, and jealousy, for example. Obviously, some of these emotions are a source of anguish. One study found that romantic lovers were likelier than friends to be the cause of depression (Berscheid & Fei, 1977).

Affectionate Love   Love is more than just passion. **Affectionate love,** also called *companionate love,* is the type of love that occurs when someone desires to have the other person near and has a deep, caring affection for the person.

There is a growing belief that the early stages of love have more romantic ingredients but that as love matures passion tends to give way to affection (Berscheid & Reis, 1998; Harvey & Weber, 2001). Phillip Shaver (1986) describes the initial phase of romantic love as a time that is fueled by a mixture of sexual attraction and gratification, a reduced sense of loneliness, uncertainty about the security of developing an attachment, and excitement from exploring the novelty of another human being. With time, he says, sexual attraction wanes, attachment anxieties either lessen or produce conflict and withdrawal, novelty is replaced with familiarity, and lovers either find themselves securely attached in a deeply caring relationship or distressed—feeling bored, disappointed, lonely, or hostile, for example. In the latter case, one or both partners may eventually seek a different close relationship.

Consummate Love   So far we have discussed two forms of love: romantic (or passionate) and affectionate (or companionate). Robert J. Sternberg (1988) described a third form of love, *consummate love,* which he said is the strongest, fullest type of love. Sternberg proposed that love can be thought of as a triangle with three main dimensions—passion, intimacy, and commitment. Passion, as described earlier, is physical and sexual attraction to another. Intimacy is emotional feelings of warmth, closeness, and sharing in a relationship. Commitment is our cognitive appraisal of the relationship and our intent to maintain the relationship even in the face of problems (Rusbult & others, 2001).

romantic love Also called *passionate love;* the type of love that has strong components of sexuality and infatuation and often predominates in the early part of a love relationship.

affectionate love Also called *companionate love;* the type of love that occurs when individuals desire to have the other person near and have a deep, caring affection for the person.

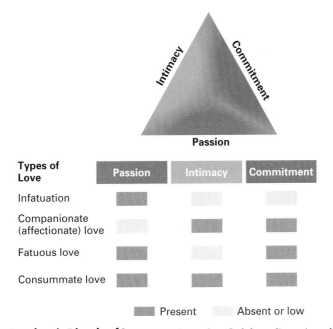

Types of Love	Passion	Intimacy	Commitment
Infatuation	�in		
Companionate (affectionate) love		▪	▪
Fatuous love	▪		▪
Consummate love	▪	▪	▪

▪ Present   ▫ Absent or low

FIGURE 16.11 **Sternberg's Triangle of Love** Sternberg identified three dimensions that shape the experience we call love: passion, intimacy, and commitment. Various combinations of the three dimensions produce particular types of love.

Sternberg's theory states that the ideal form of love involves all three dimensions (see figure 16.11). If passion is the only ingredient in a relationship (with intimacy and commitment low or absent), we are merely *infatuated*. An affair or a fling in which there is little intimacy and even less commitment would be an example. A relationship marked by intimacy and commitment but low or lacking in passion is *affectionate love*, a pattern often found among couples who have been married for many years. If passion and commitment are present but intimacy is not, Sternberg calls the relationship *fatuous love*, as when one person worships another from a distance. But if couples share all three dimensions—passion, intimacy, and commitment—they will experience consummate love. The Psychology and Life box, "What Is Your Love Like?" will help you determine what kind of relationship you have with a particular person in your life.

Relationships and Gender

Do women and men hold different views of love? One recent study found that men conceptualize love in terms of passion, whereas women think of love more in terms of friendship (Fehr & Broughton, 2001). However, both women and men view love in affectionate terms.

One aspect of relationships that seems to be linked to gender is caring (Brannon, 2002). Recall the discussion of Carol Gilligan's care perspective in chapter 4. Gilligan (1982) believes that social relationships are more important to females than they are to males and that females are more sensitive in social relationships. In contrast, she argues that males are more individualistic and self-oriented. Even as children, boys often define themselves apart from their caregivers and peers, whereas girls emphasize social ties. Researchers have indeed found that adult females often are caring, supporting, and empathic, whereas adult males are independent, self-reliant, and unexpressive (Brannon, 1999; Paludi, 1998). And, once the novelty, unpredictability, and urgency of sexual attraction in a love relationship have abated, women are more likely than men to detect deficiencies in caring that indicate the relationship has problems. Perhaps that sensitivity is why wives are almost twice as likely as husbands to initiate a divorce (National Center for Health Statistics, 1989).

Many females show a stronger interest in relationships than many males do. *What has been your experience with the gender differences in relationship orientation that have been discussed? If you are a female, do you have a strong interest in relationships? If you are a male, do you have less interest in relationships than most females you know?*

What Is Your Love Like?

Imagine the blank spaces filled in with the name of one person you love or care about deeply. Then rate each of the items from 1 to 9 with 1 = not at all, 5 = moderately, and 9 = extremely.

_____ 1. I actively support _____ 's well-being.

_____ 2. I have a warm relationship with _____ .

_____ 3. I can count on _____ in times of need.

_____ 4. _____ is able to count on me in times of need.

_____ 5. I am willing to share myself and my possessions with _____ .

_____ 6. I receive considerable emotional support from _____ .

_____ 7. I give considerable emotional support to _____ .

_____ 8. I communicate well with _____ .

_____ 9. I value _____ greatly in my life.

_____ 10. I feel close to _____ .

_____ 11. I have a comfortable relationship with _____ .

_____ 12. I feel that I really understand _____ .

_____ 13. I feel that _____ really understands me.

_____ 14. I feel that I can really trust _____ .

_____ 15. I share deeply personal information about myself with _____ .

_____ 16. Just seeing _____ excites me.

_____ 17. I find myself thinking about _____ frequently during the day.

_____ 18. My relationship with _____ is very romantic.

_____ 19. I find _____ to be very personally attractive.

_____ 20. I idealize _____ .

_____ 21. I cannot imagine another person making me as happy as _____ .

_____ 22. I would rather be with _____ than anyone.

_____ 23. There is nothing more important to me than my relationship with _____ .

_____ 24. I especially like physical contact with _____ .

_____ 25. There is something special about my relationship with _____ .

_____ 26. I adore _____ .

_____ 27. I cannot imagine my life without _____ .

_____ 28. My relationship with _____ is passionate.

_____ 29. When I see romantic movies and read romantic books I think of _____ .

_____ 30. I fantasize about _____ .

_____ 31. I know that I care about _____ .

_____ 32. I am committed to maintaining my relationship with _____ .

_____ 33. Because of my commitment to _____ , I would not let other people come between us.

_____ 34. I have confidence in the stability of my relationship with _____ .

_____ 35. I could not let anything get in the way of my commitment to _____ .

_____ 36. I expect my love for _____ to last for the rest of my life.

_____ 37. I will always feel a strong responsibility for _____ .

_____ 38. I view my commitment to _____ as a solid one.

_____ 39. I cannot imagine ending my relationship with _____ .

_____ 40. I am certain of my love for _____ .

_____ 41. I view my relationship with _____ as permanent.

_____ 42. I view my relationship with _____ as a good decision.

_____ 43. I feel a sense of responsibility toward _____ .

_____ 44. I plan to continue my relationship with _____ .

_____ 45. Even when _____ is hard to deal with, I remain committed to our relationship.

Add up your score for each of the three areas of love: 1–15 (intimacy), 16–30 (passion), and 31–45 (commitment). Below are the average scores of a group of women and men (average age = 31) who either were married or in a close relationship:

Intimacy	Passion	Commitment	Percentile
93	73	85	15
102	85	96	30
111	98	108	50
120	110	120	70
129	123	131	85

The fourth column (percentile) shows the percentage of adults who scored at that level or above. Thus, if your intimacy score is 122, your intimacy is greater than 70 percent of the adults whose scores are averaged here.

Another aspect of relationships that seems to be linked to gender is communication styles (Lips, 2003). Deborah Tannen (1990) highlighted the differences between women and men in her analyses of their talk. She reported that a common complaint women have about their husbands is "He doesn't listen to me anymore." Another is "He doesn't talk to me anymore." Lack of communication, although high on women's lists of reasons for divorce, is much less often mentioned by men.

Tannen distinguishes between rapport talk and report talk. _Rapport talk_ is the language of conversation. It is a way of establishing connections and negotiating relationships. Women prefer to engage in rapport talk. Women enjoy private conversations more than men do, and it is men's lack of interest in rapport talk that bothers many women. *Report talk* is talk that is designed to give information, which includes public speaking. Men prefer to engage in report talk. Men hold center stage through such verbal performances as telling stories and jokes. They learn to use talk as a way of getting and keeping attention.

Tannen (1990) argues that these gender differences are the result of girls and boys being socialized differently as they grow up. Mothers have participated far more in rearing children than fathers have and have modeled a stronger interest in relationships when interacting with their daughters than when interacting with their sons. Tannen (1990) and others (Levant, 2001; Levant & Brooks, 1997) recommend that men develop a stronger interest in relationships and make women feel more comfortable in public speaking contexts. Tannen (1990) also recommends that women seek more report-talk opportunities, including speaking up in groups.

Loneliness

In chapter 11, I described the importance of the motive for affiliation and relatedness. People have a basic human desire to seek the company of others. Because of this strong human tendency, people who do not interact with others in close relationships on a regular basis may feel lonely. Lonely people may feel that no one knows them very well. They might feel isolated and sense that they do not have anyone to turn to in times of need and stress.

Each of us has times in our lives when we feel lonely, but for some people loneliness is a chronic condition. More than just an unwelcome social situation, chronic loneliness is linked with impaired physical and mental health (Brehm, 2002; McInnis & White, 2001). Chronic loneliness can even lead to an early death (Cuijpers, 2001). In one recent study, lonely college students had higher levels of stress-related hormones and poorer sleep patterns than students who had relationships with others (Cacioppo & others, 2000).

Our society's emphasis on self-fulfillment and achievement, the importance we attach to commitment in relationships, and a decline in stable close relationships are among the reasons loneliness is common today (de Jong-Gierveld, 1987). Researchers have found that married individuals are less lonely than their nonmarried counterparts (never married, divorced, or widowed) in studies conducted in more than 20 countries (Perlman & Peplau, 1998).

Males and females attribute their loneliness to different sources, with men tending to blame themselves, women tending to blame external factors. Men are socialized to initiate relationships, whereas women are traditionally socialized to wait and then respond. Perhaps men blame themselves because they feel they should do something about their loneliness, whereas women wonder why no one calls.

How do you determine if you are lonely? Scales of loneliness ask you to respond to items such as "I don't feel in tune with the people around me" and "I can find companionship when I want it." If you consistently respond that you never or rarely feel in tune with people around you and rarely or never can find companionship when you want it, you are likely to fall into the category of people who are described as moderately or intensely lonely (Russell, 1996).

Loneliness and Life's Transitions   Loneliness is interwoven with how people pass through life transitions, such as a move to a different part of the country, a divorce, or the death of a close friend or family member. Another situation that often creates loneliness is the first year of college. When students leave the familiar world of their hometown and family to enter college, they can feel especially lonely. Many college freshmen feel anxious about meeting new people, and developing a new social life can create considerable anxiety. As one student commented,

My first year here at the university has been pretty lonely. I wasn't lonely at all in high school. I lived in a fairly small town—I knew everybody and everyone knew me. I was a

"What I'm trying to say, Mary, is that I want *your* site to be linked to *my* site." © The New Yorker Collection 2000. Mick Stevens from cartoonbank.com. All Rights Reserved.

member of several clubs and played on the basketball team. It's not that way at the university. It is a big place and I've felt like a stranger on so many occasions. I'm starting to get used to my life here and the last few months I've been making myself meet people and get to know them, but it has not been easy.

As this comment illustrates, freshmen rarely bring their popularity and social standing from high school into the college environment. There may be a dozen high school basketball stars, National Merit scholars, and former student council presidents in a single dormitory wing. Especially if students attend college away from home, they face the task of forming completely new social relationships.

One study found that 2 weeks after the school year began, 75 percent of 354 college freshmen felt lonely at least part of the time (Cutrona, 1982). More than 40 percent said their loneliness was moderate to severe. Students who were the most optimistic and had the highest self-esteem were the likeliest to overcome their loneliness by the end of their freshman year. Loneliness is not reserved for college freshmen, though. Upperclassmen are often lonely, as well. In one recent study of more than 2,600 undergraduates, lonely individuals were less likely to actively cope with stress than individuals who were able to make friends (Cacioppo & others, 2000).

Loneliness and Technology One of the factors that may be contributing to loneliness in contemporary society is technology. Although invention of the telephone more than a century ago seems to have decreased social isolation for many individuals and families, psychologists have found a link between TV viewing and loneliness. Correlation does not equal causation, but it does seem plausible that television can contribute to social disengagement.

Because most people isolate themselves at their computers when they use the Internet, the Internet also may increase disengagement. One study focused on 169 individuals during their first several years online (Kraut & others, 1998). In this study, greater use of the Internet was associated with declines in participants' communication with family members in the household and increases in depression and loneliness. However, some people use the Internet to form potentially strong new ties (Clay, 2000). Especially for socially anxious and lonely individuals, the Internet may provide a safe way to begin contacts that eventually lead to face-to-face meetings and possibly even intimate relationships.

Strategies for Reducing Loneliness If you are lonely, how can you become better connected with others? Following are some strategies:

- *Participate in activities that you can do with others.* Join organizations or volunteer your time for a cause you believe in. You likely will get to know others whose views are similar to yours. Going to just one social gathering can help you develop social contacts. When you go, introduce yourself to others and start a conversation. Another strategy is to sit next to new people in your classes or find someone to study with.
- *Be aware of the early warning signs of loneliness.* People often feel bored or alienated before loneliness becomes pervasive. Head off loneliness by becoming involved in new social activities.
- *Draw a diagram of your social network.* Determine whether the people in the diagram meet your social needs. If not, pencil in the people you would like to get to know.
- *Engage in positive behaviors when you meet new people.* You will improve your chances of developing enduring relationships if, when you meet new people,

you are nice, considerate, honest, trustworthy, and cooperative. Have a positive attitude, be supportive of the other person, and make positive comments about him or her.

- *See a counselor or read a book on loneliness.* If you can't get rid of your loneliness on your own, you might want to contact the counseling services at your college. The counselor can talk with you about strategies for reducing your loneliness. You also might want to read a good book on loneliness, such as *Intimate Connections* by David Burns (1985).

Review and Sharpen Your Thinking

5 *Understand the nature of relationships.*

- Describe the factors involved in attraction.
- Identify three types of love.
- Explain how gender affects relationships.
- Discuss some causes of loneliness and strategies for reducing it.

Think about the people to whom you are attracted. What is it about them that attracts you?

For study tools related to this learning goal, see the Study Guide, the CD-ROM, and the Online Learning Center.

You have arrived at the end of this book. You should be able to look back and say you have learned a lot about both yourself and other human beings. You should also see that, although many unanswered questions remain, psychology's quest to understand human behavior produces information we can use to make our lives more enjoyable and humane. What could be more intriguing and important to all of us than psychology's mission of describing, explaining, and predicting the behavior of the human species?

Reach Your Learning Goals

Social Psychology

1 SOCIAL THINKING
- Attribution
- Social Perception
- Attitudes

2 SOCIAL INFLUENCE
- Conformity and Obedience
- Group Influence
- Leadership

3 INTERGROUP RELATIONS
- Group Identity: Us Versus Them
- Prejudice
- Ways to Improve Interethnic Relations

4 SOCIAL INTERACTION
- Aggression
- Altruism

5 RELATIONSHIPS
- Attraction
- Relationships and Gender
- Love
- Loneliness

1 ***Describe how people think about the social world.***

- Attributions are our thoughts about why people behave the way they do and about who or what is responsible for the outcome of events. Attribution theory views people as motivated to discover the causes of behavior as part of their effort to make sense of it. The dimensions that we use to make sense of the causes of human behavior include internal/external, stable/unstable, and controllable/uncontrollable. The fundamental attribution error states that observers overestimate the importance of traits and underestimate the importance of situations when they seek explanations of an actor's behavior. When our self-esteem is threatened, we might depart from the fundamental attribution error and engage in a self-serving bias, attributing our successes to internal causes and our failures to external causes.

- Social perception involves the impressions we develop of others, comparisons of ourselves with others, and presentation of ourselves to others to influence others' perceptions. Our impressions of others are unified and integrated. An individual's notions of which traits go together is called implicit personality theory. We use social schemas, or prototypes, to evaluate others. We simplify our impressions by categorizing others. In some instances, though, we develop a more individualized approach to impressions. First impressions are important and influence later impressions. As for social comparison, we evaluate ourselves by comparison with others. Festinger stresses that social comparison is an important source of self-knowledge, especially when no other objective means is available. We tend to compare ourselves with similar others. Self-presentation to influence others' social perceptions includes two dimensions: impression management to present a favorable self-image and self-monitoring to fine-tune the impressions we are making.

- Attitudes are beliefs or opinions about people, objects, and ideas. We are better able to predict behavior from attitudes when the person's attitudes are strong, when the person is very aware of his or her attitudes and expresses them often, and when the attitudes are specifically relevant to the behavior. Sometimes changes in behavior precede changes in attitude. Cognitive dissonance theory, developed by Festinger, argues that we have a strong need for cognitive consistency. We change our attitudes to make them more consistent with our behavior in order to reduce dissonance. In many cases, we reduce dissonance by justifying our actions. Justification is the most intense when self-esteem is involved. Bem's more behavioral approach, called self-perception theory, stresses the importance of making inferences about attitudes by observing our own behavior, especially when our attitudes are not clear. Success in changing someone's attitudes may involve the communicator (source), the message, the medium, and the target (audience).

2 ***Identify how people are influenced in social settings.***

- Conformity involves a change in a person's behavior to coincide with a group standard. Asch's classic study on judgments of line length illustrated the power of conformity. Many factors influence whether we will conform, including normative social influence and informational social influence. Obedience is behavior that complies with the explicit demands of an individual in authority. Milgram's classic experiment demonstrated the power of obedience. Participants obeyed the experimenter's directions even though they thought they were hurting someone. As we go through our lives, we are both conformist and nonconformist, obedient and not obedient. Sometimes we are overwhelmed by persuasion. At other times, we exert personal control and resist such influence.

- Groups satisfy our personal needs, reward us, provide us with information, raise our self-esteem, and enhance our identity. Every group has norms and rules. Our performance in groups can be improved through social faciliation and lowered because of social loafing. In a group, we also can experience deindividuation—a loss of personal identity and a decrease in responsibility. The risky shift is the tendency for a group decision to be riskier than the average decision made by the individual group members. The group polarization effect is the solidification and further strengthening of a position as a consequence of group discussion. Groupthink involves impaired decision making and avoidance of realistic appraisal to maintain harmony in the group. The majority usually gets its way in group influence, but occasionally the minority has its day.

- Theories of group leadership include the great-person theory (leaders are born), the situational approach (leaders are made), and the person-situation view, known as the contingency model of leadership (leaders are people who have the ability to take charge when the situation requires it). As leaders, men tend to be more directive and task-oriented, whereas women are more likely to be more democratic and interpersonally oriented.

3 ***Discuss intergroup relations.***

- Social identity is how we define ourselves in terms of our group memberships. Tajfel proposed social identity theory, which states that when individuals are assigned to a group they invariably think of it as the in-group, or "we." Identifying with the group allows them to have a positive self-image. Ethnocentrism is the tendency to favor one's own group over other groups. Ethnocentrism can have positive or negative outcomes.

- Prejudice is an unjustified negative attitude toward an individual based on the individual's membership in a group. Among the reasons given for why people develop prejudice are an individual's personality (authoritarian), competition between groups over scarce resources, motivation to enhance one's self-esteem, cognitive processes that contribute to a tendency to categorize and stereotype others, and cultural learning. Prejudice is based on stereotyping, a generalization about a group's characteristics that does not consider any variations from one individual to the next. The cognitive process of stereotyping can lead to discrimination, an unjustified negative or harmful action toward a member of a group simply because he or she is a member of that group. Discrimination results when negative emotional reactions combine with prejudiced beliefs and are translated into behavior.

- Contact between ethnic groups, by itself, does not decrease conflict and improve relations. Two effective strategies are to set up task-oriented cooperation and for members of different ethnic groups to share intimate information.

4   *Explain how aggression and altruism characterize social interaction.*

- One view of the biological basis of aggression is that, early in human evolution, the most aggressive individuals were likely to be the survivors. Freud proposed an instinct theory of aggression, but that view has not been supported. There is some evidence for the genetic basis of aggression, however. Neurobiological factors involved in aggressive behavior include the amygdala, the neurotransmitter serotonin, alcohol's disinhibiting affects, and hormones. Psychological factors in aggression include frustrating and aversive circumstances, expectations, equity, intentions, responsibility, and reinforcement and observational learning. Sociocultural factors include cross-cultural variations and the extensive violence American children watch on TV. Gender also is a factor. Males are consistently more physically aggressive than females, but gender differences in verbal aggression are not consistent.

- Altruism is an unselfish interest in helping someone else. Reciprocity often is involved in altruism. The motivation can be altruistic or egoistic. Psychologists have studied both person and situation variables in altruism. Evolutionary psychologists stress that altruism increases the prospects of survival, as well as reproduction. Evolutionary examples involve favoritism toward kin, as well as a parental care for offspring. The bystander effect is the concept that individuals who observe an emergency help less when someone else is present than when they are alone. The altruistic behavior of college students has fluctuated over the years. When examining the link between altruism and gender, context is important. Females are likelier to help in situations that are not dangerous and involve caregiving. Males are likelier to help in situations that involve danger or in which they feel competent.

5   *Understand the nature of relationships.*

- Familiarity precedes a close relationship. We also like to associate with people who are similar to us. The principles of consensual validation and matching can explain the appeal of similarity. Physical attraction is usually more important in the early part of a relationship. Criteria for physical attractiveness vary across cultures and over time.

- Romantic love (or passionate love) is involved when we say we are "in love." It includes passion, sexuality, and a mixture of emotions, not all of which are positive. Affectionate love (or companionate love) is the type of love that usually becomes more important as relationships mature. Sternberg proposed a triarchic model of love involving passion, intimacy, and commitment. Consummate love is that in relationships in which all three elements are present.

- Females have a stronger interest in relationships than males do. Tannen suggests that another gender difference in relationships relates to communication styles. Females prefer rapport talk, and males prefer report talk.

- Men tend to blame themselves for their loneliness, whereas women tend to blame external sources. Loneliness often emerges when people make life transitions, so it is not surprising that loneliness is common among college freshmen. Technology, such as the telephone, television, and the Internet, can affect loneliness. A number of strategies can help to reduce loneliness, including participating in activities that one can do with others and taking positive steps to meet new people.

Key Terms

social psychology, p. 646
attribution theory, p. 647
fundamental attribution error, p. 648
implicit personality theory, p. 650
impression management (self-presentation), p. 651
self-monitoring, p. 652

attitudes, p. 653
cognitive dissonance, p. 655
self-perception theory, p. 655
elaboration likelihood model, p. 657
conformity, p. 658
normative social influence, p. 659
informational social influence, p. 659

obedience, p. 660
social facilitation, p. 663
social loafing, p. 663
deindividuation, p. 664
risky shift, p. 664
group polarization effect, p. 664
groupthink, p. 665
social identity, p. 669
social identity theory, p. 669

ethnocentrism, p. 669
prejudice, p. 670
stereotype, p. 672
discrimination, p. 672
altruism, p. 682
egoism, p. 683
bystander effect, p. 644
romantic love, p. 688
affectionate love, p. 688

Apply Your Knowledge

1. We're often unaware of how many attributions we make about the behavior of others. To demonstrate this to yourself, spend some time in a crowded area observing the interactions of others (or you could watch some scenes in television shows or movies). Take careful notes about the social behaviors that occur and then indicate your impression of why the people behaved the way they did. What cues did you use to make your decision about their behavior? Did your knowledge of the fundamental attribution error influence your attributions?

2. The text discusses stereotyping and prejudice as two factors affecting intergroup relations. Many of our stereotypes and prejudices are quite subtle, and we can be unaware of them. To help you better appreciate the effects of these subtle influences, take one of the tests at the following website:

http://buster.cs.yale.edu/implicit/index.html. Knowing the results, how can you use the suggestions in the text to change your attitudes or behavior?

3. Find a movie that shows an example of aggression (or altruism). Look at the scene and assess the influences that caused the characters to behave aggressively (or altruistically). In what ways are these influences consistent with those discussed in the text, and in what ways do they differ?

4. Many of the conclusions about the nature of relationships are based on correlational studies. Discuss the factors that contribute to the difficulty of conducting experiments on relationships, and describe an experiment that you might conduct to test one of the factors described as contributing to attraction or loneliness.

Connections

For extra help in mastering the material in this chapter, see the review sections and practice quizzes in the Student Study Guide, the CD-ROM, and the Online Learning Center.

Glossary

A **abnormal behavior** Behavior that is deviant, maladaptive, or personally distressful. p. 20

absolute threshold The minimum amount of stimulus energy that people can detect. p. 180

accommodation Occurs when individuals adjust their schemas to new information. p. 128

acculturative stress The negative consequences that result from contact between two distinctive cultural groups. p. 610

achievement tests Tests that measure what a person has learned or the skills that a person has mastered. p. 393

acquired immunodeficiency syndrome (AIDS) Caused by the human immunodeficiency virus (HIV), a sexually transmitted disease that destroys the body's immune system. p. 638

acquisition (in classical conditioning) The initial learning of the stimulus-response link, which involves a neutral stimulus being associated with a UCS and becoming a conditioned stimulus (CS) that elicits the CR. p. 272

action potential The term used to describe the brief wave of electrical charge that sweeps down the axon during the transmission of a nerve impulse. p. 84

activation-synthesis theory States that dreaming occurs when the cerebral cortex synthesizes neural signals emanating from activity in the lower part of the brain. p. 245

addiction A pattern of behavior characterized by an overwhelming need to use the drug and to secure its supply. p. 261

adrenal glands Important endocrine glands that are instrumental in regulating moods, energy level, and the ability to cope with stress. p. 103

affectionate love Also called *companionate love*; the type of love that occurs when individuals desire to have the other person near and have a deep, caring affection for the person. p. 688

afferent nerves Sensory nerves that transport information to the brain. p. 80

agonist A drug that mimics or increases a neurotransmitter's effects. p. 88

agoraphobia A cluster of fears centered around public places and being unable to escape or to find help should one become incapacitated. p. 528

alcoholism A disorder that involves long-term, repeated, uncontrolled, compulsive, and excessive use of alcoholic beverages and that impairs the drinker's health and work and social relationships. p. 254

algorithms Strategies that guarantee a solution to a problem. p. 357

all-or-none principle Once an electrical impulse reaches a certain level of intensity, it fires and moves all the way down the axon without losing any of its intensity. p. 83

altruism An unselfish interest in helping someone else. p. 18

amnesia The loss of memory. p. 338

androgens The main class of male sex hormones. p. 145

anorexia nervosa An eating disorder that involves the relentless pursuit of thinness through starvation. p. 436

antagonist A drug that blocks a neurotransmitter's effects. p. 88

anterograde amnesia A memory disorder that affects the retention of new information or events p. 338

antianxiety drugs Commonly known as *tranquilizers*, they reduce anxiety by making people calmer and less excitable. p. 563

antidepressant drugs Drugs that regulate mood. p. 563

antipsychotic drugs Powerful drugs that diminish agitated behavior, reduce tension, decrease hallucinations, improve social behavior, and produce better sleep patterns in people who have a severe psychological disorder, such as schizophrenia. p. 565

anxiety disorders Psychological disorders that include these features: motor tension, hyperactivity, and apprehensive expectations and thoughts. p. 527

apparent movement The perception that a stationary object is moving. p. 201

applied behavior analysis (behavior modification) The application of operant conditioning principles to change human behavior. p. 288

approach/approach conflict A conflict in which the individual must choose between two attractive stimuli or circumstances. p. 698

approach/avoidance conflict A conflict involving a single stimulus or circumstance that has both positive and negative characteristics. p. 608

aptitude tests Tests that predict an individual's ability to learn. p. 393

archetypes The name Jung gave to the emotionally laden ideas and images in the collective unconscious that have rich and symbolic meaning. p. 483

artificial intelligence (AI) The science of creating machines capable of performing activities that require intelligence when they are done by people. p. 352

assimilation Occurs when individuals incorporate new information into existing knowledge. p. 128

association cortex Region of the cerebral cortex in which the highest intellectual functions, including thinking and problem solving, occur (also called association areas). p. 98

associative learning In which a connection is made between two events. p. 269

Atkinson-Shiffrin theory The view that memory involves a sequence of three stages: sensory memory, short-term memory, and long-term memory. p. 311

attachment The close emotional bond between an infant and its caregiver. p. 136

attitudes Beliefs or opinions about people, objects, and ideas. p. 653

attribution theory Views people as motivated to discover the underlying causes of behavior as part of their effort to make sense of the behavior. p. 447

auditory nerve Carries neural impulses to the brain's auditory area. p. 209

authoritarian parenting A restrictive, punitive style in which the parent exhorts the child to follow the parent's directions and value hard work and effort. p. 139

authoritative parenting A parenting style that encourages children's independence (but still places limits and controls on their behavior), includes extensive verbal give-and-take, and warm and nurturant interactions with the child. p. 139

automatic processes States of consciousness that require little attention and do not interfere with other ongoing activities. p. 229

autonomic nervous system Division of the PNS that communicates with the body's internal organs. It consists of the sympathetic and parasympathetic nervous systems. p. 81

availability heuristic A prediction about the probability of an event based on the frequency of the event's past occurrences. p. 367

aversive conditioning A classical conditioning treatment which consists of repeated pairings of the undesirable behavior with aversive stimuli to decrease the behavior's rewards. p. 272

avoidance/avoidance conflict A conflict in which the individual must choose between two unattractive stimuli or circumstances. p. 608

axon The part of the neuron that carries information away from the cell body to other cells; each neuron has only one axon. p. 82

B **barbiturates** Depressant drugs that decrease the activity of the central nervous system. p. 255

basal ganglia Located above the thalamus and under the cerebral cortex, these large clusters of neurons work with the cerebellum and the cerebral cortex to control and coordinate voluntary movements p. 94

basal metabolism rate (BMR) The minimal amount of energy an individual uses in a resting state. p. 433

basic skills-and-phonetics approach Stresses that reading instruction should emphasize the basic rules for translating written patterns into sounds. p. 380

behavior Everything we do that can be directly observed. p. 6

behavior modification The application of operant conditioning principles to change human behavior; especially to replace unacceptable, maladaptive behaviors with acceptable, adaptive behaviors. p. 288

behavior therapy Uses principles of learning to reduce or eliminate maladaptive behavior. Emphasis on self-healing capacities. p. 574

behavioral approach Emphasizes the scientific study of behavior and asserts that behavior is shaped by the environment. p. 9

behavioral medicine An interdisciplinary field that focuses on developing and integrating behavioral and biomedical knowledge to promote health and reduce illness. p. 603

behavioral neuroscience approach Views understanding the brain and nervous system as central to understanding behavior, thought, and emotion. p. 12

belief perseverance The tendency to hold on to a belief in the face of contradictory evidence. p. 366

big five factors of personality Openness to experience, conscientiousness, extraversion, agreeableness, and neuroticism (emotional stability). p. 498

binding The bringing together and integration of what is processed through different pathways or cells. p. 193

binocular cues Depth cues that are based on the combination of the images on the left and right eyes and on the way the two eyes work together. p. 198

biofeedback The process in which individuals' muscular or visceral activities are monitored by instruments. The information from the instruments is fed back to the individuals so that they can learn to voluntarily control their physiological activities. p. 630

biological rhythms Periodic physiological fluctuations in the body. p. 233

biological therapies Treatments to reduce or eliminate the symptoms of psychological disorders by altering the way an individual's body functions. p. 562

bipolar disorder A mood disorder characterized by extreme mood swings that include one or more episodes of mania. p. 539

bottom-up processing Processing that begins with sensory receptors registering environmental information and sending it to the brain for integration and cognitive processing. p. 177

brain stem The region of the brain that includes most of the hindbrain (excluding the cerebellum) and the midbrain. p. 92

burnout A feeling of overload, including mental and physical exhaustion, that usually results from a gradual accumulation of everyday stresses. p. 609

bystander effect The concept that individuals who observe an emergency help less when someone else is present than when they are alone. p. 684

C **Cannon-Bard theory** States that emotion and physiological states occur simultaneously. p. 457

case study An in-depth look at a single individual. p. 52

catatonic schizophrenia A type of schizophrenia that is characterized by bizarre motor behavior, which sometimes takes the form of a completely immobile stupor. p. 549

catharsis The release of anger or aggressive energy by directly or vicariously engaging in anger or aggression; the *catharsis hypothesis* states that behaving angrily or watching others behave angrily reduces subsequent anger. p. 467

cell body Part of the neuron that contains the nucleus, which directs the manufacture of substances that the neuron needs for growth and maintenance. p. 82

central nervous system (CNS) The brain and spinal cord. p. 81

cerebral cortex Highest level of the forebrain, where the highest mental functions, such as thinking and planning, take place. p. 78

chromosomes Threadlike structures that contain genes and DNA. Humans have 23 chromosome pairs in the nucleus of every cell. Each parent contributes one chromosome to each pair. p. 106

circadian rhythms Daily behavioral or physiological cycles, such as the sleep/wake cycle. p. 233

classical conditioning Learning by which a neutral stimulus becomes associated with a meaningful stimulus and acquires the capacity to elicit a similar response. p. 270

classical model States that all instances of a concept share defining properties. p. 355

client-centered therapy Rogers' humanistic therapy in which the therapist provides a warm, supportive atmosphere to improve the client's self-concept and encourage the client to gain insight about problems. p. 573

cognition The way in which information is processed and manipulated in remembering, thinking, and knowing. p. 351

cognitive appraisal Lazarus' term for individuals' interpretation of events in their lives as threatening, harmful, or challenging and their determination of whether they have the resources to effectively cope with the events. p. 615

cognitive approach Focuses on the mental processes involved in knowing: how we direct our attention, perceive, remember, think, and solve problems. p. 12

cognitive dissonance A concept developed by Festinger that refers to an individual's motivation to reduce the discomfort (dissonance) caused by two inconsistent thoughts. p. 653

cognitive theory of dreaming Proposes that dreaming can be understood by relying on the same cognitive processes that are used in studying the waking mind. p. 244

cognitive therapies Emphasize that individuals' cognitions or thoughts are the main source of abnormal behavior and psychological problems. p. 582

cognitive-behavior therapy Consists of a combination of cognitive therapy and behavior therapy. p. 580

collective unconscious Jung's term for the impersonal, deepest layer of the unconscious mind, shared by all human beings because of their common ancestral past. p. 483

concepts Mental categories that are used to group objects, events, and characteristics. p. 355

concrete operational stage The third Piagetian stage of cognitive development (approximately 7 to 11 years of age) in which thought becomes operational, replacing intuitive thought with logical reasoning in concrete situations. p. 131

conditioned response (CR) The learned response to the conditioned stimulus that occurs after the CS-UCS pairing. p. 271

conditioned stimulus (CS) A previously neutral stimulus that eventually elicits the conditioned response after being associated with the unconditioned stimulus. p. 271

cones The receptors in the retina that process information about color. p. 190

confirmation bias The tendency to search for and use information that supports, rather than refutes, our ideas. p. 365

conformity Involves a change in a person's behavior to coincide more with a group standard. p. 658

connectionism (parallel distributed processing) The theory that memory is stored throughout the brain in connections between neurons, several of which may work together to process a single memory. p. 323

consciousness Awareness of external events and internal sensations, including awareness of the self and thoughts about one's experiences. p. 228

control group A comparison group that is treated in every way like the experimental group except for the manipulated factor. p. 56

controlled processes The most alert states of consciousness. p. 229

convergent thinking Thinking that produces one correct answer; characteristic of the type of thinking required on traditional intelligence tests. p. 408

coping Managing taxing circumstances, expending effort to solve life's problems, and seeking to master or reduce stress. p. 621

corpus callosum A large bundle of axons that connect the brain's two hemispheres. p. 98

correlational research Research with the goal of describing the strength of the relationship between two or more events or characteristics. p. 53

counterconditioning A classical conditioning procedure for weakening a CR by associating the fear-provoking stimulus with a new response that is incompatible with the fear. p. 274

couples therapy Therapy with married or unmarried couples whose major problem is within their relationship. p. 585

creativity The ability to think about something in novel and unusual ways and come up with unconventional solutions to problems. p. 388

critical thinking The process of thinking reflectively and productively, as well as evaluating evidence. p. 364

crystallized intelligence An individual's accumulated information and verbal skills. p. 162

culture-fair tests Intelligence tests that are intended to be culturally unbiased. p. 395

D decay theory States that when something new is learned, a neuro-chemical memory trace is formed, but over time this trace tends to disintegrate. p. 337

decision making Involves evaluating alternatives and making choices among them p. 365

deductive reasoning Reasoning from the general to the specific. p. 364

defense mechanisms The ego's protective methods for reducing anxiety by unconsciously distorting reality. p. 480

deindividuation Occurs when being part of a group reduces personal identity and the sense of responsibility. p. 664

dendrites Branches of a neuron that receive and orient information toward the cell body; most neurons have numerous dendrites. p. 82

deoxyribonucleic acid (DNA) A complex molecule that contains genetic information; makes up chromosomes. p. 106

dependent variable The factor that can change in an experiment in response to changes in the independent variable. p. 56

depressants Psychoactive drugs that slow down mental and physical activity. p. 252

depressive disorders Mood disorders in which the individual suffers depression without ever experiencing mania. p. 537

depth perception The ability to perceive objects three dimensionally. p. 198

descriptive statistics Mathematical procedures that are used to describe and summarize samples of data in a meaningful way. p. 59

development The pattern of change in human capabilities that begins at conception and continues throughout the life span. p. 119

diathesis-stress model A model of schizophrenia that proposes a combination of biogenetic disposition and stress as the cause of the disorder. p. 552

difference threshold Also called *just noticeable difference*, this concept refers to the smallest difference in stimulation required to discriminate one stimulus from another 50 percent of the time. p. 182

discrimination (in classical conditioning) The process of learning to respond to certain stimuli and not to others. p. 272

discrimination (in operant conditioning) The tendency to only respond to stimuli that signal whether a behavior will or will not be reinforced. p. 284

discrimination An unjustified negative or harmful action toward a member of a group simply because he or she is a member of that group. p. 672

disease model of addiction Describes addictions as biologically based, lifelong diseases that involve a loss of control over behavior and require medical and/or spiritual treatment for recovery. p. 261

disorganized schizophrenia A type of schizophrenia in which an individual has delusions and hallucinations that have little or no recognizable meaning. p. 549

display rules Sociocultural standards that determine when, where, and how emotions should be expressed. p. 464

dissociative amnesia A dissociative disorder involving extreme memory loss caused by extensive psychological stress. p. 535

dissociative disorders Psychological disorders that involve a sudden loss of memory or change in identity. p. 535

dissociative fugue A dissociative disorder in which the individual not only develops amnesia but also unexpectedly travels away from home and establishes a new identity. p. 535

dissociative identity disorder (DID) Formerly called *multiple personality disorder,* this is the most dramatic but least common dissociative disorder; individuals suffering from this disorder have two or more distinct personalities. p. 535

divergent thinking Thinking that produces many answers to the same question; characteristic of creativity. p. 408

dominant-recessive genes principle If one gene of a pair governing a given characteristic (such as eye color) is dominant and one is recessive, the dominant gene overrides the recessive gene. A recessive gene exerts its influence only if both genes in a pair are recessive. p. 106

double-blind experiment An experiment that is conducted so that neither the experimenter nor the participants are aware of which participants are in the experimental group and which are in the placebo control group until after the results are calculated. p. 68

dream analysis The psychotherapeutic technique used by psychoanalysts to interpret a person's dream. Psychoanalysts believe dreams contain information about the individual's unconscious thoughts and conflicts. p. 571

drive An aroused state that occurs because of a physiological need. p. 425

DSM-IV *Diagnostic and Statistical Manual of Mental Disorders,* fourth edition; the APA's major classification of psychological disorders. p. 523

dysthymic disorder A depressive disorder that is generally more chronic and has fewer symptoms than major depressive disorder. p. 538

E **efferent nerves** Motor nerves that carry the brain's output. p. 80

ego The Freudian structure of personality that deals with the demands of reality. p. 479

egoism Giving to another person to ensure reciprocity, to gain self-esteem, to present oneself as powerful, competent, or caring, or to avoid social and self-censure for failing to live up to normative expectations. p. 683

elaboration likelihood model States that there are two ways to persuade—by a central route and by a peripheral route. p. 657

elaboration The extensiveness of processing at any given level of memory. p. 309

electroconvulsive therapy (ECT) Commonly called shock therapy, this treatment is used for severely depressed individuals; it causes a seizure to occur in the brain. p. 566

emotion Feeling, or affect, that can involve physiological arousal, conscious experience, and behavioral expression. p. 455

emotion-focused coping Lazarus' term for responding to stress in an emotional manner, especially using defensive appraisal. p. 622

emotional intelligence The ability to monitor one's own and others' emotions and feelings, to discriminate among them, and to use this information to guide one's thinking and actions. p. 404

empirically keyed test Relies on items to predict some criterion that discriminates between groups individually. p. 506

encoding The way in which information gets into memory storage. p. 308

endocrine system A set of glands that regulate the activities of certain organs by releasing hormones into the bloodstream. p. 102

episodic memory The retention of information about the where and when of life's happenings. p. 316

estrogens The main class of female sex hormones. p. 146

ethnic gloss Involves using an ethnic label, such as "African American" or "Latino," in a superficial way that portrays the ethnic group as more homogeneous than it really is. p. 67

ethnocentrism The tendency to favor one's own ethnic group over other groups. p. 669

evolutionary psychology approach Emphasizes the importance of functional purpose and adaptation in explaining why behaviors are formed, are modified, and survive. p. 13

experiment A carefully regulated procedure in which one or more factors believed to influence the behavior being studied are manipulated and all other factors are held constant. p. 56

experimental group A group in a research study whose experience is manipulated. p. 56

experimenter bias The influence of the experimenter's own expectations on the outcome of the research. p. 57

explicit memory (declarative memory) The conscious recollection of information, such as specific facts or events and, at least in humans, information that can be verbally communicated. p. 316

extinction (in classical conditioning) The weakening of the conditioned response in the absence of the unconditioned stimulus. p. 272

extinction (in operant conditioning) A previously reinforced behavior is no longer reinforced, and there is a decreased tendency to perform the behavior. p. 284

extrinsic motivation Involves external incentives, such as rewards and punishments. p. 428

F **facial feedback hypothesis** States that facial expressions can influence emotions, as well as reflect them. p. 462

factor analysis A statistical procedure that examines various items or measures and identifies factors that are correlated with each other. p. 400

family therapy Group therapy with family members. p. 585

feature detectors Neurons in the brain's visual system that respond to particular lines or other features of a stimulus. p. 192

figure-ground relationship People organize the perceptual field into stimuli that stand out and those that are left over. p. 197

fixation Involves using a prior problem-solving strategy and failing to look at a problem from a new perspective. p. 358

fluid intelligence One's ability to reason abstractly. p. 162

forebrain The highest level of the brain. Key structures in the forebrain are the limbic system, thalamus, basal ganglia, hypothalamus, and cerebral cortex. p. 93

formal operational stage The fourth and final Piagetian stage of cognitive development (emerging from about 11 to 15 years of age) in which thinking becomes more abstract, idealistic, and logical. p. 133

free association The psychoanalytic technique of having individuals say aloud whatever comes into their minds. p. 570

frequency theory Perception of a sound's frequency is due to how often the auditory nerve fires. p. 207

frontal lobe The part of the cerebral cortex just behind the forehead that is involved in the control of voluntary muscles, intelligence, and personality. p. 95

functional fixedness A type of fixation in which individuals fail to solve a problem because they are fixated on a thing's usual functions. p. 358

functionalism An early school of psychology that emphasized the interaction between the mind and the outside environment. p. 8

fundamental attribution error The tendency for observers to overestimate the importance of traits and underestimate the importance of situations when they seek explanations of a person's behavior. p. 648

G **gate-control theory of pain** The spinal column contains a neural gate that can be open (allowing the perception of pain) or closed (blocking the perception of pain). p. 214

Gender role Expectations for how females and males should think, act, and feel. p. 147

general adaptation syndrome (GAS) Selye's term for the common effects on the body when demands are placed on it. The GAS consists of three stages: alarm, resistance, and exhaustion. p. 612

generalization (in classical conditioning) The tendency of a new stimulus that is similar to the original stimulus to elicit a response that is similar to the conditioned response. p. 272

generalization (in operant conditioning) Giving the same response to similar stimuli. p. 283

generalized anxiety disorder An anxiety disorder that consists of persistent anxiety over at least 1 month; the individual with this disorder cannot specify the reasons for the anxiety. p. 527

genes The units of hereditary information. They are short segments of chromosomes, composed of DNA. p. 105

genotype An individual's genetic heritage, the actual genetic material. p. 121

gestalt psychology People naturally organize their perceptions according to certain patterns. p. 197

gestalt therapy Perls' humanistic therapy in which the therapist challenges clients to help them become more aware of their feelings and face their problems. p. 573

gifted Individuals who have an IQ of 120 or higher and/or superior talent in a particular domain. p. 407

glial cells Provide support and nutritional benefits in the nervous system. p. 82

group polarization effect The solidification and further strengthening of a position as a consequence of a group discussion. p. 664

groupthink Involves impaired decision making and avoidance of realistic appraisal to maintain group harmony. p. 665

H **hallucinogens** Psychoactive drugs that modify a person's perceptual experiences and produce visual images that are not real. p. 258

hardiness A personality style characterized by a sense of commitment (rather than alienation), control (rather than powerlessness), and a perception of problems as challenges (rather than threats). p. 605

health psychology Emphasizes psychology's role in promoting and maintaining health and in preventing and treating illness. p. 603

heritability The fraction of the variance in IQ in a population that is attributed to genetics. p. 413

heuristics Strategies or guidelines that suggest, but do not guarantee, a solution to a problem. p. 358

hierarchy of needs Maslow's view that individuals' main needs are satisfied in the following sequence: physiological, safety, love and belongingness, esteem, and self-actualization. p. 429

hindbrain The lowest level of the brain, consisting of the medulla, cerebellum, and pons. p. 91

hindsight bias The tendency to falsely report, after the fact, that we accurately predicted an event. p. 36

homeostasis The body's tendency to maintain an equilibrium, or steady state. p. 426

hormones Chemical messengers manufactured by the endocrine glands. p. 102

human sexual response pattern Identified by Masters and Johnson; consists of four phases—excitement, plateau, orgasm, and resolution. p. 438

humanistic movement An emphasis on a person's capacity for personal growth, freedom to choose a destiny, and positive qualities. p. 17

humanistic perspectives Stress the person's capacity for personal growth, freedom to choose a destiny, and positive qualities. p. 490

humanistic therapies In these therapies people are encouraged to understand themselves and to grow personally. The humanistic therapies are unique in their emphasis on self-healing capacities. p. 573

hypnosis A psychological state or possibly altered attention and awareness in which the individual is unusually responsive to suggestions. p. 246

hypothalamus Forebrain structure involved in regulating eating, drinking, and sex; directing the endocrine system through the pituitary gland; and monitoring emotion, stress, and reward. p. 432

hypothesis An idea that is a testable prediction, often arrived at logically from a theory. p. 43

I **id** The Freudian structure of personality that consists of instincts, which are the individual's reservoir of psychic energy. p. 479

identity versus identity confusion Erikson's fifth psychological stage in which adolescents face the challenge of finding out who they are, what they are all about, and where they are going in life. p. 153

implicit memory (nondeclarative memory) Memory in which behavior is affected by prior experience with-out that experience being consciously recollected. p. 325

implicit personality theory The term given to the public or layperson's conception of which personality traits go together in an individual. p. 650

impression management (self-presentation) Involves acting in a way to present an image of oneself as a certain type of person, which might or might not be who one really is. p. 651

imprinting The tendency of an infant animal to form an attachment to the first moving object it sees and/or hears. p. 137

independent variable The manipulated, influential, experimental factor in an experiment. p. 56

individual psychology The term for Adler's approach, which views people as motivated by purposes and goals, being creators of their own lives. p. 484

inductive reasoning Reasoning from the specific to the general. p. 363

indulgent parenting A parenting style in which parents are involved with their children but place few limits on them. p. 139

inferential statistics Mathematical methods that are used to draw conclusions about data. p. 61

infinite generativity The ability to produce an infinite number of sentences using a finite set of words and rules. p. 363

informational social influence The influence other people have on us because we want to be right. p. 659

inner ear Consists of oval window, cochlea, and basilar membrane. p. 206

insight learning A form of problem solving in which the organism develops a sudden insight or understanding of the problem's solution. p. 295

insight therapy Encourage insight and self-awareness; includes the psychodynamic and humanistic therapies. p. 568

instinct An innate (unlearned), biological pattern of behavior that is assumed to be universal throughout a species. p. 425

instinctive drift The tendency of animals to revert to instinctive behavior that interferes with learning. p. 296

integrative therapy A combination of techniques from different therapies based on the therapist's judgment of which particular techniques will provide the greatest benefit for the client. p. 591

intelligence Problem-solving skills and the ability to adapt to and learn from life's everyday experiences. p. 388

intelligent quotient (IQ) Consists of an individual's mental age divided by chronological age multiplied by 100. p. 390

interference theory States that people forget not because memories are actually lost from storage but because other information gets in the way of what we want to remember. p. 337

intrinsic motivation Based on internal factors, such as self-determination, curiosity, challenge, and effort. p. 428

J **James-Lange theory** States that emotion results from physiological states triggered by stimuli in the environment. p. 456

K **kinesthetic senses** Provide information about movement, posture, and orientation. p. 219

L **language** A form of communication, whether spoken, written, or signed, that is based on a system of symbols. p. 368

latent content In Freud's view, the dream's hidden content; its unconscious meaning. p. 244

latent learning Unreinforced learning that is not immediately reflected in behavior. p. 295

law of effect Thorndike's concept that behaviors followed by positive outcomes are strengthened, whereas behaviors followed by negative outcomes are weakened. p. 277

learned helplessness Occurs when individuals are exposed to aversive stimulation, such as prolonged stress, over which they have no control. The inability to avoid such aversive stimulation can produce an apathetic state of helplessness. p. 489

learning A relatively permanent change in behavior that occurs through experience. p. 268

levels of processing theory States that memory is on a continuum from shallow to deep, with deeper processing producing better memory. p. 308

Limbic system Loosely connected network of structures—including the amygdala and hippocampus—that play important roles in memory and emotion. p. 93

lithium A drug that is widely used to treat bipolar disorder. p. 564

locus of control Individuals' beliefs about whether the outcomes of their actions depend on what they do (internal control) or on events outside of their personal control (external control). p. 488

long-term memory A relatively permanent type of memory that holds huge amounts of information for a long period of time. p. 315

M **major depressive disorder** Indicated by a major depressive episode and depressed characteristics, such as lethargy and hopelessness, lasting at least 2 weeks. p. 538

manifest content In Freud's view, the dream's surface content, which contains symbols that distort and disguise the dream's true meaning. p. 244

mean A statistical measure of central tendency that is calculated by adding all the scores and then dividing by the number of scores. p. 59

median A statistical measure of central tendency that falls exactly in the middle of a distribution of scores after they have been arranged (or ranked) from highest to lowest. p. 60

medical model A biological approach that describes psychological disorders as medical diseases with a biological origin. p. 520

meditation The practice and system of thought that incorporates exercises to attain bodily or mental control and well-being, as well as enlightenment. p. 629

memory The retention of information over time through encoding, storage, and retrieval. p. 306

mental age (MA) An individual's level of mental development relative to that of others. p. 390

mental processes The thoughts, feelings, and motives that each of us experiences privately but that cannot be observed directly. p. 6

mental retardation A condition of limited mental ability in which the individual has a low IQ, usually below 70, has difficulty adapting to everyday life, and has an onset of these characteristics in the so-called developmental period p. 405

mental set A type of fixation in which an individual tries to solve a problem in a particular way that has worked in the past. p. 359

meta-analysis Statistical analysis that combines the results of many different studies. p. 590

midbrain Located between the hindbrain and forebrain, a region in which many nerve-fiber systems ascend and descend to connect the higher and lower portions of the brain. p. 92

middle ear Consists of eardrum, hammer, anvil, and stirrup. p. 206

Minnesota Multiphasic Personality Inventory (MMPI) The most widely used and researched self-report personality test. p. 506

mode A statistical measure of central tendency, the score that occurs most often. p. 60

monocular cues Depth cues that can be extracted from the images in either eye. p. 198

mood disorders Psychological disorders in which there is a primary disturbance in mood (prolonged emotion that colors the individuals entire emotional state). Two main types are the depressive disorders and bipolar disorder. p. 537

morphology A language's rules for word formation. p. 368

motivation Why people behave, think, and feel the way they do. Motivated behavior is energized, directed, and sustained. p. 424

motor cortex Area of the cerebral cortex that processes information about voluntary movement. p. 97

multiple-factor theory Thurstone's theory that intelligence consists of seven primary mental abilities: verbal comprehension, number ability, word fluency, spatial visualization, associative memory, reasoning, and perceptual speed. p. 400

myelin sheath A layer of fat cells that encases and insulates most axons. The myelin sheath speeds up the transmission of nerve impulses. p. 82

N **natural selection** The principle that the organisms that are best adapted to their environment are the most likely to survive, reproduce, and pass on their genes to their offspring. p. 7

naturalistic observation Observations of behavior in real-world settings with no effort made to manipulate or control the situation. p. 50

nature An organism's biological inheritance. p. 122

need A deprivation that energizes the drive to eliminate or reduce the deprivation. p. 425

need for achievement The desire to accomplish something, to reach a standard of excellence, and to expend effort to excel. p. 447

need for affiliation The motive to be with other people. p. 452

negative punishment A behavior decreases when a positive stimulus is removed from it. p. 284

negative reinforcement The frequency of a behavior increases because it is followed by the removal of an aversive (unpleasant) stimulus. p. 281

neglectful parenting A parenting style in which parents are uninvolved in their child's life. p. 139

nervous system The body's electrochemical communication circuitry, made up of billions of neurons. p. 78

neural networks Clusters of neurons that are interconnected to process information. p. 80

neuron Nerve cell that is specialized for processing information. Neurons are the basic units of the nervous system. p. 82

neurotransmitters Chemicals that carry information across the synaptic gap from one neuron to the next. p. 85

noise Irrelevant and competing stimuli. p. 181

normal distribution A symmetrical, bell-shaped curve with a majority of the scores falling in the middle of the possible range and few scores appearing toward the extremes of the range. p. 391

normative social influence The influence that other people have on us because we seek their approval or to avoid their disapproval. p. 659

nurture An organism's environmental experience. p. 122

O **obedience** Behavior that complies with the explicit demands of the individual in authority. p. 660

observational learning Also called *imitation* or *modeling*; learning that occurs when a person observes and imitates another's behavior. p. 268

obsessive-compulsive disorder (OCD) An anxiety disorder; the individual has anxiety-provoking thoughts that will not go away (obsession) and/or urges to perform repetitive, ritualistic behaviors to prevent or produce some future situation (compulsion). p. 530

occipital lobe The part of the cerebral cortex at the back of the head that is involved in vision. p. 95

Oedipus complex In Freud's theory, the young child's development of an intense desire to replace the same-sex parent and enjoy the affections of the opposite-sex parent. p. 481

olfactory epithelium Located in the roof of the nasal cavity, a sheet of receptor cells for smell. p. 218

operant conditioning Also called instrumental conditioning; a form of learning in which the consequences of behavior change the probability of the behavior's occurrence. p. 277

operational definition A circumstance or behavior defined in such a way that it can be objectively observed and measured. p. 44

opiates Opium and its derivatives; they depress the central nervous system's activity. p. 44

opponent-process theory Cells in the visual system respond to red-green and blue-yellow colors; a given cell might be excited by red and inhibited by green, whereas another might be excited by yellow and inhibited by blue. p. 195

outer ear Consists of the pinna and the external auditory canal. p. 206

overconfidence bias The tendency to have more confidence in judgments and decisions than we should based on probability or past occurrence. p. 366

P **pain** The sensation that warns us that damage to our bodies is occurring. p. 215

panic disorder An anxiety disorder marked by the recurrent sudden onset of intense apprehension or terror. p. 528

papillae Bumps on the tongue that contain taste buds, the receptors for taste. p. 217

parallel processing The simultaneous distribution of information across different neural pathways. p. 323

paranoid schizophrenia A type of schizophrenia that is characterized by delusions of reference, grandeur, and persecution. p. 550

parasympathetic nervous system The division of the autonomic nervous system that calms the body. p. 81

parietal lobe Area of the cerebral cortex at the top of the head that is involved in registering spatial location, attention, and motor control.sensory cortex Area of the cerebral cortex that processes information about body sensations. p. 96

perception The brain's process of organizing and interpreting sensory information to give it meaning. p. 177

perceptual constancy Recognition that objects are constant and unchanging even through sensory input about them is changing. p. 201

perceptual set A predisposition or readiness to perceive something in a particular way. p. 185

peripheral nervous system (PNS) The network of nerves that connects the brain and spinal cord to other parts of the body. It is divided into the somatic nervous system and the autonomic nervous system. p. 81

personality A pattern of enduring, distinctive thoughts, emotions, and behaviors that characterize the way an individual adapts to the world. p. 477

personality disorders Chronic, maladaptive cognitive-behavioral patterns that are thoroughly integrated into the individual's personality. p. 582

phenotype The expression of an individual's genotype in observable, measurable characteristics. p. 121

pheromones Odorous substances released by animals that are powerful attractants. p. 440

phobic disorder Commonly called *phobia*, an anxiety disorder in which the individual has an irrational, overwhelming, persistent fear of a particular object or situation. p. 529

phonology A language's sound system. p. 368

physical dependence The physical need for a drug, accompanied by unpleasant withdrawal symptoms when the drug is discontinued. p. 251

pituitary gland An important endocrine gland at the base of the skull that controls growth and regulates other glands. p. 102

place theory A theory of hearing that states that each frequency produces vibrations at a particular spot on the basilar membrane. p. 207

placebo An innocuous, inert substance or condition that may be given to participants instead of a presumed active agent, such as a drug, to determine if it produces effects similar to those of the active agent. p. 58

placebo effect The influence of participants' expectations, rather than the experimental treatment, on experimental outcome. p. 58

plasticity The brain's special capacity for modification and change. p. 79

polygraph A machine that monitors changes physiological thought to be influenced by emotional states; it is used by examiners to try to determine if someone is lying. p. 456

population The entire group that the investigator wants to learn about. p. 45

positive psychology movement A strong emphasis on the experiences that people value subjectively (such as happiness), positive individual. p. 16

positive punishment A behavior decreases when it is followed by an unpleasant stimulus. p. 284

positive reinforcement The frequency of a behavior increases because it is followed by a rewarding stimulus. p. 281

post-traumatic stress disorder (PTSD) An anxiety disorder that develops through exposure to a traumatic event, severely oppressive situations, severe abuse, and natural and unnatural disasters. p. 332

prejudice An unjustified negative attitude toward an individual based on the individual's membership in a group. p. 670

preoperational stage The second Piagetian stage of cognitive development (approximately 2 to 7 years of age) in which thought becomes more symbolic, egocentric, and intuitive rather than logical; but the child cannot yet perform operations. p. 130

preparedness The species-specific biological predisposition to learn in certain ways. p. 297

primary reinforcement The use of reinforcers that are innately satisfying. p. 281

priming A type of implicit memory; information that people already have in storage is activated to help them remember new information better and faster. p. 319

proactive interference Occurs when material that was learned earlier disrupts the recall of material learned later. p. 337

problem solving An attempt to find an appropriate way of attaining a goal when the goal is not readily available. p. 356

problem-focused coping Lazarus' term for the cognitive strategy of squarely facing one's troubles and trying to solve them. p. 622

procedural memory Memory for skills. p. 318

projective test personality assessment tool that presents individuals with an ambiguous stimulus and then asks them to describe it or tell a story about it; based on the assumption that the ambiguity of the stimulus allows individuals to project their personalities onto it. p. 501

prospective memory Remembering information about doing something in the future. p. 317

prototype model People decide whether an item reflects a concept by comparing it with the most typical item(s) of that concept that they know about. p. 355

psychoactive drugs Drugs that act on the nervous system to alter consciousness, modify perceptions, and change moods. p. 249

psychoanalysis Freud's psychotherapeutic technique for analyzing an individual's unconscious thoughts. Freud believed that clients' current problems could be traced to childhood experiences, involving conflicts about sexuality. p. 570

psychodynamic approach Emphasizes the unconscious aspects of the mind, conflict between biological instincts and society's demands, and early family experiences. p. 11

psychodynamic perspectives View personality as primarily unconscious (that is, beyond awareness) and as occurring in stages. Most psychoanalytic perspectives emphasize that early experiences with parents play a role in sculpting personality. p. 478

psychodynamic therapies Stress the importance of the unconscious mind, extensive interpretation by the therapist, and the role of experiences in the early-childhood years. The goal of the psychodynamic therapies is to help individuals recognize their maladaptive ways of coping and the sources of their unconscious conflicts. p. 570

psychological dependence The strong desire and craving to repeat the use of the drug for emotional reasons. p. 251

psychology The scientific study of behavior and mental processes. p. 5

psychoneuroimmunology The field that explores connections among psychological factors (such as attitudes and emotions), the nervous system, and the immune system. p. 616

psychophysics The field that studies links between the physical properties of stimuli and a person's experience of them. p. 180

psychosurgery A biological therapy that involves removal or destruction of brain tissue to improve an individual's adjustment. p. 568

psychotherapy The process used by mental health professionals to help individuals recognize, define, and overcome their psychological and interpersonal difficulties. p. 568

puberty A period of rapid skeletal and sexual maturation that occurs mainly in early adolescence. p. 151

punishment A consequence that decreases the likelihood a behavior will occur. p. 284

R **random assignment** Assignment of participants to experimental and control groups by chance. p. 56

random sample A sample in which every member of the population has an equal chance of being selected. p. 45

range A statistical measure of variability that is the distance between the highest and lowest scores. p. 60

rational-emotive behavior therapy Based on Ellis' assertion that individuals develop a psychological disorder because of their beliefs, especially those that are irrational and self-defeating. p. 579

reasoning The mental activity of transforming information to reach conclusions. p. 000

reinforcement The process by which a stimulus or event strengthens or increases the probability of an event that it follows. p. 280

reliability The extent to which a test yields a consistent, reproducible measure of performance. p. 47

REM sleep Rapid-eye-movement sleep; stage 5 of sleep, in which most dreaming occurs. p. 236

representativeness heuristic Making faulty decisions based on how well something matches a prototype—the common or representative example—rather than on its relevance to the particular situation. p. 367

research participant bias The influence of research participants' expectations on their behavior within an experiment. p. 57

resistance The psychoanalytic term for the person's unconscious defense strategies that prevent the analyst from understanding the person's problems. p. 572

resting potential The term given to the stable, negative charge of an inactive neuron. p. 84

Reticular formation A midbrain system that consists of a diffuse collection of neurons involved in stereotypical behaviors such as walking, sleeping, or turning to attend to a sudden noise. p. 579

retina The light-sensitive surface in the back of the eye that houses light receptors called rods and cones. p. 189

retrieval The memory process of taking information out of storage. p. 326

retroactive interference Occurs when material learned later disrupts the retrieval of information learned earlier. p. 337

retrograde amnesia A memory disorder that involves memory loss for a segment of the past but not for new events. p. 339

retrospective memory Remembering the past. p. 318

risky shift The tendency for a group decision to be riskier than the average decision made by individual group members. p. 664

rods The receptors in the retina that are sensitive to light but are not very useful in color vision. p. 190

romantic love Also called *passionate* love; the type of love that has strong components of sexuality and infatuation and often predominates in the early part of a love relationship. p. 688

Rorschach inkblot test A widely used projective test; it uses an individual's perception of inkblots to determine his or her personality. p. 502

S **sample** The subset of the population that the investigator has chosen for study. p. 45

schedules of reinforcement "Timetables" that determine when a behavior will be reinforced. p. 282

schema A concept or framework that already exists at a given moment in a person's mind and that organizes and interprets information. p. 128

schizophrenia A severe psychological disorder that is characterized by highly disordered thought processes. p. 87

science In psychology, the use of systematic methods to observe, describe, predict, and explain behavior. p. 6

script A schema for an event. p. 322

secondary reinforcement Acquires its positive value through experience. p. 281

secure attachment An important aspect of socioemotional development in which infants use the caregiver, usually the mother, as a secure base from which to explore the environment. p. 137

selective attention Focusing on a specific aspect of experience while ignoring others. p. 184

self-actualization The highest and most elusive of Maslow's needs; the motivation to develop one's full potential as a human being. p. 429

self-concept A central theme in Rogers' and other humanists' views; self-concept refers to individuals' overall perceptions of their abilities, behavior, and personalities. p. 491

self-efficacy The belief that one can master a situation and produce positive outcomes. p. 488

self-esteem The person's overall evaluation of self-worth or self-image. p. 493

self-monitoring Individuals' attention to the impressions they make on others and the degree to which they fine-tune their performances accordingly. p. 652

self-perception theory Bem's theory about the connection between attitudes and behavior; stresses that individuals make inferences about their attitudes by perceiving their behavior. p. 655

self-report tests Also called *objective tests* or *inventories*, they directly ask people whether items (usually true/false or agree/disagree) describe their personality traits or not. p. 504

semantic memory A person's knowledge about the world. p. 316

semantics The meaning of words and sentences in a particular language. p. 368

semicircular canals Located in the inner ear; contain the sensory receptors that detect head motion. p. 219

sensation The process of receiving stimulus energies from the environment. p. 176

sensorimotor stage The first Piagetian stage of cognitive development (birth to about 2 years of age), in which infants construct an understanding of the world by coordinating sensory experiences (such as seeing and hearing) with motor (physical) actions. p. 129

sensory adaptation A change in the responsiveness of the sensory system based on the average level of surrounding stimulation. p. 186

sensory memory Holds information from the world in its original form only for an instant, not much longer than the brief time it is exposed to the visual, auditory, and other senses. p. 312

sensory receptors Specialized cells that detect and transmit stimulus information to sensory neurons and the brain. p. 178

serial position effect The tendency for items at the beginning and at the end of a list to be recalled more readily. p. 327

set point The weight maintained when no effort is made to gain or lose weight. p. 433

sexually transmitted diseases (STDs) Diseases that are contracted primarily through sex—intercourse as well as oral-genital and anal-genital sex. p. 638

shaping The process of rewarding approximations of desired behavior. p. 279

short-term memory A limited-capacity memory system in which information is retained for only as long as 30 seconds unless strategies are used to retain it longer. p. 313

signal detection theory Focuses on decision making about stimuli in the presence of uncertainty; detection depends on a variety of factors besides the physical intensity of the stimulus and the sensory abilities of the observer. p. 183

social cognitive behavior view of hypnosis Views hypnosis as a result of social factors associated with the hypnotic context, coupled with cognitive events involved in the efforts of the hypnotized person to immerse himself or herself in the role of the hypnotized person. p. 248

social cognitive theory States that behavior, environment, and person/cognitive factors are important in understanding personality. p. 487

social facilitation Occurs when an individual's performance improves because of the presence of others. p. 663

social identity Refers to the way we define ourselves in terms of group memberships. p. 669

social identity theory Tajfel's theory that when individuals are assigned to a group, they invariably think of it as an in-group. p. 669

social loafing Each person's tendency to exert less effort in a group because of reduced monitoring. p. 663

social psychology The study of how people think about, influence, and relate to other people. p. 21

social support Information and feedback from others that one is loved and cared for, esteemed and valued, and included in a network of communication and mutual obligation. p. 625

sociocultural approach Emphasizes social and cultural influences on behavior. p. 15

somatic nervous system Division of the PNS consisting of sensory nerves, whose function is to convey information to the CNS, and motor nerves, whose function is to transmit information to the muscles. p. 81

spontaneous recovery The process in classical conditioning by which a conditioned response can recur after a time delay without further conditioning. p. 272

standard deviation A statistical measure of variability that involves how much the scores vary on the average around the mean of the sample. p. 61

standardization Involves developing uniform procedures for administering and scoring a test, as well as creating norms for the test. p. 394

standardized test An oral or written assessment for which an individual receives a score indicating how the individual reponded relative to others. p. 51

stereotype A generalization about a group's characteristics that does not consider any variations from one individual to another. p. 672

stimulants Psychoactive drugs that increase the central nervous system's activity. p. 256

storage Ways in which information is retained over time and how it is represented in memory. p. 311

stream of consciousness James' concept that the mind is a continuous flow of sensations, images, thoughts, and feelings. p. 8

stress management programs Teach individuals to appraise stressful events, to develop skills for coping with stress, and to put these skills into use in their everyday lives. p. 629

stress The response of individuals to stressors, the circumstances and events that threaten and tax their coping abilities. p. 604

structuralism An early school of psychology that attempted to discover basic elements (structures) of the human mind. p. 8

subgoaling Involves setting intermediate goals or defining intermediate problems that put you in a better position to reach the final goal or solution. p. 357

subliminal perception The ability to detect information below the level of conscious awareness. p. 181

superego The Freudian structure of personality that deals with morality. p. 479

suprachiasmatic nucleus (SCN) A small structure in the hypothalamus that registers changes in light. p. 233

sympathetic nervous system The division of the autonomic nervous system that arouses the body. p. 81

synapses Tiny junctions between two neurons, generally where the axon of one neuron meets the dendrites or cell body of another neuron. p. 85

syntax A language's rules for the way words are combined to form acceptable phrases and sentences. p. 368

systematic desensitization A method of behavior therapy based on classical conditioning that treats anxiety by getting the person to associate deep relaxation with increasingly intense anxiety-producing situations. p. 575

T **temperament** An individual's behavioral style and characteristic way of responding. p. 138

temporal lobe The portion of the cerebral cortex just above the ears that is involved in hearing, language processing, and memory. p. 95

thalamus Forebrain structure that functions as a relay station to sort input and direct it to different areas of the cerebral cortex. It also has ties to the reticular formation. p. 94

Thematic Apperception Test (TAT) An ambiguous projective test designed to elicit stories that reveal something about an individual's personality. p. 503

theory A broad idea or set of closely related ideas that attempt to explain and predict observations. p. 42

thermoreceptors Located under the skin, they respond to increases and decreases in temperature. p. 214

thinking Manipulating information, as when we form concepts, solve problems, think critically, reason, and make decisions. p. 353

tolerance The need to take increasing amounts of the drug to produce the same effect. p. 251

top-down processing Processing of perceptual information that starts out with cognitive processing at the higher levels of the brain. p. 177

trait An enduring personality characteristic that tends to lead to certain behaviors. p. 496

tranquilizers Depressant drugs that reduce anxiety and induce relaxation. p. 255

transcendental meditation (TM) The most popular form of meditation in the United States, derived from an ancient Indian technique; involves using a mantra. p. 629

transduction The process of transforming physical energy into electrochemical energy. p. 177

transference The psychoanalytic term for the person's relating to the analyst in ways that reproduce or relive important relationships in the individual's life. p. 571

triarchic theory Sternberg's theory that there are three main types of intelligence: analytical, creative, and practical. p. 402

trichromatic theory Color perception is based on the existence of three types of receptors that are maximally sensitive to different, but overlapping, ranges of wavelengths. p. 194

two-factor theory of emotion Schachter and Singer's theory that emotion is determined by two main factors: physiological arousal and cognitive labeling. p. 400

two-factor theory Spearman's theory that individuals have both general intelligence (*g*) and a number of specific abilities (*s*). p. 400

Type A behavior pattern A cluster of characteristics—being excessively competitive, hard-driven, and hostile—thought to be related to the incidence of heart disease. p. 605

Type B behavior pattern A relaxed and easygoing personality. p. 605

U **unconditional positive regard** Rogers' term for accepting, valuing, and being positive toward another person regardless of the person's behavior. p. 492

unconditioned response (UCR) An unlearned response that is automatically elicited by the UCS. p. 271

unconditioned stimulus (UCS) A stimulus that produces a response without prior learning. p. 271

unconscious thought Freud's concept of a reservoir of unacceptable wishes, feelings, and thoughts that are beyond conscious awareness. p. 231

undifferentiated schizophrenia A type of schizophrenia that is characterized by disorganized behavior, hallucinations, delusions, and incoherence. p. 550

V **validity** The extent to which a test measures what it is intended to measure. p. 394

vestibular sense Provides information about balance and movement. p. 219

visual illusion A discrepancy or incongruency between reality and the perceptual representation of it. p. 202

volley principle A cluster of nerve cells can fire neural impulses in rapid succession, producing a volley of impulses. p. 209

W **Weber's law** The principle that two stimuli must differ by a constant minimum percentage (rather than a constant amount) to be perceived as different. p. 183

whole-language approach Stresses that reading instruction should parallel a child's natural language learning; so reading materials should be whole and meaningful. p. 380

wisdom Expert knowledge about the practical aspects of life. p. 164

wish fulfillment Freud's concept of dreaming as an unconscious attempt to fulfill needs (especially for sex and aggression) that cannot be expressed, or that go ungratified, while awake. p. 244

working memory A three-part system that temporarily holds information. Working memory is a kind of mental workbench on which information is manipulated and assembled to perform other cognitive tasks. p. 314

Y **Yerkes-Dodson law** States that performance is best under conditions of moderate arousal than under those of low or high arousal. p. 426

References

A

Abbey, A., Ross, L. T., & McDuffie, D. (1993). Alcohol's role in sexual assault. In R. R. Watson (Ed.), *Drug and alcohol abuse reviews. Vol. 5: Addictive behaviors in women.* Totowa, NJ: Humana Press.

Abelson, J. L., Weg, J. G., Nesse, R. M., & Curtis, G. C. (2001). Persistent respiratory irregularity in patients with panic disorder. *Biological Psychiatry, 49,* 588–595.

Abernethy, G., Gill, D. P., Parks, S. L., & Packer, S. T. (2001). Expertise and the perception of kinematic and situational probability information. *Perception, 30,* 233–252.

Abramson, L. Y., Seligman, M. E. P., & Teasdale, J. (1978). Learned helplessness in humans: Critique and reformulation. *Journal of Abnormal Psychology, 87,* 49–74.

Achat, H., Kawachi, I., Spiro, A., DeMolles, D. A., & Sparrow, D. (2000). Optimism and depression as predictors of physical and mental health functioning: The Normative Aging Study. *Annals of Behavioral Medicine, 22,* 127–130.

Ackerman, P. L., Kyllonen, P. C., & Roberts, R. D. (Eds.) (1999). *Learning and individual differences: Process, trait, and content determinants.* Washington, DC: American Psychological Association.

Adams, H. E., & Cassidy, J. F. (1993). The classification of abnormal behavior: An overview. In P. B. Sutker & H. E. Adams (Eds.), *Comprehensive textbook of psychopathology* (2nd ed.). New York: Plenum Press.

Adams, R. (1998). *The abuses of punishment.* New York: St. Martin's Press.

Ader, R. (1974). Letter to the editor: Behaviorally conditioned immunosuppression. *Psychosomatic Medicine, 36,* 183–184.

Ader, R. (2000). On the development of psychoneuroimmunology. *European Journal of Pharmacology, 405,* 167–176.

Ader, R., & Cohen, N. (1975). Behaviorally conditioned immunosuppression. *Psychosomatic Medicine, 37,* 333–340.

Ader, R., & Cohen, N. (2000). Conditioning and immunity. In R. Ader, D. L. Felton, & N. Cohen (Eds.), *Psychoneuroimmunology,* (3rd ed.). San Diego: Academic Press.

Adler, A. (1927). *The theory and practice of individual psychology.* Fort Worth: Harcourt Brace.

Adler, N. E. (2001). A consideration of multiple pathways from socioeconomic status to health. In J.A. Auerbach & B.K. Krimgold (Eds.), *Income, socioeconomic status, and health.* Washington, DC: National Policy Association.

Adler, T. (1991, January). Seeing double? Controversial twins study is widely reported, debated. *APA Monitor, 22,* 1, 8.

Adorno, T. W., Frenkel-Brunswick, E., Levinson, D. J., & Sanford, R. N. (1950). *The authoritarian personality.* New York: Harper & Row.

Ahasan, R., Lewko, J., Campbell, D., & Slamoni, A. (2001). Adaptation to night shifts and synchronization processes of night workers. *Journal of Physiological Anthropology, 20,* 215–226.

Aiken, L. R. (2003). *Psychological testing and assessment (11th Ed.).* Boston: Allyn & Bacon.

Ainsworth, M. D. S. (1979). Infant-mother attachment. *American Psychologist, 34,* 932–937.

Ajzen, I. (2001). Nature and operation of attitudes. *Annual Review of Psychology.* (Vol. 52). Palo Alto, CA: Annual Reviews.

Al-Issa, I. (1982). Does culture make a difference in psychopathology? In I. Al-Issa (Ed.), *Culture and psychopathology.* Baltimore: University Park Press.

Al-Mashaan, O. S. (2001). Job stress and job satisfaction in relation to neuroticism, type A behavior, and locus of control among Kuwaiti personnel. *Psychological Reports, 88,* 1145–1152.

Alan Guttmacher Institute. (2000, February 24). *United States and the Russian Federation lead the developed world in teenage pregnancy rates.* New York: The Alan Guttmacher Institute.

Alberti, R., & Emmons, M. (1995). *Your perfect right* (7th ed.). San Luis Obispo, CA: Impact.

Alberto, P., & Troutman, A. C. (1999). *Applied behavior analysis for teachers* (5th ed.). Upper Saddle River, NJ: Merrill.

Albrecht, U. (2002). Invited review: Regulation of mammalian circadian clock genes. *Journal of Applied Physiology, 92,* 1348–1355.

Alderman, M. K. (1999). *Motivation for achievement.* Mahwah, NJ: Erlbaum.

Alexander, D. A., & Klein, S. (2001). Caring for others can seriously damage your health. *Hospital Medicine, 62,* 264–267.

Alkire, M. T., Haier, R. J., & James, H. F. (1998). Toward the neurobiology of consciousness: Using brain imaging and anesthesia to investigate the anatomy of consciousness. In S. Hameroff, A. Kaszniak, & A. Scott (Eds.), *Toward a Science of Consciousness II.* Cambridge, MA: MIT Press.

Allan, K., Wolf, H. A., Rosenthal, C. R., & Rugg, M. D. (2001). The effects of retrieval cues on post-retrieval monitoring in episodic memory: An electrophysiological study. *Brain Research, 12,* 289–299.

Allan, R., & Scheidt, S. (Eds.). (1996). *Heart and mind.* Washington, DC: American Psychological Association.

Allen, D. N., Goldstein, G., & Weiner, C. (2001). Differential neuropsychological patterns of frontal- and temporal-lobe dysfunction in patients with schizophrenia. *Schizophrenia Research, 48,* 7–15.

Allen, J. J. B. (1998). DSM-IV. In H. S. Friedman (Ed.), *Encyclopedia of mental health* (Vol. 2). San Diego: Academic Press.

Allen, J. J., & Movius, H. L. (2000). The objective assessment of amnesia in dissociative identity disorder using event-related potentials. *International Journal of Psychophysiology, 38,* 21–41.

Allen, J., Kraus, N., & Bradlow, A. (2000). Neural representation of consciously imperceptible speech sound differences. *Perception and Psychophysics, 62,* 1383–1393.

Alloy, L. B., & Abramson, L. Y. (1979). Judgment of contingency in depressed and nondepressed students: Sadder but wiser? *Journal of Experimental Psychology: General, 108,* 441–485.

Alloy, L. B., Abramson, L. Y., & Francis, E. L. (1999). Do negative cognitive styles confer vulnerability to depression? *Current Directions in Psychological Science, 8,* 128–132.

Alloy, L. B., Jacobson, N. S., & Acocella, J. (1999). *Abnormal psychology* (8th ed.). New York: McGraw-Hill.

Allport, G. (1954). *The nature of prejudice.* Reading, MA: Addison-Wesley.

Allport, G. W. (1937). *Personality: A psychological interpretation.* New York: Holt.

Almagor, M., Tellegen, A., & Waller, N. G. (1995). The big seven model: A cross-cultural replication and further exploration of the basic dimensions of natural language trait descriptors.

Alterman, A. I., Gariti, P., & Mulvaney, F. (2001). Short- and long-term smoking cessation for three levels of intensity of behavioral treatment. *Psychology and Addictive Behavior, 15,* 261–264.

Altmann, E. M., & Gray, W. D. (2002). Forgetting to remember: The functional relationship of decay and interference. *Psychological Science, 13,* 27–33.

Amato, P. R., & Keith, B. (1991). Parental divorce and the well-being of children: A meta-analysis. *Psychological Bulletin, 110,* 26–46.

American Academy of Pediatrics. (2001). Health care supervision for children with Williams syndrome. *Pediatrics, 107,* 1192–1204.

American Association on Mental Retardation, Ad Hoc Committee on Terminology and Classification. (1992). *Mental retardation* (9th ed.). Washington, DC: Author.

American Psychiatric Association. (1994). *Diagnostic and statistical manual of mental disorders* (4th ed.). Washington, DC: American Psychiatric Press.

American Psychiatric Association. (2000). *Diagnostic and statistical manual of mental disorders, Fourth edition, Text revision.* Washington, DC: Author.

American Psychiatric Association. (2001). *Mental illness.* Washington, DC: Author.

American Sleep Apnea Association. (2001). *Sleep apnea: General information packet.* Washington, DC: American Sleep Apnea Association.

Amsel, E., & Byrnes, J. (2001). Symbolic communication and cognitive development. In J. Byrnes & E. Amsel (Eds.), *Language, literacy, and cognitive development.* Mahwah, NJ: Erlbaum.

Anastasi, A., & Urbina, S. (1996). *Psychological testing* (7th ed.). Upper Saddle River, NJ: Prentice Hall.

Anderson, B. A., Golden-Kreutz, D. M., & DiLillo, V. (2001). Cancer. In A. Baum, T. A. Revenson, & J. E. Singer (Eds.), *Handbook of health psychology.* Mahwah, NJ: Erlbaum.

Anderson, B. L. (1983). Primary orgasmic dysfunction: Diagnostic considerations and a review of treatment. *Psychological Bulletin, 93,* 105–136.

Anderson, B. L. (1998). Cancer. In H.S. Friedman (Ed.), *Encyclopedia of mental health* (Vol. 1). San Diego: Academic Press.

Anderson, B. L. (2000). Cancer. In A. Kazdin (Ed.), *Encyclopedia of psychology.* Washington, DC, & New York: American Psychological Association and Oxford University Press.

Anderson, B. L., Kiecolt-Glaser, J. K., & Glaser. R. (1994). A biobehavioral model of cancer stress and disease course. *American Psychologist, 49,* 389–404.

Anderson, C. A. (1989). Temperature and aggression. *Journal of Personality and Social Psychology, 106,* 74–96.

Anderson, C. A., & Bushman, B. J. (2002). Human aggression. *Annual Review of Psychology* (Vol. 53). Palo Alto, CA: Annual Reviews.

Anderson, D. R., Huston, A. C., Schmitt, K., Linebarger, D., & Wright, J. C. (2001). Early television viewing and adolescent behavior: The recontact study. *Monographs of the Society for Research in Child Development, 66* (1, Serial No. 264.)

Anderson, E. M., & Lambert, M. J. (2001). A survival analysis of clinically significant change in outpatient psychotherapy. *Journal of Clinical Psychology, 57,* 875–888.

Anderson, J. R. (2000). *Cognitive psychology* (5th ed.). New York: Worth.

Anderson, M. C., & Green, C. (2001, March 15). Suppressing unwanted memories by executive control. *Nature, 410,* 366–369.

Anderson, N. H. (1965). Primacy effects in personality impression formation using a generalized order effect paradigm. *Journal of Personality and Social Psychology, 2,* 1–9.

Anderson, N. H. (1974). Cognitive algebra: Integration theory applied to social attribution. In L. Berkowitz (Ed.), *Advances in experimental social psychology* (Vol. 7). New York: Academic Press.

Anderson, N. H. (1989). Functional memory and on-line attribution. In J. N. Bassili (Ed.), *On-line cognition in person perception.* Mahwah, NJ: Erlbaum.

Anderson, R. A. (2002). Parietal lobe. *Annual Review of Neuroscience* (Vol. 25). Palo Alto, CA: Annual Reviews.

Angers, T. (1999). *The forgotten hero of My Lai: The Hugh Thompson story.* Lafayette, LA: Arcadian House.

Angold, A., Costello, E. J., & Worthman, C.M. (1998). Puberty and depression: The roles of age, pubertal status, and pubertal timing. *Psychological Medicine, 28,* 51–61.

Antonucci, T. C. (2001). Social relations. In J. E. Birren & K. W. Schaie (Eds.), *Handbook of the psychology of aging* (5th ed.). San Diego: Academic Press.

Antonucci, T. C., Vandewater, E. A., & Lansford, J. E. (2000). Adult development and aging: Social processes and development. In A. Kazdin (Ed.), *Encyclopedia of psychology.*

Washington, DC, & New York: American Psychological Association and Oxford University Press.

Arana-Ward, M. (1997). As technology advances, a bitter debate divides the deaf. *Washington Post,* p. A1.

Archer, D., & Gartner, R. (1976). Violent acts and violent times: A comparative approach in postwar homicide. *American Sociological Review, 41,* 937–963.

Archer, D., & McDaniel, P. (1995). Violence and gender: Differences and similarities across societies. In R. B. Ruback & N. A. Weiner (Eds.), *Interpersonal violent behaviors: Social and cultural aspects.* New York: Springer.

Archer, R. P., Handel, R. W., Greene, R. L., Baer, R. A., & Elkins, D. E. (2001). An evaluation of the usefulness of the MMPI-2 F (p) sale. *Journal of Personality Assessment, 76,* 282–285.

Archibald, A. B., Graber, J. A., & Brooks-Gunn, J. (2002, in press). Pubertal processes and physical growth in adolescence. In G. R. Adams & M. Berzonsky (Eds.), *Handbook of adolescence.* Malden, MA: Blackwell.

Argyropoulos, S. V., & Nutt, D. J. (2000). Substance P antagonists: Novel agents in the treatment of depression. *Expert Opinion in the Investigation of Drugs, 9,* 1871–1875.

Arkowitz, H. (1997). Integrative theories of therapy. In P. L. Wachtel & S. B. Messer (Eds.), *Theories of psychotherapy.* Washington, DC: American Psychological Association.

Arledge, E. (Writer & Director), & Cort, J. (Writer). (2001). Cracking the code of life [Television series episode]. In P. S. Apsell (Executive Producer), *NOVA.* Boston: WGBH and Clear Blue Sky Productions.

Armitage, R., Emslie, G. J., Hoffman, R. F., Rintelmann, J., & Rush, A. J. (2001). Delta sleep EEG in depressed adolescent females and healthy controls. *Journal of Affective Disorders, 63,* 139–148.

Arnitz, A., & van den Hout, M. A. (1996). Psychological treatment of panic disorder without agoraphobia: Cognitive therapy versus applied relaxation. *Behaviour Research and Therapy, 34,* 113–121.

Arnkoff, D. B., Glass, C. R., & Shapiro, S. J. (2002). Expectations and preferences. In J. C. Norcross (Ed.), *Psychotherapy relationships that work.* New York: Oxford University Press.

Arnoux, D. (1998, September). Description of teaching experiences prepared for John Santrock's text, *Educational Psychology.* New York: McGraw-Hill.

Aron, A., & Aron, E. N. (2003). *Statistics for psychology* (3rd ed.). Upper Saddle River, NJ: Prentice-Hall.

Aron, A., & Aron, E. N. (2003). *Statistics for the behavioral and social sciences* (2nd ed.). Upper Saddle River, NJ: Prentice Hall.

Aronson, E. (1986, August). *Teaching students things they think they already know all about: The case of prejudice and desegregation.* Paper presented at the meeting of the American Psychological Association, Washington, DC.

Aronson, E. (1995). *The social animal* (7th ed.). New York: Freeman.

Aronson, E. (2000). *Nobody left to hate.* New York: Freeman.

Aronson, E., Wilson, T. D., & Akert, R. M. (1997). *Social psychology* (2nd ed.). New York: Longman.

Aronson, E., Wilson, T. D., & Akert, R. M. (2002). *Social psychology* (4th ed.). Upper Saddle River, NJ: Prentice-Hall.

Aronson, J., Cohen, G., & Nails, P. R. (1999). Unwanted consequences and the self: In search of the motivation for dissonance reduction. In E. Harmon-Jones & J. Mills (Eds.), *Cognitive dissonance.* Washington, DC: American Psychological Association.

Asch, S. E. (1946). Forming impressions of personality. *Journal of Personality and Social Psychology, 41,* 248–290.

Asch, S. E. (1951). Effects of group pressure on the modification and distortion of judgments. In H. S. Guetzkow (Ed.), *Groups, leadership, and men.* Pittsburgh: Carnegie University Press.

Ashcraft, M. H., & Kirk, E. P. (2001). The relationships among working memory, math anxiety, and performance. *Journal of Experimental Psychology: General, 130,* 224–237.

Ashcroft, D. (2003). *Personalities theories workbook (2nd ed.).* Belmont, CA: Wadsworth.

Asher, J., & Garcia, R. (1969). The optimal age to learn a foreign language. *Modern Language Journal, 53,* 334–341.

Ashida, H., Seiffert, A. E., & Osaka, N. (2001). Inefficient visual search for second-order motion. *Journal of the Optical Society of America, 18,* 2255–2266.

Astin, A. W. (1993). *What matters in college.* San Francisco: Jossey-Bass.

Atkin, J. M., & Black, P. (1997, September). Policy perils of international comparisons. *Phi Delta Kappan, 79,* 22–28.

Atkinson, D., Morten, G., & Sue, D. (1998). *Counseling American minorities* (5th ed.). New York: McGraw-Hill.

Atkinson, J. W., & Raynor, I. O. (1974). *Motivation and achievement.* Washington, DC: Winston.

Atkinson, R. C., & Shiffrin, R. M. (1968). Human memory: A proposed system and its control processes. In K. W. Spence & J. T. Spence (Eds.), *The psychology of learning and motivation* (Vol. 2). San Diego, CA: Academic Press.

Attorney General's Commission on Pornography. (1986). *Final report.* Washington, DC: U.S. Department of Justice.

Atwood, J. D. (Ed.). (2001). *Family systems/family therapy.* Binghamton, NY: Haworth Press.

Auerbach, S. M., & Gramling, S. E. (1998). *Stress management.* Upper Saddle River, NJ: Prentice-Hall.

Auger, C., Latour, S., Trudel, M., & Fortin, M. (2000). Post-traumatic stress disorder: After the flood in Saguenay. *Canadian Family Physician, 46,* 2420–2427.

Auyang, S. Y. (2001). *Mind in everyday life and cognitive science.* Cambridge, MA: MIT Press.

Averill, J. R. (1983). Studies on anger and aggression: Implications for theories of emotion. *American Psychologist, 38,* 1145–1160.

Azar, S. T. (2002). Parenting and child maltreatment. In M. Bornstein (Ed.), *Handbook of parenting* (2nd ed.). Mahwah, NJ: Erlbaum.

Azhar, M. Z. (2001). Comparison of Fluvoxamine alone, Fluvoxamine and cognitive psychotherapy and psychotherapy alone in the treatment of panic disorder in Kelantan: Implications for management by family doctors. *Medical Journal of Malaysia, 55*, 402–408.

B

Baars, B. (1999). Psychology in a world of sentimental, self-knowing beings: A modest utopian fantasy. In R. L. Solso (Ed.), *Mind and brain sciences in the 21st century.* Cambridge, MA: MIT Press.

Bachman, J. (1997). *Smoking, drinking, and drug use in young adulthood: The impact of new freedoms and responsibilities.* Mahwah, NJ: Erlbaum.

Backman, L., Small, B. J., & Wahlin, A. (2001). Aging and memory. In J. E. Birren & K. W. Schaie (Eds.), *Handbook of the psychology of aging* (5th ed.). San Diego: Academic Press.

Baddeley, A. (1992). Working memory. *Science, 255*, 556–560.

Baddeley, A. (1993). Working memory and conscious awareness. In A. F. Collins, S. E. Gatherhole, M. A. Conway, & P. E. Morris (Eds.), *Theories of memory.* Mahwah, NJ: Erlbaum.

Baddeley, A. (1998). *Human memory* (Rev. ed.). Boston: Allyn & Bacon.

Baddeley, A. (2000). Short-term and working memory. In E. Tulving & F. I. M. Craik (Eds.), *The Oxford handbook of memory.* New York: Oxford University Press.

Baddeley, A. (2001). *Is working memory still working?* Paper presented at the meeting of the American Psychological Association, San Francisco.

Baddeley, A. D., & Hitch, G. (1974). Working memory. In G. H. Bower (Eds.), *The psychology of learning and motivation* (Vol. 8). San Diego: Academic Press.

Badgaiyan, R. D., Schacter, D. L., & Alpert, N. M. (2001). Priming within and across modalities: Exploring the nature of rCBF increases and decreases. *NeuroImage, 13*, 272–282.

Baehr, E. K., Revelle, W., & Eastman, C. I. (2000). Individual differences in the phase and amplitude of the human circadian temperature rhythm with an emphasis on morningness-eveningness. *Journal of Sleep Research, 9*, 117–127.

Baillargeon, R. (1997). The object concept revisited. In C. E. Granrud (Ed.), *Visual perception and cognition in infancy.* Mahwah, NJ: Erlbaum.

Baity, M. R., & Hilsenroth, M. J. (1999). Rorschach aggression variables: A study of reliability and validity. *Journal of Personality and Assessment, 72*, 93–110.

Baker, B. (2001, March). *Marital interaction in mild hypertension.* Paper presented at the meeting of the American Psychosomatic Association, Monterey, CA.

Baker, N. L. (2001). Prejudice. In J. Worell (Ed.), *Encyclopedia of gender and women.* San Diego: Academic Press.

Baldo, M. V., Kihra, A. H., Namba, J., & Klein, S. A. (2002). Evidence for an attentional component of the perceptual misalignment between moving and flashing stimuli. *Perception, 31*, 17–30.

Baldwin, J. D., & Baldwin, J. I. (2001). *Behavior principles in everyday life.* Upper Saddle River, NJ: Prentice-Hall.

Baldwin, J. D., & Baldwin, J. I. (1998). Sexual behavior. In H. S. Friedman (Ed.), *Encyclopedia of mental health* (Vol. 3). San Diego: Academic Press.

Bales, J. (1988, December). Vincennes: Findings could have averted tragedy, scientists tell Hill panel. *APA Monitor*, pp. 10–11.

Baltes, P. B. (1993). The aging mind: Potentials and limits. *Gerontologist, 33*, 580–594.

Baltes, P. B. (2000). Life-span developmental theory. In A. Kazdin (Ed.), *Encyclopedia of psychology.* Washington, DC, & New York: American Psychological Association and Oxford University Press.

Baltes, P. B., Lindenberger, U., & Staudinger, U. M. (1998). Life-span theory in developmental psychology. In W. Damon (Ed.), *Handbook of child psychology* (5th ed., Vol. 1). New York: Wiley.

Bandura, A. (1965). Influences of models' reinforcement contingencies on the acquisition of imitative responses. *Journal of Personality and Social Psychology, 1*, 589–596.

Bandura, A. (1977). *Social learning theory.* Englewood Cliffs, NJ: Prentice Hall.

Bandura, A. (1977). *Social learning theory.* Upper Saddle River, NJ: Prentice Hall.

Bandura, A. (1986). *Social foundations of thought and action.* Englewood Cliffs, NJ: Prentice Hall.

Bandura, A. (1998, August). *Swimming against the mainstream: Accentuating the positive aspects of humanity.* Paper presented at the meeting of the American Psychological Association, San Francisco.

Bandura, A. (2000). Social cognitive theory. In A. Kazdin (Ed.), *Encyclopedia of psychology.* Washington, DC, and New York: American Psychological Association and Oxford University Press.

Bandura, A. (2001). Social cognitive theory. *Annual Review of Psychology, 52.*

Bandura, A. (1986). *Social foundations of thought and action.* Upper Saddle River, NJ: Prentice Hall.

Bandura, A. (1989). Social cognitive theory. In R. Vasta (Ed.), *Six theories of child development.* Greenwich, CT: JAI Press.

Bandura, A. (1997). *Self-efficacy.* New York: Freeman.

Bandura, A. (1997). *Self-efficacy: The exercise of self-control.* New York: Freeman.

Bandura, A. (2000). Self-efficacy. In A. Kazdin (Ed.), *Encyclopedia of psychology.* Washington, DC, & New York: American Psychological Association and Oxford University Press.

Bandura, A. (2001). Social cognitive theory. *Annual Review of Psychology* (Vol. 52). Palo Alto, CA.

Banks, J. (2002). *Introduction to multicultural education* (5th Ed.). Boston: Allyn & Bacon.

Banks, J. (2003). *Teaching strategies for ethnic studies* (7th Ed.). Boston: Allyn & Bacon.

Bannerman, K., Lemaire, M., Yee, K., Iversen, D., Oswald, P., Good, A., & Rawlins, G. A. (2002). Selective cytotoxic lesions of the retrohippocampal region produce a mild deficit in social recognition memory. *Experimental Brain Research, 142*, 395–401.

Barber, A. E., Hollenbeck, J. R., Tower, S. L., & Phillips, J. M. (1994). The effects of interview focus on recruitment effectiveness: A field experiment. *Journal of Applied Psychology, 79*, 886–896.

Barber, T. X. (1969). *Hypnosis.* New York: Von Nostrand Reinhold.

Bard, P. (1934). Emotion. In C. Murchison (Ed.), *Handbook of general psychology.* Worcester, MA: Clark University Press.

Barefoot, J. C., Siegler, I. C., Nowlin, J. B., & Peterson, B. L. (1987). Suspiciousness, health, and mortality: A follow-up study of 500 older adults. *Psychosomatic Medicine, 49*, 450–457.

Barker, L. M. (2001). *Learning and behavior* (3rd ed.). Upper Saddle River, NJ: Prentice-Hall.

Barlow, D. H. (1988). *Anxiety and its disorders: The nature and treatment of anxiety and panic.* New York: Guilford.

Barlow, D. H. (2001). *Anxiety and its disorders* (2nd ed.). New York: Guilford.

Barlow, D. H., Gorman, J. M., Shear, M. K., & Woods, S. W. (2000). Cognitive-behavioral therapy, imipramine, or their combination for panic disorder: A randomized controlled trial. *Journal of the American Medical Association, 283*, 2229–2236.

Barnett, R. C. (2002). Work-family balance. In J. Worell (Ed.), *Encyclopedia of women and gender.* New York: Oxford University Press.

Barnett, R. C. (2002). Work-family balance. In J. Worell (Ed.), *Encyclopedia of women.* San Diego: Academic Press.

Barnett, R. C., & James, J. (2001). *Career and family expectations of female and male freshmen.* Unpublished manuscript, Radcliffe College, Cambridge, MA.

Barnett, R. C., Gareis, K. C., James, J. B., & Steele, J. (2001, August). *Planning ahead: College seniors' concerns about work-family conflict.* Paper presented at the meeting of the American Psychological Association, San Francisco.

Baron, N. (1992). *Growing up with language.* Reading, MA: Addison-Wesley.

Barron, K. E., & Harackiewicz, J. M. (2001). Achievement goals and optimal motivation: Testing multiple goal models. *Journal of Personality and Social Psychology, 80*, 706–722.

Barry, H., Child, I. L., & Bacon, M. K. (1959). Relation of child training to subsistence economy. *American Anthropologist, 61*, 51–63.

Bartlett, F. C. (1932). *Remembering.* Cambridge: Cambridge University Press.

Bartlett, J. (2001, January 14). *Personal communication.* Richardson, TX: Program in Psychology, University of Texas at Dallas.

Bartlett, J. C. (2001, June). Personal communication. Richardson, TX: University of Texas at Dallas, Program in Psychology.

Bartoshuk, L. M., & Beauchamp, G. K. (1994). Chemical senses. *Annual Review of Psychology* (Vol. 45). Palo Alto, CA: Annual Reviews.

Bassett, A. S., Cohw, E. W., Waterworth, D. M., & Brzustowicz, L. (2001). Genetic insights into schizophrenia. *Canadian Journal of Psychiatry, 46*, 121–122.

Basso, M. R., Schefft, B. K., Ris, M. D., & Dember, W. N. (1996). Mood and global-local visual processing. *Journal of the International Neuropsychological Society, 2,* 249–255.

Batson, C. D. (1998). Altruism and prosocial behavior. In D. T. Gilbert, S. T. Fiske, & G. Lindzey (Eds.), *Handbook of social psychology* (4th ed., Vol. 2). New York: McGraw-Hill.

Batson, C. D. (2002). Addressing the altruism question experimentally. In S. G. Post, L. G. Underwood, J. P. Schloss, & W. B. Hurlbut (Eds.), *Altruism and altruistic love*. New York: Oxford University Press.

Battaglia, M. (2002). Beyond the usual suspects: A cholingeric route for panic attacks. *Molecular Psychiatry, 7,* 239–246.

Baum, A., & Posluszny, D. M. (1999). Health Psychology. *Annual Review of Psychology, 50.* Palo Alto, CA: Annual Reviews.

Baum, A., Revenson, T. A., & Singer, J. E. (Eds.). (2001). *Handbook of health psychology.* Mahwah, NJ: Erlbaum.

Baumeister, R. F. (1997). *Evil: Inside human violence and cruelty.* New York: Freeman.

Baumeister, R. F. (1989). The optimal margin of illusion. *Journal of Social and Clinical Psychology, 8,* 176–189.

Baumeister, R. F. (1991). *Meanings of life.* New York: Guilford.

Baumeister, R. F. (1993). *Self-esteem: The puzzle of low self-regard.* New York: Plenum Press.

Baumeister, R. F. (1997). Identity, self-concept, and self-esteem. In R. Hogan, J. Johnson, & S. Briggs (Eds.), *Handbook of personality psychology.* San Diego: Academic Press.

Baumeister, R. F. (1999). *Evil: Inside human violence and cruelty.* New York: Freeman.

Baumeister, R. F., & Bratslavsky, E. (1999). Passion, intimacy, and time: Passionate love as a function of change in intimacy. *Personality and Social Psychology Review, 3,* 2–22.

Baumeister, R. F., Bratslavsky, E., & Finkenauer, C. (2000). *Bad is stronger than good.* Unpublished manuscript, Case Western Reserve University.

Baumrind, D. (1971). Current patterns of parental authority. *Developmental Psychology Monographs, 4* (1, Pt. 2).

Baumrind, D. (1991). Parenting styles and adolescent development. In J. Brooks-Gunn, R. Lerner, & A. C. Petersen (Eds.), *The encyclopedia of adolescence* (Vol. 2). New York: Garland.

Baxter, L. R., Jr., Phelps, M. E., Mazziotta, J. C., Schwartz, J. M., Gerner, R. H., Selin, C. E., & Sumida, R. M. (1995). Cerebral metabolic rates for glucose in mood disorders: Studies with positron emission tomography and fluorodeoxyglucose F 18. *Archives of General Psychiatry, 42,* 441–447.

Baylor, D. (2001). *Seeing, hearing, and smelling the world* [Commentary]. Retrieved October 2001 from http://www.hhmi.org/ senses.

Beatty, J. (1995). *Principles of neuroscience.* New York: McGraw-Hill.

Beatty, J. (2001). *The human brain.* Thousand Oaks, CA: Sage.

Beauchamp, M. S., Less, K. E., Haxby, J. V., & Martin, A. (2002). Parallel visual motion processing streams for manipulable objects and human movements. *Neuron, 34,* 149–159.

Beck, A. (1967). *Depression.* New York: Harper & Row.

Beck, A. T. (1993). Cognitive therapy: Past, present, and future. *Journal of Consulting and Clinical Psychology, 61,* 194–198.

Beck, A. T. (1976). *Cognitive therapies and the emotional disorders.* New York: International Universities Press.

Beck, A. T., Rush, A. J., Shaw, B. F., & Emery, G. (1979). *Cognitive therapy of depression.* New York: Guilford.

Beck, J. (2002). Beck therapy approach. In M. Hersen & W. H. Sledge (Eds.), *Encyclopedia of psychotherapy.* San Diego: Academic Press.

Becker, A. J., Uckert, S., Stief, C. G., Scheller, F., Knapp, W. H., Hartmann, U., & Jonas, U. (2002). Cavernous and systematic plasma levels of norepinephrine and epinephrine during different penile conditions in healthy men and patients with erectile dysfunction. *Urology, 59,* 281–286.

Beckham, E. E. (2000). Depression. In A. Kazdin (Ed.), *Encyclopedia of psychology.* Washington, DC, & New York: American Psychological Association and Oxford University Press.

Beckman, M. (2002). Pheromone reception: When in doubt, mice mate rather than hate. *Science, 295,* 782.

Bednar, R. L., Wells, M. G., & Peterson, S. R. (1995). *Self-esteem* (2nd ed.). Washington, DC: American Psychological Association.

Behrman, B. W., & Davey, S. L. (2001). Eyewitness identification in actual criminal cases: an archival analysis. *Law and Human Behavior, 25,* 475–491.

Békésy, G. von (1960). Vibratory patterns of the basilar membrane. In E. G. Wever (Ed.), *Experiments in hearing.* New York: McGraw-Hill.

Belk, A., & Ruse, M. (2000). Why should evolutionary psychology be a science? *Psychological Inquiry, 11*(1), 22–23.

Bell, A. P., Weinberg, M. S., & Mammersmith, S. K. (1981). *Sexual preference.* New York: Simon & Schuster.

Bell, P., Greene, T., Fisher, J., & Baum, A. (2001). *Environmental psychology* (5th ed.). Belmont, CA: Wadsworth.

Bellesiles, M. A. (1999). *Lethal imagination.* New York: New York University Press.

Bellodi, L., Cavallini, M. C., Bertelli, S., Chiapparino, D., Riboldi, C., & Smeraldi, E. (2001). Morbidity risk for obsessive-compulsive spectrum disorders in first-degree relatives of patients with eating disorders. *American Journal of Psychiatry, 158,* 563–569.

Belsky, J. K. (1999). *The psychology of aging* (3rd ed.). Belmont, CA: Wadsworth.

Bem, D. (1967). Self-perception: An alternative explanation of cognitive dissonance phenomena. *Psychological Review, 74,* 183–200.

Ben-Shakhar, G., Bar-Hillel, M., Yoram, B., Ben-Abba, E., & Flug, A. (1986). Can graphology predict occupational success? Two empirical studies and some methodological ruminations. *Journal of Applied Psychology, 71,* 645–653.

Benbow, C. P., & Stanley, J. C. (1983). Sex differences in mathematical reasoning ability: More facts. *Science, 222,* 1029–1031.

Benca, R. M. (2001). Consequences of insomnia and its therapies. *Journal of Clinical Psychiatry, 62* (Suppl. 10), 33–38.

Benes, F. M., Todtenkopf, M. S., Logiotatos, P., & Williams, M. (2000). Glutamite decarboxylase (65)-immunoreactive terminals in cingulate and prefrontal cortices of schizophrenic and bipolar brains. *Journal of Chemistry and Neuroanatomy, 20,* 259–269.

Benet, V., & Waller, N. G. (1995). The big seven factor model of personality description: Evidence for its cross-cultural generality in a Spanish sample. *Journal of Personality and Social Psychology, 69,* 701–718.

Benini, A. L., Camilloni, M. A., Scordato, C., Lezzi, G., Savia, G., Oriani, G., Bertoli, S., Balzola, F., Liuzzi, A., & Petroni, M. L. (2001). Contribution of weight cycling to serum leptin in human obesity. *International Journal of Obesity and Related Metabolic Disorders, 25,* 721–726.

Benjamin, L. T. (1999). Psychology's portrait gallery: Part III. *Contemporary Psychology, 44,* 27–28.

Bennett, W. I., & Gurin, J. (1982). *The dieter's dilemma: Eating less and weighing more.* New York: Basic Books.

Bereiter, C., & Scardamalia, M. (1993). *Surpassing ourselves: An inquiry into the nature and implications of expertise.* Chicago: Open Court.

Berenbaum, S. A., & Hines, M. (1992). Early androgens are related to childhood sex-typed toy preferences. *Psychological Science, 3,* 203–206.

Berg, C. (2000). Intellectual development in adulthood. In R. J. Sternberg (Ed.), *Handbook of intelligence.* New York: Cambridge University Press.

Bergin, A. E., & Richards, P. S. (2000). Religious values and mental health. In A. Kazdin (Ed.), *Encyclopedia of psychology.* Washington, DC, & New York: American Psychological Association and Oxford University Press.

Berkman, L. F., & Syme, L. L. (1979). Social networks, host resistance, and mortality. *American Journal of Epidemiology, 109,* 186–204.

Berko, J. (1958). The child's learning of English morphology. *World, 14,* 150–157.

Berkowitz, L. (1990). On the formation and regulation of anger and aggression: A cognitive neoassociationistic analysis. *American Psychologist, 45,* 494–503.

Berlin, L., & Cassidy, J. (2000). Understanding parenting. Contributions of attachment theory and research. In J. D. Osofsky & H. E. Fitzgerald (Eds.), *WAIMH handbook of infant mental health* (Vol. 3). New York: Wiley.

Bernheim, K. F. (1997). *The Lanahan cases and readings in abnormal behavior.* Baltimore, MD: Lanahan.

Bernstein, A. B. (2001). Motherhood, health status, and health care. *Women's Health Issues, 11,* 173–184.

Berridge, C. W., & O'Neil, J. (2001). Differential sensitivity to the wake-promoting actions of norepinephrine within the medial preoptic area and the substantia innominata. *Behavioral Neuroscience, 115,* 165–174.

Berry, J. W. (1980). Acculturation as varieties of adaptation. In A. Padilla (Ed.), *Acculturation: Theory, model, and some new findings.* Washington, DC: American Association for the Advancement of Science.

Berscheid, E. (2000). Attraction. In A. Kazdin (Ed.), *Encyclopedia of psychology.* Washington, DC, & New York: American Psychological Association and Oxford University Press.

Berscheid, E., & Fei, J. (1977). Sexual jealousy and romantic love. In G. Clinton & G. Smith (Eds.), *Sexual jealousy*. Englewood Cliffs, NJ: Prentice-Hall.

Berscheid, E., & Reis, H. T. (1998). Attraction and close relationships. In D. T. Gilbert, S. T. Fiske, & G. Lindzey (Eds.), *Handbook of social psychology* (4th ed., Vol. 2). New York: McGraw-Hill.

Berscheid, E., Snyder, M., & Omoto, A. M. (1989). Issues in studying close relationships: Conceptualizing and measuring closeness. In C. Hendrick (Ed.), *Close relationships*. Newbury Park, CA: Sage.

Berschied, E. (1988). Some comments on love's anatomy. Or, whatever happened to an old-fashioned lust? In R. J. Sternberg & M. L. Barnes (Eds.), *Anatomy of love*. New Haven, CT: Yale University Press.

Best, D. (2002). Cross-cultural gender roles. In J. Worell (Ed.), *Encyclopedia of women and gender*. New York: Oxford University Press.

Betch, T., Haberstroh, S., Glockner, A., Haar, T., & Fiedler, K. (2001). The effects of routine strength on adaptation and information search in recurrent decision making. *Organizational Behavior and Human Decision Processes, 84,* 23–53.

Bettman, J. (2001). *Learning.* Unpublished manuscript, Fuqua School of Business, Duke University, Durham, NC.

Bhattacharjee, C., Smith, M., Todd, F., & Gillepsie, M. (2001). Bupropion overdose: A potential problem with the new "miracle" anti-smoking drug. *International Journal of Clinical Practice, 55,* 221–222.

Bhugra, D., & de Silva, P. (1998). Sexual dysfunction therapy. In H. S. Friedman (Ed.), *Encyclopedia of mental health* (Vol. 3). San Diego: Academic Press.

Bi, G., & Poo, M. (2001). Synaptic modification by correlated activity: Hebb's postulate revisited. *Annual Review of Neuroscience, 24.* Palo Alto, CA: Annual Reviews.

Bialystok, E. (2001). *Bilingualism in development: Language, literacy, and cognition.* New York: Cambridge University Press.

Bidikov, I., & Meier, D. E. (1997). Clinical decision-making with the woman after menopause. *Geriatrics, 52*(3), 28–35.

Billings, A. G., Cronkite, R. C., & Moos, R. H. (1983). Social-environment factors in unipolar depression. *Journal of Abnormal Psychology, 92,* 119–133.

Billman, G. E. (2002). Aerobic exercise conditioning: A nonpharmacological antiarrhythmic intervention. *Journal of Applied Physiology, 92,* 446–454.

Billman, J. (2003). *Observation and participation in early childhood setting: A practicum guide (2nd Ed.).* Boston: Allyn & Bacon.

Billmann, S. J., & Ware, J. C. (2002). Marital satisfaction of wives of untreated sleep apneic men. *Sleep Medicine, 3,* 55–59.

Birdsong, D. (Ed.) (1999). *Second-language acquisition and the critical period hypothesis.* Mahwah, NJ: Erlbaum.

Birren, J. E. (2000). Using the gift of long life: Psychological implications of the age revolution. In S. H. Qualls & N. Abeles (Eds.), *Psychology and the aging revolution.* Washington, DC: American Psychological Association.

Birren, J. E., & Schaie, K. W. (Eds.). (2001). *Handbook of the psychology of aging* (5th ed.). San Diego: Academic Press.

Bishop, S. R. (2002). What do we really know about mindfulness-based stress reduction? *Psychosomatic Medicine, 64,* 71–83.

Bjorklund, D. F. (2000). *Children's thinking* (3rd ed.). Belmont, CA: Wadsworth.

Bjorklund, D. F., Yunger, J. L., & Pellegrini, A. D. (2002). The evolution of parenting and evolutionary approaches to childrearing. In M. Bornstein (Ed.), *Handbook of parenting* (2nd ed.). Mahwah, NJ: Erlbaum.

Björkqvist, K., Österman, K., & Lagerspetz, K. M. J. (1994). Sex differences in covert aggression among adults. *Aggressive Behavior, 20,* 27–33.

Black, I. B. (1998). Plasticity. In M. S. Gazzaniga (Ed.), *The new cognitive neurosciences* (2nd ed.). Cambridge, MA: MIT Press.

Blair, C. (2002). School readiness: Integrating cognition and emotion in a neurobiological conceptualization of children's functioning at school entry. *American Psychologist, 57,* 111–127.

Blair, C., & Ramey, C. (1996). Early intervention with low birth weight infants: The path to second generation research. In M. J. Guralnick (Ed.), *The effectiveness of early intervention.* Baltimore: Paul H. Brookes.

Blair, I. V. (2001). Implicit stereotypes and prejudice. In G. B. Moscowitz (Ed.), *Cognitive social psychology.* Mahwah, NJ: Erlbaum.

Blais, F. C., Morin, C. M., Boisclair, A., Greiner, V., & Guay, B. (2001). Insomnia. *Canadian Family Physician, 47,* 759–767.

Blake, R. (2000). Vision and sight: Structure and function. In A. Kazdin (Ed.), *Encyclopedia of psychology.* Washington, DC, & New York: American Psychological Association and Oxford University Press.

Blatt, S. J. (2000). Projective techniques. In A. Kazdin (Ed.), *Encyclopedia of psychology.* Washington; DC, & New York: American Psychological Association and Oxford University Press.

Blatt, S. J., & Zuroff, D. C. (1992). Interpersonal relatedness and self-definition: Two prototypes for depression. *Clinical Psychology Review, 12,* 527–562.

Blazer, D. G., Kessler, R. C., McGonagle, K. A., & Swartz, M. S. (1994). The prevalence and distribution of major depression in a national community sample: The National Comorbidity Study. *American Journal of Psychiatry, 151,* 979–986.

Blittner, M., Goldberg, J., & Merbaum, M. (1978). Cognitive self-control factors in the reduction of smoking behavior. *Behavior Therapy, 9,* 553–561.

Block, J. (2002). *Personality as an affect processing system.* Mahwah, NJ: Erlbaum.

Bloom, B. (1985). *Developing talent in young people.* New York: Ballantine.

Bloom, F., Nelson, C. A., & Lazerson, A. (2001). *Brain, mind, and behavior* (3rd ed.). New York: Worth.

Bloom, P. (2000). *How children learn the meaning of words.* Cambridge, MA: MIT Press.

Blum, D. (1998). *Sex on the brain: The biological differences between men and women.* New York: Penguin.

Blum, H. P. (2001). Freud's private minimonograph on his own dreams. *International Journal of Psychoanalysis, 82,* 953–964.

Blundell, J. E. (1984). Systems and interactions: An approach to the pharmacology of feeding. In A. J. Stunkard & E. Stellar (Eds.), *Eating and its disorders.* New York: Raven Press.

Blyth, D. (2000). Community approaches to improving outcomes for urban children, youth, and families. In A. Booth & A. C. Crouter (Eds.), *Does it take a village?* Mahwah, NJ: Erlbaum.

Bodenhausen, G. V., Mussweiler, T., Gabriel, S., & Moreno, K. N. (2001). Affective influences on stereotyping and intergroup relations. In J. P. Forgas (Ed.), *Handbook of affect and cognition.* Mahwah, NJ: Erlbaum.

Bogaert, A. F., Woodard, U., & Hafer, C. L. (1999). Intellectual ability and reactions to pornography. *Journal of Sex Research, 36,* 283–291.

Bogatz, G., & Ball, S. (1972). *Reading with television: An evaluation of the Electric Company.* Princeton, NJ: Educational Testing Service.

Bohart, A. C. (1995). The person-centered psychotherapies. In A. S. Gurman (Ed.), *Essential psychotherapies: Theory and practice* (pp. 55–84). New York: Guilford Press.

Bohart, A. C., & Greening, T. (2001). Humanistic psychology and positive psychology. *American Psychologist, 56,* 81–82.

Boll, T. J., Johnon, B., Perry, N., & Rozensky, R. H. (Eds.) (2002). *Handbook of clinical health psychology, Vol. 1.* Washington, DC: American Psychological Association.

Bond, R., & Smith, P. B. (1994). Culture and conformity: A meta-analysis of studies using the Asch-type perceptual judgment task. *British Psychological Society 1994 Proceedings, 9,* 297–308.

Booth, A., & Crouter, A. C. (Eds.). (2000). *Does it take a village?* Mahwah, NJ: Erlbaum.

Booth, A., Johnson, D. R., & Granger, D. A. (1999). Testosterone and men's health. *Journal of Behavioral Medicine, 22,* 1–12.

Booth-Kewley, S., & Friedman, H. S. (1987). Psychological predictors of heart disease: A quantitative review. *Psychological Bulletin, 101,* 343–362.

Boraud, T., Bezard, E., Bioulac, B., & Gross, C. E. (2002). From single extracellular unit recording in experimental and human Parkinsonism to the development of a functional concept of the role played by the basal ganglia in motor control. *Progress in Neurobiology, 66,* 265–283.

Borckardt, J. J. (2002). Case study examining the efficacy of a multi-modal psychotherapeutic intervention for hypertension. *International Journal of Clinical and Experimental Hypnosis, 50,* 189–201.

Bordens, K. S., & Horowitz, I. A. (2002). *Social psychology* (2nd ed.). Mahwah, NJ: Erlbaum.

Borkovec, T. D., & Ruscio, A. M. (2001). Psychotherapy for generalized anxiety disorder. *Journal of Clinical Psychiatry, 62* (Suppl. 11), 37–42.

Bornstein, M. H. (Ed.) (2002). *Handbook of parenting* (2nd ed.). Mahwah, NJ: Erlbaum.

Bornstein, M. H., & Bradley, R. H. (Eds.) (2003). *Socioeconomic status, parenting, and child development.* Mahwah, NJ: Erlbaum.

Bornstein, M. H., & Tamis-LeMonda, C. S. (2001). Mother-infant interaction. In A. Fogel & G. Bremner (Eds.), *Blackwell handbook of infant development.* London: Blackwell.

Borrelli, B., Hogan, J. W., Bock, B., Pinto, B., Roberts, M., & Marcus, B. (2002). Predictors of quitting and dropout among women in a clinic-based smoking cessation program. *Psychology of Addictive Behaviors, 16,* 22–27.

Bou-Flores, C., & Berger, A. J. (2001). Gap junctions and inhibitory synapses modulate inspiratory motoneuron synchronization. *Journal of Neurophysiology, 85,* 1543–1551.

Bouchard, T. J., Lykken, D. T., Tellegen, A., & McGue, M. (1996). Genes, drives, environment, and experience. In D. Lubinski & C. Benbow (Eds.), *Psychometrics and social issues concerning intellectual talent.* Baltimore: Johns Hopkins University Press.

Bourne, E. J. (1995). *The anxiety and phobia workbook* (2nd ed.). Oakland, CA: New Harbinger.

Bower, G. H., Clark, M., Winzenz, D., & Lesgold, A. (1969). Hierarchical retrieval schemes in recall of categorized word lists. *Journal of Verbal Learning and Verbal Behavior, 3,* 323–343.

Bowers, T. G., & Clum, G. A. (1988). Relative contribution of specific and nonspecific treatment effects: Meta-analysis of placebo-controlled behavior therapy research. *Psychological Bulletin, 103,* 315–323.

Bowlby, J. (1969). *Attachment and loss* (Vol. 1). London: Hogarth Press.

Bowlby, J. (1989). *Secure and insecure attachment.* New York: Basic Books.

Boyer, L. B. (1999). *Countertransference and aggression.* Mahwah, NJ: Erlbaum.

Bozarth, J. D., Zimring, F. M., & Tausch, R. (2001). Client-centered therapy: The evolution of a revolution. In D. J. Cain & J. Seeman (Eds.), *Humanistic psychotherapies.* Washington, DC: American Psychological Association.

Bradbury, J. (2001). Teasing out the genetics of bipolar disorder. *Lancet, 357,* 156.

Bradford, D., Stroup, S., & Lieberman, J. (2002). Pharmacological treatments for schizophrenia. In P. Nathan & J. M. Gorman (Eds.), *A guide to treatments that work (2nd Ed.).* New York: Oxford University Press.

Brain, P. F., & Susman, E. J. (1997). Hormonal aspects of aggression and violence. In D. M. Stoff, J. Breiling, & J. D. Maser (Eds.), *Handbook of antisocial personality disorder* (pp. 314–323). New York: Wiley.

Brammer, L. M., & MacDonald, G. (1999). *The helping relationship* (7th ed.). Boston: Allyn & Bacon.

Brannon, L. (1999). *Gender: Psychological perspectives* (2nd ed.). Boston: Allyn & Bacon.

Brannon, L. (2002). *Gender: Psychological perspectives.* Boston: Allyn & Bacon.

Bransford, J. D., & Stein, B. S. (1993). *The IDEAL problem solver.* New York: Freeman.

Braun, B. G. (1985). Transgenerational incidence of dissociation and multiple personality disorder: A preliminary report. In R. P. Kluft (Ed.), *Childhood antecedents of multiple personality.* Washington, DC: American Psychiatric Press.

Breggin, P. R., & Breggin, G. R. (1995). *Talking back to Prozac: What doctors aren't telling you about today's most controversial drug.* New York: St. Martin's Press.

Brehm, S. S. (2002). *Intimate relationships* (3rd ed.). New York: McGraw-Hill.

Brehony, K. A. (1999). *Ordinary grace.* New York: Riverhead Books.

Breland, K., & Breland, M. (1961). The misbehavior of organisms. *American Psychologist, 16,* 681–684.

Brems, C. (2001). *Basic skills in psychotherapy and counseling.* Belmont, CA: Wadsworth.

Brennan, F. X., & Charnetski, C. J. (2000). Explanatory style and immunglobin A (IgA). *Integration of Physiology and Behavioral Science, 35,* 251–255.

Brennan, P., Mednick, S., & Kandel, E. (1991). Congenital determinants of violent and property offencing. In D. Pepler & K. Rubin (Eds.), *The development and treatment of childhood aggression.* Mahwah, NJ: Erlbaum.

Bressan, R. A., Jones, H. M., Ell, P. J., & Pilowsky, L. S. (2001). Dopamine d (2) receptor blockade in schizophrenia. *American Journal of Psychiatry, 158,* 971–972.

Brewer, J. B., Zuo, Z., Desmond, J. E., Glover, G. H., & Gabrieli, J. D. E. (1998). Making memories: Brain activity that predicts how well visual experience will be remembered. *Science, 281,* 1185–1187.

Brewer, M. B., & Gaertner, S. L., (2001). Toward reduction of prejudice: Intergroup contact and social categorization. In R. Brown & S.L. Gaertner (Eds.), *Handbook of social psychology: Intergroup processes.* Malden, MA: Blackwell.

Brewer, M.B., & Brown, R. J. (1998). Intergroup relations. In D. T. Gilbert, S. T. Fiske, & G. Lindzey (Eds.), *Handbook of social psychology* (4th ed., Vol. 2). New York: McGraw-Hill.

Brickman, A. L., LoPiccolo, C. J., & Johnson, S. L. (2002). Screening for bipolar disorder. *Psychiatric Services, 53,* 349.

Brickman, P., Coates, D., & Janoff-Bulman, R. J. (1978). Lottery winners and accident victims: Is happiness relative? *Journal of Personality and Social Psychology, 36,* 917–927.

Brigham, J. C. (1986). Race and eyewitness identifications. In S. Worschel & W. G. Austin (Eds.), *Psychology of intergroup relations.* Chicago: Nelson-Hall.

Brim, O. (1999). *The McArthur Foundation study of midlife development.* Vero Beach, FL: The McArthur Foundation.

Bringsjord, S., & Ferrucci, D. (2000). *Artificial intelligence and literary creativity.* Mahwah, NJ: Erlbaum.

Brink, S. (2001, May 7). Your brain on alcohol. *U.S. News & World Report, 130*(18), 50–57.

Brislin, R. (1993). *Understanding culture's influence on behavior.* Fort Worth, TX: Harcourt Brace.

Brody, N. (2000). Intelligence. In A. Kazdin (Ed.), *Encyclopedia of psychology.* Washington, DC, & New York: American Psychological Association and Oxford University Press.

Bronfenbrenner, U. (2000). Ecological systems theory. In A. Kazdin (Ed.), *Encyclopedia of psychology.* Washington, DC, and New York: American Psychological Association and Oxford University Press.

Bronfenbrenner, U., & Morris, P. (1998). The ecology of developmental processes. In W. Damon (Ed.), *Handbook of child psychology* (5th ed., Vol. 1). New York: Wiley.

Brooks, D. C. (2000). Recent and remote extinction cues reduce spontaneous recovery. *Quarterly Journal of Experimental Psychology, 3,* 25–58.

Brooks, J. G., & Brooks, M. G. (2001). *In search of understanding: The case for the constructivist classroom.* Upper Saddle River, NJ: Prentice-Hall.

Brooks-Gunn, J., & Warren, M. P. (1989). The psychological significance of secondary sexual characteristics in 9- to 11-year-old girls. *Child Development, 59,* 161–169.

Brosvic, G. M., Dihoff, R. E., & Fama, J. (2002). Age-related susceptibility to the Muller-Lyer and the horizontal-vertical illusion. *Perceptual and Motor Skills, 94,* 229–234.

Brouwer, W. H., Withaar, F. K., Tant, M. L., & van Zomeren, A. H. (2002). Attention and driving in traumatic brain injury: A question of coping with time pressure. *Journal of Head and Trauma Rehabilitation, 17,* 1–15.

Brown, A. L. (1997). Transforming schools into communities of thinking and learning about serious matters. *American Psychologist, 52,* 399–413.

Brown, A. L., & Campione, J. C. (1996). Psychological learning theory and the design of innovative environments. In L. Schuable & R. Glaser (Eds.), *Contributions of instructional innovation to understanding learning.* Mahwah, NJ: Erlbaum.

Brown, E., Deffenbacher, K., & Sturgill, W. (1977). Memory for faces and the circumstances of encounter. *Journal of Applied Psychology, 62,* 311–318.

Brown, G., Bhrolchain, M., & Harris, T. (1975). Social class and psychiatric disturbance among women in an urban population. *Sociology, 9,* 225–254.

Brown, J. D., Steele, J. R., & Walsh-Childers, K. (Eds.) (2002). *Sexual teens, sexual media.* Mahwah, NJ: Erlbaum.

Brown, L. S. (1989). New voices, new visions: Toward a lesbian/gay paradigm for psychology. *Psychology of Women Quarterly, 13,* 445–458.

Brown, R. (1973). *A first language: The early stages.* Cambridge, MA: Harvard University Press.

Brown, R. (1986). *Social psychology* (2nd ed.). New York: Free Press.

Brownell, K. A., & Rodin, J. (1994). The dieting maelstrom: Is it possible to lose weight? *American Psychologist, 9,* 781–791.

Brownell, K. D., & Cohen, L. R. (1995). Adherence to dietary regimens. *Behavioral Medicine, 20,* 226–242.

Brownlee, S. (1998, June 15). Baby talk. *U.S. News & World Report,* 48–54.

Bruner, J. S., & Tagiuri, R. (1954). The perception of people. In G. Lindzey (Ed.), *Handbook of social psychology* (Vol. 2). Boston: Addison-Wesley.

Bruning, R. H., Schraw, G. J., & Ronning, R. R. (1999). *Cognitive psychology and instruction* (3rd ed.). Upper Saddle River, NJ: Erlbaum.

Brynes, J. P. (2001). *Cognitive development and learning in instructional contexts* (2nd ed.). Boston: Allyn & Bacon.

Buchsbaum, M. S., Someya, T., Wu, J. C., Tang, C. Y., & Bunney, W. E. (1997). Neuroimaging bipolar illness with positron emission tomography and magnetic resonance imaging. *Psychiatric Annals, 27,* 489–495.

Buckley, P. F., Miller, D. D., Singer, B., & Donenwirth, K. (2001). The evolving clinical profile of a atypical antipsychotic medications. *Canadian Journal of Psychiatry, 46,* 285.

Bukatko, D., & Daehler, M. W. (2001). *Child development* (4th ed.). Boston: Houghton Mifflin.

Burgess, P. W., Quayle, A., & Frith, C. D. (2001). Brain regions involved in prospective memory as determined by positron emission tomography. *Neuropsychologica, 39,* 545–555.

Burke, G. L., Arnold, A. M., Bild, D., Cushman, M., Fried, O., Newman, A., & Robbins, C. (2001). Factors associated with healthy aging. *Journal of the American Geriatric Society, 49,* 254–262.

Burlingame, G., & Davies, R. (2002). Self-help groups. In M. Hersen & W. H. Sledge (Eds.), *Encyclopedia of psychotherapy.* San Diego: Academic Press.

Burns, D. (1985). *Intimate connections.* New York: William Morrow.

Burns, D. D. (1980). *Feeling good: The new mood therapy.* New York: Morrow.

Burnstein, E., Crandall, C., & Kitayama, S. (1994). Some neo-Darwinian decision rules for altruism: Weighing cues for inclusive fitness as a function of the biological importance of the decision. *Journal of Personality and Social Psychology, 67,* 773–789.

Bushman, B. J., & Huesmann, L. R. (2001). Effects of televised violence on aggression. In D. Singer & J. Singer (Eds.), *Handbook of children and the media.* Thousand Oaks, CA: Sage.

Buss, A. H., & Plomin, R. (1987). Commentary. In H. H. Goldsmith, A. H. Buss, R. Plomin, M. K. Rothbart, A. Thomas, A. Chess, R. R. Hinde, & R. B. McCall (Eds.), Roundtable: What is temperament? Four approaches. *Child Development, 58,* 505–529.

Buss, D. M. (1995). Evolutionary psychology: A new paradigm for psychological science. *Psychological Inquiry, 6,* 1–30.

Buss, D. M. (2000). Evolutionary psychology. In A. Kazdin (Ed.), *Encyclopedia of psychology.* Washington, DC, & New York: American Psychological Association and Oxford University Press.

Buss, D. M. (1995). Psychological sex differences: Origins through sexual selection. *American Psychologist, 50,* 164–168.

Buss, D. M. (2000). The evolution of happiness. *American Psychologist, 55,* 15–23.

Buss, D. M., & Barnes, M. (1986). Preferences in human mate selection. *Journal of Personality and Social Psychology, 50,* 559–570.

Buss, D. M., & others. (1990). International preferences in selecting mates: A study of 37 cultures. *Journal of Cross-Cultural Psychology, 21,* 5–47.

Butcher, J. N. (1999). *A beginner's guide to the MMPI-2.* Washington, DC: American Psychological Association.

Butler, G., Fennell, M., Robson, P., & Gelder, M. (1991). Comparison of behavior therapy and cognitive behavior therapy in the treatment of generalized anxiety disorder. *Journal of Consulting and Clinical Psychology, 59,* 167–175.

Byrne, S. M., & McLean, N. J. (2002). The cognitive-behavioral model of bulimia nervosa: A direct evaluation. *International Journal of Eating Disorders, 31,* 17–31.

C

Cacioppo, J. T., Ernst, J. M., Burleson, M. H., McClintock, M. K., Malarkey, W. B., Hawkley, L. C., Kowalewski, R. B., Paulsen, A., Hobson, J. A., Hugdahl, K., Spiegel, D., Berntson, G. G. (2000). Lonely traits and concomitant physiological processes: The MacArthur Social Neuroscience Studies. *International Journal of Psychophysiology, 35,* 143–154.

Cain, D. J. (2001). Defining characteristics, history, and evolution of humanistic psychotherapies. In D. J. Cain & J. Seeman (Eds.), *Humanistic psychotherapies.* Washington, DC: American Psychological Association.

Calkins, M. (1896). Association. *Psychological Review, 2* (Monograph suppl.), 4–5.

Callan, J. E. (2002). Gender development: Psychoanalytic perspectives. In J. Worell (Ed.), *Encyclopedia of women and gender.* San Diego: Academic Press.

Cameron, N. (1963). *Personality development and psychopathology.* Boston: Houghton Mifflin.

Campbell, F. A., & Ramey, C. T. (1993, March). *Mid-adolescent outcomes for high risk students: An examination of the continuing effects of early intervention.* Paper presented at the biennial meeting of the Society for Research in Child Development, New Orleans.

Campbell, F. A., Pungello, E. P., Miller-Johnson, S., Burchinal, M., & Ramey, C. T. (2001). The development of cognitive and academic abilities: Growth curves from an early childhood educational experiment. *Developmental Psychology, 37,* 231–243.

Campbell, J. D., Tesser, A., & Fairey, P. J. (1986). Conformity and attention to the stimulus: Some temporal and contextual dynamics. *Journal of Personality and Social Psychology, 51,* 315–324.

Campbell, L., Campbell, B., & Dickinson, D. (1999). *Teaching and learning through multiple intelligences* (2nd ed.). Boston: Allyn & Bacon.

Campbell, N. A., Reece, J. B., & Mitchell, L. G. (2002). *Biology* (6th ed.). Reading, MA, & Menlo Park, CA: Benjamin/Cummings.

Campfield, L. A., Smith, F. J., Gulsez, Y., Devos, R., & Burn, P. (1995). Mouse OB protein: Evidence for a peripheral signal linking adiposity and central neural networks. *Science, 269,* 546–549.

Campione, J. C. (2001, April). *Fostering a community of learners.* Paper presented at the meeting of the Society for Research in Child Development, Minneapolis.

Canadian Mental Health Association. (1984). *Links between work and home.* Toronto: Canadian Mental Health Association.

Canino, I. A., & Spurlock, J. (2000). *Culturally diverse children and adolescents: Assessment, diagnosis, and treatment.* New York: Guilford Press.

Cannon, W. B. (1927). The James-Lange theory of emotions: A critical examination and an alternative theory. *American Journal of Psychology, 39,* 106–124.

Cannon, W. B. (1929). *Bodily changes in pain, hunger, fear, and rage* (2nd ed.). New York: Appleton-Century-Crofts.

Cannon, W. B., & Washburn, A. L. (1912). An explanation of hunger. *American Journal of Physiology, 29,* 444–454.

Cantor, N., & Langston, C. A. (1989). Ups and downs of life tasks in a life transition. In L. A. Pervin (Ed.), *Goal concepts in personality and social psychology.* Mahwah, NJ: Erlbaum.

Caporael, L. (2001). Evolutionary psychology: Toward a unifying theory and a hybrid science. *Annual Review of Psychology, 52,* 607–628.

Capuzzi, D. (2003). *Approaches to group counseling.* Upper Saddle River, NJ: Prentice-Hall.

Capuzzi, D., & Gross, D. R. (1999). *Counseling and psychotherapy* (2nd ed.). Upper Saddle River, NJ: Prentice-Hall.

Capuzzi, D., & Gross, D. (2003). *Counseling and psychotherapy* (3rd Ed.). Upper Saddle River, NJ: Prentice-Hall.

Carey, L. M. (2001). *Measuring and evaluating school learning* (3rd ed.). Boston: Allyn & Bacon.

Carkenord, D. M., & Bullington, J. (1995). Bringing cognitive dissonance to the classroom. In M. E. Ware & D. E. Johnson (Eds.), *Demonstrations and activities in teaching of psychology* (Vol. 3). Mahwah, NJ: Erlbaum.

Carlson, L. E., Ursuliak, Z., Goodey, E., Angen, M., & Speca, M. (2001). The effects of a mindfulness meditation-based stress reduction program on mood and symptoms of stress in cancer outpatients: 6-month follow-up. *Supportive Care and Cancer, 9,* 112–123.

Carlson, N. (2000). Neuron. In A. Kazdin (Ed.), *Encyclopedia of psychology.* Washington, DC, & New York: American Psychological Association and Oxford University Press.

Carlson, N. R. (2001). *Physiology of behavior* (7th ed.). Boston: Allyn & Bacon.

Carnegie Council on Adolescent Development. (1995). *Great transitions.* New York: Carnegie Foundation.

Carroll, C. R. (2003). *Drugs in modern society* (6th ed.). New York: McGraw-Hill.

Carskadon, M. A., Acebo, C., & Seifer, R. (2001). Extended nights, sleep loss, and recovery sleep in adolescents. *Archives of Italian Biology, 139,* 301–312.

Carskadon, M. A., Labyak, S. E., Acebo, C., & Seifer, R. (1999). Intrinsic circadian period of adolescent humans measured in conditions of forced desynchrony. *Neuroscience Letters, 260,* 129–132.

Carskadon, M. A., Wolfson, A. R., Acebo, C., Tzischinsky, O., & Seifer, R. (1998). Adolescent sleep patterns, circadian timing, and sleepiness at a transition to early school days. *Sleep, 21,* 873–884.

Carson, R. C., Butcher, J. N., & Mineka, S. (2000). *Abnormal psychology and modern life* (11th ed.). Boston: Allyn & Bacon.

Carson, R. C., Butcher, J. N., & Mineka, S. (1996). *Abnormal psychology and life.* (10th ed.). New York: HarperCollins.

Carstensen, L. L. (1995). Evidence for a life-span theory of socioemotional selectivity. *Current Directions in Psychological Science, 4,* 151–156.

Carstensen, L. L. (1998). A life-span approach to social motivation. In J. Heckhausen & C. Dweck (Eds.), *Motivation and self-regulation across the life span.* New York: Cambridge University Press.

Carstensen, L. L., & Turk-Charles, S. (1994). The salience of emotion across the adult life span. *Psychology and Aging, 9,* 262. American Psychological Association.

Carstensen, L. L., Pasupathi, M., & Mayr, U. (1998). *Emotion experience in the daily lives of older and younger adults.* Unpublished manuscript, Stanford University.

Carstensen, L. L., Pasupathi, M., & Nesselroade, J. R. (2000). Emotional experience in everyday life across the life span. *Journal of Personality and Social Psychology, 79,* 644–655.

Carter, R. (1998). *Mapping the mind.* Berkeley, CA: University of California Press.

Caruso, J. C. (2001). Reliable component analysis of the Stanford-Binet: Fourth Edition for 2- to 6-year-olds. *Psychological Assessment, 13,* 261–266.

Carver, C. S., & Scheier, M. F. (2001). Optimism. In C. R. Synder & S. J. Lopez (Eds.), *Handbook of positive psychology.* New York: Oxford University Press.

Castro-Alamancos, M. A., & Calcagnotto, M. E. (2001). High-pass filtering of corticothalamic activity by neuromodulators released during arousal. *Journal of Neurophysiology, 85,* 1489–1497.

Cauller, L. (2001, May). *Review of Santrock, Psychology* (7th ed.). New York: McGraw-Hill.

Cavedini, P., Riboldi, G., Keller, R., D'Annucci, A., & Bellodi, K. L. (2002). Frontal lobe dysfunction in pathological gambling patients. *Biological Psychiatry, 15,* 334–341.

Ceci, S. (1996). Unpublished review of *Child Development* (8th ed.) by J. W. Santrock. New York: McGraw-Hill.

Ceci, S. J., & Gilstrap, L. L. (2000). Determinants of intelligence: Schooling and intelligence. In A. Kazdin (Ed.), *Encyclopedia of Psychology.* Washington, DC, & New York: American Psychological Association and Oxford University Press.

Center for Leadership Studies. (2000). *Multifactor Leadership Questionnaire: Norms.* Retrieved November 24, 2001, from http://cls.binghamton.edu/mlq.htm

Center for Survey Research. (2000). *Hours on the job.* Storrs, CT: University of Connecticut, Center for Survey Research.

Centers for Disease Control and Prevention. (2001). *How to quit.* Atlanta, GA: Centers for Disease Control and Prevention.

Centers for Disease Control and Prevention. (2001). *AIDS.* Atanta: Centers for Disease Control and Prevention.

Chance, P. (2003). *Learning and behavior* (4th ed.). Belmont, CA: Wadsworth.

Changeux, J., & Chavillion, J. (1995). *Origins of the human brain.* New York: Oxford University Press.

Charles, C. M. (2002). *Building classroom discipline* (7th ed.). Boston: Allyn & Bacon.

Chase, W. G., & Simon, H. A. (1973). Perception in chess. *Cognitive Psychology, 4,* 55–81.

Chastain, G., & Landrum, R. E. (1999). *Protecting human subjects.* Washington, DC: American Psychological Association.

Chaves, J. F. (2000). Hypnosis. In A. Kazdin (Ed.), *Encyclopedia of psychology.* Washington DC, and New York: American Psychological Association and Oxford University Press.

Cheasty, M., Condren, R., & Cooney, C. (2002). Altered sexual preference and behavior in a man with vascular ischemic lesions in the temporal lobe. International *Journal of Geriatric Psychiatry, 17,* 87–88.

Chen, C., & Stevenson, H. W. (1989). Homework: A cross-cultural comparison. *Child Development, 60,* 551–561.

Chen, Z. (2002). Analogical problem solving: A hierarchical analysis of procedural similarity. *Journal of Experimental Psychology, 28,* 81–98.

Cherry, K. E., & LeCompte, D. C. (1999). Age and individual differences influence prospective memory. *Psychology and Aging, 14,* 60–76.

Chess, S., & Thomas, A. (1977). Temperamental individuality from childhood to adolescence. *Journal of Child Psychiatry, 16,* 218–226.

Child Trends. (2000). Trends in sexual activity and contraceptives among teens. *Child Trends Research Brief.* Washington, DC: Author.

Children's Defense Fund (2000). *The state of America's children: 2000.* Washington, DC: Children's Defense Fund.

Chirot, D., & Seligman, M. E. P. (Eds.). (2001). *Ethnopolitical warfare.* Washington, DC: American Psychological Association.

Chodorow, N. (1978). *The reproduction of mothering.* Berkeley: University of California Press.

Chodorow, N. (1989). *Feminism and psychoanalytic theory.* New Haven, CT: Yale University Press.

Chomsky, N. (1975). *Reflections on language.* New York: Pantheon.

Chorney, M. J., Chorney, K., Seese, N., Owen, M. J., Daniels, J., McGuffin, P., Thompson, L. A., Detterman, D. K., Benbow, C., Lubinski, D., Eley, T., & Plomin, R. (1998). A quantitative trait locus associated with cognitive ability in children. *Psychological Science, 9,* 159–166.

Christensen, L. (1996). *Diet-behavior relationships.* Washington, DC: American Psychological Association.

Christian, K., Bachnan, H. J., & Morrison, F. J. (2001). Schooling and cognitive development. In R. J. Sternberg & E. L. Grigorenko (Eds.), *Environmental effects on cognitive development.* Mahwah, NJ: Erlbaum.

Christiansen, L. B. (2001). *Experimental methodology* (8th ed.). Boston: Allyn & Bacon.

Chung, K., & Chung, J. M. (2001). Sympathetic sprouting in the dorsal root ganglion after spinal nerve ligation; evidence of regenerative collateral sprouting. *Brain Research, 895,* 204–212.

Church, R. M., & Kirkpatrick, K. (2001). Theories of conditioning and timing. In R. R. Mowrer & S. B. Klein (Eds.), *Handbook of contemporary learning theories.* Mahwah, NJ: Erlbaum.

Cialdini, R. B. (1993). *Influence: Science and practice* (3rd ed.). New York: HarperCollins.

Cialdini, R. B. (2001). *Influence: Science and practice* (4th Ed.). Boston: Allyn & Bacon.

Cialdini, R. B., & Trost, M. R. (1998). Social influence: Social norms, conformity, and compliance. In D. T. Gilbert, S. T. Fiske, & G. Lindzey (Eds.), *Handbook of social psychology* (4th ed., Vol. 2). New York: McGraw-Hill.

Cialdini, R. B., Schaller, M., Houlihan, D., Arps, K., Fultz, J., & Beaman, A. L. (1987). Empathy-based helping: Is it selflessly or selfishly motivated? *Journal of Personality and Social Psychology, 52,* 749–758.

Cicchetti, D., & Toth, S. (1998). Perspectives on research and practice in developmental psychopathology. In I. E. Sigel & K. A. Renninger (Eds.), *Handbook of child psychology* (5th ed., Vol. 4). New York: Wiley.

Clark, D. M., Salkovskis, P. M., Hackmann, A., Middelton, H., Anastasiades, P., & Gelder, M. (1994). A comparison of cognitive therapy, applied relaxation, and imipramine in the treatment of panic disorder. *British Journal of Psychiatry, 164,* 759–769.

Clark, E. V. (1983). Meanings and concepts. In P. H. Mussen (Ed.), *Handbook of child psychology* (4th ed., Vol. 2). New York: Wiley.

Clark, L. A., Watson, D., & Reynolds, S. (1995). Diagnosis and classification in psychopathology. *Annual Review of Psychology, 46.* Palo Alto, CA: Annual Reviews.

Clark, N. M., & Dodge, J. A. (1999). Exploring self-efficacy as a predictor of disease management. *Health Education & Behavior, 26,* 72–89.

Clark, T. (2001). Post-traumatic stress disorder: Baby should not be thrown out with the bath water. *British Journal of Medicine, 322,* 1303–1304.

Clark-Plaskie, M., & Lachman, M. E. (1999). The sense of control in midlife. In S. L. Willis & J. D. Reid (Eds.), *Life in the middle.* San Diego: Academic Press.

Clarke, V. A., Lovegrove, H., Williams, H., & Macpherson, M. (2000). Unrealistic optimism and the health belief model. *Journal of Behavioral Medicine, 25,* 367–376.

Clay, R. A. (2000, April). Linking up online: Is the Internet enhancing interpersonal connections or leading to greater isolation? *Monitor on Psychology,* 20–23.

Clayton, A. H., McGarvey, E. L., Abouesh, A. L., & Pinkerton, R. C. (2001). Substitution of an SSRI with bupropion sustained release following SSRI-induced sexual dysfunction. *Journal of Clinical Psychiatry, 62,* 185–190.

Close, C. E., Roberts, P. L., & Berger, R. E. (1990). Cigarettes, alcohol, and marijuana are related to pyospermia in infertile men. *Journal of Urology, 144,* 900–903.

Cochran, S. D., & Mays, V. M. (1990). Sex, lies, and HIV. *New England Journal of Medicine, 322,* 774–775.

Cohen, J. A., Mannarino, A. P., & Rogal, S. (2001). Treatment practices for childhood post-traumatic stress disorder. *Child Abuse and Neglect, 25,* 123–135.

Cohen, L. A. (1987, November). Diet and cancer. *Scientific American,* pp. 128–137.

Cohen, L., De Moor, C., & Amato, R. J. (2001). The association between treatment-specific optimism and depressive symptomatology in patients enrolled in a Phase I cancer clinical trial. *Cancer, 91,* 1949–1953.

Cohen, P., Cohen, J., Kasen, S., Velez, C. N., Hartmark, C., Johnson, J., Rojas, M., Brook, J., & Streuning, E. L. (1993). An epidemiological study of disorders in late adolescence: I. Age- and gender-specific prevalence. *Journal of Child Psychology & Psychiatry, 6,* 851–867.

Cohen, R. J., & Swerdlik, M. E. (2002). *Psychological testing and assessment* (5th ed.). New York: McGraw-Hill.

Cohen, R. L., & Borsoi, D. (1996). The role of gestures in description-communication: A cross-sectional study of aging. *Journal of Nonverbal Behavior, 20,* 45–64.

Cohen, S. (1988). Psychosocial models of the role of social support in the etiology of physical disease. *Health Psychology, 7,* 269–297.

Cohen, S. (2002). Psychosocial stress, social networks, and susceptibility to infection. In H. G. Koenig & H. J. Cohen (Eds.), *The link between religion and health.* New York: Oxford University Press.

Cohen, S. I. (2002). Treatment of insomnia. *Lancet, 359,* 1433–1434.

Cohen, S., Doyle, W. J., Skoner, D. P., Rabin, B. S., & Gawaltney, J. M. (1997). Social ties and susceptibility to the common cold. *Journal of the American Medical Association, 277,* 1940–1944.

Cohen, S., Evans, G. W., Krantz, D. S., Stokols, D., & Kelly, S. (1981). Aircraft noise and children: Longitudinal and cross-sectional evidence on adaptation to noise and the effectiveness of noise abatement. *Journal of Personality and Social Psychology, 40,* 331–345.

Cohen, S., Frank, E., Doyle, W., Skoner, D. P., Rabin, B. S., & Gwaltney, J. M. (1998). Types of stressors that increase susceptibility to the common cold in healthy adults. *Health Psychology, 17,* 214–223.

Cohen, S., Glass, D. C., & Singer, J. E. (1973). Apartment noise, auditory discrimination, and reading ability in children. *Journal of Experimental Psychology, 9,* 407–422.

Cohen, S., Miller, G. E., & Rabin, B. S. (2001). Psychological stress and antibody response to immunization. *Psychosomatic Medicine, 63,* 7–18.

Colby, A., Kohlberg, L., Gibbs, J., & Lieberman, M. (1983). A longitudinal study of moral judgment. *Monographs of the Society for Research in Child Development, 48* (21, Serial No. 201).

Cole, C. F., Richman, B. A., & Brown, S. K. (2001). The world of *Sesame Street* research. In S. M. Fisch & R. T. Truglio (Eds.), *"G" is for growing: Thirty years of research on children and Sesame Street.* Mahwah, NJ: Erlbaum.

Cole, M. (1999). Culture in development. In M. H. Bornstein & M. E. Lamb (Eds.), *Developmental psychology: An advanced textbook* (4th ed.). Mahwah, NJ: Erlbaum.

Cole, M., & Cole, S. R. (2003). *The development of children* (5th ed.). New York: Freeman.

Coleman, B. L., Stevens, M. J., & Reeder, G. G. (2001). What makes recovered-memory testimony compelling to jurors? *Law and Human Behavior, 25,* 317–338.

Coleman, J. (1995, March). *Adolescent sexual knowledge: Implications for health and health risks.* Paper presented at the meeting of the Society for Research in Child Development, Indianapolis.

Coleman, P. D. (1986, August). *Regulation of dendritic extent: Human aging brain and Alzheimer's disease.* Paper presented at the meeting of the American Psychological Association, Washington, DC.

College Board. (2001). *2001 college bound seniors are the largest, most diverse group in history.* Princeton, NJ: Educational Testing Service.

Collins, M. (1996, Winter). The job outlook for '96 grads. *Journal of Career Planning,* 51–54.

Collins, W. A., Maccoby, E. E., Steinberg, L., Hetherington, E. M., & Bornstein, M. H. (2000). Contemporary research on parenting: The case for nature and nurture. *American Psychologist, 55,* 218–232.

Comarow, D. D., & Chescheir, M. W. (1999). *Talking about therapy.* Westport, CT: Greenwood.

Combs, M. (2002). *Readers and writers in the primary grades* (2nd ed.). Upper Saddle River, NJ: Prentice-Hall.

Compas, B. E., Connor-Smith, J. K., Saltzman, H., Thomsen, A. H., & Wadsworth, M. E. (2001). Coping with stress during childhood and adolescence: Problems, progress, and potential in theory and research. *Psychological Bulletin, 127,* 87–127.

Conklin, C. A., & Tiffany, S. T. (2002). Applying extinction research and theory to cue-exposure addiction treatments. *Addiction, 97,* 155–167.

Conway, M., & Rubin, D. (1993). The structure of autobiographical memory. In A. F. Collins, S. E. Gathercole, M. A. Conway, & P. E. Morris (Eds.), *Theories of memory.* Hillsdale, NJ: Erlbaum.

Cooley, E., & Toray, T. (2001). Disordered eating in college freshmen women: A prospective study. *Journal of American College Health, 49,* 229–235.

Cooper, R. M., & Zubek, J. P. (1958). Effects of enriched and restricted early environments on the learning ability of bright and dull rats. *Canadian Journal of Psychology, 12,* 159–164.

Cooper. R. P., Yule, P., Fox, J., & Glasspool, D. W. (2002). *Modeling high-level cognitive processes.* Mahwah, NJ: Erlbaum.

Corballis, P. M., Funnell, M. G., & Gazzaniga, M. S. (2002). Hemispheric asymmetries for simple visual judgments in the split brain. *Neuropsychologia, 40,* 401–410.

Coren, S., & Girus, J. S. (1972). Illusion decrement in intersecting figures. *Psychonomic Science, 26,* 108–110.

Corey, G. (1996). *Theory and practice of counseling and psychotherapy* (5th ed.). Pacific Grove, CA: Brooks/Cole.

Corey, G., & Corey, M. S. (2002). *I never knew I had a choice* (7th ed.). Belmont, CA: Wadsworth.

Cosgrave, E., McGorry, P., Allen, N., & Jackson, H. (2000). Depression in young people: A growing challenge for primary care. *Australian Family Physician, 29,* 123–127.

Cosmides, L., Tooby, J. Cronin, H., & Curry, O. (2003). *What is evolutionary psychology? Explaining the new science of the mind.* New Haven, CT: Yale University Press.

Costa, P. T., & McCrae, R. R. (1992). *Revised NEO personality inventory.* Odessa, FL: Psychological Assessment Resources.

Costa, P. T., & McCrae, R. R. (1995). Solid ground on the wetlands of personality: A reply to Black. *Psychological Bulletin, 117,* 216–220.

Costa, P. T., & McCrae, R. R. (1998). Personality assessment. In H. S. Friedman (Ed.), *Encyclopedia of mental health* (Vol. 3). San Diego: Academic Press.

Cotter, D., Mackay, D., Chana, G., Beasley, C., Landau, S., & Everall, I. P. (2002). Reduced neuronal size and glial density in area 9 of the dorsolateral prefrontal cortex in subjects with major depressive disorder. *Cerebral Cortex, 12,* 386–394.

Coupland, N. J. (2001). Social phobia: Etiology, neurobiology, and treatment. *Journal of Clinical Psychiatry, 62,* (Suppl. 1), 25–35.

Coupland, N. J. (2002). Worry WARTS have generalized anxiety attacks. *Canadian Journal of Psychiatry, 47,* 197.

Cowan, P. A., & Cowan, C. P. (2001). What an intervention design reveals about how parents affect their children's academic achievement and social competence. In J. Borkowski, S. Landesman-Ramey, & M. Bristol (Eds.), *Parenting and the child's world: Multiple influences on intellectual and social-emotional development.* Mahwah, NJ: Erlbaum.

Cowley, G. (1988, May 23). The wisdom of animals. *Newsweek,* pp. 52–58.

Cowley, M. A., Smart, J. L., Rubinstein, M., Cerdan, M. G., Diano, S., Horvath, T. L., Cone, R. D., & Low, M. J. (2001). Leptin activates anorexigenic POMC neurons through a neural network in the arcuate nucleus. *Nature, 411,* 480–484.

Coyne, J. C. (2000). Mood disorders. In A. Kazdin (Ed.), *Encyclopedia of psychology.* Washington, DC, & New York: American Psychological Association and Oxford University Press.

Crabbe, J. C. (2001). Use of genetic analysis to refine phenotypes related to alcohol tolerance and dependence. *Alcoholism: Clinical and Experimental Research, 25,* 288–292.

Crabbe, J. C. (2002). Genetic contributions to alcoholism. *Annual Review of Psychology, 53.*

Craighead, W. E., & Craighead, L. W. (2001). The role of psychotherapy in treating psychiatric disorders. *Medical Clinics of North America, 85,* 617–629.

Craik, F. I. M., & Lockhart, R. S. (1972). Levels of processing; A framework for memory research. *Journal of Verbal Learning and Verbal Behavior, 11,* 671–684.

Craik, F. I. M., & Salthouse, T. A. (Eds.) (2000). *The handbook of aging and cognition.* Mahwah, NJ: Erlbaum.

Craik, F. I. M., & Tulving, E. (1975). Depth of processing and retention of words in episodic memory. *Journal of Experimental Psychology: General, 104,* 268–294.

Cramer, P. (1999). Future directions for the Thematic Apperception Test. *Journal of Personality Assessment, 72,* 74–92.

Cramer, P., & Brilliant, M. A. (2001). Defense use and defense understanding in children. *Journal of Personality, 69,* 297–322.

Crano, W., & Brewer, M. (2002). *Principles and methods of social research* (2nd ed.). Mahwah, NJ: Erlbaum.

Crasilneck, H. B. (1995). The use of the Crasilneck bombardment technique in problems of intractible organic pain. *American Journal of Clinical Hypnosis, 37,* 255–266.

Crawford, M., & Unger, R. (2000). *Women and gender* (2nd ed.). New York: McGraw-Hill.

Crick, F., & Koch, C. (1998). Consciousness and neuroscience. *Cerebral Cortex, 8,* 97–107.

Crocker, J. (2001, August). *The costs of seeking self-esteem.* Paper presented at the meeting of the American Psychological Association, San Francisco.

Crocker, J., Major, B., & Steele, C. (1998). Social stigma. In D. T. Gilbert, S. T. Fiske, & G. Lindzey (Eds.), *Handbook of social psychology* (4th ed., Vol. 2). New York: McGraw-Hill.

Crooks, R., & Bauer, K. (2002). *Our sexuality* (8th ed.). Belmont, CA: Wadsworth.

Crosby, A. E., Cheltenham, M. P., & Sacks, J. J. (1999). Incidence of suicidal ideation and behavior in the United States, 1994. *Suicide and Life-Threatening Behavior, 29,* 131–140.

Crosby, F. J. (1991). *Juggling.* New York: Free Press.

Cross-National Collaborative Group (1992). The changing rate of major depression. *Journal of the American Medical Association, 268,* 3098–3105.

Crouter, A. C., Helms-Erikson, H., Updegraff, K., & McHale, S. M. (1999). Conditions underlying parents' knowledge about children's daily lives in middle childhood: Between- and within-family comparisons. *Child Development, 70,* 246–259.

Crowther, J. H., Sanftner, J., Bonifazi, D. Z., & Shepherd, K. L. (2001). The role of daily hassles in binge eating. *International Journal of Eating Disorders, 29,* 449–454.

Csikszentmihalyi, M. (1995). *Creativity.* New York: HarperCollins.

Csikszentmihalyi, M. (1990). *Flow: The psychology of optimal experience.* New York: HarperPerennial.

Csikszentmihalyi, M. (1996). *Creativity*. New York: HarperCollins.

Csikszentmihalyi, M., & Beattie, O. (1979). Life themes: A theoretical and empirical exploration of their origins and effects. *Journal of Humanistic Psychology, 19*, 677–693.

Csikszentmihalyi, M., & Rathunde, K. (1998). The development of the person: An experiential perspective on the ontogenesis of psychological complexity. In W. Damon (Ed.), *Handbook of child psychology* (5th ed., Vol.1). New York: Wiley.

Cueller, I., & Paniagua, F. A. (Eds.). (2000). *Handbook of multicultural health*. San Diego: Academic Press.

Cuijpers, P. (2001). Mortality and depressive symptoms in inhabitants of residential homes. *International Journal of Geriatric Psychiatry, 16*, 131–138.

Cummings, B., & DeAngelis, G. (2001). The physiology of stereopsis. *Annual Review of Neuroscience* (Vol. 24). Palo Alto, CA: Annual Reviews.

Cummings, M. (2003). *Human heredity (6th Ed.)*. Belmont, CA: Wadsworth.

Curran, K., DuCette, J., Eisenstein, J., & Hyman, I. A. (2001, August). *Statistical analysis of the cross-cultural data: The third year*. Paper presented at the meeting of the American Psychological Association, San Francisco.

Curtiss, S. (1977). *Genie*. New York: Academic Press.

Cushner, K., & Brislin, R. W. (1995). *Intercultural interactions* (2nd ed.). Newbury Park, CA: Sage.

Cutler, B. L., & Penrod, S. D. (1995). *Mistaken identities: The eyewitness, psychology, and the law*. New York: Cambridge University Press.

Cutrona, C. E. (1982). Transition to college: Loneliness and the process of social adjustment. In L. A. Peplau & D. Perlman (Eds.), *Loneliness*. New York: Wiley.

Czienskowski, U., & Giljohann, S. (2002). Intimacy, concreteness, and the "self-reference" effect. *Experimental Psychology, 49*, 73–79.

D

d'Ydewalle, G., Bouckaert, D., & Brunfaut, E. (2001). Age-related differences and complexity of ongoing activities in time- and event-based prospective memory. *American Journal of Psychology, 114*, 411–423.

DaCosta, D., Larouche, J., Dritsa, M., & Brender, W. (2000). Psychosocial correlates of prepartum and postpartum depressed mood. *Journal of Affective Disorders, 59*, 31–40.

Dadds, M. R., Holland, D. E., Barrett, P. M., & Spence, S. H. (1999). Early intervention and prevention of anxiety disorders in children: Results at 2-year follow-up. *Journal of Consulting & Clinical Psychology, 67*, 145–150.

Dalfen, A. K., & Stewart, D. E. (2001). Who develops severe or fatal adverse drug reactions to selective serotonin reuptake inhibitors? *Canadian Journal of Psychology, 46*, 258–263.

Dalton, J. H., Elias, M. J., & Wandersman, A. (2001). *Community psychology*. Belmont, CA: Wadsworth.

Damasio, A. (Ed.). (2001). *The Scientific American book of the brain*. New York: Scientific American.

Dannon, P. N., Dolberg, O. T., Schrieber, S., & Grunhaus, L. (2002). Three and six-month outcome following courses of either ECT or rTMS in a population of severely depressed individuals—preliminary report. *Biological Psychiatry, 51*, 687–690.

Darley, J. M., & Latané, B. (1968). Bystander intervention in emergencies: Diffusion of responsibility. *Journal of Personality and Social Psychology, 8*, 377–383.

Darwin, C. (1979). *The origin of species*. New York: Avenal Books. (Original work published 1859)

Darwin, C. (1965). *The expression of the emotions in man and animals*. Chicago: University of Chicago Press. (Original work published 1872)

Das, J. P. (2000). Mental retardation. In A. Kazdin (Ed.), *Encyclopedia of psychology*. Washington, DC, & New York: American Psychological Association and Oxford University Press.

Dattilio, F. M. (Ed.), *Case studies in couple and family therapy*. New York: Guilford.

Davidson, A. R., & Jacard, J. J. (1979). Variables that moderate the attitude-behavior relation: Results of a longitudinal survey. *Journal of Personality and Social Psychology, 37*, 1364–1376.

Davidson, G. C. & Neale, J. M. (2001). *Abnormal psychology* (8th ed.) New York: Wiley.

Davidson, J. E., & Callery, C. (2001). Care of the obesity surgery patient requiring immediate-level or intensive care. *Obesity Surgery, 11*, 93–97.

Davidson, P. S., Glisky, E. L. (2002). Is flashbulb memory a special instance of source memory? Evidence from older adults. *Memory, 10*, 99–111.

Davidson, R. J. (2000). Affective style, psychopathology, and resilience: Brain mechanisms and plasticity. *American Psychologist, 55*, 196–214.

Davidson, R. J. (1993). The neuropsychology of emotion and affective style. In M. Lewis & J. M. Haviland (Eds.), *Handbook of emotion*. New York: Guilford Press.

Davidson, R. J., Scherer, K. R., & Goldsmith, H. H. (Eds.). (2002). *Handbook of affective sciences*. New York: Oxford University Press.

Davidson, R. J., Shackman, A., & Pizzagalli, D. (2002). The functional neuroanatomy of emotion and affective style. In R. J. Davidson, K. R. Scherer, & H. H. Goldsmith (Eds.), *Handbook of affective sciences*. New York: Oxford University Press.

Davies, K. (2001). *Cracking the genome*. New York: Free Press.

Davis, J. H. (1996). Group decision making and quantitative judgments: A consensus model. In E. H. Witte & J. H. Davis (Eds.), *Understanding group behavior* (Vol. 1). Mahwah, NJ: Erlbaum.

Davison, G. C., & Neale, J. M. (1994). *Abnormal psychology* (6th ed.). New York: Wiley.

Davison, G. C., & Neale, J. M. (2001). *Abnormal psychology* (8th ed.). New York: Wiley.

Day, D. E., & Roberts, M. W. (1983). An analysis of the physical punishment component of a parent training program. *Journal of Abnormal Child Psychology, 11*, 141–152.

De Benedittis, G., & Sironi, V. A. (1985). Deep cerebral electrical activity during the hypnotic state in man: Neurological considerations in hypnosis. *Review of Neurology, 55*, 1–16.

de Boysson-Bardies, B. (2001). *How language comes to children*. Cambridge, MA: MIT Press.

de Jong-Gierveld, J. (1987). Developing and testing a model of loneliness. *Journal of Personality and Social Psychology, 53*, 119–128.

de Lacoste-Utamsing, C., & Holloway, R. L. (1982). Sexual dimorphism in the human corpus callosum. *Science, 216*, 1431–1432.

De Pascalis, V., Magurano, M. R., Bellusci, A., & Chen, A. C. (2001). Somatosensory event-related potential and autonomic activity to varying pain reduction cognitive strategies in hypnosis. *Clinical Neurophysiology, 112*, 1475–1485.

De Valois, K. K. (2000). *Seeing*. San Diego: Academic Press.

Deaux, K. (2001). Social identity. In J. Worell (Ed.), *Encyclopedia of gender and women*. San Diego: Academic Press.

DeBattista, C., Solvason, H. B., & Schatzberg, A. F. (1998). Mood disorders. In H.S. Friedman (Ed.), *Encyclopedia of mental health* (Vol. 2). San Diego: Academic Press.

deCharms, R. (1984). Motivation enhancement in educational settings. In R. Ames & C. Ames (Eds.), *Research on motivation in education* (Vol. 1). Orlando: Academic Press.

Deci, E. L., & Ryan, R. M. (1995). Human autonomy: The basis for true self-esteem. In M. Kernis (Ed.), *Efficacy, agency, and self-esteem*. New York: Plenum.

Deci, E., & Ryan, R. (1994). Promoting self-determined education. *Scandinavian Journal of Educational Research, 38*, 3–14.

Decruyenaere, M., Evers-Kiebooms, G., Welkenhuysen, M., Denayer, L., & Claes, E. (2000). Cognitive representations of breast cancer, emotional distress, and preventive health behavior: A theoretical perspective. *Psychooncology, 9*, 528–536.

Dehaene, S., & Naccache, L. (2001). Towards a neuroscience of consciousness: Basic evidence and a workspace format. *Cognition, 79*, 1–37.

Dell, P. F. (2002). Dissociative phenomena of dissociative identity disorder. *Journal of Nervous and Mental Disorders, 190*, 10–15.

Dell, P. F., & Eisenhower, J. W. (1990). Adolescent multiple personality disorder: A preliminary study of eleven cases. *Journal of the American Academy of Child & Adolescent Psychiatry, 29*, 359–366.

Demakis, G. (1997). Hindsight bias and the Simpson trial: Use in introductory psychology. *Teaching of Psychology, 24*, 190–191.

Dement, W. C. (1978). *Some must watch while some must sleep*. New York: Norton.

Dement, W. C. (1999). *The promise of sleep*. New York: Delacorte Press.

Demerouti, E., Bakker, A. B., Nachreiner, F., & Schaufeli, W. B. (2001). The job demands-resources model of burnout. *Journal of Applied Psychology, 86*, 499–512.

Denmark, F. L., Russo, N. F., Frieze, I. H., & Eschuzur, J. (1988). Guidelines for avoiding sexism in psychological research: A report of the ad hoc committee on nonsexist research. *American Psychologist, 43*, 582–585.

Derryberry, D., & Reed, M. (2002). Information processing approaches to individual differences in emotional reactivity. In R. J. Davidson, K. R. Scherer & H. H. Goldsmith (Eds.), *Handbook of affective sciences*. New York: Oxford University Press.

DeRubeis, R. J., & Crits-Cristoph, P. (1998). Empirically supported individual and group psychological treatments for adult mental disorders. *Journal of Consulting and Clinical Psychology, 66,* 37–52.

Deutsch, M., & Collins, M. (1951). *Interracial housing: A psychological evaluation of a social experiment.* Minneapolis: University of Minnesota Press.

DeVellis, B. M., & DeVellis, R. F. (2001). Self-efficacy and health. In A. Baum, T. A. Revenson, & J. E. Singer (Eds.), *Handbook of health psychology.* Mahwah, NJ: Erlbaum.

Devi, G., & Silver, J. (2000). Approaches to memory loss in neuropsychiatric disorders. *Seminars in Clinical Neuropsychiatry, 5,* 259–265.

Devine, P. G., Evett, S. R., & Vasquez-Suson, K. A. (1996). Exploring the interpersonal dynamics of intergroup contact. In R. M. Sorrentino & E. T. Higgins (Eds.), *Handbook of motivation and cognition: The interpersonal context* (Vol. 3). New York: Guilford Press.

Devlin, M. J., Golfein, J. A., Crino, J. S., & Wolk, S. L. (2000). Open treatment of overweight binge eaters with phentermine and fluoxetine as an adjunct to cognitive-behavioral.

Devries, L. K. (1998). *Insomnia.* New York: Harold Shaw.

Dewey, J. (1933). *How we think.* Lexington, MA: Heath.

Dickens, W. T., & Flynn, J. R. (2001). Heritability estimates versus large environmental effects: The IQ paradox resolved. *Psychological Review, 108,* 346–369.

Dickson, G. L. (1990). A feminist post-structuralist analysis of the knowledge of menopause. *Advances in Nursing Science, 12,* 15–31.

Diener, E. (2000). Subjective well-being: The science of happiness and a proposal for a national index. *American Psychologist, 55,* 34–43.

Diener, E. (1984). Subjective well-being. *Psychological Bulletin, 109,* 542–575.

Diener, E. (1999). Introduction to the special section on the structure of emotion. *Journal of Personality and Social Psychology, 76,* 803–804.

Diener, E., & Seligman, M. E. P. (2002). Very happy people. *Psychological Science, 13,* 81–84.

Diener, E., Lucas, R. E., & Oishi, S. (2001). The science of happiness and life satisfaction. In C. R. Snyder & S. J. Lopez (Eds.), *Handbook of positive psychology.* New York: Oxford University Press.

Diener, E., Suh, E. M., Lucas, R. E., & Smith, H. L. (1999). Subjective well-being: Three decades of progress. *Psychological Bulletin, 125,* 276–301.

DiGiacomo, M., & Adamson, B. (2001). Coping with stress in the workplace: Implications for new health professionals. *Journal of Allied Health, 30,* 106–111.

Dillon, K. M., Minchoff, B., & Baker, K. H. (1985/1986). Positive emotional states and enhancement of the immune system. *International Journal of Psychiatry in Medicine, 15,* 13–17.

DiMatteo, M. R., & Martin, L. R. (2002). *Health psychology.* Boston: Allyn & Bacon.

Dinsmoor, J. A. (1998). Punishment. In W. O'Donohue (Ed.), *Learning and behavior therapy.* Boston: Allyn & Bacon.

Dobzhansky, T. G. (1977). *Evolution.* New York: Freeman.

Dodd, D. K. (1995). Robbers in the classroom: A deindividuation exercise. In M. E. Ware & D. E. Johnson (Eds.), *Demonstrations*

and activities in teaching of psychology (Vol. 3). Mahwah, NJ: Erlbaum.

Dohm, F. A., Beattie, J. A., Aibel, C., & Striegel-Moore, R. H. (2001). Factors differentiating women and men who successfully maintain weight loss from women and men who do not. *Journal of Clinical Psychology, 57,* 105–117.

Dohrenwend, B. S., & Shrout, P. E. (1985). "Hassles" in the conceptualization and measurement of life event stress variables. *American Psychologist, 40,* 780–785.

Dollard, J., Doob, L. W., Miller, N. E., Mowrer, O. H., & Sears, R. R. (1939). *Frustration and aggression.* New Haven, CT: Yale University Press.

Dolphin, W. D. (2002). *Biological investigations* (6th ed.). New York: McGraw-Hill.

Domhoff, G. W. (1999). New directions in the study of dream content using the Hall/Van de Castle coding system. *Dreaming, 9,* 115–137.

Domhoff, G. W. (2001). A new neurocognitive theory of dreams. *Dreaming, 11,* 13–33.

Domhoff, G. W., & Schneider, A. (1998). New rationales and methods for quantitative dream research outside the laboratory. *Sleep, 21,* 398–404.

Domino, G. (2000). *Psychological testing.* Upper Saddle River, NJ: Prentice-Hall.

Domjan, M. P. (1996). *Essentials of conditioning and learning.* Pacific Grove, CA: Brooks/Cole.

Donnerstein, E. (2001). Media violence. In J. Worell (Ed.), *Encyclopedia of gender and women.* San Diego: Academic Press.

Dooley, D. (2001). *Social science research methods* (4th ed.). Upper Saddle River, NJ: Prentice Hall.

Doran, S. M., Van Dongen, H. P., & Dinges, D. F. (2001). Sustained attention performance during sleep deprivation. *Archives of Italian Biology, 139,* 253–267.

Dorn, L. D., & Chrousos, G. P. (1996, March). *Behavioral predictors of stress hormone responses.* Paper presented at the meeting of the Society for Research on Adolescence, Boston.

Doty, R. L. (2001). Olfaction. *Annual Review of Psychology* (Vol. 52). Palo Alto, CA: Annual Reviews.

Dougall, A. L., & Baum, A. (2001). Stress, health, and illness. In A. Baum, T.A. Revenson, & J.E. Singer (Eds.), *Handbook of health psychology.* Mahwah, NJ: Erlbaum.

Dougherty, D. M., Cherek, D. R., & Bennett, R. H. (1996). The effects of alcohol on the aggressive responding of women. *Journal of Alcohol Studies, 57,* 178–186.

Dovidio, J. E., & Penner, L. A. (2001). Helping and altruism. In M. Hewstone & M. Brewer (Eds.), *Handbook of social psychology.* London: Blackwell.

Dowd, E. T. (2002). Self-statement modification. In M. Hersen & W. H. Sledge (Eds.), *Encyclopedia of psychotherapy.* San Diego: Academic Press.

Draguns, J. G. (1990). Applications of cross-cultural psychology in the field of mental health. In R. W. Brislin (Ed.), *Applied cross-cultural psychology.* Newbury Park, CA: Sage.

Drevets, W. C. (2001). Neuroimaging and neuropathological studies of depression: Implications for the cognitive-emotional features of mood disorders. *Current Opinions in Neurobiology, 11,* 240–249.

Drobes, D. J., Miller, E. J., Hillman, C. H., Bradley, M. M., Cuthbart, B. N., & Lang,

P. J. (2001). Food deprivation and emotional reaction to food cues: Implications for eating disorders. *Biological Psychology, 57,* 153–177.

Druckman, D., & Bjork, R. A. (Eds.) (1994). *Learning, remembering, and believing.* Washington, DC: National Academy Press.

Dryfoos, J. G. (1990). *Adolescents at risk: Prevalence and prevention.* New York: Oxford University Press.

Duffy, K. (2003). *Community psychology* (3rd Ed.). Boston: Allyn & Bacon.

Duffy, K., & Wong, F. K. (2003). *Community psychology* (3rd Ed.). Boston: Allyn & Bacon.

Duka, T., Weissenborn, R., & Dienes, Z. (2001). State-dependent effects of alcohol on recollective experiences, familiarity, and awareness of memory. *Psychopharmacology, 153,* 293–306.

Dunne, M. (2002). Sampling considerations. In M. W. Wiederman & B. E. Whitley (Eds.), *Handbook for conducting research on human sexuality.* Mahwah, NJ: Erlbaum.

Dunner, D. L. (2001). Acute and maintenance treatment of chronic depression. *Journal of Clinical Psychiatry, 62* (Suppl. 6), 10–16.

Dunner, D. L., Hendricksen, H. E., Bea, C., Budech, C. B., & Friedman, S. D. (2002). Dysthmic disorder: Treatment with citalopram. *Depression and Anxiety, 15,* 18–22.

Dunnett, S. B. (1989). Neural transplantation: Normal brain function and repair after damage. *Psychologist, 1,* 4–8.

Durgin, F. H. (2000). Sensory adaptation. In A. Kazdin (Ed.), *Encyclopedia of psychology.* Washington, DC, & New York: American Psychological Association and Oxford University Press.

Durrant, J. E. (2000). Trends in youth crime and well-being since the abolition of corporal punishment in Sweden. *Youth and Society, 31*(4), 437–455.

Dutton, D., & Aron, A. (1974). Some evidence for heightened sexual attraction under conditions of high anxiety. *Journal of Personality and Social Psychology, 30,* 510–517.

Dutton, R. C., Maurer, A. J., Sonner, J. M., Fanselow, M. S., Laster, M. J., & Eger, E. I. (2002). Isoflurane causes anterograde but not retrograde amnesia for Pavlovian fear conditioning. *Anesthesiology, 96,* 1223–1229.

Dweck, C. (1996). Social motivation: Goals and social-cognitive processes. In J. Juvonen & K. R. Wentzel (Eds.), *Social motivation.* New York: Cambridge University Press.

E

Eagly, A. (2001). Social role theory of sex differences and similarities. In J. Worell (Ed.), *Encyclopedia of women and gender.* San Diego: Academic Press.

Eagly, A. (2002). Social role theory of sex differences and similarities. In J. Worell (Ed.), *Encyclopedia of women and gender.* New York: Oxford University Press.

Eagly, A. H. (1997, August). *Social roles as an origin theory for sex-related differences.* Paper presented at the meeting of the American Psychological Association, Chicago.

Eagly, A. H. (2000). Gender roles. In A. Kazdin (Ed.), *Encyclopedia of psychology.* Washington, DC, and New York: American Psychological Association and Oxford University Press.

Eagly, A. H., & Chaiken, S. (1998). Attitude structure and function. In D. T. Gilbert, S. T. Fiske, & G. Lindzey (Eds.), *Handbook of social psychology* (4th ed., Vol. 2). New York: McGraw-Hill.

Eagly, A. H., & Crowley, M. (1986). Gender and helping behavior: A meta-analytic review of the social psychological literature. *Psychological Bulletin, 100,* 283–308.

Eagly, A. H., & Steffen, V. J. (1986). Gender and aggressive behavior: A meta-analytic review of the social psychological literature. *Psychological Bulletin, 111,* 3–22.

Ebata, A. T., & Moos, R. H. (1989, April). *Coping and adjustment in four groups of adolescents.* Paper presented at the meeting of the Society for Research in Child Development, Kansas City.

Eccles, J. S., & Wiegfield, A. (2002). Motivational beliefs, values, and goals. *Annual Review of Psychology, 53,* 109–132.

Eccles, J. S., Wigfield, A., & Schiefele, U. (1998). Motivation to succeed. In W. Damon (Ed.), *Handbook of child psychology* (Vol. 3). New York: Wiley.

Eckert, E. D., Heston, L. L., & Bouchard, T. J. (1981). MZ twins reared apart. In L. Gedda, P. Paris, & W. D. Nance (Eds.), *Twin research* (Vol. 1). New York: Alan Liss.

Edinger, J. D., Wohlgemuth, W. K., Radtke, R. A., Marsh, G. R., & Quillian, R. E. (2001). Cognitive behavioral therapy for treatment of chronic primary insomnia. *Journal of the American Medical Association, 285,* 1856–1864.

Educational Testing Service (1992, February). *Cross-national comparisons of 9–13 year-olds' science and math achievement.* Princeton, NJ: Educational Testing Service.

Edwards, B. (1979). *Drawing on the right side of the brain.* Los Angeles: Tarcher.

Edwards, C. D. (1999). *How to handle a hard-to-handle kid.* Los Angeles: Free Spirit Pub.

Edwards, C. P., & Liu, W. (2002). Parenting toddlers. In M. H. Bornstein (Ed.), *Handbook of parenting* (2nd ed.). Mahwah, NJ: Erlbaum.

Edwards, J. R., & Rothbard, N. P. (1999). Work and family stress and well-being: An examination of person-environment fit in the work and family domains. *Organizational Behavior and Human Decision Processes, 77,* 85–129.

Ehrhardt, A. A. (1987). A transactional perspective on the development of gender differences. In J. M. Reinisch, L. A. Rosenblum, & S. A. Sanders (Eds.), *Masculinity/femininity: Basic perspectives.* New York: Oxford University Press.

Eibl-Eibesfeldt, I. (1977). Evolution of destructive aggression. *Aggressive Behavior, 3,* 127–144.

Eimer, B. N. (2000). Clinical applications of hypnosis for brief and efficient pain management psychotherapy. *American Journal of Clinical Hypnosis, 43,* 17–40.

Einstein, G. O., & McDaniel, M. A. (1996). Remembering to do things: Remembering a forgotten topic. In D. J. Hermann, C. McEvoy, C. Hertzog, P. Hertel, & M. K. Johnson (Eds.), *Basic and applied memory research: Practical applications* (Vol. 2). Mahwah, NJ: Erlbaum.

Einstein, G. O., McDaniel, M. A., Mazi, M., Cochran, B., & Baker, M. (2000). Prospective memory and aging: Forgetting inten-

tions over short delays. *Psychology and Aging, 15,* 671–683.

Eisenberg, N., & Murphy, B. (1995). Parenting and children's moral development. In M. H. Bornstein (Ed.), *Children and parenting* (Vol. 4). Hillsdale, NJ: Erlbaum.

Eisenberg, N., & Valiente, C. (2002). Parenting and children's prosocial and moral development. In M. H. Bornstein (Ed.), *Handbook of parenting* (2nd ed.). Mahwah, NJ: Erlbaum.

Eissenberg, T., Stitzer, M. L., & Henningfield, J. E. (1999). Current issues in nicotine replacement. In D. F. Seidman & L. S. Covey (Eds.), *Helping the hard-core smoker.* Mahwah, NJ: Erlbaum.

Ekman, P. (1980). *The face of man.* New York: Garland.

Ekman, P. (1996). Lying and deception. In N. L. Stein, C. Brainerd, P. A. Ornstein, & B. Tversky (Eds.), *Memory for everyday emotional events.* Mahwah, NJ: Erlbaum.

Ekman, P., & Friesen, W. V. (1968). The repertoire of nonverbal behavior—Categories, origins, usage, and coding. *Semiotica, 1,* 49–98.

Ekman, P., & Friesen, W. V. (1971). Constants across cultures in the face and emotion. *Journal of Personality and Social Psychology, 17,* 124–129.

Ekman, P., & O'Sullivan, M. (1991). Facial expressions: Methods, means, and moues. In R. S. Feldman & B. Rime (Eds.), *Fundamentals of nonverbal behavior.* Cambridge: Cambridge University Press.

Ekman, P., Levenson, R. W., & Friesen, W. V. (1983). Autonomic nervous system activity distinguishes among emotions. *Science, 223,* 1208–1210.

Eliasson, A., Eliasson, A., King, J., Gould, B., & Eliasson, A. (2002). Association of sleep and academic performance. *Sleep and Breathing, 6,* 45–48.

Eliot, L. (2001). *What's going on in there? How the brain and mind develop in the first five years of life.* New York: Bantam Doubleday.

Elkind, D. (1978). Understanding the young adolescent. *Adolescence, 13,* 127–134.

Ellemers, N., Spears, R., & Doosje, B. (2002). Self and social identity. *Annual Review of Psychology* (Vol. 53). Palo Alto, CA: Annual Reviews.

Elliott, B. A., Beattie, M. K., & Kaitfors, S. E. (2001). Health needs of people living below the poverty level. *Family Medicine, 33,* 361–366.

Ellis, A. (1962). *Reason and emotion in psychotherapy.* New York: Lyle Stuart.

Ellis, A. (1996). A rational-emotive behavior therapist's perspective on Ruth. In G. Corey (Ed.), *Case approach to counseling and psychotherapy.* Pacific Grove, CA: Brooks/Cole.

Ellis, A. (2000). Rational emotive behavior therapy. In A. Kazdin (Ed.), *Encyclopedia of Psychology,* Washington, DC, and New York: American Psychological Association and Oxford University Press.

Ellis, A. (2002). Rational emotive behavior therapy. In M. Hersen & W. H. Sledge (Eds.), *Encyclopedia of psychotherapy.* San Diego: Academic Press.

Ellis, H. C. (1987). Recent developments in human memory. In V. P. Makosky (Ed.), *The G. Stanley Hall Lecture Series.* Washington, DC: American Psychological Association.

Ellis, L., & Ames, M. A. (1987). Neurohormonal functioning and sexual orientation. *Psychological Bulletin, 101,* 233–258.

Ellsworth, P. C. (2002). Appraisal processes in emotion. In R. J. Davidson, K. R. Scherer, & H. H. Goldsmith (Eds.), *Handbook of affective sciences.* New York: Oxford University Press.

Elmes, D. G., Kantowitz, B. H., & Roediger, H. L. (2003). *Research methods in psychology (7th Ed.).* Belmont, CA: Wadsworth.

Empson, J. A. C., & Clarke, P. R. F. (1970). Rapid eye movements and remembering. *Nature, 227,* 287–288.

Endler, N. S. (1995). *Personality theories* (4th ed.). Fort Worth: Harcourt Brace.

Engel, A. K. & Singer, W. (2001). Temporal binding and the neural correlates of sensory awareness. *Trends in Cognitive Science, 5,* 16–25.

Enger, E., & Ross, F. (2003). *Concepts in biology* (10th ed.). New York: McGraw-Hill.

Enoch, M. A., & Goldman, D. (2002). Problem drinking and alcoholism: diagnosis and treatment. *American Family Physician, 65,* 449–450.

Enstrom, J. E. (1999). Smoking cessation and mortality trends among two United States populations. *Journal of Clinical Epidemiology, 52,* 813–825.

Ephraim, D. (2000). Culturally relevant research and practice with the Rorschach comprehensive system in Iberoamerica. In R. H. Dana (Ed.), *Handbook of cross-cultural and multicultural personality assessment.* Mahwah, NJ: Erlbaum.

Eppley, K. R., Abrams, A. I., & Shear, J. (1989). Differential effects of relaxation effects on trait anxiety. *Journal of Clinical Psychology, 45,* 957–974.

Epstein, N. B., & Baucom, D. H. (2002). *Enhanced cognitive-behavioral therapy for couples.* Washington, DC: American Psychological Association.

Ericsson, K. A., Krampe, R. T., & Tesch-Römer, C. (1993). The role of deliberate practice in the acquisition of expert performance. *Psychological Review, 100,* 363–406.

Eriksen, T. H. (2001). Ethnic identity, national identity, and intergroup conflict: The significance of personal experiences. In R. D. Ashmore, L. Jussim, & D. Wilder (Eds.), *Social identity, intergroup conflict, and conflict resolution.* New York: Oxford University Press.

Erikson, E. H. (1968). *Identity: Youth and crisis.* New York: Norton.

Erikson, E. H. (1969). *Gandhi's truth.* New York: Norton.

Erwin, B. A., Heimberg, R. G., Juster, H., & Mindlin, M. (2002). Comorbid anxiety and mood disorders among persons with social anxiety disorder. *Behavior Therapy and Research, 40,* 19–35.

Etaugh, C., & Bridges, J. S. (2001). *Psychology of women: A life-span perspective.* Boston: Allyn & Bacon.

European Agency for Safety and Health at Work. (2000). *Research on work-related stress.* Retrieved November 15, 2001, from http://agency.osha.eu.int/

Evans, D. L. (1999). Introduction: Assessing antidepressant effectiveness. *Journal of Clinical Psychology, 60,* (Suppl. 4), 3.

Evans, D. L., Herbert, J. D., Nelson-Gray, R. O., & Gaudiano, B. A. (2002). Determinants of diagnostic prototypicality judgments of the personality disorders. *Journal of Personality Disorders, 16,* 95–106.

Evertson, C. M., Emmer, E. T., & Worsham, M. E. (2003). *Classroom management for elementary teachers,* (5th ed.). Boston: Allyn & Bacon.

Eysenck, H. J. (1952). The effects of psychotherapy: An evaluation. *Journal of Consulting Psychology, 16,* 319–324.

Eysenck, H. J. (1967). *The biological basis of personality.* Springfield, IL: Thomas.

Ezzo, J., Hadhazy, V., Birch, S., Lao, L., Kaplan, G., Hochberg, M., & Berman, B. (2001). *Acupuncture for osteoarthritis of the knee: A systematic review.* Unpublished manuscript, Project LEAD, Washington, DC.

F

Faneslow, M. S., DeCola, J. P., & Young, S. L. (1993). Mechanisms responsible for reduced contextual conditioning with masses unsignaled unconditioned stimuli. *Journal of Experimental Psychology: Animal Processes, 19,* 121–127.

Fava, G. A., Rafanelli, C., Ottolini, F., Ruini, C., Cazzaro, M., & Grandi, S. (2001). Psychological well-being and residual symptoms in remitted patients with panic disorder and agoraphobia. *Journal of Affective Disorders, 65,* 185–190.

Fazio, R. H., Chen, J., McDonel, E. C., & Sherman, S. J. (1982). Attitude accessibility, attitude-behavior consistency, and the strength of the object-evaluation association. *Journal of Experimental Social Psychology, 18,* 339–357.

Fehr, B., & Broughton, R. (2001). Gender and personality differences in conceptions of love: An interpersonal theory analysis. *Personal Relationships, 8,* 115–136.

Feighner, J. P. (1999). Mechanisms of action of antidepressant medications. *Journal of Clinical Psychology, 60* (Suppl. 4), 4–13.

Fein, S., Goethals, G. R., Kassin, S. M., & Cross, J. (1993, August). *Social influence and presidential debates.* Paper presented at the meeting of the American Psychological Association, Toronto.

Feist, J., & Feist, G. J. (2002). *Theories of personality* (5th ed.). New York: McGraw-Hill.

Feldhusen, J. (1999). Giftedness and creativity. In M. A. Runco & S. Pritzker (Eds.), *Encyclopedia of creativity.* San Diego: Academic Press.

Feldman, D. H. (1997, August). *Hitting middle C: Toward a more comprehensive domain for creativity research.* Paper presented at the meeting of the American Psychological Association, Chicago.

Feldman, R. (1999, January). Commentary in Murray, B.: This architect builds a career in psychology. *APA Monitor,* p. 13.

Feng, A. S., & Ratnam, R. (2000). Neural basis of hearing in real world situations. *Annual Review of Psychology* (Vol. 51). Palo Alto, CA: Annual Reviews.

Fergusson, D. M., & Woodward, L. J. (2002). Mental health, educational, and social role outcomes of adolescents with depression. *Archives of General Psychiatry, 59,* 225–231.

Feshbach, S., & Weiner, B. (1996). *Personality* (4th ed.). Lexington, MA: Heath.

Festinger, L. (1954). A theory of social comparison processes. *Human Relations, 7,* 117–140.

Festinger, L. (1957). *A theory of cognitive dissonance.* Evanston, IL: Row Peterson.

Field, T. (2001). Massage therapy facilitates weight gain in preterm infants. *Current Directions in Psychological Science, 10,* 51–53.

Field, T. M. (1998). Massage therapy effects. *American Psychologist, 53,* 1270–1281.

Field, T. M. (Ed.) (1995). *Touch in early development.* Mahwah, NJ: Erlbaum.

Field, T. M., Grizzle, N., Scafidi, F., & Schanberg, S. (1996). Massage and relaxation therapies' effects on depressed adolescent mothers. *Adolescence, 31,* 903–911.

Field, T. M., Scafidi, F., & Schanberg, S. (1987). Massage of preterm newborns to improve growth and development. *Pediatric Nursing, 13,* 386–388.

Field, T., Schanberg, S. M., Scafidi, F., Bauer, C. R., Vega-Lahr, N., Garcia, R., Nystrom, J., & Kuhn, C. M. (1986). Tactile/kinesthetic stimulation effects on preterm neonates. *Pediatrics, 77,* 654–658.

Fielder, F. E. (1978). Contingency model and the leadership process. In L. Berkowitz (Ed.), *Advances in experimental social psychology* (Vol. 11). New York: Academic Press.

Fifer, B., & Grose-Fifer, J. (2002). Prenatal development and risk. In A. Fogel & G. Bremner (Eds.), *Blackwell handbook of infant development.* London: Blackwell.

Filley, C. M., Price, B. H., Nell, V., Morgan, A. S., Bresnahan, J. F., Pincus, J. H., Gelbort, M. M., Weissberg, M., & Kelly, J. P. (2001). Toward an understanding of violence: Neurobehavioral aspects of unwarranted physical aggression. *Neuropsychiatry, 14,* 1–14.

Fils-Aime, M. -L., Eckardt, M. J., George, D. T., Brown, G. L., Mefford, I., & Linnoila, M. (1996). Early-onset alcoholics have lower cerebrospinal fluid 5-hydroxyindoleacetic acid levels than late-onset alcoholics. *Archives of General ***

First, M. B., & Pincus, H. A. (2002). The DSM-IV text revision: Rationale and potential impact on clinical practice. *Psychiatric Services, 53,* 288–292.

Fisch, S. M., & Truglio, R. T. (Eds.). (2001). *"G" is for growing: Thirty years of research on children and Sesame Street.* Mahwah, NJ: Erlbaum.

Fischer, A. R., Jome, L. R., & Atkinson, D. R. (1998). Reconceptualizing multicultural counseling: Universal healing conditions in a culturally specific context. *Counseling Psychologist, 26,* 525–588.

Fischer, J., & Gochros, H. L. (1975). *Planned behavior change.* New York: Free Press.

Fishbein, H. D. (2002). *Peer prejudice and discrimination* (2nd ed.). Mahwah, NJ: Erlbaum.

Fiske, S. T. (1998). Stereotyping, prejudice, and discrimination. In D. T. Gilbert, S. T. Fiske, & G. Lindzey (Eds.), *The handbook of social psychology* (4th ed., Vol. 2). New York: McGraw-Hill.

Flavell, J. H., Miller, P. H., & Miller, S. A. (2002). *Cognitive development* (4th ed.). Upper Saddle River, NJ: Prentice-Hall.

Fleming, J. S., & Courtney, B. E. (1984). The dimensionality of self-esteem. *Journal of Personality and Social Psychology, 46,* 404–421.

Fleming, P. (2002, February). *AIDS and HIV prevalence in the United States.* Paper presented at the Conference on Retroviruses, Seattle.

Fletcher, J. S., & Banasik, J. L. (2001). Exercise self-efficacy. *Clinical Excellence in Nursing Practice, 5,* 134–143.

Flynn, J. R. (1999). Searching for justice: The discovery of IQ gains over time. *American Psychologist, 54,* 5–20.

Foa, E. D., & Riggs, D. S. (1995). Posttraumatic stress disorder following assault: Theoretical considerations and empirical findings. *Current Directions in Psychological Science, 4,* 61–65.

Fodor, I., & Epstein, J. (2002). Agoraphobia, panic disorder, and gender. In J. Worell (Ed.), *Encyclopedia of women and gender.* San Diego: Academic Press.

Fogel, A. (2001). *Infancy* (4th ed.). Belmont, CA: Wadsworth.

Fogoros, R.N. (2001). *Does stress really cause heart disease?* Retrieved October 10, 2001, from http://www.about.com

Folkman, S., & Lazarus, R. S. (1980). An analysis of coping in a middle-aged community sample. *Journal of Health and Social Behavior, 21,* 219–239.

Forbes, R. J., & Jackson, P. R. (1980). Nonverbal behavior and the outcome of selection interviews. *Journal of Occupational Psychology, 53,* 65–72.

Ford, J. D. (1999). Disorders of extreme stress following war-zone military trauma: Associated features of posttraumatic stress disorder or comorbid but distinct syndromes? *Journal of Consulting and Clinical Psychology, 67,* 3–12.

Forgas, J. P. (Ed.). (2001). *Handbook of affect and social cognition.* Mahwah, NJ: Erlbaum.

Forshaw, M. (2002). *Essential health psychology.* New York: Oxford University Press.

Forsyth, J. P., & Savsevitz, J. (2002). Behavior therapy: Historical perspective and overview. In M. Hersen & W. H. Sledge (Eds.), *Encyclopedia of psychotherapy.* San Diego: Academic Press.

Fortin, N. J. Agster, K. L., & Eichenbaum, H. B. (2002). Critical role of the hippocampus in memory for sequence of events. *Nature Neuroscience, 5,* 458–462.

Foulkes, D. (1993). Cognitive dream theory. In M.A. Carskadon (Ed.), *Encyclopedia of sleep and dreams.* New York: Macmillan.

Foulkes, D. (1999). *Children's dreaming and the development of consciousness.* Cambridge, MA: Harvard University Press.

Foulks, E. (2002). Cultural issues. In M. Hersen & W. H. Sledge (Eds.), *Encyclopedia of psychotherapy.* San Diego: Academic Press.

Fowler, C. A., Wolford, G., Slade, R., & Tassinary, L. (1981). Lexical access without awareness. *Journal of Experimental Psychology: General, 110,* 341–362.

Fox, B., & Hull, M. (2002). *Phonics for the teacher of reading* (8th ed.). Upper Saddle River, NJ: Prentice-Hall.

Fox, S. I. (1996). *Human physiology* (5th ed.). New York: McGraw-Hill.

Frank, J. D. (1982). Therapeutic components shared by all psychotherapies. In J. H. Harvey & M. M. Parks (Eds.), *Psychotherapy research and behavior change.* Washington, DC: American Psychological Association.

Frankl, V. (1984). *Man's search for meaning.* New York: Pocket Books.

Fraser, S. (Ed.). (1995). *The bell curve wars: Race, intelligence, and the future of America.* New York: Basic Books.

Frederich, R. C., Hamann, A., Anderson, S., & others (1995). Leptin levels reflect body lipid content in mice: Evidence for diet-induced resistance to leptin action. *Nature Medicine, 1,* 1311–1314.

Frederickson, B. L. (2001). The role of positive emotions in positive psychology. *American Psychologist, 56,* 218–226.

Frederickson, B. L., & Joiner, T. (2002). Positive emotions trigger upward spirals of well being. *Psychological Science, 13,* 172–176.

Frederickson, B. L., & Joiner, T. (2000). *Positive emotions trigger upward spirals toward emotional well-being.* Unpublished manuscript, University of Michigan, Ann Arbor, Department of Psychology.

Frederickson, B. L., & Levenson, R. W. (1998). Positive emotions speed recovery from the cardiovascular sequelae of negative emotions. *Cognition and Emotion, 12,* 191–220.

Frederikse, M., Lu, A., Aylward, E., Barta, P., Sharma, T., & Pearlson, G. (2000). Sex differences in inferior lobule volume in schizophrenia. *American Journal of Psychiatry, 157,* 422–427.

Freed, C. R., Greene, P. E., Breeze, R. E., Tsai, W. Y., DuMouchel, W., Kao, R., Dillon, S., Winfield, H., Culver, S., Trojanowksi, J. Q., Eidelberg, D., & Fahn, S. (2001). Transplantation of embryonic dopamine neurons for severe Parkinson's disease. *New England Journal of Medicine, 344,* 710–719.

Freedman, J. L. (1984). Effects of television violence on aggressiveness. *Psychological Bulletin, 96,* 227–246.

Freeman, A., & Reinecke, M. A. (1995). Cognitive therapy. In A. S. Gurman (Ed.), *Essential psychotherapies.* New York: Guilford Press.

Freeman, T. W., & Roca, V. (2001). Gun use, attitudes toward violence, and aggression among combat veterans with chronic post-traumatic stress disorder. *Journal of Nervous and Mental Disorders, 189,* 317–320.

Freud, S. (1917). *A general introduction to psychoanalysis.* New York: Washington Square Press.

Freud, S. (1953). The interpretation of dreams. In J. Strachey (Ed.), *The standard edition of the complete psychological works of Sigmund Freud.* New York: Washington Square Press. (Original work published 1900)

Friedman, H. S., & Schustack, M. W. (1999). *Personality: Classic theories and modern research.* Boston: Allyn & Bacon.

Friedman, J. I., Temporini, H., & Davis, K. L. (1999). Pharmacologic strategies for augmenting cognitive performance in schizophrenia. *Biological Psychiatry, 45,* 1–16.

Friedman, M. A., & Brownell, K. A. (1998). Obesity. In H. S. Friedman (Ed.), *Encyclopedia of mental health* (Vol. 3). San Diego: Academic Press.

Friedman, M., & Rosenman, R. (1974). *Type A behavior and your heart.* New York: Knopf.

Friedman, R., Myers, P., & Benson, H. (1998). Meditation and the relaxation response. In H.S. Friedman (Ed.), *Encyclopedia of mental health* (Vol. 2). San Diego: Academic Press.

Friedrich, F. (2001). *Cognitive psychology 3120: Online notes.* Retrieved from http://www. psych.utah.edu/friedrich/friedrich.html.

Frieman, J. L. (2002). *Learning and adaptive behavior.* Belmont, CA: Wadsworth.

Fromm, E. (1947). *Man for himself.* New York: Holt, Rinehart & Winston.

Frost, R. O., & Steketee, G. (1998). Obsessive-compulsive disorder. In H. S. Friedman (Ed.), *Encyclopedia of mental health* (Vol. 3). San Diego: Academic Press.

Fry, A. F., & Hale, S. (2000). Relationships among processing speed, working memory, and fluid intelligence in children. *Biological Psychology, 54,* 1–34.

Fu, Q., Heath, A. C., Bucholz, K. K., Nelson, E. C., Glowinski, A. L., Goldberg, J., Lyons, M. J., Tsuang, M. T., Jacob, T., True, M. R., & Eisen, M. A. (2002). A twin study of genetic and environmental influences on suicidality in men. *Psychological Medicine, 32,* 11–24.

Funder, D. C. (2001). Personality. *Annual Review of Psychology, 52.* Palo Alto, CA: Annual Reviews.

Fung, H. H., Carstensen, L. L., & Lang, F. R. (2001). Age-related patterns in social networks among European Americans and African Americans. *International Journal of Aging and Human Development, 52,* 185–206.

Furnham, A. (1988). Write and wrong: The validity of graphological analysis. *Skeptical Inquirer, 13,* 64–69.

Furth, H. (1971). Linguistic deficiency and thinking: Research with deaf subjects. *Psychological Bulletin, 75,* 52–58.

Furth, H. G., & Wachs, H. (1975). *Thinking goes to school.* New York: Oxford University Press.

Furumoto, L. (1991). "Paired associates" to a psychology of self: The intellectual odyssey of Mary Whiton Calkins. In G. A. Kimble, M. Wertheimer, & C. L. White, (1991), *Portraits of pioneers in psychology.* Washington, DC: American Psychological Association.

G

Gage, F. H. (2000). Mammalian neural stem cells. *Science, 287,* 1433–1438.

Gage, F. H., & Bjorklund, A. (1986). Cholinergic septal grafts into the hippocampal formation improve spatial learning and memory in aged rats by an atropine-sensitive mechanism. *Journal of Neuroscience, 6,* 2837–2847.

Gallup Organization (1999). *The 31st annual Phi Delta Kappa/Gallup Poll.* Princeton, NJ: Author.

Garb, H. N., Wood, J. M., Nezworski, M. T., Grove, W. M., & Stejskal, W. J. (2001). Toward a resolution of the Rorschach controversy. *Psychological Assessment, 13,* 433–448.

Garbarino, S., Beelke, M., Costa, G., Violani, C., Lucidi, F., Ferrillo, F., & Sannita, G. (2002). Brain function and effects of shift work: implications for clinical neuropharmacology. *Neuropsychobiology, 45,* 50–56.

Garcia, E. E., Bravo, M. A., Dickey, L. M., Cun, K., & Sun-Irminger, X. (2002). Rethinking school reform in the context of cultural and linguistic diversity. In L. Minaya-Rowe (Ed.), *Teaching training and effective pedagogy in the context of cultural diversity.* Greenwich, CT: IAP.

Garcia, J. (1989). Food for Tolman: Cognition and cathexis in concert. In T. Archer & L. Nilsson (Eds.), *Aversion, avoidance, and anxiety.* Mahwah, NJ: Erlbaum.

Garcia, J., Ervin, F. E., & Koelling, R. A. (1966). Learning with prolonged delay of reinforcement. *Psychonomic Science, 5,* 121–122.

Gardner, B. T., & Gardner, R. A. (1971). Two-way communication with an infant chimpanzee. In A. Schreir & F. Stollnitz (Eds.), *Behavior of nonhuman primates* (Vol. 4). New York: Academic Press.

Gardner, H. (1983). *Frames of mind.* New York: Basic Books.

Gardner, H. (1985). *The mind's new science.* New York: Basic Books.

Gardner, H. (1993). *Multiple intelligences.* New York: Basic Books.

Gardner, H. (1999). *The disciplined mind.* New York: Simon & Schuster.

Gardner, H. (2001, March 13). *An education for the future.* Paper presented to the Royal Symposium, Amsterdam.

Gardner, H. (2002). The pursuit of excellence through education. In M. Ferrari (Ed.), *Learning from extraordinary minds.* Mahwah, NJ: Erlbaum.

Garfield, S. L., & Kurtz, R. (1976). Clinical psychologists in the 70s. *American Psychologist, 31,* 1–9.

Garnets, L. D. (2002) Sexual orientation in perspective. *Cultural Diversity and Ethnic Minority Psychology, 8,* 115–129.

Garraghty, P. E. (1996, June). *Neuroplasticity: From mechanisms to behavior.* Paper presented at the meeting of the American Psychological Association, San Francisco.

Gartner, J., Larson, D. B., & Allen, G. D. (1991). Religious commitment and mental health: A review of the empirical literature. *Journal of Psychology and Theology, 19,* 6–25.

Garza, M. (1999). Review of Halonen/Santrock. *Psychology* (3rd ed.). New York: McGraw-Hill.

Gast, U., Roodewald, F., Nickel, V., & Emrich, H. M. (2001). Prevalence of dissociative disorders among psychiatric patients in a German university clinic. *Journal of Nervous and Mental Disorders, 189,* 249–257.

Gatewood, R., Perloff R., & Perloff, E. (1998). Testing and industrial application. In G. Goldstein & M. Hersen (Eds.), *Handbook of psychological assessment* (3rd ed.). Boston: Allyn & Bacon.

Gazda, G. M., Horne, A., & Ginter, E. (2001). *Group counseling and psychotherapy.* Boston: Allyn & Bacon.

Gazzaniga, M. S., Ivry, R. B., & Mangun, G. R. (2001). *Cognitive neuroscience* (2nd ed.). New York: Norton.

Gedo, J. E. (2002). The enduring scientific contributions of Sigmund Freud. *Perspectives in Biology and Medicine, 45,* 200–211.

Gehring, W. J., & Knight, R. T. (2002). Lateral prefrontal damage affects processing selection but not attention switching. *Brain Research: Cognitive Brain Research, 2,* 267–279.

Gelder, M. G., Mayou, R., & Geddes, J. (1999). *Psychiatry* (2nd ed.). New York: Oxford University Press.

Gentner, D., & Lowenstein, J. (2001). Relational thinking and relational language. In J. Byrnes & E. Amsel (Eds.), *Language, literacy, and cognitive development.* Mahwah, NJ: Erlbaum.

George, L. K. (2001). The social psychology of health. In R. H. Binstock & L. K. George (Eds.), *Handbook of the psychology of aging* (5th ed.). San Diego: Academic Press.

Gergen, K. J. (1994). *Realities and relationships: Soundings in social construction.* Cambridge, MA: Harvard University Press.

Gesell, A. (1934). *Infancy and human growth.* New York: MacMillan.

Gevins, A. S. (1999). What to do with your own personal brain scanner. In R. L. Solso (Ed.), *Mind and brain sciences in the 21st century.* Cambridge, MA: MIT Press.

Gibbons, F. X., & McCoy, S. B. (1991). Self-esteem, similarity, and reactions to active versus passive downward comparison. *Journal of Personality and Social Psychology, 60,* 414–424.

Gibbs, J. T., & Huang, L. N. (1989). A conceptual framework for assessing and treating minority youth. In J. T. Gibbs & L. N. Huang (Eds.), *Children of color.* San Francisco: Jossey-Bass.

Gibson, E. J. (2001). *Perceiving the affordances.* Mahwah, NJ: Erlbaum.

Gibson, R. L., & Mitchell, M. H. (1999). *Introduction to counseling and guidance* (5th ed.). Upper Saddle River, NJ: Prentice-Hall.

Gibson, R., & Mitchell, M. (2003). *Introduction to counseling and guidance (6th Ed.).* Upper Saddle River, NJ: Prentice-Hall.

Gigerenzer, G., & Selton, R. (Eds.). (2001). *Bounded rationality.* Cambridge, MA: MIT Press.

Gilbert, P. (2001). *Overcoming depression.* New York: Oxford University Press.

Gilbert, S. J., & Shallice, T. (2002). Task switching: A PDP model. *Cognitive Psychology, 44,* 297–337.

Giles, T. R., & Marafiote, R. A. (1998). Managed care and the practitioner. *Clinical Psychology and Practice, 5,* 41–50.

Gillani, N. B., & Smith, J. C. (2001). Zen meditation and ABC relaxation theory. *Journal of Clinical Psychology, 57,* 839–846.

Gilligan, C. (1982). *In a different voice.* Cambridge, MA: Harvard University Press.

Gilligan, C. (1996). The centrality of relationships in psychological development. In G. Noam & K. W. Fischer (Eds.), *Development and vulnerability in close relationships.* Mahwah, NJ: Erlbaum.

Gilligan, C. (1998). *Minding women: Reshaping the educational realm.* Cambridge, MA: Harvard University Press.

Gilman, S. L. (2001). Karen Horeny, M.D., 1885–1952. *American Journal of Psychoanalysis, 15,* 1205.

Gjerde, P. F., Block, J., & Block, J. H. (1991). The preschool family context of 18-year-olds with depressive symptoms: A prospective study. *Journal of Research on Adolescence, 1,* 63–92.

Gladding, S. T. (1999). *Family therapy* (2nd ed.). Upper Saddle River, NJ: Prentice-Hall.

Gladue, B. A. (1994). The biopsychology of sexual orientation. *Current Directions in Psychological Science, 3,* 150–154.

Gleaves, D. H., May, M. C., & Cardena, E. (2001). An examination of the diagnostic validity of dissociative identity disorder. *Clinical Psychology Review, 21,* 577–608.

Goddard, L., Dritschel, B., & Burton, A. (2001). The effects of specific retrieval instruction on social problem-solving in depression. *British Journal of Clinical Psychology, 40,* 297–308.

Godden, D. R., & Baddeley, A. D. (1975). Context-dependent memory in two natural environments: On land and under water. *British Journal of Psychology, 66,* 325–331.

Goenjian, A. K., Molina, L., Steinberg, A. M., Fairbanks, L. A., Alvarez, M. L., Goenjian, H. A., & Pynoos, R. S. (2001). Post-traumatic stress and depression reactions among Nicaraguan adolescents after Hurricane Mitch. *American Journal of Psychiatry, 158,* 788–794.

Goethals, G. R., & Demorest, A. P. (1995). The risky shift is a sure bet. In M. E. Ware & D. E. Johnson (Eds.), *Demonstrations and activities in teaching of psychology* (Vol. 3). Mahwah, NJ: Erlbaum.

Gold, B. (2002). Integrative approaches to psychotherapy. In M. Hersen & W. H. Sledge (Eds.), *Encyclopedia of psychotherapy.* San Diego: Academic Press.

Goldberg, R. (2003). *Clashing views on controversial issues in drugs and society* (5th ed.). New York: McGraw-Hill.

Golden, R. (2001, January 14). *Personal communication.* Richardson, TX: Program in Psychology, University of Texas at Dallas.

Goldman, S. L., Kraemer, D. T., & Salovey, P. (1996). Beliefs about mood moderate the relationship of stress to illness and symptom reporting. *Journal of Psychosomatic Research, 41,* 115–128.

Goldsmith, H. H. (2002). Genetics of emotional development. In R. J. Davidson, K. R. Scherer, & H. H. Goldsmith (Eds.), *Handbook of affective sciences.* New York: Oxford University Press.

Goldsmith, T. H., & Zimmerman, W. F. (2001). *Biology, evolution, and human nature.* New York: John Wiley.

Goldstein, E. B. (2002). *Sensation and perception* (6th ed.). Belmont, CA: Wadsworth.

Goldstein, I. L., & Ford, K. (2002). *Training in organizations.* Belmont, CA: Wadsworth.

Goldstein, J. M., Seidman, L. J., Horton, N. J., Makris, N., Kennedy, D. N., Caviness, V. S., Faraone, S. V., & Tsuang, M. T. (2001). Normal sexual dimorphism of the adult human brain assessed by in vivo magnetic resonance imaging. *Cerebral Cortex, 11,* 490–497.

Goldstein, R. B., Prescott, C. A., & Kendler, K. S. (2001). Genetic and environmental factors in conduct problems and adult antisocial behavior among adult female twins. *Journal of Nervous and Mental Disorders, 189,* 201–209.

Goldstein, R. B., Wickramaratne, P. J., Horwath, E., & Weissman, M. M. (1997). Familial aggregation and phenomenology of "early"-onset (at or before age 20 years) panic disorder. *Archives of General Psychiatry, 54,* 271–278.

Goleman, D. (1995). *Emotional intelligence.* New York: Bantam.

Goleman, D., Kaufman, P., & Ray, M. (1993). *The creative mind.* New York: Plume.

Gomez Beldarrain, M., Gafman, J., Ruiz De Velasco, J., & Pascual-Leone, A. (2002). Prefrontal lesions impair the implicit and explicit learning of sequences in visuomotor tasks. *Experimental Brain Research, 142,* 529–538.

Gong-Guy, E. (1986). *Depression in students of Chinese and Japanese ancestry: An acculturation, vulnerability and stress model.* Unpublished dissertation, University of California, Los Angeles.

Gonzales, D. H., Nides, M. A., Ferry, L. H., Kustra, R. P., Jamerson, B. D., Segall, N., Herrero, L. A., Krishen, A., Sweeney, A., Buaron, K., & Metz, A. (2001). Bupropion SR as an aid to smoking cessation in smokers previously treated with bupropion: A randomized placebo-controlled study. *Clinical and Pharmacology Therapy, 69,* 438–444.

Goodstein, I. K., & Calhoun, J. F. (1982). *Understanding abnormal behavior.* Reading, MA: Addison-Wesley.

Gorenstein, E. E. (1997). *Case studies in abnormal psychology.* New York: Longman.

Gorman, J. M., & Kent, J. M. (1999). SSRIs and SNRIs: Broad spectrum of efficacy beyond major depression. *Journal of Clinical Psychology, 60* (Suppl. 4), 33–39.

Gotesdam, K. G., & Agras, W. S. (1995). General population-based epidemiological survey of eating disorders in Norway. *International Journal of Eating Disorders, 18,* 119–126.

Gottesman, I. I., & Goldsmith, H. H. (1994). Developmental psychopathology of antisocial behavior. In C. A. Nelson (Ed.), *Threats to optimal development.* Mahwah, NJ: Erlbaum.

Gottesman, I. I., & Shields, J. (1982). *The schizophrenic puzzle.* New York: Cambridge University Press.

Gottlieb, B. H. (1998). Support groups. In H. S. Friedman (Ed.), *Encyclopedia of mental health* (Vol. 3). San Diego: Academic Press.

Gottlieb, G. (2002). Nature and nurture theories. In A. Kazdin (Ed.), *Encyclopedia of psychology.* Washington, DC, & New York: American Psychological Association and Oxford University Press.

Gottlieb, G. (2002). Origin of the species: The potential significance of early experience for evolution. In W. W. Hartup & R. A. Weinberg (Eds.), *Child psychology in retrospect and prospect.* Mahwah, NJ: Erlbaum.

Gottman, J. M. (1994). *What predicts divorce?* Mahwah, NJ: Erlbaum.

Gottman, J. M., & Silver, N. (1999). *The seven principles for making marriages work.* New York: Crown.

Gottman, J. M., Coan, J., Carrere, S., & Swanson, C. (1998). Predicting marital happiness and stability from newlywed interactions. *Journal of Marriage and the Family, 60,* 5–22.

Gottman, J. M., Katz, L. F., & Hooven, C. (1997). *Meta-emotion: How families communicate.* Mahwah, NJ: Erlbaum.

Gottselig, J. M., Bassetti, C. L., & Achermann, P. (2002). Power and coherence of sleep spindle frequency activity following hemispheric stroke. *Brain, 125,* 373–383.

Gotz, M. E., Janetzky, B., Pohli, S., Gottschalk, S., Gsell, A., Tatshchner, T., Ransmyar, G., Leblhuber, F., Gerlach, M., Reichmann, H., Riederer, P., & Boning, J. (2001). Chronic alcohol consumption and cerebral indices of oxidative stress: Is there a link? *Alcoholism: Clinical and Experimental Research, 25,* 717–725.

Gould, E., Reeves, A. J., Graziano, M. S., & Gross, C. G. (1999). Neurogenesis in the neocortex of adult primates, *Science, 286* (1), 548–552.

Gould, S. J. (1981). *The mismeasure of man.* New York: Norton.

Grabowski, J. (1999, January). Addicted to addictions? *APA Monitor,* p. 8.

Graffin, N. F., Ray, W. J., & Lundy, R. (1995). EEG concomitants of hypnosis and hypnotic susceptibility. *Journal of Abnormal Psychology, 104,* 123–131.

Graham, S. (1992). Most of the subjects were white and middle class. *American Psychologist, 47,* 629–637.

Graham, S. (1986, August). *Can attribution theory tell us something about motivation in Blacks?* Paper presented at the meeting of the American Psychological Association, Washington, DC.

Graham, S. (2001). Inferences about responsibility and values: Implication for academic motivation. In F. Salihi & C. Chiu (Eds.), *Student motivation: The culture and context of learning.* New York: Plenum.

Graham-Bermann, S., Eastin, J. A., & Bermann, E. A. (2002). Stress and coping. In J. Worell (Ed.), *Encyclopedia of women and gender.* New York: Oxford University Press.

Grau, C., Polo, M. D., Yago, E., Gual, A., & Escera, C. (2002). Auditory sensory memory as indicated by a mismatch negativity in chronic alcoholism. *Clinical Neurophysiology, 112,* 728–731.

Gray, C. (2002). Pediatricians taking a new look at corporal-punishment issue. *Canadian Medical Association Journal, 19,* 793.

Gray, C. R., & Gummerman, K. (1975). The enigmatic eidetic image: A critical examination of methods, data, and theories. *Psychological Bulletin, 82,* 383–407.

Gray, J. (1992). *Men are from Mars, women are from Venus.* New York: Harper Collins.

Gray, J. R. (2001). Emotional modulation of cognitive control: Approach-withdrawal states double-dissociate spatial from verbal two-back task performance. *Journal of Experimental Psychology: General, 130,* 436–452.

Graziano, W. J. (1995). Evolutionary psychology: Old music, but now on CDs? *Psychological Inquiry, 6,* 41–44.

Green, B. L., Lindy, J. D., Grace, M. C., & Leonard, A. C. (1992). Chronic posttraumatic stress disorder and diagnostic comorbidity in a disaster sample. *Journal of Nervous & Mental Disease, 180,* 760–766.

Greene, R. L. (1999). Applied memory research: How far from bankruptcy? *Contemporary Psychology, 44,* 29–31.

Greenfield, S. (1996, April). *Neural assemblies.* Paper presented at the conference on "Toward a science of consciousness," Tucson, AZ.

Greenglass, E. R. (1998). Gender differences in mental health. In H. S. Friedman (Ed.), *Encyclopedia of mental health* (Vol. 2). San Diego: Academic Press.

Greenough, W. (2000). Brain development. In A. Kazdin (Ed.), *Encyclopedia of psychology.* Washington, DC, & New York: American Psychological Association and Oxford University Press.

Greenough, W. T. (2001). *Commentary.* In J. W. Santrock, *Child Development* (9th ed.). Boston: McGraw-Hill.

Greenwald, A. G., & Banaji, M. R. (1995). Implicit social cognition: Attitudes, self-esteem, and stereotypes. *Psychological Review, 102,* 4–27.

Greenwald, A. G., Draine, S. C., & Abrams, R. L. (1996). Three cognitive markers of unconscious semantic activation. *Science, 273,* 1699–1702.

Gregory, R. L. (2000). Visual illusions. In A. Kazdin (Ed.), *Encyclopedia of psychology.* Washington, DC, & New York: American Psychological Association and Oxford University Press.

Greven, P. (1991). *Spare the child: The religious roots of punishment and the psychological impact of physical abuse.* New York: Knopf.

Griffin, W. A. (2002). Family therapy. In M. Hersen & W. H. Sledge (Eds.), *Encyclopedia of psychotherapy.* San Diego: Academic Press.

Grigorenko, E. (2000). Heritability and intelligence. In R. J. Sternberg (Ed.), *Handbook of intelligence.* New York: Cambridge University Press.

Grodzinsky, Y. (2001). The neurology of syntax: Language use without Broca's area. *Behavior and Brain Sciences, 23,* 1–21.

Grunberg, N. E., Klein, L. C., & Brown, K. J. (1998). Psychopharmacology. In H. S. Friedman (Ed.), *Encyclopedia of mental health* (Vol. 3). San Diego: Academic Press.

Grush, J. E. (1980). Impact of candidate expenditures, regionality, and prior outcomes on the 1976 Democratic presidential primaries. *Journal of Personality and Social Psychology, 38,* 337–347.

Guilford, J. P. (1967). *The structure of intellect.* New York: McGraw-Hill.

Gupta, P., & Dell, G. S. (1999). The emergence of language from serial order and procedural memory. In B. MacWhinney (Ed.), *The emergence of language.* Mahwah, NJ: Erlbaum.

Gutierrez-Lobos, K., Frohlich, S., Quiner, S., Haring, C., & Barnas, C. (2001). Prescription patterns and quality of information provided for consumers of benzodiazepines. *Acta Medica Austria, 28,* 56–59.

Guttman, N., & Kalish, H. I. (1956). Discriminability and stimulus generalization. *Journal of Experimental Psychology, 51,* 79–88.

H

Hahn, U., & Ramscar, M. (Eds.). (2001). *Similarity and categorization.* New York: Oxford University Press.

Hakuta, K., Butler, Y. G., & Witt, D. (2000). *How long does it take English learners to attain proficiency?* (Linguistic Minority Institute Policy Report 2000–2001). Berkeley: University of California.

Haladyna, T. M. (2002). *Essentials of standardized testing.* Boston: Allyn & Bacon.

Halford, J. C., & Blundell, J. E. (2000). Pharmacology of appetite suppression. *Progress in drug research, 54,* 25–58.

Hall, R. V., & Hall, M. L. (1998). *How to select reinforcers* (2nd ed.). Austin: Pro-Ed.

Hallahan, D. P., & Kauffman, J. M. (2003). *Exceptional learners* (9th Ed.). Boston: Allyn & Bacon.

Halpern, D. (2001). Sex difference research: Cognitive abilities. In J. Worell (Ed.), *Encyclopedia of women and gender.* New York: Oxford University Press.

Halpern, D. F. (1997). Sex differences in intelligence: Implications for education. *American Psychologist, 52,* 1091–1102.

Halpern, D. F. (1998). Teaching critical thinking for transfer across domains: Dispositions, skills, structure training, and metacognitive monitoring. *American Psychologist, 53,* 449–455.

Halpern, D. F. (2000). Critical thinking. In N. J. Smelser & P. B. Baltes (Eds.), *International encyclopedia of the social and behavioral sciences.* Amsterdam: Pergamon.

Halpern, D. F. (2000). *Sex differences in cognitive abilities.* Mahwah, NJ: Erlbaum.

Halpern, D. F. (2002). Teaching for critical thinking: A four-part model to enhance thinking skills. In S. Davis & W. Buskist (Eds.), *The Teaching of Psychology: Essays in Honor of Wilbert J. McKeachie and Charles L. Brewer.* Mahwah, NJ: Erlbaum.

Halpern, D. F. (2003). *Thought and Knowledge: An Introduction to Critical Thinking (4th Edition).* Mahwah, NJ: Erlbaum

Halpern, D. F. (1996). *Thinking critically about critical thinking.* Mahwah, NJ: Erlbaum.

Hammond, R. (2001, August). *Best practices for youth violence prevention.* Paper presented at the meeting of the American Psychological Association, San Francisco.

Hancock, P. A., & Desmond, P. A. (2000). *Stress, workload, and fatigue.* Mahwah, NJ: Erlbaum.

Handel, R. W., & Ben-Porath, Y. S. (2000). Multicultural assessment with the MMPI-2. In R. H. Dana (Ed.), *Handbook of cross-cultural and multicultural personality assessment.* Mahwah, NJ: Erlbaum.

Handler, L. (1999). Introduction to the special series on personality assessment: Classics in contemporary perspective. *Journal of Personality Assessment, 72,* 144–146.

Hanna, A., & Remington, R. (2001). The representation of color and form in long-term memory. *Memory and Cognition, 24,* 322–330.

Hannigan, J. H., Spear, L. P., Spear, N. E., & Goodlet, C. R. (Eds.). (1999). *Alcohol and alcoholism.* Mahwah, NJ: Erlbaum.

Hannon, B., & Craik, F. I. (2001). Encoding specificity revisited: The role of semantics. *Canadian Journal of Experimental Psychology, 55,* 231–243.

Hanson, R. F., Saunders, B., Kilpatrick, D., Resnick, H., Crouch, J. A., & Duncan, R. (2001). Impact of childhood rape and aggravated assault on adult mental health. *American Journal of Orthopsychiatry, 71,* 108–119.

Harkness, S., & Super, C. M. (1995). Culture and parenting. In M. H. Bornstein (Ed.), *Children and parenting* (Vol. 2). Hillsdale, NJ: Erlbaum.

Harkness, S., & Super, C. M. (2002). Culture and parenting. In M. Bornstein (Ed.), *Handbook of parenting* (2nd ed.). Mahwah, NJ: Erlbaum.

Harlow, H. F., & Zimmerman, R. R. (1959). Affectional responses in the infant monkey. *Science, 130,* 421–432.

Harmatz, M. (1997). Introduction to clinical psychology. In Santrock, J. W., *Psychology* (5th ed.). New York: McGraw-Hill.

Harris, D. M., & Kay, J. (1995). I recognize your face but I can't remember your name: Is it because names are unique? *British Journal of Psychology, 86,* 345–358.

Harris, J. R. (1998). *The nurture assumption.* New York: Free Press.

Harris, R. F., Wolf, N. M., & Baer, D. M. (1964). Effects of adult social reinforcement on child behavior. *Young Children, 20,* 8–17.

Harrison, Y., & Horne, J. A. (2000). The impact of sleep deprivation on decision making: A review. *Journal of Experimental Psychology: Applied, 6,* 236–249.

Hart, B., & Risley, T. R. (1995). *Meaningful differences in the everyday experience of young Americans.* Baltimore: Paul H. Brookes.

Harter, S. (1998). The development of self-representations. In W. Damon (Ed.), *Handbook of child psychology* (5th ed., Vol. 3). New York: Wiley.

Hartmann, E. (1993). Nightmares. In M.A. Carskadon (Ed.), *Encyclopedia of sleep and dreams.* New York: Macmillan.

Harvey, A. G. (2001). Insomnia: Symptom or diagnosis? *Clinical Psychology Review, 21,* 1037–1059.

Harvey, J. H. (1995). *Odyssey of the heart.* New York: Freeman.

Harvey, J. H., & Weber, A. L. (2002). *Odyssey of the heart* (2nd ed.). Mahwah, NJ: Erlbaum.

Hastie, R. (2001). Problems for judgment and decision making. *Annual Review of Psychology* (Vol. 52). Palo Alto, CA: Annual Reviews.

Hastie, R., Penrod, S. D., & Pennington, N. (1983). *Inside the jury.* Cambridge MA: Harvard University Press.

Hatcher, R., & others (1988). *Contraceptive technology, 1988–1989* (14th ed.). New York: Irvington.

Hauptmann, B., & Karni, A. (2002). From primed to learn: the saturation of repetition priming and the induction of long-term memory. *Brain Research: Cognitive Brain Research, 13,* 313–322.

Hawkins, F. H. (1987). *Human factors in flight.* Aldershot, England: Gower Technical Press.

Hawkins, G., & Zimring, F. E. (1988). *Pornography in a free society.* New York: Cambridge University Press.

Hayes, N. (1997, July). The distinctive skills of a psychology graduate. *APA Monitor,* p. 33.

Hayflick, L. (1997). The cellular basis for biological aging. In C. E. Finch & L. Hayflick (Eds.), *Handbook of the biology of aging.* New York: Van Nostrand.

Haythronthwaite, J. A., Lawrence, J. W., & Fauerbach, J. A. (2001). Brief cognitive interventions for pain. *Annals of Behavioral Medicine, 23,* 42–49.

Heath, A. C., Todorov, A. A., Nelson, E. C., Madden, P. A., Bucholz, K. K., & Martin, N. G. (2002). Gene-environment interaction effects on behavioral variation and risk of complex disorders: the example of alcoholism and other psychiatric disorders. *Twin Research, 5,* 30–37.

Hebb, D. O. (2002). *The Organization of behavior.* Mahwah, NJ: Erlbaum.

Hebb, D. O. (1949). *The organization of behavior: A neuropsychological theory.* New York: Wiley.

Hebb, D. O. (1980). *Essay on mind.* Mahwah, NJ: Erlbaum.

Heeger, (1997). Signal detection theory. Unpublished handout. Stanford, CA: Stanford University, Department of Psychology.

Hefferman, D. D., Harper, S. M., & McWilliam, D. (2002). Women's perceptions of the outcome of weight loss diets: A signal detection approach. *International Journal of Eating Disorders, 31,* 339–343.

Heider, F. (1958). Attitudes and cognitive organization. *Journal of Psychology, 21,* 107–122.

Heikkinen, M., Aro, H., & Loennqvist, J. (1992). Recent life events and their role in suicide as seen by the spouses. *Acta Psychiatrica Scandinavica, 86,* 489–494.

Heim, C., & Nemeroff, C. B. (2002). Neurobiology of early life stress: Clinical studies. *Seminars in Clinical Psychiatry, 7,* 147–159.

Heiman, G. W. (1995). *Research methods.* Boston: Houghton Mifflin.

Heinrichs, R. W. (2001). *In search of madness.* New York: Oxford University Press.

Heller, W., Nitschke, J. B., Etienne, M. A., & Miller, G. A. (1997). Patterns of regional activity differentiates types of anxiety. *Journal of Abnormal Psychology, 106,* 376–385.

Helmholtz, H. von. (1852). On the theory of compound colors. *Philosophical Magazine, 4,* 519–534.

Henderson, V. L., & Dweck, C. S. (1990). Motivation and achievement. In S. S. Feldman & G. R. Elliott (Eds.), *At the threshold: The developing adolescent.* Cambridge, MA: Harvard University Press.

Hendin, H. (1995). *Suicide in America.* New York: W. W. Norton.

Heppner, P., & Lee, D. (2001). Problem-solving appraisal and psychological adjustment. In C.R. Snyder & S.J. Lopez (Eds.), *Handbook of positive psychology.* New York: Oxford University Press.

Herberman, R. B. (2002). Stress, natural killer cells, and cancer. In H. G. Koenig & H. J. Cohen (Eds.), *The link between religion and health.* New York: Oxford University Press.

Herbert, J. (1988). The physiology of aggression. In J. Groebel & R. Hinde (Eds.), *Aggression and war: The biological and social bases.* New York: Cambridge University Press.

Herbert, T. B., & Cohen, S. (1993). Depression and immunity: A meta-analytic review. *Psychological Bulletin, 113,* 472–486.

Hergenhahn, B. R. (2001). *An introduction to the history of psychology* (4th ed.). Belmont, CA: Wadsworth.

Hergenhahn, B. R., & Olson, M. H. (2001). *An introduction to theories of learning* (6th ed.). Upper Saddle River, NJ: Prentice-Hall.

Herrnstein, R. J., & Murray, C. (1994). *The bell curve: Intelligence and class structure in American life.* New York: Macmillan.

Herxheimer, A., & Petrie, K. J. (2001). *Melatonin for preventing and treating jet lag* [CD-ROM]. Retrieved from Cochrane Database System 1, CD No. 001520.

Herzberg, E. (2000). Use of TAT in multicultural societies: Brazil and the United States. In R. H. Dana (Ed.), *Handbook of cross-cultural and multicultural personality assessment.* Mahwah, NJ: Erlbaum.

Herzog, H. A. (1995). Discussing animal rights and animal research in the classroom. In M. E. Ware & D. E. Johnson (Eds.), *Demonstrations and activities in teaching of psychology* (Vol. 1). Mahwah, NJ: Erlbaum.

Hetherington, E. M. (1999). *Should we stay together for the sake of the children?* Unpublished manuscript, Dept. of Psychology, University of Virginia, Charlottesville.

Hetherington, E. M. (2000). Divorce. In A. Kazdin (Ed.), *Encyclopedia of psychology.* Washington, DC, & New York: American Psychological Association and Oxford University Press.

Hetherington, E. M., & Kelly, (2002). *For better or for worse: Divorce reconsidered.* New York: Norton.

Hetherington, E. M., & Stanley-Hagan, M. (2002). Parenting in divorced and remarried families. In M. Bornstein (Ed.), *Handbook of parenting* (2nd ed.). Mahwah, NJ: Erlbaum.

Hewitt, J. P. (2001). The social construction of self-esteem. In C. R. Synder & S. J. Lopez (Eds.), *Handbook of positive psychology.* New York: Oxford University Press.

Hewstone, M., Rubin, M., & Willis, H. (2002). Intergroup bias. *Annual Review of Psychology* (Vol. 53). Palo Alto, CA: Annual Reviews.

Hidalgo, R. B., & Davidson, J. R. (2001). Generalized anxiety disorder: An important clinical concern. *Medical Clinics of North America, 85,* 691–710.

Hilgard, E. R. (1965). *Hypnotic suggestibility.* Ft. Worth, TX: Harcourt Brace.

Hilgard, E. R. (1977). *Divided consciousness: Multiple controls in human thought and action.* New York: Wiley.

Hilgard, E. R. (1992). Dissociation and theories of hypnosis. In E. Fromm & M. R. Nash (Eds.), *Contemporary hypnosis research.* New York: Guilford Press.

Hilgard, E. R. (1986). *Divided consciousness: Multiple controls in human thought and action.* New York: Wiley.

Hilgard, E. R. (1992). Divided consciousness and dissociation. *Consciousness and Cognition: An International Journal, 1,* 16–31.

Hill, C. E. (2000). Client-centered therapy. In A. Kazdin (Ed.), *Encyclopedia of psychology.* Washington, DC, & New York: American Psychological Association and Oxford University Press.

Hill, C. E., & O'Brien, K. M. (1999). *Helping skills.* Washington, DC: American Psychological Association.

Hill, P. C., & Butter, E. M. (1995). The role of religion in promoting physical health. *Journal of Psychology and Christianity, 14,* 141–155.

Hilsenroth, M. J. (2000). Rorschach test. In A. Kazdin (Ed.), *Encyclopedia of psychology.* Washington, DC, & New York: American Psychological Association and Oxford University Press.

Hines, M. (1982). Prenatal gonadal differences in human behavior. *Psychological Bulletin, 92,* 56–80.

Hirsch, B. J., Roffman, J. G., Pagano, M., & Deutsch, N. (2000, April). *Inner-city youth: Ties to youth development staff and adult kin.* Paper presented at the meeting of the Society for Research on Adolescence, Chicago.

Hobfoll, S. E. (1989). Conservation of resources: A new attempt at conceptualizing stress. *American Psychologist, 44,* 513–524.

Hobson, A. (2000). Dreams: Physiology. In A. Kazdin (Ed.), *Encyclopedia of psychology.* Washington, DC, & New York: American Psychological Association and Oxford University Press.

Hobson, J. A. (1999). Dreams. In R. Conlan (Ed.), *States of mind.* New York: Wiley.

Hobson, J. A., Pace-Schott, E. F., & Stickgold, R. (2000). Dreaming and the brain. *Behavior and Brain Sciences, 23,* 793–842.

Hodges, J. R. (2000). Memory in the dementias. In E. Tulving & F. I. M. Craik (Eds.), *Oxford Handbook of Memory.* New York: Oxford University Press.

Hofferth, S. L. (1990). Trends in adolescent sexual activity, contraception, and pregnancy in the United States. In J. Bancroft & J.M. Reinisch (Eds.), *Adolescence and puberty.* New York: Oxford University Press.

Hogan, E. H. Nornick, B. A. & Bouchoux, A. (2002). Focus on communications: Communicating the message: Clarifying the controversies about caffeine, *Nutrition Today, 37,* 28–35.

Hogan, J. (1986). *Hogan Personality Inventory manual.* Minneapolis: National Computer Systems.

Hogan, R. T. (1987, August). *Conceptions of personality and the prediction of job performance.* Paper presented at the meeting of the American Psychological Association, New York City.

Hoge, M. A. (1998). Managed care. In H. S. Friedman (Ed.), *Encyclopedia of mental health* (Vol. 2). San Diego: Academic Press.

Holaday, M., Smith, D. A., & Sherry, A. (2000). Sentence completion tests: A review of the literature and results of a survey of members of the Society for Personality Assessment. *Journal of Personality Assessment, 74,* 371–383.

Holcomb, H. H., Cascella, N. G., Thaker, G. K., Medoff, D. R., Dannals, R. F., & Tamminga, C. A. (1996). Functional sites of neuroleptic drug action in the human brain. *American Journal of Psychiatry, 153,* 41–49.

Holland, P. C. (1996). The effects of intertrial and feature-target intervals on operant serial feature-positive discrimination learning. *Animal Learning & Behavior, 24,* 411–428.

Holmes, D. S. (1988). The influence of meditation versus rest on physiological considerations. In M. West (Ed.), *The psychology of meditation.* New York: Oxford University Press.

Holmes, S. E., Slaughter, J. R., & Kashani, J. (2001). Risk factors in childhood that lead to the development of conduct disorder and antisocial personality disorder. *Child Psychiatry and Human Development, 31,* 183–193.

Holmes, T. H., & Rahe, R. H. (1967). The social readjustment rating scale. *Journal of Psychosomatic Research, 11,* 213–218.

Holtzmann, W. (1982). Cross-cultural comparisons of personality development in Mexico and the United States. In D. Wagner & H. W. Stevenson (Eds.), *Cultural perspectives on child development.* San Francisco: Jossey-Bass.

Honts, C. (1998, June). Commentary. *APA Monitor,* p. 30.

Hood, A. S., & Morrison, J. D. (2002). The dependence of binocular contrast sensitivities on binocular single vision in normal and amblyopic human subjects. *Journal of Physiology, 540,* 607–622.

Hood, D. C., Frishman, L. J., Saszik, S., & Viswanathan, S. (2002). Retinal origins of the primate multifocal ERG: Implications for the human response. *Investigative Ophthalmology and Visual Science, 43,* 1673–1685.

Hooper, J., & Teresi, D. (1993). *The 3-pound universe.* New York: Tarcher/Putnam.

Hoptman, M. J., & Davidson, R. J. (1994). How and why do the two cerebral hemispheres interact? *Psychological Bulletin, 116,* 195–219.

Horn, J. L., & Donaldson, G. (1980). Cognitive development II: Adulthood development of human abilities. In O. G. Brim & J. Kagan (Eds.), *Constancy and change in human development.* Cambridge, MA: Harvard University Press.

Horney, K. (1945). *Our inner conflicts.* New York: Norton.

Horowitz, M. J. (1998). Psychoanalysis. In H. S. Friedman (Ed.), *Encyclopedia of mental health* (Vol. 3). San Diego: Academic Press.

Horton, D. M. (2001). The disappearing bell curve. *Journal of Secondary Gifted Education, 12,* 185–188.

Hough, L. (2001). I/Owes its advances to personality. In B. W. Roberts & R. Hogan (Eds.), *Personality psychology in the workplace.* Washington, DC: American Psychological Association.

Hovey, J. D. (2000). Psychosocial predictors of acculturation stress in Mexican immigrants. *Journal of Psychology, 134,* 490–502.

Howard, K. I., Moras, K., Brill, P. L., Martinovich, Z., & Lutz, W. (1996). Evaluation of psychotherapy: Efficacy, effectiveness, and patient progress. *American Psychologist, 51,* 1059–1064.

Howard, M. W., & Kahana, M. J. (1999). Contextual variability and serial position effects in free recall. *Journal of Experimental Psychology: Learning, Memory, and Cognition, 25,* 923–941.

Howard, R. W. (2001). Searching the real world for signs of rising population intelligence. *Personality and Individual Differences, 30,* 1039–1058.

Howe, M. J. A., Davidson, J. W., Moore, D. G., & Sloboda, J. A. (1995). Are there early childhood signs of musical ability? *Psychology of Music, 23,* 162–176.

Howley, E. T. (2001). Type of activity: Resistance, aerobic and leisure versus occupational physical activity. *Medical Science and Sports Exercise, 33* (Suppl.), S364–369.

Hoyle, R. H., & Judd, C. M. (2002). *Research methods in social psychology* (7th ed.). Belmont, CA: Wadsworth.

Hsu, P., Yu, F., Feron, F., Pickles, J. O., Sneesby, K., & Mackay-Sim, A. (2001). Basic fibroblast growth factor and fibroblast growth factor receptors in adult olfactory epithelium. *Brain Research, 896,* 188–197.

Hu, M. T., Taylor-Robinson, S. D., Chaudhuri, K. R., Bell, J. D., Labbe, C., Cunningham, V. J., Koepp, M. J., Hammers, A., Morris, R. G., Turjanski, N., & Brooks, N. J. (2000). Cortical dysfunction in non-demented Parkinson's disease patients: A combined (31)P-MRS and (18)FDG-PET study. *Brain, 123,* 340–352.

Hubel, D. H., & Wiesel, T. N. (1965). Receptive fields and functional architecture in two nonstriate areas (18 and 19) of the cat. *Journal of Neurophysiology, 28,* 229–289.

Huber, D. E., Shiffrin, R. M., Lyle, K. B., & Ruys, K. I. (2001). Perception and preference in short-term word priming. *Psychological Review, 108,* 149–182.

Hublin, C., Kaprio, J., Partinen, M., & Koskenvu, M. (2001). Parasomnias: Co-occurrence and genetics. *Psychiatric Genetics, 11,* 65–70.

Huffcutt, A. I., Conway, J. M., Roth, P. L., & Stone, N. J. (2001). Identification and meta-analytic assessment of psychological constructs measured in employment interviews. *Journal of Applied Psychology, 86,* 897–913.

Humphreys, M. S. (2001). Proactive interference and complexity. *Journal of Experimental Psychology: Learning, Memory, and Cognition, 27,* 872–888.

Humphreys, M. S., Tehan, G., O'Shea, A., & Bolland, S. W. (2000). Target similarity effects: Support for the parallel distributed processing assumptions. *Memory and Cognition, 28,* 798–811.

Hunt, M. (1993). *The story of psychology.* New York: Anchor Books.

Hunt, M. (1974). *Sexual behavior in the 1970s.* Chicago: Playboy.

Hunt, R. R., & Kelly, R. E. S. (1996). Accessing the particular from the general: The power of distinctiveness in the context of organization. *Memory and Cognition, 24,* 217–225.

Hurley, S. R., & Tinajero, J. V. (2001). *Literacy assessment of second-language learners.* Boston: Allyn & Bacon.

Hurvich, L. M., & Jameson, D. (1969). Human color perception. *American Scientist, 57,* 143–166.

Huttenlocher, J., Haight, W., Bruk, A., Selzer, M., & Lyons, T. (1991). Early vocabulary growth: Relation to language input and gender. *Developmental Psychology, 27,* 236–248.

Huttenlocher, P. R., & Dabholkar, A. S. (1997). Regional differences in synaptogenesis in human cerebral cortex. *Journal of Comparative Neurology, 37* (2), 167–178.

Hy, L., & Loevinger, J. (1996). *Measuring ego development.* Mahwah, NJ: Erlbaum.

Hyde, J. S., & DeLamater, J. D. (2003). *Understanding human sexuality* (8th ed.). New York: McGraw-Hill.

Hyde, J. S., & Mezulis, A. H. (2002). Gender difference research: Issues and critique. In J. Worell (Ed.), *Encyclopedia of women and gender.* San Diego: Academic Press.

Hyde, J. S., & Plant, E. A. (1995). Magnitude of psychological gender differences: Another side of the story. *American Psychologist, 50,* 159–161.

Hyman, S. (2001, October 23). *Basic and clinical neuroscience in the post-genomic era.* Paper presented at the centennial symposium on The Celebration of Excellence in Neuroscience, The Rockefeller University, New York City.

I

Iacono, W. G., & Lykken, D. T. (1997). The validity of the lie detector: Two surveys of scientific opinion. *Journal of Applied Psychology, 82,* 426–433.

Ickovics, J. (2001). *Identity and pregnant teens prospective study of HIV risk.* Unpublished manuscript, Center for Interdisciplinary Research on AIDS, Yale University, New Haven, CT.

Idson, L. C., & Mischel, W. (2001). The personality of familiar and significant people: The lay perceiver and the social-cognitive theorist. *Journal of Personality and Social Psychology, 80,* 585–596.

Ilgen, D. R. (2000). Industrial and organizational psychology. In A. Kazdin (Ed.), *Encyclopedia of psychology.* Washington, DC, & New York: American Psychological Association and Oxford University Press.

Ilgen, D. R. (2001). Industrial psychology. In W. E. Craighead & C. B. Nemeroff (Eds.), *The Corsini encyclopedia of psychology and behavioral science* (3rd ed.). New York: Wiley.

Impara, J. C., & Plake, B. S. (Eds.) (2001). *The fourteenth mental measurements yearbook.* Lincoln, NE: U. of Nebraska Press.

Ironson, G. (2001, March). *Hostile personality and AIDS.* Paper presented at the meeting of the American Psychosomatic Society, Monterey, CA.

Ironson, G., Solomon, G., Balbin, E., O'Cleirigh, C., George, A., Schneiderman, N., & Woods, T. (2001, March). *Religious behavior, religious coping, and compassionate view of others is associated with long-term survival with AIDS.* Paper presented at the meeting of the American Psychosomatic Society, Monterey, CA.

Irwin, M. (2002). Psychoneuroimmunology of depression: clinical implications. *Brain, Behavior, and Immunity, 16,* 1-16.

Isotani, T., Tanaka, H., Lehmann, D., Pascual-Marqui, R.D., Kochi, K., Saito, N., Yagyu, T., Kinoshita, T., & Sasada, K. (2001). Source localization of EEG activity during hypnotically induced anxiety and relaxation. *International Journal of Psychophysiology, 41,* 143–153.

Iverson, G. L., & Barton, E. (1999). Interscorer reliability of the MMPI-2: Should TRIN and VRIN be computer scored? *Journal of Clinical Psychology, 55,* 65–70.

J

Jackson, L. C., & Greene, B. (2000). *Psychotherapy with African-American women.* New York: Guilford Press.

Jakel, R. J., & Marangos, W. F. (2000). Neuronal cell death in Huntington's disease: A potential role for dopamine. *Trends in Neuroscience, 23,* 239–245.

James, R. K., & Gilliland, B. E. (2003). *Theories and strategies in counseling and psychotherapy (5th Ed.).* Boston: Allyn & Bacon.

James, W. (1950). *Principles of psychology.* New York: Dover. (Original work published 1890)

Jameson, D., & Hurvich, L. M. (1989). Essay concerning color constancy. *Annual Review of Psychology* (Vol. 40). Palo Alto, CA: Annual Reviews.

Jamison, K. R. (1995). *An unquiet mind.* New York: Random House.

Jamurtas, A. Z., Goldfarb, A. H., Chung, S. C., Hegde, S., & Marino, C. (2000). Beta-endorphin infusion during exercise in rats. *Medical Science and Sports Exercise, 32,* 1570–1575.

Janis, I. (1972). *Victims of groupthink: A psychological study of foreign-policy decisions and fiascos.* Boston: Houghton Mifflin.

Jarrett, R. B., Kraft, D., Doyle, J., Foster, B. M., Eaves, G. G., & Silver, P. C. (2001). Preventing recurrent depression using cognitive therapy with and without a continuation phase: A randomized clinical trial. *Archives of General Psychiatry, 58,* 381–388.

Jausovec, N., & Jausovec, K. (2001). Differences in EEG current density related to intelligence. *Brain Research: Cognitive Brain Research, 12,* 55–60.

Jausovec, N., & Jausovec, K. (2000). Correlations between ERP parameters and intelligence: A reconsideration. *Biological Psychology, 55,* 137–154.

Jenike, M. A. (2001). An update on obsessive-compulsive disorder. *Bulletin of the Menninger Clinic, 65,* 4–25.

Jenkins, S. (2002). Race and human diversity. In M. Hersen & W. H. Sledge (Eds.), *Encyclopedia of psychotherapy.* San Diego: Academic Press.

Jennings, L., & Skovholt, T. M. (1999). The cognitive, emotional, and relational characteristics of master therapists. *Journal of Counseling Psychology, 46,* 3–11.

Jensen, A. R. (1969). How much can we boost IQ and scholastic achievement? *Harvard Educational Review, 39,* 1–123.

Jensen, S. M., Barabasz, A., Barabasz, M., & Warner, D. (2001). EEG P300 event-related markers of hypnosis. *American Journal of Clinical Hypnosis, 44,* 127–139.

Jeong, J., Kim, D. J., Kim, S. Y., Chae, J. H., Go, H. J., & Kim, K. S. (2001). Effect of total sleep deprivation on the dimensional complexity of the waking EEG. *Sleep, 15,* 197–202.

Jernigan, T. L., Ostergaard, A. L., & Fennema-Notestine, C. (2001). Mesial temporal, diencephalic, and striatal contributions to single word reading, word priming, and recognition memory. *Journal of the International Neuropsychological Society, 7,* 67–78.

Johnson, D. W., & Johnson, F. P. (2003). *Joining together: Group theory and group skills. (8th Ed.).* Boston: Allyn & Bacon.

Johnson, D. W., & Johnson, R. T. (1999). *Learning together and alone* (5th ed.). Boston: Allyn & Bacon.

Johnson, G. B. (2000). *The living world* (2nd ed.). New York: McGraw-Hill.

Johnson, G. B. (2003). *The living world* (3rd ed.). New York: McGraw-Hill.

Johnson, J. S., & Newport, E. L. (1989). Critical period effects in second-language learning. *Cognitive Psychology, 21,* 60–69.

Johnson, M. H. (2000). Infancy: Biological processes. In A. Kazdin (Ed.), *Encyclopedia of psychology.* Washington, DC, & New York: American Psychological Association and Oxford University Press.

Johnson, M. H. (2002). Functional brain development during infancy. In G. Bremner & A. Fogel (Eds.), *Blackwell handbook of infant development.* Malden, MA: Blackwell.

Johnson-Laird, P. N. (2000). Thinking: Reasoning. In A. Kazdin (Ed.), *Encyclopedia of psychology.* Washington, DC, & New York: American Psychological Association and Oxford University Press.

Johnston, L. D., O'Malley, P. M., & Bachman, J. G. (2001, December). *Drug trends in U.S. adolescents.* Ann Arbor, MI: Institute for Social Research.

Johnston, L., Bachman, G., & O'Malley, P. (1989, February 24). *Teenage drug use continues decline* [News release]. Ann Arbor: University of Michigan, Institute for Social Research.

Joiner, T. E., Steer, R. A., Abramson, L. Y., Mealsky, G. I., & Schmidt, N. B. (2001). Hopelessness depression as a distinct dimension of depressive symptoms among clinical and non-clinical samples. *Behavior Research and Therapy, 39,* 523–536.

Jones, E. E. (1998). Major developments in five decades of social psychology. In D. T. Gilbert, S. T. Fiske, & G. Lindzey (Eds.), *Handbook of social psychology* (4th ed., Vol. 1). New York: McGraw-Hill.

Jones, J. H. (1997). *Prejudice and racism* (2nd ed.). New York: McGraw-Hill.

Jones, M. (2002). *Social psychology of prejudice.* Upper Saddle River, NJ: Prentice-Hall

Jones, M. C. (1924). A laboratory study of fear: The case of Peter. *Journal of Genetic Psychology, 31,* 308–315.

Jones, N., Kemenes, G., & Benjamin, P. R. (2001). Selective expression of electrical correlates of differential appetitive classical conditioning in a feedback network. *Journal of Neurophysiology, 85,* 89–97.

Jou, J., Shanteau, J., & Harris, R. J. (1996). An information processing view of framing effects: The role of causal schemas in decision making. *Memory and Cognition, 24,* 1–15.

Judge, T. A., & Bono, J. E. (2001). Relationship of core self-evaluation traits—self-esteem, generalized self-efficacy, locus of control, and emotional stability—with job satisfaction and job performance: A meta-analysis. *Journal of Applied Psychology, 86,* 80–92.

Jung, C. (1917). *Analytic psychology.* New York: Moffat, Yard.

Jusczyk, P. W., & Hohne, E. A. (1997). Infants' memory for spoken words. *Science, 277,* 1984–1986.

Jussim, L., Ashmore, R., & Wilder, D. (2001). Introduction: Social identity and intergroup conflict. In R. D. Ashmore, L. Jussim, & D. Wilder (Eds.), *Social identity, intergroup conflict, and conflict resolution.* New York: Oxford University Press.

K

Kagan, J. (1992). Yesterday's premises, tomorrow's promises. *Developmental Psychology, 28,* 990–997.

Kagan, J. (1998). Biology and the child. In W. Damon (Ed.), *Handbook of child psychology* (5th ed., Vol. 3). New York: Wiley.

Kagan, J. (2000). Temperament. In A. Kazdin (Ed.), *Encyclopedia of psychology.* Washington, DC, & New York: American Psychological Association and Oxford University Press.

Kagan, S., & Madsen, M. C. (1972). Experimental analysis of cooperation and competition of Anglo-American and Mexican children. *Developmental Psychology, 6,* 49–59.

Kahneman, D., & Tversky, A. (1995). Conflict resolution: A cognitive perspective. In K. Arrow, R. H. Mnookin, L. Ross, A. Tversky, & R. Wilson (Eds.), *Barriers to conflict resolution.* New York: Norton.

Kales, A. (1970). Sleep patterns following 205 hours of sleep deprivation. *Psychosomatic Medicine, 32,* 189–200.

Kalichman, S. (1996). *Answering your questions about AIDS.* Washington, DC: American Psychological Association.

Kalick, S. M., & Hamilton, T. E. (1986). The matching hypothesis reexamined. *Journal of Personality and Social Psychology, 51,* 673–682.

Kamin, C. S., O'Sullivan, P. S., Younger, M., & Deterding, R. (2001). Measuring critical thinking in problem-based learning discourse. *Teaching and Learning in Medicine, 13,* 27–35.

Kamin, L. J. (1968). Attention-like processes in classical conditioning. In M. R. Jones (Ed.), *Miami symposium on the prediction of behavior: Aversive stimuli.* Coral Gables, FL: University of Miami Press.

Kandel, E. R., & Schwartz, J. H. (1982). Molecular biology of learning: Modulation of transmitter release. *Science, 218,* 433–443.

Kandel, E. R., Schwartz, J. H., & Jessell, T. M. (2003). *Principles of neuroscience* (5th ed.). New York: McGraw-Hill.

Kanner, A. D., Coyne, J. C., Schaeter, C., & Lazarus, R. S. (1981). Comparisons of two modes of stress measurement: Daily hassles and uplifts versus major life events. *Journal of Behavioral Medicine. 4,* 1–39.

Kanner, A. M., & Balabanov, A. (2002). Depression and epilepsy: How closely related are they? *Neurology, 58,* S27–S39.

Kaplan, R. M., & Kerner, D. N. (1998). Behavioral medicine. In H.S. Friedman (Ed.), *Encyclopedia of mental health* (Vol. 1). San Diego: Academic Press.

Karacek, R. (1979). Job demands, job decision latitude, and mental strain: Implications for job redesign. *Administrative Science Quarterly, 24,* 285–307.

Karau, S. J., & Williams, K.D. (1993). Social loafing: A meta-analytic review and theoretical integration. *Journal of Personality and Social Psychology, 65,* 681–706.

Kassin, S. M., Tubb, V. A., Hosch, H. M., & Memon, A. (2001). On the "general acceptance" of eyewitness testimony research. *American Psychologist, 56,* 405–416.

Katchadourian, H. (1987). *Fifty: Midlife in perspective.* New York: Freeman.

Katz, L. F. (1999, April). *Toward a family-based hypervigilance model of childhood aggression: The role of the mother's and the father's meta-emotion philosophy.* Paper presented at the meeting of the Society for Research in Child Development, Albuquerque.

Kaufman, A. S., & Llichtenberger, E. O. (2002). *Assessing adolescent and adult intelligence (2nd Ed.).* Boston: Allyn & Bacon.

Kaufmann, J. M., Mostert, M. P., Trent, S. C., & Hallahan, D. P. (2002). *Managing classroom behavior: A reflective, case-based approach* (3rd ed.). Boston: Allyn & Bacon.

Kavanaugh, D. J., & Wilson, P. H. (1989). Prediction of outcome with a group version of cognitive therapy for depression. *Behaviour Research and Therapy, 27,* 333–347.

Kawachi, I., & Kennedy, B. P. (2001). How income inequality affects health: Evidence from research in the United States. In J. A. Auerbach & B. K. Krimgold (Eds.), *Income, socioeconomic status, and health.* Washington, DC: National Policy Association.

Kay, J. (2002). Psychopharmacology: Combined treatment. In M. Hersen & W. H. Sledge (Eds.), *Encyclopedia of psychotherapy.* San Diego: Academic Press.

Kazdin, A. (2002). Behavior analysis. In M. Hersen & W. H. Sledge (Eds.), *Encyclopedia of psychotherapy.* San Diego: Academic Press.

Kazdin, A. E. (2000). *Essentials of conditioning and learning* (2nd ed.). Belmont, CA: Wadsworth.

Kazdin, A. E. (2001). *Behavior modification in applied settings* (6th ed.). Belmont, CA: Wadsworth.

Kearney, C. A., & Vecchio, J. (2002). Contingency management. In M. Hersen & W. H. Sledge (Eds.), *Encyclopedia of psychotherapy.* San Diego: Academic Press.

Keck, P. E., McElroy, S. L., & Arnold, I. M. (2001). Bipolar disorder. *Medical Clinics of North America, 85,* 645–661.

Keel, P. K., Mitchell, J. E., Miller, K. B., Davis, T. L., & Crowe, S. J. (1999). Long-term outcome of bulimia nervosa. *Archives of General Psychiatry, 56,* 63–69.

Keillor, J. M., Barrett, A. M., Crucian, G. P., Kortenkamp, S., & Heilman, K. M. (2002). Emotional experience and perception in the absence of facial feedback. *Journal of the International Neuropsychological Society, 8,* 130–135.

Kelsoe, J. R., Spence, M. A., Loetscher, E., Foguet, M., Sadovinick, A. D., Remick, R. A., Khristich, J., Mrosczkowski-Parker, Z., Brown, J. L., Masster, D., Ungerleider, S., Rapaport, M. H., Wishart, W. L., & Luebbert, H. (2001). A genome survey indicates a possible susceptibility locus for bipolar disorder on chromosome 22. *Proceedings of the National Academy of Science, 98,* 585–590.

Keltner, D., & Ekman, P. (2000). Emotion: An overview. In A. Kazdin (Ed.), *Encyclopedia of psychology.* Washington, DC, & New York: American Psychological Association and Oxford University Press.

Kempermann, G., & Gage, F. H. (1999, May). New nerve cells for the adult brain. *Scientific American,* 48–53.

Kendler, K. S., Myers, J., & Prescott, C.A. (2002). The etiology of phobias: An evaluation of the diathesis-stress model. *Archives of General Psychiatry, 59,* 242–248.

Kennaway, D. J., & Wright, H. (2002). Melatonin and circadian rhythms. *Current Topics in Medicinal Chemistry, 2,* 199–209.

Kennedy, P. G. E., & Folk-Seang, J. F. (1986). Studies on the development, antigenic phenotype and function of human glial cells in tissue culture. *Brain, 109,* 1261–1277.

Kephart, W. M. (1967). Some correlates of romantic love. *Journal of Marriage and the Family, 29,* 470–474.

Kerston, D. (2002). Shape and form perception. *Annual Review of Psychology* (Vol. 53).

Kesey, K. (1962). *One flew over the cuckoo's nest.* New York: Viking Press.

Kessler, R. C., McGonagle, K. A., Zhao, S., Nelson, C. B, Hughes, M., Eshleman, S., Wittchen, H., & Kendler, K. S. (1994). Lifetime and 12-month prevalence of DSM-III-R psychiatric disorders in the United States: Results from the National Comorbidity Study. *Archives of General Psychiatry, 51,* 8–19.

Kessler, R. C., Olfson, M., & Berglund, P. A. (1998). Patterns and predictors of treatment contact after first onset of psychiatric disorders. *American Journal of Psychiatry, 155,* 62–69.

Kessler, R. C., Stein, M. B., & Berglund, P. (1998). Social phobia subtypes in the National Comorbidity Survey. *American Journal of Psychiatry, 155,* 613–619.

Kiecolt-Glaser, J. K., Dura, J. R., Specher, C. E., Trask, O. J., & Glaser, R. (1991). Spousal caregivers of dementia victims. *Psychosomatic Medicine, 53,* 345–362.

Kiecolt-Glaser, J. K., McGuire, L., Robles, T. F., & Glaser, R. (2002a). Psychoneuroimmunology and psychosomatic medicine: Back to the future. *Psychosomatic Medicine, 64,* 15–28.

Kiecolt-Glaser, J. K., McGuire, L., Robles, T. F., & Glaser, R. (2002b). Emotions, morbidity, and mortality: New perspectives from psychoneuroimmunology. *Annual Review of Psychology, 53.* Palo Alto, CA: Annual Reviews.

Kiernan, M., Kraemer, H. C., Winckleby, M. A., King, A. C., & Taylor, C. B. (2001). Do logistic regression and signal detection identify different subgroups at risk? *Psychological Methods, 6,* 35–48.

Kihlstrom, J. F. (1992). Dissociation and dissociations: A comment on consciousness and cognition. *Consciousness & Cognition: An International Journal, 1,* 47–53.

Kikyo, H., Ohki, K., & Sekihara, K. (2001). Temporal characterization of memory retrieval process: An fMRI study of the "tip-of-the-tongue" phenomenon. *European Journal of Neuroscience, 14,* 887–892.

Kimble, G. A. (1961). *Hilgard and Marquis's conditioning and learning.* New York: Appleton-Century-Crofts.

Kimble, G. A. (1989). Psychology from the standpoint of a generalist. *American Psychologist, 44,* 491–499.

Kimbrough, S. K., Wright, D. L., & Shea, C. H. (2001). Reducing the saliency of intentional stimuli results in greater context-dependent performance. *Memory, 9,* 133–143.

Kimmel, A. (1996). *Ethical issues in behavioral research.* Cambridge, MA: Blackwell.

Kimmell, E., & Crawford, M. C. (2002). Methods of studying gender. In J. Worell (Ed.), *Encyclopedia of women and gender.* New York: Oxford University Press.

Kimura, D. (2000). *Sex and cognition.* Cambridge, MA: MIT Press.

King, H. E. (1961). Psychological effects of excitement of the limbic system. In D. E. Sheer (Ed.), *Electrical stimulation of the brain.* Austin: University of Texas Press.

King, L. A., & Pennebaker, J. (1998). *Subjective well-being.* Unpublished manuscript, Southern Methodist University, Dallas, TX.

King, R. N., & Koehler, D. J. (2000). Illusory correlations in graphological inference. *Journal of Experimental Psychology: Applied, 6,* 336–348.

Kinsey, A. C., Pomeroy, W. B., & Martin, E. E. (1948). *Sexual behavior in the human male.* Philadelphia: W. B. Saunders.

Kirsch, I. & Sapirstein, G. (1998). Listening to Prozac but hearing placebo: A meta-analysis of antidepressant medication. *Prevention and Treatment, 1,* Article 0002a, posted June 26, 1998. (Retrieved from http://www.journals.apa.org/prevention/volume1/pre0010002a.html).

Kitayama, S. (2002). Culture and basic psychological processes—Toward a system view of culture: Comment on Oyserman et al. (2002). *Psychological Bulletin, 128,* 89–96.

Kite, M. (2001). Gender stereotypes. In J. Worell (Ed.), *Encyclopedia of women and gender.* San Diego: Academic Press.

Kitzmann, K., & Gaylord, N. K. (2002). Divorce and child custody. In J. Worell (Ed.), *Encyclopedia of women and gender.* New York: Oxford University Press.

Klein, K., & Boals, A. (2001). Expressive writing can increase working memory capacity. *Journal of Experimental Psychology: General, 130,* 520–533.

Klein, S. (2002). *Learning (4th Ed.).* New York: McGraw-Hill.

Kliegel, M., Martin, M., McDaniel, M. A., & Einstein, G. O. (2001). Varying the importance of a prospective memory task: Differential effects across time- and event-based prospective memory. *Memory, 9,* 1–11.

Kline, W. B. (2003). *Interactive group work.* Upper Saddle River, NJ: Prentice-Hall.

Klinger, E. (2000). Daydreams. In A. Kazdin (Ed.), *Encyclopedia of psychology.* Washington, DC, & New York: American Psychological Association and Oxford University Press.

Klug, W. S., & Cummings, M. R. (2003). *Genetics: A molecular perspective.* Upper Saddle River, NJ: Prentice-Hall.

Kluznik, J. C., Walbek, N. H., Farnsworth, M. G., & Melstrom, K. (2001). Clinical effects of a randomized switch of patients from clozaril to generic clozapine. *Journal of Clinical Psychiatry, 62,* (Suppl. 5), 14–17.

Knight, J. A. (2000). The biochemistry of aging. *Advances in Clinical Chemistry, 35,* 1–62.

Knox, J. M. (2002). Memories, fantasies, archetypes: An exploration of some connections between cognitive science and analytical psychology. *Journal of Analytical Psychology, 46,* 613–635.

Kobasa, S. C., Maddi, S. R., Puccetti, M. C., & Zola, M. (1986). Relative effectiveness of hardiness, exercise, and social support as resources against illness. *Journal of Psychosomatic Research, 29,* 525–533.

Kobasa, S., Maddi, S., & Kahn, S. (1982). Hardiness and health: A prospective study. *Journal of Personality and Social Psychology, 42,* 168–177.

Koenig, H. G. (2001). Religion and medicine: II. Religion, mental health, and related behaviors. *International Journal of Psychiatry, 31,* 97–109.

Koenig, H. G., & Cohen, H. J. (Eds.). (2002). *The link between religion and health.* New York: Oxford University Press.

Koenig, H. G., & Larson, D. B. (1998). Religion and mental health. In H.S. Friedman (Ed.), *Encyclopedia of mental health* (Vol. 3). San Diego: Academic Press.

Kohlberg, L. (1958). *The development of modes of moral thinking and choice in the years 10 to 16.* Unpublished doctoral dissertation, University of Chicago.

Kohlberg, L. (1969). Stage and sequence: The cognitive-developmental approach to socialization. In D. A. Goslin (Ed.), *Handbook of socialization theory and research.* Chicago: Rand McNally.

Kohlberg, L. (1976). Moral stages and moralization: The cognitive-developmental approach. In T. Lickona (Ed.), *Moral development and behavior.* New York: Holt, Rinehart, & Winston.

Kohlberg, L. (1986). A current statement on some theoretical issues. In S. Modgil & C. Modgil (Eds.), *Lawrence Kohlberg.* Philadelphia: Falmer.

Kohler, W. (1925). *The mentality of apes.* New York: Harcourt Brace Jovanovich.

Kohut, H. (1977). *Restoration of the self.* New York: International Universities Press.

Kolb, B. (1989). Brain development, plasticity, and behavior. *American Psychologist, 44,* 1203–1212.

Kolb, B., & Whishaw, I. Q. (2001). *Introduction to brain and behavior.* New York: Worth.

Kolb, L. (1973). *Modern clinical psychiatry* (8th ed.). Philadelphia: W.B. Saunders.

Kolchakian, M. R., & Hill, C. E. (2002). Dream interpretation with heterosexual dating couples. *Dreaming, 12,* 1–16.

Kondziolka D., Wechsler, L., Goldstein, S., Meltzer, C., Thulborn, K. R., Gebel, J., Jannetta, P., DeCesare, S., Elder, E. M., McGrogan, M., Reitman, M. A., & Bynum, L. (2000). Transplantation of cultured human neuronal cells for patients with stroke. *Journal of Neurology, 55,* 565–569.

Kopp, C. (1984). *Baby steps.* New York: Freeman.

Kornstein, S. G., & Clayton, A. H. (Eds.). (2002). *Women's mental health.* New York: Guilford.

Koss, M., & Boeschen, L. (1998). Rape. In H. S. Friedman (Ed.), *Encyclopedia of mental health* (Vol. 3). San Diego: Academic Press.

Kosslyn, S. M. (1994). *Image and brain: The resolution of the imagery debate.* Cambridge, MA: MIT Press.

Kotani, S., Kawahara, S., & Kirino, Y. (2002). Classical eyeblink conditioning in decerebrate guinea pigs. *European Journal of Neuroscience, 15,* 1267–1270.

Kraik, K. H. (2000). Personality: Methods of study. In A. Kazdin (Ed.), *Encyclopedia of psychology.* Washington, DC, & New York: American Psychological Association and Oxford University Press.

Kramer, M. S., Cutler, N., Feighner, J., Shrivastava, R., Carman, J., Sramek, J. J., Reines, S. A., Liu, G., Snavely, D., Wyatt-Knowles, E., Hale, J. J., Mills, S., MacCoss, M., Swain, C. J., Harrison, T., Hill, R. G., Hefti, G. C., Scolnick, E. M., Casieri, M. A., Chicchi, G. G., Sadowski, S., Williams, A. R., Hewson, L., Smith, D., Carlson, E. J., Hargreaves, R. J., & Rupniak, N. M. J. (1998). Distinct mechanism for antidepressant activity by blockade of central substance P receptors. *Science, 281,* 1640–1645.

Kramer, P. D. (1993). *Listening to Prozac.* New York: Viking.

Krashen, S. D. (1996, May 9). *Bilingual education: Arguments for and (bogus) arguments against.* Paper presented at the Georgetown University Roundtable on Languages and Linguistics, Washington, DC.

Krause, J. B., Taylor, J. G., Schmidt, D., Hautzel, H., Mottaghy, F. M., & Muller-Gartner, H. W. (2000). Imaging and neural modelling in episodic and working memory processes. *Neural Networks, 13,* 847–849.

Krauss, J. K., & Jankovic, J. (2002). Head injury and posttraumatic movement disorders. *Neurosurgery, 50,* 927–940.

Kraut, R., Patterson, M., Lundmark, V., Kiesler, S., Mukopadhyay, T., & Scherlis, W. (1998). Internet paradox. *American Psychologist, 53,* 1017–1031.

Kris, A. O. (2002). Free association. In M. Hersen & W. H. Sledge (Eds.), *Encyclopedia of psychotherapy.* San Diego: Academic Press.

Krogh, D. (2000). *Biology.* Upper Saddle River, NJ: Prentice-Hall.

Krull, D. S. (2001). On partitioning the fundamental attribution error. In G. B. Moskowitz (Ed.), *Cognitive social psychology.* Mahwah, NJ: Erlbaum.

Krupa, D. J., Thompson, J. K., & Thompson, R. E. (1993). Localization of a memory trace in the mammalian brain. *Science, 260,* 989–991.

Kuch, K., & Cox, B. J. (1992). Symptoms of PTSD in 124 survivors of the Holocaust. *American Journal of Psychiatry, 149,* 337–340.

Kuhl, P. K. (1993). Infant speech perception: A window on psycholinguistic development. *International Journal of Psycholinguistics, 9,* 33–56.

Kuhl, P. K. (2000). A new view of language acquisition. *Proceedings of the National Academy of Science, USA, 97,* 11850–11857.

Kuhn, D., Weinstock, M., & Flaton, R. (1994). How well do jurors reason? Competence dimensions of individual variation in a juror reasoning task. *Psychological Science, 5,* 289–296.

Kulik, J. A., Bangert-Drowns, R. L., & Kulik, C. C. (1984). The effectiveness of coaching for aptitude tests. *Psychological Bulletin, 95,* 179–188.

Kulik, J. A., Kulik, C. C., & Bangert-Drowns, R. L. (1985). Effectiveness of computer-based education in elementary schools. *Computers in Human Behavior, 1,* 59–74.

Kutchinsky, B. (1991). Pornography and rape: Theory and practice? Evidence from crime data in four countries where pornography is easily available. *International Journal of Law and Psychiatry, 14,* 47–64.

L

La Greca, A., Silverman, W. K., Vernberg, E. M., & Prinstein, M. J. (1996). Symptoms of post-traumatic stress in children after Hurricane Andrew: A prospective study. *Journal of Consulting and Clinical Psychology, 64,* 712–723.

LaBar, K. S., & LeDoux, J. E. (2002). Emotional learning circuits in animals and man. In R. J. Davidson, K. R. Scherer, & H. H. Goldsmith (Eds.), *Handbook of affective sciences.* New York: Oxford University Press.

LaBar, K. S., Gitelman, D. R., Parrish, T. B., & Mesulam, M. M. (2002). Functional changes in temporal lobe activity during transient global amnesia. *Neurology, 58,* 638–641.

Labbe, E. E. (1998). Biofeedback. In H.S. Friedman (Ed.), *Encyclopedia of mental health* (Vol. 1). San Diego: Academic Press.

Labott, S. M., & Martin, R. B. (1990). Emotional coping, age, and physical disorder. *Behavioral Medicine, 16,* 53–61.

Laboure, H., Van Wymelbeke, V., Fantino, M., & Nicolaidis, S. (2002). Behavioral, plasma, and calorimetric changes related to food texture modification in men. *American Journal of Physiology: Regulatory, Integrative, and Comparative Physiology, 282,* R1501–R1511.

Labouvie-Vief, G. (1986, August). *Modes of knowing and life-span cognition.* Paper presented at the meeting of the American Psychological Association, Washington, DC.

Lam, L. T., & Kirby, S. L. (2002). Is emotional intelligence an advantage? An exploration of the impact of emotional and general intelligence on individual performance. *Journal of Social Psychology, 142,* 133–142.

Lamb, C. S., Jackson, L. A., Cassiday, P. B., & Priest, D. J. (1993). Body figure preferences of men and women: A comparison of two generations. *Sex Roles, 28,* 345–358.

Lamb, M. E., Hwang, C. P., Ketterlinus, R. D., & Fracasso, M. P. (1999). Parent-child relationships: Development in the context of the family. In M. H. Bornstein & M. E. Lamb (Eds.), *Developmental psychology: An advanced textbook* (4th ed.). Mahwah, NJ: Erlbaum.

Lambert, M. J. (2001). The effectiveness of psychotherapy: What a century of research tells us about the effects of treatment. *Psychotherapeutically speaking–Updates from the Division of Psychotherapy (29).* Washington, DC: American Psychological Association.

Lambert, M. J., & Ogles, B. M. (2002). The efficacy and effectiveness of psychotherapy. In M. J. Lambert (Ed.), *Handbook of psychotherapy and behavior change* (5th ed.). New York: Wiley.

Lambert, W. E., Genesee, F., Holobow, N., & Chartrand, L. (1993). Bilingual education for majority English-speaking children. *European Journal of Psychology of Education, 8,* 3–22.

Lammers, H. B. (2000). Effects of deceptive packaging and product involvement on purchase intention: An elaboration likelihood model perspective. *Psychological Reports, 86*, 546–550.

Landrine, H., & Klonoff, E. A. (2001). Cultural diversity and health psychology. In A. Baum, T.A. Revenson, & J.E. Singer (Eds.), *Handbook of health psychology*. Mahwah, NJ: Erlbaum.

Landy, M. (2002). Depth, space, and motion. *Annual Review of Psychology* (Vol. 53).

Lane, H. (1976). *The wild boy of Aveyron*. Cambridge, MA: Harvard University Press.

Lane, R. D., Reiman, E. M., Bradley, M. M., Lang, P. J., Ahern, G. L., Davidson, R. J., & Scwartz, G. E. (1997). Neuroanatomical correlates of pleasant and unpleasant emotion. *Neuropsychologia, 35*, 1437–1444.

Lang, F. R., & Carstensen, L. L. (1994). Close emotional relationships in late life: Further support for proactive aging in the social domain. *Psychology and Aging, 9*, 315–324.

Lang, P. J., Davis, M., & Ohman, A. (2000). Fear and anxiety: Animal models and human cognitive psychophysiology. *Journal of Affective Disorders, 61*, 137–159.

Lange, C. G. (1922). *The emotions*. Baltimore: Williams & Wilkins.

Langenfeld, M. C., Cipani, E., & Borckardt, J. J. (2002). Hypnosis for the control of HIV/AIDS-related pain. *International Journal of Clinical and Experimental Hypnosis, 50*, 170–188.

Langer, E. (1989). *Mindfulness*. Reading, MA: Addison-Wesley.

Langer, E. (1997). *The power of mindful learning*. Reading, MA: Addison-Wesley.

Langer, E. J. (2000). Mindful learning. *Current Directions in Psychological Science, 9*, 220–223.

Langer, E. J., & Moldoveanu, M. (2000). The construct of mindfulness. *Journal of Social Issues, 56*, 1–11.

Langer, L. L. (1991). *Holocaust testimonies: The ruins of memory*. New Haven: Yale University Press.

Langs, R. (1978). *Technique in transition*. New York: Jason Aronson.

Langston, W. (2002). *Research methods manual for psychology*. Belmont, CA: Wadsworth.

Larcerda, F., von Hofsten, C., & Heimann, M. (Eds.). (2000). *Emerging cognitive abilities in early infancy*. Mahwah, NJ: Erlbaum.

Larsen, J. P., & Tandberg, E. (2001). Sleep disorders in patients with Parkinson's disease. *CNS and Drugs, 15*, 267–275.

Larsen, R. J., & Buss, D. M. (2002). *Personality psychology: Domains of knowledge about human nature*. New York: McGraw-Hill.

Larson, R. (2000). Toward a psychology of positive youth development. *American Psychologist, 55*, 170–183.

Larson, R. J., & Buss, D. M. (2002). *Personality psychology*. New York: McGraw-Hill.

Lashley, K. (1950). In search of the engram. In *Symposium of the Society for Experimental Biology* (Vol. 4). New York: Cambridge University Press.

Latané, B. (1981). The psychology of social impact. *American Psychologist, 36*, 343–356.

Latané, B. (1996). Strength from weakness: The fate of opinion minorities in spatially distributed groups. In E. H. Witte & J. H. Davis (Eds.), *Understanding group behavior* (Vol. 1). Mahwah, NJ: Erlbaum.

Laurent, G., Stopfer, M., Friedrich, W., Rabinovich, M. I., Volkovski, A., & Abarbanel, H. D. (2001). Odor encoding as an active, dynamical process. *Annual Review of Neuroscience* (Vol. 25). Palo Alto, CA: Annual Reviews.

Lavie, P. (2001). Sleep-wake as a biological rhythm. *Annual Review of Psychology, 52*.

Lazar, S. W, Bush, G., Gollub, R. L., Fricchione, G. L., Khalsa, G., & Benson, H. (2000). Functional brain mapping of the relaxation response and meditation. *Neuroreport, 15*, 1581–1585.

Lazarus, A. A. (1996). A multimodal behavior therapist's perspective on the truth. In G. Corey (Ed.), *Case approach to counseling and psychotherapy* (4th ed.). Pacific Grove, CA: Brooks/Cole.

Lazarus, A. A., Beutler, L. E., & Norcross, J. C. (1992). The future of technical eclecticism. *Psychotherapy, 29*, 11–20.

Lazarus, R. S. (1991). On the primacy of cognition. *American Psychologist, 39*, 124–129.

Lazarus, R. S. (1993). Coping theory and research: Past, present, and future. *Psychosomatic Medicine, 55*, 234–247.

Lazarus, R. S. (2000). Toward better research on stress and coping. *American Psychologist 55*, 665–673.

Le Vay, S. (1994). *The sexual brain*. Cambridge, MA: MIT Press.

Leadbeater, B. J., & Way, N. (2001). *Growing up fast*. Mahwah, NJ: Erlbaum.

Leahy, T. H. (2001). *A history of modern psychology* (3rd ed.). Upper Saddle River, NJ: Prentice-Hall.

Leahy, T. H., & Harris, R. J. (2001). *Learning and memory* (5th ed.). Upper Saddle River, NJ: Prentice-Hall.

Leary, M. R., Nezlek, J. B., Downs, D., Radford-Davenport, J., Martin, J., & McMullen, A. (1994). Self-presentation in everyday interactions. *Journal of Personality and Social Psychology, 67*, 664–673.

Leavitt, F. (2000). *Evaluating scientific research*. Upper Saddle River, NJ: Prentice Hall

LeBoeuf, B. J., & Peterson, R. S. (1969). Social status and mating activity in elephant seals. *Science, 163*, 91–93.

Lederman, S., & Klatsky, R. (1998, June). Commentary in B. Azar's "From surgery to robotics, touch is the key," *APA Monitor*, p. 21.

LeDoux, J. (2002). *The synaptic self*. New York: Viking.

LeDoux, J. E. (2000). Emotion circuits in the brain. *Annual Review of Neuroscience, 23*, 155–184.

LeDoux, J. E. (1996). *The emotional brain: The mysterious underpinnings of emotional life*. New York: Simon & Schuster.

LeDoux, J. E. (2001). *Emotion, memory, and the brain*. Retrieved October 15, 2001, from http://www.cns.nyu.edu/home/ledoux.html

Lee, D. J., & Markides, K. S. (1990). Activity and mortality among aged persons over an eight-year period. *Journals of Gerontology: Social Sciences, 45*, S39–S42.

Lee, G., & Farhat, N. H. (2001). The bifurcating neuron network. *Neural Networks, 14*, 115–131.

Lee, I., Hsieh, C., & Paffenbarger, O. (1995). Exercise intensity and longevity in men. *Journal of the American Medical Association, 273*, 1179–1184.

Lee, Y. S., Cheung, Y. M., & Wurm, L. H. (2000). Levels-of-processing effects on Chinese character completion: The importance of lexical processing and test cue. *Memory and Cognition, 28*, 1398–1405.

Lehar, S. M. (2002). *The world in your head*. Mahwah, NJ: Erlbaum.

Leiter, M. P., & Maslach, C. (1998). Burnout. In H.S. Friedman (Ed.), *Encyclopedia of mental health* (Vol. 1). San Diego: Academic Press.

Leiter, M. P., & Maslach, C. (2001). Burnout and health. In A. Baum, T.A. Revenson, & J.E. Singer (Eds.), *Handbook of health psychology*. Mahwah, NJ: Erlbaum.

Leith, L. M. (1998). Exercise and mental health. In H.S. Friedman (Ed.), *Encyclopedia of mental health* (Vol. 2). San Diego: Academic Press.

Lemke, G. E. (2001). Glial control of neuronal development. *Annual Review of Neuroscience, 24*.

Lenneberg, E. (1967). *The biological foundations of language*. New York: Wiley.

Lenneberg, E. H., Rebelsky, F. G., & Nichols, I. A. (1965). The vocalization of infants born to deaf and hearing parents. *Human Development, 8*, 23–37.

Leon, G. R. (1990). *Case histories of psychopathology* (4th ed.). Boston: Allyn & Bacon.

Lepper, M., Greene, D., & Nisbett, R. E. (1973). Undermining children's intrinsic interest with extrinsic rewards. *Journal of Personality and Social Psychology, 28*, 129–137.

Lerner, R. (2002). *Concepts and theories of human development* (3rd ed.). Mahwah, NJ: Erlbaum.

Lerner, R. M. (2000). Developmental psychology: Theories. In A. Kazdin (Ed.), *Encyclopedia of psychology*. Washington, DC, & New York: American Psychological Association and Oxford University Press.

Lessard, N., Pare, M., Lepore, F., & Lassonde, M. (1998). Early-blind human subjects localize sound sources better than sighted subjects. *Nature, 395*, 278–280.

Lesserman, J., Golden, R. N., Petitto, J. M., Gaynes, B. N., Gu, H., Folds, J. D., & Evans, D. L. (2001, March). *Progression to AIDS: The effects of stress, social support, coping, cortisol, and viral load*. Paper presented at the meeting of the American Psychosomatic Society, Monterey, CA.

Lessow-Hurley, J. (2000). *Foundations of dual language instruction* (3rd ed.). Boston: Allyn & Bacon.

Lester, D. (1992). Cooperative/competitive strategies and locus of control. *Psychological Reports, 71*(2), 594.

Leunes, A. & Nation, J. (2002). *Sport psychology* (3rd ed.). Belmont, CA: Wadsworth.

Levanen, S., & Hamdorf, D. (2001). Feeling vibrations: Enhanced tactile sensitivity in congenitally deaf humans. *Neuroscience Letters, 301*, 75–77.

Levanen, S., Jousmak, V., & Hari, R. (1998). Vibration-induced auditory-cortex activation in a congenitally deaf adult. *Current Biology, 8*, 869–872.

Levant, R. (2001). Men and masculinity. In J. Worell (Ed.), *Encyclopedia of women and gender*. San Diego: Academic Press.

Levant, R. F., & Brooks, G. R. (1997). *Men and sex: New psychological perspectives*. New York: Wiley.

LeVay, S. (1991). A difference in the hypothalamic structure between heterosexual and homosexual men. *Science, 253,* 1034–1037.

Leventhal, H., & Tomarken, A. J. (1986). Emotion: Today's problems. *Annual Review of Psychology, 37,* 565–610.

Levin, J. S., & Vanderpool, H. Y. (1989). Is religion therapeutically significant for hypertension? *Social Science and Medicine, 29,* 69–78.

Levine, D. S. (2000). *Introduction to neural and cognitive modeling* (2nd ed.). Mahwah, NJ: Erlbaum.

Levine, J. D., Gordon, N. C., & Fields, H. L. (1979). Naloxone dose dependently produces analgesia and hyperalgesia in postoperative pain. *Nature, 278,* 740–741.

Levine, J. H., & Moreland, R. H. (1998). Small groups. In D. T. Gilbert, S. T. Fiske, & G. Lindzey (Eds.), *Handbook of social psychology* (4th ed., Vol. 2). New York: McGraw-Hill.

Levine, J. M. (2000). Groups: Group processes. In A. Kazdin (Ed.), *Encyclopedia of psychology.* Washington, DC, & New York: American Psychological Association and Oxford University Press.

Levine, R. L. (2002). Endocrine aspects of eating disorders in adolescents. *Adolescent Medicine, 13,* 129–144.

Levinson, D. (1978). *The seasons of a man's life.* New York: Knopf.

Levinson, D. J. (1996). *Seasons of a woman's life.* New York: Knopf.

Levy, L. (1979). Handwriting and hiring. *Dun's Review, 113,* 72–79.

Levy, S. M., Herberman, R. B., Lee, J., Whiteside, T., Kirckwood, J., & McFreeley, S. (1990). Estrogen receptor concentration and social factors as predictors of natural killer cell activity in early-stage breast cancer patients. *Natural Immunity and Cell Growth Regulation, 9,* 313–324.

Levy, T. M. (Ed.). (1999). *Handbook of attachment interventions.* San Diego: Academic Press.

Lewinsohn, P. (1987). The Coping with Depression course. In R. F. Munoz (Ed.), *Depression prevention.* New York: Hemisphere.

Lewinsohn, P. M., & Gotlib, I. H. (1995). Behavioral therapy and treatment of depression. In E. E. Beckham & W. R. Leber (Eds.), *Handbook of depression* (2nd ed., pp. 352–375). New York: Guilford.

Lewinsohn, P. M., Antonuccio, D. O., Steinmetz, J., & Teri, L. (1984). *The coping with depression course: A psychoeducational intervention for unipolar depression.* Eugene, OR: Castalia.

Lewinsohn, P. M., Joiner, T. E., & Rohde, P. (2001). Evaluation of cognitive diathesis-stress models in predicting major depressive disorder in adolescence. *Journal of Abnormal Psychology, 110,* 203–215.

Lewinsohn, P. M., Striegel-Moore, R. H., & Seeley, J. R. (2000). Epidemiology and natural course of eating disorders in young women from adolescence to young adulthood. *Journal of American Academy of Child and Adolescent Psychiatry, 39,* 1284–1292.

Lewis, M. (1997). *Altering fate: Why the past does not predict the future.* New York: Guilford Press.

Lewis, R. (2001). *Life* (4th ed.). New York: McGraw-Hill.

Lewis, R. (2002). *Human genetics* (4th ed.). New York: McGraw-Hill.

Lewis, R. (2003). *Human genetics* (5th Ed.). New York: McGraw-Hill.

Lewis, R., Hoefnageis, M., Gaffi, D., & Parker, B. (2002). *Life* (4th ed.). New York: McGraw-Hill.

Li, D., Chokka, P., & Tibbo, P. (2001). Toward an integrative understanding of social phobia. *Journal of Psychiatry and Neuoroscience, 26,* 190–202.

Lieber, C. S. (1997). Gender differences in alcohol metabolism and susceptibility. In S.C. Wilsnack & R.W. Wilsnack (Eds.), *Gender and alcohol.* New Brunswick, NJ: Rutgers Center of Alcohol Studies.

Light, L. L. (2000). Memory changes in adulthood. In S. H. Qualls & N. Abeles (Eds.), *Psychology and the aging revolution.* Washington, DC, & New York: American Psychological Association and Oxford University Press.

Lilienfeld, S. O., Wood, J. M., & Garb, H. N. (2000, November). The scientific status of projective techniques. *Psychological Science in the Public Interest, 1* (2).

Lindeman, M. (1998). Motivation, cognition, and pseudoscience. *Scandinavian Journal of Psychology, 39,* 257–265.

Linden, W., Lenz, J. W., & Con, A. H. (2001). Individualized stress management for primary hypertension: A randomized trial. *Archives of Internal Medicine, 161,* 1071–1080.

Lindqvist, R., & Aberg, H. (2002). Locus of control in relation to smoking cessation during pregnancy. *Scandinavian Journal of Public Health, 30,* 30–35.

Lindvall, O. (2001). Parkinson disease: Stem cell transplanation. *Lancet, 358* [Supplement], S48.

Lingjaerde, O., Foreland, A. R., & Engvik, H. (2001). Personality structure in patients with winter depression, assessed in a depression-free state according to the five-factor model of personality. *Journal of Affective Disorders, 62,* 165–174.

Lips, H. M. (2003). *A new psychology of women: Gender, culture, and ethnicity* (2nd ed.). New York: McGraw-Hill.

Lipsey, M. W., & Wilson, D. B. (1993). The efficacy of psychological, educational, and behavioral treatment: Confirmation from meta-analysis. *American Psychologist, 48,* 1181–1209.

Lister, P. (1992, July). A skeptic's guide to psychics. *Redbook,* pp. 103–105, 112–113.

Livanou, M., Basoglu, M., Marks, I. M., De, S. P., Noshirvani, H., & Lovell, K. (2002). Beliefs, sense of control, and treatment outcome in post-traumatic stress disorder. *Psychological Medicine, 32,* 157–165.

Lively, W. J. (2001). *Handbook of personality disorders.* New York: Guilford.

Lochman, J. J. (2000). A perception-action perspective on tool use development. *Child Development, 71,* 137–144.

Locke, E. A. (2001). Setting goals for life and happiness. In C. R. Snyder & S. J. Lopez (Eds.), *Handbook of positive psychology.* New York: Oxford University Press.

Locke, J. L. (1993). *The child's path to spoken language.* Cambridge, MA: Harvard University Press.

Locke, J. L. (1999). Towards a biological science of language development. In M. Barrett (Ed.), *The development of language.* Philadelphia: Psychology Press.

Loehr, J. (1989, May). (Personal communication). United States Tennis Association Training Camp, Saddlebrook, FL.

Loftus, E. F. (1975). Spreading activation within semantic categories. *Journal of Experimental Psychology, 104,* 234–240.

Loftus, E. F. (1993a). Psychologists in the eyewitness world. *American Psychologist, 48,* 550–552.

Loftus, E., & Ketcham, K. (1994). *The myth of repressed memory: False memories and allegations of abuse.* New York: St. Martin's Press.

Logie, R. H. (1995). *Visuospatial working memory.* Hove, England: Erlbaum.

Longo, D. A., Lent, R. W., & Brown, S. D. (1992). Social cognitive variables in the prediction of client motivation and attribution. *Journal of Counseling Psychology, 39,* 447–452.

Lopez, S. R., & Guarnaccia, P. J. (2000). Cultural psychopathology: Uncovering the social world of mental illness. *Annual Review of Psychology, 51.* Palo Alto, CA: Annual Reviews.

Lorenz, K. Z. (1965). *Evolution and the modification of behavior.* Chicago: University of Chicago Press.

Lott, B., & Maluso, D. (2002). Gender development: Social learning. In J. Worell (Ed.), *Encyclopedia of women and gender.* New York: Oxford University Press.

Louie, T. A., Curren, M. T., & Harich, K. R. (2000). "I knew we would win": Hindsight bias for favorable and unfavorable team decision outcomes. *Journal of Applied Psychology, 85,* 264–272.

Lucurto, C. (1990). The malleability of IQ as judged from adoption studies. *Intelligence, 14,* 275–292.

Ludolph, P. (1982, August). *A reanalysis of the literature on multiple personality.* Paper presented at the meeting of the American Psychological Association, Washington, DC.

Luria, A. R. (1973). *The working brain.* New York: Penguin.

Luria, A. R. (1968). *The mind of a mnemonist.* New York: Basic Books.

Luria, A., & Herzog, E. (1985, April). *Gender segregation across and within settings.* Paper presented at the biennial meeting of the Society for Research in Child Development, Toronto.

Lutz, D. J., & Sternberg, R. J. (1999). Cognitive development. In M. H. Bornstein & M. E. Lamb (Eds.), *Developmental psychology: An advanced textbook* (4th ed.). Mahwah, NJ: Erlbaum.

Lyall, V., Alam, R. I., Phan, D. Q., Heck, G. L., & DeSimone, J. A. (2002). Excitation and adaptation in the detection of hydrogen ions by taste receptor cells: a role for cAMP and CA (2+). *Journal of Neurophysiology, 87,* 399–408.

Lykken, D. T. (1987). The probity of the polygraph. In S. M. Kassin & L. S. Wrightsman (Eds.), *The psychology of evidence and trial procedures.* Newbury Park, CA: Sage.

Lykken, D. T. (2001). Lie detection. In W. E. Craighead & C. B. Nemeroff (Eds.), *The Corsini encyclopedia of psychology and behavioral science* (3rd ed.). New York: Wiley.

Lynch, G. (1990, June). *The many shapes of memory and the several forms of synaptic plasticity.* Paper presented at the meeting of the American Psychological Society, Dallas.

Lynn, R. (1996). Racial and ethnic differences in intelligence in the U.S. on the Differential Ability Scale. *Personality and Individual Differences, 26,* 271–273.

M

Maas, J. (1998). *Power sleep.* New York: Villard.

Macaluso, E., Frith, C. D., & Driver, J. (2002). Directing attention to locations and to sensory modalities: Multiple levels of selective processing revealed with PET. *Cerebral Cordex, 12,* 357–368.

Maccoby, E. E. (2000). Parenting and its effects on children: Reading and misreading behavior genetics. *Annual Review of Psychology, 51.* Palo Alto, CA: Annual Reviews.

Maccoby, E. E., & Jacklin, C. N. (1974). *The psychology of sex differences.* Palo Alto, CA: Stanford University Press.

MacKenzie, R. (2002). Group psychotherapy. In M. Hersen & W. H. Sledge (Eds.), *Encyclopedia of psychotherapy.* San Diego: Academic Press.

MacKinnon, D., Jamison, K. R., & DePaulo, J. R. (1997). Genetics of manic depressive illness. *Annual Review of Neuroscience, 20,* 355–373.

MacKinnon, D. F., Zandi, P. P., Cooper, J., Potash, J. B., Simpson, S. G., & Gershon, E. (2002). Comorbid bipolar disorder and panic disorder in families with a high prevalence of bipolar disorder. *American Journal of Psychiatry, 159,* 30–35.

MacLeod, C., Rutherford, E., Campbell, L., Ebsworthy, G., & Holker, L. (2002). Selective attention and emotional vulnerability: Assessing the casual basis of their association through the experimental manipulation of attentional bias. *Journal of Abnormal Psychology, 111,* 107–123.

MacWhinney, B. (Ed.) (1999). *The emergence of language.* Mahwah, NJ: Erlbaum.

Madden, D. J. (2001). Speed and timing of behavioral processes. In J. E. Birren & K. W. Schaie (Eds.), *Handbook of the psychology of aging* (5th ed.). San Diego: Academic Press.

Maddi, S. (1996). *Personality theories* (6th ed.). Pacific Grove, CA: Brooks/Cole.

Maddi, S. (1998). Hardiness. In H.S. Friedman (Ed.), *Encyclopedia of mental health* (Vol. 3). San Diego: Academic Press.

Maddux, J. (2001). Self-efficacy. In C.R. Snyder & S.J. Lopez (Eds.), *Handbook of positive psychology.* New York: Oxford University Press.

Mader, S. (2003). *Biology* (7th ed.). New York: McGraw-Hill.

Mader, S. S. (2002). *Human biology* (7th ed.). New York: McGraw-Hill.

Mader, S. S. (2003). *Inquiry into life* (10th Ed.). New York: McGraw-Hill.

Mager, R. F. (1972). *Goals analysis.* Belmont, CA: Fearon.

Mahendran, R. (2001). Characteristics of patients referred to an insomnia clinic. *Singapore Medical Journal, 42,* 64–70.

Maier, N. R. F. (1931). Reasoning in humans. *Journal of Comparative Psychology, 12,* 181–194.

Majeres, R. L. (1999). Sex differences in phonological processes: Speeded matching and word reading. *Memory and Cognition, 27,* 246–253.

Malapani, C., Deweer, B., & Gibbon, J. (2002). Separating storage from retrieval dysfunction of temporal memory in Parkinson's disease. *Journal of Cognitive Neuroscience, 114,* 311–322.

Mandler, G. (1980). Recognizing: The judgment of previous occurrence. *Psychological Review, 87,* 252–271.

Mandler, J. M. (1998). Representation. In W. Damon (Ed.), *Handbook of child psychology* (5th ed., Vol. 2). New York: Wiley.

Manes, Sahakain, B., Clark, L., Rogers, R., Antoun, N., Aitken, M., & Robbins, T. (2002). Decision-making processes following damage to the frontal lobe. *Brain, 125 (Pt. 3),* 624–639.

Mangels, J. A., Picton, T. W., & Craik, F. I. (2001). Attention and successful episodic encoding: An event-related potential study. *Brain Research, 11,* 77–95.

Manji, H. K. (2001). Strategies for gene and protein expression studies in neuro-psychopharmacology and biological psychiatry. *International Journal of Neuropsycho-pharmacology, 4,* 45.

Manji, H. K., Dreverts, W. C., & Charney, D. S. (2001). The cellular neurobiology of depression. *Nature Medicine, 7,* 541–547.

Mann, J. J., & Arango, V. (1999). The neurobiology of suicidal behavior. In D. G. Jacobs (Ed.), *The Harvard Medical School guide to suicide assessment and intervention.* San Francisco: Jossey-Bass.

Manson, S. M., Ackerson, L. M., Dick, R. W., & Baron, A. E. (1990). Depressive symptoms among American Indian adolescents: Psychometric characteristics of the Center for Epidemiologic Studies Depression Scale (CES-D). *Psychological Assessment, 2,* 231–237.

Mantere, T., Tupala, E., Hall, H., Sarkoja, T., Rasanen, P., Bergstrom, K., Callaway, J., & Tihonen, J. (2002). Serotinin transporter distribution and density in the cerebral cortex of alcoholic and nonalcoholic comparison subjects: A whole-hemisphere autoradiograph study. *American Journal of Psychiatry, 159,* 599–606.

Maratsos, M. (1999). Some aspects of innateness and complexity in grammar acquisition. In M. Barrett (Ed.), *The development of language.* Philadelphia: Psychology Press.

Marcia, J. E. (1980). Ego identity development. In J. Adelson (Ed.), *Handbook of adolescent psychology.* New York: Wiley.

Marcia, J. E. (2001). Unpublished review of J. W. Santrock's *Adolescence* (9th ed.). New York: McGraw-Hill.

Marcus, E. (2002). Psychoanalytic psychotherapy and psychoanalysis: An overview. In M. Hersen & W. H. Sledge (Eds.), *Encyclopedia of psychotherapy.* San Diego: Academic Press.

Marcus, G. F. (2001). *The algebraic mind.* Cambridge, MA: MIT Books.

Marder, S. R., Davis, J. M., & Chouinard, G. (1997). The effects of risperidone on the five dimensions of schizophrenia derived by factor analysis: Combined results of the North American trials. *Journal of Clinical Psychiatry, 58,* 538–546.

Maril, A., Wagner, A. D., & Schacter, D. L. (2001). On the tip of the tongue: An event-related fMRI study of semantic retrieval failure and cognitive conflict. *Neuron, 31,* 653–660.

Maris, R. W. (1998). Suicide. In H. S. Friedman (Ed.), *Encyclopedia of mental health* (Vol. 3). San Diego: Academic Press.

Markman, A., & Gentner, D. (2001). Learning and reasoning. *Annual Review of Psychology* (Vol. 51). Palo Alto, CA: Annual Reviews.

Markman, H. J. (2000). Marriage. In A. Kazdin (Ed.), *Encyclopedia of psychology.* Washington, DC, & New York: American Psychological Association and Oxford University Press.

Markovitz, J. H., Jonas, B. S., & Davidson, K. (2001). Psychological factors as precursors to hypertension. *Current Hypertension Reports, 3,* 25–32.

Marks, I. M. (1987). *Fears, phobias, and rituals.* New York: Oxford University Press.

Marlow, A. (1999). *How to stop time: Heroin from A to Z.* New York: Basic Books.

Marr, D. (1982). *Vision.* New York: Freeman.

Marr, D. B., & Sternberg, R. J. (1987). The role of speed in intelligence: A triarchic perspective. In P. A. Vernon (Ed.), *Speed of information processing and intelligence.* Norwood, NJ: Ablex.

Marra, M., Polito, A., De Fillippo, E., Cuzzolar, M., Ciarapica, D., Contaldo, F., & Scalfi, L. (2002). Are the general equations to predict BMR applicable to patients with anorexia nervosa? *Eating and Weight Disorders, 7,* 53–59.

Marsella, A. J. (2000). Culture and mental health. In A. Kazdin (Ed.), *Encyclopedia of psychology.* Washington, DC, & New York: American Psychological Association and Oxford University Press.

Marsland, A. L., Bachen, E. A., Cohen, S., & Manuck, S. B. (2001). Stress, immunity, and susceptibility to infectious disease. In A. Baum, T. A. Revenson, & J. E. Singer (Eds.), *Handbook of health psychology.* Mahwah, NJ: Erlbaum.

Martin, C. L. (2000). Cognitive theories of gender development. In T. Eckes & H. M. Trautner (Eds.), *The developmental social psychology of gender.* Mahwah, NJ: Erlbaum.

Martin, C. L., & Dinella, L. (2001). Gender development: Gender schema theory. In J. Worell (Ed.), *Encyclopedia of women and gender.* New York: Oxford University Press.

Martin, G., & Pear, J. (2002). *Behavior modification* (7th Ed.). Upper Saddle River, NJ: Prentice-Hall.

Martin, W. E., & Swartz-Kulstad, J. L. (Eds.). (2000). *Person-environment psychology and mental health.* Mahwah, NJ: Erlbaum.

Martini, F. (2001). *Fundamentals of anatomy and physiology* (5th ed.). Upper Saddle River, NJ: Prentice-Hall.

Masland, R. H., & Raviola, E. (2000). Confronting complexity: Strategies for understanding the microcircuitry of the retina. *Annual Review of Neuroscience,* Vol. 23. Palo Alto, CA: Annual Reviews.

Maslow, A. (1971). *The farther reaches of human nature.* New York: Viking.

Maslow, A. H. (1954). *Motivation and personality.* New York: Harper & Row.

Maslow, A. H. (1954). *Motivation and personality.* New York: Harper & Row.

Masoro, E. J., & Austad, S. N. (Eds.) (2001). *Handbook of the biology of aging* (5th ed.). San Diego: Academic Press.

Massimini, F., & Delle Fave, A. (2000). Individual development in bio-cultural perspective. *American Psychologist, 55,* 24–33.

Masson, J. M. (1988). *Against therapy.* New York: Atheneum.

Masten, A. S. (2001). Ordinary magic: Resilience processes in development. *American Psychologist, 56,* 227–238.

Masten, A. S., & Coatsworth, J. D. (1998). The development of competence in favorable and unfavorable environments: Lessons from successful children. *American Psychologist, 53,* 205–220.

Masters, W. H., & Johnson, V. E. (1966). *Human sexual response.* Boston: Little, Brown.

Matlin, M. (1988). *Sensation and perception* (2nd ed.). Boston: Allyn & Bacon.

Matlin, M. W. (2001). *Cognition* (5th ed.) Fort Worth, TX: Harcourt Brace.

Matsumoto, D. (2000). *Culture and social behavior.* Belmont, CA: Wadsworth.

Matsumoto, D. (Ed.). (2001). *The handbook of culture and psychology.* New York: Oxford University Press.

Matthews, G., & Dreary, I. J. (1998). *Personality traits.* Cambridge, England: Cambridge University Press.

Mattson, M. P. (2002). Neurogenetics: White matter matters. *Trends in Neuroscience, 25,* 135–136.

Mattys, S. L., & Jusczyk, P. W. (2001). Phonotactic cues for segmentation of fluent speech by infants. *Cognition, 78,* 91–121.

Maultsby, M. C., & Wirga, M. (1998). Behavior therapy. In H. S. Friedman (Ed.), *Encyclopedia of mental health* (Vol. 1). San Diego: Academic Press.

May, P. A., & Gossage, J. P. (2001). Estimating the prevalence of fetal alcohol syndrome: A summary. *Alcohol Research and Health, 25,* 159–167.

Mayer, E. L. (2002). Freud and Jung: the boundaried mind and the radically connected mind. *Journal of Analytical Psychology, 47,* 91–99.

Mayer, R. (2000). Problem solving. In M. A. Runco & S. Pritzker (Eds.), *Encyclopedia of psychology.* San Diego: Academic Press.

Maylor, E. A., Chater, N., & Brown, G. D. (2001). Scale invariance in the retrieval of retrospective and prospective memories. *Psychonomic Bulletin Review, 8,* 162–167.

McAdams, D. P. (1993). *The stories we live by.* New York: Morrow.

McAllister, M. M. (2000). Dissociative identity disorder: A literature review. *Journal of Psychiatric and Mental Health Nursing, 7,* 25–33.

McCann, R. S. (2001, March/April). Human factors psychology at NASA. *Psychological Science Agenda, 14,* 11.

McClelland, D. C. (1955). Some social consequences of achievement motivation. In M. R. Jones (Ed.), *Nebraska Symposium of Motivation.* Lincoln: University of Nebraska Press.

McClelland, D. C. (1978). Managing motivation to expand human freedom. *American Psychologist, 33,* 201–210.

McClelland, D. C., Atkinson, J. W., Clark, R., & Lowell, E. L. (1953). *The achievement motive.* New York: Appleton-Century-Crofts.

McClelland, J. L., & Rumelhart, D. E. (1986). *Parallel distributed processing: Explorations in the microstructure of cognition. Vol. 2: Psychological and biological models.* Cambridge, MA: MIT Press.

McConaghy, N. (1993). *Sexual behavior: Problems and management.* New York: Plenum Press.

McCrae, R. R., & Costa, P. T. (2001). A five-factor theory of personality. In L. A. Pervin & O. P. John (Eds.), *Handbook of personality.* New York: Guilford Press.

McCullough, M. E., Hoyt, W. T., Larson, D. B., Koenig, H. G., & Thoresen, C. (2000). Religious involvement and mortality: A meta-analytic review. *Health Psychology, 19,* 211–222.

McDaniel, M. A., & Einstein, G. O. (1993). The importance of cue familiarity and cue distinctiveness in prospective memory. *Memory, 1,* 23–41.

McDaniel, M. A., & Einstein, G. O. (2000). Strategic and automatic processes in memory retrieval: A multiprocess framework. *Applied Cognitive Psychology, 14,* S127–S144.

McDougall, W. (1908). *Social psychology.* New York: Putnam.

McDowell, M. J. (2001). Principle of organization: A dynamic-systems view of the archetype-as-such. *Journal of Analytical Psychology, 46,* 637–654.

McEwen B. S. (1998). Protective and damaging effects of stress mediators. *New England Journal of Medicine, 338,* 171–179.

McFarlane, T., Polivy, J., & Herman, C. P. (1998). Dieting. In H.S. Friedman (Ed.), *Encyclopedia of mental health* (Vol. 1). San Diego: Academic Press.

McGaugh, J. L., & Cahill, L. (2002). Emotion and memory. In R. J. Davidson, K. R. Scherer, & H. H. Goldsmith (Eds.), *Handbook of affective sciences.* New York: Oxford University Press.

McGrath, E., Strickland, B. R., Keita, G. P., & Russo, N. F. (Eds.). *Women and depression: Risk factors and treatment issues.* Washington, DC: American Psychological Association.

McGue, M., Bouchard, T. J., Iacono, W. G., & Lykken, D. T. (1993). Behavioral genetics of cognitive ability: A life-span perspective. In R. Plomin & G. E. McClearn (Eds.), *Nature, nurture, and psychology.* Washington, DC: American Psychological Association.

McGuire, P. A. (1999, May). Worker stress, health reaching critical point. *APA Monitor, 30,* 26–27.

McInnis, G. J., & White, J. H. (2001). A phenomenological exploration of loneliness in the older adult. *Archives of Psychiatric Nursing, 15,* 128–139.

McIntosh, A. R. (2000). Towards a network theory of cognition. *Neural Networks, 13,* 861–870.

McIntyre, C. K., Pal, S. N., Marriott, L. K., & Gold, P. E. (2002). Competition between memory systems: acetylcholine release in the hippocampus correlates negatively with good performance on an amygdala-dependent task. *Journal of Neuroscience, 22,* 1171–1176.

McIver, T. (1988). Backward masking and other backward thoughts about music. *Skeptical Inquirer, 13,* 50–63.

McKay, D., & Tryon, W. W. (2002). Behavior therapy: Theoretical bases. In M. Hersen & W. H. Sledge (Eds.), *Encyclopedia of psychotherapy.* San Diego: Academic Press.

McKelvie, S. J., & Drumheller, A. (2001). The availability heuristic with famous names: A replication. *Perceptual and Motor Skills, 92,* 507–516.

McKendree-Smith, N., & Scogin, F. (2000). Depressive realism: Effects of depression severity and interpretation time. *Journal of Clinical Psychology, 56,* 1601–1608.

McKenna, M. C, Zevon, M. A., Corn, B., & Rounds, J. (1999). Psychosocial factors and the development of breast cancer: A meta-analysis. *Health Psychology, 18,* 520–531.

McKinlay, J. B. (1999, March). *Erectile dysfunction: The most overlooked biobehavioral marker of disease.* Paper presented at the meeting of the American Psychosomatic Association, Vancouver.

McKinlay, S.M., & McKinlay, J. B. (1984). *Health status and health care utilization by menopausal women.* Unpublished manuscript, Cambridge Research Center, American Institutes for Research, Cambridge, MA.

McKnight, C. C., Crosswhite, F. J., Dossey, J. A., Kifer, E., Swafford, J. O., Travers, K. J., & Cooney, T. J. (1987). *The underachieving curriculum: Assessing U.S. school mathematics from an international perspective.* Champaign, IL: Stipes.

McLean, P. D., & Wood, S. R. (2001). *Anxiety disorders in adults.* New York: Oxford University Press.

McLoyd, V. C. (1999). Cultural influences in a multicultural society: Conceptual and methodological issues. In A. S. Masten (Ed.), *Cultural processes in child development.* Mahwah, NJ: Erlbaum.

McLoyd, V. C. (2000). Poverty. In A. Kazdin (Ed.), *Encyclopedia of psychology.* Washington, DC, & New York: American Psychological Association and Oxford University Press.

McMillan, J. H. (2000). *Educational research* (3rd ed.). Upper Saddle River, NJ: Merrill.

McMillan, J. H. (2001). *Classroom assessment* (2nd ed.). Boston: Allyn & Bacon.

McMillan, J. H., & Wergin, J. F. (2002). *Understanding and evaluating educational research* (2nd ed.). Upper Saddle River, NJ: Prentice Hall.

McNally, D. (1990). *Even eagles need a push.* New York: Dell.

McNally, R. (1994). *Panic disorder: A critical analysis.* New York: Guilford.

McNally, R. J. (1998). Panic attacks. In H. S. Friedman (Ed.), *Encyclopedia of mental health* (Vol. 3). San Diego: Academic Press.

McNeil, E. B. (1967). *The quiet furies.* Englewood Cliffs, NJ: Prentice Hall.

Meador, B. D., & Rogers, C. R. (1979). Person-centered therapy. In R. J. Corsini, *Current psychotherapies* (2nd ed.). Itasca, IL: Peacock.

Meador, K. J. (2002). Cognitive outcomes and predictive factors in epilepsy. *Neurology, 58,* S21–S26.

Mealey, L. (2000). *Sex differences: Developmental and evolutionary perspectives.* San Diego: Academic Press.

Mechler, F., & Ringach, D. L. (2002). On the classification of simple and complex cells. *Vision Research, 42,* 1017–1033.

Medin, D. L., Lynch, E. B., & Solomon, K. O. (2000). Are there kinds of concepts? *Annual Review of Psychology* (Vol. 51). Palo Alto, CA: Annual Reviews.

Medin, D. L., Proffitt, J. B., & Schwartz, H. C. (2000). Concepts: Structure. In A. Kazdin (Ed.), *Encyclopedia of psychology.* Washington, DC, & New York: American Psychological Association and Oxford University Press.

Medin, D., Ross, R., & Markham, A. (2001). *Cognitive psychology* (3rd ed.). Fort Worth, TX: Harcourt.

Meehl, P. (1962). Schizotonia, schizotypy, schizophrenia. *American Psychologist, 17,* 827–838.

Meehl, P. E. (1986). Diagnostic taxa as open concepts. In T. Millon & G.I. Klerman (Eds.), *Contemporary directions in psychopathology.* New York: Guilford.

Meichenbaum, D. (1977). *Cognitive-behavior modification: An integrative approach.* New York: Plenum Press.

Meichenbaum, D., Turk, D., & Burstein, S. (1975). The nature of coping with stress. In I. Sarason & C. Spielberger (Eds.), *Stress and anxiety.* Washington, DC: Hemisphere.

Melinder, K. A., & Andersson, R. (2001). The impact of structural factors on the injury rate in different European countries. *European Journal of Public Health, 11,* 301–308.

Melis, M., Camarin, R., Ungless, M. A., & Bonci, A. (2002). Long-lasting potentiation of GABAergic synapses in dopamine neurons after a single in vivo ethanol exposure. *Journal of Neuroscience, 22,* 2074–2982.

Meller, R., Harrison, P. J., Elliott, J. M., & Sharp, T. (2002). In vitro evidence that 5-hydroxytrptamine increases efflux of glial glutamate via 5-HT2a receptor activation. *Journal of Neuroscience Research, 67,* 399–405.

Melzack, R. (1973). *The puzzle of pain.* New York: Basic Books.

Melzack, R., & Wall, P. D. (1965). Pain mechanisms: A new theory. *Science, 150,* 971–979.

Memmler, R. L., Cohen, B. J., Wood, D. L., & Schwegler, J. (1995). *The human body in health and disease* (8th ed.). Philadelphia: Lippincott Williams & Wilkins.

Mendez, M. F., Chow, T., Ringman, J., Twitchell, G., & Hinkin, C. H. (2000). Pedophilia and temporal lobe disturbances. *Journal of Neuropsychiatry and Clinical Neurosciences, 12,* 71–76.

Mercer, J. R., & Lewis, J. F. (1978). *System of multicultural pluralistic assessment.* New York: Psychological Corporation.

Mervis, J. (1996, July). NIMH data point way to effective treatment. *APA Monitor,* pp. 1, 13.

Mesquita, B. (2002). Emotions as dynamic cultural phenomena. In R. J. Davidson, K. R. Scherer, & H. H. Goldsmith (Eds.), *Handbook of affective sciences.* New York: Oxford University Press.

Messer, W. S., & Griggs, R. A. (1989). Student belief and involvement in the paranormal and performance in introductory psychology. *Teaching of Psychology, 16,* 187–191.

Messinger, J. C. (1971). Sex and repression in an Irish folk community. In D. S. Marshall & R. C. Suggs (Eds.), *Human sexual behavior.* New York: Basic Books.

Metcalfe, J., & Mischel, W. (1999). A hot/cool system analysis of delay of gratification: Dynamics of will power. *Psychological Review, 106,* 3–19.

Meyer, G. J. (2001). Introduction to the special section in the special series on the utility of the Rorschach for clinical assessment. *Psychological Assessment, 13,* 419–422.

Meyer, G. J., & Archer, R. P. (2001). The hard science of Rorschach research: What do we know and where do we go from here? *Psychological Assessment, 13,* 486–493.

Meyer, R. G., & Osborne, Y. V. H. (1982). *Case studies in abnormal behavior.* Boston: Allyn & Bacon.

Meyer, R. G., Wolverton, D., & Deitsch, S.E. (1998). Antisocial personality disorder. In H.S. Friedman (Ed.), *Encyclopedia of mental health* (Vol. 2). San Diego: Academic Press.

Meyer, R. J. (2002). *Phonics exposed.* Mahwah, NJ: Erlbaum.

Michael, R. T., Gagnon, J. H., Laumann, E. O., & Kolata, G. (1994). *Sex in America.* Boston: Little, Brown.

Michael, W. (1999). Guilford's view. In M. A. Runco & S. Pritzker (Eds.), *Encyclopedia of creativity.* San Diego: Academic Press.

Michaels, J. W., Bloomel, J. M., Brocato, R. M., Linkous, R. A., & Rowe, J. S. (1982). Social facilitation and inhibition in a natural setting. *Replications in Social Psychology, 2,* 21–24.

Michinov, E., & Michinov, N. (2001). The similarity hypothesis: A test of the moderating role of social comparison orientation. *European Journal of Social Psychology, 31,* 549–556.

Middleton, F. A., & Strick, P. L. (2001). Cerebellar projections to the prefrontal cortex of the primate. *Journal of Neuroscience, 21,* 700–712.

Mignot, E. (2001). A hundred years of narcolepsy research. *Archives of Italian Biology, 139,* 207–220.

Mignot, E., & Thorsby, E. (2001). Narcolepsy and the HLA system. *New England Journal of Medicine, 344*(9), 692.

Miklowitz, D. J. (2002). *The bipolar disorder survival guide.* New York: Guilford.

Milgram, P., Vigehesa, H., & Weinstein, P. (1992). Adolescent dental fear and control. *Behavior Research and Therapy, 30,* 367–373.

Milgram, S. (1965). Some conditions of obedience and disobedience to authority. *Human Relations, 18,* 56–76.

Milgram, S. (1974). *Obedience to authority.* New York: Harper & Row.

Milgram, S., Liberty, H. J., Toledo, R., & Wackenhut, J. (1986). Response to intrusion in waiting lines. *Journal of Personality and Social Psychology, 51,* 683–689.

Miller, C. (2002). Flooding. In M. Hersen & W. H. Sledge (Eds.), *Encyclopedia of psychotherapy.* San Diego: Academic Press.

Miller, E. K., & Cohen, J. D. (2001). An integrative theory of prefrontal cortex function. *Annual Review of Neuroscience, 24.*

Miller, G. A. (1956). The magical number seven, plus or minus two: Some limits on our capacity for information processing. *Psychological Review, 48,* 337–442.

Miller, N. E. (1985). The value of behavioral research on animals. *American Psychologist, 40,* 432–440.

Miller, N. E. (1941). The frustration-aggression hypothesis. *Psychological Review, 48,* 337–442.

Miller, N. E. (1959). Liberalization of basic S-R concepts: Extension to conflict behavior, motivation, and social learning. In S. Koch (Ed.), *Psychology: A study of science.* New York: McGraw-Hill.

Miller, N. E. (1969). Learning of visceral glandular responses. *Science, 163,* 434–445.

Miller, P. J. (2001, April). *Self-esteem as folk theory: A comparison of ethnographic interviews.* Paper presented at the meeting of the Society for Research in Child Development, Minneapolis.

Miller-Jones, D. (1989). Culture and testing. *American Psychologist, 44,* 360–366.

Millis, R. M. (1998). Smoking. In H.S. Friedman (Ed.), *Encyclopedia of mental health* (Vol. 3). San Diego: Academic Press.

Milner, A. D., & Goodale, M. A. (1995). *The visual brain in action.* New York: Oxford University Press.

Miltenberger, R. G. (2001). *Behavior modification* (2nd ed.). Belmont, CA: Wadsworth.

Minda, J. P., & Smith, J. D. (2001). Prototypes in category learning: The effects of category size, category structure, and stimulus complexity. *Journal of Experimental Psychology: Learning, Memory, and Cognition, 27,* 775–799.

Mineka, S., & Nugent, K. (1995). Mood-congruent memory biases in anxiety and depression. In D. L. Schacter, J. T. Coyle, G. D. Fischbach, M. M. Mesulam, & L. E. Sullivan (Eds.), *Memory distortion: How minds, brains, and societies reconstruct the past.* Cambridge, MA: Harvard University Press.

Mirksy, A. F., Bieliauskas, L. M., Van Kammen, D. P., Jonsson, E., & Sedvall, G. (2000). A 39-year followup of the Genain quadruplets. *Schizophrenia Bulletin, 3,* 5–18.

Mischel, W. (1968). *Personality and assessment.* New York: Wiley.

Mischel, W. (1973). Toward a cognitive social learning theory reformulation of personality. *Psychological Review, 80,* 252–283.

Mischel, W. (1995, August). *Cognitive-affective theory of person-environment psychology.* Paper presented at the meeting of the American Psychological Association, New York City.

Mischel, W., & Moore, B. S. (1980). The role of ideation in voluntary delay for symbolically presented rewards. *Cognitive Therapy and Research, 4,* 211–221.

Mischel, W., & Shoda, Y. (2001). Integrating dispositions and processing dynamics within a unified theory of personality: The cognitive affective personality system. In L. A. Pervin & O. P. John (Eds.), *Handbook of personality.* New York: Guilford Press.

Mischel, W., Cantor, N., & Feldman, S. (1996). Principles of self-regulation: The nature of will power and self-control. In E. T. Higgins & A. W. Kruglanski (Eds.), *Social psychology: Handbook of basic principles.* New York: Guilford Press.

Mischel, W., Shoda, Y., & Mendoza-Denton, R. (2002). Situation-behavior profiles as a locus of consistency in personality. *Current Directions in Psychological Science, 11,* 50–53.

Misra, A., Arora, N., Mondal, S., Pandey, R. M., Jailkhani, B., Peshin, S., Chaudhary, D., Saluja, T., Singh, P., Chandra, S., Luithra, K., & Vikram, N. K. (2001). Relation between plasma leptin and anthropometric and metabolic covariates in lean and obese diabetic and hyperlipdaemic Asian Northern Indian subjects. *Diabetes, Nutrition, and Metabolism, 14,* 18–26.

Mittag, W., & Schwarzer, R. (1993). Interaction of employment status and self-efficacy on alcohol consumption: A two-wave study on stressful life transitions. *Psychology and Health, 8,* 77–87.

Miyake, A. (2001, September). Commentary on Carpenter, S., "A new reason for keeping a diary." *Monitor on Psychology, 32,* 68–70.

Miyashita, Y., & Hayashi, T. (2000). Neural representation of visual objects: Encoding and top-down activation. *Current Opinions in Neuroscience, 10,* 187–194.

Mizes, J. S., & Miller, K. J. (2000). Eating disorders. In M. Herson & R. T. Ammerman (Eds.), *Advanced abnormal child psychology* (2nd ed.). Mahwah, NJ: Erlbaum.

Moffitt, T. E., Brammer, G. L., Caspi, A., Fawcet, J. P., Raleigh, M., Yuwiler, A., & Silva, P. A. (1998). Whole blood serotonin relates to violence in an epidemiological study. *Biological Psychiatry, 43,* 446–457.

Monahan, J. L., Murphy, S. T., & Zajonc, R. B. (2000). Subliminal mere exposure: Specific, general, and diffuse effects. *Psychological Science, 11,* 462–466.

Monahan, J. S. (2001). Coloring single Stroop elements: Reducing automaticity or slowing color processing? *Journal of General Psychology, 138,* 98–112.

Money, J. (1986). *Lovemaps: Clinical concepts of sexual/erotic health and pathology, paraphilia, and gender transposition in childhood, adolescence, and maturity.* New York: Irvington.

Monk, T. H. (1993). Shiftwork. In M. A. Carskadon (Ed.), *Encyclopedia of sleep and dreaming.* New York: Macmillan.

Monsell, S., & Driver, J. (Eds.). (2000). *Control of cognitive processes.* Cambridge, MA: MIT Press.

Monsell, S., Taylor, T. J., & Murphy, K. (2001). Naming the color of a word: Is it responses or task sets that compete? *Memory and Cognition, 29,* 137–151.

Monteith, M. J. (2000). Prejudice. In A. Kazdin (Ed.), *Encyclopedia of psychology.* Washington, DC, & New York: American Psychological Association and Oxford University Press.

Monteith, M. J., & Voils, C. I. (2001). Exerting control over prejudiced responses. In G. B. Moscowitz (Ed.), *Cognitive social psychology.* Mahwah, NJ: Erlbaum.

Moore, D. (2001). *The dependent gene.* New York: W. H. Freeman.

Moore, D. S. (2001). *Statistics* (5th ed.). New York: Worth.

Moore, T. E. (1995). Subliminal self-help auditory tapes: An empirical test of perceptual consequences. *Canadian Journal of Behavioural Science, 27,* 9–20.

Moore-Ede, M. C., Sulzman, F. M., & Fuller, C. A. (1982). *The clocks that time us.* Cambridge, MA: Harvard University Press.

Moras, K. (2002). Research on psychotherapy. In M. Hersen & W. H. Sledge (Eds.), *Encyclopedia of psychotherapy.* San Diego: Academic Press.

Morgan, D. L. (2002). *Essentials of learning and cognition.* New York: McGraw-Hill.

Morgan, T., & Cummings, A. L. (1999). Change experienced during group therapy of female survivors of childhood sexual abuse. *Journal of Consulting and Clinical Psychology, 67,* 28–36.

Moscovici, S. (1985). Social influence and conformity. In G. Lindzey & E. Aronson (Eds.), *Handbook of social psychology* (3rd ed., Vol. 2). New York: Random House.

Moses, J., Steptoe, A., Mathews, A., & Edwards, S. (1989). The effects of exercise training on mental well-being in a normal population: A controlled trial. *Journal of Psychosomatic Research, 33,* 47–61.

Moskowitz, G. B. (Ed.). (2001). *Cognitive social psychology.* Mahwah, NJ: Erlbaum.

Muchinsky, P. M. (2003). *Psychology applied to work* (7th Ed.). Belmont, CA: Wadsworth.

Mulvihill, C. B., Davies, G. J., & Rogers, P. J. (2002). Dietary restraint in relation to nutrient intake, physical activity, and iron status in adolescent females. *Journal of Human Nutrition-Dietetics, 15,* 19–31.

Mumford, M., & Porter, P. P. (1999). Analogies. In M. A. Runco & S. Pritzker (Eds.), *Encyclopedia of creativity.* San Diego: Academic Press.

Munoz, R. F. (1998). Depression—applied aspects. In H. S. Friedman (Ed.), *Encyclopedia of mental health* (Vol. 1). San Diego: Academic Press.

Murdock, B. B. (1999). The buffer 30 years later: Working memory in a theory of distributed associative model (TODAM). In C. Izawa (Ed.), *On human memory.* Mahwah, NJ: Erlbaum.

Murphy, R. A., Baker, A. G., & Fouquet, N. (2001). Relative validity effects with either one or two more valid cues in Pavlovian and instrumental conditioning. *Journal of Experimental Psychology: Animal Processes, 27,* 59–67.

Murray, H. A. (1938). *Explorations in personality.* Cambridge, MA: Harvard University Press.

Murstein, B. I., & Mathes, S. (1996). Projection on projective techniques = pathology: The problem that is not being addressed. *Journal of Personality Assessment, 66,* 337–351.

Myers, A. (2003). *Experimental psychology* (5th Ed.). Belmont, CA: Wadsworth.

Myers, A., & Hansen, C. (2002). *Experimental psychology* (5th ed.). Belmont, CA: Wadsworth.

Myers, D. G. (2000). *The American paradox.* New Haven, CT: Yale University Press.

Myerson, J., Rank, M. R., Raines, F. Q., & Schnitzler, M. A. (1998). Race and general cognitive ability: The myth of diminishing returns in education. *Psychological Science, 9,* 139–142.

N

NAEYC. (1996). NAEYC position statement: Responding to linguistic and cultural diversity. *Young Children, 51,* 4–12.

Nakamura, J., & Csikszentmihalyi, M. (2002). The concept of flow. In C. R. Snyder & S. J. Lopez (Eds.), *Handbook of positive psychology.* New York: Oxford University Press.

Nakao, M., Fricchione, G., Myers, P., Zuttermeister, P. C., Barksky, A. J., & Benson, H. (2001). Depression and education as predicting factors for completion of a behavioral medicine intervention in a mind/body medicine clinic. *Behavioral Medicine, 26,* 177–184.

Nardi, A. E., Valenca, A. M., Nascimento, I., Mezzalama, M. A., & Zin, W. A. (2001). Hyperventilation in panic disorder and social phobia. *Psychopathology, 34,* 123–127.

Nash, J. M. (1997, February 3). Fertile minds. *Time,* pp. 50–54.

Nash, M. R. (2001). The truth and the hype about hypnosis. *Scientific American, 285,* 46–49, 52–55.

Nash, M. R., & Nadon, R. (1997). The scientific status of research on hypnosis. In D. L. Faigman, D. H. Kaye, M. K. Saks, & J. Sanders (Eds.), *The West companion of scientific evidence.* St. Paul, MN: West Publishing.

Naslund, E., Hellstrom, P. M., & Krail, J. G. (2001). The gut and food intake: An update for surgeons. *Journal of Gastrointestinal Surgeons, 5,* 556–567.

Nathan, P. E. (1994). DSM-IV. *Journal of Clinical Psychology, 50,* 103–109.

Nathan, P. E., & Langenbucher, J. W. (1999). Psychopathology: Description and classification. *Annual Reviews of Psychology.* Palo Alto: Annual Reviews.

Nathan, P., & Gorman, J. M. (Eds.) (2002). *A guide to treatments that work* (2nd Ed.). New York: Oxford University Press.

Nathan, P. E., Gorman, J. M., & Salkind, N. J. (1999). *Treating mental disorders.* New York: Oxford University Press.

Nathan, P. E., Stuart, S. P., & Dolan, S. L. (2000). Research on psychotherapy efficacy and effectiveness: Between Scylla and Charybdis? *Psychological Bulletin, 126,* 964–981.

National Advisory Council on Economic Opportunity. (1980). *Critical choices for the 80s.* Washington, DC: U.S. Government Printing Office.

National Assessment of Educational Progress (2001). *Reading gap widens between high- and low-performing fourth-grade students.* Washington, DC: National Center for Health Statistics.

National Assessment of Educational Progress. (1997). *NAEP 1996 mathematics report card for the nation and the states.* Washington, DC: National Center for Education Statistics.

National Center for Children Exposed to Violence. (2001). *Statistics.* New Haven, CT: Author.

National Center for Health Statistics (2000). *Births, deaths, marriages, and divorces.* Atlanta: Centers for Disease Control and Prevention.

National Center for Health Statistics (2000). *Prevalence of overweight among children and adolescents.* Hyattsville, MD: U.S. Department of Health and Human Services.

National Center for Health Statistics (2000). *Smoking.* Atlanta, GA: Centers for Disease Control and Prevention.

National Center for Health Statistics (2001). *AIDS.* Atlanta: Centers for Disease Control and Prevention.

National Center for Health Statistics. (2001). *Key health measures tracked in national survey.* Atlanta: Centers for Disease Control and Prevention.

National Center for Health Statistics. (1989, June). *Statistics on marriage and divorce.* Washington, DC: U.S. Government Printing Office.

National Center for Health Statistics. (1994). Advance report of final mortality statistics, 1991. *Monthly Vital Statistics Report, 42.*

National Center for PTSD (2001). *What is post-traumatic stress disorder?* Washington, DC: Author.

National Commission on Sleep Disorders Research. (1993, January). *Report of the National Commission on Sleep Disorders Research.* Report submitted to the United States Congress and to the Secretary of the U.S. Department of Health and Human Services.

National Institute for Occupational Safety and Health. (2001). *Job stress in American workers.* Washington, DC: Centers for Disease Control and Prevention.

National Institute of Mental Health (2000). *Suicide facts.* Washington, DC: Author. Retrieved January 26, 2000 from the World Wide Web: http://www.nimh.nih.gov/genpop/su_fact.htm

National Institute of Mental Health (2001c). *Post-traumatic stress disorder.* Washington, DC: Author.

National Institute of Mental Health. (2001a). *The numbers count.* Bethesda, MD: Author.

National Institute of Mental Health. (2001b). *Mental disorders in America.* Bethesda, MD: Author.

National Institute of Neurological Disorders and Stroke. (2001). *Brain basics: Understanding sleep.* Washington, DC: National Institutes of Health.

National Institute on Drug Abuse (2001). *Common drugs of abuse.* Washington, DC: National Institutes of Health.

National Research Council. (1999). *How people learn.* Washington, DC: Author.

National Sleep Foundation (2001). *2001 Sleep in America Poll.* Washington, DC: National Sleep Foundation.

Nehra, A., Blute, M. L., Barrent, D. M., & Moreland, R. B. (2002). Rationale for combination therapy of intrauerethal prostaglandin E (1) and sildenafil in the salvage of erectile dysfunction patients during noninvasive therapy. *International Journal of Impotency Research, 14* (Suppl. 1), S38–S42.

Neisser, U., & Hyman, I. E. (2000). *Memory observed* (2nd ed.). New York: Worth.

Neisser, U., Boodoo, G., Bouchard, T. J., Boykin, A. W., Brody, N., Ceci, S. J., Halpern, D. F., Loehlin, J. C., Perloff, R., Sternberg, R. J., & Urbina, S. (1996). Intelligence: Knowns & unknowns. *American Psychologist, 51,* 77–101.

Nelson, D. L., Quick, J. C., & Simmons, B. L. (2001). Preventive management of work stress: Current themes and future challenges. In A. Baum, T.A. Revenson, & J.E. Singer (Eds.), *Handbook of health Psychology.* Mahwah, NJ: Erlbaum.

Nelson, M. E., Fiatarone, M. A., Moranti, C. M., Trice, I., Greenberg, R. A., & Evans, W. J. (1994). Effects of high-intensity strength training on multiple risk factors for osteoporotic fractures: A randomized controlled trial. *Journal of the American Medical Association, 272,* 1909–1914.

Nelson, T. D. (2002). *Psychology of prejudice.* Boston: Allyn & Bacon.

Nemeroff, C. B., & Schatzberg, A. F. (2002). Pharmacological treatments for unipolar depression. In P. Nathan & J. M. Gorman (Eds.), *A guide to treatments that work (2nd Ed.).* New York: Oxford University Press.

Neverlien, P. O., & Johnsen, T. B. (1991). Optimism-pessimism dimension and dental anxiety in children aged 10–12. *Community Dentistry and Oral Epidemiology, 19,* 342–346.

Nevo, B. (1986). *Scientific aspects of graphology.* Springfield, IL: Thomas.

Newman, C. F., Leahy, R. L., Beck, A. T., Reilly-Harringont, N. A., & Gyulai, L. (2002). *Bipolar disorder: A cognitive behavior therapy approach.* Washington, DC: American Psychological Association.

Nicholls, J. G. (1979). Development of perception of own attainment and causal attribution for success and failure in reading. *Journal of Educational Psychology, 71,* 94–99.

Nicholls, J. G., Cobb, P., Wood, T., Yackel, E., & Patashnick, M. (1990). Assessing students' theories of success in mathematics: Individual and classroom differences. *Journal for Research in Mathematics Education, 21,* 109–122.

Nichols, C. D., & Sanders-Bush, E. (2002). A single dose of lysergic acid diethyamide influences gene expression patterns with the mammalian brain. *Neuropsychopharmacology, 26k,* 634–642.

Nickels, W. G., McHugh, J. M., & McHugh, S. M. (2002). *Understanding business* (6th ed.). New York: McGraw-Hill.

Nickerson, R. S., & Adams, M. J. (1979). Long-term memory for a common object. *Cognitive Psychology, 11,* 287–307.

Niehoff, D. (1999). *The biology of violence.* New York: The Free Press.

Nielson, S. L., Johnson, W. B., & Ellis, A. (2001). *Counseling and psychotherapy with religious persons.* Mahwah, NJ: Erlbaum.

Niki, K., & Luo, J. (2002). An fMRI study on the time-limited role of the medial temporal lobe in long-term topographical autobiographical memory. *Journal of Cognitive Neuroscience, 14,* 500–507.

Nisbett, R. E., & Ross, L. (1980). *Human inference.* Upper Saddle River, NJ: Prentice Hall.

Nobel, P. A., & Shiffrin, R. M. (2001). Retrieval processes in recognition and cued recall. *Journal of Experimental Psychology: Learning, Memory, and Cognition, 27,* 384–413.

Nock, S. (1995). A comparison of marriages and cohabiting relationships. *Journal of Family Issues, 16,* 53–76.

Nolen-Hoeksema, S. (1995). Gender differences in coping with depression across the lifespan. *Depression, 3,* 81–90.

Nolen-Hoeksema, S. (2000). The role of rumination in depressive disorders and mixed anxiety/depressive symptoms. *Journal of Abnormal Psychology, 109,* 504–511.

Nolen-Hoeksema, S. (2001). *Abnormal psychology* (2nd ed.). New York: McGraw-Hill.

Nolen-Hoeksema, S., & Morrow, J. (1991). A prospective study of depression and distress following a natural disaster: The 1989 Loma Prieta earthquake. *Journal of Personality & Social Psychology, 61,* 105–121.

Nolen-Hoeksema, S., Larson, J., & Grayson, C. (1999). Explaining the gender difference in depressive symptoms. *Journal of Personality & Social Psychology, 77,* 1061–1072.

Nolen-Hoeksema, S., Parker, L. E., & Larson, J. (1994). Ruminative coping with depressed mood following loss. *Journal of Personality & Social Psychology, 67,* 92–104.

Norcross, J. C. (Ed.) (2002). *Psychotherapy relationships that work.* New York: Oxford University Press.

Norcross, J. C., & Kobayshi, M. (2000). Psychotherapy: Clinical practice. In A. Kazdin (Ed.), *Encyclopedia of psychology.* Washington, DC, & New York: American Psychological Association and Oxford University Press.

Norcross, J. C., & Newman, C. F. (1992). Psychotherapy integration: Setting the context. In J. C. Norcross & M. R. Gottfried (Eds.), *Handbook of psychotherapy integration.* New York: Basic Books.

Norcross, J. C., & Prochaska, J. O. (1983). Clinicians' theoretical orientations. *Professional Psychology: Research and Practice, 14,* 197–208.

Norcross, J. C., & Prochaska, J. O. (1988). A study of eclectic (and integrative) views revisited. *Professional Psychology: Research and Practice, 19,* 170–174.

Norem, J. K., & Cantor, N. (1986). Anticipatory and post-hoc cushioning strategies: Optimism and defensive pessimism in risk "situations." *Cognitive Therapy Research, 10,* 347–362.

Norris, F. N., Bryne, C. M., Diaz, E., & Kaniasty, K. (2001). *The range, magnitude, and duration of effects of natural and human-caused disasters: A review of the empirical literature.* Washington, DC: National Center for PTSD.

North, C. S., Tivis, L., McMillen, J. C., Pfefferbaum, B., Spitznagel, E. L., Cox, J. Nixon, S., Bunch, K. P., & Smith, E. M. (2002). Psychiatric disorders in rescue workers after the Oklahoma City bombing. *American Journal of Psychiatry, 159,* 857–859.

Notman, M. T., & Nadelson, C. C. (2002). Women's issues. In M. Hersen & W. H. Sledge (Eds.), *Encyclopedia of psychotherapy.* San Diego: Academic Press.

Nottelmann, E. D., Susman, E. J., Blue, J. H., Inoff-Germain, G., Dorn, L. D., Loriaux, D. L., Cutler, G. B., & Chrousos, G. P. (1987). Gonadal and adrenal hormone correlates of adjustment in early adolescence. In R. M. Lerner & T. T. Foch (Eds.), *Biological-psychological interactions in early adolescence.* Hillsdale, NJ: Erlbaum.

Nucci, L. P. (2001). *Education in the moral domain.* New York: Cambridge University Press.

Nutt, D. J. (2001). Neurobiological mechanisms in generalized anxiety disorder. *Journal of Clinical Psychology, 62* (Suppl. 11), 22–27.

Nyberg, L., Forkstam, C., Petersson, K. M., Cabeza, R., & Ingvr, M. (2002). Brain imaging of human memory systems: between-systems similarities and within-system differences. *Brain Research: Cognitive Brain Research, 13,* 281–292.

Nystrand, A. (1996). New discoveries on sex differences in the brain. *Lakartidningen, 93,* 2071–2073.

Nystul, M. S. (1999). *Introduction to counseling.* Boston: Allyn & Bacon.

O

O'Brien, G., & Opie, J. (1999). A connectionist theory of phenomenal experience. *Behavior and Brain Sciences, 1,* 127–148.

O'Connor, E. (2001, February). Marketing medications. *Monitor on Psychology, 32,* (2), 33.

O'Donnell, B. F. (2002). Forms of attention and attention disorders. *Seminars in Speech and Language, 23,* 99–106.

O'Donnell, L., & others (1999). Violence prevention and young adolescents' participation in community service. *Journal of Adolescent Health, 24,* 28–37.

O'Hara, M., & Taylor, E. (2000). Humanistic psychology. In A. Kazdin (Ed.), *Encyclopedia of psychology.* Washington, DC, & New York: American Psychological Association and Oxford University Press.

O'Leary, V. E., & Flanagan, E. H. (2001). Leadership. In J.W. Worell (Ed.), *Encyclopedia of gender and women.* San Diego: Academic Press.

O'Neil, H. F., & Andrews, D. (Eds.). (2000). *Aircrew training and assessment.* Mahwah, NJ: Erlbaum.

Oberbauer, A. M., Rundstadler, J. A., Murray, A. D., & Havel, P. J. (2001). Obesity and elevated plasma leptin concentration in oMTIA-o growth hormone transgenic mice. *Obesity Research, 9,* 51–58.

Offer, D., Ostrov, E., Howard, K. I., & Atkinson, R. (1988). *The teenage world: Adolescents' self-image in ten countries.* New York: Plenum.

Ogbu, J., & Stern, P. (2001). Caste status and intellectual development. In R. J. Sternberg & E. L. Grigorenko (Eds.), *Environmental effects on cognitive abilities.* Mahwah, NJ: Erlbaum.

Ogilvie, R. D., & Wilkinson, R. T. (1988). Behavioral versus EEG-based monitoring of all-night sleep/wake patterns. *Sleep, 11*(2), 139–155.

Okagaki, L. (2000). Determinants of intelligence: Socialization of intelligence. In A. Kazdin (Ed.), *Encyclopedia of psychology.* Washington, DC, & New York: American Psychological Association and Oxford University Press.

Olds, J. M. (1958). Self-stimulation experiments and differential reward systems. In H. H. Jasper, L. D. Proctor, R. S. Knighton, W. C. Noshay, & R. T. Costello (Eds.), *Reticular formation of the brain.* Boston: Little, Brown.

Olds, J. M., & Milner, P. M. (1954). Positive reinforcement produced by electrical stimulation of the septal area and other areas of the rat brain. *Journal of Comparative and Physiological Psychology, 47,* 419–427.

Olff, M. (1999). Stress, depression, and immunity. *Psychiatry Research, 85,* 7–16.

Oliner, S. P. (2001). Ordinary people: Faces of heroism and altruism. In S. G. Post, L. G. Underwood, J. P. Schloss, & W. B. Hurlbut (Eds.), *Altruism and altruistic love.* New York: Oxford University Press.

Olivardia, R., Pope, H. G., Mangweth, B., & Hudson, J. I. (1995). Eating disorders in college men. *American Journal of Psychiatry, 152,* 1279–1284.

Oltmanns, T. F., & Emory, R. E. (2001). *Abnormal psychology* (3rd ed.). Upper Saddle River, NJ: Prentice-Hall.

Oltmanns, T. F., Neale, J. M., & Davison, G. C. (1986). *Case studies in abnormal psychology* (2nd ed.). New York: Wiley.

Onwuegbuzi, A. J., & Daley, C. E. (2001). Racial differences in IQ revisited: A synthesis of nearly a century of research. *Journal of Black Psychology, 27,* 209–220.

Oren, D. A., & Terman, M. (1998). Tweaking the human circadian clock with light. *Science, 279,* 333–334.

Orfanos, S. D. (2002). Relational psychoanalysis. In M. Hersen & W. H. Sledge (Eds.), *Encyclopedia of psychotherapy.* San Diego: Academic Press.

Orlinsky, D. E., & Howard, K. L. (2000). Psychotherapy: Research. In A. Kazdin (Ed.), *Encyclopedia of psychology.* Washington, DC, & New York: American Psychological Association and Oxford University Press.

Orlinsky, D. E., Grawe, K., & Parks, B. K. (1994). Process and outcome in psychotherapy. In A. E. Bergin & S. L. Garfield (Eds.), *Handbook of psychotherapy and behavior change* (4th ed.). New York: Wiley.

Osborne, L., & Pober, B. (2001). Genetics of childhood disorders: XXVII. Genes and cognition in Williams syndrome. *Journal of the Academy of Child and Adolescent Psychiatry, 40,* 732–735.

Osipow, S. (2000). Work. In A. Kazdin (Ed.), *Encyclopedia of psychology.* Washington, DC, and New York: American Psychological Association and Oxford University Press.

Ost, L. (1991). Acquisition of blood and injection phobia and anxiety response patterns in clinical patients. *Behavior and Research Therapy, 23,* 263–282.

Otte, C., Kellner, M., Arlt, J., Jahn, H., Holsboer, F., & Wiedemann, K. (2002). prolactin but not ACTH increases sodium lactate-induced panic attacks. *Psychiatry Research, 2,* 201–205.

Otten, L. J., Henson, R. N., & Rugg, M. D. (2001). Depth of processing effects on neural correlates of memory encoding. *Brain, 124,* 399–412.

Owen, A. M. (1997). Cognitive planning in humans: Neuropsychological, neuro-anatomical, and neuropharmacological perspectives. *Progress in Neurobiology, 53* (4), 431–450.

Oyserman, D., Coon, H. M., & Kemmelmeir, M. (2002). Rethinking individualism and collectivism: Evaluation of theoretical assumptions and meta-analyses. *Psychological Bulletin, 128,* 3–72.

Ozer, D. (2001). Four principles for personality assessment. In L. A. Pervin & O. P. John (Eds.), *Handbook of personality.* New York: Guilford Press.

Ozer, D. J., & Riese, S. P. (1994). Personality assessment. *Annual Review of Psychology, 45,* 357–388.

P

Pacher, P., Kohegyi, E., Kecskemeti, V., & Furst, S. (2001). Current trends in the development of new antidepressants. *Current Medicine and Chemistry, 8,* 89–100.

Padma-Nathan, H. (1999, March). *Oral drug therapy for erectile dysfunction: What have we learned from the Viagra experience?* Paper presented at the meeting of the American Psychosomatic Association, Vancouver.

Paffenbarger, O., Hyde, R. T., Wing, A. L., & Hsieh, C. (1986). Physical activity, all-cause mortality, and longevity of college alumni. *New England Journal of Medicine, 324,* 605–612.

Paivio, A. (1971). *Imagery and verbal processes.* New York: Holt, Rinehart & Winston.

Paivio, A. (1986). *Mental representations: A dual coding approach.* New York: Oxford University Press.

Paloutzian, R. (2000). *Invitation to the psychology of religion* (3rd ed.). Boston: Allyn & Bacon.

Paludi, M. A. (2002). *Psychology of women* (2nd Ed.). Upper Saddle River, NJ: Prentice-Hall.

Paludi, M. A. (1998). *The psychology of women.* Upper Saddle River, NJ: Prentice Hall.

Pan, B. A., & Snow, C. E. (1999). The development of conversational and discourse skills. In M. Barrett (Ed.), *The development of language.* Philadelphia: Psychology Press.

Panskepp, J. (1993). Neurochemical control of moods and emotions: Amino acids to neuropeptides. In M. Lewis & J. M. Haviland (Eds.), *Handbook of emotion.* New York: Guilford Press.

Park, D. C., Nisbett, R., & Hedden, T. (1999). Aging, culture, and cognition. *Journal of Gerontology, 54B,* P75–P84.

Park, N. W., Conrod, B., Rewilak, D., Kwon, C., Gao, F., & Black, S. E. (2001). Automatic activation of positive but not negative attitudes after brain injury. *Neuropsychologia, 39,* 7–24.

Pascual-Leone, J., & Johnson, J. (1999). A dialectical constructivist view of representation. In I. E. Sigel (Ed.), *Development of mental representation.* Mahwah, NJ: Erlbaum.

Pashler, H., Johnston, J. C., & Ruthruff, E. (2001). Attention and performance. *Annual Review of Psychology* (Vol. 52). Palo Alto, CA: Annual Reviews.

Passchier, W., Knottnerus, A., Albering, H., & Walda, I. (2001). Public health impact of large airports. *Review of Environmental Health, 15,* 83–96.

Pate, R. H., & Bondi, A. M. (1992). Religious beliefs and practice: An integral aspect of multicultural awareness. *Counselor Education and Supervision, 32,* 108–115.

Patterson, C. (1995). Lesbian and gay parenthood. In M. H. Bornstein (Ed.), *Handbook of parenting* (Vol. 3). Mahwah, NJ: Erlbaum.

Patterson, C. J. (2000). Family relationships of lesbians and gay men. *Journal of Marriage and the Family, 62,* 1052–1069.

Patterson, G. R., Debaryshe, B. D., & Ramsey, E. (1989). A developmental perspective on antisocial behavior. *American Psychologist, 44,* 329–335.

Paulus, P. B. (1989). An overview and evaluation of group influence. In P. B. Paulus (Ed.), *Psychology of group influence.* Mahwah, NJ: Erlbaum.

Paunonen, S., Jackson, D., Trzebinski, J., & Forserling, F. (1992). Personality structures across cultures: A multimethod evaluation. *Journal of Personality and Social Psychology, 62,* 447–456.

Paus, T., Collins, D. L., Evans, A. C., Leonard, G., Pike, B., & Zijdenbros, A. (2001). Maturation of white matter in the human brain: A review of magnetic resonance imaging. *Brain Research Bulletin, 54,* 255–266.

Pavlov, I. P. (1927). *Conditioned reflexes* (G. V. Anrep, Trans.). New York: Dover.

Payne, D. G., Lang, V. A., & Blackwell, J. M. (1995). Mixed versus pure display format in integration and nonintegration visual display. *Human Factors, 37,* 507–527.

Payne, L. R., Smith, P. O., Sturges, L. V., & Holleran, S. A. (1996). Reactivity to smoking cues: Mediating roles of nicotine and duration of deprivation. *Addictive Behaviors, 21,* 139–154.

Pearce, J., & Bouton, M. E. (2001). Elementary associative learning. *Annual Review of Psychology.* Palo Alto, CA: Annual Reviews.

Pedersen, P. B., & Carey, J. C. (2003). *Multicultural counseling in schools* (2nd Ed.). Boston: Allyn & Bacon.

Pegna, A. J., Caldara-Schnetzer, A. S., Perrig, S. H., Lazeyras, F., Khateb, A., Landis, T., & Seeck, M. (2002). Is the right amygdala involved in visuospatial memory? Evidence from MRI volumetric measures. *European Neurology, 47,* 148–155.

Penfield, W. (1947). Some observations in the cerebral cortex of man. *Proceedings of the Royal Society, 134,* 349.

Peng, J., Qiao. H., & Xu, Z. B. (2002). A new approach to stability of neural networks with time-varying delays. *Neural Networks, 15,* 95–103.

Pengilly, J. W., & Dowd, E. T. (2000). Hardiness and social support as moderators of stress. *Journal of Clinical Psychology, 56,* 813–820.

Pennebaker, J. W. (1997). *Opening up: The healing power of expressing emotions* (Rev. ed.). New York: Guilford Press.

Pennebaker, J. W. (1997). Writing about emotional experiences as a therapeutic experience. *Psychological Science, 8,* 162–166.

Pennebaker, J. W. (2001). Dealing with a traumatic emotional experience immediately after it occurs. *Advances in Mind-Body Medicine, 17,* 160–162.

Pennebaker, J. W., & Graybeal, A. (2001). Patterns of natural language use: Disclosure, personality, and social integration. *Current Directions in Psychological Science, 32,* 90–93.

Pennebaker, J. W., Kiecolt-Glaser, J. D., & Glaser, G. (1988). *Disclosure of traumas and immune function: Health implications for psychotherapy. Journal of Consulting and Clinical Psychology, 56,* 239–245.

Pennix, B. W., Rejeski, W. J., Pandya, J., Miller, M. E., Di Bari, M., Applegate, W. B., & Pahor, M. (2002). Exercise and depressive symptoms: A comparison of aerobic and resistance exercise effects on emotional and physical function in older persons with high and low depressive symptomatology. *Journal of Gerontology: Psychological Sciences, 57,* P124–P132.

Perault, M. C., Favreliere, S., Minet, P., & Remblier, C. (2000). Benzodiazepines and pregnancy. *Therapy, 55,* 587–595.

Peregoy, S., & Boyle, O. (2001). *Reading, writing, and learning in ESL* (3rd ed.). Boston: Allyn & Bacon.

Perkins, D. (1994, September). Creativity by design. *Educational Leadership,* pp. 18–25.

Perkins, K. A., Marcus, M. D., Levine, M. D., D'Amico, D., Miller, A., Broge, M., Ashcom, J., & Shiffman, S. (2001). Cognitive-behavioral therapy to reduce weight concerns improves smoking cessation outcome in weight-concerned women. *Journal of Consulting and Clinical Psychology, 69,* 604–613.

Perlman, D., & Peplau, L. A. (1998). Loneliness. In H. S. Friedman (Ed.), *Encyclopedia of mental health* (Vol. 2). San Diego: Academic Press.

Perloff, R. M. (2001). *Persuading people to have safer sex.* Mahwah, NJ: Erlbaum.

Perls, F. (1969). *Gestalt therapy verbatim.* Lafayette, CA: Real People Press.

Perner, L. (2001). *The psychology of consumers.* Unpublished manuscript, George Washington University, Washington, DC.

Perse, E. M. (2001). *Media effects and society.* Mahwah, NJ: Erlbaum.

Person, L., & Taylor, E. J. (2002). Managing pain in outpatients: There are particular challenges to pain control in outpatient settings.

American Journal of Nursing, 102, Supplement, 24–27.

Pert, A. B., & Snyder, S. H. (1973). Opiate receptor: Demonstration in a nervous tissue. *Science, 179,* 1011.

Pert, C. B. (1999). *Molecules of emotion.* New York: Simon & Schuster.

Pervin, L. A. (2000). Personality. In A. Kazdin (Ed.), *Encyclopedia of psychology.* Washington, DC, & New York: American Psychological Association and Oxford University Press.

Pervin, L. A., & John, O. P. (Eds.). (2001). *Handbook of personality.* New York: Guilford Press.

Petersen, A. (1979, January). Can puberty come any faster? *Psychology Today,* pp. 45–56.

Petersen, S. (2001). Functional brain imaging methods. *Annual Review of Neuroscience, 24.*

Petersen, S. (2001). Functional brain imaging methods. *Annual Review of Psychology, 52.*

Peterson, C. (1988). *Personality.* Fort Worth: Harcourt Brace.

Peterson, C. (2000). The future of optimism. *American Psychologist, 55,* 44–55.

Peterson, C., Seligman, M. E. P., & Vaillant, G. E. (1988). Pessimistic explanatory style is a risk factor for physical illness: A thirty-five year longitudinal study. *Journal of Personality and Social Psychology, 55,* 23–27.

Petry, N. M., Petrakis, I., Trevisan, L., Wiredu, G., Boutros, N. N., Martin, B., & Kosten, T. R. (2001). Contingency management interventions: From research to practice. *American Journal of Psychiatry, 158,* 694–702.

Pettigrew, T. F., & Tropp, L. R. (2000). Does intergroup contact reduce prejudice? Recent meta-analytic findings. In S. Oskamp (Ed.), *Reducing prejudice and discrimination.* Mahwah, NJ: Erlbaum.

Petty, R. E., & Cacioppo, J. T. (1986). The elaboration likelihood of persuasion. In L. Berkowitz (Ed.), *Advances in experimental social psychology* (Vol. 19). New York: Academic Press.

Petty, R. E., & Krosnick, J. A. (Eds.), (1995). *Attitude strength: Antecedents and consequents.* Mahwah, NJ: Erlbaum.

Petty, R. E., Wheeler, S. C., & Bizer, G. Y. (2000). Attitude functions and persuasion: An elaboration likelihood approach to matched versus mismatched messages. In G. R. Maio & J. M. Olson (Eds.), *Why we evaluate.* Mahwah, NJ: Erlbaum.

Pezdek, K., & Banks, K. W. (Eds.). (1996). *The recovered memory / false memory debate.* San Diego, CA: Academic Press.

Phaneuf, S., & Leeuwenburgh, C. (2001). Apoptosis and exercise. *Medical Science and Sports Exercise, 33,* 393–396.

Phares, E. J. (1984). *Personality.* Columbus, OH: Merrill.

Philips, H. C., & Rachman, S. (1996). *The psychological management of chronic pain* (2nd ed.). New York: Springer.

Phillips, V. L., Saks, M. J., & Peterson, J. L. (2001). *The application of signal detection theory to forensic science.* Unpublished manuscript, Arizona State University, Mesa.

Phillips, W. T., Kiernan, R. M., & King, A. C. (2001). The effects of physical activity on physical and psychological health. In A. Baum, T.A. Revenson, & J.E. Singer (Eds.), *Handbook of health psychology.* Mahwah, NJ: Erlbaum.

Phinney, J. S. (1989). Stages of ethnic identity development in minority group adolescents. *Journal of Early Adolescence, 9,* 34–49.

Phinney, J. S. (2000). Ethnic identity. In A. Kazdin (Ed.), *Encyclopedia of psychology.* Washington, DC, and New York: American Psychological Association and Oxford University Press.

Piaget, J. (1952). *The origins of intelligence in children.* New York: Oxford University Press.

Piaget, J., & Inhelder, B. (1969). *The child's conception of space* (F. J. Langdon & J. L. Lunzer, Trans.). New York: Norton.

Pickering, T. G. (2001). Mental stress as a causal factor in the development of hypertension and cardiovascular disease. *Current Hypertension Reports, 3,* 249–254.

Pikona-Sapir, A., Melamed, Y., & Elizur, A. (2001). The insanity defense: Examination of the extent of congruence between psychiatric recommendation and adjudication. *Medicine and Law, 20,* 93–100.

Pilkonis, P. A. (1999). Introduction: Paradigms for psychotherapy outcome research. *Journal of Clinical Psychology, 55,* 145–146.

Pilkonis, P. A., & Krause, M. S. (1999). Summary: Paradigms for psychotherapy outcome research. *Journal of Clinical Psychology, 55,* 201–206.

Pillow, D. R., Zautra, A. J., & Sandler, I. (1996). Major life events and minor stressors. *Journal of Personality and Social Psychology, 70,* 381–394.

Pinel, J. P. J. (2003). *Biopsychology* (5th ed.). Boston: Allyn & Bacon.

Pines, A. M., & Maslach, C. (2002). *Experiencing social psychology* (4th ed.). New York: McGraw-Hill.

Pines, M. (2001). *Seeing, hearing, and smelling the world.* Retrieved October 2001 from http://www.hhmi.org/senses.

Pinker, S. (1994). *The language instinct.* New York: William Morrow.

Pinker, S. (1999). *How the mind works.* New York: Norton.

Pintrich, P. R. (2000). The role of goal orientation in self-regulated learning. In M. Boekaerts, P. R. Pintrich, & M. Zeidner (Eds.), *Handbook of self-regulation.* San Diego: Academic Press.

Pintrich, P. R., & Schunk, D. H. (Eds.). (2002). *Motivation in education* (2nd ed.). Upper Saddle River, NJ: Prentice-Hall.

Piran, N. (2002). Eating disorders and disordered eating. In J. Worell (Ed.), *Encyclopedia of women and gender.* New York: Oxford University Press.

Pittenger, D. (2003). *Behavioral research design and analysis.* New York: McGraw-Hill.

Pittman, T. S. (1998). Motivation. In D. T. Gilbert, S. T. Fiske, & G. Lindzey (Eds.), *Handbook of social psychology* (4th ed., Vol. 1). New York: McGraw-Hill.

Plomin, R. (1999). Genetics and general cognitive ability. *Nature, 402* (Suppl.), C25–C29.

Plomin, R., & Craig, I. (2001). Genetics, environment, and cognitive abilities: Review and work in progress toward a genome scan for quantitative trait locus associations using DNA pooling. *British Journal of Psychiatry, 40,* 41–48.

Plutchik, R. (1980). *Emotion: A psychoevolutionary synthesis.* New York: Harper & Row.

Poling, A. & Carr, J. E. (2002). Operant conditioning. In M. Hersen & W. H. Sledge (Eds.), *Encyclopedia of psychotherapy.* San Diego: Academic Press.

Pollmacher, T., Schuld, A., Kraus, T., Haack, M., Hinze-Selch, D., & Mullington, J. (2000). Experimental modulation, sleep, and sleepiness in humans. *Annals of the New York Academy of Science, 917,* 488–499.

Polsky, D., Onesirosan, P., Bauer, M. S., & Glick, H. A. (2002). Duration of therapy and health care costs of fluoxetine, paroxetine, and sertraline in 6 health plans. *Journal of Clinical Psychiatry, 63,* 156–164.

Pomplum, M., Reingold, E. M., & Shen, J. (2001). Investigating the visual span in comparative search: The effects of task difficulty and divided attention. *Cognition, 81,* B57–67.

Ponterotto, J. G., Casas, J. M., Suzuki, L. A., & Alexander, C. M. (Eds.). (2001). *Handbook of multicultural counseling.* Thousand Oaks, CA: Sage.

Popham, W. J. (2002). *Classroom assessment* (2nd ed.). Boston: Allyn & Bacon.

Posner, M. I., & Raichle, M. E. (1998). The neuroimaging of human brain function. *Proceedings of the National Academy of Science, USA, 95,* 763–764.

Post, S. G., Underwood, L. G., Scholls, J. P., & Hurlbut, W. B. (Eds.) (2002), *Altruism and altruistic love.* New York: Oxford University Press.

Powell, D. R. (2001). Early intervention and risk. In A. Fogel & G. Bremner (Eds.), *Blackwell handbook of infant development.* London: Blackwell.

Powell, L. (1992). The cognitive underpinnings of coronary-prone behaviors. *Cognitive Therapy & Research, 16*(2), 123–142.

Powell, R. A., & Symbaluk, D. G. (2002). *Introduction to learning and behavior.* Belmont, CA: Wadsworth.

Pratt, M. W., Danso, H. A., Arnold, M. L., Norris, J. E., & Filyer, R. (2001). Adult generativity and the socialization of adolescents. *Journal of Personality, 69,* 89–120.

Premack, D. (1986). *Gavagi! The future history of the ape language controversy.* Cambridge, MA: MIT Press.

Pressley, M. (1995). More about the development of self-regulation: Complex, long-term, and thoroughly social. *Educational Psychologist, 30,* 207–212.

Pressley, M. (2000). What should comprehension instruction be the instruction of? In M. Kamil (Ed.), *Handbook of reading research.* Mahwah, NJ: Erlbaum.

Prieto, M., & Giralt, M. T. (2001). Effects of N-(2-chlorethyl)-N-ethyl-2-bromobenzylamine on alpha2-adrenoceptors which regulate the synthesis and release of noradrenaline in the rat brain. *Pharmacological Toxology, 88,* 152–158.

Prietula, M. J., Feltovich, P. J., & Marchak, F. (2000). Factors influencing analysis of complex cognitive tasks: A framework and example from industrial process control. *Human Factors, 4,* 56–74.

Proctor, R. W., & Wang, H. (2002). Influences of different combinations of conceptual, perceptual, and structural similarity on stimulus-response compatibility. *Quarterly Journal of Experimental Psychology, 55,* 59–74.

Provenzo, E. F. (2002). *Teaching, learning, and schooling in American culture: A critical perspective.* Boston: Allyn & Bacon.

Pukrop, R., Sass, H., & Steinmeyer, E. M. (2000). Circumplex models for the similarity relationships between higher-order factors of personality and personality disorders: An empirical analysis. *Contemporary Psychiatry, 41,* 438–445.

Punamaki, R., & Joustie, M. (1998). The role of culture, violence, and personal factors affecting dream content. *Journal of Cross-Cultural Psychology, 29,* 320–343.

Purdy, J. E., Markham, M., Schwartz, B., & Gordon, W. M. (2001). *Learning and memory* (2nd ed.). Belmont, CA: Wadsworth.

Puri, B. K., Huttson, S. B., Saeed, N., Oatridge, A., Hajnal, J. V., Duncan, L., Chapman, M. J., Barnes, T. R., Bydder, G. M., & Joyce, E. M. (2001). A serial longitudinal quantitative MRI study of cerebral changes in first-episode schizophrenia using image segmentation and subvoxel registration. *Psychiatry Research, 106,* 141–150.

Puri, B. K., Richardson, A. J., Oatridge, A., Hajnal, J. V., & Saeed, N. (1999). Cerebral ventrical asymmetry in schizophrenia. *International Journal of Psychophysiology, 34,* 207–211.

Putnam, S. P., Sanson, A. V., & Rothbart, M. K. (2002). Child temperament and parenting. In M. Bornstein (Ed.), *Handbook of parenting* (2nd ed.). Mahwah, NJ: Erlbaum.

Q

Quality Assurance Project (1990). Treatment outlines for paranoid, schizotypal, and schizoid personality disorders. *Australian & New Zealand Journal of Psychiatry, 24,* 339–350.

Qualls, P. J., & Sheehan, P. W. (1981). Electromyograph biofeedback as a relaxation technique: A critical appraisal and reassessment. *Psychological Bulletin, 90,* 21–42.

Quinlin, M., Mayhew, C., & Bohle, P. (2001). The global expansion of precarious employment. *International Journal of Health Services, 31,* 507–536.

R

Rabasca, L. (1999, May). Stress caused when jobs don't meet expectations. *APA Monitor, 30,* 24–25.

Rabasca, L. (2000, June) More psychologists in the trenches. *Monitor on psychology, 31,* 50–51.

Raikkonen, K., Matthews, K. A., Flory, J. D., Owens, J. F., & Gump, B. B. (1999). Effects of optimism, pessimism, and trait anxiety on ambulatory blood pressure and mood during everyday life. *Journal of Personality and Social Psychology, 76,* 104–113.

Rainer, G., & Miller, E. K. (2002). Time-course of object-related neural activity in the primate prefrontal cortex during a short-term memory task. *European Journal of Neuroscience, 15,* 1244–1254.

Rains, G. D. (2002). *Principles of human neuropsychology.* New York: McGraw-Hill.

Rakic, P. (2002). Neurogenesis in adult primate neocortex: An evaluation of the evidence. *Nature Reviews: Neuroscience, 3,* 65–71.

Ramesch, M., & Roberts, G. (2002). Use of night-time benzodiazepines in an elderly inpatient population. *Journal of Clinical and Pharmacological Therapy, 27,* 93–97.

Ramey, C. T., & Campbell, F. A. (1984). Preventive education for high-risk children: Cognitive consequences of the Carolina Abecedarian Project. *American Journal of Mental Deficiency, 88,* 515–523.

Ramey, C. T., & Ramey, S. L. (1998). Early prevention and early experience. *American Psychologist, 53,* 109–120.

Ramey, C. T., Ramey, S. L., & Lanzi, R. G. (2001). Intelligence and experience. In R. J. Sternberg & E. L. Grigorenko (Eds.), *Environmental effects on cognitive abilities.* Mahwah, NJ: Erlbaum.

Ramey, S. L., & Ramey, S. T. (2000). Early childhood experiences and developmental competence. In S. Danzinger & J. Waldfogel (Eds.), *Securing the future: Investing in children from birth to college.* New York: Russell Sage Foundation.

Ramphal, C. (1962). *A study of three current problems in education.* Unpublished doctoral dissertation, University of Natal, India.

Rapaport, D. (1967). On the psychoanalytic theory of thinking. In M. M. Gill (Ed.), *The collected papers of David Rapaport.* New York: Basic Books.

Rapaport, S. (1994, November 28). Interview. *U.S. News and World Report,* p. 94.

Rappaport, J. L. (1989, March). The biology of obsessions and compulsions. *Scientific American,* 83–89.

Rasmussen, K. G. (1984). Nonverbal behavior, verbal behavior, resume credentials, and selection interview outcomes. *Journal of Applied Psychology, 69,* 551–556.

Ratner, N. B. (1993). Learning to speak. *Science, 262,* 260.

Raven, P. H., & Johnson, G. B. (2002). *Biology* (6th ed.). New York: McGraw-Hill.

Raz, N., Gunning-Dixon, F., Head, D., Williamson, A., & Acker, J. D. (2001). Age and sex differences in the cerebellum and the ventral pons. *American Journal of Neuroradiology, 22,* 1161–1167.

Razdin, U., & Sidhu, T. S. (2001). Need for research on health hazards due to noise pollution in metropolitan India. *Journal of the Indian Medical Association, 98,* 453–456.

Rebec, G. V. (1996, June). *Neurochemical and behavioral insights into mechanisms of action of stimulant drugs.* Paper presented at the meeting of the American Psychological Society, San Francisco.

Rector, N. A., & Beck, A. T. (2001). Cognitive behavioral therapy for schizophrenia: An empirical review. *Journal of Nervous and Mental Disorders, 189,* 278–287.

Redd, W. H. (1995). Behavioral research in cancer as a model for health psychology. *Health Psychology, 14,* 99–100.

Reed, S. K. (2001). *Cognition* (5th ed.). Belmont, CA: Wadsworth.

Rehm, L. P. (1998). Listening to Prozac and hearing noise: Commentary on Kirsch and Sapirstein's "Listening to Prozac but hearing placebo." *Prevention and Treatment, 1,* Article 0004c, posted June 26, 1998. (Retrieved from http://www.journals.apa.org/prevention/volume1/pre0010004c.html).

Reid, P. T., & Zalk, S. R. (2001). Academic environments: Gender and ethnicity in U.S. higher education. In J. Worrell (Ed.), *Encyclopedia of women and gender.* New York: Oxford University Press.

Reid, R. C. (2000). Sensory systems. In A. Kazdin (Ed.), *Encyclopedia of psychology.* Washington, DC, & New York: American Psychological Association and Oxford University Press.

Reinisch, J. M. (1990). *The Kinsey Institute new report on sex: What you must know to be sexually literate.* New York: St. Martin's Press.

Reinitz, M. T., Morrissey, J., & Demb, J. (1994). Role of attention in face encoding. *Journal of Experimental Psychology: Learning, Memory, and Cognition, 20,* 161–168.

Rescoria, R. A. (1966). Predictability and number of pairings in Pavlovian fear conditioning. *Psychonomic Science, 4,* 383–384.

Rescorla, R. A. (1988). Pavlovian conditioning: It's not what you think it is. *American Psychologist, 43,* 151–160.

Rescorla, R. A. (1996). Spontaneous recovery after training with multiple outcomes. *Animal Learning & Behavior, 24,* 11–18.

Rescorla, R. A. (2001). Experimental extinction. In R. R. Mowrer & S. B. Klein (Eds.), *Handbook of contemporary learning theories.* Mahwah, NJ: Erlbaum.

Restak, R. M. (1988). *The mind.* New York: Bantam.

Reuter-Lorenz, P., & Davidson, R. J. (1981). Differential contributions of the two cerebral hemispheres to the perception of happy and sad faces. *Neuropsychologia, 19,* 609–613.

Revelle, W. (2000). Individual differences. In A. Kazdin (Ed.), *Encyclopedia of psychology.* Washington, DC, and New York: American Psychological Association and Oxford University Press.

Revitch, E., & Schlesinger, L. B. (1978). Murder: Evaluation, classification, and prediction. In I. L. Kutash, S. B. Kutash, & O. B. Schlesinger (Eds.), *Violence.* San Francisco: Jossey-Bass.

Rex, T. S., Lewis, G. P., Geller, S. F., & Fisher, S. K. (2002). Differential expression of cone opsin mRNA levels following experimental retinal detachment and reattachment. *Molecular Vision, 8,* 114–118.

Reynolds, C. R. (2001). Employment tests. In W. E. Craighead & C. B. Nemeroff (Eds.), *The Corsini encyclopedia of psychology and behavioral science* (3rd ed.). New York: Wiley.

Rezvani, A. H., & Levin, E. D. (2001). Cognitive effects of nicotine. *Biological Psychiatry, 49,* 258–267.

Rice, J. K. (2000, August). *Cross-cultural perspectives on divorce and the family life cycle.* Paper presented at the meeting of the American Psychological Association, Washington, DC.

Rickels, K., & Rynn, M. A. (2001). What is generalized anxiety disorder? *Journal of Clinical Psychology, 62* (Suppl. 11), 46–50.

Riggio, R. E. (1986). Assessment of basic social skills. *Journal of Personality and Social Psychology, 51,* 649–660.

Rijsdijk, F. V., & Boomsma, D. I. (1997). Genetic mediation of the correlation between peripheral nerve conduction velocity and IQ. *Behavior Genetics, 27,* 87–98.

Rijsdijk, F. V., Vernon, P. A., & Boomsma, D. I. (1998). The genetic basis of the relation between speed-of-information-processing and IQ. *Behavior and Brain Research, 95,* 77–84.

Roback, H. W., Barton, D., Castelnuovo-Tedesco, P., Gay, V., Havens, L., & Nash, J. (1999). A symposium on psychotherapy in the age of managed care. *American Journal of Psychotherapy, 53,* 1–16.

Robbins, T. W. (2000). From arousal to cognition: The integrative position of the prefrontal cortex. *Progress in Brain Research, 126,* 469–483.

Roberts, B. W., & Hogan, R. (Eds.). (2001). *Personality psychology in the workplace.* Washington, DC: American Psychological Association.

Roberts, D., Anderson, B. L., & Lubaroff, A. (1994). *Stress and immunity at cancer diagnosis.* Unpublished manuscript, Dept. of Psychology, Ohio State University, Columbus.

Roberts, J. E., Gotlib, I. H., & Kassel, J. D. (1996). Adult attachment security and symptoms of depression: The mediating roles of dysfunctional attitudes and low self-esteem. *Journal of Personality & Social Psychology, 60,* 310–320.

Roberts, R. D., & Pallier, G. (2001). Individual differences in performance on elementary cognitive tasks (ECT's): Lawful vs. problematic parameters. *Journal of General Psychology, 128,* 279–314.

Robins, L. & Regier, D. (Eds.). (1991). *Psychiatric disorders in America.* New York: Free Press.

Robins, R. W., Trzesniewski, K. H., Tracey, J. L., Potter, J., & Gosling, S. D. (in press). Age differences in self-esteem from age 9 to 90. *Psychology and Aging.*

Rodin, J. (1984, December). Interview: A sense of control. *Psychology Today,* pp. 38–45.

Rodin, J. (1993). *Body traps.* New York: Morrow.

Rodin, J., & Langer, E. J. (1977). Long-term effects of a control-relevant intervention with the institutionalized aged. *Journal of Personality and Social Psychology, 35,* 397–402.

Rodrigues, M. S., & Cohen, S. (1998). Social support. In H.S. Friedman (Ed.), *Encyclopedia of mental health* (Vol. 3). San Diego: Academic Press.

Roehrs, T., & Roth, T. (1998). Reported in Maas, J. (1998). *Power sleep.* New York: Villard, p. 44.

Rogers, C. R. (1961). *On becoming a person.* Boston: Houghton Mifflin.

Rogers, C. R. (1974). In retrospect: Forty-six years. *American Psychologist, 29,* 115–123.

Rogers, C. R. (1980). *A way of being.* Boston: Houghton Mifflin.

Rogers, R. (2001). *Handbook of diagnostic and structured interviewing.* New York: Guilford.

Rogers, T. B., Kuiper, N. A., & Kirker, W. S. (1977). Self-reference and the encoding of personal information. *Journal of Personality and Social Psychology, 35,* 677–688.

Rogoff, B. (1998). Cognition as a collaborative process. In W. Damon (Ed.), *Handbook of child psychology* (5th ed., Vol. 2). New York: Wiley.

Rogoff, B. (1990). *Apprenticeship in thinking.* New York: Oxford University Press.

Rogosch, F. A., Cicchetti, D., Shields, A., & Toth, S. L. (1995). Parenting dysfunction in child maltreatment. In M. H. Bornstein (Ed.), *Handbook of parenting* (Vol. 4). Hillsdale, NJ: Erlbaum.

Rosch, E. (1973). On the internal structure of perceptual and semantic categories. In T. E. Moore (Ed.), *Cognition and the acquisition of language.* San Diego: Academic Press.

Rose, R. J., Koskenvuo, M., Kaprio, J., Sarna, S., & Langinvainio, H. (1988). Shared genes, shared experiences, and similarity of personality: Data from 14,228 adult Finnish co-twins. *Journal of Personality and Social Psychology, 54,* 161–171.

Rosen, K. S., & Burke, P. B. (1999). Multiple attachment relationships within families. *Developmental Psychology, 35,* 436–444.

Rosenbaum, J. (2001, May 5). *Antidepressant treatment and the biology of depression.* Paper presented at the annual meeting of the American Psychiatric Association, New Orleans.

Rosenbaum, M., Leibel, R. L., & Hirsch, J. (1997). Medical progress: Obesity. *New England Journal of Medicine, 337,* 396–407.

Rosenbloom, M. (2002). Chlorpromazine and the psychopharmacological revolution. *Journal of the American Medical Association, 287,* 1860–1861.

Rosenfeld, A. H. (1985, June). Depression: Dispelling despair. *Psychology Today,* pp. 28–34.

Rosenhan, D. L. (1973). On being sane in insane places. *Science, 179,* 250–258.

Rosenthal, D. (1963). *The Genain quadruplets.* New York: Basic Books.

Rosenthal, R. (1966). *Experimenter effects in behavioral research.* New York: Appleton-Century-Crofts.

Rosenthal, R. (1994). Interpersonal expectancy effects: A 30-year-perspective. *Current Dimensions in Psychological Science, 3,* 176–179.

Rosenthal, R., & DiMatteo, M. R. (2001). Meta-analysis: Recent developments in quantitative methods for literature reviews. *Annual Review of Psychology, 52,* 59–62.

Rosenthal, R., & Jacobsen, L. (1968). *Pygmalion in the classroom.* Fort Worth: Harcourt Brace.

Rosenzweig, M. R., Bennett, E. L., & Diamond, M. C. (1972, February). Brain changes in response to experience. *Scientific American,* 22–29.

Rosnow, R. L. (1995). Teaching research ethics through role-playing and discussion. In M. E. Ware & D. E. Johnson (Eds.), *Demonstrations and activities in teaching psychology* (Vol. 1). Mahwah, NJ: Erlbaum.

Rosnow, R. L., & Rosenthal, R. (1996). *Beginning behavioral research* (2nd ed.). Upper Saddle River, NJ: Prentice Hall.

Rosnow, R., & Rosenthal, R. (2002). *Beginning behavioral research* (4th ed.). Upper Saddle River, NJ: Prentice Hall.

Ross, B. H. (2000). Concepts: Learning. In A. Kazdin (Ed.), *Encyclopedia of psychology.* Washington, DC, and New York: American Psychological Association and Oxford University Press.

Ross, C. A., & Norton, G. R. (1989). Differences between men and women with multiple personality disorder. *Hospital & Community Psychiatry, 40,* 186–188.

Rossell, C., & Baker, K. (1996). The educational effectiveness of bilingual education. *Research in the Teaching of English, 30,* 7–74.

Rossi, F., Saggiorato, C., & Strata, P. (2002). Target-specific innervation of embryonic cerebellar transplants by regenerating olivo-cerebellar axons in the adult rat. *Experimental Neurology, 172,* 205–212.

Roth, D., Eng, W., & Heimberg, R. G. (2002). Cognitive behavior therapy. In M. Hersen & W. H. Sledge (Eds.), *Encyclopedia of psychotherapy.* San Diego: Academic Press.

Rothbart, M. K., & Bates, J. E. (1998). Temperament. In W. Damon (Ed.), *Handbook of child psychology* (5th ed., Vol. 3). New York: Wiley.

Rotter, J. B. (1966). Generalized expectancies for internal versus external control of reinforcement. *Psychological Monographs, 80,* (1, Whole No. 609).

Rowe, D. C. (1994). *The limits of family influence: Genes, experience, and behavior.* New York: Guilford Press.

Rowe, J. W., & Kahn, R. L. (1997). *Successful aging.* New York: Pantheon.

Rowe, S. M., & Wertsch, J. V. (2002). Vygotsky's model of cognitive development. In U. Goswami (Ed.), *Blackwell handbook of childhood cognitive development.* Malden, MA: Blackwell.

Roy, A. (1992). Genetics, biology, and suicide in the family. In R. W. Maris, A. L. Berman, J. T. Maltsberger, & R. I. Yufit (Eds.), *Assessment and prediction of suicide* (pp. 574–588). New York: Guilford.

Roy-Byrne, P. P. & Cowley, D. S. (2002). Pharmacological treatments for panic disorders, phobias, and generalized anxiety disorder. In P. Nathan & J. M. Gorman (Eds.). *A guide to treatmentsthat work (2nd Ed.).* New York: Oxford University Press.

Royden, C. S. (2000). Motion perception. In A. Kazdin (Ed.), *Encyclopedia of psychology.* Washington, DC, & New York: American Psychological Association and Oxford University Press.

Rozanski, A., Blumenthal, J. A., Kaplan J. (1999). Impact of psychological factors on the pathogenesis of cardiovascular disease and implications for therapy. *Circulation, 99,* 2192–2217.

Rubel, E. W., & Fritzsch, B. (2002). Auditory system development: Primary auditory neurons and their targets. *Annual Review of Neuroscience* (Vol. 25). Palo Alto, CA: Annual Reviews.

Rubenzer, S., Ones, D. Z., & Faschingbauer, T. (2000, August). *Personality traits of U.S. presidents.* Paper presented at the meeting of the American Psychological Association, Washington, DC.

Rubin, D. C., & Kozin, M. (1984). Vivid memories. *Cognition, 16,* 81–95.

Rubin, Z., & Mitchell, C. (1976). Couples research as couples counseling. *American Psychologist, 31,* 17–25.

Ruby, N. F., Dark, J., Burns, D. E., Heller, H. C., & Zucker, I. (2002). The suprachiasmatic nucleus is essential for circadian body temperature rhythms in hibernating ground squirrels. *Journal of Neuroscience, 22,* 357–364.

Rudd, M. D., Joiner, T. E., & Rajab, M. H. (2001). *Treating suicidal behavior.* New York: Guilford.

Rudolf, K. I., Chang, S., Lee, H., Gottlieb, G. J., Greider, C., & DePinto, R. A. (1999). Longevity, stress, response, and cancer in aging telomerase-deficient mice. *Cell, 96,* 701–712.

Rusbult, C. E., Olsen, N., Davis, J. L., & Hannon, P. A. (2001). Commitment and relationship maintenance mechanisms. In J. H. Harvey & A. Wenzel (Eds.), *Close romantic relationships.* Mahwah, NJ: Erlbaum.

Ruse, M. (2001). Altruism: A Darwinian naturalist's perspective. In S. G. Post, L. G. Underwood, J. P. Schloss, & W. B. Hurlbut (Eds.), *Altruism and altruistic love.* New York: Oxford University Press.

Ruse, M. (2002). A Darwinian naturalists's perspective on altruism. In S. G. Post, L. G. Underwood, J. P. Schloss, & W. B. Hurlbut (Eds.), *Altruism and altruistic love.* New York: Oxford University Press.

Rushton, J. P., Fulker, D. W., Neal, M. C., Nias, D. K. B., & Eysenck, H. J. (1986). Altruism and aggression: The heritability of individual differences. *Journal of Personality and Social Psychology, 50,* 1192–1198.

Russell, D. W. (1996). UCLA Loneliness Scale (Version 3): Reliability, validity, and factor structure. *Journal of Personality, Assessment, 66,* 20–43.

Russo, N. F. (1990). Overview: Forging research priorities for women's health. *American Psychologist, 45,* 373–386.

Ryan, J. M. (2001). Pharmacologic approach to aggression in neuropsychiatric disorders. *Seminars in Clinical Neuropsychiatry, 5,* 238–249.

Ryan, R. M., & Deci, E. L. (2000). Self-determination theory and the facilitation of intrinsic motivation, social development, and well-being. *American Psychologist, 55,* 68–78.

Ryan, R. M., & Deci, E. L. (2001). On happiness and human potentials: A review of research on hedonic and eudaimonic well-being. *Annual Review of Psychology* (Vol. 52). Palo Alto, CA: Annual Reviews.

Ryan, R. M., & LaGuardia, J. G. (2000). What is being optimized? Self-determination theory and basic psychological needs. In S. H. Qualls & N. Abeles (Eds.), *Psychology and the aging revolution.* Washington, DC: American Psychological Association.

Ryan-Finn, K. D., Cause, A. M., & Grove, K. (1995, March). *Children and adolescents of color: Where are you? Selection, recruitment, and retention in developmental research.* Paper presented at the meeting of the Society for Research in Child Development, Indianapolis.

Ryff, C. D., & Singer, B. (1998). Middle age and well-being. In H. S. Friedman (Ed.), *Encyclopedia of mental health* (Vol. 2). San Diego: Academic Press.

Rymer, R. (1993). *Genie.* New York: Harper-Collins.

S

Sacks, O. (1985). *The man who mistook his wife for a hat.* New York: Summit Books.

Salkind, N. J. (2003). *Exploring research (5th Ed.).* Upper Saddle River, NJ: Prentice-Hall.

Salkovskis, P. M., Westbrook, D., Davis, J., Jeavons, A., & Gledhill, A. (1997). Effects of neutralizing on intrusive thoughts: An experiment investigating the etiology of obsessive-compulsive disorder. *Behaviour Research & Therapy, 35,* 211–219.

Salmon, D. P. (2000). Alzheimer's disease. In A. Kazdin (Ed.), *Encyclopedia of psychology.* Washington, DC, & New York: American Psychological Association and Oxford University Press.

Salovey, P., & Birnbaum, D. (1989). Influence of mood on health-relevant cognitions. *Journal of Personality and Social Psychology, 57,* 539–551.

Salovey, P., Rothman, A., Detweiler, J. B., & Steward, W. T. (2000). Emotional states and physical health. *American Psychologist, 55,* 110–121.

Salovey, P., & Mayer, J. D. (1990). Emotional intelligence. *Imagination, Cognition, and Personality, 9,* 185–211.

Salthouse, T. (2000). Adult development and aging: Cognitive processes and development. In A. Kazdin (Ed.), *Encyclopedia of psychology.* Washington, DC, & New York: American Psychological Association and Oxford University Press.

Salthouse, T. A. (1994). The aging of working memory. *Neuropsychology, 8,* 535–543.

Salthouse, T. A. (1994). The nature of the influence of speed on adult age differences in cognition. *Developmental Psychology, 30,* 240–259.

Sand, P. G., Godau, C., Riederer, P., Peters, C., Franke, P., Nothen, M. M., Stober, G., Fritze, J., Maier, W., Propping, P., Lesch, K. P., Riess, O., Sander, T., Bechmann, H., & Deckert, J. (2001). Exonic variants of the GABA (B) receptor gene and panic disorder. *Psychiatry and Genetics, 10,* 191–194.

Sandell, J. (2000). Vision and sight: Behavioral and functional aspects. In A. Kazdin (Ed.), *Encyclopedia of psychology.* Washington, DC, & New York: American Psychological Association and Oxford University Press.

Sanderson, W. C. (1995, March). Which therapies are proven effective? *APA Monitor,* p. 4.

Sangha, S., McComb, C., Scheibenstock, A., Johannes, C., & Lukowiak, K. (2002). The effects of continuous versus partial reinforcement schedules on associative learning, memory, and extinction in Lymnaea stagnalis. *Journal of Experimental Biology, 205,* 1171–1178.

Sanocki, T. (2001). *Student friendly statistics.* Upper Saddle River, NJ: Prentice-Hall.

Sanson, A., Smart, D., & Hemphill, S. (2002). Temperament and social development. In P. Smith & C. Hart (Eds.), *Blackwell handbook of childhood social development.* Malden, MA: Blackwell.

Santacruz, K. S., & Swagerty, D. (2001). Early diagnosis of dementia. *American Family Physician, 63,* 703–713.

Santrock, J. W. (2001). *Educational psychology.* New York: McGraw-Hill.

Santrock, J. W. (2002). *Life-span development* (8th ed.). New York: McGraw-Hill.

Santrock, J. W. (2003). *Child Development* (9th ed.). New York: McGraw-Hill.

Santrock, J. W., & Halonen, J. A. (2002). *Your guide to college success* (2nd ed.). Belmont, CA: Wadsworth.

Sarason, I. G., & Sarason, B. R. (2002). *Abnormal psychology* (10th ed.). Upper Saddle River, NJ: Prentice-Hall.

Sarbin, T. R., & Keen, E. (1998). Classifying mental disorders. In H. S. Friedman (Ed.), *Encyclopedia of mental health* (Vol. 1). San Diego: Academic Press.

Sarigiani, P. A., & Petersen, A. C. (2000). Adolescence: Puberty and biological maturation. In A. Kazdin (Ed.), *Encyclopedia of psychology.* Washington, DC, & New York: American Psychological Association and Oxford University Press.

Saucier, G. (2001, April). *Going beyond the big five.* Paper presented at the meeting of the Society for Research in Child Development, San Francisco.

Savage-Rumbaugh, E. S., Murphy, J., Sevcik, R. A., Brakke, K. E., Williams, S. L., & Rumbaugh, D. M. (1993). Language comprehension in ape and child. *Monographs of the Society for Research in Child Development,* Serial No. 233 (Vol. 58, Nos. 3–4).

Savage-Rumbaugh, S., Shanker, S., & Taylor, T. (1998). *Apes, language, and mind.* New York: Oxford University Press.

Savic, I. (2002). Sex differences in hypothalamic activation by putative pheromones. *Molecular Psychiatry, 7,* 335–336.

Sax, L. J., Astin, A. W., Korn, W. S., & Mahoney, K. M. (1998). *The American freshman: National norms for fall 1998*. Los Angeles: American Council on Education, UCLA.

Sax, L. J., Astin, A. W., Korn, W. S., & Mahoney, K. M. (1995). *The American college freshman: National norms for fall, 1995*. Los Angeles: University of California at Los Angeles Higher Education Research Institute.

Sax, L. J., Lindholm, J. A., Astin, A. W., Korn, W. S., & Mahoney, K. M. (2001). *The American freshman: National norms for fall 2001*. Los Angeles: Higher Education Research Institute, UCLA.

Saxe, L. (1998, June). Commentary. *APA Monitor*, p. 30.

Saxena, S., Brody, A. L., Schwartz, J. M., & Baxter, L. R. (1998). Neuroimaging and frontal-subcortical circuitry in obsessive-compulsive disorder. *British Journal of Psychiatry, 173* (Suppl. 35), 26–37.

Scafidi, F., & Field, T. M. (1996). Massage therapy improves behavior in neonates born to HIV-positive mothers. *Journal of Pediatric Psychology, 21*, 889–897.

Scalzone, F., & Zontini, G. (2001). The dream's navel between chaos and thought. *International Journal of Psychoanalysis, 82*, 263–282.

Scarborough, E., & Furumoto, L. (1987). *Untold lives: The first generation of American women psychologists*. New York: Columbia University Press.

Scarr, S. (1984, May). Interview. *Psychology Today*, pp. 59–63.

Scarr, S., & Weinberg, R. A. (1983). The Minnesota adoption studies: Genetic differences and malleability. *Child Development, 54*, 182–259.

Schachter, S., & Singer, J. E. (1962). Cognitive, social, and physiological determinants of emotional state. *Psychological Review, 69*, 379–399.

Schacter, D. L. (1999). Consciousness. In M.S. Gazzaniga (Ed.), *The new cognitive neurosciences* (2nd ed.). Cambridge, MA: MIT Press.

Schacter, D. L. (1996). *Searching for memory*. New York: Basic Books.

Schacter, D. L. (1999). The seven sins of memory: Insights from psychology and cognitive neuroscience. *American Psychologist, 54*, 182–203.

Schacter, D. L. (2000). Memory: Memory systems. In A. Kazdin (Ed.), *Encyclopedia of psychology*. Washington, DC, & New York: American Psychological Association and Oxford University Press.

Schacter, D. L. (2001). *The seven sins of memory*. Boston: Houghton Mifflin.

Schafer, G. (1999). Early speech perception and word learning. In M. Barrett (Ed.), *The development of language*. Philadelphia: Psychology Press.

Schaffer, H. R., & Emerson, P. E. (1964). The development of social attachments in infancy. *Monographs of the Society for Research in Child Development, 29* (3, Serial No. 94).

Schaie, K. W. (1983). Consistency and changes in cognitive functioning of the young-old and old-old. In M. Bergner, U. Lehr, E. Lang, & R. Schmidt-Scherzer (Eds.), *Aging in the eighties and beyond*. New York: Springer.

Schaie, K. W. (1994). The life course of adult intellectual abilities. *American Psychologist, 49*, 304–313.

Schaie, K. W. (1996). *Intellectual development in adulthood: The Seattle Longitudinal Study*. New York: Cambridge University Press.

Schaie, K. W., & Willis, S. L. (2001). *Adult development and aging* (5th ed.). Upper Saddle River, NJ: Prentice-Hall.

Schaller, M., & Conway, L. G. (2001). From cognition to culture: The origins of stereotypes that really matter. In G. Moskowitz (Ed.), *Cognitive social psychology*. Mahwah, NJ: Erlbaum.

Schank, R., & Abelson, R. (1977). *Scripts, plans, goals, and understanding*. Mahwah, NJ: Erlbaum.

Scharff, L., Marcus, D. A., & Masek, B. J. (2002). A controlled study of minimal-contact thermal biofeedback treatment in children with migraine. *Journal of Pediatric Psychology, 27*, 109–119.

Scharfman, H. E. (2002). Epilepsy as an example of neural plasticity. *Neuroscientist, 8*, 154–173.

Schaubroeck, J., Jones, J. R., & Xie, J. L. (2001). Individual differences in utilizing control to cope with job demands: Effects on susceptibility to infectuous disease. *Journal of Applied Psychology, 86*, 114–120.

Scheier, M. F., & Carver, C. S. (1992). Effects of optimism on psychological and physical well-being: Theoretical overview and empirical update. *Cognitive Therapy and Research, 16*, 201–228.

Schiffman, J., & Walker, E. (1998). Schizophrenia. In H. S. Friedman (Ed.), *Encyclopedia of mental health* (Vol. 2). San Diego: Academic Press.

Schmolk, H., Buffalo, E. A., & Squire, L. R. (2000). Memory distortions develop over time: Recollections of the O. J. Simpson trial verdict after 15 and 32 months. *Psychological Science, 11*, 39–45.

Schneider, K. J. (2002). Humanistic psychotherapy. In M. Hersen & W. H. Sledge (Eds.), *Encyclopedia of psychotherapy*. San Diego: Academic Press.

Schneider, S. L. (2001). In search of realistic optimism: Meaning, knowledge, and warm fuzziness. *American Psychologist, 56*, 250–263.

Schneiderman, N., Antoni, M. H., Saab, P. G., & Ironson, G. (2001). Health psychology: Psychological and biobehavioral aspects of chronic disease management. *Annual Review of Psychology* (Vol. 52). Palo Alto, CA: Annual Reviews.

Scholnick, E. K. (1999). Piaget's legacy: Heirs to the house that Jean built. In E. K. Scholnick, K. Nelson, S. A. Gelman, & P. H. Miller (Eds.), *Conceptual development: Piaget's legacy*. Mahwah, NJ: Erlbaum.

Scholnick, E. K., Nelson, K., Gelman, S. A., & Miller, P. H. (Eds.). (1999). *Conceptual development: Piaget's legacy*. Mahwah, NJ: Erlbaum.

Schretlen, D., Pearlson, G. D., Anthony, J. C., Aylward, E. H., Augustine, A. M., Davis, A., & Barta, P. (2000). Elucidating the contributions of processing speed, executive ability, and frontal lobe volume to normal age-related differences in fluid intelligence. *Journal of the International Neuropsychology Society, 6*, 52–61.

Schulenberg, J. (1999, June). *Binge drinking trajectories before, during, and after college: More reasons to worry from a developmental perspective*. Paper presented at the meeting of the American Psychological Society, Denver, CO.

Schulenberg, J., O'Malley, P. M., Bachman, J. G., & Johnston, L. D. (2000). "Spread your wings and fly": The course of health and well-being during the transition to young adulthood. In L. Crockett & R. Silbereisen (Eds.), *Negotiating adolescence in times of social change*. New York: Cambridge University Press.

Schultheiss, O. C., & Brunstein, J. C. (1999). Goal imagery: Bridging the gap between implicit motives and explicit goals. *Journal of Personality, 67*, 1–38.

Schultz, A., Williams, D., Israel, B., Becker, A., Parker, E., James, S. A., & Jackson, J. (2000). Unfair treatment, neighborhood effects, and mental health in the Detroit metropolitan area. *Journal of Health and Social Behavior, 41*, 314–332.

Schultz, R., & Curnow, C. (1988). Peak performance and age among superathletes: Track and field, swimming, baseball, tennis, and golf. *Journal of Gerontology, 43*, 113–120.

Schunk, D. (2000). *Theories of learning applied to education* (3rd ed.). Upper Saddle River, NJ: Merrill.

Schunk, D. H. (2000). *Learning theories* (3rd ed.). Upper Saddle River, NJ: Prentice Hall.

Schunk, D. H., & Ertmer, P. A. (2000). Self-regulation and academic learning: Self-efficacy enhancing interventions. In M. Boekaerts, P. R. Pintrich, & M. Zeidner (Eds.), *Handbook of self-regulation*. San Diego: Academic Press.

Schwartz, B. (2000). Self-determination: The tyranny of freedom. *American Psychologist, 55*, 79–88.

Schwartz, B. L. (2002). *Tip-of-the-tongue states*. Mahwah, NJ: Erlbaum.

Schwartz, T. (1999). *Kids and guns*. New York: Franklin Watts.

Scott, T. R. (2000). Taste. In A. Kazdin (Ed.), *Encyclopedia of psychology*. Washington, DC, & New York: American Psychological Association and Oxford University Press.

Sears, D. O., Peplau, L. A., & Taylor, S. E. (2000). *Social psychology* (10th Ed.). Upper Saddle River, NJ: Prentice Hall.

Sechehaye, M. (1951). *Autobiography of a schizophrenic girl*. New York: Grune & Stratton.

Sedikides, C., Campbell, W. K., Reeder, G. D., & Elliot, A. J. (1998). The self-serving bias in relational context. *Journal of Personality and Social Psychology, 74*, 378–386.

Seffge-Krenke, I. (1995). *Stress, coping, and relationships in adolescence*. Mahwah, NJ: Erlbaum.

Segal, D. L., & Coolidge, F. L. (2000). Assessment. In A. Kazdin (Ed.), *Encyclopedia of psychology*. Washington, DC, & New York: American Psychological Association and Oxford University Press.

Segrin, C. (2001). *Interpersonal processes in psychological disorders*. New York: Guilford.

Seidemann, E., Meilijson, I., Abeles, M., Bergman, H., & Vaadia, E. (1996). Simultaneously recorded single units in the frontal cortex go through sequences of discrete and stable states in monkeys performing a delayed localization task. *Journal of Neuroscience, 16*, 752–768.

Seidman, D. F., Rosecan, J., & Role, L. (1999). Biological and clinical perspectives on nicotine addiction. In D. F. Seidman & L. S. Covey (Eds.), *Helping the hard-core smoker*. Mahwah, NJ: Erlbaum.

Seidman, S. N. (2002). Exploring the relationship between depression and erectile dysfunction in aging men. *Journal of Clinical Psychiatry, 63, Supplement,* 5–12.

Seifer, R. (2001). Socioeconomic status, multiple risks, and development of intelligence. In R. J. Sternberg & E. L. Grigorenko (Eds.), *Environmental effects on cognitive abilities.* Mahwah, NJ: Erlbaum.

Sejnowski, T. (2001). *Seeing, hearing, and smelling the world* [Commentary]. Retrieved October 2001 from http://www.hhmi.org/senses.

Sekular, R., & Blake, R. (2002). *Perception* (4th ed.). New York: McGraw-Hill.

Seligman, C., Olson, J. M., & Zanna, M. P. (Eds.). (1996). *The psychology of values.* Mahwah, NJ: Erlbaum.

Seligman, M. E. P. (1970). On the generality of the laws of learning. *Psychological Review, 77,* 406–418.

Seligman, M. E. P. (2001). Positive psychology, prevention, and positive therapy. In C. R. Snyder & S. J. Lopez (Eds.), *Handbook of positive psychology.* New York: Oxford University Press.

Seligman, M. E. P. (1975). *Helplessness: On depression, development and death.* San Francisco: W. H. Freeman.

Seligman, M. E. P. (1989). Why is there so much depression today? The waxing of the individual and the waning of the common. In *The G. Stanley Hall Lecture Series.* Washington, DC: American Psychological Association.

Seligman, M. E. P. (1990). *Learned optimism.* New York: Knopf.

Seligman, M. E. P. (1994). *What you can change and what you can't.* New York: Knopf.

Seligman, M. E. P., & Csikszentmihalyi, M. (2000). Positive psychology: An introduction. *American Psychologist, 55,* 5–14.

Selye, H. (1974). *Stress without distress.* Philadelphia: W.B. Saunders.

Selye, H. (1983). The stress concept: Past, present, and future. In C.I. Cooper (Ed.), *Stress research.* New York: Wiley.

Serpell, R. (2000). Determinants of intelligence: Culture and intelligence. In A. Kazdin (Ed.), *Encyclopedia of psychology.* Washington, DC, & New York: American Psychological Association and Oxford University Press.

Servaes, P., Vignerhoets, A., Vreugdenhil, G., Keuning, J. J., & Broekhuijsen, A. M. (1999). Inhibition of emotional expression in breast cancer patients. *Behavioral Medicine, 25,* 26–34.

Service, R. F. (1994). Will a new type of drug make memory-making easier? *Science, 266,* 218–219.

Seto, M. C., & Barbaree, H. E. (1995). The role of alcohol in sexual aggression. *Clinical Psychology Review, 15,* 545–566.

Shadubina, A., Agam, G., & Belmaker, R. H. (2001). The mechanism of lithium: State of the art, ten years later. *Progress in Neuropsychology and Biological Psychiatry, 25,* 855–866.

Shakesby, A. C., Anwyl, R., & Rowan, M. J. (2002). Overcoming the effects of stress on synaptic plasticity in the intact hippocampus: rapid actions of serotonergic and antidepressant agents. *Journal of Neuroscience, 22,* 3638–3644.

Shanks, D. R. (1991). Categorization by a connectionist network. *Journal of Experimental Psychology: Learning, Memory, and Cognition, 17,* 433–443.

Sharkey, K. M., & Eastman, C. I. (2002). Melatonin phase shifts human circadian rhythms in a placebo-controlled simulated night-work study. *American Journal of Physiology: Regulatory, Integrative, and Comparative Physiology, 282,* R454–R463.

Shaughnessy, J. J., Zechmeister, E. B., & Zechmeister, J. S. (2003). *Research methods in psychology (6th Ed.).* New York: McGraw-Hill.

Shaver, P. (1986, August). *Being lonely, falling in love: Perspectives from attachment theory.* Paper presented at the meeting of the American Psychological Association, Washington, DC.

Shay, J. W., & Wright, W. E. (2000). The use of telomerized cells for tissue engineering. *Nature Biotechnology, 18,* 22–23.

Shaywitz, B. A, Shaywitz, S. E., Pugh, K. R., & others (1995). Sex differences in the functional organization of the brain for language. *Nature, 373,* 607–609.

Sheldon, K. M., Ryan, R. M., Rawsthorne, L., & Ilardi, B. (1997). Trait self and true self: Cross-role variation in the Big Five traits and its relations with authenticity and subjective well-being. *Journal of Personality and Social Psychology, 73,* 1380–1393.

Shelton, R. C., & Hollon, S. D. (2000). Antidepressants. In A. Kazdin (Ed.), *Encyclopedia of psychology.* Washington, DC, & New York: American Psychological Association and Oxford University Press.

Shepard, R. N. (1967). Recognition memory for words, sentences, and pictures. *Journal of Verbal Learning and Verbal Behavior, 6,* 156–163.

Shepard, R. N. (1996, August). *The eye's mind and the mind's eye.* Paper presented at the meeting of the American Psychological Association, Toronto.

Sher, K. J. (1993). Children of alcoholics and the intergenerational transmission of alcoholism: A biopsychological perspective. In J. S. Baer, G. A. Marlatt, & R. J. McMahon (Eds.), *Addictive behaviors across the life span.* Newbury Park, CA: Sage.

Sheras, P., & Worchel, S. (1979). *Clinical psychology: A social psychological approach.* New York: Van Nostrand.

Sherif, M., Harvey, O. J., White, B. J., Hood, W. R., & Sherif, C. W. (1961). *Intergroup cooperation and competition: The Robbers Cave experiment.* Norman: University of Oklahoma Press.

Sherwood, A., Light, K. C., & Blumenthal, J. A. (1989). Effects of aerobic exercise training on hemodynamic responses during psychosocial stress in normotensive and borderline hypertensive Type A men: A preliminary report. *Psychosomatic Medicine, 51,* 123–136.

Shevell, S. K. (2000). Color vision. In A. Kazdin (Ed.), *Encyclopedia of psychology.* Washington, DC, & New York: American Psychological Association and Oxford University Press.

Shewchuk, R. M., Johnson, M. O., & Elliott, T. R. (1999). Self-appraised social problem solving abilities, emotional reactions, and actual problem-solving performance. *Behavioral Research and Therapy, 38,* 727–740.

Shields, S. A. (1991). Gender in the psychology of emotion. In K. T. Strongman (Ed.), *International Review of Studies of Emotion* (Vol. 1). New York: Wiley.

Shields, S., & Eyssell, K. M. (2002). History of the study of gender psychology. In J. Worell (Ed.), *Encyclopedia of women and gender.* New York: Oxford University Press.

Shier, D., Butler, J., & Lewis, R. (1999). *Human anatomy and physiology* (8th ed.). New York: McGraw-Hill.

Shnek, Z. M., Irvine, J., Stewart, D., & Abbey, S. (2001). Psychological factors and depressive symptoms in ischemic heart disease. *Health Psychology, 20,* 141–145.

Shotland, R. L. (1985, June). When bystanders just stand by. *Psychology Today.* pp. 50–55.

Showers, C. (1986). *The motivational consequences of negative thinking.* Paper presented at the meeting of the American Psychological Association, Washington, DC.

Shultz, R. T., Grelotti, D. J., & Pober, B. (2001). Genetics of childhood disorders: XXVI. Williams syndrome and brain-behavior relationships. *Journal of the American Academy of Child and Adolescent Psychiatry, 40,* 606–609.

Siebner, H. R., Limmer, C., Peinemann, A., Drzezga, A., Bloem, B. R., Schwaiger, M., & Conrad, B. (2002). Long-term consequences of switching handedness: A positron emission tomography study on handwriting in "converted" left handers. *Journal of Neuroscience, 22,* 2816–2825.

Siegel, S. (1988). State dependent learning and morphine tolerance. *Behavioral Neuroscience, 102,* 228–232.

Siegle, G. J., Steinhauer, S. R., Thase, M. E., Stenger, V. A., & Carter, C. S. (2002). Can't shake that feeling: event-related fMRI assessment of sustained amygdala activity in response to emotional information in depressed individuals. *Biological Psychiatry, 51,* 693–707.

Siegler, R. S. (1998). *Children's thinking* (3rd ed.). Upper Saddle River, NJ: Erlbaum.

Siffre, M. (1975). Six months alone in a cave. *National Geographic, 147,* 426–435.

Silverman, N. N., & Corsini, R. J. (1984). Is it true what they say about Adler's individual psychology? *Teaching of Psychology, 11,* 188–189.

Silverstein, S. M., Menditto, A. A., & Stuve, P. (2001). Shaping attention span: An operant conditioning procedure to improve neurocognition and functioning in schizophrenia. *Schizophrenia Bulletin, 27,* 247–257.

Simeon, D., Guralnik, O., Knutelska, M., & Schmeidler, J. (2002). Personality factors associated with dissociation: Temperament, defenses, and cognitive schemata. *American Journal of Psychiatry, 159,* 489–491.

Simon, H. (2000). Artificial intelligence. In A. Kazdin (Ed.), *Encyclopedia of psychology.* Washington, DC, & New York: American Psychological Association and Oxford University Press.

Simon, H. A. (1996). Putting the story together. *Contemporary Psychology, 41,* 12–14.

Simon, H. A. (1969). *The sciences of the artificial.* Cambridge, MA: MIT Press.

Simpson, J. A. (1995). Self-monitoring and commitment to dating relationships: A classroom demonstration. In M. E. Ware & D. E. Johnson (Eds.), *Demonstrations and activities in teaching of introductory psychology.* Mahwah, NJ: Erlbaum.

Simpson, J. A., & Gangestad, S. W. (2001). Evolution and relationships: A call for integration. *Personal Relationships, 8,* 341–356.

Simpson, K. J. (2002). Anorexia nervosa and culture. *Journal of Psychiatric and Mental Health Nursing, 9,* 65–71.

Singer, D. G., & Singer, J. L. (1998). Television viewing. In H.S. Friedman (Ed.), *Encyclopedia of mental health* (Vol. 3). San Diego: Academic Press.

Singer, M., Gagnon, N., & Richards, E. (2002). Strategies of text retrieval: A criterion shift account. *Canadian Journal of Experimental Psychology, 56,* 41–57.

Singer, W., & Gray, C. M. (1995). Visual feature integration and the temporal correlation hypothesis. *Annual Review of Neuroscience* (Vol. 18). Palo Alto, CA: Annual Reviews.

Singh, R. P. (1984, January). Experimental verification of locus of control as related to conformity behavior. *Psychological Studies, 29*(1), 64–67.

Skinner, B. F. (1938). *The behavior of organisms: An experimental analysis.* New York: Appleton-Century-Crofts.

Skinner, B. F. (1948). *Walden Two.* New York: Macmillan.

Skinner, B. F. (1957). *Verbal behavior.* New York: Appleton-Century-Crofts.

Skinner, E. A., Wellborn, J. G., & Connell, J. P. (1990). What it takes to do well in school and whether I've got it. *Journal of Educational Psychology, 82,* 22–32.

Slavin, R. (1989). Cooperative learning and student achievement. In R. Slavin (Ed.), *School and classroom organization.* Mahwah, NJ: Erlbaum.

Slavin, R. E. (2000). *Educational psychology* (6th ed.). Boston: Allyn & Bacon.

Slife, B., & Yanchar, S. C. (2000). Unresolved issues in psychology. In B. Slife (Ed.), *Taking sides* (11th ed.). New York: Duskin McGraw-Hill.

Sloan, D. M., & Mizes, J. S. (1999). Foundations of behavior therapy in the contemporary health-care context. *Clinical Psychology Review, 19,* 255–274.

Sloan, P., Arsenault, L., Hilsenroth, M., & Harvill, L. (1996). Rorschach measures of post-traumatic stress in Persian Gulf War veterans: A three-year follow-up study. *Journal of Personality Assessment, 66,* 54–64.

Slobin, D. (1972, July). Children and language: They learn the same way around the world. *Psychology Today,* 71–76.

Smith, D. V., & Margolskee, R. F. (2001). Making sense of taste. *Scientific American, 284,* 32–39.

Smith, K. H., & Rogers, M. (1994). Effectiveness of subliminal messages in television commercials. *Journal of Applied Psychology, 79,* 866–874.

Smith, L. (2002). Piaget's model. In U. Goswami (Ed.), *Blackwell handbook of childhood cognitive development.* Malden, MA: Blackwell.

Smith, M. B. (2001). Humanistic psychology. In W. E. Craighead & C. B. Nemeroff (Eds.), *The Corsini encyclopedia of psychology and behavioral science* (3rd ed.). New York: Wiley.

Smith, M. L., Glass, G. N., & Miller, R. L. (1980). *The benefit of psychotherapy.* Baltimore: Johns Hopkins University Press.

Smith, S. M., & Fabrigar, L. R. (2000). Attitudes: An overview. In A. Kazdin (Ed.), *Encyclopedia of psychology.* Washington, DC, & New York: American Psychological Association and Oxford University Press.

Smith, S. M., & Vela, E. (2001). Environmental context-dependent memory: A review and meta-analysis. *Psychonomic Bulletin Review, 8,* 203–220.

Smyth, M. M., Collins, A. F., Morris, P. E., & Levy, P. (1994). *Cognition in action* (2nd ed.). Hove, England: Erlbaum.

Snow, C. (1999). Social perspectives on the emergence of language. In B. MacWhinney (Ed.), *The emergence of language.* Mahwah, NJ: Erlbaum.

Snow, D. E. (1998). *Preventing reading difficulties in young children.* Washington, DC: U.S. Department of Education.

Snowden, D. (2001). *Aging with grace: What the nun study teaches us about longer, healthier, and more meaningful lives.* New York: Bantam.

Snowden, D. A. (1995). *An epidemiological study of aging in a select population and its relationship to Alzheimer's disease.* Unpublished manuscript, Sanders Brown Center on Aging, Lexington, KY.

Snowden, D. A. (1997). Aging and Alzheimer's disease: Lessons from the nun study. *Gerontologist, 37,* 150–156.

Snyder, M., & Stukas, A. A. (1999). Interpersonal processes: The interplay of cognitive, motivational, and behavioral activities in social interaction. *Annual Review of Psychology* (Vol. 49). Palo Alto, CA: Annual Reviews, Inc.

Sober, E. (2001). The ABC's of altruism. In S. G. Post, L. G. Underwood, J. P. Schloss, & W. B. Hurlbut (Eds.), *Altruism and altruistic love.* New York: Oxford University Press.

Sober, E., & Wilson, D. S. (1998). *Unto others: The evolution of unselfish behavior.* Cambridge, MA: Harvard University Press.

Soderstrom, M., Dolbier, C., Leiferman, J., & Stenhardt, M. (2000). The relationship of hardiness, coping strategies, and perceived stress to symptoms of illness. *Journal of Behavioral Medicine, 23,* 311–328.

Sofroniew, M. V., & Mobley, W. C. (2001). Nerve growth factor, neuroprotection, and neural repair. *Annual Review of Neuroscience, 24.*

Soja, P. J., Pang, W., Taepavarapruk, N., & McErlane, S. A. (2001). Spontaneous spike activity of spinorecticular tract neurons during sleep and waking. *Sleep, 24,* 18–25.

Solms, M. (1997). *The neuropsychology of dreams.* Mahwah, NJ: Erlbaum.

Sommer, B. (2002). Menopause. In J. Worell (Ed.), *Encyclopedia of women and gender.* New York: Oxford University Press.

Sonnenberg, S. M., & Ursano, R. (2002). Psychoanalysis and psychoanalytic psychotherapy: Technique. In M. Hersen & W. H. Sledge (Eds.), *Encyclopedia of psychotherapy.* San Diego: Academic Press.

Sorensen, A., Adam, C. L., Findlay, P. A., Marie, M., Thomas, L., Travers, M. T., & Vernon, R. G. (2002). Leptin secretion and hypothalamic neuropeptide receptor gene expression in sheep. *American Journal of Physiology: Regulatory, Integrative, and Comparative Physiology, 282,* R1227–R1235.

Sorensen, B. K., Hojrup, P., Ostergard, E., Jorgensen, C. S., Enghild, J., Ryder, L. R. & Houen, G. (2002). Silver staining of proteins of electroblotting membrandes and intensification of silver staining of proteins separated by polyacrylamide gel. *Annals of Biochemistry, 304,* 33–41.

Sothern, M. S., Schumacher, H., von Almen, T. K., Carlisle, L. K., & Udall, J. N. (2002). Committed to kids: an integrated, 4-level team approach to weight management in adolescents. *Journal of the American Dietetic Association, 102,* S81–S85.

Spanos, N. P., & Chaves, J. F. (Eds.). (1989). *Hypnosis: The cognitive-behavior perspective.* Buffalo, NY: Prometheus.

Spearman, C. E. (1927). *The abilities of man.* New York: Macmillan.

Speca, M., Carlson, L. E., Goodey, E., & Angen, M. (2000). A randomized, wait-list controlled clinical trial: The effect of a mindfulness meditation-based stress reduction program on mood and symptoms of stress in cancer outpatients. *Psychosomatic Medicine, 62,* 613–622.

Spector, A. C., & Kopka, S. L. (2002). Rats fail to discriminate quinine from denatonium: implications for the neural coding of bitter-tasting compounds. *Journal of Neuroscience, 22,* 1937–1941.

Spence, C., Kingstone, A., Shore, D. I., & Gazzaniga, M. S. (2002). Representation of visotactile space in the split brain. *Psychological Science, 90–93.*

Spencer, M. B. (2000). Ethnocentrism. In A. Kazdin (Ed.), *Encyclopedia of psychology.* Washington, DC, and New York: American Psychological Association and Oxford University Press.

Spera, S. P., Buhrfeind, E. D., & Pennebaker, J. W. (1994). Expressive writing and coping with job loss. *Academy of Management Journal, 37,* 722–733.

Sperling, G. (1960). The information available in brief presentations. *Psychological Monographs, 74* (Whole No. 11).

Sperry, R. W. (1968). Hemisphere deconnection and unity in conscious awareness. *American Psychologist, 23,* 723–733.

Sperry, R. W. (1974). Lateral specialization in surgically separated hemispheres. In F. O. Schmitt & F. G. Worden (Eds.), *The neurosciences: Third study program.* Cambridge, MA: MIT Press.

Spetea, M., Rydelius, G., Nylander, I., Ahmed, M., Blieviciute-Ljungar, I., Lundeberg, T., Svensson, S., & Kreicergs, A. (2002). Alteration in endogenous opioid systems due to chronic inflammatory pain conditions. *European Journal of Pharmacology, 435,* 245–252.

Spiegler, M. D., & Guevremont, D. C. (2003). *Contemporary behavior therapy* (4th Ed.). Belmont, CA: Wadsworth.

Springer, S. P., & Deutsch, G. (1998). *Left brain, right brain.* New York: Freeman.

Sprinthall, R. C. (2003). *Basic statistical analysis* (7th Ed.). Boston: Allyn & Bacon.

Squire, L. (1990, June). *Memory and brain systems.* Paper presented at the meeting of the American Psychological Society, Dallas.

Squire, L. R. (1998). Interview. *Journal of Cognitive Neuroscience, 10,* 778–782.

Squire, L. R., & Kandel, E. R. (2000). *Memory: From mind to molecule.* New York: Worth.

Sroufe, L. A. (2000, Spring). The inside scoop on child development [Interview]. *Cutting through the hype.* Minneapolis: University of Minnesota, College of Education and Human Development.

Staddon, J. E., Chelaru, I. M., & Higa, J. J. (2002). A tune-trace theory of interval-timing dynamics. *Journal of the Experimental Analysis of Behavior, 77,* 105–124.

Stafford, J., & Lynn, S. J. (2002). Cultural scripts, memories of childhood abuse, and multiple identities: A study of role-played enactments. *International Journal of Experiemental Hypnosis, 50,* 67–85.

Stahl, S. M. (2002). The psychopharmacology of energy and fatigue. *Journal of Clinical Psychiatry, 63,* 7–8.

Stanley, M. A. (2000). Obsessive-compulsive disorder. In A. Kazdin (Ed.), *Encyclopedia of psychology.* Washington, DC, & New York: American Psychological Association and Oxford University Press.

Stanley, M. A., & Turner, S. M. (1995). Current status of pharmacological and behavioral treatment of obsessive-compulsive disorder. *Behavior Therapy, 26,* 163–177.

Stanovich, K. (2001). *How to think straight about psychology* (6th ed.). Boston: Allyn & Bacon.

Stanovich, K. E. (1999). *Who is rational? Individual differences in reasoning.* Mahwah, NJ: Erlbaum.

Stanovich, K. E., & West, R. E. (2000). Individual differences in reasoning: Implications for the rationality debate? *Behavior and Brain Sciences, 23,* 645–665.

Steele, C. (2001). Zyban: An effective treatment for nicotine addiction. *Hospital Medicine, 61,* 785–788.

Steele, C. M. (1996, August). *A burden of suspicion: The role of stereotypes in shaping intellectual identity.* Paper presented at the meeting of the American Psychological Association, Toronto.

Steers, W., Guay, A. T., Leriche, A., Gingell, C., Hargeave, T. B., Wright, P. J., Price, D. E., & Feldman, R. A. (2001). Assessment of the efficacy and safety of Viagra (sildenafil citrate) in men with erectile dysfunction during long-term treatment. *International Journal of Impotence Research, 13,* 261–267.

Stefanick, M. L. (1999). Estrogen, progesterons, and cardiovascular risk. *Journal of Reproductive Medicine, 44,* 221–226.

Stein, M. T., & Ferber, R. (2001). Recent onset of sleepwalking in early adolescence. *Journal of Development, Behavior, and Pediatrics, 22,* S33–S35.

Sternberg, E. M., & Gold, P. W. (1996). The mind-body interaction in disease. *Mysteries of the mind.* New York: Scientific American.

Sternberg, R. J. (1997). Educating intelligence: Infusing the triarchic theory into instruction. In R. J. Sternberg & E. Grigorenko (Eds.), *Intelligence, heredity, and environment.* New York: Cambridge University Press.

Sternberg, R. J. (2003). *Cognitive psychology* (3rd Ed.). Belmont, CA: Wadsworth.

Sternberg, R. J. (1986). *Intelligence applied.* Fort Worth: Harcourt Brace.

Sternberg, R. J. (1988). *The triangle of love.* New York: Basic Books.

Sternberg, R. J. (1994, December). Commentary. *APA Monitor,* p. 22.

Sternberg, R. J. (1997a). Inspection time for inspection time. *American Psychologist, 52,* 1144–1147.

Sternberg, R. J. (1997b). *Successful intelligence.* New York: Simon & Schuster.

Sternberg, R. J. (1999). Intelligence. In M. A. Runco & S. Pritzker (Eds.), *Encyclopedia of creativity.* San Diego: Academic Press.

Sternberg, R. J. (2000). The holy grail of general intelligence. *Science, 289,* 399–401.

Sternberg, R. J. (2001). Is there a heredity-environment paradox? In R. J. Sternberg & E. L. Grigorenko (Eds.), *Environmental effects on cognitive abilities.* Mahwah, NJ: Erlbaum.

Sternberg, R. J. (2002). Intelligence: The triarchic theory of intelligence. In J. W. Gutherie (Ed.), *Encyclopedia of education* (2nd ed.). New York: Macmillan.

Sternberg, R. J. (Ed). (1997). *Career paths in psychology.* Washington, DC: American Psychological Association.

Sternberg, R. J., & Grigorenko, E. L. (Eds.) (2001). *Environmental effects on cognitive abilities.* Mahwah, NJ: Erlbaum.

Sternberg, R. J., & O'Hara, L. A. (2000). Intelligence and creativity. In R. J. Sternberg (Ed.), *Handbook of intelligence.* New York: Cambridge University Press.

Sternberg, R. J., & Spear-Swerling, P. (1996). *Teaching for thinking.* Washington, DC: American Psychological Association.

Steur, F. B., Applefield, J. M., & Smith, R. (1971). Televised aggression and the interpersonal aggression of preschool children. *Journal of Experimental Child Psychology, 11,* 442–447.

Stevenson, H. G. (1995, March). *Missing data: On the forgotten substance of race, ethnicity, and socioeconomic classifications.* Paper presented at the meeting of the Society for Research in Child Development, Indianapolis, IN.

Stevenson, H. W. (1995). Mathematics achievement of American students: First in the world by the year 2000? In C. A. Nelson (Ed.), *Basic and applied perspectives on learning, cognition, and development.* Minneapolis: University of Minnesota Press.

Stevenson, H. W. (1992, December). Learning from Asian schools. *Scientific American,* pp. 6, 70–76.

Stevenson, H. W. (1997, August), *Bronfenbrenner award address.* Paper presented at the meeting of the American Psychological Association, Chicago.

Stevenson, H. W. (2000). Middle childhood: Education and schooling. In A. Kazdin (Ed.), *Encyclopedia of psychology.* Washington, DC, & New York: American Psychological Association and Oxford University Press.

Stevenson, H. W., Lee, S., & Stigler, J. W. (1986). Mathematics achievement of Chinese, Japanese, and American children. *Science, 231,* 693–699.

Stevenson, H. W., Lee, S., Chen, C., Stigler, J. W., Hsu, C., & Kitamura, S. (1990). Contexts of achievement. *Monograph of the Society for Research in Child Development, 55* (Serial No. 221).

Stickgold, R. (2001). Watching the sleeping brain watch us: Sensory processing during sleep. *Trends in Neuroscience, 24,* 307–309.

Stickgold, R., & Hobson, J. A. (2000). Visual discrimination learning requires sleep after training. *Nature Neuroscience, 3,* 1237–1238.

Stigler, J. W., & Hiebert, J. (1997, September). Understanding and improving classroom mathematics instruction. *Phi Delta Kappan, 79,* 14–21.

Stipek, D. (2001). *Motivation to learn* (4th ed.). Boston: Allyn & Bacon.

Stipek, D. J. (1996). Motivation and instruction. In D. C. Berliner & R. C. Calfee (Eds.), *Handbook of educational psychology.* New York: Macmillan.

Stolley, K. S. (2001). *Groupthink.* Retrieved November 24, 2001, from http://www.about.com

Stone, A. A., Neale, J. M., Cox, D. S., Napoli, A., Valdimarsdottir, H., & Kennedy-Moore, E. (1994). Daily events are associated with secretory immune response to an oral antigen in men. *Health Psychology, 13,* 440–446.

Stoner, J. (1961). *A comparison of individual and group decisions, including risk.* Unpublished master's thesis, School of Industrial Management, MIT.

Stout, S. C., Owens, M. J., & Nemeroff, C. B. (2001). Neurokinin (1) receptor antagonists as potential antidepressants. *Annual Review of Pharmacology and Toxicology, 41,* 877–906.

Straus, M. A. (1991). Discipline and deviance: Physical punishment of children and violence and other crimes in adulthood. *Social Problems, 38,* 133–154.

Strean, H. S. (1996). Resistance viewed from different perspectives. *American Journal of Psychotherapy, 50,* 29–31.

Strege, J. (1997). *Tiger: A biography of Tiger Woods.* New York: Broadway Books.

Streissguth, A. (1997). *Fetal alcohol syndrome: A guide for families and communities.* Baltimore: Brookes.

Striefel, S. (1998). *How to teach through modeling and imitation.* Austin, TX: Pro-Ed.

Striegel-Moore, R. H., Silberstein, L. R., & Rodin, J. (1993). The social self in bulimia nervosa: Public self-consciousness, social anxiety, and perceived fraudulence. *Journal of Abnormal Psychology, 102,* 297–303.

Strupp, H. H. (1989). Psychotherapy. *American Psychologist, 44,* 717–724.

Strupp, H. H. (1995). The psychotherapist's skills revised. *Clinical Psychology: Science and Practice, 2,* 70–74.

Stuart, G. L., Treat, T. A., & Wade, W. A. (2000). Effectiveness of empirically based treatment for panic disorder delivered in a service clinic setting. *Journal of Consulting and Clinical Psychology, 68,* 506–512.

Sue, D. (2002). Culture specific psychotherapy. In M. Hersen & W. H. Sledge (Eds.), *Encyclopedia of psychotherapy.* San Diego: Academic Press.

Sue, S. (1997, August). *In search of cultural competence in psychotherapy and counseling.* Paper presented at the meeting of the American Psychological Association, Chicago.

Sue, S. (2000). Ethnocultural psychotherapy. In A. Kazdin (Ed.), *Encyclopedia of psychology.* Washington, DC, & New York: American Psychological Association and Oxford University Press.

Sugarman, A., & DePottel, C. (2002). The unconscious. In M. Hersen & W. H. Sledge (Eds.), *Encyclopedia of psychotherapy.* San Diego: Academic Press.

Suhner, A., Schlagenhauf, P., Hofer, I., Johnson, R., Tschopp, A., & Steffen, R. (2001). Effectiveness and tolerability of melatonin and zopidem for the alleviation of jet lag. *Aviation, Space, and Environmental Medicine, 72,* 638–646.

Suinn, R. M. (1976, July). Body thinking: Psychology for Olympic champions. *Psychology Today, 10,* 38–41.

Suinn, R. M. (1984). *Fundamentals of abnormal psychology.* Chicago: Nelson-Hall.

Sullivan, H. S. (1953). *The interpersonal theory of psychiatry.* New York: Norton.

Sullivan, K. T., & Christensen, A. (1998). In H. S. Friedman (Ed.), *Encyclopedia of mental health* (Vol. 1). San Diego: Academic Press.

Suls, J., & Swain, A. (1998). Type A–Type B personalities. In H.S. Friedman (Ed.), *Encyclopedia of mental health* (Vol. 3). San Diego: Academic Press.

Sun, R. (2002). *Duality of the mind: A bottom-up approach toward cognition.* Mahwah, NJ: Erlbaum.

Surprenant, A. M. (2001). Distinctiveness and serial position effects in tonal sequences. *Perception and Psychophysics, 63,* 737–745.

Susman, E. J., Worrall, B. K., Murowchick, E., Frobose, C. A., & Schwab, J. E. (1996). Experience and neuroendocrine parameters of development: Aggressive behaviors and competencies. In D. M. Stoff & R. B. Cairns (Eds.), *Aggression and violence.* Mahwah, NJ: Erlbaum.

Sussman, E., Ceponiene, R., Shestakova, A., Naatanen, R., & Winkler, I. (2001). Auditory stream segregation processes operate similarly in school-aged children and adults. *Hearing Research, 153,* 108–114.

Sussman, S. (2001). School-based tobacco use prevention and cessation: Where are we going? *American Journal of Health Behavior, 25,* 191–199.

Sutker, P. B., & Allain, A. N. (1993). Behavior and personality assessment in men labeled adaptive sociopaths. *Journal of Behavioral Assessment, 5,* 65–79.

Swaab, D. F., Chung, W. C., Kruijver, F. P., Hofman, M. A., & Ishunina, T. A. (2001). Structural and functional sex differences in the human hypothalamus. *Hormones and Behavior, 40,* 93–98.

Swann, W. B., De La Ronde, C., & Hixon, J. G. (1994). Authenticity and positive strivings in marriage and courtship. *Journal of Personality and Social Psychology, 66,* 857–869.

Swanson, J. (Ed.). (1999). *Sleep disorders sourcebook.* New York: Omnigraphics.

Swartz-Kulstad, J. L., & Martin, W. E. (2000). Culture as an essential aspect of person-environment fit. In W. E. Martin & J. L. Swartz-Kulstad (Eds.), *Person-environment psychology and mental health.* Mahwah, NJ: Erlbaum.

Szasz, T. S. (1961). *The myth of mental illness: Foundations of a theory of personal conduct.* New York: Hoeber-Harper.

T

Tager-Flusberg, H. (1999). Language development in atypical children. In M. Barrett (Ed.), *The development of language.* Philadelphia: Psychology Press.

Tager-Flusberg, H. (Ed.). (1994). *Constraints on language acquisition.* Mahwah, NJ: Erlbaum.

Tajfel, H. (1978). The achievement of group differentiation. In H. Tajfel (Ed.), *Differentiation between social groups.* London: Academic Press.

Takeuchi, T., Miyasia, A., Inugami, M., & Yamamoto, Y. (2001). Intrinsic dreams are not produced without REM sleep mechanisms. *Journal of Sleep Research, 10,* 43–52.

Tamarin, R. H. (2002). *Principles of genetics* (7th ed.). New York: McGraw-Hill.

Tanaka-Matsumi, J. (2001). Abnormal psychology and culture. In D. Matsumoto (Ed.), *The handbook of culture and psychology.* New York: Oxford University Press.

Tang, Y. P., Shimizu, E., Dube, G. R., Rampon, C., Kerchner, G. A., Zhuo, M., Liu, G., & Tsien, J. Z. (1999). Genetic enhancement of learning and memory in mice. *Nature, 401,* 63–69.

Tannen, D. (1990). *You just don't understand!* New York: Ballantine.

Tapert, S. F., Brown, G. G., Kinderman, S. S., Cheung, E. H., Frank, L. R., & Brown, S. A. (2001). fMRI measurement of brain dysfunction in alcohol-dependent young women. *Alcohol: Clinical and Experimental Research, 25,* 236–245.

Tassi, P., & Muzet, A. (2001). Defining states of consciousness. *Neuroscience and Biobehavioral Review, 25,* 175–191.

Taub, E. (2001, April). *Adult brain plasticity.* Paper presented at the meeting of the Society for Research in Child Development, Minneapolis.

Tavris, C. B. (in press). *Women and health psychology.* Mahwah, NJ: Erlbaum.

Tavris, C., & Wade, C. (1984). The longest war: Sex differences in perspective (2nd ed.). Fort Worth: Harcourt Brace.

Taylor, S. (2002). Classical conditioning. In M. Hersen & W. H. Sledge (Eds.), *Encyclopedia of psychotherapy.* San Diego: Academic Press.

Taylor, S. E. (1998). Positive illusions. In H.S. Friedman (Ed.), *Encyclopedia of mental health* (Vol. 3). San Diego: Academic Press.

Taylor, S. E. (2001). Toward a biology of social support. In C. R. Snyder & S. J. Lopez (Eds.), *Handbook of positive psychology.* New York: Oxford University Press.

Taylor, S. E. (2003). *Health psychology* (5th ed.). New York: McGraw-Hill.

Taylor, S. E., & Brown, J. D. (1994). Positive illusions and well-being revisited: Separating fact from fiction. *Psychological Bulletin, 116,* 21–27.

Taylor, S. E., Klein, L. S., Lewis, B. P., Gurenewald, T. L., Gurun, R. A., & Updegraff, J. A. (2000). Biobehavioral responses in females: Tend-and-befriend, not fight-or-flight. *Psychological Review, 107,* 411–429.

Taylor, S. E., Peplau, L. A., & Sears, D. O. (2003). *Social psychology* (11th ed.). Upper Saddle River, NJ: Prentice Hall.

Teasdale, J. D., Taylor, M. J., Cooper, Z., Hayhurst, H., & Paykel, E. S. (1995). Depressive thinking. *Journal of Abnormal Psychology, 104,* 500–507.

Temple, E. C., Hutchinson, I., Lang, D. G., & Jinks, A. L. (2002). Taste development: Differential growth rates of tongue regions in humans. *Brain Research: Developmental Brain Research, 135,* 65–70.

Terman, L. (1925). *Genetic studies of genius. Vol. 1: Mental and physical traits of a thousand gifted children.* Stanford, CA: Stanford University Press.

Terr, L. C. (1988). What happens to early memories of trauma? *Journal of the American Academy of Child and Adolescent Psychiatry, 27,* 96–104.

Teti, D.M., & Candelaria, M. (2002). Parenting competence. In M. H. Bornstein (Ed.), *Handbook of parenting* (2nd ed.). Mahwah, NJ: Erlbaum.

Tetreault, M. K. T. (1997). Classrooms for diversity: Rethinking curriculum and pedagogy. In J. A. Banks & C. A. Banks (Eds.), *Multicultural education* (3rd ed.). Boston: Allyn & Bacon.

Tharp, R. G. (1991). Cultural diversity and treatment of children. *Journal of Consulting & Clinical Psychology, 59,* 799–812.

Thayer, J. F., Rossy, I., Sollers, J., Friedman, B. H., & Allen, M. T. (1996, March). *Relationships among heart period variability and cardiodynamic measures vary as a function of fitness.* Paper presented at the meeting of the American Psychosomatic Society, Williamsburg, VA.

Thelen, E. (1995). Motor development: A new synthesis. *American Psychologist, 50,* 79–95.

Thelen, E. (2000). Infancy: Perception and motor development. In A. Kazdin (Ed.), *Encyclopedia of psychology.* Washington, DC, & New York: Oxford University Press.

Thelen, E., & Smith, L. B. (1998). Dynamic systems theories. In W. Damon (Ed.), *Handbook of child psychology* (5th ed., Vol. 1). New York: Wiley.

Thiedke, C. C. (2001). Sleep disorders and sleep problems in childhood. *American Family Physician, 63,* 277–284.

Thigpen, C. H., & Cleckley, H. M. (1957). *Three faces of Eve.* New York. McGraw-Hill.

Thijssen, J. H. (2002). Relations of androgens and selected aspects of human behavior. *Maturitas, 41, Supplement,* 47–54.

Thomas, C. B. (1983). *Stress and coping.* Unpublished manuscript, Johns Hopkins University, Baltimore.

Thomas, M., Sing, H., Belenky, G., Holcomb, H., Mayberg, H., Dannals, R., Wagner, H., Thorne, D., Popp, K., Rowland, L., Welsh, A., Balwinksi, S., & Redmond, D. (2001). Neural basis of alertness and cognitive performance impairments during sleepiness: I. Effects of 24 hours of sleep deprivation on waking human regional brain activity. *Journal of Sleep Research, 9,* 335–352.

Thomas, R. M. (2001). *Recent human development theories.* Thousand Oaks, CA: Sage.

Thompson, M. J., Raynor, A., Cornah, D., Stevenson, J., & Sonuga-Barke, E. J. (2002). Parenting behavior described by mothers in a general population sample. *Child: Care, Health, and Development, 28,* 149–155.

Thompson, P. M., Giedd, J. N., MacDonald, D., Evans, A. C., & Toga, A. W. (2000). Growth patterns in the developing brain by using continuum sensor maps. *Nature, 404,* 190–193.

Thompson, R. (2000). Early experience and socialization. In A. Kazdin (Ed.), *Encyclopedia of psychology.* Washington, DC, & New York: American Psychological Association and Oxford University Press.

Thompson, S. C. (2001). The role of personal control in adaptive functioning. In C. R. Snyder & S. J. Lopez (Eds.), *Handbook of positive psychology.* New York: Oxford University Press.

Thompson, S. C., & Spacapan, S. (1991). Perceptions of control in vulnerable populations. *Journal of Social Issues, 47,* 1–22.

Thorne, B. M. (2001). Introversion-extraversion. In W. E. Craighead & C. B. Nemeroff (Eds.), *The Corsini encyclopedia of psychology and behavioral science* (3rd ed.). New York: Wiley.

Thrybom, T., Rooth, P., & Lindstrom, P. (2001). Effect of serotonin reuptake inhibitor on syndrome development in obese hyperglycemic mice. *Metabolism, 50,* 144–150.

Thurstone, L. L. (1938). *Primary mental abilities.* Chicago: University of Chicago Press.

Tinbergen, N. (1969). *The study of instinct.* New York: Oxford University Press.

Tisserand, D. J., Bosma, H., Van Boxtel, M. P., & Jolles, J. (2001). Head size and cognitive ability in nondemented older adults are related. *Neurology, 56,* 969–971.

Tobach, E. (2002). Development of sex and gender: Biochemistry, physiology, and experience. In J. Worell (Ed.), *Encyclopedia of women and gender.* New York: Oxford University Press.

Todd, G. S., & Gigerenzer, G. (2001). Precis of simple heuristics that make us smart. *Behavior and Brain Sciences, 23,* 727–741.

Tolan, P., Miller, L., & Thomas, P. (1988). Perception and experience of two types of social stress and self-image among adolescents. *Journal of Youth and Adolescence, 17,* 147–163.

Tolman, E. C. (1932). *Purposive behavior in animals and man.* New York: Appleton-Century-Crofts.

Tolman, E. C. (1948). Cognitive maps in rats and men. *Psychological Review, 55,* 189–208.

Tolman, E. C., & Honzik, C. H. (1930). Degrees of hunger, reward and non-reward, and maze performance in rats. *University of California Publications in Psychology, 4,* 21–256.

Tompkins, S. S. (1962). *Affect, imagery, and consciousness* (Vol. 1). New York: Springer.

Torgersen, S. (1986). Genetic factors in moderately severe and mild affective disorders. *Archives of General Psychiatry, 43,* 222–226.

Tracey, T. J., Sherry, P., & Albright, J. M. (1999). The interpersonal process of cognitive-behavioral therapy. *Journal of Counseling Psychology, 46,* 80–91.

Trainor, L. J., McDonald, K. L., & Alain, C. (2002). Automatic and controlled processing of melodic contour and interval information measured by electrical brain activity. *Journal of Cognitive Neuroscience, 14,* 430–432.

Treasure, D. C., & Roberts, G. C. (2001). Students' perceptions of the motivational climate, achievement beliefs, and satisfaction in physical education. *Research Quarterly on Exercise and Sport, 72,* 165–175.

Triandis, H. C. (2000). Cross-cultural psychology: History of the field. In A. Kazdin (Ed.), *Encyclopedia of psychology.* Washington, DC, and New York: American Psychological Association and Oxford University Press.

Triandis, H. C. (2001). Individualism and collectivism. In D. Matsumoto (Ed.), *The handbook of culture and psychology.* New York: Oxford University Press.

Triandis, H. C. (1994). *Culture and social behavior.* New York: McGraw-Hill.

Trimble, J. E. (1989, August). *The enculturation of contemporary psychology.* Paper presented at the meeting of the American Psychological Association, New Orleans, LA.

Triplett, N. (1898). The dynamogenic factors in peacemaking and competition. *American Journal of Psychology, 9,* 507–533.

Trivers, R. (1971). The evolution of reciprocal altruism. *Quarterly Review of Biology, 46,* 35–57.

Trowell, J., Kolvin, I., Weeramanthri, T., Sadowski, H., Berelowitz, M., Glasser, D., & Leitch, I. (2002). Psychotherapy for abused girls. *British Journal of Psychiatry, 180,* 234–247.

Tryon, R. C. (1940). Genetic differences in maze-learning ability in rats. In *39th Yearbook, National Society for the Study of Education.* Chicago: University of Chicago Press.

Tsien, J. Z. (2000). Linking Hebb's coincidence-detection to memory formation. *Current Opinions in Neurobiology, 10,* 266–273.

Tsuang, M. T., Stone, W. S., & Faraone, S. V. (2001). Genes, environment, and heredity. *British Journal of Psychiatry, 40,* (Suppl.), 18–24.

Tulving, E. (2000). Concepts of memory. In E. Tulving & F. I. M. Craik (Eds.), *The Oxford handbook of memory.* New York: Oxford University Press.

Tulving, E. (1972). Episodic and semantic memory. In E. Tulving & W. Donaldson (Eds.), *Origins of memory.* San Diego: Academic Press.

Tulving, E. (1983). *Elements of episodic memory.* New York: Oxford University Press.

Tulving, E. (1989). Remembering and knowing the past. *American Scientist, 77,* 361–367.

Tulving, E., & Thomson, D. M. (1973). Encoding specificity and retrieval processes in episodic memory. *Psychological Review, 80,* 352–373.

Turiel, E. (1983). *The development of social knowledge: Morality and convention.* New York: Cambridge University Press.

Turnbull, C. (1972). *The mountain people.* New York: Simon & Schuster.

Tversky, A., & Fox, C. R. (1995). Weighing risk and uncertainty. *Psychological Review, 102,* 269–283.

Tyler, C. (1983). Sensory processing of binocular disparity. In C. M. Schor & K. J. Ciuffreda (Eds.), *Vergence eye movements.* Boston: Butterworth.

U

U. S. Bureau of Justice Statistics. (2001). *Homicide rates.* Washington: Author.

U. S. Bureau of the Census (2000). *Marriage statistics.* Washington, DC: Author.

Ubell, C. (1992, December 6). We can age successfully. *Parade,* pp. 14–15.

UNDCP (2001). *Global illicit drugs.* Geneva, Switzerland: United Nations.

Ungerleider, L. G., and Mishkin, M. (1982). Two cortical visual systems. In D. J. Engle, M. A. Goodale, & R. J. Mansfield (Eds.), *Analysis of visual behavior.* Cambridge, MA: MIT Press.

United Nations. (1999). *Demographic yearbook.* Geneva, Switzerland: United Nations.

Uppaluri, C. R., Schumm, I. P., & Lauderdale, D. S. (2001). Self-reports of stress in Asian immigrants: Effects of ethnicity and acculturation. *Ethnic Distribution, 11,* 107–144.

V

Vadum, A. E., & Rankin, N. O. (1998). *Psychological research.* New York: McGraw-Hill.

Vaillant, G. E. (1977). *Adaptation to life.* Boston: Little, Brown.

Vaillant, G. E. (1983). *The natural history of alcoholism.* Cambridge, MA: Harvard University Press.

Vaillant, G. E. (1992). Is there a natural history of addiction? In C. P. O'Brien & J. H. Jaffe (Eds.), *Addictive states.* Cambridge, MA: Harvard University Press.

Valencia, R. R., & Suzuki, L. A. (2001). *Intelligence testing and minority students.* Thousand Oaks, CA: Sage.

Vallone, R. P., Griffin, D. W., Lin, S., & Ross, L. (1990). Overconfident prediction of future actions and outcomes by self and others. *Journal of Personality and Social Psychology, 58,* 582–592.

Van Ameringen, M., Lane, R. M., Walker, J. R., Rudaredo, C., Chooka, P. R., Goldner, E., Johnston, E., Lavallee, Y., Saibal, N., Pecknold, J. C., Hadrava, V., & Swinson, R. P. (2001). Sertaline treatment of generalized social phobia: 20-week, double-blind, placebo-controlled study. *American Journal of Psychiatry, 158,* 275–281.

Van Ameringen, M., Mancini, C., Farvolden, P., & Oakman, A. J. (2000). The neurobiology of social phobia: From pharmacology to brain imaging. *Current Psychiatry Reports, 2,* 358–366.

Van den Boom, D. C. (1994). The influence of temperament and mothering on attachment and exploration: An experimental manipulation of sensitive responsiveness among lower-class mothers with irritable infants. *Child Development, 65,* 1457–1477.

van Dielen, F. M., van 't Veer, C., Buurman, W. A., & Greve, J. W. (2002). Leptin and soluble leptin receptor levels in obese and weight-losing individuals. *Journal of Clinical Endocrinology and Metabolism, 87,* 1708–1716.

Van Elst, L. T., Ebert, D., & Trimble, M. R. (2001). Hippocampus and amygdala pathology in depression. *American Journal of Psychiatry, 158,* 652–653.

Van Goozen, S. H. M., Matthys, W., Cohen-Kettenis, P. T., Thisjssen, J. H., & van Engeland, H. (1998). Adrenal androgens and aggression in conduct disorder prepubertal boys and normal control. *Biological Psychiatry, 43,* 156–158.

van Praag, H. M. (2000). Serotonin disturbances and suicide risk: Is aggression or anxiety an interjacent link? *Crisis, 21,* 160–162.

Van Winkle, E. (2000). The toxic mind: The biology of mental illness and violence. *Medical Hypotheses, 55,* 356–368.

Vandell, D. L. (2000). Parents, peer groups, and other socializing influences. *Developmental Psychology, 36*(6), 699–710.

VandenBos, G. R. (2000). Schizophrenia. In A. Kazdin (Ed.), *Encyclopedia of psychology.* Washington, DC, & New York: American Psychological Association and Oxford University Press.

Vatcher, C. A., & Bogo, M. (2001). The feminist/emotionally focused therapy practice model: An integrated approach for couple therapy. *Journal of Marital and Family Therapy, 27,* 69–83.

Vaughn, S., Bos, C. S., & Schumm, J. S. (2003). *Teaching exceptional, diverse, and at-risk students in the general education classroom* (3rd Ed.). Boston: Allyn & Bacon.

Vernon, P. A. (2000). Determinants of intelligence: Biological theories. In A. Kazdin (Ed.), *Encyclopedia of psychology.* Washington, DC, & New York: American Psychological Association and Oxford University Press.

Vernoy, M. W. (1995). Demonstrating classical conditioning in introductory psychology: Needles do not always make balloons pop! In M. E. Ware & D. E. Johnson (Eds.), *Demonstrations and activities in teaching psychology* (Vol. 2). Mahwah, NJ: Erlbaum.

Vernoy, M. W., & Kyle, D. (2003). *Behavioral statistics in action (3rd ed.).* New York: McGraw-Hill.

Versiani, M., Cassano, G., Perugi, G., Benedetti, A., Mastalli, L., Nadi, A., & Savino, M. (2002). Reboxetine, a selective norepinephrine reuptake inhibitor, is an effective and well-tolerated treatment for panic disorder. *Journal of Clinical Psychiatry, 63,* 31–37.

Viana, del Pena, E., & Belmonte, C. (2002). Specificity of cold thermotransduction is determined by differential ionic channel expression. *Nature Neuroscience, 5,* 254–260.

Vicari, S., Bellucci, S., & Carlesimo, G. A. (2001). Procedural learning deficits in children with Williams syndrome. *Neuropsychologia, 39,* 665–677.

Viglione, D. J., & Hilsenroth, M. J. (2001). The Rorschach: Facts, fictions, and future. *Psychological Assessment, 13,* 452–471.

Villani, S., & Sharfstein, S. S. (1999). Evaluating and treating violent adolescents in the managed care era. *The American Journal of Psychiatry, 156,* 458–464.

Viney, W., & King, D. B. (2003). *History of psychology (3rd Ed.).* Boston: Allyn & Bacon.

Vogt, T. M., Mullooly, J. P., Ernst, D., Pople, C. R., & Hollis, J. F. (1992). Social networks as predictors of ischemic heart disease, cancer, stroke, and hypertension. *Journal of Clinical Epidemiology, 45,* 659–666.

Vokey, J. R., & Read, J. D. (1985). Subliminal messages: Between the devil and the media. *American Psychologist, 40,* 1231–1239.

Voudouris, N. J., Peck, C. L., & Coleman, G. (1985). Conditioned placebo responses. *Journal of Personality and Social Psychology, 48,* 7–53.

Vygotsky, L. S. (1962). *Thought and language.* Cambridge, MA: MIT Press.

W

Wachs, T. D., & Kohnstamm, G. A. (Eds.). (2001). *Temperament in context.* Mahwah, NJ: Earlbaum.

Wachs, T. D., Bishry, Z., Sobhy, A., McCabe, G., Galal, O., & Shaeen, F. (1993). Relation of rearing environment to adaptive behavior of Egyptian toddlers. *Child Development, 54,* 396–407.

Wadden, T. A., Foser, G. D., Stunkard, A. J., & Conill, A. M. (1996). Effects of weight cycling on the resting energy expenditure and body composition of obese women. *Eating Disorders, 19,* 5–12.

Wagner, A. D., Schacter, D. L., Rotte, M., Koutstaal, B., Maril, A., Dale, A. M., Rosen, B. R., & Buckner, R. L. (1998). Building memories: Remembering and forgetting of verbal experiences as predicted by brain activity. *Science, 281,* 1185–1187.

Wagner, K. D., & Ambrosini, P. J. (2001). Childhood depression: Pharmacological therapy. *Journal of Clinical Child Psychology, 30,* 88–97.

Wagner, U., Gais, S., & Born, J. (2001). Emotional memory formation is enhanced across sleep intervals with high amounts of rapid eye movement sleep. *Learning and Memory, 8,* 112–119.

Wahlsten, D. (2000). Behavioral genetics. In A. Kazdin (Ed.), *Encyclopedia of psychology.* Washington, DC, & New York: American Psychological Association and Oxford University Press.

Waldstein, S. R., Neumann, S. A., Drossman, D. A., & Novack, D. H. (2001). Teaching psychosomatic (biopsychosocial) medicine in United States medical schools: Survey findings. *Psychosomatic Medicine, 63,* 335–343.

Walker, L. E. (1999). Psychology and domestic violence around the world. *American Psychologist, 54,* 6–20.

Walker, L. J., & Pitts, R. C. (1998). Naturalistic conceptions of moral maturity. *Developmental Psychology, 34,* 403–419.

Wall, P. D., & Melzack, R. (1999). *Textbook of pain* (4th ed.). Philadelphia: Saunders.

Wall, T. L., Shea, S. H., Chan, K. K., & Carr, L. G. (2001). A genetic association with the development of alcohol and other substance use in Asian Americans. *Journal of Abnormal Psychology, 110,* 173–178.

Wallace, B. E., Wagner, A. K., Wagner, E. P., & McDeavit, J. T. (2001). A history and review of quantitative electroencephalography in traumatic brain disorders. *Journal of Head and Trauma Rehabilitation, 16,* 165–190.

Wallace, R. K., & Benson, H. (1972). The physiology of meditation. *Scientific American, 226,* 83–90.

Wallerstein, R. S. (1989). The psychotherapy research project of the Menninger Foundation: An overview. *Journal of Consulting and Clinical Psychology, 57,* 195–205.

Wallston, K. A. (2001). Conceptualization and operationalization of perceived control. In A. Baum, T. A. Revenson, & J. E. Singer (Eds.), *Handbook of health psychology.* Mahwah, NJ: Erlbaum.

Walsh, L. A. (2000, Spring). The inside scoop on child development [Interview]. *Cutting through the hype.* Minneapolis: University of Minnesota, College of Education and Human Development.

Walsh, W. B. (1995, August). *Person-environment psychology: Contemporary models and perspectives.* Paper presented at the meeting of the American Psychological Association, New York City.

Walsh, W. B., & Betz, N. E. (2001). *Tests and measurement* (4th ed.). Upper Saddle River, NJ: Prentice-Hall.

Walsh, W. B., & Betz, N. E. (1995). *Tests and assessment* (3rd ed.). Upper Saddle River, NJ: Prentice-Hall.

Walters, E., & Kendler, K. S. (1994). Anorexia nervosa and anorexia-like symptoms in a population based twin sample. *American Journal of Psychiatry, 152,* 62–71.

Ward, R. A., & Grashial, A. F. (1995). Using astrology to teach research methods to introductory psychology students. In M. E. Ware & D. E. Johnson (Eds.), *Demonstrations and activities in teaching of psychology* (Vol. 1). Mahwah, NJ: Erlbaum.

Warnecke, R. B., Morera, O., Turner, L., Mermelstein, R., Johnson, T. P., Parsons, J., Crittenden, K., Freels, S., & Flay, B. (2001). Changes in self-efficacy and readiness for smoking cessation among women with high school or less education. *Journal of Health and Social Behavior, 42,* 97–110.

Waters, E., Merrick, S. K., Albersheim, L. J., & Treboux, E. (1995, March). *Attachment security from infancy to early adulthood.* Paper presented at the meeting of the Society for Research on Adolescence, Boston.

Watkins, C. E., & Guarnaccia, C. A. (1999). Introduction: The future of psychotherapy training: Psychodynamic, experimental, and eclectic perspectives. *Journal of Clinical Psychology, 55,* 381–383.

Watkins, E., & Subich, L. M. (1995). Career development, reciprocal work/nonwork interaction, and women's workforce participation. *Journal of Vocational Behavior, 47,* 109–163.

Watkins, L. R., & Maier, S. F. (2000). The pain of being sick. *Annual Review of Psychology* (Vol. 51). Palo Alto, CA: Annual Reviews.

Watras, J. (2002). *The foundations of educational curriculum and diversity: 1565 to the present.* Boston: McGraw-Hill.

Watson, D. (2001). Positive affectivity: The disposition to experience pleasurable emotional states. In C. R. Snyder & S. J. Lopez (Eds.), *Handbook of positive psychology.* New York: Oxford University Press.

Watson, D. L., & Tharp, R. G. (2003). *Self-directed behavior* (8th Ed.). Belmont, CA: Wadsworth.

Watson, D., Wiese, D., Vaidya, J., & Tellegen, A. (1999). The two general activation systems of affect: Structural findings, evolutionary considerations, and psychobiological evidence. *Journal of Personality and Social Psychology, 76,* 820–838.

Watson, J. B. (1913). Psychology as the behaviorist views it. *Psychological Review, 20,* 158–177.

Watson, J. B. (1928). *Psychological care of the infant and child.* Philadelphia: Lippincott.

Wauters, M., Mertens, I. K., Chagnon, M., Rankinen, T., Considine, R. V., Chagnon, Y. C., Van Gaal, L. F., & Bouchard, C. (2001). Polymorphisms in the leptin receptor gene, body composition, and fat distribution in overweight and obese women. *International Journal of Obesity and Related Metabolic Disorders, 25,* 714–720.

Waysman, M., Schwarzwald, J., & Solomon, Z. (2001). Hardiness: An examination of its relationship with positive and negative long term changes following trauma. *Journal of Traumatic Stress, 14,* 531–548.

Webb, W. B. (2000). Sleep. In A. Kazdin (Ed.), *Encyclopedia of psychology.* Washington, DC, & New York: American Psychological Association and Oxford University Press.

Webster, J. M., Smith, R. H., Rhodes, A., & Whatley, M. A. (1999). The effect of a favor on public and private compliance: How internalized is the norm of reciprocity? *Basic and Applied Social Psychology, 21,* 251–260.

Wechsler, D. (1939). *The measurement of adult intelligence.* Baltimore: Williams & Wilkins.

Wechsler, H., Davenport, A., Sowdall, G., Moetykens, B., & Castillo, S. (1994). Health and behavioral consequences of binge drinking in college. *Journal of the American Medical Association, 272,* 1672–1677.

Wechsler, H., Lee, J. E., Kuo, M., & Lee, H. (2000). College binge drinking in the 1990s—A continuing health problem: Results of the Harvard University School of Public Health 1999 College Alcohol Study. *Journal of American College Health, 48,* 199–210.

Weich, S., Lewis, G., & Jenkins, S. P. (2001). Income inequality and the prevalence of common mental disorders in Britain. *British Journal of Psychiatry, 178,* 222–227.

Weidemann, G., Georgilas, A., & Kehoe, E. J. (1999). Temporal specificity in patterning of the rabbit nictitating membrane response. *Animal Learning & Behavior, 27,* 99–109.

Weine, S. M., Becker, D. F., McGlashan, T. H., Laub, D., Lazrove, S., Vojvoda, D., & Hyman, L. (1995). Psychiatric consequences of "ethnic cleansing": Clinical assessments and trauma testimonies of newly resettled Bosnian refugees. *American Journal of Psychiatry, 152,* 536–542.

Weiner, B. (1986). *An attributional theory of motivation and emotion.* New York: Springer-Verlag.

Weiner, I. B., Exner, J. E., & Sciara, A. (1996). Is the Rorschach welcome in the courtroom? *Journal of Personality Assessment, 67,* 422–424.

Weinraub, M., Hill, C., & Hirsh-Pasek, K. (2002). Child care: Options and outcomes. In J. Worell (Ed.), *Encyclopedia of women and gender.* New York: Oxford University Press.

Weisman, C. S., Maccannon, D. S., Henderson, J. T., Shortridge, E., & Orso, C. L. (2002). Contraceptive counseling in managed care. *Women's Health Issues, 12,* 79–95.

Weissberg, R. P., & Greenberg, M. T. (1998). School and community competence-enhancement and prevention programs. In W. Damon (Ed.), *Handbook of child psychology* (5th ed., Vol. 4). New York: Wiley.

Weissenborn, R., & Duka, T. (2000). State-dependent effects of alcohol on explicit memory: The role of semantic associations. *Psychopharmacology, 149,* 98–106.

Weissman, M. M., & others (1999). Prevalence of suicide ideation and suicide attempts in nine countries. *Psychological Medicine, 29,* 9–18.

Weissman, M., & Olfson, M. (1995). Depression in women: Implications for health care research. *Science, 269,* 799–801.

Wells, A., & Papageorgiou, C. (2001). Brief cognitive therapy for social phobia: A case series. *Behavior Research and Therapy, 39,* 713–720.

Wenzlaff, R. M., & Prohaska, M. L. (1989). When misery loves company: Depression, attributions, and responses to others' moods. *Journal of Experimental Social Psychology, 25,* 220–223.

Whipple, B., Ogden, G., & Komisaruk, B. (1992). Analgesia produced in women by genital self-stimulation. *Archives of Sexual Behavior, 9,* 87–99.

Whitbourne, S. K. (2000). Adult development and aging: Biological processes and physical development. In A. Kazdin (Ed.), *Encyclopedia of psychology.* Washington, DC, & New York: American Psychological Association and Oxford University Press.

White, J. W. (2001). Aggression and gender. In J. Worell (Ed.), *Encyclopedia of gender and women.* San Diego: Academic Press.

Whiting, B. B. (1989, April). *Culture and interpersonal behavior.* Paper presented at the biennial meeting of the Society for Research in Child Development, Kansas City.

Whitman, T. L., Borkowski, J. G., Keogh, D. A., & Weed, K. (2001). *Interwoven lives.* Mahwah, NJ: Erlbaum.

Whorf, B. L. (1956). *Language, thought, and creativity.* New York: Wiley.

Widiger, T. (2000). Diagnostic and statistical manual of disorders. In A. Kazdin (Ed.), *Encyclopedia of psychology.* Washington, DC, & New York: American Psychological Association and Oxford University Press.

Wiederman, M. W., & Whitley, B. E. (Eds.). (2002). *Handbook for conducting research on human sexuality.* Mahwah, NJ: Erlbaum.

Wielandt, H., Bolden, J., & Knudsen, L. B. (2002). The prevalent use of contraception among teenagers in Denmark and the corresponding low pregnancy rate. *Journal of Biosocial Science, 34,* 1–11.

Wierzbicki, M. (1999). *Introduction to clinical psychology.* Boston: Allyn & Bacon.

Wigfield, A., & Eccles, J. (Eds.). (2002). *Development of achievement motivation.* San Diego: Academic Press.

Wiggins, J. S., & Trapnell, P. D. (1997). Personality structure: The return of the big five. In R. Hogan, J. Johnson, & S. Briggs (Eds.), *Handbook of personality research.* San Diego: Academic Press.

Wilding, J., & Valentine, E. (1996). Memory and expertise. In D. Hermann, C. McEvoy, C. Hertzog, P. Hertel, & M. Johnson (Eds.), *Basic and applied memory research.* (Vol. 1). Hillsdale, NJ: Erlbaum.

Wilens, T. E., Spencer, T. J., Biederman, J., Girard, K., Doyle, R., Polisner, J., Solhkhah, D., Comeau, R., Monuteaux, M. C., & Parekh, A. (2001). A controlled clinical trial of bupropion for attention deficit hyperactivity disorder in adults. *American Journal of Psychiatry, 158,* 282–188.

Williams, C. C., & Zacks, R. T. (2001). Is retrieval-induced forgetting an inhibitory process? *American Journal of Psychology, 114,* 329–354.

Williams, J. D., & Gruzelier, J. H. (2001). Differentiation of hypnosis and relaxation by analysis of narrow band theta and alpha frequencies. *International Journal of Clinical and Experimental Hypnosis, 49,* 185–206.

Williams, P. T. (2001). Health effects resulting from exercise versus those from body fat. *Medical Science and Sports Exercise, 33* (Suppl.), S611–621.

Williams, R. B. (1995). Coronary prone behaviors, hostility, and cardiovascular health. In K. Orth-Gomer & N. Schneiderman (Eds.), *Behavioral medicine approaches to cardiovascular disease prevention.* Mahwah, NJ: Erlbaum.

Williams, R. B. (2001). Hostility (and other psychosocial risk factors): Effects on health and the potential for successful behavioral approaches to prevention and treatment. In A. Baum, T.A. Revenson, & J.E. Singer (Eds.), *Handbook of health psychology.* Mahwah, NJ: Erlbaum.

Williams, R. B. (2002). Hostility, neuroendocrine changes, and health outcomes. In H. G. Koenig & H. J. Cohen (Eds.), *The link between religion and health.* New York: Oxford University Press.

Willingham, D. B. (2001). *Cognition.* Upper Saddle River, NJ: Prentice Hall.

Willis, S. L., & Schaie, K. W. (1994). Assessing everyday competence in the elderly. In C. Fisher & R. Lerner (Eds.), *Applied developmental psychology.* Mahwah, NJ: Erlbaum.

Willis, S. L., & Schaie, K. W. (1999). Intellectual functioning in midlife. In S. L. Willis & J. D. Reid (Eds.), *Life in the middle: Psychological and social development in middle age.* San Diego: Academic Press.

Wilson, G. L. (2002). *Groups in context: Leadership and participation in small groups* (6th ed.). New York: McGraw-Hill.

Wilson, J. F. (2003). *Biological foundations of human behavior.* Belmont, CA: Wadsworth.

Wilson, J. P., Friedman, M. J., & Lindy, J. D. (Eds.). (2001). *Treating psychological trauma and PTSD.* New York: Guilford.

Winne, P. H., & Perry, N. E. (2000). Measuring self-regulated learning. In M. Boekaerts, P. R. Pintrich, & M. Zeidner (Eds.), *Handbook of self-regulation.* San Diego: Academic Press.

Winner, E. (1996). *Gifted children: Myths and realities.* New York: Basic Books.

Winner, E. (2000). The origins and ends of giftedness. *American Psychologist, 55,* 159–169.

Wise, J. A., & Hopkins, V. D. (Eds.). (2000). *Human factors in certification.* Mahwah, NJ: Erlbaum.

Wisniewski, E. (2000). Concepts: Combinations. In A. Kazdin (Ed.), *Encyclopedia of psychology.* Washington, DC, & New York: American Psychological Association and Oxford University Press.

Witelson, S. F., Kigar, D. L., & Harvey, T. (1999). The exceptional brain of Albert Einstein. *Lancet, 353,* 2149–2153.

Wolpe, J. (1963). Behavior therapy in complex neurotic states. *British Journal of Psychiatry, 110,* 28–34.

Wong, E. H., Sonder, M. S., Amara, S. G., Tinholt, P. M., Percey, M. F., Hoffman, W. P., Hyslop, D. K., Franklin, S., Porsolt, R. D., Bondignori, A., Carfagna, N., & McArthur, R. A. (2000). Reboxetine: A pharmacologically potent, selective, and specific norepinephrine inhibitor. *Biological Psychiatry, 47,* 818–829.

Wood, D. (2001). Established and emerging cardiovascular risk factors. *American Heart Journal, 141* (Suppl. 2), S49–57.

Wood, G. (1986). *Myth of neurosis: Overcoming the illness excuse.* New York: Perennial.

Wood, J. T. (2001). *Gendered lives* (4th ed.). Belmont, CA: Wadsworth.

Wood, W. (1987). Meta-analytic review of sex differences in group performance. *Psychological Bulletin, 102,* 53–71.

Woodruff-Pak, D. S. (1999). New directions for a classical paradigm: Human eyeblink conditioning. *Psychological Science, 10,* 1–3.

Wooley, S. C., & Garner, D. M. (1991). Obesity treatment: The high cost of false hope. *Journal of the American Dietetic Association, 91,* 1248–1251.

Worell, J., & Robinson, D. (1993). Feminist counseling therapy for the 21st century. *Counseling Psychologist, 21,* 92–96.

World Health Organization (2000). *The World Health Report.* Geneva, Switzerland: World Health Organization.

Worrell, J. (Ed.). (2002). *Encyclopedia of women and gender.* New York: Oxford University Press.

Wright, J. C., Huston, A. C., Scantlin, R., & Kotler, J. (2001). The early window project: *Sesame Street* prepares children for school. In S. M. Fisch & R. T. Truglio (Eds.), *"G" is for growing.* Mahwah, NJ: Erlbaum.

Wrightsman, L., Greene, E., Nietzel, M. T., & Fortune, W. H. (2002). *Psychology and the legal system.* Belmont, CA: Wadsworth.

Wu, J. C., Iacono, R., Ayman, M., Salmon, E., Lin, S. D., Carlson, J., Keator, D., Lee, A., Najafi, A., & Fallon, J. (2000). Correlation of intellectual impairment in Parkinson's disease with FDG PET scan. *Neuroreport, 11,* 2139–2144.

Y

Yalom, I. D. (1975). *The theory and practice of group psychotherapy.* New York: Basic Books.

Yalom, I. D. (1995). *The theory and practice of group psychotherapy* (4th ed.). New York: Basic Books.

Yamamoto, J., Frequet, N., & Sandner, G. (2002). Conditioned taste aversion using four different means to deliver sucrose to rats. *Physiology and Behavior, 75,* 387–396.

Yanovski, S. Z., & Yanovski, J. A. (2002). Obesity. *New England Journal of Medicine, 346,* 591–602.

Yapko, M. (2001). Hypnosis in treating symptoms and risk factors of major depression. *American Journal of Clinical Hypnosis, 44,* 97–108.

Yardley, L., Owen, N., Nazareth, I., & Luxon, L. (2001). Panic disorder with agoraphobia associated with dizziness: Characteristic symptoms and psychosocial sequelae. *Journal of Nervous and Mental Disorders, 189,* 328–331.

Yarmey, A. D. (1973). I recognize your face but I can't remember your name: Further evidence for the tip-of-the-tongue phenomenon. *Memory and Cognition, 1,* 287–290.

Yasuno, F., Nishigawa, T., Tokunaga, H., Yoshiyama, K., Nakagawa, Y., Ikejiri, Y., Oku, N., Hashiawa, K., Tanabe, H., Shinozaki, K., Sugita, Y., Nishimura, T., & Takeda, M. (2000). The neural basis of perceptual and conceptual word priming: A PET study. *Cortex, 36,* 59–69.

Yau, K. (2002). Cellular and molecular mechanisms of olfaction. *Annual Review of Neuroscience* (Vol. 25). Palo Alto, CA: Annual Reviews.

Young, E., & Korzun, A. (1998). Psychoneuroendocrinology of depression: Hypothalamic-pituitary-gonadal axis. *Psychiatric Clinics of North America, 21,* 309–323.

Young, T. (1802). On the theory of light and colors. *Philosophical Transactions of the Royal Society of London, 92,* 12–48.

Z

Zacks, J. M., & Tversky, B. (2001). Event structure in perception and conception. *Psychological Bulletin, 127,* 3–21.

Zahm, S., & Gold, E. (2002). Gestalt therapy. In M. Hersen & W. H. Sledge (Eds.), *Encyclopedia of psychotherapy.* San Diego: Academic Press.

Zaimovic, G. G., Zambelli, U., Timpano, M., Reali, N., Bernasconi, S., & Brambilla, F. (2000). Neuroendocrine responses to psychological stress in adolescents with anxiety disorder. *Neuropsychobiology, 42,* 82–92.

Zajonc, R. B. (1965). Social facilitation. *Science, 149,* 269–274.

Zajonc, R. B. (1984). On the primacy of affect. *American Psychologist, 39,* 117–123.

Zalla, T., Koechlin, E., Pietrini, P., Basso, G., Aquino, P., Sirigu, A., & Grafman, J. (2000). Differential amygdala responses to winning and losing. *European Journal of Neuroscience, 15,* 1764–1770.

Zeki, S. (1991). Cerebral akinetopsia (visual motion blindness). A review. *Brain 114,* 811–824.

Zeki, S. (2001). Localization and globalization in conscious vision. *Annual Review of Neuroscience* (Vol. 24). Palo Alto, CA: Annual Reviews.

Ziegert, K. A. (1983). The Wedisih prohibition of corporal punishment: A preliminary report. *Journal of Marriage and the Family, 45,* 917–926.

Zilbergeld, B. (1992). *The new male sexuality.* New York: Bantam Books.

Zillman, D. (1998). Anger. In H. S. Friedman (Ed.) *Encyclopedia of mental health* (Vol. 1). San Diego: Academic Press.

Zillmer, E. A., & Spiers, M. V. (2001). *Principles of neuropsychology.* Belmont, CA: Wadsworth.

Zimmerman, B. J. (2000). Attaining self-regulation: A social cognitive perspective. In M. Boekaerts, P. R. Pintrich, & M. Zeidner (Eds.), *Handbook of self-regulation.* San Diego: Academic Press.

Zimmerman, B. J. (2001). Theories of self-regulated learning and academic achievement. In B. J. Zimmerman & D. H. Schunk (Eds.), *Self-regulated learning and academic achievement.* Mahwah, NJ: Erlbaum.

Zimmerman, B. J., & Schunk, D. H. (Eds.). (2001). *Self-regulated learning and academic achievement.* Mahwah, NJ: Erlbaum.

Zisapel, N. (2001). Circadian rhythm sleep disorders. *CNS and Drugs, 15,* 311–328.

Zola, S. M., & Squire, L. R. (2001). Relationship between magnitude of damage to the hippocampus and impaired recognition in monkeys. *Hippocampus, 11,* 92–98.

Zuckerman, M. (1994). *Behavioral expressions and biosocial bases of sensation seeking.* New York: Cambridge University Press.

Zuckerman, M. (2000). Sensation seeking. In A. Kazdin (Ed.), *Encyclopedia of psychology.* Washington, DC, & New York: American Psychological Association and Oxford University Press.

Zuckerman, M., Kuhlman, D. M., Joireman, J., Teta, P., & Kraft, M. (1993). A comparison of three structural models for personality: The big three, the big five, and the alternate five. *Journal of Personality and Social Psychology, 657,* 757–768.

Zwislocki, J. J. (2002). *Auditory sound transmission.* Mahwah, NJ: Erlbaum.

Credits

Text and Line Art Credits

Chapter 1

p. 25 From Jane Halonen and John Santrock, *Psychology: Contexts and Applications, Third Edition*, McGraw-Hill, 1999. Copyright © 1999 The McGraw-Hill Companies. Reprinted with permission from The McGraw-Hill Companies.

Chapter 3

Figures 3.3, 3.4 From R. Lewis, *Life, 3rd Edition*. Copyright © 1998 by The McGraw-Hill Companies. Reproduced with permission of The McGraw-Hill Companies. **Figures 3.6, 3.18** From *Mapping the Mind* by Rita Carter, 1998. Reprinted by permission of Weidenfeld & Nicolson. **Figure 3.11** From *Brain, Mind, and Behavior* by Floyd Bloom, Charles A. Nelson, Arlyne Lazerson. Copyright © 1985, 1988, 2001 by Educational Broadcasting Corporation. Used with the permission of W.H. Freeman and Company. **Figure 3.16** From *Brain, Mind, and Behavior* by Floyd Bloom, Charles A. Nelson, Arlyne Lazerson. Copyright © 1985, 1988, 2001 by Educational Broadcasting Corporation. Used with the permission of W. H. Freeman and Company. **Figure 3.23** From John Santrock, *Psychology, 6th Edition, Module On Evolution and Heredity*, Figure 12. Reprinted with permission from The McGraw-Hill Companies.

Chapter 4

Figures 4.5, 4.16, 4.21, 4.22, 4.28, 4.29, 4.30 From John W. Santrock, *Life-Span Development, 8th Ed.*, **Figures 9.5, 12.2, 13.1, 16.4, 16.5, 16.6.** Copyright © 2002 The McGraw-Hill Companies, Inc. Reproduced with permission of The McGraw-Hill Companies. **Figure 4.20** From "The Development of Competence in Favorable and Unfavorable Environments" by A. Masten & J.D. Coatsworth, *American Psychologist*, 553, pp. 205–220. Copyright © 1998 by the American Psychological Association. Adapted with permission. **Figure 4.25** From Grant Jarding, *USA Today*, January 5, 1999, p 4. Reprinted with permission. **Figure 4.31** From "The Nature of the Influence of Speed on Adult Age Differences in Cognition" from *Developmental Psychology*, 1994, 30, 240–259. Copyright © 1994 by the American Psychological Association. Adapted with permission. **Figure 4.32** From "The Nature of the Influence of Speed on Adult Age Differences in Cognition" from *Developmental Psychology*, 1994, 30, 240–259. Copyright © 1994 by the American Psychological Association. Adapted with permission. **Figure 4.33** From "Dual-Career Couples" by R. C. Barnett, in *Encyclopedia of Women and Gender: Sex Similarities and Differences and the Impact of Society on Gender*, edited by Judith Worell. Copyright © 2001 Elsevier Science (USA). Reproduced by permission of the publisher. **Figure 4.34** From L. L. Carstensen and S. Turk-Charles, *Psychology and Aging*, 9, 262. Copyright © 1994 by the American Psychological Association. Adapted with permission. **Figure 4.35** From *Aging Well* by George Vaillant. Copyright © 2002 by George E. Vaillant, M.D. By permission of Little, Brown and Company, Inc. **Figure 4.3** From T. Field, S. M. Schanberg, F. Scafidi, C.R. Bauer, N. Vega-Lahr, R. Garcia, J. Nystrom, C.M. Kuhn, "Tactile/Kinesthetic Stimulation Effects on Preterm Neonates," *Pediatrics*, 77, 1986, p. 657, Figure 1. Reproduced with permission from the publisher.

Chapter 5

Figure 5.17 Reproduced with permission from Ishihara's Tests for Colour Deficiency published by Kanehara Trading Inc., located at Tokyo in Japan. Tests for color deficiency cannot be conducted with this material. For accurate testing, the original plates should be used. **Figure 5.18** From *Introduction to Psychology, 7th edition*, by Hilgard, Atkinson and Atkinson. Copyright © 2003 Thomson Learning. Reprinted with permission of Wadsworth, an imprint of the Wadsworth Group, a division of Thomson Learning. Fax 800 730-2215. **Figure 5.27** From *Wathern-Dunn*, Models for the Perception of Visual Form. Copyright © The MIT Press. Reprinted by permission. **Figure 5.29** From James J. Gibson, *The Perception of the Visual World*. Copyright © 1950 by Houghton Mifflin Company. Reprinted with permission. **Figure 5.36** From *Brain, Mind, and Behavior* by Floyd Bloom, Charles A. Nelson, Arlyne Lazerson. Copyright © 1985, 1988, 2001 by Educational Broadcasting Corporation. Used with the permission of W.H. Freeman and Company.

Chapter 6

p. 242 Quiz and Strategies: From *Power Sleep* by James B. Maas. Copyright © 1998 by James B. Maas, Ph.D. Used by permission of Villard Books, a division of Random House, Inc. **Figure 6.6** Reprinted with permission from H. P. Roffwarg, J.N. Muzio, and W.C. Dement, "Ontogenetic Development of Human Dream-Sleep-Cycle," *Science*, 152, 604–609. Copyright © 1966 American Association for the Advancement of Science. **Figure 6.7** From *Brain, Mind, and Behavior* by Floyd Bloom, Charles A. Nelson, Arlyne Lazerson. Copyright © 1985, 1988, 2001 by Educational Broadcasting Corporation. Used with the permission of W.H. Freeman and Company. **Figure 6.10** From John W. Santrock, *Adolescence, Eighth Edition*. Copyright © 2001 The McGraw-Hill Companies, Inc. Reprinted by permission of The McGraw-Hill Companies. **Figure 6.11** National Institute of Drug Abuse 2001, Teaching Packet for Psychoactive Drugs, Slide 9. **Figure 6.13** From *Journal of the American Medical Association*, 272, 1672–1677, 1994, data presented by H. Wechsler, Davenport, et al., *Journal of the American Medical Association*, 272, 1672–1677. With permission from the American Medical Association. **Figure 6.14** National Institute of Drug Abuse 2001, Teaching Packet for Psychoactive Drugs, Slides 12 and 13.

Chapter 8

Figure 8.11 Figure from "Retrieval Time for Semantic Memory" by A. M. Collins and M. R. Quillan in *Journal of Verbal Learning and Verbal Behavior*, Volume 3, 240–248. Copyright © 1969 Elsevier Science (USA). Reproduced by permission of the publisher. **Figure 8.12** From R. Lachman, et al., *Cognitive Psychology and Information Processing*. Copyright © 1979 Lawrence Erlbaum Associates, Inc. Reprinted with permission from the publisher. **Figure 8.13** From J.C. Bartlett, *Remembering*, Cambridge, England: Cambridge University Press, 1932. Reprinted with permission. **Figure 8.16** From B. Murdock, Jr., *Human Memory: Theory and Data*. Copyright © 1974 Lawrence Erlbaum Associates, Inc. Reprinted by permission of the author. **Figure 8.19** D. C. Rubin and M. Kozin, "Vivid Memories" in *Cognition*, 16:81–95. Copyright © 1984 Associated Scientific Publishers, Amsterdam, Netherlands. Reprinted with permission. **Figure 8.20** From Kassin, Tubb, Hosch, and Memon, *American Psychologist*, 56, 405–416. Copyright © 2001 by the American Psychological Association. Adapted with permission. **Figure 8.21** http://www.exploratorium.edu/exhibits/common_cents/index.html. Copyright © Exploratorium. With permission from the Exploratorium, San Francisco. **Figure 8.22** From Hermann Ebbinghaus, *Memory: A Contribution to Experimental Psychology*, 1885. Translated by Henry A. Ruger and Clara E. Bussenius, 1913.

Chapter 9

Figure 9.1 With permission from Dr. Ursula Bellugi. **Figure 9.7** From *The Universe Within: A New Science Explores the Human Mind*, by Morton Hunt, 1982. Copyright © 1982 Morton Hunt. Reprinted with permission from Simon & Schuster. **Figure 9.11** From John Santrock, *Children, Seventh Edition*. Copyright © 2003 The McGraw-Hill Companies, Inc. Reprinted with permission from The McGraw-Hill Companies. **Figure 9.13** From John W. Santrock, *Educational Psychology*. Copyright © 2001 The McGraw-Hill Companies, Inc. Reprinted by permission of The McGraw-Hill Companies.

Chapter 10

Figure 10.1 From John W. Santrock, *Children, Fifth Edition*. Copyright © 1997 The McGraw-Hill Companies, Inc. Reprinted by permission of The McGraw-Hill Companies. **Figure 10.4** *Raven Standard Progressive Matrices*, F-A5. Reprinted by permission of J. C. Raven Ltd. **Figure 10.6** From John W. Santrock, *Educational Psychology*.

Photographs

Chapter 1

Chapter 2

Chapter 3

Chapter 4

Images; p. 520, © AP/Wide World Photos; p. 528, © Scala/Art Resource, NY; p. 530, © AP/Wide World Photos; p. 531T, © Rex USA, Ltd.; p. 531B, © Lewis Baxter/Peter Arnold, Inc.; p. 533TL, © Catherine Ursillo/Photo Researchers, Inc.; p. 533TM, © Monica Anderson/Stock Boston; p. 533TR, © AFP/Corbis; p. 533B, © Christopher Brown/Stock Boston; p. 536, © 1974 The Washington Post. Photo by Gerald Martineau; p. 538, © Erich Lessing/Art Resource, NY; p. 541, Courtesy Lewis Baxter and Michael Phelps/UCLA School of Medicine; p. 546T, © Bettmann/Corbis; p. 546B, © Alain Benainous/Getty Images; p. 549L, *Landscape,* 1907. by August Neter. Reprinted by permission of Prinzhorn-Sammlung der Psychiatrischen Universitätsklinik Heidelberg; p. 549R, © Grunnitus/Monkmeyer Press; p. 551, © Monte S. Buchsbaum, M.D., Mt. Sinai School of Medicine, New York, NY; p. 552L, © Monte S. Buchsbaum, M.D., Mt. Sinai School of Medicine, New York, NY; p. 552R, Courtesy of the Genain Quadruplets; p. 553, © Bob Daemmrich/The Image Works p. 554, © AP/Wide World Photos

Chapter 14

p. 560, © Stacy Pickerell/Getty Images/Stone; p. 567, © W & O McIntyre/Photo Researchers, Inc.; p. 569, © Historical Pictures/Stock Montage; p. 571, © Scala/Art Resource, NY; p. 574, Courtesy Deke Simon; p. 575, © David Frazier Photo Library, Inc.; p. 576T, Courtesy Albert Bandura; p. 576B, © Mary Levin/University of Washington; p. 584, © Michael Newman/PhotoEdit; p. 585, © Bob Daemmrich/Stock Boston; p. 588, Courtesy Stanley Sue

Chapter 15

p. 600, © Philip North-Coombes/Getty Images/Stone; p. 603T, George V. Mann, Sc. D., M.D.; p. 603B, © David Stoecklein/The Stock Market; p. 609, © Superstock; p. 610, © Catherine Gehm; p. 611, Courtesy Vonnie McLoyd; p. 614, Photo by Todd Cheney. Courtesy Dr. Shelly Taylor; p. 617, © Meckes/Ottawa/Photo Researchers, Inc.; p. 628TL, © Don Smetzer/Getty Images/Stone; p. 628TR, © David Austen/Getty Images/Stone; p. 628M, © Nabeel Turner/Getty Images/Stone; p. 628BL, © David Austen/Getty Images/Stone; p. 628BR, © Bob Daemmrich/Getty Images/Stone; p. 629, © Cary Wolkinsky/Stock Boston; p. 630, © Peter Gregoire Photography; p. 633, © John P. Kelly/Getty Images/The Image Bank; p. 634, © John Elk; p. 638, © Lloyd Wolf

Chapter 16

p. 644, © Gary Conner/PhotoEdit; p. 646, © AP/Wide World Photos; p. 648, © Romilly Lockyear/Getty Images/The Image Bank; p. 650, © John P.

Kelly/Getty Images/The Image Bank; p. 659, © William Vandivert; p. 661, © 1965 by Stanley Milgram, from the film Obedience distributed by Penn State Media Sales; p. 662, © AP/Wide World Photos; p. 663T, © Scott T. Smith/Corbis; p. 663B, © Hughes Martin/Corbis; p. 664T, © Andrea Pistolesi/Getty Images/The Image Bank; p. 664B, © Jean-Marc Loubat/Photo Researchers, Inc.; p. 666T, © AP/Wide World Photos; p. 666B, © Alberto Garcia/Getty Images; p. 669L, © Reuters NewMedia Inc./Corbis; p. 669R, © Reuters NewMedia Inc./Corbis; p. 670TL, © Bob Daemmrich/The Image Works; p. 670TM, © Bill Gillette/Stock Boston; p. 670TR, © Spencer Grant/Index Stock Imagery; p. 670B, © Larry Kolvoord/The Image Works; p. 674, © Cleo Photography; p. 675, © Mary Kate Denny/PhotoEdit; p. 677T, © Bettmann/Corbis; p. 677B, © AP/Wide World Photos; p. 683L, © Kent Reno/Jeroboam; p. 683R, © David Young-Wolff/PhotoEdit; p. 685, © David W. Hamilton/Getty Images/The Image Bank; p. 687, Courtesy of the Academy of Motion Picture Arts and Sciences; p. 689, © David Young-Wolff/PhotoEdit

Name Index

Subject Index

Guide to Selected Topics